MW00809592

blished in hardcover in the U.S. in 2018 by Stackpole Books
imprint of The Rowman & Littlefield Publishing Group, Inc.
01 Forbes Blvd., Ste. 200
ham, MD 20706
w.rowman.com

stributed by NATIONAL BOOK NETWORK
0-462-6420

st published in Australia in 2006 by Leaping Horseman. This edition

more information about Leaping Horseman Books, please visit
w.leapinghorseman.com

s and illustrations by Jason D. Mark

ish Library Cataloguing in Publication Information available

rary of Congress Cataloging-in-Publication Data available

N 978-0-8117-1991-9 (hardcover)
N 978-0-8117-6619-7 (e-book)

The paper used in this publication meets the minimum requirements
merican National Standard for Information Sciences—Permanence of
er for Printed Library Materials, ANSI/NISO Z39.48-1992.

ted in the United States of America

Island of Fire

The Battle for the
Barrikady Gun Factory in Stalin

Jason D. Mark

STACKPOLE
BOOKS

Guilford, Connecticut

Dedicated to Hans Bernhart...
and to all the other soldiers,
be they German or Russian,
who died or are still missing in Stalingrad

Publisher's notes:

1. A conscious decision had been made to avoid the word 'Russian' when referring to the soldiers of the Red Army. Instead, the term 'Soviet' is used, in an effort to encompass all nationalities of the Soviet Union who fought in its armed forces.

2. German forces operating in the Soviet Union adhered to German time. From 0300 hours on 2 November, 1942, watches were set back an hour to Deutsche Winterzeit (German winter time) = GMT + 1 hour, while the city of Stalingrad was GMT + 3 hours. To ease confusion in time-zone differences, all Soviet times have been converted to German time.

3. The naming of landmarks is another tricky issue because both German and Soviet designations (and nicknames) exist for each building in the Barrikady settlement. Therefore, the following convention has been used:

   German designations are prefixed by the word 'Haus' (eg. Haus 81), Soviet ones by 'Dom' (eg. Dom 63). If a German designation is used, the Soviet term will quite often follow, eg. 'Haus 81 [Dom 63]' and vice versa.

   The workhalls of the Barrikady Gun Factory: German designations are prefixed by 'Hall', Soviet by 'Workshop'.

   Quite often, a landmark acquired a memorable nickname on both sides (eg. one building was called 'Kommissarhaus' by the Germans, 'P-shaped house' by the Soviets.) To simplify matters, one name has been selected for use throughout the book – with the exception of eyewitness accounts or direct quotes, where the original terminology is unchanged. In this case, the original term will be followed by the common name (eg. '…P-shaped House [Kommissarhaus]…').

   If in doubt with any landmark designation, please consult the large map. This has both German and Soviet terms (where known).

4. Abbreviations used throughout the footnotes: **DKiG** = Deutsche Kreuz in Gold (German Cross in Gold); **DKiS** = Deutsche Kreuz in Silber (German Cross in Silver); **EB** = Ehrenblattspange (Honour Roll Clasp); **EK1** = Eisernes Kreuz 1. Klasse (Iron Cross First Class); **EK2** = Eisernes Kreuz 2. Klasse (Iron Cross Second Class); **EL** = Eichenlaub (Oak Leaves to the Knight's Cross); **GRD** = Guards Rifle Division; **GRR** = Guards Rifle Regiment; **HoSL** = Hero of Socialist Labour; **HotSU** = Hero of the Soviet Union; **RD** = Rifle Division; **RR** = Rifle Regiment; **RK** = Ritterkreuz (Knight's Cross); **RK.z.Kvk.m.Schw.** = Ritterkreuz zum Kriegsverdienstkreuz mit Schwerter (Knight's Cross of the War Merit Cross with Swords).

TABLE OF CONTENTS

PREFACE

American historian Ralph H. Gabriel once wrote, "'History' is that image of the past which filters through the mind of the historian, as light through a window. Sometimes the glass is dirty; too often it is distressingly opaque." Every historian brings personal opinions and biases to their study, and this inevitably colours their interpretations of the past. In doing so, the historian – either knowingly or subconsciously – selects facts that suit his or her own perceptions of the truth. But no-one knows the real truth, and so it is possible that two well-intentioned historians can produce distinct hypotheses for the same events, even though each follows proper research methods.

This book – the result of four years of intensive research – is my attempt to deliver the truth about an overlooked phase of the Second World War; the grim struggle for the Barrikady Gun Factory. This battered microcosm perfectly symbolises the futility, waste and changing fortunes known as 'the Battle of Stalingrad'. For the Soviets, it was an astounding victory, the turning point in the war and is an immense source of pride to this day. As a result, hundreds of books about the battle have rolled off the presses in the last 60 years and Red Army veterans are more than willing to record their experiences in spoken or written word. Once the language barrier has been scaled, a wealth of material is available. Moreover, Russian military archives, swollen with unimaginable quantities of war diaries and other records, are slowly but surely revealing their treasures.

The issue is rather more complicated when it comes to the German perspective. While on the surface it might seem easier to obtain information from Germany than nouveau-capitalist Russia, several factors proved otherwise. Firstly, war diaries of the German units lost at Stalingrad were either burnt in the days before capitulation or else captured by the Red Army (today, these German records languish in the elusive 'Fond 500' in the Central Archive of the Ministry of Defence in Podolsk, safe under lock and key from further investigation). Vast swathes of German military records (regimental level and below) were lost forever when British bombers levelled the archives in Berlin in February 1945. Fortunately, records for divisions and above survive – albeit with gaping holes.

Secondly, emotions about Stalingrad and the war in general vary markedly: while one person will answer any question put to them, the next will say nothing while another will grow irate and even yell. Tears are not uncommon. The word 'Stalingrad' evokes painful memories for a lot of German families: many interviewed for this book still have fathers or brothers or sons listed as 'missing in action'. A stigma is attached to Stalingrad, not as a stain but more as a scar that hurts as soon as it is touched. Veterans, particularly members of panzer units, prefer to remember their armoured victories – of which they are proud, as soldiers – rather than the wretched, sacrificial fighting for a city on the very edge of Europe. One officer attended post-war reunions for over 50 years and never once told his best friend that he was at Stalingrad – even though that friend had been at Stalingrad himself.

Enormous efforts were therefore required to compile the German side of this battle. Tiny threads of information were gathered from every conceivable source ('another piece of the mosaic', I kept saying to myself). The most important sources were veterans and families, but locating them was terribly difficult, mostly due to Germany's strict privacy laws. Imaginative detective work was needed simply to establish contact with a potential lead. Weeks of searching often led to disappointment, but occasionally, a gold mine of information was opened up.

The difference in type and quality of information will be obvious throughout the book. While Soviet actions have been taken almost exclusively from detailed war diaries and combat reports, the German perspective has been gleaned from various sources. In contrast, an abundance of personal information and private photos exists for individual German soldiers but not for the Soviets. The intention has been to utilise a wide range of sources in order to provide a detailed, unbiased account of the fighting. I hope this has been achieved.

The German point-of-view would not have been possible without the tireless and diligent work of Agnes Moosmann. Never has an author been so blessed. I often thought of this youthful octogenarian as my 'secret weapon' – stubborn silences to my repeated requests for information were often breached by a single phone call from Agnes. Armed with a computer, telephone and many years of experience authoring her own books, she ensured that a steady stream of new material flowed in and conducted numerous interviews. Understandably, many Germans are reluctant to send irreplaceable family photos and documents around the world to Australia, so instead, they went to Agnes. At a conservative estimate, Agnes has scanned over 1500 items in the past three years. Any attempt to convey my gratitude to Agnes in these few lines will never do her justice, so I only hope this book fulfils her sole request of me: "Do a good job".

Locating and gathering documents from the different archives across the globe would have been prohibitively expensive without the selfless assistance of several people: Phil Logan and Tim Whistler for visiting NARA on numerous occasions to fulfil my many requests; Ute von Livonius-Ueberschär for her sterling efforts in the archives of BA-MA in Freiburg; Michael Struss for obtaining documents from DRK and WASt; Sean McIntyre for finding and copying files in the Hoover Institution; Maxim Tarutin for patiently enduring the bureaucratic procedures at TsAMO; and finally, 'AMVAS' and 'Condor' (you know who you are) for supplying countless pages of previously unseen documents from TsAMO.

Those reams of documents, of course, were all in German or Russian, which severely overtaxed my meagre translating skills. I frequently called upon the services of those gifted individuals who have command of two languages: Kamen Nevenkin for transcribing handwritten Russian documents; Yan Mann for translating many pages of Russian text; and Michael von Brasch and Howard Davies for translating German text.

The words would suffer without pictures, so I'm grateful to the following people for supplying photos: Nik Orlov for sourcing hard-to-find Russian images; Frank Gulin for his help in sourcing aerial photos in NARA; Wolfgang Kirstein, Rainer Lehmann, Ralf Anton Schäfer and Wolfgang Wiesen for permission to use several important photographs; Thomas Anderson and Akira Takiguchi for photos of the sIG33B; Phil Curme; Konni Dreier; Michael A. Hawash; Günter Hils; Vladimir Kalgine; Evgeny Kulichenko; and Kamen Nevenkin.

Proofreading a manuscript is a difficult and time-consuming task, but that did not stop Tim Whistler, Michael A. Hawash and Prof. Roy Casagranda from offering their services.

Their keen eyes and insightful suggestions markedly improved the finished text.

Many thanks to the following people for various other forms of assistance: Dr. Manfred Oldenburg for sending transcripts of lengthy interviews with three German veterans; Tom Houlihan for drawing several maps; Vladimir Kalgine for supplying invaluable reports by Soviet veterans; Evgeny Kulichenko for answering my many questions about the battlefield and locating quite a few rare books; Mike Jones for allowing me to use excerpts from his interviews with Soviet veterans; Robin Diez from Metzingen Stadtarchiv for sharing letters and documents about soldiers of 305.Inf.Div.; Heiko Klatt for his research into Major Otto Krüger's life; Konni Dreier, chairman of the Pionierkameradschaft Ulm, for providing information about Pi.Btl.45 and for putting me in contact with veterans of the unit; Gerhard Ruddenklau for sending materials about Pi.Btl.50; Karlheinz Münch and Markus Jaugitz for kindly supplying information about the elusive sIG33B; and Dieter Schäfer.

Acknowledgments would not be complete without thanking the personnel of the following institutions: Barrikady Museum in Volgograd; Bulgarian State Archives in Sofia; Bundesarchiv-Fotoarchiv in Koblenz; Bundesarchiv-Militärarchiv (BA-MA) in Freiburg; Bundesarchiv-Zentralnachweisstelle (BA-ZNS) in Aachen; Deutsche Dienststelle (DD/WASt) in Berlin; Deutsches Rotes Kreuz (DRK) in München; Tsentralniy Arkhiv Ministerstva Oborony (TsAMO – Central Archive of the Ministry of Defence) in Podolsk; United States Holocaust Memorial Museum (USHMM) in Washington, D.C.; and finally, the various Standesämter (registry offices), Stadtarchive (city archives) and Einwohnermeldeämter (resident's reporting offices) across Germany and Austria who answered my requests for information about certain individuals. There are far too many to thank individually.

I will forever be indebted to the following veterans and families who generously assisted me with photos, documents, Feldpost letters, information, anecdotes and countless other facts needed to compile this book (listed in alphabetical order):

Wife of Ludwig Apmann (2./Pz.Pi.Btl.50); son of Kurt Barth (1./Pi.Btl.162); son of Erich Bauchspiess (Stab/Pi.Btl.336); daughter of Ludwig Beigel (3./Pi.Btl.305); son of Eberhard Beyersdorff, DKiG (6./Pz.Gr.Rgt.26); son-in-law of Karl Binder (Dinafü 305); son of Andreas Bleistein (II./Gr.Rgt.577); son of Johann Bonetsmüller (2./Pi.Btl.305); daughter of Herbert Borkowski (1./Pi.Btl.336); sister-in-law of Wilhelm Braun, RK (II./Gr.Rgt.576); nephew of Eitel Brock (Sturmkompanie 44); son of Karl Brockmann (2./Pi.Btl.336); sons of Dr. Ludwig Büch (Stab/Pi.Btl.45); family of Ernst Bunte (3./Pz.Pi.Btl.50); daughter of Hans-Ludwig Eberhard, DKiG (2./Pi.Btl.389); daughter of Eugen Förschner (II./Gr.Rgt.576); wife & niece of Erwin Gast (Stab/Pz.Pi.Btl.50); son of Christian Geuenich (Pz.Pi.Btl.50); daughter of Wilhelm Giebeler (Pi.Btl.336); son of Udo Giulini (Radfahr-Schwadron 305); brother-in-law of Paul Göhner (Stab 305.Inf.Div.); daughter of Richard Grimm (2./Pi.Btl.305); daughter of Friedrich von Grolman (Stab/Gr.Rgt.578); brother of Ernst-Eberhard von Haaren (4./Stug.Abt.245); daughter of Hans Häussler (San.Kp.305); wife of Otto-Wilhelm Heinze (Stab/Pi.Btl.294); brother of Eugen Hering, DKiG (6./Gr.Rgt.576); sister of Egon Hillmann (Stab/Pz.Pi.Btl.50); grandson of Josef Hufschmid (6./Gr.Rgt.576); daughter of Hans Kempter (Stab/Gr.Rgt.576); son of Max Keppler (Stab/Pi.Btl.305); Richard Klein (Radfahr-Schwadron 305); wife of Hans Krauss (Stab/Pi.Btl.162); Karl Krauss (2./Pi.Btl.45); sister & niece of Klaus Kunze (Stab/Pz.Pi.Btl.50); sister-in-law of Erwin Kretz (II./Gr.Rgt.578); daughter-in-law of Karl-Heinz Krüder (Stab/Gr.Rgt.576); Anton Locherer (2./Pi.Btl.45);

Peter Löffler (deceased) (Stab/Gr.Rgt.577); daughter-in-law of Hermann Lundt (Stab/Pi.Btl.336); god-daughter of Franz Mäder (1./Pi.Btl.336); Franz Maier (Sturmkompanie 44); brother of Hans-Joachim Martius (II./Pz.Gr.Rgt.26); Hans Messerschmidt (4./Pz.Rgt.24); Paul Nagler (Kameradenschaft 305.Inf.Div.); family of Kurt Nippes, RK (Stug.Abt.244); nephew of Adam Pauli (2./Pi.Btl.305); daughter of Gerhard Piltz (2./Pi.Btl.336); Alban Plaum (II./Gr.Rgt.578); son & daughter-in-law of Mariano Puschiavo (248° Autoreparto pesante); son of Wilhelm Püttmann, DKiG (III./Gr.Rgt.578); Paul Reiner (3./Gr.Rgt.578); daughter of Eugen Rettenmaier (I./Gr.Rgt.578); wife of Hans Rinck (2 & 3./Pi.Btl.305); Karl-August Rombach (II./Art.Rgt.305); wife & grandson of Heinz Schaate (1./Pi.Btl.305); Dr. Hans Schellmann (III./Gr.Rgt.578); Günther Schendel (Nebelwerfer-Regiment 53); nephew of Alfons Schinke, DKiG (3./Pi.Btl.162); grandson of Paul Schmidt (12./Gr.Rgt.578); Dr. Karl Schöpf (II./Art.Rgt.305); daughter of Paul Schuboth (Gr.Rgt.576); son & grandson of Martin Schüsslbauer (6./Gr.Rgt.577); wife of Erich Skutlartz (3./Pi.Btl.45); Berthold Staiger (deceased) (3./Pi.Btl.305); Kurt Steinlen (II./Gr.Rgt.576); Ivan Ilyich Svidrov (650th Rifle Regiment); son of Alfons Thanisch (2./Pi.Btl.305); son of Wilhelm Traub (Stab/Pi.Btl.305); daughter of Josef Troiber (5./Gr.Rgt.577); sister-in-law of August Uhlendorf (Stab./Pz.Pi.Btl.50); Paul Vetter (Radfahr-Schwadron 305); wife of Karl Vögele (2./Pi.Btl.45); niece of Lothar Walter (2./Pi.Btl.45); wife of Willi Walter (2./Pi.Btl.45); Helmut Walz (7./Gr.Rgt.577); Hans von Wartburg (11./Gr.Rgt.131); Walter Weinbrecht (5./Gr.Rgt.577); niece of Wilhelm Willmitzer (Sturmkompanie 44); son of Friedrich Winkler (II./Gr.Rgt.577); Franz Winter (6./Gr.Rgt.577); son of Georg Wittmann (III./Gr.Rgt.577); daughter of Dr. Donatus Wörner (Stab/Pi.Btl.305); daughter of Walter Wroblewski (Sturmschwadron 24); Georg Zeller (Stab/Pi.Btl.305); nephew & brother of Bernhard Ziesch (3./Pi.Btl.336); Helmut Zimmermann (8./Gr.Rgt.577); sister of Hans Zorn (1./Pi.Btl.305); Josef Zrenner (Stab/Pi.Btl.305); and two German veterans and one family who requested anonymity.

The hospitality and warmth shown to my wife and I by the Krauss, Messerschmidt, Moosmann and Rettenmaier families during our visit in September-October 2005 will never be forgotten.

Lastly, my greatest thanks are reserved for Belinda, my wife. This book would never have come about if it were not for her suggestion four years ago that set me on this path. My initial response was "there's not enough information", but the fire had been kindled. Thank you for your understanding and for encouraging my passion.

Although all of these people have contributed to this book, they bear no responsibility for any errors, and all judgements and interpretations are my own. Comments, criticism, corrections or additional information are always greatly appreciated. Write to me at info@leapinghorseman.com

Jason D. Mark
Sydney, Australia
October 2006

THE IMPASSE – STALEMATE IN STALINGRAD

CHAPTER ONE

Assault guns supported the infantrymen as they pushed into the chaotic tangle of railway sidings, gutted warehouses and stacks of gun barrels that lined the western edge of the Barrikady Gun Factory, the assault guns in turn being guided on to their targets by the soldiers. Advancing warily alongside one of them was Gefreiter Helmut Walz[1]. Only four days had passed since he'd been thrown into the fighting in Stalingrad but the gruesome events that he'd already witnessed would be etched into his memory forever. Many of his comrades from 7./Infanterie-Regiment 577 had been killed or wounded right next to him. He himself had been forced to use his razor-honed spade twice, hacking at the heads and necks of enemy soldiers during brutal hand-to-hand combat, on one occasion slicing of a Soviet soldier's hand. But to 20-year-old Walz, the morning of 17 October seemed to be the culmination of horror and savagery. He watched as an infantry Leutnant stood near an assault gun and indicated a new target, but as the gun began to pivot, the Leutnant stumbled and fell. The gun crew did not see him and continued to spin their tracks, running over the Leutnant's face. An unearthly howl arose and as the assault gun lurched forward, Walz saw half of the Leutnant's ripped-off face being carried along in its track.

The desperate attack continued. Walz advanced deeper into the grounds of the Barrikady factory as part of a machine-gun team. Next to him, carrying the gun, was his mate Schappel. When bullets started to whiz past them, Walz went to ground, but Schappel kept running. Watching the bullets and ricochets fly about his comrade, Walz yelled at him to get down. Schappel collapsed into a large bomb crater. Ignoring the fusillade, Walz dashed across to the crater. His friend was lying there, wounded, his nostrils and mouth full of dirt. Walz cleaned out the muck and then looked at the wound. He went cold: he knew his friend would not survive. Shot from behind, the bullet had gone in below the left shoulder-blade, near the spine, and blown out the right side of his torso. Air whistled out of the wound. Walz knew his friend's innards were only being held in by his uniform, so he wrapped bandages completely around him, overcoat and all.

"The war's over, isn't it, Helmut," groaned Schappel.

"Yes, Schappel, the war's over. I promise I'll fetch you this evening, I promise. Lay here quietly, I'll look for a medic for you, you're very badly wounded. Do you hear the air?"

"Yes," he said.

After swathing his friend in more bandages, Walz returned to the battle still raging around him, not knowing that his own time in Stalingrad would end less than half an hour later. He heard unfamiliar voices coming from a dug-out about five metres in front of him. Russians! Walz immediately dropped down behind a massive chunk of masonry. Squatting

---

1. Walz, Obergefreiter Helmut, 7./Inf.Rgt.577; born 22 August, 1922 in Berghausen, Karlsruhe. Still alive in 2006.

Infanterie-Regiment 577, supported by assault guns of Sturmgeschütz-Abteilung 245, push into the Barrikady Gun Factory from the north on 16 October, 1942.

behind the mighty brick-and-concrete boulder, Walz shouted to the enemy soldiers to give themselves up. Nothing happened. Walz took out a stick-grenade and lobbed it into the dug-out. A dull explosion. Then, as the dust settled, a Soviet soldier staggered out of the dug-out, blood trickling from his nose, ears and mouth. No medical knowledge was needed to know that the man would not survive. Without thinking, Walz stood up and the wounded Soviet soldier pointed his submachine-gun at him. Talking calmly, Walz said, "I won't fight you." The two men were only a few metres apart. Quickly realising that he was in real trouble, Walz unholstered his pistol in one swift movement and started to take aim at his adversary. Stars flashed in front of his eyes and he stood there, numb, wondering what was wrong. He tried to call out to a comrade but could not speak. Reaching up to his face, he felt a thick ooze of blood and pieces of broken teeth. The Soviet's bullet had ripped open his cheek, shattered his teeth and smashed both his upper and lower jawbones. The entire lower right side of Walz's face was a gory mess.

One of his comrades, a Berliner, saw what had happened and flew into a rage. He ran forward, clambered up onto the massive masonry block and then, with his full weight, jumped down on the Soviet soldier, who collapsed to the ground. Still gripped by anger, the Berliner repeatedly stomped on the face of the fallen Soviet soldier, accompanied by the terrible sounds of cracking bone. The Soviet was trampled to death.

Walz's commander, Leutnant Hermann Hennes[2], helped him into a bomb crater and did his best to bind the nasty wound. When Hennes stood up, he saw enemy soldiers moving towards them, so he grabbed his rifle and lined up a shot. Lying on his back in the crater, Walz looked up at his commander, expecting him to be the first to fire. A shot rang out and Leutnant Hennes' helmet flew off his head: a Soviet sniper had nailed him from the side. His skull ruptured from back to front and Walz could see both hemispheres of his brain. Clear fluid ran out, but no blood. For an eternal second, Hennes stared down at Walz, disbelief etched on his face, then he toppled backwards into the bottom of the crater – dead.

Above: Helmut Walz as a young Gefreiter in 7./ Inf.Rgt.577 in 1942.

Below: Helmut Walz in his later years. The grievous facial wound is only barely visible. Many operations were required before Walz regained the ability to speak and chew properly.

---

2. Hennes, Leutnant Hermann, 7./Inf.Rgt.577; born 5 April, 1921. Killed in action, 17 October, 1942 in Stalingrad.

Other 7. Kompanie soldiers repelled the onrushing enemy and took care of the sniper who had slain their commander. Walz crawled to the nearby railway embankment that sidled the Barrikady factory's western boundary, slithered under a destroyed railway wagon and rolled into a trench. When the crew of a 14. Panzer-Division half-track saw the severely wounded man crawling along the ground, they stopped to pick him up and said: "Come, comrade, we'll take you to a dressing station."

At 2300 hours that evening, in a large army hospital, Walz endured the first of many operations on his shattered face. His wound was so severe that he took no further part in the war and would need an oral prosthesis for the rest of his life.

Because of his wounds, Walz was unable to keep his promise to fetch his friend Schappel. And with the death of Leutnant Hennes, no-one else knew the whereabouts of the wounded machine-gunner. Schappel almost certainly died alone and in anguish in the bomb crater, waiting for help that never came.

- - -

This tableau was one of dozens taking place throughout the grisly ruins of the Barrikady Gun Factory on the morning of 17 October, 1942. Casualties for 305. Infanterie-Division on this day were high: 2 officers killed and 2 wounded, 29 NCOs and men killed, 124 wounded and 4 missing. It was barely four days into the offensive designed to capture northern Stalingrad and the German divisions were being exsanguinated. The casualties suffered by 305. Infanterie-Division on 17 October were less than the first days of the attack but the fighting was becoming more vicious and the 'lighter' casualties were being inflicted on ever smaller numbers of combat troops.

The large-scale German offensive that started on 14 October had the objective of taking all of Stalingrad's industrial complexes. The first stage was a massive thrust through the Dzerhezinsky Tractor Factory, whereupon the left flank would be anchored to the Volga. Next, after pivoting to face south, the attack forces would push south along the river where they would capture and clear the brickworks, the Barrikady Gun Factory, Bread Factory No. 2 and the grim Krasny Oktyabr Steel Factory in succession. For this huge attack, relatively fresh divisions – at least fresh in the sense that they had not yet been blooded in the Stalingrad grist-mill – had been brought forward: 305. Infanterie-Division was moved in from defensive positions in the steppe between the Don and Volga, and 14. Panzer-Division was sent up from the Beketovka area south of Stalingrad. Also slated for the attack was 389. Infanterie-Division, a unit that had been in Stalingrad since the beginning, as well as smaller elements of 24. Panzer-Division and 100. Jäger-Division.

The first day of the offensive was a brutal and bloody affair but it ended successfully for the Germans in the early hours of 15 October when the vast tractor factory complex was in German hands. Stage one of the offensive was complete but casualties were heavy: between them, 305. and 389. Infanterie-Divisions lost 3 officers and 84 men killed, 7 officers and 276 men wounded and 15 men missing. It was a similar story with 14. Panzer-Division: 4 officers and 27 men killed, 9 officers and 96 men wounded, and 2 men missing, as well as the loss 6 Panzer III short-barrels, 15 Panzer III long-barrels, 7 Panzer IV short-barrels and 2 Panzer IV long-barrels (many of which would, however, be back in service on 16 October). For the successes achieved, several officers were awarded the Knight's Cross[3].

---

3. Domaschk, Major Erich, RK; II./Pz.Gr.Rgt.103; born 19 May, 1908 in Luckau. Died 14 February, 1974 in Bochum; and

Sauvant, Oberst Bernhard, EL, RK, DKiG; I./Pz.Rgt.36; born 25 March, 1910 in Kutten. Died 15 April, 1967 in Ludwigsburg.

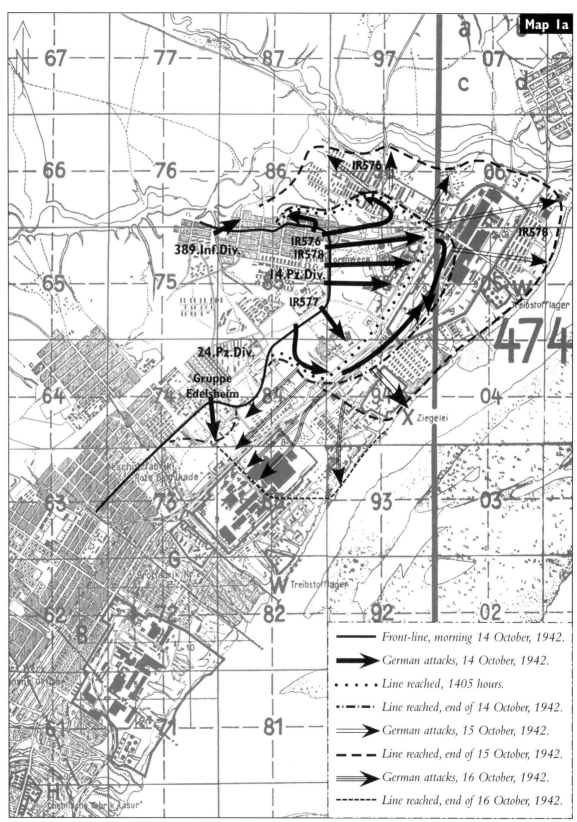

The German offensive in Stalingrad-North, 14-16 October, 1942.

Generalleutnant Arthur Schmidt[4], 6. Armee's chief-of-staff, would remember this attack as the one and only "absolutely complete success" during the attack on the city.

On 15 October, the German assault forces were realigned to face south. A few units, including most of 305. Infanterie-Division, secured the recently taken areas. They expended a great deal of time, energy and blood in mopping up stubborn Soviet resistance in the ruins of the tractor factory and its housing settlements to the west and north-east. On this day, 305. Infanterie-Division lost 53 men killed, 7 officers and 122 men wounded and 1 man missing. 14. Panzer-Division suffered many wounded but few fatalities: 3 men killed, 2 officers and 83 men wounded.

The large-scale attack continued on 16 October, sweeping south through the brickworks and into the Barrikady Gun Factory. Despite the menacing bulk of the factory's workshops, progress was quite good. The panzers of 14. Panzer-Division suffered an initial setback when they lost 17 of their number to dug-in T-34s. Nevertheless, by the end of the day, the overall balance favoured the attackers: a large section of the gun factory was in German hands, as was a lengthy stretch of the Volga cliffs east of the brickworks and tractor factory. These operational successes were not as apparent to the weary infantrymen as was the loss of so many long-time comrades. 305. Infanterie-Division lost 1 officer and 30 men killed, 5 officers and 74 men wounded, and 1 officer and 13 men missing; 14. Panzer-Division lost 2 officers and 21 men killed, 4 officers and 121 men wounded, and 2 men missing.

It was at this point that the situation turned particularly nasty for the Germans. The first elements of a fresh Soviet division, Colonel Ivan Ilyich Lyudnikov's[5] 138th Rifle Division, were transported across the Volga and thrown straight into the mangled wreckage of the gun factory. The fighting developed – or, better said, degenerated – into a vicious brawl where death or injury could come from any quarter and in any possible manner. Gefreiter Walz and Leutnant Hennes suffered their grisly fates on 17 October, the day after the arrival of Lyudnikov's riflemen. Over the next week, individual workshops were taken, lost, recaptured, blown up and demolished. The battle spiralled into an unending hell from which the only escape was a severe wound.

– – –

All thoughts of conquering Stalingrad's industrial north by sweeping south along the Volga were forgotten. A new attack, launched on 23 October, used Generalmajor Richard von Schwerin's[6] 79. Infanterie-Division, yet another German unit fatefully withdrawn from the vital Don river sector protecting 6. Armee's flanks. This attack, falling upon the Krasny Oktyabr factory from the west, effectively divided the Schwerpunkt[7] in Stalingrad-North between the two massive factories. Von Schwerin's infantry regiments were quickly flayed of their combat strength in the ruins of the Krasny Oktyabr steel works, and by the end of October, a week after being fed into Stalingrad, they were spent and no longer suitable for large assaults. However, in the Barrikady factory, the tenacious Germans achieved a modicum of success as 305. Infanterie-Division gradually prised the Soviet defenders out of

---

4. Schmidt, Generalleutnant Arthur, RK, DKiG; 6. Armee; born 25 October, 1895 in Hamburg. Died 5 November, 1987 in Karlsruhe.

5. Lyudnikov, General Ivan Ilyich, HotSU; 138th RD; born 26 September, 1902 in Krivaya Kosa. Died 22 April, 1976.

6. Schwerin, Generalleutnant Richard von, DKiG; 79.Inf.Div.; born 24 May, 1892 in Peitschendorfswerder, East Prussia. Died 23 July, 1951 in Dobrock.

7. Trans.: 'Schwerpunkt' = 'point of maximum effort'.

the demolished workhalls, crawling ever so slowly towards their objective, the Volga river, where victory presumably lay, and then – hopefully – a well-deserved rest.

– – –

The Germans believed that once they had captured most of the Barrikady's massive workhalls, Soviet resistance would lessen. After all, where else could the Soviets continue to resist? All that stood between 305. Infanterie-Division and the Volga were several rows of houses built on relatively open ground. The Germans soon discovered that these houses were fortresses, built not only from concrete and iron, but also from the unfathomable courage and determination of ordinary Soviet soldiers. The closer the Germans pushed to the Volga, the more fanatical the Soviet defence became. One example will suffice: on 24 October, Ivan Ilyich Svidrov[8], a young sergeant from 650th Rifle Regiment, was ordered to defend one of these houses along with a squad of four other soldiers. The address was Dom 31 [Haus 71] located on the corner of Arbatovskaya and Pribaltiskaya streets. This building was considered to be of paramount importance for the defence because it blocked passage from the Barrikady's rear (western) gates, covered two houses on the other side of Arbatovskaya street and also allowed a large part of Pribaltiskaya street to be controlled. Sergeant Svidrov was warned that the house had to be held at any price.

On 24 October, Svidrov and his four men took up position in the house. Senior-Sergeant Yusupov, a Kazakh, was senior in age and rank, but the gaunt black-haired Svidrov was in command[9]. The five men were armed with three rifles, two submachine-guns, a Degtyarev light machine-gun and dozens of grenades. They also carried with them a burzhuika [a small, makeshift iron stove, used during a fuel crisis] and enough water, bread and tinned food to last a few days. When the small group moved into the house, the second floor had been utterly demolished by shells, but the ground floor and cellar were still intact. Instinctively assessing the most defensible areas, Svidrov and his men braced themselves for the inevitable German onslaught. They had only been in the house for a short time when the Germans launched a series of fierce attacks that lasted until nightfall. The Soviets inflicted casualties on the Germans and, eventually, repelled all of the attacks without loss.

Above: Ivan Ilyich Svidrov, a 19-year-old Sergeant in 650th Rifle Regiment.

During the night, one of Svidrov's men – by the name of Yarokhovets – crept out of the house and supplemented the garrison's meagre arsenal by searching German corpses for food and weapons. He returned with an MP-40, two clips of ammunition and some bread. To prevent being caught by a surprise night-time raid, a line of empty cans was strung around the house. A sentry was placed while the remainder of the garrison tried to get some sleep.

The next morning, 25 October, the Germans once again threw themselves at the house. This time, the attack was paved by a volley of grenades, quickly followed up by teams of submachine-gunners. The Germans intended entering the house via the windows but were beaten back with grenades. The fierceness of the attack convinced Svidrov and his men that the

8. Svidrov, Sergeant Ivan Ilyich, 650th RR; born 26 June, 1923 in Obilnoye Sarpinsky district. Still alive in 2006.

9. Unlike the Germans, the Soviets did not strictly adhere to seniority and rank in determining who commanded a unit, as would be the case with Konovalenko commanding 344th Rifle Regiment. See pages 68-9.

Germans were drunk. Several more attacks were thrown back during the day. Later that night, as if to underline the importance of the house, the commander of 138th Rifle Division, Colonel Lyudnikov, dropped in on Svidrov's garrison during a midnight inspection tour of various strongpoints of Major Pechenyuk's 650th Rifle Regiment. Svidrov smartly reported to Lyudnikov that his garrison was performing its duty and provided numbers of German soldiers killed. Senior-Sergeant Yusupov was cooking a soldier's pilaff made from dried bread mixed

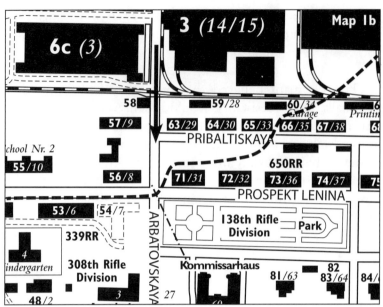

Svidrov and his garrison in Dom 31 were able to dominate the area, including the rear gates from the Barrikady factory. They anchored the left flank of the entire division: to their left was 339th Rifle Regiment (308th Rifle Division).

with tinned food. He removed the mess-tin from the cooker and said to Svidrov:

"Vanya, shall we treat the Colonel to a meal?"

Like any good host, Svidrov was embarrassed by the paltry offering. Yusupov turned to Lyudnikov and said, "When we crush Hitler, you come to our collective farm and there'll be such a pilaff that... that..."

He was at a loss for words to describe the pilaff he would give Lyudnikov. The commander thanked the soldiers, wished them success and continued on his inspection tour.

The next day passed precisely like the previous one: multiple German attacks were successfully repelled without loss to the defenders. The morning of 27 October, however, began differently from the others – no German attacks. Svidrov thought he had a good understanding of the Germans: they never attacked at night, they always enjoyed a good sleep followed by breakfast with a large measure of alcohol, as a rule they were always intoxicated when attacking... and they always launched their attacks in the morning. Perhaps Svidrov's beliefs of German tactics clouded his judgement and upset the established defensive routine, because when the Germans did finally hurl themselves at the house at noon, the Soviet defence was caught slightly off guard. The garrison repelled the first few attacks but were unable to completely regroup before the next assault rolled in. As the sun descended behind the massive workhalls, the Germans pushed right up to the house and lobbed grenades through the windows. They also advanced past the house and captured several buildings behind it, effectively cutting off Svidrov and his garrison from the rest of their regiment.

Major Pechenyuk[10], commander of 650th Rifle Regiment, rang Lyudnikov and, after reporting on the difficult situation in his sector, said, "You know that brick house where you were; it's now in the Germans' rear. But we can hear its garrison returning fire. I know these lads – they won't surrender as long as there's life in them."

---

10. Pechenyuk, Major Fedor Iosifovich, HotSU; 650th RR; born 1906 in Torchin, Zhitomir region. Died 26 January, 1965.

Lyudnikov was subsequently told that the garrison had perished.

Hours of combat had depleted almost all of the ammunition in Svidrov's house. Only a few grenades remained. The Germans gathered outside the building, hurled grenades through the windows, clambered inside and sprayed everything with automatic fire. Three men of the garrison were killed whilst valiantly trying to defend themselves without ammunition. With the Germans inside the house and also surrounding it, there was only one way for Svidrov and his mate Yusupov to escape, and that was to scurry down to the cellar via the stairwell in the middle of the house. The Germans saw the pair flee down the stairs. Cautiously approaching the stairwell entrance, they pitched half a dozen stick-grenades down into the darkness… and then did nothing. Experience had taught the Germans that it was suicide to go down into a dark cellar, especially after night had fallen. Hoping that the two Russians in the cellar were either dead or severely wounded, the Germans took no further action, and soon, their attention was diverted by other events.

Down in the dim cellar that reeked of powdered brick and cordite, Svidrov and Yusupov huddled against the rear wall, rifles in hand, grenades next to them. They were bleeding from multiple fragment wounds but both were absolutely determined to dig in their heels and sell their lives as dearly as possible. The Soviet line was still being held, even though it was underground. They could hear the Germans moving about overhead and wondered what deviousness was being planned to wheedle them out. Hours passed and still nothing happened. Suddenly, a gunfight erupted upstairs. Grenades thumped. Guttural Germanic shouts rang out, then Russian voices were heard.

"Our boys… they're here!"

An assault team led by Captain Korolev, a battalion commander in 650th Rifle Regiment, had counterattacked and reached the house. Svidrov and Yusupov crept up the stairs and entered the swirling melee. Muzzle flashes and grenade bursts illuminated the savage skirmish. Shadows flitted across the room. Screams filtered through the gunfire. Korolev's raid caught the Germans by surprise and the confusion was doubled when the two Russians from the cellar appeared amongst it all. Germans and Soviets alike were killed by grenades and blindly-fired volleys: Svidrov and Yusupov were both seriously wounded and shell-shocked, but the counterattack had been successful. Dom 31 was once again back in Soviet hands. Captain Korolev assigned a new garrison to take over the house and prepare it for defence. Stocks of food and ammunition were laid on. Thus the defence of Dom 31 was carried on, this time by a new generation of defenders.

Following their narrow escape from almost certain death, Svidrov and Yusupov were carried to a first-aid post near the water pump on the bank of the Volga river and later transported across in different boats. Neither man was in any state to report to headquarters that the garrison had carried out its mission, but both men certainly knew that they had. In hospital, Svidrov heard that he and his garrison had been considered entirely lost and their relatives had even been notified about their deaths. It was only many years later that Svidrov and Yusupov each learned that the other had survived… and only when the 20th anniversary of the battle was being celebrated in Volgograd[11] did Lyudnikov once again meet Svidrov and learn about the final heroic act of 'Svidrov's garrison'.

This was a battle for one house held by five men over a four-day period. There were

---

11. In 1961, the city of Stalingrad was renamed Volgograd as part of Nikita Khruschev's 'De-Stalinisation' program. Currently, there is a growing movement within Volgograd to rename the city Stalingrad, in memory of the rapidly disappearing Soviet veterans of the battle and the Great Patriotic War.

dozens more houses like Dom 31, many hundreds more men like Svidrov and Yusupov but only a few short weeks until the dreaded Russian winter set in. The Germans were keenly aware that once winter arrived, the initiative would swing over to the Soviets, whose men and equipment were better suited for offensive operations in the harsh Russian climate.

– – –

As October drew to a close, the German attacks ground mercilessly forward, consuming enormous quantities of manpower and ammunition for increasingly minor gains. On 27 October, 305. Infanterie-Division suffered casualties of 1 officer[12] and 12 men killed, and 70 men wounded, a total of 83 men. The next day, 28 October, 1 officer[13] and 26 men were killed, 1 officer[14] and 84 men were wounded, and 1 officer and 13 men were missing, a total of 126 men. This was an appalling number of casualties, especially for a division that had been embroiled in two full weeks of ruthless city fighting. The Volga had to be reached regardless of losses if all Soviet resistance was to be stamped out, so, on 29 October, another attack was launched. Once again the Soviet soldiers – supported by massive barrages of artillery, rocket and mortar fire – doggedly defended themselves. The German assault groups barely moved forward in bitter house-to-house combat. Only after many hours of fighting did the Germans capture several buildings in the row of houses along Lenin Prospekt, just south-east of the gun factory (grid square 83d1). 305. Infanterie-Division also had to repel determined Soviet counterattacks out of the gullies north and south of the fuel installation. The fight against rekindled nests of Soviet resistance in the fuel installation area continued well into the night.

These small gains cost the division 1 officer[15] and 37 men killed, 2 officers[16] and 93 men wounded, and 5 men missing, a total of 138 men. At the completion of the day's fighting, the division reported that without the supply of additional forms of support, they no longer possessed the strength to continue reducing the enemy bridgehead. Their attacks were therefore halted. The only positive news for the division was that a convalescent company had just arrived in Gumrak. However, it only had 260 men – barely enough to make good the losses sustained in the previous two days of inconsequential fighting.

– – –

By the end of October, the assault troops in Stalingrad could no longer be supported in the lavish manner to which they had become accustomed. Ammunition stocks were low, particularly hand grenades and mortar ammunition. Combat strengths had dropped alarmingly, so much so that on 29 October, Generaloberst Friedrich Paulus[17], commander-in-chief of 6. Armee, even suggested using excess panzer crews as infantry. Panzer officers were appalled at the suggestion of using these invaluable men in this manner: their highly

---

12. Geissler, Hauptmann Karl, 3./Gr.Rgt.578; born 14 February, 1910 in Friedberg. Killed in action, 27 October, 1942.
13. Beinert, Leutnant Jakob, 3./Gr.Rgt.577; born 17 March, 1921 in Hesselhurst. Killed in action, 29 October, 1942 in Stalingrad.
14. Fortsch, Leutnant, Stab Gr.Rgt.578.
15. Baenerle, Oberleutnant Hans, 6./Gr.Rgt.577; born 6 September, 1910 in Schopfheim. Killed in action, 29 October, 1942 in Stalingrad.
16. Denz, Major Fritz, I./Gr.Rgt.576; born 8 May, 1909 in Brunnadern. No further information known; and Kolb, Oblt. Konrad, 7./Gr.Rgt.577; born 6 October, 1913 in Stein/Franken. Died of wounds, 30 October, 1942 in Gorodische.
17. Paulus, Generalfeldmarschall Friedrich, EL, RK; 6. Armee; born 23 September, 1890 in Breitenau bei Melsungen. Died 1 February, 1957 in Dresden.

specialised training should have automatically excluded them from being tossed into the inferno in any capacity other than as panzer crews. To raise their combat strengths without resorting to Paulus's draconian measure, panzer divisions combed out rear area offices and supply trains for the requisite quantity of warm bodies, thus sparing the panzer crews from dangerous front-line duty as infantrymen.

6. Armee constantly struggled with plans on how to shift around its combat forces in Stalingrad and how to best use their limited resources to take the last major enemy bridgehead in the city. The situation east of the Barrikady Gun Factory did not affect the army's main goal of assembling enough strength to take the Lazur Chemical Factory. This was considered much more important than clearing up a few small bridgeheads in order to obtain a clean line along the Volga.

Whatever path 6. Armee chose, it was of vital importance to have the hard-hitting support of the Luftwaffe's bomber and Stuka squadrons for all offensive operations. Some members of the air arm, particularly the Commander-in-Chief of Luftflotte 4, Generaloberst Wolfram Freiherr von Richthofen[18], were critical of the army's performance. A good working relationship between the two branches was absolutely crucial for success, and some fence-mending was in order. Paulus needed to find a way to both assemble sufficient forces to take the chemical factory and placate the Luftwaffe. At 0745 hours on 1 November, Generaloberst Paulus and his chief-of-staff, General Arthur Schmidt, left Armee HQ in a plane bound for the advanced airstrip of VIII. Fliegerkorps at Razgulyayevka railway station. They had a meeting there that would eventually prove to be the genesis of the drama to follow. After landing at the airfield, they were chauffeured to the advanced command post of VIII. Fliegerkorps in the Razgulyayevka brickworks, arriving at 0830 hours. Already present was the Commanding General of LI. Armeekorps, General der Artillerie Walther von Seydlitz-Kurzbach[19], as well as his chief-of-staff Oberst i.G. Hans Clausius[20] and several other staff officers. Arriving a short time later was the fiery Generaloberst von Richthofen and the Commanding General of VIII. Fliegerkorps, Generalleutnant Martin Fiebig[21]. It is obvious from von Richthofen's own diary that he was frustrated by the slow progress in Stalingrad and it seemed he was spoiling for a fight:

> Early this morning I went to the fighter airfield and from there on to a conference with Paulus and Seydlitz. I told them that proper use of the air arm was not being made, 'because the artillery won't fire and the infantry makes no attempt at all to exploit the air raids to their advantage. We drop our bombs on enemy positions less than a hand grenade's throw from the infantry, but they do nothing.' They trotted out all the same old arguments, which are only partly true: numerical weaknesses, lack of training in this type of warfare, shortage of ammunition and so on. I said that I would place transport at their disposal for ammunition supplies and would use my influence to see that properly trained reinforcements would be forthcoming… The real explanation is to be found in the weariness of both troops and command and in that rigid army conservatism, which still tolerates only 1,000 men in the

---

18. Richthofen, Generalfeldmarschall Wolfram Freiherr von, EL, RK; Luftflotte 4; born 10 October, 1895 in Barzdorf. Died 12 July, 1945 in Bad Ischl.

19. Seydlitz-Kurzbach, General der Artillerie Walther von, EL, RK; LI. Armeekorps; born 22 August, 1888 in Hamburg-Eppendorf. Died 28 April, 1976 in Bremen.

20. Clausius, Oberst i.G. Hans, DKiG; LI. Armeekorps; born 6 May, 1899 in Wittenberg. Missing in action, 25 January, 1943 in Stalingrad.

21. Fiebig, General der Flieger Martin, EL, RK, DKiG; VIII. Fliegerkorps; born 7 May, 1891 in Rösnitz, Silesia. Executed 24 October, 1957 in Belgrad.

front-line out of a divisional ration strength of 12,000, and which leads to the generals being content merely to issue orders, without bothering to go into any detail or making sure that the preparations required for this type of fighting are properly made. That is what I told Paulus, who, of course, didn't like it, but couldn't refute the truth of it…

The harsh criticism levelled at the army and its command by von Richthofen was certainly unfair, especially when the hideous casualties suffered by the men on the ground were taken into consideration. Likewise, the fanatical doggedness displayed by Soviet soldiers was not apparent from the cockpit of a plane. Apart from a very brief mention in Paulus's trip notes that simply stated there were 'lengthy conversations', there is unfortunately no record of what Paulus, Schmidt or von Seydlitz thought about the tempestuous meeting. This 'lengthy conversation' lasted close to three hours and was only broken off because the two commanders-in-chief had other meetings.

After arranging to meet again later in the day, Paulus and von Richthofen parted ways at 1115 hours. Paulus and Schmidt headed off to inspect Sturmgeschütz-Abteilung 244 south-east of Gumrak railway station, followed by a trip to the command post of 295. Infanterie-Division for a conversation with its commander, Generalmajor Rolf Wuthmann[22]. At 1300 hours, Paulus and Schmidt arrived at von Seydlitz's corps command post at Gumrak railway station. Generaloberst von Richthofen, returning from an inspection tour, pulled up at the same moment. Again, no details about this meeting are written in Paulus's trip notes, but instead of being labelled a 'Besprechung'[23], as the morning meeting had been, this latter conference was curiously described as an 'Unterredung'[24]. Perhaps a sign of Paulus's exasperation with the hot-tempered airman? The meeting lasted for two hours. Arriving one hour into the conference – at 1400 hours – was the Commanding General of XIV. Panzerkorps, General der Panzertruppe Hans Hube[25], and the Divisionsführer of 305. Infanterie-Division, Oberst i.G. Bernhard Steinmetz[26]. The units of both these men were scheduled to play a part in Paulus's plan: Hube was there because one of his divisions – 60. Infanterie-Division (mot.) – was to be used in the city. Because it occupies a considerable number of lines in the war diary of 6. Armee, it seems that von Richthofen reiterated his earlier proposal of placing Luftwaffe transport space at the army's disposal:

> Because of the narrowness of the area along the bank of the Volga, the Luftwaffe can no longer be employed very effectively. The Luftwaffe is therefore willing to relinquish some of its railway haulage space and supply columns to the army so that more artillery ammunition can be brought forward and the artillery can then be more aggressively deployed.

Absolutely no mention of von Richthofen's other offer to "use [his] influence to see that properly trained reinforcements would be forthcoming" can be found in 6. Armee records for 1 November 1942, yet, his offer to relinquish haulage space is mentioned several times.

Was von Richthofen's offer to obtain reinforcements not taken seriously by Paulus? Had it seemed to Paulus like a passing remark that didn't merit any attention? Whatever

22. Wuthmann, General der Artillerie Rolf, RK, DKiG; 295.Inf.Div.; born 26 August, 1893 in Kassel. Died 20 October, 1977 in Minden.

23. Trans.: 'Besprechung' = conference, discussion or meeting.

24. Trans.: 'Unterredung' = 'interview' or 'discussion', but can also mean 'to parley', as with an enemy.

25. Hube, General der Panzertruppe Hans, Brillanten, Schwerter, EL, RK; XIV. Panzerkorps; born 29 October, 1890 in Naumburg an der Saale. Died 21 April, 1944 in an air crash.

26. Steinmetz, Generalleutnant Bernhard, DKiG; 305. Inf.Div.; born 13 August, 1896 in Neuenkirchen. Died 22 January, 1981 in Minden.

Paulus thought of it, and regardless of whether he agreed with it or not, von Richthofen took it upon himself to demand properly-trained units for use in Stalingrad. Soon after returning to his command post that evening, von Richthofen telephoned Generaloberst Hans Jeschonnek[27], Chief of the General Staff of the Luftwaffe, at the Führer's 'Wolfsschanze' headquarters in East Prussia and demanded the immediate dispatch of four pioneer assault battalions. Jeschonnek was von Richthofen's inside line to Hitler and enabled him to bypass all other channels and directly access the Führer himself. Jeschonnek assured von Richthofen that his request would be submitted to Hitler the next day, but – as will be shown later – the 'request' arrived on Hitler's desk shortly after their conversation. The seed had been planted.

- - -

Paulus and Schmidt left the meeting at 1500 hours and flew back to army headquarters at Golubinsky, completely ignorant of the fact that von Richthofen was about to meddle in their affairs. They were satisfied that they had touched base with the relevant commanders of those units scheduled to take part in the proposed assault. They put their plan in writing and it was as follows: fresh assault forces would be garnered by having 24. Panzer-Division lengthen its front so that 305. Infanterie-Division could be pulled out of the main fighting line on 4 to 5 November. After a few days of rest, 305. Infanterie-Division would then 'move into its winter positions' by relieving 60. Infanterie-Division on Stalingrad's northern front on 8 to 9 November. 60. Infanterie-Division (mot.) would receive a week's rest and then be ready for use in the city. This division, although on the 'quieter' northern blocking position between the Don and Volga rivers, had still suffered huge casualties whilst repelling the massive armadas of Soviet tanks that lumbered down from the north[28]. The division could not be considered fresh by any stretch of the imagination, but when compared to the battered divisions in the city, it still had quite a lot of strength[29]. It was thought that the division could bring into action 3 to 4 reinforced battalions and 9 artillery batteries for the attack on the chemical factory. Slated to help them were a regiment-sized assault group formed from elements of 295. Infanterie-Division, a reinforced regiment from 100. Jäger-Division and 3 assault companies originating from other divisions. At 1800 hours, 6. Armee chief-of-staff Generalleutnant Schmidt called General von Sodenstern[30], chief-of-staff of Heeresgruppe B, to discuss the question of "how the attack on Stalingrad can be nourished with new forces, since the strength of 79. Infanterie-Division has declined so far that it can no longer be considered for larger missions". After running through the overall assessment of the situation at Stalingrad, Schmidt then stated that, "79. Infanterie-Division was still in a position to hold its current front-line but could not lead the attack on the chemical factory". He continued: "On the other hand, we must prepare so thoroughly for this final action that we punch

---

27. Jeschonnek, Generaloberst Hans RK; Chef d.Gen.Stab d. Luftwaffe; born 9 April, 1899 in Hohensalza. Committed suicide 19 August, 1943 in Führerhauptquartier, East Prussia.

28. In the last ten days of October alone, the division lost over 130 dead and 300 wounded… and these losses were minor compared to those incurred during the August and September fighting.

29. A report from 2 November, 1942 states it had 6 grenadier battalions: 2 medium-strength, 1 average, 2 weak and 1 battle-weary, plus 9 artillery batteries: 6 light, 3 heavy. It was 'Bedingt zum Angriff geeignet' – conditionally suited for attack.

30. Sodenstern, General der Infanterie Georg von, RK, DKiG; Heeresgruppe B; born 15 November, 1889 in Kassel. Died 22 July, 1955 in Frankfurt a.Main.

right through. We can only do this by taking a division from XIV. Panzerkorps."

Schmidt then laid out the full plan of using 305. Infanterie-Division to relieve 60. Infanterie-Division so that the latter could be deployed as the main spearhead of the proposed attack. He finished by saying that the earliest the attack could begin was 15 November. General von Sodenstern's reply left Schmidt in no doubt as to what Heeresgruppe B thought of the plan: "Timewise, that is of course fairly catastrophic…" With that rebuff, Schmidt turned to the serious ammunition situation of the army and informed von Sodenstern of von Richthofen's proposal to relinquish Luftwaffe trains and supply columns so that more ammunition could be brought forward. Schmidt said: "This proposal seems to be correct from our perspective. We will of course use the intervening period to make small improvements to the front-line." Finally, General von Sodenstern told Schmidt that "the Heeresgruppe can no longer help with fresh units". Nothing had been resolved – 6. Armee was still in limbo.

– – –

Matters had not been settled to 6. Armee's liking because barely an hour later, at 1900 hours, Paulus himself phoned Generaloberst von Weichs[31], commander-in-chief of Heeresgruppe B. Paulus reiterated what his chief-of-staff had already said:

> Because the strength of 79. Infanterie-Division is no longer sufficient for the final act, we have to bring forward another division. We have therefore designated 60. Infanterie-Division.

Paulus rammed home his point by bluntly stating that without this, the 'final act' – as he called it – could not be carried out. Generaloberst von Weichs then made a suggestion he thought could solve the matter. "How would the Armee react to the proposal of receiving two regiments from 29. Infanterie-Division, but without artillery?" Paulus was pleased:

> This solution is definitely better. We only require infantry strength [author's emphasis]. We will nevertheless still try to get 79. Infanterie-Division ready for the final attack. Once the chemical factory and the bank of the Volga are in our hands, the large workhalls can be strangulated.

Finally, Paulus mentioned that Generaloberst von Richthofen's proposal was 'unselfish' and seemed to be 'very favourable' for the army, whereupon their conversation ended. Paulus was satisfied that a solution had been found.

Barely fifteen minutes later, at 1920 hours, Oberst i.G. August Winter[32], Ia of Heeresgruppe B, called General Schmidt at 6. Armee:

> In reference to the preceding discussions: 6. Armee can still implement its plan of extracting 60. Infanterie-Division regardless of whether 29. Infanterie-Division is employed for the final assault. Perhaps 60. Infanterie-Division can be supplied to 4. Panzerarmee?

Generaloberst von Weichs was somewhat reluctant to hand over two regiments from 29. Infanterie-Division because at that moment the division was one of his most powerful mobile reserves, ready to intervene in the sectors of both 4. Panzerarmee and 3. Romanian Armee. This solution put his mind at ease. All proposals, however, needed to be submitted to and approved by the Army High Command. Heeresgruppe B sent off the appropriate communiqués that evening.

---

31. Weichs an der Glon, Generalfeldmarschall Maximilian Reichsfreiherr von und zu, EL, RK; born 12 November, 1881 in Dessau. Died 27 September, 1954 in Burg Rösberg bei Bonn.
32. Winter, General der Gebirgstruppe, August, DKiG; Ia Heeresgruppe B; born 18 January, 1897 in München. Died 16 February, 1979 in München.

- - -

The seed planted by von Richthofen was quickly taking root. As with von Richthofen, Hitler too was frustrated by the snail-like progress at Stalingrad and wanted the whole affair over and done with before winter set in. When von Richthofen's 'demand' for four pioneer assault battalions landed on his desk, Hitler seized upon it immediately. It was precisely to his liking – Hitler had a penchant for unusual methods of warfare and loved specialist troops. Assault pioneers, he decided, would be just the thing to wrap up the bloody business at Stalingrad.

In his telephone conversation with Jeschonnek, von Richthofen had been assured that his request would be presented to Hitler the next day, on 2 November. All published sources implicitly state that Hitler was first presented with this request during his daily situation conference on 2 November 1942. Indeed, the OKW war diary reads as follows:

> Hitler turned down the request to supply 29. Infanterie-Division (mot.) to Stalingrad, but agreed to the proposal of the Chefs Generalstab das Heeres[33] to extract pioneer battalions from other divisions and deploy them in Stalingrad.

Previously published accounts of these events all state that Hitler was first informed on 2 November 1942. However, hard evidence from three separate and extremely credible sources clearly shows that a decision to use the pioneer battalions had been reached – and acted on – during the night of 1 November 1942. The implications are stunning. Not only must Hitler have set the ball rolling scant hours after receiving von Richthofen's request, but a veneer of propriety and impartiality had been placed over the decision by having Zeitzler formally submit the request during the situation conference. Even more stunning is the fact that Paulus's 6. Armee – as well as its superior formation, Heeresgruppe B – had absolutely zero input into the request or decision.

The first piece of evidence is the '1 November 1942' entry from the war diary of 294. Infanterie-Division:

> At 2330 hours, an order from XXIX. Armeekorps arrived by telephone stating that Pionier-Bataillon 294 should be made ready as a Sturm-Bataillon for operations in Stalingrad. Transport will probably be by lorries or by air.

It is rather strange that 294. Infanterie-Division received this order from XXIX. Armeekorps because the division was not even part of the corps' structure – in fact, it was subordinated directly to Heeresgruppe B, and had been since 25 September 1942. Admittedly, 294. Infanterie-Division was in XXIX. Armeekorps' sector, but its direct report was still Heeresgruppe B.

The second piece of evidence is the entry from the war diary of 336. Infanterie-Division for 1 November 1942:

> At 2330 hours, a message arrived from Korps, whereby the removal of Pionier-Bataillon 336 by air should be reckoned on.

The 'Korps' being referred to is the very same XXIX. Armeekorps, to which the division had been subordinated since 21 July 1942.

The third piece of proof comes from the war diary of 62. Infanterie-Division, where it reports about a message that came into its HQ in Meshkov at midnight on 1-2 November:

---

33. Zeitzler, Generaloberst Kurt, RK; Chef d. Gen.Stab d. Heeres; born 9 June, 1895 in Cossmar/Luckau. Died 24 September, 1963.

Around midnight, the chief-of-staff[54] of the German General near 8. Italian Armee[35] ordered that Pionier-Bataillon 162 should be ready by 1200 hours for transportation by air or vehicle. It is presumed that the battalion will be employed in Stalingrad.

All three of these divisions were in the area of 8. Italian Armee, which was subordinated to Heeresgruppe B. Moreover, XXIX. Armeekorps, which had issued the order to two of the divisions, was part of the Italian army. Therefore, it seems likely that all three orders to send the pioneer battalions to Stalingrad emanated from the staff of the German general attached to the Italian army, and indeed, the daily report of the German general for 3 November noted that "German pioneer battalions within the realm of 8. Italian Armee were designated for this purpose". Unfortunately, because the records of Heeresgruppe B no longer exist, it is impossible to declare with absolute certainty that it did not know about these orders being given to units under its command. However, by the content and tone of its messages to 6. Armee the next day, it seems clear that Heeresgruppe B was also in the dark. An order such as this should go from the top down, cascading through the various levels of command. At the very least Heeresgruppe B should have been informed. It seems as though they were being purposely kept out of the loop: official reporting channels were being sidestepped.

2 November, 1942

The proposal to use four pioneer battalions at Stalingrad – upon which Hitler had already acted – was formally submitted during the Führer's daily briefing, no doubt for the benefit of the others present. Also put to him were the suggestions formulated by Heeresgruppe B and 6. Armee for the continuation of the offensive in Stalingrad, namely the relief of 60. Infanterie-Division (mot.) and the supply of two regiments from 29. Infanterie-Division (mot.) for use in an attack on the chemical factory. As mentioned in the OKW war diary, Hitler turned down the request to send 29. Infanterie-Division (mot.) to Stalingrad but agreed to the proposal put forward by General Zeitzler to extract pioneer battalions from other divisions and deploy them in Stalingrad. A third proposal, to halt the attack for eight days so the troops could recover, was also knocked back. For yet another unknown reason, Heeresgruppe B and 6. Armee were not informed of Hitler's denial of their suggestions.

At an undetermined point during the day, probably mid-afternoon, OKH finally called Heeresgruppe B to inform them about the possibility of using the pioneer battalions. At 1645 hours, General von Sodenstern called General Schmidt to update him on what was happening. Von Sodenstern started out by saying that apart from the two previously discussed suggestions for the reactivation of combat in Stalingrad, there existed a third possibility, namely that 6. Armee could have four pioneer battalions flown in by air from other sectors of the army group. Schmidt replied that the best solution would be to fly in the pioneer battalions in addition to supplying the two grenadier regiments of 29. Infanterie-Division (mot.). Moreover, Schmidt continued, 60. Infanterie-Division (mot.) would be pulled out of the line regardless. From the tone of this message, it seems clear that Heeresgruppe B did not know

---

34. Nagel, Generalmajor Walter; Chef d. Gen.Stab d. dtsch. General b. d. 8. ital. Armee; born 27 February, 1901 in Hannover. No further information known.
35. Tippelskirch, General der Infanterie Kurt von, EL, RK; deutsche Generals b. d. 8. ital. Armee; born 9 October, 1891 in Charlottenburg. Died 10 May, 1957 in Lüneburg.

that the third 'possibility' had already been approved by the Führer.

At 1700 hours, only fifteen minutes after the phone call to General Schmidt, Heeresgruppe B transmitted the order to 294. Infanterie-Division that its pioneer battalion was to be sent to Stalingrad. The order stated that the battalion would make its way to the Rossosh airfield while its commander and adjutant would go on ahead via car to Kalach to make contact with 6. Armee. Heeresgruppe B also wanted to immediately know the transport strength of the battalion.

At 2030 hours, the commander of Pionier-Bataillon 336, Hauptmann Hermann Lundt[36], received the order to report to Ilovskoye airfield (Nikolayevka) at 0900 hours the next day and fly straight to 6. Armee headquarters. Although records no longer exist, it is safe to assume the three other pioneer battalions received similar orders.

At 2045 hours, after the pioneer battalions had been notified, Oberst i.G. Winter, Ia of Heeresgruppe B, finally telephoned 6. Armee to inform them that Heeresgruppe had decided to supply the Armee with five pioneer battalions:

> Pz.Pi.Btl.50 and Pi.Btl.45 (mot.) will arrive via a land march, Pi.Btl.162 via lorries of an Italian column, Pi.Btle.336 and 294 will be brought in by air.

– – –

In the midst of all this high-level manoeuvring, the bloodletting and futile assaults against the battered ruins of Stalingrad continued. It was hoped that these types of attacks would finally end once the pioneer units spearheaded a powerful attack against the Lazur factory bridgehead and wrapped up this messy Stalingrad business once and for all. Until then, pressure had to be maintained.

At 1055 hours on 1 November, LI. Armeekorps issued Korpsbefehl No. 102 which began by stating that "at daybreak on 2.11., 305. Infanterie-Division, together with the southern wing of 389. Infanterie-Division, will renew the attack and gain the Volga bank". Apart from counting on support from Korps-Art.-Gruppe Nord (Stiegler[37]), the attacking divisions were allocated additional support: 305. Infanterie-Division would receive Sturmgeschütz-Abteilung 244 with the new s.I.G.[38], one company of self-propelled anti-tank guns from Panzerjäger-Abteilung 4 (14. Panzer-Division) and a company of panzers from 24. Panzer-Division; 389. Infanterie-Division would receive Sturmgeschütz-Abteilung 245[39], and a company of self-propelled anti-tank guns from Panzerjäger-Abteilung 40 (24. Panzer-Division). Plenty of heavy direct-fire support.

Just as the sun was rising on 2 November, 305. and 389. Infanterie-Divisions hurled themselves yet again at the bulge of land that stood between themselves and the Volga. By 0930 hours, Grenadier-Regiment 576 had struck fierce resistance south of the fuel installation and was unable to reach the bank of the Volga. North of them, Grenadier-Regiment 578 was able to occupy a few blocks of houses. Further north, the attack of Grenadier-Regiment 546 (389. Infanterie-Division) south of the brickworks only made slow progress.

---

36. Lundt, Hauptmann Hermann; Pi.Btl.336; born 14 May, 1908 in Kiel. Missing in action, 2 February, 1943 in Stalingrad. See Appendix 2 (page 575) and Appendix 5 (page 584) for more details.
37. Stiegler, Oberstleutnant; Höhere-Arko 310.
38. The battalion had 3 long-barrels, 7 short-barrels and 3 s.I.G. operational, but the new sIG33Bs would not be used in this attack despite being included in 305. Infanterie-Division's assault plan.
39. The battalion had 1 long-barrel and 3 short-barrels operational.

As the battle raged, Paulus made another front-line inspection[40]. He flew into the airstrip at Razgulyayevka railway station and reached his advance command post at 0900 hours. He immediately phoned von Seydlitz, who oriented him about the progress of the attack of 305. and 389. Infanterie-Divisions. Paulus decided to visit both these divisions. At 0930 hours, he reached the command post of 305. Infanterie-Division and was briefed by the division's chief-of-staff, Oberstleutnant i.G. Heinrich Kodré[41]. Paulus learned about the slow and costly progress of the division's grenadier regiments. Paulus was on his way after only ten minutes, this time to pay a visit to Generalmajor Erich Magnus[42], the newly appointed commander of 389. Infanterie-Division. At General Magnus' advanced command post, it was reported that Grenadier-Regiment 546's

Oberstleutnant i.G. Heinrich Kodré, chief-of-staff 305. Infanterie-Division, and his commander, Generalmajor Kurt Oppenländer, during the opening days of Operation 'Blau'.

attack south of the brickworks was still in progress. As Paulus was leaving, a staff officer from Höhere-Arko 310 approached and recommended the transfer of a 15cm battery from the area of 4. Panzer-Armee.[43]

Despite the attack being supported by massive firepower, it was obviously still not enough. All suggestions and impressions gathered by Paulus during these front-line inspections would play their part in his approach toward organising later attacks. At 1010 hours, Paulus was at the command post of 14. Panzer-Division where its chief-of-staff, Oberstleutnant i.G. Bernd von Pezold[44], provided a very grave description of the strained situation resulting from the ongoing heavy casualties.

Paulus's next stop was the command post of Artillerie-Regiment 83, where he arrived at 1100 hours. Its commander, Oberst Albrecht Czimatis[45], reported about the employment

40. This trip will be covered in detail because the extreme difficulties of combat in the ruins of Stalingrad were clearly expressed to Paulus by the various units, and these must certainly have had some affect on his thinking.

41. Kodré, Oberstleutnant i.G. Heinrich, RK; 305.Inf.Div., born 8 August, 1899 in Wien. Died 22 May, 1977 in Linz.

42. Magnus, Generalmajor Erich; 389.Inf.Div.; born 31 July, 1892 in Danzig. Died 6 August, 1979 in Hamburg.

43. This was eventually ordered on 6 November 1942.

44. Pezold, Oberstleutnant i.G. Bernd von; 14.Pz.Div.; born 10 September, 1906 in Reval. Died 12 July, 1973 in Niederfüllbach.

45. Czimatis, Oberst Albrecht, DKiG; Art.Rgt.83; born 18 April, 1897 in Kattowitz. Died 22 December, 1984 in Freiburg i.B.

of the subordinated artillery. A radio post of the regiment had intercepted a Soviet radio message broadcast in the clear from a battalion staff in the steel factory. Of 550 Russian replacements that had crossed the river, only half of them reached their destination without being killed or wounded. Oberst Czimatis then gave Paulus his impression of the situation: "Stuka and artillery preparations for our own attacks could not be better. The striking power of our infantry and the training for such tasks, however, is not adequate." These were statements that von Richthofen would have wholeheartedly agreed with.

On the road again, he reached the command post of 79. Infanterie-Division in Razgulyayevka at 1140 hours. The division reported that it had sustained further heavy casualties. Also, the commander of Grenadier-Regiment 226, Oberst Andreas von Aulock[46], had dropped out due to illness. Paulus returned to his advanced command post at noon for a meeting with General von Seydlitz. He talked about his impressions gathered during the day and considered postponing the final mopping-up actions between steel factory and Volga bank until after the attack on the large railway loop at Lazur. General von Seydlitz spoke about the details of the planning and preparation for this. At 1310 hours, Paulus climbed into his plane and flew back to Armee HQ at Golubinsky.

While their commanders were talking, the troops were still caught up in savage combat. South of the brickworks, elements of 389. Infanterie-Division struggled forward to the Volga against a doggedly defending Soviet enemy. The Volga bank, from the tractor factory down to about 200 metres south of the brickworks, was in German hands. The fighting along the riverside cliff was still in progress at nightfall. Two Soviet resistance nests on the southern tip of the brickworks could not be cleared up. The units of 389. Infanterie-Division suffered heavy losses: 19 men killed, 42 men wounded and 3 men missing.

Further south, 305. Infanterie-Division slogged forward against bitter Soviet resistance that was backed up by heavy fire from the Volga island. Only a few buildings and some small patches of ground were gained. So fierce was the Soviet defence that 305. Infanterie-Division had the impression that the enemy was superior in both numbers and quantity of weapons. Once darkness fell, Soviet counterattacks against Grenadier-Regiment 576 on the division's right flank – near the fuel installation – led to the loss of some of the ground that had been seized at such cost in the morning. Casualties for the division were again high: 44 men killed, 3 officers[47] and 116 men wounded, and 1 man missing.

Holding the ground between the Barrikady Gun Factory and Krasny Oktyabr Steel Factory was 14. Panzer-Division. The terrain here consisted mostly of uneven ground, dirt roads and the remains of hundreds of wooden huts, now broken and splintered by thousands of artillery impacts. Soviet assault groups equipped with flamethrowers attacked towards the positions of Panzergrenadier-Regiment 108 but were repelled in vicious fighting. Throughout the day, the division lost 23 men killed, 1 officer and 67 men wounded, and 5 men missing.

In the northern part of the Krasny Oktyabr Steel Factory, the clearing up of the situation was hindered by a Soviet counterattack from one of the workhalls. The sudden Soviet thrust stalled the attack of 79. Infanterie-Division. The overall situation in the mutilated factory was already convoluted and only worsened when the Soviet counterattack captured one of

---

46. Aulock, Oberst Andreas von, EL, RK, DKiG; Gr.Rgt.226; born 23 March, 1893 in Kochelsdorf, Upper Silesia. Died 23 June, 1968 in Wiesbaden.

47. Bergmann, Unterarzt Dr., II./Gr.Rgt.577; Steinhauser, Hauptmann Richard, 8./Gr.Rgt.576; born 9 February, 1918 in Zell, Wiesental. Died of wounds, 2 November, 1942 in Gorodische; and Weber, Leutnant, II./Gr.Rgt.578.

the smaller workshops. Divisional staff could not obtain an accurate picture of the front-line.

At midday, two German assault groups moved off towards one another with the aim of meeting up and pinching off the Soviet intrusion. By 1630 hours, the two German groups were separated by only 100 metres and were able to shout out to each other. Any further advance, however, was hindered by ferocious Soviet resistance. Only once night fell did the two groups actually join up. The resulting pocket was scheduled to be cleaned up the next day. The weakened division had incurred further painful losses: 1 officer[48] and 26 men killed, and 1 officer[49] and 55 men wounded.

From the four divisions involved in the 2 November assaults, over 400 men became casualties, all on a day of inconsequential

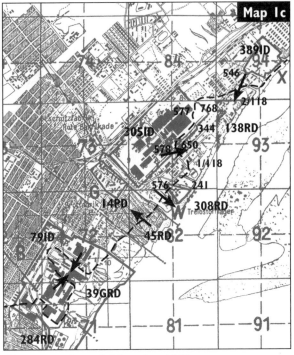

German attacks on 2 November, 1942.

fighting and minuscule gains of ground. To make matters worse for these battered divisions, the attacks were scheduled to continue the next day. The stated intention of LI. Armeekorps for 3 November was to "clean up the enemy breakthrough position at 79. Infanterie-Division" and to "continue the assault with the southern wing of 389. Infanterie-Division".

- - -

At 2200 hours, during the same evening of 2 November, Heeresgruppe B again called 294. Infanterie-Division and said that the embarkation of the battalion at Rossosh airfield was delayed and would only take place on 4 November. Half an hour later, 336. Infanterie-Division also received the official order:

> Transportation of the Pionier-Bataillon to Stalingrad on 4.11.1942.

Generaloberst von Richthofen's demand for pioneer battalions had been set in motion with surprising rapidity. After first being suggested on 1 November, it had been immediately and secretly approved by Hitler that same evening, officially approved on 2 November and orders sent out later that same day. While Heeresgruppe B and 6. Armee were quite happy at receiving the pioneers, neither thought these welcome reinforcements would be the solution to the ongoing stalemate. Both waited anxiously for word on their proposal to relieve 60. Infanterie-Division and insert two regiments from 29. Infanterie-Division into the attack plan – they harboured no illusions that the pioneer forces alone could decide the issue in Stalingrad. They received their answer the next day.

48. Greiff, Leutnant Rolf, 3./Gr.Rgt.226; born 9 November, 1922 in Wuppertal. Killed in action, 2 November, 1942 in Stalingrad.
49. Schönfeldt, Hauptmann Hans Joachim von, 4./Gr.Rgt.212; born 11 July, 1912 in Fritzlar. Died March 1943 in Frolov POW Camp.

3 November, 1942

Now that Paulus definitely knew he was getting the pioneer battalions, he needed to incorporate them into his attack plans in a way that would allow him to maximise their special training and capabilities. To do this, he needed to meet with the man who would control their deployment, General der Artillerie Walther von Seydlitz-Kurzbach. Paulus climbed into his Storch plane and flew to the command post of LI. Armeekorps north-west of Gumrak railway station, arriving there at 0915 hours.

Together with General von Seydlitz and his chief-of-staff Oberst i.G. Clausius, Paulus reviewed the requirements of the forces, the starting points and implementation possibilities for what they hoped would be the final assault on Stalingrad. Discussions moved back and forth about the ways in which the pioneer battalions could be used. General von Seydlitz laid down his opinion:

> A complete solution to this Stalingrad business is only possible through the addition of 4 grenadier battalions from 29. Infanterie-Division and the 5 pioneer battalions to the available forces. The attack must be as broad as possible. The narrow sectors of previous attacks led to a flanking effect on the core of the assault. Besides the forces on hand, if only the 5 pioneer battalions will be available – which will indeed allow a substantial improvement to the positions through the capture of individual objectives – then no final solution will be achieved.

Oberst Herbert Selle

General von Seydlitz could not have put it any more clearly. To gain a better perspective on the use of pioneers in city fighting, the Armeepionierführer, Oberst Herbert Selle[50], and the Korpspionierführer of LI. Armeekorps, Major Dr. Carl Romeis[51], were summoned, arriving at von Seydlitz's command post at 1045 hours. They reported their experiences with pioneer battalions in operations in Stalingrad. Because the pioneers were not equipped with heavy weapons, they could not take on the tasks of an infantry battalion and could only tackle their special assignments when incorporated into the framework of the infantry whom they were supporting. The opinions of these two pioneer experts gave Paulus fresh insight into the use of these specialist troops in Stalingrad. At 1145 hours, two and a half hours after the meeting started, Paulus departed.

At 1045 hours, while Paulus was away, General von Sodenstern called General Schmidt and advised him that he should definitely assume the infantry of 29. Infanterie-Division would not be made available by OKH. Heeresgruppe seemed to think that "this would not be bad at all because the army will have five pioneer battalions at its disposal". General Schmidt answered:

> The Commander-in-Chief [Paulus] has already taken this point into consideration and is discussing it with the Commanding General of LI. Armeekorps. General von Seydlitz – and the

---

50. Selle, Oberst Herbert, DKiG; A.Pi.Fü. 6. Armee; born 30 May, 1896 in Breddin. Died 18 March, 1988 in Ahrensburg.

51. Romeis, Major Dr. Carl, Ko.Pi.Fü. LI. Armeekorps; born 17 December, 1886 in München. Missing in action, 20 January, 1943 in Stalingrad.

Armee – share the point of view that the pioneer battalions can in no way be a substitute for infantry, because they are specialists. They are particularly accomplished in cracking bunkers and other larger objects, such as blocks of houses, as well as clearing gullies. However, they lack the strength of infantry. What is required in precisely this type of terrain – in accordance with the previously gained experiences in city fighting – are strong infantry forces to safeguard the flanks and to do the permanent mopping up of the area that has been broken through.

The pioneers' performance in the assault on the tractor factory on 14-15 October, 1942 had impressed von Richthofen and was the main reason why he suggested more battalions be brought in, but Schmidt pointed out the following to von Sodenstern:

> Only once during the battle for the northern part of Stalingrad has the Armee had an absolutely complete success, namely the operation against the massive tractor factory. Here, we were in a position to allow sufficient numbers of infantry to follow behind the pioneer and panzergrenadier spearheads.

General Schmidt stressed that "the army can only regard an attack without the subordination of 29. Infanterie-Division as an attempt because a definite chance for success cannot be seen with this solution". Nevertheless, he stated that everything would be done to exploit all possibilities and that apart from the 5 pioneer battalions, there would presumably still be a regiment (2 battalions) each from 295. Infanterie-Division and 100. Jäger-Division, 1 battalion from 79. Infanterie-Division and 3 assault companies (from 44. Infanterie-Division, 24. and 14. Panzer-Divisions). Schmidt concluded by stating 6. Armee's intention of withdrawing all dispensable mortars and infantry guns from the front-line and concentrating them for the attack.

General von Sodenstern immediately called Führer headquarters and put forward 6. Armee's case. No deliberation was needed: Hitler still refused to release elements of 29. Infanterie-Division. At 1100 hours, von Sodenstern called Schmidt again: "The employment of the two panzergrenadier regiments from 29. Infanterie-Division, in addition to the pioneer battalions, has been refused by the Führer." General Schmidt did not want to give up:

> Our assessment of the situation is as follows: if we are to only make do with the pioneer battalions, we'll certainly bring about a successful result, but it won't be the definitive conclusion. A remainder will be left that will require a new front to cover it. Infantry strength is lacking to initially pave the way for the pioneers up to the objectives and to subsequently take over the defence.

General von Sodenstern did not seem to be very sympathetic to 6. Armee's plight and implied that such a request was greedy:

> To begin with, LI. Armeekorps alone made the proposal, then 6. Armee said that the most important thing was to receive the panzergrenadier regiments of 29. Infanterie-Division, and then, when the possibility occurred of receiving the pioneer battalions instead, 6. Armee suddenly requests both.

Schmidt was forced to defend himself: "Casualties and experiences from the last few days have shown that 79. Infanterie-Division is finished and the pioneer battalions will not be strong enough." General von Sodenstern replied: "I cannot raise your hopes in regards to 29. Infanterie-Division. The assessment of 6. Armee, however, will of course be presented [to OKH]. What is your timetable then?" Schmidt: "We cannot begin before 9 or 10 November." General Schmidt then outlined the plans of 6. Armee:

> General von Seydlitz expressed the following opinion regarding the employment: if only the five new pioneer battalions are available, then it is arguably best to launch into the enemy from

the sides; first of all, 295. Infanterie-Division will gain the Volga bank in the south and then a thrust will be launched southward out of the steel factory. It is, however, quite possible that the Führer will order that the chemical factory be taken first with the new forces. In our opinion, this is equally important; perhaps because if one holds the chemical factory, then the rest can be taken next month. The situation will then be similar to that south of Stalingrad where we by and large hold the Volga except for some smaller bridgeheads.

Now that 6. Armee was certain it was going to receive the 5 pioneer battalions, preparations to receive them were swiftly implemented. At 1125 hours, General Schmidt sent out a written order to ensure that everything was prepared for the arrival of the first three battalions. The opening paragraph read:

> Pi.Btle.45 (mot.), 50 (from 22.Pz.Div.) and 162 (from 62. Inf.Div), which are being conveyed to 6. Armee during the course of the day, will be tactically subordinated to LI. Armeekorps upon their arrival at Kalach.

Recipients of the order included LI. Armeekorps, the three commanders of the pioneer battalions, Oberst Hans Mikosch[52], 6. Armee's Oberquartermeister[53] and its Armeepionierführer Oberst Selle. The commanders of the pioneer battalions were ordered to immediately contact LI. Armeekorps headquarters by telephone.

The main responsibility of Oberst Mikosch was to house the approximately 1400 men from these three battalions. They would be accommodated in army pioneer school lodgings in Kumenka, Pyatizbyansky and Malo-Luchka, three small riverside villages along the Don south of Kalach. If need be, the village of Kamyshevski [Kamyshi] in the steppe north of Kalach could also be used. Oberst Mikosch was granted full authority to provide accommodation for the pioneer battalions, including permission to temporarily clear out troops who were already occupying the lodgings. The arrival of the battalions would be continually reported to 6. Armee and LI. Armeekorps. Once the battalions were ready to be sent to Stalingrad, Oberst Mikosch was responsible for moving them to the east by ensuring a smooth crossing over the busy Don bridge near Kalach. The pioneers were to be given priority – all other traffic would stand back. To help him in the accomplishment of this task, Mikosch was given the appropriate decisional authority over the Kalach town commander.

Armeepionierführer Oberst Selle was responsible for the necessary arrangement and replenishment of pioneering equipment, such as flamethrowers. The pioneer battalions were directed to the army supply depot near the Chir railhead to collect rations, ammunition and fuel. In the Armeepionierschule, the battalion and company commanders would receive maps and aerial photos of their planned operational areas.

At 1130 hours, General von Sodenstern made a final call to General Schmidt, confirming once and for all the bad news for 6. Armee: "OKH has turned down the release of 29. Infanterie-Division for 6. Armee's attack." With this final pronouncement, 6. Armee was essentially denied a shot at success. Despite General Schmidt's convincing arguments that 6. Armee could not obtain a complete victory without the infantry battalions from the Falke-Division, no infantry reinforcements would be forthcoming. The conversations with General von Sodenstern earlier in the day had prepared Schmidt for this – of course there was disappointment, but 6. Armee still needed to get on with the job. Now that the matter was

---

52. Commander of 6. Armee's pioneer school. Mikosch, Generalleutnant Hans, EL, RK, DKiG; Pi.Rgt.Stab 677; born 7 January, 1898 in Kattowitz, Upper Silesia. Died 18 January, 1993 in Reichshof-Eckenhagen.

53. Bader, Generalmajor Robert, Oberquartermeister 6. Armee; born 14 March, 1899 in Lindau. Killed in action, 10 May, 1945 near Iglau, Czechoslovakia.

finally settled, the conversation again turned to where the pioneer battalions should be used. General von Sodenstern said:

> Heeresgruppe is of the opinion that the fresh pioneer battalions should first be applied to an attack on the chemical factory, and the clearing up of the bank east of the steel works and the gun factory can be left to a later time. The army must count on receiving the corresponding order.

General Schmidt replied that the army's thoughts were along the same line, even though the prior clearance of the Volga bank offered large advantages. After getting off the phone with von Sodenstern, Schmidt placed a call to Paulus at the command post of LI. Armeekorps and informed him of OKH's decision. At 1230 hours, 6. Armee sent a teletype to LI. Armeekorps:

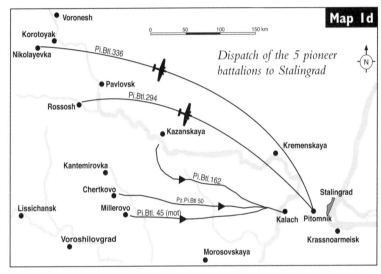

Dispatch of the 5 pioneer battalions to Stalingrad

Map 1d

> On 4.11., Pi.Btle.336 and 294 will be brought forward via air transport and subordinated upon arrival. Arrival at Pitomnik around 1000 hours. LI. Armeekorps will temporarily supply the necessary combat vehicles.

Preparations were now in place to receive the new arrivals.

– – –

At 1300 hours, the teletype printer in the staff offices of 6. Armee sprang to life and printed out the following directive from Heeresgruppe B:

> 1.) The general situation demands that the battles around Stalingrad be ended soon and without committing 29. Infanterie-Division.
> 2.) For this purpose, 6. Armee will be supplied on 4 and 5.11. with 5 pioneer battalions – organised as assault battalions – via air and ground transport. These battalions should be combined under particularly qualified staffs of grenadier regiments and be complemented by heavy companies from grenadier regiments.
> 3.) After the arrival of the pioneer battalions, the attack to seize the 'Lazur Chemical Factory' district will be carried out – after careful preparation – as soon as possible with a total of at least 10 battalions.
> Preparations are to be accelerated by all means possible.
> Troops: 5 pioneer battalions with corresponding heavy companies from grenadier regiments;
> One grenadier regiment from 295. Infanterie-Division;
> One jäger regiment from 100. Jäger-Division;
> Three assault companies (from 44. Infanterie-Division, 14. and 24. Panzer-Division).
> Time of the attack will be reported as soon as possible.
> 4.) Independent of the attack order in Figure 3.), the relief of 60. Infanterie-Division by 305. Infanterie-Division – based on the suggestions of Armee – will be carried out.

At 1825 hours, Paulus sent an order to General von Seydlitz at LI. Armeekorps via teletype confirming what had been discussed earlier in the day and echoing this order from Heeresgruppe B. Its contents set in play all the drama that was to follow.

CHAPTER TWO

Within a matter of days, five powerful and experienced pioneer battalions had come under 6. Armee's control. Seen from the distance of an army headquarters, and indeed, from the comfort of an armchair many decades later, it is easy to forget that these pioneer units were more than just abstract symbols on a map that could be used to accomplish an objective. It is important to realise that the pioneer battalions being sent to Stalingrad had long histories and were filled with experienced, well-trained soldiers, many of whom had been fighting in the war since the very beginning. To better understand the enormity of deploying these valuable soldiers in such a manner, it is worthwhile to know a little more about them.[1]

Pionier-Bataillon 45[2]

For the few months prior to being summoned to Stalingrad, Pionier-Bataillon 45 was directly subordinated to 6. Armee, its main task during that time being the construction of new defensive positions behind the allied armies holding the 500km long flank along the Don river. Two river crossings in August had given the battalion casualties, but since then, losses had been almost non-existent because their main duties consisted of backbreaking digging and construction, all under the blistering sun. Whilst it was hard and tiring work, the men enjoyed it and at least one remembers it as "by far the most wonderful time during the entire Russian campaign". It was into this relaxed atmosphere that the order arrived for the battalion – one of the oldest pioneer units in the Wehrmacht – to head to Stalingrad via Kalach. Leutnant Anton Locherer[3], battalion adjutant, would not go to Stalingrad with his battalion:

> In the evening, we received the order to drive to Stalingrad with our combat elements. The staff company would remain behind as the mission would only be for a short time. Because I became adjutant of the battalion, I would take over the staff company and remain behind. With an uneasy feeling I watched my comrades drive off the next morning – Farewell for ever?!

The men hastily gathered their equipment, climbed aboard their cars and lorries and set out from the Millerovo area in the hinterland, across the parched steppe towards Stalingrad, 350km distant. Those who had not participated in the August fighting in the Don bend were amazed by what they saw. "We passed through the steppe near Kalach and saw the results of a clash between 6. Armee and a Russian tank army", recalls Gefreiter Karl Krauss[4], "about one thousand shot up and derelict Russian tanks – from T-34s up to the 152mm equipped

---

1. Detailed histories of each pioneer battalion are contained in Appendix 1 – see page 489.
2. See page 489 for a detailed history of Pionier-Bataillon 45.
3. Locherer, Hauptmann Anton, Pi.Btl.45; born 22 June, 1920 in Ulm. See Appendix 2 (page 575) for more details.
4. Krauss, Karl Leutnant, 2./Pi.Btl.45; born 21 July, 1920 in Mehrstetten. Still alive in 2006.

Familie Vögele

Men of Pionier-Bataillon 45 pose atop one of the many Soviet tanks that littered the vast battlefield west of Kalach.

KV2s – covered the battleground, and amongst all these were countless quantities of guns and other materiel. Did Ivan still have the power to resist?"

After a dusty and gruelling drive, the battalion reached its first destination, Kalach, where it was directed into small villages on the bank of the Don river. The battalion commander, Hauptmann Dr. Ludwig Büch[5], headed to the army pioneer school for a briefing. The total number of men who made the trip was 451, which broke down to 11 officers, 1 administrative official, 43 NCOs and 396 men. Combat strength was 9 officers, 30 NCOs and 246 men equipped with 27 light machine-guns, 6 gun mounts and 6 flamethrowers. The battalion may have had more flamethrowers than officially reported because Gefreiter Krauss remembers his 2. Kompanie being equipped with 3 German flamethrowers (weighing 40kg each) and 3 Italian flamethrowers (30kg each), the latter having possibly been acquired during their brief subordination to the Italian 8. Armee.

The command structure that arrived on 4 November 1942 was as follows:

DRK/Familie Büch

Commander:	Hauptmann Dr. Ludwig Büch
Adjutant:	Leutnant Wolfgang Sartorius
Schirrmeister:	Oberschirrmeister Martin Ehret
Schirrmeister:	Oberschirrmeister Ernst Schüle
Werkmeister:	Werkmeister Kurt Dodel

Hauptmann Dr. Ludwig Büch, commander of Pionier-Bataillon 45 in Stalingrad.

5. Büch, Major Dipl.Ing. Ludwig, Pi.Btl.45; born 13 June, 1895 in Heydt. Missing in action, 23 January, 1943 in Stalingrad.
   See Appendix 2 (page 570) for more details.

1. Kompanie:	Oberleutnant Max Bunz
	Zugführer: Leutnant Emil Gräf
	Zugführer: Leutnant Manfred Kimmich
	Zugführer: Oberfeldwebel Kurt Sachse
	Spieß: Hauptfeldwebel Konrad Sturmlinger
	Schirrmeister: Schirrmeister Karl Winter
2. Kompanie:	Oberleutnant Walter Heinrich
	Zugführer: Leutnant Fritz Molfenter
	Zugführer: Feldwebel Hermann Tag
	Zugführer: Feldwebel Lothar Walter
	Spieß: Hauptfeldwebel Adolf Scheck
3. Kompanie:	Oberleutnant Eberhard Warth
	Zugführer: Leutnant Hans-Dietrich Waldraff
	Zugführer: Leutnant Erich Skutlartz
	Zugführer: Oberfeldwebel Alfred Hartmann
	Schirrmeister: Schirrmeister Eugen Nachbaur

The battalion was an excellent blend of experience and youth. Most of the officers had been soldiers or NCOs in the battalion during the Polish or French campaigns: the battalion was one of the fortunate few where men would spend their entire careers. If they were wounded, retrained or promoted, chances were very good that they would return to their beloved Pionier-Bataillon 45.

Four young platoon commanders of the battalion. From left: Leutnant Emil Gräf (1. Kp.), Leutnant Anton Locherer (2. Kp.), Leutnant Fritz Molfenter (2. Kp.) and Leutnant Karl Vögele (2. Kp.).

Panzerpionier-Bataillon 50[6]

The only Panzerpionier battalion sent to Stalingrad for the offensive was Panzerpionier-Bataillon 50 (22. Panzer-Division). This battalion differed from the others in that it was much more heavily armed and its 3. Kompanie was equipped with half-tracks. With the young Hauptmann Erwin Gast[7] still settling in as battalion commander, the order arrived for the battalion to start marching eastward for operations in Stalingrad. The command staff of 22. Panzer-Division were not surprised: the battalion was just the latest unit to be withdrawn from the divisional structure and sent elsewhere. With justified bitterness, the division remarked that "the clearance of 22. Panzer-Division continues". Fortunately for the division, Panzerpionier-Bataillon 50 would leave behind all armoured vehicles of 3. Kompanie, including its half-track platoon. The officers and men of this company were less fortunate than their vehicles because they too were on their way to Stalingrad with the rest of the battalion. Regardless of 22. Panzer-Division's own pressing needs regarding fuel[8], the division's quartermaster, Major Dietz von dem Knesebeck, gave his pioneers an ample supply

Hauptmann Erwin Gast, the youthful commander of Panzerpionier-Bataillon 50 in Stalingrad.

for the drive. And so, Panzerpionier-Bataillon 50 began its march towards 6. Armee on the Volga. The distance from their positions north of Millerovo to the Don bridge at Kalach amounted to about 250 kilometres, and the battalion covered this distance within a day, arriving late on 4 November. The battalion's first commander, Oberst Herbert Selle (who had relinquished command in 1940), was now Armeepionierführer of 6. Armee, and in a gully south of Kalach, he met his old battalion for the last time.

Gefreiter Ludwig Apmann[9] from 2. Kompanie recalls the trip:

> Mounted in our vehicles, our battalion rolled in the direction of Stalingrad, into the suburbs that were already occupied by German units. Winter was close but we still didn't have winter clothing. It looked nasty here, almost everything lying completely in ruins; we also saw many dead German soldiers…

---

6. See page 504 for a detailed history of Panzerpionier-Bataillon 50.

7. Gast, Hauptmann Erwin, Pz.Pi.Btl.50; born 18 October 1911 in Stolp. Missing in action, 2 February 1943 in Stalingrad. See Appendix 2 (page 572) and Appendix 4 (page 582) for more details.

8. On 27 October, the division's quartermaster, Major von dem Knesebeck, wrote: "Gasoline situation is intolerable! Oral requests continually come in from all units… The fuel trains are on their way". On 28 October: "Three wagons from the coming fuel train are absent. 22. Panzer-Division will therefore be allocated 30 cubic metres less fuel than needed…" The fuel train finally arrived on 9 November 1942.

9. Apmann, Gefreiter Ludwig, 2./Pz.Pi.Btl.50; born 13 November, 1920 in Achim. Died 13 September, 1992 in Hann.-Münden.

The battalion arrived in Stalingrad with a ration strength of 10 officers, 3 administrative officials, 51 NCOs and 475 enlisted men, a total of 539 men. Its combat strength was 10 officers, 44 NCOs and 405 men. An infusion of replacements in mid-October had brought the battalion completely up to strength. The command structure that arrived at Stalingrad was as follows:

Commander: Hauptmann Erwin Gast
Adjutant: Leutnant Klaus Kunze
Ordonanzoffizier: Leutnant Egon Hillmann
Paymaster: Stabszahlmeister Artur Hassler
Werkmeister: Werkmeister Walter Hinsch
Techn. Inspektor: Oberinspektor Ernst Schneider
1. Kompanie: Oberleutnant Wolfgang Ziegenhagen
                   Zugführer: Leutnant Rudolf Gottwald
                   Zugführer: Oberfeldwebel Friedrich Hellberg
2. Kompanie: Oberleutnant Walter Hardekopf
                   Zugführer: Leutnant Gerhard Thiele
                   Zugführer: Oberfeldwebel Wilhelm Müller
3. Kompanie: Oberleutnant Rindermann (?)
                   Zugführer: Leutnant Ernst Bunte
                   Zugführer: Leutnant Herbert Palmowski
                   Zugführer: Feldwebel Josef Löffler

Obergefreiter August Uhlendorf poses next to one of the battalion staff's Renault AHN trucks prior to their departure towards Stalingrad.

Formed from one of the army's oldest pioneer units, the attitude of Pionier-Bataillon 50's men altered in March 1942 when they were converted to a fully motorised unit. As older officers became casualties or were transferred, the command roles were filled by confident young officers who instilled a more aggressive spirit in their units. Belonging to a panzer division carried some prestige and the pioneers of the battalion considered themselves elite. Embodying the new character of the battalion was its commander, Hauptmann Gast. He was by far the youngest battalion commander heading to Stalingrad and like any ambitious young officer, he wanted to demonstrate his prowess to his elders on the field of battle. There could be no more daunting arena than Stalingrad.

Pionier-Bataillon 162[10]

Mark/NARA

Months of constructing defensive positions along the front-line of their Italian allies had not dulled the men of Pionier-Bataillon 162 (62. Infanterie-Division). Felling trees, digging trenches and erecting anti-tank obstacles kept the men in top physical condition, while their commander, Major Otto Krüger[11], scheduled constant training and drills, combined with occasional stormtroop operations, to hone the fighting skills of his tough pioneers (the bulk of the men hailed from Upper Silesia and were drawn from a stock of hardy farmers and workers). The most recent operation, carried out on the night of 25 October, had been small. A previous attack on 9 October had not gone as well because the infantry element of the assault groups suffered heavy casualties, but the pioneers had performed well.

A few weeks before being called to Stalingrad, the battalion was unfortunate to lose two experienced company commanders. Hauptmann Hans Gierth[12], long-time commander of 3. Kompanie, had been transferred to the staff of XXIX. Armeekorps, but taking his place was the battalion adjutant, Oberleutnant Alfons Schinke[13]. Daredevil actions had been his

Otto Krüger in 1934 as a newly-promoted Leutnant in Pi.Btl.1. In November 1942, as a Major, he commanded Pi. Btl.162 in Stalingrad.

trademark since crossing the Soviet border in June 1941. The second old company commander to leave was Hauptmann Munz[14] of 1. Kompanie, transferred back to Germany. Taking over as commander was a relative newcomer to the company, Oberleutnant Kurt Barth[15], but he had 16 years of soldiering experience under his belt. The commander of the remaining company – the 2nd – was Oberleutnant Arthur Baranski[16], still wearing the

---

10. See page 520 for a detailed history of Pionier-Bataillon 162.

11. Krüger, Major Otto, Pi.Btl.162; born 15 September, 1904 in Elbing. Died in captivity, 20 April, 1943. See Appendix 2 (page 575) for more details.

12. Gierth, Major Hans, 3./Pi.Btl.162; born 12 October, 1915 in Bromberg. Killed in action, 1 May, 1945 in Berlin. See Appendix 2 (page 572) for more details.

13. Schinke, Hauptmann Alfons, DKiG; 3./Pi.Btl.162; born 24 May 1915 in Leuber, Upper Silesia. Missing in action, 2 February 1943 in Stalingrad. See Appendix 2 (page 577) for more details.

14. Munz, Hauptmann, 1./Pi.Btl.162. No further information known. See Appendix 2 (page 576) for more details.

15. Barth, Hauptmann Kurt, 1./Pi.Btl.162; born 18 March, 1909 in Kassel. Killed in action, 18 November, 1942 in Stalingrad. See Appendix 2 (page 569) for more details.

16. Baranski, Hauptmann Arthur, 2./Pi.Btl.162; born 7 December, 1904 in Rastenburg, East Prussia. Missing in action, 5 January, 1943 in Stalingrad. See Appendix 2 (page 569) for more details.

bandages after being wounded just three weeks earlier during a stormtroop operation over the Don. Leading them all was Krüger. He had commanded the battalion for more than a year and his officers and men trusted him implicitly. His courage was beyond reproach: he was never one to command from the rear, and this attitude was passed to his company and platoon commanders.

Around midnight on 1 November, the staff of 62. Infanterie-Division received a communique from the Ia of the German General near 8. Italian Armee ordering Pionier-Bataillon 162 to be ready by 1200 hours on 2 November for transportation by air or road. It was presumed that the battalion would be employed in Stalingrad. The division wrote in its diary:

> The withdrawal of the pioneer battalion places further construction of positions seriously into question if at least a few men aren't left behind in every regimental sector to instruct the infantrymen. The division therefore orders that at least 2 or 3 men are to remain behind in every sector.

Major Krüger and his battalion began their long drive to Kalach early on 3 November. The staff and 3. Kompanie had their own vehicles but the two foot companies were temporarily motorised by 30 trucks of the Italian 248° Autoreparto pesante[17], with about 50 drivers under the command of Italian Lieutenant Giusberti. Each pioneer company took along their own field-kitchen. The battalion required almost two days to reach their destination, the bulk arriving at Kalach on 4 November and the rest the next day. Its ration strength was 8 officers, 45 NCOs and 384 enlisted men, a total of 437 men, its combat strength 7 officers, 31 NCOs and 281 men with 27 light machine-guns and 6 flamethrowers. The command structure that arrived at Stalingrad was as follows:

Commander:	Major Otto Krüger
Adjutant:	Oberfeldwebel Rudolf Gregor
1. Kompanie:	Oberleutnant Kurt Barth
	Zugführer: Leutnant Alfons Dziumbla (?)
2. Kompanie:	Oberleutnant Artur Baranski
	Zugführer: Leutnant Engelbert Kleiner (?)
3. Kompanie:	Oberleutnant Alfons Schinke
	Zugführer: Leutnant Dr. Johannes Schütze
	Zugführer: Oberfeldwebel Wilhelm Altmann
	Zugführer: Oberfeldwebel Max Giessmann

Pionier-Bataillon 162 had one distinct advantage over the other pioneer battalions being sent to Stalingrad: because the large majority of the men came from Upper Silesia, many spoke Silesian – a dialect of Polish – and also Polish itself, and could therefore understand and communicate in Russian, a very similar Slavic language. When prisoners were taken, they could talk to them and gain knowledge that was immediately useful to their current situation, rather than having to send them to higher headquarters where a Sonderführer interrogated the prisoner, as happened in most other units.

---

17. Trans.: '248th Heavy Truck Company'. This company was part of 8. ital. Armee and consisted of 150 drivers commanded by a captain.

Pionier-Bataillon 294[18]

Pionier-Bataillon 294 (294. Infanterie-Division) had also spent many months working on defensive positions along the Don River before being sent to Stalingrad. Its three companies were regularly allotted to the infantry regiments to help construct bunkers, lay minefields, erect wire obstacles and clear trees to produce open fields of fire. Orders made it clear that the defensive line along the Don River needed to be strong because large sections were being held by allied troops. The telephone in the divisional command post at Chkalova kolkhoz rang at 2330 hours on 1 November: it was an advance order from XXIX.

Armeekorps warning the division that Pionier-Bataillon 294 should be made ready as a Sturm-Bataillon for operations in Stalingrad. Transport would either be by lorries or by air. When Major Weimann[19] was advised to prepare his battalion for action in Stalingrad, he protested, citing that it was not ready for such a task. In his latest weekly report, dated 29 October, he clearly stated that "the battalion is suitable for limited offensive tasks and for defence", and he had repeatedly expressed this opinion in previous reports. The division commander, Generalmajor Johannes Block[20], was sympathetic but it was out of his hands because the order had come from much higher up. There were even rumours that it came directly from the top. The definite order to use Pionier-Bataillon 294 in Stalingrad arrived directly from Heeresgruppe B at 1700 hours on 2 November and they immediately wanted to know the transport strength of the battalion. The battalion's instructions were as follows:

Major Wilhelm Weimann, commander of Pionier-Bataillon 294 in Stalingrad.

a) the battalion will make its way to the Rossosh airfield;
b) the commander and adjutant will be sent ahead to Kalach in 2 passenger cars to make contact with 6. Armee;
c) a large part of the battalion's trucks, with the field-kitchens and a portion of the pioneering equipment, will also be sent to Kalach.

Weimann was informed right away and he dispatched messengers to his company commanders. Within a matter of minutes, the battalion's billet areas were hives of activity. Preliminary preparations had already been carried out after receipt of the advanced order but no-one expected to leave in such a hurry. Because night had fallen, it was not possible to head off to the airfield, but the trucks were loaded so they could leave early the next morning. At 2200 hours, however, Heeresgruppe B again called and said that embarkation was delayed and would only take place on 4 November. Major Weimann and his adjutant, Leutnant Walter Zimmer[21], still rose in darkness the next morning and drove to Kalach. Upon Weimann's departure, the battalion was led by its senior company commander, the popular and combat-experienced Oberleutnant Pohl[22] (1. Kompanie). He had recently run

---

18. See page 537 for a detailed history of Pionier-Bataillon 294.
19. Weimann, Major Wilhelm, Pi.Btl.294, born 15 March, 1895 in Meiderich/Duisburg. Missing in action, January 1943 in Stalingrad. See Appendix 2 (page 579) for more details.
20. Block, General der Infanterie Johannes, EL, RK; 294.Inf.Div.; born 17 November, 1894 in Büschdorf. Killed in action, 26 January, 1945 in the Baranov bridgehead.
21. Zimmer, Leutnant Walter, 2./Pi.Btl.294; born 1 June, 1915. See Appendix 2 (page 580) for more details.
22. Pohl, Oberleutnant Gerhard, 1./Pi.Btl.294; born 21 April 1915 in Hauteroda. Died of wounds, 14 November, 1942 in Stalingrad. See Appendix 2 (page 577) for more details.

an Unterführer (junior commander) training course that produced two dozen young soldiers ready to move up the ranks, and their first opportunity to prove themselves would be in Stalingrad. The other two company commanders were the newly arrived Oberleutnant Fritz Bergemann[23] of 2. Kompanie and Oberleutnant Gerhard Menzel[24] of 3. Kompanie, both of whom had been at the front since the war began.

In the last strength report filed by Pionier-Bataillon 294, four days before it left for Stalingrad, the battalion had a combat strength of 6 officers, 46 NCOs and 356 men, a total headcount of 408. It was slightly overstrength in men and a few NCOs short, but it was drastically understrength in officers… 12 in all. Major Weimann expressed his opinion about the condition of his battalion: "Morale of the troops is good. Particular difficulties exist because of the complete lack of officers as platoon commanders…" When the battalion arrived at Pitomnik airfield near Stalingrad at 1130 hours on 4 November, it only had 4 officers, 29 NCOs and 275 men, plus about 20 more men not counted as combatants. That was a total of 328 men – 80 less than reported a few days earlier (those 80 men had been left behind as a Nachkommando[25]). The command structure that flew into Stalingrad was as follows:

Commander:	Major Wilhelm Weimann
Adjutant:	Leutnant Walter Zimmer
Paymaster:	Oberzahlmeister Arndt Rudolph
Battalion Doctor:	Oberarzt Dr. Ulrich Matthäus
1. Kompanie:	Oberleutnant Gerhard Pohl
	Zugführer: Oberfeldwebel Josef Rischer
	Zugführer: Feldwebel Wilhelm Angerstein
	Zugführer: Feldwebel Bernhard Krebs
2. Kompanie:	Oberleutnant Fritz Bergemann
	Zugführer: Oberfeldwebel Max Puppel
	Zugführer: Feldwebel Oskar Dickler
	Zugführer: Feldwebel Gerhard Husmann
3. Kompanie:	Oberleutnant Gerhard Menzel
	Zugführer: Feldwebel Alfred Polenz
	Zugführer: Feldwebel Franz Kerkhoff
	Zugführer: Feldwebel Fritz Kother

Although the battalion lacked officers, one thing it was not short of was weapons: captured Soviet weapons were incorporated into the battalion's arsenal. In addition to the many PPSh submachine-guns, the battalion also had the following Soviet weapons: 1 heavy 14.5mm machine-gun, 13 light Degtyarev DP machine-guns, 5 14.5mm anti-tank rifles and 9 light mortars. Although many of the Soviet weapons, including the heavier weapons, were left behind with the Nachkommando and the battalion's POW-Pionier company, a large majority of the arsenal accompanied the battalion on the planes.

23. Bergemann, Oberleutnant Fritz, 2./Pi.Btl.294; born 22 May, 1915 in Landsberg/Warthe. Died of wounds, 12 November, 1942 in Stalingrad. See Appendix 2 (page 570) for more details.

24. Menzel, Oberleutnant Gerhard, 3./Pi.Btl.294; born 12 February, 1907 in Oebisfelde. Died 15 December, 1954 in Berlin. See Appendix 2 (page 576) for more details.

25. Trans.: 'Nachkommando' is a difficult term to translate. It can mean 'rear-guard' but in this case it means part of a unit left behind to act as a cadre and to take care of administrative matters.

Pionier-Bataillon 336[26]

Many men of Pionier-Bataillon 336 (336. Infanterie-Division) flying to Stalingrad had brand-new medals on their chests after participating in the most ferocious battle they thought they'd ever face: Korotoyak-on-Don. The command structure of the battalion that arrived in Stalingrad was vastly different to the one that emerged from that battle. Their commander, Major Richard Pavlicek[27], was on home leave and command should have passed to the senior company commander, Hauptmann Borkowski[28], but he had just been transferred to the Hungarian 2. Armee as a liaison officer. Next in line was Hauptmann Hermann Lundt[29] who had been transferred to the unit in mid-September. He was once described by a superior as a man whose military manner was "firm, energetic and soldierly". He was polite, popular and possessed the characteristics of a leader. An early wartime commander summed up Lundt in a few words: "a simple, forthright and reliable man. A soldierly personality through and through."

Hauptmann Hermann Lundt, Bataillonsführer (temporary commander) of Pionier-Bataillon 336 in Stalingrad.

Half an hour before midnight on 1 November, 336. Infanterie-Division received a communique stating that the transportation of its pioneer battalion by air to another sector should be expected. The division commander gave Hauptmann Lundt a heads-up. The tight time restrictions meant preparations had to be brief. At 2030 hours the next evening, Lundt was ordered to report to the Ilovskoye airfield near Nikolayevka at 0900 hours on 3 November. He was to fly straight to 6. Armee for a briefing at the army pioneer school in Kalach-on-Don. Two hours later, the official order arrived:

> Transportation of the Pionier-Bataillon to Stalingrad on 4.11.1942.

Lundt immediately assembled his company commanders and ordered them to prepare for aerial transport. He told them they needed to bring all available heavy weapons, including the flamethrowers. When asked where they were going, Lundt just needed to say one word: "Stalingrad". Gefreiter Wilhelm Giebeler, a cook, gathered his kitchen equipment. Together with the other elements of the battalion's supply echelon, he would reach Stalingrad by road. As he packed his gear, the pioneers around him grumbled loudly

---

26. See page 551 for a detailed history of Pionier-Bataillon 336.
27. Pavlicek, Oberstleutnant Richard, Pi.Btl.336; born 3 February, 1902 in Wilten, Austria. No further information known. See Appendix 2 (page 576) for more details.
28. Borkowski, Major Herbert, 1./Pi.Btl.336; born 20 October, 1909 in Danzig/Neufahrwasser. Died 16 July, 1995. See Appendix 2 (page 570) for more details.
29. See Footnote 36 on page 17.

about their new assignment. Giebeler had heard their griping before, on the eve of every special 'dirty job'. But since they were consummate professionals at streetfighting, he had no worries about their morale nor doubt as to their success.

The plane bearing Hauptmann Lundt and his adjutant, Leutnant Dr. Ruhl[30], left promptly at 0900 hours and landed three hours later at Pitomnik airfield. Back in the Korotoyak area, Oberleutnant Brockmann's[31] 2. Kompanie climbed into nine lorries at midday and reached the Ilovskoye airfield as the sun was casting long shadows. Formed into squads, they clambered aboard the Ju-52s. The flight went without a hitch and the company landed at Pitomnik in the late autumn darkness. A small column of lorries drove them west along the Kalach-Stalingrad railway, across the Don and into accommodations arranged for them.

Long before sun-up on 4 November, the two remaining companies were ready to move to the Ilovskoye airfield. The lorries pulled up just after 0300 hours, and 15 minutes later, having stowed all their gear and weapons, the men of Oberleutnant Hullen's[32] 1. Kompanie and Oberleutnant Ziesch's[33] 3. Kompanie squeezed into the trucks for the long drive. They drove on to the airfield at 0700 hours, jumped down from the lorries, quickly loaded their gear in the planes and then climbed in themselves. The planes were soon in the air and flew into Pitomnik airfield around 1000 hours. Trucks supplied by LI. Armeekorps picked them up and delivered them to their billet areas on the other side of the Don.

The command structure that arrived near Stalingrad was as follows:

Commander:	Hauptmann Hermann Lundt
Adjutant:	Leutnant Dr. Karl Ruhl
Battalion Doctor:	Stabsarzt Dr. Horst Gallwoszus
1. Kompanie:	Oberleutnant Karl-Heinz Hullen
	Zugführer: Leutnant Wilhelm Schmidt
	Zugführer: Oberfeldwebel Otto Grimm
	Zugführer: Oberfeldwebel Helmut Milkau
2. Kompanie:	Oberleutnant Karl Brockmann
	Zugführer: Leutnant Fritz von Velsen
	Zugführer: Oberfeldwebel Johannes Zimmermann
	Zugführer: Stabsfeldwebel Gerhard Piltz (3. Zug)
3. Kompanie:	Oberleutnant Bernhard Ziesch
	Zugführer: Stabsfeldwebel Otto Reiter (1. Zug)
	Zugführer: Leutnant Erich Oberst (2. Zug)
	Zugführer: Oberleutnant Bernd Ehringhaus (3. Zug)

30. Ruhl, Oberleutnant Dr. Karl, Stab/Pi.Btl.336; born 17 November, 1913. No further information known. See Appendix 2 (page 577) for more details.

31. Brockmann, Oberleutnant Karl, 2./Pi.Btl.336; born 18 May, 1910 in Hannover. Killed in action, 12 March, 1944 near Skalat, Tarnopol. See Appendix 2 (page 570) for more details.

32. Hullen, Hauptmann Karl-Heinz, 1./Pi.Btl.336; born 2 June, 1917 in Wethmar. Killed in action, 26 December, 1943 near Barishevka. See Appendix 2 (page 574) for more details.

33. Ziesch, Oberleutnant Bernhard, 3./Pi.Btl.336; born 19 August, 1915 in Strohschütz. Missing in action, 11 January, 1943 in Stalingrad. See Appendix 2 (page 580) for more details.

Oberleutnant Ziesch, commander of 3. Kompanie, with his staff car. All of the battalion's vehicles were left behind when it was flown to Stalingrad.

The combat strength of the battalion on 4 November 1942 was 8 officers, 38 non-commissioned officers and 336 men. Ration strength was about 20 men more. The battalion was up to strength but was lacking in flamethrowers, only having two per company instead of the regulation three. The battalion also distinguished itself by carrying an unusual weapon. Having been stationed in Belgium in May 1941, the battalion's men picked up the Browning FN (Fabrique Nationale) High-Power pistol manufactured by the Belgian state-owned company FN Herstal. Chambering the standard 9mm Parabellum, with 13 in the magazine and 1 in the chamber, the pioneers appreciated its greater capacity, and many men, particularly the officers and NCOs, opted to wear it as their sidearm. The pistols had stood the test in Korotoyak and now, two months later, the most experienced men preferred to carry it as their back-up weapon.

Korotoyak had melded Pionier-Bataillon 336 into a formidable unit and provided them with valuable experience in street-fighting and taking fortified buildings. They had all seen that a combination of flamethrowers, explosives and – above all – offensive elan were effective in taking stubborn enemy nests. Of the five pioneer battalions brought in for the offensive, Pionier-Bataillon 336 was the one with the most recent experience of combat in a built-up area and, because they had succeeded with a similar mission in Korotoyak, they were confident they would again prevail. The men thought nothing in Stalingrad could compare to what they had already seen. Their recently awarded medals kept it fresh in their memories.

– – –

The five pioneer commanders heading to Stalingrad were a mixed lot. Hauptmann Ludwig Büch (Pi.Btl.45), an old warrior from the First World War, was university-educated, mature, and very experienced; Hauptmann Erwin Gast (Pz.Pi.Btl.50), by far the youngest, was brash, confident and aggressive; Major Otto Krüger (Pi.Btl.162), the former NCO, was modest, self-conscious and reliable; Hauptmann Hermann Lundt (Pi.Btl.336), another NCO who had worked his way through the ranks, was extremely well-mannered, tactful and honest; and Major Wilhelm Weimann (Pi.Btl.294), the oldest of the five, was cautious but knowledgeable.

Five completely different commanders, five completely different units, but all were gathered for one purpose: to take the last stubborn patches of land in Stalingrad and settle the matter once and for all.

Apart from the five pioneer battalions, there were other units being sent to Stalingrad. In preparation for the final push, several of the divisions already battered and bruised during their previous deployment in the city were ordered to create Sturmkompanien (assault companies). In essence, these units were like a battalion that had been boiled down and stripped of anyone and everything that was not needed in combat: a company filled entirely by battle-hardened veterans equipped with a multitude of fast-firing automatics, bags of grenades and a plethora of heavy weapons.

Sturmschwadron 24

At 1415 hours on 4 November, 24. Panzer-Division issued Divisionsbefehl Nr. 83 which ordered the formation of a Sturmkompanie, or, as it was called in 24. Panzer-Division, a Sturmschwadron. This would be accomplished by relieving a schwadron of II./Panzergrenadier-Regiment 26. Details of its establishment were contained in an appendix to Divisionsbefehl Nr. 83 which stated that before 7 November, Panzergrenadier-Regiment 26 would form a reinforced Sturmschwadron with a strength of about 150 combatants, including a squad of pioneers. The schwadron would also be armed with heavy machine-guns and heavy mortars. At the same time, 14. Panzer-Division and 79. Infanterie-Division would form Sturmkompanien of their own. It was planned to attach these three heavily armed units to 100 Jäger-Division for an attack on the Lazur chemical factory.

Familie Beyersdorff

Leutnant Eberhard Beyersdorff, commander of the Sturmschwadron formed from Panzergrenadier-Regiment 26

The composition of the Sturmschwadron was as follows:

– a Kompanietrupp (company headquarters personnel) with the commander (an officer), a Kompanietruppführer[34] (NCO), 8 messengers and a medic.

– three assault platoons, each consisting of:

a platoon commander (NCO), Zugtruppführer[35] (NCO), 3 messengers and a medic;

three squads, each of 1 NCO and 7 men.

This totalled 1 officer, 17 NCOs and 83 men. There was also a heavy machine-gun squad, a heavy mortar platoon, an anti-tank gun and a ten-man pioneer squad. All up, around 150 men, the core of which came from 6. Schwadron. The man chosen to lead the new unit was Leutnant Eberhard Beyersdorff[36], commander of 6./Panzergrenadier-Regiment 26. Arriving as a replacement on 8 September, he had earned a reputation as a tough fighter and an excellent leader, precisely the qualities needed for an assignment of this type. The order he received regarding the formation of the unit was flexible: he was given carte blanche to select 100

---

34. Trans.: 'Kompanietruppführer' = 'leader of the company headquarters personnel'.

35. Trans.: 'Zugtruppführer' = 'leader of the platoon headquarters personnel'.

36. Beyersdorff, Oberleutnant Eberhard, DKiG; 6./Pz.Gr.Rgt.26; born 27 March, 1918 in Greifenhagen. Died 15 September, 1974 in Oldenburg. See Appendix 3 (page 581) for more details.

men from his own schwadron as well as from any of the regiment's other units. Beyersdorff had first entered the service in October 1938 as a volunteer in the famous Kavallerie-Regiment 5[37]. He had belonged to 1. Kavallerie-Division since becoming an officer in early 1941 and was with the unit throughout the first five months of Barbarossa, until the division was recalled to Germany to refit and reform as 24. Panzer-Division. As a result, he knew many of the division's veteran soldiers and was able to select the toughest and most combat-experienced men, men who had long ago proved their courage and covered the chests with medals, men who had survived month after month of savage combat on the Ostfront. Beyersdorff had no say, however, in the men who belonged to the heavy machine-gun and heavy mortar squads, the anti-tank gun crew or the pioneer squad. Nonetheless, these were all good, reliable men.

The formation was organised in assault squads. For each squad, there would be 1 light machine-gun, the rest of the squad carrying rifles, submachine-guns, hand-grenades, explosives, Russian trench periscopes, smoke pots and smoke grenades. The squads of the Sturmschwadron were equipped as follows:

Squad commander: submachine-gun, 2 hand grenades
Rifleman 1:   machine-gun, 1 50-round drum magazine, pistol, 2 hand grenades
Rifleman 2:   pistol, 4 drum magazines, 1 300-round ammunition can, 2 hand grenades
Rifleman 3:   rifle, 2 300-round ammunition cans, 2 hand grenades
Riflemen 4-5:   rifle, each with one bag of 8 hand grenades
Rifleman 6:   rifle, 1 concentrated charge, 2 hand grenades
Rifleman 7:   rifle, 1 bag with 6 smoke grenades, 1 smoke pot, 2 hand grenades

Ammunition was distributed as follows:

Per rifle: 100 rounds
Per submachine-gun: 6 magazines
Per pistol: 2 magazines
Per light machine-gun: 10 50-round drums and 2 300-round ammunition cans
Per heavy machine-gun: 12 300-round ammunition cans
Per soldier: 2 hand grenades

A 3.7cm anti-tank gun was assigned, in addition to heavy mortars and heavy machine-guns, and two rifle grenade launchers were supplied by Panzerpionier-Bataillon 40. The squad of pioneers would be sent as an intact unit from Panzerpionier-Bataillon 40, kitted out with specialist equipment for house-to-house fighting, including flamethrowers. This squad was supplied to the Sturmschwadron early on 6 November and there were strict instructions for it to be employed only as an intact unit and not be dispersed amongst the grenadiers.

On the morning of 5 November, 6./Panzergrenadier-Regiment 26 was extracted from the steel factory and sent back to a forming-up area. Throughout the morning, men assigned to the new company or personally selected by Beyersdorff arrived in dribs and drabs, other larger groups arriving in lorries from the rear areas further to the west. There was not much time for the unit to bond: the deadline for completion of training was the evening of 7 November. On that final day of training, Leutnant Walter Wroblewski[38] – wounded during the early days of

---

37. Kavallerie-Regiment 5 'Feldmarschall von Mackensen' wore the traditional cavalry Totenkopf (death's head) as originally worn by the Prussian 1st and 2nd Bodyguard Hussars because the tradition had been passed on to the 5. Reiter-Regiment in 1921. This Totenkopf insignia can clearly be seen in the photo on the previous page.

38. Wroblewski, Oberleutnant Walter, 7./Pz.Gr.Rgt.26; born 30 March, 1917 in Stettin. Died 26 December, 1994 in Isernhagen. See Appendix 3 (page 581) for more details.

the summer offensive but arriving with the latest contingent of officer replacements from Insterburg – was immediately assigned to the Sturmschwadron on account of his experience, front-line knowledge and courage. Generalmajor von Lenski[39] paid a visit to his Sturmschwadron training in the rear area. The General stood next to his Kübelwagen and watched the squads practice assault troop tactics amongst the ruins of a small village. It seemed that within two days, the men from disparate units had come together effectively and von Lenski was pleased with what he saw. The unit would soon be ready for action.

Sturmkompanie 44

In contrast to the Sturmkompanien formed by LI. Armeekorps' divisions, all of which only began to be formed on 4 November or later, the Sturmkompanie assembled by 44. Infanterie-Division was created much earlier. It was first envisaged as an 'Eingreifsreserve' (ready reaction force) as part of a winter-mobile unit and had been formed in accordance with an order issued to XI. Armeekorps by 6. Armee on 4 October, 1942. The opening paragraph of this directive stated that "after occupying winter positions, every infantry division will form an Eingreifgruppe[40], constantly enabled for independent conduct of operations, and a Stoßgruppe (assault group) in each infantry regiment". The Eingreifgruppe would consist of a battalion staff with a communications section, two rifle companies reinforced by a heavy machine-gun platoon and a heavy mortar platoon, a light howitzer battery and a heavy company with a platoon each of light infantry guns, heavy anti-tank guns and pioneers. Some of the men would receive skis while the rest would be equipped with snow shoes, wheeled vehicles would be replaced by sleighs and hand sleds would be supplied to haul the machine-guns. Every man would also receive full winter clothing. The Stoßgruppen to be formed by each infantry regiment would consist of a rifle company reinforced by a heavy machine-gun platoon and a heavy mortar squad. From the scant evidence available, it seems these Stoßgruppen were not created, but the Eingreifgruppe was formed during October. The actual formation was very close to the planned version, and indeed, consisted of the staff and communications section from Panzerjäger-Abteilung 46, two reinforced rifle companies (one each from Grenadier-Regiments 131 and 132), a light infantry gun platoon from Grenadier-Regiment 132, a pioneer platoon from Pionier-Bataillon 80, an anti-tank company from Panzerjäger-Abteilung 46 (with 6 heavy anti-tank guns, 6 heavy mortars and 6 light mortars) and an artillery battery (4./Artillerie-Regiment 96). In late October, it was decided to send the two reinforced rifle companies to LI. Armeekorps for use in the city itself, but no records exist to show why these companies – now called 'Sturmkompanie 44' – were ordered to head east to Stalingrad. The teletype message sent at 1600 hours on 28 October, 1942 by 6. Armee to the staffs of LI. Armeekorps and XI. Armeekorps, to which 44. Infanterie-Division was subordinated, read:

> Sturmkompanie 44.I.D., with an attached Sturmpionierzug of Pi.Btl.672, will be brought forward in lorries to Kamenny Buyerak on 29 October. The commander will arrive in advance and report at the command post of LI. Armeekorps. The reinforced Sturmkompanie will be subordinated to LI. Armeekorps upon its arrival. For the time being, it will be accommodated at the army's disposal in the Kamenny Buyerak area.

---

39. Lenski, Generalleutnant Arno von, DKiG; 24.Pz.Div.; born 20 July, 1893 in Czymochen. Died 4 October, 1986 in Eichwalde.

40. Trans.: 'Eingreifgruppe' = 'strike force', 'reaction force' or 'task force'.

On the morning of 29 October, the Armeepionierführer [Oberst Herbert Selle], in conjunction with XI. Armeekorps, will provide lorries to bring the company forward to Molkerei 8km east-north-east of Verkhnaya Golubaya. He is also responsible for transporting the Sturmpionierzug.

Arrival of the reinforced Sturmkompanie will be reported to Armee by LI. Armeekorps in its daily report.

At 1945 hours on 28 October, LI. Armeekorps sent a teletype message of its own to 79. Infanterie-Division:

Reinforced Sturmkompanie of 44.I.D. will arrive via lorry on 29 October in the area north-west of Kamenny Buyerak. The company will be subordinated upon arrival to 79. Infanterie-Division for troop matters and supplies. For the moment, they will be accommodated in the Kamenny Buyerak area at the disposal of Korps HQ. The Sturmkompanie commander will report to the command post of 79. Infanterie-Division at Razgulyayevka railway station. His arrival will be reported to Korps HQ.

Mentioned in the above message is a 'Sturmpionierzug'[41]. It was subordinated to Sturmkompanie 44 and ready to be deployed at the same time. This platoon, designated Heerespionierzug 672, was actually 1. Zug of 3. Kompanie from Pionier-Bataillon 672, the battalion that were the resident instructors at the nearby Armee-Pionier-Schule in Kalach. The role of Pionier-Bataillon 672 was to run courses and train others in specialised pioneer activities, such as tank destruction and assault group operations in cities[42]. Therefore, the men of Heerespionierzug 672 were extremely well versed in city-fighting tactics. None of that knowledge and practice, however, had yet been put to the test. On 28 October, no other units like Sturmkompanie 44 and Heerespionierzug 672 existed within 6. Armee.

The precise composition of Sturmkompanie 44, as well as how many men and weapons it contained, is not known, but both reinforced rifle companies and the pioneer platoon originally created for the winter-mobile task force were part of it. It is probably pedantic to speculate if it should have been called a Sturmkompanie if it contained two overstrength companies, but several sources[43] do refer to it as 'Sturmbataillon 44'. With a single exception, however, 6. Armee war diary consistently calls it a 'Sturmkompanie' and the only time that it suggests it was larger than a company is in a document dated 11 November where it states that 44. Infanterie-Division had supplied a reinforced company from Grenadier-Regiment 131 and a reinforced company from Grenadier-Regiment 132 to 6. Armee. The report then states "both grenadier companies have been handed over to LI. Armeekorps". If we tally the elements mentioned in available reports, then Sturmkompanie 44 possessed two rifle companies, each reinforced by a heavy machine-gun platoon and a heavy mortar platoon, as well as a pioneer platoon, making a total of two companies and five platoons. In any case, the Sturmkompanie was formed from elements of 11./Grenadier-Regiment 131, 2./ Grenadier-Regiment 132 and a platoon from 2./Pionier-Bataillon 80, but the strength of each element is unknown: each company could have had 150 men, or 50 men. It is this author's opinion that Sturmkompanie 44 was considerably larger than a normal company and was probably more than twice the size of other Sturmkompanien later set up by other divisions. The number of heavy weapons

---

41. Trans.: Sturmpionierzug' = 'pioneer assault platoon'
42. See page 72 for more details about Pi.Btl.672.
43. 44.Inf.Div. unit history, the division's Mitteilungsblatt (newsletter) and veteran Franz Maier.

Familie Brock

Oberfeldwebel Eitel Brock, a platoon commander in 2./ Pi.Btl.80, took charge of the pioneers attached to Sturmkompanie 44.

would also have been quite impressive. An estimate of 300 or more men would not be out of the question. For the sake of simplicity, the term 'Sturmkompanie 44' will be used when referring to this unit.

Almost all the men in the unit were young 18- to 20-year old recruits, leavened with a cadre of experienced NCOs and Landsers. For example, commander of the pioneer platoon was the vastly experienced Oberfeldwebel Eitel Brock[44]. Leading the reinforced company from Grenadier-Regiment 131 was Leutnant Wilhelm Willmitzer[45], while the leader of the company from Grenadier-Regiment 132, 35-year-old bachelor Oberleutnant Willi Kindler[46], was appointed commander of the Sturmkompanie. Unlike most of the men in 44. Infanterie-Division, Kindler was German, not Austrian, and had commanded 5./ Infanterie-Regiment 132 until heavily wounded on 10 June 1942. After recovery and recuperation in a homeland hospital, Kindler returned to his division in late October 1942.

On the morning of 29 October, the Sturmkompanie left its assembly area behind 44. Infanterie-Division's front-line facing the Kremenskaya bridgehead. While Oberleutnant Kindler headed off to LI. Armeekorps headquarters, the rest of the Sturmkompanie moved out on the lorries provided for them. In charge during Kindler's absence was Leutnant Willmitzer. The small column headed in a south-east direction, crossed the Don on the Luchinskoi bridge, passed through Vertyachii and then drove across the vast tract of featureless steppe west of Stalingrad. The reinforced Sturmkompanie reached their lodgings in Kamenny Buyerak in the afternoon but their arrival was not reported to Korps until the next day. Together with Heerespionierzug 672, they were officially subordinated to 79. Infanterie-Division on 30 October for supplies and other troop matters but could not be used on operations – they remained under the control of LI. Armeekorps.

It seems that the company had figured in the attack being planned on the Lazur chemical factory from the very beginning.

– – –

44. Brock, Oberfeldwebel Eitel, 2./Pi.Btl.80; born 19 April, 1915 in Langenberg. Killed in action, 11 November, 1942 in Stalingrad.

45. Willmitzer, Oberleutnant Wilhelm, 11./Gr.Rgt.131; born 27 January, 1918 in Krakau. Killed in action, 13 November, 1942 in Stalingrad. See Appendix 3 (page 581) for more details.

46. Kindler, Hauptmann Willi, 5./Gr.Rgt.132; born 24 December, 1906 in Durlach. Killed in action, 21 June, 1944 near Serwery, Poland. See Appendix 3 (page 581) for more details.

Although Heerespionierzug 672 would not play a role in the upcoming attack, it is worthwhile examining their formation and operations because the results must have had an effect on the wisdom of using pioneer units in the way that was now being planned. Heerespionierzug 672 had a strength of 6 NCOs and 42 enlisted men. All of them had been thoroughly schooled in house-to-house combat and indeed, were passing that knowledge on to others. Platoon commander was 29-year old Feldwebel O.A.[47] Theodor Reher[48]. On 30 October, 1942, the platoon was subordinated to 79. Infanterie-Division for supplies and troop matters. The next day, an initially successful effort by Grenadier-Regiment 226 (79. Infanterie-Division) – supported by pioneers from 1. and 3./Pi.Btl.179 – to take the Martin Furnace Hall in the Krasny Oktyabr factory turned to failure after forward elements that had reached the Volga were cut off by Soviet counterattacks and forced back. All earlier gains in the vital hall were then lost. Casualties for Grenadier-Regiment 226 were extremely high: 1 officer killed and 1 wounded; 40 NCOs and men killed, 116 wounded, 14 missing and 50 'stragglers'[49]. Casualties for the pioneers were light: 2 men killed, 1 NCO and 4 men wounded. Preparations were underway to finally conquer the Martin Furnace Hall, and because the pioneer assault groups from Pionier-Bataillon 179 had brought a hard-hitting punch to the assault, it was decided to add more pioneering strength: Feldwebel Reher's new pioneer assault platoon, trained specifically for a task like this, was the ideal choice. The platoon was tactically subordinated to 79. Infanterie-Division for operational use on 1 November, 1942. After being briefed about the forthcoming attack, the platoon was sent forward to the Krasny Oktyabr factory during the night.

To pave the way for the attack, Luftwaffe planes dropped napalm-like incendiaries for 45 minutes, beginning at 1015 hours. Most landed directly on target. The operation to capture the northern section of the Martin Furnace Hall then began. Pioneer squads from Heerespionierzug 672, 3./Pi.Btl.179 and flamethrower troops from 2./Pi.Btl.179, together with infantry storm groups, moved out of their starting positions 200 metres from the objective, the minimum safe distance from the Luftwaffe bombs. Soviet resistance in this 'safety zone' – thus still outside the targeted workhall – was much stronger than expected. These Soviet defenders slowed down the attack for several hours and it was only toward 1500 hours that the assault groups actually reached the hall itself. Resistance in the hall was just as strong as on the previous day, preventing the assault groups from getting inside. After a quick regrouping, the attack was relaunched at 1530 hours. Vicious fighting continued until nightfall, when the German troops pulled back. Results of the attack were negligible: the objective had not been seriously threatened, no significant gain of ground had been made and only 5 prisoners were taken. Casualties were not too serious amongst the 79. Infanterie-Division units involved: Grenadier-Regiment 226 had 3 NCOs and men killed, 17 NCOs and men wounded and 1 man missing, while Pionier-Bataillon 179 had 1 man killed, 2 men wounded and 1 man missing. On the other hand, Heerespionierzug 672 suffered grievous casualties: its commander, Feldwebel Reher, was killed, as were five of his men[50], 17 NCOs

---

47. O.A. = 'Offizieranwärter' - officer candidate.

48. Reher, Leutnant Theodor, 3./Pi.Btl.672; born 20 April, 1913 in Nordkirchen. Killed in action, 1 November, 1942 in Stalingrad.

49. Men separated from their units in action.

50. Pionier Robert Guthing, born. 25 July, 1923 in Siegen; Gefreiter Josef Otterbein, born 4 May, 1908 in Bad Salzschlirf; Gefreiter Johannes Hans Schulze, born 20 October, 1921 in Braunschweig; Pionier Willi Ziems, born 14 June, 1923 in Blumenholz; plus one other unknown man

and men were wounded and 1 man was missing. That means 24 of the platoon's 48 men became casualties – an appalling rate of 50%. Squad commander Feldwebel Hölker took command of the remnants of the platoon. Heerespionierzug 672 was immediately released from tactical subordination to 79. Infanterie-Division, pulled out of the Krasny Oktyabr factory and sent into reserve positions on the western outskirts of Stalingrad. It was returned to Sturmkompanie 44 in Kamenny Buyerak on 3 November, 1942.

The use of Heerespionierzug 672 in a completely devastated industrial area should have been a cautionary tale. Even well-trained pioneers, additionally schooled in the brutal art of city-fighting, had failed to make significant headway.

Sturminfanteriegeschütz 33B

Apart from these 'experimental' units, there was also a new piece of unproven technology sent to Stalingrad for Operation Hubertus. This was the Sturminfanteriegeschütz 33B mounting a 150mm heavy infantry gun. The development of this vehicle had been orchestrated and overseen by Hitler himself. It was his baby. Plans for creating this vehicle were first discussed during Hitler's conference on 20 September, 1942. It was stated that:

> Fighting in Stalingrad has clearly resulted in the necessity of having a heavy gun in a heavily armoured vehicle to fire high explosive shells capable of destroying entire houses with only a few rounds. It doesn't have to have long range or be able to drive swiftly. However, good armour protection is decisive. Everything is to be immediately lined up to produce 12 such vehicles if possible but at least start with 6 within 14 days at the latest. If it isn't possible to mount a s.I.G. in the turret of a Pzkpfw. III or IV, attempts must be made to install this gun in an assault gun.

Notes from Hitler's conference on 22 September state that "Hitler is extremely satisfied with the report that 6 s.I.G. would be installed in assault guns on 7 October and a further 6 on 10 October. An additional 12 assault guns will be outfitted with s.I.G. in October".

Anderson

Anderson

The 15cm s.I.G.33/1 was already available from Skoda, having been designed and a production series started for mounting this weapon as a self-propelled gun on a Pzkpfw. 38t chassis. Within two days of receiving the directive, Alkett had expediently designed a box-shaped superstructure to be mounted on a Sturmgeschütz chassis. The design was based on the chassis of the Stug. III Ausf. B but the first 12 production models were built on the Stug. III Ausf. E and the final 12 on the F/8 chassis[51]. It was certainly not a pretty vehicle: weighing in at 21 tonnes, it was 2.90 metres high, 5.40 metres long and 2.90 metres wide, and looked like a steel box with a pipe sticking out of it. Armament consisted of a 150mm L/11.4 heavy infantry gun and a hull-mounted MG-34 7.92mm with storage space for only thirty 150mm rounds and 600 rounds of machine-gun ammunition. Two MP-38s (with 384 rounds) were also carried for use if the crew bailed out. The five-man crew was formed by a commander, gunner, two loaders and a driver. Armour thickness ranged from 80mm on the hull and superstructure front, to 50mm on the sides and down to 16mm on the engine decks. Propelling the vehicle was a water-cooled V-12 Maybach that pushed it along at a top speed of 20km per hour. Fuel capacity of 310 litres enabled a maximum range on roads of 110km, or 85km cross country. It was slow, had a limited range and possessed fairly good armour protection… exactly as Hitler had ordered.

In Hitler's conference on 13 October, 1942, it was reported that 12 s.I.G. as Sturmgeschütz with 80mm frontal armour had been delivered and assembly was to begin immediately on an additional twelve.

The Heeres Waffenamt reported the completion of 24 's.I.G. auf Fgst.Pzkpfw.III (Sfl.)' in October 1942, with 12 released for issue in October and a further 12 in November. It was noted that this was a single Versuchserie (experimental series) using rebuilt chassis.

---

51. A total of 24 s.I.G.33 auf Fgst. Pz.Kpfw.III (Sfl.) were eventually produced. Chassis number 90101 to 91400.

The Ia Abteilung of Armee-Oberkommando 6 sent the following teletype message to XIV. Panzerkorps at 2020 hours on 21 October, 1942:

> On the Führer's orders, Panzer-Kompanie 616[52] – Trip Nr. 430 238 – with 6 Stug. mit s.I.G. will be supplied to Stug.Abt.177. Arrival at Chir railway station around 23.10.
> It is dependent on Chef H.Rüst u. BdE[53] whether the 6 crews be given transport or set in march to Stug.Abt.177. The crews will be transferred to Stug.Abt.177. The arrival of the assault guns is to be communicated to OKH by AOK6.

At the same time, a similar message was sent to LI. Armeekorps:

> Stug.Abt.244 will shortly be supplied with Panzer-Kompanie 627 – Trip Nr. 430 255 – with 6 Stug. mit s.I.G. at Chir railway station. Chef H.Rüst u. BdE has assigned to the shipment 1 driver, 1 gunner and 1 loader per gun, as well as armoury personnel. The crews will be transferred to the battalion. Stug.Abt.244 will supply the remaining crew members at Chir railway station. The arrival of the assault guns will be communicated to OKH/GenStdH.,Org. Abt. by Ia of AOK6.

The estimated date of arrival stated in 6. Armee's message – 23 October – was a little optimistic. The twelve vehicles did not actually leave the Alkett factory on Berlin's outskirts until the middle of October, and it would take much longer than a week to cross the several thousand kilometres between Berlin and Stalingrad. The Quartiermeister records of 6. Armee logged the arrival of the first batch of vehicles as follows:

> 27.10.: Pz.K.616 – Fahrt.Nr.430 238 – arrived at Chir railway station on 27.10.1942. 8 wagons panzer.

This train contained the 6 s.I.G. and crews for Stug.Abt.177, as well as two other unspecified armoured vehicles. The second shipment of six s.I.G. with crews for Stug. Abt.244 arrived the next day. Again from the Quartiermeister records:

> 28.10.: Pz.K.627 – Fahrt.Nr.430 255 – arrived at Chir railway station on 28.10.1942. 6 wagons Sturmgeschütze.

On the day the second half dozen vehicles arrived, 6. Armee sent messages to the two Korps to which the Sturmgeschütz-Abteilungen were subordinated. The following is what was sent to LI. Armeekorps and XIV. Panzerkorps at 1935 hours on 28 October:

> Stug.Abt.177 and 244, after each being supplied with 6 Stug. mit s.I.G. at Chir, will be employed in the fighting around Stalingrad as soon as possible. This will be the first time that this new weapon has been employed, so a short experience report will be submitted after their first operation.

Early on the morning of 29 October, officers from both Stug.Abt.177 and 244 were dispatched by their commanders to the Chir railway station to take receipt of the new vehicles and their crews. Going with them were some of their own technical personnel and other men who had been selected to become crew members. The six sIG33Bs assigned to Stug.Abt.177 headed to the command post area east of Gorodische, while the other six drove to Stug.Abt.244's leaguer south-east of Gumrak railway station. LI. Armeekorps reported their arrival in an interim report at 1700 hours.

---

52. Tanks and assault guns being sent to the front were organised as temporary companies.

53. 'Chef H.Rüst u. BdE' = Chef Heeresrüstung und Befehlshaber der Ersatzarmee (Chief of Army Equipment and Commander of the Reserve Army).

One of the brand-new sIG33B supplied to Sturmgeschütz-Abteilung 244 rolls past Gumrak railway station on 29 October, 1942. This photo was taken by a soldier of 79. Infanterie-Division. It is quite possible that the officer standing on the engine deck (in a greatcoat) is Generaloberst Paulus himself.

The six new behemoths of Stug.Abt.177 took much longer to arrive because one of them broke down. They did not arrive until after sundown. In its daily report to 6. Armee at 2210 hours that evening, XIV. Panzerkorps reported: "Sturmgeschütze with s.I.G. arrived at the battalion workshop, one of which had temporarily broken down due to damage during transport."

One of Generaloberst Paulus' front-line visits took him to LI. Armeekorps' command post north-west of Gumrak railway station on the morning of 29 October. A meeting with von Seydlitz that began at 0915 hours ended half hour later with the Korps commander reiterating the difficulty of capturing the Volga shoreline east of the gun factory, bread factory and steel factory. At that moment, almost as if it was a divine sign, the convoy of six sIG33Bs and attendant vehicles drove by on their way to Stug.Abt.244 headquarters south-east of Gumrak station. It is not recorded whether Paulus conducted an impromptu inspection of the new vehicles but there is a gap of an hour in his usually to-the-minute trip notes, so it is likely he did just that. At 1045 hours, he placed a call to his chief-of-staff back at army headquarters and ordered that all six of the newly arrived sIG33Bs allocated to Stug.Abt.244 be employed in an artillery role, particularly in the difficult terrain near the Volga bank.

That order, however, would have to wait because even though the six sIG33Bs were listed as part of Stug.Abt.244's battle strength on 30 October, the next day it was reported that, "the 6 s.I.G. (Sfl.) of Stug.Abt.244 are still in a non-operational state 2km west of Bezugspunkt 447[54]."

On 1 November, 1942, the six s.I.G. assigned to Stug.Abt.177 left that battalion's workshops, arrived at battalion headquarters and were declared ready for battle. They were formed into three platoons, two vehicles in each, and integrated into 3. Batterie. Further south, Paulus was paying a visit to Sturmgeschütze-Abteilung 244 south-east of Gumrak railway station. He arrived at 1115 hours and was shown the newly arrived guns. The battery commander was not shy in voicing his disappointment about the new vehicle. He pointed out various shortcomings and was of the opinion that the gun was a makeshift solution and not yet ready for deployment.

Left: Generaloberst Paulus converses with his Sturmgeschütz-Abteilungen commanders. From left: Major Dr. Josef Gloger (Kommandeur Stug.Abt.244), Generaloberst Friedrich Paulus and Major Hans Zielesch (Kommandeur Stug.Abt.245).

54. Bz.Pkt.447 was Stalingradski (see map on page 99).

Visibility was poor for both the driver and radio operator/machine-gunner, the gun itself had negligible traverse and the vehicle's overall vulnerability would not allow the same types of operations as an assault gun. Nevertheless, it seems many were keen to see them used immediately. An order issued by 305. Infanterie-Division on 1 November for an attack the next day shows that some of the guns were to support the infantry: an s.I.G. platoon (2 guns) from Stug.Abt.244 was assigned to Grenadier-Regiment 576 while another platoon of 2 guns would support Grenadier-Regiment 578. No records exist to categorically prove whether or not the guns participated in the attack, but circumstantial evidence, particularly the lack of any mention in daily reports, suggests that they were not.

On 2 and 3 November, Stug.Abt.244 only had 3 s.I.G. operational. After declaring on 1 November that all six vehicles were ready for action, Stug.Abt.177 only had 3 operational on 3 November: the other three were returned to the workshops. The reasons for the vehicles' unreliability became startlingly clear after experienced mechanics thoroughly inspected the machines. In a report to 6. Armee at 0900 hours on 3 November, Sturmgeschütz-Abteilung 177 made the following deficiencies known: old assault gun mounts had been used, all of which displayed considerable technical defects that had to be repaired before they were operational. The mounts displayed typical symptoms of old age in the chassis and engines, such as steering brakes, carburettors, fuel pumps, rollers and tracks. There was also no means of observation for the gun commander, apart from him poking his head out of the hatch, so the use of a scissors telescope was the temporary solution. Hitler was only informed on 7 or 8 November 1942 that the first 12 vehicles did not have Scherenfernrohre 14 Z (scissors periscopes). Finally, no firing tables for the 150mm gun or operating instructions for the vehicle in general were available.

Apart from all the problems with the vehicle, there were also shortcomings with the men that had been sent along with them as crewmen. Of the 12 men sent along with the vehicles, 7 had been trained as drivers after steering nothing more than a horse. They went straight from horseback to assault guns. These 7 men, as well as a further three, had not been trained on the s.I.G. That means only two men had experience handling the horse-drawn s.I.G. However, none of the men had been given any instruction on the self-propelled s.I.G. The drivers were completely without experience and had only taken their driving licence examinations the day before they left Germany. Sturmgeschütz-Abteilung 244 had similar problems with their new men. In addition, they also noted that the men sent with the vehicles were all from a replacement battalion. They had been detailed for 6 days to the Alkett factory, where the guns were manufactured, but apart from seeing their future mounts being assembled, they were neither trained on the driving panzer nor the gun.

The absence of a manual and firing tables for the green crews meant that the maximum impact could not be obtained from the new vehicles and the crews were placed in danger. Both booklets provided essential information for the safe and effective operation of the vehicle because if used properly, it could be a devastating weapon. Its 38kg shells could be fitted with the s.Igr.Z.23 impact fuse which possessed the option of being fired with a half-second delay, long enough to penetrate the target before exploding. But there were vital facts the crews needed to know about the fuse: it was dangerous to stow such fuse-armed shells or drive around without their safety-pins in; the possibility of ricochets existed at certain impact angles; the shells should not be fired if the fuses were even lightly damaged; and extreme care had to be taken to ensure that the flight path in front of the barrel was clear of all obstacles, including twigs and leaves, because the fuses were highly sensitive after leaving the barrel and could prematurely detonate, endangering the crew. The crews also needed to know other things. The powder charges had to be protected from humidity (rain, show and fog) because increased moisture resulted in shells falling short. After every shot, even at night, the barrel should be looked through to see if there were remnants of the powder charge or other foreign bodies, and if so, they should be removed, otherwise, stoppages would result. These matters would have been second nature with an experienced crew but the youngsters assigned to these sIG33Bs were underprepared, undertrained and did not even possess the manuals so desperately needed to ensure the safe operation of their vehicles. The only saving grace was the allocation of experienced men from the Sturmgeschütz-Abteilungen, particularly the vehicle commanders. These battle-hardened NCOs and officers worked feverishly to whip their crews into shape and to come to grips with the new assault gun themselves.

- - -

Courtesy of a supreme effort by the maintenance personnel, five of Sturmgeschütz-Abteilung 244's new guns were ready for action the next day, 4 November. Together with 4 long-barrels and 6 short-barrels, they were set in march to 79. Infanterie-Division to take part in Operation 'Hubertus'. The other gun required more extensive repairs and so remained behind in the battalion workshop. Sturmgeschütz-Abteilung 177 had 4 guns ready on this day, although one of those still had a damaged radio. On 5 November, this battalion was informed that its new problem children were scheduled for use elsewhere. The following message was sent to XIV. Panzerkorps at 1550 hours:

> The 6 s.I.G. (Sfl.) of Sturmgeschütz-Abteilung 177 will be placed under LI. Armeekorps on 8.11. for 'Hubertus', when the situation on the north front of XIV. Pz.K. allows it. An Einweisungskommando[55] will be dispatched to LI. A.K.

Sturmgeschütz-Abteilung 245 was subsequently informed that it would probably receive these six guns on 8 November. After devoting a week to repairing the vehicles and getting them ready for action, Sturmgeschütz-Abteilung 177 had been ordered to hand the vehicles over. Before then, Major Bochum[56,] the new commander of the battalion, wanted to see the guns in operation. A minor demonstration was prepared against a live target.

The man to lead the s.I.G. battery was Oberleutnant Dr. Karl-Otto Mai[57], who barely two weeks earlier had been in a replacement battalion in Schweinfurt:

> I was only transferred to Stalingrad on 27 October, 1942 and arrived there after a train journey lasting 10 days and nights, battling bedbugs all the way.

His diary entry for 5 November – the day of his arrival – reads:

> Lorry trip (hitchhiker): Chir – Karpovka – Gumrak railway station – Gorodische (battalion command post). Reported to Major Bochum,

Oberleutnant Dr. Mai

---

55. Trans.: 'Einweisungskommando = 'party of guides'.

56. Bochum, Major Gerhard, Stug.Abt.177; born 30 July, 1902 in Rapitz. Died in the mid 1970s.

57. Mai, Oberleutnant Dr. Karl-Otto, Stug.Abt.177; date of birth unknown. Died in 2001.

Battalion Commander, who has just been transferred to Sturmgeschütz-Abteilung 177 to replace the ill Major Käppler[58]. Battalion in operations on the north front of Stalingrad.

Oberleutnant Dr. Mai had a good idea why he had been selected for the job:

Apparently I'd received a good evaluation, both earlier on the heavy artillery and later with the mountain guns (3. Gebirgs-Division), and should lead the deployment of the 15cm s.I.G. in city combat. This occurred on 8 and 9 November 1942 from positions in the tractor factory against the Soviet bridgehead in the Spartakovka worker's settlement north of the Orlovka Brook.

Four guns were available to Mai on 8 November. They trundled through the ruins of the tractor factory's worker's settlement, drove along the western boundary of the factory itself and took up positions at the very northern tip of the factory. They had a good view of their targets and proceeded to hurl 15cm projectiles into the designated enemy buildings. The good results prompted XIV. Panzerkorps to order an attack the following day which would utilise the confusion and destruction caused by another direct bombardment. The next day, 9 November, the guns returned to the emplacements north of the tractor factory and, at the appointed time, opened fire. From Oberleutnant Dr. Mai's diary:

9.11. Attack on enemy positions north of the Orlovka Brook, in particular on the school in Spartakovka (15cm s.I.G.).

He elaborated in a post-war account:

The targets, such as the school in Spartakovka, were – in as much as their walls were still standing – destroyed. For all that, however, the grenadiers attacking into the settlement's gardens from the west made no progress. Armoured vehicles were knocked out by enemy anti-tank rifles. The Soviet bridgehead in Spartakovka (extending about 300 metres from the west bank of the Volga) could not be crushed, whereas in the tractor factory we had occupied the workhalls and held the west bank of the Volga.

The daily report of XIV. Panzerkorps for 9 November 1942 makes no mention of this operation. Immediately after this, about 1200 hours, all six sIG33Bs were sent south to 305. Infanterie-Division for eventual incorporation into Sturmgeschütz-Abteilung 245. For some strange reason, Oberleutnant Dr. Mai, the specialist who had been sent 'on special assignment' from Germany to lead the experimental assault guns, did not accompany them. In its evening report at 2130 hours, LI. Armeekorps reported: "6 Sturmgeschütze mit s.I.G. from Stug. Abt.177 arrived near 305.Inf.Div." Once there, they went into reserve in preparation for the attack on 11 November.

The sIG33Bs assigned to Sturmgeschütz-Abteilung 244 were also put through their paces on 8 November. These minor actions were extremely beneficial to the green crew members because they operated the vehicle under combat conditions and fired at live targets. It was decided to use the new guns in the Krasny Oktyabr factory, where 79. Infanterie-Division had been taking grievous casualties since 23 October. A large proportion of the casualties – both in the factory and in the hinterland – were caused by Soviet artillery fire, while most angst amongst the weary grenadiers was due to enemy snipers. And both of these could be linked to the massive chimneys still looming over the factory. Apart from attempts to demolish the stubborn chimneys, there was no way for the Germans to prevent

58. Käppler, Oberstleutnant Erich, DKiG; Stug.Abt.177; born 22 January, 1906 in Gräfentonna. No further information known.

enemy forward artillery observers and snipers from installing themselves in the tower-like smokestacks which offered a commanding view over the battlefield. The chimneys formed an integral part of the Soviet defences and were practically impenetrable because roomy subterranean smoke ducts ran from the massive Martin electro-furnaces to the chimneys, allowing soldiers to climb up inside the chimneys without ever leaving the safety of the underground defences. It was now the job of the sIG33Bs to eliminate some of these troublesome observation posts. The guns were temporarily subordinated to Gruppe Schwerin (79. Infanterie-Division) for this assignment.

Four guns moved carefully into position in the rear of Grenadier-Regiment 208 under cover of darkness early on the morning of 8 November. Once in position, they waited for the sun to come up and illuminate their targets. Being the tallest objects in the factory, the chimneys were bathed in sunlight long before the rest of the factory. This was the moment selected for commencement of the bombardment. The guns flung high-explosive shells at several different chimneys. A report from Grenadier-Regiment 208 (79. Infanterie-Division) sums up the quite credible results:

> The s.I.G. self-propelled guns subordinated to Gruppe Schwerin placed 3 chimneys in the Martin Furnace hall under direct fire, whereby 5 known enemy observers were destroyed.

Later that evening, LI. Armeekorps reported this success to 6. Armee:

> In the steel factory… enemy observation posts in the Martin Furnace Hall were destroyed by s.I.G. auf Sfl.

Strength reports filed the next day indicate that the sIG33Bs suffered no losses. Oberkanonier Walter Kretz, a radioman and loader in Sturmgeschütz-Abteilung 244, recalls the operation:

> There was a crossroads in Stalingrad that was always overlaid with artillery fire whenever a Wehrmacht vehicle drove along the street, even though it was not observed by the enemy. It was always worse for horse-drawn vehicles because they moved too slowly. It was determined that Russian observers equipped with radios in the factory chimneys were able to see the junction. The gun commanders of 244 then received the task of flattening the chimneys. They succeeded in knocking down 4 or 5 of them. A Russian artillery observer went down with one of the chimneys. A Croatian major from Kroat-Regiment 369[59] who saw the shooting presented Croatian medals to the gun commanders.[60]

After this operation, all of Sturmgeschütz-Abteilung 244's guns were withdrawn from subordination to 79. Infanterie-Division and returned to their battalion leaguer near Gumrak station.

After these minor operations, the guns underwent further maintenance so as to be ready for the big attack on 11 November.

4 November, 1942

At 1825 hours the previous evening, 6. Armee had issued the attack order to LI. Armeekorps. The objective was determined to be the northern section of the chemical

---

59. This would almost certainly have been Major Tomislav Brajkovic, who commanded the combat troops of Infanterie-Regiment 369 in the Krasny Oktyabr factory

60. Unfortunately, a search in the Croatian State Archives did not yield a list of these gun commander's names, despite the records of recipients of Croatian decorations being well-organised.

factory and the pioneer battalions would be subordinated to particularly qualified regiment staffs. For the time being, the deadline for the attack was set for 9 or 10 November. LI. Armeekorps had to regroup its forces to carry out this task. Therefore, at 0700 hours on 4 November, LI. Armeekorps issued Korpsbefehl No. 105 to prepare for Operation 'Hubertus'. This was the very first time this code word was used. The opening paragraph stated: "LI. Armeekorps will initially transition to defence for a short time while preparing an attack to wrench the district around the 'Lazur' Chemical Factory out of the enemy bridgehead (code word 'Hubertus')." The text explaining the tasks for all divisions – which included some stirring words that could have been penned by Stalin himself – went as follows: "The divisions will hold the positions, fortify them with as much energy as possible and promote the construction of obstacles in front of their lines by all means available. Should the enemy actually carry out an attack on the anniversary of his revolution (7 November), then there is only one thing to do: Not one step back! What has been gained in sacrificial struggle must be unconditionally held under all circumstances." Another instruction was to "mislead the enemy with well-prepared operations, particularly by well-trained assault groups…"

100. Jäger-Division was already in the correct position for the assault, so it was not really mentioned in the order. Other nearby units, however, needed to be regrouped and repositioned. The Korpsbefehl ordered the formation of Gruppe Schwerin under the command of Generalmajor von Schwerin, commander of 79. Infanterie-Division. Belonging to it – apart from 79. Infanterie-Division – would be combat groups from both 14. and 24. Panzer-Divisions which would be created by assembling all combat-ready soldiers and weapons of the panzer divisions deployed in the combat zone. In addition, 14. Panzer-Division had an artillery battalion and a panzer company as a reserve force while the other two divisions of the Gruppe – 24. Panzer-Division and 79. Infanterie-Division – were both setting up Sturmkompanien with a strength of 150 men equipped with heavy machine-guns and heavy mortars.[61] The assumption of command by Gruppe Schwerin was set for 0800 hours on 5 November. Accordingly, 14. Panzer-Division ordered the formation

---

61. Formation of these was to be completed by 7 November. 79. Infanterie-Division's Sturmkompanie – formed from Grenadier-Regiment 212 – ended up having a strength of 3 officers, 28 NCOs and 146 men, a total of 177 men. This Sturmkompanie, commanded by Oberleutnant Krah, contained some excellent men, particularly the Stoßzugführer (assault platoon commanders), all of whom were extremely experienced NCOs. All three, plus the Kompanietruppführer, wore the highly coveted German Cross in Gold – a high concentration of valuable and experienced medal-winners in one small company. They were: Kompanietruppführer Feldwebel Ernst Neunecker, German Cross in Gold on 6 November, 1942; 1. Stoßzugführer Oberfeldwebel Karl Hess, German Cross in Gold on 7 March, 1942; 2. Stoßzugführer Unteroffizier Josef Krieger, German Cross in Gold on 28 July, 1942 and 3. Stoßzugführer Oberfeldwebel August Janson, German Cross in Gold on 9 October, 1942. In addition to these, the officer leading the heavy weapons of the Sturmkompanie, Leutnant Anton Link, would be awarded the German Cross in Gold on 29 January, 1943. The Sturmkompanie was armed with 9 light MGs, 2 heavy MGs, 4 heavy mortars and two 3.7cm anti-tank guns.
Krah, Hauptmann, Heinrich, 5./Gr.Rgt.212; born 4 January, 1914 in Neuwied. Missing in action, 8 January, 1943 in Stalingrad.
Neunecker, Oberfeldwebel Ernst, DKiG; 5./Gr.Rgt.212; born 20 March, 1916 in Erbes. Died of wounds, 15 December, 1942 in Stalingrad.
Hess, Oberfeldwebel Karl, DKiG; I./Gr.Rgt.212; no further information known.
Krieger, Unteroffizier Josef, DKiG; 5./Gr.Rgt.212; born 17 January, 1917. Missing in action, January 1943 in Stalingrad.
Janson, Oberfeldwebel August, DKiG; 10./Gr.Rgt.212; born 19 February, 1914. Missing in action, January 1943 in Stalingrad.
Link, Leutnant Anton, DKiG; Gr.Rgt.212; born 12 December 1914 in Fladungen. Killed in action, 11 December, 1942 in Stalingrad.

of 'Kampfgruppe Seydel'[62] and 24. Panzer-Division for 'Gruppe Scheele'[63]. Both divisions shifted their dispensable elements to the rear.

Further preparations for the big attack were contained in the order. 14. Panzer-Division was ordered to release Jäger-Regiment 54 and return it to 100. Jäger-Division. To free up forces for 295. Infanterie-Division, 71. Infanterie-Division was ordered to prepare to take over the southern wing of 295. Infanterie-Division up to but not including the 'Markthallen', as well as quickly forming a reserve force to be placed behind the boundary with 295. Infanterie-Division. The artillery, nebelwerfer units and Sturmgeschütz-Abteilungen also received orders in preparation for 'Hubertus', the latter being 'strongly recommended' to get as many assault guns operational as possible.

– – –

Later that morning, the Commanding General of LI. Armeekorps, General von Seydlitz, and his chief-of-staff Oberst i.G. Clausius arrived at Armee headquarters in Golubinsky, a small village on the west bank of the Don north of Kalach. In a meeting with Paulus and Schmidt, the possibilities and intentions for the forthcoming attack in Stalingrad were discussed. A discussion subsequently took place with the Commanding General of VIII. Fliegerkorps, Generalleutnant Martin Fiebig.

– – –

Pionier-Bataillone 294 and 336 arrived via aerial transport in the area of LI. Armeekorps and were subordinated to 100. Jäger-Division. These two battalions, plus Pionier-Bataillon 45 (mot.) and Panzerpionier-Bataillon 50, were all placed under LI. Armeekorps.[64]

In a letter to his wife, the paymaster of Pionier-Bataillon 336, Oberzahlmeister Erich Bauchspiess[65], wrote:

> The quickest journey in my life is behind me. In two and a half hours I have covered 500km and with me, the whole battalion, other than the baggage train. It was a great experience but now the time of discomfort and strain begins again. At the moment, I'm waiting with another battalion for a truck that was assigned to me to collect rations. It's already dark (it is now 1500 hours) so I must finish up. I am well.

The elements of the battalion that could not be transported by air – such as the field-kitchens, baggage trains and lorries with equipment, ammunition and rations – finally arrived late the next day after many hours of strenuous driving.

5 November, 1942

The arrival of the pioneer battalions caused a ripple of excitement to run through the ranks of the exhausted front-line soldiers. The common Landser respected the skill and bravery of the pioneer troops and breathed a sigh of relief whenever they arrived with their

---

62. Trench strength (without staffs and heavy company): 11 officers, 60 NCOs and 507 men. 2. Weapons: 43 light machine-guns, 13 machine-guns, 5 heavy mortars, 9 light infantry guns, 3 3.7cm Pak, 6 5cm Pak, 5 7.5cm Pak, 6 Panzer III long-barrels, 1 Panzer IV short-barrel. Panzergrenadier-Regiment 103 and 108 were practically battalion strength while Kradschützen-Bataillon 64 had sunk to company strength.

63. Strength: 23 officers, 121 NCOs and 640 men.

64. Pi.Btl.162 would be subordinated to LI. Armeekorps on 5 November.

65. Bauchspiess, Oberzahlmeister Erich, Stab/Pi.Btl.336; born 8 January 1913. Died 1989 in Hamburg-Fulsbüttel. See Appendix 2 (page 569) for more details.

flamethrowers and demolition charges. An attack carried out with the assistance of pioneers always stood a better chance of succeeding, especially when the objective was a fortification or other type of fiercely defended position. The arrival of the five battalions even raised a glimmer of hope amongst other pioneer units that the fighting in Stalingrad might soon end. On 5 November, Hauptmann Helmut Welz[66], commander of Pionier-Bataillon 179 of 79. Infanterie-Division, had just given one of his staff NCOs an order and dismissed him. The door had barely closed behind the NCO when it again flew open. Oberleutnant Paul Fiedler[67] practically fell into the room, his face red and with beads of sweat on his smooth forehead. Oberleutnant Fiedler, commander of the battalion's 3. Kompanie, quickly saluted. His pale blue eyes twinkled as he blurted out, "Have you heard about the new pioneer battalions?"

His words struck Welz like a circus fanfare. A triumphal note was in his voice. "What battalions do you mean?" replied Welz, who had absolutely no idea what Fiedler was talking about.

"Those, the ones that arrived yesterday. The strongest battalions were pulled out everywhere. From the Crimea, the Don, up north. Loaded aboard planes or lorries and sent to Stalingrad. Now they're here and will sort things out. I have just heard it from the infantry."

"That sounds highly unlikely," said Welz doubtfully.

"But it's true. They'll mount their first attack tomorrow. I believe on the Tennis Racket. After that, the Red October, and then the rest."

"If everything goes according to plan! That's short notice!" said Welz, who immediately grasped the implications – once the pioneers succeeded in capturing the Tennis Racket, they would then be employed in the Krasny Oktyabr factory. And that's where his companies were deployed. They would no doubt be called upon to help their newly arrived brothers, so Welz had to think about an attack on Hall 4.

Oberleutnant Fiedler was still in awe: "Wow, five full battalions, pioneer battalions, that adds up. But it does annoy me that they've only come now, at the end, when everyone is worn out and they can grab the glory."

"That hasn't happened yet. But I'll look into it. Wait a moment, I'll check things out." Welz picked up the phone and called various staffs to clear up the situation. Welz later wrote:

> It was just as Fiedler had said. Five fresh pioneer battalions had arrived and would straighten out the Tennis Racket... That was the area between Red October factory and central Stalingrad. The railway line passed around this district in a circular loop, running back in the same alignment. The line drawn on the map looked like a tennis racket. Hence the name. Oil tanks and smaller workshops were here, gullies cut through the terrain, differences in ground levels needed to be overcome. Extensive reconnaissance would be needed...

– – –

Because Welz and his battalion weren't scheduled to be part of Operation Hubertus, he wasn't privy to the planning, which was in full swing. LI. Armeekorps issued a revised order for Operation 'Hubertus' at 1430 hours. In Korpsbefehl Nr. 107, the goal of the attack was succinctly explained:

> 'Hubertus' is the attack of LI. Armeekorps on x-day on the Lazur Chemical Factory district with a breakthrough to the Volga.

---

66. Welz, Major Helmut, Pi.Btl.179; born 20 August, 1911 in Thorn. Died in 1979.

67. Fiedler, Hauptmann Paulus, 3./Pi.Btl.179; born 19 January, 1906 in Limburg. Missing in action, 22 January, 1943 in Stalingrad.

It stated that "all preparations must be completed so that the attack can begin at daybreak (y-hour) on 10.11.". The division that would bear the main burden of the attack was 100. Jäger-Division. For this assault, all five of the newly-arrived pioneer battalions would be subordinated to it, plus three Sturmkompanien[68] and copious amounts of artillery and nebelwerfer support. Two of the pioneer battalions and Sturmkompanie 44 were scheduled to be reserves that could nourish the later stages of the assault. Accompanying the attack would be one reinforced grenadier regiment from 295. Infanterie-Division and Gruppe Schwerin would participate in the later stages of the attack. One important paragraph in this order explains how the pioneers were to be used: "Pioneer forces will be provided to all assault groups for the attack and will be held ready to clear minefields, to create crossings over railway lines blocked by trains and to clear the way through rubble."

– – –

At 2315 hours, General von Sodenstern called General Schmidt and related the following: the Führer had expressed the opinion that the ground east of the steel and gun factories should be taken before the attack on the chemical factory. The corresponding order from OKH (Chef des Generalstab des Heeres)[69] had arrived at Heeresgruppe B. Before forwarding this order to 6. Armee, they wanted to explain to OKH the reasons why both Heeresgruppe B and 6. Armee wanted to attack the chemical factory first.

General von Sodenstern had already pointed out to Generaloberst Kurt Zeitzler, the Chief of the Army General Staff, that 6. Armee would consume so much strength during the attacks east of the gun and steel factories that it would no longer be in a position to take the chemical factory, the most difficult part.

General Zeitzler had agreed to talk to the Führer again but requested answers to the following questions:

1.) When can the attack on the chemical factory be implemented with the forces now made available for it?

2.) When can the attack on the ground east of the steel factory and east of the gun factory be carried out?

3.) Which reasons argue in favour of the army conducting the attack on the chemical factory before the other attacks?

6 November, 1942

To the questions posed the previous night by the chief-of-staff of Heeresgruppe B regarding the attack in Stalingrad, Paulus answered with lengthy comments that highlighted the pros and cons of whether it was better to first clear up the ground east of the gun factory and metallurgical works or to conduct the attack on the chemical factory first. Paulus's conclusion re-emphasised that it was not certain whether one solution or the other was more likely to lead to the ultimate goal of seizing the chemical factory because the forces available to the army were extremely limited. In either case, it would be better if more infantry forces were placed at the army's disposal. This had become even more necessary because the Soviets had brought fresh forces into Stalingrad during the previous few days.

---

68. From 24.Panzer-Division, 44. and 79.Infanterie-Divisions.

69. Trans.: 'Chef des Generalstab des Heeres' = 'Chief of the Army General Staff'.

Paulus replied to General von Sodenstern's questions as follows:

1.) The assault on the chemical factory can be expected to be carried out on 10 November.

2.) The assault on the area east of the steel factory and the gun factory can likewise be conducted on 10 November. An earlier implementation is probably not possible because the infantry assault forces and heavy weapons have already begun to regroup for the attack on the chemical factory and would have to be cancelled.

3.) I have no cause to raise objections to an order by the Führer to carry out a preliminary attack on the terrain east of the steel factory and the gun factory.

Below are 6. Armee's reasons for conducting it first of all:

a) The army would obtain a clear front along the Volga prior to implementing the attack on the chemical factory;

b) It would be easier than the previous postponements to lengthen certain sectors and release forces within the army;

c) If the attack on the chemical factory can no longer be carried out in the foreseeable future because of a shortage of forces, the front in Stalingrad will be easier to defend if the Volga shore east of the steel factory and gun factory is in our hands. If an attack on the chemical factory is unsuccessful, the danger exists that the army will have to hold a very extended front in the city.

Against this solution are the following reasons:

a) The chemical factory is actually the most difficult object to attack in Stalingrad. It can only be taken if sufficient – and also fresh forces – are employed.

The army believes that the currently available forces (12-14 concentrated battalions, including 5 unused pioneer battalions) are barely sufficient to achieve success around the chemical factory. Even before the beginning, these forces – weak in comparison to the object – must reckon on the possibility that the assault will not be quickly and completely pushed through. It should not be carried out, however, if the forces employed for it are still weakened by preceding combat. From previous experience with similar attacks, the assault troops must reckon on casualties of 30-50%.

b) In an attack on the chemical factory, a relatively battleworthy infantry regiment from both 295. and 100. Jäger-Division can launch attacks out of their present positions with little prior shifting.

If the terrain east of the steel factory and gun factory is to be attacked beforehand, however, regrouping with reliefs must be carried out because defence against daily attacks on our positions around the chemical factory could be jeopardised.

c) If heavy casualties are suffered during an attack on the chemical factory, the possibility still exists to later take the terrain east of the steel factory and gun factory.

In summary, I again come to the previously expressed opinion that it is not certain whether one solution or the other – with the ultimate objective of the chemical factory – can succeed because the army has very few forces at its disposal and that's why it would be better in any case if the army were provided with more infantry units. This is thought more necessary because the Russians have again thrown fresh forces into Stalingrad in the last few days.

Having just dictated Paulus's reply to General von Sodenstern, General Schmidt added the following remark: "Give us a decision and an order, and we'll carry it out!"

The Ia of Heeresgruppe described the opinion of the commander-in-chief of Heeresgruppe as follows:

We regard several small bridgeheads to be less dangerous than the one large bridgehead around the Lazur chemical factory, particularly once the Volga has frozen over. This large bridgehead may then represent a certain operational threat. The Armee chief-of-staff confirms that this is also the view of the Armee.

At 1940 hours, Oberst Winter, Ia of Heeresgruppe B, phoned 6. Armee and spoke to Oberstleutnant Elchlepp, Ia of 6. Armee. Oberst Winter said: "We've got the decision from the OKH operations department; the Führer has ordered that the first decision retains validity, whereby the 'lesser evil' (the bridgeheads east of the gun factory and metallurgical works) should be eliminated first."

Half an hour later, at 2010 hours, the following resolution regarding the attack in Stalingrad arrived via teletype from Heeresgruppe B:

> The Führer has ordered the following: before resuming the attack to capture the Lazur chemical factory, the two sections of the city still held by the enemy east of the gun factory and east of the steel factory are to be taken. Only after the bank of the Volga there is entirely in our hands will the assault on the chemical factory begin.

With that, Operation Hubertus – an attack that 6. Armee hoped would settle the Stalingrad situation once and for all by eliminating the biggest and most dangerous Soviet bridgehead – was aborted. This was stated unequivocally in the opening sentence of Korpsbefehl Nr. 108 issued by LI. Armeekorps at 1015 hours the next day: "Operation Hubertus is postponed".

It is open to speculation what would have happened had Paulus got his way by receiving the infantry units he'd requested and attacked the main Soviet bridgehead based around the Lazur chemical factory.

– – –

Pionier-Bataillone 45, 50 and 162 were set in march from Kalach in the direction of Karpovka. By the evening of 7 November, Pionier-Bataillone 45 and 50 were in quarters near Razgulyayevka, while Pionier-Bataillon 162 arrived south of the Pilot's School. Gefreiter O.A. Karl Krauss recalls the trip toward Stalingrad:

> As we approached the city region, the temperature was still 12 degrees. Light rain fell from a dull sky. Within ten hours we experienced a temperature drop of 24 degrees: it suddenly plummeted to -12° when we reached the edge of the city! Our vehicles slipped around, they no longer had any grip. We had to install snow chains because the rain turned to ice and formed a thick coating of ice on the loamy earth.
> We now hoped to at least find decent accommodation in this large city. In vain, everything was unsurveyable destruction! Information: dig your foxholes and dug-outs in the gullies!

Puschiavo Family

After dropping off 1./ and 2./Pionier-Bataillon 162, the Italian drivers and heavy trucks of 248° Autoreparto pesante tarried in the rear: they had been ordered to wait until Pionier-Bataillon 162 had completed its assignment. Then, the Italian trucks were to transport the pioneers back to the sector of 62. Infanterie-Division along the Don river. Little did the men from sunny Italy know that they were going to be trapped in an icy hell.

Italian drivers of 248° Autoreparto pesante. Third from left in the upper row is Mariano Puschiavo. Fourth from left is an officer, possibly Lieutenant Giusberti.

7 November, 1942

All the toing and froing by 6. Armee and LI. Armeekorps about which objective should be taken first by the assembled pioneer units had ultimately been determined by the Führer. 'Hubertus' had been postponed. Details regarding the subordination arrangements of units gathered for the attack were contained in Korpsbefehl Nr. 108 issued at 1015 hours on 7 November 1942. Pionier-Bataillon 336 and the Sturmkompanien from both 44. Infanterie-Division and 24. Panzer-Division remained subordinated to 100. Jäger-Division for troop matters and supplies. The training of the Sturmkompanien and pioneer battalions in streetfighting techniques was to continue as planned. Sturmkompanie 79. Infanterie-Division remained subordinated to Gruppe Schwerin. The panzer company from 14. Panzer-Division and panzer schwadron from 24. Panzer-Division were to be kept ready by the panzer divisions for use by LI. Armeekorps. Pionier-Bataillone 45, 50 and 162 were still subordinated to the Korpspionierführer of LI. Armeekorps[70] for troop matters and supplies but were ordered to be moved into their allocated areas and accommodate themselves according to meteorological conditions. 295. Infanterie-Division and 100. Jäger-Division placed the requisite billeting areas at their disposal.

LI. Armeekorps submitted a proposal by teletype to 6. Armee about the planned implementation of the attack on 11 November. The intention was to make an assault on the Martin Furnace Hall in the Krasny Oktyabr factory and the Volga bank east of the gun factory. Continuation of the attack would begin on 13 November at the earliest to gain the bank of the Volga east of the steel factory after being supplied with units freed up after 305. and 389. Infanterie-Divisions had attained their objectives. This was certainly optimistic and allowed absolutely no room for error. Nevertheless, at 1030 hours, LI. Armeekorps issued Korpsbefehl No. 109 containing details of how this attack was to be carried out. The forces that had been gathered for 'Hubertus' were now to be split up for two separate attacks: the Martin Furnace Hall in the Krasny Oktyabr factory would be taken by Gruppe Schwerin; 305. Infanterie-Division and the southern wing of 389. Infanterie-Division would conquer the bank of the Volga east of the gun factory. Instead of concentrating all available forces on one objective, they would now be divided into the following groups:

Gruppe Schwerin: two pioneer battalions, half a Sturmgeschütz-Abteilung with three of the new sIG33B assault guns, one heavy and two light Werfer battalions. 305. Infanterie-Division: two pioneer battalions, one Sturmgeschütz-Abteilung with 6 new sIG33B, Sturmkompanie 44, one panzer company from 14. Panzer-Division, one s.I.G.-Zug from 71. Infanterie-Division, one s.I.G.-Zug from 14. Panzer-Division and 6 heavy mortars from Pionier-Regiment 604.

389. Infanterie-Division: one pioneer battalion, half a Sturmgeschütz-Abteilung with three new sIG33B assault guns and Sturmschwadron 24.

General von Seydlitz did not appear to be 100% behind this proposal, however, because it was withdrawn by his Ia[71] during a telephone call with the Ia of 6. Armee[72]. General von Seydlitz wanted to make a new proposal based on consultations with his division commanders

---

70. Major Dr. Carl Romeis.

71. Sprenger, Oberstleutnant i.G. Leo, LI. Armeekorps; born 16 September, 1904 in Dresden. Killed in action, 25 January, 1943 in Stalingrad.

72. Elchlepp, Oberst i.G. Hans-Heinrich, 6. Armee; born 3 October, 1902 in Freiburg im Breisgau. Missing in action, 25 January, 1943 in Stalingrad.

who were of the opinion that splitting up the available forces – which were meagre at best – would be a serious mistake. As famous panzer leader General Guderian was found of saying: 'Klotzen, nicht kleckern!'[73] Seydlitz was in agreement. After all the consultations, LI. Armeekorps annulled Korpsbefehl No. 109 and re-issued a revised version at 1435 hours in which the conquest of the bank of the Volga and the capture of the Martin Furnace Hall were again ordered but were now chronologically staggered. It began by stating: "Advanced order for the continuation of the assault on 11.11. Korpsbefehl Nr. 109 (issued at 1015 hours on 7.11.) is invalid and is superseded by the following order". The main objective was for "305. Infanterie-Division and 389. Infanterie-Division (south wing) – after thorough preparation – to conquer the bank of the Volga east of the gun factory on 11.11."

305. Infanterie-Division now had the lion's share of available forces: three pioneer battalions, one Sturmgeschütz-Abteilung with 6 sIG33Bs, Sturmkompanie 44, one panzer company from 14. Panzer-Division, one s.I.G.-Zug from 71. Infanterie-Division, one s.I.G.-Zug from 14. Panzer-Division and 6 heavy mortars from Pionier-Regiment 604. 389. Infanterie-Division was allocated two pioneer battalions, one Sturmgeschütz-Abteilung with 6 sIG33Bs and Sturmschwadron 24. Gruppe Schwerin, after thorough preparations, would only carry out their missions[74] after 14 November. The timing was still tight but the available forces had been concentrated to take one objective.

- - -

The experiences and lessons learned from transporting a battalion by air were compiled in a report by the staff of 294. Infanterie-Division and sent to Heeresgruppe B on 7 November:

Experiences during the conveyance of Pionier-Bataillon 294 via air transport
1.) Preparations for the transportation of the pioneer battalion were adversely affected from the beginning by the fact that it was left open as to whether the battalion would be transported by vehicular means or by air. If transported by lorries, the possibilities to supply the battalion are favourable because no field-kitchens can be taken along when transported by air. The division can help – if they decide on air transportation – by allowing the bulk of the pioneer battalion's lorries with field-kitchens, rations and part of the equipment to be sent ahead to the probable operational area.
2.) Because the commander of the pioneer battalion was only able to head off in his vehicle one day before the transportation of the battalion and had to cover a stretch of 400km (as the crow flies), he barely arrived in the operational area before his battalion. It is therefore advisable that the commander be transported by air the day before. The machines were heavily weighed down by the freight of the staffs, possibly a part of the equipment. The commander therefore has the possibility to establish an early connection with the superior offices and can possibly still give orders to his battalion to bring along certain equipment, etc.
3.) It has proved unsuitable that the Luftwaffe agency providing transport be in direct contact with the pioneer battalion regarding the loading of the personnel and material strength of the battalion. Thus it came about that the commander of the pioneer battalion – without the knowledge of division – provided information for the transport of equipment weighing about 5 tonnes, while in actuality about 18 tonnes was required. Through the intervention

---

73. Translation of this famous quote varies widely but 'Mass, not driblets!' is probably the most succinct. Guderian's philosophy – although he applied it to panzer operations, it was also relevant to most military operations – was to employ forces en masse and not split them up into smaller groups.

74. First objective: assault on Martin Furnace Hall. Second objective: assault to occupy the bank of the Volga east of the steel factory. Subordinated for this: 5 pioneer battalions, 2 Sturmgeschütz-Abteilungen with 12 sIG33Bs, Sturmkompanien 24. Panzer-Division and 44. Infanterie-Division, and heavy mortars from Pionier-Regiment 604.

of the division, the appropriately adjusted requisition was able to be delivered to Luftflotte 4 in time.

4.) In preparation for loading, it is vital that every individual piece of equipment (machine-gun cases, weapons, flamethrowers, ammunition crates etc.) carry accurate designations (company, platoon, squad), because it was necessary to arrange the loading of equipment of different companies and platoons in different transport aircraft.

5.) Smaller pieces of equipment must be packed in crates, sacks or something similar and designated with the unit or owner's names, otherwise, difficulties will arise in the distribution and location of equipment after loading.

6.) During the loading of equipment, it must be remembered that the loads should be mixed on the transport aircraft, otherwise, the loss of an aircraft that was, for example, loaded only with ammunition, would mean the troops would arrive in the disembarkation area without ammunition. On the other hand, it must be considered that related equipment which is not operational if one part of the equipment is missing, for example the flamethrowers, should actually be loaded on one transport aircraft because the assembly of equipment would be made unnecessarily difficult during unloading.

7.) The battalion was set down at the airport, camouflaged against aerial observation and prepared to split itself up for embarkation. By sending an officer ahead who can make contact with the leader of the transport planes, a partitioning of the battalion into scheduled loading strengths corresponding to each aircraft could have taken place before they were dropped off at the airfield. These groups could then move to the airstrip individually, and in this way, an efficient dispersal during embarkation would be attained. It is recommended that a leader of the transport aircraft be employed on the edge of the airstrip as a marshal to direct the approaching groups to the assigned aircraft.

8.) Because this is the first time the bulk of the army members have set foot on an airfield or used an airplane, it is recommended that it be pointed out to the troops that smoking is forbidden in the vicinity of the aircraft and in the planes themselves.

8 November, 1942

At 1010 hours, the army announced its intentions to Heeresgruppe B for the attack in Stalingrad. To begin with, the bank of the Volga east of the gun factory would be attacked with all available forces. For this, the following units were supplied to 305. and the southern wing of 389. Infanterie-Division:

7 companies of infantry assembled from several divisions[75]

2 divisional pioneer companies of the Armee[76]

5 newly supplied pioneer battalions

2 Sturmgeschütz-Abteilungen, including the sIG33Bs

1 panzer company from 14. Panzer-Division

In addition, heavy infantry weapons and the bulk of the artillery from the sector of LI. Armeekorps.

VIII. Fliegerkorps would support the attack with strong forces.

Beginning of the attack: early on 11 November. The systematic reduction of Soviet artillery on the east bank of the Volga had already begun on 7 November. After the conquest of the Volga bank, regrouping for the attack on the area east of the steel factory would follow and be implemented on 15 November at the earliest.

---

75. Grenadier-Regiments 544, 546, 576, 577 and 578, plus Sturmkompanie 44 and Sturmschwadron 24.

76. Pionier-Bataillone 305 and 389.

- - -

After renewed discussions with 6. Armee, the order for the attack had to be changed once again, so in Korpsbefehl No. 110 issued at 1400 hours, the capture of the Martin Furnace Hall and the bank of the Volga within the sector of Gruppe Schwerin was no longer mentioned. This order was definitive and was titled "Korpsbefehl Nr. 110 for the attack to capture the Volga shore east of the gun factory". The opening sentence made it perfectly clear that this attack was not going to be a pushover:

> The enemy fights with undiminished toughness around the remnants of Stalingrad's city sectors and has a continuous supply of fresh forces.

The objective of the attack was clearly explained: "LI. Armeekorps will capture the Volga shore east of the gun factory from the fuel installation (inclusive) to the south-west area of the brickworks". The missions allocated to the units themselves were more explicit:

> 305. I.D. and the southern wing of 389. I.D. will launch a surprise attack at daybreak (Y Hour) along a broad front with grenadier regiments reinforced by strong pioneer forces and capture the Volga shore.
> Through deep deployment and the readiness of strong reserve forces, it will be ensured that they approach the forward line again and again, conserve their fighting strength and maintain sufficient forces to remove bypassed enemy nests and clean out the cellars of conquered houses. The pioneer battalions are not to be employed in a single pioneer regiment or battalion, but will be attached to the infantry and will work in the closest co-operation with them and their heavy weapons.
> Extensive use of every method of smoke generation.

The mission of the other divisions of LI. Armeekorps was simple:

> 71., 295., 100. J.D. and Gruppe Schwerin will carry out well-prepared stormtroop operations to deceive the enemy about the extent of the assault front…Gruppe Schwerin [also] has the task, from the beginning of the attack, to eliminate every flanking effect from the area in front of the left wing of Gruppe Schwerin against the right attack wing of 305. I.D. by heavy fire from infantry weapons and artillery.

The definitive list of subordinated units was as follows:
a) Subordinated to 305. Infanterie-Division:
    Sturmkompanie 44. Infanterie-Division
    a heavy infantry gun platoon from both 71. Infanterie-Division and 14. Panzer-Division[77]
    6 heavy mortars from Pionier-Regiment 604
    Sturmgeschütz-Abteilung 245 with the sIG33Bs of Sturmgeschütz-Abteilung 177
    one panzer company from 14. Panzer-Division
    staff of Pionier-Bataillon 672
    Pionier-Bataillone 50, 294 and 336
    staff of Werfer-Regiment 53 with 2 light Werfer-Abteilungen
b) Subordinated to 389. Infanterie-Division:
    Sturmschwadron 24. Panzer-Division
    Sturmgeschütz-Abteilung 244 with sIG33Bs
    Pionier-Bataillone 45 and 162

---

77. One platoon each from 13./Grenadier-Regiment 211 and 13./Panzergrenadier-Regiment 103 respectively.

There was also an additional order for the pioneers:

As a precaution, pioneers are to be kept ready to produce crossings over the railway embankments, to blast passages in barricaded streets and to clear mines, particularly for the movement of the assault guns and the panzers.

- - -

Based on the above order, 24. Panzer-Division issued Divisionsbefehl Nr. 84 at 2130 hours concerning further aims from 8 November onwards. A schedule of LI. Armeekorps' upcoming operations were listed, as follows:

The first was set for 11 November in front of and north of the gun factory with 389. Infanterie-Division.

The second was an assault on the Martin Furnace Hall (Hall 4) in the north-east sector of the steel factory, scheduled to start some time after 14 November.

The third was an attack on the Volga shore east of the steel factory with Gruppe Schwerin, to which Gruppe Scheele belonged.

Leutnant Beyersdorff's Sturmschwadron 24 was allocated to 389. Infanterie-Division and sent to that division's command post in Gorodische on 8 November. It would be formally subordinated upon the arrival of Leutnant Beyersdorff. The Sturmschwadron was only tactically subordinated to 389. Infanterie-Division: it would still draw supplies from its parent division.

- - -

The German forces had been gathered. An array of first-class units had been brought up to reduce the bridgehead east of the Barrikady. Only the final preparations needed to be carried out before the attack was launched.

CHAPTER THREE

7 November, 1942

With his furlough now over, Hauptmann Eugen Rettenmaier[1], commander II./Grenadier-Regiment 578, returned to his unit in Stalingrad. The last time he had seen his men was in defensive positions in the steppe a long way west of the city:

> The leave train to the front had long stops in Yasinovataya and Lichaya railway stations north of Rostov. Transport trains carrying wounded men stood at both stations. On every wagon, I asked after members of the Bodensee Division, and there were many that made themselves known. Their reports were shocking. The Stalingrad terminus was at Chir, the line not going any further. The distance to Stalingrad-North amounted to about 150 kilometres. There was no system in place to bring men returning from leave back to the front. I found transportation with an ammunition column.

> I arrived in Stalingrad on 5 November. It was a sad reunion with the unit. Oberst i.G. Steinmetz had taken the place of General Oppenländer[2] and the position of chief-of-staff Kodré had been taken by Oberstleutnant Paltzo[3]. The commander of Grenadier-Regiment 578, Oberst Winzer[4], had been killed. II. Bataillon had lost almost all of its officers[5], and the companies numbered 7, 9, 12 and 13 men respectively. To the many, many questions of 'Where is this person, where is that person' – I got the same answer over and over: 'Killed, wounded, missing'. I was returning to a foreign environment.

During his absence, Rettenmaier's battalion had been commanded by Hauptmann Georg Althenn[6]. Since the death of Oberst Willy Winzer on 17 October, the regiment had been led by the commander of III. Bataillon, Hauptmann Wilhelm Püttmann[7], but seniority in rank meant that Hauptmann Rettenmaier took command of the regiment upon his return. It was small consolation for Rettenmaier now that his II. Bataillon barely even existed. In a letter to

1. Rettenmaier, Major Eugen, II./Gr.Rgt.578; born 9 December, 1891 in Wört. Died 7 January, 1965 in Schwäbisch Gmünd.
2. Oppenländer, Generalleutnant Kurt, RK, DKiG; 305.Inf.Div.; born 11 February, 1892 in Ulm. Died 17 March, 1947 in Garmisch (POW camp).
3. Paltzo, Oberst Rudolf, DKiG; 305.Inf.Div.; born 29 October, 1904 in Lötzen. Died 1985 in München.
4. Winzer, Oberst Willy, RK; Gr.Rgt.578; born 10 August, 1894 in Teveren. Killed in action, 17 October, 1942 in Stalingrad.
5. All three company commanders had been wounded in Stalingrad: Oberleutnant Wolfgang Rabenau, DKiG, 5./Gr.Rgt.578; Hauptmann Josef Meyer, DKiG, 6./Gr.Rgt.578; and Oberleutnant Stutz, 8./Gr.Rgt.578. Also wounded was the battalion adjutant, Oberleutnant Wingenfeldt.
6. Althenn, Hauptmann Georg, 14./Gr.Rgt.578; born 20 October, 1907 in Leihgestern. Died 27 March, 1943 in Speziallager Nr. 3655, Arsk.
7. Püttmann, Major Wilhelm, DKiG; III./Gr.Rgt.578; born 28 February, 1910 in Speyer. Missing in action, January 1943 in Stalingrad.

his wife on 6 November, Rettenmaier wrote:

> I am now in a room of a large factory along the Volga. I can no longer find any of the officers from my battalion. The packages that I brought with me are given to the comrades of those to whom they were addressed. Hurlebaus[8] and Tham[9] are dead, Maier[10] and Zink[11] wounded. I temporarily command the regiment. The war in this sector is terrible. There's a concentration of destructive weapons on both sides. Whoever comes out of this hell will never forget their days in Stalingrad. It is a stark contrast coming from my beautiful furlough into this[12]. In any case, one must not lose heart…

Rettenmaier was one of the oldest men in the division, and certainly the most senior combat commander. Born in the tiny village of Wört on 9 December 1891, his life began ordinarily enough as an elementary school teacher. In 1912, he entered the service in Grenadier-Regiment 119 and was made a Feldwebel

Familie Rettenmaier

Hauptmann Eugen Rettenmaier, commander of II./Gr.Rgt.578, returned from furlough and was put in charge of the regiment for the assault on 11 November, 1942.

shortly before the First World War began. As a young Leutnant he experienced the Great War from the very first day, received both grades of the Iron Cross and was wounded five times. Despite his wounds, he only returned home after the war. He married in 1919, returned to his teaching profession, and had five children – four sons and a daughter. All four sons would serve in the army during the war. On the very first day of the Second World War, 1 September 1939, Rettenmaier was recalled to the military. In 1941, he became a company commander in 305. Infanterie-Division, and later a battalion commander. In May 1942, he received the terrible news that his eldest son, Ottokar, had been killed on the Eastern Front. In a small note, his division commander sent him a personal message:

---

8. No further information known.
9. No further information known.
10. Probably referring to Meyer, Oberleutnant Josef, 6./Gr.Rgt.578, wounded on 22 October, 1942.
11. Zink, Oberleutnant, 12./Gr.Rgt.576, was wounded on 14 October, 1942.
12. The period of Rettenmaier's return in early November was the quietest time for his division during the entire battle, so while Rettenmaier describes it as 'hell' now, it would soon get much worse.

My dear Rettenmaier!

I have just heard of the heroic death of your eldest son. I know you are suffering from so heavy a loss. My special sympathy belongs to you, the courageous soldier, who is now taking part in the second war in the front-line. Your pain, however, must be borne like a soldier.

In comradely solidarity.
Your division commander [signed Oppenländer]

As can be imagined, the loss affected Rettenmaier, and it rammed home with razor sharp clarity the fact that every one of his men was someone's son or father. He genuinely cared for his men. Rettenmaier led his battalion throughout the entire summer campaign and saw many of his officers and men killed. After leading a successful assault against the Serafimovich bridgehead, Rettenmaier headed home for some well deserved furlough, only to return to Stalingrad and find his division had been bled white. He felt guilty that he had been enjoying himself back in the homeland while his comrades were being killed and mutilated in Stalingrad.

– – –

The division was fortunate to have three good men leading its grenadier regiments. While Hauptmann Rettenmaier temporarily commanded Grenadier-Regiment 578, the other two regiments were led by Oberstleutnant Brandt[13] and Major Braun[14].

Like Rettenmaier, Oberstleutnant Hans-Georg Brandt of Grenadier-Regiment 577 cared deeply for his men. One example will suffice. On 2 July, Gefreiter Franz Winter[15], a messenger on the staff of 6. Kompanie in Brandt's II. Battalion, witnessed a shocking event during a Soviet tank attack that would ultimately demonstrate how Brandt felt about his men:

> We had a good view over the battlefield from our elevated position. What we saw happening there caused the blood to freeze in our veins: to the left of us, in the hollow of a valley, the third platoon of our fifth company was attacked. We saw how they surrendered and ran towards the tanks with their hands above their heads. These monsters circled around our comrades, opened fire and pulped them under their tracks.

Winter's unit was ordered to fall back and the situation gradually eased. It was then that Winter and his comrades saw Major Brandt:

Oberstleutnant Hans-Georg Brandt, commander of Gr.Rgt.577.

13. Brandt, Oberst Hans-Georg, RK; Gr.Rgt.577; born 4 November, 1903 in Grimma. Died of wounds, 4 January, 1943 in Stalingrad.

14. Braun, Oberstleutnant Willi, RK; II./Gr.Rgt.576; born 6 February, 1902 in Hasenweiler. Missing in action, 2 February, 1943 in Stalingrad.

15. Winter, Gefreiter Franz, 6./Gr.Rgt.577; born 17 July, 1922 in Hochdorf. Still alive in 2006.

Sitting in a roadside ditch, surrounded by officers, was our battalion commander, a beaten man. I had never seen a German officer in such a state. A person who was otherwise seen by us ordinary soldiers to be head and shoulders above us, in appearance and conduct, now sat there and we could see that he was also only a human, like us, how he was depressed and tormented by anxiety. He had observed the tragedy down below through binoculars. He probably also felt responsible for it.

Brandt had commanded his battalion in Grenadier-Regiment 577 from the first day of its creation. In fact, it is probably correct to say he even commanded it before that because he led III./Infanterie-Regiment 520, the unit which was transferred en masse on 4 December 1940 to form II./Infanterie-Regiment 577. When regiment commander Oberst Max Voigt[16] was transferred home at the end of September 1942 due to heart problems, Major Brandt took over as Regimentsführer and led the regiment in an exemplary manner. The fighting in Stalingrad-North had been a severe test but his superiors were impressed by his performance and he received a promotion to Oberstleutnant in November.

Orlov

Familie Braun

The third Regimentsführer was Major Willi Braun, an avid sportsman who excelled at swimming, skiing, marksmanship and horseriding, the latter bringing him to grief in May 1939 when a fall during a tournament put him out of action for two months. He was also a keen motor enthusiast and was one of the first in his home town of Hasenweiler to own a private car. He began his career as a police officer and it lasted for 13 years, until he was transferred over to the army in October 1935. Various postings followed until he was transferred in late November 1940 into the newly-forming 305. Infanterie-Division as commander of II./Infanterie-Regiment 576. And he had commanded that battalion ever since. The entire summer campaign had been difficult but

Left: Major Willi Braun, commander of II./Gr.Rgt.576, and temporary regiment commander throughout November 1942.

16. Voigt, Oberst Max, DKiG; Gr.Rgt.577; born 25 September, 1893 in Markranstädt. Missing in action, January 1945 near Warthbruecken.

it all paled into insignificance compared to the weeks in Stalingrad. When the regiment commander, Oberstleutnant Karl-Heinz Krüder[17], went on leave in October, and the substitute commander Oberstleutnant Werner Gunkel[18] was transferred in late October, Braun took temporary control of the regiment.

These were the three men leading the German attack against the Soviet bridgehead.

- - -

Major Fedor Iosifovich Pechenyuk, commander of 650th Rifle Regiment.

Their opposite numbers were a diverse group of men. The most accomplished was Major Fedor Iosifovich Pechenyuk, commander of 650th Rifle Regiment. According to Lyudnikov, he was "distinguished for his bravery and was gifted with that priceless intuition in war which enabled him to take bold decisions and carry them into effect". Pechenyuk was born to a Christian family in 1906 in Torchin village in Zhitomir province and was Ukrainian by nationality. He completed 8 years of school and became a member of the Communist Party in 1927. He worked as a secretary of the agricultural union in the town of Rusanovka in Zhitomir province but joined the Red Army in 1928. He graduated from the state infantry academy, fought in the Finnish Winter War of 1939-40 and had participated in the Great Patriotic War since July 1941. He commanded 834th Rifle Regiment of 400th Rifle Division until transferred to 650th Rifle Regiment on 29 May 1942 as its commander. He was a toughened commander greatly respected by his subordinates for his personal bravery and wise military decisions.

Almost the polar opposite of Pechenyuk was the commander of 768th Rifle Regiment, Major Grigory Mikhailovich Gunyaga[19]. Neurotic, panicky and preferring to lead from his command post, Gunyaga believed that a commander should control his units from headquarters, where more information was available, rather than in a hands-on manner. After all, that's what subordinate commanders were for. Lyudnikov graciously described him as "overcautious" but "his calm foresight […] had produced good results". He took command of the regiment on 29 May 1942 and had led it in his nervous manner ever since.

The third regiment commander was by far the youngest but perhaps the most adored. Captain Vladimir Anufrievich Konovalenko[20] was born 22 April, 1917 in Skrebni village in Vitebsk province to a Russian Christian family. Completed 9 years of school, joined the Red Army in 1937 and fought in the

Major Grigory Mikhailovich Gunyaga, commander of 768th Rifle Regiment.

Orlov

---

17. Krüder, Oberst Karl-Heinz, Gr.Rgt.576; born 14 October, 1895 in Lehe/Wesermünde. Died 29 April, 1943 in Lager Nr. 97 Yelabuga.
18. Gunkel, Oberstleutnant Werner, II./Gr.Rgt.576; born 13 August, 1896 in Baumgarten. No further information known.
19. No further information known.
20. Konovalenko, Major Vladimir Anufrievich, HotSU; 344th RR; born 22 April, 1917 in Skrebni village. Killed in action, 19 March, 1944.

Captain Vladimir Anufrievich Konovalenko, commander of 344th Rifle Regiment.

Finnish Winter War. He graduated from the Sukhumi infantry academy in 1941 but had only participated in the Great Patriotic War since January 1942. He became a member of the Communist Party later that year. As a senior-lieutenant and assistant to the divisional chief of operations, he accompanied 650th Rifle Regiment across the Volga on the night of 15 October and was one of the first division members to set foot on the tortured soil of Stalingrad.

On 17 October, the commander of 344th Rifle Regiment, Colonel Dmitri Aleksandrovich Reutsky[21], was severely wounded when a German shell struck his observation post. Major Vladimir Betlamovich Mikaberidze[22] took temporary command of the regiment but Lyudnikov had his eye on a commander who was as brave as Pechenyuk and as prudent as Gunyaga: Senior-Lieutenant Konovalenko.

Konovalenko was very young and junior in rank to many officers in the regiment. Colonel Reutsky's wounding had strongly affected him. Lyudnikov once heard Konovalenko arguing with his superior, Major Rutkovsky[23], that Reutsky would not have been hurt had he, Konovalenko, been in 344th Rifle Regiment.

"My, what a guardian angel you are!" said Rutkovsky sarcastically.

"That's not the point!" the usually calm Konovalenko angrily exclaimed. "I crossed to this bank before the others and I knew what the situation was like here and where the regimental commander's observation post could be set up."

Konovalenko had often accompanied Lyudnikov around the regimental sectors so that the division commander could see for himself how observation posts and strongpoints had been set up and communications between them organised. It was on these inspection tours that Lyudnikov came to appreciate the inherent military talent of his young escort. In a meeting with his military council that night, Lyudnikov turned to his chief-of-staff, Lieutenant-Colonel Shuba[24], and said:

"The 344th Regiment needs a commander who will have to be appointed from your staff."

Shuba was slightly taken aback: "Whom do you have in mind?"

"Konovalenko."

No-one said a word. Colonel Kurov[25], the division's deputy commander, was the oldest and Lyudnikov waited to see what he would say: "Konovalenko is an intelligent commander but," said Kurov, making a helpless gesture, "what about subordination? The regiment has captains and majors: how can a senior-lieutenant take command?"

Kurov's objection was overruled and they sent for Konovalenko. He reported in field dress, assuming that he was to go to the regiments on some job or the other. He was embarrassed and overjoyed at the confidence shown in him. He looked at Lyudnikov and said slowly: "If you're sure I'll be able to cope…"

21. Reutsky, Colonel Dmitri Aleksandrovich; 344th RR; no further information known

22. Mikaberidze, Major Vladimir Betlamovich; 344th RR; Killed in action, 19 November, 1943.

23. Rutkovsky, Major Konstantin Romanovich, 138th RD; Killed in action, 21 November, 1942 in Stalingrad.

24. Shuba, Lieutenant-Colonel Vasili Ivanovich, no further information known.

25. Kurov, Colonel Ivan Ivanovich, 138th RD; no further information known.

"Don't you dare think you won't cope!" the divisional commissar butted in. "Or we'll all be in the soup."

Promoted to Captain and given command of the regiment on 25 October, Konovalenko quickly repaid the trust placed in him by proving to be a first-rate leader respected by all his subordinates. Of course, as a young officer with little experience in leading a large formation, he occasionally made mistakes. For example, on 3 November, he submitted his plans on paper for the coming day, the main objective being to probe the German defences to establish where their main strongpoints were located. This would be accomplished by sending out three storm groups. Apparently, Lyudnikov thought Konovalenko should already know this. In red pencil, Lyudnikov scrawled across Konovalenko's memo: "What are you doing that you don't know the enemy's firing positions?" Obviously agitated, Lyudnikov scribbled "in charge of" next to Konovalenko's title of "Commander 344th Rifle Regiment", thereby putting Konovalenko in his place by clearly indicating to him that he led the regiment only by Lyudnikov's good grace. It should be noted that this is the sole occasion in which any tension can be found between the two. In all other documents, and particularly in post-war memoirs, Lyudnikov has nothing but glowing praise for his 25-year-old regiment commander.

– – –

The heart and soul of the Soviet defence, however, was the division commander, Colonel Ivan Ilyich Lyudnikov. He took command of 138th Rifle Division on 16 May, 1942 and had become its keystone, its driving force, from the very first day. Others had commanded the division before him: Major-General Yakov Andreyevich Ishchenko[26] (14 March 1941 – 22 September 1941); Colonel Pavel Maksimovich Yagunov[27] (25 September 1941 – 23 March 1942); and Colonel Mikhael Yakovlevich Pimenov[28] (24 March 1942 – 15 May 1942). But it was Lyudnikov who inspired his subordinates to achieve the impossible, led them, shared the concerns of his soldiers and counselled them with sage advice. Russian by nationality, Lyudnikov was born on 26 September, 1902 in the village of Krivaya Kosa, located in the Novoazovskiy district of the Donetsk province. His father was a harbour worker down at the Azov Sea. The family's dire financial situation forced Lyudnikov to begin working in a coal mine as an 11-year old boy. He had an innate military talent and the violent upheavals of war

Orlov

Colonel Lyudnikov in his observation post during the fighting in December 1942.

26. Ishchenko, Major-General Yakov Andreyevich, 138th RD; date of birth unknown. Died 1 April, 1970.

27. Yagunov, Colonel Pavel Maksimovich, 138th RD; born 10 January, 1900 in Cheberchina. Killed in action, 5 July, 1942.

28. No further information known.

and revolution in Russia and the Ukraine soon allowed him to demonstrate this. He became a member of the Red Guards in 1917, as a 15-year old. A year later, he joined the regular Red Army as a soldier. "From this moment on", said Lyudnikov, "my beloved life as a soldier began." He participated in the Russian Civil war, first as a Red cavalryman, then a sailor with the Azov Flotilla and finally a machine-gunner on a Tatschanka[29]. After the Civil War, he aspired to enter an artillery school, however, his third grade village education was not sufficient for the artillery. He graduated from the Odessa infantry academy in 1925 as one of the school's best officers and became a member of the Communist Party that same year. He graduated from the M.V. Frunze Military academy in 1938 where he had learned so well that he was offered a teaching position there. Lyudnikov chose to return to the troops. The war confirmed that this was his proper place and he fought in the Great Patriotic War from June 1941. He first commanded the 200th Rifle Division (26 June 1941 - 14 September 1941) of the Kiev Special military district, then the 16th Independent Rifle Brigade (24 December 1941 - March 1942) and finally the 390th Armenian Rifle Division (March 1942 - April 1942) in the Crimea. However, it was his leadership of 138th Rifle Division during the Stalingrad fighting that would earn him eternal glory amongst the Soviet people.

8 November, 1942

By order of 305. Infanterie-Division, the remnants of Grenadier-Regiment 578's battalions were lumped together to form 'Kampfgruppe 578'. Hauptmann Rettenmaier was appointed temporary commander until the arrival of Oberstleutnant Max Liesecke[30], who had been given command of the regiment effective from 1 November, 1942, but who in actuality wouldn't arrive for some considerable time. On 8 November, Oberstleutnant Paltzo, divisional chief-of-staff, made the perilous journey through the demolished factory to visit the regimental commanders and suggest they make plans and preparations for an attack. His first stop was at Major Brandt's bunker near Hall 3 on the Kommissarstrasse. Next, he went to Hauptmann Rettenmaier's command post in one of the workhalls. He discussed general matters. Just as he was leaving, Paltzo said casually: "You might want to give some thought as to how we could get through to the Volga".

Such was the advanced order received by Rettenmaier. The remaining regimental commander, Major Braun of Grenadier-Regiment 576, received his 'advanced order' in a similar fashion. Hauptmann Rettenmaier immediately got to the task at hand. Questions already put to his men upon his return – in order to orient himself – had clearly shown that there were two major enemy strongpoints in his sector:

> The course of the front was approximately as follows (starting from Kampfgruppe 578): between the gun factory and the Volga were two rows of houses, mostly shops or exhibition halls constructed in a crude fashion. One building used to be in our possession and stood to the left of some open ground. We called it the Apotheke[31]. The distance to the cliffs of the Volga bank was about 300 to 400 metres. Close to the steep slope stood Haus 79.
>
> About 200 metres to the left of the Apotheke and a bit further back was the Kommissarhaus. It was a fortress-like, red brick construction that dominated the gently sloping foreground to

---

29. A horse-drawn machine-gun carriage of the Red cavalry.

30. Liesecke, Oberstleutnant Max, Gr.Rgt.578; born 2 October, 1898 in Passau. Missing in action, January 1943 in Stalingrad.

31. Trans.: 'Apotheke' = 'chemist's shop'. The Russian designation for this building was 'Apteka'.

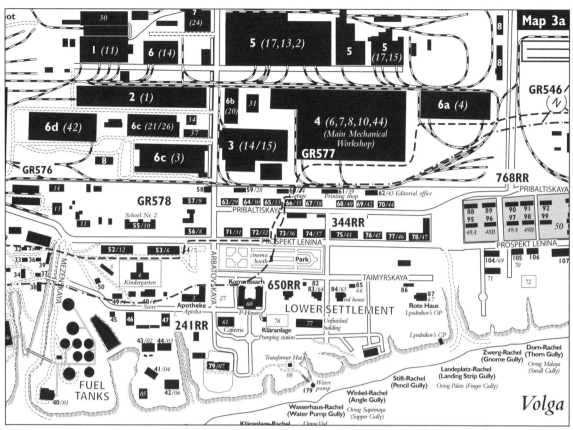

Course of the German and Soviet front-lines, 8 November, 1942.

the Volga. From there, the front-line jumped back a distance of about 800 metres from the river and then curved to the left, back to the Volga bank. The neighbouring regiment to the left was the 577th, to the right the 576th. Regiment 578 had a direct connection with this regiment: the command posts were on the ground floor of the same factory building.

Jotting down a few brief words to his wife that night, Rettenmaier wrote:

I don't have much time for a letter. The entire day was spent thinking and planning... The battle for Stalingrad continues and will claim further sacrifices.

– – –

With so many pioneer battalions being concentrated for the attack, it was thought necessary to put someone in overall charge of them. Someone who would ensure they were properly utilised. Someone, in other words, who knew the pioneers intimately. Armeepionierführer Oberst Herbert Selle was the man responsible for choosing the overall commander:

Assigned by me to provide care and pioneer-technical advice for their employment was the reliable commander of Pionier-Bataillon 672, Major Linden[32].

Choosing Linden to oversee the attack on the Barrikady bridgehead was a wise move. Major Josef August Linden was a man whose exploits with 6. Armee in Russia would

32. Linden, Major Josef, Pi.Btl.672; born 9 February, 1904 in Essen. Died 26 March, 1981 in Essen.

become legendary. Born and educated in Essen, Linden entered federal police service in Hannoverisch-Münden on 29 April, 1926. He was called to active duty almost a decade later, on 16 March, 1936, and received the rank of Oberleutnant in Pionier-Bataillon 36, a unit newly activated in Mainz. He was sworn in that very day. On 6 October the same year, he was assigned to 2./Pionier-Abteilung 29[33] in Hann.-Münden. He was promoted to Hauptmann on 31 July, 1937 and attended a pioneer unit commanders course with Pionier-Bataillon 49 from 1 August to 11 October, 1937, where he received training on how to command a motorised pioneer company. Upon completion of the course, he took command of 3./Pionier-Bataillon 16[34] with which he served up to May 1940. Just prior to the French campaign, he was transferred to the OKH Führerreserve while simultaneously assuming duties of the Kommandeur of Pionier-Bataillon 256. He was acting CO until the new commander arrived. He led the battalion through Belgium but relinquished command after twelve days, on 21 May, 1940. On the same day, he was awarded the Iron Cross Second Class for his actions as temporary commander. On 30 May, 1940 he took command of Pionier-Bataillon 672, a position he would hold until called up for the special operation in Stalingrad. He received a promotion to Major on 18 January, 1942, effective from 1 January, and was awarded the Iron Cross First Class on 15 September, 1941. After playing a role in building and maintaining the vital bridges over the Don in late August and throughout most of September, Linden and his battalion were moved to Kalach-on-Don, about 90 kilometres west of Stalingrad.

The Armee was setting up a Pionierschule whose main purpose was to instruct troops throughout the coming autumn and winter: Linden and his men were selected to become the school's resident training battalion. In a short amount of time, the Armee-Pionier-Schule was set up in a former sanatorium on the Don hills near Kalach under the command of Oberst Hans Mikosch[35]. Linden was the 'deputy principal' of the new school. Under his guidance, a complete program of different pioneer courses was created to cater to all ranks and arms of service. Among the courses on offer were 'Construction of field fortifications', 'Tank destruction' and 'Assault troop training for house-to-house combat', the latter becoming increasingly in demand as weeks spent in the ruins of Stalingrad turned into months. The area around the Armee-Pionier-Schule was an ideal training ground for every pioneering purpose. The trenchworks and fortifications constructed on the Don hills during the training courses were later used by German units during the Soviet counteroffensive. The hulks of hundreds of T-34s lying destroyed or abandoned on nearby battlefields – lost by the Soviets during the massive battles in the Don bend in July and August – served as 'practice dummies' for the tank destruction courses. Five or six T-34s were even repaired and made operational so that students could practice their new skills on moving targets.[36] Assault troop tactics were rehearsed in the ruins of nearby villages and lessons gleaned from the vicious fighting just over the horizon in Stalingrad were rapidly integrated into both the theoretical

33. Also in this battalion at the same time were Oberfeldwebel Lundt, later Hauptmann and Führer of Pionier-Bataillon 336, and Oberfeldwebel Kurt Barth, later Oberleutnant and company commander in Pionier-Bataillon 162. Linden would meet both men again in Stalingrad.

34. This battalion was also at Stalingrad under its new designation: Panzerpionier-Bataillon 16 (16. Panzer-Division)

35. Mikosch, Generalleutnant Hans, EL, RK, DKiG; Pi.Rgt.677; born 7 January, 1898 in Kattowitz. Died 18 January, 1993 in Reichshof.

36. These tanks would inadvertently play a crucial role during the Soviet counteroffensive in November when German sentries at the Kalach bridge mistook a genuine Soviet tank pack for these friendly T-34s.

and practical aspects of the training. Major Linden was the one man who knew more than anyone else in 6. Armee about how to use pioneers in city fighting – he was the perfect choice. Linden recalls the moment he learned of his new assignment:

> The layover in Kalach was soon interrupted for me, however, when I received the following order by telephone from the Armeepionierführer (naturally with camouflaged terms and reference points) on the evening of 6 November: 'You will report to reference point X at 0900 hours on 7 November with your adjutant and several men that you will require to carry out a special task. Duration of the assignment will be 6–8 days. The battalion will remain in its current location and continue training.'

> I arrived at the designated place at the ordered time with my men (adjutant[37] and 6 men[38]) – it was the command post of 305. Infanterie-Division in Stalingrad. Here, the Divisionsführer, Oberst i.G. Steinmetz, and his chief-of-staff, Oberstleutnant Paltzo, informed me of what was being planned.

Steinmetz and Paltzo apprised Linden of the situation: the battles that had flowed back and forth in the Barrikady for the last three weeks, the current front-line, what was known about the enemy, plus many other crucial pieces of information needed by Linden to formulate his plan of attack. Linden was temporarily attached to 305. Infanterie-Division as Pionier-Führer and was informed that he had the following battalions placed at his disposal: Panzerpionier-Bataillon 50, Pionier-Bataillon 162, Pionier-Bataillon 294, Pionier-Bataillon 305 and Pionier-Bataillon 336. The two pioneer battalions belonging to the northern neighbour, Pionier-Bataillon 45 and Pionier-Bataillon 389, were ordered to co-operate. Linden looked over the strength figures for all seven battalions:

> With the exception of Pionier-Bataillon 305 and 389, the battalions were completely combat-ready. Pionier-Bataillon 305 was at about one-third strength and Pionier-Bataillon 389 about one-half combat strength. All battalions had Eastern Front experience from many battles and were fully qualified for their impending task.

Having received a rough outline of the task that stood before him, Linden called together the pioneer battalion commanders, all of whom had been ordered to be at 305. Infanterie-Division's HQ in the Schnellhefter Block at 0930 hours.

The crisp frostiness of a November morning still freshened the air. The glorious sun warmed the battalion commanders as they tarried around their cars, waiting to be summoned by Linden. They introduced themselves to each other, shook hands, and discussed common acquaintances. A few had met each other before, mostly in pre-war training exercises, but none were close friends.

> The battalion commanders, who had reported themselves to me in the meantime, were briefly oriented and received the order: 'Readiness for pioneer assault groups – commanders will be at my disposal in 3 hours at the advanced command post of 305. Infanterie-Division for a reconnaissance.' For the battalions, this brief order signified a careful preparation for the members of the assault groups and likewise good preparations for the weapons and pioneer combat equipment, particularly the flamethrowers, concentrated and elongated charges with the requisite ignition fuses, hand grenades and smoke-pots – moreover, an inspection of pioneer tools like axes, pick-axes, hatchets, spades and wire-cutters. These preparations had to be carefully met if everything was to work in action – every movement must be exactly right.

---

37. Adjutant was Leutnant Stahl. Stahl, Oberleutnant Horst, Stab Pi.Btl.672; born 16 June, 1902 in Gera. Died of wounds, February 1943 in Stalingrad.

38. Two of the 6 men were Schirr-Unteroffizier Georg Wagenpfeil and Gefreiter Erich Conrad.

After concluding the meeting with his battalion commanders, Linden met up again with Oberst Steinmetz, and together with the artillery commander, Major Erich Würker[39], drove the short distance to the Barrikady. They first surveyed the factory from an observation post situated on the dominating ridgeline. They then carefully worked their way down into the shattered industrial complex using trenches and paths through the wreckage, hidden from enemy view. There, they were joined by the three regiment commanders – Major Braun of 576, Oberstleutnant Brandt of 577 and Hauptmann Rettenmaier of 578 – to reconnoitre the attack area. They met with the various sector commanders who, thoroughly versed in the landmarks and enemy defences in their respective areas, briefed their high-level visitors. Once Linden obtained an accurate overview, he was able to ask:

What did the situation offer me?

305. Infanterie-Division was in constant operations and had suffered considerable casualties. The average trench strength of an infantry company was about 25–35 men.

The attack width of the division was about 2–2.5kms.

Armaments and ammunition were sufficient.

The enemy had elite troops in the bridgehead who defended themselves toughly, bitterly and cunningly. Through their army commander and his political commissars, who were likewise at the front in the bridgehead, discipline was brutally maintained – according to statements from deserters and prisoners. There is no land over the Volga. The Russians constantly received supplies of men and material at night-time from the other shore. He also received fire support from heavy weapons over there.

The terrain in the gun factory area was a gigantic field of rubble that gently fell away to the Volga – right up to the steep slope of the river bank. The ruins of the numerous workhalls were still partly standing with their steel frameworks and individual corrugated iron walls. Loosely hanging corrugated panels creaked eerily with each gust of wind, frequently clapping together and being pierced by shrapnel. A noise that couldn't be forgotten. The houses in the immediate vicinity of the factory were ruins, whose floors had mostly collapsed. The underground vaults of the workhalls and the cellars of the houses had been turned into command posts and strongpoints. Iron parts, wreckage of machines, gun barrels of all calibres scattered about in enormous quantities, T-beams, corrugated iron and massive craters made the entire terrain impassable. Panzers could not operate in this terrain. Trenches, which on the whole served as approach routes to the forward positions because the positions on the forward slope could be seen by the enemy, were constantly being improved by further construction.

With regards to the climatic conditions, it could be said that the Russian winter had in the meantime set in, the temperature getting lower and lower each day, and the inclemency of the weather could adversely affect the objective of the attack.

After my reconnaissance, I made my proposal to use the pioneers. Because the division had employed its three infantry regiments in the forward line and the division commander placed the attack Schwerpunkt with the middle regiment, I proposed that each infantry regiment be supported by a pioneer battalion in the following order: Pionier-Bataillon 294, Pionier-Bataillon 50, Pionier-Bataillon 336 with 305. Infanterie-Division and Pionier-Bataillon 162 and 389 with 389. Infanterie-Division. I placed Pionier-Bataillon 305 behind Pionier-Bataillon 50 in the sector of the spearhead regiment of 305. Infanterie-Division as a reserve.

The assault would be launched on 11 November, 1942. For the time of the attack, I chose the first light of day after the appropriate preparatory fire. Strong pioneer assault groups (at least

---

39. Würker, Oberstleutnant Erich, Art.Rgt.305; born 14 July, 1896 in Reichenbach. Died 18 March, 1943 in Lager Nr. 97 Yelabuga.

platoon strength) would push themselves into their starting positions under the protection of this fire, then the artillery would be abruptly advanced: after this, the pioneers would advance as the first wave and penetrate to their objectives while overcoming the enemy in known positions. Once there, they would immediately set themselves up for defence. Infantry would follow as the second wave and clear the enemy from the intermediate ground and subsequently take over the defensive line.

My proposal was accepted and details of its implementation were discussed with the regiment commanders. – Never before during the war had so many pioneer battalions been concentrated for a single attack in so small an area. – The commanders of the pioneer battalions employed on the sector of 305. Infanterie-Division were precisely briefed on site by me about boundaries, objectives and known enemy positions. Connections with the commanders of the attached weapons was taken up. From the advanced observation posts (towering ruins of houses and workhalls), the Russian positions 100 metres away (sometimes even closer) could be seen. Firing was not permitted from here, however, so as not to reveal the observation posts. The commanders had now briefed their company commanders on their assignments. All care had to be taken while doing this so that the Russians did not notice movements in the front-line and discern our attack objectives. A precise briefing of the neighbouring pioneer battalion to the left was taken over by 389. Infanterie-Division in its sector.

During the time of reconnaissance, the pioneers had the opportunity to conclude their preparations and experience the atmosphere of Stalingrad for themselves. There was no break in the fighting here in Stalingrad, something was always going on: the duel by artillery and infantry weapons from both sides, in addition to the special interlude by our rocket-launchers or the other side's 'Stalin Organ', the hail of bombs in the air from the air forces of both sides, each time met with a hurricane of anti-aircraft fire. Yes, a new kind of atmosphere dominated here. One only needed to look at the faces of the soldiers or the smoking ruins to know what was happening.

– – –

After the briefing and discussion of objectives, the officers of Pionier-Bataillon 336 noted the remarkable geographic similarities between Stalingrad and Korotoyak and were somewhat taken aback when they saw that a few Soviet strongpoints bore the same names as those in Korotoyak… 'Red House', 'White House'. But they knew this task was easily within their abilities. They were confident. Some would even say cocksure.

– – –

On the afternoon of 7 November, Hitler left his 'Wolfsschanze' headquarters near Rastenburg, East Prussia, and headed for München to celebrate the Beer Hall Putsch of 1923 with his old beer-drinking minions and the party faithful. It had become an annual Nazi tradition for him to deliver a major speech but in November 1942, with crises looming on several fronts, it would have been prudent for him to remain at Führer headquarters. Cancellation of the speech, however, would have indicated to the public that something serious was happening on one of the fronts. So, on 8 November, Hitler entered the Bürgerbräukeller to the ecstatic roar of a zealous crowd. Soon, they were belting out the Nazi party song 'Horst Wessel'. Hitler, kitted out in a brownshirt uniform with a swastika armband on his left sleeve, stood on the stage, chin in the air, and accepted the table-rattling salute:"Sieg Heil! Sieg Heil! Sieg Heil!" He then launched into a rousing speech: "My fellow German countrymen and women! Party comrades…" He began by talking about the good old days, such as his assumption to power 10 years earlier. He then hit out at the Jews, slammed Roosevelt and mocked the British. After several rabid minutes, he mentioned Stalingrad. It is worth quoting this section of his speech at length – and verbatim – because the tragic events that followed at Stalingrad would come back to haunt Hitler:

> If you read the Russian communiques since 22 June, you will read the following every day: 'Fighting of unimportant character' or maybe 'of important character'. 'We have shot down three times as many German planes'. 'The amount of sunken tonnage is already greater than the entire naval tonnage, greater than all types of German tonnage before the war'. They have so many of us missing that they amount to more divisions than we can ever muster. But above all, they are always fighting in the same place. Here and there they then say modestly, after 14 days, 'We have evacuated a city'. But in general they have been fighting since 22 June in the same place, always successfully; we are constantly being beaten back, and in this continued retreat we have slowly come to the Caucasus. I say 'slowly'!

> I should say that for my enemies, not for our soldiers. For the speed with which our soldiers have now traversed territory is gigantic. Also what was traversed this year is vast and historically unique. Now, I do not always do things just as the others want them done. I consider what the others probably believe, and then do the opposite on principle. So if Mr. Stalin expected that we would attack in the centre, I did not want to attack in the centre, not only because Mr. Stalin probably believed I would, but because I didn't care at all about it any more. But I wanted to come to the Volga, to a definite place, to a definite city. It accidentally bears the name of Stalin himself, but do not think that I went after it on that account.

> Indeed, it could have an altogether different name. But only because it is an important point, that is, there, 30 million tonnes of traffic can be cut off, including about 9 million tonnes of oil shipments. There, all the wheat pours in from those enormous territories of the Ukraine, of the Kuban territory, then to be transported to the North. There, the manganese ore was forwarded. A gigantic terminal was there; I wanted to take it. And do you know, we're modest: that is, we have it; there are only a couple of very small places left there.

> Now the others say: why aren't you fighting there? Because I don't want to make a second Verdun but would rather do it with very small shock units. Time plays no part here. No ships come up the Volga any more – that is the decisive thing.

> They have also reproached us, asking why it took us so long at Sevastopol? Because there, too, we did not want to cause an enormous mass murder. Blood is flowing as it is – more than enough. But Sevastopol fell into our hands, and the Crimea fell into our hands. We have reached goal after goal, stubbornly, persistently.

> And if the enemy, on his part, makes preparations to attack, don't think I want to forestall him there, but at the same moment, we let him attack also. Because then defence still is less expensive. Then just let him attack; he'll bleed to death that way, and thus far we have always taken care of the situation anyhow.

> At any rate, the Russians are not at the Pyrenees or before Seville; that, you see, is the same distance as for us to be in Stalingrad today, or on the Terek, let us say; – but we are there; that can really not be disputed. That is a fact, after all.

> Naturally, when nothing else will do any more, they also say it's a mistake. Then they suddenly turn around and say: 'It is absolutely a mistake for the Germans to have gone to Kirkenes, or to have gone to Narvik, or now perhaps to Stalingrad – what do they expect to do in Stalingrad? For Stalingrad is a capital mistake, a strategic mistake'. We will just wait and see whether that was a strategic mistake…

'I don't want to make a second Verdun but would rather do it with very small shock units… Time plays no part…' These words underplayed the sacrifices already made in

Stalingrad. More importantly, these words condemned five fresh pioneer battalions to hellish house-to-house combat from which few would survive. Hitler's boastful bragging committed him to completely capturing and holding Stalingrad, come what may. What is more, his speech – among the most conceited and vainglorious in history – was heard by many in 6. Armee who were barely days away from sacrificing their lives in pursuit of the Führer's goal.

– – –

In a letter home, Gefreiter Willi Füssinger[40], a member of the supply train of 1./Pionier-Bataillon 305, reports about the conditions affecting the common soldier in Stalingrad:

> "It has now already become quite cold near us. It is somewhat unpleasant on the open plains! We should have received a rest long ago but it is not yet completely finished at Stalingrad. Only a small strip, along the Volga, is still occupied by the Russians.

> "At present, men on leave from the east are at home. Want to see what's awaiting me. Today, one would be happy if a bed and a house was seen again. No more houses are standing here in Stalingrad and the city will not rise again for 20–30 years.

> "Now we hope for the best for the future, in particular that this slaughter here also stops…"

Füssinger's wish would not be granted. A more senseless slaughter was soon to begin.

9 November, 1942

Paulus decided to pay a visit to LI. Armeekorps to check on preparations for the coming assault. He departed in his plane from 6. Armee headquarters at 0915 hours and landed half an hour later at the command post of LI. Armeekorps north-west of Gumrak railway station. Oberst i.G. Clausius, chief-of-staff of LI. Armeekorps, presented a compilation of prisoner and deserter statements out of which emerged the mood, condition and casualties of the Russian troops employed in Stalingrad. Paulus then left and headed east, towards the city. At 1015 hours, he arrived at the command post of 305. Infanterie-Division located in the Schnellhefter Block west of the gun factory. The division commanders of 305. and 389. Infanterie-Divisions talked about the attack on 11 November, of whose success they were convinced. While the pioneer battalions allocated to 305. Infanterie-Division were incorporated into the grenadier regiments, at 389. Infanterie-Division they remained directly subordinate to the division. The equipping of the pioneer battalions with flamethrowers appeared to be too little. Paulus and his entourage departed at 1030 hours and drove north-east to the Dzerhezinsky Tractor Factory where Paulus looked over the devastated factory and talked to Major Wilhelm Knetsch[41], commander of Grenadier-Regiment 545, which had no role in the forthcoming offensive. Paulus left at 1215 hours for the return trip to Korps command post, arriving back there at 1315 hours. Paulus examined the assault plan for 11 November with General der Artillerie Seydlitz-Kurzbach. He ordered that the Korpspionierführer or Armeepionierführer help out with the flamethrowers. He requested – as far as was possible – the earliest selection of a manpower calculation for the attack on the

---

40. Füssinger, Obergefreiter Willi, 1./Pi.Btl.305; born 1 January, 1909 in Mohrhaus. Missing in action, January 1943 in Stalingrad.

41. Knetsch, Oberst Wilhelm, RK, DKiG; Gr.Rgt.545; born 26 February, 1906 in Marburg a.d. Lahn. Died 27 March, 1982 in Garmisch-Partenkirchen.

Lazur Chemical Factory. At 1400 hours, Paulus climbed into his Storch plane and headed back to his command post in Golubinsky.

On Stalingrad's outskirts, the newly arrived pioneers tried to explain to their families where they were now located. Oberzahlmeister Erich Bauchspiess, Pionier-Bataillon 336, wrote to his wife:

> You'll be able to imagine where we are now stuck. To be precise, in a focal point of the highest magnitude. Things appear so crazy here, as I have never before seen. Only a very few houses could be patched up to become habitable. You can't really talk of houses here, other than a couple of industrial or office buildings, because they are the same huts as in every other little place. There is absolutely nothing directly behind the city. After 40km there is the first small village. That is where my supplies are. This 40km stretch is a flat plain where neither trees nor shrubs grow. All undeveloped land.

> Rumbling above our heads day and night is artillery of every calibre and aircraft of all types unloading their stuff during the day. At night, which have now become very long, the Russians also drop their bombs. We hope we are able to contribute to a decision in the next few days. Unfortunately, it became very cold four days ago. Last night it was 16 degrees below. But the period of mud, thank God, did not come, because it would have brought everything here to a standstill…

Krauss

With the start of the attack rapidly approaching, the pioneers arranged their equipment, readied their weapons and were distributed into storm groups. Gefreiter Karl Krauss, 2./Pionier-Bataillon 45, recalls the arrangements carried out by his battalion:

> Preparations for the attack and organisation of assault detachments (into 20 man strong groups). The objectives of the attack were first shown to us with the aid of aerial photographs of the rubbled landscape. Our reliable company commander, Oberleutnant Walter Heinrich[42], divided the Kompanie into three assault groups and one reserve group that would remain behind under Leutnant Anton Locherer. Combat strength of the Kompanie was about 90 men.

Left: Oberleutnant Walter Heinrich, the much-loved commander of 2./Pi.Btl.45, as a Leutnant in 1941.

---

42. Heinrich, Major Walter, DKiG, EB; 2./Pi.Btl.45; born 6 April, 1918 in Ulm. Died 13 February, 1997 in Ulm/Donau. See Appendix 2 (page 573) for more details.

The grenadier regiments received the official attack order late in the piece. Hauptmann Rettenmaier remembers the moment:

> On 9 November came the order for the attack to the Volga bank. The order stated: 'The bank of the Volga is to be taken securely into our hands and the encircled enemy destroyed. As reinforcement, Kampfgruppe 578 has received Pionier-Bataillon 50 and allocated Pionier-Bataillon 305.' For the attack, all batteries made available would operate on the attack area or suppress the enemy's artillery positions. Multiple connections and cross-connections were secured to all of these batteries.

After receiving his verbal 'advanced order' from Paltzo on 8 November, Rettenmaier had talked it over with some of his men who knew the Soviet methods in Stalingrad. He was therefore prepared when the official order arrived:

> The assault was planned as follows: the Apotheke and the Kommissarhaus would be taken in a surprise attack. The attack of Regiment 576 on the fuel installation would begin at the same time, and after reaching a pre-determined point in advance of the attack area of Regiment 578, a thrust through the gully on to the Volga bank and to Haus 79 would take place. The artillery would suddenly open fire at the beginning of the attack, suppressing and screening the designated targets with smoke. All Infanteriegeschütz and mortars would be kept ready to combat enemy resistance in the area.

> The following Kampfgruppen were formed from Regiment 578:

> 1. A group, reinforced by Pi.Btl.305; Mission: take the Apotheke in a surprise attack.

> 2. Pz.Pi.Btl.50; Mission: take the Kommissarhaus. (The commander expressly waived being supported by infantry.)

> 3. A group, reinforced by Pi.Btl.305; Mission: thrust through to the Volga, reach the water's edge of the Volga and press further up the river along the Sandbank.

> 4. A reinforced battalion; Mission: prepare to attack Haus 79. The beginning of the attack would be separately ordered for both the last groups.

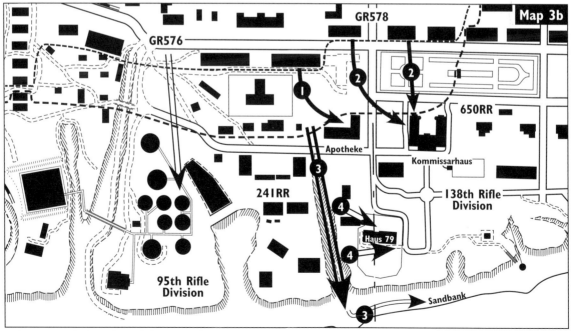

Objectives and plan of attack for Grenadier-Regiment 578's four combat groups. Note that the attack would strike the boundary between 138th and 95th Rifle Divisions.

Bundesarchiv

The battlefield. The Barrikady Gun Factory and its lower settlement looked like this (above) on 13 August, 1942, prior to any bombing raids or fighting within its boundaries. After the battle, it was a scene of utter devastation (below). Not one building would be left intact after the most concentrated, vicious fighting the world would ever see.

Mark/NARA

The months of fighting would take place in the 'Lower Settlement' of the Barrikady Gun Factory, a small housing estate east of the massive industrial complex. Residing in this settlement were the factory's upper management, such as workshop heads, engineers, and craftsmen. The factory director also lived in a grand residence there and ran operations from his head office, called the 'factory administration building' but better known by the German name of the 'Kommissarhaus'. It was a comfortable area, complete with a shady park, gardens, a theatre, a club, schools and a kindergarten. A technical college was also being constructed. The factory workers lived in much humbler dwellings – rows of wooden shacks south-east of the Barrikady and in the massive 'Upper Settlement' west of the factory. All of their lives were turned upside down on the morning of 24 August, 1942, when German planes rained tonnes of deadly bombs and incendiaries on the factory. The ground shook from the explosion of massive demolition bombs. The houses in the lower settlement were quickly set ablaze, but no-one asked to save their own houses: they were all busy saving the factory. According to incomplete information, from 24 August to 6 September, 150 high-explosive bombs and more than 2,500 incendiaries were dropped on the factory. Nevertheless, the workers stoically remained at their work stations and churned out several dozen 76mm guns for the front a few kilometres away. The Barrikady not only helped the front with guns. Often, together with the cannon, went gun crews, formed by the factory workers. And as the fighting moved closer, the workers were formed into militia brigades.

Right: The factory as viewed from the high ground on its western boundary – positions that would soon be occupied by German artillery observers. The pylon – known as 'Hühnerleiter' (chicken roosts) to the Germans – carried electricity from the StalGRES plant south of Stalingrad to a substation that served the factory. The Barrikady also had its own power generators.

Below: The lower settlement during its construction in 1916, as seen from the roof of Workshop 1 (Hall 2). The open ground on the left would soon be filled by Workshop 14/15 (Hall 3), while a railway line and concrete boundary wall would be laid down between the lower settlement and the factory.

Barrikady Museum

Barrikady Museum

Familie Püttmann

Wilhelm Püttmann as an Oberleutnant in 1941 (photo taken in the 'Englischen Garten' in München).

The infantry units made preparations to accommodate the pioneers. Hauptmann Wilhelm Püttmann, the commander of III./ Grenadier-Regiment 578, issued a handwritten order to his battalion for its relief by Panzerpionier-Bataillon 50:

1.) Relief by Pionier-Bataillon 50 on 10.11.1942, 1900 hours. By 1900 hours, Pionier-Bataillon 50 (mot.) will assume responsibility for the front-line in the blocks of houses, boundary on the right Gruppe Meier[43], boundary on the left Gruppe Düthorn[44]. After relief, Gruppe Meier will go to Kampfgruppe Kretz[45]. Kampfgruppe Frank[46] will move to Meier cellar as regimental reserve. Leutnant Zorn[47] will remove the S-mines after darkness has fallen. Confirmation of operation to battalion command post by 1800 hours.

2.) Successful relief and deployment in new locations will be immediately reported to battalion command post."

– – –

In contrast to the other pioneer battalions, which were almost at full strength and had received detailed guidelines for planning their attack, Pionier-Bataillon 389 was to play a relatively minor role but had greater latitude in formulating its assault plan. The key player in Pionier-Bataillon 389 was Oberleutnant Hans-Ludwig Eberhard[48], commander of its 2. Kompanie. The combat strength of the battalion was so low that every available men from 1. and 3. Kompanie was placed under Eberhard's control. After recovering from a severe bout of jaundice, Eberhard returned to Stalingrad on 28 October and was shocked by what he found:

---

43. Meier – Either Mayer, Oberfeldwebel Anton, III./Gr.Rgt.578; or Maier, Unteroffizier Ernst, 1./Gr.Rgt.578.

44. Düthorn, Unteroffizier Josef, 7./Gr.Rgt.578; born 16 June, 1915. Killed in action, 11 October, 1944 in Italy.

45. Kretz, Oberleutnant Erwin, Gr.Rgt.578; born 18 August, 1917 in Rastatt. Killed in action, 13 November, 1942 in Stalingrad

46. Frank, Hauptfeldwebel Albert, 11./Gr.Rgt.578.

47. Zorn, Oberleutnant Hans, 1./Pi.Btl.305; born 11 January, 1921 in Pforzheim. Died 16 September, 1989 in Frankfurt am Main. See Appendix 2 (page 580) for more details.

48. Eberhard, Hauptmann Hans-Ludwig, DKiG; Pi.Btl.389; born 9 June, 1917 in Shanghai, China. Died 30 November, 2002 in Rheinbach. See Appendix 2 (page 571) for more details.

Oberleutnant Hans-Ludwig Eberhard, commander of 2./ Pi.Btl.389 and provisional battalion commander, as a Feldwebel in 1937.

After an adventurous trip, I rejoined my company on the outskirts of Stalingrad. Since my departure, they had sunk to a fighting strength of 1 NCO and 11 pioneers. It was the same thing with the first and third companies. The battalion no longer had any officers. In the rest positions in a gully, the supply train was now combed out. In addition, through several men returning from field-hospitals, and by absorbing the remnants of the other two companies, the combat strength of my company grew to 2 NCOs and 30 pioneers. They were the last levy. My Hauptfeldwebel, together with two men and the Sanitäts-Unteroffizier, formed the 'supply section'.

One of Eberhard's two available NCOs was Unteroffizier Wilhelm Iffland[49], a valiant soldier who had already earned both grades of the Iron Cross in the 6 months the battalion had been on the Ostfront. Eberhard continues:

During my absence, the division had taken the suburban settlement of the tractor factory in Stalingrad and the factory itself. Now, they were only a few hundred metres from the Volga.

Our gully had been made very comfortable. Resourceful pioneers had built a wind wheel, removed a dynamo and batteries from a shot-up tank and so provided our dug-outs with electric lighting.

The rest period lasted until 9 November. During this time, we trained keenly for assault troop missions in house-to-house combat. I believed I had found the right mixture of men and equipment. We formed two assault detachments, each with two flamethrowers teams. Everyone else had two bags slung around their necks, filled with hand grenades. In addition, everyone carried a submachine-gun, mostly of the Russian type[50].

If the moment for the attack could be freely chosen, then we would opt for early in the morning, which meant still under cover of darkness, so that the objective could be reached when dawn was breaking. In this way, even the range of our submachine-guns would be adequate.

Oberleutnant Eberhard was informed that a large-scale operation was being planned to wipe out the Soviet bridgehead east of the Barrikady Gun Factory and that his battalion would take part:

The time had come. The division, still deployed in the northern part of the city, would attack again on 11 November and seize the Volga bank. The units to the right of us, that is, more towards the centre of the city, had to cope with much greater difficulties than we did. The width of the city was considerably greater there. To make progress, the army had strengthened the units deployed there with five pioneer battalions that had been flown in.

Much to his delight, Eberhard was told that his unit would not be playing the main role in the upcoming assault:

I was glad that our division – and as a result 'my Restbataillon' – was only directed to cooperate. This allowed me a certain freedom in the operational planning. And I was able to act independently... well, almost independently. I had my reasons for that. The new pioneer battalions attacking in the neighbouring sector wanted to employ assault guns, an excellent

49. Iffland, Unteroffizier Wilhelm, Pi.Btl.389; born 13 August, 1914 in Warstein. Killed in action, 11 November, 1942 in Stalingrad. Awarded the Iron Cross Second Class on 29 May, 1942, the First Class on 17 August, 1942.

50. German troops were quite fond of the Soviet PPSh submachine-gun, its main advantages being the 71-round drum magazine and the ability to fire from a prone position.

weapon, but in my estimation unsuitable for streetfighting, and even more so in darkness. Besides that, they easily made their presence known because their engines needed to be warmed up in the cold weather.

Having been informed where his battalion would attack, Eberhard ventured to the front to undertake a personal reconnaissance:

> On the evening of 9 November, I called on our infantry in the most forward positions and asked them to fill me in. It was relatively quiet. In hindsight, I believe the enemy had completely positioned himself for heavy combat in the city centre and made his preparations by neglecting our sector. During the orientation, while I was surveying the terrain from an advanced machine-gun post, a few civilians formed themselves into small groups. The machine-gun team leader chuckled: that happened every evening. Women and children came out of the cellars and headed down to the Volga to fetch water. They would be back in half an hour. I quickly decided to join the water carriers with my escort. After about a hundred metres I could discern the gullies that led down to the river bank. The enemy positions also had to be there. It was time to head back, because I didn't need to know any more, and I was also feeling uneasy.

– – –

Despite Linden's earlier assertion that "panzers could not operate in this terrain", quite a few armoured vehicles had been allotted for the assault. Apart from the assault guns of Sturmgeschütz-Abteilung 244 (5 long-barrels, 7 short-barrels, 6 sIG33B) and Sturmgeschütz-Abteilung 245 (2 long-barrels, 2 short-barrels, 6 sIG33B), there was a company of panzers from 14. Panzer-Division. It belonged to Oberleutnant Paul Schuknecht's[51] II./Panzer-Regiment 36 (Schuknecht was commander of 8. Kompanie but was temporarily commanding the battalion). It has not been possible to determine the name of the officer who commanded the panzer company subordinated to 305. Infanterie-Division, but it might well have been Schuknecht himself. The other candidate is Oberleutnant Hans-Günther Twisselmann[52], commander of 6./Panzer-Regiment 36. In any case, this panzer support company possessed 6 Panzer III long-barrels and 1 Panzer IV long-barrel. On 5 November, the panzers had been held in reserve in the Bread Factory (grid square 73d), ready to intervene in the fighting, but a few days later they were pulled back to the edge of the city (grid square 65d) to rest and refit. In preparation for the attack, Oberleutnant Schuknecht conducted reconnaissance of the proposed battleground and the route his panzers needed to take to get there. His report makes for interesting reading and conveys a tanker's perspective about the wisdom and efficacy of deploying panzers in city fighting:

> Approach route: Edge of the city (grid square 65d) to the operational area
>
> Distance: 3km
>
> Operational terrain: Extremely difficult technical driving through piles of rubble, bomb- and mortar-craters. (Only very low speeds are possible, extremely poor turning possibilities, no possibility for united deployment).
>
> Operations of panzers must therefore be carried out in small groups (about 2 panzers). Driving in darkness in cratered terrain impossible.

---

51. Schuknecht, Oberleutnant Paul, DKiG; 8./Pz.Rgt.36; born 27 January, 1919. Killed in action, 19 November, 1942, near Manulin in the Stalingrad area.
52. Twisselmann, Oberleutnant Hans-Günther, EB; 6./Pz.Rgt.36; born 3 September, 1918. Missing in action, 18 January, 1943 in Stalingrad.

Operational possibilities of the weapon: The fields of rubble and shell-pocked ground offer good concealment to enemy infantry, so as a result, the flat trajectories of cannon and machine-guns have restricted possibilities. Firing at the walls themselves with the 7.5cm has little or no effect.

Approaching close to the steep cliffs of the Volga bank is not promising because of good enemy observation and the poor freedom of movement for our panzers, as well as enemy armour-piercing defensive weapons located on the island.

Operations by the panzers to secure our own front-line are only promising when used as a ready reaction force from sheltered assembly positions.

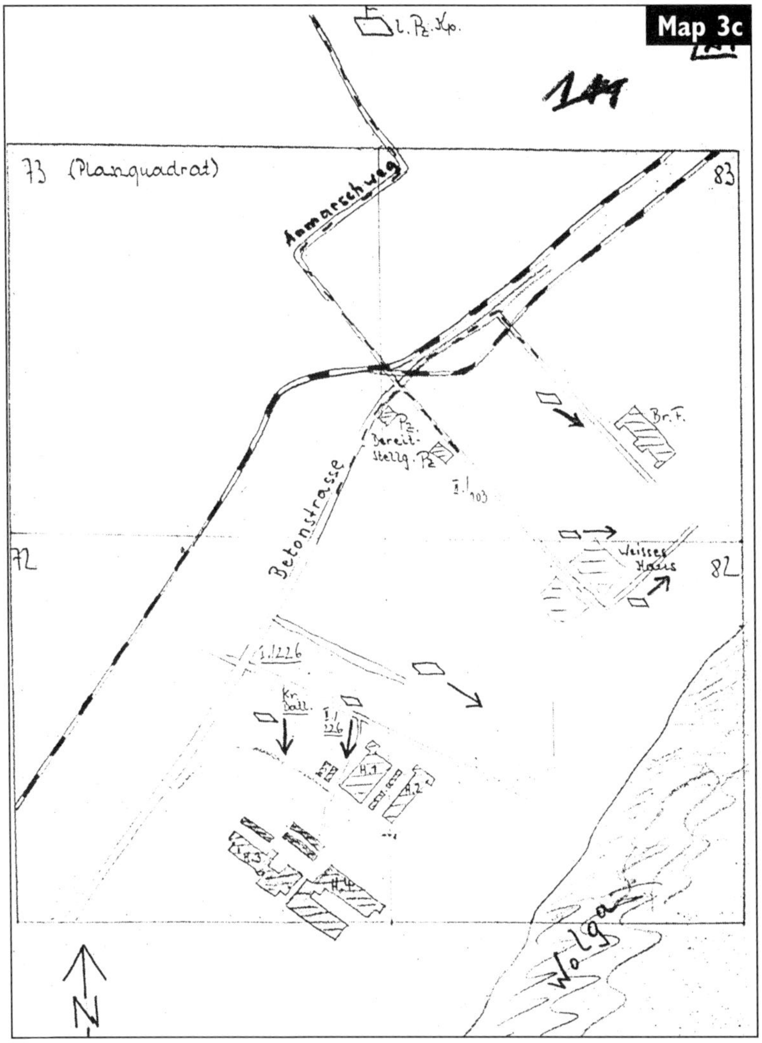

Addition concerning the approach route: The approach will be adversely affected by the narrowness of the railway crossing as a result of the destroyed freight trains standing on the rails because it is only possible to drive slowly over the crossing under enemy observation. The company requests that the crossing be broadened and levelled.

The sketch accompanying Schuknecht's report shows the planned approach routes. The building labelled 'Br.F.' in the upper right is Hall 6e (Workshop 32) in the Barrikady factory and the road running to the south of it – Stalnaya street – is the road the panzer company would use to reach their area of operations.

Oblt. und Abt.Führer

(signed Schuknecht)

The panzer men of the support company were therefore fully aware of the difficult terrain and conditions in which they would be operating.

– – –

Once night had fallen, Leutnant Zorn and his pioneer of 1./Pionier–Bataillon 305 crept outside their buildings and removed several S-mines so that the newcomers of Panzerpionier-Bataillon 50 would not walk into them. While they were carrying out the delicate task, an ongoing firefight continued between both sides: fiery strings of machine-gun bursts swept through the darkness and splashed off building facades; detonating mortar rounds fleetingly lit up walls and ruins of walls; the red glare of signal rockets illuminated the area, throwing everything into darkness and light. Lying on their stomachs, Zorn and his men took advantage of this light, disconnecting trip wires and removing detonators from the mines. Task completed, they crawled back and Zorn immediately called the command post of III./Grenadier-Regiment 578 to confirm that the mines had been rendered safe.

Despite the enormous amount of activity and preparations being carried out in and behind the German line, their Soviet opponents did not detect any of it, and, in fact, the rifle regiments remarked about the lessening amount of activity. On 8 November, 650th Rifle Regiment wrote in its combat journal:

> With the onset of winter, the enemy is building fires in the buildings and basements and keeping them going around the clock.

The next day, they noted that "the enemy hasn't been seen running from house to house; we see smoke of fires coming from every structure".

Leutnant Hans Zorn took command of 1./Pi.Btl.305 immediately upon his arrival in late October 1942.

10 November, 1942

To be in the best position to observe and control the attack, Oberst Steinmetz and his chief-of-staff, Oberstleutnant Paltzo, transferred the forward command post of 305. Infanterie-Division even further forward, from the Schnellhefter Block to an artillery observation post in the Barrikady's upper settlement. This post, located on the very edge of a ridge that dominated the Barrikady factory from the west, had absolutely commanding views of the entire factory, its lower settlement, the Volga and the opposite bank. No other site in northern Stalingrad offered better observation possibilities, which explained why dozens of observation posts had been installed along this ridgeline, both in bunkers and in several massive buildings. Oberleutnant Friedrich Waldhausen[53], a 24-year-old battery commander in Artillerie-Regiment 305, was the man who had to billet the divisional commander and his retinue in his beloved bunker. In a letter to his family, Waldhausen wrote about the number of high-ranking guests who had visited his post:

> I've already written to you that I have the best observation post in the entire northern part of the city. [On 9 November], our commanding general[54] and his chief-of-staff[55] arrived so that

53. Waldhausen, Hauptmann Friedrich, Art.Rgt.305; born 19 July, 1918 in Lixheim. Killed in action, 30 January, 1943 in Stalingrad.

54. General der Artillerie von Seydlitz-Kurzbach, LI. Armeekorps.

55. Oberst i.G. Clausius

they could see the battlefield for themselves from an observation post. And since [10 November], living in my comfortable bunker, is the division commander and his chief-of-staff, who will control the fighting in the city from here for several days. A lot of pride for our small battalion, but also a lot of commotion. We'd also invited the General and his staff for tea and even had to put the samovar on twice because he liked it so much…

Oberleutnant Richard Grimm,[56] Kompanieführer 2./Pionier-Bataillon 305, was very ill. He recorded his impressions in a postcard to his wife on 9 November:

After 21 days of fighting in Stalingrad, I must leave the battlefield. I'm suffering badly from stomach and intestinal infections and my new battalion commander, who was my predecessor, has – as already demonstrated – more sympathy for me. I have been so miserable since then that I cannot write, let alone read. Today, however, I will be able to dictate. At the request of my new boss, the division has authorised sick leave for me. My train will leave on the 19th of this month and will presumably be on the rails for 6 to 8 days. Until then, I hope to regain a bit of health. Perhaps I will be home before this card.

He was therefore flabbergasted when he received new instructions:

I was not a little astounded […] to receive the order that I was subordinated to Major Braun, II./Inf.Rgt.576, for the attack on 11 November. We already knew each other from France. I was ordered to support the infantry after reaching the steep cliff of the Volga bank. I reported at his command post the day before. My route to him in the gun factory, in which I'd been for weeks, was about 150 metres. A guide led me to a massive annealing and tempering furnace which had large, broad heating chambers, an overhead coal supply and an underfloor receptacle for ashes and slag. Next to it were gigantic presses and drop forges. It is simply unimaginable how impressed I was to read upon them the names of German companies in embossed, red-lacquered letters… The finished, pressed-out baseplates, probably for Russian heavy mortars, had been dragged by our infantrymen to the entrances of their dug-outs, as overhead cover. It was suspiciously quiet and there was no immediate enemy action. By candlelight, under the furnace, where there was even a serving tray-sized trestle table set up with a seat for me, I received the following order: for the s.I.G. auf Selbstfahrlafette, employed for the first time during the war, a crossing over the railway tracks was to be immediately readied so that they avoided damaging

Zeller

Oberleutnant Richard Grimm as a Leutnant in 1941, before the rigours of the Ostfront took their toll.

56. Grimm, Hauptmann Richard, 2./Pi.Btl.305; born 17 May, 1913 in Kirchheim/Teck. Died 24 May, 1990 in Kirchheim/Teck. See Appendix 2 (page 572-3) for more details.

their tracks. Flamethrowers (2 units), rolls of plain wire, explosives and several anti-tank mines were brought up during the night and placed in readiness. A shelter was set up in heating ducts, under the collapsed ceiling joists of the workhall (about 15-20 metres high). This was able to be carried out without casualties and I stayed with Major Braun in his command post under the annealing furnace.

– – –

All along the front, the pioneer battalions were making their final preparations. Gefreiter Karl Krauss, 2./Pionier-Bataillon 45, recalls the day before the big attack:

> As the last Unteroffizier vom Dienst (duty sergeant) of the still intact company, I reported to the commander: 'Assault company ready and equipped for tomorrow's attack!'

> Equipment of the assault groups: flamethrowers, demolition charges (3kg of TNT), Stangenladungen (pole charges) for bunker fighting, hand grenades and other close-combat equipment. My question: how will our attack be prepared by heavy weapons?

> Because the dovetailed front-line could not be surveyed, such an operation was not at all possible. The distance to the enemy often amounted to only 15 metres. I was assigned to the second assault group.

> As I stood in front of the combat-ready Kompanie, I thought that with these magnificent, well-equipped men, we could drag the devil himself out of hell!

Hauptmann Dr. Büch, commander of Pionier-Bataillon 45, decided to move his men into position during daylight hours. Because their starting positions were in the massive Hall 4, it was quite easy – and relatively safe – to move them in without being observed. Gefreiter Krauss clearly remembers the reception they received from the haggard infantrymen:

> We were warmly greeted by the units already there: the pioneers had arrived to throw Ivan into the Volga! One further surprise was that we were employed in the sector of the Swabian 305. Infanterie-Division (Bodensee-Division, from the area south of Ulm).[57]

> Our operational area was now the 'Red Barricades' industrial complex, formerly a gun factory, now an indescribable landscape of rubble. Enclosing it in this northern part of the city was the tractor factory to the north and the Red October Steel Factory to the south. All around were giant, hard-fought-over factory buildings. From now on, our positions were fields of rubble and half-destroyed cellars.

> Stukas flew over the Volga with fighter protection and dropped countless bombs in the impenetrable primeval forests lying on the opposite bank. The horrifying screaming of their sirens during their dives was clearly audible. I was astonished by the massive Russian air defence in the forests on the Volga islands and the eastern bank. For the first time I could see the legendary large river of Russia: it was a tremendous watery labyrinth divided by many islands. However, had I – in spite of sheer curiosity – raised my head a second time in the same spot to have another look, it would have been my death due to the invisible enemy snipers lurking everywhere. Coming as a reciprocal gesture at night were the enemy 'sewing-machines'[58] which dropped their parachute flares and bombs unhindered.

---

57. Pionier-Bataillon 45 was actually subordinated to 389. Infanterie-Division, not 305. Infanterie-Division, but infantry from both divisions were positioned in Hall 4.

58. Nickname for the Soviet biplanes that plagued the Germans at night. The sound of its engine was quite peculiar. Other monikers included 'Leukoplast bomber', 'duty sergeant', 'coffee grinder', and the female pilots which often flew the planes were coined 'night witches'.

Oberleutnant Eberhard and his men of Pionier-Bataillon 389 had gathered all their equipment, weapons and ammunition, and were waiting until the appointed time to start marching to the front. Eberhard then had a surprise visitor:

> On the evening of 10 November, my Hauptfeldwebel was suddenly standing in front of me. His request: 'I want to take part in tomorrow's operation. What should I answer at home when I'm asked what it was like in Stalingrad when I've never set foot in the city, let alone been in action.' He could not be dissuaded and I therefore promised that I would take him with me with the warning that he should stay as close to me as possible.

Stabsfeldwebel Leonhard Lang[59], 42-years-old from Nürnberg, was not a desk warrior. He'd been in the field many times during 'Blau', and indeed, had been awarded the Iron Cross Second Class on 17 August 1942. His desire to be involved in this operation may be difficult to understand, particularly when he must have been perfectly aware of the savage nature of the fighting in Stalingrad and the hideous casualties suffered by his battalion. In his mind, the future pressures of being asked 'what did you do in the war?' far outweighed the current danger of being wounded, permanently maimed or killed. So, during the tense night of 10 November, he shouldered his gear and walked into Stalingrad with Oberleutnant Eberhard and the other 30-odd men of Pionier-Bataillon 389.

– – –

The pioneers moved into position. Panzerpionier-Bataillon 50 took over the positions of Püttmann's III./Grenadier-Regiment 578 at 1900 hours. One of Püttmann's men recalls his nocturnal extraction from the front-line:

> The sky was clear and frost set in. […] Our unit was pulled out, pioneers relieved us, and we had to go back to the company command post in a tunnel. We grabbed ammunition and hand grenades, hand grenades. Tomorrow, we would chuck out the Russians in front of us…

In the dark of night, the pioneers moved into their dangerous positions east of the gun factory. A soldier from Pionier-Bataillon 336 recalls that evening:

> We marched along the railway tracks… Hovering over the northern edge of the business district were signal flares, and salvoes of artillery were coming down in the vicinity of the former pilots school of Stalingrad.
>
> It was still quiet at our position. We scurried over an open space strewn with debris. A Sturmgeschütz had gone into position in one of the entrances. The crewmen were smoking behind a tarpaulin. Others, wrapped in blankets, squatted near the vehicle.
>
> We moved forward in single file and reached the factory grounds after a short time. Our Leutnant squatted behind a stack of ingots and waved us into cover.
>
> 'There – to the right, near the workhall! There it is!'
>
> The Leutnant continued, and we followed him. A flare climbed upwards. I threw myself to the ground and cracked my nose against a girder. It caused a fair bit of pain and tears ran from my eyes. The factory hall was now drawn in all clarity in the blazing light of the flare. Then it was dark again and we continued forward. Only no noise! Ivan was sitting everywhere around here.
>
> We remained lying short of the factory hall and observed the terrain. Nothing stirred. Together with the Leutnant, I leapt up, wormed my way between several pipes and ran up to the hall.

---

59. Lang, Stabsfeldwebel Leonhard, Pi.Btl.389; born 9 April, 1900 in Nürnberg. Killed in action, 11 November, 1942 in Stalingrad.

Then we ducked behind an iron girder. The hall appeared to be deserted. In the centre ran a two metre deep by three metre wide brick-constructed trench. Metal casting moulds stood around the casting pit. The Leutnant gave me a signal. I crept back and fetched the others.

They came up, one after another. The moonlight gleamed dimly on their steel helmets. The faces of the men were emaciated and covered with stubble. Their bodies were bowing under the burden of their equipment. We had explosive charges. In addition to them, there were wire-cutters, mine probes and hand grenades.

The Leutnant led us along the left wall of the hall. Without warning, a blaze of fire flashed through the night. Then a loud explosion ripped apart the nightmarish silence. High-pitched, shrill screams echoed through the twilight.

It must have been mines. One of our groups had obviously gone into a minefield. We lay on the ground and held our breath. All of a sudden, there was howling in the air above us. Shells howled in and ripped the roof to pieces. Mixed in with the orgiastic bursting of the explosions was the dry launching noise of mortars.

We leapt up and ran on. Then we found our Leutnant again. Both of his legs had been torn off by the mine explosion. We not only found him, however. Within several seconds, we had lost eighteen comrades. And that was still on the march to the starting positions! ”

Unteroffizier Ernst Wohlfahrt of Grenadier-Regiment 577, to which Pionier-Bataillon 336 had been subordinated, was one of the first to arrive at the horrific scene in Hall 3. Dashing in from an adjoining room, he was met by a gory sight: strewn along the wall were piles of dead and wounded men, many with severed limbs and bellies split open. Others,

sprayed by jagged shrapnel, lay tattered and bleeding on the rubble-strewn floor. As the smoke from the explosion drifted up to the twisted rafters, groaning filled the chilly air. Medics were called and were soon moving from body to body, checking for signs of life. The wounded were extracted from the bloody chaos and treated on the spot. The dead were left where they lay, to be collected later and sent to the rear for burial.

With several weeks of first-hand experience in the Barrikady under his belt, Wohlfahrt had been pessimistic about the upcoming attack, despite the confidence of the pioneers. Now, as he looked around at the stunned faces of the survivors, he could see they were crestfallen, their ardour dampened. The men of Oberleutnant Karl Brockmann's 2./Pionier-Bataillon 336 were the unfortunate victims of the Soviet mine. Several sources state that 18 men were lost in this incident, and available documents show that 7 men from 2./Pi.Btl.336 were wounded by a mine on 10 November. They were:

Oberleutnant Karl Brockmann, commander of 2./Pi.Btl.336

Pionier Stefan Bartkowski[60], Gefreiter Adolf Dietrich[61], Obergefreiter Willi Gruhl[62], Obergefreiter Rudolf Ickert[63], Pionier Hans Kühn[64], Obergefreiter Karl Sebastian[65] and Oberpionier Werner Thiele[66]. This means that 11 men were killed, but it is not possible to state with certainty who they were because their bodies were only collected the next day and their dates of death were therefore registered as 11 November, not 10 November.[67]

- - -

In the southern half of the factory, Oberleutnant Grimm, 2./Pionier-Bataillon 305, was still lodged in Major Braun's command post beneath the furnace. His face was ashen: intestinal troubles were draining his strength. Six months of constant operations on the Ostfront had stripped every ounce of fat from his diminutive, robust frame, but it was the last three weeks in Stalingrad that had taken the greatest toll. Physical exhaustion, compounded by the grief and mental burden of witnessing the ghastly death and wounding of most of his men, had drastically weakened his immunity and opened the door for illness.

> During the night, I once again considered the thought that this would be my last attack because I was so exhausted that I could not even think of climbing back up the steep river bank. My men were to blow up the entrenchments to the left and right and erect a makeshift blockade with wire and mines down to the waterline.

- - -

Colonel Lyudnikov and his commanders were not aware that a massive German hammer blow was about to fall upon them, but defensive precautions were always a necessity. Combat Order No. 81 was sent out to all regiments at 2100 hours:

> Fire with all weapons to prevent the enemy from attacking; reinforce the front-lines and depth of the front. Set up round-the-clock observation of the enemy, create a network of observation points and posts with the aim of not only observing the front-line of the enemy but its depth as well.

More active measures were also planned. In Combat Report No. 195, sent to 62nd Army headquarters, Lyudnikov laid out a plan and sought permission to carry it out:

> It has been established by observation and reconnaissance that the movement of enemy groups and individual soldiers has noticeably reduced along the division's front. The overwhelming majority of soldiers have no winter clothing and therefore huddle in the dug-outs and cellars on the territory of the Barrikady factory.
>
> Senior-Lieutenant Klyukin[68], one of the commanders in the army blocking detachment, has questioned 8 assistant engineers about protection in the Barrikady factory. The factory has plenty of cellars, tunnels and dug-outs able to be used by the enemy. In terms of shelter, the

---

60. Bartkowski, Pionier Stefan, 2./Pi.Btl.336; born 2 September, 1919 in Slawoschin. No further information known.
61. Dietrich, Gefreiter Adolf, 2./Pi.Btl.336; born 17 October, 1910 in Nirkendorf. No further information known.
62. Gruhl, Obergefreiter Willi, 2./Pi.Btl.336; born 20 February, 1910 in Walddorf/Löbau. No further information known.
63. Ickert, Obergefreiter Rudolf, 2./Pi.Btl.336; born 16 August, 1911 in Niederstrahwalde. No further information known.
64. Kühn, Pionier Hans, 2./Pi.Btl.336; born 24 September, 1908 in Erfurt. No further information known.
65. Sebastian, Obergefreiter Karl, 2./Pi.Btl.336; born 24 September, 1918 in Gössnitz. Killed in action, 6 November, 1944 in Huertgen Forest.
66. Thiele, Oberpionier Werner , 2./Pi.Btl.336; born 29 March, 1920 in Ottmannsdorf. No further information known.
67. Despite extensive research, it has not proved possible to find the name of the Leutnant who had both his legs torn off by the mine, which is rather odd considering the fact that the casualty lists for 2./Pi.Btl.336 are quite detailed.
68. Klyukin, Senior-Lieutenant Leonid Mitrofanovich, 650th RR; born 1908 in Altsy. No further information known.

A bomber's perspective of the battlefield. The Luftwaffe was occasionally called upon to assist the troops but in the forthcoming battle, the two adversaries would be barely metres apart, effectively neutralising the Germans' most potent weapon.

cellars, dug-outs and tunnels which have the most significant capacity are shown on the representational schematic.

I request your instructions on dealing with the specified areas by bombers during the day and missions of destruction by large-calibre artillery.

– – –

During the night of 10 November and the very early morning hours of 11 November, the Red Air Force conducted numerous sorties and bombing raids on positions in the city and the hinterland but Soviet artillery only occasionally laid down heavy harassing fire. In contrast, the Germans suppressed 13 Soviet batteries on 10 November and throughout the night with artillery and Luftwaffe bombardments. As a result, in one place on the east bank of the Volga, there were continual explosions and long lasting fires.

This isolated conflagration was symbolic of the fighting to come. While other fronts in Stalingrad were greyed out in a state of mutual exhaustion, the battlefield east of the Barrikady blazed with the most violent and profligate clash the world would ever see. Stalingrad is without doubt the epitome of hand-to-hand fighting, and nowhere was it more brutal, more savage, more relentless, than in the Barrikady.

Lyudnikov had been wise to arrange his precautionary measures, for the very next day, a concentrated thrust by a crack force of German specialists would ferociously attack his precarious stronghold… and would continue to attack until they took it. His soldiers would need every ounce of courage to simply survive the onslaught. Seven battalions of carefully trained pioneers, backed by several thousand battle-wise veterans, were about to engage the courageous Soviets in one last, spectacular, roll of the dice.

CHAPTER FOUR

The Barrikady Gun Factory was eerily silent in the early morning darkness of 11 November. A layer of frost glazed the mounds of rubble. Frigid air enveloped the entire factory and amplified the smallest sound. Thousands of men cautiously and quietly shuffled through the gloom of the devastated workhalls toward their jumping-off positions. Their breath hung in the air. Having reached their assembly positions, they huddled behind anything offering shelter and waited for the artillery preparation to begin.

– – –

The unit history of Werfer-Regiment 51 recounts the first moments of the German preparatory barrage:

> Beginning at 0340 hours in the icy cold of first dawn was the short but concentrated burst of fire from all heavy weapons. The bright impacts splashed in front of the murky sky.

Looking back from the east, from the front-line, the grenadiers, pioneers and Soviet riflemen saw countless flashes strobing behind the western horizon. The distant rumble of heavy artillery and the wailing of rocket-launchers was clearly audible to the soldiers crouched in buildings and workhalls along the eastern edge of the factory. Moments later, the first wave of rockets and shells came screeching in over the heads of the German soldiers and fell upon the Soviet positions, both directly in front of them and on Zaitsevsky Island and the opposite river bank. The cannonade continued… strobe, screech, explosion… strobe, screech, explosion… until the entire area east of the factory, including the river and Zaitsevsky Island, was a seething cauldron into which more projectiles were hurled.

The formidable firepower of Oberst Hans-Joachim Meix's[1] Artillerie-Kommandeur 153 – the control organ for the many independent artillery battalions subordinated to LI. Armeekorps[2], and, for this assault, the artillery of non-attacking divisions – was brought to bear on Zaitsevsky Island and the forested east bank of the Volga. One 210mm Mörser battalion was being used to support the assault of 79. Infanterie-Division in the Krasny Oktyabr factory. However, the Arko's main task, and therefore the main weight of its firepower, was in the area of 305. Infanterie-Division. Its goal was to suppress the Soviets, combat their artillery and prevent anything interfering with the German attack – a gargantuan and practically impossible task. Constant observation, surveillance and triangulation by observation battalions over the previous days had pinpointed the locations of many Soviet batteries on the other bank, but

---

1. Meix, Oberst Hans-Joachim, Arko 153; born 10 December, 1891 in Landeck. Died 5 April, 1943 in Frolov POW Camp.
2. The artillery units under Meix's control were as follows: Artillerie-Regiment Stab 783, II./Art.Rgt.64 with 10cm Kanone, schw.Art.Abt.430 with 10cm Kanone, II./Art.Rgt.59 with sFH, schw.Art.Abt.101 with sFH, Art.Rgt.Stab z.b.V. 41, schw. Art.Abt.616 with 21cm Mörser, schw.Art.Abt.733 with 21cm Mörser, and schw.Art.Abt.855 with 21cm Mörser.

German troops form up in one of the shattered workhalls. Many thought that taking the housing settlement east of the factory would not be difficult compared to the costly fighting that had been required to clear the factory's workhalls.

there were dozens more lurking unnoticed. The Stukas and bombers of VIII. Fliegerkorps made regular appearances during the day and dropped their payloads on Zaitsevsky Island and the opposite bank. Throughout this first day of the attack, 8 batteries were combated by observation battalions, 6 by aerial spotters and 29 by VIII. Fliegerkorps. Artillery also sunk two landing barges and one 400-tonne boat east of the steel factory[3].

The next stratum of artillery gathered for this attack were the divisional artillery regiments. The guns of Major Erich Würker's Artillerie-Regiment 305 and Oberst Kurt Schuster-Woldan's[4] Artillerie-Regiment 389, strengthened by two light battalions of rocket-launchers from Werfer-Regiment 53, laid down their barrages closer to the front-line, guided on to targets by forward observers distributed along the forward line. By collaborating closely, these two commanders had clearly demarcated their respective target areas and harmonised the impact of their artillery. To negate the demoralising effect of shells dropping short, their target areas were well in front of the German main line, mostly along the cliff line and on Zaitsevsky Island. Some of the rocket-launchers had the important task of firing smoke shells into the attack area.

Finally, joining in this deadly cacophony of Korps and divisional artillery were the 81mm mortars of the grenadier regiments, plus six heavy mortars of Pionier-Regiment 604, all nestled in emplacements within the tangled wreckage of the factory itself. Further back,

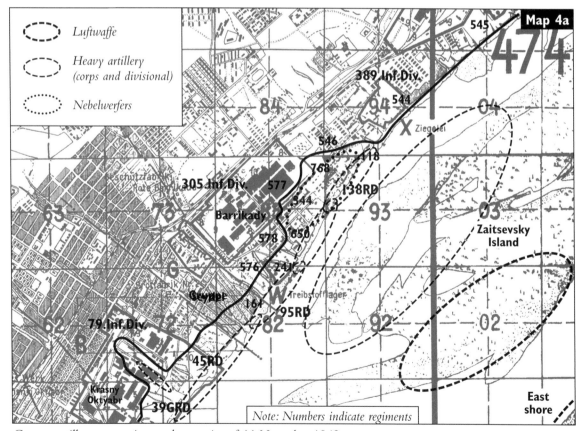

German artillery preparation on the morning of 11 November, 1942.

---

3. Soviet records show that Minesweeper No. 343 was sunk by artillery fire east of the steel factory on 11 November, 1942.

4. Schuster-Woldan, Generalmajor Kurt, DKiG; Art.Rgt.389; born 30 July, 1893 in München. No further information known.

behind the low ridge that overlooked Barrikady from the west, were several platoons of heavy 150mm infantry guns drawn from units on 'quieter' sections of the front: a platoon each from Grenadier-Regiment 211 (71.Inf.Div.), Grenadier-Regiment 517 (295.Inf.Div.) and Panzergrenadier-Regiment 103 (14.Pz.Div.), as well as the heavy gun platoons of 305. and 389. Infanterie-Divisions.

General Krylov[5], 62nd Army chief-of-staff, sat in a command post considerably removed from the focal point of this artillery barrage but still remarked on its fierceness:

> At 0400 hours on 11 November, enemy artillery came down on our positions with heavy fire that had not been seen on any day in the past two weeks. The deafening thunder of the exploding shells blotted out all other sounds and the ground trembled beneath our feet. It was immediately clear: a new storm would have to be weathered.

It was not a one-sided affair, as Hauptmann Rettenmaier recalls:

> The artillery fire began abruptly. However, it was not successful in eliminating the enemy batteries; they soon reciprocated with lively disruptive fire on the command posts and our jumping-off positions. It was a surprise that the enemy had far more batteries available than we had previously known. His ammunition supplies seemed inexhaustible.

The forward command post of Major Braun was beneath a furnace in Hall 6e (Workshop 32).

5. Krylov, Lieutenant-General Nikolai Ivanovich, HotSU; 62nd Army; born 29 April, 1903 in Galyayevka. Died 9 February, 1972.

Soviet counterfire was unexpectedly swift and heavy. Oberleutnant Grimm, 2./Pionier-Bataillon 305, was still in Major Braun's shelter under the furnace:

> I suspected that the Russians had been expecting our attack because a destructive artillery barrage began. Large calibre shells slammed into our furnace. The light went out and Major Braun grabbed me every now and then and shouted 'Are you hit?'. Our exits were buried by piles of brickwork… it took quite a while to clear these, with the assistance of those outside. We didn't know what had been happening with the attack…

Combat records from 295th Artillery Regiment – the organic artillery of Lyudnikov's division – show that they fired a total of 50 rounds at the Barrikady during the night but did not begin their counterfire until 0430 hours. Therefore, it seems the heavy fire at 0400 hours was most likely army-level artillery on the east bank. However, artillery reports from 62nd Army prove that the heavy counterfire was not pre-planned, despite German suspicions that the Soviets had foreknowledge of the attack. The artillery bombardments planned by 62nd Army for 11 November were not scheduled to begin until 0800 hours, and even they were targeting the tractor factory and its housing settlements. The artillery of 138th Rifle Division was also to add its voice to these bombardments by laying down a 20-minute barrage on the brickworks and the tractor factory. The German preparatory bombardment, however, alerted the Soviets, and with admirable promptitude and decisiveness, they laid down their own accurate and devastating fire.

– – –

Before the main attack is discussed, the many small raids and feint attacks launched by the other German divisions – and their effect on the Soviets – will first be examined. Even though they were mere pin pricks compared to the main assault, they still rate a mention in the memoirs of both the commander and chief-of-staff of 62nd Army, albeit within the scope of the main assault. First Krylov:

> The infantry and panzers attacked at 0430 hours. On an approximately 5km wide sector between Volkhovstroyevskaya Street in the north and Banny Gully in the south, five German infantry divisions (79, 100, 295, 305 and 389) as well as 24. Panzer-Division – thus six of the eight divisions facing our army – launched an attack. We later learned from captured documents that battalions of two other divisions that had participated in the attack were brought in by air.

General Chuikov[6], commander-in-chief of 62nd Army, wrote along the same lines:

> The [five kilometre] front along which the offensive was launched ran from Volkhovstroyevskaya Street to Banny Gully. Although the majority of these German divisions were not up to strength (they had been given a sound thrashing in the recent fighting)… Paulus was obviously intending to crush Lyudnikov's, Gorishny's[7], Sokolov's[8], Guriev's[9] and Batyuk's[10] divisions with one blow, and reach the Volga.

---

6. Chuikov, Colonel-General Vasili Ivanovich, HotSU; 62nd Army; born 12 February, 1900 in Serebryanye Prudy. Died 18 March, 1982 in Moscow.

7. Gorishny, Lieutenant-General Vasili Akimovich, HotSU; 95th RD; born 29 January, 1903 in Pavlograd. Died 15 February, 1962 in Simferopol.

8. Sokolov, Major-General Vasili Pavlovich, HotSU; 45th RD; born 17 June, 1902 in Kamenets. Died 7 January, 1958.

9. Guriev, Major-General Stepan Savelyevich, HotSU; 39th GRD; born 1 August, 1902. Killed in action 22 April, 1945 near Königsberg.

10. Batyuk, Major-General Nikolai Filipovich, 284th RD; born in 1905 in Akhtyrke Sumskoi. Killed in action, 28 July, 1943 near Orel.

As can be seen, the German plan to launch localised raids and multiple feint attacks in order to confuse the Soviet defence and take the focus off the true Schwerpunkt worked perfectly. Even decades later, Krylov and Chuikov never seem to have recognised the limited extent of the main attack. Although relatively minor in a tactical sense, these 'localised raids' and 'feint attacks' fulfiled their main strategic goal. All along the German front-line that ran through the ruins of the city, from central Stalingrad in the south to Rynok up north, the assault groups moved out. Their actions are summarised as follows:

71. Infanterie-Division: two storm groups broke into a Soviet position and cleared two strongpoints, taking two prisoners. Casualties for the division on this day were extremely light: 4 men wounded.

295. Infanterie-Division: strong assault groups pushed into a group of houses in 51c and blew up 7 bunkers. Casualties were heavier for this division: 1 officer wounded[11], 1 man killed, 12 men wounded and 5 men missing.

100. Jäger-Division: carried out 5 successful operations. Nineteen bunkers were destroyed and 15 prisoners taken. This minor 'success' came at a high cost: 13 men killed, 58 men wounded and 1 man missing.

79. Infanterie-Division: the operation planned by this division was considerably larger and was launched with the expectation of obtaining a major victory. The Krasny Oktyabr could only be completely suppressed once the keystone of its defence, the Martin Furnace Hall (Hall 4), had been taken. Pionier-Bataillon 179, reinforced by the experienced pioneers of 3./Panzerpionier-Bataillon 40 (24. Panzer-Division), conducted the assault. Divided into four attack wedges, the stormtroops moved against the western part of the workhall but ran into a simultaneous Soviet attack. Some of the spearheads experienced initial success but once the Soviets recovered from the surprise, they reacted with swift and ferocious resistance. The Germans faltered in the tangled mess inside the workhall and despite the ample application of flamethrowers, satchels charges and grenades, the pioneers could simply not overpower the Soviet defenders. The operation failed and the assault groups pulled back to their starting positions. Casualties were bloody: 23 men killed, 101 men wounded and 10 men missing.

XIV. Panzerkorps, positioned in the very north-east corner of Stalingrad, also carried out stormtroop operations against Spartakovka, Pechetka and Rynok to support the attack of LI. Armeekorps.

94. Infanterie-Division: storm groups succeeded in assaulting 2 machine-gun nests, 4 earth bunkers and 1 Soviet position in Spartakovka. Fifteen prisoners were brought back. Casualties were reported as 'negligible'. The front-line was moved forward into the captured Soviet positions. Casualties for the division at the end of the day: 1 officer wounded, 9 men killed and 39 men wounded.

16. Panzer-Division: after strong artillery preparation, two storm groups thrust towards Rynok from the north and north-east. They succeeded in approaching to within 200 metres of the village. Thick defensive fire prevented further progress. Casualties were 1 man killed and 7 men wounded.

---

11. Löhr, Hauptmann Wilhelm, 12./Gr.Rgt.516; born 15 June, 1901 in Usingen. Died of wounds, 11 November, 1942 in Stalingrad.

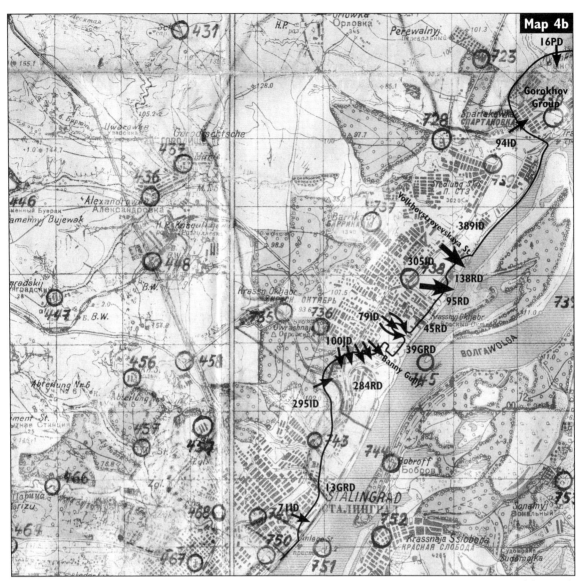

Localised German raids were launched on 11 November, 1942, to deceive the Soviets about the true extent of the attack.

Although the actual physical gains from these raids were extremely minor, the deception and confusion caused to the Soviets was what really counted. An interim report sent to Heeresgruppe B by 6. Armee said:

> Our stormtroops have been active along the entire army front, particularly in the southern part of Stalingrad where over 30 bunkers were destroyed and a large number of prisoners brought in… Stormtroop operations of 71., 295., 100.JD and 79.ID cleared enemy bunkers and strongpoints with bloody casualties for the enemy, as well as several prisoners being taken.

– – –

Now we turn our attention to the main assault of Infanterie-Divisions 305 and 389 with the attached pioneer battalions. At 0355 hours, the first wave of pioneer assault groups, weighed down by satchel charges, flamethrowers and bags of grenades, pressed forward.

The attack of Grenadier-Regiment 576 with Pionier-Bataillon 294 and 2./Pionier-Bataillon 305:

As streams of artillery shells whined over their heads, Sturmkompanie 576, together with the pioneer assault groups of Pionier-Bataillon 294 and Grimm's 2./Pionier-Bataillon 305, crept out of their lying-up positions in Halls 6d and 6e and, bent double, ran across to the concrete wall that girdled the factory. A swirling orange haze, illuminated internally by flashes of gunfire and detonations, backlit the gaunt ruins of School No. 2, Haus 52 and 53 to their front left. The northern combat group reached their designated starting position via a tortuous route through metre-high stacks of gun barrels, over a railway embankment and into another gun barrel storage area. The central group had it easier: they simply filed through a deep trench that passed under the railway embankment. The southern group moved straight out of Hall 6e, skirted several massive craters and formed up in the gun barrel junkyard. The movement of hundreds of soldiers, helmets gleaming under the flickering light of explosions and flares, was not missed by the Soviet defenders.

Major Braun's objective was to capture the fuel installation and reach the Volga. He and his men had reached the fuel installation on 2 November but only succeeded in capturing the two westernmost tanks. The Soviet defence managed to hold on by mobilising its last reserves, and even pushed the Germans back a hundred metres or so, but Braun was not discouraged. He shifted his command post into the furnace directly behind his regiment's forward line and explored the assault possibilities in this area on his own initiative. When Oberstleutnant i.G. Paltzo gave him the advanced order on 7 November, Braun already had his plan of attack. Four days later, he was able to put it into effect.

Major Braun's assault groups moved out of their starting positions in Halls 6e (left) and 6d (right).

Still opposing him were the resilient riflemen of Major Ivan Kuzmich Kalmykov's 241st Rifle Regiment. They had been defending this area since early November and despite suffering bloody casualties – 23 killed and 97 wounded on 5 November, 4 killed and 27 wounded on 7 November, and 79 men just the previous day – the regiment displayed a stubbornness that infuriated the Germans. The steadily mounting losses naturally took a toll on the regiment's combat strength: facing the German attack this morning were only 340 'active bayonets' in two battalions. Very few would survive the day.

– – –

The artillery barrage walked forward and continued to batter the rear area of 241st Rifle Regiment until 0440 hours. In Combat Report No. 40, 95th Rifle Division described the initial attack on this sector:

> At 0400 on the sector of 241st Rifle Regiment, the enemy opened up intensive artillery and mortar preparation. Under cover of his artillery and mortar fire and supported by 3 tanks, the enemy force of more than a battalion went on the offensive towards the fuel tanks.

Escorted by a battery of assault guns, the pioneer assault groups set off. They were immediately met by a hail of bullets. There were no large buildings in this area, so the fire only came from the front, rather than from above. One of the first to be killed was Gefreiter Werner Mähnert[12], 2./Pionier-Bataillon 294, struck in the head by a bullet at 0400 hours. With well-practiced movements, the pioneers crawled ahead in small groups and knocked out a few strongpoints. A Soviet report states that "at 0430, they broke through the front-line and a group of 20-25 men filtered through to the bank of the Volga. Having cut off this group, they were surrounded and destroyed".

The boundary between 241st and 161st Rifle Regiments straddled a small railway spur atop an embankment. It was at this sensitive location that the southern group aimed its spearhead, as a Soviet report makes clear:

> …concentrated on the boundary between 241st and 161st Rifle Regiments, along the factory spur railway, was up to a battalion of infantry which fired on the right flank of 161st Rifle Regiment. A battalion of enemy infantry advanced towards the front of 161st Rifle Regiment. The approaching infantry were beaten off by our units' fire.

The pioneers pushed on. They were supported by well-placed fire laid down by the right neighbour, Kampfgruppe Seydel[13]. Mortars, artillery, machine-guns and heavy infantry guns pounded the field of ruins in front of Panzergrenadier-Regiment 103, as well as smothering the Volga cliff and shoreline. Guns from Artillery-Regiment 179 also added their voice. Part of a panzer company dug in just behind the panzergrenadiers' front-line added their considerable firepower to the destruction. Kampfgruppe Seydel reported its actions in several reports throughout the morning: "The night passed quietly. Enemy artillery harassment fire. A weak enemy recon patrol repulsed on the left wing." Later, it reported that "the advance of the left neighbour was supported by heavy infantry weapons". Through their actions, Soviet flanking fire from the south was lessened and Major Braun's assault groups could concentrate on dealing with the enemy ahead of them instead of worrying about their flanks.

---

12. Mähnert, Gefreiter Werner, 2./Pi.Btl.294; born 9 October, 1919 in Leutzsch/Leipzig. Killed in action, 11 November, 1942 in Stalingrad.

13. This Kampfgruppe, commanded by Oberstleutnant Peter Seydel (commander of Panzergrenadier-Regiment 103), contained all the combatworthy elements of 14. Panzer-Division.

Despite this neighbourly support, the attack only moved forward slowly. Major Braun was still trapped beneath the furnace at this point, so the initial assault lacked his drive and energy. Also, each Soviet strongpoint needed to be assaulted individually but momentum slowed as casualties mounted. One of the assault group leaders from Pionier-Bataillon 294, Feldwebel Franz Kerkhoff[14] of 3. Kompanie, was killed. Obergefreiters Walter Demme[15] and Erich Döbler[16], both from 1. Kompanie, also fell at this time, the former by a head shot. Offensive impetus completely disappeared, however, when three of the supporting armoured vehicles were pummelled in quick succession: two went up in flames and the third limped back into the factory.

Responsible for destroying them was anti-tank rifleman Fedor Filippovich Manenkov. The earth shuddered from the explosion of bombs. Shells from guns and mortars, fire from machine-guns and submachine-guns – everything merged into an intolerable roar. The German behemoths moved towards Manenkov and a handful of men. One of the tanks, shrouded in smoke, brewed up and stopped, while the others moved inexorably towards the building defended by Manenkov and his comrades. Shells crashed through the building, bricks showered down, beams collapsed, but Manenkov did not leave his position. After his commander and all of his comrades were killed, Manenkov continued to fire his anti-tank rifle at the German assault guns. When the attack was over, it was reported that six tanks and one armoured car lay knocked out in front of him.[17] For his courage and heroism displayed in battle, Manenkov was awarded the Order of Lenin.

The attack ground to a temporary halt on this sector.

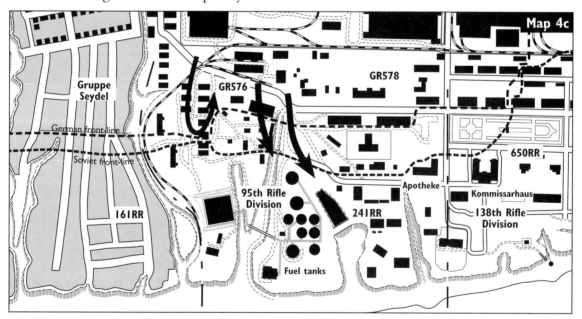

Initial stages of the attack: Grenadier-Regiment 576 with Pi.Btl.294 and 2./Pi.Btl.305.

---

14. Kerkhoff, Feldwebel Franz, 3./Pi.Btl.294; born 4 February, 1913 in Uedem. Killed in action, 11 November, 1942 in Stalingrad.

15. Demme, Obergefreiter Walter, 1./Pi.Btl.294; born 3 August, 1911 in Dölzig/Leipzig. Killed in action, 11 November, 1942 in Stalingrad.

16. Döbler, Obergefreiter Erich, 1./Pi.Btl.294; born 9 September, 1913 in Gross Zschepa. Killed in action, 11 November, 1942 in Stalingrad.

17. Figures of tank kills vary widely in every battle, mainly due to exaggeration and mistaking disabled tanks for destroyed ones. Combat Report No. 40 of 95RD confirms that "1 heavy and 1 medium tank" were knocked out on this sector.

The attack of Grenadier-Regiment 578 with Panzerpionier-Bataillon 50, 1./Pionier-Bataillon 305 and part of Sturmkompanie 44:

Protected by the artillery barrage screeching overhead, a battle group of Grenadier-Regiment 578, strengthened by Leutnant Zorn's 1./Pionier-Bataillon 305, quietly filed out of their jumping-off positions in Haus 53. Moving swiftly across a narrow expanse of open ground, they slithered into shell craters and old trenches. To their right was the Kindergarten, a relatively intact two-storey building unoccupied by either side.[18] A waist-high fence enclosing the Kindergarten and its rectangular yard had been shredded long ago by shrapnel. Careful observation showed Hauptmann Rettenmaier that the entrances to the L-shaped Apotheke were clogged with rubble, making it difficult for his assault groups to enter the building, so he decided to create his own doorways:

> The most important thing was to create new openings into the house. We had the means for it. Enormous explosive charges would be positioned and detonated at the scheduled time.

Lying down behind their guns, the infantry covered the pioneers as they stole up to the Apotheke. Skilled hands rapidly positioned the explosives and inserted detonators and igniters. The pioneers – trailing the electrical detonation cables – then dashed back to the infantry, wound up the internal springs of the exploders, connected all leads to the terminals and then inserted winding keys into the detonation sockets. Then they waited.

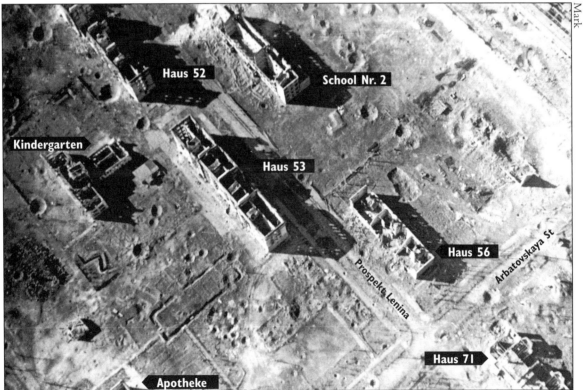

Haus 53: starting point for the attack on the Apotheke and Hauptmann Rettenmaier's command post. Its proximity to the Apotheke (barely visible at bottom of photo) is evident.

---

18. The Kindergarten (the building actually was a kindergarten – known as a 'detsad' in Russian) was easily overlooked by the Germans in Haus 52 and 53, and the Soviets in the Apotheke. Both sides knew it was an exposed position that would be hard to hold without first capturing the dominating enemy strongholds behind it.

- - -

The Soviet defenders of the Apotheke – men from 241st Rifle Regiment – remained silent. At precisely 0355 hours, the signal was given. The soldiers that gripped the exploders twisted the winding keys… and massive explosions momentarily drowned out the roar of the artillery barrage and enveloped the Apotheke in smoke and dust. The assault groups charged the building and bounded through the smoking holes. The Soviet garrison was caught by surprise. The pioneers fanned out, overwhelmed any signs of resistance and rapidly cleared the building floor by floor. Infantry from Grenadier-Regiment 578 supported the pioneers by following close on their tails, taking part in the clearing actions and setting up defences in the conquered building. A total of 45 prisoners were taken in the building's four storeys. With the pre-dawn greyness still covering the battlefield, a messenger left the Apotheke and ran across the open ground to Hauptmann Rettenmaier's command post in Haus 53. Rettenmaier remembers that "the first reports of success came from the Apotheke. The surprise attack completely succeeded here; the garrison was captured." The enemy in the basement of the Apotheke, however, had not given themselves up. Volleys of bullets whipped up the cellar staircases every time a German showed himself at the entrance. Grenades were tossed down. When Soviet fire continued, demolition charges were heaved down the stairs. Smoke, dust and the cloying stench of TNT and picric acid explosives swirled up the stairwells. A few more grenades, then the infantry warily descended into the basement. Incredibly, some of the resilient Soviet defenders had survived the blasts and opened fire. The leading infantrymen were hit. Their comrades hastily dragged them to the surface. The decision was taken to not make any further attempts at storming the basement.

While the assault on the Apotheke proceeded according to plan, the infantry securing the right flank and keeping pace with Grenadier-Regiment 576 were experiencing the same difficulties as their southern neighbour, as one of Hauptmann Püttmann's soldiers reports:

> As it became light, the action started. Despite the frost, our overcoats were taken from us so that we could run quicker. The artillery fired and the Russians answered. We attacked, but even without our overcoats, we moved no further than twenty metres. It was a battle with hand grenades. On the second or third attempt to move out of our foxholes, one exploded right next to me. My boot, ankle and right calf were nothing but holes. I was amazed what a human could endure. […] I looked around and then called over to an Unteroffizier: 'I'm hurt!' I crawled into the nearest crater, pulled off my boot, tipped out the blood and had a look to see what was happening. 'Beat it', said the Unteroffizier, after I had crept over to him. Beat it, but how? How could I get out of the crater on one foot? There was another wounded man and I said to the other idiot: 'Come on! We can help each other.'

- - -

Before the pioneers of 1./Pionier-Bataillon 305 had detonated their explosive charges placed outside the Apotheke, the assault groups of Panzerpionier-Bataillon 50 courageously approached the Kommissarhaus, setting off from the area of Haus 56 [Dom 8] and Haus 54 [Dom 7]. Supporting them were part of Sturmkompanie 44 (mainly members of 11./Grenadier-Regiment 131) which moved out from Haus 72 [Dom 32]. The pioneer groups also planned on using demolition charges to gain access to their objective. After being persuaded by Hauptmann Gast that his pioneers could take their objective without infantry support, Rettenmaier watched their attack go in from his observation post in Haus 53:

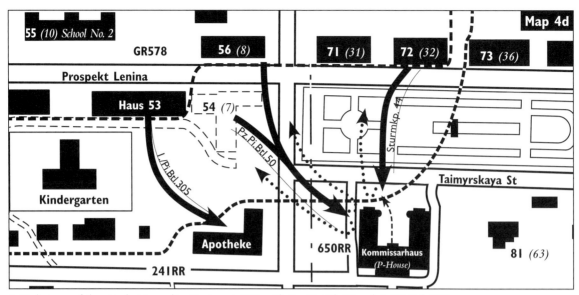

Initial stages of the attack: Grenadier-Regiment 578 with Pz.Pi.Btl.50 and 1./Pi.Btl.305.

Armed with mines and other explosives, they plunged into the darkness to place them in and around the house. They tried to find an entrance or other opening into which they could place their charges. However, nothing could be found because everything was bricked up or so skillfully camouflaged that any search in the dark was in vain. For that reason, the pioneers waited for the dim light of dawn.

The pioneers thought that a bit more light would enable them to plant their demolition charges, so they hunkered down in craters to await the coming dawn. The area surrounding the castle-like building was relatively flat and coverless, and the observant defenders of the building noticed the Germans skulking outside their fortress. Rettenmaier recalls the first shots: "The enemy was vigilant. At first there were isolated bursts of fire, but it quickly swelled and claimed an unmerciful sacrifice." Through this uninterrupted fire, the pioneers were forced into complete cover, most being banished to the craters from which they could no longer move. The attack had faltered.

The defenders of the Kommissarhaus – the remnants of the Barrikady workers militia plus several platoons from Pechenyuk's 650th Rifle Regiment – noticed that the Germans had gathered in shell craters in front of and to the left of the building. It was immediately obvious that the danger had not yet passed because it seemed that the Germans were regrouping for another attack. Their destruction or repulsion was therefore necessary. Militiaman Ivan Fedin grabbed some grenades, dashed out into the central courtyard and ran up to the corner of the southern wing. Covering him from one of the windows was submachine-gunner Putirin, who started firing long bursts at the pioneers huddled in the craters. Putirin's elevated position enabled him to fire into the nearest craters. As the Germans hugged the bottom of their shell holes, Fedin proceeded to lob grenades at them. Some of the pioneers recoiled, jumped out of their shell-holes and scurried back to German lines. Fedin chased the retreating Germans with volleys of grenades but was soon hit and wounded. Still covered by his comrades, he managed to stagger back into the building.

Junior-Lieutenant Mikhail Ilyich Senchkovsky, commander of the NKVD blocking detachment assigned to safeguard the river bank behind 138th Rifle Division, had nothing but praise for the defenders of the P-shaped house [Kommissarhaus]:

On 11 November, 1942, the fascists were all fired up to capture the factory administration building. A company of Germans concentrated in shell craters not far from the defences of our building. Their destruction was necessary because they were assembling their attack. For this task, militiaman Fedin grabbed some grenades, left the building and under the cover of his submachine-gunner Putirin, tossed grenades at the Germans, forcing the survivors to give up and then take flight. Even though they were now further away, we did not lose our heads. Fedin was wounded in this fighting but stopped advancing forward and carried on fighting. Many of the militia died bravely in defence of the Barrikady factory.

Crouching in one of the shell craters was Gefreiter Ludwig Apmann along with four other soldiers of 2./Panzerpionier-Bataillon 50. Although young in years, Apmann was experienced in the ways of the Eastern Front and had been with the battalion in Yugoslavia, the Crimea, Sevastopol and now Stalingrad. Initially deployed with the battalion's bridging column, he served as a 'lifeguard' on the long pontoon bridges, then became a motorcycle messenger, and finally ended up as a combat pioneer. Huddled in the crater, Apmann sensed the hand grenades landing closer and closer until the inevitable happened. A grenade sailed directly into their crater and seriously wounded all five men. Apmann's back was sprayed with shrapnel, mostly tiny slivers of metal, but he was able to make it back to a dressing station and was eventually transported to a homeland hospital.[19]

Gefreiter Ludwig Apmann

As with many soldiers in the Barrikady, Unteroffizier Albert Heitzmann of Panzerpionier-Bataillon 50 remembers one aspect of the Soviet defenders above all others:

> The worst thing was not the shells or the machine-gun fire or the hand grenades. The worst thing was the Soviet snipers! They were so well hidden because they wore camouflaged hoods. Again and again comrades collapsed around me with shots to the head and chest. With a couple of dozen single shots these experts caused more harm than hundreds of shells!

From his advanced command post, Rettenmaier witnessed the panicky retreat of Panzerpionier-Bataillon 50:

> Many pioneers fell, lifeless, far more crept back, exhausted and bleeding, and formed up for a trip to the hospital. They had achieved nothing here, except for perhaps gaining the experience that this way would not result in them obtaining their objective.

Casualties for Gast's men had been quite heavy. Four NCOs and 13 men killed, 1 officer, 8 NCOs and 52 men wounded. Fortunately, no-one was missing and all bodies were eventually recovered. Among them were Unteroffizier Erich Pischko[20] and Unteroffizier Heinz Stadie[21] from 3. Kompanie, and Pionier Heinrich Markus[22] and Pionier Erich Wilm[23]

---

19. Several splinters could never be removed from his back and they remained there until his death in 1992.

20. Pischko, Unteroffizier Erich, 2./Pz.Pi.Btl.50; born 19 April, 1914 in Adorf. Killed in action, 11 November, 1942 in Stalingrad.

21. Stadie, Unteroffizier Heinz, 3./Pz.Pi.Btl.50; born 22 February, 1920 in Berlin-Lichtenberg. Killed in action, 11 November, 1942 in Stalingrad.

22. Markus, Pionier Heinrich, 3./Pz.Pi.Btl.50; born 6 April, 1923 in Oberfell. Killed in action, 11 November, 1942 in Stalingrad.

23. Wilm, Pionier Erich, 3./Pz.Pi.Btl.50; born 10 November, 1912 in Witten-Annen. Killed in action, 11 November, 1942 in Stalingrad.

Barrikady Museum

The fortress-like facade of the Kommissarhaus. This pre-war photo clearly shows the difficult task facing the pioneers. On the morning of 11 November, the basement windows and all doors were clogged by rubble.

from 2. Kompanie. Casualties for Sturmkompanie 44 are unknown but Gefreiter Georg Reigl[24] was killed and Obergefreiter Philipp Eichhorn[25] was severely wounded and died later in the day in the Gorodische dressing station. A huge loss for the Sturmkompanie was the death of Oberfeldwebel Eitel Brock, commander of its pioneer platoon.

It is significant that the repulsion of the attack of Panzerpionier-Bataillon 50 and Sturmkompanie 44 against the Kommissarhaus did not even rate a mention in the combat journal of 650th Rifle Regiment. Of far more concern – and rightly so – was the critical situation around the Apotheke, or as it is referred to in the journal, the 'L-shaped building'. Here is an excerpt from the entry for 11 November:

> At 0330, the enemy undertook advances in separate groups from Dom 32 [Haus 72] and 33 [Haus 65] and from Dom 7 [Haus 54] in the direction of the P-shaped structure [Kommissarhaus] with the strength of up to a platoon of infantry under the command of an officer trying to approach from the left. Artillery preparations were started at the same time. The regiment, defending its front-line, is in battle with the enemy. The mortar battalion is firing on groups of the enemy in the direction of Dom 32, 33, and 7…

> From 0330 hours, the enemy, with the strength of two companies and supported by seven tanks, repeatedly attacked our front-line and that of our neighbours, throwing a group of 15-20 submachine-gunners into the breach. The attacks were aided by the tanks, as well as by methodical mortar and artillery fire on our formations. The main area targeted by the enemy was the left flank of the front, in the area of the L-shaped building and the fuel tanks, which was the junction between our formation and the neighbour. Their aim was to cut off the neighbours to our left and reach the Volga river. As a result of the fighting, the enemy pushed through the front-lines of 241st Rifle Regiment, took the L-shaped structure and pushed on to the fuel tank area.

---

24. Reigl, Gefreiter Georg, StuKp.44; born 6 February, 1923 in Wien-Oberlaa. Killed in action, 11 November, 1942 in Stalingrad.
25. Eichhorn, Obergefreiter Philipp, StuKp.44; born 12 September, 1908 in Offenbach. Died of wounds, 11 November, 1942 in Stalingrad.

Knowing that Panzerpionier-Bataillon 50's attack on the Kommissarhaus had completely failed, a request was made for the waiting assault guns of Sturmgeschütz-Abteilung 245 to be brought into action. Major Josef Linden, overall commander of the pioneer operation, recalls the use of armoured support:

> Assault guns were employed now and then during the pioneer attacks. Nevertheless, approach routes for the missions had to be precisely reconnoitred beforehand because of the impassable terrain. The assault guns could not follow up the attacks of the pioneer assault groups and operated only from the rear as fire support. Even doing this, losses in assault guns occurred on our side because the Russians also had heavy defensive weapons in their forward line that were skillfully camouflaged…

And that is what happened when the assault guns were awkwardly employed on this first morning of the attack. Their task was to screen the Kommissarhaus with smoke so that the remaining pioneers could retreat. All available guns of Major Zielesch's[26] battalion, including the battery of six brand-new 150mm sIG33Bs commanded by Oberleutnant Alfred Beckmann[27], left their reserve positions near the Barrikady's central gates. A short drive east along Arbatovskaya Street, then the gloomy Kommissarhaus appeared between the shattered birch trees in the park. Some of the guns turned left at Haus 71 [Dom 31] into Prospekt Lenina, crawled forward a short distance and then pivoted on their tracks so that they were facing the building. They then proceeded to hurl shells into the hulking fortress. The other guns, for some reason, continued east and turned into Taimyrskaya Street, which ran directly in front of the Kommissarhaus.

Leonid Mitrofanovich Klyukin, politruk of the Barrikady militia company commanded by Junior-Lieutenant A.P. Fedotov, recalls when the assault guns attacked the building:

> The Germans held a building just across the street from us. They fired cannon at us. The shells penetrated the thick walls and exploded inside the rooms. Machine-guns showered us with lead rain… the enemy [then] threw tanks and infantry against us. The first to engage the enemy tanks were the anti-tank riflemen of comrade Danilin's group. They used Molotov cocktails to burn out the first tank. The second tank manoeuvred to bypass us in an attempt to crush the mortar battery north of the house. The anti-tank riflemen lay amidst the rubble of the building's central stairwell. They opened fire but the tank continued to fire its gun. Soon the anti-tank rifle fell silent.
>
> What had happened? Company commander Fedotov crawled to the positions of the anti-tank riflemen. Heavily wounded, they lay unconscious as two more tanks approached the building. Fedotov himself positioned the anti-tank rifle and burned out a tank as it was turning in front of the house. The Germans quickly began getting out of the vehicle. Several enemy soldiers from a nearby basement ran

Lieutenant Leonid Mitrofanovich Klyukin, politruk of the Barrikady factory's militia unit.

---

26. Zielesch, Major Hans, Stug.Abt.245; born 1 March, 1896 in Dar Es Salaam. Died 19 December, 1979 in Berlin.

27. Beckmann, Oberleutnant Alfred, Stug.Abt.245; born 27 October, 1917 in Kronheide. Died 25 March, 1949 in Zaporoshy POW camp, Ukraine.

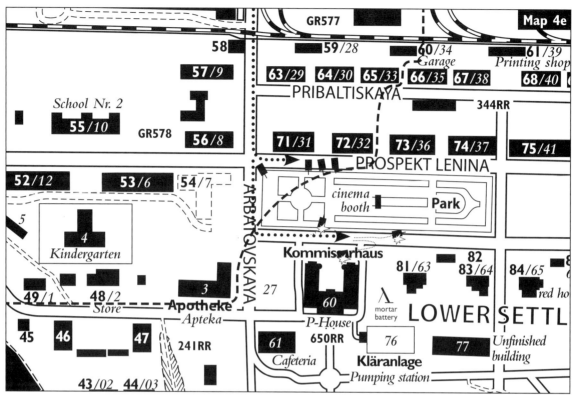

Deployment of Sturmgeschütz-Abteilung 245 against the Kommissarhaus. Three knocked-out Stug. are shown.

out to assist them. We cut them down with submachine-gun fire and burned out another tank. The fourth vehicle turned back. The enemy infantry which followed the tanks dispersed in numerous directions. At this time, an enemy machine-gun, which was situated in a window covered up with bricks, opened up just across from us. Our anti-tank riflemen soon silenced the gun.

The amateur tactics of the assault guns are almost inexplicable: moving right up to the target had been a disastrous manoeuvre. Photographic evidence[28] of the destroyed vehicles shows that panic and desperation must have gripped the crews. Destroyed were 1 Sturmgeschütz long-barrel[29], as well as 2 of the new sIG33Bs and their inexperienced crews. The loss of these two experimental vehicles was reported in 6. Armee's war diary: "East of the gun factory, two of the new sIG33Bs were knocked out by direct hits and were consequently total losses." Another 2 of these vehicles did not appear on the battalion's strength report for 12 November, so it is likely that they were damaged during the fighting on 11 November and had been sent for repairs. Oberleutnant Grimm, commander of 2./ Pionier-Bataillon 305, also reports that an officer commanding one of these new assault guns was wounded:

> I learned from the regiment's doctor that the commander of a sIG33B, an Oberleutnant who had reported with me yesterday, had been struck in the backside by a piece of shrapnel, totally harmless, but he almost died of shock.

28. See photos on page 392 and 396 in Chapter 8.

29. Strength returns show that Sturmgeschütz-Abteilung 245 had 1 long-barrel and 2 short-barrels less on 12 November than they did at the start of the day on 11 November

Records of opposing sides rarely coincide because the enemy's intentions are misconstrued and his fatalities grossly exaggerated. In this case, the entry concerning Pechenyuk's 650th Rifle Regiment in the combat journal of 138th Rifle Division – apart from the inaccurate tally of German dead – meshes precisely with eyewitness accounts and available German documents:

> From 0430 hours 650th Rifle Regiment, together with 241st Rifle Regiment, is in combat with an enemy infantry regiment supported by ten tanks. Throughout the course of the day all enemy attacks were repelled. 400 Germans have been wiped out, 3 tanks have been burned out and one was knocked out.

The tally in the combat journal of 650th Rifle Regiment, however, was much closer to the truth: "…during the fighting, [the enemy] lost 4 tanks and 180 soldiers and officers killed and wounded, but was able to destroy 4 of our light machine-guns."

With the Kommissarhaus still in Soviet hands, the full attainment of German objectives was exceedingly difficult. This building was by far the most important in the entire lower settlement because of its strategic location. From there, the surrounding area in all directions could be easily covered by fire and just as easily observed. Even though Rettenmaier's men had all but captured the Apotheke, they now faced a dilemma. Accurate sniping from the Kommissarhaus had cut them off from all other German units. The 45 prisoners taken earlier in the morning were still under guard in the Apotheke. Rettenmaier recalls:

> Daylight came and our pioneers could no longer leave the house or let themselves be seen in any doorway because death lurked behind every opening. Who were the prisoners now?

The attack of Grenadier-Regiment 577 with Pionier-Bataillon 336, 3./ Pionier-Bataillon 305 and part of Sturmkompanie 44:

After their nightmarish introduction to the Barrikady, the assault groups of Pionier-Bataillon 336 warily congregated in their starting positions along the inner eastern walls of Hall 3 and Hall 4, together with elements of Sturmkompanie 44 (mainly members of 2./Grenadier-Regiment 132). Leading the combat groups of Grenadier-Regiment 577 were two experienced battalion commanders: Hauptmann Georg Wittmann, III./Gr.Rgt.577[30], and Oberleutnant Friedrich Winkler[31], II./Gr.Rgt.577.

The unnamed soldier from Oberleutnant Brockmann's 2. Kompanie continues his report by describing his company's attack on their objective, Haus 66 [Dom 35]:

> It did not take long until our own artillery began to fire. In front of the factory hall, a wall of flame rose into the air. Under the protection of the rolling barrage, we moved forward. Following behind us were our comrades from the infantry, who were employed as the second wave.
>
> We fought our way up to a large block of houses. Although the building was already half-destroyed, we were lashed by massive defensive fire. We tossed explosive charges into the cellar windows and bounded down the staircase. We climbed over dying Russians and intended

---

30. Wittmann, Hauptmann Georg, III./Gr.Rgt.577; born 27 March, 1910 in Neumarkt/Oberpfalz. Died 18 September, 1997 in Neumarkt/Oberpfalz.

31. Winkler, Hauptmann Friedrich, II./Gr.Rgt.577; born 22 August, 1909 in Worms. Died between 8–10 February, 1943 in Beketovka POW camp. Winkler's face has become one of the most recognisable images captured during the battle for Stalingrad. See pages 114–15 for more information.

Familie Grimm

Before the massive attack on 14 October, Oberleutnant Grimm had this 'final' photo taken of himself, in case he was killed. From left: Oberleutnant Berthold Staiger (then a member of 2./Pi.Btl.305 but later commander of 3./Pi.Btl.305), Oberleutnant Richard Grimm (commander 2./Pi.Btl.305) and Grimm's orderly, Obergefreiter Paul Nuoffer. After being wounded on 10 January, 1943 and flown out on 13 January, Nuoffer would be the last man of the battalion to escape the Stalingrad pocket. In the background is the white church at Gorodische, a landmark known to all soldiers in Stalingrad-North. The church was used as a dressing station and was surrounded by large German cemeteries.

going to the upper floor. We did not succeed. We attempted it four times but the Russians always threw us back.

After a short time, reinforcements arrived. Hand grenades rolled down the staircase. We caught them and threw them back up. The hurricane of fire from the artillery raged all around the building. When we finally succeeded in the fight for control of the house, many of my comrades lay dying next to the Russians.

The Reds fought to the last man. Several even leapt down from the roof of the house.

Supporting the attack on the building was Oberleutnant Berthold Staiger[32] and his 3. Kompanie of Pionier-Bataillon 305. As a platoon commander, Staiger had been physically and emotionally traumatised by an event that took place on 30 June near Volchansk:

I was deployed on the Oskol, a tributary of the Dnepr, in the summer of 1942. During the advance into enemy territory, a bridge over which our troops would push forward had to be held. Together with my Kompaniefeldwebel Janzik[33], I went with an advanced troop to look for mines on and around the bridge. This was an extremely difficult task to undertake because we guessed they would be dangerous 'Zugzünder' (pull igniters), as we called them. Despite every precaution, there was suddenly a violent explosion from a mine not too far away from

32. Staiger, Oberleutnant Berthold, 3./Pi.Btl.305; born 13 March, 1914 in Rottweil. Died 21 February, 2006 in Reutlingen. See Appendix 2 (page 578) for more details.

33. Janzik, Feldwebel Siegfried, 3./Pi.Btl.305; born 9 December, 1915 in Castrop. Killed in action, 30 June, 1942 near Krassnoye Polyana.

me. Feldwebel Janzik was torn into unrecognisable shreds. I have been unable to banish this image of my comrade from my life. It was quite simply dreadful. That the eardrums in both my ears had burst was only noticed later when I saw shells exploding but did not hear the detonations or the cannon fire of enemy tanks. I'd become completely deaf and was put into hospital until it returned, to some extent. Still, I remained hard of hearing and should have found another assignment but I requested that I be returned to my troops.

At the end of September / beginning of October, while the Stalingrad pocket was still open, this was authorised. When I arrived at the Pitomnik airfield, our unit was positioned in front of Stalingrad.

The half-deaf Staiger was assigned to Oberleutnant Grimm's 2. Kompanie but Grimm kept him in reserve as leader of a flamethrower troop. Mounting casualties, in particular the heavy loss of officers, forced Staiger to be employed as commander of 3. Kompanie. Since that time, he had led his company through weeks of vicious scuffles in the gun factory. Now, he led his men through the curtain of artillery fire to assist the pioneers of Bataillon 336. One of his NCOs was hit by a large piece of shrapnel:

A Feldwebel by the name of Heiduk[34] was in my battalion. His name sticks in my memory because he suffered a grievous stomach wound from a shell, a wound from which he could not be saved. He knew that and said to me that if I made it home, could I locate his bride and bring her his final wishes. This bride was a nanny working for a high Nazi.[35]

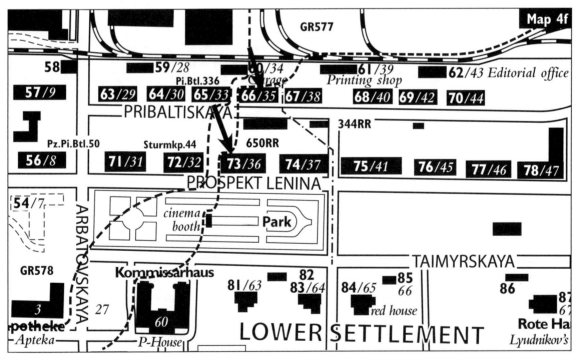

Initial stages of the attack: Grenadier-Regiment 577 with Pi.Btl.336 and 3./Pi.Btl.305.

---

34. Heiduk, Unteroffizier Rudolf, 3./Pi.Btl.305; born 17 October, 1908 in Königshütte. Died of wounds, 12 November, 1942 in Stalingrad.

35. This 'high Nazi' was Martin Bormann. Heiduk's bride worked as a nanny at the Bormann house in München. When Staiger drove there in order to bring her the message, he found the house protected and surrounded by barbed wire. He was not allowed inside into the house. When he asked for the girl, he was told that she would come to the garden gate so she could receive the message. Staiger did not meet Martin Bormann face to face.

Staiger and his men reached the building and, as he recalls, the men of Pionier-Bataillon 336 were "only on the lower floor. [We] could not capture more. The Russians were on the two upper floors. The Russians, however, were only a mob of stragglers." Fighting together, the pioneers from the two different battalions were able to capture the rest of the house.

The building being attacked by Oberleutnant Brockmann's 2./336 and Oberleutnant Staiger's 3./305 – Haus 66 [Dom 35] – was on the right flank of 650th Rifle Regiment, and in fact, was the rightmost building held by Pechenyuk's men. The neighbouring building, Haus 67 [Dom 38], held by Lieutenant I.S. Pogrebnyak and 7 men, was Strongpoint No. 4 of 1st Battalion, 344th Rifle Regiment. Haus 66 [Dom 35], as well as two other buildings (Haus 73 [Dom 36] and Haus 74 [Dom 37]), were held by units of 650th Rifle Regiment. Positioned in this area was Captain Vasili Trofimovich Piven and his company from Pechenyuk's regiment:

On 11 November, 1942, my company was situated not far from the Barrikady factory. We beat back enemy attacks throughout the day. Although we only had a small amount of ammunition and a small number of men in the company, the Germans were not able to move even one metre forward. At that point the Germans brought tanks into the battle. Our troops blew up three tanks with Molotov cocktails and anti-tank grenades. Dying in this battle was Komsomol member Nikolai Semendyayev, who threw himself under a tank with grenades in his hands. The tank blew up. From a close distance, Ivan Vinogradov threw himself on a tank with Molotov cocktails and set it on fire[36]. I had to take the disk off a light machine-gun and swing it like a bat, to beat back heavy attacks in hand-to-hand combat. The Germans did not pass!

Captain Vasili Trofimovich Piven

Another officer in this area was Senor-Lieutenant Mikhail Andreyevich Danilenko, from the medical services of 650th Rifle Regiment:

During the war I was in 3rd Battalion of 650th Rifle Regiment. As a senior medical assistant, I not only provided medical assistance to wounded soldiers but in desperate moments of fighting even went into the attack with weapon in hand, grabbing rifles and grenades to defend the city of Stalingrad. I exterminated 10 Germans with a sniper rifle and during the battle of Stalingrad carried at least 70 wounded men out of the fighting and provided them with first-aid. In one of the fiercest fascist attacks on 11 November, 1942, I was wounded and left the unit…

Snr.-Lt. Mikhail Andreyevich Danilenko, a medical officer who took rifle in hand.

Unfortunately, Piven and Danilenko do not specifically mention in which buildings they were located. The events in this area are very briefly mentioned in the combat journal of 650th Rifle Regiment:

On the right flank, the enemy has the intention of taking over Dom 36 [Haus 73], capturing the movie theatre and in this way cutting off 2nd Rifle Battalion from the 1st and 3rd Rifle Battalions.

---

36. It is difficult to verify these claims as others sources, particularly photographic evidence, show that the acknowledged Germans losses of armoured vehicles took place during the attack on the Kommissarhaus.

Familie Winkler

Right: After many years of research, the identity of this unknown officer – whose face is now synonymous with the futile German attacks in the factories – has finally been established. His name is Friedrich Konrad Winkler, born 22 August, 1909 in Worms. His Erkennungsmarke (dog-tag) number was -4-1.I.R.14. He was a 'Zwölfender' (literally a 'twelve-point buck', a soldier committed to twelve years of military service). Promoted to Oberleutnant with effect from 1 November, 1941 (RDA 786) and to Hauptmann with effect from 1 December, 1942 (RDA 313). He began the war in Inf.Rgt.56 (later Jäg. Rgt.56) and was transferred to 305. Infanterie-Division in mid-1942, initially commanding the Stabskompanie of Inf. Rgt.577. When the famous photo was taken on 16 October, 1942, Winkler was commanding 6./Inf.Rgt.577 as it pushed through the northern gates of the Barrikady Gun Factory. It can be seen that half of Winkler's Infantry Assault Badge has been broken off. One might think this happened in battle but in most cases, this damage was done intentionally. A man wearing a broken badge could be recognised as someone who fought out of a sense of duty but was still combat-ready, thus a 'genuine, trustworthy guy', despite his opinion that the war was lost. Because the troops were not allowed to openly express this, they were able to make their feelings known in this way.

Above left: On the day of his marriage, 21 September, 1935, to Mathilde. The Winklers had two sons (the first born in June 1936, the second in July 1942). The stripes on his cuff signify two shooting accomplishments – the horizontal stripe is a marksmanship grade, the chevrons both a grade and a qualification as a sharpshooter.

Familie Winkler

Left: Winkler as a Leutnant and platoon commander in Jäg.Rgt.56 shortly before Operation Barbarossa. He was the first in his unit to receive the Iron Cross First Class. One of his soldiers, Gefreiter Josef Troiber, a Kompaniemelder from 5./Gr.Rgt.577, recalls that Winkler was "ein prima Chef" (a fantastic commander). Winkler would survive four months of fighting in Stalingrad, only to be captured in early February 1943 during an attempt to break out of the Stalingrad pocket. He died 8-10 February 1943 in Beketovka POW camp. The photo to the right was the last image his family ever saw of him. It appeared in numerous magazines and his sons cut out the picture and wrote "Our dear dad in Stalingrad in October 1942" on the back. Only in late 1948 did his family learn about his death.

Nothing is mentioned about the loss of Haus 66 [Dom 35]. However, confirmation appears in a report issued at 0800 hours by Captain Konovalenko, commander of 344th Rifle Regiment. Combat Report No. 48 to divisional staff states:

> At 0400 on 11.11.42, after artillery preparation, the enemy, in up to platoon-strength, went on the offensive on the left flank of the regiment's defensive positions, but organised fire from small arms, machine-guns and mortars threw the enemy back to his starting positions. At 0420, with a strength of up to 2 companies, the enemy again tried to attack the regiment's entire defensive position. He was able to break through the neighbouring formation's front-line and capture Dom 35 [Haus 66], hit the flank with a separate group and strike the main defensive line…

Based on this combat report, it seems that this regiment escaped the full brunt of the German assault, despite the division's combat journal recording that "from 0400, 344th Rifle Regiment has been repelling fierce enemy attacks originating in Workshops 4 and 14". Most of the action was taking place on both of the regiment's flanks. In summarising its actions up to 0800 hours, Konovalenko informed division that "all enemy attacks on the regiment's defensive line were beaten off. We are continuing to hold the foremost front-line defences and continue to fight the enemy groups who had advanced earlier. Losses are heavy, but they are still being calculated, as is the damage inflicted on the enemy. Enemy artillery fire destroyed 5 of our mortar positions."

As can be seen in the last sentence, five of 344th Rifle Regiment's seven 82mm mortars were knocked out by the preliminary German artillery barrage.

The attack of 389. Infanterie-Division with Pionier-Bataillone 45, 162 and 389:

The first moments of the attack are clearly remembered by Gefreiter Karl Krauss, a member of the second assault group formed by 2./Pionier-Bataillon 45:

> With fixed bayonets, we crept silently towards what we supposed were the Russian positions. Objective: the so-called 'White House', the command post of a Russian commander that lay in a gully. After a few metres, hand grenades and Molotov cocktails came flying towards us out of the darkness. Did the Russians know about our attack? A simultaneous crash from both sides, then machine-guns chattered and rifles cracked… but the enemy remained invisible. Screams, curses, explosive shells… there was no longer a front and a rear.
>
> Gefreiter Willi Walter[37], the flamethrower-operator assigned to my group, was shot during the advance in the darkness. The pressure in the thrower caused the container to burst. The viscous Flamm-Öl[38] completely engulfed him, particularly his face. He collapsed and lay on the ground, motionless. Fortunately the oil did not catch fire, otherwise he would have been hopelessly burnt.[39] He was carried back by his comrades. I feared that he had been blinded. His face was completely black and thickly encrusted, and he was close to suffocating. Would he survive?[40]

---

37. Walter, Gefreiter Willi, 2./Pi.Btl.45; born 1922. Died 1998 in Saarbrücken. Krauss fondly remembers Walter's ability to recite Goethe's 'Faust' from heart and Walter's wife recalls that her husband "always wanted to change things and make the world a better place".

38. A black oil smelling like creosote.

39. The reason the oil did not catch fire was because of the ignition system used on the Model 42 flamethrower. Whereas the Model 41 used a hydrogen jet, the newer model used a cartridge system which consisted of a magazine loaded with ten rimless, blank 9mm pistol cartridges which loaded, fired and ejected in automatic succession at each pull of the trigger. Since the fuel ejection and firing mechanism were operated by the same trigger, the result was 'hot-firing', where the jet of fuel was set afire the instant it left the nozzle. There were no naked flames unless the trigger was pulled.

40. Karl Krauss recalls: "About 40 years later, I learned through many detours that he was still alive, and had further established that he even still had his eyesight. Our reunion was full of gratitude and joy."

Now that it was light, we took fire from all sides from an invisible enemy. Ivan sat in chimneys, between the wreckage of machines, under the ground in sewerage canals, and we were almost without cover. Then a counterattack began, supported by snipers. It was -15° but there was still no snow. The attack was repulsed with casualties for the enemy. The ground we had gained was small, perhaps 50–60 metres. Any careless movement was punished with a head shot. I noticed that the neighbouring assault group under Feldwebel Walter[41] had made better progress than mine. As it later turned out, however, not one single man from that assault group survived because they walked into a trap and were badly injured by enemy fire and hand-to-hand fighting, and were then bestially mutilated (because no prisoners should be taken?).[42]

Flamethrower-operator Gefreiter Willi Walter, 2./Pi.Btl.45.

Then the area-bombardment Stalin Organs came into effect behind us.

Soldat Bertold Paulus[43], also in the same company as Krauss, recorded his experiences of this attack in a letter home to his family:

And now the latest: you already know that I am in Stalingrad. Luckily, I have survived my first attack and my first assault group. Unfortunately, many of my comrades did not.

And now compose yourself, because my comrade and friend Hartmut[44] was killed at 0400 hours on the morning of 11 November as leader of an assault group. Here's the details of what

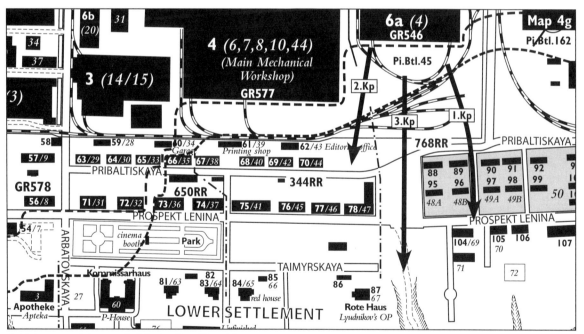

Initial stages of the attack: Pionier-Bataillon 45.

41. Walter, Leutnant Lothar, 2./Pi.Btl.45; born 1 May, 1920 in Leutkirch. Killed in action, 11 November, 1942 in Stalingrad. See Appendix 2 (page 579) for more details.

42. As a footnote, Krauss wrote: "The snipers used by the Russians were, in part, well-trained woman, and woe betide the soldier who fell alive into the hands of those Furies!"

43. Paulus, Soldat Bertold, 2./Pi.Btl.45; born 9 February, 1923 in Kastel/Saar. Missing in action, January, 1943 in Stalingrad.

44. Müller, Unteroffizier Hartmut, 2./Pi.Btl.45; born 16 September, 1917 in Kastel. Killed in action, 11 November, 1942 in Stalingrad.

happened: our platoon was split into two assault groups. The platoon was led by a Leutnant[45], and Hartmut led a squad with 10 men.

At 0230 hours in the morning, we readied ourselves for the attack in the 'Red Barricades'[46] Gun Factory. The attack began at 0330 hours. We had to take a piece of ground about 500 metres long by 200 metres wide. Every 10 metres was a bunker and all of them were occupied by snipers. We used machine-guns, demolition charges, hand grenades and flamethrowers. Then frightful combat began. Always hand-to-hand combat. No Russians gave themselves up. No prisoners were taken.

Now I will tell you how Hartmut found a heroes death.

He moved forward 50 metres with his squad. Then they received heavy fire from the bunkers and from snipers perched in the roofs. He formed up his squad to launch an attack on the bunker. Twenty metres in front of the bunker he suddenly fell forward and was dead on the spot. He had a head wound. He did not utter a word. Only then did we notice he was dead. I can tell you it was a hard and frightful battle.

Above: Soldat Bertold Paulus.

Below: Unteroffizier Hartmut Müller.

The attack of Pionier-Bataillon 45 struck at the boundary of two of Lyudnikov's regiments: the right flank of 344th Rifle Regiment and the left flank of 768th Rifle Regiment, the most formidably fortified sector of the Soviet line.

In his morning report, Captain Konovalenko stated that "on the right flank, the enemy broke through the defences of 768th Rifle Regiment and began to advance in individual groups in the direction of Dom 47 [Haus 78] and towards the command post via the gully".

This attack by Feldwebel Walter of Pionier-Bataillon 45 seriously threatened the command post of Major Gunyaga, commander of 768th Rifle Regiment, located a few dozen metres north of Palets Ovrag (Finger Gully). Dawn coloured the sky and cast a pale light over the drab battlefield as the pioneers approached the broad, deep gully. Lieutenant-Colonel Shuba, chief-of-staff of 138th Rifle Division, reported to Lyudnikov that Major

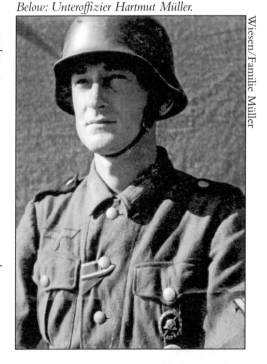

Gunyaga was waiting to speak to him on the telephone. The regiment was having trouble containing the German attack. Punctuating every word as usual, but with a voice trembling

---

45. This was almost certainly Molfenter, Oberleutnant Fritz, 2./Pi.Btl.45; born 12 August, 1919 in Ulm. Missing in action, 23 January, 1943 in Stalingrad. See Appendix 2 (page 576) for more details.

46. The original text says 'Red October'.

with anxiety, Gunyaga reported:

"The enemy has broken through to the regimental command post and is showering it with hand grenades. What are we to do?"

Lyudnikov replied incredulously: "What are you to do? Throw him back and destroy him, but do not retreat a single inch. You, of course, are aware that command post personnel not only direct the units but also fight."

"I appreciate that, Comrade Divisional Commander, but our headquarters has suffered considerable losses and we just don't have the men."

"Alright. Stand by. In five minutes Comrade Tychinsky[47] will hit the enemy in front of your regiment and in the region of your command post. But bear in mind that some of the shells may land on your command post. Therefore, take cover, be careful and do not lose contact."

After ten minutes of shelling, during which the Soviet artillery coped splendidly with its task, Major Gunyaga again telephoned Lyudnikov and reported that he and his men were grateful to the artillerymen. Two shells landed squarely in the trench at the command post, but no one had been hurt. Heavy losses had been inflicted on the Germans and the situation had now been restored.

At 0800 hours, Major Gunyaga sent in a combat report to division command. The confused situation and low combat strengths of his regiment are obvious:

> At 0340, the enemy on our right flank – with the strength of up to a platoon of infantry and supported by artillery and mortar fire – went on the offensive, breaking through the front-line into our defences. His right flank is on the entrance of the gully that comes out towards the north-east corner of Taimyrskaya street and his left flank is 150 metres further to the right, along the road that runs to the right from the end of the gully. In meeting the attack, our group of 20-25 men, which was made up of logistical troops and mortarmen, beat off the enemy. A group of 8-10 enemy soldiers is located in a shell crater and in the ruins of the second house to the right of the ravine across from the eastern corner of factory square. The combat ranks laid down heavy fire from machine-guns and mortars.

> After repulsing the enemy, the regiment's formations took up defensive positions as follows: on the right flank in the area of the road which runs from the ravine exit and then 200-250 metres to the right, a group of 9 men closer to the ravine on this same road, then a group of 12-14 men, and to the left, level with the spot where the railroad tracks run next to a crane located 150 metres east of the right corner of the main mechanical workshop, is a group of 6 men. We have not been able to establish communications with the battalion that was located on the previous defensive line. Right now we are undertaking all measures to establish communications and we have taken measures to destroy the fritzes who are located in the crater to the right. The mortar battalion is located in its previous fire positions. There are dead and wounded, up to 20 men, we continue to count our losses.

– – –

A large amount of the pressure applied to Gunyaga's 768th Rifle Regiment was caused by the aggressive assault of Major Krüger's Pionier-Bataillon 162. They had formed up in the relatively open area north of the gun factory where the terrain consisted of rubbled single-story buildings, churned-up earth and hundreds of shell craters. The Soviet front-line in this area straddled a slightly elevated railway embankment, which gave the defenders –

---

47. Tychinsky, Colonel Sergei Yakovlevich, would be killed in 1945, shortly before the end of the war.

tough survivors of Zholudev's[48] 37th Guards Rifle Division and riflemen from Major Gunyaga's 768th Rifle Regiment – a minor advantage. Bolstering the Soviet defences on this sector were five immobilised tanks from 84th Tank Brigade that had been dug into the ground. The most recent report about enemy strength released by the Ic Abteilung[49] of 6. Armee stated that the once powerful 37th Guards Division now consisted only of the extremely weak 118th Guards Rifle Regiment whose 2nd company had 15 men, while its 6th still had 23 men. Another report stated that 1st company of 768th Rifle Regiment had 54 men. The true figures were vastly different – Soviet combat strengths were much lower but their tenacity was incalculable – and this information was all the Germans had as they prepared for battle. Major Krüger passed on this information to his company commanders.

The battalion's assault groups moved out a few minutes before the bombardment began at 0340 hours. As with all of the pioneer battalions subordinated to 389. Infanterie-Division, they preferred to preserve the element of surprise by foregoing any artillery preparation on their objectives, in contrast to their southern neighbours. Krüger's pioneers furtively crept across the churned earth towards the railway embankment and swiftly overwhelmed the Soviet defenders there just as the first artillery volley erupted. As Major Gunyaga would later report, "our company holding the defences along the front-line was swept away...". With artillery and rockets screeching overhead towards the Volga, the pioneer detachments pushed on, blasting and flaming their way east, towards the river. Their attack pressed right on the

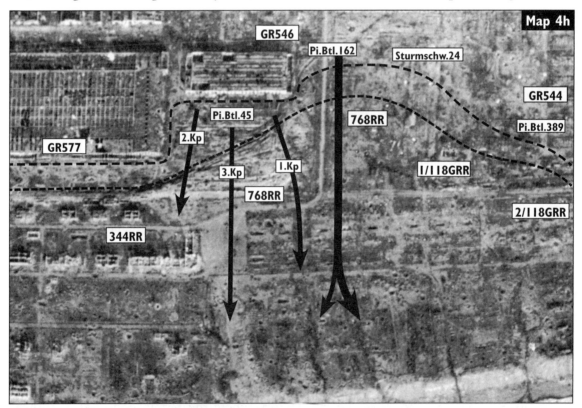

Initial stages of the attack: Pionier-Bataillon 162.

---

48. Zholudev, Major-General Viktor Grigoryevich, HotSU; 37th GRD; born 22 March, 1905 in Uglich. Killed in action, 21 July 1944 near Minsk.
49. Ic Abteilung = counter-intelligence department.

boundary between 768th Rifle Regiment and 118th Guards Rifle Regiment. Having taken heavy casualties, the guardsmen continued to hold their line after beating off numerous attacks by 'drunk Hitlerites', but the annihilation of each Soviet defensive position permitted the German pioneers to intrude deeper into the vulnerable flanks of both rifle regiments. Resistance slowly but surely stiffened and the pioneers on the right, facing Gunyaga's regiment, eventually halted along a street that ran in front of them. Assault groups to the left were able to keep moving along the junction. Moving side by side with these pioneers was Leutnant Beyersdorff's Sturmschwadron. Together, they punched right through the Soviet defences and reached the river near 'Dorn Rachel' (Thorn Gully). 138th Rifle Division's combat report states that "at 0830 hours, the enemy brought fresh forces into the fighting and crushed the insignificant remnants of 1/118th Guards Rifle Regiment – reaching the Volga river". The regiment, now encircled, continued to stoically repel German attacks. The Germans widened their breakthrough but resistance to the south was so fierce that attacks in this direction were halted. Inroads were made to the north, into 118th Guards Rifle Regiment, but they were small and inconsequential. The Germans ceased their attacks so that they could regroup.

Following up behind the first wave were assault groups formed from the remaining infantrymen of Grenadier-Regiment 546. They dealt with any stragglers or resistance nests left behind. Countless bunkers and dug-outs studded the area and each needed to be checked and, if still occupied, mopped up.

The attacks on Lieutenant-Colonel Kolobovnikov's 118th Guards Rifle Regiment were accurately recorded in 138th Rifle Division's combat report:

> From 0400, 118th Guards Rifle Regiment was attacked by the enemy with a strength of two battalions from the following directions: first attack group – one battalion from the eastern edge of Volkhovstroyevsk against 2/118th Guards Rifle Regiment; second attack group – one battalion from the western edge of Volkhovstroyevsk into the boundary between 768th Rifle Regiment and 1/118, striking 1/118th Guards Rifle Regiment in the flank.

The second attack group was Grenadier-Regiment 546 supported by Pionier-Bataillon 162, while the first group was Oberleutnant Eberhard's Pionier-Bataillon 389 and Grenadier-Regiment 544.

The commander of this latter regiment, Oberstleutnant Colmar von Debschitz[50], recorded his impressions of the fighting and highlights how troublesome Lyudnikov's strongpoints were:

> The buildings on the river bank still occupied by the Russians represented a constant threat to our flank and […] were scenes of particularly violent and obstinate fighting in which a combat group formed from members of the regiment, under the command of Oberleutnant Schlüter[51], […] was deployed several times. In this combat, carried out with the employment of all sorts of weapons including panzers and flamethrowers, the tough defensive will of the Russian troops was revealed. The German infantry, pioneer battalions and assault gun units deployed there bled themselves to death in terror-filled attacks and only gained ground with extraordinary casualties.

Furthest north of all the pioneer battalions and deployed in the sector of Oberstleutnant von Debschitz's regiment was the combat group formed from Pionier-Bataillon 389. The

---

50. Debschitz, Oberstleutnant Colmar von, DKiG; Gr.Rgt.544; born 17 January, 1900 in Berneuchen. Died 7 October, 1980 in Erlangen.
51. Schlüter, Oberleutnant Max, Gr.Rgt.544; born 25 May, 1910. Missing in action, 22 January, 1943 in Stalingrad.

leader of this pioneer battle group, Oberleutnant Hans-Ludwig Eberhard, vividly remembers the morning of the attack:

> Everything was arranged, both with the infantry and also with the neighbour on the right. It would all start before dawn. Arriving in the jump-off positions, I had to take a couple of deep breaths. I hesitated: had everything been thought through properly? Was everything right? I pulled myself together and whispered: 'Come on!'
>
> We ran down the street and dispersed into the two gullies. It was still quiet. Only when the fire of the flamethrowers lit up the gully did the first tentative shots ring out. They were answered by the dull thud of hand grenades. I ran along the upper edge of the gully – as best I could in the field of ruins – towards the Volga. Reaching the riverside cliff, I slid down it and after a few metres stood on the edge of the river. It was like a dream. I stood there for a few seconds, oblivious to everything. Night-time darkness still lay over the water, but slowly, I could make out the silhouette of the large island standing opposite. I recovered from my stupor. In the meantime, fighting had broken out for every position. It was also quite lively on the island. The bombardment of the rocket-launchers and artillery located there had begun: it was unpleasant. I ran back into the gully from which the dull thump of hand grenades still predominated.
>
> In order not to get caught up in our own attack, I quickly clambered up the slope. Reaching the top, my Kompaniefeldwebel jumped up from behind the ruins of a wall and ran up to me. Meanwhile, it was already almost light, dawn would soon be here.
>
> 'Herr Oberleutnant, the Volga, we've reached it!' He stood up, then suddenly sank back down. Head shot. My euphoria disappeared. I asked two soldiers running past to pick up the fatally

Rinck/Grimm

The ground east of the brickworks – the sector occupied by Pi.Btl.389 – was exposed and possessed very few buildings, offering scant defensive opportunities for the guardsmen of Lt.-Col. Kolobovnikov's 118th Guards Rifle Regiment.

Initial stages of the attack: Pionier-Bataillon 389.

wounded Hauptfeldwebel because I lacked the heart to do it. My Sanitäts-Unteroffizier[52] later reported to me that he died an hour later without having regained consciousness. I turned away. Because I was alone, I started blubbering hysterically.

Pionier-Bataillon 389 succeeded in slicing off part of 2/118th Guards Rifle Regiment in the extreme northern point of the Soviet bridgehead. In a post-war account, Lieutenant-Colonel Nikolai Efimovich Kolobovnikov, commander of 118th Guards Rifle Regiment, recalls the attack on his guardsmen:

> The enemy was readying his assault with superior forces. I only had Tolin's[53] battalion and a reserve company of reinforcements. We were not afraid of the enemy. Every guardsman could fight for 5 men. I myself was at the command post together with officer Zhatko and a few message runners where I ordered everything to be burned, including papers, maps and reports, so that they would not fall into enemy hands. We knew that we would have to fight to the death. An artillery barrage began at six in the morning, followed by an attack. Then a second and third after it. The guardsmen held their ground. They fought off attacks all day but took losses. Commanders themselves manned machine-guns, replacing fallen soldiers.

The net result of 389. Infanterie-Division's attack was that the right flank of Major Gunyaga's 768th Rifle Regiment was overrun by Pionier-Bataillon 162 and Sturmschwadron 24 and forced back into some battered ruins north of Finger Gully, while Lieutenant-Colonel Kolobovnikov's 118th Guards Rifle Regiment was cut off from the main body. The encircled guardsmen held their new line… but for how long?

---

52. Grünbaum, Sanitäts-Unteroffizier Leonhard.

53. Tolin, Guards Captain K.T., 2/118 GRR. Killed in action, 11 November, 1942 in Stalingrad.

Mid-morning: the assault continues

Paulus landed at an advanced airstrip near Razgulyayevka railway station at 0845 hours. Soviet artillery shells fell at frequent intervals. An hour later, Paulus arrived at the forward command post of 305. Infanterie-Division in the artillery observation post and was oriented about the situation by Oberst Steinmetz. Details from the front-line were still sketchy but it was obvious that the expected successes had not eventuated, so Steinmetz reported that the attack was progressing very slowly. 389. Infanterie-Division informed Paulus that it was gaining ground only against obstinate enemy resistance. After fifteen minutes, Paulus started discussing other matters with Seydlitz and Clausius, namely the discovery of strong Russian forces on the army's left flank.

At 1140 hours, 6. Armee gave Heeresgruppe B a brief progress report over the phone. Oberstleutnant Elchlepp, Ia of 6. Armee, informed Oberst Winter:

> In Stalingrad, 305. Infanterie-Division has only gained a small amount of ground, several hundred metres near the fuel installation. 389. Infanterie-Division has made somewhat better progress. The resistance is extraordinarily tough. On the remaining fronts in Stalingrad, successful stormtroop operations were undertaken which have shown that the Russians are in strength everywhere.

So, by mid-morning, the German attack had barely made any progress. All along the line, fierce Soviet resistance stalled the pioneer-led assaults. Grenadier-Regiment 576 had been halted outside the fuel installation, Grenadier-Regiment 578 had seized one important building (Apotheke) but failed to secure the most vital one, the Kommissarhaus, the linchpin of the Soviet defence, while Grenadier-Regiment 577 had captured one objective (Haus 66) but was unsuccessful in its assaults against the other targets. Grim resistance, powerful counterattacks and relentless artillery strikes sapped the gusto from the German attacks. The Soviets were always tough opponents but their almost suicidal defiance was beyond anyone's expectations. But the attack had to continue.

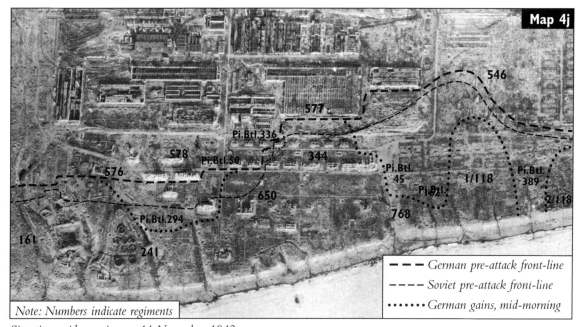

Situation, mid-morning on 11 November, 1942.

After regrouping, the Germans – now led by Major Braun – launched a new attack towards the fuel tanks. The reserves of 241st Rifle Regiment and remnants of its 1st Battalion girded themselves for the onslaught. They managed to contain the Germans and then drive them back. Wounded Soviet soldiers had themselves hastily bandaged, collected grenades and then returned to their units, ready to throw back the next frenzied assault.

At 0930 hours, the Germans gathered all their reserve forces and again went on the offensive against the right flank of 241st Rifle Regiment, held by the battered and bleeding men of Senior-Lieutenant Selifanov's 1st Rifle Battalion. The remnants of the battalion absorbed the mighty impact and took a nasty toll on the German attackers. Playing a major role in this advance was a flamethrower section of 2./Pi.Btl.305. An unnamed soldier from that company recounts the action:

> One of our best-trained men was an Obergefreiter; he got out when he was wounded, and he was killed in Italy in 1944.
>
> It must have been about 11 November. Obergefreiter M., from Upper Franconia, he was a specialist, was given orders to attack the sewage system, that's to say go down every manhole, the entire length of the street. The Russians were causing us a lot of trouble there, they had barricaded themselves in the cellars, and in the sewage canals, and that's where we started…
>
> He climbed in; we gave him cover, good cover, with rifle fire, and he climbed in and cleaned up the entire length of the sewage canal. They have to do that alone. What they do is carry the liquid container on their backs and hold the flamethrower itself, the equipment, in front of them. Exactly like a fireman using a hose.
>
> [He] worked his way along [the entire street] and cleaned everything up. After that, of course, we could resume the attack.

Although the man is not named, it is almost certainly Obergefreiter Franz Müller[54]. In a letter written in June 1943, Müller briefly described his actions:

> During my operations in Stalingrad as a flamethrower-operator, I was in action 6 times with success, the last time on 11 November with the assault pioneers of 294 under Feldwebel Dickler[55].

Müller's story is one of the most remarkable to emerge from the Stalingrad battle. He was the father of seven children, one of the few circumstances which excused a man from front-line duty. Yet, here he was, in the most dangerous sector of the entire Eastern Front, performing the most dangerous tasks with the most fearsome weapon. Only in a post-war account did Oberleutnant Grimm – who described Müller as "a difficult fellow" – reveal why he had been assigned to the combat troops:

> Gefreiter Müller was supplied to 2. Kompanie as a replacement 'on probation', as far as I can remember, only after the Don crossing. The papers were with the unit train and I was verbally informed about it by my Spieß (Hauptfeldwebel). As the father of seven children, he must have committed numerous criminal offences to be sentenced to 'probation at the front'. To ensure that nothing affected him, the Spieß and I had to keep silent about his probation.
>
> I continually received complaints about his uncomradely behaviour towards other men, so I put him into another squad. The NCOs and platoon commanders complained about my 'problem child'. Only in my presence did he show himself to be a courageous man… When I took Müller to task, he said "they accuse me of things, which they are not allowed to mention at all", and with an eloquence that could, in my opinion, only have been learned through many

---

54. Müller, Obergefreiter Franz, 2./Pi.Btl.305; born 17 April, 1907 in Bruchsal. Died 6 March, 1944.

55. Dickler, Feldwebel Oskar, 2./Pi.Btl.294; no further information known.

court appearances. I therefore kept him behind the front-line in a flamethrower section. Only during the conquest of Hall 6 in the gun factory were both our flamethrowers brought into action and during two attacks – in my presence – he notably proved himself.

Müller was fortunate to survive his hazardous tasks. The other flamethrower-operator, Obergefreiter Schwarzer[56], was not so lucky: he was killed in Hall 6 on 25 October. Grimm's estimation about the flamethrower as a weapon was not positive:

> The flamethrower primarily had a moral effect, forcing the enemy to flee, but our own losses were disproportionately high. The perceptions about it are, in my opinion, wrong and they should not have been manufactured any more. I can only shake my head about reports which reached my ears after the war.

After the way had been burned clear by the flamethrower section, the attack of Grenadier-Regiment 576 continued. The men of 1/241st Rifle Regiment did not abandon their line and continued to fight heroically for several hours, but they were hopelessly outgunned. Having now lost up to 95% of its personnel, the remnants of the battalion – reduced to 15 men – withdrew to the east and occupied a line 50-70 metres from the river. The battalion commander, Senior-Lieutenant Selifanov, had been surrounded in his observation post by a group of about 45 Germans, but having organised the defence, he managed to throw them back and escape from the encirclement with a few men. Collecting and organising the remnants of his battalion, he again entered the battle.

A soldier of the security platoon of 241st Rifle Regiment – the only survivor of a detachment defending the regimental command post – was wounded. His right hand was smashed, so he could no longer hold his weapon. He went down into the bunker and had it bandaged, but upon hearing that there were no reserves left, he filled his cap with grenades. "I can throw these with my left hand," he explained. He returned to battle with the enemy pressing towards him.

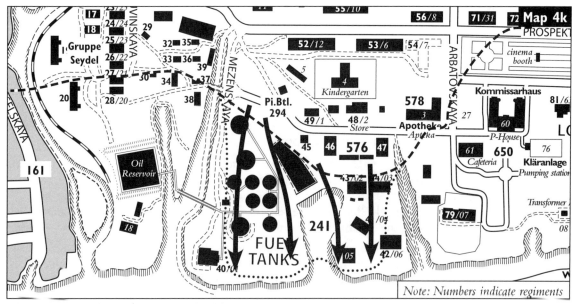

The attack on the fuel tanks and Volga bank by Grenadier-Regiment 576, 11 November, 1942.

---

56. Schwarzer, Obergefreiter Karl, 2./Pi.Btl.305; born 7 September, 1913 in Wien, Austria. Killed in action, 25 October, 1942 in Stalingrad.

The 2nd Rifle Battalion and regimental reserves were brought into action to restore the position. An order also went out to the neighbouring 161st Rifle Regiment: "Using reserves – up to 1 company – strike the enemy's flank from the south to cut them off, push them back to the west, and restore the position on 241st Rifle Regiment's sector". An ambitious and optimistic directive, to say the least. Hindering the Soviet defence was the fact that from 1000 hours, their artillery occasionally lowered its rate of fire because of ammunition shortages.

At 1130 hours, Major Braun's men again plunged forward with the aim of reaching the Volga. By this time, there were very few men left in the companies of 241st Rifle Regiment. Despite that, the Germans were met by heavy fire and suffered losses. The Soviet remnants fought back courageously but Major Braun – with thrilling impetus – dashed into the fuel tanks at the head of his grenadiers and overpowered the Soviet riflemen there in hand-to-hand fighting amongst the crumpled cylinders. Further north, German troops pushed on to the riverside cliff, finally reaching the Volga 300 metres north of the fuel tanks.

The Germans quickly spread out and occupied the small peninsula bordered to the north and south by enemy-occupied gullies. Groups of pioneers slid down the loamy slopes but discovered that the bunkers in the cliffside were stubbornly defended. The pioneers of Oberleutnant Grimm's 2./Pionier-Bataillon 305, temporarily led by Feldwebel Adam Pauli[57], had orders to begin erecting wire obstacles down to the waterline and laying mines on what the Germans called the 'Sandbank', but it was far too dangerous to be carried out at that moment.

Four soldiers, all that remained of a platoon of 241st Rifle Regiment, huddled in a pipe that emptied into a gully north-east of the fuel tanks. Their ammunition had run out and they were encircled by about 60 Germans. A wounded man somehow made it back with the message: "Begin shelling our position. In front of us is a large group of fascists. Farewell comrades, we did not retreat." The artillery and rockets came down upon them. They perished but did not retreat.

– – –

Concurrent with the attack of Grenadier-Regiment 576 against the fuel installation was the next phase of Grenadier-Regiment 578's plan. When the first of the fuel tanks was reached towards 0930 hours, Hauptmann Rettenmaier gave the order for his third and fourth assault groups (Balka and Haus 79) to advance. The two assault groups left the relative safety of their starting positions in the Kindergarten and the Apotheke and moved toward the gully they called 'Zeigefinger Rachel' (Index Finger Gully). The third assault group (Balka), commanded by Hauptfeldwebel Albert Frank, led the way with a barrage of grenades. The fourth assault group followed behind, ready to clear up bypassed enemy nests. Machine-gunners and riflemen in the upper floors of the Apotheke covered their advance. Obstinate resistance at the gully entrance was broken with a combination of fire and movement. The men of both assault groups were keen to get into the gully to escape the menacing glare of the Kommissarhaus, and this desire gave them impetus. The floor of the 100-metre long gully sloped gently from the southern side of the Apotheke down to the riverside beach, providing an easy route to the river… if the enemy defences were discounted. And the surviving defenders of 241st Rifle Regiment certainly had no intention of letting the Germans waltz down to the river. Foxholes and dug-outs had been driven deep into the steep slopes. Still covered by their comrades in the

---

57. Pauli, Feldwebel Adam, 2./Pi.Btl.305; born 20 December, 1917 in Hessenthal. Missing in action, January 1943 in Stalingrad.

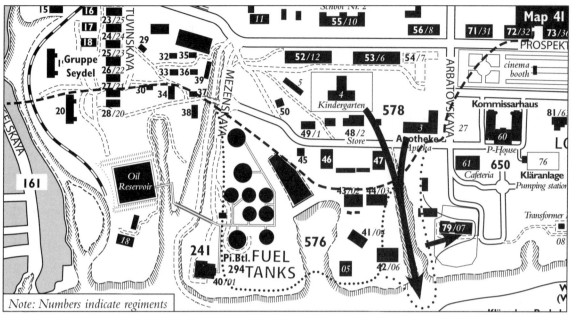

The attack towards the Volga and Haus 79 by Grenadier-Regiment 578, 11 November, 1942.

Apotheke, Kampfgruppe Frank suppressed one enemy position after another. They soon reached the river bank and consolidated their hold on the gully mouth and surrounding areas. After cleaning up enemy stragglers, Kampfgruppe 4 formed up for the attack on Haus 79 – a building of vital importance to both sides.

The man leading the fourth Kampfgruppe, and the attack on Haus 79, was 25-year-old Oberleutnant Erwin Kretz, a bespectacled company commander from II. Bataillon of Grenadier-Regiment 578. His combat group consisted of an infantry battalion reinforced by heavy machine-gunners and pioneer squads. Leading the battalion-sized combat group was a responsible task that needed the cool head and acumen of an experienced officer... and that officer was Kretz. According to Leutnant Alban Plaum, a young platoon commander, Kretz was a "courageous, fair-minded and ever helpful officer, and a good comrade". Kretz began the war as an Unteroffizier in 9./Infanterie-Regiment 34 but was transferred around various units for the next two years. Contained in his letters home, apart from many attempts at poetry, were constant lamentations that he had not yet been in action, neither in the Polish campaign,

Oberleutnant Erwin Kretz, company commander in II./Grenadier-Regiment 578.

the French campaign, nor anywhere else. Only when the Russian campaign began did Kretz get his chance. Sixteen months later, when his unit arrived in Stalingrad in October 1942, he was an Oberleutnant with the Iron Cross First Class and Infantry Assault Badge pinned to his left breast and was one of Grenadier-Regiment 578's most experienced and popular company commanders. The next month of gruelling combat in the ruined city whittled down the officer ranks. Since arriving on the Eastern Front in May 1942, his regiment had lost just under thirty company commanders[58] – eleven of those in Stalingrad alone – to death, wounds or an unknown fate, and Kretz was one of the few to make it through to the end of October. In a letter to his aunt, dated 30 October, 1942, he described his surroundings:

> You can obviously see from the soiled writing paper that I am not living in the cleanest of houses. I'm sitting in a building that's been blasted to pieces. The Volga flows 300 metres in front of me and shells are cracking all around me, planes zoom overhead and the earth trembles under the bombardments. Lying behind us is the 'Red Barrikade' Gun Factory. It's a pile of rubble. Not one of the large workhalls is still intact, everything is destroyed, girders sag down and block the way. The ground is ploughed up, impact upon impact, shell crater upon shell crater. It is a tough battle here in Stalingrad which surpasses all my previous front-line experience.

> That's as much as I'm able to collect myself to give a short description. I'm dreadfully tired because I'm not getting much sleep…

Bundesarchiv

'Girders sag down and block the way'… wrote Oberleutnant Kretz. The devastation in Barrikady's workhalls was total. During quiet moments, expeditions were undertaken through the massive halls. The troops marvelled at and examined the mostly German-made lathes, drill-presses and drop-forges.

---

58. Both Kompaniechef (company commanders) and Kompanieführer (temporary company commanders).

Up front as always, Kretz led his assault group up and out of the gully. Cover-fire from the Apotheke lashed the long western facade of Haus 79 and kept down the heads of its Soviet defenders. Oberleutnant Kretz and his assault troops dashed across twenty metres of open ground and burst into the ground floor of the two-storey building. The Soviet riflemen were caught off guard as the Germans swept through the house. The attack on Haus 79 succeeded surprisingly well although losses were heavy. Any further advances, however, miscarried: the Kommissarhaus dominated the vacant foreground.

- - -

Numerous appeals for assistance from Colonel Gorishny's 95th Rifle Division to its northern neighbour (138th Rifle Division) could not be heeded as Lyudnikov and his men were themselves in an exceedingly difficult situation. To close the breach that had formed was not possible at that moment because the reserves of 241st Rifle Regiment had been completely exhausted, including one and a half platoons sent from 161st Rifle Regiment. Every last man was combed out of headquarters and sick bays to fill holes in the shredded line of 241st Rifle Regiment. Because 95th Rifle Division's other sectors were quiet, units were withdrawn from those and thrown into the chaos: the divisional reconnaissance company with 25 men, a sapper company with 18 men and 50 men from the reserves of 161st Rifle Regiment.

The disintegration of its northern neighbour left 161st Rifle Regiment with a wide open flank. It had repelled three German attacks on its sector, each one by a company-strong force, and also participated in the repulsion of an attack on the left flank of 241st Rifle Regiment, but its line had held. By bending its right flank back along the railway line to the north-east, 161st Rifle Regiment was able to hold its defensive sector.

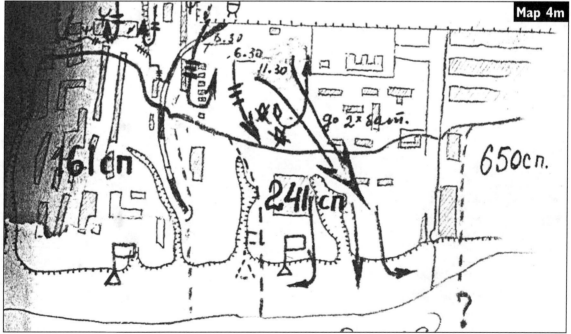

A sketch drawn by 95th Rifle Division shows the succession of attacks that led to the Germans reaching the Volga. Also shown are the two panzers knocked out by Manenkov (represented as diamonds, below the arrow showing the 1130 attack). (Note: the times shown on these sketches are in Russian time, not German time.)

A stunning blow had been dealt to the Soviet defence. In his memoirs, 62nd Army chief-of-staff General Krylov wrote:

> After a short pause and a new preparation by his artillery, the enemy - who had achieved nothing in the morning hours – renewed his attack shortly before 1000. At this time, he employed his reserves, mainly on the sector south of the Barrikady Factory, with a main attack direction along the axis of Mezenskaya Street. Two German divisions rushed towards the two regiments of Gorishny's division defending this area. The regiment on the right flank was rolled out of its positions.
>
> The Germans penetrated here between 95th Rifle Division and 138th Rifle Division, occupied the southern part of the Barrikady Factory grounds and reached the Volga.

Lyudnikov and his 138th Rifle Division were now cut off from the rest of the army. After consolidating their hold on the Volga at the breakthrough position, German combat groups thrust north and south, both along the river bank and atop the escarpment. Leading the way in these attacks was Pionier-Bataillon 294. After brief but intense fighting, they joined up with Grenadier-Regiment 578 at Index Finger Gully. The conquest of the fuel installation had cost Pionier-Bataillon 294 dearly and the number of dead, many to head shots, was very high.[59]

---

59. From 1. Kompanie: Soldat Fiedler, assault group leader Feldwebel Krebs (head shot) and Unteroffizier Schaarschmidt (killed near the Volga by a head shot). From 2. Kompanie: Gefreiter Friedel, Obergefreiter Herzog (bullet), Soldat Erich Klötzer (bullet), Soldat Martin Klötzer (bullet), Gefreiter Kubitschke (bullet), Soldat Morgenstern (bullet), Soldat Pieke (head shot near the fuel installation), Obergefreiter Schmarsel (bullet near the fuel installation), Obersoldat Schultz (head shot near the fuel installation) and Gefreiter Walter (shrapnel). From 3. Kompanie: Soldat Jahn, Gefreiter Kittler (head shot), Gefreiter König (head shot) and Gefreiter Riedel (bullet). In addition, Unteroffizier Bätz was severely wounded near the fuel installation and died of his wounds while being transported to hospital, and Obergefreiter Chadima from battalion staff died in a casualty collection point in Karpovka from a stomach wound.

Fiedler, Soldat Gerhard, 1./Pi.Btl.294; born 11 February, 1922 in Chemnitz. Killed in action, 11 November, 1942 in Stalingrad.

Krebs, Feldwebel Bernhard, 1./Pi.Btl.294; born 20 September, 1914 in Dresden. Killed in action, 11 November, 1942 in Stalingrad.

Schaarschmidt, Unteroffizier Kurt, 1./Pi.Btl.294; born 5 November 1914 in Gross-Rückerswalde. Killed in action, 11 November, 1942 in Stalingrad.

Friedel, Gefreiter Arno, 2./Pi.Btl.294; born 25 July, 1914 in Lichtenstein. Killed in action, 11 November, 1942 in Stalingrad.

Herzog, Obergefreiter Oskar, 2./Pi.Btl.294; born 27 January, 1913 in Neugersdorf. Killed in action, 11 November, 1942 in Stalingrad.

Klötzer, Soldat Erich, 2./Pi.Btl.294; born 9 October, 1917 in Werdau. Killed in action, 11 November, 1942 in Stalingrad.

Klötzer, Soldat Martin, 2./Pi.Btl.294; born 7 March, 1922 in Mittelsdorf. Killed in action, 11 November, 1942 in Stalingrad.

Kubitschke, Gefreiter Erich, 2./Pi.Btl.294; born 18 June, 1910 in Waldenburg. Killed in action, 11 November, 1942 in Stalingrad.

Morgenstern, Soldat Manfred, 2./Pi.Btl.294; born 30 September, 1922 in Kleinhartsmannsdorf. Killed in action, 11 November, 1942 in Stalingrad.

Pieke, Soldat Rudolf, 2./Pi.Btl.294; born 2 May, 1914 in Herrnskretschen. Killed in action, 11 November, 1942 in Stalingrad.

Schmarsel, Obergefreiter Franz, 2./Pi.Btl.294; born 26 August, 1912 in Kreiwitz. Killed in action, 11 November, 1942 in Stalingrad.

Schultz, Obersoldat Helmut, 2./Pi.Btl.294; born 27 February, 1914 in Weida. Killed in action, 11 November, 1942 in Stalingrad.

Walter, Gefreiter Alfred, 2./Pi.Btl.294; born 16. July, 1915 in Gebirgsneudorf. Killed in action, 11 November, 1942 in Stalingrad.

Jahn, Soldat Walter, 3./Pi.Btl.294; born 10 June, 1922 in Jüdenberg. Killed in action, 11 November, 1942 in Stalingrad.

Kittler, Gefreiter Robert, 3./Pi.Btl.294; born 15 December, 1922 in Halle. Killed in action, 11 November, 1942 in Stalingrad.

König, Gefreiter Felix, 3./Pi.Btl.294; born 6 March, 1920 in Muschwitz. Killed in action, 11 November, 1942 in Stalingrad.

Riedel, Gefreiter Erich, 3./Pi.Btl.294; born 19 January, 1920 in Reppen. Killed in action, 11 November, 1942 in Stalingrad.

Bätz, Unteroffizier Kurt, 3./Pi.Btl.294; born 9 September, 1920 in Schwemsal. Died of wounds, 11 November, 1942 in Stalingrad.

Chadima, Obergefreiter Erhard, Stab/Pi.Btl.294; born 21 May, 1916 in Bischofswerda. Died of wounds, 11 November, 1942 in Stalingrad.

A further advance up the river from the Sandbank, however, was not possible. The Soviets had constructed what the Germans called 'Kanzeln'[60] in the steep cliffs, which could not be got at from the Sandbank. As the Germans were soon to discover, some of these small unassuming 'hides' were unconquerable strongholds.

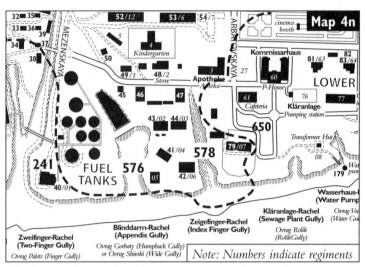

The German line on the afternoon on 11 November, 1942.

The Germans now held a sweep of river bank stretching from the fuel tanks in the south up to the midpoint of Index Finger and Kläranlage (Sewage Treatment Plant) Gullies. The width of this breakthrough amounted to about 500 metres. The Germans continued their efforts to drive south. By 1320, having lost almost all of its manpower, 241st Rifle Regiment retreated further to the south, to the headquarters of 95th Rifle Division. It had been totally annihilated. Every man Gorishny could find now had a rifle in his hands and was in the front-line halting the German march south. The withdrawal of 241st Rifle Regiment also exposed the left flank of Pechenyuk's 650th Rifle Regiment. Fighting would continue on this flank deep into the night.

– – –

General Chuikov was not able to offer much help to Lyudnikov's embattled troops. Any movement of land forces during the day brought down a murderous reaction from German artillery and ground attack aircraft. In any case, he did not have a reserve of manpower upon which to draw, and the remaining units of the army were stretched thin enough as it was. The German diversionary attacks had served their purpose but it would not be long before the Soviets recognised where the main danger lay. The Red Air Force only played a minor role during the day. German observers noted that until noon, only two Soviet sorties – each consisting of 6 bombers protected by fighters – had appeared over the battleground. In the early stages of the fighting, the air force was nowhere to be seen. The only way Chuikov could effectively assist Lyudnikov was with artillery. Battery upon battery was emplaced in the thick scrub east of the Volga. Comparatively safe behind their broad moat and with secure supply lines, they could deliver devastating blows.

– – –

During the morning, Pionier-Bataillon 336 took several large houses but had to relinquish some of them around 0800 hours, as reported by one of the unit's veterans:

> After four hours of fighting, we had to give up the block. The infantry assigned as the second wave had apparently been trapped by artillery fire. We pulled back because our ammunition was exhausted. A short time later, we learned that our battalion had suffered casualties of 60 men.

---

60. Trans.: 'Kanzeln' = A hunting term, meaning 'a raised hide'.

Whether knowingly or not, the Soviet strategy for retarding the German attack was working: artillery fire blanketing the front-line prevented reinforcements and supplies from moving up, thus starving the assault troops of manpower and ammunition. Pionier-Bataillon 336 was unfortunate because it struck at the most formidable section of the Soviet defensive line. Captain Konovalenko and his battalion commanders had created a solid web of mutually-supporting strongpoints interconnected by trenches. If one strongpoint fell, favourable opportunities existed to retake it immediately: forces needed for the counterattack could assemble in relative safety and overwhelming, close fire support could be placed on the targeted building. Four hours after losing the buildings, Konovalenko's riflemen were able to retake them. The entire morning's gains for Pionier-Bataillon 336 evaporated.

After a swift regrouping, the pioneer assault groups moved out again. The daily report of 138th Rifle Division mentions the actions of these groups:

> By 0930, small groups of enemy submachine-gunners had managed to penetrate the front-line on the regiment's left flank and infiltrate deep into the defences. Combat with the enemy submachine-gunners who had broken through into the depth of the defences and against the groups continuously attacking from the front continued until 1400. By this time, the group that had broken through had been wiped out.

In Combat Report No. 49 issued at 1600 hours, Konovalenko summarised the position of his regiment:

> Throughout the day, 344th Rifle Regiment beat back ceaseless enemy attacks that assaulted the front-line. From 1400, we destroyed enemy groups that had broken through and now defend our previous defensive line.

> Connection with 650th Rifle Regiment still exists, the right flank is open, 768th Rifle Regiment fell back from its previous line. Groups of the enemy, up to 30 men, went on the offensive from the direction of building 48 into the rear of the right flank – one rifle company.

The final German actions against the regiment are covered in the division's daily report:

> At 1540, the enemy renewed his attacks on the centre of the regiment's defensive line. All enemy attacks were successfully repelled with stable and well-coordinated fire by 344th Rifle Regiment's units. The regiment continues to hold the previously occupied line.

In a special announcement later in the evening, Lyudnikov recognised the magnificent effort of Konovalenko and his men:

> On 11 November, 1942, the enemy brought in fresh reserves and began heavy attacks along the entire front of the division from 0400. Units of the division, offering fierce defence against the enemy forces, destroyed a good number of the damned fritzes. Soldiers, commanders, and political workers all fought bravely.

> Fighting especially persistently and heroically – with heavy losses for the enemy – were the soldiers, commanders, and political workers of 344th Rifle Regiment, the blocking battalion and the divisional security company.

> On behalf of the armed forces, I give thanks to all personnel of 344th Rifle Regiment, the blocking battalion and the divisional security company for their stubbornness in battle.

> Commemoration: for the experienced command of the battle – and brotherly assistance to their neighbours – of the commander of the 344th Rifle Regiment, Captain Konovalenko, his deputy for political affairs Commissar Fomin, his assistant Senior-Politruk Scherbak, and regimental chief-of-staff Captain Maslov[61].

---

61. Maslov, Major, Nikolai Mikhailovich, would command the regiment later in the war, until wounded in February 1945.

For the quick and experienced liquidation of the enemy submachine-gunners that broke through, to the commander of the blocking detachment of the division, Senior-Lieutenant Ozerov, and his deputy for political affairs, Politruk Kalentyev.

To the glorious artillerymen of the 295th and 499th Artillery Regiments who were able to provide huge help to the infantry with their small number of guns.

To the chief-of-staff of 292nd Guards Mortar Regiment, Major Lyesnikh, for his excellent work in completing the mission given to 292nd Guards Mortar Regiment.

Coming up against Konovalenko's impressive defences was Hauptmann Lundt's pioneer battalion, which suffered devastating losses in these futile attacks. Although the total number of casualties was almost the same as the other pioneer battalions, the number of dead was twice as high (37 dead and 36 wounded) and many of the wounded suffered terrible injuries. Losses incurred by the mine incident during the morning contributed to the tally, but it was the swirling combat inside the buildings and the smothering artillery outside that took the greatest toll. The casualties were harder to bear because there was nothing to show for it.

Amongst the wounded was Oberleutnant Karl Brockmann, commander of 2. Kompanie, struck in the left eye by a shell splinter. He was evacuated to hospital and was able to get a short telegram to his wife on the morning of 16 November:

Wounded in the left eye on 11.11.42. In hospital.[62]

Command of 2. Kompanie was assumed by its senior platoon commander, Leutnant Erich Oberst.[63]

The casualties of Sturmkompanie 44 are not known but they certainly suffered fatalities: documents found on bodies left behind on the battlefield showed that Grenadier-Regiment 132 was operating on Lyudnikov's sector.

Brockmann, after being fitted with a glass eye.

– – –

With the attack of Pionier-Bataillon 45 stalled, many men remained stranded in no-man's land. Gefreiter Karl Krauss was one of them:

For over four hours, I lay in a shallow shell crater while being constantly pelted by hand grenades and incendiary bottles. Small pieces of shrapnel from explosive shells clattered on my helmet. The slightest change of position would mean certain death. Hopefully the runny, burning concoction of the Molotov cocktails would not flow into my crater. Many defenceless comrades were picked off in this manner. Luckily, the projectiles thrown at me only reached the edge of my crater. The Russians then counterattacked again. I was barely able to defend myself from my cover and the enemy pulled back. Now my submachine-gun stopped working. This miserable, touchy hunk of metal was far inferior to the Russian PPSh!

– – –

After a brief regrouping, the attack of Pionier-Bataillon 162 was relaunched at 1100. They pushed south along the Volga. As always, Oberleutnant Schinke was at the head of his men, charging into the enemy defences. The pioneers bypassed the right flank of Gunyaga's

---

62. Brockmann was later flown out of the Stalingrad pocket and eventually fitted with a glass eye.

63. Oberst, Leutnant Erich, 2./Pi.Btl.336; born 21 November, 1910 in Schenkendorf. Missing in action, January 1943 in Stalingrad. See Appendix 2 (page 576) for more details.

768th Regiment, infiltrated into their rear area and pressed towards Finger Gully. They were exposed to Soviet guns across the river but these withheld their fire for fear of hitting their own men. Lyudnikov sensed the danger in this attack and effected immediate countermeasures. A hastily gathered force comprised of divisional and company staffs, logistical troops and all staff workers, were thrown at the German intrusion. The commander of Gunyaga's signals company, Senior-

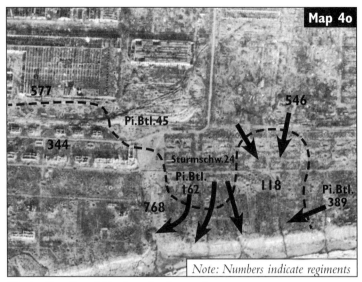

Note: Numbers indicate regiments

Pionier-Bataillon 162 relaunches its attack.

Lieutenant S.M. Bushuyev, repelled an attack by a German platoon with only two soldiers. Running from one place to another in the trench, the officer and his soldiers fired and threw grenades at the attacking enemy, creating the impression of a large number of defenders in the line and thus holding off the Germans.

Whilst defending against one of the attacks, the commander of 768th Rifle Regiment's mortar company was killed, and platoon commander and company politruk R.B. Zarkayev was wounded. But he did not leave the battlefield and took command of the company himself. When the Germans relaunched the attack, Zarkayev stood upright and with the exclamation "For the Motherland, forward, comrades!", rushed towards the Germans. The soldiers swept along behind him and halted the Germans in hand-to-hand fighting.

A group of 12 men from 344th Rifle Regiment had also been sent to bolster the line. Leading them was Senior-Lieutenant Fedor Anisimovich Lesin, a replacement who had crossed into Stalingrad the previous day and been immediately appointed company commander by Konovalenko:

> We soon took up defence on the right side of a gully that ran from the Barrikady factory down to the Volga… The Germans aimed to throw us into the gully, and then into the river. Letting the Germans approach to within 15-20 metres, we opened fire on them, they dropped to the ground and then retreated. The Germans left six dead and wounded men on the battlefield.
>
> In the evening […] the Germans played records of Strauss's waltzes and others. 'Russians, you'll soon be blowing bubbles in the Volga! Ivan, surrender, come into captivity', the Germans shouted.
>
> Certainly, the Germans managed to win a piece of Stalingrad's earth, but they could not break the iron will of the defenders of the Barrikady factory and no-one from our regiment gave themselves up.

Vicious close quarters fighting rippled along the clifftops. Leutnant Beyersdorff led his Sturmschwadron into the fray. Unbeknownst to Beyersdorff, he was being lined up by a Soviet anti-tank rifleman as he charged forward. From a distance of only 20 metres, the Soviet soldier fired and the heavy 14.5mm armour-piercing projectile smashed into Beyersdorff's left arm, pulverising his elbow and causing massive tissue damage.

Several other old-timers from the Sturmschwadron became casualties, including Oberwachtmeister Hans Roeder[64], an experienced 32-year old cavalryman who had been with the division when it was mounted on horseback. Roeder was leading one of the assault platoons. He was struck and died on the battered cliffs above the Volga.

This German advance was checked and Soviet sources state that "by 1300, the enemy group that had broken through was completely eliminated". However, most of the German troops were able to pull back and regroup for the next attack. This began at 1330 and was the fifth attack of the day on 768th Rifle Regiment. The war diary of 138th Rifle Division states that "the enemy had moved up fresh forces, again in a state of intoxication". This new attack on Gunyaga's regiment was very powerful. It crushed the Soviet defences. German assault groups then broke through the line and continued moving along the Volga, both atop the cliffs and down along the bank itself. The regiment's remaining 24 men, including the mortarmen, continued to defend a group of buildings 150 metres east of the north-eastern corner of the Barrikady factory. The alarm was raised in Lyudnikov's nearby command post. "The Germans are attacking! They're approaching along the bank!"

Major Rutkovsky, chief of the operations department, rushed into Lyudnikov's command post. The order from his assistant, Captain Gulko's[65], was already pealing:

"To the guns! Everybody to the guns!"

Lyudnikov went outside. To the left of the command post, near the water line, machine-guns were firing. The wind wafted shouts. Two machine-guns in the trench leading from the headquarters to the river were turned northward to face the German threat.

"We have inspected the headquarters of 768th Regiment", Shuba reported to Lyudnikov. "I just talked to Gunyaga on the phone. He's complaining: 'They shower grenades on me'. But I think that this attack on Gunyaga is just a feint. A diversion group has penetrated here."

Lyudnikov called for Captain Andrei Vasilyevich Kosarev[66], commander of the division's sapper battalion: "How many soldiers have you got left?"

"Eighteen. I'm the nineteenth."

"Take protection of the headquarters under your control. Act fast."

As the night battle continued, two colonels remained near the machine-guns: the division commander and his deputy, Kurov. Captain Kosarev returned an hour later and brought the documents of dead Germans. There were forty-two documents, and all of them were issued by the headquarters of the special Magdeburg field engineer battalion.

"Sapper met sapper. Diamond cut diamond!" Kosarev said angrily. His battalion had decreased to seven soldiers. The guards of the headquarters grew thin too.

Lyudnikov returned to his office and called Gunyaga, in whose sector the Germans had burst through. To avoid trouble, Gunyaga began to complain to the division commander: "The fascists shower grenades upon me. We are under fire…"

Gunyaga had earlier asked to shift his command post but Lyudnikov refused. Now Gunyaga hoped that his commander would sympathise.

"Why does the enemy throw grenades at you?" asked Lyudnikov with deliberate naivete, knowing beforehand what Gunyaga would answer. "Why are you under attack, not them?"

"Comrade 'One'", said the voice in the receiver, sounding dispirited, "I'm not in a

64. Roeder, Oberwachtmeister Hans, 2./Pz.Gr.Rgt.26; born 3 August, 1910 in Girrchlischken. Killed in action, 11 November, 1942 in Stalingrad.
65. Gulko, Captain Peter Vlasovich, 138th RD; date of birth unknown. Killed in action, 20 November, 1942 in Stalingrad.
66. Kosarev, Major Andrei Vasilyevich, HotSU; 179th Sap.Bat.; born 1913 in Kanino. Killed in action, November 1943.

trench. It's headquarters here. Documents. I have to command, and instead I am repulsing the attack just like a private…"

"Enough!" snapped Lyudnikov. "Stop grumbling about your destiny. I'm coming to you, you hear me? We'll beat off the enemy together."

They had to repulse enemy attacks on the way to 768th Regiment headquarters. Petukhov[67], a young scout, perhaps the most courageous in the Barrikady, accompanied Lyudnikov. Kolya Petukhov knew all the labyrinths of trenches and underground passages and penetrated into the German rear more than once, snatching prisoners and valuable information. Petukhov warned his division commander that the most dangerous sector was the trench leading to Gunyaga's command post. The Germans were showering grenades upon the trench, but rarely got them into the narrow slit. Lyudnikov and the scout were bending down until they reached the trench. From there to the command post they were followed by grenade explosions. Lyudnikov counted six of them. When there was just a few metres left to the dug-out, Petukhov threw a grenade at the Germans and, together with his division commander, ran forward and turned the corner. The sentry had been warned that Lyudnikov would be arriving, and so let him through. Petukhov stayed with the sentry to guard the command post.

Major Gunyaga, ready to meet the division commander, began with the usual report, but stopped suddenly:

"Are you wounded, Comrade Colonel?" Gunyaga exclaimed. "Overcoat! Look at your overcoat! No, not there! On your chest…"

Only then did Lyudnikov notice a wide cut on his overcoat, and when he unbuttoned it, he saw a similar cut on his soldier's blouse. A grenade splinter went through the left pocket of the blouse. Lyudnikov took a leather case out of his pocket and opened it. A cut corner of the first page of his Party membership card fell out of the case.

"I'll have to save it." Lyudnikov picked up the corner from the floor and tucked it away. "It's evidence. You, Major, will be my witness at the Party committee, otherwise, they won't exchange it…"

But Gunyaga was not in the mood for joking.

"Why did you come here?" Gunyaga yelled, although he understood that such a tone was not allowed in conversations with the division commander. "While I'm here, at the command post, I'm the boss. I'm responsible for the regiment. And for your life, comrade Colonel!"

"Don't make noise! No one, Major, is encroaching upon your rights. And don't wait for sympathy, although you really are being attacked by the Germans. But their cannon do not fire at your front-line, and planes do not bomb you. Can you see the advantage?"

But Gunyaga was prepared to give up this 'advantage' and answered darkly: "I need normal conditions for the work of the regiment headquarters. And I don't have them. You can see that."

"I know", Lyudnikov confirmed. "Here, at the Barrikady, nothing is normal in relation to the standards of war. But we broke the rules ourselves! We forced the enemy to carry out war in a way they don't want to. You may think I'm cruel, but I prohibit changing the command post. Pro-hi-bit!"

After this statement, Gunyaga stopped arguing. However, his silence did not mean consent with the commander's decision, and Lyudnikov felt that. Gunyaga tended to think

---

67. Petukhov, Sergeant Nikolai Ivanovich, 155th Recon.Co. Petukhov became a legend in 138th Rifle Division and today a memorial in Volgograd – dedicated solely to him – stands on on the battlefield east of the Barrikady factory, where he performed his most famous exploits.

that his division commander was being unfair.

"Tell me, you think that I'm cruel?"

Lyudnikov understood the difference between cruel necessity and cruelty, and wanted Gunyaga to understand it too.

"We are cut off from our people and we are our own judges. Do you know, Gunyaga, what your strength is now? Your command post." Major Gunyaga looked at the division commander, surprised, and the commander repeated: "Yes, we are strong because we have our command posts. Our soldiers know Chapayev[68] and remember what he said about the role of the commander in the battle. The conditions are different but the essence has not changed, do you understand? The soldier sees your post near his trench. The soldier knows how hard it is for you, but you don't leave. Why? Because you, regiment commander, trust the soldier. And he won't give up! There's nothing dearer in the world for him than this trust."

– – –

The intensity of the German attack even caused Lyudnikov's most able commander to have a Gunyaga-like moment of pessimism. The conversation between Lyudnikov and Pechenyuk was overheard by Junior-Sergeant Vasili Andreyevich Kamyshanov, a signaller from 650th Rifle Regiment:

> It was 11 November, 1942. I repaired a broken cable from the regiment staff to the divisional observation post. Regiment commander F.I. Pechenyuk reported to division commander Lyudnikov: "I report that the 650th no longer exists. What is to be done…" In response to him, Ivan Ilyich [Lyudnikov] said: "As long as there is a connection, that means the regiment exists". But reserves of cable had run out.

> Under cover of darkness, I went in search of some cable, ran into the Germans, slaughtered some and stretched it toward the P-shaped house.

– – –

After Pionier-Bataillon 162, Sturmschwadron 24 and infantry assault groups of Grenadier-Regiment 546 had reached the Volga, the situation for 118th Guards Rifle Regiment became increasingly desperate. The guardsmen valiantly held their line but the number of defenders was whittled down by each attack. Only at the end of the day, when almost every man had fallen, did the Germans completely seize the line of 118th Guards Rifle Regiment. The regiment's commander, Lieutenant-Colonel Kolobovnikov, continues his report:

> By evening, when we had only a handful of men left, the Germans began the most powerful attack. This was the ninth or tenth by our count. Our battalion commander K.T. Tolin was killed. The guardsmen fought on hand to hand. The Germans broke through to the railway line and approached the command post. All of us, including the runners, lay in a group firing

---

68. Vasili Ivanovich Chapayev (28 January, 1887 – 5 September, 1919) was immortalised as a hero of the Bolshevik Revolution in a popular book and 1934 movie. The film was a run-away success and a staggering proportion of the country saw it. In one of the film's most memorable sequences, Chapayev berates an officer for being wounded in battle and, using some potatoes, a pipe and an upturned bowl, proceeds to give an impromptu lesson on where a commander should stand when his troops go into battle. After regurgitating the military tactics taught to him by the Communist Party, the wounded officer laughs and dismisses Chapayev's lecture, pointing out that no matter what the situation, Chapayev leads his men from the front. One night, Chapayev's men are surprised by the monarchist Whites and Chapayev, rather than making an easy escape, stays behind at a machine-gun to ward off the enemy and eventually has to be dragged away from the gun, cursing that 'Chapayev never retreats'.

at point-blank range – preventing the Germans from reaching our rear. We halted the enemy, but within a moment a mortar blast seriously wounded me. Officers Zhatko, Glotov and a few other men were with me…

The trapped guardsmen had fought toughly, but now, seven wounded men tried to reach the main part of Lyudnikov's force while carrying their commander. The evacuation of a wounded commander was no easy task. A recon team sent by Lyudnikov ran into the Germans to the south of the factory. They could not reach the river crossing, and besides, ice floes were moving down the Volga, so crossing by small boat was impossible. The remaining guardsmen found a way out –

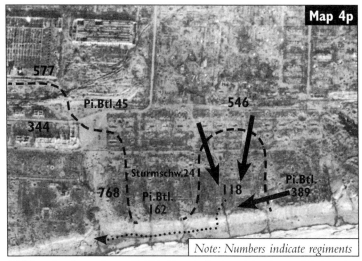

Kolobovnikov's guardsmen (118th Guards Regiment) break out of their pocket.

they decided to break out along the river bank and reach the crossing. Great bravery was shown on the part of soldier V.I. Bugrov. As the group was moving towards the river bank, it ran into a German machine-gun nest. "Halt" someone yelled. The guardsman wasted no time and immediately went into action. He crawled to within a short distance of the nest and lobbed a grenade. The machine-gun was silenced. Leading the way was V.F. Kuznetsov while Zhatko's group followed behind, carrying their commander on a stretcher. They reached the crossing and loaded him onto a boat. The next morning, already in hospital, he had a complex operation performed on him together with a blood transfusion. Kolobovnikov's life was in danger for a long time.

The regiment had been wiped out. Only seven guardsmen, all wounded, remained on the west bank. They were incorporated into the ranks of 768th Rifle Regiment.

– – –

After the capture of a bunker during the morning, in which his friend Unteroffizier Hartmut Müller had been killed, Soldat Bertold Paulus and the remaining men of his group from 2./Pionier-Bataillon 45 consolidated themselves:

> After we had stormed the bunker, we immediately went over to the defence. The Russians attacked when darkness was falling but they were repulsed. It was a day that I'll never forget. You see comrades falling to the right and left but you cannot go over to help because you must shoot and defend yourself…

The Soviet twilight counterattack was also experienced by Gefreiter Krauss and a few other men of Pionier-Bataillon 45 still marooned in the middle of no-man's-land:

> Fortunately, dusk had almost arrived. However, the enemy was coming again. I was alone, everyone around me was either dead or wounded, or had retreated, and on top of all that, my gun was jammed. With a rolling dive, I leapt out of my crater. I only had one way of defending myself: hand grenades and a bayonet from the abandoned rifle of a fallen comrade. A shell landed near me, I was flung through the air and – with shredded clothes – landed on a Russian earth bunker. Rolling over to the side, I searched for cover so that I could repel the onrushing

enemy with hand grenades. Then – an awful blow. A shell exploded right next to me, quickly followed by another. Probably mortar shells. Heavily wounded, I dropped to the ground, still wanting to defend myself with a pistol and a bayonet. The attacking Ivans were only about 10 metres away from me. Would I be defencelessly beaten or stabbed to death? I screamed out of rage and despair because I was helpless and could no longer move by myself… and just then I heard German voices. With a yell, my courageous company commander Oberleutnant Heinrich and quite a few comrades fell upon the Russians and dealt with their attack in hand-to-hand fighting. Oberleutnant Heinrich's face was scratched a short time later in this hand-to-hand combat.

For the moment, I was rescued. Under violent artillery fire, I was carried in a tarpaulin through the rubble to a dressing-station behind the front-line. The dressing-station was in a deep earth bunker. The next destination was a makeshift field hospital set up in a deep hollow. The doctors and medics looked liked butchers.

Gefreiter Karl Krauss

Result: two gunshot wounds in my legs and over 35 shrapnel wounds on my entire body. A Russian dictionary and my Soldbuch in the left breast pocket were punctured three times and a metal uniform button was shot flat. Before the attack, I stashed these small books into my pocket as protection for my heart – in tribute of Friedrich the Great's tobacco case.

Despite some setbacks, particularly near Pionier-Bataillon 45, 389. Infanterie-Division had gained the Volga shore along a 500-metre front, taking the streets north-east of the gun factory and destroying five dug-in tanks in the process. It then cleaned out the entire area. Oberleutnant Eberhard had a theory about why his division had been successful and 305. Infanterie-Division had not:

The attack of the neighbouring division remained stuck halfway. Perhaps the enemy, by focusing his operations in the neighbour's sector, had made it possible for us to reach the river bank along the entire breadth of the divisional sector without the heaviest resistance.

About 90% of Stalingrad was in German hands. I was convinced that in a short amount of time, the remaining sectors of the city would be conquered. Our mission seemed to be fulfiled.

As tensions eased, I came to see that I had underestimated the after-effects of my jaundice. Because peace had returned to our sector, I had a break, as urgently suggested by the doctors. When the division later announced that a successor for me was already on his way, I took home leave.[69]

– – –

The weather remained favourable for the first day of the new offensive. Clear skies had permitted aerial support but contributed to heavy frosts that coated the battlefield and forced temperatures down, a long way down, below zero. Wind chill made it just a bit more miserable for the troops. For the Germans, the supply of winter equipment and uniforms was erratic and depended entirely upon random luck: while one unit received warm clothing, their neighbour went without. After directing artillery fire all day, Oberleutnant Waldhausen of Artillerie-Regiment 305 penned a letter home during the evening:

I'm awfully tired today but tomorrow I'll be able to send a letter via courier-post, so I want to make use of that. – Winter has now arrived. It was kind enough to wait until I had my fur coat but also exactly long enough until winter kit had arrived for our men. Long fur pants,

---

69. Eberhard left Stalingrad on the evening of 18 November. Together with his driver, he drove throughout the night, across the Don bridge and – unwittingly – escaped the pocket closing behind him.

felt overboots, fur-lined undervests, warm headgear, etc. And then [the temperature] fell to minus 15° at night. On top of that, a fairly unpleasant wind is blowing. But it's bearable. You'd be reassured if you saw this winter equipment. Not every soldier has a long fur coat, of course, but we have enough so that we're able to kit out those who have to be outside as sentries or on the scissors-telescope. I wear a pair of beautiful fur trousers over my underwear as a second layer. And over the top of that a pair of long cloth pants. And under my service coat is a rabbit-fur jacket, so that I don't even need an overcoat.

The day had not been easy for the artillerymen. The confused nature of the fighting compelled them to be more accurate than usual, plus they had to contend with deadly Soviet counter-battery fire. The same applied to the crews of the light infantry guns of 13. Kompanien. Most at risk were the forward observers who advanced with the combat troops. Killed in this role was Leutnant Otto Schwarzmaier[70], Artillerie-Regiment 305, and Hauptmann Paul Lechner[71], commander 13./Grenadier-Regiment 577. Some observers were posted in the chimneys and upper floors of the factory but others were further forward, as Oberleutnant Karl Ring[72], platoon commander in Oberleutnant Hannemann's[73] 13./Grenadier-Regiment 517 (295. Infanterie-Division), reports:

Kirstein/Ring

Oberleutnant Karl Ring

On 11 November, I participated in an attack near the Red Barricades Gun Factory with the heavy platoon while Infanterie-Regiment 517 remained in its positions… Hannemann […] explained to me what was happening and said: 'You will lead the operation of the platoon as an expert because a specialist task has fallen to the heavy platoons. I will brief you on the situation then and there.' Only when I made contact with the battalion commanders up front would I learn about their anxieties and problems: the Russian units had solidly clawed themselves into the Volga cliff and constructed their dug-outs there, so that they could not be reached by our shells. Our shells slipped cleanly over the high edge without causing any appreciable damage. On the other hand, they also couldn't smash through the thick layer of earth over the dug-outs. Only aerial bombs could do that. Fourth platoon made a change of position to the north […] near the Red Barricades Gun Factory in old gun emplacements (from October 1942). Every heavy infantry gun was taken there by ten harnessed panje ponies. The gun emplacements were basically in order.

Russian positions dug into the ground of Stalingrad's inner defensive line – which was overwhelmed by us in October – served well as quarters for the platoon. We could be satisfied with them. However, they had one severe disadvantage: they were lice-ridden. [Nearby] stood another 10 guns from other regiments.

The ammunition supply was centrally regulated for everyone. Ammunition was available in sufficient quantities. Hannemann briefed me in the terrain sloping from the hills down to the Volga. We crawled under burnt-out wagons, over railway tracks, passed over a dud 10 cwt aerial bomb in the Bread Factory Nr. 2 area and then reached the Red Barricades Gun Factory. Hannemann described the forward line to me and showed me our scheduled target area. We fired. I sat on the slope almost directly under the flight path of the shells. I saw them flying over us and could follow their trajectory until they impacted. I therefore had no difficulties arranging

70. Schwarzmaier, Oberleutnant Otto, Art.Rgt.305; born 5 September, 1915 in Tieringen. Killed in action, 11 November, 1942 in Stalingrad.
71. Lechner, Hauptmann Paul, 13./Gr.Rgt.577; born 27 April, 1909 in Tann. Killed in action, 11 November, 1942 in Stalingrad.
72. Ring, Oberleutnant Karl, 13./Gr.Rgt.517; born 1914. Still alive in 2006.
73. Hannemann, Oberleutnant Karl-Ernst, 13./Gr.Rgt.517.

the exact azimuth for each target shortly before the impact. As the range to the targets increased, the shells scattered and either struck the lip of the Volga cliff or slipped past this ledge so that a cloud of smoke appeared from down on the river bank. I then worked my way forward to the command posts of the pioneer battalions. A battalion commander explained to me: 'The Russians wait out the heavy gun fire in their bunkers but as soon as the shelling stops or advances, they are outside – ready to counterattack and throw us back. We've had high casualties because we're playing right into their hands. It's madness, it can't be done.' He was right about that. The repetition of the attack here was pure insanity. We had to think hard if we were to solve this problem. I explained to the battalion commander: 'We have at least 10 heavy infantry guns on this sector. You can select ten targets, one for each gun. Then, for each target, we can assign varying numbers of shells to keep the targeted enemy under cover. We therefore know, for example, that no eleventh shell will fall after the tenth one. The Russians, however, will know nothing and will be waiting for the next shell. With this steady rate of fire, your men have some time to approach the bunker before the garrison is outside and ready for combat. Then, independently of that, the neighbouring target will continue to be shelled, until the fifteenth shell, for example. I can take over the adjustment fire of targets chosen by your men. In the meantime, we can work out the necessary details based on this model.' My proposal was clear to him. He spoke with his commanders and all of a sudden I was Kampfgruppführer of more than 10 heavy infantry guns in the Barrikady area.

The role of such a Kampfgruppführer – at least in the beginning, like here – was that he didn't need to be concerned about ammunition supplies or rations for his men. […] In other words, it was a temporary concentration of firepower for a determined purpose as dictated by combat requirements. This arrangement started. To gain an overall perspective for myself, I climbed up a staircase – half-destroyed by aerial bombs – to the first floor of a house ruin. This endeavour failed. I did not even succeed in seeing more of the field of ruins through a cracked wall because a chunk of masonry crashed down on my helmet. Just then a shot lodged in the wall. Had I dared to look over the window ledge, I would have been a dead man. I bolted down the shattered staircase just as the ruins were smashed apart by bursts of fire. Observation from the battalion command post was impossible to imagine under these conditions. Moving even closer to the front was also not advisable. This meant that each day we were only able to fire on a single target, or perhaps two targets at best. But we did not have much time: that's why I now carried a telephone with a connection that lead to the assault troops at the very front. They best knew the targets that were causing them the greatest trouble. The assault troop commander transmitted to me where he wanted the heavy infantry guns to fire and I translated that into instructions for the Infanteriegeschütz-Zugführer [infantry gun platoon commander] or the Stellungsunteroffizier [gun position NCO]. In this way, every heavy platoon was responsible for two targets and if necessary each gun could answer for the other. After the results of the shelling from the first day, we said that we thought our plan would be ready to be performed on other days.

– – –

Hauptmann Rettenmaier sums up the situation at Grenadier-Regiment 578:

The balance in the evening was not pleasing. During the advance, we had covered forty and more kilometres daily between repeatedly breaking enemy resistance. The casualties, however, were never as high as they were today. Here, we moved one or two houses and around three to four hundred metres of ground. We had to realise that it was a different type of warfare that we had to conduct here. The pocket was formed and with that, about 2000 Russians were encircled; the division rated this success very highly.

Until darkness, the Volga bank east and north-east of the fuel installation, as well as the gully north of it, were cleared of Soviet remnants and blocked to the south by barricades and mines. These barriers were erected by the men of Oberleutnant Grimm's 2./Pionier-Bataillon 305, now led by Leutnant Erwin Hingst.[74]

At 1715 hours, Seydlitz sent a progress report to 6. Armee:

The attack of 305. and 389. Infanterie-Divisions have had no decisive success. 305. Infanterie-Division gained the Volga cliffs east of the fuel installation and then advanced to the next gully north of there. 389. Infanterie-Division won the bank of the Volga along a 500 metre front, joining it up with the previously occupied river bank. The assaults of both divisions were halted in the face of bitter and obstinate enemy resistance… Objective for 12 November: prepare for the continuation of the attack east of the gun factory on 13 November.

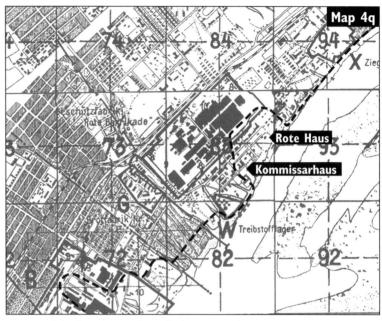

Course of the front-line at the end of 11 November, 1942.

The new German front-line ran as follows: old forward line to the fuel installation – south corner of the fuel installation – top of the Volga cliff – steep slope to gully in grid square 83d3 – corner house (Apotheke) – from there to the old forward line to the north-east corner Hall 4 – north-east corner gun factory – steep slope of the Volga near 93a3 (small gully) – cliff top to the old forward line. As can be seen in the accompanying map, the gains of ground were small compared to the size and potency of the forces employed. Nevertheless, the attack would continue so as to clean up the small Soviet bridgehead. At 1820 hours, LI. Armeekorps issued Korpsbefehl Nr. 111 in preparation for continuation of the assault:

In courageous and tough combat, 305. and 389. Infanterie-Divisions and their attached pioneers have wrenched a substantial portion of the bridgehead east of the gun factory from the enemy.

General Seydlitz realised some time was needed to regroup:

The attack will continue on 13 November. 305. and 389. Infanterie-Divisions will complete their preparations on 12 November. Proposal for the time of the assault (Y-Hour) will be immediately transmitted to corps.

Objectives for 305. Infanterie-Division: Kommissarhaus and the area between this and the Volga. For 389. Infanterie-Division: Rotes Haus.

With good successful progress of the attack along the Volga, both assault groups will meet and then destroy the remaining nests of resistance. Pionier-Bataillon 162 is subordinated to 305. Infanterie-Division with immediate effect.

Remaining divisions will conduct small assault troop operations to tie down the enemy. Objectives will be reported to corps.

---

74. Hingst, Oberleutnant Erwin, 2./Pi.Btl.305; born 14 September, 1908 in Hameln/Weser. Missing in action, 2 February, 1943 in Stalingrad. See Appendix 2 (page 574) for more details.

Artillery support and aerial support by VIII. Fliegerkorps on 13 November would be almost the same as on 11 November, while 12 November would be used for destructive fire with targeted single shots.

In compliance with the Korpsbefehl, Major Krüger and his battalion handed over their sector along the Volga to the infantry of Grenadier-Regiment 546 and then carefully filed back into the northern part of the Barrikady factory during the night. They were given no chance for recuperation. The day's operation had cost them 20 dead, 70 wounded and 1 missing, a total of 91 from a pre-attack combat strength of 319 men (7 officers, 31 NCOs and 281 men), but the successful conduct of their attacks and attainment of objectives gave them confidence and they were certain they would prevail in their new sector.

– – –

Once combat operations died down, LI. Armeekorps was able to tot up the numbers of prisoners and booty taken during the day: 202 prisoners, of those 11 were deserters, 5 dug-in tanks destroyed, 3 machine-guns, 1 anti-tank gun, 2 mortars, 16 anti-tank rifles and 9 submachine-guns captured. In addition, two landing craft and a 400-tonne boat were destroyed on the Volga east of the steel factory by infantry guns and artillery.

In Combat Report No. 195 issued at 1700 hours, 138th Rifle Division reported :

> Losses inflicted on the enemy by small-arms fire: a total of 9 prisoners were taken, about 750 hitlerites[75], 4 machine-guns and one gun were destroyed, 3 heavy tanks were burnt out and one light tank was knocked out.

When compared to the meagre results, German casualties were alarmingly high:

305.Inf.Div. with reinforcements (Pi.Btle. 50, 294 and 336)
2 officers killed and 3 officers wounded
83 NCOs and men killed, 271 NCOs and men wounded.

305.Inf.Div. without reinforcements:
2 officers killed and 1 officer wounded
11 NCOs and men killed, 118 NCOs and men wounded.

389.Inf.Div. with reinforcements (Pi.Btle.45, 162 and Sturmschwadron 24):
2 officers killed, 3 officers wounded, 1 officer missing
46 NCOs and men killed, 149 NCOs and men wounded, 180 NCOs and men missing

Casualties of the pioneer battalions on 11 November:
Pionier-Bataillon 45:
1 officer killed, 1 officer wounded, 1 officer missing
18 NCOs and men killed, 68 NCOs and men wounded, 44 NCOs and men missing
Panzerpionier-Bataillon 50:
1 officer wounded
4 NCOs killed, 8 NCOs wounded
13 men killed, 52 men wounded
Pionier-Bataillon 162:
4 NCOs killed, 6 NCOs wounded
16 men killed, 53 men wounded, 1 man missing

---

75. German casualties were around 750 men, so this figure is quite accurate.

Pionier–Bataillon 294:
5 NCOs killed, 7 NCOs wounded
13 men killed, 51 men wounded
Pionier–Bataillon 336:
1 officer wounded
5 NCOs killed, 3 NCOs wounded
32 men killed, 32 men wounded
Total casualties:
1 officer killed, 3 officers wounded, 1 officer missing.
110 NCOs & men killed, 280 NCOs & men wounded, 45 NCOs & men missing.
= 5 officers and 435 NCOs & men.

With casualties of 440 men from the 1753 men at the beginning of the attack, the pioneers suffered a 25% casualty rate on the first day alone. It is not possible to calculate the overall German casualty rate for 11 November because manpower figures for the infantry units prior to the attack are not available.

– – –

Soviet casualties were severe, particularly when related to the total manpower:
344th Rifle Regiment (had a total of 207 active soldiers prior to the attack):
3 officers killed, 2 officers wounded
3 NCOs killed, 8 NCOs wounded
8 men killed, 38 men wounded
= 5 officers, 11 NCOs and 46 men, a total of 62
650th Rifle Regiment (had a total of 167 active soldiers prior to the attack):
1 officer killed, 15 officers wounded, 6 officers 'other'[76]
5 NCOs wounded, 2 NCOs 'other'
8 men killed, 45 men wounded, 16 men 'other'
= 22 officers, 7 NCOs and 69 men, a total of 98
Total casualties for 138th Rifle Division (without 118th Guards Rifle Regiment):
8 officers killed, 40 officers wounded, 6 officers 'other'
7 NCOs killed, 34 NCOs wounded, 2 NCOs 'other', 1 NCO evacuated
31 men killed, 207 men wounded, 16 men 'other', 2 men missing, 1 man evacuated
= 55 officers, 43 NCOs and 257 men, a total of 355 men

With casualties of 355 men from the 1288 men of 138th Rifle Division who were actually on the Stalingrad side of the Volga river, Lyudnikov's division suffered 27% casualties on this first day of the offensive. The division also lost 7 mortars, two 76mm guns and one 45mm gun.

The losses for 95th Rifle Division were devastating. Of its 420 men, 161st Rifle Regiment lost 100 of them (24%), but that paled compared to the bloodbath that swept through the ranks of 241st Rifle Regiment: from a pre-attack strength of 340 men, it lost 400 men.[77] An unbelievable casualty rate of 117%.

At 1500 hours, the strength of Lyudnikov's division was as follows: total number of people in the division – 2226. Of those, 928 were on the west bank of the Volga. From them, 333

---

76. The term 'other' is used in Soviet reports in lieu of the term 'captured' or 'missing'.

77. The regiment's casualties were higher than its strength due to the fact that it lost most of its original complement as well as many reinforcements that had arrived during the fighting.

were active soldiers. Armament: 290 rifles, 4 heavy machine-guns, 1 heavy anti-aircraft gun (DShK), 6 light machine-guns, 106 PPSh, 10 mortars, 4 anti-tank guns and 9 anti-tank rifles.

– – –

That evening, Gorishny requested artillery fire on the following sectors: the L-shaped house [Apotheke], the E-shaped house [School Nr. 2 / Haus 56], and the central section and south-east corner of the Barrikady factory up to fuel tanks. The aim was to suppress German emplacements and to prevent reserves being brought forward from the factory to the east, to the sector of the breach. He also issued a directive to his units:

"1. Prevent the expansion of the enemy breakthrough in a southern direction. 2. After the arrival of 3rd Battalion of 92nd Separate Rifle Brigade, restore the position on the sector of 241st Rifle Regiment and establish direct communication with the neighbour to the right – 138th Rifle Division."

At 2000 hours, the indomitable men of 241st Rifle Regiment launched a small attack that cleared the Volga bank and drove the Germans 70 metres back from the cliff.

– – –

The vagaries of fate determined what became of the many wounded soldiers. Each had his own story to tell. A few examples will suffice:

Gefreiter Karl Krauss, 2./Pionier-Bataillon 45:

A medic silently re-applied the dressings but by the doctor's facial expression, I saw that I was no longer worthy of 'repair'. I was wrapped in a Finnish paper bag and placed on the cold stone floor of a half-destroyed church that was nearby. Already lying in this building were about 300-400 wounded comrades. In my thoughts I was with my Kompanie and feared that nearly half of my comrades-in-arms were already dead or wounded.

Oberleutnant Richard Grimm, 2./Pionier-Bataillon 305:

Whether by chance or by orders, I don't know, I was spoken to by a doctor whom I immediately recognised because you were still glad to meet someone who had been [with the division] in France. He suggested that I go back to the regiment command post and get through to division HQ by phone. Because of enteritis and blood in my stools, he wanted to have me admitted to the hospital in Kalach but didn't get away with it, and I also didn't want that because I would then not be returned to my unit.

An unnamed soldier from Hauptmann Püttmann's III./Grenadier-Regiment 578:

When the fire died down, I took a couple of steps on one leg and looked for the next piece of cover. I eventually reached a block of houses where the medics were, and as I hobbled down to the cellar, wounded men already lay everywhere. I did not get myself bandaged. First, I took the cover off my canteen, stuck it in the fire, scorched it and heated up the tea inside. I also ate a piece of bread. And then I said to a medic: "Alright, you can bandage me now."

In the cellar, I met up with a buddy from my squad, a Swabian, father of two small children, who had the same type of wound as me. In the evening, we both moved off and limped to the dug-out of the battalion doctor. This was also full of the wounded and dying. The doctor looked at us and asked: "You already have bandages?" "Yes." "What do you want here then? Look around. You cannot stay here. We also can't carry you off, we have no more men, so you must see to it yourself that you get to the main dressing station." They gave us yet another injection… We had to make our way back to the front, back to the medics in the cellar. You wanted to be under a roof. It was cold…

The next morning, we said to each other that we couldn't remain here. With a couple of fence palings as crutches, we hobbled through the ruins of houses. It was awful on the open expanses [because] the fire of Russian artillery lay upon them. We dragged each other through a long gully up to a brick building… Exhausted, we sat in a corner and then a plump Sanitäts-Feldwebel came up to us and asked: "What' up here then?" "We both can't go on." "Well" he said, "the next ambulance will come soon."

The ambulance drove me and my pal a couple of kilometres to Gorodische, to the main dressing station. They got to work and cut off my boot. My foot was already completely black. I hopped up on to the operating table and was looking at my foot and the doctor snapped at me: "Lie down! You don't need to see." When I came to after the operation, they hung a red card around my neck and took me to the church where the severely wounded lay. For how long, I don't know exactly, perhaps I lay in the straw there for one or two days. From time to time the medics woke me up and gave me some tea.

It was a bright day when I was taken to the airfield at Pitomnik. First I was placed in a tent and then in a plane, lying on straw. I was not with it most of the time. But I still know that I had a thick, old black wool shawl, it could almost move on its own it was so full of lice.

– – –

With the Germans ensconced along the cliffs on both flanks, Lyudnikov and his division were in a precarious situation, so Lyudnikov gathered his brains trust: "At midnight, we gathered in a 'small military council' to summarise the day's fighting and to make some conclusions." The opening point of the division's final daily combat report sums up the eventful day:

At 0400, after a strong half hour artillery barrage, the enemy, with a strength of three infantry regiments and two sapper battalions, went on the offensive along the entire division's front-line.

From the north and north-west advanced 544th and 546th Infantry Regiments and 45th Separate Sapper Battalion against the right flank and the centre of the division (118th Guards Rifle Regiment and 768th Rifle Regiment). Advancing on the left flank of the division (344th Rifle Regiment, 650th Rifle Regiment and 241st Rifle Regiment of 95th Rifle Division) were 577th Infantry Regiment and 336th Sapper Battalion.

According to captured soldiers and officers, as well as from documents taken from bodies, it was established that 45th and 336th Sapper Battalions had arrived at full strength in Stalingrad from 5 to 10 November 1942, the first on motor vehicles from Millerovo, the second by plane from Rossosh.

The offensive by enemy infantry was supported by aircraft, artillery and – on the left-flank – a group of 10 tanks.

Lyudnikov continues:

The division bravely repulsed strong enemy attacks. Konovalenko commanded his units in a confident and calm manner. Vasili Ivanovich [Shuba] said that sometimes, remembering the past, he would request to be sent to the battalions. Shuba addressed this request to me but […] the situation simply wouldn't allow it.

What was the conclusion? We repelled strong enemy attacks, including those from fresh forces. Pechenyuk and Konovalenko sent over twenty 14-round 'Browning' pistols – captured from the recently arrived sappers.[78] My objective was for all the commanders to check their defences and to note the units which we would be combating the next day.

---

78. These pistols no doubt came from Pionier-Bataillon 336.

'Sergei Yakovlevich,' I addressed Tychinsky, 'tomorrow, we will focus on artillery. The enemy will resume his attack but our artillery must stop it in its tracks before it begins. Make concise orders for your artillerymen. If the enemy reaches the divisional command post, then it must be targeted. In this case, I order all of the division's artillery to open fire on the command post.' The chief-of-staff cautioned the staff to be ready for battle.

12 November, 1942

The newly-won German positions were covered by Soviet artillery and mortar fire. Gorishny's divisional artillery bombarded German troop concentrations near the fuel tanks, the L- and E-shaped houses and throughout the factory. Also, throughout the night, 25 Soviet sorties were counted by 6. Armee, the bombing being restricted mainly to the gun factory area. This did not prevent nocturnal German attacks: north-east of the fuel installation, Haus 80 was taken into possession in a daring assault by a pioneer assault group. This small gain considerably strengthened the German hold on the river bank.

Fighting continued further south too. At 2000 and 2300 hours the previous night, and at 0100 on 12 November, the Germans north of the fuel tank area tried to advance south along the river bank with a force of 100 men. All three attempts were repulsed. Being in close proximity to the forward line of 241st Rifle Regiment, the Germans laid down heavy small-arms and machine-gun barrages and used copious amounts of hand grenades.

Plans had been put into effect during the night to bring some relief to Lyudnikov's division and eventually break through to them. The 3rd Battalion of 92nd Rifle Brigade – filled with tough marines – arrived on Gorishny's sector to help his units punch through to Lyudnikov. The first attack was launched at 0730 hours. Several German positions were overrun and 2 heavy machine-guns were captured, but the attackers were

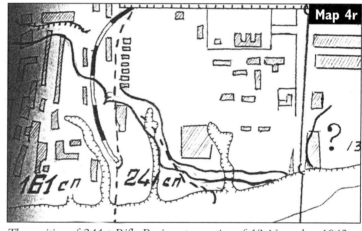

The position of 241st Rifle Regiment, morning of 12 November, 1942.

easily repelled. LI. Armeekorps reported to 6. Armee that an "enemy assault on the south-east edge of the fuel installation (82b1) was repulsed". As Gorishny's men were about to discover, retaking the fuel tanks and establishing contact with Lyudnikov would be no easy task. General Krylov reports on these attacks:

> Parts of the Gorishny division and the subordinated battalion of 92nd Rifle Brigade fought stubbornly around an advantageous position on the riverside cliff next to the fuel tanks. Nevertheless, they could not establish themselves there. The Germans offered furious resistance and the fuel tanks changed hands repeatedly.

The next attack was delivered at 0930 hours. After artillery preparation, an assault group led by the deputy commander of 2/241st Rifle Regiment, Politruk Zuyev, surged forward and captured the fuel tanks at 1000 hours, also seizing 9 German machine-guns during the conquest. They quickly consolidated. At 1015, a German company-strength force attacked but was repelled by fire. At 1130 the Germans repeated the attack towards the fuel tanks – this time in battalion strength. This was also beaten off. Taking losses, the German attackers pulled back to their starting positions. Assisting in the repulsion of these counterattack was 161st Rifle Regiment, which fired into the flanks of the attacking Germans.

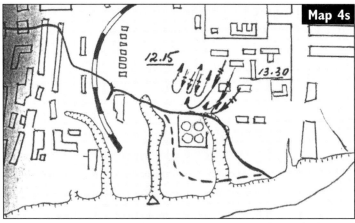

The fuel tanks are recaptured and German counterattacks repulsed. (Note: the times shown on these sketches are in Russian time, not German time, which is used throughout the book.)

At 1400 hours, a German battalion-strength force – covered by artillery and mortar fire – went on the offensive against the right flank of 241st Rifle Regiment and on the sector of 3/92nd Rifle Brigade, seizing the fuel tanks. At 1440, two German infantry platoons tried to reach the Volga from the fuel tanks but a Soviet storm group of 8 soldiers stopped them cold. Sustaining losses, the German group pulled back to the fuel tanks. A second group of two companies pushed down Appendix Gully, reached the Volga and then pushed south

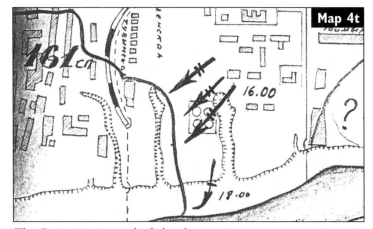

The Germans recapture the fuel tanks.

along the river bank, attacking 3/92nd Rifle Brigade. At 1550 their advance was smothered by Soviet firepower and the attack receded.

A small group of 3/92nd Rifle Brigade, led by the commander of the anti-tank rifle company, Lieutenant Shport, was cut off by the German attack at 1400 hours on the Volga cliff 200 metres north of the fuel tanks. Despite being encircled, they continued to fight. Communications with the small group was lost.[79]

The Pacific Fleet marines in 92nd Rifle Brigade fought like lions, further enhancing their formidable reputation. Black-and-white striped shirts worn under their uniforms were a potent symbol of their esprit de corps and earned them the epithet of the 'striped death' amongst the Germans. Chuikov vividly recalls the marines' feats on this day:

> German soldiers, drunk or mad, came on and on. The Far East seaman who had come to reinforce Gorishny's infantry division showed the enemy what was what and how the famous Red Navy men could fight. The petrol tanks on Tuvinskaya Street changed hands several times. In the heat of the battle the Red Navy men threw off their greatcoats and in their singlets and hats beat off the attacks and then went on to the offensive themselves.

79. It is not known what became of Shport's group of marines. It is probable that most perished during the fierce fighting but a German source indicates that at least a few were captured. See Hauptmann Traub's account on page 193.

According to one of the marines, Boris Mikhailovich Dmitriev, less than a quarter of the men survived these counterattacks. Dmitriev then received a new assignment: with 12 Red Army men, he was entrusted with halting the German advance. Carrying out this order, Dmitriev and his comrades occupied a pillbox on a small rise and managed to contain the fierce German onslaughts. They were eventually cut off but held their ground for the next 14 days, with very little food and water. Despite grievous wounds – 5 bullet and shrapnel wounds to his head, a bayonet wound to his chest, concussion and 'poisoning by gas' (most likely German smoke or phosphorous grenades) – Dmitriev was credited with killing numerous German soldiers and was awarded the Order of the Red Banner for his efforts. He spent more than a year in hospital before being invalided home.

The war diary of 62nd Army had this to say about the fighting:

> 95th Rifle Division, having repulsed three enemy attacks with forces of up to two battalions, engaged in stubborn fighting with the enemy for the restoration of the position on the right flank at the fuel tanks. During the day, they changed hands several times. At 1400, the enemy, having again thrown in reserves of two battalions, launched an attack, crumpled the right flank of 241st Rifle Regiment and again seized the fuel tanks. Fighting for the restoration of this position continues.

At the end of the day, 241st Rifle Regiment had 23 active bayonets; 161st Rifle Regiment had 235 and 3/92nd Rifle Brigade had 15. Losses were again heavy and 241st Rifle Regiment's were estimated at 90%.

– – –

The fearful casualties, bitter Soviet resistance and incomplete attainment of objectives were the cause of many discussions and much soul-searching amongst the German upper command echelons. As had been pointed out right from the very beginning, the strength of infantry was required to hold the initial gains, no matter how many well-trained pioneer battalions were crammed into the operational area. The man responsible for the well-being of the pioneers, Major Linden, had no misconceptions of why the attack had failed:

> The pioneers felt at a disadvantage in this fighting because in this most difficult terrain, they had to lug their bulky and heavy tools and equipment, in addition to their weapons. Because of this, the conveyance of sufficient infantry weapons and ammunition sometimes had to be dispensed with. While trying to traverse this barely negotiable terrain, they frequently had to pay more attention to the obstacles than to the enemy who lay in wait behind cover for any movement and unfortunately found many rewarding targets. When the pioneers then nevertheless advanced to their objectives and the infantry did not follow up in time, they soon wore themselves out repelling Russian counterattacks and sometimes a newly-won position bought with sacrifices had to be given up. Experiences from the first day of the attack showed that the pioneers could only carry out their difficult task if strong infantry support was available. This support was not provided in the necessary quantities by the exsanguinated infantry regiments, even though the heroic fighting conducted by the infantry was exemplary. Manpower was lacking – the meagre infantry forces that were available found themselves constantly in action. There was no rest for them. Any breaks in the fighting had to be used to consolidate positions, to reconnoitre, to obtain ammunition and supplies, etc.

Major Linden was called to a meeting being held at the advanced command post of 305. Infanterie-Division in the basement of one of the Schnellhefter Block's multi-storey buildings. Once there, he reported about the attack on 11 November to the Commanding General of LI. Armeekorps, General von Seydlitz, in the presence of his chief-of-staff, Oberst i.G. Clausius, the Divisionsführer of 305. Infanterie-Division, Oberst i.G. Steinmetz and his chief-of-staff, Oberstleutnant Paltzo. Linden didn't hold back in his appraisal of the situation:

"To achieve quick results in this difficult terrain, with such a strong enemy, it is essential to bring up an infantry regiment to reinforce 305. Infanterie-Division. This difficult task can only succeed with the help of these fresh forces. I know that the divisions on the Volga have all had heavy casualties and are tied down in their sectors, but it should be possible to fly in a reinforced infantry regiment, just as the pioneer battalions were brought by air to Stalingrad."

General von Seydlitz replied: "There is no infantry available. Our reconnaissance shows that the Russians are moving up large motorised formations against the sectors of our neighbouring armies. The few panzer divisions at our disposal must remain as corset-stays behind the Romanians, Italians and Hungarians. Nothing can be taken from these panzer divisions."

To that, Linden replied: "Herr General, the pioneer battalions employed here must be regarded as a specialist force. In the present circumstances these battalions will bleed to death if the immediate supply of infantry forces is avoided. Next spring, when full-scale operations are resumed, we shall miss these pioneers. It is my duty to draw attention to this now."

General von Seydlitz replied: "Our task now is to consolidate and hold the positions we have reached on the Volga. All the forces at our disposal must be employed to achieve this. When spring comes, we shall have to think again."

Linden later wrote: "I sometimes thought about this conversation, both in the Stalingrad pocket and during the course of my seven years of captivity." What Linden did not know was that over the previous one and a half weeks, von Seydlitz had fought hard to obtain infantry forces and been unsuccessful. All that now remained for von Seydlitz was to be a good soldier and carry out his orders.

In a communique to Heeresgruppe B, 6. Armee summed up the previous day's operation… an operation from which many people expected great things:

> On their first day of operations, the 5 pioneer battalions supplied to LI. Armeekorps have together lost 440 men, that's 30% [of their strength]. In further combat alone until 15 November, they will lose at least a further 25% and will then be so weak – especially in junior commanders – that they will no longer be capable of a difficult mission, if it turns out to be the Martin Furnace Hall.

The heavy-handed gambit of employing many demolition experts and close combat specialists against one sector had failed – and it was the pioneers paying the price.

– – –

Whether Linden liked it or not, the attack was to continue, seemingly regardless of the losses incurred by the pioneer battalions. At 1530 hours, Seydlitz sent out an addendum to Korpsbefehl Nr. 111, which had been issued at 1820 hours the previous day. It began:

> The attack will be continued in a sequence of systematic assault troop operations. It will therefore rely on thorough preparation, rigid command and systematic new dispositions of forces when a target is reached.

Instructions stated that only as many assault troops be deployed in the forward line as there was room available to use them to full effect. Remaining forces would be held further back and moved up only if required. On no account should massed forces be displayed or come to a standstill in areas where artillery and mortar fire could strike them. Where bypassed resistance nests had come back to life, assault troops made available would be immediately applied. Captured houses, bunkers and cellars would – on principle – be mopped up once again.

On the basis of reports filed by 389. Infanterie-Division, the assault on the Rote Haus would only be carried out on the evening of 14 November or early on 15 November. It would be at 305. Infanterie-Division's discretion to postpone the attack on the Kommissarhaus – scheduled for the evening of 13 November – in order to synchronise all attacks in its area with that of 389. Infanterie-Division on the Rote Haus. Intentions would be reported to LI. Armeekorps.

The operations ordered for the remaining divisions – to tie down the enemy – could be halted if no suitable objective was available and large casualties were expected without a corresponding success. Their artillery, however, would continue to suppress Soviet forces with active destructive fire and barrages, and furthermore, would stand at the Arko's disposal for artillery suppression or to work in conjunction against the east bank of the Volga during the attacks of 305. and 389. Infanterie-Divisions. By laying down heavy fire, Gruppe Schwerin would prevent Soviet relief attacks against 305. Infanterie-Division.

Oberst Meix and his Artillerie-Kommandeur 153 continued to be assigned a cooperative role with 305. and 389. Infanterie-Divisions. Besides artillery suppression, heavy barrages on the Volga island and the east bank of the Volga opposite the steel factory were a priority. For observed single fire, the 'on call' 210mm howitzers of 305. and 389. Infanterie-Divisions were placed at Artillerie-Kommandeur 153's disposal.

General von Seydlitz also declared that it was of decisive importance to stop the arrival of enemy reinforcements – and, if possible, his supplies too – into the bridgehead east of the gun factory. For that purpose, 305. and 389. Infanterie-Divisions would use artillery and heavy weapons to drop barrages on the bank lying opposite and the stretch of river lying in front of it. During the night, active illumination, as well as active harassment fire, would be carried out.

Finally, a fundamental method to reduce casualties was ordered: sufficient approach trenches and communications trenches would be dug so that troops could move up to and along the front-line without having to expose themselves to deadly artillery and mortar barrages, machine-gun fire and accurate sniping. Construction of the trenches was a high priority. Prisoners of war would be employed.

At 1645 hours, LI. Armeekorps reported its objective for 13 November to 6. Armee:

> Continuation of the attack with assault group methods until the final capture of the Volga bank east of the gun factory.

Major Linden reports:

> Another large-scale attack was ordered for early 13 November... The Russians had reinforced their bridgehead garrison in front of our sector and it was necessary to undertake a regrouping of our forces. Pionier-Bataillon 294 would be left behind on the right wing of 305. Infanterie-Division because the enemy was constantly launching harassing attacks on this area from the south. The Schwerpunkt regiment of the division, however, would receive reinforcements, which could only be done by taking Pionier-Bataillon 162 from 389. Infanterie-Division and employing it next to Pionier-Bataillon 50. This was possible because the enemy remained quiet in the neighbouring division's sector. The regrouping of the pioneers took place on 12 November, therefore only small local attacks occurred on this day.

– – –

In an interim report, LI. Armeekorps reported that "clearance of the last bunkers in the steep riverside cliffs of the Volga east and north-east of the fuel installation is in progress from 1300 hours." The grim reality of capturing some of these 'last bunkers' would soon be forced upon the Germans.

Numerous holes riddled the steep cliff. Some were only shallow caves burrowed out of the hard loam, while others were large dug-outs driven deep into it. Checking and clearing each one would be a nightmare. Fortunately for the Germans, most had been abandoned, but the few which remained caused an inordinate amount of trouble. The most stubborn position in the steep cliffs was that of the 'Rolik' group. Rolik didn't belong to any of the rifle regiments. It became the collective name of four soldiers from 138th Rifle Division's 203rd Separate Signals Battalion who operated a small telephone exchange. 'Rolik' – which translates as 'Roller' – was their call sign. Their position looked hopeless: located halfway up the sides of a semi-circular crevice were their small caves, one on either side, each sheltering two men. The positioning of the two dug-outs, however, allowed them to support and cover one another: the southern pair could fire on enemy soldiers appearing on the clifftop above the northern pair, and vice versa. The steepness of the cliff also meant the Germans had to dangerously expose themselves if they wanted to fire at the Soviet caves.

When the Germans moved north along the top of the cliffs, they stopped at the steep bank near the crevice. A German soldier lay down and peered over the side, down into the crevice. One of the Rolik group was waiting and immediately shot him in the head. The rest of the Germans pulled back. They then circumvented the crevice, crawled up without reaching the crest and raised an improvised periscope. Through it they saw an overhanging cliff wall with a large hole dug into it. One end of a wire led down to the Volga while the other led to the opposite side of the crevice. The Germans found the second wire and cut it. They now realised that they had stumbled upon a communications post between two units. Contact had now been cut off with the left neighbour – 95th Rifle Division – and 62nd Army.

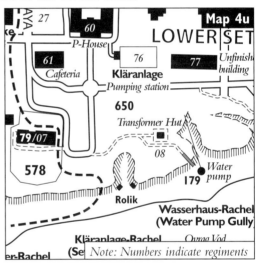

The Rolik gully

In the two holes dug into the sides of the crevice sat the four signalmen: the commander Junior-Sergeant Nikolai Nikiforovich Kuzminsky, Junior-Sergeant Aleksandr Semyonovich Kolosovsky and soldiers Andrei Nikonorovich Vetoshkin and Semyon Konstantinovich Kharaziya. No one gave them an order to retreat and thus they remained at their positions – maintaining one-way communications with their division's command post.

Junior-Sergeant Kuzminsky contacted their commander, Senior-Lieutenant Ozerov, and reported on their situation and observations of the enemy. He then said: "We can see the Germans but they can't see us. They know where we are but they can't get us out of here. As long as we have ammunition and food, Rolik will keep spinning."

Ozerov reported the situation to Lyudnikov and at midnight Junior-Sergeant Kuzminsky was summoned to the command post. He told the commander that the Germans were digging a trench above his position. "The enemy is just over our heads but he is only able to

The Rolik gully as seen in 1947 (the structure atop the cliffs is a memorial built to commemorate the Rolik group). The cave on the left is clearly visible but the one on the right is hidden by the bushes. The power pole is post-battle addition.

shoot at a few metres between us and the Volga. Beyond that, his fire is harmless.' Kuzminsky also thought that this was the best place for boats to land safely.

'We won't let the Germans reach the river bank…"

He wanted to add "while we're alive" but didn't, so as to not upset his commander. Lyudnikov now understood the kind of problem Rolik was for the front-line German positions. Let the Germans see if they can remove this thorn from their side. The commander wrote down the names of the four men into his notebook and also asked about their age, how long each man had been fighting and how many medals each of them had. Then the commander and the junior-sergeant decided on measures to be taken in case of a life-threatening emergency – should communication with the command post be severed.

"Tell your men exactly how the situation is," said Lyudnikov, bidding farewell to the sergeant. "There is no one to the left of Rolik. It is only you, the Volga and the Germans. Rolik became our cut-off point and it will become our meeting point. I believe in this and I believe in you just as much!"

- - -

LI. Armeekorps would later report that "cleaning actions in attained areas were successfully carried out during the day, particularly on the steep slopes and shore of the Volga east and north-east of the fuel installation. The toughly defending enemy lost 30 prisoners and numerous dead."

German casualties figures show just how bitter the fighting was. 305. Infanterie-Division (discounting the subordinated pioneer battalions) lost more men killed on this day than they did the previous day. [80]

---

80. 21 dead compared to 13 dead on 11 November.

Some of the individual units suffered heavy losses. Incredibly, Leutnant Zorn's 1./Pionier-Bataillon 305, which had not lost one man during the previous day's heavy fighting in and around the Apotheke, now shed blood during the small local attacks to clear remaining nests of enemy resistance. Two of his men – Gefreiter Valentin Warth[81] and Pionier Ernst Kruse[82] – were killed, while Gefreiter Paul Merk, Gefreiter Helber and Gefreiter Josef Bertsch were wounded. Leutnant Zorn was wounded too, hit in the upper left arm.

Pionier-Bataillon 294 took bloody losses during their attacks in the morning, the repulsion of the Soviet assaults near the fuel tanks and whilst clearing enemy bunkers in the cliffs. It was Oberleutnant Bergemann's 2. Kompanie and Oberleutnant Menzel's 3. Kompanie that faced the brunt of these actions and all of the casualties. Oberleutnant Bergemann was severely wounded and died later in the day in a hospital near Gorodische. Leutnant Walter Zimmer, the battalion adjutant, took command of 2. Kompanie.[83]

– – –

Because great things had been expected of it, many people – from Hitler and Paulus to the Alkett workers – were interested in the debut performance of the new sIG33B. When the crews of the new vehicles returned from action, they filed reports on how well the vehicles had performed. Most were not happy with it. The salient points were compiled in a report entitled 'A brief preliminary experience report about the s.I.G'. This is what it said:

> A very effective weapon, if it continues to be developed. They provide a suitable complement to the assault gun batteries.
>
> Until now, the s.I.G. (Sfl.) were either employed in formation together with the assault guns, whereby the assault guns took over the fire protection, or driven up individually to prepared covered positions in front of a fixed target and, after combating it with direct fire, were pulled back.

81. Warth, Gefreiter Valentin, 1./Pi.Btl.305; born 7 July, 1920 in Haueneberstein. Killed in action, 12 November, 1942 in Stalingrad.

82. Kruse, Pionier Ernst, 1./Pi.Btl.305; born 3 August, 1922 in Tribsees. Killed in action, 12 November, 1942 in Stalingrad.

83. Other members of the company killed on this day were Gefreiter Pohl (shrapnel in the head) and Soldat Schindler. In addition, the following company members were missing: Obergefreiter Claus, Obergefreiter Lehmert, Obergefreiter Leunert and Soldat Otte. Killed from 3 Kompanie were Gefreiter Bauer, Unteroffizier Hentzschel, Obersoldat Lindner (bullet in the lung), Gefreiter Lowin (killed by a hand-grenade on the Volga cliff) and Obergefreiter Paula. Also, Gefreiter Werner was missing in action.

Pohl, Gefreiter Erich, 2./Pi.Btl.294; born 31 July, 1914 in Demnitz-Thumitz. Killed in action, 12 November, 1942 in Stalingrad.

Schindler, Soldat Karl, 2./Pi.Btl.294; born 26 December, 1922 in Brüx. Killed in action, 12 November, 1942 in Stalingrad.

Claus, Obergefreiter Alfred, 2./Pi.Btl.294; born 21 June, 1919 in Blosswitz. Missing in action, 12 November, 1942 in Stalingrad.

Lehmert, Obergefreiter Erwin, 2./Pi.Btl.294; born 19 July, 1918 in Lichtenhain. Missing in action, 12 November, 1942 in Stalingrad.

Leunert, Obergefreiter Erich, 2./Pi.Btl.294; born 8 October, 1919 in Hermsdorf. Missing in action, 12 November, 1942 in Stalingrad.

Otte, Soldat Herbert, 2./Pi.Btl.294; born 9 August, 1923 in Sandersdorf. Missing in action, 12 November, 1942 in Stalingrad.

Bauer, Gefreiter Gerhard, 3./Pi.Btl.294; born 17 November, 1921 in Annaberg. Killed in action, 12 November, 1942 in Stalingrad.

Hentzschel, Unteroffizier Kurt, 3./Pi.Btl.294; born 12 January, 1910 in Ammendorf. Killed in action, 12 November, 1942 in Stalingrad.

Lindner, Obersoldat Heinz, 3./Pi.Btl.294; born 6 September, 1922 in Leipzig. Killed in action, 12 November, 1942 in Stalingrad.

Lowin, Gefreiter Paul, 3./Pi.Btl.294; born 17 May, 1912 in Gelsenkirchen. Killed in action, 12 November, 1942 in Stalingrad.

Paula, Obergefreiter Franz, 3./Pi.Btl.294; born 17 May, 1916 in Greppin. Killed in action, 12 November, 1942 in Stalingrad.

Zeun, Gefreiter Werner, 3./Pi.Btl.294; born 17 February, 1915 in Dresden. Missing in action, 12 November, 1942 in Stalingrad.

Anderson

A destroyed sIG33B captured by the Soviets and subsequently used for testing.

Good results from shooting, observation possibilities insufficient, fitting of a scissors telescope was necessary.

Chassis is too weak, therefore making it possible to take along only a few rounds of ammunition. The thickness and shape of the armour-plating is in need of improvement. Range of traverse is too small; view for the driver is not sufficient, cannot see the entire roadway. Loading tray is absent, therefore allowing only two shots per minute at present.

During the attack east of the gun factory on 11 November, two were total losses through direct hits.

Recommendation: send an officer of the Sturmgeschütze Abteilung to the manufacturing factory, to help on the spot in evaluating the experiences.

– – –

At 2150 hours, LI. Armeekorps sent its daily report to 6. Armee:

After the attacks in the morning against the gully position on the north wing of 100. Jäger-Division and the attacks in the steel factory, enemy combat activity abated, apart from the usual harassment fire. With the onset of darkness, harassment fire with heavy artillery on the hinterland and roads approaching the steel factory and bombing raids on the city area.

Clearance of the steep slope and shoreline along the Volga east and north-east of the fuel installation was carried out. The toughly defending enemy lost 30 prisoners and numerous dead.

The corps captured 57 prisoners, 9 of them deserters. Interrogation of prisoners captured the previous day revealed some very interesting information. A riflemen from 241st Rifle Regiment stated that prior to the attack, his regiment had about 700 men but sustained severe casualties. A soldier from 650th Rifle Regiment revealed that his regiment was very weak at the beginning of the attack: it only had 200-250 men before taking heavy losses. Finally, a man from 768th Rifle Regiment said that 32 men, all that remained of 339th Rifle

Regiment (308th Rifle Division), had been incorporated into the regiment. These reports encouraged the Germans. The Soviets also received encouragement of their own, as Lyudnikov reports:

> In the evening, Captain Konovalenko, commander of 344th Rifle Regiment, brought me a letter that was found on the body of a dead German officer. The letter, dated 11 November, said: 'There is only one kilometre to go to the Volga but nothing we do brings us any nearer to it. We're fighting longer for this kilometre that we fought for the whole of France. We've killed more troops here than in the battle of Sevastopol, but the Russians stand like rocks. It seems to me that they have decided to fight to the last man.'
>
> He was not mistaken. We did indeed decide to fight to the last man.

Other important information was also found on the German corpses, as noted in 62nd Army's war diary:

> Documents from dead bodies confirm the presence of new units: 336th Infantry Regiment of 161st Infantry Division, 132th Infantry Regiment of 44th Infantry Division, 162nd Sapper Battalion of 162nd Infantry Division and 294th Sapper Battalion of 294th Infantry Division.

Although the report was not faultless, three of the four units were correctly identified, and the fourth was nearly so. What Soviet intelligence had not yet discovered was the presence of Pionier-Bataillone 45 and 50.

Casualties for 12 November, 1942:	
138th Rifle Division:	9 killed, 16 wounded, 6 for other reasons, a total of 31 men
305. Infanterie-Division:	21 men killed, 1 officer and 20 men wounded, 1 man missing

– – –

"On 12 November, […] holding the sector was not easier than on the previous day," remembers General Krylov.

> Half of 92nd Brigade and a regiment of the Gorishny division – on which we were counting – still found themselves on the other side of the Volga: the transport ships could not overcome the ice floes. Soon after that, the ice ripped apart the cable connections and we remained without a telephone connection to the east shore. The description in the army war diary for this date concluded as follows: 'The non-arrival of reinforcements and the delays with the transport of the battalions from the 92nd Separate Rifle Brigade and 90th Rifle Regiment have placed the army in an extremely difficult situation. Only the extraordinary heroism of the personnel and their steadfastness in combat allowed the army to hold its present positions, to shatter the enemy attacks with his considerably superior forces and to inflict large casualties on him…'

The daily entry from 138th Rifle Division's combat journal reveals that the division was to receive some reinforcements:

> 12 November. After the fighting on 11 November, the enemy spent the whole day regrouping. The 138th Rifle Division fought off small enemy reconnaissance probes. The 138th Rifle Division received 289 men – the remnants of 193rd Rifle Division. The command staff of that division was relocated to the left bank of the Volga.

The problem was that these men could not get through to Lyudnikov. His army commander, General Chuikov, recalls how even this small reinforcement was scraped together, and how it would be used:

We had to find, or rather squeeze out, some resources or other among our units on the right bank. The Army Military Council decided primarily to incorporate all the units of Smekhotvorov's division into one regiment, the 685th, and, concentrating it on the right flank of Gorishny's division, to counterattack northward along the Volga to join up with Lyudnikov's division. In all of Smekhotvorov's units we managed to collect only 250 able-bodied men.

At 1430 hours, 62nd Army issued Combat Order No. 237 "for the destruction of the enemy group that has reached the Volga". It read:

> The composite regiment of 193rd Rifle Division will concentrate in the area directly north of the mouth of Banny Gully by 0500 on 13.11.42, where the regiment will be operationally subordinated to the commander of 138th Rifle Division.
>
> The mission of the composite regiment:
> 1. Combined operations with units of 95th Rifle Division to destroy the enemy groups that have reached the bank of the Volga in the area of the fuel tanks and Mezenskaya Street, and to restore the position on the boundary between 138th and 95th Rifle Divisions.
> 2. Establish a direct connection between units of 138th and 95th Rifle Divisions.

The combat journal of 685th Rifle Regiment, commanded by Lieutenant-Colonel Evgeny Ivanovich Drogaitsev, describes the preparations for their new mission:

> For the liquidation of the breakthrough and to secure the delivery of ammunition and food to 138th Rifle Division, in accordance with the order of the Commander of 62 Army, 685th Rifle Regiment took in the personnel of 883rd Rifle Regiment, 895th Rifle Regiment and the special command and control elements of the staff of 193rd Rifle Division – in all, a strength of 258 men[84] – and marched off to carry out its mission together with units of 95th Rifle Division.
>
> For the march to its area of operations, the regiment was formed into three echelons which in turn were organised into march units (rifle platoons) with intervals of 100 metres between them, and they moved directly along the river bank. As a result, losses from mortar fire during the march were less even though the density of fire along the river bank was greater.

Chuikov continues:

> With this composite regiment and the right flank of Gorishny's division, which was gradually reinforced with soldiers and small groups of soldiers coming over from the left bank, we counterattacked northward [...] with the aim of linking up with Lyudnikov's men. Our counterattacks, it is true, did not restore the position, but neither was the enemy able to wipe out Lyudnikov's division.

Lieutenant-Colonel Drogaitsev's composite regiment would launch the first of its many attacks at midnight.

The situation for Lyudnikov and his men was dire but signs that became evident during the day caused some optimism amongst the staff of 62nd Army, as General Krylov recalls:

> Towards the end of 12 November, still no statement lay in front of me about the casualties we had inflicted on the enemy on this day. However, we were already certain of something that was more important than the numbers on which we were waiting. One division commander after another reported that to all appearances the enemy was worn out and could not continue the assault tomorrow. This conclusion – which seemed to be correct – had also been reached at army staff. The German November offensive could be thought of as defeated.

---

84. Of these, only 100 were active bayonets. The composite regiment was armed with 24 PPSh, 1 light machine-gun, one 45mm anti-tank gun, eight 82mm mortars and two 120mm mortars.

CHAPTER FIVE

13 November, 1942

Soviet artillery laid down sporadic harassment fire throughout the night with large-calibre guns, mostly on positions in the north of the city but also stretching all the way inland to Gorodische. The Soviet air force also flew numerous sorties over that same area, terrorising the Germans below with high-explosive bombs and incendiaries.

Lieutenant-Colonel Drogaitsev's composite 685th Rifle Regiment began their assault at midnight, as its combat journal notes:

> Having reached the defensive sector of 241st Rifle Regiment (95th Rifle Division) […] the regiment, on the verbal orders of the Commander of 95th Rifle Division and in accordance with the operational instructions from 62nd Army staff, began offensive operations […] without any assistance from 241st Rifle Regiment.

> The assault begun at 2400 on 12-13.11.1942. During the assault, the regiment was formed up with 2nd and 3rd Rifle Battalions in the forward echelon and 1st Rifle Battalion on the boundary between them but 100 metres behind.

The Soviet riflemen pushed north and threw themselves into a battle that lasted throughout the morning.

– – –

Units were shifted around during the night in readiness for continued operations. Elements of Pionier-Bataillon 45 were pulled out of the line for a few days. Soldat Bertold Paulus wrote home that "the fighting continued uninterrupted from 0330 hours on the morning of 11 November until 0600 hours on 13 November. We were then relieved and returned with 1 Leutnant, 1 Unteroffizier and 10 men. We had 9 dead and 24 wounded, all with head shots." Pionier-Bataillon 162 was moved into the battle sector of Grenadier-Regiment 578 as a further reinforcement. The objective: constriction of the pocket. Grenadier-Regiment 576 (with Pionier-Bataillon 294) would fend off Soviet relief attacks from the south, Grenadier-Regiment 577 (with Pionier-Bataillon 336) would take some of the stubbornly defended houses along Pribaltiskaya Street and Prospekt Lenina, and Grenadier-Regiment 578 would renew the assault against the Kommissarhaus with Panzerpionier-Bataillon 50 and Sturmkompanie 44, and penetrate along the Volga – into the Soviet rear – with Pionier-Bataillon 162. Regiment 578 also had the task of widening its hold along the Volga. Major Linden recalls the conditions facing his pioneers:

> There were isolated ruins here that had to be eliminated at all costs because of their flanking effect. Between these ruins and the Volga was a flat, undeveloped area that fell away with a steep drop to the river bank. The Russians had built dug-outs halfway up this cliff which were

protected by emplacements along the top edge of the cliff which could rake the open ground in front of them with effective fire. They also received accurate fire support from the other bank of the Volga. An attack here was therefore very difficult…

The objective of 138th Rifle Division was simple: defend the front-line to prevent the Germans reaching the Volga and fight to the last man, if need be. Lyudnikov had ordered all his unit commanders to mobilise every resource to fulfil this objective. He even issued Stalin's catchcry: 'Not a step back'. His units, which had increased observation of German activities, detected that the Germans were readying a new offensive throughout the day and night of 12 November. Infantry and armoured units had concentrated along the division's front-line and especially at the factory's central gates.

The German attack began at 0345 hours, half an hour before the sky had begun to lighten and a full eighty minutes prior to the first glimpse of the sun. The plan was to use darkness to surprise, overwhelm and capture the Soviet defences along the Volga before the defenders of the Kommissarhaus could intervene. If the daring thrust up the river was successful, the Soviet strongpoints would be cut off from the rear. The primary launch pads for this northward assault were Haus 79 and the Apotheke. Artillery heralded the fighting. Heavy artillery and mortar fire, including volleys from the nebelwerfers, bracketed the attack area. The German assault groups moved out. Departing from Haus 79 itself was the group of Oberleutnant Erwin Kretz, the man who had led the successful assault on the building two days earlier. He again stormed forward at the head of his troops. As they approached the Soviet defence line strung between the Kommissarhaus and the Rolik gully, Kretz came

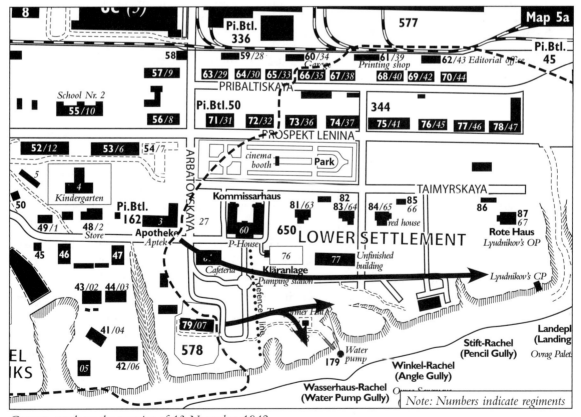

German attack on the morning of 13 November, 1942.

upon an occupied bomb crater. A submachine-gun rattled and Kretz crashed to the ground. His final words were: "Regards to my comrades, regards to the homeland!" To honour his memory, the house which he and his men had captured – and in front of which he died – was later named 'Kretzhaus'.

At first, the German attack went according to plan. The assault groups slipped through the darkness, taking out Soviet sentries, blasting dug-outs, but always pushing toward their objectives. Pechenyuk's 650th Rifle Regiment reported:

> The enemy went over to the offensive at 0345 hours in the morning. The strength of the enemy is not known but he throws grenades into the P-shaped structure [Kommissarhaus]. The enemy is laying down heavy rifle and machine-gun fire and periodically fires his mortars and artillery. From the Red House [Haus 79] he is firing into our rear and in the direction of the Volga river. The enemy is trying to encircle us. The regiment holds its defensive positions and continues to give battle to the advancing enemy.

Haus 79 and the Apotheke were used as firebases from which to cover the assault groups. Pionier-Bataillon 162 kept pushing up the Volga. This sudden attack along the top of the riverside cliff towards Lyudnikov's command post took the Soviet defence by surprise. In a

Kalgine/Gorbatenko

post-war report, Senior-Sergeant Alexei Iosifovich Gorbatenko[1], a member of Major Pechenyuk's staff, recalls this surprise raid. He begins by describing the location of the regiment command post in Haus 83 [Dom 64]:

Command posts and staffs were accommodated in two-storey houses in the lower settlement. Behind us was an unfinished building[2], towards which a communications trench was dug at night. In front was the park. On the ground floor of our building was a grand piano which was sometimes played by Dubov and others. Ivan Vasiliyevich Dubov[3], a veteran of the regiment, was very agile, always lively and an energetic staff worker. Windows on the second floor were prepared by the soldiers.

All the time there were less and less soldiers in the battalions. The Germans were already in the park. Everyone on the second floor was continuously on duty. In fact, absolutely everyone was on duty: Datsyuk, Tolkach, the reconnaissance guys, Dubov, myself and others.

Post-war photo of Alexei Iosifovich Gorbatenko, 650th Rifle Regiment.

Gorbatenko then describes the morning when Pionier-Bataillon 162 broke through:

In the morning, chemical defence chief Datsyuk raised the alarm. It was not yet dawn. 'Germans in the rear, between us and the Volga!', he said. Everyone grabbed rifles. We rushed into the unfinished building. We saw silhouettes of people running past the windows. They were moving in the direction of the divisional command post – a lot of them. Datsyuk asked: 'Who are they?' 'It's the Germans! Fire!' We did so without pause. Artillery fire came from the right. We later learned that this was Charashvili and his artillery.

– – –

1. Gorbatenko, Senior-Sergeant Alexei Iosifovich, 650th RR; born in 1922 in Khrabrov, Vitebsk. No further information known.

2. The building was to become a technical college.

3. Dubov, Ivan Vasiliyevich, 650th RR; born 7 June, 1914 in Timersyan. No further information known.

Post-war photo of Ivan Georgiyevich Charashvili, 90th Rifle Regiment.

Senior-Lieutenant Ivan Georgiyevich Charashvili originally commanded the artillery battery of 90th Rifle Regiment (95th Rifle Division) but was now part of 650th Rifle Regiment. He had fought in many battles since arriving in Stalingrad on 19 September; back then, his unit had charged right into the fighting on Mamayev Kurgan (Hill 102). Charashvili suffered his first wound during this assault but he returned to his unit the next day, his face swathed in bandages. He continued to lead his battery during the storming of Mamayev Kurgan and corrected artillery fire for the divisional guns against the water tanks on top of the hill until 30 September. During a mission on Mamayev Kurgan, Charashvili came as close as he ever would to losing his life: he was positioned in one of the round water tanks with his scouts and signalmen when a large-calibre German shell crashed through, slid around the inside wall of the tank a few times and landed at Charashvili's feet. During the fighting for Mamayev Kurgan, he lost half his personnel and one gun. His division was transferred to other sectors and in mid-October participated in fierce combat south of the tractor factory. 95th Rifle Division lost almost all of its men. While the 90th Rifle Regiment headquarters crossed to the east bank of the Volga to reform, the regiment's survivors were handed over to other formations still defending Stalingrad. It was as this stage that Charashvili and his battery began supporting 138th Rifle Division. Charashvili recalls:

Around 4-5 November, 1942, we were told that our regimental artillery battery was now part of 161st Rifle Regiment of 95th Rifle Division, but to get our artillery to 161st Regiment was impossible up to this time because of heavy artillery fire and systematic sorties by Ju-87s. The battery's guns, as well as my men, were fired on, and all that was left was one gun without sights and a few rounds, plus 11 men.

We were given a new order on 8 November, 1942; see the commander of 650th Rifle Regiment of 138th Rifle Division. On the same day, at 1500, I arrived at the command post, which I think was set up on the ground floor of a two-storey house. From the south it was covered by long 2-3 storey buildings, it seemed open to the north, with only brick chimneys from burned down wooden buildings poking up here and there, while to the rear, that is, to the west, also stood dilapidated buildings. Out in front, to the east, at about a distance of 50-100 metres, stood an unfinished brick U-shaped building[4]. A communications trench to a depth of 80 centimetres and a width of half a metre had been dug between this U-shaped premises and the command post of 650th Rifle Regiment. This U-shaped house was no more than 100 metres from river bank.

The guns of our battery on this sector of 650th Rifle Regiment were totally destroyed by 11 November and the soldiers of the battery were either killed or severely wounded in heavy combat with the enemy.

The battle of 13 November, 1942, deserves special mention. On this day, early in the morning, from the eastern side of the unfinished U-shaped building, I noticed a large number of soldiers

---

4. In Russian, Charashvili calls it the 'P-shaped building', but to prevent confusion with the more well known P-shaped building (Kommissarhaus), the English equivalent – 'U-shaped building' – will be used in Charashvili's account. Elsewhere in this book, this same building is referred to as the 'unfinished building'. See page 232 for a description.

in holes hiding from bombs and artillery shells. The Germans, seemingly without our knowing it, approached this building and sat in the holes, apparently waiting until it was fully light.

There were ten or eleven of us in this building and I took the initiative in this battle. Because of the situation we were in and to get reinforcements, I sent a senior-sergeant to the regiment commander, so there was only ten of us left. Because there was no time to lose, we had to act decisively, we had to determine how many of the enemy there was and we had to then go into battle. Dawn broke and I saw two strapping German officers about 100-120 metres away, heading towards the bank of the Volga. I decided not to let them go. I grabbed a rifle, loaded one bullet, shot the first officer, the German shook, then shot the second officer and he fell, the first turned around and started moving toward us but I shot him again and he collapsed.

The Germans in the holes did not move, apparently they were waiting for some kind of signal. The reinforcements were late, we didn't see the senior-sergeant, but time did not allow us the luxury of waiting. I decided to go into battle: first we threw grenades into the holes, where there were a large number of Germans, after that, when the Germans got up from the holes, we shot them down with all our small arms (we had Russian rifles, some submachine-guns, dozens of grenades and our pistols).

The German assault group that was reputedly destroyed was 3. Kompanie of Pionier-Bataillon 162, about 70 in number, led by its daring commander Oberleutnant Alfons Schinke. This silent and swift attack was typical of Schinke. They hurtled forward, disregarding nests of resistance – as had been ordered. They pushed further north, towards Lyudnikov's headquarters, and actually succeeded in infiltrating to the command post. Lyudnikov and his staff were fully aware of the danger facing them. "Stand to!", ordered Colonel Lyudnikov. Every possible man was gathered to stymie this impudent German raid. All of the division's staff officers, including Lyudnikov, together with the 12 remaining men of Captain Kosarev's 179th Separate Engineer Battalion, 6 from the security company led by Senior-Lieutenant Vladimir Ivanovich Grichina[5] and some lightly wounded soldiers with female medical assistant S.Z. Ozerova, rose up into a counterattack screaming "For the Motherland!", "For Stalin!" and "Hurra!". They flung themselves at the surprised German group. Russian records state that the German infiltrators were eliminated in the ensuing hand-to-hand fighting and the position was restored two hours

Oberleutnant Alfons Schinke, commander of 3./Pi. Btl. 162, led the daring attack that seriously threatened Colonel Lyudnikov's command post.

later. Awarded the Red Star for their actions were Senior-Lieutenant Petr Pavlovich Pechenkin, a company commander in 203rd Separate Signals Battalion, and Senior-Sergeant

---

5. Grichina, Senior-Lieutenant Vladimir Ivanovich, 69th Recon Co.; born 5 August, 1916 in Bronislav. Still alive in 2003 in Volgograd.

Stepan Nikolayevich Radygin and Red Army man Ivan Nikonovich Ivanov, both from 179th Separate Engineer Battalion, while platoon commander Lieutenant Sergei Vasilyevich Panovalov and Red Army men Surik Aleksandrovich Avetisyan and Kalir Aloyev – all three also from Kosarev's battalion – received the 'For Bravery' medal.

In the unfinished building, in 650th Rifle Regiment's sector, Senior-Sergeant Gorbatenko and his men were still firing on the marauding Germans:

> It started to get light. A concerted 'Hurra' came from the division staff. Our counterattack struck the Germans from the rear. The fascists were confused. Any ability to resist disappeared. Their complete destruction was simply and successfully carried out.

Senior-Lieutenant Charashvili and his artillerymen also participated:

> On my command, we threw almost 50 hand grenades (most of them were lemon grenades, and they were German) into the holes at the same time. After we threw the grenades, some Germans stood up from the holes and began to run in all directions towards the bank of the Volga. We started to shoot at them from a distance of 10-15 metres. There was not one shot from the German side. They got tangled up in some brush and weren't able to run, and arriving at this time were staff workers from 650th Regiment and their regiment commander, Major Pechenyuk, who himself carried a German submachine-gun, and they started to shoot the Germans. After a few minutes I yelled 'For the Motherland! For Stalin! Urrah… Comrades, after me!' And I jumped from the building. Almost everyone followed me, and they continued to chase down and shoot the Germans. From the left flank, with a yell of 'Urrah!' a small group of 12 men began to fire on the Germans. The battle lasted around 10-15 minutes. It is possible to say without exaggeration that not one Hitlerite from this German battalion or company escaped, they were all killed. When everything quietened down, we returned to the unfinished brick U-shaped building. I remember quite clearly that from our forces, not one man was killed. We took trophies from the Germans, the most valued by me was the food and cigarettes, and it goes without saying the captured weapons too.

> I remember well that in this small sector we were able to pick up 15 light machine-guns, 49 submachine-guns, 8 or 9 of which were fully loaded, around 136 rifles, and many hand-grenades, 11 'Parabellum' pistols and a few binoculars.

Captain Piven from 650th Rifle Regiment also describes this attack:

> In the early morning, the regiment commander Pechenyuk arrived and told me that the artillery battery of the Georgian Senior-Lieutenant I.G. Charashvili was encircled by German submachine-gunners and that immediate help was needed. I took a few soldiers, Major Pechenyuk gave me a German submachine-gun and we began to annihilate the Germans that had broken through our lines. A heavy battle began there, which turned into hand-to-hand fighting. As a result, the Germans were annihilated and Charashvili's battery was saved.

> On the battlefield were around 40 dead Germans and many submachine-guns and grenades, which served us in later battles. Senior-Sergeant V. Reshetnikov was killed in this battle, as was another officer. Charashvili was also wounded…

In a situation report issued later in the day, 138th Rifle Division reported:

> The group of submachine-gunners that had broken through was destroyed, only individuals managing to escape…

While the entire group was not wiped out by the Soviet counterattack, and casualties were not as grievous as Soviet accounts suggest, losses were nevertheless high. Complete documentation is not available for all of Pionier-Bataillon 162's companies to show the total number of casualties but at least 9 men from Schinke's 3. Kompanie were killed.[6] In any case, the audacious but reckless advance up the Volga had failed. Based on statements from prisoners and seized documents, Lyudnikov would learn that the reinforced 305. Infanterie-Division had the goal of penetrating into the flank and reaching the Volga river in the rear of the division, near the command post.

Later in the day, a German managed to exact a bit of revenge on Senior-Lieutenant Charashvili and his men in the unfinished building:

> After a few hours, a German sniper – within the span of about 5-6 minutes – killed 4 of our men, 3 of them were sergeants and one officer. I spotted the German sniper sitting between a brick chimney and some metal on the roof, not far from us (60-70 metres). I settled down with my single-shot rifle and with one shot, under the eyes of Major Pechenyuk, killed the German sniper on the roof.

The German breakthrough on the left flank of 650th Rifle Regiment had completely scattered the covering force deployed there. Any available man was sent to that open flank. Once the assault had been shattered, offensive momentum dwindled and the attack eventually came to a standstill. This gave Soviet units the courage to counterattack. Haus 79 was almost going to be lost. A machine-gunner posted in the second storey of the house recognised the danger in time and forced the Soviets into complete cover with his fire. An immediately organised counterthrust restored the situation. By 1000 hours, the situation on the left flank of 138th Rifle Division had settled down. A menacing lull loomed over the cold, clear morning. The Soviets felt the Germans had not finished with them yet.

– – –

While Pionier-Bataillon 162 struggled to gain ground along the Volga, a new attack was launched by Grenadier-Regiment 577, Pionier-Bataillon 336 and Sturmkompanie 44. The objectives of their attack remained the same as two days earlier: the complete capture of Haus 73 [Dom 36], Haus 67 [Dom 38] and Haus 66 [Dom 35], all important Soviet strongpoints that prevented further progress. Haus 67 [Dom 38] was garrisoned by Lieutenant I.S. Pogrebnyak and several men from 1st Rifle Battalion of 344th Regiment. The other two buildings were held by the battered remnants of 2nd and 3rd Rifle Battalions of 650th Rifle Regiment. Each of these 'battalions' was nothing more than a handful of exhausted men who

---

6. They were: Gefreiter Helmut Böhm, Gefreiter Anton Bulenda, Gefreiter Kurt Grauer, Soldat Otto Hackerschmied, Gefreiter Richard Hoffmann, Unteroffizier Richard Irrgang, Gefreiter Ernst Kattelans, Soldat Gerhard Kirsch and Soldat Fritz Schmude. Obergefreiter Gerhard Nowak was severely wounded and would succumb to his wounds the next day.
Böhm, Gefreiter Helmut, 3./Pi.Btl.162; born 6 June, 1922 in Neundorf. Killed in action, 13 November, 1942 in Stalingrad.
Bulenda, Gefreiter Anton, 3./Pi.Btl.162; born 31 May, 1912 in Gregorsdorf. Killed in action, 13 November, 1942 in Stalingrad.
Grauer, Gefreiter Kurt, 3./Pi.Btl.162; born 19 January, 1921 in Massel. Killed in action, 13 November, 1942 in Stalingrad.
Hackerschmied, Soldat Otto, 3./Pi.Btl.162; born 16 May, 1923 in Dux. Killed in action, 13 November, 1942 in Stalingrad.
Hoffmann, Gefreiter Richard, 3./Pi.Btl.162; born 16 September, 1920 in Rankau. Killed in action, 13 November, 1942 in Stalingrad.
Irrgang, Unteroffizier Richard, 3./Pi.Btl.162; born 9 January, 1921 in Eckartswaldau. Killed in action, 13 November, 1942 in Stalingrad.
Kattelans, Gefreiter Ernst, 3./Pi.Btl.162; born 20 April, 1921 in Uedem. Killed in action, 13 November, 1942 in Stalingrad.
Kirsch, Soldat Gerhard, 3./Pi.Btl.162; born 16 March, 1923 in Chemnitz. Killed in action, 13 November, 1942 in Stalingrad.
Schmude, Soldat Fritz, 3./Pi.Btl.162; born 9 March, 1922 in Liegnitz. Killed in action, 13 November, 1942 in Stalingrad.
Nowak, Obergefreiter Gerhard, 3./Pi.Btl.162; born 28 October, 1911 in Klosterbrück. Died of wounds, 14 November, 1942 in Stalingrad.

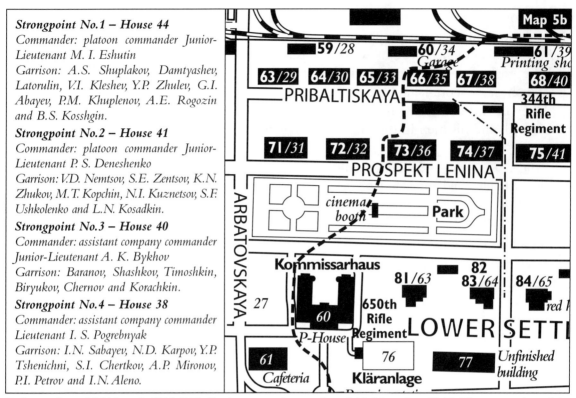

Defensive line of 344th and 650th Rifle Regiments on the morning of 13 November, 1942. The strongpoints of 1st Battalion of 344th Rifle Regiment are also shown.

had courageously – but barely – retained control of their buildings during the German attack on 11 November. In fact, the entire regiment only had 90 men at the beginning of the day, including the few replacements scraped together from staffs and rear echelon units. As for weaponry, it had 61 rifles, 2 heavy machine-guns, 3 light machine-guns, 2 anti-tank rifles, 13 PPSh and 7 mortars. Now, they once again prepared to throw back a furious assault.

Leading the attack of Pionier-Bataillon 336 was 3. Kompanie, commanded by Oberleutnant Bernhard Ziesch. By comparison, 3. Kompanie had suffered the least on 11 November: only 6 dead and 3 wounded. During the night of 12-13 November, the 70-odd men of 3. Kompanie had silently filed through trenches and craters to form up in their starting position – the cellar of Haus 65 [Dom 33]. Part of Oberleutnant Kindler's Sturmkompanie 44 gathered in Haus 72 [Dom 32]. At 0345 hours, in conjunction with the attack of Grenadier-Regiment 578 and Pionier-Bataillon 162, they moved off.

Russian sources state that at 0400 hours, a group of German submachine-gunners – up to 70 men – managed to break through along Prospekt Lenina to the gun pits of 344th Rifle Regiment's mortar battery. True, the battery had no operational tubes because all seven mortars had been destroyed in the previous two days, but the pits were still manned. The Germans began lobbing grenades into the emplacements. Hand to hand fighting erupted. A group of mortarmen commanded by Lieutenant Bechaykin, together with some riflemen, were able to repel the German attack. The mortarmen then launched a counterattack. They killed ten of the German attackers, forced the rest to flee and captured 4 light and 1 heavy machine-gun, 18 rifles and a submachine-gun.

The combat journal of 650th Rifle Regiment makes no mention of the attack on two of its strongpoints, so unfortunately, there is very little information about the struggle for Haus 73 [Dom 36] and Haus 66 [Dom 35]. All that is available is a brief statement in the daily report of 138th Rifle Division: "By the end of the day, the enemy had occupied Dom 35 and 36 […] after completely wiping out their garrisons." In regards to the third targeted building, however, we have Combat Report No. 51 of 344th Rifle Regiment, which does describe the attack near Haus 67 [Dom 38]:

> At 0415 hours, an enemy group of up to 70 men attacked the 3rd rifle company. This attack was beaten off with fire and grenades, part of the enemy being annihilated and the rest thrown back to their starting positions in a counterattack. Altogether, up to 60-70 soldiers and officers were destroyed and 1 prisoner was taken.

Very heavy casualties were suffered by Oberleutnant Ziesch's 3. Kompanie in these assaults: 10 killed and 11 wounded. Killed were Obergefreiter Franz Gedusch[7], Obergefreiter Josef Herzig[8], Unteroffizier Rudolf Lang[9], Feldwebel Arthur Menzel[10], Gefreiter Josef Pfeiffer[11], Obergefreiter Helmut Reichel[12], Pionier Franz Rüprich[13], Obergefreiter Rudolf Schmied[14], Obergefreiter Max Urban[15] and Gefreiter Erich Winter[16]. Wounded were Obergefreiter Hans Ehren[17], Gefreiter Kurt Falk[18], Pionier Gerhard Gäbler[19], Obergefreiter Rudolf Koch[20], Pionier Heinrich Osterkamp[21], Unteroffizier Kurt Richter[22], Pionier Paul Schiller[23], Gefreiter Alfred Seelig[24], Obergefreiter Herbert Sittner[25], Gefreiter Arno Zimmermann[26] and Pionier Helmut Zwadlo[27]. Also killed was Gefreiter Alfred Willy Strauch[28] of 2. Kompanie[29].

---

7. Gedusch, Obergefreiter Franz, 3./Pi.Btl.336; born 13 July, 1911 in Tilsit-Gumbinnen. Killed in action, 13 November, 1942 in Stalingrad.
8. Herzig, Obergefreiter Josef, 3./Pi.Btl.336; born 4 March, 1908 in Seidenschwanz. Killed in action, 13 November, 1942 in Stalingrad.
9. Lang, Unteroffizier Rudolf, 3./Pi.Btl.336; born 6 October, 1910 in Reichenbach. Killed in action, 13 November, 1942 in Stalingrad.
10. Menzel, Feldwebel Arthur, 3./Pi.Btl.336; born 27 March, 1914 in Halle. Killed in action, 13 November, 1942 in Stalingrad.
11. Pfeiffer, Gefreiter Josef, 3./Pi.Btl.336; born 19 July, 1909 in Prening-Passau. Killed in action, 13 November, 1942 in Stalingrad.
12. Reichel, Obergefreiter Helmut, 3./Pi.Btl.336; born 30 July, 1918 in Ursprung. Killed in action, 13 November, 1942 in Stalingrad.
13. Rüprich, Pionier Franz, 3./Pi.Btl.336; born 23 October, 1922 in Steuden. Killed in action, 13 November, 1942 in Stalingrad.
14. Schmied, Obergefreiter Rudolf, 3./Pi.Btl.336; born 23 August, 1911 in Chemnitz. Killed in action, 13 November, 1942 in Stalingrad.
15. Urban, Obergefreiter Max, 3./Pi.Btl.336; born 15 November, 1908 in Lauska bei Löbau. Killed in action, 13 November, 1942 in Stalingrad.
16. Winter, Obergefreiter Erich, 3./Pi.Btl.336; born 15 May, 1909 in Hohnbach. Killed in action, 13 November, 1942 in Stalingrad.
17. Ehren, Obergefreiter Hans, 3./Pi.Btl.336; born 17 July, 1910 in Menzelen.. Missing in action, December 1942 in Stalingrad.
18. Falk, Gefreiter Kurt, 3./Pi.Btl.336; born 23 June, 1912 in Oberplanitz. No further information known.
19. Gäbler, Pionier Gerhard, 3./Pi.Btl.336; born 30 August, 1922 in Dresden. Missing in action, September 1943 near Melitopol.
20. Koch, Obergefreiter Rudolf, 3./Pi.Btl.336; born 7 February, 1911 in Remse. No further information known.
21. Osterkamp, Pionier Heinrich, 3./Pi.Btl.336; born 29 November, 1908 in Hameln. Killed in action, 4 June 1943, west of Russkoye
22. Richter, Unteroffizier Kurt, 3./Pi.Btl.336; born 27 May, 1910 in Kemnitz. Died 17 January, 1946 in France as a POW.
23. Schiller, Pionier Paul, 3./Pi.Btl.336; born 7 October, 1919 in Eibenstock. No further information known.
24. Seelig, Gefreiter Alfred, 3./Pi.Btl.336; born 27 May, 1913 in Kleinzschocher. Died of wounds, 2 December, 1942 in Berdichev.
25. Sittner, Obergefreiter Herbert, 3./Pi.Btl.336; born 28 July, 1910 in Oberwiera. No further information known.
26. Zimmermann. Gefreiter Arno. 3./Pi.Btl.336; born 14 January, 1909 in Ottewig. No further information known.
27. Zwadlo, Pionier Helmut. 3./Pi.Btl.336; born 4 December, 1912 in Danzig-Langführ. No further information known.
28. Strauch, Gefreiter Alfred. 2./Pi.Btl.336; born 28 March, 1912 in Chemnitz. Killed in action, 13 November, 1942 in Stalingrad.
29. Another source says he was missing in action on 11 November, 1942.

At the same time as the attacks of Pionier-Battalione 162 and 336, the boundary position along the Volga was being widened in both directions. Despite the death of Oberleutnant Kretz almost immediately, the assault spearheads continued pushing north along the clifftops and the flat, sandy beach, known to the Germans as the 'Sandbank'. Hauptmann Rettenmaier observed the attack going in across the open ground:

> Russian resistance stiffened enormously. With the advance to the Volga bank, the supply of those surrounded was cut off. The final result depended on whether this stretch of river bank could be retained. The Russians directed all their strength there. He placed well-aimed artillery fire on this particular funnel for the entire day. The Russian's firing was incredibly accurate. Our attack moved up from the south with panzer support. The panzers went up in flames.

Major Linden recounts that an advance along the cliffs "succeeded by approaching the river through a trench, and in this way we broadened our positions along the Volga. The Russians should now have been thrown out of the rest of the bridgehead, but they brought in new men and material time and again. The result of the attack we conducted was unsuccessful because the enemy was skilled and obstinate. The hand grenades we threw rolled down the steep slope and exploded at the bottom with no effect. The same thing happened with the shells from the heavy weapons. Most of these also landed in the Volga."

The situation down on the Volga river bank was just as tricky. "From the squad that lay on the Sandbank, only one man returned, wounded," recalls Hauptmann Rettenmaier, "and he brought back news of the fate of the others. An Unteroffizier who was listening to this information volunteered to occupy the position there with his squad. In a short time, they was also worn down to three men. It was pointless to sacrifice any more men there. The posts were withdrawn into the outlet of the gully and the entire stretch of the Sandbank was, wherever possible, mined."

AKG Images

Zaitsevsky Island as seen from a German machine-gun post. From their cliff-top positions, German machine-gunners easily controlled the river. Here, Luftwaffe bombs plaster Soviet artillery emplacements hidden amongst the thick brush.

Further south, in the sector of Grenadier-Regiment 576 along the Volga near the fuel installation, it was the German's turn to be on the defensive. Drogaitsev's riflemen had been attacking since midnight. At 0850, Gruppe Seydel observed "an enemy attack of about 250 men toward the fuel installation. The attack was repulsed." The German estimate of Soviet strength was extremely accurate. Estimates of German forces facing Drogaitsev's regiment were reported as follows:

> On the sector being attacked by the composite regiment of 193rd Rifle Division, the enemy defends with about 100-120 infantrymen and lays down artillery and mortar fire on the combat ranks of the composite regiment.

The diary of 685th Rifle Regiment records the results of their first attack against the fuel installation, and includes a higher estimate of Germans opposing them:

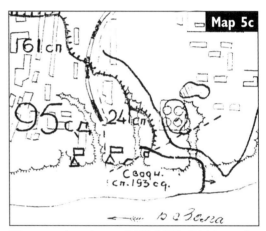

The composite regiment of 193rd Rifle Division pushes north along the Volga.

> By 0900 on 13.11.42, the regiment, involved in a slugging match, drove the enemy out of ten foxholes, trenches and dug-outs and pushed 200 metres to the north, but any further advance was stopped by heavy fire from artillery, mortars and machine-guns, as well as hand grenades from the area of the fuel tanks, the head of the gully and the northern slopes of the gully, so it dug in on the attained line. At the same time it was replenished with ammunition issued from Banny Gully during the assault (especially grenades).

The initial offensive battle showed that the assessment of enemy forces as specified by 95th Division staff was incorrect – 30-80 men different from the facts. In front of the attacking regiment, the enemy had on average 200-250 men with time to dig in properly and consolidate by making use of dug-outs and trenches left the day before by 241st Rifle Regiment.

The enemy's system of fire was set up in such a way that not one opportunity presented itself to cross the gully north of the fuel tanks without the suppression of firing points. The regiment's assault came to a halt […] because fire came not only from the front, but also mainly from the area of the fuel tanks and the head of the gully that lies to the north of them.

The war diary of 62nd Army reported the regiment's progress thus:

> The composite regiment of 193rd Rifle Division, deployed on the right flank of 95th Rifle Division, was stopped on the line of Mezenskaya Street and east of there to the Volga after meeting strong enemy fire resistance. Fierce fighting continues.

At 1100, Gruppe Seydel reported that "the focal point of enemy artillery has shifted to the north, to the left neighbour (305. Infanterie-Division), whose assault we must support with our artillery, upon request". In its midday report, Artillerie-Regiment 179 recorded: "Ferry traffic on the Volga. Shortly before midday, our bombers bombed the river bank along the front-line from the gun factory down to the level of Hall 4 in the steel factory. Orientation from left neighbour: 'our attack is only progressing very slowly, only individual assault troop operations possible…'"

After its first attack was repulsed, 95th Rifle Division renewed its assault at midday. Fighting would continue amongst the gullies and fuel tanks until nightfall. Combat Report No. 47 records the outcome:

The composite regiment of 193rd Rifle Division reached the gully mouth north-east of the fuel tanks but a further advance was not possible under the effect of enemy firing points on the northern face of the gully and in houses.

The division's actions warranted a brief mention in 62nd Army's war diary:

All attempts by the enemy to expand the site of his breakthrough along the riverbank to the south have been beaten off. Units hold their positions but have not restored the situation on the right flank of 241st Rifle Regiment.

The division's losses were as follows: 685th composite regiment – 45 men; 241st Rifle Regiment – 10 men; 3/92nd Rifle Brigade – 5 men; 161st Rifle Regiment – 30 men.

- - -

By 1000 hours, having concentrated large numbers of men in buildings throughout the Barrikady factory settlement, the Germans resumed their offensive on the left flank of the 650th Rifle Regiment with a strength of at least two infantry battalions and supporting armour. The objective was no less than the Kommissarhaus itself.

The first assault on the Kommissarhaus had been a bitter lesson for Hauptmann Gast. When they had approached the building, the last thing they expected was to not find an entry point: for such a large building, there were very few ways of getting in. The many windows on the southern face were too high off the ground, the knee-level basement windows were clogged with rubble and the main entrances were securely blocked by Soviet defences. With the benefit of hindsight, Gast realised he should have observed the target more thoroughly and not been so pigheaded about refusing support from Rettenmaier's infantry… For this renewed assault on the Kommissarhaus, the pioneer assault groups were equipped with guides, men from Grenadier-Regiment 578 who had thoroughly studied the building and knew the best way to approach it. Scheduled to go in against the Kommissarhaus with Gast's pioneers was part of Oberleutnant Kindler's Sturmkompanie 44.

Barrikady Museum

The Kommissarhaus – or the 'factory administration building', as it was known to the Barrikady's workers – during the final stages of its construction in 1916. Its fortress-like attributes are readily apparent.

The Kommissarhaus was a grim, stocky fortress. No other civil building could have been more suitable as a strongpoint than this one. Leonid Mitrofanovich Klyukin, deputy chief of the Barrikady factory militia, recollects the building:

> Before the war, this building was one of the most beautiful in the area. Built decades earlier, it was notable for its unusual architectural form, patterned brick towers and ornamental windows.

Construction of the building was completed in early 1916 and it was therefore one of the oldest buildings in the area. It served as the main office of the gun factory from the very beginning. By 1942, its many offices were lined with bookshelves and filing cabinets. Everything was there to enable the director of the factory, Lev Robertovich Gonor[30], and his board to control production and output of the mighty factory. The official designation of the head office was the 'factory administration building' but to Lyudnikov's soldiers it was simply known as the P-shaped building[31]. It was later designated Dom 60. To the Germans, it was known as the Kommissarhaus, but this name was only coined in November. It came about because captured Soviet soldiers revealed that some of the building's garrison were from an NKVD blocking detachment, and furthermore, several politruks were also present. To the Germans, a politruk was just another name for a commissar, and the term 'Kommissarhaus' quickly stuck[32].

Hawash

The walls of the Kommissarhaus were tremendously strong, in some places a metre thick. The floors were constructed from steel-reinforced concrete and beneath the building was a labyrinth of cramped cellars and garages connected by narrow passageways. What's more, about a metre below ground level was a tunnel linking the building with the factory. In peacetime, the tunnel – about two metres wide and just as high – had been used by foremen and factory administrators to shuttle back and forth, but in wartime, it obviously served a more martial purpose.

The ends of both wings were buttressed with stout structures that

The immense thickness of the Kommissarhaus's walls can be seen in this modern photo. In the background is the rebuilt Dom 31 [Haus 71].

---

30. Gonor, Lev Robertovich, HoSL; born 15 September, 1906. Died 13 November, 1969. He was only 33 years old when appointed director of the Barrikady Gun Factory, one of the biggest defence enterprises in the Soviet Union. When the Germans captured almost all of Stalingrad in late autumn 1942, the Barrikady engineers and workers were transferred to the Urals where a new artillery plant was built and Gonor appointed its director. Gonor had the rank of Major-General, was decorated many times and awarded the title of 'Hero of Socialist Labour' in 1942. From August 1946 to August 1950 he was a leading figure in the manufacture of long-range ballistic rockets. He was arrested in 1952 and accused of espionage and links with the Jewish Anti-Fascist Committee. He was tortured during interrogation and suffered from the damage done to his health for the rest of his life. Only the death of Stalin saved him.
31. Because of its resemblance to the Cyrillic letter 'P'.
32. For the sake of clarity, the term 'Kommissarhaus' will be used throughout the book.

strongly resembled a castellated keep. Both keeps, decorated with ornate brick trimming along the roofline and around the windows, were veritable fortresses. The few windows were extremely narrow, much like the lancet windows on medieval castles, and inside both were stairwells leading up to the second floor and down to the cellars. The two external entrances on each keep were small and easily defensible. One entrance was on the curved wall facing the courtyard and could therefore be covered from windows on the opposite wing, while the other entrance faced the park. Trying to gain entry here would create problems of another sort. A few stairs led into a narrow anteroom, a useful architectural feature in the fearsome depths of winter that enabled

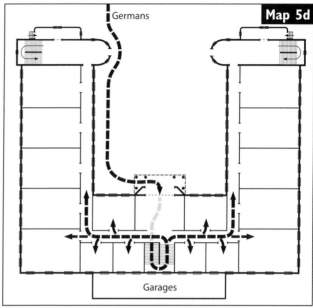

German attack on the Kommissarhaus, 13 November, 1942. Access was gained via the main entrance and central stairwell. German assault groups then quickly moved up to the second floor.

the main sections to retain warmth while permitting frequent usage by visitors. When incorporated into the building's defences, however, attackers would need to funnel into the constricted anteroom – a natural killing zone – before they could even penetrate into the building itself.

Klyukin recalls the defences of the mighty building:

> At the beginning of November, the workers-militia, together with soldiers, took up defence in this house. Machine-guns were placed in vacant window openings. Mortars were positioned on the second floor. Boxes of ammunition were delivered at night from the bank of the Volga. Placed on hand near the windows were hand grenades, cartridges and bottles filled with an incendiary mixture. During those days, documents from a German killed in the factory came into our hands. We found photos amongst some papers, including some that made the blood boil in our veins. The photos showed a scene of monstrous punishment that the Germans inflicted on women and children in a village street. The Germans crushed them under the tracks of their tanks... I remember how militiaman Vanya Mukhortov, having seen these pictures, said: 'We must beat them! Destroy the fascists!'

A unit of the Barrikady militia practise marching in formation. These factory workers fought courageously but very few would survive the battle.

Continuous attacks were repulsed until 1300 hours, but by this time, 650th Rifle Regiment's front-line had been severely mauled and the Kommissarhaus dreadfully battered by artillery and German assaults. Klyukin describes these difficult hours:

> The Germans stormed the factory administration building in which our civil guardsmen fought together with the soldiers of 138th Rifle Division. The Germans fired at this bastion with artillery and mortars. Every window and breach in the walls was under the sights of hostile snipers. Flaring up in one place or the other in the building were fires. Dense, suffocating smoke spread throughout every storey. Filing cabinets filled with Whatman drawing papers, books and furniture blazed. Anything flammable burned. Ripping the quilted jackets and shirts from their shoulders, the soldiers smothered fires in rooms, corridors, and on the staircases. They also continued to fight. From the factory citadel shrouded by smoke, our mortars continued to fire, bursts from our machine-guns and submachine-guns were heard and hand grenades rained down. Wave after wave of German submachine-gunners reeled back… The garrison also beat off tank attacks. I remember how soldiers from Danilin's squad threw bottles filled with an incendiary mixture at a tank approaching the building. Flames blanketed the enemy armoured vehicle.

At 1310 hours, the Germans sent in ten more panzers to batter the building. This time, the assault on the Kommissarhaus would be preceded by massive and overwhelming direct firepower. Prior to the departure of the pioneers, these vehicles – the remnants of the company from Panzer-Regiment 36, as well as the three of the new sIG33Bs and few assault guns of Sturmgeschütz-Abteilung 245 – moved into position directly opposite the building, on the other side of the shredded park. Their assignment: destroy the top floor of the Kommissarhaus. On the given signal, each tank and assault gun sent high-explosive shells directly through the narrow windows. Volley after volley chiselled the upper storey. Armour-piercing shells were interspersed. The bulky fortress seethed under the iron pummelling. Clouds of grey smoke and red dust wept out of every opening. Most of the top floor garrison were obliterated but a few surviving mortarmen abandoned their crushed weapons and staggered down the stairs to seek shelter. The top floor was destroyed and had been swept clean of Soviet defenders.

The German plan of attack was cunningly simple, yet was calculated to catch the Soviet defenders off guard. Major Josef Linden:

> A large-scale attack was renewed… The side entrances could not be penetrated because they were secured by effective enemy flanking fire from concealed positions, so Pionier-Bataillon 50 launched a frontal attack…

Instead of vainly attacking the well-defended entrances at the end of each wing, the pioneers and grenadiers of Sturmkompanie 44 dashed past the entrances of the southern keep and worked their way along the inner wall of the partially enclosed forecourt, hurling grenades through windows as they went. This daring move caught Klyukin and his men off guard, for there were now precious few defenders positioned at the windows overlooking the courtyard. The pioneers swiftly formed up outside the portico of the central entrance. Others, kneeling down, covered the main group by aiming their weapons at the many leering windows. The large doors of the central entrance had been bolted shut, reinforced, and blocked by debris. Depositing their powerful demolition charges, the pioneers blasted apart the obstruction and created a ragged opening. Hand grenades were tossed through the smouldering hole, and after these volleys exploded, the pioneers warily clambered inside.

Crossing the threshold into the thick-walled building, the Germans felt the clamour of battle evaporate with a sudden hush. No whine of shrapnel. No chirping of bullets. Even the omnipresent cannonade became a muted rumble. Inside the Kommissarhaus, there was just a crypt-like silence. With furiously pounding hearts, the pioneers and grenadiers cautiously spread out, expecting at any moment to be struck by Soviet fire. Leading them were junior officers, like Leutnants Ernst Bunte[33] and Herbert Palmowski[34], platoon commanders from 3./Panzerpionier-Bataillon 50, and Leutnant Wilhelm Willmitzer, originally Führer of 11./Grenadier-Regiment 131 but now part of Sturmkompanie 44. They moved into the building's main foyer. Directly opposite was a thick concrete staircase, the kind with an intermediate landing. Heading off laterally to the left and right were hallways to the outer wings. Several doorways opened directly into the main foyer. The interior was gloomy, illuminated only by slanting beams of orange light from the hallway windows facing the courtyard. An

Familie Bunte

Leutnant Ernst Bunte, a platoon commander in 3./Pz.Pi.Btl.50, was killed during the fighting in the Kommissarhaus.

acrid smog from smouldering drafting plans, mixed with the smell of burnt paper and brick dust, hung in the air. Many walls and ceilings were blackened by smoke and the floor was covered in debris, mainly detached stucco and thousands of charred, trampled documents.

Reconnaissance, observation and the abortive attack on 11 November had shown that the Soviet defences were concentrated on the ground floor with only support weapons based on the second floor. Accordingly, the German plan was straightforward: outflank the Soviet defences from above. Prior to the attack, the decision had been made to clear the Kommissarhaus from top to bottom. With purposeful movements, the pioneers set up barricades and strongpoints to block the hallways, equipped them with machine-guns, then cautiously proceeded up the staircase. Their hearts pounded in their chests. The silence was nervewracking. Then, grenades were hoisted up onto the next floor, bursts of fire from a cover squad lashed the same area while a knot of pioneers stormed up the stairwell. The sound of German jackboots echoed hollowly through the empty halls. A perimeter was established and the pioneers fanned out, covering both hallways while the first few offices were checked. The only Soviet defenders found were those lying torn and distorted amongst the smoking rubble. Reaching this second – and topmost – floor of the Kommissarhaus had only taken a few minutes. Down below, a machine-gun of the ground floor strongpoint

---

33. Bunte, Leutnant Ernst, 3./Pz.Pi.Btl.50; born 13 October, 1912 in Holzhausen. Killed in action, 13 November, 1942 in Stalingrad. See Appendix 2 (page 570) for more details.

34. Palmowski, Leutnant Herbert, 3./Pz.Pi.Btl.50; born 11 September, 1911 in Kl. Kleeberg. Died of wounds, 13 November, 1942 in Stalingrad. See Appendix 2 (page 576) for more details.

started hammering. Russian shouts then rang out, closely followed by bursts of submachine-gun fire and the crack of rifles. Hand grenades thudded and the German machine-guns opened up a continuous fire. The noise was absolutely deafening within the enclosed confines of the building.

The Soviet defenders realised what was happening and launched furious counterattacks down the hallways. The danger of the German intrusion was obvious. Some of the Soviet soldiers, workers at the Barrikady factory until a few months ago, had visited the building prior to the battle, but it was the last two weeks spent defending the building that enabled them to possess intimate knowledge of its layout. They now crept through offices and crawled through mouseholes knocked in the walls, trying to catch the Germans unaware.

As their compatriots downstairs held off the Soviet counterattack, the pioneers on the top floor assembled into two combat groups and simultaneously moved in opposite directions down the hallways. Down on the ground floor, Klyukin and his men fought desperately:

> Hitlerite submachine-gunners managed to break into the stairwell of the central entrance. Combat began inside the building. Mortarmen fought in the right wing of the factory administration building. Soldiers' hand grenades beat off fascist attack which made their way along the second floor corridors… the civil guardsmen and Red Army soldiers held one floor while the fascists controlled the other. There was fighting for each room, each stairwell, each cellar. Many of our civil guardsmen died the death of the brave here. I want to talk about worker Vanya Mukhortov. Everyone loved him for his cheerful disposition and kind heart. He fought bravely in every battle, encouraged his comrades and came to the aid of wounded men. Vanya Mukhortov carried on fighting steadfastly in the ranks of the garrison that protected the factory administration building. He was severely wounded there. Bleeding profusely, Vanya found the strength in the last minutes of his life to throw a grenade at the charging fascists. Dying here too was worker of the security detail, former border guard Ivan Fedin. Never to fade from my memory is the moment during the fighting when he moved a machine-gun from one end of the building to the other, repulsing enemy attacks. There were ever less defenders remaining in the citadel above the Volga.

The pioneers quickly captured the second floor and secured the top of each staircase. To descend these and attempt to take them was another matter. Using hollow charges, the pioneers blasted holes through the ferro-concrete floor and dropped grenade after grenade down onto the ground floor. Flamethrowers nozzles were also poked through, projecting fearsome streams of fire into the downstairs rooms. 138th Rifle Division later reported that "the enemy has blown up the house from the top floor down and set it on fire". With the Germans holding the staircase in the

Mark/Kulichenko

One of the Kommissarhaus's cellars. As can be seen, the building did not have floorboards (the statement 'pioneers ripped up the floorboards to attack the enemy', as reported in several books, is wrong). Instead, the floors were made of thick concrete reinforced by steel girders. After the war, local residents bricked up most passages in the cellars so that they could be used as secure garages or store rooms, but this dark underworld attracted unsavoury characters (drug addicts) and was a favoured hide-out for those on the run from the police.

centre of the building, the two remaining stairwells in the end of each wing were the Soviet garrison's only means of escaping down to the cellars. Pressured from above and by the German group in the centre of the building, the garrison immediately realised that they were about to be cut off, so Klyukin and his militiamen, together with the remaining mortarmen of 650th Rifle Regiment, tumbled down the stairwells into the cellars. The radio over which the mortarmen previously received target coordinates was now used to request that Soviet artillery open fire on them. This was done. Artillery batteries on Zaitsevsky Island and the east bank of the Volga dropped shells around and onto the building. Several mortar batteries also joined in. While this was a shock to the Germans, there was relatively little danger because all men were down from the second floor. The desperate request by the Soviet garrison only delayed the inevitable.

The pioneers commenced actions against the Soviets lurking in the cellars. Again, holes were blown through the floor, grenades by the dozen were dropped through, flamethrowers poured in fire, but the Germans were still unable to penetrate the cellars. Downstairs, Klyukin and his men waited, knowing full well that the Germans would try anything to get them out. The severely wounded gathered in the underground tunnel where they were safe from explosives and flames. The able-bodied soldiers concentrated on defending the stairwells. Conditions in the cellars were horrifying. Feeble spokes of light from the elevated windows – from the very few unclogged by rubble – highlighted rubbish-strewn floors and bodies slumped in corners. A suffocating haze of smouldering flame-oil, gunpowder fumes and concrete dust rasped at the defenders' throats and made their eyes water. And at any moment they could be obliterated when the ceiling erupted above their heads. The only thing going for them was the layout of their subterranean stronghold: individual rooms of the compartmentalised cellar helped contain the blast and flames of each German intrusion.

At 1400 hours, the pioneers decided to up the ante. Satchel charges were crammed through the holes. Their stupendous detonations shook the building's foundations. Next, petrol-filled jerry cans with explosive charges strapped to them were lowered on ropes. The resulting fireballs roared through the underground passageways and sucked the oxygen out of the foetid air. From the outside, the house seeped smoke. Concussed, stunned and suffering from painful burns, the few remaining Soviet defenders retreated to the furthest corners of the cellars. Klyukin describes what happened next:

> The fascists then used thermite hand grenades against our soldiers. The caustic smoke took our breath away and soldiers almost went blind.

It is not known exactly what these 'thermite grenades' were but they were probably frangible glass smoke grenades. These grenades, known as Blendkörper, resembled a large electric light bulb filled with 260 grams of amber-coloured titanium tetrachloride. The Blendkörper were designed to be thrown against tanks so that the glass containers smashed, allowing the chemicals to create a spontaneous volatile reaction. Target areas were any openings leading to the main crew compartment. The caustic smoking mixture would penetrate to the interior of the tank and either incapacitate the crew or force them to abandon their vehicle. The effect of the Blendkörper was potent in confined spaces. After ten minutes of this fearsome bombardment, Klyukin and nine other men, all wounded and burnt, managed to escape the building's charred ruins.

The commander of the NKVD blocking detachment, Junior-Lieutenant Senchkovsky, recalls the stoicism and bravery of Klyukin and his men:

Something special that I can describe from memory was the patriotism displayed by the workers militia units from the Barrikady factory. When the German invaders daringly captured part of the factory territory, they turned towards our workers group defending their factory, amongst whom was communist Leonid Mitrofanovich Klyukin, who had asked to become part of our unit. Naturally, I could not refuse him. Every one of the workers declared that they were prepared to defend their beloved factory until their last ounce of strength.

In practice, they kept their word during the fighting, helping our unit maintain its line and inflicting losses on the enemy. In spite of everyone being wounded, no-one left his post. Here's an example: when the Germans repeatedly attacked the defences of our unit in the former factory administration office, using tear-inducing grenades, many of the people defending there, including militiamen Klyukin, Kleimyatov and Fedin, were blinded, and afterwards Klyukin was wounded…

A messenger arrived at Hauptmann Rettenmaier's command post in Haus 53 to report that the Kommissarhaus was completely taken:

Only in the evening did the Russians disappear from the cellar and escape through an exit facing towards the enemy. There was universal delight at the command post when the first messenger came from there because during the day, only radio contact had been possible.

The paucity of German records means that it is not possible to provide accurate figures of the casualties sustained during the vicious fighting for the building. LI. Armeekorps would later report that losses had been 'very heavy'. In a preliminary statement, 305. Infanterie-Division reported casualties of 80 men without the attached pioneer battalions. Panzerpionier-Bataillon 50 suffered many killed and wounded: amongst the dead were two platoon commanders from 3. Kompanie, Leutnants Ernst Bunte and Herbert Palmowski (seriously wounded and died a short time later), and Pionier Hermann Paelchen[35] from 2. Kompanie, but there were certainly many others. Sturmkompanie 44 lost one of its officers, Leutnant Wilhelm Willmitzer, during the storming of the Kommissarhaus. The bodies of young Austrians littered the battlefield and the scorched ruins of the Kommissarhaus. Situation Report No. 190 of 138th Rifle Division, issued at 1500, described 305. Infanterie-Division being "strengthened by units from 131st and 132nd Infantry Regiments and 80th Sapper Battalion of 44th Infantry Division". This intelligence definitely originated from documents gathered from corpses but also possibly from interrogation of prisoners because quite a few men of Sturmkompanie 44 were declared MIA.

At 1620 hours, LI. Armeekorps reported to 6. Armee:

Stormtroops of 305. Infanterie-Division broke two houses (73[36] & 66) out of the enemy bridgehead and are clearing out the Kommissarhaus. The enemy in the bridgehead is supported by artillery, flak and mortar fire from the Volga island and the east bank of the Volga…

For such a momentous day, the daily entry from the combat journal of 650th Rifle Regiment is rather brief and uninformative and mentions nothing about the loss of the regiment's most important defensive bastion. Exact numbers of Soviet casualties in the Kommissarhaus are not known, but 650th Rifle Regiment as a whole lost 55 of its 90 men to death and wounds throughout the day. The militiamen were essentially wiped out. Only

---

35. Paelchen, Pionier Hermann, 2./Pz.Pi.Btl.50; born 6 December, 1923 in Schmarse. Killed in action, 13 November, 1942 in Stalingrad.

36. The war diary of 6. Armee states that it was 'Haus 71' but that is definitely an error because this building was already in German hands prior to the beginning of the offensive.

Klyukin and one other man were absorbed into the new defensive line along the clifftop. The others, most severely burnt, made their way to the hospital bunker next to Lyudnikov's command post. Left behind in the tunnel linking the Kommissarhaus and the factory were many wounded men. Nothing is known about how they met their fate but it is certain that they all perished. Evidence suggests that the tunnel entrance collapsed, entombing the men inside, and that the Germans knew nothing about its existence.[37]

Above: The ruins of the Kommissarhaus were demolished on 27-28 July, 2003, despite protests from local veterans' groups (the ruins had not been registered as a memorial). Once most of the rubble was removed, however, the tunnel linking the building with the factory was exposed.

Below: Interior view of the rubble-clogged tunnel.

– – –

While the drama being enacted in the Kommissarhaus was almost coming to an end, fighting still swirled around the fuel tanks on the sector of Grenadier-Regiment 576. The relief attacks by Gorishny's division were intended to draw off some of the heat from Lyudnikov's beleaguered units. At 1415 hours, a fresh attack was launched by a group of 200 Soviets, this time aimed at the left wing of Gruppe Seydel. All attacks in this area were only repelled in hand-to-hand combat once night began to fall.

An account by Valentina Ivanovna Vlasenko, a surgeon from 103rd Medical Battalion of 95th Rifle Division, describes the conditions under which surgery was performed and also mentions the Germans' use of Blendkörper:

> An operating theatre was set up in one of the dug-outs sunk into the cliff of the high bank of the Volga. It is difficult to relate under what conditions it was necessary to operate. The constant shudder dislodged dirt from the walls and ceiling. Both were covered by bed sheets but this also didn't always help. 'Stalingrad' lights – lamps made from a shell casing and filled with petrol – provided a little light, but they often flared up, setting hands on fire, especially

37. Decades after the war, during the excavation of a narrow trench for a pipe in the park facing the Kommissarhaus, the tunnel was rediscovered. When workers broke into it, they discovered numerous skeletons, weapons and equipment. The breach was sealed up and the 'mass grave' left in peace. Only many years later was the tunnel re-opened and bodies retrieved for proper burial. If the Germans knew about the tunnel, they would surely have removed the bodies so that it was useable to them.

in small dug-outs where there was not enough oxygen. It was necessary to operate by the light of burning telephone wires that had been braided into bunches. Innovation was close at hand. Wounded men had it hard, were in continuous fighting for a long time, in trenches and dug-outs, tired, exhausted, dirty, and some were wounded several times. Many were burnt – the Germans tossed glass spheres filled with an inflammable liquid. Planes dropped tablets of inflammable phosphorus. The wounded men, being under the influence of continuous fighting, the constant danger of death, were hyped up and continued 'to be at war' on the operating table, describing in detail what they had been through. They required not only medical aid, but also attention, sympathy, a kind word.

In November, the difficult conditions become more complicated when the freezing period also began on the Volga, starting with slush ice. Communications with the left bank were interrupted, there were no bandages, there were no rations. Evacuation of wounded men stopped, many accumulated, and it was necessary to cover, warm, feed and tend to all of them. And all of this under continuous barrages, bombardments, close to sharp end. They were accommodated in dug-outs and crevices dug into the steep bank of the Volga, but there was no longer sufficient space there. Then a tent was erected under the ledge of the river bank. A drum-oven was set up in it and the wounded men were brought in. Warm and hot water came from the drum. But during the day the tent burnt down. All the wounded men were rescued in time.

– – –

With the neutralisation of the Kommissarhaus, which hung over any northward movement like the sword of Damocles, the Germans gained a substantial amount of operational freedom. Strong attacks by German infantry and armoured forces continued until the onset of darkness. As twilight set in, Pionier-Bataillon 162 relaunched its attack and again pushed along the Volga. Resistance was fierce and they were only able to occupy about another 70 metres of prestigious Volga frontage. The battalion only had a small base on the Volga, however, and this would have to be broadened by all means possible. Once darkness fell, small groups of German infantry operated against the reduced front-line of the Soviet bridgehead and continued to do so late into the night. The entire defensive sector of 138th Rifle Division was fired on by strong artillery, mortar and automatic machine-gun fire.

At 2030 hours, LI. Armeekorps reported to 6. Armee:

> In addition to two houses fortified like strongpoints, 305. Infanterie-Division gained the Kommissarhaus and about 70 metres of the Volga shoreline north-east of the fuel installation after tough fighting.

The entire corps took 53 prisoners, including 3 deserters, during the day. Most of those came from the Barrikady area. Later in the evening, 6. Armee reported to Heeresgruppe B that the objective of LI. Armeekorps for 14 November was to "clear out the conquered territory east of the gun factory and regroup for another attack on 15 November". This time, however, there would not be another large-scale attack. Tactics were revised. It was decided to concentrate efforts on capturing individual structures.

As the light faded from the cold sky, three days of unforgiving combat ended for Lyudnikov and his mauled riflemen. Lyudnikov later wrote that "fighting with grenades on individual floors and rooms became very important. The Germans often blew up those brave soldiers in the stairwells who did not surrender." The division noted in its daily report:

> During the course of the day, 138th Rifle Division waged fire fights and repulsed numerous attacks by superior enemy forces with fire and counterattacks, but by the end of the day, owing

to the utter annihilation of the garrisons of Dom 35, 36 and the P-shaped building – and not having any reserves to replenish the garrisons – the enemy occupied those buildings.

From documents found on bodies and statements made by prisoners, Lyudnikov established that several new units were operating against his division: elements of 131. and 132. Infanterie-Regiments, as well as Pionier-Bataillon 80, of 44. Infanterie-Division – which were the three components of Sturmkompanie 44 – and Pionier-Bataillon 162, whose previous deployment against Lieutenant-Colonel Kolobovnikov's guardsmen on 11 November had gone unnoticed by Soviet intelligence.

The division had been cut off from the rest of 62nd Army and its supplies. Despite sustaining huge losses, the Germans had captured the Tuvinsk area and gained control over the bank of the Volga, upsetting the usual delivery of supplies and reinforcements. Instead, everything had to be transported by hand throughout the night, and the division was forced to allocate up to 35% of its strength for this task. Cut off from the rest of the army, the division was in more and more need of war materials and rations. Without supplies, the division would wither and die. Ammunition and food supplies were critically low, so much so that at the end of the day, there was only enough left for a further 24 hours. Resupply in the foreseeable future was doubtful because conditions on the river rapidly deteriorated. A thick slurry of ice covered the river's surface and ice floes logjammed in certain sectors, threatening not only 138th Rifle Division but also the entire 62nd Army with starvation of ammunition, food and replacements. Two tugboats, 'Emelyan Pugachev' and tugboat No. 2, attempted to deliver 90th Rifle Regiment to Banny Gully but the vessels could not make their way through the ice floes on the Kuropatki River and so turned back to Tumak. The regiment would only be delivered to the west bank two days later – on 15 November.[38]

Throughout the entire day, the Germans laid down intensive artillery and mortar fire on the river crossings, along Zaitsevsky Island and on the east bank of the Volga. More than one and a half thousand mortar rounds were fired.

Lyudnikov's division estimated the losses it had inflicted on the Germans: captured were 1 prisoner, 1 heavy machine-gun, 4 light machine-guns, 45 rifles and 5 submachine-guns. Destroyed were 450 soldiers and officers, an anti-tank gun, two mortars, 5 machine-guns, one tank was knocked out and a mortar battery was suppressed.

In return for those minor successes, the division suffered appalling casualties: 5 officers, 2 NCOs and 14 enlisted men killed, 6 officers, 13 NCOs and 72 enlisted men wounded, and 6 officers, 4 NCOs and 23 enlisted men who suffered other fates[39], a total of 145 men.

Combat and numerical strength of the division as at 1700 hours:

Total number of people in the division – 2051, but of those, only 750 were on west bank of the Volga. Active soldiers on the west bank were as follows:

344th Rifle Regiment: 157 men, 130 rifles, 22 PPSh, 1 heavy machine-gun, 4 anti-tank rifles and 2 light machine-guns.

650th Rifle Regiment: 35 men, 24 rifles, 9 PPSh, 1 heavy machine-gun, 1 anti-tank rifle and 6 mortars.

768th Rifle Regiment: 49 men, 41 rifles, 1 DShK, 5 PPSh, 1 45mm gun and 2 mortars.

230th Anti-Tank Battalion: 2 anti-tank guns.

---

38. On that day, 'Spartakovets' and 3 armoured boats delivered 1500 men. Those same boats evacuated 543 wounded men.
39. Soviet documents are loathe to use the terms 'missing' or 'captured'.

At 1840 hours, LI. Armeekorps ordered that the panzer company supporting 305. Infanterie-Division be relieved. The teletype message said:

> The panzer company of 14. Panzer-Division participating in the scheduled operations of 305. Infanterie-Division on 14 November will subsequently be relieved and released to Gruppe Seydel so that it can be returned to 14. Panzer-Division as quickly as possible. 24. Panzer-Division will detach one panzer schwadron to 305. Infanterie-Division. Arrival on the afternoon of 14 November. Supply is to be directly arranged with 305. Infanterie-Division.

There was slight confusion as to whether the company from 14. Panzer-Division could still be used for actions planned for 14 November. A telephone called at 2135 hours clarified the matter:

> The panzer company of 14. Panzer-Division will still participate in the operation on 14 November but will then be released by 305. Infanterie-Division to Gruppe Seydel. Gruppe Seydel will set the panzer company in march to 14. Panzer-Division as soon as possible.

That night, Oberzahlmeister Erich Bauchspiess, paymaster of Pionier-Bataillon 336, wrote a letter home:

> Our brief detachment that was to have only been for a short period will take longer. The fighting for the last ruins of St[alingrad] is shaping up to be the most bitter ever witnessed. Less than one third of the city is still to be taken. Every ruined house must be taken individually and every operation requires lengthy preparation, making out the enemy nests and then supplying the assault troops with sufficient fire protection. Throughout the day and night, planes and artillery drop bombs and shell after shell into the rubble. We have achieved some splendid successes, as yesterday's Wehrmacht report states, but it only goes forward step by step. Temperatures of -20 degrees naturally hamper our attack tempo. Well, even if it takes weeks, Stalingrad will fall. Then, what we are longing for is a withdrawal back to our lovely bunkers. The weather has been exceptionally fair for my responsibilities. The roads are firm, no snow has fallen and today a still warming sun shines, so for me the weather could not be better. Until now, everything has gone all right…

One of Bauchspiess's men in the rear echelon, Gefreiter Wilhelm Giebeler, a cook, began to realise that things were not going 'all right' for the battalion. Working at his field-kitchen in the rear, west of the Barrikady, Giebeler waited for the arrival of his friend, a messenger, who would come to collect the evening meal for his company. Ever since the battle for the Barrikady began, this friend had kept him informed of the action at the front. The first day, he had come back and told him everything was going well; the next he had returned with snapshots, letters, and other personal effects of men Giebeler had known well. He told the cook to send them on to their next-of-kin. By now Giebeler had hundreds of small bundles to mail back to Germany. Listening to the symphony of shells and grenades exploding to the east, he thumbed through the letters and pictures and waited for his friend to make his nightly visit. But the man did not appear. Giebeler new saw him again – nor any other soldier of Pionier-Bataillon 336.

Casualties for 13 November, 1942:	
138th Rifle Division:	21 killed, 91 wounded, 33 for other reasons, a total of 145 men
305. Infanterie-Division:	about 80 men without the pioneer battalions (partial report only)
389. Infanterie-Division:	2 men killed and 4 men wounded

14 November, 1942

An unnamed soldier from 2./Pionier-Bataillon 336 reports: "On the morning of 14 November came the news that Pionier-Bataillon 162 had reached the Volga. We were regrouped and added to the breakthrough position with the remnants of other units. The pioneers of Pionier-Bataillon 162 were breathing easier when we arrived there. We immediately saw how critical the situation was. The Russians had entrenched themselves in the bunkers along the river bank. Shells from the Soviet artillery on the other bank roared over toward us incessantly."

– – –

At 0830 hours, 62nd Army commander Chuikov ordered 95th Rifle Division and the composite regiment of 193rd Rifle Division to attack northward during the day so as to create a front and link up with 138th Rifle Division. Combat Order No. 241 read as follows:

> The enemy, having broken through the front of 95th Rifle Division's defensive sector, has reached the bank of the Volga. 241st Rifle Regiment, having abandoned its positions, has exposed the left flank of 138th Rifle Division and through that created a threat to its emplacements.
>
> Attached to 95th Rifle Division is 3/92nd Rifle Brigade, a company of submachine-gunners from 92nd Rifle Brigade and a composite rifle regiment of 193rd Rifle Division. During the course of 14.11.42, strike north with the right flank along the Volga bank to restore the front-line within 95th Rifle Division's boundaries and gain direct communication with units of 138th Rifle Division.
>
> The Army artillery chief will support the operations of 95th Rifle Division with artillery fire.

Gorishny sent back a progress report to 62nd Army:

> The division has commenced implementation of Combat Order No. 241. It consists of: 241st Rifle Regiment – 70 men; 3/92nd Rifle Brigade – 22 men; composite regiment of 193rd Rifle Division – 149 men, plus some removed from the sector of 161st Rifle Regiment – 125 men.[40]
>
> The company of submachine-gunners from 3/92nd Rifle Brigade with 79 men, which has arrived, was intended for 241st Rifle Regiment but is now transferred to the control of the commander of the composite regiment of 193rd Rifle Division.
>
> Beginning of the attack: 2000 on 14.11.

The artillery regiment of Gurtiev's[41] 308th Rifle Division, the 1011th, had distinguished itself in earlier battles through its extraordinarily high accuracy. It remained in its emplacements on the eastern bank after the remnants of the rifle units had been handed over to 138th Rifle Division in early November and the remaining command elements withdrawn. Its regiment commander, Major G.A. Fugenfirov, was – as always – at the front in his observation post, now ready to bring down the devastating fire of his 122mm and 76mm guns in support of Gorishny's Division.

General Krylov describes how a few units were scraped together to help Gorishny:

> Initially, it was still hoped that Lyudnikov would not be cut off for long. To reinforce 95th Rifle Division, which had turned its front to the north, the composite regiment of the

---

40. Two companies were extracted and sent to 241st Rifle Regiment.

41. Gurtiev, Major-General Leonty Nikolayevich, HotSU; 308th Rifle Division; born 14 July, 1891 in Shemakha. Killed in action, 3 August, 1943 near Orel.

Smekhotvorov Division – which had until now been protecting the ferry landing – was sent with all haste, as were two battalions of 92nd Rifle Brigade that had been replenished with Pacific Fleet marines and had already arrived on our bank. They were our reserve for the counterattack being prepared against Mamayev Kurgan and the Krasny Oktyabr factory. All these troops had the task of pushing the Germans back from the Volga and re-establishing a continuous front across the breakthrough position.

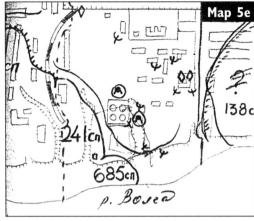

The situation around the fuel tanks, 14 November, 1942. German mortar and MG positions are shown.

The 62nd Army war diary summed up the actions on this sector:

> 95th Rifle Division, with 3/92nd Rifle Brigade and the composite regiment of 193rd Rifle Division, took part in intense fighting for the restoration of the position on the sector of 241st Rifle Regiment with the purpose of regaining a continuous front-line and establishing direct contact with units of 138th Rifle Division. Fighting continues in the area of the fuel tanks. Left-flank units of the division conduct combat from their previous positions.

The composite regiment recorded the course of the attack in its journal:

> By the morning of 14.11.42, a company of submachine-gunners from 92nd Rifle Brigade (75 men) had arrived as reinforcements for the regiment and the regiment attacked once more – on its own – without the assistance 95th Rifle Division.

> We went over to the offensive at 0930, preceded by 15 minutes of artillery preparation by three artillery regiments and one army regiment, but in view of insufficient orientation of the artillerymen about target acquisition by rifle commanders and observation posts, the artillery fire provided almost no advantage. All attempts by the regiment to break through the gully were again beaten back by enemy firing points. At 1400 on 14.11.42, on the regiment's area of operation, the enemy launched a counterattack with a company of infantry but pulled back to their starting positions after suffering losses of up to 55 men. At the same time as this, enemy forces in company strength that began an attack near the fuel tanks on the sector of 241st Rifle Regiment were not beaten off.

> After repulsion of the enemy attack, the regiment remained on the line reached on the morning of 13.11.42.

– – –

The Germans did not launch their attacks at dawn this time. Instead, the morning hours were used to bombard the Soviet positions with copious quantities of artillery and mortar rounds. Particular attention was paid to the front-line bastions but all buildings in the area were softened up. Panzers and assault guns stood back in covered positions and sent shell after shell into their brick targets while sheafs of machine-gun fire swept through the narrow defensive sector. Soviet garrisons waited out the bombardments in their cellars. Major Pechenyuk's command post in Dom 64 received a savage mauling from artillery and tank fire. The structure was totally destroyed and the roof of the basement heavily damaged.

At 0930 hours, the same time as the Soviet attack on the fuel tanks, the Germans finally launched their attack from the area of Halls 3 and 4 of the Barrikady factory. Spearheaded by two companies from Pionier-Bataillon 336 – Oberleutnant Karl-Heinz Hullen's 1.

Kompanie and Oberleutnant Bernhard Ziesch's 3. Kompanie – and elements of Oberleutnant Kindler's Sturmkompanie 44, the attack was aimed directly at two houses on the boundary between Konovalenko's 344th Regiment and Pechenyuk's 650th Regiment. Their targets: Dom 37 and 38. Dom 37 was defended by the remnants of all three rifle battalions from 650th Rifle Regiment. Men from Captain Toporkov's 1st Rifle Battalion were the original garrison but they had incorporated soldiers from the other two battalions who had fallen back after the loss of Dom 35 and 36 the previous day. Dom 38, on the other hand, belonged to 344th Rifle Regiment, and had been designated 'Strongpoint No. 4' in 1st Rifle Battalion's chain of four redoubts. The garrison of the house had never been numerous: on 9 November, it consisted of seven soldiers plus their garrison chief, assistant

Above: Pre-war Pribaltiskaya Street. From left: Haus 63 [Dom 29], Haus 64 [Dom 30], Haus 65 [Dom 33], Haus 66 [Dom 35] and Haus 67 [Dom 38].
Below: Immediately after the war. Instead of demolishing the ruins, local authorities 'renovated' the buildings by patching up holes and missing sections with new brickwork. This measure saved time and valuable resources (every brick was needed for the reconstruction of the city).

company commander Lieutenant I.S. Pogrebnyak. A few of those men had become casualties in the previous three days but a few reinforcements had taken their place.

Of the two targets, Dom 37 was definitely the more formidable. It was twice the size of Dom 38, had larger fields of fire and was more easily supported by garrisons in other buildings. Also, Dom 38 would be easier to take second rather than vice versa. The decision was taken to seize Dom 37 first.

At 0930 hours, darting forward under a shroud of artillery support, the German assault groups swiftly crossed the open ground and found their routes unhindered by obstacles, mines or wire. The combat journal of 138th Rifle Division states that "the enemy undertook an offensive with the strength of up to a company of infantry, organised into groups of 30-40 soldiers each, and supported by tanks". The violent artillery barrages had effectively levelled any barricades, while the around-the-clock fusillade from machine-guns and small-arms had prevented Soviet engineers from erecting effective defensive barriers. At Dom 37, the pioneer squads reformed in the lee of the building and systematically blasted their way into the ground floor. The Soviet garrison was forced into the cellar. A few offered some resistance in the central stairwell but making headway up to the ground floor was near impossible in the face of the heavily armed pioneers. The death of several riflemen in the massive blast of a demolition charge was a grim harbinger of what awaited them all if they remained down in the cellar, therefore, the survivors decided to abandon the building. Carrying their wounded, they exited the cellar using a trench that cut across the road to Dom 41, a major strongpoint of the neighbouring 344th Rifle Regiment. With that, the house passed into German hands.

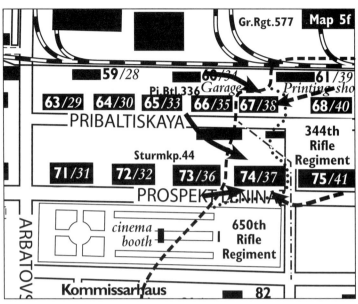

Battle for Dom 37 [Haus 74] and Dom 38 [Haus 67], 14 November, 1942.

The next assault began at 1100 hours. Artillery and tank fire had thoroughly smashed Dom 38. Its second storey had been abraded down to floor level, leaving the ground storey supporting nothing but chunks of masonry and occasional remnants of internal walls. Lieutenant Pogrebnyak's tiny garrison, stupefied and benumbed by the countless large-calibre strikes on their bastion, still offered stubborn resistance when the German assault groups pushed in through the windows. Soviet observers estimated that the Germans employed 150 men against the building: the true figure was approximately half that. A combat report later written by 344th Rifle Regiment stated that their garrison in Dom 38 had been wiped out but evidence proves that Lieutenant Pogrebnyak managed to survive and fall back to the main positions. Others with him probably did the same. Lyudnikov reported to 62nd Army: "Dom 38 was destroyed at 1030. The Germans have rushed into the ruins of the house. The small garrison fought fiercely for one and a half hour with the hitlerites that had broken in. Again and again we are convinced that each survivor counts for ten." The new German tactic of storming one building at a time seemed to be paying dividends. 305. Infanterie-Division sent off a report to LI. Armeekorps stating that they had easily captured Dom 67 and 74.

The soldiers of 1st Rifle Battalion, under the command of Lieutenant G.V. Tolkachev[42], distinguished themselves. After the heavy artillery strike a group of German infantry, together with some panzers, managed to break into the rear of the battalion, creating the threat of encirclement. But not one of the soldiers wavered. Accurate fire from the machine-gun of Sergeant Z.K. Yamshchikov shot away at the enemy. Wounded, and losing consciousness, he fired until his last breath and died, but did not let go of his weapon. A group of German submachine-gunners got into a building's garage and laid down flanking fire. Senior-Sergeant Z. I.Goryukhin crept up to the building with five soldiers and threw grenades at the Germans. Tolkachev skillfully directed the fighting, appearing where it was most intense and where his presence was needed. Tolkachev himself quite often took submachine-gun in hand and – together with his men – threw the Germans back. He counted numerous German corpses after fighting near a dug-out.

---

42. Tolkachev, Major Grigory Vasiliyevich, HotSU; 1/344th RR; born 1919, killed 15 November, 1943 near Zhitomir.

The refugees of 650th Rifle Regiment from Dom 37 used their asylum in Dom 41 to plan a counterattack. No time could be lost in recapturing it because they knew the Germans would be feverishly preparing it for defence. At noon, together with groups from 2nd Rifle Battalion of 344th Rifle Regiment, they launched a well-organised counterattack against the new occupants in Dom 37. Covered by heavy fire from Dom 41, they rushed the building with the aim of gaining entry through the windows because their old escape route through the northern cellar wall had been promptly blocked and mined. The pioneers had made effective use of the two and a half hours that had elapsed since they captured the building: apart from blocking the trench leading into the cellar, they rigged explosive charges in the main entrance facing Prospekt Lenina, installed booby-traps in some windows and laid a few mines. The Soviet storm groups stumbled across some of these devices. Trip-wires connected to S-mines brutally slay several riflemen trying to clamber through one window. Despite the heavy toll caused by the mines, the Soviets managed to get into the house and – after a short but violent struggle – forced the Germans out. At 1220 hours, the building was returned to Soviet possession.

At 1300 hours, Lieutenant Tolkachev's 1st Rifle Battalion of 344th Rifle Regiment launched a counterattack to regain their lost strongpoint, the crumbling Dom 38. The actions of this storm group were supported by the artillery emplaced on Zaitsevsky Island. The artillerymen fired 200 rounds. 138th Rifle Division later reported that "excellent use of mines by the enemy slowed down operations".

Tolkachev's riflemen prevailed and reclaimed ownership of the battered building by 1320 hours. For courage shown during the fighting, every soldier and officer of the battalion – no more than a couple of dozen – were distinguished with government awards, and Tolkachev was the first bearer of the Alexander Nevsky award in the division. Konovalenko reported that the Germans in both buildings had been destroyed but the truth was somewhat different: 305. Infanterie-Division reported that "in the face of an enemy counterattack with superior forces, the assault groups had to be pulled back to their starting positions". During the battle, Konovalenko's men captured 1 heavy and 3 light machine-guns, more than 25 rifles, numerous grenades and about 40 kilograms of explosives. They also stated that they had inflicted heavy casualties on the enemy, annihilating up to 85 officers and soldiers.[43]

---

43. Precise German casualty figures are not available, but what is known is that Oberleutnant Ziesch's 3. Kompanie suffered losses of 2 killed and 8 wounded. The dead were Pionier Anton Chowanietz and Obergefreiter Horst Rasche. The wounded were Pionier Wilhelm Deubner, Stabsgefreiter Werner Frey, Gefreiter Kurt Körner, Gefreiter Erich Lehmann, Gefreiter Heinz Mothes, Gefreiter Werner Oltscher, Pionier Heinz Pfeifer and Obergefreiter Walter Töpfer. The casualties of Oberleutnant Hullen's 1. Kompanie are not known, but it seems no fatalities were incurred. Hullen himself was wounded by a bullet through his right upper arm and sent to a field-hospital. Oberleutnant Bernd Ehringhaus, a platoon commander in Ziesch's 3. Kompanie, was appointed commander of 1. Kompanie.

Chowanietz, Pionier Anton, 3./Pi.Btl.336; born 15 October, 1909 in Chorzow. Killed in action, 13 November, 1942 in Stalingrad.

Rasche, Obergefreiter Horst, 3./Pi.Btl.336; born 10 March, 1914 in Stolpen. Killed in action, 13 November, 1942 in Stalingrad.

Deubner, Pionier Wilhelm, 3./Pi.Btl.336; born 12 July, 1908 in Hannover. No further information known.

Frey, Stabsgefreiter Werner, 3./Pi.Btl.336; born 30 October, 1914 in Tilsit-Gumbinnen. No further information known.

Körner, Gefreiter Kurt, 3./Pi.Btl.336; born 18 January, 1909 in Brunndöbra. No further information known.

Lehmann, Gefreiter Erich, 3./Pi.Btl.336; born 8 December, 1911 in Holzhausen. No further information known.

Mothes, Gefreiter Heinz, 3./Pi.Btl.336; born 30 April, 1922 in Aue. Missing in action, 28 August, 1944.

Oltscher, Gefreiter Werner, 3./Pi.Btl.336; born 26 January, 1913 in Neundorf bei Plauen. No further information known.

Pfeifer, Pionier Heinz, 3./Pi.Btl.336; born 2 June, 1922 in Kleinzschocher. No further information known.

Töpfer, Obergefreiter Walter, 3./Pi.Btl.336; born 7 October, 1910 in Leimbach. No further information known.

Ehringhaus, Oberleutnant Bernd, 1./Pi.Btl.336; born 7 September, 1917. Missing in action, 6 January, 1943 in Stalingrad, but probably survived captivity. See Appendix 2 (page 571) for more details.

The commander of Sturmkompanie 44, Oberleutnant Willi Kindler, was heavily wounded during the day's fighting and was evacuated from the battlefield. It is not certain who took command of the Sturmkompanie because the only other officer, Leutnant Willmitzer, had been killed the previous day. Another officer, Leutnant Hans von Wartburg[44], commander of 11./Grenadier-Regiment 131 back on 44. Infanterie-Division's defensive line along the Don river, had been assigned to the Sturmkompanie but a blessing in disguise saved him from the carnage in the Barrikady:

> On the day of my detachment, I was ill with a severe case of jaundice and had a temperature of 41°. I stayed with my company until 20 November and only then was I admitted to the divisional hospital. In any case, I did not serve one day with the Sturmkompanie.

Leutnant von Wartburg was flown out of the pocket on the afternoon of 1 December, 1942. As for the new commander of the Sturmkompanie from 14 November onwards, it is possible that the role was taken on by the remaining senior NCO, Unteroffizier Kurt Janssen[45].

On the Soviet side, losses for 138th Rifle Division had not been light: 22 killed and 93 wounded, a total of 115 men. Particularly heavy casualties were caused by rocket projectiles. Throughout the day, the Luftwaffe circled over the division and attacked Zaitsevsky Island, the east bank of the Volga and Lyudnikov's divisional command post. 344th Rifle Regiment also lost 1 heavy machine-gun and a 45mm artillery piece.

Active soldiers in the rifle regiments: 244 men with 164 rifles, 70 PPSh, 2 light machine-gun, 5 anti-tank rifles, 2 heavy machine-guns, 6 mortars and 2 anti-tank guns.

At 1600 hours, the Germans started softening up the front-lines of 344th and 650th Rifle Regiments and methodically laying down artillery and mortar fire. The forward line was under heavy machine-gun fire. Pechenyuk's observers spotted individual soldiers and small groups of Germans running about near the 5-storey white house, the fuel tanks and towards the bank of the Volga.

At 1640 hours, LI. Armeekorps reported to 6. Armee: "At the moment, an attack (about 50 men) from the south-east towards the fuel installation."

– – –

Lyudnikov's division would certainly not have survived without its excellent artillery support. Lyudnikov recalls the herculean feats performed by his divisional artillery:

> In all these grim days and nights, side by side with the infantrymen, machine-gunners, engineers and signalmen, miracles of courage and an ability to carry on accurate, telling, and timely fire were displayed by our artillerymen. But towards the evening of 14 November they too ran out of ammunition, while the enemy prepared a fresh attack. That is a moment I shall always remember. Lieutenant-Colonel Tychinsky, our division's artillery commander, was standing beside me and telephoning orders to commanders of artillery units to open up with a barrage along the front held by 344th Rifle Regiment in order to halt the Germans. He insisted on regimental commanders repeating how much ammunition they had, and I saw the frown on his face deepening. Finishing the conversation, he replaced the receiver, took his cap off and all but threw it to the ground.
>
> 'No more', he said angrily.

---

44. Wartburg, Leutnant Hans von, 11./Gr.Rgt.131; born 20 August, 1920 in Salzburg. Still alive in 2005. See Appendix 3 (page 581) for more details.

45. Janssen, Unteroffizier Kurt, 11./Gr.Rgt.131; born 7 April, 1910 in Ürdingen. Died April 1943 in Frolov POW camp.

'What's no more?' I asked.

'No more shells. All batteries report zero.'

I knew that artillery units always left a small emergency supply of shells
for self-defence. Our division's artillery was positioned on the east bank
of the Volga, and I decided that the situation called for the use of this
reserve. I said to Tychinsky: 'Time does not wait. The Germans are
about to attack. Order your men to use their emergency supply.'

Within minutes our artillery delivered a devastating barrage. The
enemy was thrown back with huge losses. The news that our artillery
had repulsed the enemy with zero shells quickly spread throughout
the division and from that day on, whenever the talk was about
artillerymen, the troops of our division would say affectionately:
'Those boys can beat back the Nazis even with zero shells.'

*Colonel Sergei Yakovlevich
Tychinsky, artillery commander
of 138th Rifle Division.*

The divisional and attached artillery units occupied positions
on the left bank of the Volga in the area of Starenky farm. In
addition, two batteries of 292nd Separate Mortar Battalion were
emplaced on Zaitsevsky Island. Artillery units were assigned to the rifle regiments and had
observation posts within the combat ranks of the infantry. Their presence allowed swift
reactions to changing conditions. Supporting 344th Rifle Regiment with its 76mm guns
was Captain V.G. Sokolov's 295th Artillery Regiment (138th Rifle Division); supporting
650th Rifle Regiment were the 76mm anti-tank guns of Captain N.S. Koshelevich's 397th
Tank Destroyer Artillery Regiment; and supporting 768th Rifle Regiment with its 122mm
and 76mm guns was Guards Major Yurov's 86th Guards Artillery Regiment (37th Guards
Rifle Division). Directly subordinated to 138th Rifle Division were 292nd Separate Mortar
Battalion with its 25 or so 120mm mortars, and the remnants of Senior-Lieutenant
Aleksandr Vladimirovich Istratov's 230th Anti-Tank Battalion, now consisting of only two
45mm guns and 16 men. However, the gunners performed sterling service, knocking out
several German tanks and numerous machine-guns. Later in the month, Istratov was
awarded the Red Star, while Lieutenant Yakov Ivanovich Rutikov, Senior-Sergeant Afanasi
Ivanovich Sinegub and Red Army man Dmitri Matveyevich Mikhailenko received the 'For
Bravery' medal.

General Krylov had a very good opinion of 397th Tank Destroyer Artillery Regiment:
"Located in the positions of 138th Rifle Division was the observation post of the anti-tank
regiment of Captain N.S. Koshelevich, which had cooperated earlier with this division. He
belonged to our best anti-tank regiment. His artillery observers, equipped with radio
equipment, secured very effective support." And one of Captain Koshelevich's best men –
battery commander Senior-Lieutenant Nikolai Petrovich Stepanov – was soon to receive
the Red Star.

After General Zholudev's 37th Guards Division was seriously mauled by the fierce
German assaults from 14 October onward, the surviving remnants were eventually lumped
together in Lieutenant-Colonel Kolobovnikov's 118th Guards Rifle Regiment. In early
November, this composite regiment was subordinated to Lyudnikov's division and assigned
a sector next to Gunyaga's 768th Rifle Regiment. Both were supported by artillery fire from
Major Yurov's 86th Guards Artillery Regiment. As we have seen, with the exception of 7
men, Kolobovnikov's guardsmen were all killed off on 11 November. Despite the fact that it
no longer had any of its own men to support, the staff of 86th Guards Artillery Regiment

stayed in Stalingrad. The regiment continued to give supportive fire to the units of Lyudnikov's division and remained in its positions on Zaitsevsky Island. Major Yurov later reported to 37th Guards Division's chief-of-staff Brushko:

> The enemy moved closer all the time. There was 300 metres of river bank to the right our command post, water could not be taken from the Volga. There was no food…

The German encirclement of Lyudnikov's division and their ability to control the river caused General Zholudev to lose contact with his artillerymen still in Stalingrad. He therefore ordered that the lines of communication be re-opened:

> During the night of 13 to 14 November 1942, deliver a motor boat or dinghy by any means possible to the area of the command post of artillery commander Major Yurov (command post in its previous position) to establish communications with the artillery commander and to evacuate the wounded Second-Lieutenant Lavrenev and Letukov… The route along the riverbank from Ferry No. 62 to Major Yurov is cut off by the Germans…

It is unknown whether Lavrenev and Letukov were rescued.

In general, communications were maintained via radio. Fire control of the division's artillery was centralised and handled by Lieutenant-Colonel Tychinsky and his staff from the divisional command post. General Krylov thought highly of him:

> Colonel Lyudnikov was particularly proud of his division's artillery regiment and its first-rate artillery commander, S.Y. Tychinsky. Now, as the army artillery commander Pozharski had discovered, the division commander fixed a special signal for his artillery to request that they fire on his command post. He demanded from them that they immediately take this target under fire in case of the signal.

- - -

At 2035 hours, LI. Armeekorps summed up the day's events for 6. Armee:

> The stormtroop operations of 305. Infanterie-Division had no success as a result of counterattacks by superior enemy forces. Continual and heavy artillery and mortar fire on our forward line east of the gun factory. An attack against the fuel installation from the south-east was repulsed. Our artillery successfully combated crossing sites, enemy bunkers, rocket-launchers and artillery batteries. One Volga rowboat was sunk.
>
> Aim for 15 November: storm group operation of 305. Infanterie-Division against Haus 81 and 85, 389. Infanterie-Division against 'Rote Haus'.

- - -

At the end of the day, 344th Rifle Regiment only had enough cartridges and grenades left for one day of fighting. The same applied for rations. 138th Rifle Division had used up most of its supplies, so increasing use was to be made of those captured from the Germans. The situation was becoming increasingly dire and 62nd Army staff were growing concerned. Army chief-of-staff General Krylov wrote:

> In front of me lies a photocopy of a report sent by army commander Chuikov to the Front War Council on the evening of 14 November: 'I'm worried about 138th Rifle Division. The enemy is attacking them with large forces. We're really helping them with artillery and Katyushas, but we do not have more forces…' Chuikov requested that cartridges, hand grenades and chocolate be dropped on the division's positions by airplanes and ordered the

garrison on Zaitsevsky Island to construct a landing stage there (between Zaitsevsky Island and the small Lyudnikov 'bridgehead' lay the small arm of the river called Denezhnaya Volozhka, which froze earlier than the rest of the Volga).

A report on a blank form received from the Front command post had the following resolution from General A. I. Yeremenko[46] in spirited letters: 'The enemy should not be allowed to wipe out 138th Rifle Division…' Then followed instructions about strengthening support for the severed division by the Front artillery and other means of assistance.

From the combat journal of 138th Rifle Division:

Considering that the division is now fighting without food or war materials, the defence being offered by the men of the division, defending the right bank of the Volga, is the perfect example of heroism.

In one battle, Sergeant-Major Belotyukov and Sergeant Makhmudov each killed three Germans and took one prisoner. Other soldiers followed their example and, not even heeding the fact that they had been wounded numerous times, launched themselves into counterattacks, throwing back the maddened occupiers. Through these deeds they were accepted into the Communist Party and given military decorations.

Political agitator of 344th Rifle Regiment, Lieutenant Vechaiken, teaches Communists throughout the battle through his own deeds. He personally shot seven Germans with his rifle.

Together with the heroic actions of the soldiers of 138th Rifle Division, there were also actions which were the opposite. Sergeant-Major Shpak, Communist Party candidate, had earlier been awarded the 'For Bravery' medal, but upon receiving an insignificant wound, left the field of battle and crossed to the east bank of the Volga. The division commander took away his medal and reduced his rank to private. Sergeant-Major Shpak lost his candidacy for the party.

– – –

In the German rear, life continued for the vast bulk of men for whom the fighting was but a dull rumble on the horizon. Fallen comrades, burgeoning cemeteries and fleeting glimpses of torn bodies in ambulances, however, brought home the bloody drama being played out. Gefreiter Willi Füssinger belonged to the supply train of 1./Pionier-Bataillon 305 and was spared the perils of front-line duty, but every evening he undertook the dangerous job of bringing supplies forward to his company in position near the Apotheke. In a letter home, he wrote:

Gefreiter Willi Füssinger, 1./Pi.Btl.305.

The kilo package with winter things arrived safely in these days, as well as the small package with gingerbread and writing paper. Many thanks for it all. The winter things are already needed, it is 20 below here. In the last few days, my health did not leave a lot to be desired, I couldn't eat anything for 4 days, but everything is now back in order. Hans Bernhart[47,48] is now back here again, has come back into this right mess. However, I have still not met up with him but my

46. Yeremenko, Marshall of the Soviet Union Andrei Ivanovich, HotSU; Stalingrad Front; born 14 October, 1892 in Markovka. Died 19 November, 1970.

47. Bernhart, Stabsgefreiter Hans 1./Gr.Rgt.578; born 20 July, 1908 in Bodnegg. Missing in action, January 1943 in Stalingrad.

48. Füssinger and Bernhart came from the same close-knit municipality of Bodnegg.

Rations are brought forward to the combat troops. Each company detailed a few men to carry supplies to the front. Apart from a food container on his back, the first soldier carries a pair of boots – either repaired or new – for a comrade up front. The second man carries a tent-quarter full of bread over his shoulder. Despite their relaxed appearance, these men are close to the front-line: on the left is Hall 2 [Workshop 1], in the middle is Hall 6c [Workshop 21/26].

company is located next to his unit up front along the Volga. Every evening I hope to meet him when I take supplies forward. I will probably only see him when we are finally finished in Stalingrad, with these few metres where the Russian still sit. Nobody can imagine the fighting in Stalingrad, it is the heaviest in this war, and whoever has experienced it and still gets out will be able to proudly say that they had a guardian angel, and many have learned to pray here. Taking supplies to the front is always very difficult…

Füssinger's commander was also in the rear. After three days of tough fighting, Hauptmann Wilhelm Traub[49], commander of Pionier-Bataillon 305, returned to his headquarters in Gorodische in the Stalingrad hinterland, and no-one begrudged him this because 14 November was his birthday. He recorded his thoughts in a letter to his wife:

Early today, after four days in Stalingrad, I returned to our quarters, one good reason being to thoroughly wash myself and shave for my birthday. The other reason is that I wanted to read my incoming birthday mail and finally, tonight, as a celebration for the day, I want to get a good night's rest.

Early today I thoroughly completed my washing and shaving and feel reborn; with the birthday mail there was unfortunately nothing of value, neither from you nor anyone else. I now hope to get the expected mail tomorrow. I will get a good sleep tonight and not allow myself to be disturbed by the Russian pilots.

49. Traub, Major Wilhelm, Pi.Btl.305; born 14 November, 1895 in Helmstedt. Missing in action, February 1943 in Stalingrad. See Appendix 2 (page 579) for more details.

In the past days we have had heavy combat. We had to take each house one by one from the Bolsheviks in hand-to-hand combat. In the remaining houses, the Russians have turned them into fortresses. Despite this we have reached the Volga in some places and I believe the fighting in our sector will end within a week at the latest. Then, the metallurgical works and chemical factory south of us must be captured, which will take somewhat longer, and then Stalingrad will be completely conquered. The fighting here – and everyone agrees about this – will be the high point of this present war and can certainly be compared with the battle of Verdun in the First World War.

Tonight I invited the adjutant, another Leutnant and the Zahlmeister[50] to a small birthday celebration. The two remaining officers that I have in the battalion[51] are in their positions at the front. The third company is led by a Feldwebel[52]. However, I hope that some of the lightly wounded officers will soon return.

Captured by LI. Armeekorps on 14 November: 50 prisoners, including 16 deserters.

Casualties for 14 November, 1942:
138th Rifle Division: 22 killed, 93 wounded, a total of 115 men
305. Infanterie-Division: 17 men killed, 1 officer and 57 men wounded
389. Infanterie-Division: 2 men killed and 2 men wounded

15 November, 1942

In the next letter to his wife, Hauptmann Traub recounted his birthday celebrations from the previous evening:

Today the many letters I have been ardently awaiting have arrived… In addition, my birthday parcel also arrived, for everything my thanks. Now my promotion to Major can proceed, I have enough epaulets, thank you. I celebrated my birthday yesterday evening with the adjutant, the doctor and the Zahlmeister, enjoying a number of bottles of wine. We finally closed the festivity by drinking a bottle of Sekt. The other three officers – more I don't have in the battalion – were at their posts and naturally could not be with us.

I wanted to go to the front this afternoon but have an appointment with the divisional commander this evening. I'll drive out again tomorrow. I slept well last night. There were no enemy planes, I would not have heard them anyway, I was too tired.

He also described other personal aspects affecting him:

Familie Traub

Hauptmann Wilhelm Traub, commander of Pionier-Bataillon 305.

50. Keppler, Oberzahlmeister Max; Pi.Btl.305; born 7 March, 1909 in Kirchheim. Missing in action, January 1943 in Stalingrad. See Appendix 2 (page 574) for more details.
51. These two officers were Leutnant Hingst commanding 2. Kompanie and Oberleutnant Staiger commanding 3. Kompanie.
52. Feldwebel Langendörfer took command of 1. Kompanie after the wounding of Leutnant Zorn on 12 November, 1942.

We are at present well supplied with tobacco and alcohol. I don't have any problem with you keeping the cigarettes so when I am next on leave, I think it will be February or March, I'll have something to smoke at home… The weather here is quite tolerable. We have about 10° of frost but the wind has eased, so one can bear it reasonably well. We are well supplied with warm clothing. I have not yet begun to wear my good pullover, I'll wait until it becomes colder… We still believe, however, that the Russians are at the end of their tether. Some days ago we took prisoners from a naval NCO school in Vladivostok[53]. It is noteworthy that they have to put such people into action.

- - -

The night generally passed quietly. Strengthening Soviet harassment fire came down on the fuel installation. A small Soviet assault north along the Volga bank against the right wing of 305. Infanterie-Division was repulsed.

The combat journal of 650th Rifle Regiment reports about the beginning of the German attacks on this day:

> After a short artillery preparation, the enemy – with a strength of up to a company of infantry – undertook an advance on our left and right flank at 0410 from the direction of the P-shaped structure, Dom 35 and 36 in an attempt to take over Dom 37, the structure earlier used as a command post and the unfinished building, which is 60-70 metres from the Volga.

Senior-Lieutenant Charashvili and his artillerymen were still positioned in the ruins of the unfinished building:

> In the morning the Germans began uninterrupted mortar and artillery shelling on the unfinished U-shaped building, as well as the command post of 650th Rifle Regiment. With an anti-tank rifle, I was able to hit two German tanks – one next to the command post, 10-15 metres from the structure, the other next to the P-shaped house, from which the Germans had been able to force us out of on 13 November, 1942.

Grenadier-Regiment 578, with subordinated units, moved out to assault its objective: Haus 81, close by the Kommissarhaus. The initial penetration succeeded by going in through the cellar. Leading the attack was 2. and 3. Kompanie of Panzerpionier-Bataillon 50. Rettenmaier wrote "A further surprise awaited us there. The enemy had demolished the staircase leading to the upper floor. What other pieces of devilry could he think of?" The Soviets weren't the only ones employing 'pieces of devilry'. The combat journal of 650th

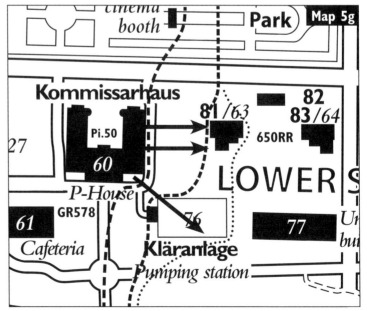

The attack on Haus 81 [Dom 63], 15 November, 1942.

---

53. These were marines from the 3rd Battalion of 92nd Rifle Brigade supporting Gorishny's northward attacks.

Rifle Regiment records that "the enemy is employing smoke chemicals which are causing our soldiers to choke and sneeze as well as causing tears and affecting their vision. These chemicals are being used to smoke out the soldiers and commanders from buildings." One of Lyudnikov's soldiers remembers that "it was necessary to moisten clothes with water and hold damp pieces of cloth to your face so as not to choke".

The intensity of the fighting in Haus 81 is conveyed in a few sentences by Hauptmann Rettenmaier: "The entire day had to be spent fighting from room to room. It was a struggle for both sides with scarcely imaginable exasperation and tenacity."

During the assault, Oberleutnant Hardekopf's[54] 2. Kompanie suffered the loss of three experienced NCOs: Unteroffizier Werner Friedrichs[55], Feldwebel Herbert Griep[56] and Feldwebel Ernst Peters[57]. Also killed from that company were Obergefreiter Georg Brauns[58] and Obergefreiter Karl Steinl[59]. Losses from 3. Kompanie were lighter: killed were Schirr-Unteroffizier Hans-Otto Ehlers[60] and Obergefreiter Willi Engel[61].

- - -

While 305. Infanterie-Division and its retinue attacked Lyudnikov's division from the south, 389. Infanterie-Division came toward them from the north. Spearheading this attack was Pionier-Bataillon 45, Sturmschwadron 24 and combat groups from Grenadier-Regiment 546. Supporting them were the assault guns and sIG33Bs of Sturmgeschütz-Abteilung 244. Available strength at the beginning of the day was 7 long-barrels, 7 short-barrels and 5 sIG33Bs. Leading one of the sIG33B platoons was future Knight's Cross winner Leutnant Kurt Nippes[62].

The objective of the attack was to seize Haus 87, better known to the Germans as 'Rote Haus', on the other side of the large gully. This building stood there like a brick sentinel, guarding against any approach from the north and providing a firm anchor upon which the Soviet defences could be moored, and as a result, it became the centre of attention of German preparatory fire. Artillery and mortar fire roughed up the building. Hull-down in the churned terrain to the north, the assault guns and sIG33Bs heaved high-explosive shells into the stout edifice, shells from the latter being particularly effective. Great chunks of masonry were split off and several sections of the building collapsed. Later in the day,

---

54. Hardekopf, Oberleutnant Dipl. Ing. Walther, 2./Pz.Pi.Btl.50; born 8 August, 1902 in Lübeck. Missing in action, December, 1942 in Stalingrad. See Appendix 2 (page 573) for more details.

55. Friedrichs, Unteroffizier Werner, 2./Pz.Pi.Btl.50; born 6 January, 1916 in Hamburg. Killed in action, 15 November, 1942 in Stalingrad.

56. Griep, Feldwebel Herbert, 2./Pz.Pi.Btl.50; born 25 February, 1915 in Hamburg. Killed in action, 15 November, 1942 in Stalingrad.

57. Peters, Feldwebel Ernst, 2./Pz.Pi.Btl.50; born 3. August, 1915 in Hamburg. Killed in action, 15 November, 1942 in Stalingrad.

58. Brauns, Obergefreiter Georg, 2./Pz.Pi.Btl.50; born 6 December, 1910 in Hemsbünde. Killed in action, 15 November, 1942 in Stalingrad.

59. Steinl, Obergefreiter Karl, 2./Pz.Pi.Btl.50; born 5 April, 1910 in Graslitz. Killed in action, 15 November, 1942 in Stalingrad.

60. Ehlers, Schirr-Unteroffizier Hans-Otto, 3./Pz.Pi.Btl.50; born 17 June, 1916 in Kiel. Killed in action, 15 November, 1942 in Stalingrad.

61. Engel, Obergefreiter Willi, 3./Pz.Pi.Btl.50; born 20 December, 1917 in Klein Wüstenfelde. Killed in action, 15 November, 1942 in Stalingrad.

62. Nippes, Oberleutnant Kurt, RK; born 19 June, 1917 in Düsseldorf. Killed in action, 10 December, 1943 in Bechi, north-east of Kiev. Nippes would be posthumously awarded the Knight's Cross on 29 January, 1944 for actions with Sturmgeschütz-Abteilung 276.

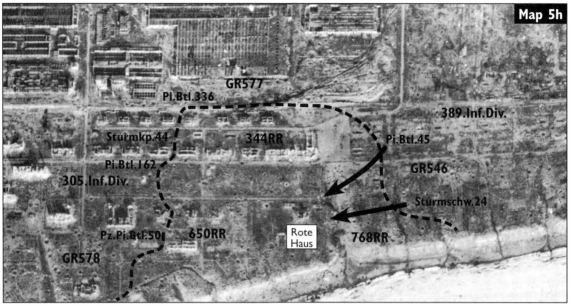

The attack of 389. Infanterie-Division from the north, 15 November, 1942.

6. Armee would report to Heeresgruppe B that the building had been 'battered down'. The sIG33B was finally living up to its envisaged purpose.

Under the cover of this fusillade, the infantry and pioneers pushed forward, overwhelming the defensive line of Gunyaga's riflemen. They rushed on, towards the gully and Rote Haus. The terrain was carved up by trenches and craters. Savage encounters developed as German clearing groups burst into Soviet dug-outs. Grenades exploded. Murderous scuffles whirled about in dim bunkers. The pioneers were in heavy demand with their satchel charges and flamethrowers. In the forefront as usual was Oberleutnant Heinrich's 2./Pionier-Bataillon 45. Right beside them were the experienced panzergrenadiers of Sturmschwadron 24, now led by Leutnant Walter Wroblewski. In a letter to his brother who previously belonged to the same unit, the adjutant of Panzergrenadier-Regiment 26, Oberleutnant Hans Joachim Martius[63], describes the ferocity of the fighting faced by Sturmschwadron 24:

> Beyersdorff is now in hospital for the third time – wounded in the arm. Soon there will be no more men left. The 5th [Schwadron] has today lost its seventh commander! All hell's been let loose in the city. We face each other at 20 metres. Between so much steel and iron that Hermann [Göring] could get randy about it!!![64] Our men often hit the Russians on the head with spades. Yesterday, a soldier pulled at one end of a machine-gun, a Russian at the other. A hand grenade finished it off…

While brutal clashes continued behind them, the lead assault groups charged on, descending into Finger Gully. Their sudden appearance stirred up a hornet's nest. The gully was lined with dug-outs, and Red Army soldiers, mostly clerks, medics and other rear echelon personnel, poured out and engaged the Germans. The carnage in the gully was appalling. Hand grenades and satchel charges took a fearful toll among the Soviet defenders.

---

63. Martius, Oberleutnant Hans Joachim, Pz.Gr.Rgt.26; born 23 May, 1920 in Bonn. Killed in action, 25 December, 1942 in Stalingrad. See Appendix 3 (page 581) for more details.

64. Göring was in charge of the 5 year plan which was directed towards utilising Germany's limited natural resources.

Even though their objective – the Rote Haus – was just over the crest, the German shock troops could not wade any further through the Soviet resistance. The attack stalled. To remain where they were would be suicidal. Therefore, the German groups ebbed back, picking up individual soldiers and separated groups as they went, until they reached a defensive line hastily established in some captured Soviet trenches.

Total losses suffered by 389. Infanterie-Division in this attack were heavy: 16 men killed, 1 officer and 43 men wounded and 15 men missing.[65] On the morning of 16 November, Sturmgeschütz-Abteilung 244 reported a strength of 5 long-barrels, 5 short-barrels and 4 sIG33Bs. This would indicate that 2 long-barrels, 2 short-barrels and 1 sIG33B were lost during the fighting on 15 November. However, later strength returns suggest that none of these vehicles were totally destroyed: on the morning of 19 November, the battalion reported a strength of 7 long-barrels, 7 short-barrels and 6 sIG33Bs.

– – –

At 1145 hours, Hauptmann Hermann Lundt, commander of Pionier-Bataillon 336, sent a teletype message via 100. Jäger-Division back to his parent division, 336. Infanterie-Division. It was a very brief report about casualties sustained during the assault from 12 November until 1600 hours on 14 November:

---

65. Casualties suffered by Pionier-Bataillon 45 were painful and almost debilitating coming so soon after the hideous losses inflicted on 11 November. From Oberleutnant Bunz's 1. Kompanie, Pionier Willi Mathieu, platoon commander Oberfeldwebel Kurt Sachse, Gefreiter Eugen Waldenmaier and Gefreiter Ludwig Zipf were killed, platoon commander Leutnant Manfred Kimmich was wounded, Gefreiter Karl Fässer was missing and Gefreiter Michael Rittenbacher was reported as being captured by the Soviets (however, one contemporary document suggests he was killed). From Oberleutnant Heinrich's 2. Kompanie, Unteroffizier Ernst Nickel and Obergefreiter Franz Fischer were killed. From Leutnant Skutlartz's 3. Kompanie, Unteroffizier Theobald Böhm, Pionier Jakob Kohn and Unteroffizier Hermann Schärr were killed – Böhm and Schärr both being killed by hand grenades – while Obergefreiter Karl Koch was missing.
Bunz, Oberleutnant Max, DKiG, 1./Pi.Btl.45; born 10 July, 1914 in Ulm/Donau. Missing in action, 23 January, 1943 in Stalingrad. See Appendix 2 (page 570) for more details.
Mathieu, Pionier Willi, 1./Pi.Btl.45; born 21 March, 1923 in Neuhütten. Killed in action, 15 November, 1942 in Stalingrad.
Sachse, Oberfeldwebel Kurt, 1./Pi.Btl.45; born 4 December, 1914 in Wuppertal. Killed in action, 15 November, 1942 in Stalingrad.
Waldenmaier, Gefreiter Eugen, 1./Pi.Btl.45; born 3 August, 1921 in Loosburg. Killed in action, 15 November, 1942 in Stalingrad.
Zipf, Gefreiter Ludwig, 1./Pi.Btl.45; born 9 November, 1910 in Schminden. Killed in action, 15 November, 1942 in Stalingrad.
Kimmich, Oberleutnant Manfred, 1./Pi.Btl.45; born 23 January, 1920 in Sobald Sulz a.N. Died 20 October, 1944 in POW camp No. 3655, Arsk. See Appendix 2 (page 574) for more details.
Fässer, Gefreiter Karl, 1./Pi.Btl.45; born 6 July, 1909 in Hohenwettersbach. Missing in action, 15 November, 1942 in Stalingrad.
Rittenbacher, Gefreiter Michael, 1./Pi.Btl.45; born 14 December, 1920 in Tschurndorf, killed in action, 15 November, 1942 in Stalingrad.
Nickel, Unteroffizier Ernst, 2./Pi.Btl.45; born 23 July, 1914 in Bochum. Killed in action, 15 November, 1942 in Stalingrad.
Fischer, Obergefreiter Franz, 2./Pi.Btl.45; born 20 January, 1920 in Kappelrodeck. Killed in action, 15 November, 1942 in Stalingrad.
Skutlartz, Oberleutnant Erich, 3./Pi.Btl.45; born 14 April, 1916 in Lahr-Dinglingen. Died 30 December, 2001 in Breisach. See Appendix 2 (page 578) for more details.
Böhm, Unteroffizier Theobald, 3./Pi.Btl.45; born 27 October, 1915 in Obersheim. Killed in action, 15 November, 1942 in Stalingrad.
Kohn, Pionier Jakob, 3./Pi.Btl.45; born 6 February, 1908 in Weidenstetten. Killed in action, 15 November, 1942 in Stalingrad.
Schärr, Unteroffizier Hermann, 3./Pi.Btl.45; born 26 December, 1915 in Ulm/Donau. Killed in action, 15 November, 1942 in Stalingrad.
Koch, Obergefreiter Karl, 3./Pi.Btl.45; born 20 November, 1917 in Söflingen. Missing in action, 15 November, 1942 in Stalingrad.

Oblt. Hullen, 1. Kp. wounded. 1. Kp. now commanded by Oblt. Ehringhaus.
Casualties: 2 NCOs and 10 men killed, 3 NCOs and 30 men wounded.[66]
New replenishment of the pioneer battalion is requested.

signed Lundt, Hptm.

- - -

While Germans and Soviets grappled in a life and death struggle for Haus 81, the next building to the north, Haus 83, was also undergoing its own trial. Major Pechenyuk's command post was in this building. Instead of being in the rear, the regiment staff found themselves in the front-line. Senior-Sergeant Alexei Iosifovich Gorbatenko was still inside the building after the repulsion of Schinke's attack on 13 November:

> The battle for the regiment command post began in the middle of November. German tanks attacked. A German tank was burning by the wall of our house.[67] At midday I was standing at the ready with soldiers on the second floor. We fired two cartridges toward the Germans. When the third jammed, snipers hit the soldiers at the embrasures. Bullets ripped up the plaster on the walls. Then tracers were fired. Shells began to explode on the house. Heavy shelling destroyed the staircase. The cellar, where the staff was housed, had holes knocked in it. Dying at their desks were working and off-duty reconnaissance men. Pechenyuk received permission to relocate to the Volga bank. Defence of the house was led by Junior-Lieutenant Kalinin, regiment adjutant, and Datsyuk, chief of the chemical defence department. Members of the garrison: Geraskin, the regiment's chief engineer; Dubov, senior reconnaissance chief; myself, and a few more people. The regimental chief engineer died during the fighting. Shrapnel, about a 10cm piece, struck his neck. He was standing at a window firing his rifle. The next thing I know, his head rolled across the floor. The piece of shrapnel lodged itself in the wall near the piano. Artillery fire. Attacks one after another. We began to sing the 'Varyag', 'Katyusha', the 'Internationale', and continued to hold out.

The merciless brutality of the hand-to-hand struggle was obviously disturbing Hauptmann Rettenmaier. Normally so verbose in his letters home, all he could manage on this day was a few short lines, even though it had been a week since his last letter:

> I know you have been waiting for news from me. It is a monstrous war of uninterrupted bleeding and dying. There is no respite or rest. I can't tell you anything because I don't know where to start. Later perhaps...

With the light fading from the sky, Major Pechenyuk requested artillery fire on the Apotheke, the Kommissarhaus, Haus 79, Haus 53 (Rettenmaier's command post) and the central gates of the Barrikady Factory. This bombardment rated a mention in the interim report of LI. Armeekorps submitted to 6. Armee at 1545 hours:

> In the fighting around the enemy bridgehead east of the gun factory, 305. Infanterie-Division won Haus 81 and pushed its front-line forward to the sewage treatment plant east of Haus 81–Haus 73. The mopping up of Haus 81 has not yet ended. Heavy enemy artillery fire on the area around the Kommissarhaus and gun factory.

---

66. Of the casualties mentioned in the report, all twelve dead had been suffered by Oberleutnant Ziesch's 3. Kompanie, while the tally of 33 wounded broke down as follows: Oberleutnant Hullen's 1. Kompanie, 2 NCOs and 11 men; Leutnant Oberst's 2. Kompanie, 1 man; Oberleutnant Ziesch's 3. Kompanie, 1 NCO and 18 men. The total number of casualties suffered by the battalion since arriving in Stalingrad was 7 NCOs and 42 men killed, and 2 officers, 6 NCOs and 62 men wounded, a total of 119 men.

67. This must be one of the two tanks destroyed by Senior-Lieutenant Charashvili (see page 193).

389. Infanterie-Division won the gully and some of the ground north of 'Rote Haus'.

Roughly an hour later, 6. Armee sent a situation report to Heeresgruppe B:

In Stalingrad, storm groups of 305. Infanterie-Division took a large house north-east of the Kommissarhaus in hard fighting and pushed the front-line further to the north-east. Storm groups of 389. Infanterie-Division pushed up to the 'Rote Haus' (grid square 93a). Enemy assaults at several positions were thrown back.

In a conversation a few minutes later, 6. Armee's Ia Oberstleutnant Elchlepp conversed with Ia of Heeresgruppe B, Oberst Winter. Elchlepp began by summarising the day's events: "In Stalingrad, our stormtroop operations east of the gun factory were successful; the Russian positions were pushed back a little. Several buildings east of the Party House [Kommissarhaus] were taken. In the sector of 389. Infanterie-Division, the large, so-called 'Rote Haus' was battered down. The assault detachments pushed up to the house."

Oberst Winter then posed a question: "What is now intended for the further occupation of the gun factory?"

Elchlepp replied, "A small piece will be chipped away from the north and south every day until they join hands…"

The entire scope of 6. Armee's intentions are revealed in this small conversation. Gone were the days of throwing several battalions against the Soviet line in the hope of achieving a large-scale victory. Enormous casualties for minuscule gains had forced the German commanders to come to the realisation that such attacks would swiftly deplete their strength. Now, they would focus their energy on obtaining small, attainable objectives upon which the full weight of German firepower could be concentrated.

– – –

Back in Haus 83, where the garrison had withstood a full day of German attacks and bombardments, the situation was dire. Major Pechenyuk had dashed out of the building with a few members of his staff to set up a new command post in a dug-out in the Volga cliff. Left behind were a small group of men, including Senior-Sergeant Gorbatenko:

In the evening, our garrison divided into two. Kalinin remained at the command post. Datsyuk and I left for the unfinished building, and Dubov was with us. In the unfinished building, I.V. Dubov was wounded by shrapnel from a shell.

As with most soldiers, Dubov clearly remembers being wounded:

The last defensive site of our 650th Rifle Regiment was a two-storey building located two hundred metres from the bank of the Volga. On orders from Captain Datsyuk, the chief of this garrison, my friend Stepanov and I defended one of the rooms of this building. We noticed German submachine-gunners running from one house to another with the goal of attacking us after they regrouped. Firing at them with rifles, comrade Stepanov and I destroyed about twenty Germans. The Germans noticed us and they aimed straight at us with tanks. The second shot fired by the tank fatally wounded my friend and I was wounded on the left side of my chest. This splinter – 'a gift' of the Stalingrad battle – has never been

Ivan Vasiliyevich Dubov

taken out of my body. Dressing the wound with anything available – there was absolutely no bandaging material, so I used the singlet from a dead man – I did not leave the battlefield but continued to carry on fighting for four more days…

With the departure of Gorbatenko, Datsyuk and Dubov, only four men were left in the former command post. One of them, regiment adjutant Junior-Lieutenant Kalinin, commanded the small garrison. His position was hopeless. The Germans held nearby buildings, effectively cutting them off from Lyudnikov's main forces. They were an island within an island. By all rights they should have been immediately overwhelmed but they were able to keep a hold on the building for a few more days.

– – –

Lyudnikov's units had taken a severe battering on this day. Losses were 64 killed and 137 wounded, a total of 201 men. On this heaviest of days, 138th Rifle Division was incapable of submitting a detailed situation report. The events of the entire day were contained in one sentence: "During the day, the enemy conducted active offensive actions along the entire front-line of the division." A few more details are found in the division's combat journal:

> The enemy has been attacking heavily throughout the day, capturing the flanks of the division. The enemy made many heavy attacks, most of which are repelled by the steadfastness of our soldiers. With the coming of night the enemy began to concentrate on the flanks of our division.

At the end of the day, the combat structure of the division was as follows: 768th Rifle Regiment with its command section – 15 men; 650th Rifle Regiment with its command section – 31 men; 344th Rifle Regiment with its command section – 123 men. All of the submachine-gun cartridges and hand grenades had been used up, and there were only 20 or 30 cartridges for each rifle. The men fought mainly with German weapons and ammunition. The soldiers of the division received food once but after that there was no more. In a large bunker next to the division command post, 250 wounded had already accumulated. The division commander asked the Army Commander to take immediate action so that the division could be replenished in terms of materials and rations, as well as having its wounded evacuated. General Krylov, chief-of-staff of 62nd Army, sent an encoded radiogram to the staff of 138th Division: "Designate the front-line with bonfires. Planes will arrive at night and drop their cargo."

The front-line had acquired the outline of an irregular horseshoe shape. The greatest depth from the front-line to the Volga was about 300-400 metres. At night, fires were ignited along the forward line, outlining the 'Island' with a ring of fire. Three PO-2 planes trundled over the Volga towards the Barrikady. Lyudnikov knew that aerial supply would not be easy:

> Attempts were made to supply us with the help of PO-2 aircraft. But this, too, was a difficult undertaking. Flying low over the right bank, a pilot would shut off his engine and ask if he could drop his load. If he was given permission, he would drop bags filled with ammunition and food.

The target area was so small that even the slow-flying PO-2s struggled to drop their cargo accurately. Lyudnikov recalls that "most of these bags would fall into the river, and some would be seized by the Germans. Moreover, a portion of the cartridges were useless because the bags were dropped without parachutes and the cartridges were knocked out of shape by the impact against the ground." Commissar Pavel Grigoryevich Tyupa, deputy commander of 1/650th Rifle Regiment, remembers that some supplies were parachuted to them:

Our PO-2 aircraft dropped ammunition and food to us by parachute but these mostly fell either behind enemy lines or into the Volga. When crates of ammunition were thrown to us, they struck the ground, deforming the cartridges and rendering them unsuitable for firing.

The aerial resupply was seen by the Germans as a sign of hope because they thought that the stubborn Soviet hold-outs could not last much longer, as Hauptmann Rettenmaier reports:

We experienced a surprise in the evening. Two Russians airplanes circled at a low altitude over the positions. Something suddenly detached from them, but we saw that they did not look like bombs. They were sacks, some of which fell in our territory. They contained bread and fat. The need of those surrounded must already be very great. Delight prevailed amongst us as we now hoped for a speedy complete success. We thought hunger would force the surrounded men to capitulate.

After dropping bags with crackers and cartridges, the PO-2s headed back to their airfields to pick up new cargo. When they appeared over the Barrikady a second time, however, the pilots no longer saw an outline of the front-line that was familiar to them. The Germans had quickly caught on to what was happening and lit fires of their own. Now, it was impossible for the pilots to distinguish the course of the front-line. Switching off his motor, the commander of the PO-2s flew low along the river bank. As he passed above Lyudnikov's dug-out, those on the ground heard his voice: "Hey, Lyudnikov's Island! Put out the fires!" The fires within the divisional area were immediately extinguished and the resulting black semi-circle of land upon which pilots could dump their cargo was still clearly designated before the Germans had time to extinguish their fires. Nevertheless, most of the bags fell to the Germans and other cargo fell into the river. The bridgehead, named 'the island' by the pilots, was too small to supply from the air. Lyudnikov decided it was necessary to refuse the flights of planes.

– – –

In the unfinished building, Senior-Lieutenant Charashvili, now in his seventh week in Stalingrad, was shot through the thigh:

At 1300 or 1400 hours, in heavy hand-to-hand combat, I was severely wounded in the ruins of the unfinished brick U-shaped building. I was taken away from the field of battle by a worker of the Barrikady, whose last name I don't remember, and by Private Maisuradze, I think he was the cook at the command post of 650th Rifle Regiment.

On the precipice above the bank of the Volga, a rather large tunnel had been dug for the wounded so that they could be tended. I was taken there to be bandaged. I clearly remember that I was looked over by a senior doctor, I don't remember his last name, and was told that the senior doctor was a Jew (the wounded for some reason didn't like this doctor), under him worked an Azerbajani by the last name of Aliyev. There also appeared a nurse, 'our' Valya-Valentina.

In the tunnel the medics first took away all my weapons, my pistol, and then bandaged my thigh, in which Valentina also took part. After the bandaging, Valentina walked with me along the river bank, in the direction from which I had come. With one arm I was holding myself up with a piece of wood and the other was around Valentina's shoulder. In this fashion we passed all the wounded, there was no free space for me to sit and so I was led even further. I was unable to walk. I was put in a space with around 20 other wounded, mostly commanders. I was sitting in this place because I could not lay down since it was so tightly packed. We did not eat until 20-22 November, we were very hungry.

With his wounding, the former artillery battery of 90th Rifle Regiment ceased to exist as a separate entity. Charashvili's few remaining artillerymen were incorporated directly into Pechenyuk's regiment. Senior-Lieutenant Charashvili recalls that "from the officer ranks of my battery, apart from myself and Lieutenant A.A. Midyuk, everyone else died in the fighting and were buried near the Barrikady factory."

– – –

In its evening report, LI. Armeekorps reported that "in the afternoon, Grenadier-Regiment 576 repulsed several enemy attacks (150 men). At night, enemy forces crossed towards the fuel installation." This attack against Grenadier-Regiment 576 was just the latest in a series that would continue until Soviet forces had broken through to Lyudnikov. Each assault, although unsuccessful, benefited Lyudnikov by drawing away German units – or at least tying them down – and thereby relieving some pressure. The war diary of 62nd Army said the following about the attack:

> At 1130, after half an hour of artillery preparation, parts of 95th Rifle Division with 3/92nd Rifle Brigade and the composite regiment of 193rd Rifle Division, launched an attack with the task of restoring the position in the Mezenskaya Street area. Despite exceedingly strong fire resistance, our units moved slowly ahead. The fierce fighting in the area of the fuel tanks came down to hand-to-hand combat. The area of the fuel tanks changed hands repeatedly.

> By the end of the day the enemy, having thrown in fresh forces, launched an attack and recaptured the area of the fuel tanks. Fighting continues.

The combat journal of 685th Rifle Regiment reports about the attack in greater detail:

> At 1130 on 15.11.42, for the assault on the fuel tanks, 241st Rifle Regiment received 1st Rifle Battalion of 90th Rifle Regiment as a reinforcement. 685th Rifle Regiment, having received reinforcements – two rifle platoons – went over to the offensive in the previous direction after a 30-minute artillery preparation.

> The assault this time was formed as follows: all personnel were divided up into groups of 8-10 men with the task of successively cutting across the gully to blockade dug-outs and trenches in which the enemy has consolidated. One such storm group managed to negotiate the heavy fire of mortars, machine-guns and grenades and pushed across the gully, but it was not possible to complete the storming of the first dug-outs because all the men were lost to fire from snipers and submachine-gunners located on the slopes of the gully. Consequently, at this time, the attacks of 685th and 241st Rifle Regiments were repelled. At 1330, the enemy, with a strength of two platoons, again launched a counterattack on the regiment's sector, but having lost up to forty men, they fell back. At 2000 and throughout the night, the regiment, together with 241st Rifle Regiment, repeatedly tried to break through to the gully but enemy fire repulsed all our attempts.

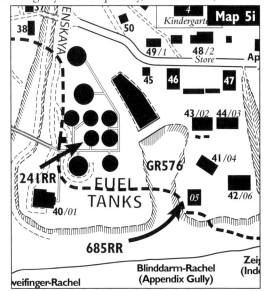

Failed attack across Appendix Gully, 15 November.

In a period of self-analysis after being withdrawn from the battle on 22 November, the regiment commander, Lieutenant-Colonel Drogaitsev, and his chief-of-staff, Major Korshunov, recorded the reasons for the failure to cross the gully:

> The enemy, having pressed back the units of 95th and 138th Rifle Divisions, reached the Volga river, captured trenches and dug-outs from these units and organised defence, not only having firing

points on the slopes but also on the floor of the gully itself, enabling them to have the power to hit everything that entered the gully – especially those trying to infiltrate it – with fire of increasing force. The majority of the firing points tucked away in the gully could not be surveyed before the assault and were naturally only vulnerable in a small way to our fire.

The enemy made widespread use of trenches and reinforced concrete pipes which enabled him to manoeuvre personnel and throw in reinforcements. The enemy employed hand grenades and jumping mines on a large scale, which we estimate has caused about 50-60% of our casualties in these battles. Apart from that, the trenches and pipes enabled the enemy to temporarily abandon individual defensive sectors with an immediate alert by a system of signal rockets for mortars and artillery fire.

The enemy employed snipers in this fighting on an especially wide scale, placing them in hides on all defensive sectors so that every area ahead of the front-line and river bank was exposed to their fire.

For the regiment's part, mortars and grenades were widely used: the mortar company – with six 82mm mortars – was in continual communication with the regimental command post and rifle units, knew the reference points precisely after adjusting them in advance, and opened immediate fire during the course of the fighting in any direction necessary. The greatest effect from the mortar fire was on enemy concentrations and during the moment of a counterattack.

At the time of crossing the gully, the prime means of fighting the enemy were hand grenades and submachine-guns. Every soldier had no less than 4-5 grenades on hand, which were continuously brought forward from ammunition dumps and stored on the departure line for the attack. Grenades destroyed enemy groups in 12 occupied dug-outs and trenches.

The outcome of the fighting on 15 November was summed up by 62nd Army: "The position on the sector of 241st Rifle Regiment has not been restored." Chuikov issued an order aimed at helping Lyudnikov and his encircled men:

> Night actions by units of 95th Rifle Division and the composite 685th Rifle Regiment will destroy the enemy that has reached the river bank in the area east of Mezenskaya Street and will establish contact with units of 138th Rifle Division. Positions on other fronts will be held. I obligate units of the Fortified District on Zaitsevsky Island to deliver ammunition to 138th Rifle Division and to organise the evacuation of wounded across the Denezhnaya Volozhka channel.

The good news for 95th Rifle Division was that its third regiment – Major Borisov's[68] 90th – had arrived on the Stalingrad bank. While its 1st Rifle Battalion had already been committed to the northward assaults, its 3rd battalion took up defensive positions on the boundary between 161st and 241st Rifle Regiments.

– – –

A report released by the Ic (Enemy Intelligence) Department of 6. Armee at 2000 hours contained interesting statements by Soviet prisoners:

> It is reputed that from 14 November, all forces employed behind the battle line in Stalingrad would be deployed on the front-line. No supplies for 5 days, no rations for 3 days. Of 3 supply parachutes dropped so far, only one has landed correctly. There is a high number of commissars and officers in the bridgehead.

The fierceness of the fighting over the previous four days – together with the difficulty and blood required to capture even a single building – forced a rethink amongst the

---

68. Borisov, Colonel Mikhail Semyonovich, HotSU; 90th RR; born 21 January, 1904 in Barskoye-Rykino. Killed in action, 9 February, 1944.

Germans. There had to be a better way. Even when attacks were prepared with heavy, accurate artillery bombardments and carried out by experienced pioneers armed with flamethrowers and demolition charges, success was not guaranteed. An interesting confidential document reached 6. Armee headquarters at 2025 hours. It said:

> 6. Armee will have the following unit immediately supplied and subordinated for operations in Stalingrad:
> 1. Gem.Kp./Pz.Abt.301 (Sprengstoffträger).

This '1. Gem.Kp./Pz.Abt.301 (Sprengstoffträger)' was the 1st combined Kompanie of Panzer-Abteilung 301 (demolition carriers). This unit was better known as Kompanie Abendroth: it had been formed as a special overstrength remote-control unit. The bulk of the unit came from 2./Panzer-Abteilung 301 with additional personnel (a Sonderführer, maintenance crews and 84 drivers) from 1./Panzer-Abteilung 301 and the headquarters company, as well as a platoon of 'Goliaths' from 3. Kompanie. Leading the unit was Oberleutnant Ferdinand von Abendroth[69].

Panzer-Abteilung 301 – previously Panzer-Abteilung 300 (Fernlenk) – was stationed in the Leningrad area when it received the order to send Kompanie Abendroth south. After being deployed with some success in the capture of Sevastopol in June 1942, the battalion spent most of July with 1. Panzer-Armee attacking towards the Donets, the lower Don and Rostov. Then, after a brief rest period, the battalion entrained on 6 August and was transported in a north-west direction, toward Leningrad. After the fall of Sevastopol, units of von Manstein's experienced 11. Armee – conquerors of Sevastopol – were tasked with carrying out Operation 'Nordlicht' [Northern Lights], the reduction and capture of Leningrad. Proposed attack date was 11 September, 1942. Major Soviet assaults launched on 27 August, however, upset this plan by achieving a deep penetration, and forcing the deployment of 11. Armee to restore the situation. Manstein's units succeeded in smashing the Soviet forces and recapturing the lost ground but ammunition and reserves built up for 'Nordlicht' had been expended and the proposed attack on Leningrad was therefore postponed. The battalion was involved in positional fighting through October and into the middle of November. It was at this moment that Kompanie Abendroth received the order to transfer to the area of Heeresgruppe B.

Kompanie Abendroth employed two different types of demolition carriers: the Borgward BIV, a small 3.6 tonne radio-controlled tank that could deposit a 450 kilogram explosive charge[70] next to an objective, whereupon the carrier automatically shifted into reverse gear and backed out of the blast zone at high speed; and the 'Goliath', a wire-guided miniature tank that weighed 370 kilograms and carried a 60 kilogram charge. The power of the Borgward BIV had first been demonstrated to Hitler at his 'Wolfsschanze' headquarters at the end of March 1942. Leutnant Jus Fischer, a platoon commander in 2./Panzer-Abteilung 300 (Fernlenk), conducted the demonstration for the benefit of Hitler, Keitel[71], several generals and senior party functionaries. Immediately after the explosion against a massive

69. Abendroth, Major Ferdinand von, DKiG; 1./Pz.Abt.301; born 4 January, 1916 in Kössern. Died of wounds, 16 July, 1944 in Lemberg.

70. The explosive used was Ekrasit, a stable compound that was relatively safe to handle. If no detonator was fitted the charge could be struck by small-calibre fire without exploding. If the explosive caught fire, it slowly burned itself up.

71. Keitel, Generalfeldmarschall Wilhelm, RK; Chef OKW; born 22 September, 1882 in Helmscherode bei Gandersheim. Hanged 16 October, 1946 in Nürnberg.

anti-tank barrier set up specifically for the demonstration, Hitler was driven up in a command and control panzer to inspect the results. Leutnant Fischer wrote in his memoirs:

> Hitler climbed out of the tank at the crater and walked with me toward Keitel. He spoke in chopped staccato (something like): 'I am imagining… their use in Sevastopol. First… the small Goliaths… attack on a broad front… into the infantry positions and trench systems… then… break in with the big demolition-charge carriers…! That's how we will break through this complex system of positions!'

Whenever Hitler paused, Keitel bowed his head and said, "Jawohl, mein Führer" – "Jawohl, mein Führer" – "Jawohl, mein Führer." Fischer knew that would be the worst thing for remotely-controlled BIVs because tracked vehicles easily became caught up in wire entanglements and trench systems. After Keitel's last "Jawohl", Fischer said, "Mein Führer, the success of this first mission will depend on the terrain. We need terrain which is definitely favourable for tanks." Hitler, almost shocked, stared straight ahead, even looking past Keitel. After a brief pause, Hitler said to Keitel: "Please look into this."

Despite Fischer's knowledgeable and courageous interjection, the demolitions carriers were nevertheless used at Sevastopol and, as forewarned by Fischer, their opportunities for deployment were limited by the terrain and Soviet defences. Many were destroyed by artillery fire, while others stumbled into craters or minefields. However, they were extremely effective when they did actually reach Soviet trench-lines and blockhouses. Two BIVs destroyed a bunker each while four others eliminated well dug-in Soviet infantry positions, including one which had previously resisted three infantry assaults. The massive explosions levelled trenches for a dozen or so metres and the lethal effect was many times that distance. Dead Soviet infantry were later found lying in trenches, bleeding from the mouth and nose.

No evidence has yet surfaced as to who initially suggested that the demolition carriers be used in Stalingrad. There is absolutely no hint that 6. Armee requested them, and even though the records of Heeresgruppe B are practically non-existent, von Weichs and his staff would have discussed this new measure with 6. Armee in some way prior to requesting them. It seems rational to assume that the Führer himself was behind it. Hitler ordered the demolition carriers to be used at Sevastopol and later had them sent north for the attack on Leningrad, so there is no reason to believe he did not also think of using them at Stalingrad after Operation Nordlicht had been cancelled.

Heinz Prenzlin, a radio operator with Kompanie Abendroth, recorded in his diary the moment he learned they were being transferred:

> 16 November, 1942: The entire company is filled with a curious uneasiness. Scarcely an officer to be seen. As well, contrary to what we are used to, the Spieß is much calmer today. At 1200 hours we had to fall in. We were told to pack at once, we are being moved but no-one knows where. Much debate. Some claim to have heard we were going to Germany. Some say to Kurland. Yet others say we're going to Stalingrad. This unit is frightfully strict on secrecy…

Preparations for departure were completed and Kompanie Abendroth moved out at 1200 hours on 17 November, reaching Gachina at 1600 hours where they entrained. The Kompanie was equipped with ten command and control Panzer IIIs and a mix of Borgward BIVs and Goliaths. The train pulled out of the station at midnight. When it arrived in Dünaberg at 2030 hours on 19 November, Prenzlin wrote ecstatically in his diary:

> We celebrate, we're going home.

The excitement lasted until 21 November, when the train changed direction and started heading east. Prenzlin noted sombrely:

> We are all disappointed; we're not going home. There are murmurs that we are headed for Stalingrad.

The rumours were true. Fate, however, would spare them from fighting in the rubble-strewn streets of Stalingrad.[72]

It is interesting to speculate what effect Kompanie Abendroth would have had on the fighting. There is no doubt the demolition carriers would have caused severe damage to the defences of 138th Rifle Division. The nature of the terrain forced Lyudnikov's men to be concentrated in tight groups within their fortified buildings, making each defensive strongpoint a high-value target against which several demolition carriers could be expended. The elimination of a single building would have opened a sizeable gap in the line, all at low-cost of life to the Germans. Would the explosions have been effective? The massively-thick walls of the buildings might have absorbed the brunt of an explosion but it is hard to imagine a Soviet garrison being unaffected by the detonation of a 450 kilogram charge, let alone several, on their front doorstep. How would the terrain have affected the deployment of the demolition carriers? The latticework of trenches, rubbled streets and overlapping craters would no doubt have hampered operations, but panzers and assault guns were used in the area, so there is no reason why the demolition carriers could not also have been employed. Distance to the targets was very small, so the man behind the radio control would have had no problem guiding the carrier up to a specified building. One wonders what would have happened if several BIVs had been sent up against the Kommissarhaus or if a Goliath or two had been dropped into the Rolik gully. Would Lyudnikov's bridgehead have been completely subdued if the Germans had knocked out all the major strongpoints with the demolition carriers? Would Kompanie Abendroth have arrived as a deus ex machina, an all-conquering power, to solve the seemingly insoluble and bloody deadlock? No-one can say for sure… all we have is speculation and a tantalising 'what if' scenario.

- - -

In the meantime, back in the dark and twisted ruins of Stalingrad, there were several matters involving Hitler's other baby, the sIG33B. In Korpsbefehl Nr. 113 issued at 1945 hours, the following was ordered:

> Stug.Abt.244 with s.I.G. auf Sfl. will be released from 389. Infanterie-Division on 19.11. and be placed at Gruppe Schwerin's disposal. Two assault guns will remain with 389. Infanterie-Division for operations against the 'Rote Haus'.

Stubborn Soviet resistance was throwing German plans into disarray. The capture of the Barrikady bridgehead should have been completed and the forces freed-up for redeployment in a forthcoming operation with Gruppe Schwerin that would crush the Krasny Oktyabr bridgehead. Yet, Lyudnikov and his men held on, necessitating von Seydlitz to keep the majority of his forces marshalled around 'the Island'. The only unit that von

---

72. Kompanie Abendroth arrived at Oblivskaya railway station at 1500 hours on 26 November. They were bound for Chirskaya station, the last stop before Stalingrad and the main railhead for 6. Armee, but could go no further because Soviets units were only a few kilometres away. The Soviet counteroffensive at Stalingrad prevented Kompanie Abendroth from reaching its destination and using its demolition carriers against Lyudnikov's stubborn redoubts.

Seydlitz could send to Gruppe Schwerin was Sturmgeschütz-Abteilung 244, and even that was to leave two of its guns behind.

At 2000 hours, 6. Armee called LI. Armeekorps:

> At the end of November, an officer from a Sturmgeschütz-Abteilung who has gathered personal practical combat experience with the s.I.G. (Sfl.) will be dispatched to make a report to OKH. Presentation in front of the Führer and forwarding to the construction firm is possible.
>
> LI. Armeekorps will select a suitable officer who will be thoroughly prepared for this task. He must have participated in an attack himself and must be confident with the tactical operations and all technical aspects of the weapon.
>
> Korps will report when the officer is expected to conclude his preparations.

The officer selected for this mission was Leutnant Kurt Nippes from Sturmgeschütz-Abteilung 244. It is telling that an officer from this battalion was chosen, rather than from Sturmgeschütz-Abteilung 245 whose sIG33Bs had suffered heavy losses during the gruelling fighting around the Kommissarhaus.

– – –

At 2000 in Chkalova kolkhoz, in the Rossosh sector far away from Stalingrad, the staff of 294. Infanterie-Division received a teletype message from Hauptmann Weimann, commander of Pionier-Bataillon 294. Weimann reported that his battalion had completed its mission of thrusting from the Stalingrad Gun Factory through to the Volga and mopping up the river bank. This assignment had caused severe casualties. The battalion had lost 3 officers, 13 NCOs and 134 men, of those, 1 officer, 5 NCOs and 27 men had been killed. The division commander, Generalmajor Block, and his staff officers were stunned. The battalion had lost almost half its effective strength in a few days. More than a third of the experienced NCOs had become casualties and – even worse – three of the four line officers had been taken out of action. The state of affairs regarding the officers was actually worse than Block realised. One of the two wounded officers, Oberleutnant Gerhard Pohl of 1. Kompanie, had succumbed to his severe wounds in hospital the previous day but Weimann was unaware of that when he sent his report. And the only uninjured officer still at the front, Oberleutnant Gerhard Menzel of 3. Kompanie, was himself quite ill. The battalion's combat groups were being led by combat-hardened NCOs like Feldwebel Wilhelm Angerstein of 1. Kompanie and Feldwebel Oskar Dickler of 2. Kompanie.

– – –

At 2030 hours, LI. Armeekorps sent its daily report to 6. Armee:

> With storm groups, 305. Infanterie-Division took the sewage treatment plant, Haus 81 and the terrain between Haus 81 and 73 firmly into possession. Grenadier-Regiment 576 repulsed several enemy attacks (150 men) in the afternoon. At night, enemy forces crossed toward the fuel installation.
> 389. Infanterie-Division gained some ground north of the Rote Haus.
> In the evening, enemy artillery fire in the area around the Kommissarhaus.
> Forward line: Unaltered apart from negligible changes near 305. and 389. Infanterie-Divisions.

The corps captured 44 prisoners, including 16 deserters, on this day.

In a report compiled about the enemy situation, 6. Armee's enemy intelligence department remarked about the aerial supply of Lyudnikov:

Of 15 supply parachutes dropped during the night of 15/16 November, only 5 landed in the bridgehead east of the gun factory.

This report was fairly accurate. Situation Report No. 193 of 138th Rifle Division, dated 16 November, recorded that "the help rendered by the planes was insignificant. The planes dumped 6 bags of products, 8 boxes of 45mm shells and 2 boxes of 82mm mortar rounds. Four bags landed on enemy territory."

Casualties for 15 November, 1942:	
138th Rifle Division:	64 killed, 137 wounded, a total of 201 men
305. Infanterie-Division: 3 men killed and 40 men wounded	
389. Infanterie-Division: 16 men killed, 1 officer and 43 men wounded, 15 men missing	

16 November, 1942

At 0555 hours, LI. Armeekorps reported to 6. Armee that "the enemy east of the gun factory repeatedly advanced against our front-line during the night with assault groups. He was supplied from the air during the night…"

650th Rifle Regiment reported that "from 0130 hours, the enemy opened fire with machine-guns and submachine-guns, and periodically shot from artillery and mortars".

German units reported artillery harassment fire throughout the night and during the morning, particularly on the sector of Grenadier-Regiment 576 and Gruppe Seydel.

In a situation report, 138th Rifle Division noted that "the enemy continued to concentrate in the area of the eastern part of the Barrikady factory, and west and the north of the fuel tanks". For the moment, Lyudnikov and his men could take a breather as the German units facing them regrouped and prepared to relaunch the attack. On this day, 16 November, most of the action was to take place further south, around the hotly-contested fuel tanks being held by Grenadier-Regiment 576 and attacked by Gorishny's various units.

At daybreak, Gorishny's division succeeded in breaking into German positions along the Volga bank south-east of the fuel installation. Grenadier-Regiment 576 immediately launched a counterattack, sealed off the penetration and captured one Soviet officer and 35 men in the process. Gorishny's riflemen and marines renewed their attacks at 0900 hours and 1100 hours with their surviving forces, supported by tanks and flamethrowers. Their aim – as always – was to break through to Lyudnikov's men trapped behind the Barrikady. All attacks failed, however, and one of the tanks was destroyed. The war diary of 79. Infanterie-Division records:

> 1115 hours: Everything quiet in front of Gruppe Seydel. One flamethrowing tank was combated by heavy infantry weapons.

Artillerie-Regiment 179 also reported that the Soviet attack near 305. Infanterie-Division was thrown back with the support of its III. Bataillon. In its daily report, the regiment summed up its actions:

> At midday, the enemy attacked with strong forces out of 82a4 along the Volga towards the right wing of 305. Infanterie-Division. The regiment combated the assembly areas in 82a4 and heavy infantry weapons on the island. The attack was repulsed. The focal point of enemy artillery fire lies on the forward line of 305. Infanterie-Division…

In a call to Oberst Winter at Heeresgruppe B later in the afternoon, Oberstleutnant i.G. Elchlepp described the situation: "On the southern front of the fuel installation, a flamethrowing tank was thrown into the fighting. Stormtroops of Oberst Steinmetz also had to be deployed to the south for this attack."

Soviet records about this day's attack are brief and unfortunately offer no detail about tanks or men lost the Germans as prisoners. The combat journal of 685th Rifle Regiment states:

> From the line of departure, the regiment – with fire from mortars and rifles – provided cover for the approach march of subunits of 90th Rifle Regiment (95th Rifle Division), which arrived from the river crossing, and their attack on the fuel tanks and gully mouth north of the fuel tanks, but all attempts by 90th Rifle Regiment to cut across the gully during the course of the day were repulsed by enemy fire.

The war diary of 62nd Army provides a clearer view of the situation around the fuel tanks:

> Units of 95th Rifle Division, with 3/92nd Rifle Brigade and the composite regiment of 193rd Rifle Division, continue to counterattack in the Mezenskaya Street area with the aim of restoring the position. The enemy offered stubborn resistance. Combat came to hand-to-hand fighting with the widespread use of grenades. The enemy threw in fresh forces at the end of the day.

> Situation on the sector of 241st Rifle Regiment has not been restored. Fighting along the line of Mezenskaya Street continues.

Instrumental in throwing back the attack was Oberleutnant Eugen Hering[73], commander of 6./Grenadier-Regiment 576, and his few remaining men. In the close-quarters fighting, Hering was lightly wounded in the thigh and the ball of his right foot by a hand grenade. "He did not go to the rear, however, because he did not want to leave his comrades in the lurch during those difficult hours," wrote his wife in a letter to her family.

> Although I wanted him to go back with every fibre of my being, I completely understand why he didn't. He is an officer in the truest sense of the word and the Lord will certainly reward him for his courage. Eugen also told me that as the fighting becomes more frightful, their food gets better; they receive special additions. This seems to me like the last meal for a condemned man.

After the repulsion of all heavy attacks, Major Braun, commander of Grenadier-Regiment 576, ordered the men of Pionier-Bataillon 294 and 2./Pionier-Bataillon 305 to block the Volga bank with T-mines and S-mines. This was done: the beach and surrounding cliffs and gullies were thickly sewn with the deadly devices. At 1400 hours, the front-line was again firmly in German hands. Throughout the day, Pionier-Bataillon 294 lost several men: Obergefreiter Walter Günther[74] and Obergefreiter Horst Hönicke[75] both went missing, while Gefreiter Ernst Kochanek[76] was killed when struck in the head by a bullet.

In an effort to help Grenadier-Regiment 576 and its attached units, von Seydlitz decided to relieve some of the burden of repelling the increasingly fierce and determined attacks coming from the south by reducing the size of its sector. At 1625 hours, Grenadier-Regiment 576 was

73. Hering, Hauptmann Eugen, DKiG; 6./Gr.Rgt.576; born 24 September, 1915 in Lauterbach. Died of wounds, 19 December, 1942 in Rostov.

74. Günther, Obergefreiter Walter, 3./Pi.Btl.294; born 18 August, 1911 in Thum. Missing in action, 16 November, 1942 in Stalingrad.

75. Hönicke, Obergefreiter Horst, 2./Pi.Btl.294; born 3 March, 1921 in Dresden. Missing in action, 16 November, 1942 in Stalingrad.

76. Kochanek, Gefreiter Ernst, 2./Pi.Btl.294; born 13 December, 1921 in Peiskretscham. Killed in action, 16 November, 1942 in Stalingrad.

ordered to hand over part of its sector to Gruppe Schwerin on the night of 17/18 November. Carrying this out would be Gruppe Seydel, the combat group formed from 14. Panzer-Division. Grenadier-Regiment 576 would retain the fuel installation, Zweifinger Rachel (Two Finger Gully) and half of the spit south of the gully. The new dividing line between Gruppe Seydel and Grenadier-Regiment 576: broad street grid square 64b – 74c – south-west edge of the southern Hall 6 of the gun factory – centre of the playground – centre of the spit south-east of the playground.

It was hoped this measure would share the burden and bring the increased firepower of Gruppe Schwerin into play.

Note: Numbers indicate regiments

New boundary between 305. Infanterie-Division and Gruppe Seydel.

– – –

Back on Lyudnikov's Island, the relative calm was interrupted by a few minor clashes.

At 1210 hours, the storm groups of Grenadier-Regiment 577 and Pionier-Bataillon 336 undertook an attack on the right flank of 650th Rifle Regiment from the direction of Dom 35 [Haus 66], 36 [Haus 73] and Workshop 14/15 [Hall 3]. Pechenyuk was not sure of the strength of the German groups. His men held their positions in Dom 37, despite the fact that the German attackers threw grenades into the building. Pionier-Bataillon 336 suffered light casualties: from 2. Kompanie, Gefreiter Gerhard Richter[77] was killed and Pionier Walter Knödel[78] wounded, while in 3. Kompanie, Pionier Otto Rubel[79] was killed and Pionier Heinrich Claus[80] was wounded.

Pechenyuk's men noticed ominous signs in their opponent's sector. In the evening of 15 November, they had heard the deep grumbling of engines, probably panzers. And in the area of the Kommissarhaus and behind the front-line on the left flank, the Germans had grouped together up to 200 men. They knew it was only a matter of time before this assemblage hurled themselves at the thin line. 138th Division noted in its journal that "the enemy continues to gather strength".

At 1400 hours, small groups tried to infiltrate through the main defensive line into the combat ranks of 138th Rifle Division's units.

– – –

77. Richter, Gefreiter Gerhard, 2./Pi.Btl.336; born 6 February, 1910 in Weifa. Killed in action, 16 November, 1942 in Stalingrad.

78. Knödel, Pionier Walter, 2./Pi.Btl.336; born 15 July, 1909 in Buchholz. No further information known.

79. Rubel, Pionier Otto, 3./Pi.Btl.336; born 26 January, 1909 in Gommern. Killed in action, 16 November, 1942 in Stalingrad.

80. Claus, Pionier Heinrich, 3./Pi.Btl.336; born 1 July, 1909 in Geithain. No further information known.

The four signalmen of the Rolik group were still holding out in their cliffside dug-outs right under the very noses of the Germans. Word of Rolik's daring and sangfroid had rapidly spread throughout the division and every morning the Soviet defenders of the Barrikady asked themselves: "How is our Rolik? Is he holding on?" The sound of gunfire and explosions from the far left flank answered their questions: 'Rolik is spinning, Rolik is firing. That means that they are well off and fighting!'

The Germans had tried numerous times to destroy Junior-Sergeant Kuzminsky and his men. Dozens of grenades were hurled at the dug-outs but they either sailed harmlessly by or bounced down the slope and exploded at the base of the cliff. When the Germans tried to fire at the signalmen, they did so by peaking over the crest and therefore silhouetted their heads against the skyline, offering easy targets for Rolik. The group was in a perfect defilade position. When the Germans tried to get them with mortars, they moved deeper into their dug-outs from where they could still cover each other. As soon as the bombardment stopped, they moved closer to the dug-out entrances, ready to nail any foolish German who'd exposed himself. One time, the Germans wheeled an anti-tank gun onto the crest just as a bombardment ended. They quickly discovered that the barrel could not be depressed low enough to strike the dug-outs and were only able to get off a few hasty shots before the Rolik group – exploiting the few quiet seconds when the gun was being reloaded – sprayed the gun with submachine-gun fire. Most of the German crew were killed or wounded.

And throughout all this, Rolik maintained contact. Only once, on 16 November, was communication with the division command post broken. On line-repairs was Junior-Sergeant Kolosovsky. The route to the breakage was blocked by a group of German soldiers. Well-aimed shots hit two of them, the third was wiped out with a grenade, then Kolosovsky repaired the damage to the line. He was later awarded the Order of the Red Star for this feat.

Rolik was the southernmost defensive position on Lyudnikov's Island. The next one heading north along the cliffline was the remnants of the Barrikady militia group – those that had survived the terrible furnace in the Kommissarhaus on 13 November – and the NKVD blocking detachment under their commander Senchkovsky. Amongst this motley collection was Politruk Leonid Klyukin, still singed and battered after his ordeal at the Kommissarhaus:

> In mid-November, our group held the line between the Rolik signal group and the units of 138th Rifle division, on this division's left flank. Three teams from our group and 650th regiment held defensive positions in the pumping station and in the neighbouring gully. My team was situated near the steep bank, north of the pumping station. The company commander was wounded and I was forced to take his place.
>
> 'Lyudnikov's Island' had three gullies. It was by way of these gullies that the Germans tried to reach the Volga. How many enemy attacks petered out on the approaches to our positions! I remember our neighbours – the soldiers of the Rolik group. The enemy made his fiercest attacks on them but could do nothing to overcome the brave defenders.
>
> 'Rolik is alive!' Our soldiers rejoiced – having just found out about the neighbours' repulsion of the latest attack. At one point, Rolik fell silent. Detachment commander Senchkovsky summoned me and gave me, together with chief-of-staff Finogenov, the task of finding Rolik. When we finally found the signalmen and saw them with our own eyes, we became very happy. After the repulsion of the last attack, the Rolik men were resting.
>
> 'Do either of you comrades have a smoke?' asked one of the men. We shook our heads. We too suffered from a lack of cigarettes. On the way back, as we ran across the gully, the enemy opened fire with mortars. Finogenov was wounded in the leg. We reached the command post with great difficulty. The next day, the Germans mounted another attack. 'Rus, bul, bul… but if you don't want… surrender!', they hollered.

We let the Germans approach closely before opening fire. The Germans never managed to reach our trenches. Several officers and men came from the command post to assist us. The enemy did not succeed this time.

Slightly north of Klyukin were the worn-out remnants of 650th Rifle Regiment. After being forced to vacate his command post in Haus 83, Major Pechenyuk had settled into one of the ubiquitous riverside dug-outs. His few remaining men embedded themselves in cleverly sited positions along the very edge of the precipice. These positions offered the narrowest of targets to artillery and mortars, yet could easily cover the open ground between the cliff and the buildings. The foxholes and trenches were also interconnected by tunnels. Commissar Tyupa, deputy commander of 1st Rifle Battalion, recalls:

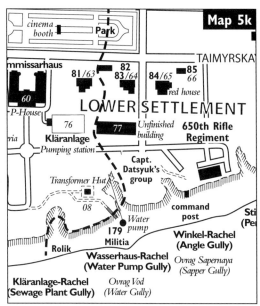

Defensive positions of 650th Rifle Regiment.

> We held on to the steep Volga bank […] and ruined houses close to the Volga. We repulsed enemy submachine-gunners who filtered through us to the rear, along the Volga… our position became significantly more complicated. We stopped getting ammunition and food. We captured weapons and ammunition to fight the Germans.

Only a few people were left and almost everyone else was wounded, but they were still divided into storm groups of 3 to 5 men. Storm groups maintained the defence, filtered through the enemy positions and destroyed his personnel while taking weapons, ammunition and food.

Senior-Sergeant Gorbatenko tried to supply his comrades with some sustenance:

> In the evening […] defence was organised along the bank of the Volga. I dropped into every staff and contacted division administration. Supplies: sugar for 4-8 people and a piece of lard – these were the rations for twenty-four hours.

– – –

After the fruitless attack against the Rote Haus, Pionier Bertold Paulus, 2./Pionier-Bataillon 45, jotted off another letter to his anxious parents, dated 16 November:

> I am healthy and lively, as I hope is the case with all of you…

> I will tell you shortly what is happening here. I've already written to you in my letter from the 13th how Hartmut was killed. On the 16th we buried him and ten other comrades with military honours at the Heroes Cemetery. Don't say anything to his parents until the company has written to them.

> I was again in action from the 13th to the 16th. We attacked two days, and on the 20th we'll attack again. We're now only a very small mob. Many comrades are dead, and most are wounded. I've been lucky so far. Hopefully it stays that way.

> I had never visualised war as being so terrifying. If I have good luck and come home, then I will tell you about Stalingrad. What I have seen so far cannot be described. One can still be satisfied with the weather – it is cold and dry. We have averages of -12 to -22°. I am well-supplied with winter equipment…

In the meantime, stocks of foods on 'the Island' were running out. Lyudnikov was compelled to introduce the following daily ration for each man and officer: 25 grams of dry bread (like crackers), 12 grams of grain and 5 grams of sugar. Lyudnikov dictated this order when only two of eighteen fishing boats that set sail from Zaitsevsky Island arrived on the west bank of the Volga near the Barrikady. Sixteen boats were smashed when they were riddled by fire on the Volga channel.

The current brought in two boats. Lying in each were wet bags of crackers and tins of pork fat. And in each boat was three dead men: the helmsman and two oarsmen. The 'Islanders' accepted this gift from the dead, and Lyudnikov strictly ordered that everyone receive a share of this gift.

Lyudnikov dictated the order, pressing a flask of hot water to his right hip. Before the war he had been ill with a stomach ulcer, then the ulcer had cicatrised, but the meagre rations had caused an aggravation of the illness. Lyudnikov told no-one about it, and only the nurse on staff, Sima Ozerova, who supplied the division commander with hot water, knew how it troubled Lyudnikov. The division commander grudgingly told his chief-of-staff about his illness. Lieutenant-Colonel Shuba consulted with the deputy division commander, Colonel Kurov, and they went to Lyudnikov together.

Barrikady Museum

"We soldiers are able to tighten our belts in a famine", Lyudnikov said, handing the order for 42 grams of food a day to Shuba. "It's a pity about the wounded men… There is no medicine, no bandages. How many wounded men with us?"

Shuba answered: "More than three hundred. And also one who is seriously ill with an aggravated stomach ulcer. To risk the health of this patient…" said Shuba, significantly emphasising the last words, "…we have no right. If the boats come on a return trip tonight…"

"Enough, Lieutenant-Colonel! I did not ask you about that patient, and this damned gossiping…"

The conversation was now entered by Colonel Kurov: "Ivan Ilyich, we absolutely officially…"

Lyudnikov lifted his hand and Kurov stopped short. He knew the division commander well enough to understand that gesture and that stare, a penetrating glare from under his dense eyebrows that formed one line. But Lyudnikov's voice still remained quiet. "Absolutely

Lieutenant-Colonel Vasili Ivanovich Shuba, chief-of-staff of 138th Rifle Division.

officially as commander of this division, I demand to stop this conversation."

Kurov remained in the background, but Shuba, hurt by such a conversation with the division commander, did not want to give up: "I consider it my duty to inform army staff about the illness of the division commander."

"If that's how you understand your duty – inform them! By the way, it will be your last message as divisional chief-of-staff."

Shuba had become confused. There was a long pause.

"Sit down", said Lyudnikov in a reconciliatory tone, and his gaze become warmer. "I do not apologise for my abruptness because you've caused it."

"Ivan Ilyich!" exclaimed Kurov. "Forgive us, we did it out of the best motives."

"I understand. However, what motives can there be now, except for one: to stand our ground and win? We formed the division together, we are at war together. Apparently we know one another, but do we really know? We as soldiers should learn sincere frankness", said Lyudnikov, his face brightening, though still remaining anxious. "Two soldiers will sit in a trench at night and will soon know everything about one another. Where they lived and what they did, who they loved, what they liked doing… Last night I dreamed about my uncle, Andrei Lyudnikov. Shall I tell you about my uncle?"

Kurov and Shuba exchanged glances, surprised by the unusual turn the conversation had taken. Devoid of any sentimentality, Lyudnikov just needed to pour his heart out. All of them would understood when he finished his story. He started with memories of his distant childhood in a fishing village on the Sea of Azov. In spring and autumn, strong easterly winds blew across the Azov, and the most skilled fishermen would dare to head out to sea. Among the helmsmen, Andrei Lyudnikov was considered the best. And so, when the winds blew, the fishermen waited to see how Uncle Andrei acted. If he continued out to sea, it meant it was possible for others to raise their sails. Such a person would not risk himself in vain, not set a bad example for the people. "Apparently, I did not dream in vain about Uncle Andrei," said Lyudnikov, continuing his story. "I saw his barge float across the Volga, struggling against all calibres, and then it moored safely on the bank just next to our dug-out. Uncle Andrei said, 'Just don't forget your fishing ancestry, Vanyusha. Don't let go of the rudder while you're still alive! As I was at the fishing co-operative, so you are at the division. If you show weakness, if your heart trembles and you rush to Volga, yes to the Volga, far away from the enemy – all Russia will be orphaned.' And after these words it's as if he dissolved: he was no longer there."

Kurov and Shuba now understood. "When a ship capsizes, the captain is the last to leave," said Lyudnikov, "but there will be no such capsizing with us. It is impossible for us to drown. We're on the unsinkable island of Barrikady."

- - -

138th Rifle Division steadily held its positions while repelling numerous but small German attacks. The day had turned out to be a pause in the intense attacks against the division. It was apparent to Lyudnikov that the Germans were in no position to continually attack as they had previously done from 11 to 13 November. Because of the steadfastness of 138th Rifle Division's troops, it was necessary for the Germans to take a few days off in order to prepare future offensive actions. Lyudnikov needed his superiors to undertake immediate measures to ease the pressure on his division, in accordance with the fact that a new German advance was expected on the morning of 17 November. Lyudnikov's division was dangerously weak. It had a total of 800 men on the western bank and of those, 450 were soldiers and command staff, 350 were wounded men. More were added on this day: the division suffered losses of 3 killed and 15 wounded, a total of 18 men. Grenades, PPSH cartridges, medicine and dressing materials were not available. There was also no food. The power supply for the radio set was also getting dangerously low. The division's dire situation simply had to be reported but the solitary radio set could not transmit and even reception was only available for very limited periods. Lyudnikov ordered the reconnaissance chief, Major T.M. Batulin, to make ready the sort of scout who could reach army staff and report on the conditions which had developed in the division. He chose the legendary Sergeant Nikolai Ivanovich Petukhov, a scout who specialised in penetrating into the German rear using tunnels, sewerage pipes and conduits. He got behind the German line almost every night, sowing panic, killing soldiers, destroying equipment and capturing 'tongues' – Russian slang for enemy prisoners. Recently, he destroyed a German machine-gun atop the steep Volga cliff that was firing at the river crossing, and had so far captured ten prisoners who revealed that new units had been transferred from other sectors of the front. Petukhov was eventually awarded the Order of Lenin for his combat feats in Stalingrad.

Now Petukhov put forward a risky and dangerous plan to reach 62nd Army HQ: he would lie down in a boat covered with a white smock and drift with the Volga current down to the area of army staff.

– – –

The day had been miserable: temperatures never rose above freezing and the morbid sky never once permitted the sun to shine through. Chunks of ice moved down the river. By night-time, the temperature had fallen well below freezing and larger ice floes had formed, making so much noise that the Germans didn't hear two fishing boats depart near the Rolik dug-out. One of the boats was carried downstream. Petukhov laid down in the boat to hide himself. At the same time, the other boat headed towards Zaitsevsky Island. At night, the floating ice developed an eerie fog-like appearance. The fishing boats, having been wrapped in wet canvas to form ice, also began to resemble floes. From the Rolik position, they watched the first boat – now surrounded by ice – disappear behind a bluff near the Krasny Oktyabr factory. The second boat became immobilised in the middle of the channel. What had stopped it? Perhaps the wet canvas was pulling the boat downstream. The Rolik group then saw the boat reach clear water at which point the man stood up and jumped overboard. The Germans then opened fire on the boat and sunk it soon after[81]. Soviet artillery opened intensive fire on German positions in an effort to disrupt their attempts at eliminating the brave man. The Rolik group did not know the fate of the man who had jumped into the water. They reported their observations to the divisional staff.

On the same night, the chief of staff of engineer units of the Stalingrad Front summoned the commander of the 107th Separate Pontoon Battalion from Zaitsevsky Island. Before the chief-of-staff sat a politruk dressed in a new greatcoat that was not fit for his rank. The politruk's face was thin and had a look of exhaustion to it. Surely he had been brought there after going through a heavy illness.

"This is Politruk Zuyev. He came here from Lyudnikov's Island", said the chief-of-staff to the battalion commander. "Before you receive orders, I want you to speak with Zuyev and then the two of you will depart to the pontoon battalion. I want the pontoon unit to see this man and hear what he has to say." Senior-Politruk Mikhail Timofeyevich Zuyev – the editor of the divisional newspaper 'Patriot of the Motherland' and a fine sportsman – had volunteered to swim to Zaitsevsky Island to report on the needs of his imperilled division. He risked his life in the icy waters, knowing that there was no other way to establish contact. The pontoon unit had been aware of the situation of 138th Rifle Division but, after listening to Zuyev, they fully understood the difference between a real island like the one they were on and the 'Island' from where Zuyev had come and to where he would return.

Petukhov's operation also succeeded. Based on his report, Chuikov called the military council of the Stalingrad Front: "I am afraid for 138th Rifle Division. The enemy presses

---

81. In the evening report of LI. Armeekorps at 2100 hours, it was reported that "one rowboat with 20 men was sunk by artillery of 389. Infanterie-Division. Perhaps an exaggerated claim by the division?

them with large forces. Realistically, I can only help them with artillery and Katyushas..."

– – –

The period of drift-ice would be a dangerous time for 62nd Army. The fear that the Germans would successfully exploit the serious disruption to Soviet supplies caused by the ice floes was very real. It was more serious than officially acknowledged. Chuikov had hoarded a small reserve but it was not very much:

> For several days before the period of heavy drifting ice and the beginning of the new enemy offensive, the army laid in ammunition... I also had my own secret store. Colonel Spasov was in charge of it. In it was the army's emergency stores – about twelve tons of chocolate. I reckoned that in a difficult moment, by giving out half a bar per man at a time, we could survive a week or two, until the Volga had frozen over and regular supplies could be delivered.

Unfortunately for Lyudnikov and his hungry men, two German regiments and hundreds of metres of occupied river bank lay between them and this stash. More important than food was a connection between Lyudnikov's Island and the rest of 62nd Army. Chuikov wrote:

> We had the task of trying to help Lyudnikov's division, cut off from the main army. Its position had become extremely serious: it was under enemy pressure from the north, the west and the south and on the east was cut off by the Volga, with its non-stop floating ice... I cannot omit to mention the courage of the encircled division's commanders, led by Colonel Ivan Ilyich Lyudnikov. In spite of the extraordinarily difficult situation, they remained calm and confident. Telephone links, of course, had been broken. Our only communication was by radio. I several times had a personal, uncoded conversation with Lyudnikov over the radio. We recognised each other's voices and did not call each other by name. I had no hesitation in telling him that help would be forthcoming, and that we would soon be joining up with him. I hoped he would understand why I was talking openly to him, and that our troops could in fact give him no help. He also said we would be meeting soon. In this way we tried to mislead the enemy.

At the same time, however, Chuikov set up special armoured posts, consisting of heavy machine-gunners, hand machine-gunners and anti-tank guns, on Zaitsevsky Island, to try and forestall a German breakthrough and encirclement. The implications are that he feared Lyudnikov's Island would be lost and the Germans would then encircle the broken remnants of 62nd Army and finish the job.

It unexpectedly became warmer in the evening, so the drift-ice on the Volga became less dense and powerful. This enabled an immediate increase in ferry transportation to 62nd Army. Delivery of food and ammunition to 138th Rifle Division, however, proceeded only by plane. On Chuikov's order, PO-2 aircraft again dropped small amounts of supplies to the division during the night. Of the 13 parcels dropped, only 8 were retrieved, the rest falling behind German lines or into the Volga. Received were four bales of food, two bales of 45mm shells and two bales of 82mm shells. The division was still critically short of ammunition, mortar shells and rations.

Captured by LI. Armeekorps on 16 November: 69 prisoners, including 21 deserters.

Casualties for 16 November, 1942:	
138th Rifle Division:	3 killed, 15 wounded, a total of 18 men
305. Infanterie-Division:	26 men killed and 42 men wounded
389. Infanterie-Division:	2 men killed and 2 men wounded

17 November, 1942

Throughout the night, there was continual strong artillery harassment fire on the entire sector of the gun, bread and steel factories, but particularly on the forward line of Kampfgruppe Seydel and Grenadier-Regiment 576. Otherwise, there were no special occurrences. From the point of view of 650th Rifle Regiment: "The enemy did not partake in any active measures throughout the night and day, apart from methodically firing on the front-line and periodically firing his machine-guns and submachine-guns…" There was little activity on both sides. The most notable occurrence on this day was the first heavy fall of snow later in the evening.

- - -

After more than a full month in Stalingrad for 305. Infanterie-Division, and even longer for 389. Infanterie-Division, both divisions were completely spent. Hundreds of officers and thousands of men had been stripped from both divisions by death and wounds. The moment was rapidly approaching when they could no longer function effectively, so 6. Armee decided an urgent remedy was needed. They had sent a teletype message to Heeresgruppe B at 2045 hours the previous evening:

> The army demands the raising and speedy dispatch of a replacement battalion for 389. Infanterie-Division.
>
> On 15 November, the division had a total combat strength of 3530 men, but of that, the combat strength of the infantry is only about 1600 men.
>
> The replacements previously supplied to the division were numerically far below the average number of replacements supplied to other divisions. 389. Infanterie-Division is the only division of the army that is not expecting any further replacements out of the homeland for the time being.

At 1120 hours on the current day, Oberstleutnant i.G. Elchlepp at 6. Armee telephoned Oberstleutnant i.G. Schulze at Heeresgruppe B:

> Deployed in the front-lines of Stalingrad are 389. and 305. Infanterie-Divisions. 389. Infanterie-Division has not received a replacement battalion for a long time, so the danger exists that this division will bleed to death. We therefore request the accelerated delivery of replacements.
>
> 305. Infanterie-Division received about 1000 replacements but there are no junior commanders amongst them. It is barely possible to train these men because NCOs are missing. These missing men must be supplied by the fastest possible means, even if that entails bringing them in by air.

One division received no replacements while the other had, but even then they were merely human materiel, a group of naive young men not yet soldiers. And 305. Infanterie-Division simply had no experienced NCOs to train them. Those not buried in the ground or lying in a hospital bed were desperately needed at the front. Sending the untrained replacements into the brutal hell of Barrikady would accomplish nothing except needless deaths. To be of any worth, the men needed to be drilled, not just in streetfighting tactics, but also in ordinary basic training. Hauptmann Rettenmaier was pulled out of the front-line on 18 November and sent to the rear to help incorporate the new replacements into his regiment: "At the moment I am in the rear of Stalingrad. Replacements are coming in and the regiment must be reformed, this being my task over the next few days."

Anecdotal evidence seems to show that training of the replacements was at the discretion of each unit. While the grenadier regiments conducted rudimentary training, Pionier-Bataillon 305 put them straight into the line, as Gefreiter Josef Zrenner[82] recalls:

> We received reserve units in the middle of November and they were parcelled out, but unfortunately I must say that they were quickly trained men. They therefore had no experience of any form. They were young men, and we assigned them, proportionately, according to the individual strengths still remaining in the companies.
>
> They were first briefed by the staff. They were then split up amongst the individual combat groups. They were instructed by the staff and told exactly how to behave by those men already at the front, and then at night, they were directed into the battle line, into the foremost position, and there, 2, 3, 4 soldiers were each assigned to the strongpoints at the front. There was no uniform combat line […] but only individual strongpoints, and they were assigned to those, two there, two there and two there. The familiarisation was therefore done at the front by a man who had combat experience.
>
> I have to say that these replacements were not a reinforcement for us. I received approximately ten, fifteen new men for a unit, and among them was an officer, and I can still clearly remember saying to him, 'Herr Leutnant, take off your epaulets because if they are still there, then the snipers there, with the Russian units, if they see those, then you will quickly fall victim'. So he removed his epaulets and we moved the group forward during the evening, into the front ranks, the front position, and on the next day when I came forward and asked for the Leutnant, he was already missing, was already gone. Nothing more was found. And the young men, some of them had already fallen, either wounded, or generally could not be found because they'd gone astray in the positions. They had to know that our units were stationed on one side of the building and the road, Russian units were on the other side, and it moved back and forth. We could no longer advance any further because the forces available to us were lacking.
>
> It was unfortunate that these quickly trained young men were thrown into this fighting. As a consequence of this, which was shocking for me, after two, three days I noticed that these young men were not up to the fighting. They came back and some were mentally stressed, they had discarded their weapons, they were insane, they spoke insanely, thus they were like that, and I say this mildly, they had gone crazy because of the fighting, and they were not able to bear the strain. We had to disarm them, we had to take them into our care by force, those lying out in the snow. They could not be approached, they were totally insane, and reasoning with them did not help. One of them aimed his weapon at us, at himself, we had to disarm him, some of the others simply lay down in the snow, others ran ahead and as much as it was possible we took them back to the main dressing station and handed them over to the medics. However, all of this happened before the encirclement, and afterwards, when there was a pocket, beginning from 21 November, we could no longer care for these people, it was no longer possible.

Despite the grim situation along the Volga, the troops still put on a brave face for their loved ones at home. Stabsgefreiter Hans Bernhart, 1./Grenadier-Regiment 578, wrote that "I'm as fit as a fiddle, as much as one can be here. We don't have any snow but it is very chilly…"

– – –

During the morning, a Führer Decree concerning the capture of Stalingrad arrived at 6. Armee HQ:

> The following Führer Decree is to be communicated by word of mouth to all commanding officers engaged at Stalingrad down to and including regiment commanders:

---

82. Zrenner, Gefreiter Josef, Stab/Pi.Btl.305; born 5 December, 1920 in Neustadt, Still alive in 2006.

'I am aware of the difficulties of the fighting in Stalingrad and of the diminishing combat strengths. Ice drifting on the Volga, however, now poses even greater difficulties for the Russians. If we exploit this time span, we shall avoid a great deal of bloodshed later on.

'I therefore expect that the leadership and the troops will once more, as they often have in the past, devote all their energy and spirit to at least breaking through to the Volga at the gun factory and at the steel works, and occupying these sections of the city.

'Luftwaffe and artillery must do all they can to prepare and support this attack.

'The Führer'

Paulus sent back a limp reply:

I beg to report to the Führer that the commanders in Stalingrad and I are acting entirely in the spirit of this order to exploit the Russians' weakness occasioned during the past several days by the drift-ice on the Volga. The Führer Decree will give the troops fresh impulse.

Before forwarding the Decree to his subordinates at 1315 hours, Paulus added his own appeal: "I am confident that this order will give our brave troops fresh impetus!"

Hitler's expectations had become smaller. No longer were there strategic sweeps of his hand over a map of the Soviet Union; now, he was happy to conquer a few hundred metres of battered riverside real estate. General Seydlitz, the corps commander under whose aegis the gun and steel factories fell, was appalled when the decree arrived: "After all of our efforts, I received this order as a slap in the face."

- - -

At 2337 the previous evening, 62nd Army staff issued Order No. 220 directing a part of its forces to counterattack the German group in the area east of Mezenskaya and join up with 138th Rifle Division. The task fell to 95th Rifle Division and its subordinated units and support would be provided by artillery groups of 62nd Army. In preparation for the attack, a schedule of artillery strikes began at 0500 and continued until 1145 with the aim of destroying German pillboxes and firing points near the fuel tanks before finishing off with a 15-minute crescendo prior to the infantry going in at midday.

Languid tendrils of fog draped around the mutilated ruins of the Barrikady and across the river. Noises were dampened by the grey blanket. Occasional shells whined over and down into the ruins, but the following detonations were muffled, muted. Sporadic volleys of rifle and machine-gun fire rippled along the front-line. Both sides strained their eyes and ears into the fog. Things were quiet around the boundary of Lyudnikov's Island. As over the past few days, the focal point of artillery bombardments and attacks had shifted south, to the cratered plateaux and gullies around the fuel installation. Soviet artillery placed their harassment fire over the entire sector from 0500 hours in the morning and the Katyushas joined in at 1000 by placing volleys into the south-eastern section of the factory in an effort to destroy German personnel and any reserves positioned close behind the lines. At about 1130 hours, however, a violent surprise barrage landed right on Grenadier-Regiment 576 and the left sector of Kampfgruppe Seydel. The Germans estimated that the fire came from at least two heavy batteries, several light battalions and numerous rocket-launchers. Artillerie-Regiment 179 reported:

Assembly positions and enemy movements in front of Gruppe Seydel's sector were effectively shelled with concentrated fire… The regiment placed massive harassment fire on the assigned areas.

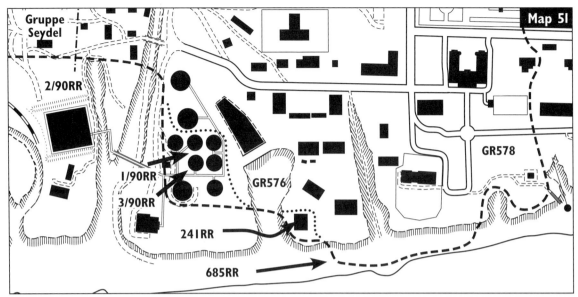

Soviet attacks around the fuel tanks, 17 November, 1942.

The heavy, concentrated artillery, mortar and rocket-launcher fire moved on to the German front-line defences at 1145 hours and continued to pound those sectors until 1200 hours, when it shifted to the depths of the German defences. One final volley of rockets came down on the fuel tank area. At that moment, Gorishny's units set off to attack the right wing of 305. Infanterie-Division in the fuel installation.

Heavy Soviet artillery fire, which dropped back from the attack area, stretched from the left wing of Gruppe Schwerin to the right of 389. Infanterie-Division and continued until 1300 hours. The Katyushas threw salvoes into the south-eastern section of the Barrikady until 1400 hours. LI. Armeekorps reported to 6. Armee that "our own artillery could only return fire within the limits of the inadequate stocks. Fighting is still in progress." This ammunition shortage was not noticed by the Soviets: it was stated in Combat Report No. 51 that "the enemy, laying down drum-fire on the Volga bank, tries to stem the advance of the attacking infantry at Shiroki (Wide) Gully".

The combat in the fuel installation area was becoming increasingly ferocious. Grenadiers and pioneers had entrenched themselves as best they could. Barbed-wire entanglements were strung along the front-line positions and mines densely laid, especially along the Volga beach and in the gullies. German defences were constructed around the bases of the fuel tanks and along the rim of Two-Finger Gully. The cornerstone of the defence was a squat but powerful transformer station [Dom 05] on the northern side of Appendix Gully: from its windows, machine-guns could easily control the shallow plateau below the fuel installation. The fuel tanks themselves were nothing but crumpled, charred cylinders reeking of burnt petrochemicals. The main avenue of advance for Gorishny's riflemen and marines was along the river bank and up the gullies. Open expanses were avoided, if possible.

Colonel Vasili Akimovich Gorishny, commander of 95th Rifle Division, controlled all of these attacks from his command post situated in a dug-out in the cliffs a few hundred metres south of the fuel tanks. From an observation post in front of his dug-out, he was able to watch the attacks go in along the approximately 20-metre wide river bank, but the fuel tanks further north were hidden behind the cliffline. Tasked with breaking through to Lyudnikov,

The precarious position of 95th Rifle Division, 17 November, 1942.

Gorishny and his men were in a precarious position themselves: their sector was a narrow finger of land clamped between the Volga and the parallel German front-line only a few hundred metres back from the water. Worse than that, however, was the fact that their link with the rest of 62nd was extremely tenuous… cutting directly across their rear was 'Ovrag Glubokaya' (Deep Gully), a broad, steep-sided ravine that stretched all the way inland to the bread factory. To the Germans it was known as 'Bandwurm Rachel' (Tapeworm Gully) or simply the 'Brotfabrik Rachel' (Bread Factory Gully). Soviet soldiers, however, had a more grisly name for it. Fierce fighting had been raging along the ravine since 23 October and many German attempts to reach the Volga had come to grief within its loamy walls, and as a result, so many corpses and so much destroyed materiel filled it that Soviet soldiers nicknamed it the 'Gully of Death'. In mid-November, the German line here, held by Gruppe Seydel, was only 400 metres from the Volga and the entire length of the gully was exposed to their rifle and machine-gun fire. It was only possible to reach 95th Rifle Division – and Gorishny's command post – by moving along the riverbank and crossing the mouth of the 'Gully of Death' in a commando crawl, hugging the ground as closely as possible. Even then the German bullets found victims. To avoid losses, Soviet engineers erected a double palisade across the gully and filled the resulting space with stones and sand. This log-and-dirt fence proved indispensable and Soviet soldiers could move back and forth in its protection, safe from German machine-gun fire.

Meanwhile, on the southern flank of Grenadier-Regiment 576, Soviet troops launched an attack at noon. Obscured by the fog, they surged along the river bank and up the gullies. Mines and blindly-aimed German machine-gun fire down the gullies took a heavy toll. The combat journal of 685th Rifle Regiment describes the combat on their narrow sector:

> The regiment, with its remaining forces, together with subunits of 3rd Rifle Battalion of 92nd Rifle Brigade, tried to break through the gully. A group of 8 men managed to filter across but were destroyed by the fire of machine-guns, submachine-guns and grenades from dug-outs and trenches located directly on the bank of the Volga and the northern slopes of the gully.

Despite the setback, Soviet groups from 90th Rifle Regiment were able to punch through the German line into the fuel installation. German machine-guns in the large buildings north-west of the tanks sprayed the ghostly figures as they flitted through the milky haze. Grenades thumped. Shouts rang out and machine-guns started to hammer. The fuel installation area was a warren of trenches, craters and foxholes, so the Soviet intruders were able to disappear below ground level. The grenadiers around the penetration

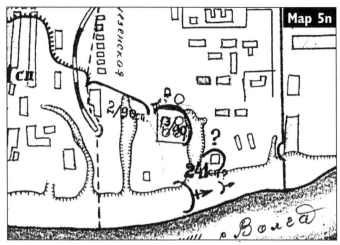

241st, 90th and 685th Rifle Regiments push north along the Volga and near the fuel tanks, 17 November, 1942.

immediately recognised the danger and pulled back. The capture of the fuel tanks was recorded in 95th Rifle Division's Combat Report No. 51:

> At 1200, having gone over to the offensive, 1st and 2nd Battalions of 90th Rifle Regiment suffered heavy losses but by 1350 had seized the fuel tanks, where they consolidated and continued to develop the success in a north-easterly direction.

The German garrison in the transformer were one of the main targets of Gorishny's attack. The battle for the strongpoint is mentioned in the same combat report:

> After an artillery and mortar preparation, 241st Rifle Regiment launched an attack on the firing points in Shiroki (Wide) Gully and by 1350 had seized the house on the corner of the cliff and the gully but had suffered heavy losses and could not advance. Communications was lost.
>
> A platoon thrown in under the command of the deputy regiment commander to boost the advance and offer assistance did not achieve any positive results.

Gorishny's men took a bit more ground amongst the buckled fuel tanks but further progress disintegrated in the face of vicious machine-gun fire. The 62nd Army war diary reported on the fighting:

> At 1200, after an artillery preparation, 95th Rifle Division's forces of 241st, 90th and 685th Rifle Regiments attacked the enemy in the area to the east of Mezenskaya. Having overcome stiff enemy resistance, 90th Rifle Regiment captured the fuel tanks and individual groups moved ahead to the north.
>
> 241st and 685th Rifle Regiment captured a gully 150 metres north-east of Mezenskaya and continued attacking towards the bank of the Volga. The enemy threw reserve troops into the battle. The intensity of the fighting is increasing.

Casualties amongst the German units were moderate and most of those had been caused by the preliminary barrage. The brunt of the attack was taken by Grenadier-Regiment 576 and 2./Pionier-Bataillon 305. Obergefreiter Franz Müller, father of seven and Grimm's 'problem child', was in the thick of the action. He wrote:

> We held a position for 7 days, from 11 to 17 November, where I was employed as a squad leader under platoon commander Feldwebel Pauli. The position was taken by the Russians with

overwhelming superiority from which Feldwebel Pauli, Obergefreiter Danner and myself emerged as the only survivors [of 2. Kompanie]… Feldwebel Pauli promised me that I'd get the Iron Cross First Class.

Müller barely escaped with his life when his bunker collapsed from a direct hit. He was buried alive but was eventually dug out and sent to the rear for medical treatment.

Hauptmann Weimann's Pionier–Bataillon 294 also suffered losses. Gefreiter Georg Huf[83], 1. Kompanie, was killed by a direct hit from a mortar. Soldat Paul Basan[84] from 2. Kompanie disappeared in the chaos and was never seen again. At 1355 hours, Hauptmann Weimann reported in to his parent division:

> Bataillon in infantry operation to hold the attained objective.
> Casualties since previous report:
> 1 officer sick and in hospital – Oblt. Menzel
> 2 Uffz and 12 men, of those 2 men dead
> Oblt. Pohl dies of his injuries.
>
> Pi.Btl.294
> signed Weimann, Hauptmann und Bataillon Kommandeur

Feldwebel Adam Pauli, 2./Pi.Btl.305

– – –

On Lyudnikov's Island, the situation was eerily calm. The adversaries were grateful for the breather but they still faced each other warily – enemy lines were just too close to tolerate any kind of carelessness. Every now and then a machine-gun would burst to life, a mortar round would sail in or a single shot would ring out. Both sides feared and respected the opposing snipers. One of the Germans who would meet his fate at the hands of these invisible killers was 19-year-old Grenadier Franz Maier[85], one of the few remaining members of Sturmkompanie 44:

> We were in the large factory workhalls in Stalingrad and could see the Volga from our positions. Our two storm companies and one platoon of pioneers had to attack again and again, about 50 to 60 men. There were only a few left, many wounded but most were dead. We collected the bodies of the dead, amassed them in bomb craters, removed their dog-tags and handed them over to the officers.

> At 9 o'clock in the morning of 17 November, while on guard duty in a communications trench, I was in the left

Grenadier Franz Maier, Sturmkp. 44.

83. Huf, Gefreiter Georg, 1./Pi.Btl.294; born 15 June, 1913 in Hesseldorf. Killed in action, 17 November, 1942 in Stalingrad.
84. Basan, Soldat Paul, 2./Pi.Btl.294; born 29 June, 1921 in Bochum. Missing in action, 17 November, 1942 in Stalingrad.
85. Maier, Grenadier Franz StuKp. 44; born 6 October, 1923 in St. Pölten. Still alive in 2006.

elbow and took a bullet through my lungs. A comrade next to me was killed by a head shot. There were snipers everywhere.

Unconscious, Maier was taken to a first-aid post and the next day was driven by ambulance into the rear area near Kalach. He was fortunate to be sent further west by train before the Soviet counteroffensive. Other wounded men from the Sturmkompanie were not so lucky, particularly those with severe injuries who were forced to remain in the field-hospital at Gorodische. Amongst them were Gefreiters Johann Kuhmayer[86] and Karl Kimmeswenger[87], the former dying of his wounds on Gorodische on 21 November, the latter on 25 November.

– – –

The entry in Lyudnikov's divisional combat journal for the day was brief: "Throughout the day, the enemy – with small groups of submachine-gunners – tried many times to slip by unnoticed to the Volga on the left flank of the division. 138th Rifle Division took up battle during the day." Losses were light: 3 killed, 10 wounded, a total of 13 men. Combat structure of the division: active bayonets: 344th Rifle Regiment – 82 men; 650th Rifle Regiment – 28 men; 768th Rifle Regiment – 28 men. Wounded – 358 men.

– – –

It did not take long for the Germans – masters of the counterattack – to strike back at the fuel installation. Their assault groups crunched into the western side of the penetration, swamped several Soviet positions and subjugated a few riflemen. The breach was partially sealed off but the inchoate Soviet line around the small penetration held. Conditions in the combat zone worsened throughout the afternoon. Rain squalls and snow flurries drenched the battlefield and quickly froze over in the sub-zero weather. This greatly hampered the Soviets because they needed to clamber up and down gully walls now slick with ice. Harassment fire from Soviet light artillery still covered the entire sector.

At 1635 hours, General Schmidt spoke to Oberst Winter at Heeresgruppe B and informed him of the situation:

> Towards midday in Stalingrad, the Russians conducted fierce attacks against the southern front of the fuel installation with heavy artillery support. The outcome of this operation is still uncertain at the moment because of disrupted telephone connections. Korps is of the view that 305. Infanterie-Division will straighten everything out.

At 1700 hours the Soviets relaunched the attack. Also, after darkness had fallen, they laid down continuous strong artillery fire. It was calculated that 50 barrages from rocket-launchers had fallen on the area around the gun factory during the day. The Soviet rocket fire, which began at 1000, was intended to destroy German personnel and reserves located in the south-eastern section of the factory. One of those who felt the effect of the rockets was Obergefreiter Peter Löffler[88], leader of the Fernsprechtrupp (telephone section) on the staff of Grenadier-Regiment 577. Löffler had only taken control of the section a few days earlier when his commander, an Unteroffizier whom Löffler considered to be a coward, had "lied

---

86. Kuhmayer, Gefreiter Johann, 11./Gr.Rgt.131; date of birth unknown. Died of wounds, 21 November, 1942 in Stalingrad.

87. Kimmeswenger, Grenadier Karl, 11./Gr.Rgt.131 born 5 July, 1923 in Seitenstetten. Died of wounds, 25 November, 1942 in Stalingrad.

88. Löffler, Obergefreiter Peter, Stab/Gr.Rgt.577; born 14 May, 1916 in Stetten am Kalten Markt. Died 25 May, 2006 in Ötigheim.

and cheated his way into hospital". On this day, Löffler was once again called upon to perform his most hazardous duty – locating and repairing breaks in the telephone lines:

Löffler

> It was very cold during the night of 16-17.11.42. The soil froze rock hard. Boughs and wires were arm-thick with frost. Searches for breaks in the line were again requested. With Soldat Fink, I left the regimental command post on Kommissarstrasse in the direction of the transformer station, which housed a first-aid post. Just as I was about to seek cover – because I had heard the rumbling and grumbling of approaching shells – a hail of Stalin Organ[89] projectiles came down upon us. A projectile exploded to my left front. Standing on the edge of a crater, I was sprayed by many pieces of shrapnel which smashed the lower parts of both my legs, but a shard also struck me near the heart. It cut through my uniform but became lodged in a relatively thick 'Feldgottesdiensttheft' [field church service book] which was kept safe, together with a note pad, in a leather case in my left

Obergefreiter Peter Löffler, Gr.Rgt.577

> breast pocket. There wasn't even any kind of damage to the skin! This small book was my guardian angel, otherwise, a pea-sized piece of metal would have struck me right in the heart. My left leg was broken and shattered above the ankle by shrapnel, while the right had two shell splinter impacts in the calf bone.

> The wounding happened at 1030 hours, about 50 metres from the first-aid post. Fink immediately went there to fetch some help and came back with 2 Russian Hiwis[90] and a stretcher. I had barely been placed upon it when a second hail of shells came in.

> I was taken to the dressing station. At 1100 hours in the first-aid post, emergency dressings were applied. Boots and clothing were cut off, surface shrapnel removed. In the evening I was transported back to the next dressing station, about 500 metres away. Wounds were cleaned out again, shrapnel removed and a plaster cast applied to both legs up to my stomach. During the night I was placed in a very large vaulted cellar and remained there all alone, plagued by pain and thirst. My canteen had been taken from me. Nobody was there or came into the room and I thought that I'd been forgotten. Nevertheless, early the next morning, I was transported via ambulance to Feldlazarett 1/542. Several large tents. A lot of severely wounded men lay there and there was only one medic to care for them. The doctors did not know where to begin. The first snow fell during the night, about 40cm of it.

Obergefreiter Löffler was flown out by Ju-52 to Rostov on 1 December 1942. When his casts were painfully removed, it was discovered that gangrene had set in. His infected right leg was amputated on 17 December, 1942 and a major operation on his left leg on 21 January, 1943 removed 900ml of pus, but it was saved. He remained in various hospitals until late 1944 and was invalided out of the army in March 1945.

– – –

Gruppe Seydel wrote in its daily report that "the takeover of the ordered sector from 305. Infanterie-Division will start with the onset of darkness". This measure would certainly help Grenadier-Regiment 576 as a shortening of its line would enable it to form larger reserves

---

89. 'Stalin Organ': German nickname for the Soviet Katyusha multiple rocket launcher.

90. Trans.: 'Hiwi' = '<u>Hilfswilliger</u>'. Soviet POWs or deserters employed by the Germans as auxiliary volunteers in roles such as drivers, cooks, stretcher bearers, ammunition carriers, etc. As the battle wore on, they were frequently employed as front-line soldiers. Some estimates put the number of Soviet Hiwis in the service of 6. Armee at Stalingrad at 50,000.

for counterattacks, and, because it was blindingly obvious that the Soviets would not stop launching attacks at the fuel installation, they needed all the help they could get. The number of casualties fluctuated every day, but there was nevertheless a steady draining of combat strength, mainly from losses caused by artillery and mortars. Gruppe Seydel had also been under the barrages but they in no way matched the intensity of bombardments ploughing up the fuel installation. Now, they were to take over part of Grenadier-Regiment 576's sector. The takeover was supposed to have been initiated at nightfall but the crisis in the fuel tanks delayed it until much later in the night. Visibility was still severely impeded by heavy fog.

– – –

To provide some fire support to the troops holding back the Soviet relief attempts, several anti-tank guns of Panzerjäger-Abteilung 305 had been moved into position several days earlier near the Kindergarten, just west of the Apotheke. During the early stages of the summer offensive, captured T-60 and T-70 tanks had been modified by the battalion's workshop for use as towing vehicles by having their turrets removed and couplings welded to their lower rear plates. They served admirably throughout the summer and came with the battalion to Stalingrad but proved unsuitable for use in city fighting. During operations in the factories, the couplings were ripped off by projecting obstacles, particularly railway lines. Since that time, the gun crews were forced to manhandle their guns into position around the factory district. Under cover of darkness, they had laboriously heaved and dragged their guns through the tortuous ruins of the Barrikady factory, emplaced them in the lee of the Kindergarten and then camouflaged them. One of the panzerjäger, Gefreiter Richard Bäuerle[91], recalls this operation:

> I was a G-Schütze. Each gun had G-Schützen to protect them from enemy infantry…We were shifted in the direction of Volga, into a kindergarten, and there we were 100 metres away from the Volga and every day we would fire over the Volga with our anti-tank gun. It was a completely imbecilic order for these anti-tank guns because they practically fired in a straight line. And we were now supposed to fire indirectly over the Volga at the other side. The Volga was 3km wide at this spot and our guns fired out to 2500 or 3000 metres at the most. All of the shells went into the water. Still, we had to carry out our set task each day. And there I was with 4 men, in one blow 5 men were caught by a mortar. There was still 10 men in the company, who were in the house. And I can remember that when I was wounded, I did not want to go back at all because cigarettes were being handed out. That was our ration and everyone smoked them like chimneys, so that they could get away from everything. And because of that I did not want to go back. Then they said, go back anyway, you'll be glad. And then I reached the main dressing station. Once there, someone stood up, ran through the dressing station and sang out: 'Blessed are those who gain ground to the rear because they will see the homeland again'.

Bäuerle would be lucky to escape the encirclement set to befall 6. Armee in a few days.

> I then went back in a ambulance, faster than I had thought. Normally there were two, three plank beds inside them. However, everything had been ripped out, everyone was chucked into the ambulance, which took off. I believe there were 15 men inside it. There were head injuries and everyone came in, foot injuries, arms, even those who should have been lying down, everyone came in. There were screams like in a lunatic asylum. And then we went cross-country in the direction of Kalach.

---

91. Bäuerle, Gefreiter Richard, Pz.Jäg.Abt.305; born 18 November, 1922. Still alive in 2004.

Several days later, once the massive Soviet counteroffensive was in full swing, a train leaving from Chir railway station under Soviet mortar fire would carry Bäuerle and other wounded men to safety. Although he did not know it at the time, Bäuerle was one of the last German troops to escape Stalingrad by land.

– – –

Late in the afternoon, LI. Armeekorps had reported its intention for the following day: "If the situation with 305. Infanterie-Division allows it, continuation of the assault troop operations on 18 November against the enemy bridgehead east of the gun factory." After consultations with 305. Infanterie-Division, however, this intention firmed up that evening. At 2020 hours, LI. Armeekorps stated that the "the plan is to break further parts out of the enemy bridgehead east of the gun factory with assault troops".

The German build-up did not escape the notice of Lyudnikov and his men. From the divisional war diary:

> The enemy continues to gather strength in the area of Workshop 14/15, the main workshop, Dom 35, 36 and especially 200 metres east of the Barrikady central gate… The division commander has judged the division's position to be a very difficult one. The actions taken to get supplies and rations to the division via boats were not successful. At the end of the day, there are around 380 wounded in the area of divisional headquarters. The enemy, with both flanks on the Volga, has laid down rifle and machine-gun fire on our divisional formations which defend an area 400 metres in length and 300 metres in depth.

> The Volga is being fired on day and night with concentrated fire from machine-guns, artillery and mortars. During the last 5 days, 138th Rifle Division continued to fight, for the most part with captured equipment and ammunition, and in these difficult circumstances the division held its line, while the enemy was only able to advance 200 metres at the cost of many lives.

Lyudnikov would later write: "The position of the wounded, of whom we had up to 380 by 17 November, was particularly difficult. There was neither medicine nor qualified medical assistance." The Germans were fully aware of this. Numerous Soviet prisoners described the difficult supply situation for the 'enemy group east of the gun factory' and the increasing number of insufficiently supplied wounded soldiers. In the evening of 17 November, Lyudnikov almost had a mutiny on his hands. Lyudnikov was with his chief-of-staff Shuba discussing their dire supply situation. Everything, including the reserves in men and ammunition, had its limits. In verification of this fact, Lieutenant-Colonel Shuba simply gave his commander number after number. Lyudnikov listened so intently that he did not hear a knock at the door. Nurse Ozerova entered in tears and began pleading with the commander to visit the wounded men before they 'scattered'.

"And where exactly would they go?" asked Lyudnikov. "On foot into the Volga?"

"You must hear what they are saying! They told me to leave and not come back without the commander. 'We ask for the commander and not your feminine sympathy,' they told me. I cannot reason with them at all."

Lyudnikov set out to visit the wounded. They were located next to the divisional command post, inside a specially constructed dug-out. "Hello soldiers! How's life? Tell me."

The wounded men, it seemed, had already decided on how they would speak with command. A soldier with a shattered left hand stepped forward. His hand was wrapped in a shirt and hung from his shoulder with a belt. Notwithstanding, the soldier saluted the commander with his other hand and then proceeded to motion in the direction of all the men. "Comrade Colonel! I will speak on their behalf!" he announced loudly. He then lowered his voice and with all due respect, stated the following: "We are grateful that you have called us soldiers. For nurse Sima we are but wounded men, but to you, comrade Colonel, we are still soldiers. As soldiers we were, so as soldiers we will die! Those of us who are not critically wounded demand to be given weapons and put back into formation… on the front-line."

"No, I won't allow it! I refuse your demand!"

It was difficult for Lyudnikov to say such a thing to such a determined group of men. He sighed heavily and then proceeded to walk the interior of the dug-out. Trying to discern the faces of the wounded men in the semi-darkness, he only saw eyes with an expression that asked: 'Why won't you let us, Colonel?'

"Do you know my last name?"

"We know it… it's a famous name," answered the men in unison. The spokesman of the wounded men then added with a hint of disappointment: "Why would you doubt us, comrade Colonel? I cannot name the number of the division, but how can I not know that I am fighting on 'Lyudnikov's Island' under the command of Lyudnikov?"

"The division has so few people left. I am almost without men, and you want me to send the last heroic veterans to the merciless enemy?! Soldier, you do not think well of your commander. There is something else I must inform you of: we have no ammunition for you. Just as well you are not fit for a bayonet attack. Are there any other questions?"

A long silence filled the dug-out. Finally, someone in the darkest corner spoke out: "There is one more question: what awaits us?"

Many did not like the question and a slight commotion began. Then, the same voice clarified: "We are not afraid of death, comrade Colonel… the Barrikady has showed it to us all too well. But still I wonder if they know about us beyond the Volga? Or have they already put us into our graves? Could they wait until the Volga freezes over?"

A commotion commenced again: "We will die before the river freezes over!"

"Pathetic!" "Be quiet!"

"That was not the point of our discussion! We ask to be put back onto the front-line."

And thus they began discussing the fate of the 'Island'. In those difficult times, its fate concerned more then just the wounded. For the men on the front-line, there was no time to think of such things. With every spare moment, they slept, knowing that the sound of battle would put them on their feet again. But the wounded men in the dug-out liked to argue and even hold meetings.

Lyudnikov raised his hand and the arguing ended abruptly. In the silence, only the heavy breathing of the wounded was heard.

"So, you have one question: what awaits us? There is only one answer – victory. As long as the soldier fights, there is no death… and we aren't waiting until the Volga freezes. We are fighting! They can hear the thunder from the Barrikady in the army staff headquarters, at the front headquarters. They too are waiting for the river to freeze. Perhaps not on this night, but on the next, the boats will come – bringing us ammunition, and then they will deliver you to the other bank. Such is the truth and I never hid it from you. It's no secret, there is a brave man who would swim down the river to reach Chuikov. There is a politruk who would swim across the Volga to reach Yeremenko and Khruschev. Help will come! And when it does, my friends, I will need your help. Anyone can sign up for a volunteer group that will unload the boats. The staff is not up to this undertaking on its own and I cannot pull anyone off the front-line. We will have to work under enemy fire. Whoever survives will receive a 'For Bravery' medal from my own hands. For the dead on this small land there is only one thing: eternal glory! Are you satisfied with my answer?"

"We are! Thank you comrade Colonel!"

At 2110 hours, LI. Armeekorps reported to 6. Armee that Sturmgeschütz-Abteilung 245 had no operational sIG33Bs, while those subordinated to Sturmgeschütz-Abteilung 244 would be withdrawn from the front and made ready for new employment. Immobilised assault guns still lying in the forward line were ordered to be recovered by all means possible, but that was easier said than done. The next morning, the two battalions lodged the following strength returns:

Sturmgeschütz-Abteilung 244:

Operational:	7 long-barrels, 7 short-barrels, 4 sIG33B
In for short-term repairs:	1 long-barrel, 5 short-barrels, 2 sIG33B
In for long-term repairs:	0 long-barrels, 0 short-barrels, 0 sIG33B

Sturmgeschütz-Abteilung 245:

Operational:	2 long-barrels, 0 short-barrels, 0 sIG33B
In for short-term repairs:	0 long-barrels, 3 short-barrels, 2 sIG33B
In for long-term repairs:	6 long-barrels, 5 short-barrels, 1 sIG33B

- - -

At 2135 hours, LI. Armeekorps issued Korpsbefehl Nr. 114, which finally gave the go ahead for the attack east of the steel factory, the attack that had been continuously postponed because the pioneer battalions and assault guns were still tied up near Lyudnikov's Island. In conjunction with this attack, 305. and 389. Infanterie-Divisions would launch their own assaults:

Operation Schwerin I will be carried out on the morning of 20 November. Time still to be ordered.

With an assault group, 305. Infanterie-Division will accompany the attack of Gruppe Schwerin, clearing out the gully on the south-western edge of the fuel installation together with the right neighbour and gaining the Volga bank near the 'Fabrik'.

On 21 November, 389. Infanterie-Division will capture the 'Rote Haus' and the Volga bank south-east of the house. After this operation, Sturmkompanie 24.Pz.Div. will be withdrawn and placed at the disposal of Korps.

Generalmajor von Schwerin and his staff had carefully planned his namesake operation down to the smallest detail. Ten assault groups would puncture the Soviet defences and finally take the riverbank into possession.

- - -

Captured by LI. Armeekorps on 17 November: 18 prisoners, including 12 deserters.

Casualties for 17 November, 1942:	
138th Rifle Division:	3 killed, 10 wounded, a total of 13 men
305. Infanterie-Division:	2 men killed and 11 men wounded
389. Infanterie-Division:	2 men killed and 4 men wounded

German troops were exhausted after weeks of fighting in the Barrikady: unshaven, dirty and benumbed by the roar of shells and unending combat, but the end was in sight. A few more days and they would prevail. Or so they thought. This man from 305. Infanterie-Division typifies the appearance of the soldiers in mid-November 1942.

At 2330 hours, after a certain fragile calm had settled upon the pockmarked fuel installation, Gruppe Seydel took over the assigned sector from its left neighbour: from the large gully, previous left border of Gruppe Schwerin, up to the promontory at the Gabelschlucht (Fork Gully) [also known as Two-Finger Gully] south of the fuel installation.

With the Germans preparing for yet another push, Lyudnikov knew that his only hope of salvation lay on Zaitsevsky island. Various attempts were made to reach 138th Rifle Division, and deep in the night of 17-18 November, two boats from 327th Army Engineer Battalion were prepared for the dangerous undertaking. Loaded with food, medicine and ammunition, they had not yet departed from the island when the Germans opened mortar fire on them. One boat was completely smashed by a direct hit but fortunately for the crew, they were not injured because they were far from the boat at that moment. The second boat safely departed from the bank and managed to make its way through the ice to reach 138th Rifle Division. It delivered 6 boxes of ammunition and batteries for the portable radio set. When this boat returned, it came under German bombardment. Of the five members of the boat crew, two soldiers – Zakharov and Suvorov – were killed, and two – Sergeant Yeremenko and Red Army man Aleksandrov – were wounded.

Earlier in the day, 107th Independent Pontoon-Bridge Battalion had received the order from the Chief of Engineers of 62nd Army to organise a boat ferry from Zaitsevsky Island to 138th Rifle Division. 327th Army Engineer Battalion transported cargo intended for 138th Rifle Division from the east bank of the Volga to Zaitsevsky Island, but the task of delivering this cargo to Lyudnikov's 'Island of Fire' was now in the hands of 107th Independent Pontoon-Bridge Battalion.

Another attempt was made later in the night to deliver ammunition and food. Ten pairs of coupled fishing boats, all brimming with cargo, set out from Zaitsevsky Island toward the Barrikady. The passage of these boats was covered by the artillery on Zaitsevsky Island and the east bank of the Volga. Battling the powerful current, pack-ice and German artillery, six of these small craft managed to reach Lyudnikov and his men. These vessels and their crews did not supply enough food, or enough ammunition, but they did deliver something more important – hope. The tenuous link across the ice-clogged channel signified to Lyudnikov's exhausted soldiers that they were no longer on their own. Communications had been re-established and this gave them the courage, if not yet the means, to fight on.

CHAPTER SIX

18 November, 1942

Colonel Lyudnikov decided to give responsibility for the left flank, down to the river itself, to Major Pechenyuk. In Order No. 85 from 138th divisional headquarters, it was stated that 650th Rifle Regiment would have the following subordinated to it: the group of Senior-Lieutenant Petrenko, the army blocking detachment under Lieutenant of State Security Senchkovsky, Captain Zorin's group, and the artillerymen of 241st Rifle Regiment with their 45mm guns. Whilst this sounds like a rather generous addition to Pechenyuk's combat strength, the opposite was actually true. The groups were nothing more than rag-tag collections of a few weary men, survivors of units that had melted away long ago in fiery combat. The strongest of these groups was Lieutenant Senchkovsky's NKVD blocking detachment. By gathering all disparate groups on the shattered left flank under one commander, Lyudnikov was hoping the defence there would stabilise, form a cohesive line and prevent the Germans from levering the division away from the river and its watery lifeline. The fate of the entire division was depending on it. Lyudnikov could not have placed the burdensome responsibility in more capable hands than those of 650th Rifle Regiment's commander, Major Pechenyuk. Lyudnikov would later write: "Major Pechenyuk […] was distinguished for his bravery and was gifted with that priceless intuition in war which enabled him to take bold decisions and put them into effect". Those skills were about to be put to the acid test.

Each attack was now meticulously prepared by the Germans. Individual buildings were singled out and bludgeoned by both indirect fire, from artillery and mortars, and by direct fire from panzers and anti-tank guns. The tank company assigned to support the attacks was pivotal in the new assault methods. While this was not the best employment for such a valuable offensive weapon, they were quite effective when kept behind the forward line to pound the targets from a distance. The tank company from Panzer-Regiment 36 (14. Panzer-Division) had suffered heavy losses when subordinated to 305. Infanterie-Division from 11 to 14 November, but the unit which replaced it – Oberleutnant Hans Messerschmidt's[1] Schwadron from Panzer-Regiment 24 (24. Panzer-Division) – fared much better, mostly because of the new style of assaults and Messerschmidt's skills in using his panzers correctly. Messerschmidt recalls how he used his panzers to attack the buildings of Lyudnikov's Island:

> At night, our panzers were parked in the shelter of 3- to 4-storey concrete apartment blocks that were constructed parallel to the Volga in a north–south direction. Most of them were burnt-out. These blocks had cellars and beneath them were deeper cellars. In these cellars we suspended steel mattress frames from the ceiling and could lie on them somewhat comfortably

---

1. Messerschmidt, Rittmeister Hans, 4./Pz.Rgt.24; born 27 July, 1919 in Beerendorf. Still alive in 2006.

and get some sleep. These apartment blocks protected our panzers and us in the cellar from aerial bombardment and artillery fire from the other bank of the Volga.

The Soviets on the east bank of the Volga fired at any movement on the east-west streets with anti-aircraft, anti-tank and artillery guns. We therefore developed the following procedure: before daybreak, we drove our panzers along these streets in an easterly direction. The Russians of course heard the noise of our tracks but they could only send out unaimed fire. This procedure was arranged every morning with the respective assault troops. The large buildings behind the factory were numbered on our city maps and a particular block was attacked each day. Our panzers (Panzer IVs with 7.5cm long- and short-barrels) drove out of cover and supported the attacking troops, assault gun-style. We prepared the attack on a building (as agreed) with our cannon fire. We fired into window openings, behind which the enemy lurked, ready to fire on our infantry assault troops. Our attacks were mostly prepared by artillery and large-calibre howitzer fire, as well as by Stuka bombs. On a signal, the infantry would storm forward.

Oberleutnant Hans Messerschmidt, 4./Pz.Rgt.24.

The Germans began to attack at 0400 hours. A hailstorm of shells and bullets struck the designated targets. Pechenyuk's men observed a group of about 100 German soldiers gathering 20 metres south-east of the Kommissarhaus. These were combat groups formed from Panzerpionier-Bataillon 50 and Pionier-Bataillon 162. At 0420 hours, these groups began to advance on the Soviet left flank and seemed to have the goal of capturing the unfinished house and emerging in the rear on the bank of the Volga river. One of Messerschmidt's panzers drove up to the southern corner of the Kommissarhaus and opened fire on the unfinished building. Maintaining defence positions inside it were the refugees from 15 November, Captain Datsyuk, Senior-Sergeant Gorbatenko and regimental clerk Dubov, the latter still swathed in bandages made from a dead man's singlet. Small groups of reinforcements had been sent into the building over the previous three days but the garrison was never very large. Their fortress, named the 'unfinished building', was exactly that: it was in the process of being built and had not been completed when war forced a halt to construction. It was to be a technical college but the building had never been fitted out. The cellar, thick outer facade and internal walls had all been finished but no roof had been installed. Not that it mattered because by November 1942, no building in the lower settlement had its roof. Trenches emanating from the northern end of the cellar connected the building to the river bank and other strongpoints. Now, as German shells smacked into it, the garrison waited out the fierce bombardment in the cellar. The fire from Messerschmidt's panzers and the assault guns was particularly effective. Their shells sailed through the windows and burst inside. At the same time, on the other side of the park, Dom 37 [Haus 74] was undergoing the same treatment. In its combat journal, 650th Rifle Regiment noted that "the attacks are helped by 3 tanks, which are destroying buildings". The divisional war diary stated that "the German attacks are accompanied by 5 to 7 tanks". The shelling continued throughout the entire morning and served to distract the garrisons while German combat groups pushed north along the edge of the Volga cliff and combated the tenacious defenders composed mostly of militiamen, staff soldiers and NKVD troops of the blocking detachment.

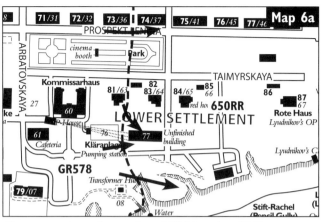

German attack on the morning of 18 November, 1942.

– – –

The Germans observed an incident on this day which forces an examination of a difficult and controversial subject: the role of the 'zagrad otryadi' – the infamous blocking detachments. Due to a popular movie and several widely-read books, the generally perceived impression of these blocking detachments is that they were positioned behind Soviet units with machine-guns, ready to scythe down anyone who retreated without orders. As soon as the words 'blocking detachment' appear, the crude image of leering NKVD soldiers aiming their guns at the backs of ordinary Soviet soldiers arises. Is there any truth to this?

The event which has sparked this line of inquiry was a letter home, dated 20 November, 1942, from Hauptmann Eugen Rettenmaier, wherein he described an incident he witnessed on the morning of 18 November, before he left for the rear:

> A few days ago, we observed wild shooting across in the Russians' territory. To begin with we could make no sense of it or what it meant. Then we began to understand. Some Russians wanted to retreat from the front-line. They were simply gunned down by their commissars[2] who were in position behind them. On top of this, a cannon bombarded them from across the Volga, whirling and hurling their corpses grotesquely about in the air. This approach is of course effective. Their tough resistance is thus explained.

The evidence which supports the account will first be examined.

Rettenmaier's other letters and reports have proven very reliable and are quite often backed up by documents and other corroborating evidence. His former profession as a teacher gave him a perceptive eye and a commonsense interpretation of what he saw and experienced. And he was never one to make wild accusations. Perhaps his statement about retreating Russians being 'simply gunned down' could be ignored if it wasn't for the fact that circumstantial evidence supports Rettenmaier, or at the very least provides the basic conditions for the event to have happened. We know from the previous week's fighting that a blocking detachment was located directly opposite Rettenmaier's regiment – if it had not been in position behind Pechenyuk's 650th Rifle Regiment, Rettenmaier's statement could be quickly discounted. Yet it was there. On this very day, 18 November, 138th Rifle Division issued an order which subordinated the blocking detachment directly to 650th Rifle

---

2. The mention of 'commissars' is the way German soldiers referred to the Soviet political officers, even though the institution of commissars had been abolished on 9 October, 1942 by Stalin's order and all political officers demoted in rank and given roles as regular officers.

Regiment. This is from the regiment's combat journal: "Order No. 085 received from divisional headquarters: Subordinated to the commander of the 650th Rifle Regiment is the […] blocking detachment of Junior-Lieutenant of State Security Senchkovsky…"

Rettenmaier was in the front-line and actually observed the event. His observation post would have offered a superb view of the incident, especially if he used binoculars. It was odd that Soviet soldiers were firing, but not at the Germans. What were they firing at? It was this fact that brought the incident to Rettenmaier's attention. Perhaps this is one of those incidents that is only reported from the enemy point-of-view? For example, in 138th Rifle Division's combat journal, an attack is mentioned where German troops were driving Russian men and women in front of them. Should this be discounted because we can find no mention of it in German veterans' accounts or in German reports?

Despite the aforementioned evidence, there are reasons to discount Rettenmaier's statements. First and foremost, it can be argued that his account is somewhat vague and speculative. It is impossible for Rettenmaier to state with 100% certainty what the source was for the wild gunfire behind Soviet lines. No mention of this incident appears in any 138th Rifle Division documents or in any other records. However, blocking detachments were under army control, so their reports were submitted directly to Army HQ. On top of all that, the Soviet regime was the past master of hushing up controversial events, so it is impossible to say the incident could not have happened.

The reason this unit was behind 650th Rifle Regiment was due to the fact that the regiment had the most precarious front-line of all Lyudnikov's rifle regiments. As reliable NKVD soldiers, the detachment could be counted on to hold their positions to the last.

The manpower situation of 138th Rifle Division was critical, so the men of the blocking detachment were being used as infantry to bolster the division's defences. It would make no sense for them to gun down Soviet soldiers in such a desperate situation. If reinforcements were being drawn from any available units like field bakeries, clerical offices, etc., so why couldn't a special unit take on such a role in a time of crisis? It's designated purpose does not have to belie its use as a combat unit.

True, Rettenmaier was an eyewitness, but from the enemy point-of-view. Misunderstandings and misconceptions happen, particularly during battle. An identical account from the Soviet perspective would be much more convincing and almost impossible to discount. An eyewitness account by the commander of the blocking detachment – Junior-Lieutenant Mikhail Ilyich Senchkovsky – does exist, but he does not write in detail about the 'normal' functions of a blocking detachment, such as detaining deserters, dealing with enemy infiltrators or 'machine-gunning his own countrymen'. Of course, nothing was normal on Lyudnikov's Island during the heavy days of November 1942. Every man was needed simply to keep the Germans from the Volga. Senchkovsky's account is purely about his detachment's military operations on Lyudnikov's Island and a brief summary of where it had been located:

> I was not a member of 138th Rifle Division but had been transferred with a detachment for a separate assignment and was under the direct command of the war council of 62nd Army. The detachment that I commanded was in the defence of the city of Kalach-on-Don, in Vertyachi-on-Don, on Mamayev Kurgan, but when the enemy broke through to the Volga on approximately 20 October, 1942, we received orders from the Army war council to transfer to the area of the Barrikady factory's lower settlement, where 138th Division was already situated.

The rest of his report is about his detachment's participation in the defence of Lyudnikov's Island, excerpts of which appear throughout this book.

Some may think the fact Senchkovsky does not mention the incident reported by Rettenmaier simply means that he has conveniently omitted the facts from his own narrative. This leads to a thorny situation: selecting facts that suit one's own argument. No matter how many accounts state that blocking detachments never fired at their own men, many will refuse to believe them. On the other hand, as soon as an account surfaces that paints a much more sinister picture, this more dramatic account will be the one cited to the exclusion of all other contrary evidence.

The truth about the blocking detachments is an extremely complex subject. Quite often, there is more myth than actual fact. Detailed information about individual units is sparse because most of it is still classified, but it is possible to obtain general information about them. The name 'blocking detachment' is very suggestive, and indeed, their defined role was to block units from retreating... but not by shooting them down with machine-guns. They simply had to detain those retreating and send them back to the front-lines. In a way, the blocking detachments were like military police but with greater powers. The detachments were placed in the second line to form the final defensive position because they were reliable NKVD troops. A veteran from a penal battalion reports that they also actually built secondary defensive positions behind the front-line. General P.N. Laschenko[3] writes that blocking detachments were always situated behind the front-line, but doesn't specify how far. Judging by the wording, it was probably more than several hundred metres. General Laschenko writes that aside from detaining deserters, blocking detachments also had to deal with possible enemy infiltrators, spies and diversionary incursions. These detachments were the precursor of SMERSH[4], which came into being in 1943.

The blocking detachments were formed in accordance with Stalin's infamous Order No. 227, issued on 28 July, 1942. This lengthy memorandum was read to all troops and certain sections are worth quoting in order to gain a better understanding of the circumstances surrounding the creation of the blocking detachments:

> The enemy throws new forces to the front without regard to heavy losses and penetrates deep into the Soviet Union, seizing new regions, destroying our cities and villages, and violating, plundering and killing the Soviet people... The population of our country, who love and respect the Red Army, start to be discouraged in her, and lose faith in the Red Army, and many curse the Red Army for leaving our people under the yoke of the German oppressors, and itself running east. Some stupid people at the front calm themselves with talk that we can retreat further to the east, as we have a lot of territory... But such talk is falsehood, helpful only to our enemies. Each commander, Red Army soldier and political commissar should understand that our means are not limitless... it is necessary to eliminate talk that we have the capability to retreat endlessly, that we have a lot of territory, that our country is great and rich, that there is a large population, and that bread will always be abundant. Such talk is false and parasitic, it weakens us and benefits the enemy, if we do not stop retreating we will be without bread, without fuel, without metal, without raw materials, without factories and plants, without railroads. This leads to the conclusion that it is time to stop retreating. Not one step back! Such should now be our main slogan. It is necessary to defend each position, each metre of our territory, up to the last drop of blood... We should establish in our army the most stringent order and solid discipline if we want to salvage the situation and keep our Motherland. It is impossible to tolerate commanders and commissars permitting units to leave their positions. It is impossible to tolerate commanders and commissars who admit that some panic-mongers

---

3. Laschenko, General Pyotr Nikolayevich, HotSU; born19 December, 1910 in Turya. Died 21 April, 1992.
4. Acronym: SMERSH = <u>Sm</u>ert <u>sh</u>pionam ('Death to Spies').

determined the situation on the battlefield by leaving with other soldiers and thus opening up the front to the enemy. The panic-mongers and cowards should be exterminated on the spot. Henceforth the solid law of discipline for each commander, Red Army soldier, and commissar should be the requirement – not a single step back without orders from higher command...

Following this rousing oratory were differing orders from the Supreme General Headquarters of the Red Army directed at Front military councils, Army military councils and commanders and commissars of corps and divisions. Section 2b of the order, relevant to army military councils in general and to army commanders in particular, deals with the blocking detachments. It is worth quoting verbatim: 'Within each army, form 3 to 5 well-armed blocking detachments (up to 200 men in each) and position them directly behind the least reliable divisions and order them, in case of disorderly retreat of the division, to shoot cowards and panic-mongers on the spot, thus helping honest soldiers of the division perform their duty for the Motherland.' Section 3b of the order, directed at commanders and commissars of corps and divisions, instructs them to 'help and support in any way possible the army's blocking detachments in their task of strengthening order and discipline in the units'.

The creation of penal companies (at army level) and penal battalions (at Front level) was also ordered.[5] In the popular imagination, penal units and blocking detachments are inextricably linked, and it is supposedly behind the penal units that the blocking detachments set up their machine-guns. In several interviews, veterans of penal units do mention the blocking detachments, but when asked if penal soldiers were ever intentionally machine-gunned by the detachments, all of the veterans stated that such things were unheard of... at least on their sector of the front. It's possible that in extreme cases this could have happened, especially in the summer of 1942, but there is no concrete proof and no validation from the veterans. Many accounts are available of deserters being executed on the spot but not a single veteran's account exists of blocking detachments gunning down groups of soldiers. If veterans recall on-the-spot executions, why doesn't anyone remember the latter? While there is no doubt that the detachments executed men – and thousands of them, to be sure – they were an extremely minor percentage compared to the numbers they detained and returned to their units. Evidence exists for this. In a memorandum of 15 October, 1942 regarding the activities of blocking detachments of the Stalingrad and Don Fronts, we read the following:

> In accordance with NKO Order No. 227, as of 15 October, 1942, 193 blocking detachments were formed within the Red Army. Of this number, 16 detachments are among the units of the Stalingrad Front, while 25 detachments are among the units of the Don Front, all of which are subordinated to NKVD special departments belonging to the Fronts' armies.
>
> Between 1 August and 15 October, the blocking detachments detained 140,755 soldiers that were supposed to be on the front-line. Of this number, 3,980 were arrested, 1,189 were executed, 2,776 were sent to penal companies, 185 were sent to penal battalions, and the remaining 131,094 men were sent back to their units and distribution points.
>
> Most of the arrests and detentions were conducted by the blocking detachments of the Stalingrad and Don Fronts.

---

5. The Front-level penal battalions would be sent mid-range and senior commanders and political commissars of equivalent rank from all arms of the service who have been guilty of a breach of discipline due to cowardice or shakiness. These battalions would be put on the most difficult sectors of the front so that the men would 'have the opportunity to repay their crimes against the Motherland in blood'. The army-level penal companies would be sent privates and junior commanders for the same reasons and they would also have the same 'opportunity' to redeem themselves.

Statistics for the Don Front: 36,109 were detained, 736 were arrested, 433 were executed, 1,056 were sent to penal companies, 33 were sent to penal battalions, and 32,933 men were sent back to their units and distribution points.

Statistics for Stalingrad Front: 15,649 were detained, 244 were arrested, 278 were executed, 218 were sent to penal companies, 42 were sent to penal battalions, and 14,833 men were sent back to their units and distribution points.

It should be noted that the blocking detachments, especially those of the Stalingrad and Don Fronts, did play their positive role during the heavy fighting in the business of upholding discipline and order in the units and preventing unorganised retreats from defended positions, and returning considerable numbers of servicemen to their units.

Several examples of the work done by individual blocking detachments were mentioned in the memorandum. It is worth quoting some of them here:

On 29 August, the staff of 29th Rifle Division of 64th Army of the Stalingrad Front was encircled by enemy tanks that broke through our lines; divisional units lost their leadership and began a chaotic retreat. The blocking detachment under Lieutenant of State Security Filatov, which was positioned behind the divisional lines, stopped the fleeing units and returned them to the defences.

And another more drastic example:

On 14 September, the enemy attacked units of 399th Rifle Division of 62nd Army that was defending Stalingrad. Personnel of 396th and 472nd Rifle Regiments panicked and began to retreat, leaving their positions. The commander of a blocking detachment (Junior-Lieutenant of State Security Elman) ordered his troops to *fire above the heads of the retreating units.*[6] As a result, personnel of these regiments halted and in two hours had returned to their positions.

The memorandum also noted several occasions in which blocking detachments were not used as intended. Considerable numbers of these units were employed as regular line formations and consequently took casualties. For example, one suffered 65% casualties and had to be disbanded while another incurred losses of 70%, whereupon it too was disbanded and its personnel distributed to rifle regiments. Others suffered casualties that caused them to be pulled back, in order to refit.

So, if the blocking detachments weren't used in the way commonly perceived, and often fought courageously, how has the misconception arisen and why was the common Soviet soldier so fearful of them? Fear of the detachments was enough to keep most soldiers in the line. To begin with, every Red Army soldier knew about the detachments, Order No. 277 having been read to every unit. Rumours and actual sightings of on-the-spot executions quickly rammed home the 'Not one step back' message. As an ordinary soldier wrote:

We talked about the significance of Order 227. This directive certainly served to simplify things a good deal. When there was a halt, we all halted together. There was no longer any uncertainty. Every soldier knew that when he stopped, his neighbour stopped too. Indeed, everyone stopped, prepared to die right there, knowing that no-one would run. The order provided a strong psychological incentive for the men. As did the knowledge that there were special blocking detachments in the rear, authorised to shoot anyone who actually did drop back...

Thanks to a common perception that is constantly being reinforced, scenes of Soviet troops being treacherously mown down from behind immediately spring to mind as soon

6. Author's emphasis.

as the words 'blocking detachment' appear. This perception leads to the unjust opinion of many that Soviet troops could only fight if they had guns to their heads. There was no need to coerce or threaten the defenders of Lyudnikov's Island. Of all locations in Stalingrad, this was the place where they were at their most courageous, their most defiant. Yet, that heroism might have been tarnished if there was a single incident where troops retreated and were fired on by their own side. Surely a division commander like Lyudnikov or a regiment commander like Pechenyuk would have considered it shameful if their men had fallen back and been fired on by the blocking detachments?

Perhaps the last word can be left to the man who commanded the NKVD detachment on Lyudnikov's Island and the role it actually performed. Lieutenant Senchkovsky:

> Cut off from the main supply base, we noticed the shortage of food, but especially noticed the shortage of ammunition. However, nobody – neither soldiers nor commanders – ever dreamt about abandoning the bridgehead, but instead fought steadfastly for every piece of ground, keeping an oath to not give up the Volga. Every day the German invaders launched furious attacks with a superiority in personnel and material that was simply not available to us. Our brave soldiers left mountains of enemy corpses and their ammunition on the battlefield, and in this way, by taking advantage of this booty, we replenished our supplies of weapons and ammunition.

The full story of the blocking detachments has yet to be told.

– – –

The vicious fighting around the fuel tanks continued. The Soviet riflemen of Major Borisov's 90th Rifle Regiment dug themselves in as best they could during the night but German machine-guns laid down overlapping fields of fire on the small foothold, while mortars constantly plastered the gullies and river bank. Soviet losses were high but Colonel Gorishny was determined to hold on to the small piece of ground because it was an ideal rally point for attacks toward Lyudnikov's men. They seemed within easy reach.

The German determination to throw the Soviets out was just as strong. A new counterattack had been planned during the night and the assault groups moved off at 05.30 hours, covered by mortar and artillery fire. Soviet artillery responded, raising a fiery curtain west of the fuel tanks. This first attack was repelled but a second followed twenty minutes later, from the same north-western direction. Another came in at 0630 hours from the south-west. According to Soviet reports, all attacks were repelled and the Germans pulled back to their starting positions.

At 0535 hours, units of 241st Rifle Regiment engaged in hand grenade duels in Appendix Gully north-east of the fuel tanks. At the same time, the noise of motors was heard from the Barrikady factory. At 0630 hours, a company-strong German force attacked 241st Rifle Regiment, 685th Rifle Regiment and 3/92nd Rifle Brigade along the Volga bank from the north. At 0825 hours, a group of 12-15 Germans trying to infiltrate through Appendix Gully was destroyed.

Soviet records are adamant that they held the fuel tanks but German sources are equally insistent. The morning report (0600 hours) of LI. Armeekorps stated:

> The enemy only suspended his attacks towards the fuel installation at 0100 hours. Weak elements still hold out on the south-east corner of the fuel installation and on the Volga bank. Mopping up has started.

And at 1635 hours:

305.Inf.Div. cleaned the remaining enemy out of the fuel installation…

Apart from the combat reports of 95th Rifle Division (from which the timeline of German attacks was obtained), we have the diary of 62nd Army, which explicity states that its units still held the fuel tanks:

95th Rifle Division repelled enemy attacks of over a battalion near the fuel tanks. 90th Rifle Regiment held the fuel tanks, where it consolidated. 241st and 685th Rifle Regiment consolidated on the line of the gully 150 metres north-east of Mezenskaya.

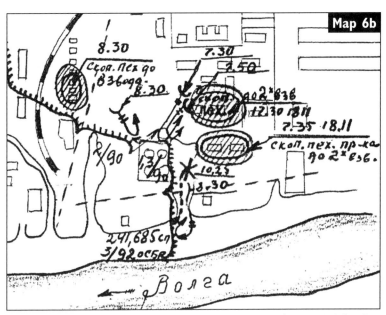

The situation on 95th Rifle Division's sector, 18 November, 1942. The three shaded areas show where Soviet artillery scattered German troop concentrations. Also shown are the repulsion of several attacks on the fuel tanks and a penetration down Appendix Gully. There is no indication on this sketch that the Germans retook the fuel tanks. (Note: times shown are Russian time, not German time.)

The combat journal of 685th Rifle Regiment offers no further clues:

Throughout 18.11.42, the regiment undertook defensive combat to repel attempts by small enemy groups to filter across to the south of the gully.

Subsequent Soviet actions seem to suggest that the fuel tanks may have been in German hands – albeit temporarily: Soviet artillery proceeded to hammer the fuel tanks and surrounding area in the afternoon. It is the author's opinion that both sides believed it was they who held the fuel tanks and the repeated change of ownership did not help because both sides submitted messages claiming that the fuel tanks had been recaptured.

– – –

A sense of the utter misery and deprivation being experienced by the German troops around the fuel tanks can be found in a letter written by Obergefreiter Paul Späth[7,] a machine-gunner from 12./Grenadier-Regiment 576. Although he does not mention the counterattack, the conditions being experienced are perfectly clear:

I want to drop you a line from here. First of all, I want to thank you for the second 1 kilo package, which reached me in good condition and has pleased me greatly. Don't worry about sending me anything else because we have enough to eat and drink, want for almost nothing and couldn't put it anywhere anyway. The reason for this is because today we still have 16 men in our company, and lose more every day, but we continually receive the packages of those who have been killed or wounded. Because of this, we have enough to eat. The postal service no longer sends these parcels back and we have so much to smoke that we don't want any at all. Therefore, you only need to send me letters, that's enough for me. – Now I want to tell you

---

7. Späth, Obergefreiter Paul, 12./Gr.Rgt.576; born 23 July, 1910 in Bommen. Missing in action, 11 December, 1942 in Stalingrad.

something about our combat situation. It's brutal what we have to do here. We were the first division to reach the Volga here in Stalingrad and the other divisions are not able to take what we have. Nevertheless, we have almost no men left. The division has had 95% casualties, more than half of those are dead, and today the Russian heavy weapons on the other side of the Volga shelled us with such a drumfire; after 5 weeks, this has almost become more than anyone can bear. A fresh battalion is thrown against us every 3-4 days but it is ripped apart in a short time. We sit close to the Volga, [in the] north of Stalingrad, and the Russians lie below us in the cliffs along the river and can't be driven out. We are only able to get things done with hand grenades, therefore we are only 20-30 metres away from each other. Our positions here are terrible and one shell crater overlaps another. The nasty winter weather has also arrived here now, it's -25 to -30° and at night we have to lie out in the open as advanced sentry posts. I can't think why we're fighting here. Everyone is sick. We know of no hour when someone is not buried or wounded. The Volga here is 3-4km wide and thickly covered with drift-ice. The Russians attack 2-3 times a day and cause us heavy casualties. Behind us lies factory after factory, everything totally shot to pieces. They are gun-, tractor-, gunpowder- and tank factories, kilometres long. We look like Jews, 15-20cm long hair, beards also 5cm long, haven't seen water since 8 weeks ago. We are covered in filth, that is a disgrace, and I do not know when we are getting out of here. I probably won't receive furlough for the time being because every single man is needed. You don't need to send anything else… In the time that I have been writing this letter, at least 200 shells have landed around us here. They land all around. Now I will finish up and trust in God the Lord for a safe return! Tomorrow 6.00 am is daybreak, 3.00 pm is nightfall. Best wishes to you all. Your son Paul.

– – –

During the counterattacks on the fuel tanks, Pionier-Bataillon 294 did not escape from casualties… no unit could escape them in the cratered frozen, hell around the fuel tanks. The deluge of shells on this exposed stretch of ground, from friend and foe alike, meant that even dug-outs and foxholes were no guarantee of safety. The battalion lost at least three more men: Gefreiter Karl Bödecker[8] and Gefreiter Franz Müller[9], both from 1. Kompanie, were missing, and Gefreiter Rudi Richter[10], 2 Kompanie, was killed by a bullet to the head. The number of wounded is unknown. This constant bloodletting was of great concern to 294. Infanterie-Division. The following entry appears in the divisional war diary:

> Due to the heavy casualties of the pioneer battalion in Stalingrad, the possibility of calling up replacements from within the ranks of the division must be considered. It is intended to relieve the pioneer commando that is still active at the division staff and to again thoroughly comb the Restkommando for dispensable people. In addition, there are pioneers from the last Marschbataillon now with the infantry pioneer platoons who could not be placed in the pioneer battalion at that time because it was already totally filled out with personnel. It is hoped that in this way, about 70 pioneers under the command of the previous leader of the Restkommando, Oberleutnant Benad, can be set in march to the battalion in Stalingrad.

Another levy of 294th pioneers was to be sent to the blood-soaked Barrikady.

– – –

8. Bödecker, Gefreiter Karl, 1./Pi.Btl.294; born 13 February, 1911 in Altseggebusch. Missing in action, 18 November, 1942 in Stalingrad.
9. Müller, Gefreiter Franz, 1./Pi.Btl.294; born 20 April, 1914 in Kommern. Missing in action, 18 November, 1942 in Stalingrad.
10. Richter, Gefreiter Rudi, 2./Pi.Btl.294; born 24 May, 1920 in Kreischa/Dresden. Killed in action, 18 November, 1942 in Stalingrad.

On Lyudnikov's Island, 650th Rifle Regiment continued to beat back the Germans in the area of the unfinished building and along the cliffs. The pioneers were heavily relied upon to dig the Soviets out of the cliff. Major Josef Linden describes the difficulties they faced:

> The Russian dug-outs halfway up the cliff were often connected to one another by tunnels. Powerful means were therefore applied here and it was through mining and blasting that an improvement of our forward position on the Volga was achieved.

Particularly tough combat took place around two gullies. The southernmost, known to the Germans as 'Wasserhaus Rachel' (Water House Gully) and to the Soviets as 'Ovrag Vod' (Water

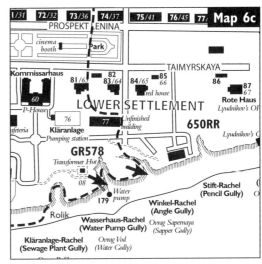

Fighting for the gullies, 18 November, 1942.

Gully), was held by Klyukin and the remnants of the Barrikady worker's militia: with the Germans placed around the rim of the gully, their position was precarious. The next gully north – known as 'Winkel Rachel' (Angle Gully) to the Germans and 'Ovrag Sapernaya' (Sapper Gully) to the Soviets – was fiercely fought over along its southern edge. This was the last natural obstacle between the Germans and Lyudnikov's command post, so furious resistance was offered. It was because of the bloody combat and German casualties suffered there that the Soviets named it 'Sapper Gully'.

Grenadier-Regiment 578 and its subordinated pioneer battalions gained more ground in these assaults, shifting the front-line 100-150 metres further north along the Volga cliff. This of course could not happen without penalty. Oberleutnant Kurt Barth, commander 1./Pionier-Bataillon 162, was killed during these attacks. One of his men, Oberpionier Walter Hanke[11], was severely wounded and carried back to the Kommissarhaus but died of his wounds there, while Obergefreiter Herbert Bischof was missing.

– – –

Major Pechenyuk lost communications with his battalions that were spread out from the Volga shore to Dom 37. The Germans continued to attack the left flank, throwing small groups of 15-20 men into the battle. Combat groups of Panzerpionier-Bataillon 50 finally broke into the unfinished building. Vicious skirmishes erupted in each room. As a result of the unending assaults against the building and the hand-to-hand fighting inside it, there were only 4 Soviet defenders left in the structure, but before the Germans could destroy them, they scurried down through the cellar and out along a trench to the north-east, taking up defensive positions about 50 metres away. By the end of the day, the Germans had penetrated deep into the defences of 650th Regiment. Fighting would continue throughout night and by morning the front-line was just 150 metres from the divisional command post. The division staff once again prepared to defend themselves. The east bank artillery, fearing friendly-fire, ceased firing on the German front-line.

650th Rifle Regiment estimated that the Germans lost 50 men dead and wounded on their sector. That figure is close but probably a bit high. A precise breakdown of German

---

11. Hanke, Oberpionier Walter, 1./Pi.Btl.162; born 15 June, 1922 in Obersoor. Died of wounds, 18 November, 1942 in Stalingrad.

casualties by unit is not available, but what is known is that Panzerpionier-Bataillon 50 lost at least five men killed: Oberpionier Kurt Schönherr[12] and Obergefreiter Kurt Wilhelmy[13] from 1. Kompanie, Pionier Heinrich Höbel[14] from 2. Kompanie and Soldat Heinrich Behnke[15] and Pionier Stanislaus von Kuczkowski[16] from 3. Kompanie. The true figure is higher. The number of wounded is unknown.

Unteroffizier Georg Moorkamp[17], 1./Panzerpionier-Bataillon 50, wrote a letter home:

> Good evening. A few short lines to fill you in. I'm still going perfectly. The weather is bearable. There is a thaw at present. Frosts at night. Things are progressing slowly in Stalingrad. House after house must be fought for. You just cannot imagine what that means...

Unteroffizier Georg Moorkamp

– – –

Safe for the moment in the rear, Hauptmann Rettenmaier jotted off a quick letter home:

> I am still well. Here, behind the hills of Stalingrad, one can reasonably endure the conditions, especially since the weather is rather foggy, which stops the visits by enemy planes. Such hard fighting as we experience here I never endured during World War I. But it will all end by being a success.

Grenadier-Regiment 578 bid farewell to Hauptmann Friedrich von Grolman[18], who had been temporarily assigned to it as part of his ongoing General Staff training. Grolman began his career in cavalry and panzer units, belonging to Reiter-Regiment 7 prior to the war, then commanding panzer companies, first in Panzer-Regiment 2 (16. Panzer-Division) during the Polish and French campaigns, and then in Panzer-Regiment 18 (18. Panzer-Division) during Barbarossa. It was during the latter assignment that he became one of the first soldiers to be awarded the German Cross in Gold (on 27 October, 1941). He then began his General Staff training.

Hauptmann Friedrich von Grolman

12. Schönherr, Oberpionier Kurt, 1./Pz.Pi.Btl.50; born 13 October, 1914 in Aue/Saale. Killed in action, 18 November, 1942 in Stalingrad.

13. Wilhelmy, Obergefreiter Kurt, 1./Pz.Pi.Btl.50; born 27 August, 1919 in Essen. Killed in action, 18 November, 1942 in Stalingrad.

14. Höbel, Pionier Heinrich, 2./Pz.Pi.Btl.50; born 19 December, 1908 in Lindenfels. Killed in action, 18 November, 1942 in Stalingrad.

15. Behnke, Soldat Heinrich, 3./Pz.Pi.Btl.50; born 6 December, 1908 in Bleckede. Killed in action, 18 November, 1942 in Stalingrad.

16. Kuczkowski, Pionier Stanislaus von, 3./Pz.Pi.Btl.50; born 22 December, 1923 in Sophienwalde. Killed in action, 18 November, 1942 in Stalingrad.

17. Moorkamp, Unteroffizier Georg, 1./Pz.Pi.Btl.50; born 12 February, 1916 in Lindern/Oldenburg. Missing in action, December 1942 in Stalingrad.

18. Grolman, Major i.G. Friedrich von, DKiG; Stab Gr.Rgt.578; born 7 July, 1913 in Altenburg. Died 5 July, 2004 in Bonn.

He was detailed to the staff of LXXXVIII. Armeekorps on 10 April, 1942, then to the staff of 305. Infanterie-Division on 5 August, 1942 where he assumed the role of O1. After Leutnant Könnings[19], adjutant of Infanterie-Regiment 578, was severely wounded on 17 October, 1942, Hauptmann von Grolman filled the vacancy:

> From the middle of October to the middle of November I took over the position of regiment adjutant in one of the infantry regiments that fought in the gun factory of Stalingrad-North. On 18 November I received my transfer orders to go to the Kriegsakademie in Berlin. Thus I escaped the encirclement of 6. Armee. When I was reporting my departure to Generaloberst Paulus the next morning, he said to me: 'Boy, you're lucky to get out. The Russians will surround us and I don't know where I'll get reserves from…'

Hauptmann von Grolman bade farewell to his pessimistic army commander and managed to drive west before the Soviet jaws clamped shut around Stalingrad.

– – –

In its evening report to 6. Armee, LI. Armeekorps stated that "305. Infanterie-Division moved their front-line forward about 100 metres to the north along the Volga cliffs and created the prerequisites for the continuation of storm group operations against the enemy strongpoints in Houses 83 and 74". This statement shows the new methods being employed. Instead of attacking many targets at once, each movement was carefully prepared to achieve the overall goal. By capturing the unfinished building, Haus 83 had effectively been outflanked and was now ripe for the picking, but more importantly, the potentially troublesome strongpoint – which could have easily fired into the flanks of any attack going in against Haus 83 – had been

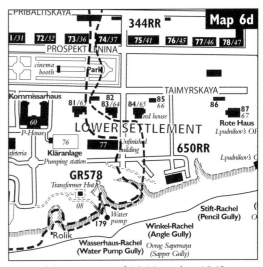

Forward lines, evening of 18 November, 1942.

eliminated, further paving the way for the attack. The German plan of nibbling away at the base of the Soviet bridgehead seemed to be working.

– – –

As always, before night fell, the armoured vehicles were withdrawn because they were easy targets once darkness covered the battlefield. Oberleutnant Messerschmidt recalls:

> In the evening, as darkness was falling, we drove back to our protective apartment blocks to provision ourselves with fuel, ammunition and rations. Every night, the Russians came out of the riverside cliffs on the west bank of the Volga… These riverside cliffs protected the enemy and could not be reached be either our Luftwaffe or our artillery.

The previous week's fighting amply demonstrated the seeming invincibility of this most unlikely defensive bastion. Military doctrine places great emphasis on holding the high ground, but on Lyudnikov's Island – as in many other locations in Stalingrad – the riverside cliff was tactically crucial and constituted a formidable last line of defence. Various schemes

19. Könnings, Hauptmann Felix, Stab Gr.Rgt.578; born 13 May, 1915 in Tangerhütte. No further information known.

were devised to deal with the cliff and one of the most ambitious was suggested to Oberleutnant Messerschmidt:

> A reserve officer, an Oberstleutnant[20], made the following proposal to me: he wanted his pioneers to blow up a section of the riverside cliff and thus create a ramp. I would then drive down this with my panzers and shell the cliffs to destroy the enemy forces taking cover there. I thought the idea was marvellous but invited the Oberstleutnant to come along on this trip as my loader. I did not get an answer and never again heard anything about this potentially Knight's Cross-winning notion.

The panzer schwadron was not to be used for this daring purpose. The war diary of 24. Panzer-Division noted: "Panzer Schwadron Messerschmidt will remain with 305. Infanterie-Division to continue to support them during the clearing actions east of the gun factory". At 1820 hours, LI. Armeekorps issued Korpsbefehl Nr. 115:

> The panzer schwadron employed with 305. Infanterie-Division will remain with the division.
>
> Sturmgeschütz-Abteilung 244 from 389. Infanterie-Division will set in march to Gruppe Schwerin on the morning on 20 November: two assault guns will stay behind for operations against the 'Rote Haus' (Red House) near 389. Infanterie-Division.
>
> As far as the weather situation permits it, VIII. Fliegerkorps will support the attack of 305. Infanterie-Division with strong forces by smashing the 'Weisshausen' (White Houses) and wearing down the enemy inside the bridgehead. Begin on 19 November.

- - -

The war diary of 138th Rifle Division sums up the day's fighting:

> Throughout the entire day, enemy groups larger than a platoon – supported by artillery fire and accompanied by 5-7 tanks – attacked the centre and left flank of the division. Regardless of heavy losses the enemy aimed to get into the area of divisional headquarters. These attacks continued throughout the entire day but were repulsed every time by the steadfastness of our troops.
>
> Defence is taken up by everyone, signallers, commanders of regiment staffs and division staff. Due to the shortage of medicine and the fact that evacuation of the wounded was impossible, deaths from wounds increased.
>
> The position of the division is getting worse, becoming catastrophic. Rations were and are gone, war materials are gone, and rifle ammunition is less than half the daily allowance.
>
> Batteries for radios are ending; because of this, requesting artillery fire from the left bank of the Volga is becoming impossible.

The situation was dire. The division lost 6 killed and 24 wounded, a total of 30, but it was the mass of wounded that concerned Lyudnikov most. Even though the drift-ice on the river was weaker than the previous day, it was still not possible to ferry the wounded men to the left bank. It was calculated that there were 357 wounded men with the division on this day. The combat strength of the rifle regiments was shockingly low: Captain Konovalenko's 344th Rifle Regiment had 74 men, Major Pechenyuk's 650th Rifle Regiment had 25 men and Major Gunyaga's 768th Rifle Regiment had 28 men.

The German attack had seriously disrupted Pechenyuk's lines of communication with his units. Telephone wires had been destroyed and runners faced great perils when dashing

---

20. Unfortunately, Messerschmidt does not remember his name.

across the open expanses between the buildings and the river bank. Once night fell, it was decided to ascertain if particular units still held their buildings. Small patrols were sent out. One of them included Senior-Sergeant Gorbatenko:

> Pechenyuk entrusted Tolkach, leader of regimental communications, with the task of finding out whether or not our soldiers were still in the former command post, now a destroyed two-storey house[21]. The house turned out to be in the rear of the Germans. Tolkach insisted I accompany him. We handed in our documents and armed ourselves with pistols and grenades. We set off at night to cross the front-line. A dark night. Only silhouettes of the buildings could be seen. We skirted round to the right of the unfinished building. We jumped into a trench and imperceptibly crept up to our former house. A sentry could be seen in an aperture in the wall. But whose sentry?

> Tolkach knocked the sentry down with his fist. In response – Russian cursing. One of ours. Tolkach scolded the sentry. The sentry then led us through a hole into the cellar. Kalinin was there and with him were 2 or 3 soldiers. They defended the ruins of the house and provided themselves with ammunition and food.

Junior-Lieutenant Kalinin, adjutant of 650th Rifle Regiment, and three soldiers had been defending the building since it was evacuated by Major Pechenyuk and his staff on 15 November. They provisioned themselves by living off the land, as Gorbatenko reports:

> Kalinin reported that parachutes dropped by the PO-2s landed between him and the Germans. While being covered by his soldiers, Kalinin crawled out to the parachute, cut it and formed it into straps. He then dragged it back into the cellar. It contained ammunition.

> The houses nearby, defended by men like Kalinin, were from the neighbouring 344th Regiment of Konovalenko. We visited them and made a list of the defenders of those garrisons and returned to Pechenyuk with the report. The moon was rising when we returned. Upon reaching a neutral area, the Germans opened fire on us.

The garrisons of Pechenyuk's strongpoints were very weak. The situation in Dom 37 was desperate. The garrison there – remnants of all three rifle battalions – knew it was only a matter of time before the Germans assailed them again.

– – –

PO-2 planes continued to drop sacks to the division containing ammunition, food, medicine and other necessities. During the night, 138th Rifle Division only received 5 sacks: 1 with food products and 4 with cartridges for PPSH, rifles and anti-tank rifles. Four sacks fell into Volga and 6 on to Zaitsevsky island.

The same night (18-19 November) two boats of 107th Independent Pontoon-Bridge Battalion made two trips to Lyudnikov and delivered a small amount of ammunition and food.

Captured by LI. Armeekorps: 6 prisoners, including 1 deserter. Two tanks destroyed.

Casualties for 18 November, 1942:		
138th Rifle Division:	6 killed, 24 wounded, a total of 30 men	
305. Infanterie-Division:	1 officer and 10 men killed, 1 officer and 41 men wounded	
389. Infanterie-Division:	1 officer and 15 men wounded	

21. This was Dom 64 [Haus 83].

19 November, 1942

In its morning report at 0540 hours, LI. Armeekorps informed 6. Armee that "enemy reconnaissance patrols against the fuel installation in 82b1 were repulsed. Encircled enemy group east of the gun factory was supplied from the air."

The morning dawned grey and foggy. The river bank already had light covering of snow, and the Volga – on which the ice floes continued to drift – lay under a misty veil. The bad weather grounded planes and brought the Soviets in Stalingrad some relief because they were unmolested by aerial attacks. However, it was now the Soviets that required good flying weather: their massive counteroffensive, with the lofty objective of surrounding 6. Armee, was scheduled to begin at 0530 hours. Fog hindered their fighter-bombers…

The sky was overcast with low-hanging clouds and the temperature was just above freezing. The German attack began at 0430 hours. Their first target was Haus 74. Preceding the attack was a heavy artillery bombardment on several buildings, all with the aim of annihilating the garrisons of the houses.

Oberleutnant Messerschmidt and his panzer schwadron had returned. His panzers left their leaguer in the Schnellhefter Block a few hours before the attack commenced. He had to be very careful where he led his panzers:

> Rubble and shell craters were very obstructive and damaged our tracks. We always drove around the Barrikady Gun Factory. It was a wasteland of rubble inside. We crossed over the railway tracks and deployed east of there. We always worked as a combined unit – not split into smaller groups, and the panzers were never used individually. We had only 5 to 6 panzers on average.

Familie Niedringhaus

Most of his panzers were powerful Panzer IVs, both long- and short-barrels, but he also had a Panzer III. In a report about the use of panzers in Stalingrad, prepared in early November after many valuable yet painful lessons had been learned, those panzers had the following pros and cons: the 7.5cm long-barrel was best used only against armoured targets because the gun was too easily damaged. The short-barrel 7.5cm was the best weapon. Delayed-fuse shells had an excellent effect against bunkers and houses. Armour-piercing rounds were good against masonry while smoke shells were proven against totally obstinate enemy resistance and to blind enemy snipers.

The long-barrel Panzer IV '432' of Wachtmeister Niedringhaus. The barrel was shot off during house-to-house fighting in the Barrikady. None of the crew were injured and the barrel was replaced a few days later.

When asked if the use of panzers in assault gun-like missions was misuse of a valuable weapon, Messerschmidt replied: "Not a misuse, but our panzers, with their cannon in revolving turrets (as opposed to the assault guns, which could only laterally pivot their guns a little), could not satisfy the mission. Mostly, the cannon were too long to be rotated in the house ruins and rubble."

The report by 24. Panzer-Division covers panzer deployment in some detail:

Terrain difficulties such as house ruins, bomb craters, narrow streets, minefields, tank barriers and obstacles largely limit the manoeuvrability and observation possibilities of panzers so that in principle, operations of panzer units in city combat must be avoided. The casualties incurred bear no comparison to the success of this most valuable weapon of the army. The main weapon of the panzers, 'fire and movement', cannot be used properly. They present a target and see very little.

The panzer is not suited for city fighting when operating in formations such as regiments or battalions. Panzer operations are often useful on the edge of the city and in completely disintegrated sectors of the city, especially when the enemy has no time to set up his defences.

To support weak and battleweary panzergrenadiers and infantry units, a panzer support schwadron (as the largest tactical formation) can be employed as an exception.

Their employment should adhere to the following guidelines:

A departure from these too easily exposes the few employed panzers to destruction by dug-in, well-camouflaged enemy tank-killing weapons.

Attack: while the panzers will support the experienced panzergrenadiers, they will only be employed to co-operate with foreign infantry because the bulk of infantry in the German army are unschooled and unaccustomed to fighting alongside panzers.

Before the beginning of an attack, a precise reconnaissance of the target area and the enemy situation (enemy tanks, anti-tank guns, mines, etc.) must be carried out.

Exact establishment of the plan of attack and implementation of this attack is to be discussed together with all of the employed commanders.

The operations of panzers will be in platoons and squads, mixed Panzer IIIs and IVs, on specific streets. Operations by single panzers are refused because as a rule, mutual support by cover-fire is not guaranteed. Prior to the beginning of the attack, enemy tanks and anti-tank guns will be eliminated by a Panzer IV long-barrel directed on foot into a concealed position.

Panzer platoons and squads will not fight in front of the panzergrenadiers, only in or behind them because only then is mutual communication possible.

The panzers will be used for covering fire and not as assault guns.

The infantry will not be allowed to advance bunched up behind the panzer but must comb through the terrain on a broad front under the cover-fire of the panzers. In the city, panzers attract all types of fire.

Operations by panzers in known and uncleared minefields, as well as in impassable terrain, destroyed factories and city sectors in Stalingrad churned by bomb craters, has led to exceptionally high losses of employed panzers. The successes in no way offset the losses sustained, especially when cooperating with untrained infantry. The latter place impossible demands on the panzers.

Based on experience of fighting in Stalingrad, employment of panzers for city combat must in principle be avoided and only be viewed as an emergency measure.

An enforced operation in a critical situation with experienced panzergrenadiers can succeed in exceptional cases when following the guidelines shown above.

The infantry must learn to cooperate better with panzers and the infantry commander must recognise the limitations of the panzers. They are not assault guns with double armour protection!

Several weeks had passed since this report was written but panzers were still being employed in the shattered ruins of Stalingrad, and mostly with other divisions. However, lessons had been learnt and the panzers were now used more circumspectly. They were employed in schwadrons – as the largest tactical formation – and placed under the most capable commanders. Only remnants of the original schwadrons remained, so instead of being organised in numbered schwadrons, the panzers were gathered into new schwadrons named after their commanders, for example, Panzer Schwadron Messerschmidt. The safety and survival of a panzer and its crew depended more on tactics and organisation than individual measures taken by the crews. "Spare tracks were quite often affixed to the front of the panzer", recalls Messerschmidt, "otherwise, there were no special precautions. Hand grenades and submachine- guns were carried in the panzers – but not on the men themselves. The guns were taken along for self-defence when bailing out after our panzers were hit." A close call earlier in the battle, on the outskirts of Stalingrad, demonstrated to Messerschmidt how these weapons should be used from a panzer:

Messerschmidt

Panzer commanders of 4./Pz.Rgt.24 who survived Stalingrad (photo taken in 1944). From left: Wachtmeister Rudolf Niedringhaus (born 2 October, 1915 in Friedewalde, died 28 September, 2002 in Friedewalde) and Wachtmeister Siegfried Freyer (born 11 February, 1917 in Wotnassen, still alive in 2005), the regiment's first Knight's Cross winner. Freyer was severely wounded in the Barrikady when struck in the neck by an anti-tank bullet while observing from the cupola of Panzer '434'. Miraculously, nothing vital was hit. Some think that the Soviet anti-tank rifleman was aiming for his Knight's Cross. The other two men in the photo are unidentified.

During an attack on Stalingrad – thus on open ground (without buildings) – I could see from my cupola two Soviets in a foxhole, about 3 to 4 metres in front, aiming an anti-tank rifle at our panzer. Because the cannon could not be used at such a short distance, I got my loader to pass me an egg-grenade. I pulled the pin and threw it towards the two Soviets. One of them stood up, caught the grenade and threw it back. I quickly closed my hatch. The grenade exploded on the turret roof in front of my cupola – without any noticeable effect. Such a hand grenade should not be thrown too quickly. They required 3 to 5 seconds before the explosion. In the excitement, I had thrown it too early after pulling the pin. I got the panzer to back up and finished the Soviets off with the submachine-gun.

That was more than two months earlier. Since then, Messerschmidt and his crews had amassed huge amounts of experience in how to fight in cities. Such tactics were never taught in the panzer schools. Now Panzer Schwadron Messerschmidt was positioned amongst the ruined buildings at the southern end of Theatre Garden, their guns aimed at Haus 74, waiting for the order to fire.

For every day of attack, one of the buildings (which were numbered on our maps) was selected. At the end of the night or very early in the morning, the targeted building was softened up for the attack by Stukas and heavy artillery (also 36cm mortars). I had to give my few panzers – and sometimes the assault guns – instructions over the radio about the target before the bombardment commenced. The assault guns and our panzers, which had moved into position during darkness, stopped firing when a light signal was shown.

All of Messerschmidt's panzers concentrated their fire on the target. "The effect of our tank shells was variable", remembers Messerschmidt. "Our assault troops, together with flamethrower-equipped pioneers who often supported them, lay under cover until then. They then stormed through the rubble into the building. This always cost a lot of blood."

With a strength of two companies and supported by the panzers and assault guns, the attack along Pribaltiskaya Street struck 344th Rifle Regiment and the right flank of 650th Rifle Regiment. The core of the assault was formed by Pionier-Bataillon 336 with a few men from 3./Pionier-Bataillon 305 and the concentrated remnants of Grenadier-Regiment 577. From the comparative safety of his cupola, Messerschmidt watched the pioneers go to work on the outer walls of the building:

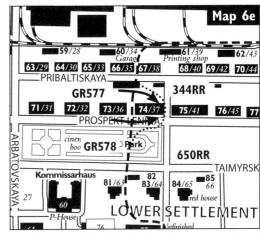

Attack on 344th Rifle Regiment's sector, morning of 19 November, 1942.

> The pioneers used explosives to blast holes through the approximately 30cm thick concrete floors. They formed the explosives into a bell shape, covered their ears and detonated them. Immediately after the explosion – in which all the force of the blast was directed into the hole – the pioneers tossed in hand grenades.[22] The hole created by the explosives had a diameter of about 40-50cm, so a man could not get through, only hand grenades and smoke canisters. In these last attacks in the Barrikady, flamethrowers were successfully deployed. We could see the pioneer-flamethrowers from our panzers. The pioneers poked their flamethrowers through the holes that had been blasted through. After that, the 'smoked out' cellar was successfully taken by the pioneers and assault infantry. The Soviets would sometimes launch counterattacks out of the cellars.

That was not to be at Haus 74 [Dom 37]. It was utterly devastated by the bombardment and occupied by the Germans at 0800 hours. The combat journal of 138th Rifle Division recorded that "our garrison in the house was destroyed". The combat journal of 650th Rifle Regiment, however, makes it clear that a couple of men did escape from the ruins: "Fire from tanks and artillery totally destroyed Dom 37 […] and some defenders left the structure". In any case, the rifle units of 650th Rifle Regiment defending the house no longer existed – the few survivors dragged themselves over to Dom 41 and were incorporated into the defences of Captain Nemkov's 2nd Rifle Battalion of 344th Rifle Regiment.

– – –

At 0520 hours, the artillery of the Soviet 5th Tank Army, in the Serafimovich bridgehead on the Don about 180km north-west of Stalingrad, and 21st Army's artillery, on the Don west of Kletskaya, received the alert code word 'Siren'. Thousands of Soviet artillerymen loaded their guns. Ten minutes later, the command to fire came through and 3,500 guns and mortars opened a massive 80-minute bombardment. As it continued, Soviet tanks and infantry moved up into the line. The guns fired their last salvo at 0648 hours; at 0650 hours, the first infantry echelon – 5th Tank Army's 14th and 47th Guards Rifle Divisions and 119th and 124th Rifle Divisions – went on the attack. The entire breadth of the attack was 320km, but the three designated breakthrough sectors totalled only 23km. Despite the heavy fog, which would only dissipate at about 1000 hours, the attack made good progress. Fifth Tank Army and 21st Army had both cracked the line of General Dumitrescu's[23] 3. Romanian

---

22. "Foolhardy!" said Messerschmidt during an interview with the author.

23. Dumitrescu, Generaloberst Petre, EL, RK; OB 3rd Romanian Army; born 18 February, 1882 in Dobridor, Dolj. Died 15 January, 1950 in Bucharest.

Armee by 1000 hours, and 5th Tank Army's 1st and 26th Tank Corps began to move through between 1100 and 1200 hours. They were followed by the 8th Cavalry Corps. Individual Romanian units still offered stout resistance in some sectors – and did so for several days – but the majority fell back and suffered terrible cases of 'tank fright'… trails of discarded weapons and equipment marked the panic-stricken Romanian retreat across the naked steppe. The die had been cast. Heeding their instructions to avoid resistance and strike for Kalach with all possible speed, the mobile Soviet units charged on.

The German troops still slogging it out in the city had no idea of the drama unfolding on the steppe far to their west.

– – –

Back at Lyudnikov's Island, events continued as before. Soviet units reported that German submachine-gunners and snipers were very active. At 0830 hours, on Pechenyuk's sector, a group of 50-60 Germans attacked from the direction of the Kommissarhaus towards the river. Soviet artillery was quickly called in and as a result of the accurate fire, the Germans went to ground and entrenched themselves. At 1130, the German storm groups, now amply covered by heavy mortar and machine-gun fire, tried to capture the water tower. An assault gun cautiously edged toward the Volga cliff until the red brick tower was in its sights. It then proceeded to hurl shells into it. German grenadiers and pioneers, lined up along the lip of the gully and cliff, also threw grenades and

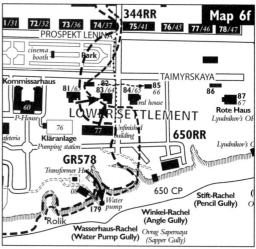

Attack on 650th Rifle Regiment's sector, morning of 19 November, 1942.

bottles of chemical mixture at the tower. Politruk Klyukin and his men vigorously defended the water tower and its adjacent gully. A grenade exploded not far from Klyukin and temporarily blinded him. Although sightless, Klyukin remained in the line, weapon in hand, encouraging his men. This group of 9 men, most of them NKVD soldiers from the blocking detachment, continued to defend the water tower.

The defensive line of 650th Rifle Regiment consisted entirely of these small groups of men, and they weren't front-line riflemen by any means – they were clerks, staff officers and any redundant men that could be found. And the overwhelming majority were officers. One group defended Sapper Gully, which ran from the unfinished structure to the Volga River. This group included Captain Datsyuk and the remnants of the regiment's security platoon. Beneath this defensive line, deep in a dug-out, was Pechenyuk's regimental HQ. Further inland, in Haus 83 (the former regiment command post), was Junior-Lieutenant Kalinin and three men. After the destruction of Dom 37 [Haus 74], it was now their turn to face the brunt of the focused German attack.

After a brief delay in which Haus 74 was consolidated and the armoured vehicles redeployed, a mighty barrage fell upon Haus 83. Unfortunately, other than the outcome, no details exist about the struggle inside the building: after a short fight, Kalinin and his garrison were overwhelmed. The Germans gained tenancy of the battered structure. The courageous resistance of Kalinin's garrison was over.

The loss of two vital defensive strongpoints was reported rather candidly in the combat journal of 650th Rifle Regiment:

> Fire from tanks and artillery totally destroyed Dom 37. The building is completely destroyed and our defenders left the structure, as they did the former regimental command post. The soldiers left after the final destruction of Dom 37 and the former regimental command post, and the annihilation of its two garrisons, is 5 men. They were not able to hold on to the buildings and were forced to go over to Dom 41.

It is unknown whether or not the valiant junior-lieutenant was amongst the few survivors from 'Kalinin's garrison'.

The pressure did not ease on Pechenyuk's men. The regimental combat journal noted that "the enemy, regardless of his losses, is undertaking countless attacks against our defensive line, trying to capture the territory from the unfinished building down to the Volga river and the water tower. We observed a group of about 80 enemy soldiers near the P-shaped structure and the unfinished building."

LI. Armeekorps reported to 6. Armee that "the daily objectives of 305. Infanterie-Division's assault groups, Haus 83 and 74, were reached. Both houses, the area east of Haus 83 and the area between both buildings, was cleared with negligible casualties." The good news was quickly passed on to Heeresgruppe B: "In Stalingrad, storm groups of 305. Infanterie-Division took 2 large house blocks (grid square 83d2) with low casualties and cleared out both sides of the terrain."

– – –

Further south, around the hotly-contested fuel tanks, the ebb and flow of attack and counterattack continued. In the morning, with a strength of 60 men, Gorishny's men again attacked towards the fuel installation, supported by artillery and rocket fire. Grenadier-Regiment 576 easily fended off this thrust. That was not the end of the Soviet attacks for the day. It could not be the end – as long as 138th Rifle Division was cut off from the rest of the army, the relief attacks would continue. Every evening, Colonel Gorishny renewed efforts to re-establish contact with his right neighbour. General Krylov, 62nd Army chief-of-staff, writes:

> The decision of the army commander for 19 November, already written in the war diary, said: 'Undertake a counterattack with a part of your forces and join up with 138th Rifle Division.' This 'part of your forces' (apart from this, everything else was also mobilised for further counterattacks on this sector) was nevertheless not very large. In the previous days, Gorishny's Division had suffered 400 dead and wounded.

> The attempts to fight through to Lyudnikov from the positions of the army's main forces and re-establish a continuous front along the bank were not suspended because the enemy in the Mezenskaya Street area had to be pushed back from the Volga. It repeatedly seemed to be successful at any moment. The units on the right flank of the Gorishny Division were finally able to entrench themselves within the fuel tank sector. They were separated from Lyudnikov's Island by only a couple of hundred metres. However, those on the 'Island' were unable to advance in the necessary direction.

Krylov and the army staff were aware that Gorishny's forces were not strong enough to punch through on their own: "As always, we strived to strongly support the weakened infantry as much as possible with artillery. A special plan, corrected day by day, was issued for the artillery support of the advance of 95th Rifle Division to fight through to 138th Rifle Division."

In an intermediate report, Artillerie-Regiment 179 stated that "at 1215 hours, the enemy concentrated strong artillery, mortar and rocket-launcher fire on the right wing of the left neighbour. Based on our own observations, a large part of the fire lay on the Russian forward line." Gruppe Seydel's report was the same: "At 1215 hours, the enemy made a strong surprise barrage on the left sector of the Kampfgruppe, from the forward line back to the western edge of the bread factory. Later, the enemy attacked the left neighbour, also with flamethrowers. The defence against this attack was supported by heavy infantry weapons and artillery of Gruppe Seydel."

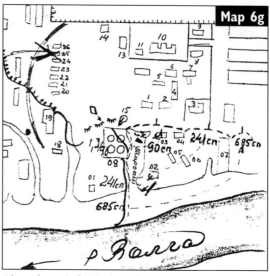

Plan of attack for 95th Rifle Division to link up with 138th Rifle Division. The results were vastly different.

Under destructive artillery fire, the weary men of Grenadier-Regiment 576, ably guided by their courageous leader, Major Braun, firmly held the conquered river bank against the Soviet counterattacks. Standing side by side with them were the exhausted soldiers of Pionier-Bataillon 294. More losses were suffered: Soldat Heinrich Hellgoth[24] and Soldat Josef Schimunek[25], both from 2. Kompanie, were struck and killed by bullets.

The combat journal of 685th Rifle Regiment describes the attack thus:

At 1230 the regiment again mounted an attack, in coordination with units of 95th Rifle Division, but all efforts to take the fuel tanks and cross the gully throughout the day had no success, and at 1600 the regiment transitioned to the defence…

Soviet units also melted quickly in the fierce fighting, as attested by General Krylov:

After renewed bitter fighting in the area of the fuel tanks, the situation there had still not changed: we held our positions, though we did not succeed in fighting through to Lyudnikov's Island. Towards the end of the day, the Gorishny Division, together with the other units subordinated to it, had 708 men…its three rifle regiments numbered 212, 91 and 330 men, the battalion from 92nd Brigade subordinated to Gorishny had 44 men. The composite regiment formed from the remnants of the Smekhotvorov Division did not have much more.[26] All of these units could naturally only advance as small combat groups…

The war diary of 62nd Army summarises the events on this sector:

Units of 95th Rifle Division fought to restore the position on the sector of 241st Rifle Regiment and establish a direct connection with units of 138th Rifle Division. The enemy launched strong counterattacks in the evening and threw parts of 95th Rifle Division back to their starting positions. 90th Rifle Regiment held the area of the fuel tanks. 241st and 685th

---

24. Hellgoth, Soldat Heinrich, 2./Pi.Btl.294; born 12 August, 1908 in Droyssig/Zeitz. Killed in action, 19 November, 1942 in Stalingrad.

25. Schimunek, Soldat Josef, 2./Pi.Btl.294; born 27 September, 1921 in Mattersdorf. Killed in action, 19 November, 1942 in Stalingrad.

26. The figures are mostly correct. The following comes from the army war diary: "Remnants of units: 161st Rifle Regiment – 330 men, 241st Rifle Regiment – 91 men, 90th Rifle Regiment – 212 men, 685th Rifle Regiment – 77 men, 3/92nd Rifle Brigade – 44 men." This makes a total of 754 men, not 708 as Krylov reported.

Rifle Regiments held the gully 150 metres north-east of Mezenskaya. The fight to restore the position on the sector of 241st Rifle Regiment continues.

At 1640 hours, LI. Armeekorps reported to 6. Armee that "at the moment, the enemy has renewed the attack in still unknown strength, supported by artillery and rocket-launchers". This attack was repulsed with counterattacks.

- - -

As the dim afternoon wore on, a thin mist formed on the battlefield. Ice lightly covered the rubble and visibility was slightly affected. The Germans retained the upper hand and continued their assaults. The large groups spotted by Pechenyuk's men now threw themselves against another building: this time it was Haus 84. It lay just across the street from Haus 83, and indeed, firmly thrown grenades could reach it. After a brief barrage from mortars and machine-guns, the German assault groups that had assembled in Haus 83 rushed Haus 84. Resistance was weak. A few minutes was all that was needed to take the building. Soviet units were utterly exhausted.

At the same time, on Pribaltiskaya Street, a new attack was also launched. The objective was Haus 67 [Dom 38]. This house, designated 'Strongpoint No. 4' of 1st Rifle Battalion of 344th Rifle Regiment, had originally been held by Lieutenant Pogrebnyak and seven other men on 11 November. The house was captured by the Germans on 14 November but had been quickly retaken in a skilful counterattack. Since then, the house had remained firmly in Soviet hands. Few of Pogrebnyak's original garrison survived the initial loss of the house, so a new garrison now defended the structure.

The German assault was well-planned. Despite the Soviet expectation of such an attack, the German stormtroops broke into the building from both sides and quickly cleared the entire building. LI. Armeekorps informed 6. Armee: "In the afternoon, 305. Infanterie-Division took Haus 84 and Haus 67 with storm group attacks".

During these attacks, Lyudnikov's men witnessed a new German tactic. This is from the divisional combat journal:

> The enemy air force, in small groups, flies very low to the ground and feigns attacks on our troops, but they don't fire because they're afraid that they will hit their own men due to the fact that they are so close to ours.

The capture of Haus 74 [Dom 37] and Haus 67 [Dom 38] on Grenadier-Regiment 577's sector were rightly seen as victories, and measured against the Stalingrad yardstick, they had come at low cost to the Germans. However, there were losses. Pionier-Bataillon 336 lost at least 3 killed and 3 wounded: Unteroffizier Alfred Szaks[27], 1. Kompanie, was killed instantly by a direct hit from an artillery shell; Unteroffizier Martin Philipp[28] and Gefreiter Wilhelm Petermann[29], both of 2. Kompanie, were also killed. Also from that company, Obergefreiter Arthur Quint[30] and Pionier Franz Tetzlaff[31] were both severely wounded, while Gefreiter Fritz Köhler[32] of 3. Kompanie suffered lighter wounds.

---

27. Szaks, Unteroffizier Alfred, 1./Pi.Btl.336; born 10 January, 1910 in Tilsit. Killed in action, 19 November, 1942 in Stalingrad.
28. Philipp, Unteroffizier Martin, 2./Pi.Btl.336; born 26 March, 1914 in Neusalza Spremberg. Killed in action, 19 November, 1942 in Stalingrad.
29. Petermann, Gefreiter Wilhelm, 2./Pi.Btl.336; born 26 August, 1912 in Coesfeld. Killed in action, 19 November, 1942 in Stalingrad.
30. Quint, Obergefreiter Arthur, 2./Pi.Btl.336; born 4 May, 1910 in Chemnitz.
31. Tetzlaff, Pionier Franz, 2./Pi.Btl.336; born 14 February, 1922 in Neustadt.
32. Köhler, Gefreiter Fritz, 2./Pi.Btl.336; born 9 December, 1912 in Zwickau.

Casualty figures for 3./Pionier–Bataillon 305 are not available but at least one of them was wounded: Gefreiter Peter Teichelkamp[33] was hit in the hip by a bullet. Teichelkamp later reported that at the time of his wounding, his company still had 15 men, 1. Kompanie had 7 men and 2. Kompanie had 6 men.

Teichelkamp was witness to several extraordinary events during the previous week. In his opinion, the discipline of the German units in Stalingrad, which had been on operations for a long time, was no longer particularly good. He once saw some soldiers refuse to follow a Hauptmann's order and act in such an insubordinate way that the Hauptmann started thumping the men with his rifle butt. The situation was only resolved by the fact that the Soviets attacked at that precise moment. On another occasion, Teichelkamp saw four combat pioneers hiding in a cellar when they were supposed to be attacking.

– – –

Lyudnikov and his division were stunned by the German attacks. Long gone were the broad offensives of several battalions supported by copious amounts of artillery and armour. Now, the German attacks were precise, well-planned and expertly executed. Instead of trying to attain grand objectives, the Germans focused their efforts on small, achievable targets. Aiding their cause was the emaciated state of the Soviet defenders. The combat journal of 138th Rifle Division reveals the unvarnished truth: "For three days now, the division has had no rations and ammunition. Three days that people have not slept. The ranks of the soldiers are getting thinner every day. Each new day becomes more catastrophic than the last." The combat journal of 650th Rifle Regiment has more of the same: "War materials are almost finished; there are no grenades or foodstuffs. The wounded are not evacuated."

Losses for the division on this day were high: 24 killed and 28 wounded, a total of 52. According to the division's strength return submitted at 1500 hours, 344th Rifle Regiment had 62 men, 650th Rifle Regiment had 29 men and 768th Rifle Regiment had 40 men. The number of able-bodied soldiers on the west bank was only 371. In addition, the number of wounded men was 357. Once 23 men from other units are taken into account, the total strength on the Stalingrad bank was a mere 811 men.

Lyudnikov's division lost four crucial strongpoints during the day. At 1700 hours, the division held the line "150 metres north of the division command post, Dom 47, 43, 39, 41, and along the street that runs from Dom 38 to the Volga." The loss of Haus 84 [Dom 65] had not been accounted for. The front-line of 650th Rifle Regiment is described in its combat journal: "The regiment, with groups of the blocking detachment (14 men), group Petrenko (10 men), some reinforcements and the remnants of the regiment, is defending the area from the unfinished building down to the river and the water tower and the stretch of river bank 100 metres north of the water tower."

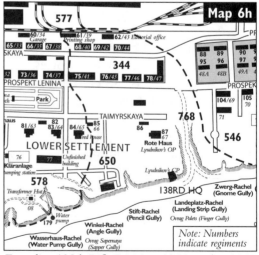

Front-line 138th Rifle Division, 19 November, 1942.

33. Teichelkamp, Gefreiter Peter, 3./Pi.Btl.305; born 10 April, 1910. No further information known.

In a letter home, Oberzahlmeister Erich Bauchspiess, paymaster of Pionier-Bataillon 336, mentions a small trifle that was symptomatic of much larger problems:

> Because of restricted paper availability, I must write to you now and in the future on a small card. Not counting upon such a long action, we have as a consequence been running short of many things. We have to manage as best we can, which naturally is unpleasant and causes a lot of work. Well, even this will come to an end. The only good thing is that we get fantastically good rations as never before. We can be satisfied with the weather. The fog keeps the temperature around the freezing point…

Before operations in Stalingrad, the men of the five pioneer battalions fully expected to complete their task in a week or two and then return to their previous positions. As a result, they did not bring many items that could make their lives a bit more comfortable. Only necessities had been taken along. For the divisions already stationed in the city, with their established supply lines, it was a different matter, as is apparent in a letter written by Hauptmann Traub to his wife:

> Early today I returned from our forward positions, washed myself properly, had a shave and am now feeling human again. If nothing else comes up, I'll go forward again the day after next. But first I'll write to you… In the meantime I have eaten supper. Actually, it is only 5 o'clock and now I want to make things comfortable for myself. The shack is nice and warm and a bottle of red wine is standing ready. This is how one can endure the war. As I wrote you some days ago, there are no shortages of liquor at present. Additionally, for commanders, there was a special allowance and I currently have an excellent cellar. I'll send you a bottle of Cacao liquor tomorrow. This will be my Christmas present to you. I wish I could give you other things but there is nothing to be had here. Anyway, you can be happy that – apart from air raids – you have been spared the war. In Stalingrad, despite the silly shooting and firing, there are still Russian civilians. They live in cellars, in sewerage pipes and potter about half-starving, pursuing their miserable existence. As my interpreter told me today and by way of an example, some days ago they found a four year-old girl in a shell crater who for two days had been lying next to her dead mother killed by a shell splinter. There are many such shocking fates. But we have become insensitive to them and are no longer touched by such events…
> We have apparently been lucky with the weather this winter. The heavy frosts have again eased. The weather is mild at the moment. We are experiencing 4 degrees Celsius, hopefully we won't get rain. If it falls here it will be very bad… At the moment I have enough cigars and cigarettes to smoke. Other than female company, we are not starved of any physical pleasures. The night before last, we sat in our cellar by feeble candlelight and played a lively game of Doppelkopf. Fourteen days ago, the last of our personnel returned from leave. They told us about getting an ample food parcel at the border station, 4 pounds of butter, a pound of flour and other nice goodies. If only it was my turn, but this is out of the question before February 1943.

– – –

In a special memorandum, 6. Armee noted the following:

Führer presentation about sIG33B:

Leutnant Nippes, Sturmgeschütz-Abteilung 244, will present an intermediate report to 6. Armee and later set in march for a presentation to OKH.

It is unknown whether Nippes ever made his presentation to 6. Armee because the performance of a new vehicle would soon be the last thing on the army's mind. The survival of the entire army was at stake. In addition, Leutnant Nippes was needed with his sIG33Bs because Sturmgeschütz-Abteilung 244 were ordered out of the ruins and sent west, over the

Don, to parry the Soviet armoured spearheads coming down from the north-west. On 24 November, Nippes was heavily wounded during an armoured clash and later flown out of the pocket. It is unlikely he ever made his presentation to OKH.

- - -

Calamity was unfolding out in the steppe. The Romanian 3. Armee had collapsed and Soviet tanks, against which the Romanians had no anti-tank weapons heavier than 47mm, completed their rout. By nightfall, Soviet spearheads had pushed forward almost 20 kilometres.

Gefreiter Teichelkamp, 3./Pionier-Bataillon 305, bearing a painful hip wound, was brought out of the forming pocket in a car to Chir railway station after an adventurous trip in all directions. During conversations with wounded comrades in Budyenny, Gefreiter Teichelkamp learned that the Soviets had broken through near the Romanians… The Romanians only had a few heavy weapons. In Chir, Teichelkamp had seen that they had no more heavy weapons, saw them clinging to vehicles and screaming loudly to be taken along. He thought that the Soviets knew to attack precisely near the Romanians. Teichelkamp was of the opinion that, in general, the Romanians were better soldiers than the Italians, despite the chasm existing between ranks: Romanian field-kitchens prepared three separate meals, one for officers, one for NCOs and one for the men, who only received a little to eat.

At 2130 hours, Weichs sent the following message to 6. Armee:

> The development of the situation at Romanian 3. Armee compels radical measures to secure forces to protect the deep flank of 6. Armee. All offensive operations in Stalingrad are to be halted at once.

Along with the message came an order to take two mobile units, an infantry division, and, if possible, another mobile division out of the city, place them under XIV. Panzerkorps and deploy them behind the army's left flank to meet the attack, protect the deep flank and secure the Lichovskoi railway line and Chir railway station. This order could only have been given with Hitler's consent. Because he had ordered the continuation of the attack in Stalingrad on 17 November, only two days earlier, it can therefore be presumed that it only took place with Zeitzler's intervention.

Shortly thereafter, at 2205 hours, LI. Armeekorps issued Korpsbefehl Nr. 116 to its subordinate units. It first of all addressed Operation Schwerin, the attack being planned to eliminate the bridgehead in the Krasny Oktyabr factory:

> Korps must reckon that the attack against the enemy bridgehead will not be continued for the time being on the orders of the supreme command. As a result, Operation Schwerin I will not take place. In any case, the instructions for 305. Infanterie-Division and 389. Infanterie-Division still stand.

Immediate steps were also taken to get armoured units to the scene of the crisis:

> On 20 November, 24. Panzer-Division will shift Panzer-Regiment 24 with all operational panzers (including the employed panzer schwadrons), one company of Panzerjäger-Abteilung 40 and IV./Panzerartillerie-Regiment 89 into the Vertyachii-Peskovatka area.

> If the order is given to carry out the withdrawal of the panzer division, the following changes in subordination will take place: a) Sturmgeschütz-Abteilung 244 will be subordinated to 305. Infanterie-Division, two assault guns will remain with 389. Infanterie-Division. b) Werfer-Regiment 53 with 2 light battalions will remain subordinated to 305. Infanterie-Division. c) Werfer-Regiment 2 will remain near 100. Jäger-Division. Missions only during heavy enemy attacks.

At 2245 hours, LI. Armeekorps reported to 6. Armee:

> The assault actions in Stalingrad – apart from the stormtroop operations east of the gun factory – are suspended with immediate effect. LI. Armeekorps will immediately withdraw 14. and 24. Panzer-Divisions and Sturmgeschütz-Abteilung 244 and set them in march in the direction of the Don river bridge at Luchinskoi.

Panzer Schwadron Messerschmidt, which had earlier received orders to continue supporting 305. Infanterie-Division, was included in the order to 24. Panzer-Division to mobilise all of its operational panzers. Messerschmidt vividly recollects that evening:

Messerschmidt

> During the night of 19 to 20 November, the loud sounds of battle far to the north-west of Stalingrad could not be ignored and plenty of flashes were to be seen. The front-line in the city was exceptionally quiet compared to that. That night, we received the order to disengage from the enemy in the city and drive in the direction of Kalach-on-Don. The roads were icy, it was very foggy, very cold and it was snowing, so much so that the man driving in front could barely be seen.

With that, Messerschmidt and his panzers left the blood-soaked arena.

Oberleutnant Messerschmidt led his panzers from the Barrikady into the snowy steppe outside Stalingrad.

– – –

In its evening report, Artillerie-Regiment 179 stated that "towards 1900 hours, a motor boat approaching the shore in the area of Tapeworm Gully was forced to turn around by artillery fire". The evening report of Gruppe Seydel mentioned the same thing: "Towards 2000 hours, an enemy boat landing at the mouth of Tapeworm Gully in the sectors of Bataillon Domaschk (left) and Steffen (right) was combated by artillery and thereupon forced to turn back out on to the river".

The ice-choked river and ferocious German reaction to any river traffic was starving 138th Rifle Division of even the most basic needs. Each bullet and grenade was precious. Something needed to be done. Commander of the Stalingrad Front, General-Colonel Yeremenko, gave an order to Rear-Admiral D.D. Rogachev[34]: the Volga Flotilla was to deliver 60 tonnes of ammunition and 20 tonnes of rations to Colonel Lyudnikov's division and take off all the wounded men there. To carry out this order over the coming days, Volga Flotilla command would organise four voyages by armoured boats and icebreakers in the hope of providing enough supplies to enable Lyudnikov to hold on.

Casualties for 19 November, 1942:
138th Rifle Division: 24 killed, 28 wounded, a total of 52 men
305. and 389. Infanterie-Divisions: no figures available

---

34. Rogachev, Rear-Admiral Dmitri Dmitriyevich; Volga Flotilla; born 20 September, 1895 in Bolshaya Roslyakovka. Died in 1963 in Zelenodolske.

20 November, 1942

At dawn, south of Stalingrad, the 64th, 57th and 51st Armies of General Yeremenko's Stalingrad Front deployed along a 200km front. They would form the southern prong of the massive pincer set to close behind 6. Armee. However, fog and the resulting poor visibility delayed the assault. A tense Stavka order from Moscow commanded Yeremenko to get on with it, but he replied that he was on the spot and it was his decision. At 0720 hours, the fog lifted, and at 0800, the Soviet artillery opened up. The offensive then began. General-Lieutenant F.I. Tolbukhin's[35] 57th Army and General-Lieutenant N.I. Trufanov's[36] 51st Army easily broke through the Romanian VI. Korps along the chain of salt lakes south of Beketovka. The Romanian corps crumbled. Hoth's[37] 4. Panzerarmee recorded that the Romanian corps disintegrated so rapidly that all measures to stop the fleeing troops had become useless before they could be carried out. The advance of General Tanaschishin's[38] 13th Tank Corps was halted when it ran into Generalmajor Leyser's[39] 29. Infanterie-Division (mot.), but it soon renewed its advance when Leyser was ordered to withdraw to the west to protect the rear of Heeresgruppe B. General Volsky's[40] 4th Mechanised Corps met almost no resistance but progress was cautious and slow as they probed north in fierce blizzards.

There was a flurry of activity in the German camp, but none of it involved Lyudnikov's Island. Hastily issued orders were sent out so that forces could be gathered to block the Soviet spearhead pushing down behind 6. Armee. The increasingly precarious situation worsened when news arrived about another Soviet offensive south of Stalingrad. Their objective was blindingly obvious. Even a casual glance at a map revealed that 6. Armee was in mortal danger. LI. Armeekorps had the lion's share of the army's divisions, so it was ordered to extract as many units as possible from the ruins of Stalingrad and send them west. At 0945 hours, it sent a teletype message to Gruppe Schwerin:

> While firmly holding the previous front-line, the following will be withdrawn as quickly as possible and set in march:
>
> 1.) From Gruppe Schwerin: a) Gruppe Seydel of 14. Panzer-Division. The previously withdrawn elements will move off on 20 November. b) Gruppe Scheele of 24. Panzer-Division. With that, Gruppe Schwerin is disbanded.
>
> 2.) From 305. Infanterie-Division: the heavy infantry guns of 14. Panzer-Division will be sent to 14. Panzer-Division without delay.
>
> 3.) From 389. Infanterie-Division: Sturmgeschütz-Abteilung 244 to Luchinskoi during the course of 20 November. Sturmkompanie of 24. Panzer-Division is to be speedily supplied to Gruppe Scheele.

- - -

35. Tolbukhin, General-Lieutenant Fedor Ivanovich, HotSU; 57th Army; born 16 June, 1894 in Androniki. Died 17 October, 1949.

36. Trufanov, General-Lieutenant Nikolai Ivanovich, 51st Army; born 2 May, 1900 in Velikoye. Died 21 February, 1982 in Kharkov.

37. Hoth, General der Panzertruppe Hermann, Schw., EL, RK; OB 4. Panzerarmee; born 12 April, 1885 in Neuruppin. Died 25 January, 1971 in Goslar.

38. Tanaschishin, General-Major Trofim Ivanovich, 13th Tank Corps; born 1903. Killed in action, 2 April, 1944.

39. Leyser, Generalmajor Hans-Georg, RK, DKiG; 29.Inf.Div.(mot.); born 16 June, 1896 in Worin. Died 18 April, 1980.

40. Volsky, General Vasili Timofeyevich, 4th Mechanised Corps; born 10 March, 1897 in Moscow. Died 22 February, 1946 in Moscow.

It was quieter than normal on Lyudnikov's Island. The divisional combat journal noted that "in the first half of the day, the enemy did not attack at all". The combat journal of 650th Rifle Regiment tells a slightly different story:

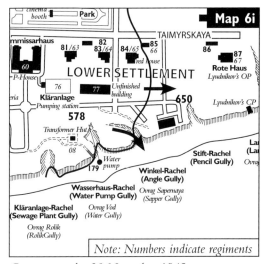

German attacks, 20 November, 1942.

> The enemy, with up to 40 men, went over to the offensive at 0245 from the direction of the unfinished building, at the same time grouping his infantry near the structure with the goal of moving up to the line from the unfinished building to the Volga river.

In the second half of the day, the Germans – in about platoon strength – launched attacks against the left flank of 650th Rifle Regiment in the area of Sapper Gully. They were still trying to break into the dispositions of Pechenyuk's regiment but artillery and rifle fire repulsed the attacks. German artillery and mortars continued to pound the combat ranks of 138th Rifle Division and Zaitsevsky Island.

At 1700 hours, once darkness had fallen, up to 50 Germans attacked the centre of the line of 650th Rifle Regiment, but the Soviet riflemen did not let the Germans pass their line. At 1830, battles still raged in the centre of 650th Rifle Regiment's sector. The combat journal of 138th Rifle Division noted:

> Our defence is especially good. There are more headquarters staff in the defence line than there are soldiers. We have no rations and ammunition. Our position has worsened. Our air force doesn't drop any supplies to us. Rations and ammunition being sent over the river were not successful. Five boats laden with supplies were caught on ice floes and carried down the Volga. Irrespective of all this, the soldiers still fight like lions. Where there is at least one soldier alive, the enemy is not able to advance even an inch.

The division's losses on this day were 4 killed and 4 wounded. The combat structure of the division was as follows: on the west bank of the Volga were 793 men. Of those, 348 were wounded men, and there were 83 men who were not part of the division.

– – –

The situation around the fuel tanks was fairly quiet. The 62nd Army war diary reads:

> 95th Rifle Division repelled two enemy attacks in company-strength from the direction of the fuel tanks. Units held their previous positions. The remnants of 685th Rifle Regiment and 3/92nd Rifle Brigade are poured into the framework of 241st Rifle Regiment.
> Remnants of units: 241st Rifle Regiment – 72 men, 90th Rifle Regiment – 60 men, 161st Rifle Regiment – 162 men.

The combat journal of 685th Rifle Regiment noted that "at 2200, in accordance with 62nd Army's order, the personnel of the regiment were handed over to 95th Rifle Division".

Based on the previous day's strength figures, each of 95th Rifle Division's three regiments had considerably less manpower: 90th Rifle Regiment had 152 men less, 161st Rifle Regiment had 168 men less and 241st Rifle Regiment – even after absorbing 685th Rifle Regiment and 3/92nd Rifle Brigade – had 121 men less. These shortfalls are most likely because of casualties suffered in the brutal fighting on 19 November.

One of Hauptmann Rettenmaier's soldiers, Stabsgefreiter Hans Bernhart, 1./Grenadier-Regiment 578, wrote a letter to his fiancee:

I'm sitting here in a deep cellar[41], I could almost sing, I just need a barrel of wine. Your soldier and many comrades are still living under the unbelievable piles of rubble in this city, in candlelight both day and night. Of course we go out into the fresh air, which has got a bit more pleasant over the past few days. We've completely thrown the Russians out of our sector and now have sentries posted on the Volga beach. The air is quite fresh but I'm rugged up for it. I haven't taken your jacket off since I got back here. The colour's changed a bit, but what the hell, it all matches. We don't wash or shave any more. Our faces are covered in beards and soot, so everyone looks strange. We're hoping for a quick relief to come. It's still too cold to snow; I've got no great wish for that… We are on guard again at 5 am and the whole day tomorrow and then every other day. You've certainly read about the Red Barricade… I'm not allowed to write anything more…

Well, everything passes and May comes again[42]… The rations will soon be here and then I'm on duty.

Bernhart's good friend, Gefreiter Füssinger from 1./Pionier-Bataillon 305, could not hide his despondency in his lines home:

First of all, many thanks for the three small packages with candy, cigarettes and knee-warmers. The latter will be well used this winter. Now, by the time you receive my lines, Christmas will already be close. For us it will be a sad celebration here in shitty Russia. Ninety percent of our comrades are wounded or dead and an atmosphere like All Souls' Day prevails. Hours of happiness have almost become unknown us.

Disconsolate thoughts and feelings were not restricted to the enlisted men. Hauptmann Rettenmaier expressed himself in a letter to his loved ones:

I was not a little surprised to receive a parcel from you yesterday. Many thanks for your kind thoughts. I will really enjoy the gingerbread and the splendid sausage. The sugar is also much in demand here. Unfortunately I don't have any comrades with which to share these goodies. Everything is smashed into miserable little pieces… For the last few days, I've been out of the front-line area, charged with reforming the regiment.

The official army report only contains very brief messages: 'Assault troop activity in Stalingrad'. But those who have not actually been involved in the action here cannot imagine what is hidden behind these few short words . Day after day our assault groups must endure the hellish fire deluging them while having to undertake dangerous missions almost every day. To get an accurate picture of the doggedness of the Russians, one has to be here at the front… However, we are starting to be convinced that the enemy in our sector is slowly becoming more brittle. He has been cut off for days from all outside communications and is being hemmed into an ever tighter pocket. Behind the enemy lies the Volga along a breadth of around 150 metres. He is now unable to ferry anything across it here. Planes come at night and drop ammunition, rations and medical supplies to them by parachute, but most of it lands within our lines. Thus the situation of our foe in our sector becomes ever more impossible and within a few days he will be utterly destroyed. Then we are hoping for quieter days. The front will never be totally peaceful in our region… there will always be something happening. Further south the enemy is bunkered down in the city. But even there he will be defeated.

---

41. A line from 'Im kühlen Keller sitz ich hier', an old student drinking song. Bernhardt is trying to express the contrast between his current situation and earlier, better times.

42. Another line from a song, this time "Es geht alles vorüber". It was created during the war and was popular with soldiers because it led them to believe that 'everything passes' and they would soon be at home with their loved ones.

It was a huge contrast for me to be thrown directly into the fighting after just having come back from leave. It is always hard until one has coped with the first few days and begun to know the enemy's units. I am now familiar with the environment and make an effort to do as well as I can in the performance of my duty, aware that a great deal of the outcome of this war will be decided here.

Regarding the weather, Rettenmaier optimistically wrote that "I am well-equipped for the winter. It isn't yet especially cold, though we did once have a temperature of minus 16 degrees. As we have become used to this temperature, however, we no longer find it quite as grim as we once would have in our normal lives at home."

– – –

During the night, Sturmschwadron 24 was pulled out of its perilous front-line trenches opposite the northern face of Lyudnikov's Island. Its latest commander[43], Oberleutnant Martius[44], described the relief in a letter dated 21 November:

Familie Martius

> After a spin as Sturmschwadronsführer, I've again landed as adjutant. I went along there, 130 metres west of the Volga river bank, and simply received the order to withdraw the schwadron. Since the schwadron was subordinated to another division and they had just received chocolate, I telephoned the regiment commander because of the same matter – and in the evening, fetched four thick bars of chocolate for each man of the schwadron. Loud cheers. In addition, schnaps was supplied and the mood was saved, even though it was bloody cold. When I arrived like Santa Claus with a whole load of enormous bags, one of them said 'It's like Christmas!' and began to sing 'Ihr Kinderlein kommt' [Come, little children]. Nevertheless, the soldiers are in good spirits. The withdrawal was somewhat difficult because it had just snowed and everything took place on the forward slope – the Russians were 20 metres away. We came out of it with four wounded…

Oberleutnant Hans Joachim Martius, adjutant II./Pz.Gr.Rgt.26 and last commander of Sturmschwadron 24.

– – –

At 2150 hours, at the faraway Rossosh railway station, the reinforcements assembled for Pioner-Bataillon 294 were loaded aboard a train. Oberleutnant Johannes Benad led the 70 pioneers on their icy railbound odyssey toward Stalingrad. The division commander was despondent to see his last pioneers needlessly dispatched to the Stalingrad grist-mill. Intermittent reports filed by Hauptmann Weimann made it patently clear that the battalion had suffered ghastly casualties and there was no reason for Generalmajor Block to think that the latest batch of replacements would escape this same fate.

43. Its previous commander, Leutnant Wroblewski, was wounded by hand grenade shrapnel on 18 November, 1942. Wroblewski, Oberleutnant Walter, 7./Pz.Gr.Rgt.26; born 30 March, 1917 in Stettin. Died 26 December, 1994 in Isernhagen.

44. Martius was three-eighths Jewish and just prior to his promotion to Leutnant, had been requested to guarantee – in writing – that he would not remain an officer after the war. According to a secret OKW directive from 8 April, 1940, a 50% 'Mischling' (literally 'half-breed') was not allowed to serve, while those with 25% Jewish blood could – with conditions. The promotion of each such man required the Führer's approval. While fighting for Germany, Martius was killed on 25 December, 1942 by a direct mortar hit. His younger brother, Friedrich (born 2 September, 1922 in Bonn) also died for the Fatherland, succumbing on 25 September, 1944 to severe wounds suffered a day earlier.

At 2250 hours, LI. Armeekorps issued Korpsbefehl Nr. 117, which ordered its units to transition to the defence:

> Strong enemy forces have achieved a deep penetration against the neighbouring army to the west. It must be reckoned that the enemy will attempt to extend this penetration with armoured forces. Countermeasures have been initiated by the army under cessation of the attack in Stalingrad. LI. Armeekorps will discontinue its attack in Stalingrad, organise itself for defence and hold the entire front-line that has been won in heavy fighting...

The mission for the two divisions girdling Lyudnikov's Island were as follows:

> 305. Infanterie-Division will continue storm group operations until the final destruction of the enemy group in the tightly compressed area east of the gun factory. For this, Sturmgeschütz-Abteilung 245 will detach its operational assault guns and sIG33Bs. The subordination of heavy infantry guns and heavy mortars from other divisions remains in effect until completion of the mission.

> 389. Infanterie-Division will prepare for the attack to capture the 'Rote Haus' and carry it out in agreement with 305. Infanterie-Division. In addition, the division must reconnoitre so that it can take over the southern sector of 94. Infanterie-Division up to the Orlovka mouth, which must be reckoned on after the destruction of the enemy group east of the gun factory.

Although crisis was looming in the rear, the German attacks on the 'Island of Fire' would continue. 6. Armee command had begun to recognise the strategic danger but tactical efforts were still being made to invest the last Soviet strongholds in Stalingrad.

Soviet post-war memoirs seem to suggest that they were aware of German intentions. Army chief-of-staff Krylov wrote:

> It was only proven on the night of 20 November that the enemy had decided to give up any further attempts to completely take Stalingrad. He suspended the attacks in the city (apart from Lyudnikov's sector, where he continued to attack throughout the day of 21 and even 22 November) and began to withdraw certain troops. Especially panzer units.

– – –

Once darkness had well and truly fallen, the first of the supply trips organised by Rear-Admiral Rogachev and his Volga Flotilla left Tumak at 1735 hours. This first fleet consisted of Armoured Boats No. 61, 63, 12[45] and a tugboat of the ice-breaking type, 'Kochegar Hetman' (commander Captain E.V. Masleyev, Commissar Gavrilov). The tugboat moved at the head of the fleet to cut a passage through the ice. On the armoured boats were 15 tonnes of ammunition and 5 tonnes of rations. Supervising this small fleet from Armoured Boat No. 63 (commander Warrant Officer V.G. Korotenko) was the commander of the 2nd Armoured Boat Detachment, Captain-Lieutenant A.I. Peskov. This armoured boat was second in line, directly behind the tugboat. Following in the wake of Armoured Boat No. 63 was Armoured Boat No. 61 (temporary acting commander Junior Politruk D.P. Medvedev) and Armoured Boat No. 12 (commander Lieutenant V.I. Cherednichenko) brought up the rear.

---

45. All armoured boats (colloquially known as 'river tanks') deployed during these supply operations were of the '1125' type. Designed in 1934 under the direction of Y.Y. Benua. In 1936 the prototype boat was tested and accepted for large-scale production. On some armoured boats the 76.2mm gun consisted of a 'T-28' tank turret. Boats constructed during the war were armed with 76.2 mm Lendera guns. Displacement: 26.5 tonnes. Dimensions: 22.65 long x 3.55 metres wide. Petrol-driven internal combustion engine, 720–800 HP. Speed of 15 knots (28kph), range of 400kms. Armour plating on hull and cabin: 4-7mm. Armament: 1 x 76.2mm in a T-34 tank turret, 1 x 12.7mm and 2 x 7.62mm machine-guns. Crew: 13 men. For more information about each individual armoured boat and its history, see Appendix 8 (page 594).

Route of the supply boats from Tumak up the Volga to 'Lyudnikov's Island' east of the Barrikady Gun Factory.

When the fleet reached the northern suburb of Krasny Oktyabr at 1930, it was fired on but no damage was inflicted on the boats. The fleet continued to head towards the Barrikady. The night was black and somewhat windy. The gunboats cleaved their way through the thin ice towards the 'Island'. The most dangerous sector was ahead of them. They had to negotiate the cramped, ice-choked Denezhnaya Volozhka channel, hemmed in on the right by Zaitsevsky Island and on the left by the German-occupied clifftops. To cover their approach, machine-guns on Zaitsevsky Island laid down a heavy barrage. Lines of tracers arched over the Volga, forming a luminous canopy. Sentries from Grenadier-Regiment 578 detected the Soviet boats moving up the river. No-one needed to be told that they were bringing help to 138th Rifle Division. Hauptmann Rettenmaier ordered two 75mm anti-tank guns to be brought forward and emplaced on the very edge of the steep cliff. Although the guns were in position near the Kindergarten, it was backbreaking work to manually manhandle them across the cratered terrain, and as a result, they would not arrive in time for the evening's events.[46]

Half an hour after being fired on near Krasny Oktyabr, the armoured boats approached the bank near Lyudnikov's command post. Unloading parties sheltered in cliffside dug-outs, waiting for them to arrive. Since manpower was at a premium, no front-line soldier was spared for this dangerous duty. Instead, the temporary stevedores consisted of staff personnel and wounded soldiers. Darkness concealed traffic on the river but the arrival of the boats caused a deadly pyrotechnics show to erupt. Huddled beneath the cliffs, the unloading parties watched the boats pull into shore. Explosions bracketed the vessels. Shrapnel whizzed through the air. The cargo was desperately needed so there was no choice but to abandon cover and venture out into the maelstrom.

---

46. Rettenmaier mistakenly wrote that this happened on 16 November, but Russian sources on this matter are extremely accurate and it is from those that the chronological order is based.

Unloading the boats was no easy task. Mortar bursts walked up and down the river bank, blindly seeking out the boats and those trying to offload the cargo. Artillery shells howled in. Machine-guns atop the cliffs to the south and the north sent long bursts into the moored vessels. Parachute flares, hissing and sputtering above the water, lit up the scene. Men dashing down to the water would abruptly crash to the ground, as only fatally wounded men do. Death came randomly. The assistant to the Divisional Chief of Operations, Captain Peter Vlasovich Gulko, was killed while unloading supplies. So were many others, including some of the wounded men who had courageously volunteered. Lyudnikov estimated that his divisional headquarters alone lost 25 men and officers.

The trench leading from Lyudnikov's command post down to the water's edge. On the right is an entrance to a bunker.

While the crews of the armoured boats helped offload the cargo and carry the wounded aboard, the boat commanders sought out Colonel Lyudnikov. They warned him that the ice east of Zaitsevsky Island was becoming dangerous and that soon crossings would no longer be possible.

"The Germans won't stop us, but the ice…" said the boatmen helplessly.

"The Germans cannot stop us either," said Lyudnikov, "But we have no control over the weather. And still, if it is possible that you come tomorrow night… and if my words mean anything to you, comrade boatmen…"

"Comrade Colonel, there is no reason to even ask us!" said the boatmen as they interrupted Lyudnikov. "Every trip we take to your 'Island' is an honour for us."

"The division needs at least another such reinforcement, such as the one you delivered to us today. Another such reinforcement and our crisis will be over…"

Despite all the difficulties, only 45 minutes were needed to unload the boats and quickly carry 100 wounded men aboard. The price had been high, but as Lyudnikov later wrote, "our greatest difficulty, that of receiving ammunition and food, and of evacuating the wounded, had been solved".

Until this moment, all the burdens for the care of the wounded were placed on the shoulders of the medical assistant of 203rd Separate Signals Battalion, Lieutenant of Medical Service S.Z. Ozerova. About 400 wounded men had accumulated in tunnels, dug-outs and deep fissures in the Volga cliff. Despite being fatigued, stressed and under constant enemy fire, she visited dug-outs and rendered the necessary help to wounded men. Lyudnikov highly valued Ozerova's commitment and bravery. She would later be awarded the Order of the Red Star and two 'For Courage' medals.

At 2120 hours, the armoured boats departed from the bank. At the head of the group again was the tugboat 'Kochegar Hetman'. As soon as the fleet came within range, the Germans immediately opened fire on them with artillery, mortars and machine-guns. The armoured boats struck back with their cannon and machine-guns, aiming at the muzzle flashes of the German guns.

Grenadier-Regiment 576 managed to hit 'Kochegar Hetman' with at least two anti-tank shells. One of the rounds smashed into the wheelhouse and fatally wounded Senior-Lieutenant I.I. Peryshkina. The same shell disabled the steering mechanism and the tugboat lost navigation. The second shell penetrated the engine room and put the vessel out of action.

Having lost navigation and propulsion, the tugboat was carried towards the shallows by the current. Then its captain requested help over the radio. Captain-Lieutenant Peskov ordered the skipper of Armoured Boat No. 12, Lieutenant Cherednichenko, to assist the stricken tugboat. Under German fire, 'Kochegar Hetman' was reined in by Armoured Boat No. 12, pulled from the shallows and towed back to base.

As the drama over the tugboat played out, the Germans continued to fire on the other vessels. Armoured boat No. 61 was also hit by two shells. One of them penetrated the cabin, killing the helmsman Sergeant A.N. Yemelin and severely wounding Senior-Lieutenant B.N. Zhitomirsky and Junior-Politruk D.R. Medvedev.

With nobody left in the cabin to pilot the vessel, it performed senseless manoeuvres. Seeing that something was wrong, Red Navy man J.K. Samoilov ran to the wheelhouse and grabbed the controls. Noticing at the same time that No. 61 was in distress, Captain-Lieutenant Peskov came to their aid in Armoured Boat No. 63. Realising that the damaged vessel was in danger of being lost, Peskov transferred to it and took command. The armoured boats then moved out from under the bombardment and returned to Tumak at midnight.

During this voyage, 1 man was killed and 9 were wounded on the armoured boats, while 1 man was killed on the tugboat 'Kochegar Hetman'.

Despite the damage inflicted on the boats, this inaugural supply run was seen as a success. Apart from the delivery of 15 tonnes of ammunition and 5 tonnes of food, 100 wounded men had been evacuated, and, more importantly, an effective supply line had been opened… albeit temporarily. The race was on to deliver more supplies before the Volga iced over.

Casualties for 20 November, 1942:
138th Rifle Division: 4 killed, 4 wounded, a total of 8 men
305. and 389. Infanterie-Divisions: no figures available

21 November, 1942

At 0100 hours, the takeover of Gruppe Seydel's sector was completed by Oberstleutnant Richard Claassen's[47] Grenadier-Regiment 517 (295. Infanterie-Division) reinforced by a pioneer company from Pionier-Bataillon 295. With that, Gruppe Seydel departed from the units of Gruppe Schwerin and played no further part in the fighting near the fuel tanks. Grenadier-Regiment 517 now held the sector from the 'Burg' up to the large gully near the fuel installation.

Early in the morning, 305. Infanterie-Division's attempts to finish off Lyudnikov's division began in earnest. At 0430 hours, with the strength of about a company and supported by five tanks with artillery and mortar fire, the Germans went on the offensive

47. Claassen, Oberstleutnant Richard, RK; Gr.Rgt.517; born 4 January, 1900 in Berlin. Died 26 May, 1943 in Frolov POW camp, near Stalingrad.

against 344th Rifle Regiment. At 0815, they attacked Haus 68 [Dom 40] and Haus 75 [Dom 41], while three assault guns cruised along the street, approached these building and opened fire on them. The attack was beaten off.

There was also action on Pechenyuk's sector. At 0500 hours, the Germans threw grenades into the water tower and at the Rolik group. Pechenyuk reported that the Germans "then tried to seize the gully 50 metres east of the gardens[48], but not having success in the face of Soviet fire, were compelled to pull back, sustaining heavy losses". German machine-guns and mortars then opened up on recognised Soviet positions, while artillery and heavy mortars shelled Zaitsevsky Island. From the south of 650th Rifle Regiment and the north of 768th Rifle Regiment, German heavy calibre machine-guns controlled the Volga and fired at any movement on Zaitsevsky Island.

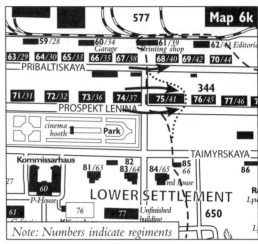

German attack on Haus 75 [Dom 41], morning of 21 November, 1942.

A short time later, Soviet observers spotted a group of about 70-80 Germans moving about in the unfinished building and the gardens south-east of the Kommissarhaus. Pechenyuk requested artillery fire on the unfinished building. Artillery shells soon whined in and smashed into the building and the surrounding area. The Germans went to ground – their attack had miscarried even before it had begun. German artillery then started up. Both sides took casualties.

A modern photo shows the proximity of the opposing sides' strongpoints: Haus 74 [Dom 37] on the left, Haus 75 [Dom 41] on the right. The impressive dimensions of the latter can be appreciated in this photo.

48. The Rolik gully.

At 0900 hours, the Germans resumed their attack against Konovalenko's regiment, trying to cut off the groups of soldiers in Haus 68 [Dom 40] and Haus 75 [Dom 41]. Only at 1020 hours, after almost an hour and a half of fighting and suffering heavy casualties, were the Germans able to annihilate the garrison and take over Haus 75 [Dom 41]. The loss of this large house, one of the Soviet's most formidable strongpoints – and former command post of regiment commander Konovalenko – was a severe blow to the defence. It was the largest building along that sector of Prospekt Lenina and projected into Konovalenko's defences like a dagger. Only a week earlier, it had seemed like an impossibility to take this building. The Germans quickly funnelled in reserves to hold it, extra machine-guns were positioned and copious amounts of ammunition and grenades were laid on. No time was wasted in improving the trench between this building and Haus 74. Fire fights continued. Like a static dreadnought, the new German strongpoint exchanged broadsides of machine-gun fire with the surrounding Soviet fortresses. During the coming nights, Haus 75 was further fortified with thick belts of barbed wire and dense minefields.

After the German capture of Haus 75 [Dom 41] (left), the survivors of the Soviet garrison took refuge in Haus 76 [Dom 45] (right). These modern buildings have the exact same layout, design and architectural features as the wartime ones because they were rebuilt using the old ruins and foundations. In the background is the Barrikady factory.

For the day, 138th Rifle Division suffered losses of 25 killed and 26 wounded, a total of 51 men. It claimed it inflicted the following losses on the Germans: one tank burnt out and another knocked out; 2 heavy and 3 light machine-guns destroyed; an ammunition depot blown up; as many as 100 soldiers and officers killed; and one serviceable light machine-gun captured.

At the end of the day, the combat strength on the west bank was 407 men, plus another 83 men from other units. The number of wounded stranded on Lyudnikov's Island now numbered 348, almost equalling the number of able-bodied men.

German attacks also came in near the fuel tanks. The constant Soviet counterattacks from the south were a bloody nuisance, so it was decided to forestall the next one by launching a pre-emptive attack. The massive artillery strike began at 0300 hours and the assault groups – issuing from the Apotheke and School Nr. 2 – moved out at 0850 hours. Several hours of hard fighting followed but 90th Rifle Regiment finally repelled the Germans at 1015 hours. The regiment lost 13 men. Krylov later reported that "the Gorishny Division and its subordinated troops threw back German attacks in the fuel tank area and on Mezenskaya Street and had suffered 200 dead and wounded since daybreak. Almost the entire position of the army lay under methodical harassment fire." The war diary of 62nd

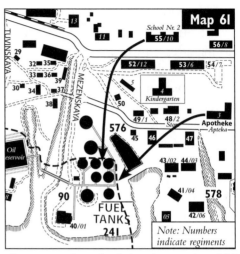

German attack on the fuel tanks, morning of 21 November, 1942.

Army stated that "95th Rifle Division repelled attacks by small groups of enemy infantry, held the previous positions and exchanged fire". Counterattacks were launched and Gorishny reported that his soldiers had taken several houses on Mashinnaya Street.

– – –

The fog persisted throughout the morning and was followed by heavy snow. Towards 1000 hours, the sound of heavy gunfire could be heard in Stalingrad. The implications to the staff of 62nd Army were clear. They realised the Germans would be surrounded, so Krylov implemented measures to pre-empt a German reaction:

> I got in contact with the division commanders and advised them to carefully observe the Germans and to not miss the beginning of a possible retreat. I also spoke in code with Lyudnikov by radio and told him the same thing. Lyudnikov replied that a retreat would not need to be looked for at this moment because the fascists were attacking. The same thing was also reported in other sectors.

Lyudnikov immediately issued Order No. 086. His units were to closely observe the enemy, be ready to pursue retreating enemy formations and capture a 'tongue' during the night. The salient points of the order were to "create careful observations of the enemy's actions, gathering points, and movements, actively fire on the enemy with all arms and in the case of an enemy withdrawal, report to the divisional command post and be ready to follow the enemy units that are withdrawing. Mobilise all strength for the organisation of a reconnaissance patrol with the goal of capturing prisoners on the night of 22-23.11.42."

– – –

As the fighting in Stalingrad ground to a halt, it was time for 305. Infanterie-Division to take stock, regroup its forces and make plans to raise its combat strength. Attending these conferences was Hauptmann Rettenmaier:

> We had a meeting at the division today. The new regimental commander[49] has arrived. We discussed how to distribute the expected replacements and bring them forward. 1,700 men

---

49. Oberstleutnant Max Liesecke.

should be joining the division: they are from Ostmarke [Austria], the Rhineland and a Württemberger Marschbataillon. The railway line at Kalach has been hit. Bringing them in by rail is therefore not possible. A convoy of trucks will be deployed and Hauptmann Schwarz[50] is made responsible for their transportation. We are delighted about the news of these replacements and now we will be able to relieve our deployed troops operating in Stalingrad.

The pioneer battalions contemplated their strengths. Worried about the grievous casualties being inflicted on his battalion, Hauptmann Lundt voiced his concerns to 305. Infanterie-Division and requested that he be able to speak to his parent division. In the following conversation, Lundt discussed long-term measures with 336. Infanterie-Division to replenish the battalion.

– – –

Throughout the day, the Volga Flotilla prepared their armoured boats for the next voyage to Lyudnikov's Island. The tugboat 'Kochegar Hetman' – battered from the previous night's effort – was put in for repairs in Tumak but would only return to action on 24 November, 1942 after a herculean effort by a work team from the Stalingrad shipyards. Before the armoured boats set out, however, a fleet of a smaller kind was at work. Ordinary fishing boats were also being used to supply 138th Rifle Division. The command of 107th Independent Pontoon-Bridge Battalion (commanded by Captain Lutsky), to which the supply of 138th Rifle Division had been entrusted, sent a company under Senior-Lieutenant Lapeto to Zaitsevsky Island on 20 November to organise a boat ferry. Also sent on 21 November were 15 more men led by Lieutenant Shibayevim. Soldiers crossed by boat to 138th Rifle Division at 1700 hours.

By order of the Front Soviet, all boats were to be used in crossing operations at the Barrikady factory. Captain Lutsky's pontoniers assembled 23 small boats near the upper end of the Akhtuba River. These were brought to the Volga on trucks and then sent across the main branch of the Volga to Zaitsevsky Island, where they were dragged through the thick scrub to the banks of the Denezhnaya Volozhka channel. This was thought better than steering the boats around the island because that would lead to unnecessary losses. The assistant commander for support in 138th Rifle Division, Major M.S. Shustov, the divisional quartermaster Major A.P. Gusev, and workers of the division's rear organised supplies for the journey. Ammunition and rations from the divisional depot located near Tumak farm (12km east of Stalingrad) were forwarded to a transshipment base on Zaitsevsky Island. Under incessant fire, soldiers of 400th Separate Machine-Gun and Artillery Battalion of 156th Fortified District loaded the ammunition and rations aboard the boats which would set out from the western bank of the island, a few hundred metres from the Germans atop the cliffs.

To ensure accurate navigation, E.V. Shestopalov, P.S. Trubachev and R. Dyusenov were ordered to install a beacon upon which the boats crossing the channel at night could aim. Besides that, they needed to agree with division command about which cargo had priority and the evacuation of the wounded.

Dense slush covered the channel. Ice floes collided with each other and, when their edges broke off, they hissed as they were ground into powdery ice. Shestopalov controlled the boat. He sat on bags of food, occasionally giving orders to his comrades who pushed the

50. Schwarz, Hauptmann Helmut, II./Gr.Rgt.578; born 16 November, 1915 in Hassental, Schwäbisch-Hall. Killed in action, 17 January, 1943 in Stalingrad.

boat between ice floes. Sometimes the vessel got caught between larger floes which tried to carry it downstream. The soldiers strained with all their might to get to the 'Island of Fire', all while under fire from German machine-guns. In the boat was a portable radio set, boxes with cartridges and bags with food. This supply task was carried out because it was necessary to deliver the most urgently needed supplies. A reference point for the pontoniers was the front-line separating the Germans from Lyudnikov's positions. Flashes from bursts of machine-gun and rifle fire, as well as tracer bullets, were clearly visible from the river. Since Soviet soldiers were counting every bullet, the crews knew that the fire was mostly German.

When the bank was still 100–150 metres away, a burst of machine-gun fire slashed across the boat. None of the soldiers were hit, and the boat, having made one last jerk forward, finally reached the shore.

Lyudnikov praised the daredevils and, having approved their idea of installing a beacon, allocated the necessary number of soldiers to help the pontoniers.

The beacon was to be set up so that it was visible only to boats crossing the channel. One soldier suggested building the fire in a cave dug into the cliff of the high Volga bank. His idea was quite sensible because such a fire was only visible from the channel and Zaitsevsky Island and not visible at all to the Germans. Soldiers from the division started the fire while the pontoniers and boat crews prepared for the hazardous crossing.

The first group of boats to cross was Captain Korikov's 1st Pontoon Company. This company had already distinguished itself during the September crossings to the main landing stage in the city centre. Korikov ordered his company to assemble in formation. He reminded them that previous attempts to reach Lyudnikov's Island had been unsuccessful.

The cloud-filled sky began to clear up. The group needed to hurry before the moon shone through. "Get aboard!" The boats pushed noisily through the ice floes into open water. Fortunately, the Germans did not notice that the crossing had begun. The moon began to peek through from behind a cloud. The black, ice-filled river began to shine – making the boats and men discernible. The Rolik group was the first to notice the crossing. The group made a signal and Major Rutkovsky, who had been appointed by Lyudnikov to head all crossing operations, alerted the entire divisional staff.

A group of volunteers exited the dug-out where the wounded had been kept and headed towards the river through a deep trench. Artillery fire from both banks began to sound. The division's flanks were now being lit up by tracer fire. As the boats navigated through the watery corridor, the men could see the outline of the 'Island'. It was being continually lit up by more and more gunfire. Until the boats reached the west bank and the relative safety of its cliffs, there was nowhere for them to hide from the German guns. They rowed as fast and as hard as they could. The brave pontoniers were provided with artillery cover by 17th, 348th and 400th Separate Machine-Gun and Artillery Battalions which shelled German positions whenever they revealed themselves. The 'Islanders' knew that the German fire would never completely cease. Even when the boats reached the west bank and unloading commenced, German machine-guns and mortars continued to harass the undertaking. Then, once the boats were loaded up, they would return along the same fiery corridor. The 'Islanders' knew that not every bullet or shell would hit its mark. This was the only thing they counted on. Nevertheless, a significant number of boats were destroyed, the shattered vessels sinking together with their crews and cargo, others with severely wounded oarsmen were carried away downstream. Despite the crippling losses, the crossings continued. The pontoniers displayed rare courage. Guided by the signal fire, the boats made trips across the channel all night long. Only 14 of the original 23 boats survived the two-way mission. Thus the 'boat bridge' across the channel was established by 107th Independent Pontoon-Bridge Battalion. The crossing was so perilous that men who completed the trip twice were awarded the 'For Courage' medal and those who made four successive trips received the 'Red Star'. Very few of the latter were handed out.

As a result of these desperate supply missions, Lyudnikov's division received a much needed replenishment of food and ammunition – but the crossings came at an almost unbearable cost, for the bodies of the heroic men of 107th Battalion were buried not only on Zaitsevsky Island, but were entombed under the dark, cold waters of the Volga as well.

- - -

The second voyage of the armoured boats to 138th Rifle Division began at 1730 hours. Heading there this time were two boats, No. 13 (commander Lieutenant S.Z. Vashchenko) and No. 63 (commander Warrant Officer V.G. Korotenko). The job of guiding the armoured boats through the ice was taken on by tugboat No. 2, which moved ahead of the fleet. On board the armoured boats were 127 soldiers as reinforcements, 4 tonnes of ammunition and 6 tonnes of rations.

Artillery support would be provided by Armoured Boats No. 12 and No. 61 from a point off the southern tip of Zaitsevsky Island. Prior to this, these two boats delivered 200 reinforcements and 10 tonnes of various cargo to the Banny Gully moorings.

As they approached the Barrikady, Armoured Boats No. 13, No. 63 and tugboat No. 2 were fired on. Replying with fire from their own guns, the armoured boats stayed on course. Armoured Boats No. 61 and No. 12 fired on German emplacements south of the Barrikady.

Armoured Boats No. 13 and No. 63 reached 138th Rifle Division. The unloading of ammunition and rations, as well as the loading of the wounded, was again carried out under heavy mortar, rifle and machine-gun fire. Lyudnikov wrote:

> Divisional HQ personnel helped to unload the boats. Our bank was under enemy mortar fire but we had to save what could still be saved. The men pitched themselves into the very thick of the explosions.

During the unloading of the boats, the chief of loading and unloading, Major Konstantin Romanovich Rutkovsky, Commander of Operations Department of the Division, was killed. The nurse on the divisional staff, Lieutenant Sima Orezov, saw the Major slump into the slush-filled river. She ran down to him and began pulling his fatally wounded body from the water but was hit in the right eye by a splinter from a mortar shell. She began to lose consciousness and nearly fell into the water after the Major. There was only one person on the river bank who watched after her in this hell – her husband. Senior-Lieutenant Ozerov pulled his wife from the water and carried her into a dug-out. The salvage of the Major's body fell to others. One of them was Lieutenant N.G. Epishin[51]:

> Armoured boats moored on our bank near the command post of divisional staff under intense enemy fire and division command ordered all staff members to help unload the boats. Taking part in unloading the cargo were the Chief of 1st Department of the divisional staff, Major K.R. Rutkovsky, and other officers and soldiers of the staff. Unloading took place under intense enemy machine-gun fire and Major Rutkovsky was fatally wounded in the heart. Being on the spot, myself, together with officers and the senior clerk of 4th Department,

---

51. Epishin, Guards Lieutenant-Colonel Nikolai Grigoryevich, staff 138th Rifle.Div.; born 18 October, 1913. Still alive in 1979.

Sergeant Fedor Vasilyevich Zagrebeny, managed to carry the dead body of Rutkovsky in a tarpaulin into the divisional command post.

Work on the crossings was considered a combat mission, and with good reason. Officers and soldiers were decorated with awards and medals for it. The Red Star was bestowed upon the editor of the divisional newspaper, Politruk M.T. Zuyev, who had only recently returned from his icy swim across the Volga. While carrying out the function of commissar at the crossing, he replaced Major Rutkovsky at the critical moment and skilfully supervised all work, neglecting the danger.

The division staff took heavy losses during the unloadings. Rutkovsky's assistant, Captain Gulko, had been killed the previous evening. Lieutenant-Colonel Shuba's orderly, Red Army man Kocherga, as well as five volunteers from the group of lightly wounded men, also met their end. They were all interred in a large soldier's grave. There were several such graves.

Having unloaded all the supplies and taken aboard 78 wounded men, the boats headed back. On the journey south from the Barrikady, the fleet of boats had to run another gauntlet of fire. Waiting for them were Hauptmann Rettenmaier's two 7.5cm anti-tank guns. The guns hacked into the ships from above. The German gunners were jubilant when one of the Soviet ships started blazing. Armoured Boat No. 13 had taken a direct hit in its engine room that ruptued a fuel line and caused a fire to flare up. The armoured boat also veered off course. The fluttering flames ripped away the protective veil of darkness and the Germans clearly saw the frantic movements on the deck of the stricken vessel. They were sure the boat was finished yet they continued to rake the vessel with rifle and machine-gun fire. The blaze in the engine room was eventually extinguished but the motor was damaged and the boat remained motionless. Coming to their aid was Armoured Boat No. 63, which took it under tow and pulled it out from under the bombardment. The fleet returned to base at 2230 hours. This second trip reached 138th Rifle Division carrying 127 reinforcements, 4 tonnes of ammunition and 6 tonnes of food. They evacuated 78 wounded men.

- - -

The 127 men who had arrived as reinforcements were immediately distributed to the rifle regiments. They gathered in the large hospital bunker next to the divisional command post. Captain Konovalenko's orderly, Sergeant Zlydnev, an obstinate but courageous man who had been temporarily appointed while he recovered from a leg wound, briefed the new arrivals in his own inimitable way. Lyudnikov witnessed it:

> Ivan Zlydnev doted on his regimental commander. I recall more or less verbatim Zlydnev's conversation with a batch of new recruits – the first small reinforcement for the 344th Regiment. They had been transported to us at night by armoured launch and Zlydnev had escorted them from the bank to the dug-out along a trench. Regimental Commissar Fomin and I were in the dug-out and, unnoticed in the darkness, we witnessed Zlydnev's 'political talk' to the new recruits.
>
> What is the fighting like here?" one of them asked Zlydnev. "Does the front-line really run along the river bank?"
>
> "Rubbish!" replied Zlydnev. "The Germans are about 200 metres away."
>
> "Is that all?" was the chorus of alarm.
>
> "Don't be afraid! A metre is something special at the Barrikady."
>
> "Is it true that we're to be sent to Konovalenko's famous regiment?" asked another newcomer. "On the other bank we were told you've got a real hero as commander!"

The talkative Zlydnev started telling them how he had been one of the first to set foot on the Volga's right bank and how he had fought as 'garrison commandant', but then, after his wound, he had been made orderly to Captain Konovalenko himself. And you wouldn't find another commander like Captain Konovalenko along the whole front.

"Warfare is very simple here," Zlydnev enlightened the newcomers. "A railway line runs along our front-line. We have sunk our teeth into the rails so hard that we can't be shifted. And if you've got weak teeth, you're not good enough for Konovalenko's regiment."

"You don't mean it!" doubted Zlydnev's audience.

"When you've fought as long as I have in Captain Konovalenko's regiment, you won't say that."

– – –

One and a half hours after the previous fleet returned to base, the third voyage to Lyudnikov's Island had been organised.

Heading to the Barrikady this time were Armoured Boats No. 12 and No. 61, with 14 reinforcements and 10 tonnes of rations and ammunition aboard. Escorting the armoured boats through the ice was the launch 'Erik' (Captain N.I. Yezushin). Their breakthrough to the Barrikady was supported by direct fire from Armoured Boats No. 53 (commander Lieutenant I.D. Karpunin) and No. 63 (commander Warrant Officer V.G. Korotenko).

The fleet came under fire south of the Barrikady. On the launch 'Erik', one member of the crew was killed and Captain N.I. Yezushin was lightly wounded by a splinter. Shrapnel from the shell also wounded the commander of Armoured Boat No. 12, Lieutenant V.I. Cherednichenko.

Despite German fire, the boats continued to make their way toward the Barrikady and eventually reached the bank near Lyudnikov's command post. After unloading the reinforcements and cargo and embarking the 133 wounded men, the armoured boats returned to base at 0330 hours on 22 November without loss. This third trip reached 138th Rifle Division carrying 14 reinforcements, 6 tonnes of ammunition and 4 tonnes of food. They evacuated 133 wounded men.

After receiving deliveries from the fishing boats and both armoured boat fleets, the position of the division was significantly eased.

Casualties for 21 November, 1942:	
138th Rifle Division:	25 killed, 26 wounded, a total of 51 men
305. Infanterie-Division:	5 men killed, 1 officer and 42 men wounded, 4 men missing

22 November, 1942

After being absorbed into 241st Rifle Regiment, the command elements of Lieutenant-Colonel Drogaitsev's 685th Rifle Regiment were not required and therefore returned to their parent division. The regiment's combat journal noted:

At 0100, the regiment staff, command platoon and communications company crossed over to the Volga's east bank and came under the control of the commander of 193rd Rifle Division.

It summed up the results of its ten days of combat as follows:

As a result of the offensives in the previous area of operations, the regiment lost 210 men in dead and wounded. It captured 3 German heavy machine-guns, suppressed the fire of 2 heavy machine-guns and one mortar battery, and destroyed six dug-outs and up to 180 soldiers and officers of 294th Sapper Battalion of 294th Infantry Division.

Only 44 of the regiment's men emerged from the fighting unscathed.

Soviet attacks continued on this sector. At 0900, 95th Rifle Division went on the offensive with the task of seizing Tuvinskaya. The units slowly advanced against tough German resistance. By 1600 hours they captured a group of buildings on Mashinnaya Street.

– – –

The war diary of 138th Rifle Division reported that "at 2240 [the previous night], the enemy – with 15-20 soldiers – tried to filter through the battle formations of 344th Rifle Regiment and attack the gun pits of the mortar unit, but finding so many of our troops, they lost 11 dead and withdrew to their starting position".

At 0430 hours, an enemy group with a total strength of 120 soldiers – from the area of Dom 41, 38 and the main mechanical workshop, and heavily supported by artillery and mortar fire as well as fire from tanks – resumed their attack against the garrison defending Dom 40. A small enemy group managed to penetrate into the depth of 344th Rifle Regiment's defences. Counterattacks and organised fire by 344th Rifle Regiment repulsed the enemy attacks. The enemy, having lost 60 soldiers killed, pulled back.

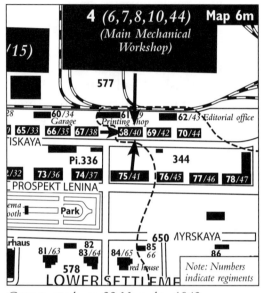

German attacks on 22 November, 1942.

Leading the way in these attacks were Grenadier-Regiment 577, supported by Pionier-Bataillon 336 and 2./Pionier-Bataillon 305. Losses for Pionier-Bataillon 336 were as follows: 2. Kompanie lost Obergefreiter Martin Bauer[52] and Oberpionier Ernst Vopel[53] killed, while Gefreiter Alfred Herbig[54], Gefreiter Alfred Kunz[55] and Gefreiter Karl Lugert[56] were wounded; from 3. Kompanie, Pionier Max Börner[57], Pionier Walter Gernegross[58], Obergefreiter Kurt Hoppstock[59] and Pionier Karl Steier[60] were wounded.

– – –

In their final efforts to destroy the stubborn defenders of Lyudnikov's Island, the Germans renewed their attacks against the Rolik group – but this time with fresh tactics. Rolik had been plaguing the Germans since 11 November. From that moment, the entire 138th Rifle Division had carefully watched after them. When Rolik went quiet, the situation became

---

52. Bauer, Obergefreiter Martin, 2./Pi.Btl.336; born 29 March, 1909 in Chemnitz. Died of wounds, 29 November, 1942 in Stalingrad.
53. Vopel, Oberpionier Ernst, 2./Pi.Btl.336; born 16 January, 1920 in Alsleben. Killed in action, 22 November, 1942 in Stalingrad.
54. Herbig, Gefreiter Alfred, 2./Pi.Btl.336; born 9 November, 1905 in Bernstadt.
55. Kunz, Obergefreiter Alfred, 2./Pi.Btl.336; born 17 March, 1911 in Vielau. Killed in action, 4 October, 1944 in Poland.
56. Lugert, Gefreiter Karl, 2./Pi.Btl.336; born 26 August, 1912 in Chemnitz.
57. Börner, Pionier Max, 3./Pi.Btl.336; born 4 November, 1909 in Pockau.
58. Gernegross, Pionier Walter, 3./Pi.Btl.336; born 28 December, 1922 in Rothenthal.
59. Hoppstock, Obergefreiter Kurt, 3./Pi.Btl.336; born 10 May, 1912 in Glaucha.
60. Steier, Pionier Karl, 3./Pi.Btl.336; born 12 October, 1922 in Obergeorgenthal.

tense. When Rolik fired, the mood lifted. The division's soldiers used to say: "Rolik is spinning and he won't let the enemy past the crevice to the river."

At 0430 hours on this morning, however, a huge fireball erupted over Rolik's position and a massive explosion shook the entire 'Island'. The commander of the division's signals battalion, Senior-Lieutenant Ozerov, reported that Rolik had fallen silent. He was quiet and not transmitting any sort of signal. Within an hour, another massive explosion was heard from the direction of the crevice.

"My men are dead!" decided Ozerov. He immediately set out to ask Lyudnikov for permission to take a number of volunteers to the crevice at night to learn the fate of the four men.

Just as Ozerov stepped up to the entrance to the commander's room, another explosion was heard. A second later, the telephone began to ring. Rolik had called the commander.

"Hello, 'First'! I cannot hear you! I can't hear anything…"

It was Kuzminsky's voice. He was quickly trying to explain what had happened and why Rolik had gone silent: "The Germans are trying to lower explosive charges into our dug-outs. In the meantime, we

Top right: The Rolik position with all four signalmen. On the right is Kharaziya. The man third from left is emerging from one of the caves. The Germans were in trenches at the top of the cliff.

Middle right: Part of the Rolik memorial today. The gully is at the bottom left of the photo. Note the width of the river – the damming of the Volga caused water levels to rise, making the river much wider today than it was in 1942. Large parts of Zaitsevsky Island are now underwater.

Bottom right: The gully as it appears today, overgrown by trees and scrub, but sadly, also littered with rubbish.

shoot the ropes with our rifles and the explosives fall downwards. A big explosion and we are all deaf… and then they are lowering another one. What? I said we're all deaf… I can't hear anything. At night we'll come to fetch some ammunition… I can't hear anything! Hello 'First'! Can you understand me? Hello?"

"I understand. I hear you…" whispered Lyudnikov, knowing that the sergeant wouldn't hear him. "I'll give you ammunition! For you – I will!"

Ammunition was carefully rationed on Lyudnikov's Island. No one, not even the commander, broke this rule. But for Rolik, Lyudnikov couldn't refuse. The sergeant would come at night and leave with his ammunition. Then it would be

The newer Rolik memorial. Note the four gold stars, symbol of the 'Hero of the Soviet Union' medal but used here simply as a graphic device to represent the 'hero signalmen'. Many people erroneously – but understandably – believe that each man was awarded this rare decoration.

morning. Once again, all along the front-line, fighting would resume… and Rolik would be the one to begin it. The soldiers would hear the gunfire from the very left flank and it would put smiles on their faces:

"Rolik is spinning… and death can't take him!"

The German attempts to destroy Rolik and the other cliffside dug-outs and command posts were unsuccessful. Only one Soviet soldier was wounded during the furious demolition. Pionier Josef Zrenner, from the staff of Pionier-Bataillon 305, clearly remembers the difficulty in attacking these cliffside positions:

> The Russians were dug in down below and we were up above, so it was not actually possible to combat them. The worst thing, however, was that the Russians were suddenly not only below us, but were also behind us because they came out of the city's sewage canals and attacked us from behind.
>
> The sewer system in Stalingrad was very well developed. And the Russian troops also used the sewer system as a means of combat. When we thought our troops were further forward, the Russians suddenly emerged from the rear, through the sewer system, and attacked our positions. After that, one of the pioneer

Gefreiter Josef Zrenner, Stab/Pi.Btl.305.

units was assigned to clean out the sewers with flamethrowers so that no further intrusions were possible. But the sewers, in particular those in certain districts, were fully developed, and the Russians utilised them.

The Germans were unaware of the full extent of Soviet subterranean operations. Even Lyudnikov was completely unaware until he visited one of his regiment commanders:

> During my visit to Captain Konovalenko's command post I saw an unusual map which had been given to Konovalenko by Tyalichev, an engineer at the Barrikady factory. On it were marked the factory's large underground system of wells, pipes and tunnels which afforded access to enemy-held workshops. Intelligence officers and sappers had already begun underground warfare. They penetrated into the enemy's rear, made surprise attacks and vanished. Every one of these sorties was risky and only volunteers made them. Konovalenko supervised their training personally, gave them final briefings, saw them off on their missions.

The Germans tossed grenades at the Soviet defensive line throughout the day. They also tried to reach the Volga river in small groups via Water and Sapper Gullies. On a small elevation opposite the water tower, the Germans placed one light machine-gun and a heavy calibre machine-gun.

On Pechenyuk's right flank, the Germans tried to reconnoitre his lines but were forced into battle. The German patrol had about 11 men but they were bested in the melee and as a result suffered casualties of one dead. The Soviets captured 3 rifles and one submachine-gun. The division later reported that it had inflicted the following losses on the Germans: 1 ammunition depot blown up, 1 battalion and 3 company mortars destroyed, as were 1 heavy and 3 light machine-guns.

– – –

In his diary notes, Hauptmann Rettenmaier recorded the arrival of the reinforcements and the news they carried with them:

> One hundred and thirty men arrived for the regiment. Some of them are young soldiers, fearlessly gazing around, while others are older chaps with which little can be done. They bring rumours with them that the Russians have broken through the Romanian lines south of Stalingrad and our allies are in wild disarray and flight. Beyond the Don the Russians are attacking towards the south from the Kalmuck steppe. This could get sticky. Any written communications about this are forbidden. Are we really encircled?

Now that the seriousness of the overall situation was fully realised, the German commanders could see the folly of launching any more attacks against Lyudnikov's Island. The units of 305. Infanterie-Division received the order: "The assaults of 305. Infanterie-Division will cease until further notice!"

– – –

Once darkness descended, the ferrying of supplies to Lyudnikov's Island began anew. During the night, 107th Independent Pontoon-Bridge Battalion sent 6 boats to 138th Rifle Division loaded with ammunition and rations. They reached the west bank safely and delivered all cargo to its destination. Eleven trips were made this night. For the two nights of 21 and 22 November, 15-16 tonnes of cargo and 40 reinforcements were transported, while 40 wounded men were evacuated. While carrying out this dangerous task, Junior-Sergeant S.M. Kletsko and Red Army man I. Gorovenko were killed, while soldiers A.J. Shcheglov, M.M. Pavlyuk, I.J. Boldyrev and others were wounded.

The fourth and final supply voyage to 138th Rifle Division also set out. Contained in the fleet were Armoured Boats No. 12 (commander Lieutenant D.F. Lukin) and No. 13 (commander Lieutenant S.Z. Vashchenko). Escorting them through the ice again was the launch 'Erik' (Captain N.I. Yezushin) with artillery support provided by Armoured Boats No. 61 and No. 53.

Despite fierce German bombardments, the fleet safely reached 138th Rifle Division and delivered 14 reinforcements and 9 tonnes of rations and ammunition. On the return trip the boats took 155 wounded men and reached base at 2330 hours.

Armoured Boats No. 61 and No. 53 destroyed 7 German emplacements with direct fire.

This fourth trip delivered 14 reinforcements, 5 tonnes of ammunition and 4 tonnes of food, and evacuated 155 wounded men. Thus, in four voyages to 138th Rifle Division, the armoured boats delivered 49 tonnes of cargo (30 tonnes of ammunition and 19 tonnes of food) and 155 reinforcements, and evacuated 466 wounded men. This means that almost all of the wounded had been evacuated. A great weight was lifted off Lyudnikov's shoulders.

The task set by the commander of the Stalingrad Front had been carried out in exceptionally difficult conditions. The crews of the armoured boats displayed unsurpassed courage, an iron will for victory, highly-developed fighting skills and persistence in achieving the set objective.

While giving due courage to the crews of the armoured boats, it is also necessary to mention the heroism of the medics who, together with wounded men, endured the burdens of combat, cold and famine. Taking part in all of the voyages was nurse Tania Kirillov. She was 19 years old at the time but under enemy fire, this fearless young woman carried dozens of wounded Red Army soldiers on her shoulders. Kirillov was wounded during the last voyage and sent to hospital, but after recovery, she returned to her armoured boat. For displaying bravery and courage, the commander of 62nd Army awarded Kirillov the 'For Services in Combat' medal.

Shortly after this last large voyage, the river – which had temporarily thawed for a few days – again became covered by a thick icy sludge. The daily supply problem became just as acute. Individual armoured boats continued to make the perilous journey for as long as conditions permitted.

Casualties for 22 November, 1942:	
138th Rifle Division:	9 killed, 29 wounded, a total of 38 men
305. Infanterie-Division:	no figures available

23 November, 1942

Once all German offensive actions had been suspended, a disquieting lull gradually enshrouded the battlefield. At 0200 hours, Pechenyuk's men noted that German small arms and machine-gun fire slackened, but they did not withdraw from their positions, as some Soviets officers thought they would. Furthermore, German sentries did not send up any flares to illuminate the river bank. The inky blackness that now cloaked the Volga was a dramatic contrast to the previous three nights of frenetic activity along the river bank. Now, there were no tracers, no flares, no mortars. Nothing but the hiss and scrape of ice floes grinding their way downriver.

When day broke frosty and clear, the Germans lobbed the occasional grenade at the water tower and fired their mortars irregularly, but that was it. They were to stay put. The combat journal of 138th Rifle Division recorded that "during the day, the enemy did not show any offensive actions along the front of the division. It was limited to occasional small arms and machine-gun bombardments of the combat ranks of the division."

For Lyudnikov's division, defence now turned to offence. Small reconnaissance groups of 768th Rifle Regiment improved the position by advancing 150-200 metres in a north-west direction. The same happened on the left flank: 650th Rifle Regiment fulfilled its orders by moving some groups forward. The leftmost group took up a new position and began to dig in. Not everything went according to plan. A recon group working around the Kommissarhaus was fired upon by the Germans with small arms and machine-guns, losing 2 dead and 4 wounded.

After weeks of grim defensive fighting, even the smallest gain was joyfully welcomed. In his memoirs, General Krylov wrote:

> On several sectors of our army, we were able to push the Germans back on 23 November, and although it was difficult, it succeeded slowly and at best around a dozen metres was gained. For the first time, even a regiment of 138th Rifle Division moved forward a little, although there was a severe shortage of soldiers on Lyudnikov's Island.

Regarding the situation around the fuel tanks, 62nd Army war diary noted:

> 95th Rifle Division conducted small but powerful reconnaissance raids and fought to improve the position. Personnel: 241st Rifle Regiment – 230 men, 161st Rifle Regiment – 303 men.

The daily entry in the combat journal of 138th Rifle Division was somewhat more positive than any in the previous two weeks:

> The enemy made no movements throughout the day. Morale in the division is high because information about Red Army successes on the Stalingrad Front is giving rise to high emotions about continuing with the offensive. Supplies and rations are coming in by armoured boat, on which reinforcements for the division are also arriving.

The division had held on. Just. It was a mighty feat of endurance and courage. At the end of the day, the combat structure of the division was as follows: 516 men on the west bank of the Volga, and of those, 50 were wounded. There were also 77 men who were not part of the division. Armament: 344 rifles, 2 heavy machine-guns, 19 light machine-guns, 66 PPSh, 3 anti-tank rifles, 3 45mm guns and 1 anti-aircraft machine-gun.

The division estimated that it had inflicted the following losses on the Germans: 20 soldiers and officers killed, not including the actions of artillery. Trophies captured included 1 large-calibre machine-gun and one domestic 45mm gun.

- - -

The Soviet artillery caused some havoc in the rear, particularly around Razgulyayevka and Gorodische, two small villages in which Pionier-Bataillon 305 had its headquarters and rear echelon. Hauptmann Traub described the events in a letter to his wife:

> The Russians heavily shelled our village. We were just able to quickly dive into a bunker. Afterwards we discovered that a few mighty shell splinters had shattered my palace, so that even my jacket, which was hanging over a chair, received a couple of respectably-sized holes. Our Zahlmeister, who was standing near the impact zone of an incoming shell, remarkably escaped with just a scratch, however his truck, which was standing in front of another one belonging

The aftermath of a Soviet artillery strike on the small village of Razgulyayevka, 23 November, 1942.

to the battalion, went up in bright flames. Unfortunately, the truck was loaded with a lot of explosives which, after about ten minutes, went up with a loud bang, causing a lot of damage to my shack, reminiscent probably of your experiences during a bombing raid.[61] But now everything has returned to normal. Strange, but the Russians did not continue with their shelling afterwards. Besides the Zahlmeister, two men were lightly wounded, but they remained with the troops.

– – –

To the Germans in the Barrikady, it felt like defeat had been snatched from the jaws of victory... a Pyrrhic victory, yes, but even that was far better than their current predicament. An inordinate amount of blood had been shed and now there was nothing to show for it. They were certain that the Soviet defence would have crumbled completely in a few more days. The previous days had clearly demonstrated that the Soviet power to resist had almost disappeared: although the Germans themselves were weak and exhausted, thoroughly-planned and well-executed attacks succeeded in taking fearsome bastions that would have been considered almost unattainable only a week earlier. Barely a few hundred metres separated the leading positions of 305. Infanterie-Division from the defensive line of 389. Infanterie-Division... a few hundred metres of open ground blocked only by the keystone of Lyudnikov's bridgehead, the indomitable Haus 87, or 'Rote Haus' as the Germans called it. The official Soviet designation was 'Dom 67' but the defenders erroneously called it 'Lyudnikov's command post'[62], even though he had never had his headquarters there. He did,

61. Traub's home town of Bremerhaven was repeatedly bombed by the British.
62. The building – which still exists as a ruin today – is still labelled as such.

however, use it as an observation post. A secret tunnel connected the cellar to the river bank and enabled Lyudnikov to reach the building with total immunity. The formerly grand two-storey building, once the residence of the factory director Lev Gonor, had been hewn down to a grotesque tower-like sculpture by torrents of bombs and shells from three directions. All that remained was the cellar covered by massive mounds of red masonry, a few jagged walls, some remnants of the steel and concrete floors, and the building's central stairwell, now its citadel, a thick-walled observation post. Rubble had been cleared from around the small cellar windows and enabled the garrison to easily cover the open ground around the building. The Germans came close to capturing it on 15 November and the building had been scheduled to be attacked by 389. Infanterie-Division on 21 November but circumstances had forced the cancellation of that operation. With the successes achieved by 305. Infanterie-Division during the last days of the attack, it was entirely possible that 389. Infanterie-Division could have equalled them by capturing the Rote Haus, and with that, completing the encirclement of Lyudnikov's valiant defenders.

But it was the Germans, not the Soviets, who were now surrounded. It was a bitter realisation. Rettenmaier wrote in his diary: "Kalach should be back in our hands. The maintenance company in our rear is supposed to have been attacked by advancing enemy armour. The Chir River is occupied by the Russians. Those advancing from the Volga to the Don and those coming south from the Don bend have joined hands. The ring is closed. We are sitting in a cauldron. Our replacements can no longer come through, they are caught up in the fighting far behind us. And what of us? Preparations are being made to fight through to the south."

Above: The ruins of 'Red House' immediately after the battle. Below: The ruins today, showing its thick walls.

Casualties for 23 November, 1942:	
138th Rifle Division:	10 killed, 15 wounded, a total of 25 men
305. Infanterie-Division: no figures available	

24 November, 1942

In the morning, Lyudnikov's troops tried to go over to the offensive. Small groups started attacking but the Germans opened up a high volume of artillery and flanking machine-gun fire. The Soviet troops dropped to the ground and defended themselves. Their main priority was to still keep German movements under surveillance and maintain constant fire on German emplacements. The war diary of 62nd Army noted:

> At 0800, after an artillery strike, the army went over to the offensive on all fronts but met strong enemy fire resistance. Units only moved ahead slowly.

> 95th Rifle Division met strong enemy fire resistance from the area of the south-eastern edge of the Barrikady factory but by 1500 hours had captured the western edge of Mashinnaya Street, the right flank overcoming the wire entanglements to the west of Mashinnaya Street.

> One dug-in tank was destroyed. Personnel: 241st Rifle Regiment – 325 men, 161st Rifle Regiment – 217 men and 90 Rifle Regiment – 320 men.

The Germans did not attack at all. They limited themselves to the occasional artillery and mortar barrage on Lyudnikov's divisional command post and Zaitsevsky Island, as well as lashing the Soviet line every now and then with machine-gun and small arms fire. It was obvious that the primary German concern was now defence. An interesting perception of the German defences appears in the combat journal of 650th Rifle Regiment:

> Along the regiment's front-line, the enemy has created a system of strongpoints with overlapping fields of fire. There is a dug-out with a light machine-gun under a tractor 60-70 metres to the right of the unfinished house.

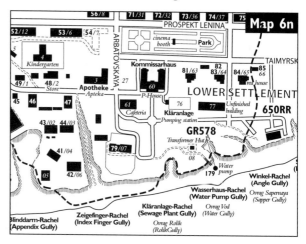

> In the unfinished building is 1 light machine-gun and up to 10 infantrymen. In the transformer hut are 2 light machine-guns and up to 15 infantrymen, while 4 light machine-guns, 1 large-calibre machine-gun and up to 20 infantrymen are in the long red house [Haus 79] and on the south-east precipice of the circular ravine. A heavy machine-gun is on the south-east edge of the kindergarten, another is in the P-shaped building [Kommissarhaus] while a third one is in the L-shaped building [Apotheke]. A mortar battery is located 75 metres north-west of Workshop 14 [Hall 3] in the Barrikady factory.

- - -

At 1445 hours, LI. Armeekorps ordered its subordinate units to hold their current positions and told them that Korpsbefehl Nr. 118 was invalid. This Korpsbefehl, issued the previous day, instructed the divisions to ready themselves for a possible break-out. Corps commander General von Seydlitz had taken it upon himself to force Paulus's hand. Although Paulus had made repeated requests to Hitler for freedom of action – meaning he wanted to break out of the pocket – von Seydlitz knew that time was of the essence and the army needed to act quickly if it was to save itself. Paulus had waited in vain throughout 23 November for a decision from Hitler. General von Seydlitz had already concluded that a break-out was inevitable and issued the order to his divisions in the north-east corner of the pocket to pull back. General von Seydlitz hoped this would be the first domino: after this withdrawal, others divisions would pull back and Paulus would be forced to order a break out to the south-west. The withdrawal of the divisions in the north-east corner took place on the evening of 23 November but it turned into a minor debacle when Soviet soldiers noticed the manoeuvre and immediately attacked 94. Infanterie-Division. Casualties were high.

Generaloberst Friedrich Paulus, Commander-in-Chief of 6. Armee.

The next morning, 24 November, when Hitler heard about the withdrawal, he demanded a full report and forbade any further retreats. It was explained to Hitler that the troops had been taken back to prepared positions and in this way, a division had been gained for employment elsewhere. Hitler was not convinced and, suspecting that Paulus was behind the withdrawal[63], gave von Seydlitz – the man who was actually responsible – command of the northern front of the pocket. When Paulus received this signal, he visited von Seydlitz's nearby headquarters without his imperious chief-of-staff. Naturally, Paulus had words with von Seydlitz about his independent actions, but in a quite matter-of-fact way, without any personal acrimony. Paulus then handed von Seydlitz the latest signal and added ironically: "Now that you have your own command, you can break out." Seydlitz could not hide his embarrassment. Feldmarschall von Manstein managed to smooth things over with Hitler and command of the Stalingrad pocket eventually reverted to Paulus's sole control.

Hitler's decision, written before he learned about the withdrawal, reached 6. Armee at 0830 hours. As predicted, he ordered the army to hold out until a relief attack reached what he now termed 'Fortress Stalingrad'. He explicitly ordered the current front along the Volga and the current northern front of LI. Armeekorps to be held under all circumstances. General von Seydlitz's presumptuous gambit had directly conflicted with Hitler's wishes and the northern front of LI. Armeekorps was now nothing but hastily dug positions anchored on several low hills.

At 1115 hours, Paulus issued an Armeebefehl to his subordinate corps explaining and expanding the Führer's decision. LI. Armeekorps was to hold its current positions, including the new line in the snow, whatever the circumstances. This is what prompted von Seydlitz to issue the order at 1445 hours. But he was not happy. He put pen to paper and produced one of the most extraordinary documents to come out of the Stalingrad battle. Dated 25 November, the memorandum expounded von Seydlitz's thoughts about why it was a mistake not to break out immediately. It began:

---

63. In his memoirs, von Seydlitz wrote: "With a noble attitude, Paulus took responsibility on himself for my independent actions. I've always credited him very highly for that. On the other hand, I must stress that I never avoided full responsibility for it, not even one word."

In receipt of the Armeebefehl of 24.11.1942 for the continuation of fighting, and fully aware of the seriousness of the situation, I feel obliged to resubmit – in writing – my opinion, which has been further strengthened by events during the past 24 hours.

The army is faced with a clear either/or situation:

Either break out to the south-west in the general direction of Kotelnikovo or face destruction in a few days.

This assessment is based on a sober evaluation of the actual conditions.

What followed was a comprehensive and damning analysis of the situation. He stated that supplies, which had already been running short before the counteroffensive began, would decide the issue. "The numbers speak for themselves," he wrote. To found any hopes on air supply, he added, was to grasp at straws because only 30 Ju-52s were available, and even if a further 100 could be assembled, the army's full requirements could still not be met. Point by point he emphasised the dire situation and the folly of holding on.

The OKH order to hold out in hedgehog positions until help arrives is obviously based on false assumptions. It is therefore not feasible and would inevitably lead the army to disaster. If the army is to be saved, then another order must be immediately issued, or another decision immediately taken.

In March and April 1942, von Seydlitz had led the relief effort which eventually freed the Demyansk pocket and he noted that this type of combat was "extremely difficult". Of the commanders in Stalingrad, it was he who had the most experience with this type of situation. His final, extraordinary paragraph was a call to mutiny, to ignore Hitler's directive and to answer what General Strecker called "the most difficult question of conscience for every soldier: whether to disobey his superior's orders in order to handle the situation as he deems best":

Unless the OKH promptly rescinds the order to hold out in the hedgehog position, then my own conscience and responsibility to the army and the German people imposes the imperative duty to seize the freedom of action prevented by the previous order and to use what little time is left to avoid utter disaster by launching our own attack. The complete destruction of 200,000 soldiers and all their equipment is at stake.

There is no other choice.

Paulus told Seydlitz to keep out of affairs that were not his concern. Army chief-of-staff Schmidt noted that they did not worry the Führer with Seydlitz's memorandum, and anyway, General von Seydlitz was not the army's commander-in-chief. Nevertheless, Paulus basically agreed with von Seydlitz and on 26 November, in a personal letter to von Manstein, again asked for freedom of action. Knowing Hitler's thinking on the matter, von Manstein could not give Paulus what he was seeking.

With this, 6. Armee was condemned to hold its icy 'fortress' at Stalingrad.

- - -

Once night fell, rations were again brought over to Lyudnikov's Island by boat. The combat structure of the division at the end of this day was as follows: 462 men, 344 rifles, 69 PPSh, 19 light machine-guns, 2 heavy machine-guns, 3 anti-tank rifles and 3 45mm guns.

Casualties for 24 November, 1942:	
138th Rifle Division:	2 killed, 20 wounded, a total of 22 men
305. Infanterie-Division:	2 men killed and 23 men wounded

25 November, 1942

Out in the icy wastes, Oberleutnant Benad and his group of replacements from Pionier-Battalion 294 were still on their way to Stalingrad. The successful Soviet encirclement meant that these men could not reach the battalion in Stalingrad and the command of 294. Infanterie-Division quickly made the decision to get them back. An order was dispatched for them to halt at Lichaya railway station. The divisional quartermaster was directed to arrange the return of Oberleutnant Benad and his kommando to the division via rail or vehicular transport. Benad and his men narrowly escaped the frigid fate awaiting the other men of Pionier-Bataillon 294.

- - -

Despite von Seydlitz cancelling his advanced order to prepare for a break-out, it seems that the order had not filtered down very far. Hauptmann Rettenmaier wrote in his diary:

> The order to 'reorganise' has arrived. On the code word, everything will begin to roll. There is no concealment of information. We ready ourselves for the withdrawal. What is to be taken along is ammunition, which is the most important item, then rations and winter clothing. There will be two field-kitchens and for each company three vehicles. More isn't possible. We don't have any more horses. Everything else: motorcycles – vehicles – the kits for the horses – all private possessions will be collected for destruction. There is a lot, even a great quantity of valuable items. And what will happen to our guns? They can't be moved; even the artillery doesn't have horses and petrol is no longer available. It would be a crying shame if the guns had to be blown up. In the afternoon the situation is judged somewhat more positively. There is a Führer Decree: 'Stalingrad will remain occupied by us, the necessary measures will be undertaken so that our situation here does not become too flammable'. It would make one weep if we had to give up the ground in Stalingrad that has cost us so much blood.

He reiterated similar thoughts in a letter home:

> During these past days we completed preparations to break out to the south, but the Führer Decree came, informing us that we must remain in Stalingrad. Austerity and economies have been decreed in every area. Our few available starving horses are our living reserve of meat. But we continue to be confident and hope that the sun will once again shine upon us.

- - -

Relative peace still reigned on Lyudnikov's Island. The combat journal of 138th Rifle Division recorded:

> The enemy is not active. He occasionally fires on the divisional formations with his small arms and machine-guns. During the course of the day the enemy continued with engineering works to improve his defences.

Soviet observations were accurate. The replacements recently received by Grenadier-Regiment 578 were sent forward to the Volga to construct positions. The harsh conditions in the front-line trenches were a shock for the youngsters, and the work was hazardous. As the combat journal of 650th Rifle Regiment states, "the regiment fires machine-guns at enemy emplacements and running individuals, and keeps the enemy under round-the-clock observation". Any careless movement, a moment of curiosity, was punished by accurate Soviet fire. The division claimed to have destroyed about 50 German soldiers and 1 heavy machine-gun, but 305. Infanterie-Division's casualties of 3 dead and 12 wounded show that figure to be an exaggeration. In addition, 138th Rifle Division also claimed the following were destroyed by artillery fire: 2 lorries and 1 automobile with submachine-gunners were knocked out, two machine-gun nests, 2 guns with crews and 1 dug-out with infantry were destroyed, while a mortar battery was suppressed.

Combat structure of 138th Rifle Division was as follows: number of men on the west bank of the Volga was 505, and of those, 25 were wounded men. There was also 91 men who were not part of the division, making a total of 596 men in the division's combat sector.

- - -

Small storm groups of 95th Rifle Division, pushing through heavy artillery, mortar and light machine-gun fire from the Barrikady factory, overcame wire entanglements and captured individual German pillboxes. In doing so, the rifle regiments suffered heavy casualties: 241st Rifle Regiment had a shortfall of 125 men, 90th Rifle Regiment 60 men and 161st Rifle Regiment 22 men. At the end of the day, their combat strengths were as follows: 241st Rifle Regiment – 200 men, 90th Rifle Regiment – 260 men and 161st Rifle Regiment – 195 men.

Casualties for 25 November, 1942:	
138th Rifle Division:	3 killed, 6 wounded, a total of 9 men
305. Infanterie-Division:	3 men killed and 12 men wounded

- - -

At 2230 hours, LI. Armeekorps issued Befehl Nr. 119 in which the following was ordered:

305. Infanterie-Division will disband Pionier-Bataillone 162, 294 and 336 and out of them, set up one or two pioneer battalions.

389. Infanterie-Division will incorporate Pionier-Bataillon 45 into its own pioneer battalion.

The same arrangement is valid for Sturmkompanie 44, which will be absorbed into one of 305. Infanterie-Division's grenadier regiments.

Combat had taken its toll on the pioneer battalions. Major Josef Linden later wrote:

The offensive in the gun factory area had greatly weakened the battalions with the daily attacks and the high casualties resulting from those. When the enemy launched his large counteroffensive to encircle 6. Armee, our operations were no longer a priority. The attack was suspended and the pioneers, because of their high casualties, were formed into one battalion under the command of Major Krüger, commander of Pionier-Bataillon 162, and employed in an infantry role on a sector of 305. Infanterie-Division.

The disbandment of the pioneer battalions and subsequent reformation created a surplus of staffs, although Linden's statement that the pioneers were formed into one battalion was not totally correct. Available evidence suggests that only Pionier-Bataillone 162 and 305 were combined into a new battalion. In a letter to the wife of a missing comrade, Gefreiter Albrecht Löffler, 1./Pionier-Bataillon 305, wrote that "towards the end of November, our battalion and another pioneer battalion were dissolved and combined into one battalion, whereby each company was about 60 men strong. These companies also contained members of the supply train and our battalion staff…"

Some of the original staff of Pionier-Bataillon 305, including Hauptmann Traub, were set aside for special assignments while Major Krüger – as the highest-ranking pioneer officer – took over control of the composite battalion with his staff. In his letters home, Traub never mentioned to his wife that he no longer commanded his beloved battalion: his silence on the matter shows he was somewhat humbled by this demotion, but he bore absolutely no animosity to Krüger. Both officers were respected and loved by their respective battalions, and soon, the men of Pionier-Bataillon 305 came to regard Krüger as highly as they did Traub. The reformed battalion was quite strong and possessed five companies; 1. Kompanie had 1 officer (unknown), 5 NCOs and 75 men with 6 light machine-guns; 2. Kompanie had 1 officer (Leutnant Hingst), 6 NCOs and 65 men with 6 light machine-guns; 3. Kompanie had 1 officer (Oberleutnant Staiger), 5 NCOs and 83 men with 6 light machine-guns; the company formed from Pionier-Bataillon 162 contained 1 officer (Oberleutnant Schinke), 3 NCOs and 29 men with 3 light machine-guns; and finally, a company formed from Soviet POWs had a strength of 270 men, 35 of whom were German, including its commander Leutnant Hubert Homburger[64]. It seems the men of Pionier-Bataillon 162 were spread throughout the three companies while a small core of the old battalion, forming a fourth company, was left intact, perhaps as a Restkommando.

It is unknown what roles were allocated to the other three battalion commanders (Gast, Weimann and Lundt) and their staffs, but it is clear that they still existed as separate entities and were not dissolved for use as replacements. Each of their battalions were condensed into one company with a line officer as commander and attached to a grenadier-regiment: Panzerpionier-Bataillon 50 to Grenadier-Regiment 578, Pionier-Bataillon 294 to Grenadier-Regiment 576 and Pionier-Bataillon 336 to Grenadier-Regiment 577. In each case, they were subordinated to the regiments they had been supporting over the previous two weeks. Panzerpionier-Bataillon 50 had a combat strength of 1 officer, 6 NCOs and 92 men with 2 heavy and 7 light machine-guns; Pionier-Bataillon 294 had 1 officer, 7 NCOs and 40 men with 6 light machine-guns; Pionier-Bataillon 336 had 1 officer, 4 NCOs and 95 men with 7 light machine-guns.

Also now part of Pionier-Bataillon 305 were the 50 Italian drivers and 30 lorries of 248° Autoreparto pesante (248th Heavy Truck Company). After delivering Pionier-Bataillon 162 to the city in early November, their orders were to wait around and bring the battalion back after completion of its mission. The assignment was never completed, so the hapless Italians were caught in the Soviet mousetrap. Driver Mariano Puschiavo[65] wrote home:

> We are attached to the Germans but we do not understand what they are saying and what they are doing. We have to dig foxholes to get some shelter.

Sturmkompanie 44 was incorporated into Grenadier-Regiment 578. Lacking officers, it was led by Unteroffizier Janssen, a battle-hardened NCO.

There were also changes in the grenadier regiments. Each consisted of two grenadier battalions, supported by their usual 13. and 14. Kompanien (heavy infantry guns and anti-tank guns respectively), as well as a new pioneer company and a dedicated artillery battalion from Artillerie-Regiment 305 (I. Abteilung to Grenadier-Regiment 578, II. Abteilung to

---

64. Homburger, Leutnant Hubert, le.Pi.kol./Pi.Btl.305; born 23 November, 1907 in Reiselfingen. Killed in action, 22 December, 1942 in Stalingrad. See Appendix 2 (page 574) for more details.

65. Puschiavo, Autiere Mariano, 248° Autoreparto pesante; born 2 March, 1911 in Bologna. Missing in action, January 1943 in Stalingrad.

Grenadier-Regiment 577 and III. Abteilung to Grenadier-Regiment 576). In addition, Grenadier-Regiment 577 had an infantry company formed from excess artillerymen: it was a numerically strong unit with 3 officers, 36 NCOs and 253 men with 10 light machine-guns. Furthermore, in the rear was Lehrbataillon (training battalion) Schwarz, formed from II./Grenadier-Regiment 578. This unit, led by the very capable regiment adjutant, Hauptmann Schwarz, was set up to prepare newly-arrived replacements for combat in the Barrikady. Later on, as the situation became more desperate, it would also retrain artillerymen, musicians, clerks – basically any superfluous soldier – in the fine art of city combat. Hauptmann Schwarz had a difficult task but he carried it out with verve and aplomb.

A similar reconstruction was occurring at 389. Infanterie-Division, although it was much simpler there. Hauptmann Büch's Pionier-Bataillon 45 was absorbed into Pionier-Bataillon 389. Soldat Bertold Paulus from 2./Pionier-Bataillon 45 wrote home:

> On the night of 25 November, our battalion had to destroy its precious vehicles. We are no longer Pionier-Bataillon 45 but pioneer soldiers of 389. Infanterie-Division. We are now part of the Rheingold Division. On the night that we destroyed everything, it was said that Stalingrad would be given up and we would try to bust open the ring to get out. There are still 3 men from the 30 that came to the company with me. Our old battalion is only at half-strength, which is why two battalions have been made into one. Therefore, our Feldpostnummer has also changed. It is now 44509.

Hauptmann Büch took command of the battalion.

– – –

This amalgamation of pioneer battalions provides a clear-cut finishing point to our detailed examination of their offensive actions. No longer are they the main players in the deadly drama in the Barrikady: from this point forward, the emphasis shifts to the Soviet perspective, for it is they who now held the initiative. The pioneer battalions still figure in the months of fighting ahead, but on this day, they essentially lost their individual identities, their field-post numbers, and became part of the Bodensee-Division.

– – –

One of the first tasks given to the newly-reformed 305. Infanterie-Division was the construction of a new defensive position in the rear. Major Linden, recently made unemployed by the cessation of attacks east of the Barrikady, would oversee the construction. The new line was based on the heights around Gorodische. Other divisions in the city received similar orders. Major Linden was ordered to submit a proposal of the planned construction by 1800 hours on 27 November. The labour force would come from different units: Pionier-Bataillon 305 would supply 60 pioneers and 135 POWs, division staff 23 men, Panzerjäger-Abteilung 305 45 men, Nachrichten-Abteilung 305 40 men and the artillery regiment 40 men.

This new task signalled a dramatic and permanent shift in the German mindset. No longer was everything geared toward the offensive, toward pushing on to the Volga, toward capturing Stalingrad. Now, defence was the highest prerogative. A week earlier, the Germans – so close to clutching the rest of the rubbled city – could not have imagined that the roles would be reversed, that it would be them building reserve defensive lines and being ordered to hold positions in Stalingrad at any cost. A new phase of the battle had been entered.

CHAPTER SEVEN

26 November, 1942

Unbeknownst to the Soviets, and indeed, to most of the German rank-and-file, the reorganisation and consolidation of the battered German units was a prerequisite for a break-out. If they were to have any chance of surviving a gruelling march across the steppe, the divisions needed to be lean and unencumbered by excess baggage. With each passing day, the Soviet grip on the pocket tightened and the chances of a successful German withdrawal diminished. Hitler had never been warm to the idea of breaking out and now become decidedly cold to any notion of 'abandoning' Stalingrad, as he saw it, because that would mean simply giving up all the gains paid for with so much blood during the preceding three months. The Führer therefore decreed that the army was to stay put and hold its positions until relieved.

Of course, none of this was known to the Landsers huddled in their dingy cellars or frostbitten trenches. Even their officers knew very little, and what they did know was based on rumour and hearsay. In his daily notes, Hauptmann Rettenmaier recorded his impressions: "The front was noticeably quieter this morning. Attacks are again in progress to the south. Everything is relatively quiet near us. We heard a report that one of our divisions destroyed their vehicles too hastily."[1]

– – –

In the meantime, the usual happenings – recorded by Rettenmaier as being "noticeably quieter" – were being played out in the Barrikady. Throughout the night, the Germans fired on Lyudnikov's men and Zaitsevsky island with small arms, machine-guns and the occasional mortar shell. In Pechenyuk's sector, infantrymen of Grenadier-Regiment 578 holding the trench that ran along the top of the cliff threw grenades at the water pump and the Rolik group. Mortar fire harassed the front-line defences of 650th Rifle Regiment, particularly near the water pump and its gully. In return, Soviet units pelted German strongpoints with frequent flurries of small arms and machine-gun fire, as well as volleys of hand grenades. The artillery also fired methodically, interspersing their normal patterns of fire with frequent surprise barrages. After two weeks of the bloodiest combat, this activity was indeed 'noticeably quieter' to the weary soldiers of both sides.

Observers from Pechenyuk's regiment established that the Germans had set up 3 mortars between the Kommissarhaus and Haus 83. A light machine-gun had also been spotted 15-20 metres to the right of Haus 84. As always, Soviet units kept German movements under

---

1. He is referring to 94. Infanterie-Division's disastrous withdrawal on the night of 23-24 November, 1942.

round-the-clock observation. Pechenyuk's regiment received Order No. 27 from divisional headquarters in preparation for an attack first ordered on 23 November:

> Order: The regiment will organise forces and resources for thorough engineering work. For this operation, defences of enemy buildings will be thoroughly examined with the aim of detecting mines.

– – –

Once its offensive operations were halted, 305. Infanterie-Division arranged its strongpoints for long-term defence. Minefields around the buildings were thickened, extra layers of barbed wire were strung out, trenches were deepened and ammunition was stockpiled. Machine-guns were sited for maximum effect, mortars registered on likely enemy approach routes and reserves positioned in cellars of buildings behind the line, ready to launch immediate counterattacks. All measures were undertaken to ensure the line was held. Occupying the most forward strongpoints could quickly wear the nerves of the men, so regular reliefs were rostered. Hauptmann Rettenmaier wrote in his diary:

> At around 1000, I will relieve Hauptmann Püttmann at his post along the Volga. Then drop in at the regimental command post at 1200 and return to our battalion command post at 1330. I'll inspect our positions at about 1900 hours.

The relief of Püttmann's III. Bataillon by Rettenmaier's I. Bataillon was almost certainly noticed by Soviet observers because in its daily report submitted that evening, 138th Rifle Division noted:

> [The enemy] continued construction of his dug-outs. During the day, the enemy along the division's front did not show any offensive actions. The movement of small groups of enemy soldiers suggests that the enemy may be preparing an offensive against various divisional units.

With the encirclement barely five days old, measures needed to be taken to ensure that 6. Armee could hold its positions, and one of the most important was the conservation of ammunition and food. Immediate rationing was introduced. Rettenmaier noted that "we have been directed to be very thrifty with our expenditure of ammunition and rations. Only as much as is necessary to maintain our strength has been issued. The bread ration is 375 grams. In the next few days we'll again get some horsemeat. Supplies can only come through by air. Who can escape this windy spot?"

At 1900 hours, LI. Armeekorps issued Korpsbefehl Nr. 120. Its opening point certainly left no doubt as to the situation that had developed since the beginning of the Soviet counterattack a week earlier:

> The army, surrounded by enemy forces due to events in neighbouring sectors, will hold its positions until the very last. The task of each division is determined by this: not one step back! Whatever is lost must be recaptured without delay. Relief is being initiated. Supplies will be brought in by air.

Then followed several points that list how the divisions should economise on ammunition expenditure and raise combat strengths:

> For this fighting, it is essential that all available forces – down to the last man and the last weapon – be gathered and put into action. The most economical use of ammunition, the scrupulous and reasoned consumption of fuel and the careful husbanding of all remaining supplies, even down to candles and paper, must be made during this struggle in a hedgehog

position, irrespective of the time we are in it. All available inventory stocks will be collected in order to utilise the entirety in a reciprocative comradely equalisation.

Every soldier must be adjusted to these demands by his superiors in order to fit decisively, courageously and obediently into the whole. Any offence against these demands is a betrayal of the firm resolution to hold out to the very last and must be punished, even including the destruction of the offender.

The positions will be further improved and strengthened by all available means. They will above all be well protected by obstacles and minefields dominated by firepower. Fatigue and exhausting combat will not be allowed to delay the upgrading of the positions. This will be strictly implemented. This work will be recompensed by lighter casualties and an increased power of resistance in the positions.

Division commanders are authorised to consolidate formations in order to gain combatworthy forces and units, and to reduce the number of personnel in the supply trains, etc. Intentions will be reported…

Economy in ammunition consumption. Targets will only be combated with the corresponding – that is, sufficient – weapon. When a heavy infantry gun will suffice, artillery will not be deployed. Economise on the number of shots.

Ammunition lying around will be collected. Every shell is precious! With some attention, a considerable quantity can be brought together.

Economy with fuel consumption! As long as the present situation persists, every unnecessary kilometre driven is a crime! Messengers will make more use of their feet, bicycles or horses. Trips necessary for individuals will be combined and used simultaneously for several purposes.

And finally, to underline the gravity of the situation, one of the final points addressed the 'last son' policy:

At the moment, no regard can be given to last sons, etc, because the situation demands that everyone who can be drawn upon for combat will be.

– – –

Having taken over one of the most potentially dangerous sectors in Stalingrad, Hauptmann Rettenmaier undertook an inspection tour of his battalion's positions. His front-line sector began on the isthmus between Appendix and Index Finger Gullies, ran along the top of the Volga cliff, around the Rolik ravine, and up to Water House Gully where a tiny brick transforming station formed the cornerstone of the defence. The front-line of Grenadier-Regiment 578 then swung back to the west where it took in the unfinished building and Haus 84, and ended in a maze of trenches and dug-outs in the middle of the park. Behind the line, Haus 79, 83, 81 and the Kommissarhaus formed formidable bastions that could swamp any Soviet attack with machine-gun fire. In his diary notes, Hauptmann Rettenmaier wrote:

At 1900 hours, Oberleutnant Rominger[2] and I inspected the positions. There was a bright full moon, a sharp wind and snowfall. The positions are at the extreme edge of the river. The gullies are well protected. Nearly everywhere the Russian sits nearby within hand grenade distance of us. The anti-tank guns are in the forward positions to stop boat traffic on the Volga. In the middle of our sector, where the front bends to the north, our men are working on the construction of a trench to reach the edge of the riverside cliff, to get the better of the enemy. They only have five to eight metres left to dig.

2. Rominger, Oberleutnant Ludwig, 13./Gr.Rgt.576, German Cross in Gold on 25 January, 1943.

The Kommissarhaus is an enormous complex with many cellars. I myself am sitting in a cellar under Haus 53 that was once part of the heating installation. A hole in the ceiling and a ladder form the entrance to my abode. On top of it looms the remnants of a 10-metre-high brick wall. We have the option, if the need arises, of creating exits through the walls.

The men take advantage of the opportunity to write letters and I do the same. We think more than usual about our loved ones.

To hold his sector, Rettenmaier had a total of 66 combat soldiers, as indicated by a memorandum sent to 6. Armee on 26 November[3] which reported the number of combat soldiers employed in the front-line. For 305. Infanterie-Division, the figures were as follows: II./576 (Major. Braun) – 76 men, III./576 (Hptm. Kempter[4]) – 75 men, II./577 (Oberleutnant Winkler) – 132 men, III./577 (Hauptmann Wittmann) – 131 men, I./578 (Hptm. Rettenmaier) – 66 men, division reserve II./578 (Hptm. Schwarz) – 172 men, III./578 (Hptm. Püttmann) – 77 men, Pi.Btl.305 (Hptm Traub) – 45 men, Pi.Btl.162 (Major Krüger) – 99 men, Pi.Btl.294 (Major Weimann) – 40 men, Pi.Btl.336 (Hptm. Lundt) – 92 men and Sturmkompanie 44 (Uffz. Janssen) – 38 men[5].

For the northern neighbour, 389. Infanterie-Division, the strengths were as follows: I./544 – 195 men, III./544 – 220 men, I./545 – 86 men, III./545 – 90 men, I./546 – 88 men, III./546 – 139 men and Radfahr-Abteilung 389 – 53 men[6].

Facing them was 138th Rifle Division with 508 men on the west bank of the Volga, of those, 42 were wounded men. Additionally, there were 91 men who were not part of the division. The total strength in the division's combat sector was 599 men. Its armament consisted of 344 rifles, 69 PPSh, 19 light machine-guns, 2 heavy machine-guns, 3 anti-tank guns, 3 anti-tank rifles and 1 anti-aircraft machine-gun.

Casualties for 26 November, 1942:	
138th Rifle Division:	no figures available
305. Infanterie-Division:	7 men killed, 1 officer and 17 men wounded

27 November, 1942

Ensconced in the relatively safety of their cellars and unoccupied with offensives, many Germans became introspective and turned their thoughts to their loved ones. "It is 0500," wrote Hauptmann Rettenmaier, "and my family is at home, still sleeping sweetly and snugly. This is good, they don't need to know how things are with us because it would only make them more anxious and increase their worries. The main hospital can no longer accept any sick men with fevers of 39 or 40 degrees Celsius, at least until 29 November."

The German hospitals and aid stations were overflowing with wounded men. Since the pocket had formed, the only chance for the wounded to receive first-rate treatment was to be flown out and admitted to larger hospitals in the Russian hinterland. The first planes started landing on 23 November but there were simply not enough to make a dent in the

---

3. However, it should be noted that these figures seem to be based on strengths and compositions prior to the reshuffle of forces ordered on 25 November.

4. Kempter, Major Hans, III./Gr.Rgt.576; born 11 August, 1895. Died 12 July, 1980 in Landshut.

5. For some reason, Pz.Pi.Btl.50 does not appear in the list.

6. Pi.Btle.45 and 389 do not appear in the list.

number of wounded. For the first five days of the airlift, a total of 119 flights landed in the pocket (29, 20, 31, 27 and 12 respectively), all of them being Ju-52s, Ju-86s and Ju-290s. Unfortunately, no figures exist to show the number of wounded flown out on these days, but it was certainly less than a thousand.[7] The number of casualties arriving at first-aid posts far outstripped the number of wounded evacuated on the planes. It was a worrying situation for the army, the medical staff attending the wounded and commanders like Hauptmann Rettenmaier who cared deeply for the welfare of their men.

– – –

27 November was even quieter than the previous day. 138th Rifle Division continued to hold its previous line and the Germans displayed absolutely no offensive intentions. Throughout the day, the Germans occasionally placed mortar fire on the Soviet defensive line and continued throwing grenades at the water pump and the Rolik group. German machine-gun emplacements worked briskly, methodically raking the terrain with automatic fire, particularly one heavy and one light machine-gun emplaced to the right of the unfinished house. Another light machine-gun, sited on the south-east precipice above the circular Rolik gully, also caused trouble. German snipers were also active and the mortars sited between the Kommissarhaus and Haus 83 dropped barrages every now and then. The three Soviet regiments placed rifle and machine-gun fire on active German strongpoints and continued observing their movements. Lyudnikov's division had been alerted that some German units in other sectors were withdrawing but the Soviets were concerned that the retreating Germans might reverse and attack Gorokhov's group to the north. Therefore, Lyudnikov ordered his men to report even the slightest hint that the opposing German units were pulling back.

In the afternoon, at 1340 hours, the normal routine was interrupted when a German Ju-88 flew over the Barrikady battlefield, from south-east to north-west, without dropping any bombs. Both sides stopped for a few seconds to look up at the low-flying visitor, and as it droned off into the distance, rifle fire started up again. Scattered Soviet artillery bombardments howled in throughout the afternoon.

Strength of 138th Rifle Division: number of all people on the west bank – 517 men. Of those, 42 were wounded men. Men who were not part of the division – 89. Total in the division's combat sector – 606 men. Armament: 344 rifles, 69 PPSh, 19 light machine-guns, 2 heavy machine-guns, 4 anti-tank guns, 3 anti-tank rifles and 1 anti-aircraft machine-gun.

– – –

In the evening, Rettenmaier was still in a reflective mood:

At dinner, (we get everything for the whole day in the evening), I received two newspapers dated 31 October and 6 November, along with a letter from home dated 6 November. Whilst reading it, my thoughts were entirely of home, every corner of the apartment appeared before my eyes, one constructs every detail authentically and home is where one would prefer to be, with the wife and children, rather than here. It is difficult to come to terms with one's thoughts. But we must remain here and stand and fight for our loved ones at home. Outside, there is an icy cold east wind with a light snowfall.

---

7. By 9 December, a total of 741 flights had been made to the pocket and 6441 wounded men flown out, making an average of between 8 and 9 wounded men per flight.

Gefreiter Hans Luz, 1./Panzerjäger-Abteilung 305, was a crew member on one of the 7.5cm anti-tanks dug in atop the cliffs. His gun chief was Unteroffizier Walter Knittel[8]:

On 22 November, we took over a completely dangerous position on the Volga that was only open from the rear. Consequently, the Russians were around us on three sides. The distance from us to the Russians was about 80 metres. We had the task of disrupting shipping traffic on the Volga and holding the position against enemy attacks. You can probably imagine that it was always very lively. We fought there for just a week, with success. On 27 November, however, fate dealt us a severe blow. On this evening, 4 men from our gun crew were felled by a mortar. Two comrades, [Unteroffizier Knittel] and myself were active on the gun when the enemy shell exploded directly on the gun. I was immediately thrown to the ground with quite a few pieces of shrapnel in my body. Despite this, however, I still had all my senses and immediately looked around for my comrades. Unfortunately, [Unteroffizier Knittel] lay next to me with a massive shrapnel wound to his right thigh. Uninjured comrades immediately carried him into our bunker and gave him first aid. They brought me in a short while later. Another comrade had been killed outright and another was lightly wounded. Then the men uncovered the wounds of [Knittel] and myself. Unfortunately, [he] lost consciousness after a few minutes and so died a hero's death from loss of blood. I remained in Stalingrad until 28.12.42 and was then brought out of the pocket by plane to Salsk.

The deteriorating situation meant that many of the wounded, like Gefreiter Luz – and even many from the first stages of the November offensive – were trapped inside the pocket for a long time. Gefreiter Karl Krauss, 2./Pionier-Bataillon 45, grievously wounded on 11 November, still lay on the cold stone floor of the Gorodische church:

I now no longer know for how long I lay in this building. In the meantime, 6. Armee had been completely surrounded!

Because of my many injuries, I could only move my arms and my head. I was carried to a waiting ambulance by medics but instead of being taken to an escaping aircraft, I was put down into an open cellar. There I was, still surrounded by groans and cries, but there was no care and no food.

Again and again quite a few were carried out, and I was envious of them, especially because I believed they were being transported to the airfield. It was only later that I unfortunately found out that quite a number of these comrades were already dead. The cold plunged even further, down to -20° to -25°. I no longer remember how long I lay in this open rat's hole. The paper bag enclosing me, together with my high fever, saved me from freezing to death.

Then I was finally carried away, carried to a wooden shed lying in a hollow. Snow blew in through gaps in the boards. It was an improvised operating theatre. My bandages were finally removed. An old doctor, with a greying beard, examined me.

Diagnosis: Apart from many injuries, gangrene had already set in. What this meant was clear to me. A death sentence?

Doctor: 'Lad, you're lucky you came into my hands. I'm one of the few gangrene specialists from the First World War who treats it without amputation.' The operation followed under ether anaesthetic but because of shortages, I quickly regained consciousness as the pain was unbearable. (I later received three further operations outside the pocket, all of which succeeded). To this day I still have all my limbs!

I was subsequently brought to a large hospital tent (probably near Stalingradski). Russian infantry broke through, bullets whizzed through the tent and the medics went into defensive positions around the tents. Suddenly, a drone of motors and howling sirens, accompanied by frightful crashing – German Stukas saved us.

---

8. Knittel, Unteroffizier Walter, 1./Pz.Jäg.Abt.305; born 2 November, 1914 in Metzingen. Killed in action, 27 November, 1942 in Stalingrad.

We were looked after by German Red Cross sisters. I was sorry these brave young girls had decided to remain with us. After a long time we again received tea and crispbread, with about 25 grams of horseflesh. Dead, frozen horses were cut up with axes. Constant weeks-long fever of 41.3° to 41.8°. The 'sewing-machines' came at night and dropped bombs indiscriminately, without any regard for the medical tents. What was in store for us if Ivan broke through was clear to all of us: on the assumption that Kalach was still free, a hospital train headed west, then the first Russian tank moved to the entrance of the railway station. All the wounded, together with the personnel, were thrown off the train and in -25° temperatures had water poured over them!

Calmly and silently, Russian prisoners carried me out of the tent to a waiting ambulance. It was the trip to Gumrak airfield! To me, the waiting Ju-52 was a machine with angel's wings. Icy Siberian snowstorm! Quite a few aircraft started in the growing darkness, although mine didn't because its engines refused to turn over due to the cold. The pilot was fuming! A solitary flight meant the chances of being shot down were considerably higher because there would not be a fighter escort. After much fruitless effort, there was at last a magic noise from the engines. He had not allowed the engines to switch off. These aircraft were almost defenceless when exposed to the Russian Ratas. We made it through thanks to the darkness. This was my first flight[9]. We landed in Morosovskaya, in the area where we had spent many beautiful days in the past autumn. The accommodation was a two-story building. Only a few windows and doors still remained. I was placed on the ground floor. Aisles and stairs were completely covered with frozen human fluids and sodden bandages. After long hours, we were placed in a medical tent on open ground, ready for further transportation. Constant aerial attacks and bombing raids over the city and the many Red Cross tents. Our most popular man, the chaplain from Vienna, was killed in a tent with all the wounded. We wept. The Russians broke through the Chir front…

Casualties for 27 November, 1942:	
138th Rifle Division:	none
305. Infanterie-Division:	19 men wounded[10]

28 November, 1942

During the quiet of the night, when the Germans were least active, a medal presentation ceremony took place in the sector of 650th Rifle Regiment. 'For Courage' medals were bestowed upon Sergeant Nikolai Fedorovich Baranov, Sergeant Iosif Andreyevich Motamev, Red Army soldier Grigory Ivanovich Ploskonos, Red Army soldier Nikolai Mikhailovich Smirnov and Red Army soldier Filip Mikhailovich Timofiyev. Toasts were drunk and the men went back to their positions.

– – –

At 0300 hours, 138th Rifle Division reported that "along the front of the division, the enemy continues to lay down methodical fire with small arms, machine-guns and occasionally mortars. Active operations and movements by the enemy were not seen." Pechenyuk's 650th Rifle Regiment reported that the "enemy is situated in his former nests of resistance. During the course of the previous night and day he fired aggressively, especially

---

9. For his 80th birthday, Krauss' sons arranged a flight on one of the very few Ju-52s still in operation. Needless to say that Karl Krauss' second trip on a Ju-52 was less eventful than his first.

10. For unknown reasons, the death of Unteroffizier Knittel and another identified man from 1./Pz.Jäg.Abt.305 do not appear in the division's daily casualty figures, usually submitted each morning.

with small arms and machine-guns. Grenades were occasionally thrown at Rolik and the water pump." All regiments doubled observation of German fire in order to pinpoint their emplacements and earmark them for special attention. Soviet artillery on the east bank of the Volga fired on targets of opportunity and German firing points that had been detected. For the night just past, all three Soviet regiments reported that no casualties had been suffered.

At 0600 hours, LI. Armeekorps reported the nocturnal events that had occurred in 305. Infanterie-Division's sector:

> East of the gun factory, enemy assault groups were repulsed and the gully south-west of the fuel installation was cleared of infiltrating enemy groups.

– – –

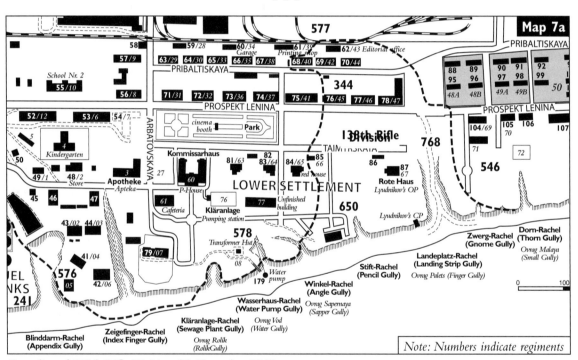

Front-line of 138th Rifle Division, 28 November, 1942.

Despite there being less pressure since the encirclement of the Germans, Lyudnikov and his men were still in a precarious position. Their forward defensive line was as follows:

768th Rifle Regiment – bank of the Volga river up to Dom 48, junction of Prospekt Lenina with the gully south-east of Dom 48, gully at the north end of Taimyrskaya.

344th Rifle Regiment – 50 metres north-west of Dom 47, along the factory spur railway, Dom 40, (excluding) Dom 41, Prospekt Lenina.

650th Rifle Regiment – southern edge of the garden, 150 metres to the east of Dom 41, bank of the Volga river at the water-pump gully.

In addition, 138th Rifle Division reported to 62nd Army that "the delivery of ammunition and rations by boat, protected by heavy bombardments, is not fulfiling the requirements of the units. The crossing is made difficult by the floating ice." The Germans tried their utmost to prevent any boats crossing the Volga in their own sectors, but

Grenadier-Regiment 578's advanced position on the Volga cliff enabled it to survey vast stretches of the river. Hauptmann Rettenmaier reported that "at midday, getting towards 1300 hours, the Russians some two kilometres south of us set out to cross the Volga in boats. We ourselves can't do anything about it, so I reported this incident to regiment." The regiment passed this information on to 79. Infanterie-Division, in whose sector the boats were crossing, but that division's own observers had already spotted the small craft. Of much more concern was another development that had been spotted: Artillerie-Regiment 179 reported that "on the opposite bank of the Volga, brisk lorry and vehicular traffic has been observed. One lorry was carrying pontoons… Smaller boats crossed over several times. The construction of a landing stage has been established in grid square 80a. The Volga carries pack-ice along its edges."

The last thing the Germans needed was for the Soviets to erect a bridge across the river, but as winter wore on, the Volga ice would become thicker and thicker, and soon, the whole mass would freeze over and form a natural bridge across the broad Volga. It was only a matter of time. Until then, everything would be done to hinder Soviet crossings.

- - -

The Soviet tactic of concentrating their fire on active German embrasures was having an effect, as briefly mentioned by Rettenmaier:

> Our opponent is causing us discomfort at the moment. There are casualties every day… Führer Decree: 'Hold the bulwark on the Volga; he will do everything in his power to ease the burden of our situation.' The Army commander General Paulus added his own words to the order: 'From tomorrow, there will only be half rations.'

The Führer Decree was transmitted to all 6. Armee divisions on 27 November: "Stalingrad, with its positions, will be held until relieved." Paulus's addendum stated that the army had been surrounded but its positions would not be given up: measures were being initiated to break through to them from the outside. For the first time, the troops were fully aware of the perilous situation they were in. Hauptmann Rettenmaier struggled with the conflicting messages from higher command and tried to make sense of it all. The conflict between hope, conviction of the need to perform one's duty and the visibly deteriorating conditions caused him angst. Rettenmaier had a paternal relationship with his soldiers and at 51 years of age, he was in fact older than many of their fathers. His sons were in the same age groups as his own soldiers, and this, combined with his decades as a teacher, made him see them almost as his own children. He felt a massive responsibility to look after them, provide for them and guide them, so Hitler's 'hold on' order promised to lighten his burden by providing some direction to the confused situation. They just needed to sit tight and wait for help to come. In reality, however, his men would have to 'hold on' with half rations because on 26 November, LI. Armeekorps issued a directive to its subordinate divisions reducing the daily ration scale. With immediate effect, each man's daily ration would consist of: 400 grams of bread (normally 750 grams); 120 grams of meat or horseflesh; half the standard allocation of vegetables (normally 250 grams); 30 grams of fat (normally 60 grams) or three-fifths of the standard allocation of jam (normally up to 200 grams); the evening meal was still the full standard allocation, as was sugar (40 grams); salt was half of the standard allocation (normally 15 grams); three servings of beverages, thinned, if need be; and finally, the soldier's staple, cigarettes and cigars, were issued in half portions (normally 7 cigarettes or 2 cigars). Divisions were to report the quantities of their existing stock to LI. Armeekorps by 29 November.

On top of the reduced rations was the order to cut back ammunition consumption. LI. Armeekorps issued a memorandum to this effect at 2240 hours the previous evening. It stated:

> Because the operational measures of OKH require a certain amount of time, the fate of the army depends, in the first instance, on ammunition. Together with the supply expected to arrive via aerial transport, ammunition stocks must be conserved by extreme thriftiness so that there is enough to last until the ring of encirclement is broken open. If that does not happen, then a state of defencelessness will arise, that is, the army will be destroyed. Everyone must be made clear about that. It is therefore essential to achieve the greatest possible benefit with the smallest usage of ammunition. This must be instilled in every soldier!

After this, several specific points were raised:

> Ammunition is only to be fired in order to destroy a target. Each larger target that is destroyed (mortars, anti-tanks guns, machine-guns, large numbers of men, etc.) is to be reported to regiment etc. and expenditure of ammunition specified.

> Only definitely recognised targets – not supposed ones – are to be combated.

> Fire is only to be opened at an effective range. Keep calm! Aim accurately or establish firing data. Strict fire discipline!

> Allow enemy concentrations to approach and then catch them with surprise fire. The effect is then so much larger, ammunition consumption so much smaller.

> Particularly valuable to us is the artillery ammunition transported in small quantities by air. The guidelines provided therefore apply to it to a great extent. Hold back with barrage fire. Only use artillery fire if infantry fire is not sufficient. Under no circumstances fire at individual people or reconnaissance patrols with artillery. Preferably only on recognised enemy concentrations, preparations or heavy weapons at favourable distances. I ask that ammunition consumption be monitored with special attention and strictness to ensure that tight fire discipline is applied in accordance with these guidelines.

> Success will then not be absent: the army will repel all hostile attacks and hold out until the relief armies are near.

Ample evidence from Soviet records, however, shows that the Germans ranged around Lyudnikov's Island did not ease back on the trigger. For example, an entry from the war diary of 138th Rifle Division states:

> The enemy continues to lay down methodical fire from his small arms and machine-guns. Due to heavy fire on the boats, they were unable to bring sufficient rations and ammunition for the division. The crossings are also being hindered by ice on the river. Communication with neighbouring formations of 138th Rifle Division are non-existent.

The Soviet ferry traffic was a 'definitely recognised target' and it seems the German fire had some success, as recorded by Rettenmaier: "[During the] night, the Russians tried to storm our positions but were repulsed in hand-to-hand combat. On the Volga we destroyed two boats, one with an anti-tank shell and the other by machine-gun fire."

Casualties for 28 November, 1942:	
138th Rifle Division:	no figures available
305. Infanterie-Division: 1 man killed, 1 officer and 6 men wounded	

29 November, 1942

The Germans did not cease persistent machine-gun fire on the river crossings by day or by night. In the darkness, outposts high on the Volga cliff raked the channel with fire whenever they heard what they supposed was an oar splashing or a rowlock squeaking. Most of the time, however, it was ice floes scraping together, causing small chunks to break off and drop into the water… but the German gunners sometimes got lucky. As soon as they were sure they'd caught a boat, streams of bullets arched down on to the hapless boat and its crew. Surprisingly, more often than not, the boat escaped when it slowly pushed into the dead-angle of the cliffs or behind an intervening bluff. By these means, 138th Rifle Division received a trickle of supplies, just enough to keep it alive. Soon, even this life-line would shut down. It was only a matter of time. The division nervously noted in its daily report: "Ice floes have appeared on the Volga, which hindered the crossing of the boats."

– – –

As was becoming the daily routine, German machine-guns fired on the Soviet formations. An increase in German artillery fire was also reported, and this was compounded when Soviet artillery fire fell short and landed within Soviet lines, mostly along the river bank. Two men of the platoon guarding Lyudnikov's command post were wounded.

Throughout the day, Grenadier-Regiment 578 fired on the forward defensive area of 650th Rifle Regiment with mortars from Haus 84, the Kindergarten and the unfinished building. Snipers and submachine-gunners were also active. Grenades were thrown at the Rolik group and the water pump. Pechenyuk's riflemen spotted individual German soldiers and groups of 3-5 men running in the area of the transformer hut: they were immediately taken under fire. All Soviet regiments, whilst continuously keeping a watch on the Germans, returned small arms and machine-gun fire and directed heavy bursts of fire at German emplacements. Two of Pechenyuk's men were wounded by snipers and mortar fire.

– – –

In his diary notes, Hauptmann Rettenmaier recorded that day's events:

For us, today was just a day like any other… Slamming down in the ruins around us – as on every day between 0900 and 1200 – are artillery shells. Great chunks of masonry pelt down upon our weakly protected cellar roof. The men sit or sleep around the oven. It's cold outside: 15 to 21 degrees below zero. We do have a receiver, which keeps us in touch with what is going on at home. We eavesdrop on the same melodies as our loved ones at home… if only we could speak to them over the ether or just briefly say: 'We are alive'.

Our situation is just like that of a condemned man who has a stay of execution and does not know when the judgement will be carried out. Yet, we are confident. The Führer will break us out of this encirclement.

Initially, most of the division's men believed they would escape the Stalingrad mousetrap, but that belief changed as the days wore on. Oberleutnant Staiger of 3./Pi.Btl.305 recalls:

Our morale became miserable after the encirclement. We spoke openly amongst each other, saying that this war would ultimately be lost even though we believed in the catchphrase: 'The army is surrounded. Hold on, the Führer will get you out!' But even that hope very soon disappeared.

Casualties for 29 November, 1942:
138th Rifle Division and 305. Infanterie-Division: no figures available

30 November, 1942

The small groups of Germans seen running about near the transformer hut the previous day had a specific purpose. Fully aware that boats crossing the river were safe once they entered the dead-angle of the Volga cliffs, German sector commanders decided to position several machine-guns closer to the water to interdict the river traffic. It was easier said than done because the cliffs and river bank below the transformer hut were Soviet-held territory and intrusion was at great risk to one's life. Regardless, a squad of intrepid machine-gunners and grenadiers set out. In its daily report, 138th Rifle Division wrote: "In the area of the transformer hut, a small enemy group with two light machine-guns tried to get down to the Volga to prevent the supply boats from crossing but 650th Rifle Regiment totally annihilated them."

The transformer hut still exists today and still occupies a dominant position atop the cliffs.

Little did those brave but doomed German machine-gunners know that no boats would arrive during the night. The frost and drift-ice had increased and became especially dense, preventing the boats from getting through to Lyudnikov. The rowboats certainly could not completely satisfy the division's ammunition and rations needs, but they rendered considerable aid. 107th Independent Pontoon-Bridge Battalion, which provided the crews for these boats, sustained heavy losses. In the 10 day period from 21 to 30 November, 1942, the battalion lost 6 dead and 18 wounded. For these same days, they made 23 boat trips, transported 80 reinforcements, two portable radio sets and corresponding battery packs, 13 tonnes of ammunition and food, and evacuated 70 wounded men. Boldly carrying out the dangerous task each night were the boat crews of Lieutenant Kalyanov, Military Technician 1st Rank M.V. Bondarchuk, and also soldiers Shestakov, Dyusenov, Voloshin, Shibayev, Grebenyuk, Myshkin, Yeremeyev and Osipov – all of whom were eventually decorated for valour. On 30 November, 1942, thick drift-ice again curtailed the supply runs. Recollecting the heroic voyages to 138th Rifle Division, Lyudnikov later wrote that the "veterans of 138th Red Banner Rifle Division bow their greying heads before the bright memory of the soldier-pontoniers and seamen of the Volga flotilla. Forwarding us cargo by fishing boats and armoured boats, they knew what we needed…"

– – –

The Germans did not launch any attacks during the day but occasionally fired on the Soviet formations. They targeted the defensive formations of 650th Rifle Regiment with mortars from the unfinished building and heavy mortars from the Barrikady factory. Machine-guns in Haus 79 and a nest located 40-50 metres north of the unfinished building kept the Volga under fire. Individual Germans were again spotted running about near the transformer hut. Snipers were also active. Pechenyuk's regiment lost five men to wounds.

– – –

Hauptmann Rettenmaier recorded his thoughts in another letter:

In four weeks time the days of Christmas will lie behind us. Yesterday was the first day of Advent. Let Advent continue to retain its meaning for us and let it ring out in the bright light of our regained freedom.

Russians planes drop leaflets: 'You are encircled and the Red Army has the mission to destroy you'. Thereafter, the text follows with the usual offer to desert.

When the food-carriers come at night, they are bombarded with questions. What is the situation, how is it looking? They want to know if a Hungarian cavalry division is on its way (from the Kalmuck steppe). Yesterday, the Russians came across the Volga in several boats. This time they were further upstream and a heavy machine-gun opened fire. The neighbour on our left did not stir. Just now, at around 1000 hours, the Russian cannon begin to curse us again.

Casualties for 30 November, 1942:	
138th Rifle Division:	no figures available
305. Infanterie-Division:	3 men killed, 15 men wounded

1 December, 1942

At midnight, Soviet observers spotted activity near the unfinished building. Apparently, the Germans there were receiving reinforcements. Lyudnikov also used the opportunity to plug a few holes in his defensive line. At 0200, Major Pechenyuk received Order No. 088 from divisional headquarters:

Close the gap between the left flank of 344th Rifle Regiment and the right flank of 650th Rifle Regiment by putting a group of 5 men, led by a mid-level commander, in the area of the destroyed tank.

This gap between the two regiments lay in the pulverised park alongside Prospekt Lenina. Sitting mangled and abandoned on the road was the hulk of a German assault gun knocked out during one of the final assaults. It was a dangerous sector for Soviet defenders because the Germans in Haus 75 [Dom 41] easily observed any movement in the park and could lash the area with fierce automatic fire. Nevertheless, it was a gap in the defensive line and Lyudnikov wanted it filled.

Once again, the day passed relatively quietly. The war diary of 138th Rifle Division states:

The enemy continues to fire with machine-guns and rifles against our divisional formations. The division's units exchanged small arms and machine-gun fire with the enemy.

The combat journal of 650th Rifle Regiment provides further detail:

In front of the regiment's defence line, the enemy has created a greater number of resistance nests, reserve positions and berms above the Volga river and its island, arranging his firing points along an advantageous line.

Machine-gun fire comes from the transformer hut, the long red house, the unfinished building and further to the right from under the broken tractor. Activity shown by enemy snipers. The barking of dogs is heard periodically from the enemy's direction.

The regiment, holding its defensive line, keeps a close watch on enemy movements and directs small arms and machine-gun fire at his emplacements.

Personnel of the regiment staff received hot food two times during the day.

The supply situation was still strained. As noted on the previous day, the ice floes on the Volga were getting larger and larger. With the first day of December, however, the Volga became covered by a thin layer of ice through which only one boat was able to push through with much difficulty.

– – –

The sombre mood of the encircled Germans lifted during the day, at least temporarily. Hauptmann Rettenmaier wrote that "the Führer Decree was announced to everyone. It is clear and confident. It proclaims that just as at Kharkov, this assault will also end with the Russians' destruction. The closing sentence of the Army order begins by saying: 'The army is encircled. Comrades, it is not your fault. Remain where you stand, the Führer will smash through the ring and release you'."

The full text of Hitler's edict reads:

The fight for Stalingrad is reaching its climax, the enemy has broken through the rear of the German troops and is desperately trying to regain possession of this decisive bulwark on the Volga.

In this hour, my thoughts, and those of the entire German nation, are with you.

You must under all circumstances hold the conquered positions in Stalingrad, captured under the leadership of your energetic generals and with so much blood.

It must be our unshakeable resolve, as in the spring at Kharkov, to see that this Russian breakthrough will in the end – through our initiated measures – lead to their destruction.

What lies within my power will be done to support you in your heroic struggle.

Paulus's addendum to Hitler's decree went as follows:

The army is encircled. It is not your fault. Tough as always, you have prevailed, even when the enemy is located in our rear. We have overcome him here. He will not attain his goal of destroying us here.

I must demand much from you: along with exertions and privations in the cold and snow, you must remain firm and cheerful, resisting all attacks by their superior numbers.

The Führer has promised help. We must hold on until it arrives. If the whole army stands together, we will make it.

Therefore hold out, the Führer will break us out.

These two announcements boosted morale but it was another piece of news that dispelled gloomy thoughts, as Rettenmaier notes:

It is also said that a radio message has been received which said: 'Hold on, I'm coming! von Manstein'. We are confident, even if we need to endure a few days longer and have to restrict ourselves in all things, because knowing with certainty that help is on its way allows us to endure anything.

With a great weight lifted off his shoulders and his spirit enlightened, Rettenmaier paid a visit to his front-line troops, and even risked calling in on the garrison of the transformer hut:

> For us the night was quiet. I was with comrades in another position. Every night the hand grenades fly. At the moment, we are only 15 metres from the enemy. We are digging ever closer towards him. It is now 2030. Our foe today commenced his artillery fire an hour earlier than on previous days. At 2300 hours there is irregular interdiction fire, for us it appears unplanned but it has been cunningly calculated.

Casualties for 1 December, 1942:	
138th Rifle Division:	no figures available
305. Infanterie-Division:	3 men killed, 4 men wounded

2 December, 1942

In the early morning hours, while it was still dark, the commander of Grenadier-Regiment 578, Oberstleutnant Max Liesecke, paid a visit to the front-line. He also chanced an inspection of one of the most advanced – and crucial – strongpoints: Haus 79. It had sweeping vistas covering almost 270 degrees and machine-gun fire could be just as easily laid down on any part of that arc. Further steps had been taken to reinforce the building: a long trench was dug towards it, windows and doorways were solidly barricaded and telephone lines were securely laid. While Liesecke was in the building, the Soviets began their fireworks display quite early. Liesecke rode out the storm and only then returned to his command post.

Liesecke's regiment was ordered to give up a small part of its strength on this day. Order Nr. 123, issued by Gruppe Seydlitz[11], ordered that "Sturmkompanie 44.ID be extracted from 305.I.D. and returned to its division in Baburkin. The division will receive another Romanian company in return".

In a strength report on 26 November, the Sturmkompanie still possessed 38 men. On 3 December, they were extracted from their positions east of the Barrikady and – according to the divisional history of 44. Infanterie-Division – "returned from the operations in Stalingrad with about 30 men" under the command of Unteroffizier Janssen. In recognition of their efforts, the following men of the Sturmkompanie would be awarded the Iron Cross Second Class on 26 December, 1942: Obergefreiter Josef Egerth, Gefreiters Walter Simanovsky[12], Josef Schuster and Georg Boemisch[13], Grenadiers Johann Hoh, Georg Reigl, Paul Kappel, Emil Hertel[14] and Emil Appelt[15], Oberpionier Martin Stumvoll[16], and Pioniers

---

11. A temporary designation for Seydlitz's LI. Armeekorps
12. Simanovsky, Gefreiter Walter, StuKp. 44; born 20 January, 1922 in Koszicken. Killed in action, 14 December, 1942 in Stalingrad.
13. Boemisch, Gefreiter Georg, StuKp. 44; born 21 April 1922. Killed in action, 28 May, 1944 in Italy.
14. Hertel, Grenadier Emil, StuKp. 44; born 30 December, 1923 in Schönwald-Rehau. Killed in action, 16 December, 1942 in Stalingrad.
15. Appelt, Grenadier Emil, StuKp. 44; born 11 June, 1922 in Rauschenfeld. Killed in action, 7 January, 1943 in Stalingrad.
16. Stumvoll, Oberpionier Martin, StuKp. 44 (3./Pi.Btl.80); born 11 September 1921. Died 2004 in Wien.

Josef Summer and Johann Hoffmann. Their wounded commander, Oberleutnant Willi Kindler, was awarded the Iron Cross First Class on the same date.

It was a case of out of the frying pan and into the fire for the 30-odd survivors of the Sturmkompanie. The Austrians of 44. Infanterie-Division faced brutal fighting in the snowy expanses west of Stalingrad, and nowhere was it fiercer than around Baburkin. Gefreiter Walter Simanovsky was killed there on 14 December, Grenadier Emil Hertel on 16 December and Grenadier Emil Appelt on 7 January, 1943. After performing valiantly in the devastated gun factory and surviving the most fearsome combat, the remaining members of the Sturmkompanie faded away in the icy wastes. Only those fortunate enough to be wounded and flown out bear witness to the Austrians' sacrifice in the Barrikady.

– – –

In accordance with Lyudnikov's order to plug a hole on the regimental boundary, a group of five men from 650th Rifle Regiment, under the command of Lieutenant Miroshchnichenko, moved into the park 100 metres to the east of Haus 76 [Dom 45]. The stately birch trees were now just splintered trunks and the ground between them was riven by craters, trenches and dug-outs. Beams and planks salvaged from nearby houses were used to reinforce the shelters but relentless artillery fire had churned everything into the earth. Lieutenant Miroshchnichenko and his men set up a defensive site and established communications with 344th Rifle Regiment through a trench that ran across Prospekt Lenina. The fate of the lieutenant and his men is unknown.

– – –

The situation along the front-line did not change. The Germans continued to dig in and occasionally fired rifles and machine-guns. For the destruction of the German firing points and formations, Lyudnikov ordered his artillery to act offensively and – in the first instance – annihilate each and every enemy artillery and mortar emplacement. His rifle regiments received a similar order. At 1230 hours, Order No. 089 was issued by divisional headquarters: "Destroy observable enemy targets and keep firing every type of weapon at probable targets. Force the enemy to expend his ammunition more quickly." By this time, the Soviets were aware of the German supply problem and their need to conserve ammunition.

In its combat journal, 650th Rifle Regiment noted:

> The enemy ground troops along the regiment's front-line did not carry out any active actions, limiting himself to occasional gun and mortar fire. By observation it was established that the enemy is working on strengthening his resistance nests. A group of 15 enemy soldiers, in camouflage, was spotted running from the white 5-storeyed house[17] into the former command post house [Haus 83] that lies north-east of the P-shaped building [Kommissarhaus].
>
> The regiment continues to hold its defence line. Continuous observation of enemy movements is conducted and small arms and machine-gun fire is sent out.
>
> Total losses from all units is 14 men, of those, 5 are wounded.

– – –

A fortnight after being encircled, the Germans were astounded that Soviet soldiers were still absconding from their units, as noted by Rettenmaier in his diary: "At 2100 hours, two

17. Possibly the Apotheke.

deserters came over to us. They crawled through our lines near the neighbour's position (fuel depot)." It is amazing to think that with the Germans under siege, in trouble and beginning to starve, any Soviet would go over to the enemy. And this phenomenon would continue well into January. The ordinary Soviet soldier must have been terrorised or severely disillusioned with the Red Army and the Soviet state. They had been lied to so often that they simply could not believe it was the Germans who were surrounded: they thought their officers were misleading them and that it was they themselves who were encircled.

Casualties for 2 December, 1942:	
138th Rifle Division:	no figures available
305. Infanterie-Division:	2 men killed, 8 men wounded

3 December, 1942

Since the morning, 62nd Army had begun the final destruction of the encircled German forces. The remnants of 95th and 138th Rifle Divisions would also play their part. Lyudnikov had Order No. 090 sent out to 650th and 768th Rifle Regiments to ready themselves for offensive actions that had been planned since 23 November. The artillery preparation commenced at 0600 hours and, according to German sources, continued for three hours, as noted in Rettenmaier's diary:

> Now in these morning hours (0600 – 0900), the interdiction fire rises at times to a crescendo. It suggests an attack will be imminent. At 0815 hours there is a hand grenade battle to our right. In the rear the ring remains closed. There is still no freedom, still no mail getting through. In the morning we look down at the Volga. With satisfaction we realise that it is not frozen over. What if the pressure from across the frozen river were also to increase? Our mission is to prevail or die at the place upon which we now stand.

Rettenmaier's fatalistic tone shows that most of the men accepted their mission but were worried that they would soon have to withstand heavy attacks from across the Volga as well. For the moment, however, and for the first time, they had to repel Soviet attacks from a defensive posture. At 1030 hours, small storm groups on the right and left flanks of 138th Rifle Division went on the offensive. The groups from 768th Rifle Regiment forced the Germans out of some bunkers 100 metres south-east of Dom 49 and moved forward 70 metre, losing 1 dead and 12 wounded. The attack by 650th Rifle Regiment did not go so well. Their available forces were few and their objectives were grand: they had orders to capture the unfinished house, the transformer hut, the Kommissarhaus and the Apotheke. Four heavily armed and fortified strongpoints. When the storm group of Senior-Lieutenant Shkarina rose up, they were immediately struck by overwhelming machine-gun fire and suffered heavy losses. Pent-up German frustration was vented upon the attackers. Pechenyuk later reported that "during the moment of our group's advance, an enemy assault troop opened up heavy fire". In a matter of minutes, Shkarina's group lost 8 men, about 60% of its strength. The assault failed utterly. Senior-Lieutenant Toporkov's group attempted to go on the offensive but also could not advance. The regiment's losses were 2 men killed, plus 3 officers, 2 NCOs and 4 men wounded, a total of 11 men.

At 1100 hours, after the miscarriage of the attack, the Germans continuously bombarded the forward Soviet defensive line with machine-gun and mortar fire. German emplacements sent out sweeping fire, raking any actual or supposed Soviet position.

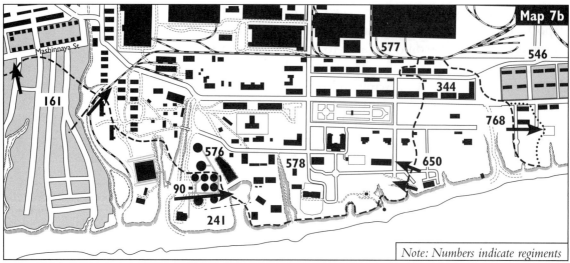

The assaults of 95th and 138th Rifle Divisions, morning of 3 December, 1942.

The hand grenade battle mentioned by Rettenmaier was in fact the attack of 95th Rifle Division. Rather than coordinating their attacks, the two Soviet divisions staggered their starting times. The following is from the combat journal of 95th Rifle Division:

> Implementing army staff's Order No. 202 and divisional Order No. 27, 1 and 2/90th Rifle Regiment and 161st Rifle Regiment launched an attack at 0800. Having reached the wire entanglement, they were stopped by well-sited small-arms and machine-gun fire.

> 90th Rifle Regiment operated in small groups. A group of 10 men had captured a dug-out near the fuel tanks by 1100.

> The left flank of 161st Rifle Regiment advanced 25-30 metres and approached an emplacement on Mashinnaya Street where they were stopped by machine-gun fire.

> 241st Rifle Regiment held its previously occupied positions and provided cover fire for the storm groups of 90th Rifle Regiment.

Casualties were serious for the meagre results: 161st Rifle Regiment lost 41 dead and wounded, 90th Rifle Regiment lost 27 and 241st Rifle Regiment lost 5 men. One of those, however, was its commander, Major Ivan Kuzmich Kalmykov, who was killed. He had commanded the regiment since 28 September, 1942 after the previous commander, Major Dannil Vladimirovich Dunayevsky, had been wounded. Kalmykov had steered the regiment through its most difficult ordeals. Taking command of the regiment after his death was Major Nikolai Petrovich Budarin[18]. Born in May 1910 in Chakino, in the Tambov province of Siberia, Budarin was a passionate athlete with uncommon organisational abilities. He served in the Soviet Army from 1932-1934, and then from 1939 onwards, participating in the Winter War in Finland from 1939-1940 as a battalion politruk. He was at the front from the very first day of Barbarossa and fought around Moscow in late 1941. With his dashing appearance and aggressive spirit, he invigorated the combat-weary men of 241st Rifle Regiment.

Casualties for 3 December, 1942:	
138th Rifle Division:	3 killed, 21 wounded, a total of 24 men
305. Infanterie-Division:	11 men killed, 14 men wounded, 4 men missing

18. Budarin, Major Nikolai Petrovich, HotSU; 241st RR; born May 1910 in Chakino. Died of wounds, 6 November 1943.

4 December, 1942

"Last night the food carrier brought some news," Rettenmaier wrote in his diary, "and as of tomorrow, we will receive our full rations; the mail should also arrive, the ring has been broken open. We don't know for certain if the news is correct. However, we believe it because it is our most fervent hope. We can breathe again. The nightmare feeding upon our nerves has retreated."

This false and ultimately cruel piece of information raised hopes and, when eventually proven untrue, produced an even deeper depression amongst the men. To top it all off, Rettenmaier's fear about the Volga freezing over – voiced in his diary only the previous day – came true. Throughout the night of 3-4 December, the channel between the west bank and Zaitsevsky Island iced over solidly. This was an event that was equally welcomed and dreaded by the Soviets. The obvious benefit was that the dangerous period of floating ice was over and supplies could now be brought directly across the frozen channel. In fact, regular communications with Zaitsevsky Island began immediately during the night but because of accurate enemy sniper fire, the movement of people over the Volga and communications with the opposite bank was getting harder. It was practically impossible during the day. However, this easing of Lyudnikov's supply and communications situation was offset by the fact that 62nd Army staff, Chuikov in particular, held the fear that Lyudnikov's Island might be lost when the ice froze because the Germans could use this moment to capture the real island in the Volga, Zaitsevsky Island. One of Chuikov's staff officers, Lieutenant Anatoli Mereshko[19], remembers there was an even bigger fear that the Germans could do the same thing in the south of city by capturing Golodny Island and then continue on to encircle the entire 62nd Army and, in Mereshko's blunt phrase, 'cart us all away'. In order to prevent the enemy from encircling 138th Rifle Division, Chuikov had ordered the 400th Machine-Gun and Artillery Battalion to take up defence on Zaitsevsky Island back in November. But the Germans did not even make the attempt. Even at this stage of the battle, when the Germans had been surrounded for a fortnight, the threat of fresh attacks being thrown against their depleted units was still very palpable to the Soviets.

– – –

The situation was without change on Lyudnikov's Island. The Germans lay down heavy rifle and machine-gun fire and prevented the movement of Soviet units. Throughout the day, 650th Rifle Regiment's defensive sector was fired upon by machine-guns from the direction of the transformer hut, 30-40 metres to the south-east there, and by barrages from company mortars out of the area of the unfinished house. Observers noticed that every day, one medium tank and one 'tankette'[20] would approach the Kommissarhaus. It was presumed that ammunition and rations were being brought forward to the building's garrison in these tanks. Shortly after, the tanks would crawl forward, fire at the water pump, and then trundle off back into the Barrikady factory.

Lyudnikov ordered that the NKVD blocking detachment and reconnaissance company – which were holding defensive sectors in 650th Rifle Regiment's area – be replaced. The reason for this is not clear because Pechenyuk's regiment was very weak: the group of

---

19. Mereshko, Colonel-General Anatoli Grigoryevich, staff 62nd Army; born 7 August, 1921 in Novocherkassk. Still alive in 2006.

20. This could be one of the T-60 or T-70 tanks used by 305. Infanterie-Division

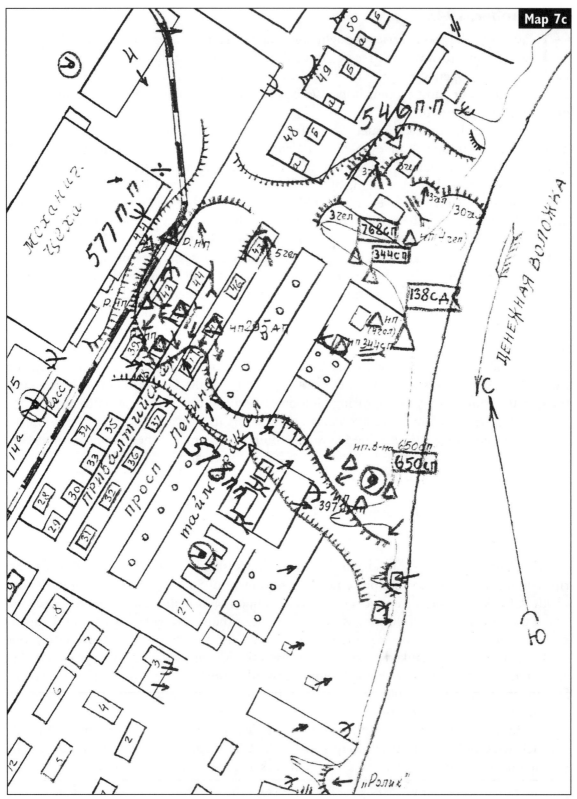

A sketch by 138th Rifle Division shows their situation, 4 December, 1942. German and Soviet weapons are depicted (arrow = light MG; semi-circle with stroke = heavy MG), as are Soviet observation posts (depicted as triangles).

Senior-Lieutenant Toporkov had 9 men, the group of Captain Mironov had 6 men and the Rolik group had 10 men. The strongest unit available to Pechenyuk was the NKVD blocking detachment, which still had a strength of 33 men. Later in the day, the regiment received a further order from divisional headquarters:

> During the course of the night of 5-6 December, the remnants of the engineer battalion that occupy a sector within 650th Rifle Regiment's area will be relieved.

– – –

Hauptmann Rettenmaier wrote up another entry in his diary:

> The enemy is still restless today but he is by no means as wasteful with his ammunition as he was yesterday. When the ammunition supply has been secured again, we will perform our former activities. Only when we get the enemy out of our face will we take up quieter winter quarters.

Casualties for 4 December, 1942:	
138th Rifle Division:	22 killed, 36 wounded, a total of 58 men
305. Infanterie-Division:	5 men killed, 16 men wounded

5 December, 1942

Taking advantage of the thin ice bridge across the Volga channel during the night, 138th Rifle Division received replacements in the form of 120 men from 149th Reserve Rifle Regiment. The ice sheet then slipped underwater and halted further crossings. Lyudnikov ordered that all enemy snipers interfering with the movement of people across the channel from Zaitsevsky Island be eliminated by nightfall.

One of those snipers was Oberleutnant Hans Wegener[21], commander 1.(Radfahr) Schwadron of Major Heinrich Siedentopf's[22] Panzerjäger-Abteilung 389. He and his men were in position along the Volga cliff north of Lyudnikov's Island and had unhindered views over the river and Zaitsevsky Island:

> When the pocket formed around Stalingrad, the two panzerjäger companies were detailed to the Don, together with my heavy machine-gun section. I never heard anything from them again. Major Siedentopf remained in the pocket but I had practically nothing to do with him because my Schwadron, or I should say the remnants of it, were continually subordinated to other units, which was not a lot of fun. We had the possibility of shooting over the Volga with our telescopic-equipped carbines. We German snipers were at least as good as the Russians!

Oblt. Hans Wegener, 1.(Radf.)/Pz.Jäg.Abt.389.

21. Wegener, Oberleutnant Hans, 1./Pz.Jäg.Abt.389; born 22 January 1912. Still alive in 2003.
22. Siedentopf, Major Heinrich, Pz.Jäg.Abt.389; born 17 April, 1904 Jerxheim. Died 28 April, 1943 in Oranki POW camp.

Lyudnikov's Island, as viewed from the positions of 389. Infanterie-Division to the north. Many landmarks can be recognised: 1. Transformer hut; 2. Haus 79 [Dom 07]; 3. Unfinished building; 4. Buildings along Taimyrskaya Street; 5. Theatre Park; and 6. Buildings along Prospekt Lenina. The importance of the first two strongpoints is obvious.

In its combat journal, 650th Rifle Regiment recorded the day's events:

> Enemy forces did not show an offensive actions during the day. The regiment's defensive area was periodically fired on by machine-guns and by mortar from the area of unfinished house. Grenades were thrown at our forward line. Regimental formations continue to improve the defences – separate entrenchments and communication passages were dug. Small arms and machine-gun fire were also placed on enemy firing points.

Pechenyuk's 'regiment' had a total headcount of 89 men on west bank of the Volga equipped with 65 rifles, 15 PPSH, 1 mortar, 2 anti-tank rifles and 6 light machine-guns. Their ammunition stocks were 7000 rifle cartridges, 7500 PPSH cartridges, 110 mortar rounds, 50 anti-tank rifle cartridges, 200 grenades and some signal rockets.

Its losses were 1 sergeant and 2 men wounded, plus 1 sergeant-major evacuated due to illness, a total of 4 men.

– – –

"Throughout the entire day, the enemy has been quieter than usual," recalls Hauptmann Rettenmaier. "There were two deserters during the night. They have had enough of the war. In Russia it appears that the people must often go hungry. Food cannot be obtained by using money, only by trade. We have not received mail and our austerity as well as economy measures remain in place. Yet everyone at his post remains confident."

Despite some disappointment at the higher-level commands for allowing the situation to develop, most Germans were convinced it would be resolved in their favour. Oberzahlmeister Bauchspiess, Pionier-Bataillon 336, expressed the thoughts of many:

This detour to Stalingrad could have become bad for us. A mighty battle has raged around us for 14 days now and our supply is restricted to air transportation. There should already be lanes broken through and soon it will be the Russians, rather than us, who are encircled.

The situation was very bad for days. One rumour chased another, until news finally arrived about the situation and the rations, then the men calmed themselves down again. We are well provisioned, so with some restrictions we can hold out for a long time. Direct danger is still far away. Given the worst, we can still break out.

At the two week mark since being surrounded, cumulative casualty figures were reported to 6. Armee for the period 21 November to 5 December: 305. Infanterie-Division had incurred 268 while their northern neighbour had 162.

Casualties for 5 December, 1942:	
138th Rifle Division:	3 killed, 10 wounded, a total of 13 men
305. Infanterie-Division:	3 men killed, 7 men wounded

6 December, 1942

Despite the worsening supply situation, it seems that 305. Infanterie-Division were profligate with their use of ammunition. This from the war diary of 138th Rifle Division:

The enemy continues to fire at the division's formations with mortars, rifles and machine-guns. He sometimes also shoots at the division command post and Zaitsevsky Island with six-barrelled mortars.

And from the combat journal of 650th Rifle Regiment:

The enemy undertook no offensive actions during the day. Small arms and machine-guns from the ruins of Dom 39 and 38, and also from the P- and L-shaped buildings to the south, fire on the Volga river and the island. The Rolik group has grenades periodically thrown at them. The regiment conducts round-the-clock observation of enemy movements and bombards the front-line and enemy firing points. No movement is noticed. The regiment has no losses.

German units continued to entrench themselves deeper into the Barrikady soil. Also, according to Rettenmaier, they readied themselves for an 'operation':

Foggy weather, thawing snow. We are digging approach and communication trenches and preparing for the next operation. Hopefully we will attain our goal quickly without spilling too much blood. The rumour goes as follows: when we attain our objective, we will go to either the Crimea or France.

Unfortunately, no German records exist to show if there were plans for some sort of offensive operation or whether this was just another rumour doing the rounds.

- - -

Further south, around the fuel tanks, matters were quiet, except for a small German raid, as reported in the combat journal of 95th Rifle Division:

The enemy has strengthened mortar bombardments on the combat ranks of our units. At midnight, on the sector of 241st Rifle Regiment, up to 6 enemy soldiers tried to approach our forward line. But small-arms and machine-gun fire partially destroyed the group, the others dropped back into Shiroki (Wide) Gully.

Holding part of this sector was Oberleutnant Eugen Hering, commander 6./Grenadier-Regiment 576 but now temporary battalion commander. A letter he penned to his parents shows the way many men coped with the difficult conditions:

> I'm writing these lines to you from a cellar of a city of ruins in which I have my battalion command post. In a few days I will return to my company because there is still a Hauptmann in the regiment who can run this battalion… At the moment, I have a proper full beard, and you would definitely be startled if you could see me. We have enough winter clothing, every man has a pair of felt boots and it has so far not been that cold here.
>
> Come what may, we will fight here until the final victory of our beloved Fatherland. In my opinion, it is not far away. […]
>
> I am so glad that I have such deep faith in our Lord because I would have despaired many times without him. I call to him when I'm in the greatest need and he has helped me again and again. Every day I pray to our Saviour that he will safely deliver me back to my dear wife and to you. Dear parents, please don't ever be sad, our Saviour will make things right and hear our prayers.

Oberleutnant Eugen Hering, 6./Gr.Rgt.576.

- - -

Combat groups were hastily formed throughout the pocket to deal with local crises. Unit integrity was a low priority: if a hole needed to be plugged, the nearest available unit was deployed. Panzerjäger battalions were particular favourites for piecemeal use – because of their tank-killing capabilities – and those that belonged to divisions defending the Volga frontage were continually parceled out to other sectors. Unteroffizier Richard Klein[23] was with Radfahrschwadron 305, which belonged to Panzerjäger-Abteilung 305. The schwadron was known as the 'Schmalspurdivision'[24] by its men:

> At the beginning of August 1942, the schwadron lay in the large Don bend in a fairly battle-weary state. I was supposed to carry out a recon patrol with my squad but I came down with a very high fever and was taken to a dressing station on a motorcycle-sidecar and from there to a field-hospital on the steppe. Dysentery was suspected. After about 2 weeks I went by train via Millerovo and Kharkov to a hospital in Poltava. A feeding tube was inserted because there was almost no gastric acid left. Despite hydrochloric acid being administered, I continued to suffer from diarrhoea. On top of all that was a high heart rate and a moderate fever. In mid- to late-October I was barely back on my feet again.
>
> With my marching orders and instructions for the army doctors ('light food, hydrochloric acid capsules and only conditionally suitable for employment') I headed towards Stalingrad. End of

---

23. Klein, Unteroffizier Richard, Radf.Schw./Pz.Jäg.Abt.305; born 18 December, 1919 in Berkheim. Still alive in 2006.
24. Trans.: 'Schmalspurdivision' = 'amateur division' or 'lightweight division'.

the line was Chir railway station. I hitched a ride with supply trucks to an assembly and distribution point in the Gorodische Gully. Following a signpost, I found a signals group of 305. Infanterie-Division. There, I learned that my Radfahr Schwadron no longer existed. Oberleutnant Giulini[25] was with the panzerjägers, Leutnant Teubert (schwadron commander during the summer) was unknown to them. Purely by chance, I found my deputy squad commander, Unteroffizier Hans Kühnert, and several men up front, attached to the infantry as a Kampfgruppe. Back with my comrades at last! A Feldwebel gave me several men and a light machine-gun. We secured an area in the forefield of the gun factory. This was about the end of November 1942. Because I felt wretched and had chronic diarrhoea a medic took me and a lightly wounded man to a dressing station in the rear. It belonged to 100. Jäger-Division. I showed a doctor my medical report. He could only shake his head.

Then I lay in some ruins with other wounded and sick men. With tea, crispbread, porridge and small pieces of meat, I got back on my feet and after a few days was attached to a squad that belonged to 100. Jäger-Division. On the night of 5-6 December I reconnoitred in front of our positions with a Leutnant. In the meantime, a firefight

Unteroffizier Richard Klein. The photo was taken in October 1942, in Poltava, just after his recovery from serious illness and shortly before heading to Stalingrad.

broke out and it intensified at daybreak. With a light machine-gun, my squad lay along the piled up remnants of a brick wall. An anti-tank gun was in position not far away. Several Russian tanks rolled diagonally toward us. Distance about 400 metres. We fired on the escorting infantry. Then a high-explosive shell detonated between the machine-gun and myself. I was just about to let loose with a captured Maxim machine-gun when I was struck by shrapnel on my left forearm and the back of my hand. My helmet was also hit. A medic was able to bandage my arm. A half-track driving past was stopped and I was loaded aboard and taken to the dressing station of a panzer division. An Unterarzt from Stuttgart looked after me and I was placed in an adjacent room. Tea and Kommissbrot were provided, and a medic gave me my 'emergency rations'. While eating, I noticed that I could only taste things quite badly. Then I came down with a fever. Days later, a swab was taken from my throat and after another two days a card was hung around my neck: diphtheria. Everything now happened quickly. I was driven to the airfield with a couple of other contagious patients. During the trip, I was repeatedly jabbed in the backside with syringes. On 16 December, I flew for the first time in my life, and indeed, flew back into my life…

Casualties for 6 December, 1942:	
138th Rifle Division:	4 killed, 7 wounded, a total of 11 men
305. Infanterie-Division:	3 men killed, 6 men wounded

---

25. Giulini de Giulino, Rittmeister Udo Karl Conte, Radf./Pz.Jäg.Abt.305; born 12 February, 1918 in Hamburg. Died 5 August, 1995 in Heidelberg.

7 December, 1942

During the night, the Volga channel again acquired a thick covering of ice capable of bearing foot traffic. Lyudnikov immediately initiated a roster for his soldiers to visit a bathhouse on Zaitsevsky Island. It was an almost unimaginable luxury. The soldiers steamed themselves for hours, received fresh clothes and underwear, and spent the night in warm lodgings. The next day they would return to the 'Island', invigorated, clean and ready to take on the Germans. No such facility was available to the Germans and the soldiers became ever thinner and ever dirtier. Nevertheless, it was still a perilous journey for those heading to the bathhouse because the Germans continued to fire methodically on the river crossing with small arms and machine-guns.

Casualties for 7 December, 1942:	
138th Rifle Division:	2 killed, 4 wounded, a total of 6 men
305. Infanterie-Division:	2 men killed, 18 men wounded

8 December, 1942

In the pitch dark night, while crossing the main channel of the Volga River which had not yet been covered by ice, a motor boat of Lyudnikov's division slammed into a large ice floe and promptly sank, taking six men with it.

Also under the cover of darkness, a group of reconnaissance men under the command of Senior-Lieutenant Novikov went out to capture a tongue in a trench they had pinpointed earlier. The group was not successful because the Germans had pulled back from the forward trenches for the night. The group came back under heavy fire but suffered no losses.

The day passed according to the now standard routine. The Germans did not undertake any offensive actions but covered Soviet defences with small arms and machine-gun fire, as well as mortar bombardments aimed mainly at the crossing site. In return, the Soviet rifle regiments held their line and fired light machine-guns and mortars at German emplacements attempting to restrict the river crossings. Pechenyuk's regiment had no losses.

- - -

Hauptmann Rettenmaier poured out his thoughts about the situation in a letter home:

Tomorrow is my birthday. I thought about where and how it was celebrated in the past and it seems as though it was not as 'great' as here.

We are still in a sticky situation. Help is on its way and is already having an impact. But it will be a few weeks yet until we are relieved in our corner of the world. The snow does hamper the rapid movement of our vehicles. There is supposed to be a gap in our rear but the road is under enemy fire. Supply can only be achieved by using aircraft. And how many would be required to supply a whole army! We still have to make sacrifices for a long time. I remember the very stupid expression: 'They must make do with what they get.' Stupidity and pride are closely wedded but what is even more bitter for us is that we must fight and sacrifice here in Stalingrad for those who think this way. Our rations are not being increased, no, quite the opposite: they are being decreased. It is necessary and we accept it even if we only get little piece of bread or several grams of horse-meat during the day. As long as it is enough to keep up our strength. The main thing is that we free ourselves. The enemy is gradually applying more pressure. The section of the Volga in front of us is frozen over and we can no longer interrupt his resupply at night. His artillery hits us ruthlessly and mercilessly. Our own artillery must economise and is only allowed to fire in an extreme emergency. It is not a good feeling to find oneself in this pocket and nothing worse can be demanded from a soldier. But we remain confident and hope once again to become cheerful. The enemy is very restless tonight. He attacked to the right and left of us. For a couple of days he has been trying to push forward against us. Every day there are casualties.

I am still in good health. If only one had more diversions. Old newspapers from early November are continually picked up and re-read. In these circumstances, Christmas will be a day like any other, but we will remind one another that our loved ones are sitting at home beneath the Christmas tree and probably thinking about us. Hopefully you at home are healthy and fresh so that any other worries besides those for your soldiers aren't a burden to you!

– – –

As the weeks dragged by and rescue seemed more distant than ever, morale amongst the trapped Germans slowly but steadily plunged. Disciplined units commanded by popular officers withstood the corrosive effects of dispiritedness and fatalism far better than poorly-led ones. A unit's commanding officer was the keystone, the source of its spirit, but even some of them were finding it difficult. Oberleutnant Staiger, 3./Pi.Btl.305, remembers:

> Most officers showed outer bravery even though they had given up hope on the inside. Naturally there were also those who covered their despondency and effected an outer arrogance. However, I once saw an officer crying bitterly about the miserable situation of his troops and from fear of what he saw coming. He had truly broken down. It was enough to make you cry! I was able to pull myself together again. We must bear in mind, however, that this was still in December, before I was wounded and flown out. What must it have been like in January?

The Germans tried to retain some sense of normality in the grim ruins of Stalingrad, not just for morale but because it also broke the monotony that set in after weeks of holding positions in the same sector. One way they did this was marking special events, like Christmas, the New Year and birthdays. In letters home, Hauptmann Rettenmaier recorded in detail how his birthday of 9 December was celebrated:

> I am still fit and well and in good health. I was able to wash and shave […] yesterday. My beard was becoming too itchy. It was an overcast day, otherwise I would have had a picture taken. In Russia there are scratchy dads – as Ottokar once said as a child. Don't worry about me as the horizon is becoming brighter, even if we must starve for a while and celebrate a less than wonderful Christmas – also without presents. This isn't important, as long as matters return to normal… I stayed up like I do most nights, even though it is dark at around 1400 hours. A Leutnant, one of the last in the regiment, kept me company. Just before midnight, I poured him a shot of cognac and when it was time, according to my watch, we drank a toast. He then stood up, rummaged around in a dark corner, found a bottle of champagne and gave it to me with best wishes from himself and his men of 4. Kompanie. It was the first surprise of the day and really gave me enormous pleasure because I never assumed that any of the soldiers knew that it was my birthday. We sampled the bottle of champagne immediately. Then the soldiers filed past and congratulated me. Thus the evening was a very pleasant surprise for me.

Rettenmaier was a popular officer and his men held him in regard. This little gathering was just the men from one company… the celebrations would continue the next day, on the day of his actual birthday.

Casualties for 8 December, 1942:	
138th Rifle Division:	6 killed, 15 wounded, a total of 21 men
305. Infanterie-Division:	4 men killed, 9 men wounded

9 December, 1942

Rettenmaier continues: "On my birthday, my commanding officer invited me for a glass of wine with him. In the afternoon a dispatch came from Hauptmann Schwarz with a bottle and a nice letter. And in the evening they brought me with my meal a bottle of wine, a box of cigars, and to eat: braised beef and macaroni. It really tasted great! The day, despite the miserable circumstances, was indeed very nice for me."

Rettenmaier thought so much of the nice letter from Hauptmann Schwarz that he tucked it in an envelope with one of his own and sent it home:

Hauptmann Rettenmaier poses for a birthday snap outside his command post in Haus 53.

> Dear Mr. Rettenmaier!
>
> It gives me the greatest pleasure to wholeheartedly wish you all the best for your birthday tomorrow. With my personal wishes I combine the no less heartfelt wishes of the entire remaining II. Bataillon for their dear old commander.
>
> In particular we all wish that the new year of your life keeps you just as healthy and resilient, so that we young men will continue to have such an example and role model.
>
> Our second fondest wish is that the new year of your life brings you fresh successes with I. Bataillon and that soldier's luck continues to remain true to you.
>
> If this evening you are now among your soldiers in a cellar or dug-out, even if your birthday is being celebrated under some 'formal' conditions, then you should know that your old battalion is with you with heartfelt wishes and hopes to make the hours somewhat more homely with this small greeting.
>
> Yours H. Schwarz

- - -

Gefreiter Willi Füssinger from Pionier-Bataillon 305 was adjusting to life in a new company and his thoughts were already turned toward Christmas:

> Hope and the belief for better times is our most ardent Christmas wish. We hope that by Christmas a light will begin to sparkle for us by being able to see better times. Here in Russia there is only life or death. But the blessing of the All Mighty will bestow us with continued life.
>
> Due to the disbandment of my company I unfortunately lost my previous occupation, therefore, I am now practically in field work again. Fortunately, however, in my new company, to which we temporarily belong, I have received a lovely task: a large number of sleighs must be built for the division. There are still some carpenters who can help with that. My previous company will be re-established in the foreseeable future and then I will have my old work to do.

- - -

138th Rifle Division summed up the day as follows:

The enemy has not moved over to the offensive. His artillery fire has discontinued. The enemy occasionally lays down heavy mortar fire on the area of the division command post. The enemy air force was not active. The enemy is entrenching in front of the division. 138th Rifle Division is sending methodical small arms and machine-gun fire against the enemy, forcing him to expend his ammunition.

The combat journal of 650th Rifle Regiment offers more detail:

Throughout the day, the enemy fired at the combat ranks of our formations with small arms and machine-guns and at the Denezhnaya Volozhka channel crossing with six-barrelled mortars from the area of Workshop 14 [Hall 3] and machine-gun fire from the P-shaped building [Kommissarhaus].

During the course of the day, our formations fired on enemy emplacements with small arms, machine-guns and mortars, and brought artillery fire down on enemy batteries located amongst the workshops and on enemy emplacements near the P-shaped building (machine-gun fire). As a result of this artillery fire, one enemy heavy machine gun with crew was destroyed in the area of the separate small house and one enemy sniper south-west of the water pump was eliminated. Our losses on this day totalled 10 men.

At the end of the day, the regiment's strength was 91 men, plus 30 who were not part of the unit. Armament consisted of 75 rifles, 6 light machine-guns, 1 heavy machine-gun, 2 82mm mortars, 1 50mm mortar, 25,241 rifle cartridges, 12,100 PPSH cartridges, 110 82mm shells and 70 50mm shells.

The division as a whole possessed 425 rifles, 77 PPSh, 17 light machine-guns, 2 heavy machine-guns, 1 DShK anti-aircraft machine-gun, 5 anti-tank rifles, 6 82mm mortars, 4 50mm mortars, 3 45mm guns and 2 ampulomets.

From 1830 to 2000 hours, the leader of the divisional artillery, Lieutenant-Colonel Tychinsky, used heavy artillery to destroy several bunkers and emplacements on the right flank of 768th Rifle Regiment that were firing on the river crossings. These German machine-gunners caused a great deal of trouble and continued to do so, despite the Soviets' best efforts.

- - -

During a quiet period, Colonel Lyudnikov presented medals to distinguished soldiers and commanders. The Order of the Red Banner was awarded to Sergeant Nizametan Nagamonovich Alimuzin, a squad commander from 650th Rifle Regiment. The same medal was awarded to Senior Sergeant Aleksandr Aleksandrovich Kanunnikov, a squad commander from 768th Rifle Regiment. The Order of the Red Star was given to Private Ivan Petrovich Belokopitov, a mortarman from 650th Rifle Regiment, and to Lieutenant Mikhael Leontevich Levin, a company commander from 344th Rifle Regiment. Going back to the front, those who received decorations swore to defeat the enemy and stand until death on the banks of 'Mother Volga'.

Casualties for 9 December, 1942:	
138th Rifle Division:	6 killed, 18 wounded, a total of 24 men
305. Infanterie-Division:	1 man killed, 10 men wounded

10 December, 1942

The Germans were generally quiet, apart from the occasional burst of small arms and machine-gun fire. They fired on the Denezhnaya Volozhka channel crossing from the Kommissarhaus and the transformer hut. In return, Pechenyuk's regiment conducted small arms, machine-gun and mortar fire – as well as fire from ampulomets – on German emplacements on their left flank. This is the first recorded instance of this weapon being used in the Barrikady. These ampulomets – literally 'ampoule throwers', but sometimes known as Molotov projectors – were unusual pieces of weaponry. The ampulomet, weighing in at 28kg including tripod, was a crude mortar-like weapon with a smooth bore that was muzzle loaded and threw spheres filled with an incendiary mixture based on white phosphorous. It could be fired at a rate of about eight rounds per minute but was neither very accurate nor very lethal when fighting tanks. It was served by a crew of three. A loader inserted the 125mm diameter projectiles down the bore, while the gunner lined up the targets and pulled the trigger, which fired a blank cartridge that sent the sphere on its way. Trajectory of the ampoule was not high like a mortar or flat like an anti-tank gun… it arced toward the target a few metres off the ground. It could also be aimed at steeper angles in order to land the ampoule behind a wall or in a trench. Maximum range was 250 metres – more than enough in the Barrikady. The ampulomets were normally gathered into one platoon of 2 to 4 weapons, with one such platoon per rifle battalion. The division first received ampulomets – a total of 2 – the previous day, and they were handed over to 650th Rifle Regiment. The regiment reported that with all types of fire, they destroyed two German emplacements and suppressed the transformer hut. The inaugural deployment of the weapon certainly caused surprise and consternation amongst the grenadiers holding the dangerously advanced positions around the transformer hut.

– – –

There was a small surprise for the inhabitants of the Barrikady at 0920 hours. Two German transport planes roared over the factory and were pounced upon by Soviet fighter planes. The outcome was not recorded.

From 1100 to 1300 hours, methodical German mortar fire continued to come from the main mechanical workshop of the Barrikady factory.

– – –

The dire situation forced married men to contemplate the future and quell the fears of their wives and families at home. Rettenmaier wrote:

> My letters […] may not give you much relief from your worries. These must be endured and I have the feeling that for all you have had to endure so far, there will be some future compensation of happiness. Here we still have much to bear and we must continue to take further casualties, but the Führer will not leave us in the lurch. There was an announcement today that 614 enemy tanks were destroyed in our army's area for the period 20 November to 9 December. With this result a substantial portion of the enemy's strength has been shattered. In the current terrain and weather conditions we cannot storm forward with the quick tempo we had during the summer. We are confident and hope for the best. Waldemar and Gerhard[26] will also be on the march. They say help is coming from France. One of them could be with the relief force.

---

26. Two of Rettenmaier's sons who were also in the Wehrmacht.

He also discussed another matter. A few days earlier, regiment staff informed him that the wife of Oberst Willy Winzer, the former regiment commander killed on 17 October, wished to write directly to him:

Familie Göhner

> I am curious as to what the Oberst's wife will request. On that day, I went immediately to the cemetery. His grave lies among his comrades. As I walked along the rows I read so many familiar names on the crosses, many whose

From left: Oberst Willi Winzer (Gr.Rgt.578), Obstlt. i.G. Kodré (Div. Ia) and Generalmajor Oppenländer (Div.Kdr.) during a briefing on 16 August, 1942. All three were not with the division from November 1942 onward.

fate of having fallen was unknown to me. It was very sad. And how the cemetery has grown!

Two days later, he mentioned this matter again:

> The Oberst's wife requested my Feldpost number. I am curious as to what she wants to know. About his death I can only report what I heard from others.

Such requests from families of men killed in action were not uncommon. When a man was killed, a family usually received two forms of notification: an official notice from an agency in Germany, usually the dead man's Wehrkreiskommando [military area headquarters], and a more comprehensive letter from the dead man's superior. The first was a simple letter composed mainly of cliched terms like 'fallen on the field for Volk und Reich' and contained very little information except for the date of death. The second notification, from the man's commanding officer, included more details about the circumstances of the death but were always carefully worded to avoid causing any upset to the grieving family. A lot of deaths – even those that were lingering and painful – were reported to the family as being quick and painless, for obvious reasons. Sometimes, a family member would press for more details by sending letters to other members of the unit, as was the case with the widow Winzer. Perceptive tact was required when imparting unpleasant facts, despite declarations from families that they could handle the truth. Oberleutnant Richard Grimm, 2./Pionier-Bataillon 305, learned this the hard way. When one of his men was blown to shreds while dismantling a mine, Grimm dutifully informed the man's wife but spared her the gruesome details. While on furlough, Grimm met with the wife, who asked for more information and also enquired about the personal effects, such as the wedding ring and watch. Grimm was forced to give the poor woman more details about her husband's death. She seemingly took it well but Grimm later learned that after their conversation, she had killed herself.

Casualties for 10 December, 1942:	
138th Rifle Division:	4 killed, 7 wounded, a total of 11 men
305. Infanterie-Division:	2 men killed, 6 men wounded

11 December, 1942

Sleighs came over the ice of the Volga at night bringing ammunition and rations to 138th Rifle Division, while the wounded were evacuated via the same method. Soldiers and commanders of 138th Rifle Division continued to go over to Zaitsevsky Island to use the bathhouses and pick up new winter clothing before they returned to their positions.

General Chuikov, 62nd Army commander, ordered 138th and 95th Rifle Divisions to organise the systematic destruction of the enemy and his firing points between the left flank of 138th Rifle Division and the right flank of 95th Rifle Division. For this, a system of cross-fire was created. Three fixed machine-guns were assigned from 138th Rifle Division and four from 95th Rifle Division.

In addition, powerful and coordinated strikes by army artillery were readied to batter the German protrusion. Slated for this task were 1011th Artillery Regiment with ten 122mm howitzers and twelve 76mm guns, 292nd Guards Mortar Battalion with twelve 120mm heavy mortars, and two 82mm mortar batteries of 138th Rifle Division with twelve tubes. Controlling this artillery grouping was the commander of 1011th Artillery Regiment, Major Fugenfirov.

– – –

Oberleutnant Eugen Hering, 6./Grenadier-Regiment 576, who prayed to God every day for deliverance, was struck down by shrapnel from a mortar round and suffered severe wounds. Shell splinters blinded his right eye and another fragment struck him in the neck, right between his clavicles, damaging important blood vessels. He was flown out of the pocket on 14 December to a field-hospital, then transferred on 16 December to Kriegslazarett-Abteilung 603, a major hospital in Rostov, for specialist treatment. He seemed to be doing fine and even wrote a letter to his wife on 17 December. His condition then deteriorated rapidly and signs of meningitis manifested themselves, seriously threatening his life. He slipped into feverish fantasies and constantly rambled about combat actions on the front-line, calling out orders, pointing out the enemy and preparing imaginary attacks. In occasional moments of lucidity he prayed. Suddenly, at 2230 hours on 19 December, he died. A wounded soldier in the bed next to him reported that he was singing 'Silent Night' shortly before his death and his final words were the last verse from the song: "Christ, the Saviour is born". He was buried with full military honours in the Heroes Cemetery set up in the forecourt of the former Rostov Institute for Engineering. He was posthumously promoted to Hauptmann, backdated to 1 December, 1942, and awarded the German Cross in Gold on 25 January, 1943 for his actions in Stalingrad, particularly his involvement in taking and holding the fuel tanks during the November offensive.

– – –

The Germans were inactive during the day except for occasional machine-gun and mortar fire on the Soviet formations. Grenades were thrown at an observation post on the left flank of 650th Rifle Regiment. Pechenyuk's men reciprocated throughout the day with heavy fire from small arms, machine-guns, mortars and ampulomets on German emplacements in the area of the Kommissarhaus and the transformer hut. Fire from these weapons, combined with artillery, was reported to have destroyed three firing points, while two communication trenches were bombarded with grenades. Pechenyuk lost 1 officer to death and 3 other ranks to wounds.

Although it has been seen that the combat strengths of Lyudnikov's rifle regiment was very low, it is interesting to look at the breakdown of those numbers. For example, on this day, 650th Rifle Regiment had a total of 83 men, but that was composed of 31 officers, 21 NCOs and 31 other ranks. There were as many officers as there were enlisted men.

– – –

Soviet observers also reported the following signs of German activity:

At 0800 hours, two groups, each of 12-15 men, tried to run from Workshop 3 [Hall 6c] into the area of Dom 38 [Haus 67]. Pechenyuk's men fired on the Germans next to the L-shaped building [Apotheke], destroying half of them and forcing the other half to run away.

At 1000 hours, four German soldiers were seen carrying boards from Dom 37 [Haus 74] to Dom 36 [Haus 73]. At 1030 hours, in the area of Workshop 14/15 [Hall 3], the Germans were more lively and the movement of up to 30 soldiers was observed to Dom 9 [Haus 57] and from there to the Volga River.

– – –

In a letter home, Hauptmann Rettenmaier reported about a new menace:

A short greeting as a sign of life. I'm still well and in good health. The only thing is the vermin are multiplying at an alarming rate and becoming a nuisance. But we will also triumph over this enemy, even if the hunt does not promise to be 100% successful under the paltry light in the bunker.

Hauptmann Rettenmaier briefs his NCOs in his battalion command post in the cellar of Haus 53. Despite extensive research, only one other man has been identified: (far right) Obergefreiter Konrad Hönig, 3./Gr.Rgt.578; born 14 September, 1912 in Czechoslovakia. Missing in action, January 1943 in Stalingrad.

Casualties for 11 December, 1942:	
138th Rifle Division:	5 killed, 8 wounded, a total of 13 men
305. Infanterie-Division:	4 men killed, 20 men wounded

12 December, 1942

Fugenfirov's artillery grouping began to fire on the German front between 138th and 95th Rifle Divisions from 12 December, 1942. They had orders to annihilate German firing points up to the depth of 300 metres from the Volga bank while offensive actions were being organised by 138th and 95th Rifle Divisions to clear the Germans located along the Volga bank between them. The artillery bombardment began at 0700 hours. The ten 122mm howitzers fired 2 shells per minute each, for a total of 1080 rounds, while the twelve 76mm guns and twelve 120mm mortar each fired a shell per minute, also for a total of 1080. Chuikov would later write:

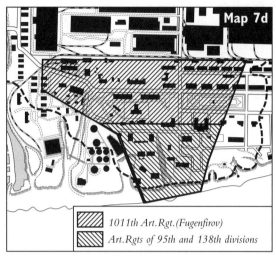

Soviet artillery preparation, 12 December, 1942.

> We could not destroy the enemy who had reached the Volga in the area of the Barrikady factory merely by attacks with our infantry regiments: we had neither tanks nor reserves. What were we to do? How could we help Lyudnikov's division?
>
> The artillery we had installed on the left bank of the Volga now came to our aid. To use this artillery we did not have to ferry ammunition across the Volga. We decided to wipe out the enemy by artillery fire. But to do this involved difficulties, which seemed insuperable: we needed to organise absolutely accurate fire on every enemy position, we needed artillery and mortar marksmen. We had such marksmen, but to correct their fire from the right bank was difficult – telephone links were being continually broken by the ice, and radio communication was weak and unreliable. Studying all these factors, we worked out and started to implement the following method of destroying the enemy who had broken through to the Volga.
>
> We marked out the area occupied by the enemy from north and south and from the Volga to the farthest point in the front-line, indicating landmarks which were clearly visible from the left bank. This gave us a 650-850 yard corridor occupied by the Germans. Our artillerymen, seeing this corridor clearly, could fire accurately at the enemy's firing positions.
>
> Spotters on the right bank watched the firing. They indicated and watched the targets, and errors in the gunners' aim. All this was communicated to the artillery observation posts, and then in turn transmitted to the firing positions.

In preparation for the artillery fire, some of the most exposed Soviet positions were pulled back. The war diary of 138th Rifle Division even reported that "the left flank group (Rolik) was moved 100 metres in a northern direction into the area of the waterworks on the bank of the Denezhnaya Volozhka channel". Not all of the fire landed accurately. The combat journal of 650th Rifle Regiment records that "army artillery lay down powerful artillery fire along our forward defensive line and on enemy emplacements. Destroyed by this artillery fire were two of our own dug-outs and three enemy emplacements in the area around the transformer hut". Fortunately for the regiment, there were no fatalities. Total losses for the day were two men wounded.

The beginning of the Soviet attritional fire did not have much impact on Hauptmann Rettenmaier:

> There is nothing new to report. Economy and austerity in all areas remain in effect. Otherwise everything is all right. Just now at 0700 – 0800 they again methodically plastered our entire sector.

At 1300 hours, Fugenfirov's artillery opened up again. The twelve 76mm guns and twelve 82 mm mortars each fired two shells per minute, for a total of 3600 shells. Exactly 5760 rounds were fired in the two one-hour bombardments. The same program would be implemented the next day.

Events took the usual course throughout the rest of the day with Soviet units placing heavy small arms, machine-gun and mortar fire on the front-line German defences. In one case, mortar crews from Pechenyuk's regiment destroyed a German emplacement near the transformer hut.

– – –

Life in the German rear was also becoming more hazardous. Soviet planes had been carrying out nocturnal bombing runs since the battle began in late autumn, even when the Germans had aerial supremacy, but their activities rapidly increased once there was little fear of retaliation. The same applied to Soviet artillery, which could now bombard any sector of Stalingrad with virtual impunity. Based in Gorodische, Hauptmann Traub, former commander of Pionier-Bataillon 305 but now tasked with special assignments, described these strikes and other concerns affecting those in the rear:

> Everything here is much the same for us. The Russians are pretty active and frequently shell us with their artillery and their planes are just as active at night. Just now, at 1615 hours, an ace among them dropped two bombs which lightly shook and rattled my excellent shack. Last night, at around 2200 hours, as I stepped out, they dropped two incendiaries which caused no damage. I have also had a bunker built, which I will move into tomorrow afternoon. It isn't safe from bombs, but one has a certain sense of security when sitting below ground for a while. Actually, I hope the bunker can be well heated. With the frequent north-easterly winds my shack is becoming pretty cold. There are absolutely no trees here on the steppe; every vehicle that goes into Stalingrad must bring back wood. But there must be a time when it is no longer possible to demolish any more houses in Stalingrad. And I fear this may happen much sooner than the end of this winter. Equally bad is the situation with the lighting. My carbide lamp has been broken for a long time. I had collected a nice supply of candles but yesterday night to my shock I discovered there were only two left. At Christmas I probably won't be celebrating under candlelight but in the dark. To be positive, yesterday there was a rumour that for the first time even parcels are coming through the mail. Now we hope that our Christmas parcels will arrive. As before only letters and airmail are being processed at the moment. Even official administrative mail remains unshipped and so there is little wonder my promotion to Major has not come through. From where I sit it should have come through from the [High Command's] personnel administration a long time ago.
>
> My hut is very comfortable tonight. The wind has eased, the stove is crackling nicely and at around 1700 hours my orderly, who has just finished his watch, is coming again and I will eat my supper. I cannot have more than two slices of bread, otherwise there would be nothing for the morning. You cannot get fat on it but it's enough for me. Eating a great deal is just a habit. God be praised, I still have a carton of cigars and something to drink and these help you get through. Our Zahlmeister confirmed today that he kept a box of cigars in reserve, because I once told him that I could become hellishly difficult if I had nothing to smoke. We have been lucky so far, not having really experienced the bitter cold. I believe that until now we have not had more than 15 degrees below. Hopefully St. Peter will show his understanding and be merciful with us this winter.

Casualties for 12 December, 1942:	
138th Rifle Division:	1 killed, 9 wounded, a total of 10 men
305. Infanterie-Division:	5 men killed, 1 officer and 14 men wounded

13 December, 1942

The carrying of ammunition and rations to 138th Rifle Division from the rear was accomplished by boats along the Volga to Zaitsevsky Island, and then from there to the right bank of the Volga over the ice of Denezhnaya Volozhka channel.

From 0600 until 1100 hours, in the right corner of the mechanical workshop [Hall 4], German soldiers continued to dig themselves in by excavating trenches, foxholes and earthen bunkers, and also creating a machine-gun firing point.

According to the war diary of 138th Rifle Division, the Germans were particularly active:

There is ceaseless firing throughout the entire day. From 0700 until 1100 hours, the enemy methodically fires his mortars at the division command post and against our artillery positions on Zaitsevsky Island.

The entry in the combat journal of 650th Rifle Regiment is similar:

During the course of the day, the enemy fired methodically on the regiment's defences with small arms and machine-guns and bombarded the area around the water pump with mortars. No movement in the enemy's area has been observed.

The regiment holds its previous line of defence. During the course of the day, it conducted small arms and machine-gun firing. The defences are continually strengthened in any spare moments, but because of the lack of engineers, the work progresses very slowly. The regiment has no losses.

Through a trickle of replacements, the headcount of the regiment rose slightly. It had 101 men, of those, 5 were wounded men. In addition, there were 34 men who were not part of the regiment. This made a total combat strength of 135 men.

- - -

Fugenfirov's artillery replayed its barrages from the previous day, for an hour at 0700 and an hour at 1300. In two days, a total of 11,520 shells had pummelled the German positions between 95th and 138th Rifle Divisions.

Casualties for 13 December, 1942:	
138th Rifle Division:	3 killed, 4 wounded, a total of 7 men
305. Infanterie-Division:	8 men killed, 23 men wounded

14 December, 1942

Generaloberst Paulus arrived at the command post of 305. Infanterie-Division at 1020 hours but only the chief-of-staff, Oberstleutnant i.G. Paltzo, was present. Paltzo reported that there had been lively and well-aimed artillery harassment fire in the last few days and it had caused heavy casualties. Also, the Unterführer (junior commander) course being run by the division had produced only about 35 combat-ready junior commanders from 50 participants. The infantry combat strength of the division amounted to only 1350 men. This meant that a decreasing number of men were holding the positions against an increasingly bold and aggressive enemy, as Hauptmann Rettenmaier wrote in a letter:

The burdens here are enormous… At present there are massive exertions of strength on all fronts. Our manpower reserves are not limitless. Therefore, the utmost is demanded from each individual, in many cases the almost unbelievable and apparently physically impossible. This is how it must be, however, if we want to survive.

Soviet supply runs across the channel from Zaitsevsky Island throughout the night were hampered by heavy German flanking fire. Reinforcements and supply troops dragging sleds across the frozen channel repeatedly dropped to the ground when they saw the twinkling muzzle bursts atop the dark cliffs and heard bullets hissing past them. The heavy machine-gun and mortar fire continued during daylight. Machine-guns north of the water pump and in the transformer hut raked any visible Soviet solder and focused on any movement across the Denezhnaya Volozhka channel. Pechenyuk's regiment attempted to neutralise these particular emplacements that covered the crossing.

The reinforcements that arrived during the night were distributed to the formations.

In the area of Rolik a German wearing a Red Army uniform was killed.

– – –

Towards the end of the day, Lyudnikov received the following order from army commander General Chuikov:

> During the course of three days, the division's forces have disrupted the defensive works of the enemy in the area between 138th and 95th Rifle Divisions while also destroying some enemy firing posts.
>
> Task: 138th Rifle Division will advance in a south-east direction and deliver the hardest blow to the enemy with its left flank. Upon reaching Taimyrskaya Street, meet up with the right flank forces of 95th Rifle Division and establish a solid front.
>
> The commander of 138th Rifle Division has decided to attack with 650th Rifle Regiment in the direction of the P-shaped building to annihilate the enemy defensive works south of Taimyrskaya Street and to meet up with the right flank forces of 95th Rifle Division.
>
> The beginning of the attack is scheduled for 1200 on 15 December, 1942.

From 62nd Army staff came the representative assistant to the Commander of Operations, Captain Kolyakin, and from 95th Rifle Division came the assistant operations officer, Senior Lieutenant Poyelov. In turn, the representative from the operations department of 138th Rifle Division, Captain Chudin, left for 95th Rifle Division.

The division regrouped its forces at night and gathered strength for the offensive. During the night of 14-15 December, more reinforcements came across the ice of the Denezhnaya Volozhka channel – a total of 222 men.

– – –

To help them in their destruction of German strongpoints, the Soviet defenders of Lyudnikov's Island were sent two 76mm guns. The heaviest weapons available to Lyudnikov in his small bridgehead were a few 45mm anti-tank guns. That lack was about to be remedied. A detachment of two 76mm regimental guns were ready and waiting on the east bank of the Volga… waiting until the ice on the river was stable enough to bear the 900kg weight of the guns. Leading the small group was Lieutenant Vasili Andreyevich Dvoryaninov, a platoon commander in 295th Artillery Regiment. He reports about his mission:

> In December, the defenders of Stalingrad were assigned a mission – to switch from defence over to the offensive in order to draw the noose tighter, to exterminate or surround all the hitlerites. And to attack – this meant to clear the fascists from house after house, cellar after cellar, which they had transformed into fortified defensive strongholds.
>
> For the successful performance of this combat assignment, what was required was the sort of artillery that could accompany infantry and be in the battle formations of the rifle units. And

an artillery platoon, which I commanded at that time, was assigned a mission – to collect new regimental 76mm guns from the Army's rear and at the first appearance of stable ice on the Volga get them across to the right bank for destruction and suppression of enemy emplacements with direct fire.

The frosts began to get more severe in the middle of December. On 13 December, we determined that the ice was already stable enough and that it was necessary to begin the crossing. We brought the guns up to the bank with horses in the evening of 14 December, sent the horses back to the rear, and then began implementing the risky assignment – crossing the guns over the thin ice from Zaitsevsky Island to Lyudnikov's Island.

Though the ice, in our opinion, was stable enough, we nevertheless decided to adopt the necessary safety precautions and to roll the guns not en masse but in a chain. For this purpose, we attached a long rope to the limber of each gun, and then took hold of it, with approximately 5-6 metres between each other. Pulling on the rope, we easily shifted the first gun from its berth and rolled it onto the slippery ice. At a distance of approximately 100 metres, the second gun slid onto the ice in a similar manner. I moved ahead of this procession, indicating a route for the gun crews…

And then the first gun reached the river bank. Everyone managed it safely. And we felt like shouting 'hurrah' and falling into each others arms, but this was not done, in order to prevent being observed because sudden attacks were possible at any moment and aimed fire could break up this operation. The second gun also rolled along successfully. Literally a few paces remained before it too would roll onto bank, but these paces appeared fateful. Alongside the river bank, having probably found a hole, the gun suddenly dropped to the bottom, sinking into a metre of water. What to do? There was no time to waste. It was vital to move into firing position by morning and to support the attacking

Kalgine/Dvoryaninov

Lieutenant Vasili Andreyevich Dvoryaninov

infantry, and now we had this misfortune. I ordered both gun crews to pull the gun out of the water. They grabbed it, pulled it, but it was stuck fast. I had to get into the icy water with four soldiers so as to grab hold of the wheels and push the gun from behind. We pulled… but still the gun remained stuck. Suddenly a flare hissed, burst into illumination and the Germans opened fire on us with mortars. It was necessary to lay low and wait out the bombardment…

It is possible to imagine the mood I was in when I was compelled to go to the divisional command post to report to Colonel S.Y. Tychinsky about what had happened. Listening to my unpleasant report, the colonel ordered firing positions to be taken up that night by only one of the forwarded guns, and to leave the second one in the Volga for the time being.

With both gun crews, we wheeled the gun up to the gully which separated the right flank of our division from the German salient. It wouldn't be simple to roll it uphill along the floor of a gully upon whose right crest the fascists were positioned. While we did try to remain silent, the Germans nevertheless noticed us and opened fire, throwing hand grenades at us from above and shooting with submachine-guns. A few of the soldiers were wounded but fortunately no-one was killed. So, in fits and starts, under the whistling of bullets and the crash of exploding grenades, we rolled the gun up onto the flat ground, and then into Dom 47. We were met there by a representative of 344th Rifle Regiment who immediately pointed out to us enemy emplacements that needed to be suppressed. It turned out that German machine-gunners had positioned themselves on platforms erected inside the factory chimneys, while openings that had been knocked out of the brick wall of the chimney at an estimated height of 20 to 30 metres above the ground served as embrasures for the machine-guns.

And from these vantage points they showered our rifle units with lead 'rain', not allowing us to raise our heads.

To more successfully suppress such unusual firing points, we – including the gun commander Sergeant Skabinym – decided to put the gun on the second floor landing. Because we had two gun crews, there was more than enough gunners, so we quickly and successfully concluded this mission. Two boards were found, they were placed over the treads of the staircase and the gun was put on top of them. After such preparatory work, not much effort was required by us to heave the gun up to the second floor and position it near a smashed window opening. Ammunition was brought up…

With his solitary gun in position, Lieutenant Dvoryaninov and his gunners waited until the signal was received to open fire.

Casualties for 14 December, 1942:	
138th Rifle Division:	2 killed, 11 wounded, a total of 13 men
305. Infanterie-Division:	5 men killed, 19 men wounded

15 December, 1942

From 2100 the previous night until midday, the moment of the Soviet attack, the Germans continued to dig trenches in the area of the right corner of the main mechanical workshop and fired methodically on Soviet units from Haus 67 [Dom 38] and Haus 73 [Dom 36]. Little did the German garrison in Dom 38 know that they were one of the prime targets for the attack that would be launched in the afternoon.

During the period before the beginning of the Soviet offensive, German artillery and mortars fired at the river bank and the crossings. Occasionally, machine-guns and submachine-guns were fired at the Soviet defensive line and methodical artillery and mortar fire was dropped on the west bank and the Denezhnaya Volozhka crossing.

In accordance with 62nd Army's plan, artillery units – Fugenfirov's 1011th Artillery Regiment and all artillery of 95th and 138th Rifle Divisions – began softening up the German defences at 0500 hours. The artillery concentration was formidable: 295th Artillery Regiment with seven 76mm guns; 292nd Guards Mortar Battalion with 24 120mm mortars; 86th Guards Artillery Regiment with ten 120mm howitzers and 19 76mm guns; 1011th Artillery Regiment with ten 122mm howitzers and twelve 76mm guns; 397th Tank Destroyer Regiment with an unspecified number of 76mm guns; the guns of the Volga Flotilla; plus numerous 50mm and 82mm mortars of the batteries from the rifle regiments of both 95th and 138th Rifle Divisions. Attritional fire continued until 1135 hours, when the full might of the artillery was unleashed for five minutes. At 1140 hours, it eased back into slow attritional fire until 1155 hours, when it rose to a five-minute crescendo preceding the attack.[27]

At noon, Lyudnikov's division transitioned to the offensive, having received the task of producing a connection with the left neighbours. Lieutenant Dvoryaninov, whose single gun had been positioned in Dom 47, supported the attack of Konovalenko's men:

---

27. See accompanying table and map on page 328 for targets and rates of fire.

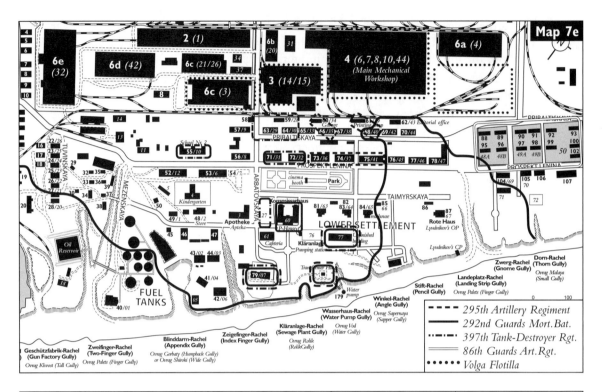

	Attritional fire (0500–1135 hours)	Barrage (1135–1140 hours)	Attritional fire (1140–1155 hours)	Barrage (1155–1200 hours)
295th Artillery Regiment	*300 shells* Dom 37, 39, 40[28], 41, 34, 35 & 36	*120 shells* Dom 40, 41, 39, 37, 35 & 36	*60 shells* Hall 15/14 Dom 28 & 29	*120 shells* Dom 37, 39, 40 41, 34, 35 & 36
292nd Guards Mortar Battalion	*360 rounds* Transformer hut, P-house, Krasny Dom & unfinished building	*240 rounds* Transformer hut, P-house, Krasny Dom & unfinished building	*60 rounds* Dom 8, 9, 28, 29, 30 & 31	*240 rounds* Transformer hut, P-house, Krasny Dom & unfinished building
397th Tank Destroyer Regiment	*600 shells* Dom 28, 30, 32, 31, 29, 27, central gates, E-shaped house, transformer hut, Krasny Dom & unfinished building	*300 shells* Dom 28, 30, 32, 31, 29, 27, central gates, E-shaped house, transformer hut, Krasny Dom & unfinished building	*120 shells* Dom 3, 4, 5, 7, 6, 12 & 2	*300 shells* Dom 28, 30, 32, 31, 29 & 27
86th Guards Artillery Regiment	*320 shells* Finger-shaped gully, Dom 48, 49, 50, 51 guitar-shaped balka	*200 shells* Finger-shaped gully, Dom 48, 49, 50 & 51	*60 shells* Dom 52	*200 shells* Finger-shaped gully, Dom 48, 49, 50 & 51
Volga Flotilla	*120 shells* Shops 3, 14/15 & main mechanical hall		*40 shells* 30 metres north of main mechanical hall	*120 shells* Shops 3, 14/15 & main mechanical hall

28. The Soviet garrison of Dom 40 [Haus 68] temporarily abandoned their house prior to the bombardment.

We walloped first one, then the second chimney. In a few minutes rifle units rose up, went on the attack and without particular casualties captured some houses, now that these enemy firing posts in the chimneys had been silenced.

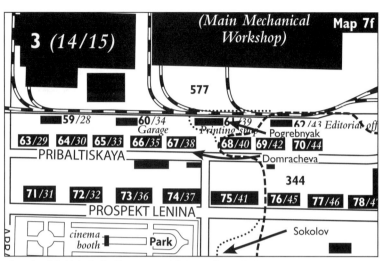

Attack of 344th Rifle Regiment, 15 December, 1942.

The advance was nowhere near as easy as Lieutenant Dvoryaninov implies. The German troops offered fierce defence, firing from all sorts of weapons. Upon seeing Konovalenko's groups attacking, intensive artillery and mortar fire also came from Hall 3 [Workshop 14/15] and the main mechanical workshop, right into the flanks of the storm groups. Moreover, in the direction of the advance, the groups encountered minefields, craters, dug-outs, houses and their approaches, barbed wire entanglements and trip-wires with booby traps. The pioneers had been working on these defences for weeks and this was their first true acid test. The groups advanced in the direction of Dom 38 and 39. Through quick and decisive actions, a group under the command of Lieutenant I.S. Pogrebnyak captured Dom 39. Under heavy machine-gun fire, a group led by Lieutenant Domracheva took two dug-outs 15-20 metres from Dom 38 and then became embroiled in a lengthy firefight. A group under the command of Lieutenant Sokolov, operating in the direction of Dom 41 and the building north of the Kommissarhaus, forced the Germans out of a dug-out 30 metres south-east of Dom 41 and consolidated themselves upon the attained line. They suffered heavy losses.

Relying upon their system of man-made obstacles, deviously booby-trapped wire entanglements and ferocious fire, Grenadier-Regiment 577 easily retained control of Dom 41, 38, and 37. Soviets soldiers who made it to the forward German line had grenades thrown at them, which effectively halted their advance. Captain Konovalenko's 344th Rifle Regiment achieved insignificant successes: they captured Dom 39, two dug-outs 15 metres north-east of Dom 38 and one dug-out 15 metres south-east of Dom 41. The regiment reported:

> Throughout the day, up to 30 enemy soldiers and officers were annihilated, 5 machine-guns were wiped out, 6 dug-outs were destroyed by direct hits, and Dom 38 was smashed by artillery fire from the 76mm guns.

In return for this minor success, their casualties had been heavy: 2 officers and 5 men killed, 1 NCO and 23 soldiers wounded, a total of 31 men. At the end of the day, the regiment had a total of 163 men, but only 64 of those were fighting on the front-line. They were equipped with 129 rifles, 2 heavy machine-guns, 7 light machine-guns, 22 submachine-guns, 3 anti-tank rifles, 2 82mm mortars and 3 50mm mortars, and in their ammunition stocks had 18,000 rifle cartridges, 6000 submachine-gun cartridges, 250 anti-tank rifle cartridges, 30 82mm mortar shells, 35 50mm mortar shells and 300 grenades. Also, food for 4 days.

The situation was no better for 650th Rifle Regiment. In fact, it was worse. At the scheduled time of 1200 hours, 1st Rifle Battalion began its offensive under strong machine-gun, mortar and automatic fire. The Germans firmly held their defensive line and offered immediate and strong resistance with heavy machine-gun fire from the transformer box, the unfinished building and the red building [Haus 84]. Straining against an angry hailstorm of bullets, the men of 1st Rifle

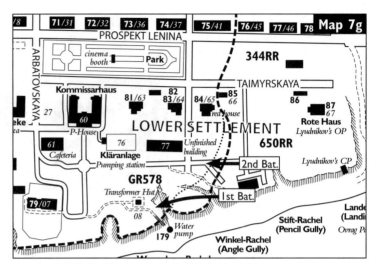

Attack of 650th Rifle Regiment, 15 December, 1942.

Battalion collapsed with alarming rapidity. Where seconds before there had been several dozen men, now there was nothing but crumpled bodies leaking blood into the dirty, torn-up snow. Several men, either brave or foolhardy, clawed their way forward and overwhelmed some German outposts, but most of the riflemen – those still uninjured – were face down in the snow. After advancing 30 metres, the attack stalled and the battalion was incapable of advancing any further.

2nd Rifle Battalion, on the other hand, did not even carry out its order. An attempt to attack miscarried from the very beginning. The extremely heavy German machine-gun, mortar and automatic fire swept everything and did not allow an opportunity to arise.

The net gain for 650th Rifle Regiment: its left flank moved forward 30-50 metres. Lyudnikov later wrote: "We valued winning back even such a small area but not at the price the regiments were suffering. I ordered the attack to be stopped."

The casualties of 650th Rifle Regiment were 60 men, including 6 by friendly artillery fire…devastating losses for a regiment that had reported a total combat strength of 135 men two days earlier. A sizeable proportion of the 222 replacements received by the division the previous day had been sent to 650th Rifle Regiment (and these are not included in the above combat strength), but a comment in the regiment's journal makes it very clear that these new arrivals were of dubious value in this attack: "The reinforcements were not prepared, operated sluggishly, and hid in dug-outs because of the heavy losses they had taken." At the end of the day, the regiment had 28 officers, 12 NCOs, 100 soldiers, plus 24 men not part of the regiment.

– – –

Colonel Gorishny's 95th Rifle Division advanced in a north-western direction with the task of reaching Taimyrskaya Street and joining up with units of 138th Rifle Division. Prior to the attack, the regiments had the following strengths: 161st Rifle Regiment had 363 men (1st Rifle Battalion – 84 men, 2nd Rifle Battalion – 106 men, 3rd Rifle Battalion – 8 men); 90th Rifle Regiment had 238 men (2nd Rifle Battalion – 60 men, 3rd Rifle Battalion – 56 men); and 241st Rifle Regiment had 230 men (1st Rifle Battalion – 62 men, 2nd-3rd Rifle Battalions – 9 men).

The outcome of their attack is recorded in Combat Report No. 106:

> Carrying out Order No. 221, 90th and 241st Rifle Regiments launched their attacks at 1200.
>
> Emerging from Humpback Gully, 241st Rifle Regiment was stopped by enemy machine-gun and submachine-gun fire, especially by large-calibre machine-guns from pillboxes in Dom 02, 05, 04, 06. Capturing 4 dug-outs, it continues to blockade enemy firing points.
>
> 90th Rifle Regiment has carried out its assigned task, seizing 3 enemy trenches and 6 dug-outs, reaching the line: right flank 60 metres west of the fuel tanks, left flank captured the red house that lies 40 metres west of the fuel tanks. They consolidated upon the attained line.

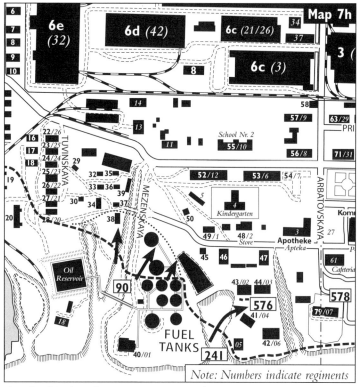

Attack of 95th Rifle Division, 15 December, 1942.

161st Rifle Regiment continued to hold its previous positions, using fire from 45mm guns, mortars and machine guns to support the attacks of 241st and 90th Rifle Regiments.

The artillery and mortars tried to suppress and destroy enemy emplacements that barred the units from advancing. The guns of 57th Artillery Regiment worked well: owing to the small-calibre guns, however, enemy firing points – being in pillboxes and 1 masonry structure – could not be destroyed (Dom 02, 04, 05 and 06).

It was also reported that "defending in front of 90th Rifle Regiment, near the fuel tanks, were two companies of 3rd battalion, 576th Infantry Regiment of the enemy 6th Army". With mortar fire, 241st Rifle Regiment destroyed 1 heavy and 2 light machine-guns. The regiment's 45mm guns also destroyed 1 pillbox. Eleven prisoners[29] were taken and the following was captured: 1 heavy machine-gun, 4 light machine-guns, 2 company mortars, 25 rifles, 5 submachine-guns, 10 grenades and 2800 cartridges. The division's losses had been heavy for the minor gains achieved: 241st Rifle Regiment had casualties of 47 men, 90th Rifle Regiment lost 19 men (3 killed) while 161st Rifle Regiment lost 3 men to wounds.

The strength of the German strongpoints in the thick-walled brick buildings and the ineffectiveness of Soviet artillery in destroying them – or even temporarily subduing them – forced Colonel Gorishny to submit a request to 62nd Army:

> I request that one battery of large-calibre artillery – for the destruction of enemy pillboxes in masonry houses – be placed at my disposal, and that reinforcements be sent to fill up the personnel of 241st and 90th Rifle Regiments to 150–200 men each.

29. The war diary of 62nd Army states: "Five prisoners were taken, 2 Germans and 3 Romanians, all from Grenadier-Regiment 576." The reason for the discrepancy is unknown but it is possible that some of the prisoners were killed. Whatever the case, the daily casualty figures for 305. Infanterie-Division did not report any of its men missing.

Reconnaissance, documents gathered from corpses and prisoner interrogations revealed the disposition of German units to their opponents, as described in 62nd Army's war diary:

From the eastern edge of the factory to the bank of Volga – 577th and 578th Infantry Regiments of 305th Infantry Division. Up to a battalion of 578th Infantry Regiment maintains defence along the river bank up to the fuel tanks.

Defending in the area of the fuel tanks are 294th and 50th Sapper Battalions.

From the fuel tanks up to Motrosskaya Street – 576th Infantry Regiment of 305th Infantry Division and 672nd Sapper Battalion.

Soviet intelligence also revealed an interesting German tactic near the fuel tanks:

It was noted that near the fuel tanks, the enemy uses sentry dogs for auxiliary protection on approach routes to prevent the infiltration of our reconnaissance groups into his combat ranks.

– – –

Small Soviet units continued to carry out their tasks after nightfall. Groups of 344th Rifle Regiment carried out operations in the direction of Dom 38 until about 1600 hours. Throughout the day, 138th Rifle Division calculated that it had annihilated over 100 Germans and 8 machine-guns, while destroying one dug-out and 3 houses. Losses of the division based on preliminary data: 51 killed and 106 wounded, a total of 157 men. The small defensive line and insignificant depth of the division, which was easily covered by German fire, gave steady rise to losses in the division.

The attack of 138th Rifle Division and its repulsion did not make many waves in the German camp. In fact, it was the attack by 95th Rifle Division that made a slightly bigger impact. At 2045 hours, LI. Armeekorps reported to 6. Armee that "after several fruitless attacks south-east of the gun factory, the enemy succeeded with a local penetration near the fuel installation. A counterattack will be launched during the night."

Casualties for 15 December, 1942:	
138th Rifle Division:	51 killed, 106 wounded, a total of 157 men
305. Infanterie-Division:	17 men killed, 4 officers and 94 men wounded

16 December, 1942

At 0430 hours, a German platoon attacked units of 241st Rifle Regiment on the northern slopes of Appendix [Humpback] Gully with the aim of recapturing the five dug-outs lost the previous day. Using machine-guns and hand grenades, the Soviet riflemen repelled the German attackers who left behind many dead when they scattered into dug-outs. At 0810 hours, 241st Rifle Regiment sent out small recon patrols which captured two dug-outs on the northern slopes of the gully.

At 0950 hours, Soviet observers spotted about 100 German soldiers pushing forward from the Apotheke and School No. 2 in communication

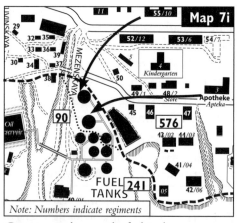

German attacks near the fuel tanks.

trenches and dispersing into a network of trenches and dug-outs north-west of the fuel tanks. They were fired on by Soviet artillery and partially scattered.

During the day, 90th Rifle Regiment was involved in heavy grenade fighting west of the fuel tanks. Operating with small groups under the cover of ampulomets, machine-guns and mortars, storm groups seized two dug-outs but they changed hands several times. By the end of the day, the Soviet riflemen retained control of one of them. The regiment's storm groups were supported by the 45mm guns, mortars and machine-guns of their southern neighbour, 161st Rifle regiment. Fire from 57th Artillery Regiment demolished 6 German dug-outs and destroyed 2 machine-guns.

The casualties of 95th Rifle Division were quite a bit heavier than the previous day: 241st Rifle Regiment lost 58 men, 90th Rifle Regiment 60 men and 161st Rifle Regiment 1 man. The division suffered further casualties but they were self-inflicted: at 1115 hours, Soviet artillery on the east bank mistakenly dropped a barrage near the divisional command post, killing 5 men and wounding 6. Among the dead was the assistant chief of divisional communications, Captain Ivanov, while Lieutenant Mironenko and Junior-Lieutenant Novikov were wounded. In addition to its battlefield casualties, 241st Rifle Regiment lost 4 killed and 13 wounded to this 'friendly fire'.

– – –

Along the front-line of 138th Rifle Division, the Germans occasionally sent out automatic, machine-gun and mortar fire. Methodical fire fell upon the battle formations of 344th Rifle Regiment. 650th Rifle Regiment shot up active German emplacements with with small arms, machine-guns, mortars, automatics and anti-tank rifles. This task was carried out with such gusto that by the end of the day the regiment reported that its two 82mm mortars only had 10 rounds left, while the sole 50mm had completely depleted its supply. The division's defensive line remained the same but added to it was Dom 39 and the three dug-outs that had been captured the previous day. In accordance with its orders, Lyudnikov's division made plans to launch an infantry attack at 1100 hours, and up to that time, it fired machine-guns and submachine guns at the Germans, forcing them to halt construction of barricades and other obstacles.

At 1100 hours, 344th and 650th Rifle Regiments went on the offensive while 768th Rifle Regiment continued to fire on the closest enemy positions. When the 15-man strong storm group of 344th Rifle Regiment advanced in the area of Dom 38 [Haus 67], the Germans opened up intensive machine-gun fire, forcing them to ground. The group was pinned down and lay in the snow for almost half an hour. At 1130 hours, from the direction of Workshop 14/15 [Hall 3], a group of 12-15 Germans counterattacked the storm group but were stopped

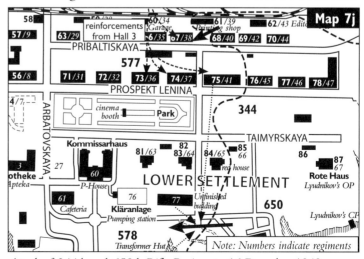

Attack of 344th and 650th Rifle Regiments, 16 December, 1942.

by machine-gun and rifle fire. The German group then consolidated themselves in Dom 38 [Haus 67], 36 [Haus73], 37 [Haus 74] and 41 [Haus 75]. They must have been reinforcements sent to strengthen the garrisons of those houses. The Soviet storm group laid down fire and pulled back to their starting positions.

The Germans on Pechenyuk's sector stubbornly defended their positions. Fire from the unfinished building, the transformer hut and Dom 41 [Haus 75] struck 1st Rifle Battalion. At 1100 hours, that battalion went on the offensive and gained a few metres but quickly staggered to a halt under heavy fire from small arms, machine-guns and automatics, as well as the occasional mortar round. The regiment's losses were 1 officer and 1 soldier killed, 8 soldiers wounded, a total of 10 men.

Both groups had met with extremely heavy fire and remained without success. The German defences were simply too formidable. Soviet artillery suppressed German weapons emplacements, destroyed dug-outs and exterminated personnel. Losses of the division were 4 killed and 21 wounded, a total of 25 men.

Again, the attack did not greatly affect the Germans and barely registered as a serious threat. At 1715 hours, LI. Armeekorps reported to 6. Armee that "several attacks with strong artillery support south-east and east of the gun factory were partially repulsed with high enemy casualties".

With the onset of nightfall, a German machine-gunner in Haus 75 shot up Dom 40 and 42 with belt after belt of ammunition.

Casualties for 16 December, 1942:	
138th Rifle Division:	4 killed, 21 wounded, a total of 25 men
305. Infanterie-Division:	13 men killed, 39 men wounded

17 December, 1942

During the night, ammunition began to be brought up to Lyudnikov's Island from the rear. Cargo from Zaitsevsky Island was delivered on man-drawn sleds. Those same sleds evacuated wounded men. With each passing night, this life-line functioned more effectively, bringing in larger quantities of supplies and reinforcements, and more quickly evacuating the wounded. New blood and fresh energy flowed into the veins of 138th Rifle Division.

– – –

LI. Armeekorps reported to 6. Armee that night-time counterattacks to straighten out local penetrations south-east of the gun factory had so far only been partially successful. Each German counterattack was recorded in 95th Rifle Division's Combat Report No. 110:

> Reserves that had been moved up in the night of 16 to 17.12 tried to restore the previous position. The attack was launched towards the fuel tanks seven times from the L- and E-shaped houses[30] on the sector of 90th Rifle Regiment. At 2035 on 16.12 with a platoon, at 2042 with about 70 soldiers, at 2100, 2130, 2145 with a platoon, at 2240 with about 60 soldiers and at 0330 with a platoon. All enemy attacks were repulsed with heavier losses for him. After these unsuccessful attacks, they pulled back to their former line and threw grenades at the trenches of 90th Rifle Regiment.

---

30. The Apotheke and School No. 2 respectively.

After heavy preparation by artillery, Gorishny's units again attacked near the fuel installation. Combat Report No. 110 again provides the details:

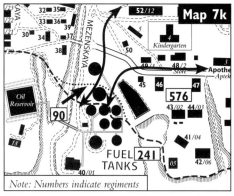

> At 1200, having repelled the enemy attacks, 90th Rifle Regiment carried out its order to wage battle for the conquest of the dug-outs north-west of the fuel tanks, but meeting stubborn resistance, the dug-outs changed hands repeatedly.

> Especially distinguishing themselves during the fighting for the fuel tanks was the commander of 3rd Rifle Battalion, Captain Slutsky, the deputy regiment commander, Captain Maksimov, company commander Lieutenant Lebedev and the deputy battalion commander for political affairs, Politruk Pavlenko.

German counterattacks during the night of 16-17 December, and the attack of 90th Rifle Regiment at midday on 17 December, 1942.

- - -

Relying on their organised system of fire, German units held their line and methodically fired on Lyudnikov's division with small arms, machine-guns and the occasional mortar round. On the sector of 650th Rifle Regiment, the Germans fired with small arms and machine-guns, as well as mortars and anti-tank rifles, from the unfinished building, Dom 41 and the transformer hut. The regiment returned fire throughout the day, particularly concentrating on the stubborn German defenders in the area of the red building [Haus 84] and the unfinished building.

Soviet observers reported that the Germans continued work on their entrenchments in the area of the Barrikady factory from 0700 to 1000 hours.

In preparation for an assault by 650th Rifle Regiment, artillery methodically destroyed German emplacements and personnel, focusing both on the front-line defences and the rear. Pechenyuk's 1st Rifle Battalion, attacking in the direction of the red building [Haus 84] and the unfinished building, came under strong fire from small arms, machine-guns and automatics, as well as erratic mortar barrages. They went to ground 20 metres from the red building. In small groups of 2-3 men, they bypassed the red building on the right with the aim of suppressing the firing point in the pillbox some 10 metres from that house. During the attack, the Germans put out an enormous amount of fire which caused the attack to collapse. As a result, 18 men were wounded. The German defenders were not without loss. Losing his life during this attack was Hauptfeldwebel Karl Wezel[31], commander of 3. Kompanie in Hauptmann Rettenmaier's I./Grenadier-Regiment 578. Wezel was one of the many rear echelon soldiers who had been quickly schooled in the art of city combat and sent into the front-line. Together with other retrained supply soldiers, young Austrian replacements and a few combat veterans, Wezel and others like him held the perilous strongpoints arrayed around Lyudnikov's Island.

The attack is not even mentioned in any German report. At 2020 hours, LI. Armeekorps reported that there was "no combat activity in the afternoon except for isolated enemy raids against the fuel installation and sporadic animated artillery activity. During the day and since the onset of darkness, brisk enemy aerial activity."

---

31. Wezel, Hauptfeldwebel Karl, 3./Gr.Rgt.578; born 25 February, 1916 in Mühlheim. Killed in action, 17 December, 1942 in Stalingrad.

Lieutenant Dvoryaninov, 295th Artillery Regiment, made the perilous journey from Dom 47 down to Volga to organise the rescue of his gun that had fallen through the ice on the night of 14-15 December:

> By means of a crane, our 'drowned woman' was raised up and delivered to the gun position, and to be at war with two guns made us more cheerful. Soon, however, two more guns arrived, and I was appointed battery commander in the ranks of 650th Rifle Regiment...

From an inauspicious beginning, Dvoryaninov's 'drowned woman' would go on to become a revered icon of the Great Patriotic War:

> Gun No. 14042, which fell into the water on 15 December, served Soviet soldiers well, not only in Stalingrad, but also on the Orlovsk-Kursk bulge, the crossing of the Desna, Dnepr, Dnestr, during the clearing of such cities as Glukhov, Bazmach, Zhitomir, Korosten, Vinnitsa, Zhmerinki, Kamenets-Podolsk, etc. This gun of our glorious battery annihilated and wounded over a thousand hitlerites, suppressed hundreds of firing points, brewed up and knocked out some tens of enemy tanks and motor vehicles.
>
> This gun, named 'Stalingrad' by us, reached the Carpathians, but was then taken away and put in one of the museums of the Soviet army.

Casualties for 17 December, 1942:	
138th Rifle Division:	5 killed, 16 wounded, a total of 21 men
305. Infanterie-Division:	8 men killed, 52 men wounded, 16 men missing

18 December, 1942

Heavy fighting again flared up near the fuel tanks during the night. A nocturnal German counterattack in the fuel installation threw Gorishny's riflemen out of the breach and recaptured the old front-line, with the exception of one strongpoint that was still being fought over when dawn arrived. Combat Report No. 112, prepared by 95th Rifle Division, describes the savage combat in detail:

> On the sector of 3/90th Rifle Regiment at 2210 on 17.12.42, the movement of a group of about 60 enemy soldiers from the Krasny Oktyabr factory towards the Barrikady factory was noticed. It is assumed that they will be put into action near the fuel tanks. At 2225 a group of about 30 soldiers was tracked crawling from the south-east corner of the Barrikady factory along an embankment before disappearing into dug-outs.... Mortars, machine-guns and artillery opened fire on them.
>
> At 2315 the enemy, with 45 soldiers, launched an attack on the sector of 90th Rifle Regiment between the fuel tanks and Humpback Gully. As a result of the hand-to-hand and grenade fighting, the enemy managed to capture one dug-out near the cone-shaped tank, after which he deployed sentry dogs.
>
> At 0225 on the sector of 241st Rifle Regiment, near the fuel tanks, a platoon of enemy infantry attacked dug-outs on the southern slopes of Humpback Gully, but suffering losses from machine-gun fire and grenades, they withdrew.
>
> From 0225 until 0500, 241st Rifle Regiment laid down fire and fought the attacking enemy infantry with grenades on the southern slopes of Humpback Gully, and as a result of the fighting, the enemy suffered losses and withdrew.
>
> To restore the position, two storm groups of 90th Rifle Regiment, supported by ampulomets, mortars and machine-guns, attacked the dug-outs captured by the enemy west of the fuel tanks. As a result of the fighting, one dug-out was taken, consolidated and fire continues to be exchanged with the enemy.

On the night of 17-18 December, 138th Rifle Division received reinforcements of 361 men together with staff officers. From 0100 until 0300 hours, the Germans fired on the crossings where supplies were being brought over. The breakdown of the reinforcements received was 10 officers, 49 NCOs and 302 enlisted men. These reinforcements were distributed to the regiments. The strength of Pechenyuk's regiment rose to 225 men.

Lyudnikov's divisional war diary reported that "from 0600 until 1300 there were frequent movements of single soldiers from Workshop 3 [Hall 6c] to Dom 9 [Haus 57] and from there to the Volga. After we opened up with rifles and machine-guns, these movements stopped." Oberleutnant Staiger, commander of 3./Pionier-Bataillon 305, was one of the many German soldiers moving toward the front-line:

> Because of the snipers, we could only move to the front or towards the rear in trenches which were sometimes quite narrow. On one occasion, things were moving too slowly for me, so I overtook by jumping up out of the trench with the plan of taking a few steps and then cutting back in further in front. Suddenly I was hit in the right wrist by a bullet. This was in the middle of December. If I had not been so impatient and did not attempt to overtake the patient transport moving far too slowly in front of me, it probably would not have happened. But I was hasty and […] the projectile hit me. It was not very far to the aid station and I went there on foot. I did not take this wound very seriously

Oberleutnant Berthold Staiger, 3./Pi.Btl.305.

The narrowness of the German trenches is clearly shown in this photo from February 1943. This was the main German trench into the southern part of the factory. The girders on the left belong to an outbuilding of Hall 1 [Workshop 11/14]. In the background is Hall 2 [Workshop 1]. The men are former upper management returning to inspect their factory.

but our commander, Hauptmann Traub, was of a different opinion and said: 'You're flying out of here. With your injuries, you're of no use to us any more. You'll only be another mouth to feed.' It was clear to me that he meant no harm because Hauptmann Traub was an officer respected and loved by all; he wanted me to escape from the encirclement in time. Thus I returned to the airfield where I had arrived, and was flown out on [a] Ju-52.

A few days later, Hauptmann Traub mentioned this incident in a letter to his wife:

Some days ago one of our battalion officers was wounded by a shot in the hand. Of the old guard who were together in France, there are now only three; myself, the adjutant[32] and the technical inspector[33]. Fortunately, most of the officers were only wounded. They have written to me from homeland hospitals. Anyway, our grand, proud battalion has been pretty much plucked. It must be time that we are withdrawn from the front for a few weeks so we can be refreshed and refitted, but it is certainly not the time to think about that now.

– – –

At midnight on 17–18 December, 138th Rifle Division received the following order:

The division will annihilate enemy positions in the central and southern parts of Pribaltiskaya Street, Prospekt Lenina and Krasny Dom, reach the line Dom 39, 28, 29, and 27 and join up with 95th Rifle Division.

For this attack, Lyudnikov knew he had to come up with a better way of capturing the thorny German strongpoints. Normal offensive strategies would not suffice in the Barrikady. New measures would be needed in order to capture individual buildings. Lyudnikov later wrote that "we decided to revise the tactics of our offensive and in every company set up assault groups which in turn consisted of storm, capture and reserve groups. The size of the group was decided by the commander and depended on the objective." Lyudnikov regrouped his forces. Konovalenko's and Pechenyuk's regiments prepared for the offensive. Now, in the combat ranks of these regiments, there were no longer sections, platoons and companies – only assault groups. Each group knew its task precisely. These assault groups would strike suddenly and swiftly. Lyudnikov continues:

Every regiment was equipped with sand tables – models of the terrain and the assault objective. There was nothing new in this but we managed to create favourable conditions for these groups to operate by lulling the enemy into relaxing his vigilance. In this case the psychological factor also had its part to play. We sent two officers to Zaitsevsky Island, where our gunners and mortarmen were positioned, for observation and communication. As soon as a signal, which was invisible to the enemy, was given from the division's command post with a pocket torch, three red flares soared over the island. Thereupon we pounded the right bank with a ten-minute artillery assault. At first the enemy retaliated with mortar fire, but then gradually became accustomed to the fact that our red flares did not herald an attack but were merely a signal for our gunners. German soldiers simply took cover to avoid casualties during the artillery assault. Prisoners' evidence later confirmed what we had been counting on. One prisoner would later say: 'When your flares go up we know that the Russians will open fire for ten minutes. And when the artillery attack finishes, we resume our positions.'

The conditioned reflex was working faultlessly and the Germans even gloated about the Soviet's simple tactics. "Come on, Ivan, get on with it!" they joked each time three red rockets

---

32. The adjutant was Fritz, Oberleutnant Max, 2./Pi.Btl.305; born 11 March, 1918 in Stuttgart. Killed in action, 22 December, 1942 in Stalingrad. See Appendix 2 (page 571) for more details.
33. The technical inspector was Zeller, Techn.Inspektor Georg, Stab Pi.Btl.305; born 4 December, 1915 in Alzenau. Still alive in 2006. See Appendix 2 (page 580) for more details.

flew up into the sky. They left their emplacements for a while during the artillery raid, but ten minutes later, as soon as the batteries on Zaitsevsky Island ceased fire, they came back and occupied their positions. Now all Lyudnikov had to do was take advantage of it.

Lyudnikov prepared draft combat instructions. As with any combat order, these instructions were laconic, stating with exhaustive clearness the purpose of the forthcoming battle. At the same time, Lyudnikov gave his commanders some scope to display initiative and daring. Starting positions could be changed to take advantage of the preparatory bombardment. Whatever the case, the purpose of the assault would be constant from the opening to the closing stage and would need to be completely understood by every fighting man.

On a page of his pocket notebook Lyudnikov formulated the task of his division thus:

Strictly observe camouflage. Continue with the same sequence of shelling from Zaitsevsky Island up to the beginning of attack, to catch the enemy unaware.

Suddenness and swiftness – the basis for the success of storm groups and capture groups.

Purpose of the offensive: strike forces will attack in the direction of Pribaltiskaya Street to destroy enemy strongpoints and completely capture not only Pribaltiskaya Street, but also Prospekt Lenina, and then Taimyrskaya Street. In a gap punched by strike forces, introduce reserves for a decisive push to the south-west so as to join up with the right flank of 95th Division and through that restore a continuous front.

Lyudnikov underlined the last four words: "Restore a continuous front."

A continuous front. Almost forty days earlier, Lyudnikov's division had been cut off from the army and from its rear. Appearing above the stretch of ground designated by fires were the quiet PO-2s with switched-off engines whose pilots were the first to call this island after the name of the division commander: "Hey, Lyudnikov's Island, put out the fires!"

Then there was famine and heavy losses, but the defenders of the Barrikady never lost the belief that a continuous front would be restored. Above all, the German 6. Armee had threatened them with complete encirclement and a fierce fight to the death continued on at the Barrikady.

– – –

In the afternoon, Pechenyuk's men noticed individual women moving toward the Volga bank and trying to reach the river. It turned out that the Germans were dressing in women's clothes and attempting to get to the Volga. It was obvious that the Germans were experiencing problems with potable water. In 650th Rifle Regiment, volunteers were selected to track down these thirsty Germans.

A heavy firefight continued between the two sides in the second half of the day. While working on strengthening their strongpoints even further, the Germans placed machine-gun fire on the battle formations of Lyudnikov's division. On Pechenyuk's sector, the Germans laid down heavy fire from the transformer hut, the unfinished building and the red building. The division fired back, destroying dug-outs and wiping out German personnel. Pechenyuk's groups placed fire from small arms, machine-guns and automatics on emplacements and communication trenches in the area to the north of the transformer hut and to the south of the Kommissarhaus.

Soviet artillery placed barrages on German emplacements in an effort to destroy dug-outs and exterminate personnel. Unfortunately, a few rounds fell short and hit Pechenyuk's command post, damaging it and wounding two men.

The morale of Lyudnikov's division was good. Twenty-eight lightly wounded men decided to stay in their positions instead of being evacuated and taken to the hospital. Losses of the division during the day amounted to 9 wounded.

- - -

Gefreiter Josef Zrenner recalls that "in December, things had already gone so far that the individual companies were dissolved, initially the first company of our battalion, then the third company, then the second company, and they were consolidated into combat teams. Thus we were already decimated by the middle of December despite the replacements we'd received in November. Losses were very high during this fighting."

- - -

German attention was still focused on the confused situation around the fuel tanks. At 1700 hours, LI. Armeekorps reported:

> In the fuel installation, the enemy – supported by prolonged artillery fire and fire from all weapons – was able to attack, and in some areas broke into the front-line that had been recaptured the previous night. A counterattack is being prepared.

And later, at 2050 hours:

> Counterattack to recapture the old front-line in the fuel installation remains unsuccessful. Further attacks were discontinued. Division controls the line: gully fork 82a2 – the two most western fuel tanks inclusive – course of the gully on the northern edge of the fuel installation to the Volga, and holds this position.

> Also in the afternoon, persistent heavy harassment fire on the steel factory and the fuel installation.

One such shell landed near Gefreiter Paul Reiner[34], 3./Grenadier-Regiment 578, a young soldier who had only joined the regiment in September. The blast threw shrapnel at him and lodged some chunks in his right thigh and shoulder. More unfortunate was his squad commander, Unteroffizier Uhrig, who was struck in the neck and chest. Uhrig, remembered by Reiner as a 'great guy', died shortly afterwards. Reiner made it to a first-aid post, then a hospital, and was flown out of the pocket the next day.

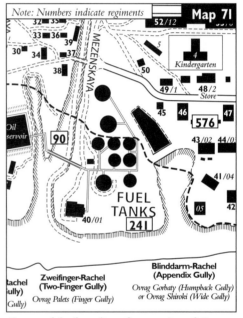

Course of the front-line after cessation of German counterattacks in the fuel tank area, 18 December, 1942.

Casualties for 18 December, 1942:		
138th Rifle Division:	9 wounded	
305. Infanterie-Division: 21 men killed, 1 officer and 99 men wounded, 7 men missing. The overall tally was later revised up to 155. With that, the division had suffered bloody losses of 741 men in the previous 7 days.		

34. Reiner, Gefreiter Paul, 3./Gr.Rgt.578; born 29 January, 1923 in Heilbronn. Still alive in 2005.

19 December, 1942

The 3-story corner building had been destroyed by a bomb. The shock wave effectively gutted the house. On the inside, walls and corridors crumbled. Three walls still remained intact. The house stood presenting its bare staircases and rooms. From the trenches of the 650th Regiment, Pechenyuk's soldiers could see closets with mirror doors, beds, tables covered by sheets and family photographs on the walls. When the Germans captured the house, everything disappeared in the course of one night. The autumn winds whined along the bare walls of the ruined house. Soon the winter snows filled its empty spaces. Covered as it was with white snow, black holes from shells still shone through. No longer did it look like a habitable house.

For artillery observers, this corner house served as a good orientation point because it was situated almost on the boundary of the German 'wedge'. On Pechenyuk's map, the house was marked as an enemy strongpoint. German soldiers were lodged in the basement where they manned two machine-gun points.

Scout Nikolai Petukhov's interest towards this corner house was caused by the fact that the Germans had dug a trench from the house to the river. Every day at dawn, a woman of enormous height and strange figure appeared from there and ran towards the Volga to get water with a bucket. This peculiar woman with a thirst for Volga water was what drew the attention of scouts Petukhov and Grigoriev.

The German dressed in women's clothes offered no resistance to the two scouts. Having turned into the trench, he stumbled onto the muzzle of a submachine-gun. On the whispered order 'Hande hoch!', he dropped his bucket and raised his hands. The scouts tore the wool shawl off the German's head and removed the dress so as to make running easier. They then tied two ropes to his belt. Grigoriev held one rope while Petukhov held the other. "Schneller und stiller!" commanded Petukhov in German "Move quickly and quietly… or else… verstehen?"

"Jawohl, jawohl…" muttered the terrified German as Petukhov led him from behind. Grigoriev was in front. They had just approached the first trench positions of 650th Regiment when machine-gun fire suddenly erupted from the basement of the corner house. Snipers also opened fire from the same building. Grigoriev managed to quickly jump into the trench, dragging the 'tongue' behind him. Petukhov was hit by a sniper's bullet. He released his rope and fell near the trench. The German sniper shot him two more times.

Grigoriev managed to quickly pull his wounded comrade into safety.

"Leave me here…" said Petukhov quietly; and having taken a breath of air, began to writhe in pain.

"Get the 'tongue' out of here!" he managed hoarsely.

"Damn this 'tongue'!" said Grigoriev as he tore open Petukhov's bloody camouflage suit and searched for the wound.

Scout Nikolai Petukhov and his divisional commander, Colonel Lyudnikov.

"Just wait a bit, brother…" The captured German began looking around nervously but he did not move.

"Get him out of here, Vasili…" Petukhov pleaded to Grigoriev. It was obvious that the presence of the German caused him the most pain.

"Don't bandage me… there's no reason to…"

The 'tongue' was Heinrich Hess[35] from 12./Grenadier-Regiment 578, and under interrogation, he mercilessly abused the Führer and his commander Hauptmann Püttmann, who had given the order to 'not fire without a command'. Hauptmann Püttmann had reduced the allocation of bullets for the mounted machine-guns. And Hess also said that the division received limited amounts of supplies because everything came in by transport planes. It was the first news the Soviets received about famine in the German camp.

- - -

As usual, the Germans were placing sporadic machine-gun and mortar fire on the combat ranks of 650th Rifle Regiment. To keep up appearances, the regiment returned fire on enemy emplacements in the area to the north of the transformer hut and the unfinished building. At 1100 hours, a relatively calm time, two storm groups – commanded by Lieutenant Chulkov and Sergeant Lyutin – began an advance in the direction of Taimyrskaya Street. It was not a full-blooded assault, merely a reconnaissance attack with two purposes: to feel out the enemy and to discover if the storm groups were prepared for an offensive. The attack began without any artillery preparation, but when the men started moving, guns of the 397th Tank Destroyer Regiment laid down

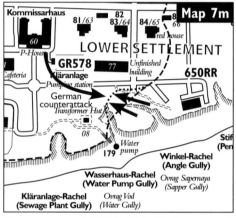

Storm groups of 650th Rifle Regiment attack German dug-outs, 19 December, 1942.

suppressive fire on German emplacements in order to support the operation. As soon as the storm groups showed themselves, however, the Germans put up fierce resistance. Covered by a ceiling of machine-gun fire, the Germans tried to launch a counterattack from the Kommissarhaus but were beaten off. Distinguishing themselves in the fighting were the first three to rush into the German trenches and dug-outs: Junior-Lieutenant Koretkovsky, Senior-Sergeant Ivanitsyn and Red Army man Svishchensky. Others followed their example. Two dug-outs were immediately blockaded by the Soviet attackers and the German garrisons trapped inside were eventually killed in vicious hand-to-hand struggles. With that, the dug-outs were captured.

Contrary to what Lyudnikov had ordered for offensive operations, capture and reserve groups had not been deployed for some reason. The storm groups therefore lacked heavy weapons, and ammunition was being rapidly expended. Immediate and fierce German counterattacks began. The storm groups held on until more men arrived. By nightfall, a total of four counterattacks were launched in an attempt to push back the storm groups and retake the dug-outs. All German counterattacks were repulsed. During the defeat of the counterattacks the following soldiers stood out: Captain Svenchkovsky knocked out a 37mm gun and blew up its ammunition supply with five shots from an anti-tank rifle;

---

35. Hess, Soldat Heinrich, 12./Gr.Rgt.578; born 22 September, 1918 in Essen. Missing in action, December 1942 in Stalingrad.

Geraskin, the senior representative of the NKVD special-purpose section with 650th Rifle Regiment, together with the two remaining soldiers of his detachment, beat back a counterattack of 20 Germans, personally killing six of them; Lieutenant Krashin killed one observer, two snipers and a soldier within the space of two hours. The storm groups, however, suffered dead and wounded – twelve soldiers in all. While others took over defence of the newly acquired dug-outs and trench section, Lieutenant Chulkov and Sergeant Lyutin returned to the main Soviet lines with their storm groups. 650th Rifle Regiment recorded German losses as 1 heavy machine-gun, 1 light machine-gun with its crew, 2 dug-outs and 3 covered foxholes to the north of the water tower in the area of the transformer box from artillery and mortar fire, while 138th Rifle Division had them at 64 Germans killed, 3 dug-outs and 5 metres of wire entanglement destroyed and 3 machine-guns suppressed. Trophies captured during the raid were 2 light machine-guns, 18 rifles, 2 submachine-guns, 1 heavy machine-gun, 900 hand grenades, 1 shovel and 1 flare pistol.

– – –

It was an attack by Gorishny's men, not the assault by Lyudnikov's division, that caught the Germans' attention, as LI. Armeekorps reported:

> On the right wing of 305.Inf.Div., in the area of the fuel installation, five enemy raids were repulsed. The enemy here is placed very close to our front-line.

Grenades duels took place near the fuel tanks both at night and in the morning, but that was normal. The storm groups of 241st and 90th Rifle Regiments prepared for the attack while 161st held the line, the latter even laying 105 anti-personnel mines in Korotky (Short) Gully and along the railway line during the night.

At 1100 hours, Gorishny's indomitable storm groups moved out, advancing in a north-west direction. The Germans offered stubborn resistance, especially with powerful fire from large-calibre machine-guns and mortar and artillery bombardments. The riflemen pressed on and the fighting turned into a hand-to-hand struggle. The left flank of 241st Rifle Regiment moved 30-40 metres forward and its storm groups brawled with the Germans for dug-outs and a communications trench on the south and south-western slopes of Appendix Gully. Individual dug-outs changed hands several times. Meanwhile, a short distance away, 90th Rifle Regiment attempted to conquer some dug-outs west of the fuel tanks. The

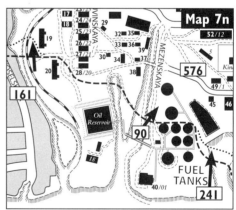

Storm groups of 241s and 90th Rifle Regiments attack German dug-outs, 19 December, 1942.

offensive spirit also seized a few small groups from 161st Rifle Regiment, who advanced 20-30 metres, reached a pillbox and seized one dug-out along the railway embankment. At noon the Germans dropped mortar rounds close to Gorishny's command post and on the mortar pits of 241st Rifle Regiment.

Throughout these attacks, Gorishny's men deployed 17 ampulomets – with good results. Upon bursting, the ampoules released dense clouds of smoke, blinding the Germans and preventing them from replying with aimed fire. These new weapons were reported to have incinerated three dug-outs. Found inside were 20 charred German corpses.

Once the smoke eventually cleared, the Soviet storm groups had captured three trenches and a few dug-outs. As the new occupants from 90th Rifle Regiment settled in and prepared for the inevitable counterattacks, their sappers discovered that German corpses left behind in the dug-outs had been booby-trapped, as had 1 light and 1 heavy machine-gun. The pioneers of Panzerpionier-Bataillon 50 had had enough time to carry out their devious handiwork before pulling back. Unfortunately for them, they also left behind many dead comrades and two men who were taken prisoner. One of them was Oberpionier Gerhard Holz from 1./Panzerpionier-Bataillon 50 and he was interrogated that same evening. Perhaps in an effort to placate his captors, Holz talked about certain activities which were seen by the Germans as capitalising on the 'spoils of war' but were later used as evidence by the 'Extraordinary State Commission to Investigate German-Fascist Crimes':

> German officers also plundered the population. For example, our former battalion commander, Oberstleutnant Ermeler, who lives in Berlin, had me take linen, cloth, etc. with me when I went on leave in August this year. I brought parcels to his wife with textiles and a letter. I brought 20 packages of tea with 50 grams in each one, 2 kilograms of soaps and various things.

Niggling attacks continued until night fell. LI. Armeekorps later reported:

> Two probes near the fuel installation were repulsed in the afternoon with bloody casualties for the enemy. Two enemy probes from the bridgehead east of the gun factory were repulsed. A third raid led to a local break-in, which has been partly straightened out. All enemy raids were supported by fierce artillery and mortar fire.

During the night, Soviet riflemen noticed small groups of German soldiers – 2 to 3 in number – moving from Dom 05 to the east and back to the Barrikady factory. At 2100 hours they saw wounded men being carried from Dom 04 [Haus 41] to the Barrikady factory.

– – –

After the veil of darkness fell upon the Barrikady, Lyudnikov left his dug-out to begin an inspection of his regiments' front-lines. His first stop was Konovalenko's command post.

"Hello, Commissar!"

"Good health, comrade Colonel!" said Battalion Commissar Fomin, welcoming Lyudnikov. "Do you want me to send for Captain Konovalenko? He's visiting the soldiers."

"That's not necessary, and I too need to go to soldiers, only from another regiment. Check into it, commissar, that there are communists and Komsomol members in each assault group. Maintain communication with Shuba because I won't be back to the staff until this evening."

"Yes, I know!" said Fomin, without thinking.

"You already know that, commissar?" Fomin was confused. Lyudnikov's eyebrows rose in a surprised expression: he looked forward to hearing this.

"Our orderly, Zlydnev – you know our Zlydnev, don't you? – was recently at the neighbours and brought back news: soon, he said, we'll be going on the offensive. I asked Zlydnev: 'Where'd you learn that?' And he answered: 'On the soldier's telegraph, from a sure sign – the Colonel will tour the front-line. We veterans know that if our Colonel inspects the front-line, the Germans had better look out.'"

– – –

Lieutenant Chulkov and Sergeant Lyutin maintained that their groups had exterminated about fifty Germans in the dug-outs. Pechenyuk, however, knew that the division commander did not like reports containing terms such as 'believed' and 'about', and he would also be quite distressed by the losses suffered by the storm groups. That is why for Lyudnikov's arrival Pechenyuk gathered all of the storm groups' trophies in one place: 2 light machine-guns, 2 submachine-guns, 7 rifles and 3 pistols. Once the dug-outs had been blocked, the Germans could not escape. And it would convince the division commander that the trophies had been taken after fierce and deadly combat with the enemy.

Lyudnikov listened to Pechenyuk's report and examined the weapons.

"Your men fought well!" he said to Pechenyuk. "Let's go see them, I wish to meet the future medal bearers."

Pechenyuk, flattered by such praise, led the division commander into a dug-out where the submachine-gunners of the two assault groups were resting. Catching sight of the Colonel, Lieutenant Chulkov – as was peculiar to recent military school graduates – quickly reported on the fulfilment of the combat mission.

And here the Colonel dumbfounded everyone with a question:

"How is it, my storming heroes, that you allowed the enemy to beat you?"

Lieutenant Chulkov's mood darkened and he looked questioningly at the regiment commander. But Pechenyuk too had been confused by the colonel's question and could not find an answer.

"But we completed the mission," said Chulkov, suppressing his anger. "We wrote off fifty Germans in those dug-outs. They…" he pointed to the submachine-gunners, "let them tell you…"

"You attacked valiantly. Honour to the soldiers. You'll receive medals. And you, Chulkov, and Sergeant Lyutin, won't miss out either. However, it is necessary to have both medals on your chest and a head on your shoulders. You knew there was not enough support! You knew! You should make your own – provide cover with a machine-gunner…Then the men would be saved. And what men! Twelve daring lads in exchange for fifty foul Germans already doomed to death or captivity? This, brothers, is not 1941! That is now an unacceptable ratio for the world-renowned heroes of the Barrikady. Do you agree with me?"

Pechenyuk was encouraged a little, Chulkov's spirit lifted and the soldiers became cheerful.

- - -

The constant Soviet attacks gradually wore down the Germans. Their effects are tangible in Hauptmann Rettenmaier's almost-daily letter:

> The Russians continue to rage uninterruptedly against us. Our situation has not become rosier. How long can it continue! The demands on each one are enormous. We hardly get any mail. From time to time a letter flutters in for one or another of us. I have not received any news from home for three weeks. I would just be happy if I was certain that you are getting regular news from me. I am well as long as I can master everything in this current situation. 'I must demand still more from you…', our army commander wrote to us then. We had no idea at that time what this actually meant. We had not imagined it like this. If we had able people and reliable leaders in sufficient numbers things may be better, but gradually we are going short. Whoever has even half their capacities still remaining must redouble their exertions. For us here it is the achievement of securing the decision, and we hope that in these days of privation and need, there will come a time for being able to enjoy oneself again!

A month after the Soviet counteroffensive had been launched, and with no sign that their release was even within sight, the Germans crouching in the miserable, dirty, frozen ruins of Stalingrad sunk ever so slowly into despair. Signs of confidence in the Führer's ability to rescue them became more seldom in letters sent from Stalingrad, as did hope of ever seeing Germany and their families again. Rettenmaier again:

> The change in the situation after the encirclement was noticed by us first of all in the increasing activity of the enemy. Close on top of that, however, was something else: the strict rationing of everything was felt by the soldiers. It was suddenly clear to everyone what it meant to be surrounded and cut off from the homeland. Loud conversations in the dug-outs were silenced; everyone wanted to be alone with their thoughts. Letter after letter was written. Everyone had to pour their hearts out in some way. The premonition of an utterly terrifying fate crept in and everyone sought release in a dialogue with his family. Mail from home arrived in dribs and drabs. They were read and then read again, and repeatedly taken out. These lines from home seemed to radiate a secret strength.

The Barrikady Gun Factory, once a bustling complex where billowing smokestacks kept watch over thousands of industrious workers, was now a thoroughly alien world, a grotesque junkyard of twisted girders and frozen piles of gun barrels. The bone-achingly cold wind swept through the iced-up ruins, whipped up snow flurries, hurled icy particles into exposed faces and caused loose sheets of corrugated iron to clap incessantly. Everything was drained of colour: the heavy grey sky that slumped like a wet blanket, the red bricks glazed with frost and filth, and even men's faces, now pallid, devoid of colour. In the front of every German soldier's mind was the knowledge that they were cut off, far from the main German line and even further from Germany. Letters from home were their only contact with loved ones… and they needed them now more than ever because of the strength that could be taken from them. Most important of all was the feeling of being connected in some way with the beloved Fatherland, and therefore, to their families. To the homesick German soldiers, any trace of Germany, any at all, was seized upon as a sign of hope, a link back to Germany. Such a sign existed in the bleak and battered Barrikady. In the half-wrecked tool shop of Hall 3c, positioned amongst other machines, was a lathe. In clear German block letters was the name of the manufacturer: Gustav Wagner, Reutlingen.[36] The letters seemed to be like a greeting from home. The machine received frequent visits, even from those who knew nothing about lathes. They acted as if they were interested in the machine; in reality, they only wanted to caress the cold iron with their hands. Others would just stare at the machine, and, as if it were some kind of medium, be transported home in their thoughts. 'Would you still be able to use it?' 'Could the Russians put it back into service if we weren't here?' 'Where's Reutlingen?' asked the non-Swabians. This machine, created by German hands, became a shrine to the lonely soldiers of the Bodensee Division.

– – –

By Lyudnikov's order, three red rockets – the signal which gave the artillery the go ahead to bombard the Germans – were sent up from Zaitsevsky Island during the night of 19 to 20 December.

Casualties for 19 December, 1942:	
138th Rifle Division:	8 killed, 14 wounded, a total of 22 men
305. Infanterie-Division:	19 men killed, 44 men wounded

---

36. The firm 'Gustav Wagner Maschinenfabrik', founded in 1890, declared itself bankrupt in 1994 and closed down.

20 December, 1942

During the night, units of 650th Rifle Regiment repulsed four counterattacks that were trying to restore the position by recapturing the lost dug-outs and trench. Second Rifle Battalion was involved in heavy grenade fighting in the trenches from 0200 to 0400 hours. Despite the brutal combat, the regiment firmly held its new defensive line. Small groups of Germans were spotted moving from the unfinished building to the gully 50 metres north of the water tower. What the Soviets needed most were sappers with explosives to undermine a German dug-out and a 15-metre long trench that were making their new positions almost untenable. From 0200 to 1600 hours, small arms and machine-guns were occasionally fired and grenades were thrown. Losses of 650th Rifle Regiment were 2 officers and 13 soldiers killed, plus 4 officers, 5 NCOs and 35 soldiers wounded, a total of 59 men.

The Germans undertook no actions on the other sectors of 138th Rifle Division but often fired on the river crossings with rifles and machine-guns. The division took up better positions and prepared for the next assault. With the onset of darkness, the Germans laid down heavy machine-gun fire on the river crossing and Soviet artillery conducted methodical fire on the German front-line and rear. Soviet losses throughout the day were 16 killed, 33 wounded, plus 14 lightly wounded men who were still in action, having refused evacuation. A total of 63 men, all but 4 of those coming from Pechenyuk's regiment.

LI. Armeekorps reported that "since 1730 hours, an enemy attack with flamethrowers had been in progress east of the gun factory". No mention of this attack, let alone flamethrowers, can be found in Soviet records, but it may well have been a very small action. The use of flamethrowers always attracted disproportionate amounts of attention.

– – –

305. Infanterie-Division held its positions firmly, having created a system of obstacles and masses of emplacements. The backbone of the German defence on the sectors of 344th and 650th Rifle Regiments was a group of buildings in the southern part of Pribaltiskaya Street and Prospekt Lenina. The main stronghold was the Kommissarhaus. The other formidable fortresses were Dom 38 [Haus 67], 41 [Haus 75], 37 [Haus 74], the red building [Haus 64] and the transformer hut. The strong redoubts themselves were furnished with large numbers of machine-guns, company mortars and a few anti-tank guns, and were linked by communication trenches and interconnected by a system of dug-outs, blockhouses and pillboxes. Spaces between buildings and dug-outs were mined and secured with wire entanglements, Bruno spirals and trip-wires. The forward line of the German defences was scored by communication trenches that allowed free passage from dug-out to dug-out and from building to building during assaults.

The enormous casualties suffered by 305. Infanterie-Division during the previous two months of fighting for the Barrikady factory, both in attack and defence, forced it to base its defence on the principle of creating serious obstacles, engineering works, and providing skilfully organised systems of fire of the thickest density. Owing to heavy losses in personnel, the grenadier regiments were equipped with an excess of automatic weapons, mainly light and heavy machine-guns and submachine-guns. Specific conditions of battle in urban areas and the extreme proximity of the Soviet front-line resulted in the widespread use of grenades. Despite the dire need for ammunition and strict limitations in its expenditure, grenades were available in large quantities. Stacked in each house-cum-strongpoint were at least 200 hand grenades, while every dug-out had several boxes available. The Germans strove to hold the occupied line at any cost, the main objective being to ensure that Gorishny's 95th Rifle Division did not break through from the south. The German policy was to replace personnel with automatic weapons and create defensive works with pioneers. By providing the main line of defence with high-density fire, man-made obstacles and engineering works, however, 305. Infanterie-Division was forced to forego the creation of defence in depth. They could not withdraw, but being in dug-outs, blockhouses and pillboxes, the garrisons displayed stubborn resistance in the face of utter annihilation.

Lyudnikov's units, literally defending a small patch of territory, were caught in difficult circumstances. The heavy saturation of German firepower, amplified by the small area being held, prohibited daylight operations. This painful lesson had been learnt on 15 December. Even the appearance of a solitary soldier during daylight was cause for German machine-gunners to immediately open fire with pinpoint accuracy. Also, the Denezhnaya Volozhka channel, which was the one and only route for communicating with the rear and for delivery of ammunition and rations, was regularly raked by artillery and mortar fire.

- - -

The goal of 138th Rifle Division was simple: join up with 95th Rifle Division. To accomplish this they needed to subjugate some, if not all, of the German strongpoints. Overcoming this formidably protected line, however, would be no simple undertaking.

344th Rifle Regiment received the task of striking in the direction of Pribaltiskaya Street to destroy enemy strongpoints in the area of Dom 38, 34, 36, 37, reach the objective line of Dom 39, 28, 29, 31 and firmly consolidate there with a front to the west and south-west.

The mission of 650th Rifle Regiment was to destroy enemy strongpoints in the area of the red, unfinished and P-shaped buildings, completely clear this area and join up with units of 241st Rifle Regiment.

Gunyaga's 768th Rifle Regiment would hold their positions.

The orders issued by the two assault regiments were as follows:

In Combat Order No. 094 issued by 344th regimental headquarters at 1500 hours on 19 December, Captain Konovalenko ordered that "a surprise attack be carried out in the direction of Pribaltiskaya to destroy enemy strongpoints in the area of Dom 38, 35, 34, 37, 36 and the dug-outs adjoining them. Sweeping operations by storm groups will seize buildings 28, 29, 31 and then consolidate on the line 39, 34, 28, 29, 31."

To accomplish this, Konovalenko would deploy two battalions, Senior-Lieutenant Tolkachev's 1st Rifle Battalion and Senior-Lieutenant Berbeshkin's[37] 2nd Rifle Battalion. The orders to the battalions were as follows:

> 1st Rifle Battalion will advance in the direction of Pribaltiskaya Street with the task of destroying enemy strongpoints in the area of Dom 38, 35, 34, 37, 36 and reach the objective area 29, 28 and consolidate there with a front to the south and south-west. The forming-up position of the groups will be in the area of Dom 39, 40 and 42.
>
> a) 1st storm group with 51 men, of them, 10 are submachine-gunners, 2 light machine-guns. Task. Surprise attack from the direction of the west side of Dom 38 to destroy the enemy in Dom 35, 34, 33. Without removing individual enemy emplacements, rapidly seize Dom 30, 29, 28, consolidate there with a front to the west and south-west and facilitate the mopping-up of the enemy in Dom 32 and 31 together with the storm groups of 2nd Rifle Battalion.

37. Berbeshkin, Major Aleksandr Andreyevich, HotSU; 2/344th RR; born 13 July, 1916 in Karavaino. Killed in action, 17 April, 1944.

b) Capture group with 35 men, 2 light machine-guns.
Task: Operating simultaneously behind the storm group, annihilate the enemy in Dom 38 and the dug-outs to the west of it, completely clear the enemy from Dom 35, 34 and 33, and consolidate along the line Dom 34, 28, 30 with a front to the west.

c) Reserve group: 25 men with 1 light machine-gun, 1 heavy machine-gun, an anti-tank rifle and 2 company mortars.
Task: Protect the right flank of the storm and capture groups in the direction of Dom 39 and 34, and be ready to repel enemy counterattacks from the direction of Workshop 14/15 and the main gate.

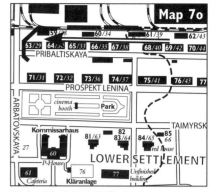

Task of 1/344th Rifle Regiment.

And to Berbeshkin's battalion:

a) Storm group with 30 men, of them, 15 are submachine-gunners, 1 light machine-gun.
Task: Operating from the direction of Dom 45 toward Taimyrskaya Street, very quickly annihilate the enemy in Dom 36, 32, seal off the dug-outs near Dom 37, seize Dom 31, and consolidate in Dom 31 and 32 with a front to the south and south-east.

b) Capture group with 20 men and 1 light machine-gun.
Task: Destroy the enemy in the dug-outs east of Dom 37, leave behind part of the force in Dom 37 facing in the direction of Dom 41, and completely clear and consolidate in Dom 37 and 36.

c) Reserve group in Dom 45: 15 men, 1 heavy machine-gun, 1 anti-tank rifle, 1 company mortar.
Task: 1) Supportive fire operations for capture groups of 1st and 2nd rifle battalions.

2) Be ready to repel enemy counterattacks from the direction of the P-shaped building.

3) In co-ordination with the capture groups of 1st and 2nd Rifle Battalions, destroy the enemy in Dom 41.

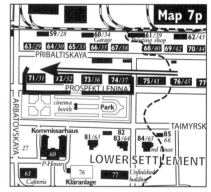

Task of 2/344th Rifle Regiment.

Up to the beginning of the assault, direct-firing artillery will destroy embrasures, suppress firing points and break open apertures in targeted houses so that grenades can be thrown into them and so that they can be infiltrated.

Requested artillery fire:

1) On Dom 38, 37, dug-outs east of Dom 37, 41 and to the west of 38.

2) From 19.12.42, mortars of 768th Rifle Regiment will switch position to fire on enemy emplacements in Krasny Dom, P-shaped building and Dom 41 and 37.

3) Reserve group of submachine-gunners from 768th Rifle Regiment will be held ready in Dom 43 [Haus 70] to repel enemy counterattacks from the main mechanical workshop.

– – –

Major Pechenyuk also issued a directive to his regiment:

I order that a sudden blow be launched on the red building, along Taimyrskaya Street and towards the P-shaped building so as to destroy enemy emplacements and dug-outs in the red, unfinished and P-shaped buildings. Battalions will be formed into assault, capture and reserve groups.

1st Rifle Battalion with a 45mm gun will strike suddenly to destroy emplacements in the area of red, unfinished and P-shaped buildings, then reach and consolidate upon a line extending from Dom 31 to the P-shaped building.

Deployed for this were three assault groups, two capture groups and reserves, whose main task was to carry grenades. This reserve group consisted of one in three of the regiment's soldiers and shows the importance Pechenyuk placed on hand grenades in the forthcoming battle:

> 1st assault group will launch a stunning surprise attack to neutralise the emplacement 15 metres north-west of the red building, aggressively reach Taimyrskaya Street and, after consolidating in the western side of the P-shaped house, firmly hold on until the arrival of the capture group. Front to the north-west.

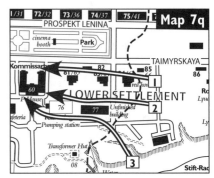

> 2nd assault group will swiftly attack to neutralise the emplacement 10 metres south-west of the red building. From the western side of the unfinished building – in co-operation with 1st group – burst into the P-shaped building and together with the commander of the 1st group, stubbornly hold on until the arrival of the capture group.

> 3rd assault group will neutralise the emplacement on the southern side of the unfinished building and emerge on the southern corner of the P-shaped building.

Assault groups were ordered to continue advancing forward, to disregard any unsuppressed emplacements and to carry out the missions as set down. The first capture group would destroy the enemy in red building and Kommissarhaus on Taimyrskaya Street and clear these same areas. Towards the end of the day, Lyudnikov received a further 79 men as reinforcements (2 officers and 77 NCOs and men) and the bulk of these went to 650th Rifle Regiment: 1 officer, 2 NCOs and 47 enlisted men, a total of 50. The regiment then reported a strength of 49 officers, 28 NCOs and 126 soldiers, a total of 203 men.

- - -

While 138th Rifle Division was preparing for the big attack, 95th Rifle Division carried out a preliminary operation. Artillery and mortars had fired on German emplacements north of Appendix Gully throughout the day, and at 1600 hours, storm groups of Major Budarin's 241st Rifle Regiment began an assault on the northern slopes of this gully. Twenty minutes later, after the liberal use of hand grenades, they seized Dom 05, the mighty transformer station that had caused them trouble for over a month. As soon as the building was lost, the Germans launched an immediate counterattack with 35 men. It failed. Attacks were repeated at 1720 and 2100 hours, each in platoon strength, but both were beaten off. Russian sources state that the Germans suffered heavy losses during the fighting, leaving over 60 corpses on the battlefield. Soviet losses were about a dozen men. The storm groups also captured 5 dugouts and 2 pillboxes. Budarin's riflemen held the vital building throughout the night.

After a month of static warfare in which the roles of attacker and defender had slowly but surely reversed, the front was about to be set in flux. The offensive impetus was in Soviet hands. The Germans could only wait. The hunter was about to become the hunted.

Casualties for 20 December, 1942:
138th Rifle Division: 16 killed, 33 wounded, plus 14 lightly wounded men who were still in action, having refused evacuation. A total of 63 men
305. Infanterie-Division: 18 men killed, 1 officer and 77 men wounded, 2 men missing

21 December, 1942

Night and silence reigned over the Barrikady. German machine-guns drummed occasionally, overlaid with the echoing snaps of rifle fire. Then silence returned. By the flickering light of random flares, Soviet observers spotted groups of German soldiers moving about. At one point, further north, from the direction of buildings 51, 50 and the ravine to the north-east, German machine-guns and mortars fired intensively on the Denezhnaya Volozhka channel. Nothing was out of the ordinary. Gunners on Zaitsevsky Island played a fifteen minute 'overture' at midnight and then stopped. The Germans returned to their firing positions after this bombardment because they knew it would be followed by almost three hours of restful sleep.

It was silent along the front-line before dawn. But Lyudnikov and his staff did not sleep. Regiment staffs were awake. Storm and capture groups had already assumed their starting positions. The hour hands on watches – synchronised beforehand by everyone involved – counted down the last seconds until 0240 hours. Lyudnikov left his dug-out. From the wintry sky fell light snow, so light in fact that it was not visible. Only if one's face was lifted to the sky was it possible to feel the pleasant tickling of snowflakes. The luminous second hand of Lyudnikov's watch clicked onto the much anticipated time. Two hours and forty minutes had passed. A blue flare hissed into the sky from the ravine in Gunyaga's sector, three red flares from Zaitsevsky Island answered it, and, as usual, one gun fired, followed by others, and then the overture was joined by howitzers and mortars.

The Germans had become inured to the artillery fire from previous nights, so after seeing the red rockets, they pulled back from the forward line to seek cover. All was as usual for them. This night, however, was unusual for the Soviets because they were aware that in two minutes sharp, the gunners on Zaitsevsky Island would transfer their fire to the depth of the German defences. And a minute after that, a second rocket would arch out over the Volga towards Zaitsevsky Island. The gunners would see it and, as if obeying a conductor's baton, would instantly halt their fire. The Germans would be startled and try rush back to their strongpoints but it would already be too late.

One minute, another, a third... the planning of each storm group's actions down to the tiniest detail by the division commander, all the lengthy and secret preparations for the offensive and all the stockpiling of weapons, shells and cartridges laboriously transported and transferred from the rear to Zaitsevsky Island and the west bank of the Volga – everything now came down to these three minutes. On the third minute, the guns and mortars would stop, and those who initiated the battle and aimed to secure victory would already be silently assaulting the opponent's strongpoints.

The cannonade suddenly ceased, as if severed by an axe, and in trenches, dug-outs and cellars, submachine-guns and grenades started talking, bayonets and daggers started flashing...

The storm groups of 138th Rifle Division broke into the forward German positions. After swiftly annihilating firing posts and sentries, they continued to move ahead. The first reports came in. Konovalenko's storm groups, advancing in the direction of Pribaltiskaya Street, had broken through the barbed wire entanglements and captured a row of trenches and dug-outs next to Dom 36 [Haus 73] and 37 [Haus 74] without a struggle. Dom 38 [Haus 67] and 35 [Haus 66] were also quickly seized and the storm groups successfully moved ahead to Dom 34 [Haus 60], 33 [Haus 65] and 36 [Haus 73]. Some of the groups even reached the Barrikady's central gates while it was still dark. Dom 41 [Haus 75] and 37 [Haus 74] – a twin-embrasured pillbox – were blockaded by capture groups.

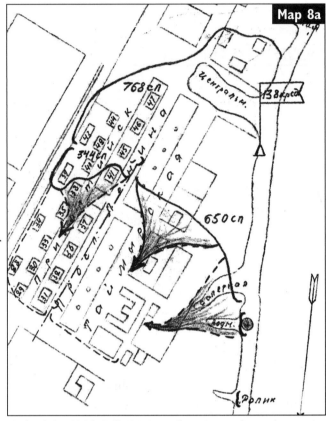

A sketch by 138th Rifle Division shows its attacks on the morning of 21 December, 1942.

"I don't see the Germans yet," reported Konovalenko by phone. This apparent enemy absence ended upon the word 'yet' because at 0300 hours, the Germans recognised the Soviet advance and began offering stubborn resistance. They tried to stop the movement of Soviet storm groups with counterattacks and fire. LI. Armeekorps later reported to 6. Armee that "since 0300 hours, enemy attacks are in progress from the bridgehead east of the gun factory".

Germans troops laid down furious flanking fire from the direction of Workshop 14/15 [Hall 3] and fire from the front, from Dom 9 [Haus 57] and 10 [Haus 55/School No. 2], effectively cutting off Konovalenko's storm groups from their capture groups. Even so, the storm groups continued to move forward and threw themselves into hand-to-hand combat with stubborn German defenders. Fighting continued in the area of Dom 36, 34, 33 and 32. Those grappling with the Germans in the darkness of workhall cellars and in the factory tunnel did not notice when dawn broke.

A soldier brought to the battalion aid station after being wounded in Dom 35 was the first to deliver some news: the storm groups had moved quite far forward and paralysed the enemy up to the central gates of the Barrikady factory.

Fierce and numerous German counterattacks began on all fronts. They were launched with groups of 25-30 submachine-gunners supported by mortars and a large number of heavy and light machine-guns. Particularly active fire and counterattacks developed from the direction of Workshop 14/15 and Dom 8, 9 and 10. All attacks were beaten off with heavy losses for the Germans.

At 0500 hours, with the grey dawn wanly illuminating the battlefield, German observers were able to bring down a hurricane of mortar fire, interfering with the advance of the capture groups. This, together with increasingly accurate machine-gun fire, completely cut off the storm groups and communication with them was lost. At 0530 hours, the storm groups in Dom 36, 34, 33, and 32 – cut off from the capture groups – went over to hand-to-hand combat in trenches and dug-outs.

– – –

Once the artillery shifted forward just after 0240 hours, the three storm groups of 650th Rifle Regiment advanced towards the Kommissarhaus. Each had an initial objective but their final goal was to capture this formidable strongpoint.

The first assault group launched themselves out of trenches and silently broke into Dom 65 [Haus 84], also known to the Soviets as the 'red building'. As envisaged by Lyudnikov, the German defenders had left their firing positions and were sheltering in the cellar. Once they realised they had intruders in their house, they acted swiftly, but it was too late. Grenades were exchanged in the cellar stairwell. The German garrison of Dom 64 [Haus 83] tried to intervene but the pre-dawn gloom mixed with a powdery haze meant it was risky to fire at shadowy figures in and around Haus 84. German reinforcements sent along the trench to Haus 84 were halted by well-placed volleys of grenades. The German garrison of Haus 84 knew they'd been bested. They burst out of the cellar and along the trench into Haus 83, harried all the way by Soviet fire. Pechenyuk's men were the new masters of Haus 84. Several nearby dug-outs were also taken out.

The second assault group pushed past Haus 84 and took a bunker south-east of it, now easily captured because the German garrison was seeking shelter in the building. When the Germans came back through the trench towards their bunker, they were stopped cold by a wall of rifle and machine-gun fire. The surviving Germans retired to Haus 83 and were incorporated into its defences. The Soviet storm group then used German trenches to penetrate the unfinished building, so facilitating the advance of the third storm group. They swept into the cellar and a vicious hand grenade duel started. Both sides used up box after box. Soviet reserve groups ensured that a steady supply of grenades reached the storm groups. The German garrison of the unfinished building eventually pulled back to Haus 81 and the Kommissarhaus. With three strongpoints now in their possession, Pechenyuk's capture groups thoroughly cleared all of them and began the slow and deadly process of subjugating the

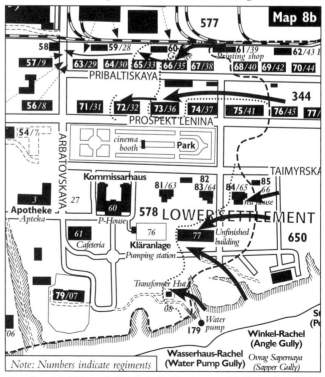

Attacks of 344th and 650th Rifle Regiments, 21 December, 1942.

Orlov

To keep in close contact with his assault troops, Lyudnikov positioned himself in his observation post in Dom 67 [Haus 87]. Calls constantly came in reporting on the progress of the storm groups. The female telephonist is G.A. Sharova.

numerous bunkers and dug-outs that led off the communications trenches, and prepared to fend off the imminent German counterattacks.

The third assault group, welling up from Water and Sapper Gullies, charged towards the transformer hut and unfinished building. Scything machine-gun fire chopped down many of them but the rest leapt into the German front-line trenches. The lack of cellars in this area meant the Germans weathered the artillery bombardments in their bunkers and so reacted much more quickly. The Soviet assault troops slogged their way along each trench, capturing each dug-out in sinister scuffles in the darkness. Slowly but surely the Soviet troops moved forward through the network of trenches but progress became costlier the closer they moved to the Kommissarhaus: machine-guns on its upper floor could fire into certain sections of the trench. Back at the clifftop, a successful assault was launched on the transformer hut and

Lyudnikov observes the attack from his observation post.

this hated pillbox was soon in Soviet hands. Also captured were two anti-tank guns that had made life difficult for the Rolik group and the armoured boats back in November.

The new reinforcements, some of whom had only set foot on Stalingrad soil a day or two earlier, fought extremely well. Amongst them were some 'shtrafnikov', men from penal battalions. Senior-Sergeant Gorbatenko remembers one of them:

> The regiment began to receive reinforcements in December. Amongst the arrivals were men of unusual physical strength, such as brave Sergeant-Major Perepich. He carried an anti-tank rifle as his personal weapon when he burst into the German trenches and cellars. Scores of them fell. His courage surprised everyone. He was unassailable at the closest distance. His fists and gun butt killed the Germans. In Stalingrad, his previous conviction was overturned. In a frank conversation, he somehow told me that 'he was convicted for running over a child with an automobile, with a fatal outcome for the child'. The child always ran alongside the machine.

Perepich redeemed himself in Stalingrad, particularly in these first battles to capture the German strongholds, and he was subsequently bestowed the Red Star and other medals. During the Kursk fighting in 1943, he destroyed some Tigers and self-propelled guns with an anti-tank rifle, but died later in the year during a bombardment.

In a report filed at 1500 hours, 138th Rifle Division wrote about the activities of Pechenyuk's regiment:

They destroyed over 80 hitlerites, took prisoner two soldiers from Grenadier-Regiment 578, captured some buildings to the north of the P-shaped house, the transformer hut and dug-outs 100 metres east of the P-shaped house and emerged on the left flank of the Rolik group.

The strength of the German strongpoints is clearly demonstrated by the amount of weapons destroyed and captured by Pechenyuk's storm groups. Whilst only three light machine-guns and one 37mm gun were destroyed, the following trophies were captured: one 75 mm anti-tank gun with 60 shells, 17 light machine-guns, 2 mortars, about 50 rifles and over 250 grenades.

– – –

On the right wing of the division, 768th Rifle Regiment's main task was to hold the line, but they also launched assault group operations of their own. As the groups moved off at 0240 hours, German mortars in Workshop 4 [Hall 6a] opened fire and bracketed the attacking troops. They were showered by hand grenades as they approached the German trenches. When they forced a small penetration, a German counterattack threw them back immediately. The operation was unsuccessful and the groups, taking further losses, withdrew to their starting line and defended their previous positions. Casualties were heavy: 6 killed and 27 wounded. At the end of the day, Gunyaga's strength was 112 men, 80 of those being deployed on the front-line.

– – –

Concurrent with these attacks was the northward advance of 95th Rifle Division. The capture of Dom 05 – the transformer station – the previous night had greatly simplified the division's task. At 0300 hours, the storm groups pushed out of the building to take some German fortifications along the cliff tops, specifically two pillboxes connected by narrow trenches to Dom 06 [Haus 42]. They met stiff resistance and went to ground. Over the next few hours, they worked their way forward and overwhelmed individual German dug-outs and foxholes. At 0600 hours, a group of about 20 Germans was seen heading towards the transformer but they were forced back by heavy fire. By 1000 hours, the Soviet storm groups had seized several dug-outs north-west of Dom 05.

Progress was also slow on the other regiments' sectors. The storm groups of 90th Rifle Regiment were met by vicious fire from the Apotheke and Dom 12 [Haus 52] and therefore had no success. At 1100 hours, individual German soldiers, numbering about 40 men, were observed moving from the Barrikady factory towards the green fuel tank in an effort to bolster the defences there. Storm groups from 161st Rifle Regiment threw grenades at a German pillbox on the railway embankment and captured a heavy machine-gun.

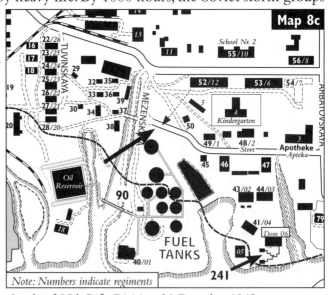

Attacks of 95th Rifle Division, 21 December, 1942.

The divisional artillery fired on German emplacements east and south-east of the factory, but it was the smaller weapons that proved more effective in the close-quarters fighting: by 1000 hours, mortars, ampulomets and 45mm guns had destroyed 4 pillboxes and 10 dug-outs near Dom 04 [Haus 41], knocking out 3 machine-guns in the process.

– – –

The few available documents from official German sources provide a good impression of the attacks and the difficulties they caused. First, a report sent to 6. Armee at 1640 hours by LI. Armeekorps:

> Since the early hours of the morning, very focused enemy attacks against the positions of 305. Infanterie-Division east of the gun factory. On the southern and northern wings, the attacks were defeated with high casualties for the enemy (in one spot, 45 enemy dead were counted). In the centre (grid square 83b4), 3 houses were lost with – at times – our own significant losses.

It was later reported to Heeresgruppe Don that the "break-in near 305. Infanterie-Division has so far been sealed off by the use of the last local reserves. Enemy attacks continue." At 1820 hours, 6. Armee sent a more detailed appraisal of the situation:

> On 21.12., strong enemy attacks in Stalingrad east of the gun factory. After our own forces employed there were battered by strong artillery and mortar fire, the enemy captured 3 houses. Forces needed to counterattack are not available. Breakthrough position has been sealed off. Our casualties have again been substantial. All battalions employed there only have available a Bataillonsführer [battalion leaders] with one adjutant each, the latter also leading one of the subordinated companies at the same time. Two battalions have Bataillonsführer only.

Finally, at 2045 hours, LI. Armeekorps sent its evening report to 6. Armee:

> The repeated strong attacks east of the gun factory in the afternoon were repulsed. Heavy artillery, mortar and rocket fire on the steel factory and gun factory, which decreased from 1500 hours. East of his gun factory bridgehead, the Russians constructed a wood and ice barricade over the Volga arm, apparently to protect his crossing traffic.

– – –

As a result of the nocturnal attack, 344th and 650th Rifle Regiments were able to finally break through the German front-line, push it back up to 200 metres in some places and completely annihilate the garrisons of the captured buildings and dug-outs. All further attacks, however, were met by fierce resistance. The German ability to rapidly mobilise reserves and launch powerful counterattacks thwarted any Soviet attempts to capitalise on the initial success. Nevertheless, the capture of four buildings, each one a fearsome fortress abundantly equipped with automatic weapons and grenades, was seen as a great achievement. On top of that, 14 pillboxes and 10 dug-outs had been seized and 18 dug-outs completely destroyed. The division calculated the loss of enemy materiel and personnel through infantry fire, artillery and hand-to-hand combat to be over 250 men, 9 heavy and light machine-guns and one 37mm anti-tank gun. Captured were one 75mm anti-tank guns, 3 mortars, 21 light machine guns, over 50 rifles, 300 grenades, up to 100 shells and nearly 5000 cartridges. Two soldiers from Grenadier-Regiment 578 were captured.

The war diary of 62nd Army provides an excellent overall view of the day's fighting, including the northward attack of Gorishny's division:

21 December. Since 0300 hours Lyudnikov's division has continued its attack in a south-westerly direction. In spite of strong enemy opposition, our units have occupied four buildings, and on the right flank advanced between 100-120 metres. Three enemy counterattacks have been beaten off. Five heavy machine-guns and two prisoners of 578th Infantry Regiment of 305th Infantry Division have been captured.

Since 0300 hours, Gorishny's division has been attacking in a north-westerly direction. Overcoming stiff enemy resistance, they have surrounded and wiped out individual enemy garrisons. After hand-to-hand fighting (with extensive use of hand grenades) units occupied a transforming station which the enemy had turned into a pillbox. One building, six dug-outs and two blockhouses have been captured. Fighting is continuing. The enemy is trying to restore the position, launching counterattacks, which have been successfully repulsed.

Equipment captured: 3 machine-guns, 6 submachine-guns, 35 rifles, 380 hand grenades; 4 blockhouses destroyed. In the captured dug-outs the enemy has left behind 40 dead…

The amount of equipment captured by 95th Rifle Division was later revised to 12 machine-guns, over 80 rifles, 15 submachine-guns, 400 hand grenades and 10,000 cartridges. The division suffered the following casualties: 241st Rifle Regiment − 14 men; 90th Rifle Regiment − 12 men; 161st Rifle Regiment − 7 men.

Casualties for 21 December, 1942:		
138th Rifle Division:	40 killed, 171 wounded, a total of 211 men (preliminary data)	
305. Infanterie-Division: 16 men killed, 3 officers and 126 men wounded, 6 men missing		
389. Infanterie-Division: 1 officer and 5 men killed, 5 men wounded, 1 man missing		

22 December, 1942

The brutal fighting did not ease during the night. Gunfire and explosions, muffled by the confines of the buildings, echoed across the city. Flares occasionally sizzled into the smoky night, machine-guns let loose at shadows and men on both sides stared towards the enemy with terror-filled eyes. At 2230 hours, storm groups of 344th Rifle Regiment continued active actions to try to take complete control of Dom 41, 37, 36, and 35. At 2300 hours, Senior-Lieutenant Berbeshkin and his storm group were in complete control of Dom 41 and captured two prisoners from Grenadier-Regiment 577. Berbeshkin particularly distinguished himself during this fighting. A few minutes later, Dom 37 and 3 dug-outs were also secured, and two men from Pionier-Bataillon 305 were taken prisoner. Savage combat still raged through Dom 35 and 36.

At 2330 hours, the Germans stepped over to the counteroffensive from Workshop 14/15, trying to

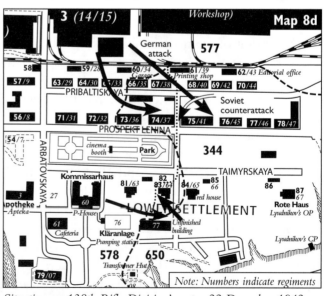

Situation on 138th Rifle Division's sector, 22 December, 1942.

recapture their old positions, the freshly captured Dom 41 being most under threat. Aspiring to recapture it, the Germans launched a powerful counterattack and surrounded Berbeshkin's group but Konovalenko skilfully manoeuvred his reserves, strengthened the capture group that was cut off from Berbeshkin and then led it into battle himself. The Germans did not manage to withdraw to the factory workshops: their path was cut off and they were pressed back against a wall of the house by fire from both Konovalenko's and Berbeshkin's groups. The Germans went to ground and then melted away, creeping back to other strongpoints. Konovalenko was the first to get into the basement of Dom 41 with his men. While the German counterattack had not been successful in recapturing Dom 41, it did succeed in driving the Soviet storm groups from Dom 35, 36, 37, 38 and the 3 dug-outs captured only a few minutes earlier.

Also during the night, a storm group of 650th Rifle Regiment managed to penetrate Dom 64 [Haus 83], their former regimental command post. A bitter hand-to-hand struggle began. At 2300 hours, the Germans launched a counterattack with up to 30 soldiers from the Kommissarhaus towards the unfinished building and Haus 83. Heavy covering fire emanated from the Kommissarhaus. Suffering casualties, the Germans were forced to retreat to their departure position. Combat groups of 650th Rifle Regiment, now consolidated in captured dug-outs, were able to beat back a total of four counterattacks from that direction.

At 0610 hours, LI. Armeekorps reported to 6. Armee that "further attacks during the night against the centre of 305. Infanterie-Division east of the gun factory were repulsed".

– – –

The night also didn't pass quietly near 95th Rifle Division. At 0030 and 0300 hours, the Germans launched attacks three times on the sector of 90th Rifle Regiment, near the fuel tanks, each time with a strength of 15-20 soldiers. They were all repelled.

Having concentrated all ampulomets – using thermite spheres – and divisional artillery on 241st Rifle Regiment's sector, the storm groups set out at 0300 hours in a north-western direction. In the area of Dom 04, 06 and to the west of the fuel tanks, the Germans laid down thick sheets of rifle and machine-gun fire. The 9 storm groups of 241st Rifle Regiment pushed on. Three groups moved along the river bank, one towards 138th Rifle Division and the other two to take Dom 06 from the rear. Atop the cliffs, another three groups overcame German defences and by 0400 hours had captured dug-outs and pillboxes north-west of Dom 05. At the same time, the two groups moving along the shore headed up Zeigefinger Gully, surprised the garrison of Dom 06 from behind and captured it after brutal hand grenade duels. The three remaining storm groups, on left flank, developed the assault on Dom 04 and by 0400 hours had seized dug-outs to the west of Dom 05, where they consolidated. During the fighting, the

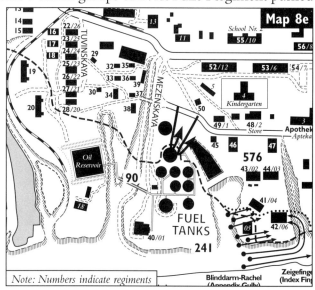

Advance of 241st Rifle Regiment's storm groups, 22 December, 1942.

Germans tried to restore the position by counterattacking the regiment's left flank twice but had no success. Sustaining heavy losses, they took up defence. One of the counterattacks was launched by 2./Pi.Btl.305 under the command of the battalion's former adjutant, Oberleutnant Max Fritz, who now led the one company consolidated from all three companies. It pressed towards the Volga and – according to Obergefreiter Franz Müller, who was employed as a machine-gunner – was successful. For his efforts, Müller was promised the Iron Cross First Class by Fritz. Nevertheless, this 'successful' counterattack did not have much of an impact because Soviet records state that it was beaten off.

At 0300 hours, small groups from 90th Rifle Regiment launched their attack towards German emplacements near Gorbaty (Humpback) Gully and the green fuel tank. They were met by heavy machine-gun fire and grenades. To their left, 161st Rifle Regiment provided fire support and carried out demonstrative actions.

– – –

German nebelwerfers fired all night long at the river bank and the area around the Rolik group. Sergeant Kuzminsky and his signalmen still sat in their holes in a steep ravine of the Volga bank. Above them, in trenches, the Germans fired in all directions. Pechenyuk's storm groups moved closer to Rolik, and from the left came Gorishny's soldiers. Kuzminsky carefully listened to the approaching battle and maintained communications with division staff for as long as the connection was available.

After a heavy artillery strike the line was damaged and Vetoshkin crept out of the hole, following the wire to find the break. Overhead, a series of red rockets flashed up from a German trench. The nebelwerfers immediately stopped firing and for an instant, all was silent. Vetoshkin looked back. Above the precipice loomed German silhouettes. Germanic shouts were replaced by a booming Russian 'hurrah' and the silhouettes disappeared. From the sound of the shots, Vetoshkin determined that the fighting was taking place in the trench above Rolik. He wanted to turn back, but having recalled the order of Sergeant Kuzminsky, he started to run forward bolt upright. Vetoshkin did not let the wire out of his left hand and the broken end eventually slipped through. Then he began to search for the other end of the wire to which to connect it.

In the crackling of rifle fire, Vetoshkin did not hear that someone was creeping up on him from behind. "Ah, you rat!" croaked Vetoshkin when he was clamped in someone's arms and driven to the ground. Vetoshkin floundered under the weight of a huge body, vainly trying to free himself and, in a fit of temper, tried to bite the hands of the one who was squeezing him tightly. The hands, however, unexpectedly released him.

A meeting of 138th Rifle Division veterans in 1978. From left: L.M. Klyukin (militia), G.A. Sharova (div. staff), I.I. Svidrov (650th Rifle Rgt.), N.I. Kravchuk and S.K. Kharaziya (Rolik group). Miffed by the fact that he was not a 'Hero of the Soviet Union' despite the gold stars on the Rolik memorial, Khazariya refused to attend functions in Volgograd (modern day Stalingrad).

Barrikady Museum

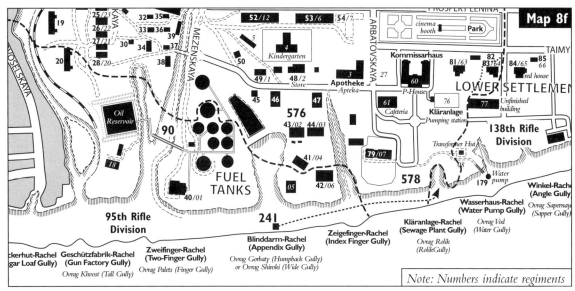

The link-up of 95th and 138th Rifle Divisions, 22 December, 1942.

"No way, one of ours!" said the tall soldier, lifting the puny Vetoshkin from the ground and turning him around toward himself. "I was going to knock you on the head with my submachine-gun… Where did you come from, as if out of nowhere?"

"Where from!" Vetoshkin shivered at the thought that having by near miracle survived the enemy and waiting for their own to arrive, he could have been killed by one of them. "Praise you to the sky, giant, but you're a dimwitted yak… I'm a signalman from Rolik…"

"From Rolik!" said the inexpressibly pleased soldier. "Let's go! To Lieutenant Chulkov!"

"Wait up, I need to establish communications…"

When Lieutenant Chulkov's group approached Rolik, the storm group from Budarin's 241st Rifle Regiment was already there, having arrived at 0340 hours. Still excited by the recent battle, Budarin's submachine-gunners went down into the ravine and stood in front of the two caves for a long time, not believing that they'd reached the signals post where for forty days and forty nights, four soldiers of 138th division – with the call-sign 'Rolik' – had continued to operate.

"Rolik here! Rolik here! Can you hear me? Received… Stand still, you devils!" Sergeant Kuzminsky shouted to the soldiers, tearing the receiver away from his ear. "I'm about to speak to 'First'…"

The soldiers became silent and Sergeant Kuzminsky again started talking on the phone. He informed Lyudnikov about who had left Rolik and when, and how at this point soldiers of two divisions had joined up. Then Kuzminsky several times repeated the short and joyful "Yes sir" – probably receiving orders from the staff in a heart-to-heart chat – and finally, after a final exclamation: "Yes sir, comrade 'First'!", Kuzminsky very carefully and in silent awe hung up the receiver, turned to the soldiers and quietly, as if to himself, repeated the last words of the divisional commander: "That which we conceived has come true. There is no longer an 'island'… I order you to establish two-way communications!"

Only now did the soldiers understand what they achieved this night. After remaining with Rolik for half an hour, the men of 241st Rifle Regiment returned to their main lines, dragging a telephone wire behind them. After that, there was no direct human contact with

Gorishny's division but at least radio and telephone communications now existed with them. General Krylov later wrote:

> Thus ended the 40 day history of 'Lyudnikov's Island'. Its defenders had basically decimated two German divisions, the 305. and 389th Infantry Divisions, which had tried again and again – in vain – to throw them into the Volga. Our 62nd Army again had a continuous front from the Barrikady Factory to the city centre…

– – –

One of the German defenders positioned in the area above Rolik's gully was Gefreiter Paul Schmidt,[1] a machine-gunner from 12./Grenadier-Regiment 578. He had been with the unit from the very beginning and was almost certainly one of the few surviving originals. In a letter home, he wrote:

> It's hard here. Yesterday, I was the only one from the entire platoon to return to the unit. As long as the war is still going, I cannot tell you any more. Because if I did tell you more, you wouldn't be able to sleep.

During the fighting on 22 December, a Stalin Organ rocket crashed down and Schmidt received a nasty wound to his jaw and several shrapnel wounds in his back. Provisional medical treatment was applied on the spot and Schmidt was fortunate to be flown out a few days later.

Gefreiter Paul Schmidt

– – –

Lyudnikov was not displeased with the result so far. Naturally he would have preferred to have captured all of the targeted buildings, but the significance of the small gains was to be found in their future implications. Firstly, physical contact had been established with Gorishny and therefore the rest of 62nd Army. Secondly, and possibly more importantly, the German stranglehold around his 'Island' had been broken. The chain of German strongpoints, all mutually supportive and linked by webs of trenches, had proven almost impregnable because overwhelming firepower could be heaped upon any Soviet attack. The first step, of cracking it and driving in a wedge, was always going to be the most difficult. With the Germans off-balance and forced to fall back upon reserve strongpoints – even though these were also imposing – Lyudnikov and his men were keen to push on and roll up the German strongpoints one after another, to suppress and capture them by blowing them up, blockading them and storming them. Whilst preparing for the next stage of the attack, the division ensured its old defensive line was held and that the recaptured positions were consolidated.

While the glory and casualties were being claimed by its two sister regiments, 768th Rifle Regiment held its former line, conducted observation and exchanged fire with Grenadier-Regiment 546 and its subordinated units. The Germans occasionally fired mortars at Gunyaga's men from the direction of the main mechanical workshop [Hall 4] and Workshop 4 [Hall 6a], and sporadically fired automatic weapons and machine-guns from forward entrenchments and dug-outs. At 0900 hours, Gunyaga's mortars destroyed a large-calibre

---

1. Schmidt, Gefreiter Paul, 12./Gr.Rgt.578; born 13 June, 1911 in Ehningen. Killed in action, 6 January, 1945 in Monte Armato, Italy.

German machine-gun in the garret of the mechanical workshop. With a rifle, Sergeant Ponamarev, a former shtrafnikov, killed a German submachine-gunner who was firing from the right corner of the mechanical workshop, destroyed the crew of a light machine-gun and knocked out a machine-gun firing from a trench that ran between that workshop and Workshop 4.

The regiment's casualties for the day were 3 men killed and 6 wounded. Its strength was 105 men, and of those, 78 were active bayonets. Its armament consisted of one 82mm mortar, two 50mm mortars, 1 DShK machine-gun, 7 light machine-guns, 12 PPSh, one 45mm anti-tank gun, 112 rifles and 2 anti-tank rifles. Ammunition stocks were forty 82mm mortar rounds, sixty 50mm mortar rounds, 9000 PPSh cartridges, 14,000 rifle cartridges, 480 DShK cartridges, 320 anti-tank rifle cartridges and 320 hand grenades.

Sergeant A. V. Ponamarev

– – –

The dramatic events on the Barrikady sector received little coverage in the official reports of 6. Armee, usually nothing more than a sentence or two. At 1615 hours, LI. Armeekorps reported that "repeated attacks during the night and morning against the positions of 305. Infanterie-Division south-east and east of the gun factory were repulsed". And at 2030 hours that "near 305. Infanterie-Division, an enemy attack east of the gun factory has been in progress since 1730 hours". With the survival of an entire army at stake, it is understandable that this strategically inconsequential fighting was so briefly reported, and those few concise sentences conveyed nothing of the misery and suffering being endured by the grenadiers and pioneers of 305. Infanterie-Division. Two examples will suffice. First, Hauptmann Rettenmaier describes the incomprehensible savagery of the fighting for one building:

> In Haus 83, one room was fought over for two days. Hand grenades from both sides flew into the no-mans-room. Thick smoke filled all the rooms. A man from there arrived at the command post. He wanted to fetch some hand grenades. His behaviour was still utterly dictated by the course of the fighting and he looked like someone who had just stared death in the face. 'Hand grenades, I must take them back to Haus 83, my comrades are waiting for me,' he said hurriedly. The doctor who was present, however, looked more closely at the man and said: 'You're eyes are completely bloodshot; you may go blind. I cannot be responsible for that. You must stay here.' Answer: 'The others back there can hardly see a thing but we must have grenades.' Only when a soldier from the messenger section volunteered to take the hand grenades did the man calm down.

The second example is a few of the events and casualties pertaining to Major Krüger's Pionier-Bataillon 305. In the evening, Obergefreiter Franz Müller, Grimm's 'problem child', who had been part of the 'successful' counterattack in the morning, was wounded. It was his third wound suffered in Stalingrad but this one was severe enough to warrant a ticket out of the pocket. Far less fortunate was his company commander, Oberleutnant Max Fritz, who jumped into a trench filled with Soviet soldiers. Some say he was beaten over the head, others that he was shot, but in any case he was killed. His death was a severe loss for the battalion. Max Fritz had been one of the battalion's original members, was an experienced officer, an adjutant without parallel and respected by all. On 27 December, the previous battalion commander, Hauptmann Traub, wrote in a letter to his wife:

Sadly, in the last few days, we have had some losses in the battalion, among them two officers: one through a direct hit from a bomb on his quarters and the other my former adjutant, the commander of 2. Kompanie, falling in action on the front-lines during a Russian attack. I have written to the wife of the first fatality. Now I have to write to the parents of our previous adjutant, Oberleutnant Fritz. These are always difficult letters to compose, but one cannot avoid this duty.

The officer killed by a direct bomb hit was Leutnant Hubert Homburger, commander of both the battalion's light pioneer column and a company formed from Soviet POWs. The battalion's technical inspector, Georg Zeller, recalls that Homburger and his entire staff were killed when the bomb plunged straight through the roof of their dug-out and exploded inside. Even though Hauptmann Traub was engaged with other tasks and was not leading the battalion in battle, he still had to carry out what some considered to be the most difficult function of a commander: writing the dreaded 'I regret to inform you…' letters.

The unexpected ferocity of the Soviet attacks and the resulting gaps in the German ranks meant that any able-bodied man was sent to the front. One of them was Gefreiter Wilhelm Füssinger from the supply train of 1./Pionier-Bataillon 305. His brief tenure as a front-line soldier was recorded in a letter home:

> On 21 December, I was deployed in the fighting in Stalingrad, and by 22 December had already been wounded in the right hand. Since then, I find myself back at the supply train so I can heal. At least I will not have to spend Christmas in the trenches.

Among the 57 wounded suffered by the division on this day were quite a few from the pioneer battalion. The fates of those later flown out of the pocket are known: Obergefreiter Klemens Bastian[2], 1. Kompanie, was struck in the right elbow by a shell splinter. He was flown out of the pocket on 3 January, 1943. Gefreiter Hermann Gamsjäger[3], 2. Kompanie, was struck in the left upper arm and both thighs by shrapnel and flown out on Christmas Day. Gefreiter August Gramling[4], 2. Kompanie, was struck in the right thigh by a bullet and also flown out on Christmas Day. Pionier Karl Kornhuber[5], 1. Kompanie, suffered phosphorous burns to the left side of his face in close combat and was flown out on 4 January, 1943. Pionier Erich Zimmermann[6], 1. Kompanie, was struck on the left side of his body by shrapnel and was flown out on 4 January, 1943 too. Another casualty was Oberschirrmeister Paul Botta[7], from the light pioneer column, whose body finally succumbed after weeks of pain. He'd been living with a hernia but on this day, his appendix burst and he required an urgent operation which could not be performed in the primitive conditions existing in the pocket, so he was put on a plane the very next day and flown out. Although Botta had not been directly involved in combat, he had rendered valuable service by transporting ammunition and pioneering specialties (explosives, detonators, etc.) directly to his men in the front-line and ensuring the operational readiness of the flamethrowers.

The variety of nasty wounds was the result of the battalion's struggle with Gorishny's men. Employed as a shock troop, the pioneers were thrown in where it was hottest. The

---

2. Bastian, Obergefreiter Klemens, 1./Pi.Btl.305; born 9 September, 1918 in Illingen bei Rastatt. Died 24 January, 1995 in Steinmauern bei Rastatt.

3. Gamsjäger, Gefreiter Hermann, 2./Pi.Btl.305; born 5 June, 1923 in Holzhüttenboden. No further information known.

4. Gramling, Gefreiter August, 2./Pi.Btl.305; born 23 September, 1912 in Mönchberg. Died 28 January, 1994 in Mönchberg.

5. Kornhuber, Pionier Karl, 1./Pi.Btl.305; born 25 May, 1921 in Kematen a.d.Krems. No further information known.

6. Zimmermann, Pionier Erich, 1./Pi.Btl.305; born 29 March, 1911 in Stuttgart. No further information known.

7. Botta, Oberschirrmeister Paul, le.Pi.kol./Pi.Btl.305; born 27 May, 1913 in Oberglogau. No further information known.

awesome spectacle of exploding phosphorous ampoules stunned the pioneers, especially after the first painful wounds were inflicted. The Soviets were naturally impressed by it:

> During the fighting, good results were shown by the ampulomet platoon and thermite spheres, as a result of whose application it was possible to force the enemy from dug-outs and trenches. It was reckoned that they burnt up 5 dug-outs, 4 pillboxes and up to 40 enemy soldiers. As a result of their use, the ampulomets and thermite spheres have earned special prestige amongst the soldiers and commanders. Using thermite spheres in a platoon of 241st Rifle Regiment was Red Army man Noskov who distinguished himself by destroying 2 dug-outs and 4 enemy soldiers.

The war diary of 62nd Army summarised the fighting on Gorishny's sector:

> As a result of the hand-to-hand fighting, the units captured one building and 4 pillboxes. The right flank advanced 150 metres north along the Volga bank. The enemy tried four times to restore the lost positions by counterattacking the division's right flank. Fighting continues. The enemy has lost 100 soldiers and officers, and ampulomets burnt out 5 dug-outs and 4 pillboxes.

Combat Report No. 119 of 95th Rifle Division provides more details:

> As a result of fierce fighting that lasted for nearly 9 hours, 241st Rifle Regiment took the following trophies: 12 heavy and light machine-guns, 120 rifles, 15 submachine-guns, 400 hand grenades and about 10,000 cartridges. It captured 6 pillboxes and 16 dug-outs.

Russian records put German losses on the sector of 241st Rifle Regiment as 150 dead, and on the sector of 90th Rifle Regiment as 30 men. Losses in 95th Rifle Division were as follows: 241st Rifle Regiment – 39 men; 90th Rifle Regiment – 14 men; 161st Rifle Regiment – 2 men. Snipers from 161st Rifle Regiment claimed 13 German soldiers.

Nightfall did not halt the fighting. 305. Infanterie-Division was determined to recapture its lost positions, so the remnants of Pionier-Bataillon 305 again entered the battle. Soviet records state that "at 1700 hours, up to a platoon of enemy infantry, in a state of intoxication, attacked the subunits of 241st Rifle Regiment in the area of Dom 06". This was the attack in which Obergefreiter Müller was wounded and Oberleutnant Fritz jumped into a trench filled with Soviet soldiers. Although he was reported as being shot or clubbed to death, there is some doubt as to whether this is true, because of the following excerpt found in Combat Report No. 121 of 95th Rifle Division:

Leutnant Max Fritz (in peaked cap) surrounded by the NCOs and enlisted men of the battalion staff, France 1941.

At 1730 on 22.12, on the sector of 241st Rifle Regiment, an officer – a lieutenant of the sappers of 305th Infantry Division – was captured and sent to the political department of army staff.[8]

At 2110 hours, a German unit in platoon-strength repeated the attack in the same area but suffered heavy losses and pulled back to their starting positions. Budarin's riflemen held on to their new possessions.

– – –

Under the cover of darkness and supported by cover-fire from Dom 41, storm groups of 344th Rifle Regiment pushed into Dom 37, which they had held for a few minutes in the morning before losing it to a German counterattack. Nightmarish struggles raged through the stygian gloom and only at 2130 hours, after an explosion was set off by Soviet sappers, was the house captured. Also taken were 3 dug-outs next to the building and two prisoners – including an Obergefreiter – belonging to Grenadier-Regiment 577.

– – –

Soviet records claim that on 138th Rifle Division's sector, more than 100 Germans were annihilated and the following trophies were captured: 1 heavy machine-gun, 7 light machine-guns, 3 mortars, 9 submachine-guns, 35 rifles, 300 grenades, 3 anti-tank rifles, more than 2000 rounds of rifle ammunition and 3 telephone sets. The amount of booty is probably correct but the number of casualties is exaggerated, as can be seen by the official German figure, which also includes losses suffered during the fighting with Gorishny's men.

Casualties for 22 December, 1942:	
138th Rifle Division:	23 killed, 62 wounded, a total of 94 men
305. Infanterie-Division:	1 officer and 8 men killed, 57 men wounded, 5 men missing

23 December, 1942

The morning report of LI. Armeekorps covered the combat during the night: "Since 0200 hours, the enemy – strongly supported by artillery, mortar and anti-tank fire – is attacking numerous positions […] east of the gun factory. The enemy achieved local penetrations in […] 82a1, along the Volga bank north of the fuel installation and east of the gun factory. Defensive combat still in progress."

The Soviet penetration near 82a1 was achieved by 161st Rifle Regiment of Gorishny's division, while 241st Rifle Regiment went into action along the river bank north of the fuel tanks. Gorishny was desperate to widen the breach but stubborn German strongholds with their stubborn German defenders stymied all attempts.

The Soviet attacks from Lyudnikov's Island were parried by German counterattacks. Combat Report No. 240, issued by 138th divisional headquarters, reported that "counterattacks were launched six times by groups of 20-70 soldiers from Dom 60

8. Extensive research has shown that no other officers from Pionier-Bataillon 305 were killed, wounded or missing on this date and German sources indicate quite clearly that Fritz was killed. Surviving veterans have the same opinion. However, the fact that Fritz was 'killed' at the same time and in the exact same place that a German pioneer officer was captured leaves some room for doubt. Indeed, Fritz's family were never convinced: in a post-war letter, one veteran noted that "his next-of-kin do not completely believe it and go to fortune-tellers". Why did they doubt it? Fritz's death was recorded on 22 June, 1943 at Standesamt (Registry Office) Stuttgart under No. 3207/1943.

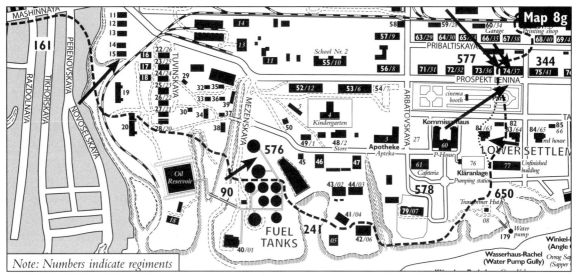

Soviet attacks and German counterattacks, 23 December, 1942.

[Kommissarhaus] and 35 [Haus 66], and Workshop 14/15 [Hall 3]. All counterattacks were beaten off with heavy losses for them." Three of those counterattacks were aimed at Dom 37 [Haus 74], including one that originated from the Kommissarhaus. The German group was halfway across the pulverised park when it was turned back by concentrated machine-gun fire.

– – –

The vicious fighting in Haus 83 continued. It was a pure hand-to-hand contest. Artillery and mortars of the two adversaries refrained from intervening. The building was a death-pit into which both sides sent their men. Haus 83 lay between the German-held Haus 81 and the Soviet-held Haus 84, and was connected to both by deep trenches, so it was easy for fresh blood to be fed in. The building, formed around an L-shaped hallway with entrances facing Haus 81 and the Volga, consisted of 5 or 6 rooms on each storey. The demolished stairwell prohibited easy access to the upper level, so the fighting was confined to the cellars and ground floor. Smoke leaked from the sub-basement windows. Grenades exploded in brief flashes in the pitch-dark rooms. Distorted bodies sprawled across the rubble-strewn floors. The wounded were hastily dragged out of the slaughter and hauled back through the trenches. One side would recapture a room after pitching in dozens of grenades, only to lose it a short while later when the enemy did the same. Pechenyuk's men, those of Toporkov's 1st Rifle Battalion, were determined to regain their old regimental command post.

The protracted struggle slowly crawled to its conclusion. Hauptmann Rettenmaier sent his men in piecemeal. He was morally conflicted at sending in the young reinforcements but his orders were explicit: every position had to be held to the last. The devoted father and devout Catholic had tears in his eyes as he sent in more men, knowing that they would only come back as corpses or, at best, severely wounded:

> The young reinforcements (Austrians) were soon used up. The supply trains and orderly offices were now combed out and every dispensable man was put in the front-line. As no more officers were available, Hauptfeldwebeln had to take their place. It must be said that everyone deserves praise; they fought with exemplary courage and many of them were decorated with the Iron Cross First Class a few days later. Artillery survey troops and artillerymen were trained by Hauptmann Schwarz and these also bled to death in the forefield of the gun factory.

Eventually, however, common sense prevailed and the decision was taken to abandon Haus 83. Before they left, the pioneers prepared a nasty surprise for the future occupants. They secreted their remaining stock of explosives – several hundred kilograms of it – into a niche in a basement wall and rigged it with a J-Feder 504 long-delay clockwork fuse. The delay was set for precisely two weeks, then the whole charge was thoroughly camouflaged to avoid detection. It was set to explode fourteen days later, at 1300 hours on 6 January.

After this final act of resistance, the grenadiers of Regiment 578 quit Haus 83 for good, leaving behind most of the dead: a difficult decision for the pious Swabians and Austrians. The small Haus 82 was also ceded to the Soviets.

As the fighting east of the Barrikady continued, higher staffs paid more attention to the fates of individual buildings. In its afternoon report, LI. Armeekorps reported:

> The enemy continued his attacks against our positions east of the gun factory… From 0500 hours, the enemy repeatedly attacked our position in 83d3 [Hauptmann Rettenmaier's Haus 79] that projects to the Volga from the south and north as well as house positions in 83d2 [Haus 83 and 81]. All attacks, which were strongly supported by artillery and mortar fire, were repulsed.

After falling back to Haus 81, the Germans barely had time to prepare themselves for defence. Soviet storm groups from Toporkov's battalion moved forward after dusk and tried to roll up the German position. The building had the same architectural style and layout as Haus 83, only a mirror image of it. And as in Haus 83, the fighting was conducted almost solely with grenades. Once again, life and death struggles revolved around the possession of solitary rooms. Snipers in the Kommissarhaus picked off any Soviet soldier foolish enough to leave the confines of the building. The fighting for Haus 81 continued throughout the night.

– – –

As can be imagined, Hauptmann Schwarz did not endear himself to some men simply because of the nature of his assignment. Unteroffizier O.A. Karl-August Rombach[9] from the Nachrichtenzug of II./Artillerie-Regiment 305, who had experienced a run-in with Schwarz during the summer advance, was one of them:

> Because the infantry had suffered higher-than-average casualties, artillerymen had to be handed over to them. I received the order to take about 50 artillerymen from our battalion to the infantry. When I arrived there, I was received by an 'old acquaintance', namely Hauptmann Schwarz… He was glad about our unexpected reunion and immediately appointed me as a platoon commander in his company. I called the division staff and asked for the adjutant, that is Leutnant Hämmerle[10], whom I knew well. I told him that Hauptmann Schwarz had employed me as a platoon commander against the orders of my commander. Leutnant Hämmerle gave the Hauptmann the order to let me go.

Unteroffizier O.A. Karl-August Rombach, II./Art.Rgt.305.

---

9. Rombach, Unteroffizier Karl-August , II./Art.Rgt.305; born 23 May, 1919 in Titisee/Neustadt. Still alive in 2006.

10. Hämmerle, Leutnant Hans-Martin, 305.Inf.Div.; born 3 November, 1921 in Müllheim. Killed in action, 4 January, 1943 in Stalingrad.

While 768th Rifle Regiment defended its former positions, gave fire support and secured the right flank of Konovalenko's regiment, assault groups from 344th and 650th Rifle Regiments continued to probe the German defences. However, the defenders were more than ready for them. Relying on their heavily reinforced strongpoints, they offered obstinate resistance with machine-guns and mortars, especially from Halls 3 and 4, Haus 67, 66, 71 and the Kommissarhaus. Their intention was to limit the movements of the Soviet storm groups. German reserves were shifted around to meet real and supposed Soviet attacks: at noon, the Germans were seen running around, 30 of them, from Dom 9 [Haus 57] into Workshop 3 [Hall 6c]. Continuous firefights erupted along the entire

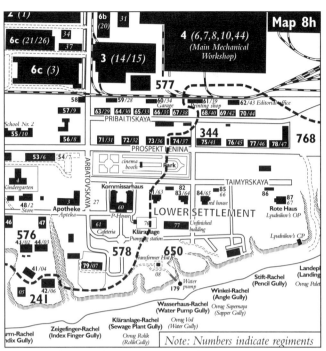

Situation along the front-line, 23 December, 1942.

front-line. Progress was almost impossible for the Soviets on this day. Apart from the capture of Dom 37 [Haus 74] and three dug-outs – taken the previous night by 344th Rifle Regiment – and Dom 64 [Haus 83] after the Germans finally relinquished control in the afternoon, the only other conquest made was one solitary pillbox by 650th Rifle Regiment. Dom 63 [Haus 81] had been penetrated, and 138th Rifle Division's daily report even said it had been captured, but it was by no means entirely in Soviet hands. The fighting was costly: on this day, the division lost 31 killed and 46 wounded, a total of 77 men.

After the capture of the buildings north of the Kommissarhaus, 650th Rifle Regiment was deployed as follows: Senior-Lieutenant Toporkov's 1st Rifle Battalion garrisoned 3 houses with 27 men from Group Milomailenko, guaranteeing a secure boundary with 344th Rifle Regiment. The battalion had 11 lightly wounded, and a total strength of 48. Second Rifle Battalion garrisoned 2 houses with 29 men, and from the unfinished building to the Rolik group with 12 men. It had 7 lightly wounded men, and also had a total headcount of 48. The Rolik group consisted of 9 men. The 24 remaining men of the NKVD blocking detachment, essentially a part of the regiment since early November, were relocated on division's orders due to the "transition to a new disposition"[11]. This dramatically reduced the strength available on the left flank of the regiment and the assault groups had to spread out to fill the gap. Pechenyuk alerted Lyudnikov to the fact that there was now no opportunity to allocate assault groups for the capture of the Kommissarhaus and he immediately requested replacements to replenish his battalions.

Throughout the day, the division took prisoner one Obergefreiter and two soldiers, destroyed 7 German machine-guns and 3 dug-outs, and captured 9 light machine-guns,

---

11. A nebulous way of saying that because defence had turned to offence, the defensive specialities of the blocking detachment were no longer required.

16 rifles, 20,000 cartridges and 15 boxes of grenades. The quantities of weapons and ammunition captured from the under-supplied Germans were staggering. In only two houses captured by 344th Rifle Regiment, Dom 37 [Haus 74] and Dom 41 [Haus 75], the following was seized: 9 light machine-guns, 1 heavy machine-gun, 9 submachine-guns, 30 rifles, 1 mortar, 400 grenades and nearly 20,000 rifle cartridges. And since the beginning of the attack on 21 December, a total of about 140 boxes of grenades had been found in captured dug-outs, pillboxes and buildings. Needless to say that these were utilised by Soviet troops.

– – –

An extract from a 62nd Army report provides an overall glimpse of the situation:

> Lyudnikov's division has continued its south-westerly attack. The enemy has put up stiff resistance and counterattacked twice with a strength of over two companies. The enemy suffered heavy losses and his attacks were beaten off.

> Two buildings were captured [Dom 37 and Dom 64], in one of which the enemy had left behind 30 dead. Other storm groups are continuing their attack to gain possession of the big rectangular building [Dom 07 / Haus 79] on the bank of the Volga.

> Gorishny's division has continued its north-westerly attack. In spite of strong enemy resistance, our units have slowly advanced. Direct communication with Lyudnikov's division has now been established.

Apart from reinforcing their positions, Gorishny's division concentrated on conquering emplacements west of Dom 06 [Haus 42] and the fuel tanks. Their artillery and mortars fired on the Apotheke while shells from direct-firing 45mm guns set fire to a dug-in German tank near Dom 03 [Haus 44]. The division's losses for the day were low: 241st Rifle Regiment – 6 men; 161st Rifle Regiment – 7 men; 90th Rifle Regiment – none.

The 'big rectangular building' mentioned in 62nd Army's report was Haus 79. This strongpoint now stood squarely in the way of a secure junction between Gorishny's and Lyudnikov's divisions. The evening report of LI. Armeekorps at 2040 hours talked about Haus 79, the 'enclosed house':

> East of the gun factory, enemy attacks from the north-east since 1300 hours against our position still projecting to the Volga. The security detachments placed along the Volga cliff had to be pulled back to the level of the enclosed house in 83d3/4.

Despite this well-defended stumbling block, Lyudnikov and his staff rated the first three days of this offensive highly. The results of the attack and lessons learned were written up in a lengthy 'summary report'. It began by summarising their opponent:

> Along the division's front, defence is still maintained by the remnants of 305th Infantry Division, reinforced by sappers from 45, 50, 80 and 336 sapper battalions.

> Being caught in a ring of encirclement, the enemy has undertaken essential arrangements, strengthening defences and enabling fighting by insignificant forces against the division's attacking units.

> Observation, reconnaissance, combat and statements from prisoners established:

> Along the division's front, 577, 578 and parts of 576 Infantry Regiment of 305th Infantry Division, filled up by means of artillerymen, specialists from divisional units and sappers, had previously been smashed by the division's operations during the battle from 11 to 23.11.42. In the regiments there are about 350-400 soldiers and officers, and of those, more than 3/4 of the manpower are active bayonets.

Next, it covers the planning and preparations for the assault:

Numerous aggressive operations attempted by 95th Rifle Division to join up with the division's units did not bring results. Carrying out the decree ordering the connection with 95th Rifle Division, the division prepared to advance.

Fundamentally, the decision fell upon the idea of suddenly attacking the enemy strongpoints with the purpose of utterly annihilating them and clearing the enemy from the conquered territory.

Combat groups of units were formed into two echelons.

First echelon - assault groups – 50% of the strength; 2nd echelon – clearing groups – 25%; the reserve – 25 % of the strength.

The storm groups had the following task: one and a half hours before dawn, suddenly and violently break through deep into the enemy's defences, stun them with audacious actions right up to and including hand-to-hand combat and ensure the seizure of the attack objectives by the clearing groups.

The clearing groups, moving forward behind the storm groups while keeping them in sight, had the task of completely annihilating enemy personnel and firepower and immediately securing the captured territory.

The reserves were assigned the task of eliminating counterattacking enemy groups.

To prepare units for implementation of the plan, three concerns were addressed: 1. procurement and integration of reinforcements; 2. preparation of line officers; 3. provision of units' operations with ammunition and foodstuffs.

During the period from 18 to 20 December, distribution of the reinforcements and their familiarisation with the terrain was carried out.

Division command conducted four briefings with the regiment commanders, assistant regiment commanders, chiefs of staff and battalion commanders.

At the same time, familiarisation of the terrain by company commanders, platoon commanders and junior officers was carried out.

In the meantime, units were completely supplied with ammunition, mainly grenades.

The results of the attack were summed up as follows:

Combat during the period of 21 to 23 December has shown that the concept of destroying strong enemy redoubts with surprise nocturnal attacks fully justifies itself. As a result of the attack on 21.12, it was possible for 344th and 650th Rifle Regiments to break through the enemy's main line of resistance along a 500-metre front, completely destroy the garrisons of the captured dug-outs, pillboxes and blockhouses, and seize a significant quantity of trophies.

For the period from 21 to 23.12, the division's units exterminated over 400 hitlerites; wiped out 18 dug-outs; and destroyed three 37 mm guns, 2 heavy and 9 light machine-guns, 5 mortars, 4 anti-tank rifles and an ammunition dump.

For the same period, the following trophies were seized: 1 37 mm and 1 75 mm gun, 5 mortars, 2 heavy and 38 light machine-guns, 18 submachine-guns, 130 rifles, 14 pistols, over 3000 grenades, 480 mortar rounds, about 300 shells, over 30,000 cartridges, 6 telephone sets and other material.

Taken prisoner were 9 soldiers and 1 Obergefreiter.

Then lessons learned were discussed:

As a result of the three-day battle, units of the division broke down the enemy's defences and captured his most heavily fortified strongpoints. After appropriate preparation, the remaining unconquered powerful strongpoint in the area, Dom 60 [Kommissarhaus], will be destroyed, despite its fierce resistance.

The division has only carried out the first part of its combat mission. This can be accounted for, first of all, by the inadequate preparation of the personnel for offensive actions against a solidly entrenched enemy amid an urban environment, in conditions coming very close to attacking a fortified region.

Providing that we be allowed a lengthier preparation, even a space of 5 days, combat groups could be hammered together, platoon and company commanders could be more carefully prepared for independent actions and could learn surprise techniques to destroy the enemy in an urban area.

Finally, the report finished off with the following paragraph:

Resumption of active operations – which is conditional upon overcoming the main defensive line – is extremely necessary in the near future. However, the division requires reinforcements of personnel which it would be desirable to receive within two days.

– – –

The enormous number of wounded men flooding into German aid stations and hospitals overwhelmed medical staff. Bandages and medicine were alarmingly low. Proper facilities for operations and the care of the wounded were simply a pipe dream. Some of these hospitals were not far from the command post of 305. Infanterie-Division in a gully 500 metres south-west of Point 447. Oberst Steinmetz visited one of these 'hospitals':

Within the sector of 305. Division lay a few deplorably squalid Russian farmhouses. Set up in them were dressing stations of several divisions, including the dressing station of 305. Infanterie-Division. I viewed these places of misery several times. During one of these visits I met with the advisory surgeon of the army. He was Oberstarzt Dr. Gross from Stuttgart. He was also shaken by the conditions, the lack of physicians, medicine and all necessary resources. I asked him if he could help by being on the army staff or could he not help much more by being on the spot. Upon his answer that he could not desert from the army staff, I urged him, he only needed to say 'yes' and I would arrange everything else with Generaloberst Paulus. And so he arrived in a couple of days.

Among the patients was a soldier who had lost an eye and whose evacuation by airplane had been rejected. That's how difficult it was to get a ticket out! During a later visit, when I saw him still lying rather miserably on a straw bed, I concocted a white lie with the divisional surgeon. I got him to bandage both eyes. In that way, he was able to reach the homeland.

Casualties for 23 December, 1942:	
138th Rifle Division:	31 killed, 46 wounded, a total of 77 men
305. Infanterie-Division:	16 men killed, 92 men wounded, 1 officer and 27 men missing

24 December, 1942

The usual machine-gun and rifle exchanges oscillated along the front-line during the night. Ammunition and rations continued to come across the ice to Lyudnikov's division but they were assailed by machine-gun and automatic fire from German positions near 'Dorn' (Thorn) Gully, or 'Malaya' (Small) Gully as it was known to the Soviets, on the right flank of 768th Rifle Regiment. Heavy artillery from the direction of Gorodische methodically fired at Zaitsevsky Island, the Denezhnaya Volozhka crossing and the divisional command post. Lyudnikov's command post also received multiple hits from six-barrelled mortars. In return, Soviet artillery covered the German artillery and mortar positions in the Gorodische area and Barrikady factory with fire strikes.

On the sector of 650th Rifle Regiment, there was heavy machine-gun fire from the Kommissarhaus and occasional mortar fire from Workshop 14/15. Hand grenades also showered their front-line.

During the night, the division lost 2 enlisted men and the chief-of-staff of 768th Rifle Regiment, Senior-Lieutenant Silchenko. His replacement was Senior-Lieutenant Demkov.

– – –

During the night, the Germans tried to restore the position on the sector of 90th Rifle Regiment, near the fuel tanks. From 2000 hours the previous night until 0200, German groups of 15-20 men launched attacks three times on Soviet dug-outs north-west of the fuel tanks. All attacks were beaten off with heavy losses for them. In the morning, small storm groups from 90th Rifle Regiment set out to capture individual strongpoints near the fuel tanks. At 1100 hours, ampulomets set a German dug-out north-west of the fuel tanks on fire. After seizing a few positions, the storm groups returned with 2 light machine-guns and 1 Soviet DP light machine-gun as trophies. On 161st Rifle Regiment's sector, 120mm mortars destroyed a German dug-out near Dom 21 and suppressed a heavy machine-gun.

The losses of 95th Rifle Division for the day: 241st Rifle Regiment – 9 men; 90th Rifle Regiment – 10 men; 161st Rifle Regiment – 1 man.

– – –

There was never-ending firefights with rifles and machine-guns during the entire day. Movements on either side were doused by accurate fire. The German machine-gunners and riflemen were on edge. Cloistered inside their brick fortresses, they vigilantly peered out of embrasures and observation slits at the chaotic landscape around them, searching for any hint that a Soviet attack was about to be launched. They concentrated particularly on neighbouring buildings. Down in the miasmic cellars, off-duty troops tried to get some rest while other groups kept alert, ready to be thrown into a counterattack.

Combat Report No. 241, prepared by Lyudnikov's headquarters, provides a

A German sentry keeps watch from the basement of a sturdy building, his MP-40 at the ready in front of him.

good description of the intricate German defences still facing the division:

> Along the division's front, the enemy continues to resist stubbornly with the remnants of 546th, 577th and 578th Infantry Regiments, which each have about 350-400 men. Along the 1500-metre long front, resistance nests have been created from numerous cellars of buildings and workhalls, pillboxes, dug-outs and trenches, all connected by a dense network of trenches and communication passages, the majority with an overlapping, organised system of fire which resist obstinately by saturating our soldiers with automatic weapons fire. Heavy artillery from the direction of Gorodische and heavy mortars from the direction of the main mechanical workshop [Hall 4] and Workshop 14/15 [Hall 3] have, during the last three days, placed methodical fire on the combat ranks of the division's units, Zaitsevsky Island and the Denezhnaya Volozhka crossing in the area of the divisional command post.

> When our combat groups transition to the attack, strong resistance is revealed by heavy fire from machine-guns and mortars in Dom 38 [Haus 67], 36 [Haus 73], 35 [Haus 66], 60 [Kommissarhaus] and Workshop 14/15 [Hall 3].

> While consolidating upon the recaptured line, the troops prepare for forthcoming operations to clear the enemy from captured territory and establish a connection with 95th Rifle Division.

> 768th Rifle Regiment – defends former positions and prepares for the capture of enemy pillboxes with an assault group.

> 344th Rifle Regiment – consolidates on the attained line and connects communication trenches to the captured Dom 41 [Haus 75] and 37 [Haus 74]. Prepares for the explosion and capture of Dom 36 [Haus 73].

> 650th Rifle Regiment – consolidates in the captured positions and prepares for the explosion and capture of Dom 60 [Kommissarhaus].

– – –

The fighting heated up in the afternoon. The intermittent struggle in Haus 81 [Dom 63] was renewed with extreme determination by the Soviets. Pechenyuk's primary objective was to capture the Kommissarhaus but that would not be possible until he eliminated any and all resistance in Haus 81. The German garrison had effectively been cut off by Toporkov's 1st Rifle Battalion. Their only lifeline was a narrow trench that stretched back to the Kommissarhaus like an umbilical cord but even this was within range of Soviet hand grenades. The fighting was unforgiving. The Soviet tactic was to "capture stairwells in targeted buildings", according to the divisional war diary.

While 1st Battalion launched attacks to destroy the surrounded garrison, 2nd Rifle Battalion held the previous defence line that stretched to the river. It built defensive works and used every type of firepower at its disposal to destroy German emplacements. Particularly bothersome was the heavy rifle and machine-gun fire from the Kommissarhaus. Heavy mortars were instructed to fire on the building and observers reported that some firing points in the Kommissarhaus were destroyed. Anti-tank rifles took out German soldiers by firing through narrow embrasures.

In the meantime, in Haus 81, the Soviets tried a new method to end the hours of fighting. Sappers brought in hundreds of kilograms of explosives and rigged up a massive charge close to the German-occupied part of the house. They then vacated the building and moved back to Haus 83. No doubt the German garrison thought they had prevailed. The charge exploded but it is not known how many – if any – Germans were killed. The consequences, however, were recorded in the evening report of LI. Armeekorps:

East of the gun factory, after two hours of hard hand-to-hand combat, the enemy partially succeeded in blowing up a house in 83d2. The house thereupon had to be abandoned.

Hauptmann Rettenmaier recalls that "in view of the fact that we would no longer be undertaking offensive actions in the current situation, Haus 83 and 81 were abandoned". According to 650th Rifle Regiment's combat journal, "Group Toporkov seized the house that lies in front of the P-shaped building [Kommissarhaus] and consolidated in it". From the number of 'trophies' captured (1 machine-gun, 1 submachine-gun and some rifles) and the lack of bodies, it would seem that most of the German garrison made it back to the Kommissarhaus. After capturing Haus 81, Toporkov's men blew up an ammunition depot in the trench that ran from the building to the Kommissarhaus.

At the end of the day, the regiment possessed a strength of 44 officers, 28 NCOs and 99 soldiers, a total of 171 men. Of those, 11 were lightly wounded.

– – –

Some of the German casualties on this day belonged to Pionier-Bataillon 305. The wounds were typical of those suffered during close quarters fighting. Stabsgefreiter Ignaz Kainz[12], 3. Kompanie, was wounded when struck in the right shoulder by shrapnel and shot through the right forearm. He was flown out of the pocket on 4 January, 1943. Gefreiter Max Lattner[13], 3. Kompanie, suffered phosphorous burns in close combat and was flown out on 30 December, 1942. Gefreiter Gottfried Riegler[14], 3. Kompanie, was wounded in the left upper arm, left shoulder and face by shrapnel and flown out on 4 January, 1943. All three were replacements that had arrived just before the Soviet counteroffensive on 19 November, but while Lattner and Riegler were young, inexperienced Austrians, 30-year-old Kainz was an 'old hare'.

– – –

War or not, the Germans were determined to celebrate one of the holiest days of their calendar... but it was not always possible. Leutnant Hans B.[15], adjutant III./Grenadier-Regiment 577, remembers a Soviet attack on this holy evening:

> It was Christmas Eve 1942. Outside in the snow I heard clear voices, they there were running at our house and screaming 'hurra'.
>
> They did not know that on the railway embankment, in a small hut, we had sited a machine-gun with a Romanian Unteroffizier in charge, and he mowed them down like wheat in a field. The next day, we saw them lying in front of our house, dozens of them lying there, all shot and frozen in the snow. The Russians suffered terrible casualties there.

Stabsfeldwebel Martin Schüsslbauer[16], career soldier and platoon commander in 6./Grenadier-Regiment 577, wrote about some horrific events in a pessimistic Christmas letter to his wife:

> Today, on Christmas Eve, my Oberleutnant was killed and I had to stand in for him until a replacement arrived. They still wanted to promote me but I turned it down. I am now the last man of the entire company that came to Russia from France. All the others are dead or

---

12. Kainz, Stabsgefreiter Ignaz, 3./Pi.Btl.305; born 29 January, 1912 in Gr.Radischen. No further information known.
13. Lattner, Gefreiter Max, 3./Pi.Btl.305; born 10 April, 1923 in Aigen. Killed in action, 18 November, 1944 in Italy.
14. Riegler, Gefreiter Gottfried, 3./Pi.Btl.305; born 17 June, 1922 in St. Thomas. No further information known.
15. Name withheld at family's request.
16. Schüsslbauer, Stabsfeldwebel Martin, 6./Gr.Rgt.577; born 27 January, 1904 in Gebenbach. Missing in action, December 1942 in Stalingrad.

wounded. Fifteen of my men wanted to desert but I desperately dissuaded them. Despite that, they went into captivity, without my knowledge. Today, on Christmas Eve, we found them. Eyes gouged out, ears and tongues cut off, as well as their genitals. A few were still alive.[17] I'm not going to let myself die that way, dear Fanny. I've got a bullet with which I'll kill myself. If Stalingrad falls, dear Fanny, then I'll be dead, you won't need to wait for me…

This was the last time Schüsslbauer's family would hear from him.

Stabsfeldwebel Martin Schüsslbauer

The importance of Christmas to the Germans cannot be over-emphasised, and even more so during the war. It was the year's most important feast day and almost everyone began thinking about it and their absence from home. The solemness and purity of the religious festival juxtaposed harshly with the murderous nature of combat and the appalling conditions in which the Germans now found themselves. Christmas became a time of introspection and reflection for most soldiers in Stalingrad, and each experienced it in a slightly different way than his comrades. Morale just prior to the holiday certainly dipped for the men stranded in Stalingrad. In a letter to his family on 27 December, Hauptmann Eugen Rettenmaier, I./Grenadier-Regiment 578, describes his Christmas experience:

> Our Christmas was absolutely wretched but we did get a little something: for three consecutive days, everyone received a bar of chocolate, and one time there was even some schnapps. There was, however, no sight of our Christmas parcels and there was not even any mail. It is pretty grim and we had to miss out in this respect.

Oberzahlmeister Erich Bauchspiess from Pionier-Bataillon 336:

> Today is Christmas. Though we have to celebrate it with the most primitive means, it is still lovely. The worst thing is that no mail has reached us for Christmas. It has now been over 7 weeks since we've received any. Hopefully you have received my sparse mail. We crafted a little tree out of thin twigs and decorated it with cotton wool, silver paper and a couple of candle stumps. Yesterday evening it illuminated our little room wonderfully and in a solemn mood thoughts wandered to home and my wish was for you and all the loved ones to have a happy and jolly atmosphere. We spent Christmas Eve with a small schnapps and a good cup of coffee. Outside, an icy wind hurls ice particles against the window. The front around us is pretty quiet…

Hauptmann Wilhelm Traub, Pionier-Bataillon 305, in a letter to his wife:

> For Christmas Eve, I invited over our doctor, who has currently been transferred to an infantry regiment. I collected something to drink and his refreshing presence helped to remove my sense of loneliness. We talked about home. The doctor has a practice in East Prussia and also two children. There were many subjects of common interest.

> Naturally there was no mail. Who knows where at Christmas they are stuck and there was not even a letter for me. Well, maybe next time. Hopefully you at least received a letter from me. How did you enjoy Christmas Eve? I hope the boys were satisfied with the Christmas spread. I barely dare to hope that the cacao liqueur arrived for you after today hearing that large quantities of parcels have not even been shipped by our postal services.

---

17. These claims of Soviet atrocities are impossible to verify.

Despite your parcel not arriving, I still had a small exchange of gifts here. From one company I received a sausage and two pork cutlets, from the other a packet of cigars, a fried piece of filet and a bottle of cognac. I was very happy with these presents. From this experience one can see the bond between us old comrades. In addition I have the feeling that the companies are of the mind that they must do something to help kept me fed. They are probably scared that one day I might go into hospital for malnourishment. I sometimes hear various remarks that I have become fearfully thin. But I feel very well even in my becoming very slim. Otherwise there is little new to report. We still have hard combat with the Russians and, sadly, casualties. Who knows when it will be different...

Oberst Steinmetz recalls his Christmas experience in a post-war account:

When I visited the command post of the Panzerjäger-Abteilung several days before the celebration, I saw some pine trees in front of the shelter. They were quite a rarity because firewood was hard to come by. When I asked the battalion commander about them, he told me that the sentries at the command post kept watch over these trees so that they could celebrate Christmas in a homelike way[18]. On the day before Christmas Eve a messenger from the battalion brought a few pine branches to the division staff as a Christmas present. We celebrated Christmas Eve in the room of a Russian farm house, squeezed in together with a field-kitchen. From the radio came some Christmas music first of all, then after that – oh what a horror! – Goebbels spoke. One look at the operator was enough, the radio was switched off and the mood was restored. And then came a big surprise: through the door came a giant bowl of doughnuts. The resourceful soldiers had lifted up the floorboards in a house and discovered a bag of grain. The grain was milled in a coffee grinder and baked together with the rest of the sugar and fat. The joy was great, even if strong teeth – and soaking with some tea – were necessary to break the doughnuts into smaller pieces.

A special surprise was also in store for Rittmeister Udo Giulini[19], commander of the Radfahr Schwadron of Panzerjäger-Abteilung 305:

Schnapps was available right up to the end. We had a special mixture made from Cointreau and gin. We also carried out a successful nocturnal expedition for flour and with the help of a baker and his home-made oven, we were able to bake a small loaf of bread for Christmas for every one of our men, distributed it with schnapps and cigarettes, and so brought a Christmas spirit the likes of which I had never felt so intensively in my entire life.

Starlit night, bitingly cold weather, the bunker doors open so that the candle light shines outside. The doors to the shelters were then closed, Christmas carols rang out and everyone in the circle of men had small surprises for the comrade beside them. Thus my men had crafted a liquor service for me, which included small schnapps glasses individually turned from shells cases and engraved upon them all were combat days that had significance for me and everyone else.

Familie Giulini

Rittmeister Udo Giulini, Radfahr Schwadron 305.

---

18. It was Rittmeister Udo Giulini who kept watch over the trees: "My bunker lay on a hill near Gorodische, the only wooded elevation that was covered with firs and whose stock of trees I jealously defended in the pre-Christmas period from those looking for Christmas trees."

19. Giulini de Giulino, Rittmeister Udo, Radf./Pz.Jäg.Abt.305; born 12 February, 1918 in Hamburg. Died 5 August, 1995 in Heidelberg.

Feldarzt Dr. Karl Schöpf, II./Artillerie-Regiment 305, prepared a veritable feast for Christmas:

> We had already fed ourselves for a long time on deep-frozen horses that appeared in the snow as small mounds. We in 305. Infanterie-Division, that is, the artillery, had 2 camels that we had already eaten up. On the camels we had two sacks of wheat that we stored in a gap in some rocks. I remembered the sacks and had them fetched. In a shot-up house, the soldiers saw a small hand-mill, which they fetched at night despite the fact it was minus 30 degrees. They also brought back a dead dog. In a foundry on the edge of Stalingrad I discovered a liquid in open vats that tasted sweet. I had others sample it and established that it was some type of syrup but it also contained some diesel fuel and floating in it were tiny metal shavings. To make the syrup palatable, I heated it, scooped the gel off the top and strained it through some gauze. In addition there was some shredded wheat, so we had something 'special' to eat on Christmas Eve. The day before we had made meatballs from horse meat and stored them outside in a large pile of snow that we hollowed out (a 'deep freezer'). A branch served

Feldarzt Dr. Karl Schöpf

Familie Schöpf

as an ersatz Christmas tree, decorated with wads of cotton wool and strings of thread from packets of dressings. Because only a few candles were still available, I filled a box with Vaseline and stuck a rolled-up piece of bandage into it so that it served as a substitute candle.

> When the above-mentioned Christmas feast had finished, we sang carols. Shell impacts could be heard during this. When we looked outside, our 'deep freezer' with the meatballs had been hit and none of them could be found.

Whether it be fact or fiction, author Heinz Schröter conveys a melancholic image of Christmas in the Barrikady factory:

> Many dead soldiers lay about the 'Red Barricades' factory. Four of them had been buried by their friends beneath a tank, which had been blown up on Christmas Eve. They had been buried there because there was no snow under the tank. For a few hours a single candle burned upon the wreckage. There are many graves, but here was the loneliest Christmas in all the world.

Casualties for 24 December, 1942:	
138th Rifle Division:	7 killed, 23 wounded, a total of 30 men
305. Infanterie-Division:	9 men killed, 24 men wounded

25 December, 1942

Trouble was still brewing for LI. Armeekorps at the fuel installation. Its morning report stated that "east of the gun factory, at 0200 hours, an attack against the fuel installation was repulsed. Enemy movements and preparations in 82a3 were combated with artillery and heavy infantry weapons." The attack was launched by 241st Rifle Regiment. Combat Report No. 125 of 95th Rifle Division describes the assault:

> At 0100, supported by the artillery of 57th Artillery Regiment, 241st Rifle Regiment – after the preparatory work – used individual storm groups to seize Dom 04 [Haus 41], and also captured 1 dug-out and 1 pillbox. Distinguishing themselves during the fighting were Red Army man Babayev, Lieutenant Rykulin and Junior-Politruk Muravev – they were the first to rush into the enemy pillbox, throwing grenades.

As a result of this operation, the following trophies were taken: 1 heavy machine-gun, 1 light machine-gun, 15 rifles, about 2000 rifle cartridges and 1 telephone set. An Austrian Obergefreiter from Pionier-Bataillon 305 was also taken prisoner. The losses of 241st Rifle Regiment were 3 dead and 7 wounded, leaving 144 active bayonets. The division's two other regiment held their positions. At 0020 hours, on the sector of 90th Rifle Regiment, mortars opened fire on a concentration of Germans – about 10 men – spotted to the west of the green fuel tank. Otherwise, there was nothing to report.

- - -

The nocturnal chorus around the 'Island of Fire' played out as it normally did. Periods of icy silence ruptured by solitary rifle reports, quickly followed by a flurry of machine-gun fire. The pyrotechnics continued for a few minutes, then the icy silence returned. A short time later, the performance was repeated. Shells would occasionally howl in. The resonant thump of German mortar rounds launched from the workhalls was heard in the few clear seconds before they whistled past the top of the cliff and exploded on the river bank.

In Situation Report No. 259 issued at 0300 hours, 138th Rifle Division reported that one of its units had captured a damaged German tank during the night.

Thus dawned Christmas morning, frosty and cold, the snow stained by soot and brick dust. Mercifully for both sides, it was to see little combat activity. LI. Armeekorps reported that there were "no enemy attacks east of the gun factory". Instead, the Germans and Soviets restricted themselves to hammering each other with artillery, mortars and machine-guns: at 0830 hours, 3rd Battery of 295th Artillery Regiment fired 18 rounds at a German gun in Workshop 4 [Hall 6a]. From 0930 to 1030 hours, 2nd Battery of 295th Artillery Regiment bombarded Dom 33 [Haus 65] and 35 [Haus 66] with 83 rounds. Observers reported that 5 Germans were killed. At 1350 hours, 1st and 2nd Batteries of 295th Artillery Regiment fired 24 rounds at a front-line German trench, reportedly killing 10 soldiers.

The Kommissarhaus was a favourite target on this day: the 120mm mortars of 292nd Separate Mortar Battalion dropped 78 rounds on to it, while the 45mm guns of 230th Anti-Tank Battalion threw 47 shells at visible machine-gun flashes in the building.

At 1426 and 1500 hours, a battery of German nebelwerfers emplaced near the tractor factory made strikes on Zaitsevsky Island.

In general, Soviet artillery and 120 mm mortars laid down fire throughout the day to destroy German emplacements and annihilate personnel in the area of Dom 60 [Kommissarhaus], 38 [Haus 67], 35 [Haus 66], 36 [Haus 73], 32 [Haus 72], Workshop 14/15 [Hall 3] and the main mechanical workshop [Hall 4].

- - -

While the artillery slugged it out, units of Lyudnikov's division prepared themselves for active operations scheduled to begin later in the night. At 1300 hours, Combat Order No. 096 was issued and would govern the actions of the regiments over the coming days. Its opening paragraph summed up their opponents:

> The enemy: remnants of 305th Infantry Division – strengthened by sappers – are fiercely contesting the offensive actions of our forces with orders to implement a well-prepared system of firing zones and engineered obstacles in order to hold their positions at all costs.

768th Rifle Regiment was to destroy emplacements in the area 100 metres east of Dom 49 and attain positions on a small gully 100 metres east of Dom 50.

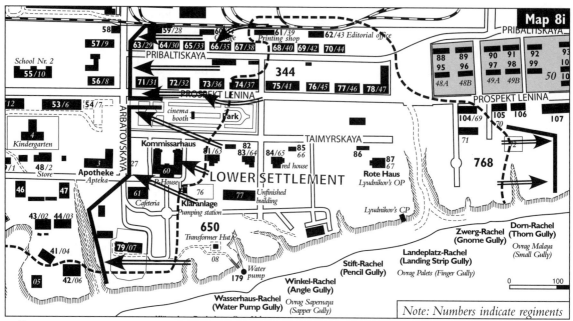

Offensive intentions of 138th Rifle Division, 25 December, 1942.

344th Rifle Regiment was to seize Dom 35 [Haus 66] and 36 [Haus 73] by the night of 26 December and reach Dom 28 [Haus 59], 29 [Haus 63], 31 [Haus 71] and Prospekt Lenina by 28 December.

650th Rifle Regiment was to seize Dom 60 [Kommissarhaus] by the night of 26 December and reach Prospekt Lenina, Dom 27 and the gully south-east of Dom 07 by 28 December.

Throughout the course of the day, the artillery would lay down intensive barrages in order to suppress and destroy German firing positions in the vicinity of the bunkers east of Dom 50, and in Dom 51, 50, 49, 48, the mechanical workshop, Workshop 14/15 and Workshop 3. With the commencement of the infantry attack, the artillery would provide fire support on the boundaries of the mechanical workshop, Workshop 14/15, Workshop 3, Dom 9, 8, 7 and 3.

Our units must act with great speed and flexibility in order to suppress and destroy the enemy with a decisive stroke," declared the order. The infantry attack would begin at 1600 hours. Only 768th Regiment would launch its operation on time.

The task facing Major Pechenyuk and his men was daunting. The Kommissarhaus could not have been better designed as a stronghold. Stout walls, narrow windows, compartmentalised cellars and an advantageous siting, coupled with the accoutrements of positional warfare like barbed wire, mines, booby traps and machine-guns. This meant that only an extraordinarily well-planned attack carried out by courageous men stood even the remotest chance of succeeding. The Germans were fully aware of the strategic importance of the building: it was the anchor for their defensive line. Without it, they would struggle to hold their positions east of the factory. According to Rettenmaier "the Kommissarhaus was defended with characteristic Swabian pigheadedness". No expense in men, weapons or ammunition would be spared to keep it.

In preparation for the storming of the Kommissarhaus [P-shaped house], Major Pechenyuk issued an order to his men:

The enemy stubbornly defends the P-shaped house, having transformed it into a stronghold. He mounts intense fire resistance and strives to hold it at any cost.

The regiment, having seized the heavily fortified strongpoints immediately next to it, has approached close to the P-shaped house. I therefore order that:

1. The fire system of the enemy in the P-shaped house be suppressed and his personnel destroyed.
2. The house be blown up in two places, on the south-east and north-west corners. Two storm groups – the 1st from Dom 63 and the 2nd from the cistern that lies to the south-west of the unfinished building – will swiftly burst into the P-shaped house after the explosion, use grenades, bayonets and fire to annihilate enemy personnel, and then consolidate in the building.

Signal for the attack – explosion in the P-shaped house. Battalion commanders will allocate one assault group with 9 men. They will be armed with grenades and automatic weapons.

The strength of 650th Rifle Regiment was 45 officers, 25 NCOs and 90 other ranks, a total of 160 men. As can be seen in Pechenyuk's order, the storm groups designated for the attack were very small. Previous attacks had shown the folly of throwing huge numbers of men at the house. It was far better to break into the target with a few men and only then follow up with larger groups that could clear the enemy and consolidate the position.

The combat journal of 650th Rifle Regiment reports about the day's events in its sector:

The enemy obstinately defends the P-shaped house, having transformed it into a centre of resistance that offers stiff opposition. During the day, he offers heavy fire from small arms, machine-guns and automatics, as well as periodic fire from heavy mortars and artillery.

The regiment, having seized the heavily protected strongpoint, will approach right up to the P-shaped house, continue to hold the occupied line and conduct small arms, machine-gun and mortar fire on enemy emplacements.

The immensity of the task forced Pechenyuk to postpone the attack until thorough preparations had been completed. The same concerns caused Konovalenko's 344th Regiment to do the same.

– – –

A summary of the day's events is captured in the 62nd Army war diary:

138th and 95th Rifle Divisions, having repelled attacks by individual groups of enemy infantry, continue to fight with small storm groups to capture individual enemy strongpoints.

Operations by individual groups of 95th Rifle Division seized Dom 04 and captured 3 dug-outs and one pillbox. Trophies: 1 heavy machine-gun, 1 light machine-gun, 15 rifles and 20,000 rifle cartridges. Taken prisoner: an Obergefreiter – an Austrian – of 305th Infantry Division and a German soldier of 305th Infantry Division.

Another Soviet attack struck this area at 1830 hours. A storm group from 90th Rifle Regiment attacked a German trench on the spur of Appendix Gully but was deluged by volleys of grenades. Not having success, they pulled back to their starting positions and proceeded to destroy the German emplacement with machine-gun and small-arms fire. Casualties: 1 dead and 8 wounded. The assaults by 95th Rifle Division were having an effect on the German line. Every now and then, a house, dug-out or trench would be conquered and then absorbed into the Soviet positions. On this holiest of days, Leutnant Rudolf Gottwald[20], a platoon commander from 1./Panzerpionier-Bataillon 50, was severely wounded during the fighting in this area and died in an aid station later in the day.

---

20. Gottwald, Leutnant Rudolf, 1./Pz.Pi.Btl.50; born 30 June, 1915 in Hamburg. Killed in action, 25 December, 1942 in Stalingrad. See Appendix 2 (page 572) for more details.

Some new reinforcements arrived for 305. Infanterie-Division: a company from Hauptmann Kahnert's[21] Festungs-Bau-Bataillon 16[22], just released from subordination to the southern neighbour, 79. Infanterie-Division.

– – –

Hauptmann Hans Kempter[23], commander of the Stabskompanie of Grenadier-Regiment 576, was fortunate to be in lodgings behind the city. He had already served time in the ruins of the city: on 22 October, he assumed command of III. Bataillon after its commander, Major Emendörfer, fell ill. Kempter led the battalion for two weeks of cruel combat in the Barrikady factory, until he was wounded on 2 November by shrapnel to the left side of his head. Although his injuries were not serious, the old Great War warrior was pulled back to regimental staff to recover. His long-awaited furlough was postponed by events and now – instead of spending Christmas with his wife and daughter – he celebrated the holy day with his men:

Hauptmann Hans Kempter, Gr.Rgt.576. This photo was taken in October 1942.

> In the afternoon, I visited an ill Hauptmann of the regiment who was nearby. At 1500 hours (it's already dark) I gathered the few remaining men (about 20) of my society around me in a horse bunker that had been freed up for us. A long wooden table covered in white cloth, an oven, the walls covered by blankets so that the bare earth could not be seen, an advent wreath and two carbide lamps on the table. That's how it looked. The room was therefore in the correct style of Bethlehem. The little donkey – ours was a horse – was taken out earlier and came back to us via the field-kitchen. In this room, we had a delicious meal, consisting of 3 meat patties and a mess tin full of a good noodle soup. After I made a short speech, there was tea with schnapps. No-one became full and that was good. As gifts, everyone received 2 small packets of biscuits, 20 cigarettes and 2 cigars. That's how we spent the hours… I then went into my bunker with my Oberleutnant. Here, I heard through the field-telephone a large part of the 'Ringsendung Front-Heimat'[24] and Goebbels' speech being broadcast in another bunker. The words out of Stalingrad must surely have been heard by you, everyone is thinking of us, the focal point of the entire front.

– – –

The freezing conditions hampered normal activities, with even the simplest tasks requiring an effort, as Hauptmann Traub reports:

21. Kahnert, Hauptmann Bruno, Fest.-Bau-Btl.16; born 6 October 1903. Missing in action, February 1943.

22. Trans.: 'Festungs-Bau-Bataillon 16' = 'Fortress Construction Battalion 16'.

23. Kempter, Major Hans, III./Gr.Rgt.576; born 11 August 1895. Died 12 July, 1980 in Landshut.

24. Trans.: 'Ringsendung Front-Heimat' = 'Hookup front-home'. The infamous broadcast at 1900–2000 hours on Christmas evening. Soldiers on all fronts sent live greetings back to Germany and after hearing reports come in from Narvik and Africa, many in Stalingrad were astonished to hear: 'This is Stalingrad. The front on the Volga.'

I had to go over to the office just now. It is only some 50 metres away from my quarters but in undertaking this, I got really clammy hands. Again we have an icy east wind. The moon is very clear and it will certainly be a cold night. Here in my quarters there is comforting warmth. The stove (made out of bricks) heats wonderfully. Even in the morning it is warm despite the fact that I let the fire go out before I go to sleep.

– – –

With the onset of darkness, 768th Rifle Regiment launched its attack on German emplacements with small combat groups. Encountering strong resistance, the storm groups lobbed a few grenades and returned to their starting positions. At 2100 hours, fire from an anti-tank rifle destroyed an ammunition depot.

Casualties for 25 December, 1942:	
138th Rifle Division:	2 killed, 14 wounded, a total of 16 men
305. Infanterie-Division:	1 officer and 5 men killed, 25 men wounded

26 December, 1942

German machine-guns and mortars occasionally fired during the night. At midnight, on Gorishny's sector, the left flank of 161st Rifle Regiment was fired on by German mortars and tracer shells from an anti-tank gun on the south-east corner of the factory. A few artillery rounds were also fired at Lyudnikov's command post, Zaitsevsky Island and the Denezhnaya Volozhka crossing. A reconnaissance patrol from 768th Regiment probing northward was opened up on by machine-gunners in the area of Dom 49 and 50.

The Germans opposite 344th and 768th Rifle Regiments did not undertake active operations but a platoon-sized force from the Kommissarhaus twice tried to counterattack the positions of 650th Rifle Regiment. The counterattacks were beaten off with small arms and machine-gun fire and grenades. Both sides suffered very few casualties. By 0100 hours, four 76mm guns of the 1927 type had been dragged across the ice to the Stalingrad bank. They were the 4th and 5th Batteries of Captain Ivanov's 295th Artillery Regiment.

– – –

The daylight hours passed with little combat and only occasional German fire. Soviet weapons, on the other hand, kept up a constant fire on the German defences. The methodical fire of artillery and 120mm mortars destroyed German emplacements, personnel and equipment in preparation for nocturnal offensive actions. Lyudnikov's divisional war diary states that "rifle and machine-gun fire was exchanged with the enemy who continues to suffer high casualties in the basements of the ruined houses". Desultory German artillery fire kept Soviet units on their toes. At 1140 hours, two nebelwerfers from the direction of Aeroportovsk fired a volley at Zaitsevsky Island. At 1340 hours, German mortars made a fire strike on the area around Lyudnikov's command post.

A summary of 138th Rifle Division's actions is as follows:

768th Rifle Regiment destroyed three dug-outs with mortars.

344th Rifle Regiment destroyed one dug-out, suppressed one emplacement and shot up 3 embrasures in Dom 38 [Haus 67]. It continued laying down fire to produce the prerequisites for nocturnal offensive actions.

Apart from repelling the two night-time German counterattacks from the Kommissarhaus, 650th Rifle Regiment smashed two embrasures in the building and covered German emplacements with fire. According to its combat journal, it also "exterminated two [enemy] deserters". The regiment continued to destroy emplacements, to exterminate enemy personnel and equipment, and to prepare for nocturnal actions with storm groups. It lost 4 enlisted men to wounds throughout the day. Its strength was then 48 officers, 25 NCOs and 91 other ranks, a total of 164 men. The entire division had 840 men on the right bank, plus 51 who were not part of the division, making a total of 891 men. Of those, 550 were active bayonets. The division was armed with 657 rifles, 126 submachine-guns, 23 light machine-guns, 1 heavy machine-gun, 1 DShK anti-aircraft machine-gun, 17 mortars, 8 anti-tank rifles, 3 anti-tank guns, 4 76mm guns and 4 ampulomets.

- - -

The fuel tank sector was unnervingly quiet during the day. While holding their positions, all three of Gorishny's regiments reinforced their trenches and dug-outs, carried out reconnaissance and occasionally exchanged fire with the Germans. At 1140 hours, three men from 161st Rifle Regiment were wounded by fire from their own 120mm mortars.

- - -

The evening report of LI. Armeekorps recorded that there was "no combat activity east of the gun factory". The furious Soviet artillery and machine-gun bombardments proved to be bluster. The German troops were quite safe in the thick-walled cellars and casualties were low. Amongst the 16 wounded suffered on this day was Gefreiter Johann Breimschmidt[25], 2./Pionier-Bataillon 305, who was struck in the right knee by shrapnel. He was flown out of the Kessel on 30 December, 1942.

Casualties for 26 December, 1942:	
138th Rifle Division:	2 killed, 18 wounded, a total of 20 men
305. Infanterie-Division:	1 man killed, 16 men wounded

27 December, 1942

The combat journal of 650th Rifle Regiment recorded that "throughout the night, the enemy placed heavy machine-gun, mortar and artillery fire on our combat ranks and on the crossing over the Denezhnaya Volozhka channel". In the morning, the Germans placed heavy nebelwerfer barrages on Lyudnikov's command post and artillery emplacements on Zaitsevsky Island. They occasionally fired small-arms, machine-guns, mortars and artillery at Soviet units, on the Denezhnaya Volozhka crossing and on Zaitsevsky island. However, they did not launch any counterattack and, indeed, rarely left the protection of their cellars and dug-outs.

Conducting reconnaissance in the direction of the Kommissarhaus, units of 344th Rifle Regiment captured a German dug-out and a communications trench. 650th Rifle Regiment combat reconnaissance simulated an attack in order to detect and destroy German firing points. The patrols suffered 2 wounded.

25. Breimschmidt, Gefreiter Johann 2./Pi.Btl.305; born 6 May, 1908 in Baden bei Wien. No further information known.

The ruined houses along Pribaltiskaya Street and the railway embankment are clearly visible in this photo. The dominance of the workhalls is also apparent – German snipers and machine-gunners in the roof could easily cover Soviet positions. Note the German trench running from Hall 4, through the railway embankment, into Haus 66 [Dom 35].

From 0700 hours, small Soviet reconnaissance groups carried out observation with the aim of revealing German groupings, emplacements and systems of fire along the front-line and in the depth of the defence. Fire from artillery and infantry weapons wiped out a dug-out and an emplacement. While 768th Rifle Regiment continued to improve its positions and fired at German personnel with machine-guns and mortars, 344th Rifle Regiment used infantry weapons and direct-firing 76mm and 45mm guns to destroy embrasures in Dom 60 [Kommissarhaus], 35 [Haus 66] and 38 [Haus 67]. The pounding received by the Kommissarhaus was brutal: from 0800 to 1100 hours, the 76mm guns of 4th and 5th Batteries of 295th Artillery Regiment pumped 300 rounds into the building. In return fire, 3 of the artillerymen were wounded. Sections of the northern facade of the Kommissarhaus collapsed and Soviet observers claimed that 12 Germans were killed and one machine-gun was destroyed. Leutnant Walter Birkmann[26], a company commander in Grenadier-Regiment 578, was severely wounded and died later in the day.

After this partial destruction by cannon fire, the Kommissarhaus was attacked at 1230 hours by two storm groups of 650th Rifle Regiment. The German garrison immediately opened up heavy fire. The building was surrounded by barbed wire and its approaches were mined. A Soviet platoon commander and one of the storm groups' soldiers were blown up on them. Lacking success, the groups returned to their positions. At 1630 hours, LI. Armeekorps reported to 6. Armee:

> At 1305 hours, after heavy artillery and mortar preparation, an enemy attack against the centre of 305. Infanterie-Division (Kommissarhaus) was repulsed. Renewed attack in progress since 1400 hours.

A surprise was experienced by both sides at 1330 hours when three German Ju-52s flew directly over the battlefield in a south-west direction. Gorishny's division reported that they

---

26. Birkmann, Leutnant Walter, Gr.Rgt.578; born 22 February, 1917 in Nürnberg. Died of wounds, 27 December, 1942 in Stalingrad.

dropped cargo by parachutes. At 1530 hours, another three transport planes came in, circled above the factory and then flew away in a north-west direction.

After the rebuff, sappers from Pechenyuk's regiment completed preparations to blow up the Kommissarhaus via a novel method: they would roll two barrels filled with 600 kilograms of explosives into it. Storm groups would be ready to attack the building.

In its evening report, LI. Armeekorps wrote:

> An attack against the Kommissarhaus near 305. Infanterie-Division collapsed in defensive fire. Further preparations recognised there were combated. [There is] continued strong artillery, mortar and anti-tank fire but it is decreasing.

- - -

The morning was fairly quiet on 95th Rifle Division's sector but that changed in the afternoon. The German garrisons of the Apotheke and Haus 55[27] covered 241st and 90th Rifle Regiments with small-arms and machine-gun fire. At 1430 hours, 18 German soldiers were spotted moving from the south-western corner of the factory towards Dom 1 and 2 [Haus 48], both of which were strongpoints close behind the front-line. Soviet machine-guns opened up on them. Ampulomets and mortars of 241st Rifle Regiment reportedly incinerated a pillbox and 3 soldiers. Exacting a heavier toll, however, were the regiment's snipers. Throughout the day, they claimed to have killed 12 enemy soldiers. Sniper Varapayev was credited with 6, sniper Krasov with 4, while snipers Evdomikov and Yurovsky claimed one each. Snipers of the neighbouring 90th Rifle Regiment fired at pillbox embrasures and single soldiers, claiming 5 Germans.

Gorishny's 95th Rifle Division had only recently begun to make widespread use of snipers. A report, compiled by the division's chief-of-staff, Lieutenant-Colonel Klimenko at the behest of 62nd Army, stated that "the division's units have snipers, but not enough. That being said, I present the list of the snipers and their personal tallies since 1 December."

No.	Surname, name, patronymic	Rgt.	Year of birth	Year of call up	Their weapon	No. of Germans killed
	Snipers of 95th Rifle Division					
1.	Fetisev, Alexei Petrovich	241	1908	1942	Rifle	4
2.	Sergazinov, Cheyboknan	161	1918	1942	Sniper rifle	5
3.	Kukorsky, Grigori Davidovich	161	1918	1939	SMG	2
4.	Jun-Lt. Glazyrin, Nikolai Grigoryevich	161	1923	1942	SMG	4
5.	Kudryavtsev, Yakob Andreyevich	161	1920	1942	SMG	2
6.	Agapov, P.P.	161	1921	1942	Rifle	3

27. Known by several names to Soviet forces: either Dom 10, the E-shaped house or School No. 2. This building still exists today and continues to function as a school. The building's chequered floor-tiles bring back vivid memories to Soviet veterans and a small museum inside commemorates the battle in the area.

Klimenko summarised by saying that a cadre of snipers had not been included in the divisional formations prior to operations but "steps have been implemented to prepare snipers". Towards the end of month, the snipers were coming into their own, particularly within the constricted confines of the battlefield.

One of their victims was Leutnant Gerhard Bofinger[28], commander of 11./Grenadier-Regiment 576. He died the next day as a result of his wounds.

– – –

Oberleutnant Bernhard Ziesch, commander of 3./Pi. Btl.336, sent a letter home which shows the bleakness of the situation in Stalingrad:

Familie Ziesch

> Today you would have celebrated the third day of Christmas. We haven't been able to celebrate Christmas this year. True, a couple of odds and ends were given as Christmas gifts, but apart from that, no-one has thought about Christmas. I'll tell you more when I'm on furlough.
>
> Healthwise, things have again taken a turn for the worse. But that is no wonder. For days on end I find myself sitting in a very draughty cellar. Outside, it is 25-30° below zero. My nose runs as if it wants to run away. My cough has also re-appeared. The fever, thank God, is not excessively high. Hopefully things will soon get better…

Oberleutnant Bernhard Ziesch

Hauptmann Rettenmaier described another discomfort which exacerbated the misery of the German troops hunkering down in the foetid cellars:

> The vermin torment us terribly. As soon as you lie down on the bunk to rest, the crawling begins all over your body, from your feet right up to the neck. I am very sensitive to this and am barely able to sleep. To 'hunt' them in my present surroundings is impossible, at least while in the dug-out. If we step out into the open we can certainly take action, but at - 20 degrees Celsius, this also has certain difficulties.
>
> I changed my clothes but the lice infestation returned in a very short space of time. One has no peace from these monsters.

He added more detail about the utterly miserable conditions in a post-war account:

> Personal hygiene was no longer thought about. The incessant combat activity allowed no time for it. Beards sprouted. In the cellars, the cylindrical iron stoves were fuelled by oil-soaked wood paving taken from factory buildings. These produced dreadfully thick clouds of smoke and a layer of black soot covered everything[29]. The entire garrison looked the same. On top of that, faces became more and more distorted by hunger. Eye sockets were larger and the look in one's eyes took on a peculiar expression. Vermin gained the upper hand and did not allow exhausted bodies any rest. Relief could only be had when one sought out a quiet spot somewhere in the open and – despite the icy cold – removed the clothes and scraped off the pests with the flat of one's hand. This helped for at least an hour.

The reason why the Germans endured these conditions – and continued to do so – can be found in a simple explanation proffered by Hauptmann Traub to his wife:

---

28. Bofinger, Leutnant Gerhard, 11./Gr.Rgt.576; born 19 December 1919. Died of wounds, 28 December, 1942 in Stalingrad.

29. Feldarzt Dr. Schöpf noted an unforeseen consequence of this: "Many soldiers had small makeshift stoves that produced a lot of smoke. Conjunctivitis developed in the eyes because of these."

We must hold out, otherwise Germany will endure a terrible disaster. Hopefully our children will have it better than we do and experience their own lives without war.

Casualties for 27 December, 1942:	
138th Rifle Division:	1 killed, 9 wounded, 1 evacuated, a total of 10 men
305. Infanterie-Division:	3 men killed, 1 officer and 22 men wounded

28 December, 1942

The Germans did not display any special activity during the night. There was the periodic fire of small arms, machine-guns and mortars, mainly directed at the Denezhnaya Volozhka crossing and Zaitsevsky island. The greatest concentration of fire came from the main mechanical workshop [Hall 4], Workshop 14/15 [Hall 3], and Dom 27, 60 [Kommissarhaus], 35 [Haus 66] and 36 [Haus 73]. Working under the mesh of German tracers were small Soviet recon patrols that probed the the defences, revealing firing points, groupings, systems of fire and defensive works along the front-line and in the depth of the defence. The results, as described in Reconnaissance Report No. 101, show the typical night-time pattern beginning at dusk on 27 December:

> Through combat, reconnaissance and observation, the following was established:
> At 1730 and 2000, an 81mm mortar in the mechanical workshop fired upon 650th Rifle Regiment. At 2220, heavy machine-gun fire from Workshop 14/15 hit the right flank of 344th Rifle Regiment. At 2230, from the south-west section of the mechanical shop [Hall 4], a 75mm cannon occasionally fired at the battle formations of 344th Rifle Regiment. At 0200, an 81mm mortar in the mechanical workshop fired on the Denezhnaya Volozhka crossing.

More importantly for the scouts, and for the division, they were able to positively identify the German unit opposite:

> At 1910, a recon patrol removed – killed – a soldier positioned at a sentry outpost between Dom 36 [Haus 73] and 35 [Haus 66] via a communications trench. The documents collected from the dead man confirm the presence of 578th Infantry Regiment of 305th Infantry-Division across from 650th Rifle Regiment.

The report also offers a portrait of the German defence:

> The enemy at the front, defending against our divisional units, does not show any activity [...] but places methodical mortar fire on our battle formations and on the area of the divisional command post. He continuously rakes the main line of defence with automatic-machine-gun fire and during the night he fires at the Denezhnaya Volozhka crossing with individual machine-guns and illuminates the district with flares. He stubbornly defends Dom 60 [Kommissarhaus] and has partially reconstructed the destroyed pillboxes and communication trenches west of Dom 60.

German planes of an unknown type were heard buzzing overhead during the night. At 0500 hours, in the Skulpturny Park area, a platoon of German infantry and 6 motor vehicles was observed, as was entrenching work in the area of Dom 38 [Haus 67].

On the right flank of the division, Red Army man Aldoshinim, operating within the framework of a reconnaissance patrol of 768th Rifle Regiment, captured a light German machine-gun and two boxes of ammunition.

Throughout the night, 138th Rifle Division suffered 4 dead and 1 wounded.

Thus a typical night passed in the fiery positions east of the gun factory.

The situation was static on Gorishny's sector. Both sides held their positions and duelled with rifles and machine-guns. Using its 45mm anti-tank guns, mortars and machine-guns, 241st Rifle Regiment suppressed known German emplacements, claiming the destruction of 3 dug-outs and about 20 soldiers. It suffered no losses and itself possessed 141 active bayonets. The snipers of 90th Rifle Regiment claimed another 7 enemy soldiers. One of them was Obergefreiter Max Albert[30] from 2./Panzerpionier-Bataillon 50. And with fire from 45mm guns, mortars and machine-guns, 161st Rifle Regiment suppressed recognised German firing points near the school in front of the forward line of 61st Rifle Regiment (Colonel Sokolov's 45th Rifle Division), assisting its offensive actions. It destroyed 1 pillbox and 3 dug-outs and killed about 15 soldiers, 7 of them with snipers. Its losses were 3 men wounded and it had 79 active bayonets.

– – –

Throughout the entire day there was heavy rifle and machine-gun fire and Soviet observers noticed groups of Germans moving from houses to the workhalls in the Barrikady factory. It was presumed that the Germans were regrouping with reinforcements received from the rear and relieving some of their formations. Fire from heavier German weapons was light during daylight hours: at 1110 hours, from the direction of Skulpturny Park, a nebelwerfer launched two volleys at Zaitsevsky Island; and at 1500 hours, an 81mm mortar in Workshop 14/15 [Hall 3] fired upon the area of Lyudnikov's command post.

Lyudnikov's men continued to improve the captured positions and used small-arms, machine-guns, mortars and direct-firing 76mm and 45mm guns to batter Dom 60 [Kommissarhaus], 36 [Haus 73], 35 [Haus 66] and 38 [Haus 67], plus various emplacements and dug-outs. In addition, 120mm mortars on Zaitsevsky Island pounded the Kommissarhaus and its outlying breastworks. The defences in this area were being worked over in readiness for another attack but it is clear from the combat journal of Pechenyuk's regiment that they knew it was not going to be an easy task:

Decision of the commander of 650th Rifle Regiment: storm the P-shaped building.

The enemy has transformed the P-shaped building into a stout fortification, gathered all his personnel into this stronghold […] and offers fierce resistance. Despite repeated treatment by artillery, the P-shaped building still has a large number of firing points in the semi-basement level in the northern part of the building. There are three light machine-guns and one heavy machine gun located on the second floor, as well as submachine-gunners and men throwing grenades. Judging by the presence of defensive posts and enemy fire […], the enemy has a strength of over 50 men.

For implementation of the combat mission to seize the P-shaped building I order the following: Small storm groups from 1st and 2nd Rifle Battalions will attack the P-shaped building. 1st Rifle Battalion will create three groups:

a) covering group – will cover to the west of the P-shaped building

b) storm group

c) capture group – will operate in trenches from its own house, attack the western part of the right wing of the P-shaped building and clear the right wing.

2nd Rifle Battalion will reinforce the storm groups of 1st Rifle Battalion, pin down the enemy in the north-east corner of the P-shaped building and be ready to repel sudden counterattacks out of the park.

---

30. Albert, Obergefreiter Max, 2./Pz.Pi.Btl.50; born 24 August, 1911 in Kirchenlamitz. Killed in action, 28 December, 1942 in Stalingrad.

Detachments with light machine-guns will cover the operations of the groups. All soldiers will be provided with sufficient numbers of hand grenades, anti-tank grenades and thermite spheres.

In order to suppress enemy emplacements, operations by heavy artillery are desired.

The evening report of LI. Armeekorps from 2050 hours mentions the attack that took place on the Kommissarhaus during the night:

East of the gun factory, after heavy artillery and anti-tank shelling, an attack is in progress at the moment against our positions in 83d Mitte (Kommissarhaus) from the north-east. Throughout the entire day and since darkness fell, enemy air activity has been lively with bombings and strafing from onboard weapons on the forward line and rear area.

The fighting would continue deep into the next day.

Casualties for 28 December, 1942:	
138th Rifle Division:	3 killed, 16 wounded, a total of 19 men
305. Infanterie-Division:	7 men killed, 27 men wounded

29 December, 1942

Situation Report No. 267, issued by 138th divisional headquarters at 0200 hours, briefly covers the assault on the Kommissarhaus:

344th Rifle Regiment provided one assault group and covers the operations of 650th Rifle Regiment with strong fire. Pechenyuk's storm groups conduct battle to conquer Dom 60 [Kommissarhaus], which is a heavily strengthened enemy strongpoint. Fighting continues.

By this time, losses of 4 dead and 7 wounded had been registered.

No mention can be found in Soviet records about the implementation of their plan to roll two barrels of explosives into the Kommissarhaus. The 4th and 5th Batteries of 295th Artillery Regiment fired a total of 76 rounds at the Kommissarhaus and surrounding emplacements. They claimed the destruction of 16 Germans and 1 heavy machine-gun, blew up a supply dump and suppressed the fire of two heavy machine-guns.

At 0610 hours, LI. Armeekorps reported to 6. Armee that "during the night, two attacks on the Kommissarhaus east of the gun factory were repulsed". The combat journal of 650th Rifle Regiment states that "the enemy, placing heavy machine-gun fire and mortar bombardments on the regiment, has put up fierce resistance in the area of the P-shaped building", while Combat Report No. 246 of 138th Rifle Division records that "the greatest amount of enemy fire is seen in the area of the combat operations of 650th Rifle Regiment's storm groups". The first attempts to break into the Kommissarhaus under cover of darkness failed. Not to be discouraged, the storm groups prepared themselves for yet another attack.

- - -

The Germans continued to carry out engineering work at night to strengthen their positions. As before, there was intermittent rifle and machine-gun fire throughout the night. Crossings over the Denezhnaya Volozhka channel were under constant German artillery and mortar fire guided in by forward observers in Haus 79. Any kind of movement over the ice was only possible during the night. Soviet artillery and 120 mm mortars fired to suppress and destroy German emplacements. Others sectors in the Barrikady remained fairly quiet. The action on this day centred around the Kommissarhaus.

- - -

Gorishny's men noticed the Germans moving about in the dark of night, no doubt to avoid the lethal sniper fire. At 0100 hours, on 161st Rifle Regiment's sector, a group of 5-6 Germans tried to approach the forward Soviet line but they were repelled by machine-gun fire. And in the area of Dom 12, individual Germans were frequently spotted moving from the factory towards Humpback Gully. In daylight, Soviet units continued to wear down German strongpoints with attritional fire. While 241st Rifle Regiment exchanged fire with the garrisons of Dom 02 [Haus 43], 03 [Haus 44] and 07 [Haus 79], their artillery and mortars destroyed 2 pillboxes near the latter. Mortars of 90th Rifle Regiment destroyed a dug-out near the green fuel tank but German fire wounded two of their men and damaged one of their mortars. Amongst the German casualties was Obergefreiter Leonhard Meissner[31], 2./Panzerpionier-Bataillon 50, who was killed.

- - -

Pechenyuk's 'regiment' stormed the Kommissarhaus during the first half of the day. They were supported by fire laid down by 344th Rifle Regiment to the west and elements of 2nd Rifle Battalion positioned near the cistern. The storm group of 1st Rifle Battalion burst out of Dom 63 [Haus 81] and succeeded in dashing across the fire-swept patch of land in front of the Kommissarhaus. The northern facade of the building was a shambolic pile of masonry chunks and crumbling concrete slabs. Collapsed sections of wall exposed glimpses of the building's innards but the cellars were blocked in by the mounds of rubble. The storm group

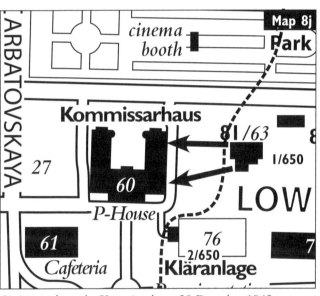

Soviet attack on the Kommissarhaus, 29 December, 1942.

scrambled up the ramp of rubble and leapt inside. Grenades were the weapon of choice and a grim struggle began inside the ghastly ruins. The German garrison defended themselves valiantly. Counterattacks surged down the hallways but they were driven back by a stream of grenades. German reinforcements dashed through trenches into the building. Troops of 2nd Rifle Battalion still outside the building did everything possible to prevent this. The group covering the park prevented help reaching the Germans from that direction. Soviet artillery played its part in cutting off the Kommissarhaus from outside help: at 0940 hours, 3rd Battery of 295th Artillery Regiment – still positioned on the other bank of the Volga – fired 12 rounds at a group of Germans near the Apotheke [Dom 3] who were preparing to reinforce the Kommissarhaus. They reported that they killed 5 Germans. Despite all these measures, reinforcements still made it into the building.

---

31. Meissner, Obergefreiter Leonhard, 2./Pz.Pi.Btl.50; born 22 April, 1916 in Hohenelbe. Killed in action, 29 December, 1942 in Stalingrad.

After the initial Soviet break-in, capture groups followed up and entered the building. With their strength bolstered, the Soviets managed to capture most of the first and second floors of the building's northern wing, but German resistance was fierce – and getting fiercer. Their defences held firm in the stout cellars and the Soviets faced extreme difficulties getting them out. The Germans were not invulnerable in the cellars, of course, as Sergeant Gorbatenko recounts:

> Chalykh and Konoputov took part in the assault on the P-shaped house in the Barrikady factory at the end of December. Konoputov made a hole through the floor into the cellar, where the Germans were, showering them with grenades and scorching them with a flamethrower.

The Germans' knowledge of the building's layout, however, gave them an advantage. They had held the cellars throughout the scuffle and now used them to attack the Soviets from two directions. While some counterattacked along the hallways, from room to room, others scurried through the cellars and came up the stairwell at the western end of the northern wing – effectively in the Soviet rear. Attacked from two directions, the Soviets had no firm anchoring point in the building, but they held steady.

A view from inside the Kommissarhaus across the park to Haus 72 [Dom 32] and the Barrikady factory beyond. This hole through the tremendously thick wall was almost certainly as a result of German attacks in November 1942.

Another view from the Kommissarhaus, this time towards Haus 53 (Rettenmaier's command post). On the right is School Nr. 2 and in the background is Hall 6e Note the long-barrel Stug. III of Stug.Abt.245 in the park on the right, knocked out on 11 November. Another armoured vehicle is next to Haus 53.

The exhausting room to room struggle continued for hours. Dozens of German hand grenades pummelled the Soviet-occupied rooms. Situation Report No. 268 of 138th Rifle Division from 1400 hours states:

> On the left flank of the division, storm groups of 650th Rifle Regiment are fighting to take possession of Dom 60. Fighting is being carried out in the northern wing of the building. The enemy lays down heavy fire from machine-guns, automatics and mortars on the area of our storm troop operations.

The division's daily report recorded that "fighting with grenades continues inside the building". Casualties at this stage were 8 dead and 40 wounded.

One of the Soviet officers in the Kommissarhaus – mentioned in Gorbatenko's account – was Senior-Lieutenant Ivan Gavrilovich Chalykh, who remembers this attack, for good reason:

> I was fortunate to be a defender of the city of Stalingrad, mainly at the Barrikady factory within the ranks of 138th Red Banner Rifle Division, holding a post as the propagandist of

650th Rifle Regiment… As the regiment propagandist, all my time was spent together with the soldiers in the companies. All our soldiers and officers heroically stood to the death.

The P-shaped house in the Barrikady factory was fought over for a long time and it was there that I was severely wounded in the head on 29 December, 1942 – 18 fragment wounds in the skull. I was only treated in the medical battalion for 12 days before returning to the unit…

The tide turned in the Kommissarhaus. The Germans gained the upper hand and forced Pechenyuk's men back. The finale is recorded in his regiment's combat journal:

Kalgine/Chalykh

Ivan Gavrilovich Chalykh

> Toporkov's group seized the first and second floors in the northern part of the building, but by the end of the day – suffering casualties – they were compelled to leave the building and consolidate themselves in the ruins on the northern side of the building. The group tried several times to restore the situation, but in view of the fact that there was very few of them, they withdrew every time. Grenades are running short.

The first successful Soviet penetration into the Kommissarhaus had failed. At 1630 hours, LI. Armeekorps reported to 6. Armee that "east of the gun factory, all of the repeated enemy attacks in the morning against the Kommissarhaus were repulsed". Casualties for both sides were almost even.

The final act on this day was carried out by the Germans. From 1900 to 2100 hours, their mortars made two sudden strikes on Pechenyuk's regiment.

Casualties for 29 December, 1942:	
138th Rifle Division:	8 killed, 49 wounded, a total of 57 men
305. Infanterie-Division:	9 men killed, 35 men wounded

30 December, 1942

In the frigid depths of the night, the southern defensive area of 305. Infanterie-Division was seriously threatened by the Soviets. At 0130 hours, storm groups of 2/61st Rifle Regiment (45th Rifle Division) broke through the front-line at 82a3, pushed to the north-west between Bayonet and Tapeworm Gullies, and captured the 'Fliegerhaus', a large school building south of the southern point of the bread factory. Although this strongpoint belonged to Grenadier-Regiment 226 of the neighbouring 79. Infanterie-Division, this move seriously threatened to unhinge the entire German defensive line in the Barrikady area. The blood-soaked defences east of the factory – solidly anchored on Haus 79 and the Kommissarhaus – formed a precarious bulge in the German line that could be easily outflanked or even cut off from the south.

The morning report of Grenadier-Regiment 226 described the loss of the strongpoint:

> Position east of the Fliegerhaus cleared up twice with counterattacks. After a thorough preparation with heavy mortars, the enemy pushed towards the position in the Fliegerhaus and took it. Left wing pulled back to Bayonet Gully to face the Fliegerhaus. Left wing placed on

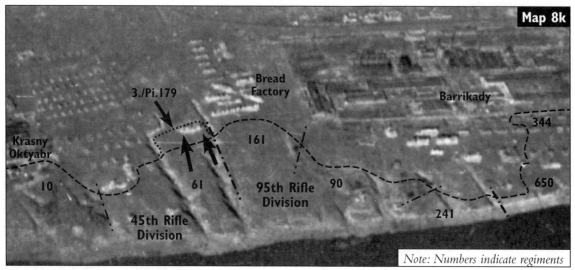

Soviet attack and German counterattacks on the 'Fliegerhaus', 30 December, 1942. The importance of the building is obvious. If the Bread Factory was then captured, the entire German position in the Barrikady would be seriously threatened.

the old position. Counterattack with assault guns and 3./Pi.179 scheduled to recapture the Fliegerhaus and establish a connection with the elements on Bayonet Gully.

The counterattack was launched at 0705 hours with Oberleutnant Paul Fiedler's 3./ Pionier-Bataillon 179 and three long-barrel assault guns of 2./Stug.Abt.245, which had been subordinated to 79. Infanterie-Division for use as a 'fire brigade'. After some initial success they came to a halt in heavy Soviet barrage fire. A group of about 40 Soviet soldiers then launched their own counterattack from the Fliegerhaus and the German force fell back to their starting positions. Fiedler lost 1 man dead, and 1 NCO and 8 men wounded. The Soviet penetration was sealed off by occupying the southern edge of the bread factory and the outlets of Bayonet Gully. The assault guns skulked in the southern part of the bread factory to monitor the situation and were kept ready to throw back any further intrusions. The fighting here was only warming up.

– – –

In darkness, a storm group of 650th Rifle Regiment and a demolitions squad from the sapper battalion undertook preparatory work to take possession of the Kommissarhaus. Small-arms and machine-gun fire, plus mortar bombardments, were directed at German emplacements in support of the sappers' operations. During the course of the night, the Germans laid down heavy small arms and machine-gun fire so that the sappers could not get too close. This was not successful. The experienced sappers managed to crawl up to the Kommissarhaus, unseen, lodge their explosives and then get back to their own lines. The remaining Soviet units were poised in a combat-ready posture. At 1000 hours, the sappers blew up the north-west corner of the Kommissarhaus. It was not followed up by an attack.

Also working under night's protective blanket were small recon patrols that continued to carry out reconnaissance on the Germans and their positions. A group of scouts from the divisional reconnaissance company attacked a German emplacement at dawn, killing one German, bringing away a machine-gun, one belt of cartridges, a rifle and a flare pistol with one bag of rockets, and returned to their positions without loss.

The night-time activities cost 138th Rifle Division 2 dead and 4 wounded.

– – –

At 0820 hours, a storm group of 161st Rifle Regiment tried to seize a pillbox on Mashinnaya Street, just to the right of the recently captured Fliegerhaus. The German counterattack was instant but it failed. Ten minutes later, a German attack with about 30 soldiers tried to recover the school [Fliegerhaus]. It struck the boundary between 161st (95th Rifle Division) and 61st Rifle Regiments (45th Rifle Division). Fire from 45mm guns, mortars and machine-guns repelled the counterattack. A Romanian soldier was taken prisoner and sent off for interrogation. The losses of 161st Rifle Regiment were 7 wounded, leaving it with 67 active bayonets.

– – –

The rest of the day passed as it usually did. The Germans occasionally fired small arms, machine-guns and mortars. Soviet units hit back harder, using direct-firing cannon and infantry weapons to destroy German-occupied buildings, emplacements, dug-outs and generally just wear down German personnel on the front-line and in the depth of the defences. LI. Armeekorps noted that there was "strong fire at times on positions east of the gun factory, but without infantry attacks".

Soviet observers spotted excavations and up to 10 explosions in the area of Workshop 4 [Hall 6a] and about 500 metres north of the Barrikady factory. This was in the sector of 389. Infanterie-Division. The German prerogative was still to build better and deeper defences. With ammunition becoming scarcer, the easiest and most effective way to hold the line was to keep men safe from Soviet bullets and shells and have them use their ammunition in the most efficient manner. The limited stocks being flown in never got close to satisfying the units' daily requirements, so the troops scrounged for whatever they could, as reported by Hauptmann Rettenmaier:

> Our situation in regards to the supply of ammunition was very serious. During the days of combat in October, a lot was left lying around in the houses and factory workhalls. It was now eagerly gathered and every unit was glad if they found some mortar shells or hand grenades or some rifle ammunition. An order arrived on 1 January, 1943: 'From now on, one shell will be allotted every second day for a heavy infantry gun and daily for each light infantry gun'. And the Russians were downright wasteful with their shells; their artillery and Stalin Organs almost completely covered us with fire. More and more every day, the ring getting ever narrower. We had to patiently endure it.

– – –

To bolster the defences of Grenadier-Regiment 226 near the bread factory and around the Fliegerhaus, III./Grenadier-Regiment 191 (71. Infanterie-Division) was subordinated to the division in the afternoon. Every man was needed on this sector because throughout the afternoon, the Soviets brought more men forward into the area of the Fliegerhaus. During the coming night, one company (9./191) would relieve the company on the left wing of Grenadier-Regiment 226. A second company (10./191) would relieve the right company of the regiment during the night of New Year's Eve. A further company (11./191), commanded by Oberleutnant Martin Crusius[32] would remain as regimental reserve.

---

32. Crusius, Oberleutnant Martin, DKiG; 11./Gr.Rgt.191; born 30 August, 1919 in Breinum. Missing in action, January 1943 in Stalingrad.

On this day, 138th Rifle Division submitted a report detailing the losses it had inflicted on the Germans in the period from 15 October to 30 December, 1942. While some figures – particularly the number of German soldiers killed and equipment destroyed – seem slightly dubious, others seem to be quite accurate.

> Annihilated: 9460 officers and soldiers, 24 tanks (destroyed and burnt out), 3 armoured cars, 24 artillery pieces of all calibres, 32 automobiles (cars and trucks), 54 mortars, 164 machine-guns, 4 anti-tank rifles and over 1000 rifles. German defences destroyed: 29 pillboxes, 62 dug-outs, 1 centre of resistance (a system of bunkers, pillboxes and dug-outs) and 6 ammunition depots blown up. Trophies: two 75 mm guns, one 45mm gun, one 37mm gun, 6 mortars, 91 machine-guns, 3 anti-tank rifles, 97 automatic rifles, 468 rifles, 112 submachine-guns, over 300 artillery shells, 400 mortar rounds, 3000 hand grenades and 96,200 rifle cartridges. Taken prisoner: 8 officers, 27 NCOs and 54 soldiers, a total of 89 men.

These statistics did not bode well for the long-suffering Germans, but for the Soviets, they were merely an appetiser. When the Red Army was finally satiated, these numbers would pale in comparison to the utter devastation wrought upon 6. Armee.

Casualties for 30 December, 1942:	
138th Rifle Division:	2 killed, 7 wounded, a total of 9 men
305. Infanterie-Division:	6 men killed, 23 men wounded

31 December, 1942

A demolition squad from the sapper battalion carried out another operation to destroy the garrison of the Kommissarhaus. At night they triggered an explosion in the northern wing and claimed to have killed 10 Germans and destroyed a light machine-gun. The sappers and their infantry escort from 650th Rifle Regiment suffered no losses. The primary objective of the regiment, set six days earlier, still remained the capture of this stubborn building. The regiment's men carried out defensive works during the night and also placed small-arms, machine-gun and mortar fire on German emplacements. The daily entry from the regiment's combat journal also reveals the debut of a new German strongpoint:

> During the course of the night, the enemy conducted small-arms and machine-gun fire from the P-shaped house, the cinema booth and Dom 07, and also fired mortars at our combat ranks from the area of Workshop 14/15.

The 'cinema booth', or the 'theatre' as the Germans called it, was a brick structure located in the middle of the park. The

On the left is the cinema booth. More noteworthy, however, is the derelict sIG33B, knocked out in the battle on 11 November, 1942. The constant fighting meant that damaged or destroyed vehicles could not be recovered.

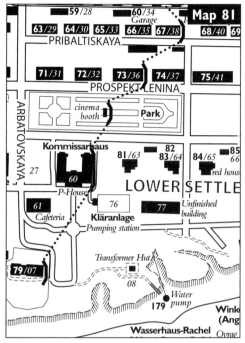

The defence line formed by German strongpoints.

two-storey edifice, painted white, had served as a theatre for the factory's upper management. Remarkably, it had so far retained its iron roof. Perhaps the Germans had been positioned in it for a long time but it was only now noticed – or at least noted – by the Soviets. It possessed great importance because it formed another strongpoint in the north-facing German defensive line, although its field of fire was obstructed by a tangle of mutilated birch trees in front of it.

At 1240 hours, Soviet observers spotted a group of 27 German soldiers running from Workshop 3 [Hall 6c] across to Dom 60 [Kommissarhaus]. The group was partially destroyed.

Lyudnikov's division reported that "our formations, while still firing at the enemy, are trying to improve their positions in some buildings. The enemy continues with his earthworks in front of the division and continues to fire on the river crossing over the Denezhnaya Volozhka channel."

– – –

LI. Armeekorps reported to 6. Armee about the situation near the bread factory:

Two attacks launched at dawn with several assault groups against the right sector of 305. Infanterie-Division were repulsed in hand-to-hand fighting. Heavy artillery and mortar fire on this sector.

Combat Report No. 137 of 95th Rifle Division describes the attack:

At 0430 two storm groups of 161st Rifle Regiment, support by a battery of anti-tank guns, mortars and ampulomets, blockaded an enemy emplacement on Mashinnaya Street. By 0435 the groups pushed forward 10-15 metres but were met by small-arms, submachine-gun and machine-gun fire. Using a communications trench, the enemy appeared on the left flank of the group and showered it with grenades. The groups, suffering casualties, returned to their starting position and continued to exchange fire. Losses: 7 dead, 9 wounded, 1 heavy machine-gun damaged. Active bayonets: 47.

As a result of the loss of the Fliegerhaus and orders to be more vigilant, the German garrisons on this sector were very edgy. They fired on Gorishny's forward line with small-arms, machine-guns and mortars from Haus 43, 44, 79, the Apotheke and the green fuel tank. Hand grenades were occasionally thrown in the fuel tank area and the river bank was hit every now and then by 'D-40' type mortars. Reinforcements were also seen moving about. At 1445 hours, about 25 Germans with a light machine-gun were observed running towards the green fuel tank, while at 1500 a second group, consisting of 10-15 men, moved from the same area towards the Fliegerhaus but were struck by machine-gun and mortar fire. The riflemen of 241st Rifle Regiment battered German emplacements near Dom 02 [Haus 43], 03 [Haus 44] and 07 [Haus 79] with fire from its entire arsenal, including the ampulomets. It lost 2 men to wounds and possessed 122 active bayonets. Its neighbour, 90th Rifle Regiment, also suffered 2 wounded and was left with 68 active bayonets.

The site where 95th and 138th Rifle Divisions had joined up early in the morning of 22 December was still a hotly contested area. The river bank had been completely retaken, as had a few dozen metres of land running atop the cliff, but Hauptmann Rettenmaier and his soldiers stubbornly held out in Haus 79. Their crumbling two-storey strongpoint with its thick masonry walls and stout cellars was endlessly pummelled by mortars, artillery and machine-guns. Rettenmaier clearly remembers the savage combat that swirled about his isolated fortress atop the Volga cliff:

> Attacks followed in quick succession, day and night, by surprise or after heavy artillery preparation. The Russians conjured up real fire magic with phosphorous bombs thrown with the aid of a catapult device. Fighting the enemy was often man against man, grabbing the collar, ripping the clothes off each other and smashing one another on the head with hand grenades. There were heavy casualties every day; it was a dreadful crucible for the troops. It was necessary to have a garrison of 30 to 35 men there. Often, there was only 10 to 15 men left in the evening. Officers were there for 2 to 3 days on average. Then, they were either dead or wounded. I think in particular of Oberleutnant Rominger of Grenadier-Regiment 576 and Leutnant Baumeister of Grenadier-Regiment 577; they were both wounded by Russian grenades in hand-to-hand combat.

The shortage of officers forced the promotion of reliable NCOs and enlisted men. Such was the case with Stabsgefreiter Hans Bernhart of 1./Grenadier-Regiment 578, whose lack of a secondary school education had hindered advancements in his military career, even though he was highly intelligent and had years of soldiering experience under his belt. His promotions therefore stopped when he reached the rank of Stabsgefreiter. The situation in Stalingrad, however, invalidated normal procedures and men were promoted on merit alone. Bernhart became an Unteroffizier and simultaneously allotted the status of Kompanieführer.

Rettenmaier's position was certainly unenviable: surrounded on three sides, the Soviets south of him in the fuel tank area, Zeigefinger and Blinddarm gullies were even able to fire along the rear wall of Haus 79. Still worse was the fact that Soviet fire from Haus 83 and the pumping station could almost – but not quite – be directed through the windows on this rear wall. The result was that the house was effectively cut off by this fire, imprisoning Rettenmaier's young Swabian and Austrian soldiers inside. Their only connection with the rest of the division were two trenches that snaked their way towards the Apotheke and the Kommissarhaus, but they were tenuous links at best. Soviet mortars were registered on them and the northernmost trench – that which ran to the Kommissarhaus – was within hand grenade range of Soviet positions. Nevertheless, Haus 79 was an enormous obstacle to continued progress for Gorishny

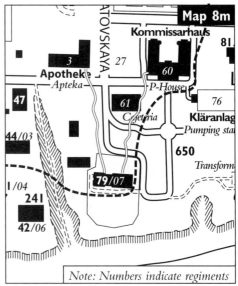

Situation around Haus 79.

and Lyudnikov: it was the quintessential 'thorn in the side'. This stubborn breakwater prevented any further widening of the corridor. With its removal, the front-line could easily be forced back a hundred metres or so, back to the Apotheke and Kommissarhaus, and this would create the breathing space so desperately needed. Capturing this strongpoint – or simply blotting it out of existence – was a high priority for both 95th and 138th Rifle Divisions.

In any case, the Germans were not on the Volga any more and signalmen from Rolik pulled a line towards the signalmen of Gorishny's division. Beyond that, the army wire already operated.

On this wire, the following order was received from army staff:

> Division commander, Colonel Lyudnikov, will come to the command post of army staff when the path along the Volga bank becomes safe.

Lyudnikov was with Pechenyuk's regiment at this time. Pechenyuk's reserves successfully repelled all German counterattacks and firmly consolidated themselves on the newly-won line. Towards evening, Lyudnikov returned to his command post where Chuikov's order was conveyed to him.

The Germans still methodically fired at the river bank. Everyone had got used to such bombardments over a long time, and Lyudnikov began to get ready for the trip. He threw on a padded jacket and put on an overcoat. The hand-sewn repair on the breast of his overcoat – where shrapnel from a grenade had ripped through – was easy to spot and would draw the commander's attention. This embarrassed Lyudnikov.

"There's no need to be ashamed of such scars. It is necessary to be proud of them!" said Kurov, but his reasonable comment had the opposite effect. Lyudnikov took off his overcoat and passed it to Kurov:

"I look like a refugee with such scars. So, please, give me yours."

They were same rank and height, so they exchanged overcoats.

Twilight thickened over the Volga, and Lyudnikov, together with divisional commissar Titov and artillery chief Tychinsky, got under way. South of 'Saperny' gully the river bank curved abruptly. Behind the bend gaped the Rolik crevice. Above it – where once there had been fighting in the trenches – silhouettes again loomed. They were soldiers from a burial detail removing corpses. The division commander and commissar wanted to pop in on Rolik but Tychinsky convinced them to do it on the return trip. It was already getting dark, it was necessary to go two more kilometres along the cluttered river bank, and Chuikov and his staff were waiting for them.

On Gorishny's sector, sentries called out to the three commanders of 138th division. Having received the answer to the password, the sentries escorted the commanders to the sector of Colonel Sokolov's 45th Rifle Division. In this way, in a chain from sentry to sentry, Lyudnikov and his travelling companions reached the dug-out of army staff. Like their own dug-out back at the Barrikady, it resembled an adit with two entrances facing the Volga.

The person on duty conveyed them into a spacious room where the Army Military Council and division commanders had gathered: General Rodimtsev, Colonels Batyuk, Sokolov and Gorishny. Constraining any emotion, Lyudnikov started to head toward the commander to officially report that he, commander of the 138th Rifle Division, had arrived as ordered… But Chuikov, by rights the senior of the two, broke the usually accepted protocol. He rushed towards Lyudnikov, tightly embraced him and then kissed him. Encouraged by such a joyful meeting, this really gave everyone free reign to express their feelings. And when everything that concerned operations had been reported, clarified and explored, the speeches began. The centre of attention were the visitors from the Barrikady, who had been awaited for so long and whose destiny excited all of 62nd Army.

"Where has it been seen in war that a commander did not meet a division commander for seventy days, even though they were fighting right next to one another?" said Chuikov, not shifting his admiring gaze from Lyudnikov. "Such curious things are only possible here, in Stalingrad. Well, why are you silent? Now tell us how you lived and fought."

"As if you don't know..." Embarrassed by the attention being paid to him, Lyudnikov really did not know what to say. He was surrounded by courageous, boundlessly brave commanders who had witnessed all sorts of things. What could surprise them? "We beat the Germans in a fight to the death. And without respite. We didn't even notice that autumn had passed and winter had arrived... We, of course, copped it too..."

"Copped it!" Chuikov was surprised, most of all by Lyudnikov's everyday tone. "No, just think about it! Two German divisions, plus other units subordinated to them, got stuck into one Soviet division, two experienced Germans generals couldn't cope with the battle against one Soviet colonel..."

Chief-of-staff Krylov whispered something to the commander, but Chuikov did not consider it necessary to disclose that which had not yet become a decree. He shook his head and with conviction, deliberately emphasised and repeated:

"Yes, with one colonel! And with his ordinary, run-of-the-mill, rifle division..."

Lyudnikov hid a smile behind his hand. If not for such a celebratory occasion, he would have objected a little to the commander, for the sake of his division's honour. Only a few, including Chuikov, knew this 'ordinary, run-of-the-mill, rifle division' well. Chuikov had seen it in combat on the Aksai and on other sectors of the Don steppe, and knew its commanders and distinguished soldiers. In October, when the second crisis during the Stalingrad battles came to a head, Chuikov asked the Front military council for this 'ordinary' division to be transferred from the reserve. Lyudnikov knew how much had been done by Chuikov, and the Commander of the Stalingrad Front Yeremenko, and personally by Khrushchev, member of the Military Council of the Stalingrad Front, to get his 'run-of-the-mill' division fighting in the fiery ring of Barrikady, where it stood its ground and won. And he, Lyudnikov, and his subordinate commanders, and the soldiers entrusted to him, carried out their duty in a self-sacrificing way. Lyudnikov now regretted only one thing: at this joyful hour, he wanted his division's veterans, the heroes of Barrikady, to learn how highly the command valued their feat.

Meanwhile the table had been laid. Light from the kerosene lamps gleamed dimly in glasses, knives and forks. To Lyudnikov, it all seemed extraordinarily elegant and festive. Soon the New Year would arrive, and to welcome it, the staff and regiments of 138th Rifle Division would lay tables too... It was now possible... And in fact, only recently, he had cancelled the order for 100 grams of food for all fighting men. No, this evening would not be saddened by memories about the past and what they had been through. In any case, it was impossible for the commanders to sit up too long. All the division commanders knew their tasks for the forthcoming day and hurried back to their units.

"What do you need, dear Ivan Ilyich?" asked Chuikov. Lyudnikov was the last to leave the army staff. "I mean your personal request. In fact I know everything. I know about the raid on your dug-out by saboteurs and about your party membership card sliced by shrapnel, and even about your stomach ulcer... Perhaps a short rest is necessary?"

"Short?" Lyudnikov seized upon that word. "If I may, I'd like to visit the division's rear echelon. There's also a bathhouse on the left bank. An excellent bathhouse! With hot steam and birch switches. And by the time it's dark tomorrow, I shall be back on this bank, with the division."

"You ask for so little, Ivan Ilyich…" sighed Chuikov, once again embracing Lyudnikov, and after escorting him to the entrance of the dug-out, added: "We have achieved victories in Stalingrad today. Tell that to your soldiers."

– – –

The German side was also welcoming the New Year, albeit in a much more humble and introspective way. In a letter to his wife, Hauptmann Traub wrote:

> I invited the gentlemen from my staff for a glass of schnapps. They left around 10.00 pm. Then I read a little until 12.00 pm and went peacefully to bed. Around 1.00 am there was loud shooting. The Russians had attacked, but were stopped and slaughtered, suffering heavy casualties.

Oberzahlmeister Bauchspiess, Pionier-Bataillon 336, likewise jotted down his thoughts for his wife:

> Bernd[33] and I lit the Christmas tree once more and let the candle stumps burn down. We had a couple of glasses of schnapps and listened to Goebbels' speech. As we had nothing more to drink and weren't in the mood for New Year's Eve, we both lay down on our beds. Bernd soon fell asleep because being awake still exhausts him, but I remained awake for a long time and my thoughts wandered yearningly towards home.

Up front, another soldier of the battalion was killed. Hauptfeldwebel Kurt Wenk[34], 1./Pionier-Bataillon 336, was felled by a bullet in the Barrikady factory.

Division commander Steinmetz recalls the day:

> I remember New Year's 1942-43 very clearly. It was a wonderful snowy day with a sunny sky. For the commanders of the division, I had set aside a few bottles of grain as well as some cigars. They were rarities of the rarest sort. I had received them from a cousin who had been flown out of the pocket in December for employment elsewhere.

> Thus I conducted an inspection tour to the command posts and brought my best wishes for the new year, not suspecting that I would be the first to withdraw from this tour because of heavy wounding.

– – –

A small fireworks display was being prepared for the Germans east of the Barrikady, and especially for the garrison of the Kommissarhaus. LI. Armeekorps reported that "south-east of the gun factory, after very strong artillery preparation from 2030 - 2200 hours, the enemy attacked with the strength of 100 men. Attack on the Kommissarhaus at 2230. All attacks were repulsed."

Unfortunately, no details of these failed attacks can be found in Soviet records. For another attack that would take place early in the morning of 1 January, 1943, however, we have any eyewitness account.

Casualties for 31 December, 1942:	
138th Rifle Division:	4 wounded
305. Infanterie-Division:	5 men killed, 17 men wounded

---

33. Leutnant Bernhard Ehringhaus, 1./Pi.Btl.336. See Appendix 2 (page 571) for more details.
34. Wenk, Hauptfeldwebel Kurt, 1./Pi.Btl.336; born 24 June, 1914 in Seefeld. Killed in action, 31 December, 1942 in Stalingrad.

1 January, 1943

Senior-Lieutenant Fedor Anisimovich Lesin, a company commander from 344th Rifle Regiment, was part of the force which attacked the Kommissarhaus:

I was summoned by regiment commander Konovalenko and given the order that I was included in a storm group consisting of seven men, including an artillery lieutenant placed at the disposal of 1st Battalion of 344th Rifle Regiment, which was defending the Barrikady factory.

On the evening of New Year's Eve, we crawled to our destination under enemy fire, over corpses, over ground deformed and impregnated by gunpowder. On duty at the entrance of the staff headquarters stood a wounded soldier, with his head and hand bandaged, who called the battalion commander. Soon, the battalion commander – Captain Tolkachev – came out to us. Having greeted us, he invited us into the destroyed building, where he read the letter that I had just brought to him. 'It is good to have you two officers. But there is nobody to command,' said the battalion commander. And later, addressing us, he said: 'Tomorrow, before dawn, we will attack the Germans ensconced in the cellar of the big P-shaped house which is located 20-30 metres from our defences'.

'Who are we going to attack with?', asked one of the new arrivals. The battalion commander smiled and, pointing his finger at us, answered: 'You and me, that is, the entire battalion'.

Senior-Lieutenant Fedor Anisimovich Lesin

We asked for some water but there was none in the battalion area. It was necessary to gather snow in our helmets but it was all stained with gunpowder residue and mixed with dirt and chips of brick. 'After the assault, we will see in the new year,' said the battalion commander, encouraging us, 'and I will bring you pure water from the Volga myself'.

At approximately three o'clock in the morning the battalion commander signalled us to get ready. He set the task, not in the form of an order, but in a friendly tone: prepare to attack with grenades and for hand-to-hand fighting. Command was entrusted to me. Soon, with a strength of six soldiers, we crept up to the house and, upon a sign from the battalion commander, rushed towards apertures and threw grenades into the cellar. Caught by surprise, the Germans panicked and began to escape from a door opposite us, leaving behind 4 dead soldiers.

We captured the cellar and suddenly, from another room of the cellar, we heard Germans speaking. Running into the room, we saw five or six wounded officers lying on a rug. One of them, speaking in broken Russian, suggested that we treat ourselves to cigarettes and French rum. Soon, a staff officer with a translator arrived from division and we were ordered to return to the Barrikady factory.

In the morning, when the first rays of sunlight of the new year shone upon the ground, we greeted the new year of 1943. We drunk 100 grams of vodka. Thoughtfully, a sergeant-major – a Muscovite named Andrei Krikanov – treated us to some long-forgotten hot and tasty food, but the main thing was pure water from the river – the mother Volga. The wise sergeant-major only gave us small doses of water, to preserve us from the cold.

Everyone's mood was cheerful and, sitting around a small fire, we quietly started singing a song: 'It is so hard for me to come to you, and here there are four steps to death…'"[35]

The Soviet intrusion into sections of the Kommissarhaus's cellars must only have been temporary because available records from both sides make it clear that the building was still controlled by the Germans. The combat journal of 650th Rifle Regiment mentions the Kommissarhaus several times:

> During the course of the day, the enemy placed heavy small-arms and machine-gun fire, as well as frequent mortar and artillery fire, on the combat ranks of the regiment from the P-shaped house and Workshop 14/15.

> By observation, it was established that the enemy constructed defensive works, dug trenches into the eastern part of the P-shaped building and on the southern and western sides trench networks outlined by bits and pieces of iron were noticed.

Most of the day was spent shooting up German embrasures and laying down barrages on occupied buildings. The regiment's losses were light: only 3 soldiers were wounded. It had a strength of 48 officers, 28 NCOs and 46 other ranks, a total of 122 men. Armament consisted of 86 rifles, 21 PPSH, 1 heavy machine-guns, 1 82mm mortar, 8 light machine-guns, 4 ampulomets and 3 anti-tank rifles. It calculated German losses as 1 light machine-gun destroyed, up to 10 soldiers killed in Dom 07 [Haus 79], and a German deserter was killed, whereupon selected documents were forwarded to divisional staff.

– – –

Familie Förschner

Haus 79 and its garrison were caught in a cross-fire from Pechenyuk's regiment to the north and Budarin's regiment to the south. Throughout the morning, units of 241st Rifle Regiment laid down machine-gun, mortar and artillery fire to suppress German emplacements near Dom 02, 03, 07 [Haus 79], 1, 2 [Haus 48], 3 [Apotheke]. At the same time, they prepared to capture Dom 07. The division's snipers reported a tally of 3 dead Germans.

One of those 3 soldiers may well have been Feldwebel Eugen Förschner[36] from Major Braun's II./Grenadier-Regiment 576. Förschner was one of the many dispensable rear-area personnel caught in the comb-outs that harnessed manpower for the front. In his last letter home, dated 30 December, 1942, Feldwebel Förschner wrote:

> It has just turned 1 o'clock in the morning and I am sitting in my bunker, on watch, as on most nights. So far I am still healthy and will come through everything with God's help, will I not, my dear little wife. We will

Feldwebel Eugen Förschner

---

35. The song was 'Zemlyanka', written by Alexei Surkov in 1941 during the battle for Moscow, and was considered unpatriotic: 'You are now very far away / Expanses of snow lie between us / It is so hard for me to come to you / And here there are four steps to death.' Nevertheless, it was a very popular song with Soviet troops.

36. Förschner, Feldwebel Eugen, II./Gr.Rgt.576; born 25 September, 1913 in Schramberg. Killed in action, early January 1943 in Stalingrad.

be relieved this evening and will head back for 7 days of rest. If you could see me now you would be startled, my beard has been growing since 13.12. and I have not washed properly [...] but that doesn't matter, as long as one is still alive.

Unteroffizier Kurt Steinlen[37], the Bataillon-Schreiber, provided the details of Förschner's death in a sworn declaration from 1950:

I was on the staff of II./Grenadier-Regiment 576 as an Unteroffizier during the Russian campaign. In the ration supply train of this battalion was Feldwebel Eugen Förschner. At the end of December or beginning of January 1943 – I no longer remember exactly – he was sent into the forward positions, indeed, into the forefield of the Stalingrad Gun Factory, due to the reductions in the supply train. There, after only a very brief time, Förschner was killed by a head shot from a Russian sniper.

I was the Bataillon-Schreiber (clerk) and know that the commander at that time, Major Braun, informed the wife about the death of her husband. It is certain that mail was still being flown out of the Stalingrad pocket at this time. It's possible that the airplane was shot down and that the notification of death did not reach Förschner's widow.

I emphatically stress that I did not see the body of Kamerad Förschner; I only know that I forwarded the notification of death myself. The adjutant at the time, Oberfeldwebel Rall[38], who in any case was killed later on, had confirmed Förschner's death to me by telephone during the fighting.

Förschner's widow therefore knew nothing about her husband's death and was under the impression that he was missing, presumed captured and in Soviet imprisonment. A courageously forthright but sympathetic letter written by Steinlen on 19 April, 1950, after his release from Soviet captivity, demolished any and all hope that Förschner was still alive: "I received your letter from 12 April, 1950 and am stunned that you know nothing about the death of your husband". Steinlen told Frau Förschner what he knew and added that "your husband suffered a very painless and swift death" and that "all remaining members of the battalion who went into captivity with me also died or starved to death [and] I therefore believe that you shouldn't hold any hope of receiving further news about your husband". His final words attempted to console the poor lady: "I feel with you in your pain and know how difficult such a blow of fate is to bear."

Behind each figure of a 'kill tally' was a similar story of overwhelming grief caused to a family back home.

– – –

In the afternoon, individual storm groups from 241st Rifle Regiment moved out to capture the dug-outs south-east of Dom 07 [Haus 79]. In addition, they continued to carry out the sapping of Dom 07. Resistance from the German fortress was fierce and the Soviet storm groups were forced to keep their distance, but their plan on this day was to subjugate a number of dug-outs that were causing trouble. Combat Report No. 2, issued by 95th Rifle Division at 1800 hours, sums up the results:

241st Rifle Regiment's storm groups conducted fire fights with the enemy in the area of Dom 07 and during the fighting seized 10 dug-outs east and south-east of Dom 07. Work was also carried out on the underground tunnel in preparation to storm Dom 07. Mortar fire destroyed one enemy dug-out. Losses: 12 men wounded. Active bayonets: 110.

---

37. Steinlen, Unteroffizier Kurt, II./Gr.Rgt.576; born 10 September, 1914 in Stuttgart. Still alive in 2006.
38. Rall, Oberfeldwebel Walter, II./Gr.Rgt.576; date of birth unknown. Killed in action, 1 February, 1943 in Stalingrad.

A report from the next day gave a precise tally of the Soviet gains:

On 1.1.43, in the area of Dom 07, 241st Rifle Regiment captured 3 pillboxes, and in dug-outs captured earlier picked up 10 rifles, 2 flare pistols, 75 signal flares and 3000 cartridges.

In a report by LI. Armeekorps at 1630 hours, it was stated that "east of the gun factory, several assault group thrusts against the enclosed house in 83d3/4 were repulsed".

The fighting for Dom 07/Haus 79 was only just starting to heat up.

– – –

Further south, around the hotly-contested fuel tanks, the day was relatively quiet. Grenades had been tossed about during the night but in daylight, 90th Rifle Regiment was content to observe German movements and suppress the fire of mortars and machine-guns. Later in the day, 1 and 2/90th Rifle Regiment exchanged heavy fire with the German units in the area of the green fuel tank and Soviet artillery and mortar fire destroyed a German trench north-west of this same fuel tank.

The command of 79. Infanterie-Division realised there was no serious prospect of retaking the Fliegerhaus, so the decision was taken to use some precious rounds of 21cm Mörser 18 ammunition set aside for emergencies. Each high-explosive shell weighed 113kg, so there was absolutely no possibility that more could be flown in. From 0815 to 0840 hours, nine rounds were fired at the Fliegerhaus and six were direct hits. Large sections of the building were demolished but III./Grenadier-Regiment 191 – which had officially taken over the sector at 2200 hours the previous night – made no move to capitalise on the momentary confusion. Every man and bullet was needed to hold the existing line.

– – –

On this day, it was announced that the Divisionsführer of 305. Infanterie-Division, Oberst Steinmetz, was made Kommandeur of the division with a simultaneous promotion to Generalmajor with effect from 26 December, 1942.

Casualties for 1 January, 1943:	
138th Rifle Division:	no figures available from this time forward
305. Infanterie-Division:	11 men killed, 54 men wounded

2 January, 1943

The riflemen of 241st Rifle Regiment spent the night digging trenches to strengthen the pillboxes and dug-outs captured the previous day while 161st and 90th Rifle Regiments carried out reconnaissance on German emplacements, suppressing them with fire from mortars and machine-guns.

In general, the day passed with little action. German artillery and mortars occasionally dropped salvoes around Lyudnikov's divisional command post and Soviet artillery replied by targeting the German gun emplacements. On the sector of 650th Rifle Regiment, the Germans sent out small-arms, machine-gun and automatic fire from the Kommissarhaus and periodically fired mortars from the main mechanical workshop and Workshop 14/15. In turn, Pechenyuk's regiment placed fire on the Kommissarhaus and Dom 07, killing an estimated 12 German soldiers, destroying 2 light machine-guns and suppressing the fire of German mortar batteries with their own 50mm mortar. The regiment received reinforcements during the night and now had a strength of 52 officers, 38 NCOs and 72 enlisted men, a total of 162 men, and was armed with 379 rifles, 48 PPSH, 1 heavy machine-gun, 2 82mm mortars, 1 50mm mortar, 1 anti-aircraft machine-gun, 4 ampulomets, 23 light machine-guns and 5 anti-tank rifles.

At midday, a German plane flew over the territory of the Barrikady factory at a height of 700-800 metres on a north-west course.

At 1600 hours, German mortars fired on units of 95th Rifle Division from the area of Dom 04 and 05, but Soviet observers saw no movements of personnel.

All in all, a very quiet day.

– – –

Gefreiter Johann Bonetsmüller

Gefreiter Johann Bonetsmüller[39], 2./Pi.Btl.305, wrote to his wife to tell her the good news about his promotion to Obergefreiter. He was happy not because it was an advancement in his military but – like most men – because it entitled him to higher wages, in Bonetsmüller's case, an extra 30 Reichsmarks per month. Although they were at the front, men were still heads of their families and had to provide for their wives and children. Many tucked relatively large sums of cash into their letters. After discussing financial matters, Bonetsmüller turned to his current situation in the Stalingrad pocket:

> We still haven't received any mail. I am getting worried about how long it is taking. It has now been 7 weeks since I received mail from you. Mail call is every second day but it is always only a few letters. There is generally nothing worth talking about anyway. But we hope for the best. We are glad and thank our Lord that we are still alive here in this Hexenkessel[40]. Otherwise I am still going well. I'm still with the field-kitchen, hopefully for a long while yet.

After this, the Bonetsmüller family was met only by silence. No more letters arrived from Johann in Stalingrad. Days with no news turned into weeks. Only with the announcement of the fall of Stalingrad did his family – and hundreds of thousands of others – learn that a catastrophe had befallen 6. Armee and claimed their loved one.

On 3 April, 1943, Frau Bonetsmüller received a letter from Gefreiter Nuoffer, the last man of the battalion to leave the Stalingrad pocket. He reported that Johann was still alive and well on 10 January and was not in action. But he could say for certain if he was still alive.[41]

Casualties for 2 January, 1943:
305. Infanterie-Division: no figures available

---

39. Bonetsmüller, Obergefreiter Johann, 2./Pi.Btl.305; born 7 April, 1907 in Westendorf. Died 23 January, 1997 in Gailling.
40. Trans.: 'Hexenkessel' = 'witch's cauldron'.
41. See Epilogue (page 480) for more information about the fate of Johann Bonetsmüller.

3 January, 1943

Throughout the night, the Germans laid down fire from machine-guns and automatic weapons on the Denezhnaya Volozhka crossing, Lyudnikov's command post and the division's battle formations. They also sent up streams of rocket flares to illuminate the district and continued to hit Zaitsevsky Island and the left bank of the Volga with artillery and mortars. Mortar fire also came from Haus 73 [Dom 36]. Pechenyuk's regiment undertook engineering-defensive works and sprayed the Kommissarhaus frequently with small-arms and machine-gun fire, while a battery of 82mm mortars dropped barrages on the Kommissarhaus, Dom 07, the cinema booth and other German dug-outs and communication trenches. Soviet estimates placed German losses at 12 soldiers killed and a heavy machine-gun in Dom 07 destroyed. One enlisted man from Pechenyuk's regiment was wounded during the night.

It was quieter on the sector of 95th Rifle Division, at least during darkness. The Germans did not show any activity prior to dawn but at 0430 hours made a fire strike with a mortar – up to 8 rounds – on the cone-shaped fuel tank. And at 0440 hours, on the sector of 241st Rifle Regiment in the area of Dom 07, six German soldiers tried to move closer to the front-line, firing at 1st Rifle Battalion with submachine-guns. The group was dispersed by machine-gun fire and two were killed. Apart from this brief flash of excitement, 241st Rifle Regiment spent the night strengthening and improving captured positions and firing on German emplacements near Dom 07, 02 and 03. The division's other two regiments, 90th and 161st, held their lines, exchanged small arms and machine-gun fire with the enemy, and opened up periodic mortar fire on emplacements that had been located. The entire division suffered no losses.

– – –

No unusual events marked the day. The combat journal of 650th Rifle Regiment sums up the day's actions:

> During the course of the day, the enemy conducted fire with small arms, machine-guns and automatics from the P-shaped building [Kommissarhaus] and Dom 07 [Haus 79], and with battalion mortars from the mechanical workshop [Hall 4] and Workshop 14/15 [Hall 3].
>
> The regiment, while defending the occupied line, places fire from small arms, machine-guns, artillery and mortars on the P-shaped building, Dom 07 and Workshop 14/15.
>
> Losses inflicted on the enemy: 15 soldiers and officers killed, 3 light machine-guns suppressed.

In the sector of 95th Rifle Division, it was a similar story. Situation Report No. 6, issued at 1500 hours, states that "units of 241st Rifle Regiment fired on enemy emplacements in the area of Dom 02, 03, 1, 2 [Haus 48], 3 [Apotheke] and 07 [Haus 79]. Fire from a 120mm mortar battery suppressed the fire of two mortars and destroyed a dug-out in the area of Dom 1. A 45mm gun destroyed 4 dug-outs in the area of Dom 07." The regiment suffered no losses. Fire from a 120mm mortar battery of 161st Rifle Regiment destroyed 2 German dug-outs, at the fork of Korotky (Short) Gully.

At the end of the day, 95th Rifle Division's regiments had the following strengths: 241st Rifle Regiment – no losses. Active bayonets: 96. 90th Rifle Regiment – 1 killed, 1 wounded. Active bayonets: 66. 161st Rifle Regiment – 1 wounded. Active bayonets: 49.

Casualties for 3 January, 1943:
305. Infanterie-Division: 10 men killed, 22 men wounded

4 January, 1943

Despite the deep cover of night, Soviet observers discovered that the Germans were still feverishly digging trenches and bunkers. The solid web of defences was constantly being thickened. Fully aware that the Soviet bridgehead was being reinforced by a constant flow of men and materiel across the frozen river, German troops kept the crossing points under systematic cross fire from machine-guns. The war diary of 138th Rifle Division reported that "movement over the ice from Zaitsevsky Island to the right bank is only done at night". Flares frantically hissed into the frigid darkness, illuminating the frost-bound ruins or the snowy wastes of the river in twitching circles of shadow and light. Peculiar movements immediately drew fiery arcs of machine-gun fire. On Pechenyuk's sector, automatic fire occasionally spurted from the Kommissarhaus, Haus 79 [Dom 07] and Haus 72 [Dom 32]. The Soviets retaliated against those same buildings with barrages of machine-gun and mortar fire. They estimated that they killed 12 Germans soldiers and suppressed a light machine-gun, while another light machine-gun was destroyed by an anti-tank rifle. The regiment lost 1 man to wounds. According to 241st Rifle Regiment of 95th Rifle Division, German reinforcements had arrived in their sector and posed a potential risk to the southern flank of 650th Rifle Regiment.

Throughout the night, 95th Rifle Division was also struck by German small arms and submachine-gun fire, as well as the occasional mortar bombardment. Placing machine-gun and mortar bombardments on emplacements in the area of Dom 02, 03 and 07, 241st Rifle Regiment killed five German soldiers with no losses of its own. Near Dom 04, one Romanian soldier voluntarily came into captivity.

The southern face of the German bulge that pushed towards the Volga was anchored on its western point by the bread factory. Gorishny's men of 90th and 161st Rifle Regiments held their positions, placed small arms and machine-gun fire on the Germans and constantly pushed and probed the defences. As a result, they were on the bread factory's eastern perimeter and in Tapeworm Gully on its immediate southern boundary. At 0600 hours, Soviet observers noticed three German soldiers carrying timber heading from the bakery in the direction of Hill 107.2, where trenching work was also spotted. On the sector of 161st Rifle Regiment, an anti-infantry obstacle – wire hedgehogs – were discovered 100 metres ahead of their front-line. In the afternoon, a 76mm battery of the same regiment fired on a German kitchen and observation post discovered in the Mashinnaya Street area. The three regiments suffered no losses. At the end of the day, 61st Rifle Regiment, had 46 active bayonets, while 90th Rifle Regiment had 66 (1st Battalion 44, 2nd Battalion 22) and 241st Rifle Regiment had 90. Throughout the day, the latter regiment collected German and domestic weapons in its sector, a total of 15 rifles and 100 grenades.

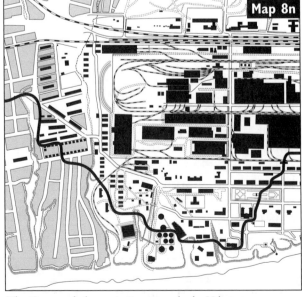

The German bulge projecting towards the Volga.

Nuisance fire and surprise barrages were a fact of life in the Barrikady. A tight grouping of shells could shriek in at any moment. Single rounds dropped down all day. Everyone became inured to it. Every now and then, however, a painful blow was dealt, as Rettenmaier describes:

An event that deeply shocked us should not be left unmentioned. The division commander, Oberst i.G. Steinmetz, Oberstleutnant Brandt and Ordonnanzoffizier Hämmerle, visited a command post in Hall 3c. The division commander wanted to personally receive the wishes of his troops. On the way back they walked into a surprise barrage. Oberstleutnant Brandt and Ordonnanzoffizier Hämmerle died of their wounds on the same day. Oberst Steinmetz took several pieces of shrapnel but was able to carry himself to the dressing station of Regiment 577. The wounded division commander was flown out. He had only led the division for a short time but we all thought the same: one felt at ease with him. He asked of his troops only what he would ask of himself in regards to privations or his personal combat-readiness. Everyone that knew him greatly regretted his departure.

The circumstances surrounding his wounding remained forever clear to Steinmetz:

During a meeting at the front on 4 January, 1943, I was severely wounded by a single mortar shell (nuisance fire). My companions, Oberstleutnant Brandt, commander of an infantry regiment, and my Ordonnanzoffizier Leutnant Hämmerle, as well as another orderly, were struck even more severely and died of their wounds at a dressing station on the same day. After several days I was flown out of the pocket on 8 January in a Ju-52 that had arrived during the night.

Steinmetz took the brunt of the shrapnel on his right side, particularly on his shoulder, arm and fingers. He fondly remembers the excellent care he received from Oberstarzt Dr. Gross, the senior doctor he had convinced to help with the deplorable medical situation:

When I was admitted in January with severe wounds, he stood at the entrance and bandaged me with touching carefulness. So well, in fact, that when I was admitted to the military hospital in Magdeburg[42] after four days of transportation, mostly by Ju-52, the doctors there were doubtful as to whether I had actually come from Stalingrad. The dressings on me were nearly of peacetime quality, so none of them were changed. I visited Dr. Gross 20 years later in his hospital in Stuttgart and thanked him personally. He then reported to me that his time in our first-aid station had been extraordinarily instructive for him. During his life, he had always been able to work with unlimited resources. There, he always had to improvise. He had learned a lot and was able to help a lot.

Steinmetz would be in hospital for the next 9 months. Leutnant Hans B., adjutant of III./Gr.Rgt.577, was close by when Steinmetz and his escort were caught:

Early one morning in January, [General Steinmetz and Oberstleutnant Brandt] visited my unit. We were deployed in one of the gun factory's workhalls. On the way back to the command post of our Regiment 577 they received a direct hit from a Russian crash-boom cannon. My medics administered first aid. Besides a couple of dead, General Steinmetz was heavily wounded and Oberstleutnant Brandt was very seriously wounded. I learned a couple of days later that Brandt died in the main dressing station and Steinmetz was flown out.

Leutnant Hans B., adjutant III./577.

---

42. Reserve Lazarett I Magdeburg.

Brandt's death stunned his men. He had been with the regiment from the very beginning, first commanding a battalion and then the regiment. Leutnant B. was particularly aghast at seeing Brandt lying in a gory mess in the snow because he had been his adjutant for almost a year. Brandt left behind a widow and two daughters. He was buried on 6 January in the Heroes Cemetery at Gorodische. In recognition of his valiant yet circumspect leadership, Brandt was promoted to Oberst and awarded the coveted Knight's Cross on 22 January, 1943. The proposal for the award was succinct:

> Oberstleutnant Brandt led his regiment in an exemplary manner during the battle for Stalingrad. The grim fighting in the ruins of the northern part of the city demanded oversight and constant operations. Hans-Georg Brandt is no longer alive for the bestowal of the Knight's Cross.

The name of the new regiment commander is difficult to determine but it may have been Oberstleutnant Rudolf Wutte[43]. Forty-five-year old Wutte – who was married and had two sons – was one of the unfortunate officers flown into the Kessel to become part of 6. Armee's 'Regimentsführer-Reserve', a pool of high-ranking officers who could assume command of leaderless units. After recovering from an inflammation to his gastro-intestinal tract in August and then attending a training course for regiment commanders in September-October, Wutte was transferred to Heeresgruppe B and subsequently to 6. Armee. He arrived in the Kessel in December 1942. Two sources – his personnel file and a casualty card – show that he belonged to Grenadier-Regiment 577 on 6 January, 1943, the date of his last letter from Stalingrad, and he was certainly the highest-ranking officer in the regiment. However, confirmation has not been found regarding his tenure with the regiment, let alone if he actually commanded it. Information provide by a modern German government agency states that he belonged to Jäger-Regiment 54 (100. Jäger-Division) on 22 January, 1943[44]. The final weeks in Stalingrad were a confusion of bloody battles, hastily assembled combat groups and the wholesale destruction or capture or written records, so trying to disentangle the threads of information regarding who commanded what unit is nigh on impossible.

The death of Steinmetz's O1, Leutnant Hans-Martin Hämmerle, deeply affected those who knew him. In a letter on 8 January, Rittmeister Giulini wrote:

> The small Leutnant, the last O1 with our Division [...] was buried by us yesterday. It shook us all very much. But here, in this regard, one becomes stubborn and hard. It happens too often. With him our new general was heavily wounded. Now we have our fourth commander.

– – –

Gefreiter Wilhelm Füssinger, 1./Pionier-Bataillon 305, records the increasingly despondent situation in a letter home:

> I have not received mail since 20 November and the Christmas packages did not reach any of us. We have now known for over 6 weeks what hunger really means. And the hope for better times still remains a long way off. Lent has arrived early for us! And so, at midday, we receive a watery soup with horse flesh, 100 grams of bread in the evening and coffee with cigarettes for breakfast. My birthday [1 January] was spiced with the humour that dominates at the moment. Now we hope that everything will get better soon.

---

43. Wutte, Oberst Rudolf, Gr.Rgt.577; born 3 April, 1897 in Leitring, Austria.
44. Oberst Armin Weber commanded this regiment and went into captivity with his men, so Wutte could only have been a battalion commander in the unit. Weber, Oberst Armin, Jäg.Rgt.54; born 12 February, 1895 in Augsburg. Died 4 September, 1973 in Balzano, Italy.

This was the last time Füssinger's family would ever hear from him. Hauptmann Rettenmaier also mentioned the dire food situation in one of his letters:

> The little bit of bacon that I kept in my knapsack is disappearing. One keeps getting thinner. I can wear a fur vest under my jacket without straining it. A daily ration of 200 grams of bread is very little and our horses will soon be eaten up.

Casualties for 4 January, 1943:
305. Infanterie-Division: 1 officer and 4 men killed, 2 officers and 5 men wounded

5 January, 1943

After the severe wounding of Oberst Steinmetz, a new division commander was needed, so a suitable candidate was searched for within the army's own ranks. A replacement was quickly found in the form of Oberst Dr. Ing. Albrecht Czimatis, commander of Artillerie-Regiment 83 of 100. Jäger-Division. According to that division's unit history, "on 5 January (1943), Oberst Czimatis handed over command of Artillerie-Regiment 83 to its most senior battalion commander and assumed command of 305. Infanterie-Division, which he would lead until the end". He had been promoted to Oberst on 20 November, 1940 with effect from 1 December, 1940, so he held seniority over all remaining officers in 305. Infanterie-Division, and was quite possibly the next officer in line within the pocket to take over a division. In an evaluation from 22 March, 1942 by his previous division commander, Czimatis was described as an "outstanding personality, of high

Oberst Dr. Ing. Albrecht Czimatis, the new commander of 305.I.D.

intellect, versatile, very skilful, energetic and cool. His bold personal employment in the front-line is to be particularly emphasised". He was recommended as being suitable for a divisional command. When Generalmajor von Hartmann[45], commander of 71. Infanterie-Division, was scheduled to go on leave from 21 November until 28 December, 1942, his substitute was to

45. Hartmann, General der Infanterie Alexander von, RK; 71.Inf.Div.; born 11 December, 1890 in Berlin. Killed in action, 26 January, 1943 in Stalingrad.

be Oberst Czimatis, but the Soviet counteroffensive forced the cancellation of furloughs, even for generals. Czimatis had a good friendship with von Seydlitz, the corps commander: the two had known each other since 1926 and had met frequently during the pre-war years. There were murmurs that his close relationship with von Seydlitz was the main reason for this prestigious career move. Czimatis was no stranger to forming and capitalising on personal connections. Barely a week earlier, although he didn't yet know it, an honour court had found him guilty of a serious breach of conduct. In the second half of 1941, Czimatis had shown extreme favouritism to the son of a wealthy industrialist by awarding him both grades of the Iron Cross and granting frequent furloughs, and then, when another officer, Leutnant Zippelius, lodged several complaints about it, Czimatis punished Zippelius with confinement, a block on promotions and general condemnation. The courageous Leutnant pursued the matter and eventually brought it to the attention of higher authorities. The verdict against Czimatis stated that he "lacked the impartiality required by a superior towards his subordinates" and was punished by having any further promotions blocked. This prevented him from reaching the rank of Generalmajor. Notification of the proceedings and verdict reached 6. Armee on 6 January, the day after Czimatis took command of 305. Infanterie-Division. It is quite possible that Czimatis would have been denied leadership of the division had the verdict arrived sooner.

– – –

Firefights continued throughout the entire day and in the thick of it were the Kommissarhaus and Haus 79. Pechenyuk reported that German mortars were firing from within both buildings. Small arms fire also came from both buildings, as well as from Dom 36 [Haus 73] and the cinema booth. Pechenyuk's men kept these German strongpoints under tight observation and periodically sprayed them with machine-gun fire. Most attention was paid to Dom 07 [Haus 79] and the regiment reported that it killed 7 German soldiers and suppressed a mortar and a heavy machine-gun in the building. Major[46] Rettenmaier's garrison inside the battered brick strongpoint were lambasted from opposite directions and would soon face a more serious trial by fire. During the morning, units of 241st Rifle Regiment had been firing on German emplacements in the area of Dom 07, 03 and 02. Not long afterwards, artillery fire destroyed a dug-out west of Dom 07. The culmination of the attack came when ampulomets fired on the building and set it alight, causing it to burn for 2 hours, according to Combat Report No. 9 of 95th Rifle Division. At 1000 hours, a heavy machine-gun suppressed a German machine-gun firing from the second floor of Dom 07. This bludgeoning was designed to erode the building's defences, weaken the Germans' spirit and pave the way for a later assault. Rettenmaier's men, however, had a few tricks of their own, as described in Situation Report No. 12 of 95th Rifle Division:

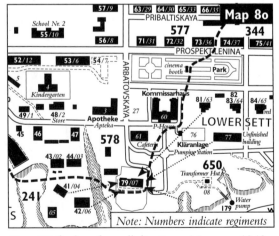

Haus 79 fired on from all directions, 4 January, 1943.

---

46. Rettenmaier was promoted to Major with effect from 1 January, 1943. The recommendation for this promotion had been submitted back in September.

In the area of Dom 07, it was observed that the enemy were using sack dummies for the purpose of revealing our fire systems.

A soldier from 305. Infanterie-Division reported that "we worked with decoys; as soon as you raised a decoy, it was shot down by Russian snipers. [These decoys looked] like the targets we had on rifle ranges, with a bit of dirt for camouflage. We knew a trick or two."

The garrison devised another method of defeating the accurate Soviet fire but it too was detected, as noted in the combat journal of 650th Rifle Regiment:

> The enemy has punched out some loopholes from within the walls of Dom 07 and lays down small arms and machine-gun fire from them in the direction of the unfinished building and the Rolik group.

In a letter dated 31 December, 1942, Rettenmaier remarked on his precarious strongpoint:

> My position still lies alongside the Volga, the Russians surround it on three sides, in part only some 30 metres away. They have recently not dared to attack here. There would be grounds for filming the weekly newsreel here!

– – –

Realising that the German defences around Lyudnikov's bridgehead were going to be tough to crack, particularly because they were tied to several formidable strongpoints, the Soviets gradually shifted the emphasis south, into Gorishny's and Sokolov's sectors. The front-line there zigzagged from the large concrete oil reservoir back to the bread factory, passing through a vast district that was nothing but a field of flattened wooden houses, shells craters and trenches. And the Germans of Grenadier-Regiment 576 certainly defended themselves with desperate tenacity. However, there were no large masonry buildings upon which the Germans could anchor their defensive line. Gorishny's storm groups were able to nibble away at the line, taking a dug-out here, pushing forward slightly there. Attacks from this direction offered a better prospect of success: a decisive thrust into the Barrikady factory itself would mortally endanger the entire German defensive sector facing Lyudnikov's division. It was normal procedure to keep an eye on enemy movements and defensive improvements but Gorishny's men now watched over the Germans like hawks. Even the smallest occurrence was noted: from 0600 until 0645 hours, Soviet observers spotted 13 Germans soldiers in three groups moving from the bakery towards the Barrikady factory; a new German dug-out was located north of Dom 21; three groups of German soldiers, with a total strength of 15 men, were seen moving from Hill 107.2 in the direction of Dom 106 at 0840 hours; two horse-drawn wagons moved in the same direction; a German pillbox was discovered by 161st Rifle Regiment to the east of Dom 102, so a battery of 76mm guns was quickly ordered to fire upon it. Apart from observation, constant harassment fire was of course maintained. The men of 90th Rifle Regiment suppressed German emplacements in the area of the railroad line and the green fuel tank. In doing so, one of their anti-tank guns destroyed a dug-out near the houses north-west of the green fuel tank. Units of 241st Rifle Regiment fired all kinds of weapons at German emplacements near Dom 07, 03 and 02, thereby destroying a dug-out and setting fire to a house near Dom 07.

At the end of the day, the strength and losses of the three regiments of 95th Rifle Division were as follows: 241st Rifle Regiment, no losses, 90 active bayonets; 90th Rifle Regiment, losses of 2 men wounded, 65 active bayonets; 161st Rifle Regiment, losses of 1 man killed and 1 man wounded, 46 active bayonets.

On Lyudnikov's sector, a group of up to 25 German soldiers were seen running from Workshop 4 [Hall 6a] into the main mechanical workshop [Hall 4] at midday. The group was scattered by submachine-gun fire.

– – –

At 2000 hours, a three-man recon patrol of 241st Rifle Regiment launched a raid near Dom 07. They showered a German trench with hand grenades, seized a light machine-gun, 2 rifles and 2 containers of ammunition, then returned to their positions. One of the men was wounded.

Casualties for 5 January, 1943:
305. Infanterie-Division: 8 men killed, 1 officer and 15 men wounded

6 January, 1943

With the exception of minor skirmishes on Gorishny's sector, the night passed quietly. While 161st and 241st Rifle Regiment exchanged fire with the Germans, 90th Rifle Regiment engaged in occasional hand grenades duels near the fuel tanks. The combat journal of 650th Rifle Regiment reports about the night-time activity:

> The enemy places occasional fire from small arms, machine-guns and mortars on the forward defensive line from Dom 07, 32, 36, the cinema booth and the P-shaped building. No offensive actions are exhibited. It was noticed that engineering work was carried out during the night.

The war diary of 138th Rifle Division reported that at 0630 hours, a "medium German tank moved from the area of the Barrikady factory towards the L-shaped building [Apotheke], fired one shot at the division command post, and then left". This 'tank' was almost certainly an assault gun of Sturmgeschütz-Abteilung 245. The morning report of LI. Armeekorps stated that the battalion had a strength of 3 long-barrels, 3 short-barrels and 3 sIG33Bs, so it could have been any one of these.

– – –

The day passed as usual and Soviet units reported on German activity. Pechenyuk's men established that the Germans were firing mortars from the area south of the Kommissarhaus and the Apotheke while nebelwerfers fired from the northern side of Haus 57 [Dom 9] and 53 [Dom 6]. There was also a light mortar on the southern side of the Kommissarhaus and heavy machine-guns were firing from Haus 73, 72 and the cinema booth. Submachine-gun fire also came from the latter. Unusual activity was seen between the buildings: groups of 3-5 German soldiers dashed from Haus 72 to Haus 73 and back again. At 1230 hours, up to 40 German soldiers began to move but were scattered by Soviet fire. The day may have seemed normal to the Soviets but the Germans – particularly those from Grenadier-Regiment 578 – had been looking forward to it with malicious satisfaction. It had been two weeks since Haus 83 had been abandoned and a massive delay-fused explosive charge left behind as a house-warming present. It was set to go off at 1300 hours. Ten minutes before it was due, however, the Germans heard a dull thump emanate from the building and saw smoke rise up. What had happened? Had the charge failed to detonate properly? Cooler heads averted disappointment amongst the German soldiers by telling them to wait until after the expected time of detonation. At the turn of the hour, an ear-shattering blast erupted from deep inside Haus 83. As the echo of the mighty explosion rolled across the city, a dirty mushroom cloud bloomed over the building and an entire section collapsed into the cellar. The Germans thought that it had probably taken care of the Russians. Surely no-one had survived the blast. The combat journal of 650th Rifle Regiment shows otherwise:

> At 1250 and 1300, there were explosions in the former regimental command post (Dom 64). There were casualties: 4 men killed and 3 wounded. The explosion at 1450 occurred from the inept handling of an anti-tank grenade in the hands of the deputy commander of 1st Rifle Battalion, Captain Perepelkina.
>
> There was a second explosion at 1500. Massive damage to the eastern facade of Dom 64. The wall and overhead (iron-concrete) ceiling were destroyed. This weakened its stability.
>
> 1) The blast occurred from an explosion of about 200–300kg of explosives.
>
> 2) A device was packed into the building (in the centre).
>
> 3) The smell of TNT was detected in the surrounding area after the explosion.
>
> The explosion was caused by the enemy leaving behind a delayed-action demolition mine in the building.

Several factors prevented the incident from turning into a bloodbath for Pechenyuk's men. Firstly, the sector held by the regiment was manned by an extremely low number of combatants, for example, at the end of the day, the regiment had a combat strength of 51 officers, 22 NCOs and 41 enlisted ranks, a total of 114 men. This meant that the garrisons of each building were quite small. Secondly, and probably more importantly, Captain Perepelkina's accident with the anti-tank grenade – whilst no doubt causing painful casualties of its own – forced almost everyone out of the cellar, for fear of further explosions and to tend to the dead and wounded. Perepelkina's ineptitude probably saved lives.

It is unclear whether the earlier German movements between Haus 72 and 73 were forces being amassed for an attack that would exploit the confusion caused by the blast. Nevertheless, even hours later, Soviet observers noticed groups of Germans being shifted around the factory, as reported in the war diary of 138th Rifle Division:

> At 1430, there was movement of up to 50 enemy soldiers from Workshops 4 [Hall 6a] and 14/15 [Hall 3] into the main mechanical workshop [Hall 4] of the Barrikady factory.

– – –

In a letter to his wife, Leutnant B., adjutant III./Grenadier-Regiment 577, reveals the conditions under which he now lived and worked:

> For most of the day it is night-time for us. It is already dark at about 1500, so considerably earlier than near you. Our lighting is primitive and simple. The Landser invent everything possible and impossible. We can simply no longer imagine electric lights. In general, the trappings of a civilised world are becoming quite foreign to us. Lice hunting is part of the daily activities so that the beasts do not gain the upper hand. Nevertheless, one must still maintain a sense of humour because that makes everything much easier to accept. And after every December May comes around again, as is said so profoundly in that beautiful song.
>
> Chin up and keep a stiff upper lip, that is our motto. We want to remain faithful and never bow before our fate that will put us to a severe test.

– – –

Familie B.

A unique photo taken inside the cellar of a German strongpoint on Pribaltiskaya Street. On the phone is Leutnant B. [name withheld], adjutant III./Gr.Rgt.577. He provided a caption to the photo in a letter home:

'My dears!

'The first photo from the area in which we've fought for months has come into my hands by accident.

'I know you're quite worried about that, so that's why I've sent it to you, because a photo says more than a thousand words. I will say something about it for you:

'As I often am, I'm on the phone every day and maintain contact with the commandants of the individual strongpoints, receive reports, give orders and directives from the commander and share the joy, suffering and every worry of the men about the enemy.

'Location of the picture: Bunker command post about 60 to 80 metres from the Russians. You'll notice that I even have a table on which to write and a bit of my old beard is also left over.

'The warm fur jacket never goes astray and the same applies to the inevitable cigarette in my hand.

'Behind my back is the radio, keeping an ear out, almost our only connection to the outside world, to home.

'The old smile still shines through on my face.'

Continual fighting around the entire perimeter of the Stalingrad Kessel drained combat strengths but ration returns showed that there was ample manpower in the pocket to adequately replenish depleted units. Most men of 6. Armee were in non-combat roles. New measures were constantly being implemented to remedy this situation: at the turn of the year, two divisions – 94. and 384. Infanterie-Divisionen – had been disbanded, their remnants allotted to other divisions and their division staffs flown out. Individual corps and divisions were encouraged to raise combat strength by any means they saw fit. Battalions and companies were consolidated, dissolved or reinforced with men freed from other duties. The tooth-to-tail ratio throughout the entire army needed a dramatic re-adjustment: what was the point of having 20 or 30 men in a company supply train supporting 4 or 5 front-line soldiers? With this is mind, LI. Armeekorps sent a report to 6. Armee on this day:

We will free up soldiers by amalgamating staffs and supply trains, dissolving unused supply units and reducing those not operating at full capacity. It is proposed that the average training time of these men will be 14 days. Training has already begun.

The number of soldiers freed up for the infantry in 305. Infanterie-Division was 11 officers, 131 NCOs and 577 men, and the total number made available throughout LI. Armeekorps was 47 officers, 2 officials, 622 NCOs and 3415 men.

305. Infanterie-Division was set to receive another massive boost in strength but it would come at the expense of another division. During the day, General von Schwerin's 79. Infanterie-Division received an order from LI. Armeekorps stating that it was to be split up. Most of the remaining elements would be concentrated into a reinforced infantry regiment and subordinated to 305. Infanterie-Division, while part of the divisional staff would be flown out of the pocket to take command of other units. In an order sent out to its units that night, 79. Infanterie-Division stated that "to gain a further number of combatants for the defence of the fortress, a far-reaching simplification of the command apparatus along the Volga front has been ordered. As a result of these measures, 79. Infanterie-Division will be disbanded, the troops of the division consolidated and then subordinated to other divisions, the bulk going to 305. Infanterie-Division. A later reformation of the division is intended."

Each of 79. Infanterie-Division's three grenadier regiments would form a battalion, each consisting of a battalion staff, 2 grenadier companies and a heavy company. These would then be consolidated into a new Grenadier-Regiment 212[47]. As regimental troops, there would be 13. and 14. Kompanien, as well as a staff company with signals and pioneer platoons. Artillerie-Regiment 179 would retain its staff and 2 battalions at previous compositions (each battery had 4 guns) and be subordinated to 305. Infanterie-Division. A third battalion would be disbanded and made available for use as infantry (the three batteries of IV. Abteilung had already been shared amongst the other three battalions on 1 January, 1943). Pionier-Bataillon 179 would likewise be dissolved and – after forming a pioneer platoon for the new Grenadier-Regiment 212 – the remaining personnel would be transferred to Pionier-Bataillon 295. Its Russian-Kompanie, Hiwi-Kompanie and Romanian-Kompanie would be supplied to 305. Infanterie-Division. Panzerjäger-Abteilung 179 was to be handed over to 389. Infanterie-Division, Radfahr-Abteilung 179 incorporated into the battalion being formed from Grenadier-Regiment 226, and Nachrichten-Abteilung 179 disbanded so as to replenish Nachrichten-Abteilung 305, all surplus men being deployed to the infantry, except for radio specialists. 'Ausbildungsstab 208' (Training Staff 208), currently employed in retraining dispensable men as infantry, would remain untouched, but in any case would be subordinated to 305. Infanterie-Division. The supply troops were divided up amongst 71., 100. Jäger, 295. and 305. Infanterie-Divisions, but the latter gained control of 79. Infanterie-Division's two ammunition dumps.

Casualties for 6 January, 1943:
305. Infanterie-Division: 4 men wounded

---

47. See Appendix 7 (page 592) for an Offizier-Stellenbesetzung [officer staffing roster] of Grenadier-Regiment 212.

7 January, 1943

The previous day had been unnervingly quiet and both sides suffered very few casualties. During the night, however, small Soviet attacks began in earnest. In its morning report, LI. Armeekorps stated that "in the evening hours […] an attack against the centre of 305. Infanterie-Division was repulsed. An enemy attack at 0330 hours against the Kommissarhaus was also repulsed."

Lyudnikov's division did launch an attack but not against the Kommissarhaus, as can be seen in the entry from its war diary:

> The enemy is firing heavily with his artillery. Active measures began at 0300 when our storm groups tried to capture Dom 36 [Haus 73], but the enemy gave heavy fire from Dom 32 [Haus 72], 35 [Haus 66] and 60 [Kommissarhaus], and counterattacked multiple times. At night the enemy tried to put barbed wire between the buildings but thanks to fire from our battle groups this came to nothing. 344th Rifle Regiment continues preparations to take Dom 36.

An interim report from LI. Armeekorps, issued at 1640 hours, stated that "three enemy thrusts in the sector of 305. Infanterie-Division were repulsed".

– – –

Peace was not to be had on Gorishny's sector either. At 2120 hours the previous night, the movement of small groups of German soldiers was observed in the area of the housing quarter of Mashinnaya Street. At 2320 hours, on the sector of 161st Rifle Regiment, individual German soldiers set up cheval-de-frise in front of embrasures and ahead of their own emplacements. Soviet riflemen opened up small arms and machine-gun fire on these individual soldiers. Combat Report No. 13 noted that "the enemy fires at our combat ranks with all kinds of weapons. At night, not having illumination flares, chaotic firing and the throwing hand grenades intensified in the area of the fuel tanks." On the battlefield, the men of 90th Rifle Regiment picked up the following trophies: 15 boxes with belts of machine-gun ammunition and 300 hand grenades of different makes. The salvaged ammunition was put to use by the Soviet soldiers.

From 0900 to 1000 hours, 1/90th Rifle Regiment was bombarded by artillery fire but of the 12 German shells that landed, not one exploded. Units of 241st Rifle Regiment placed methodical fire from all kinds of weapons on German emplacements in the area of Dom 03, 02 and 07. Ampulomet fire during the day burnt out 2 dug-outs. 161st Rifle Regiment disseminated pamphlets with ampulomets and destroyed a dug-out near Dom 100 with fire from a 45mm battery. At the end of the day, the strength and losses of the three regiments of 95th Rifle Division were as follows: 241st Rifle Regiment, no losses, 84 active bayonets; 90th Rifle Regiment, losses of 1 man wounded, 90 active bayonets; 161st Rifle Regiment, losses of 1 man wounded, 50 active bayonets.

– – –

The partitioning of 79. Infanterie-Division and the formation of a new Grenadier-Regiment 212 continued. During the coming night, Hauptmann Gerhard Münch's[48] III./Grenadier-Regiment 194 (71. Infanterie-Division) would replace Grenadier-Regiment 212 on the front-line. During the time of reformation, Grenadier-Regiment 226 would take command of the entire divisional sector.

---

48. Münch, Major i.G. Gerhard, DKiG; III./Gr.Rgt.194; born 2 December, 1914 in Vettelschoss. Still alive in 2004.

Familie Gast

A truly remarkable photograph and undoubtedly the last of Panzerpionier-Bataillon 50 in Stalingrad. Shown here are the officers of battalion staff in Razgulyayevka, 7 January, 1943 (same location as photo shown on page 280). From left: Leutnant Hans Meyer (leader of the pioneer column), Oberinspektor Ernst Schneider (battalion Inspektor), Hauptmann Erwin Gast (commander), Stabszahlmeister Artur Hassler (paymaster) and Werkmeister Walter Hinsch. Note that they are all wearing felt boots and seem well-equipped for the cold weather. A strong wind is whipping across from right to left. None of these men made it home: they are all still listed as 'missing in action'

Meyer   Schneider   Gast   Hassler   Hinsch

Further reinforcements were injected into the division, as noted by Oberleutnant Friedrich Waldhausen, Artillerie-Regiment 305, in his final letter home:

> I received three new officers for my battalion, three proficient chaps. One originates from Lüschow's old battery[49]. A valuable enrichment of my officer corps!

– – –

In his final letter home, Rettenmaier summed up the steadily worsening privations being endured in the pocket:

> It is a terrible time but we are confident and hopeful that we will be compensated for these days of deprivation and sacrifice. No-one outside the pocket can have any idea of the conditions. Our horses have been devoured. Now the Führer has instructed the most powerful person in the field to ensure our resupply. Despite this, there won't be full portions for quite some time, but if we get enough, we can maintain our strength.
>
> For two days I have been with the Tross (support echelon). I have been given four days leave to relax. It is wonderful to be without worries and not burdened with responsibilities and to be able to rest, thoroughly wash oneself, change ones clothes and be able to move about freely. Tomorrow night the days of relaxation are over.

Casualties for 7 January, 1943:
305. Infanterie-Division: 1 man killed, 28 men wounded

8 January, 1943

On Lyudnikov's sector, the Germans laid down heavy machine-gun fire, particularly from the Apotheke and the Kommissarhaus, as well as occasional mortar fire. Heavy mortars emplaced near Hall 3 [Workshop 15] fired on the channel and Zaitsevsky Island. During the night, Pechenyuk's soldiers observed a German 'tank' being dug in near Dom 07, saw soldiers dashing in and out of the Apotheke and the Kommissarhaus, and noticed that they were trying to erect wire entanglements between the Apotheke and Dom 07, and from Dom 07 to the Kommissarhaus. The Soviet riflemen fired upon the Germans carrying out this work in order to prevent them successfully erecting the new wire barricade.

At 0530 hours, a small group from 138th Rifle Division's reconnaissance company approached some German dug-outs on the right flank of 768th Rifle Regiment and captured an Obergefreiter from 546. Infanterie-Regiment.

On Gorishny's sector, observers spotted individual German soldiers with mess-kits moving from the bakery towards Dom 106. The soldiers of 241st Rifle Regiment also noticed the installation of the wire entanglement in area of Dom 07. Every opportunity was being used by the German garrison to fortify and protect their strongpoint. It seems they sensed that an attack was imminent. With the coming of light, they halted their construction work and pulled back into their pulverised bastion.

During the day, Dom 07 and the Apotheke were constantly sprayed with fire from all weapons. The combat journal of 650th Rifle Regiment reports:

> A mortar battery laid down fire on enemy trenches, dug-outs and firing points near Dom 07 [Haus 79], 11, L-shaped building [Apotheke], Dom 31 [Haus 71], 32 [Haus 72] and 36 [Haus 73]. With mortars, small arms and machine-guns, we suppressed the fire of two mortars near

---

49. II./Artillerie-Regiment 17.

the L-shaped house, destroyed 1 light machine-gun, demolished 1 dug-out, and exterminated 9 soldiers and officers, 2 submachine-gunners, 1 sniper and 2 observers. Observation of enemy movements was increased. The regiment had losses; one NCO was wounded.

– – –

Under the cover of darkness, the relief took place in the sector of 79. Infanterie-Division and Grenadier-Regiment 212 reported its successful conclusion without incident at 0030 hours. In the morning, the hand over of the remnants of the division to 305. Infanterie-Division occurred. At 1300 hours, tactical command of 79. Infanterie-Division's sector and all of its men was assumed by 305. Infanterie-Division, as was the duty of continuing to split up 79. Infanterie-Division. Generalleutnant Schwerin and his command staff were now out of jobs. The operations section of the staff had been ordered to fly out of the Kessel and so, with hand luggage only, they headed to Pitomnik airfield and flew out in the evening, destination Novocherkask. There were 70 lucky men in total – 15 officers, 7 officials, 14 NCOs and 34 enlisted men, including a Hiwi. The rest of the division remained behind and became members of the Bodensee-Division. Not all of the divisional staff were flown out, as Major Helmut Poetsch, commander I./Grenadier-Regiment 212, remembers:

> On 7 January, 1943, the divisional staff were flown out on the army's orders: of them, both divisional priests, Dr. Altendorf[50] and Lange, remained behind in the Kessel, as did the divisional adjutant, Oberleutnant Hallier[51].

Also on a plane out of the pocket during the night was Generalmajor Steinmetz. At 1130 hours, while on an inspection tour, Commander-in-Chief Paulus had dropped in at the main hospital in Gorodische to meet the wounded commander of 305. Infanterie-Division. After saying goodbye to Generalmajor Steinmetz, Paulus returned to his command post. Hours later, Steinmetz was taken to the airfield and flown out.

– – –

At 1100 hours, 2/90th Rifle Regiment moved a 45mm gun forward into an exposed position to fire directly at targets. Its fire destroyed 2 German dug-outs. Under cover of smoke from exploding ampoules, both dug-outs and a communications trench were seized in a swift rush, resulting in the death of 5 German soldiers. According to Situation Report No. 16 of 95th Rifle Division, two Romanian soldiers working in the dug-outs under the supervision of German soldiers – who prevented them from running away – voluntarily came into captivity during the artillery fire. The men of 2/90th Rifle Regiment consolidated in the captured dug-outs. An interim report by LI. Armeekorps at 1655 hours mentions the loss of the dug-outs:

> In grid square 82a2, the enemy succeeded in capturing a machine-gun nest. A counterattack is being prepared.

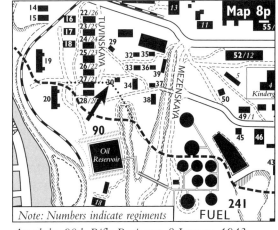

Note: Numbers indicate regiments

Attack by 90th Rifle Regiment, 8 January, 1943.

50. Altendorf, Kriegspfarrer (ev.) Dr. Erich, Stab 79.Inf.Div.; born 24 November, 1902 in Pirmasens. Died in 1984 in Kirchberg.

51. Hallier, Oberleutnant Joachim, Stab 79.Inf.Div.; born 15 December, 1903 in Diedehofen. Missing in action, January 1943 in Stalingrad.

The Soviet soldiers consolidated in the captured dug-outs and carried on fighting with hand grenades. The evening report of LI. Armeekorps stated that "the machine-gun nest in 82a2 lost in the morning was won back in a counterattack", but there is no mention of its recapture in Soviet records. At 1800 hours, 90th Rifle Regiment reported that it had lost 2 dead and 16 wounded, and still had 56 active bayonets. The division's two other regiments, 241st and 161st, held their positions while carrying out reconnaissance raids against German emplacements and suppressing them with fire from 45mm guns and mortars. Both remained without loss, 241st Rifle Regiment possessing 149 active bayonets while 161st Rifle Regiment had 60.

Casualties for 8 January, 1943:
305. Infanterie-Division: 10 men killed, 44 men wounded

9 January, 1943

Late in the night of 8 January, storm groups of 2/241st Rifle Regiment hurled themselves at Haus 79. German suspicions were accurate but tactical genius was not required to realise that the Soviets coveted the building. Every effort had been made to ready the house and its garrison for the inevitable Soviet attack. Rettenmaier's men were amply stocked with automatic weapons, ammunition and grenades. Nothing was denied to the barbican of 305. Infanterie-Division's defensive line. When the Soviet storm groups surged up out of Index Finger Gully, the calls of the German sentries immediately brought

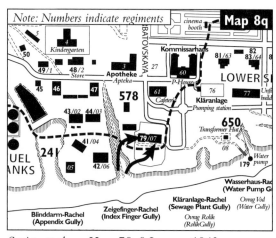

Soviet attack on Haus 79, 9 January, 1943.

every man to the loopholes. Combat Report No. 17 of 95th Rifle Division provides details of the attack:

> Having received the order to capture Dom 07, three previously prepared storm groups undertook numerous attacks on the house but met strong fire resistance and suffered heavy losses. They also had no success in the subsequent hand grenade duels in the trenches on the approach routes to the house.

By 2200 hours, the storm groups had lost 9 dead and 18 wounded. It was also noted that "the enemy, firmly holding his positions by relying on strongpoints with organised systems of fire saturated with automatic weapons, continues to offer stubborn fire resistance to attacks by our units and storm groups". The muzzle flashes seen during the night fighting indicated to the Soviets that three heavy, one light and one large-calibre machine-guns were installed in Dom 07.

Despite their costly failure, the storm groups of 241st Rifle Regiment courageously launched another attack at 0200 hours, but this too sank to the ground in the face of murderous fire. Pechenyuk's men saw their southern neighbours futilely attack the building and observed "animated activity of small enemy groups in the area of Dom 07. From 0200 the enemy began actively firing with small arms and machine-guns from Dom 07." Combat

Report No. 18 of 95th Rifle Division stated that "particularly intensive fire came from the area of Dom 07, the L-shaped building and the group of houses north-west of them". The renewed attempt cost another 4 dead and 14 wounded. The morning report of LI. Armeekorps from 0555 hours recorded that "two night-time attacks launched against the enclosed house east of the gun factory (83d3) were repulsed. Heavy artillery, mortar and anti-tank fire on forward line east of the gun factory".

After this bloody rebuff, the men of 241st Rifle Regiment were content to hold their positions and fire on German emplacements near Dom 07, 02 and 03. The regiment still had 139 active bayonets, only 10 fewer than the previous day despite the ghastly deficit of 13 dead and 32 wounded, but this was due to an influx of fresh reinforcements.

– – –

As the wan light of dawn gradually illuminated the wintry battleground, the combatants of both sides disappeared from sight into cellars, dug-outs and bunkers, and resumed the normal daytime routine: steady exchanges of fire that randomly escalated to frenzied shoot-outs, desultory mortar bombardments and occasional salvoes from rockets and artillery. As noted in 138th Rifle Division's war diary: "There was never-ending rifle and machine-gun fire along the entire front-line of the division during the entire day." 650th Rifle Regiment used machine-guns and mortars to prevent the Germans carrying out engineering-defensive works and from placing obstacles and barricades along the front and on the flanks. They also fired their mortars in the direction of Dom 07 and claimed the annihilation of a group of 6-7 Germans. The regiment's combat journal also recorded two interesting incidents on this day: Medic Nikolayev, from 2nd Rifle Battalion, threw grenades into an enemy trench, killing 4 Germans; and work was started on the construction of mine galleries. These galleries would be sunk deep into the sides of the Volga cliff until they were below a German strongpoint. Then, they would be packed with explosives and detonated as a prelude to the capture of the objective. Why this tactic was not used earlier is inexplicable.

Lyudnikov's sector witnessed a few noteworthy events in the afternoon. At 1500 hours, on the left flank of Pechenyuk's regiment, there was strong fire from small arms and machine-guns in Dom 07 and the Apotheke. Then, two motorcycles drove up to the Kommissarhaus. The reason for their visit is unknown but it must have been of some significance to risk such a dangerous drive and to warrant the use of valuable petrol. Some time later, the rumble of tracked vehicles was heard from the area of Hall 3. Gorishny's division also reported hearing the noise of motors at 0530 hours in the area of the bakery and the Barrikady factory. It may well have been the assault guns of Sturmgeschütz-Bataillon 245. While it still had 3 long-barrels, 3 short-barrels and 2 sIG33Bs available on the morning of 9 January, with a further 1 sIG33B and 3 short-barrels in for short term repairs, it had been ordered to supply a battery to 297. Infanterie-Division. The ominous build-up of Soviet forces around the perimeter of the Stalingrad pocket was not easily missed and the defensive positions of 297. Infanterie-Division on the southern edge of the pocket – simply trenches and bunkers sunk into the deep snow – were a prime target for Soviet armoured attacks. Sturmgeschütz-Bataillon 245 was therefore forced to relinquish its 2. Batterie with all three combat-ready long-barrels. The absence of the heavy-hitting guns was regretted by the battalion but their anti-tank capabilities were desperately required out on the steppe, to blunt a Soviet tank charge. The long-barrels would not be sorely missed by the infantry divisions, however, if an excerpt from the war diary of 79. Infanterie-Division from 2 January, 1943 is anything to go by:

2./Stug.Abt.245 with 3 long-barrels was exchanged for 3. Batterie with 2 short-barrels and 1 sIG33B because of the negligible possibilities for use as a 'fire brigade' in the fields of rubble.

The sound of tracked vehicles heard by the Soviets was probably 2. Batterie being pulled out for use near 297. Infanterie-Division and the remaining assault guns being shifted around. Soviet artillery observers called in fire on the presumed location of the armoured vehicles. The bombardment must have been rather heavy because it was noted in a report by LI. Armeekorps at 1715 hours: "…heavy anti-tank barrages on positions north-west of Hall 3 in the sector of 305. Infanterie-Division. Lively artillery and mortar harassing fire on entire divisional sector."

– – –

Now that 305. Infanterie-Division had Grenadier-Regiment 212 under its control, it decided to get its own house in order. The barbarous and merciless fighting had been steadily siphoning off the manpower of its three regiments since 21 December, and despite the constant efforts to bolster combat strengths with levies of hastily trained rear echelon personnel, it was becoming increasingly hopeless to maintain three regiments. When considered clinically, the only choice was to disband one of them and use its components to replenish the other two, so the decision was made to dissolve Grenadier-Regiment 578 and split it up amongst 576 and 577. Unfortunately, no documents or eyewitness accounts exist to show precisely how the regiment was partitioned and what roles were allocated to its commander, Oberstleutnant Liesecke, and three battalion commanders, Major Rettenmaier, Hauptmann Schwarz and Major Püttmann. It is probable that Rettenmaier and his I. Bataillon were handed over to Grenadier-Regiment 576, Major Püttmann and III. Bataillon to Grenadier-Regiment 577, while Hauptmann Schwarz and II. Bataillon remained in the rear and continued to carry on its task of training men for use in the front-line.

Casualties for 9 January, 1943:
305. Infanterie-Division: 14 men killed, 1 officer and 25 men wounded, 18 men missing

10 January, 1943

During the night, the first companies of 400th Separate Machine-Gun and Artillery Battalion arrived in Lyudnikov's sector to begin the process of taking over the division's defensive line. Another company relieved 241st Rifle Regiment, which then moved further south to slot into position between 161st and 90th Rifle Regiments. The arrival of 400th Battalion signalled a dramatic shift in Soviet thinking. Battalions such as the 400th were primarily defensive units and were inserted into the front-line to hold positions while offensives were launched in other sectors. With good progress being made south and south-west of the Barrikady factory by the left flank of 95th Rifle Division and Sokolov's 45th Rifle Division, it made no sense to keep throwing Lyudnikov's and Gorishny's weak forces against the sturdy breakwater of German defences east of the factory. The German strongpoints – particularly Haus 79 and the Kommissarhaus – were just too formidable. Despite being surrounded for over 6 weeks and making do with supplies that had been flown in or already existed in the pocket, the enfeebled and malnourished German defenders resisted with bloody-minded determination and launched repeated counterattacks whenever a position was lost. The fact that all of the surviving men of 138th Rifle Division were now being pulled out and deployed further south, in the Krasny Oktyabr sector, was grudging recognition of the Germans' staying power and their absolute resolve to hold on – no matter the cost.

- - -

The final Soviet push to retake Stalingrad began in the morning with a tremendous 55-minute barrage from 7,000 artillery pieces, mortars and rocket-launchers. On 8 January, General Rokossovsky[52], commander of the Don Front, had sent Paulus a surrender ultimatum. It was turned down flat. The next day, the Soviets dropped leaflets on 6. Armee giving terms of surrender, but Paulus wouldn't budge. Hitler made it clear that surrender was out of the question. On the morning of 10 January, Operation Koltso (Ring) was launched by Rokossovsky's Don Front, which controlled the perimeter with seven armies. Its goal was the liquidation of the Stalingrad pocket. The initial objective was to split the pocket on a west–east axis but this would be done in stages rather that by a single stroke. The main effort was concentrated against the weaker western and southern faces. The first day brought gains of four or five kilometres, which was disappointing for Rokossovsky but an alarming portent for 6. Armee. The Germans would manage to prevent an outright breakthrough over the next two days but the writing was on the wall – 6. Armee's days were numbered.

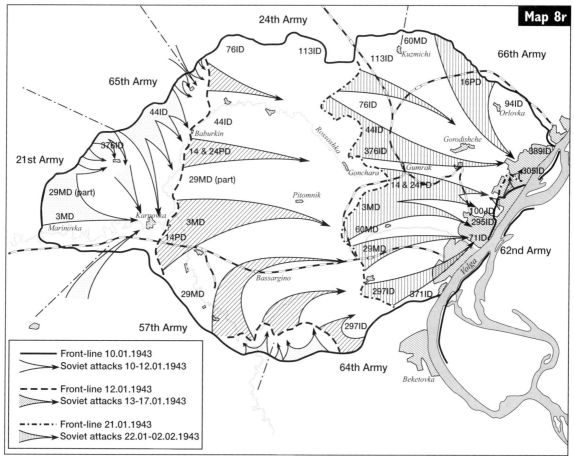

Operation Koltso: the liquidation of the Stalingrad pocket, 10 January to 2 February, 1943.

---

52. Rokossovsky, General Konstantin Konstantinovich, HotSU; Don Front; born 21 December, 1896 in Velikie Luki. Died 3 August, 1968.

Back in the ruins of Stalingrad, most Soviet units launched small attacks to tie down the German divisions but 138th Rifle Division was busy regrouping and preparing to be relieved. Even then it seemed like business as usual, as can be seen by the combat journal of 650th Rifle Regiment:

The enemy did not show any activity along the regiment's front. He placed heavy small arms and machine-gun fire on the left flank. Enemy snipers were actively operating. Mortar fire was conducted from the area of the 5-storey white house. Observation established enemy movements in the area of the Dom 36, 38 and the large five-storey house. A six-barrelled mortar was detected in the area of Workshop 4 [Hall 6a]. [...] Artillery and mortar fire suppressed 3 enemy mortars and 2 machine-guns. The enemy lost 20 soldiers and officers killed. The regiment lost 1 NCO killed.

The shattered interior of Workshop 4/Hall 6a.

The action was hotter on the sector of Grenadier-Regiment 212, faced by Sokolov's 45th Rifle Division and Guriev's 39th Guards Rifle Division. LI. Armeekorps reported that "at 0600 hours, the enemy attacked in battalion strength [...] on the boundary between 100. Jäger-Division and 305. Infanterie-Division. Counterattacks are still in progress."

Forward of the defensive area of 95th Rifle Division, the Germans still occupied a tactically important area from which they delivered withering fire. Gorishny had ordered a storm group to capture it but all previous attempts had been unsuccessful. Then, at the initiative of engineer D.A. Zabolotsky, combat engineers dug a 28-metre underground tunnel, running it up under one of the huge fuel tanks. The job was performed by the men of the divisional 48th Combat Engineer Battalion, commanded by Captain A.A. Arbuzov. They performed the task under extraordinarily difficult conditions, digging through heavy, oil-impregnated earth, but nevertheless completed the task on schedule. The fuel tank explosion fleetingly threw the Germans into confusion and served as the signal for the Soviet troops to commence the assault. The time was 0700 hours. Combat Report No. 19 stated that "with the beginning of the infantry attack, the enemy strengthened his bombardment, especially from mortars of the D-40 type from the area of the south-east corner of the Barrikady factory and the railway fork". The progress of the attacks of each regiment were as follows:

At 0700 hours, after the green fuel tank was blown up, the Germans near it fled in panic and abandoned a few positions, but they soon rallied. The left-flank group of 90th Rifle Regiment advanced 20-25 metres and captured a dug-out. In doing so, they lost 5 dead and 8 wounded. They then held the line and carried on hand grenade duels until 1000 hours to hold on to the captured dug-out. At 1000 hours, a German force of about 30 soldiers attacked from the factory and captured a dug-out north-east of the green fuel tank. An assault on this second dug-out was counterattacked and had no success. By the end of the day, the regiment lost another 8 men killed and 8 wounded, and was left with only 23 active bayonets.

161st Rifle Regiment began their attack successfully at 0700 hours. They suffered losses of 2 dead and 5 wounded. By 0810 hours, 1st Rifle Battalion had seized several communication trenches and one pillbox on Mashinnaya Street. The 2nd Rifle Battalion struck from the area of the school along Korotky (Short) Gully and with machine-gun and mortar fire successfully destroyed a machine-gun post in the area of Dom 115 and a pillbox that lay 100 metres south-east of Dom 101. In continuing to push forward to Dom 107 and 108, they also ran into a minefield and a barbed-wire entanglement but bypassed them to the left and by 1030 hours had reached Dom 109 where they were pinned down by heavy German fire from the Barrikady factory and the bakery (Dom 110). Exchanges of fire continued and the battalion suffered losses. To exploit the success of 2nd Rifle Battalion, 2/90th Rifle Regiment was committed to action at 1120 hours. It advanced in the direction of Dom 118 and made contact with units of 45th Rifle Division. Losses for 161st Rifle Regiment were heavy: 69 men killed and wounded, leaving 43 active bayonets.

After an artillery assault, 241st Rifle Regiment launched their attack at 0720 hours. Meeting persistent fire resistance from the south-east corner of the Barrikady factory, they moved forward slowly. Two men were wounded. The regiment continued to take ground, advancing 50-60 metres and seizing several communication trenches under heavy fire from machine-guns and mortars. Combat with artillery and mortars continued, suppressing German emplacements that had been located. The regiment lost a further 5 men killed and 18 wounded, leaving 115 active bayonets.

It was estimated that German casualties were about 100 soldiers but Gorishny had also lost a substantial portion of his combat strength. He lodged a request for his division's units to be replenished with 250-300 riflemen. Nevertheless, the attacks would continue. He issued the order to his units: During the night of 10 to 11 January, they would continue to destroy the Germans in houses and pillboxes south of the Barrikady factory, and from 0300 hours on 11 January, 161st Rifle Regiment, together with units of 45th Rifle Division, would continue to advance with the task of reaching Tupikovaya Street.

– – –

Apart from these battles with 95th Rifle Division, the far right flank of Grenadier-Regiment 212 was still coping with the large Soviet attack that struck the boundary between it and 100. Jäger-Division. At 2050 hours, LI. Armeekorps reported:

> On the boundary between 100. Jäger-Division and 305. Infanterie-Division, the counterattack on the left wing of 100. Jäger-Division to recapture the old positions is only making slow progress. On the right wing of 305. Infanterie-Division, the old front-line is again back in our hands with the exception of two advanced machine-gun posts. A raid by enemy assault troops south-east of the bread factory was repulsed.

Casualties for both divisions were extraordinarily high.

Casualties for 10 January, 1943:	
305. Infanterie-Division:	1 officer and 48 men killed, 2 officers and 81 men wounded, 21 men missing
100. Jäger-Division:	4 officers and 14 men killed, 2 officers and 64 men wounded (preliminary report)

Lyudnikov and his officers inspect the battlefield on the 'Island', here strolling through the torn up Theatre Park between Prospekt Lenina and Taimyrskaya Street. This photo must have been taken after the fighting had ended because to walk around openly like this during the battle would certainly have been a death sentence. One wonders what Lyudnikov thought about his division's inability to completely dislodge the Germans from their strongpoints around his bridgehead. Starving, short of ammunition and constantly besieged by the Red Army, the men of 305. Infanterie-Division held on.

Barrikady Museum

- - -

The attempts by Lyudnikov's and Gorishny's men to crack the German defences around the 'Island of Fire' had failed. Soviet forces within the city were reshuffled to continue attacks on sectors where German resistance was less stubborn and progress was being made. Nevertheless, the death knell had been sounded for all Germans in Stalingrad when the stasis around the pocket's perimeter was broken by Operation Koltso. The men of 305. Infanterie-Division would continue to resist until the very end but their defensive efforts were now focused on their right flank, on the sectors of Grenadier-Regiments 576 and 212 which ran from the fuel tanks on the Volga bank, along the southern boundary of the gun factory, encompassed the bread factory and meandered south to the outskirts of the Krasny Oktyabr factory. In 22 days, it would all be over.

CHAPTER NINE

11 January, 1943

The morning report of LI. Armeekorps at 0615 hours chronicled the small scuffles that flared up along the sector of 305. Infanterie-Division, as well as a few other events:

An enemy raid at 0200 hours on the left wing of 100. Jäger-Division was straightened out by 0430 hours. Our attack along the boundary has so far not been able to recapture the lost positions. One enemy raid north of the broad street was repulsed. During the night, 3 enemy tanks drove over the Volga and into the bridgehead east of the gun factory. At 0400 hours, Pionier-Bataillon 389 departed for Pitomnik.

The presence of Soviet tanks in Lyudnikov's old bridgehead posed a threat, particularly because the long-barrels of Sturmgeschütz-Abteilung 245 had been shifted to another sector. Loud engines noises were repeatedly heard east of the gun factory. However, it seems this was a Soviet tactic designed to draw attention away from other sectors.

- - -

The night of 10-11 January and the following morning were punctuated by brief but violent skirmishes, mostly emanating from 95th Rifle Division's sector. From 2300 to 0020 hours, on the sector of 241st Rifle Regiment, small German groups undertook five attacks – one after the other – with the aim of recapturing the dug-out lost on 10 January. All five attacks were repulsed and Soviet records claim that up to 30 Germans were killed. Closer to the river, on the sector of 90th Rifle Regiment, there was fighting with hand grenades in the fuel tank area. One Soviet soldier was wounded.

At 0525 hours, after preparatory work, 241st Rifle Regiment went over to the offensive and seized 5 dug-outs on Mashinnaya Street to the north of Dom 83 before being stopped by organised German fire. It then conducted hand grenade fighting. The regiment had casualties of 17 men.

161st Rifle Regiment went on the offensive at 0400 hours towards the railway bridge and seized a wooden house near the railway embankment at 0540. They were pinned down by intense machine-gun and mortar fire from the bakery and the houses on Tupikovaya Street. The regiment had casualties of 15 men.

The Germans smothered the advancing storm groups with fire from the south-east edge of the Barrikady factory and from Dom 83, 84, 108 and 110. Regardless, the two Soviet regiments relaunched their attacks at 0900 hours after a minor artillery assault. The storm groups of 241st Rifle Regiment surged ahead, advancing 100-120 metres and bypassing Dom 84 on the right, and occupied another 10 dug-outs in which they consolidated and prepared to capture Dom 83 and 84. The regiment captured 2 German and 2 Romanian soldiers. By 1600 hours the regiment had taken 30 dug-outs and trenches. To exploit this

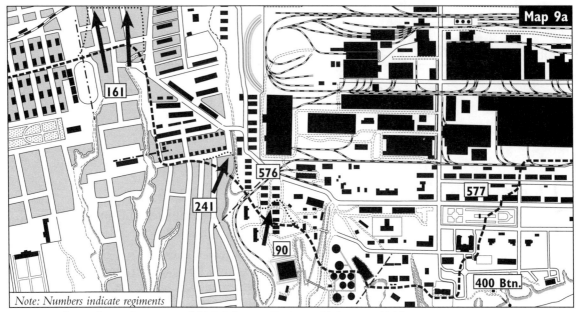

Soviet attacks on the southern sector of 305. Infanterie-Division, 11 January, 1943.

success, a group of scouts and sappers were thrown into the battle at 1400 hours. The storm groups continued offensive actions but were forced to repel two platoon-strength German counterattacks from the southern part of the Barrikady factory. Russian records show that as a result of the fighting, 7. (Infanterie) and 8. (Maschinengewehr) Kompanien of Grenadier-Regiment 576 were defeated. 241st Rifle Regiment found about 50 German corpses on its sector alone. At 1710 hours, LI. Armeekorps reported that "between the bread factory and the fuel installation, the enemy broke into two strongpoints in 82a1 at 1100 hours. A counterattack has been launched." Later, at 2110 hours, it noted that "between both gullies south-east of the bread factory (82a1), the Russians were able to roll up another 3 strongpoints. After being successfully sealed off, the counterattack has so far remained without success." The losses of 241st Rifle Regiment were 36 men wounded plus an unspecified number of dead. Active bayonets, including scouts and sappers, was 35 men.

Before also going on the offensive at 0900 hours, 161st Rifle Regiment regrouped its forces. After handing over the defensive sector on Mashinnaya Street to a group of scouts, 1st Rifle Battalion was shifted to 2/161st Rifle Regiment's sector on the railway embankment to facilitate the further advance. At 0900 hours, having moved its firepower forward, 161st Rifle Regiment continued the attack. Individual storm groups overcame the railway embankment by 1500 hours and engaged in fire fights. During the fighting, 4 dug-outs and 1 house were destroyed, 8 pillboxes were captured. Mentions of this engagement in the reports of LI. Armeekorps are brief: "Two attempts to attack south of the bread factory were broken up by concentrated artillery fire." Sixteen men of 161st Rifle Regiment became casualties and at the end of the day it possessed 50 active bayonets.

While its sister regiments attacked, 90th Rifle Regiment shot up German emplacements and prepared to capture some trenches and dug-outs near Dom 22-24. In doing so, it incurred losses of 4 dead and 2 wounded and ended up with only 20 active bayonets.

As a result of its attacks, 95th Rifle Division estimated it had inflicted about 110 casualties on the Germans. In addition, it captured 15 machine-guns, 8 mortars, about 200 rifles, and took prisoner 6 Romanian and 4 German soldiers. According to statements extracted from these prisoners-of-war, 8./Grenadier-Regiment 576 had arrived in the area of the Barrikady Factory on 8 January from Alexandrovka with a strength of 45 men and armed with 6 heavy machine-guns, 3 of which were operational. The company had been almost completely destroyed and at last count possessed only 10 men. From the 40 men of 6. Kompanie of the same regiment, only 2 men remained.

At 1800 hours, Colonel Gorishny issued an order: 241st Rifle Regiment would clear the enemy from the captured sector and consolidate; 161st Rifle Regiment would further develop the attack to reach Tupikovaya Street – and then consolidate; 90th Rifle Regiment – minus one battalion – would carry out demonstrative actions during the night to wear down the enemy and hold him on their sector.

– – –

Apart from dealing with the incessant attacks from Gorishny's division, Oberst Czimatis and 305. Infanterie-Division had to contend with niggling raids on their far right flank, on the sector running from the bread factory to the southern edge of the Krasny Oktyabr settlement. LI. Armeekorps summed up these attacks as follows:

> Against the right wing of 305. Infanterie-Division, which has had to be bent back to No. 52, enemy attacks have been in progress in 62c since 1445 hours. More detailed reports are still outstanding. Enemy preparations west of B (62b) were smashed by artillery fire. In an attack at 0800 hours, the enemy – with a strength of 80 men – succeeded in capturing 4 houses in 72a Mitte. The breach has been sealed off.

This last attack was carried out by the division's old arch nemesis – Colonel Lyudnikov and his 138th Rifle Division. They had moved out of their positions east of the gun factory and assembled in the Krasny Oktyabr factory by 0400 hours. Konovalenko's 344th and Pechenyuk's 650th Rifle Regiments went on the offensive at 1130 hours north of the factory.

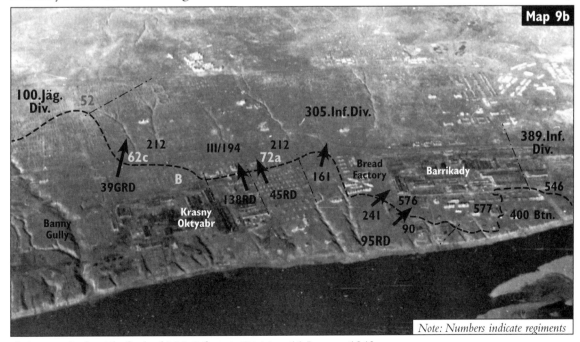

Actions on the far right flank of 305. Infanterie-Division, 11 January, 1943.

Some units reached Znamenskaya Street but dropped to the ground after encountering minefields and heavy German resistance. Lyudnikov's men claimed to have destroyed 46 Germans, suppressed the fire of three machine-gun positions and captured 1 light machine-gun, 5 submachine-guns, 4 rifles and two houses. The division did not escape casualties: 650th Rifle Regiment alone lost 9 killed and 13 wounded.

Nonetheless, each small Soviet raid captured a house here, seized a dug-out there, and maintained constant pressure that wore down the Germans and took a toll on manpower, weapons and ammunition. Large-scale successes were rare but the net effect was the steady attrition of German combat effectiveness. A memorandum sent to Heeresgruppe Don by 6. Armee at 1945 hours was a frank admission of this:

> Stalingrad: weakening power of resistance among the men has led to the constant crumbling away of the front-line in house-to-house fighting. Renewed enemy raids were mostly repulsed. Break-in on the boundary between 100. Jäger-Division and 305. Infanterie-Division.

Casualties for 11 January, 1943:
305. Infanterie-Division: 1 officer and 28 men killed, 1 officer and 103 men wounded, 4 men missing (full total to be reported later)

12 January, 1943

Utilising the cover of darkness, German units attempted to recover what had been lost during the day. At 1700 and 2100 hours on 11 January, a platoon-strength force from the Barrikady factory tried to counterattack the right flank of 241st Rifle Regiment, but fire from mortars and artillery repelled the attack. At 2245, 2300 and 0005 hours, another platoon-strength force tried three times to attack 161st Rifle Regiment from a group of houses south-west of the railway fork. All German attacks were supported by machine-gun and mortar fire from the south-east corner of the Barrikady factory, the bakery, the housing quarter south of the bakery and Buguruslanskaya Street. The German attacks were repulsed and pulled back to their starting positions.

The war of attrition was continued by 95th Rifle Division in the early morning. While 90th Rifle Regiment carried out demonstrative actions during the night, the other two regiments launched themselves at the German positions. Storm groups of 241st Rifle Regiment, both during the night and at dawn, continued the battle to conquer Dom 83 but were pinned down by flanking fire from the south-east corner of the Barrikady factory. And at 0245 hours, 161st Rifle Regiment, after regrouping, renewed their attack together with 61st Rifle Regiment (45th Rifle Division). By 0400 hours, they reached Tupikovaya Street near the railway bridge where they consolidated in houses and carried on the fight. During the battle 161st Rifle Regiment captured about 10 houses, 10 dug-outs and several pillboxes. Taken prisoner were 2 German soldiers, while 1 anti-tank gun, 1 light machine-gun, 1 submachine-gun and about 10 rifles were captured.

These losses were not taken idly by 305. Infanterie-Division. The loss of each strongpoint, whether it be large or small, ate away at the integrity of the defensive line, so counterattacks were launched. And no army was more proficient at counterattacks than the Wehrmacht. At 0630 hours, a group of about 70 Germans was noticed moving from Buguruslanskaya Street towards the left flank of 161st Rifle Regiment but artillery and mortar fire scattered them. At 0815 hours, a company of German infantry with two tanks was observed on

Feodoseyevskaya Street. All sorts of firepower then fell upon them. No doubt these 'tanks' were assault guns of Sturmgeschütz-Abteilung 245 which possessed 4 short-barrels and 1 sIG33B on this morning. This German force tried to counter-attack 161st Rifle Regiment twice from 0830 to 0920 hours. At 1430 hours, another counterattack was defeated when part of the Germans were destroyed by artillery, mortar and rocket fire. The surviving Germans pulled back to the school on Buguruslanskaya and Tiraspolskaya Streets. Throughout the day, the Germans counter-attacked 161st Rifle Regiment's positions five times but were beaten off every time. The regiment lost 15 men and possessed 90 active bayonets at the end of the day.

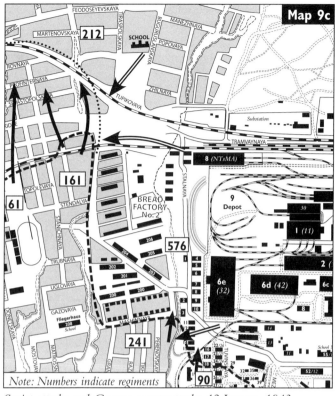

Soviet attacks and German counterattacks, 12 January, 1943.

To their east, 241st Rifle Regiment fought for control of Dom 83 with small groups and in doing so, captured 16 dug-outs and trenches in which it consolidated and repelled German attacks. It lost 17 men and ended up with only 18 active bayonets.

Apart from carrying out demonstrative actions to attract enemy fire, 90th Rifle Regiment also undertook reconnaissance raids on German emplacements on their left flank, and through this, seized 3 trenches and consolidated in them. No losses were suffered and it still had 21 active bayonets.

Combat Report No. 24 of 95th Rifle Division summarised the effect on the Germans:

During the day, the enemy recoiled under the blows of our storm groups that were attacking his units, but by relying on his system of strongpoints, he displayed stubborn resistance by laying down machine-gun, submachine-gun and mortar bombardments on our soldiers from the Barrikady factory, the bakery and the housing quarter on Buguruslanskaya Street.

The division estimated German casualties at about 125 men. They also took 3 German soldiers prisoner and captured 1 anti-tank gun, 2 light machine-guns, 1 heavy machine-gun, 3 mortars, 6 submachine-guns and about 30 rifles.

Gorishny's order to his regiments was simple:

During the night of 12.1 to 13.1, 90th and 161st Rifle Regiments will carry out active reconnaissance towards the Barrikady factory. 241st Rifle Regiment will continue to destroy the enemy south and south-west of the Barrikady factory.

– – –

Lyudnikov's 138th Rifle Division also struck another blow against 305. Infanterie-Division. Lyudnikov clearly remembers the attack:

After 11 weeks of ceaseless fighting we left the [Barrikady Factory] where every square metre of land was soaked in the blood of our men and commanders. […] We now started preparing a new attack.

The German 71st Infantry Division […] was the third division we engaged in Stalingrad.

We were advancing towards Tsentralnaya and Zaraiskaya streets from the west of the Krasny Oktyabr works. In the first day we advanced 150 metres. Ahead lay a minefield covered by German fire. To spare lives we took the enemy in the flank. The Germans had dug their heels in the factory apprenticeship school and the Lenin Club and in order to clear these buildings we could not avoid bloodshed. Here, Ivan Zlydnev, Konovalenko's orderly, was shot dead; here, too, we lost two 'Rolik' signallers and the gallant assault group commander Lieutenant Chulkov…

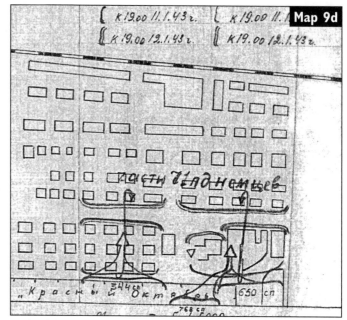

A sketch by 138th Rifle Division shows their attack west of the Krasny Oktyabr on 12 January, 1943.

And this from the division's war diary:

During the day the enemy offered heavy resistance and fire against the advancing units of the division. Fire from six-barrelled mortars was directed at the division command post, while rifle and machine-gun fire, as well as artillery, struck our storm groups.

At 1515, before the storming of the FZU building, the enemy ran in disorder toward the Lenin Club. By 1700 the division had captured the FZU building and reached Ordzhonikidze Street with its left flank. Trophies and 12 Germans were captured in the FZU building. Eight prisoners were killed by the storm groups, while 4 were taken to the division command post. Questioning of the prisoners revealed that they were part of 71. Infanterie-Division.

At 1800 hours, 344th and 768th Rifle Regiments captured the Lenin Club. The advance of our storm groups continued during the night of 12-13 January.

The matter-of-fact statement about the killing of German prisoners signifies the utter ruthlessness of the struggle and is perhaps a sign of the pent-up frustration of Lyudnikov's men who had been bottled up on their small 'island' for months with few opportunities to exact revenge. The prisoners from 71. Infanterie-Division were part of Hauptmann Münch's III./ Grenadier-Regiment 194, now attached to 305. Infanterie-Division and operating on its far right flank. The prisoners must have told their captors their commander's name because Münch was soon personally singled out by a Soviet politruk who used a loudspeaker to blare out his name: "German soldiers, drop your weapons. It makes no sense to continue. Your Captain Münch will also realise one day what is going on. What this 'super-Fascist' tells you isn't right anyway. He will recognise it. One day we'll seize him." After every mention of his name, Münch went out and visited his men, joked with them about the personal comments, but always watched carefully to gauge their reactions. Although the ruse was meant to unnerve the men, they never seemed disheartened or terrorised.

One of Münch's trusted NCOs, Unteroffizier Theodor Gerecke[1], was one of the very fortunate group of men who were later flown out of the pocket courtesy of a 6. Armee order which saved 1 officer, 1 NCO and 1 enlisted man from every division. Gerecke reported the following when he was interviewed shortly after his rescue:

> I had been in Stalingrad with my unit since 14 September. […] During the night of 7-8 January we were deployed in the Red October factory and lay opposite the southern part of Hall 4. Strength: 1 officer and 40 men, plus 20 Romanians. Equipment: 8 light machine-guns, a heavy mortar and 2 heavy machine-guns. Ammunition was available in sufficient quantities. On 10 January the mortar was useless because of a lack of ammunition. Opposite us lay two enemy companies. The enemy was equipped with anti-tank guns, rocket-launchers, 7.62 crash-boom guns and heavy artillery. He fired almost without interruption since 8 January. The soldiers were well-equipped and well-provisioned. The enemy noticed our relief during the night of 7-8 January. In the morning, about 0430 hours, about 80 Russian infantrymen attacked without artillery preparation. This attack was beaten off with heavy enemy casualties. When the Russians attacked again in the afternoon, we had to evacuate part of our positions. We then vacated the rest of the Red October voluntarily and pulled back approximately 300 metres. Early on 9 January at 1000 hours, the Russians attacked for the third time after mortar preparation. Because we suffered large casualties, we pulled back a further 50 metres, to the level of the company command post. From 10-12 January the Russians lay down harassing fire with heavy weapons. With the Romanians, we now only had 25 men. On the afternoon of 12 January, the attack was renewed after artillery, mortar and anti-tank preparation. Because our left and right flanks were open, we had to vacate our positions and pull back to prepared rear positions along the railway line. There were still 2 NCOs and 7 men. The battalion was assembled and it still had 17 men, who were newly deployed for defence along the railway line. There, the enemy covered us the entire time with fire from his heavy weapons. The enemy carried out storm troop operations to penetrate our positions at dawn and in the evening. All these break-in attempts were repulsed. During these attacks, the enemy approached to within 10 metres of our positions and fought us with hand grenades. We smashed them back with the fire of our carbines, a heavy machine-gun and 2 light machine-guns. I was in this position until the 21st, when I received the order from the army [to be flown out]. We made our way to a makeshift airfield on a snow-covered piece of steppe 5km south-east of Gumrak, an He-111 aircraft arrived, bringing in supplies and flying out the wounded. We flew out with a crew that had crashed on landing. We flew out with 16 men, of those, 2 were wounded and 4 were being flown out, the rest were air crewmen.

Casualties for 12 January, 1943:
305. Infanterie-Division: no figures available from this date onward

13 January, 1943

At 0550 hours, the morning report of LI. Armeekorps stated that "an enemy raid near 305. Infanterie-Division was repulsed. Otherwise, the night passed quietly". With this entry ends all official reports about the operations of 305. Infanterie-Division in Stalingrad. The division's final days can only be constructed from eyewitness account and mentions in Soviet records.

At 0330 hours, the right flank of 241st Rifle Regiment began advancing forward and by 0700 hours individual storm groups reached the pipe bridge across the ravine south of the Barrikady factory. They seized several dug-outs, knocked out a tankette and then

---

1. Gerecke, Unteroffizier Theodor, III./Gr.Rgt.194; born 9 September, 1918 in Magdeburg. No further information known.

consolidated themselves there. At 0730 hours, a force of 15-20 Germans counterattacked the storm groups from the south-east corner of the Barrikady factory but they were beaten off with artillery and mortar fire. Having filled up the storm groups with replacements, the attack was relaunched at 0800 hours, Dom 83 was seized as were a number of houses to the west of it, on Mashinnaya Street. The storm groups then consolidated upon the attained line. Losses in the regiment were 20 men, leaving 28 active bayonets.

At 0315 hours, 161st Rifle Regiment commenced reconnaissance raids towards the bakery but met heavy submachine-gun and machine-gun fire. At 0345 hours, a platoon of Germans, supported by machine-gun and mortar fire from the bakery, counterattacked the advancing groups of the regiment, which then pulled back to the south along the railway and assumed defence 200 metres south of the bakery. Concentrations of German infantry – up to 3 platoons – were observed at 1030 hours near the houses south-east of the bakery and at 1100 hours near the transformer hut close to the south-western corner of the Barrikady factory. They were scattered by artillery and mortar fire. At 1500, up to three platoons of German infantry had again concentrated in the same area. Artillery and rocket fire was directed on them and they scattered. One German tank was spotted on Buguruslanskaya Street at 1500 hours. The losses of 161st Rifle Regiment were 9 men but the arrival of reinforcements meant it had 111 active bayonets.

A storm group deployed on the left flank of 90th Rifle Regiment seized some dug-outs south of the railway spur line. Artillery and mortar fire destroyed 2 German dug-outs and an observation post. Casualties were light: 1 man wounded. Active bayonets: 21.

Gorishny's division claimed about 60 German soldiers killed and captured 4 heavy machine-guns, 3 light machine-guns, 30 rifles, 1 stereo telescope, 5 boxes of grenades, 60 signal flares and about 1500 rifle cartridges.

– – –

Further south, 138th Rifle Division claimed a larger booty:

> The enemy pulled back behind the railroad line, 400 metres west of the Krasny Oktyabr factory, but continues to offer stiff resistance.
>
> At 1400, the movement of about 100 enemy soldiers was noticed.
>
> Units of the division are readying themselves by conducting reconnaissance during the battles and preparing for continued offensive actions. For the day the enemy lost 200 men in dead alone, 1 heavy machine-gun and two dug-outs. Trophies: two 75mm guns, one 37mm gun, two 82mm mortars, two 50mm mortars, 4 heavy machine-guns, 8 light machine-guns, 65 rifles, more than 200 rounds of 37mm ammunition, over 1000 mortar rounds, 550 grenades and more than 1500 rifle rounds.

Right: A sketch by 138th Rifle Division shows their attack west of the Krasny Oktyabr on 13 January, 1943.

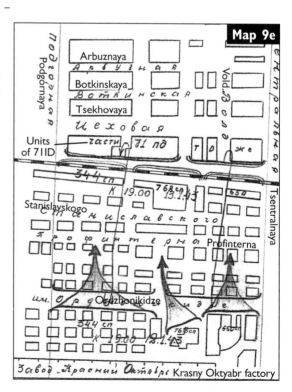

14 January, 1943

Combat Report No. 28 of 95th Rifle Division begins as follows: "Continuing to offer persistent resistance, the enemy places submachine-gun, machine-gun and mortar fire on the soldiers of our attacking units from the Barrikady factory, the bakery and the housing quarter on Feodoseyevskaya Street, and then launches counterattacks."

If the Soviets were expecting progress to be easier as the Germans grew weaker, then they were in for a nasty shock. Sheaths of fire descended upon each attack, murderous resistance was offered at every turn and counterattacks were relentlessly launched to retake lost positions. There would be no easy victories here.

During the day, 90th Rifle Regiment held its defensive sector and fired on German soldiers and emplacements near the south-eastern corner of the Barrikady factory and the green fuel tank. At 0400 hours, reconnaissance revealed a platoon of German infantry on the south-eastern corner of the Barrikady factory. Movement of individual soldiers from the factory to the trenches and back was observed at the same time. No losses in 90th Rifle Regiment. Active bayonets: 21. During the night, the regiment would hand over its sector alongside the Volga bank to 400th Battalion and 241st Rifle Regiment and move into position next to 161st Rifle Regiment, in the workers settlements west of the railway line.

Storm groups of 241st Rifle Regiment continued their advance towards the bakery and captured Dom

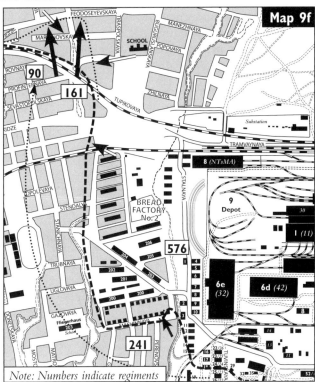

Attacks by 95th Rifle Division, 14 January, 1943.

84 after stubborn fighting. Losses: 7 men. Active bayonets: 39.

Moving ahead towards Feodoseyevskaya Street, 161st Rifle Regiment was struck by heavy fire from the bakery, the railroad tracks, the fork in the road and the houses on Feodoseyevskaya Street. At 0430 hours a storm group of 161st Rifle Regiment was counterattacked from the bakery but they beat it off. The left flank reached Feodoseyevskaya Street but then faced a succession of German counterattacks: at midday, a platoon-strength German force counterattacked 161st Rifle Regiment from the direction of Feodoseyevskaya Street; at 1305 hours, up to 50 German soldiers were seen moving along the railway line towards the bakery but this group was scattered by artillery and mortar fire; at 1430 hours, a concentration of up to one and a half companies of Germans was noticed near the school between Tiraspolskaya and Buguruslanskaya Streets. The process of repelling these determined Germans attacks meant that the losses of 161st Rifle Regiment were heavy: 60 men, but another transfusion of fresh blood left it with 115 active bayonets. German losses were estimated at about 110 soldiers.

– – –

The storm groups of 138th Rifle Division made better progress and inflicted more damage on the German defences:

> Our storm groups slowly but surely moved forward, destroying and smoking the enemy out of the basements of ruined buildings.

> At 1400 an enemy group of about 80 soldiers with two medium tanks counterattacked 344th Rifle Regiment on our left flank from Podgornaya Street. This enemy counterattack was beaten off with heavy losses for them. One of the German tanks in the counterattack was burnt out by our fire.

> Overcoming the enemy defences, the right flank of 138th Rifle Division reached the intersection of Tsentralnaya and Dublinskaya Streets, while the left flank reached the intersection of Podgornaya and Tsekhovaya Streets.

> All regiments of the division continue to move in a western direction, destroying the enemy.

> Master Sergeant Ponamarev, of 768th Rifle Regiment, rushed into the enemy dug-outs, bayoneted 8 Germans and shot 14 more with his submachine-gun. He single-handedly captured 3 light machine-guns and took one German prisoner. The captured German had been moved to this sector on 10 January from 305. Infanterie-Division. Trophies for the day: 9 mortars, 3 heavy and 9 light machine-guns, 4 submachine-guns, up to 100 rifles, 1000 mortar rounds, over 1000 grenades and up to 2000 rifle cartridges.

Attack of 138th Rifle Division, 14 January, 1943.

Sergeant A.G. Ponamarev, a squad commander in 768th Rifle Regiment, together with four soldiers, was the first in his regiment to cross the German line along the railway embankment. Working his way under some railroad wagons, Ponamarev used grenades to blast his way toward a German trench and destroyed a machine-gun there. Ponamarev's group seized several dug-outs and took three prisoners. Ponamarev was awarded the Order of Lenin. Lyudnikov's storm groups continued to press into the German defences.

Also operating skilfully during the assault were gunners and mortarmen who deployed their guns alongside the infantry so as to support them with fire. A 45mm gun of the artillery battery of 344th Regiment, commanded by Sergeant P.G. Ratanova, moved forward with the infantry and surprised the German defenders from a distance of 100-150 metres. The gunner, Junior-Sergeant G.G. Garbuz, and crewmen Privates V. Rabakidze and I. Mershchinsky, worked quickly and dexterously, destroying a tank, 2 machine-guns and over 10 Germans.

15 January, 1943

The day was quieter than normal. Whilst firmly holding their defensive line, units of 90th Rifle Regiment placed machine-gun and mortar barrages on German positions that had been detected. The regiment had no losses and possessed 21 active bayonets.

241st Rifle Regiment continued to defend the recently acquired Dom 83 and 84, laid down heavy fire to suppress German emplacements, scattered a group of 20 German soldiers and destroyed 2 dug-outs near the green fuel tank. The regiment lost 4 men and was left with 35 active bayonets.

The men of 161st Rifle Regiment continued to strengthen their defensive sector, bombarded German emplacements and reconnoitred towards the bakery while at the same time preparing to

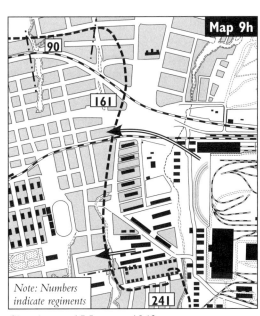

Note: Numbers indicate regiments

Situation on 15 January, 1943.

capture it. However, the Germans were loathe to let the regiment have any peace. At 0130 hours, a German platoon counterattacked its right flank from the south-western corner of the Barrikady factory and the red houses south of the bakery. The counterattack was beaten off at 0300 hours. At 0930, the movement of individual groups and single soldiers near Dom 99 and 100 was observed. Soviet records reckoned German losses at about 40, plus one gun and two machine-guns knocked out.

– – –

Major Poetsch, I./Grenadier-Regiment 212, reports about the transfer of his unit:

The last units of the division[2] were transferred on 15 January, 1943 into the previous baggage train area of Grenadier-Regiment 226, west of the 'White House', with a front to the west. All elements of the division were consolidated into Grenadier-Regiment 212; at the end of January, the division wouldn't even have the strength of a battalion.

2. Former 79. Infanterie-Division

Amongst others still alive at this time were Oberst Eichler[3], Majors Buchholz[4], Gottsmann[5], Liedtke[6], Poetsch, Schuchardt[7] and pioneer Hauptmann Welz, as well as Hauptmanns Gordner[8] and Krah, Rittmeister von Braband[9], von Lucke[10] and von Raab, Oberleutnants Hess, Nittler[11], Ries, Sander and Reissner, Leutnant Bretz, Oberfeldwebel Stumpf and Feldwebel Wolff[12] from 5./212.

16 January, 1943

While the two other regiments held the line, 161st Rifle Regiment launched a fresh attack on the bakery. During an advance towards the railway fork at midnight, two of its storm groups were counterattacked by a group of about 40 German soldiers from the south-western corner of the Barrikady factory. The counterattack was repeated at 0230 hours when a platoon-strength force struck the regiment's storm groups but fire from machine-guns, mortars and artillery repelled the Germans. In the face of heavy fire from several directions, the storm groups continued to advance towards the group of houses south of the bakery and managed to seize one, in which it consolidated and prepared to take the bakery itself. Losses of 20 men were incurred. The regiment still possessed 93 active bayonets. The

The ruins of the settlement south of Bread Factory No. 2. Sections of the streets have collapsed into the sewers.

3. Eichler, Oberst Richard, RK, DKiG; Gr.Rgt.212; born 3 April, 1943 in Frankenberg. Missing in action, 31 January, 1943 in Stalingrad.
4. Buchholz, Major Walter, DKiG; Gr.Rgt.212; born 17 April 1906 in Wiesbaden. Missing in action, January 1943 in Stalingrad.
5. Gottsmann, Major Hans, I./Art.Rgt.179; born 9 October 1913. Missing in action, January 1943 in Stalingrad.
6. Liedtke, Major Oskar, II./Art.Rgt.179; born 8 August, 1905, in Rosenberg. Died 9 May, 1943 in Yelabuga POW camp.
7. Schuchardt, Oberstleutnant Siegfried, DKiG; Gr.Rgt.226; born 3 April, 1894 in Görng. Missing in action, January 1943 in Stalingrad.
8. Gordner, Hauptmann Friedhelm, DKiG; Gr.Rgt.212; born 11 April 1915. Missing in action, January 1943 in Stalingrad.
9. Braband, Rittmeister Karl, Radf.Abt.179; born 24 May, 1917 in Neustadt. Missing in action, January 1943 in Stalingrad.
10. Lucke, Rittmeister Hans von, Radf.Abt.179; born 22 January, 1912 in Mückenhain. Missing in action, February 1943 in Stalingrad.
11. Nittler, Oberleutnant Robert, RK; 3./Gr.Rgt.212; born 8 March, 1921 in Dillingen. Killed in action, 14-16 January, 1943 in Stalingrad.
12. Wolff, Oberleutnant, Rudolf, Stab Gr.Rgt.208; born 3 March, 1919 in Weidenthal. Missing in action, January 1943 in Stalingrad.

Soviet riflemen kept an eye on the Germans opposite and noticed what seemed to be reinforcements arriving or forces being redeployed: at 0800 hours, a group of 16-20 German soldiers ran towards the south-western corner of the Barrikady factory; at 1405 hours, two groups of Germans, 7 and 15 in number, were seen moving from there to the bakery.

Using its entire arsenal, 90th Rifle Regiment fired upon the German front-line to draw their fire so as to support the offensive actions of 161st Rifle Regiment. It lost 1 man to wounds and possessed 25 active bayonets at the end of the day.

241st Rifle Regiment carried out demonstrative actions and active reconnaissance, destroyed two German dug-outs with artillery and mortar fire, seized them and then consolidated in them. It also lost 1 man to wounds. Active bayonets: 34 men.

German losses were estimated to be about 50 soldiers. Two machine-guns were captured and 4 dug-outs were destroyed by artillery and mortar fire.

17 January, 1943

The storm groups of 95th Rifle Division overcame persistent German resistance and slowly moved ahead. Most German fire was coming from the bakery, the south-western corner of the Barrikady factory, Dom 111, 112 and the railway fork.

241st Rifle Regiment continued to defend its previous positions, placed fire on German soldiers and firing points, and supported the attack of the division's other units. It destroyed two dug-outs with mortars and suffered losses of 1 dead and 9 wounded. Active bayonets: 24.

Overcoming stubborn German resistance, 161st Rifle Regiment regrouped its storm groups for an advance towards Skulpturny. Covered by fire from all kinds of weapons, they slowly moved forward. Its position on the division's left wing exposed it to the brunt of the German defences and counterattacks. At 0100 hours, a platoon of Germans counterattacked the storm groups from the houses south of the bakery. Mortar fire at 0205 hours repelled the counterattack with heavy losses for the Germans. At 1420 hours, the movement of about 50-60 German soldiers in camouflaged parkas was noticed near the school. At 1440 hours, about two platoons of German infantry were noticed on Tiraspolskaya and Buguruslanskaya Streets. All signs pointed towards fiercer German counterattacks. At the end of the day, the regiment's losses and strength were still being counted.

Units of 90th Rifle Regiment carried out reconnaissance and slowly moved forward by destroying German emplacements with machine-gun and mortar fire. The division's estimate of German losses was about 60 soldiers, while 1 machine-gun and 3 dug-outs were destroyed.

- - -

One of the German counterattacks was led by Hauptmann Helmut Schwarz, former adjutant, one-time commander of II./ Grenadier-Regiment 578 and mostly recently the man responsible for turning rear echelon men into combat-ready soldiers. Major Rettenmaier recounts what befell him:

> The fate of the regimental adjutant, Hauptmann Schwarz, should be recorded. In a self-sacrificing manner, he carried through the retraining of men from the supply trains and artillery. After this assignment was completely finished, he reported himself at the front on 12 January and was allocated a sector on the division's right boundary. The Russians had trickled through a long gully (Baumschlacht) [Tree Gully] and

Hptm. Helmut Schwarz

occupied the white houses (Teehäuser). He wanted to recapture these houses with a few men. In doing so, he was killed by a heart shot on 17 January. With him, his parents had lost their third and last son[13]. Hauptmann Schwarz was a nobleman, a marvellous character, someone you had to admire for his knowledge and ability. His death affected everyone – both officers and men – very deeply.

- - -

The war diary of 138th Rifle Division notes an interesting occurrence on this day:

> On 17 January, 344th Rifle Regiment took 4 prisoners from 545th Infantry Regiment of 389th Infantry Division, which was formed into a separate company of 130 men on 14 January, 1943 and moved over to our sector from another part of the front.

Unit integrity was now a low priority for the Germans. The divisions' defensive lines were being constantly punctured by Soviet attacks and they found themselves unable to hold certain sectors with a sufficient density of men. This was remedied by extracting units from quieter areas and inserting them into the tormented front-line in the Barrikady and Krasny Oktyabr settlements.

- - -

At 1120 hours, a German transport plane dropped 7 cargo parachutes in the Krasny Oktyabr settlement. The previous day, a plane had even landed near Hill 107.2 and on 18 January, at 1405 hours, seven transport planes would land near Vishnevaya Gully. The pressure being applied to the western face of the Stalingrad pocket by Rokossovsky's armies had led to the loss of Pitomnik, the main German airfield, on the morning of 16 January, and seriously threatened Gumrak airfield. On 17 January, landings at Gumrak were temporarily suspended when a pilot erroneously reported that German troops were retreating past it. This forced aircraft to use Stalingradski, a small airfield on the western fringes of the city. Unteroffizier Rombach, Artillerie-Regiment 305, witnessed the calamitous loss of Pitomnik airfield:

> Because our allies, particularly the Romanians, had no heavy weapons, no modern artillery pieces, the II. Abteilung – meaning us – were shifted to Pitomnik to support the Romanians and defend the airfields located there. We experienced the entire drama of the surrounded soldiers there. The runway was bombed again and again by aircraft and shot up by artillery. The pioneers were just able to keep the runway in working order to some degree. When a plane landed, the sick and wounded soldiers came over to the machine to be flown out of the pocket. The field police tried to prevent an onrush on the planes by force of arms. Horrific scenes were played out there. As a consequence of ammunition shortages and Russian superiority, we had to give up the airport together with the Romanians soldiers. We moved back into our old positions in Stalingrad-North near the tractor factory.

Amongst the pioneer units that had kept Pitomnik functional was Pionier-Bataillon 389, which also included the remnants of Hauptmann Büch's Pionier-Bataillon 45. Inspiring their men as always was the indefatigable and all but indestructible Oberleutnant Walter Heinrich, commander of 2. Kompanie, and the equally valiant Oberleutnant Max Bunz[14], commander of 1. Kompanie. Maintaining the runway was an exhausting business,

---

13. Of his two younger brothers, Herbert was killed but his body could not be recovered, so was declared dead by Amtsgericht Stuttgart, while Johann was killed in a fatal accident on 16 July, 1941 in Agouleme, France.

14. Bunz, Oberleutnant Max, DKiG; 1./Pi.Btl.45; born 10 July, 1914 in Ulm/Donau. Missing in action, 23 January, 1943 in Stalingrad. See Appendix 2 (page 570) for more details.

particularly on the ever-shrinking rations. On 13 January, the unthinkable happened: a Soviet shell exploded not far from Oberleutnant Heinrich and he collapsed. For an instant his men feared the worse but they saw him moving. Miraculously, he had not been killed but had suffered severe shrapnel wounds to his right leg. His chances of survival were slim: the appalling conditions in the dressing stations offered little hope of first-class treatment, despite the doctors' best efforts, and aircraft were only able to fly out a minuscule proportion of the wounded. Heinrich lay in hospital for almost 10 days, until the possibility of being flown out had realistically vanished. Then, his guardian angel once again intervened: one of the pilots was an old school mate from Ulm, and so, on 22 January, Heinrich escaped the Stalingrad pocket by the slimmest of margins.

– – –

On 17 January, Rokossovsky called a halt so his forces could regroup. The German troops out on the steppe gained a small breathing space. But not for long. The final stage of Operation Koltso would begin on 22 January, 1943.

18 January, 1943

Units of 90th Rifle Regiment began carrying out Combat Order No. 08. They overcame German resistance, moved ahead 250-300 metres and captured two houses and some dug-outs in which they consolidated. Its losses were 5 killed and 7 wounded.

241st Rifle Regiment held their defensive sector, improved it with engineering methods and carried out demonstrative actions. It had no losses.

At 0200 hours, 161st Rifle Regiment began a surprise attack with two storm groups but was struck with small arms and machine-gun fire from Germans in the school – the area between Tiraspolskaya and Buguruslanskaya Streets – the railway fork and the south-western corner of the Barrikady factory. At 0240 hours, a German force of about one and a half companies counterattacked 161st Rifle Regiment from the school and the factory's south-western corner. They approached to within grenade-throwing distance but were beaten off by violent fire and volleys of grenades. The Germans were reported to have lost about 60 men killed while the rest scattered. The storm groups overcame stubborn resistance, moved slowly forward, dislodged the German defenders from three houses and then consolidated in them. Fire from mortars and artillery also destroyed 4 pillboxes and dug-outs. Especially distinguishing themselves in this fighting were Junior-Sergeant Burlakov, who was the first to rush a house in which he killed 15 Germans with grenades and captured a light machine-gun, and Junior-Politruk Rodin, who killed 12

Attack of 90th and 161st Rifle Regiment, 18 January, 1943.

German soldiers with his submachine-gun and grenades. At 0850 hours, a concentration of Germans was noticed, up to a battalion in strength, near the south-eastern edge of the Barrikady settlement. Rocket fire was quickly called in on them and they scattered. The Germans struck back in the afternoon: at 1410 hours, the command post of 161st Rifle Regiment was fired on by an anti-tank gun; and at 1600 hours, a force of 150 Germans launched a counterattack from the railway fork and the school. It was eventually repelled with artillery and mortars. The units of 161st Rifle Regiment were then filled up with replacements to implement Order No. 02. Losses of the regiment: 22 men.

German losses were calculated at about 170 soldiers, while one 81mm mortar, 3 light machine-guns, 34 rifles, 6 submachine-guns and 2 telephone sets were captured.

19 January, 1943

The men of 241st Rifle Regiment held their defensive sector and carried out demonstrative actions. Two storm groups of 161st Rifle Regiment surmounted stubborn German resistance, advanced 150 metres, captured 5 houses, destroyed 2 dug-outs with artillery and mortar fire, consolidated upon the attained line and then reconnoitred German emplacements in preparation to continue its mission. Losses were high, 26 men, but the regiment still had 156 active bayonets.

Overcoming stiff fire on its left flank, 90th Rifle Regiment advanced 300 metres and captured some structures at the crossroads of Kazachya and Aivazovskaya Streets, consolidated in them, and carried out reconnaissance for forthcoming actions. Losses for the day were 10 killed and 21 wounded. At 1015 hours, observers spotted up to 2 companies of German infantry south of the Barrikady settlement, in the area of the cemetery. They were scattered by artillery and mortar fire. And at 1320 hours, near the letter 'M' of Melitopolskaya Street, a platoon of German infantry was observed.

Russian sources place German losses at 70 soldiers, while artillery and mortar fire destroyed 8 emplacements and knocked out a 37mm gun with a direct hit. One heavy machine-gun, 1 light machine-gun and 1 37mm gun were captured.

- - -

The fierce fighting on 138th Rifle Division's sector was summed up in two sentences: "During the day, heavy battles continued which often turned into hand-to-hand combat. We moved forward a little."

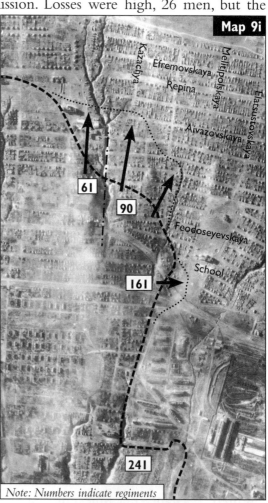

Note: Numbers indicate regiments

Situation south of the Barrikady, 19 January, 1943.

20 January, 1943

Using every weapon at its disposal, 241st Rifle Regiment placed fire on the German front-line to support the attacks of 161st and 90th Rifle Regiments. It suffered no losses.

At 2230 the previous night, a dozen Germans clad in camouflaged parkas tried to approach the forward line of 161st Rifle Regiment by crawling on all fours. The Soviet soldiers waited until they were close before tossing grenades at them. The Germans were wiped out. Early in the morning, the regiment carried out an attack with three storm groups, blockaded two buildings and at 0400 hours swiftly seized them and two nearby dug-outs. They advanced a further 30 metres to Feodoseyevskaya Street: they were struck by flanking machine-gun fire, pinned down and forced to dig in where they lay. Its losses were 8 men. Active bayonets were 135.

With two storm groups, 90th Rifle Regiment captured two buildings on Aivazovskaya Street. Overcoming German resistance, the right flank reached the crossroads of Aivazovskaya and Melitopolskaya Streets but was pinned down by heavy fire. The left flank had no success, so it held its previous positions. Casualties were severe: 10 killed and 28 wounded, leaving the regiment with 78 active bayonets. At 1000 hours, a group of 12 Germans tried to approach the regiment's line, but 10 of them were killed by machine-guns and mortar fire, while only two made it back.

Combat Report No. 40 from 95th Rifle Division noted that "the enemy offers stubborn fire resistance, clinging to each building while placing small arms, machine-gun and methodical mortar fire on our attacking units from the south-western corner of the Barrikady factory, the school and the bathhouse". It reported German losses as about 30 soldiers, fewer than it had suffered. Based on specific data for 19 January, the following trophies were captured: 3 light machine-guns, 5 rifles, 3500 cartridges and other materiel.

– – –

Further south, 138th Rifle Division also found the going very tough: "The enemy offers strong resistance and lays down murderous rifle and machine-gun fire. Our battle groups overcame the enemy defences and moved forward."

21 January, 1943

While defending its sector, 241st Rifle Regiment closely observed the Germans and then placed small arms and machine-gun fire on emplacements and personnel that had been detected. Losses in the regiment were light: 2 wounded. Active bayonets: 89.

On 161st Rifle Regiment's sector, small groups of Germans were noticed in the bakery and on the south-western edge of the Barrikady factory at 0300 hours, but no attacks eventuated. During the day, the regiment's storm groups captured 15 houses on Feodoseyevskaya Street which had been turned into pillboxes. Most German fire on this sector came from the school, the Barrikady factory, Efremovskaya Street and the bathhouse. From 1100 hours, the storm groups consolidated upon the attained line and then carried out preparations for the furtherance of its combat mission. Losses of regiment personnel were 22 men, leaving 153 active bayonets.

On the sector of 90th Rifle Regiment, the Germans tried to launch a counterattack at 0220 hours with small groups towards Elatsustovskaya and Efremovskaya Streets but they were beaten off. The regiment's storm groups carried out their mission by driving the

Germans from their dug-outs and trenches. They advanced 200 metres and seized Repina Street. German attempts to counterattack were repulsed and the regiment consolidated upon the attained line. Its casualties were 13 men and it still had 52 active bayonets.

Trophies captured by 95th Rifle Division were 1 37mm anti-tank gun, 1 81mm mortar, 5 light machine-guns, 10 rifles, 1 submachine-gun, 3000 rifle cartridges and also 8 prisoners.

At 1030 hours, there was an unusual occurrence, an event that used to be the norm. German bombers made two bombing runs on the eastern bank of the Volga. Damage to Soviet installations was light but the main effect was to slightly boost German morale.

22 January, 1943

While 241st Rifle Regiment held its positions (and suffered no losses), the other two regiments continued to chip away at the German defences. Throughout the day, storm group of 161st Rifle Regiment reached Gdovskaya Street at the letter 'K', where they blockaded 6 small houses, captured them and consolidated in them. At 1300 observers noticed small groups of German soldiers dashing from the railway fork to the nameless ravine. The regiment lost 4 men and possessed 119 active bayonets.

At 0630 hours, a new German strongpoint was detected on the sector of 90th Rifle Regiment – a 37mm gun near the bathhouse fired into the regiment's left flank. During the day, storm groups carried out their assigned mission. In swift attacks, they advanced 50-70 metres along Repina Street, pushed through German fire coming from Elatsustovskaya and Efremovskaya Streets and consolidated upon the attained line. Losses in the regiment were 7 dead and 5 wounded, active bayonets were 40.

– – –

Out on the steppe, the final stage of Operation Koltso began. Rifle units of 57th Army pressed in from the south-west on a 4km-wide front along the railway line, broke through at Voroponovo Railway Station and marched towards Stalingrad-South. The German units were simply incapable of closing the yawning gap. On that sector, ammunition was low and troops could not be brought in from other areas. The end was coming and Paulus knew it. That night, he sent a message to Hitler via OKH:

> Rations exhausted. Over 12,000 unattended wounded in the pocket. What orders should I give to troops who have no more ammunition and are subjected to mass attacks supported by heavy artillery fire? The quickest decision is necessary since disintegration is already starting in some places. Confidence in the leadership still exists, however.

Hitler's reply was blunt:

> Surrender is out of the question.
> The troops will defend themselves to the last. If possible, the size of the fortress is to be reduced so that it can be held by the troops still capable of fighting.
> The courage and endurance of the fortress have made it possible to establish a new front and begin preparing a counteroffensive. Thereby, 6. Armee has made an historic contribution to Germany's greatest struggle.

The German defensive front to the west began to fall apart and soon, the remnants of once proud divisions would retreat to the east, streaming into the horrific ruins of the city to seek shelter until the nightmare was over.

23 January, 1943

The gruelling battle for each building continued in Stalingrad-North. During the day, 241st Rifle Regiment placed methodical fire from 45mm guns and mortars on German emplacements, while volleys from 120mm batteries scattered and partially destroyed two German groups near the bakery and suppressed fire from three emplacements on the factory's south-eastern corner. A feint attack was also carried out with a smoke screen that lasted for an hour. As the smoke covered the battlefield, the Soviets fired every sort of weapon at the German front-line. The regiment's losses were 3 men and it still had 86 active bayonets.

At 0800 hours, storm groups of 90th Rifle Regiment – supported by 45mm and 76mm guns and mortars – began blockading emplacements and houses but as a result of heavy fire, particularly from a flanking machine-gun, it had no success. They continued to carry out reconnaissance, suppression and destruction of German emplacements holding up the advance. The regiment lost 4 men and was left with 36 active bayonets.

In the face of German defensive fire, units of 161st Rifle Regiment advanced 50 metres along Gdovskaya Street, captured 3 houses and destroyed their garrisons (about 20 soldiers). They then consolidated, carried out reconnaissance and worked over German emplacements with artillery in preparation for continuation of the task. One man became a casualty. The regiment still possessed 179 active bayonets.

German losses were put at about 30 soldiers, with 3 light machine-guns and 20 rifles captured. It was also reported that the ampulomet platoons had incinerated 3 houses and a dug-out, and deluged the Germans with 1500 propaganda leaflets fired in glass jars. At 1500 hours, a German transport plane dropped 5 supply parachutes in the area of 241st Rifle Regiment and the neighbouring 400th Separate Machine-Gun and Artillery Battalion.

Combat Report No. 46 of 95th Rifle Division contains an informative summary of the German units facing its three rifle regiments:

> Along the division's front, the stubbornly defending battered elements of 305th Infantry Division continue to fight in the following groupings: on the sector of 241st Rifle Regiment is 2nd Battalion/576th Infantry Regiment; on the sector of 161st Rifle Regiment is 212th Infantry Regiment; on the sector of 90th Rifle Regiment is also 212th Infantry Regiment and on the left flank of 90th Rifle Regiment are units of 3rd Battalion/194th Infantry Regiment of 71st Infantry Division. They rely on strongpoints in the south-eastern corner of the Barrikady factory, the bakery, the south-western corner of the Barrikady factory and the railway fork, all overwhelmingly backed by automatic weapons.

24 January, 1943

The units of 241st Rifle Regiment held their positions and suppressed German firing points with 45mm guns, mortars and machine-guns. It suffered no losses. After first suppressing 5 emplacements with artillery and mortars, units of 161st Rifle Regiment tried to advance in a north-western direction against heavy fire, especially flanking machine-guns in the school and the bakery, but without success. Losses were 3 wounded. During the day, 90th Rifle Regiment carried out its mission. After direct-firing 45 and 76mm guns silenced German emplacements, a sudden attack seized two small houses on Repina Street and gained 30-50 metres. Observers spotted movement on neighbouring Efremovskaya Street when a group of 30 German soldiers was discovered in some dug-outs from which individual soldiers had earlier been seen running back and forth. The regiment lost 4 dead and 7 wounded, and was left with 47 active bayonets. German losses were estimated at 30 men, and 3 light machine-guns, 7 rifles and 1 mortar were captured.

At 0900 hours, a German transport plane dumped 5 bales of ammunition by parachute, two of which landed near Gorishny's command post and the other three in no-man's-land.

25 January, 1943

The Germans were quiet during the day and only reacted when attacked. Any Soviet movement was met by fire from small arms, machine-guns and, occasionally, mortars. Gorishny's regiments were also uncharacteristically sedate on this day. The men of 241st Rifle Regiment destroyed German emplacements near the bakery and the south-western corner of the Barrikady factory with direct-firing 45mm guns. Also, the regiment continued to improve its defences and doubled observation. Losses of the regiment were 1 dead and 2 wounded. It had 83 active bayonets. 161st Rifle Regiment defended and improved its sector, carried out reconnaissance by observation and fired on German emplacements and personnel. No losses were incurred. 90th Rifle Regiment defended its captured sector, established minefields on probable directions of German attacks, strung out barbed wire and kept the Germans under fire. No losses. Active bayonets: 47.

All German movements were of great interest to Soviet observers. Gorishny's men established that 6 German vehicles carrying soldiers were seen moving towards the Silikat factory near a group of houses between a ravine and garden close to the factory itself. A German tank was also located at the south-western corner of the garden.

26 January, 1943

While 95th Rifle Division prepared to implement Combat Order No. 3, its regiments also carried out their normal daily tasks. 241st Rifle Regiment held its positions and bombarded German emplacements detected near Dom 99, 100, the bakery and the Barrikady factory. No losses were incurred. 161st Rifle Regiment improved its defences while simultaneously firing all kinds of weapons at German troop concentrations and emplacements. The regiment carried out reconnaissance from 1100 hours, suffering losses of 2 wounded. 90th Rifle Regiment held the line and destroyed German personnel and emplacements. Fire from its mortars and artillery destroyed one motor vehicle and suppressed the fire of four emplacements. One man was wounded.

– – –

Down south, other units of 62nd Army took Mamayev Kurgan once and for all. Tanks of 21st Army – coming from the west – linked up with Rodimtsev's guardsmen in the Krasny Oktyabr settlement and split the pocket in two. Army commander Chuikov poignantly describes the union between his troops and those of Rokossovsky's Don Front:

> January 26 dawned – the day of the long-awaited link-up between the troops of 62nd Army and units of Batov's[15] and Chistyakov's[16] armies, advancing from the west. This was how the meeting took place.

---

15. Batov, General-Lieutenant Pavel Ivanovich, HotSU; 65th Army; born 1 June, 1897 in Filisovo. Died 19 April, 1985.

16. Chistyakov, Colonel-General Ivan Mikhailovich, HotSU; 21st Army; born 27 September, 1900 in Otrubnivo. Died 7 March, 1979.

The link-up of 21st Army with 62nd Army, 26 January, 1943.

At dawn it was reported from an observation post that the Germans were rushing about in panic, the roar of engines could be heard, men in Red Army uniforms appeared… Heavy tanks could be seen coming down a hillside. On the tanks were inscriptions: 'Chelyabinsk Collective Farmer, Urals Metal-Worker…

Guardsmen of Rodimtsev's division ran forward with a red flag.

This joyous, moving encounter took place at 7.20am near the Krasny Oktyabr settlement. Captain A.F. Gushchin handed representatives of the units of Batov's army the banner, on the red cloth of which was written: 'A token of our meeting on 26.1.1943'.

The eyes of the hardened soldiers who met were filled with tears of joy.

Guards Captain P. Usenko told General Rodimtsev, who had now arrived, that he had accepted the banner from his renowned guardsmen.

'Tell your commander,' said General Rodimtsev, 'that it is a happy day for us: after five months of heavy and stubborn fighting we have finally met!'

Heavy tanks came up, and the crews, leaning out of the turrets, waved their hands in greeting. The powerful machines rolled on, towards the factories."

– – –

Rittmeister Udo Giulini, adjutant of Panzerjäger-Abteilung 305, clearly remembers when the defences in his area dissolved and units took flight:

It was brilliantly clear and bitterly cold as I stood in front of my bunker and observed the area. I had a wide outlook because my bunker lay on a hill near Gorodische, the only wooded elevation that was covered by firs and whose stock of trees I had jealously defended in the pre-Christmas period against those looking for Christmas trees. I was taking in the panorama through binoculars when my heart suddenly stopped: on the snow plains, under the blazing sun to the west, I recognise a marching column. I alerted my commander and together we observed and asked each other what it could probably be. Two of our own panzer divisions were deployed in this direction and both still possessed a few tanks, but they had to be available in their own sectors. Why would they suddenly come back? We called our own division but they knew nothing. Of course. And nothing was known about disengagements.

We called out and signalled but this column continued to march on, undeterred. Suddenly, I noticed that the column was marching in rows of four, like the Russians. Germans always march in rows of three. I got a terrible fright. They were Russians! And already they deployed themselves for combat from the column. They swarmed out, shots fell, machine-guns were brought into position.

Those of us who stood with our front to the east now had to turn around 180 degrees. We mobilised everything that had legs and that could move. The Russians immediately entrenched themselves in the snow. We cleared out during the following night, away from Gorodische and into Stalingrad.

The road was no longer a road, it was a stream of refugees. Panzers rattled past, soldiers were rolled over because they were wounded and could not get out of the way quickly enough. The tank drivers could not make them out in the shoving and crowding, and following tanks then rolled over the men that had already been flattened. They lay flat, like thick paper in the snow. You scurried over them, nobody paid any attention to them. […] Similar too were the dead, frozen as stiff as a board, which we had seen on the infinite snow plains on the advance from the Don to the Volga. German and Russian could barely be differentiated from each other. Such figures were stood upright in the snow. Like signposts. A macabre joke…

– – –

The German pocket had been split in two. This event caused ripples of panic to spread amongst the Germans and Gorishny's observers – ignorant of the fact that the link-up had occurred – recorded the effect on nearby Germans:

At 0730 the movement of individuals and small groups of enemy soldiers from the west into the area of the Barrikady factory was observed.

These groups were covered by artillery fire, part of them being destroyed, the others scattered.

At 1200, south-west of the school on Buguruslanskaya Street, the movement of motor vehicles with trailers in a northern direction was noticed, and 2 enemy tanks were discovered there. Also observed was the chaotic movement of enemy infantry into the areas of Skulpturny and 'Ilyich' hospital, towards the Barrikady factory.

At 1510, near the Silikat, the movement of an enemy column with up to 1000 soldiers was noticed.

At 1540, to the south of Silikat, an enemy group of up to 20 men dug trenches.

Cut off from the rest of 6. Armee, General Strecker's XI. Armeekorps took command of all units in the northern pocket.

27 January, 1943

The formation of the northern pocket really had no effect on the defensive capabilities of 305. Infanterie-Division because its units were holding the same positions, but the inrush of bedraggled and desperate newcomers overwhelmed the rear areas as they sought shelter in overcrowded cellars and tried to acquire any form of sustenance. Rittmeister Giulini recalls this despondent task – and how he found a solution:

Search for accommodation in the city. The only possibility was cellars. Everything else had already been destroyed. The lucky owners of cellars resisted us – against this unwanted influx – with all means. One asked friends, but friendships, as always in desperate situations, are cheap. You rant and raise your voice. Who's that impressing? You threaten to withdraw the only tank defence squads and anti-tank gun platoons and 'lend' them to others. And you know, that helped. We got hold of a small, dirty room beneath a collapsed apartment block, which used to be five-storeys tall.

This had inestimable advantages. Because these apartments blocks consisted of brick walls but had concrete ceilings and concrete floors, this collapsed heap of bricks with sandwich-like layers of concrete between them offered secure protection against bombs and shells of all calibres. Even against direct hits. The whole thing was elastic, it flexed with the impacts, but nothing pierced it; during bombardments, however, the oven doors had to be kept shut so that the air pressure did not spray the oven's burning contents into our nice parlour.

Our shelter in the cellar of this apartment block withstood the heaviest direct attacks. This protection offered by bricks and concrete slabs should be kept in mind. It swayed, to be sure, and teetered and trembled, but nothing got through it.

Like Giulini and his men, most of the German refugees found shelter in the buildings of the Schnellhefter Block. This vast complex was located almost in the centre of the northern pocket and was basically the rear area of all units manning the perimeter. Many staffs also took refuge in the Schnellhefter Block.

– – –

South of the Barrikady factory, it was business as usual for Gorishny's men. Throughout the day, 241st Rifle Regiment fired incessantly at German emplacements and increased observation. Volleys from 82mm mortars suppressed the fire of three German emplacements in the western section of the Barrikady factory, destroying a mortar. Two of the regiment's men were killed, leaving 81 active bayonets.

By 0500 hours, 161st Rifle Regiment had blockaded houses on the approach routes to the school, advanced 50 metres and consolidated upon the attained line. From then on, all fire means were used to suppress and destroy German personnel. In cooperation with 90th Rifle Regiment, it prepared to implement its combat mission. Its losses for the day were 3 killed and 7 wounded. It still possessed 164 active bayonets.

After handing over its sector to 45th Rifle Division and redeploying in new starting positions for the advance, units of 90th Rifle Regiment launched their attack at 0900 hours in individual storm groups and in so doing captured two houses. It seems the Germans withdrew because no trophies were captured. Fire from a mortar battery suppressed two German emplacements. Casualties were 3 killed and 4 wounded, leaving 47 active bayonets.

Observation revealed more German movements: at 0620 hours, in the area of the P-shaped house and south-east of there, a group of soldiers numbering about 80 men was noticed; and during the day, in the area of 'Ilyich' hospital, the movement of individual German infantrymen was observed. Three large groups, each of 10-20 soldiers, were observed moving from the hospital towards the Barrikady factory.

28 January, 1943

In the dark of night, courageous bands of 305. Infanterie-Division soldiers attacked the Soviet positions. At midnight, a counterattack by 20 men from the letter 'G' of Buguruslanskaya Street was beaten off by Gorishny's men, as was another platoon-strength attack at 0100 hours from Okhotnaya Street.

- - -

"After the main body of our army turned its front to the north," wrote General Krylov, "the territory ahead of us – the Barrikady factory and its settlement, with Skulpturny Park – was the scene of our combat operations. The situation here was exactly as it was earlier on the territory of Krasny Oktyabr and enemy resistance was even more bitter. Fighting took place around every clearing, the enemy concealing himself behind every work bench and piece of machinery. In many places we could only make progress with flamethrowers. When we had cleared out a workhall, we still also had to drive the enemy out of the cellars.

"Only on 28 January did our assault troops begin to sink their teeth into the enemy defences on the grounds of the Barrikady factory."

The division that "sank its teeth" into the Barrikady was Gorishny's division but their fangs were blunted by the fierceness of the German defence. The three rifle regiments began their attack at 1100 hours. Having redeployed, 241st Rifle Regiment advanced upon the south-eastern corner of the Barrikady factory. By 1400 hours two storm groups had rushed Workshop 32 [Hall 6e]. German counterattacks continuously crashed into the storm groups from the depot, the stockyard, Workshop 11 and Workshop 42 [Hall 6d], and as a result, the storm groups – which entered the factory with a total of 31 men – lost 13 killed and 17 wounded. Only one soldier survived unscathed. Total losses in the regiment were 45 men, leaving 35 active bayonets.

90th Rifle Regiment advanced towards the bakery, Stalnaya Street and the Barrikady factory. It received a new order at 1425 hours: to follow up the attack of 241st Rifle Regiment. Losses for the tiny unit were heavy: 34 men. Only 13 active bayonets were left.

161st Rifle Regiment advanced towards the south-western corner of the Barrikady factory with the task of capturing the workshops, the depot, the stockyard and Workshop 11. Having pushed through heavy enemy fire from the western part of the bakery they advanced to the edge of the Barrikady factory. They suffered casualties of 43 men but still possessed 124 active bayonets, of which 13 were 82mm mortarmen and 60 were 76mm and 45mm gunners.

The summation of the day's events by 95th Rifle Division was as follows:

> The enemy offers stubborn fire resistance to our advancing storm groups from Workshops 42 [Hall 6d], 32 [Hall 6e], the south-western corner of the Barrikady factory, and flanking fire from the green fuel tank and the school on Buguruslanskaya Street.

General Krylov reported that "on 28 January, we moved forward noticeably, in fact, about 300 to 700 metres. Soldiers of Gorishny's division pushed into the factory grounds and captured the advantageously positioned Workshop 32 in the south-eastern

Riflemen of 95th Rifle Division push towards Hall 6e [Workshop 32] from the south.

Orlov

Above: Soviet troops faced the difficult task of dislodging German units from the tangled wreckage of the factory.

Below: The nightmarish jumble of railway sidings and gun barrels in front of Hall 6d. The railway embankment and concrete boundary fence can be seen cutting diagonally across the bottom left of the photo.

Despite gaining a foothold in the factory by capturing Workshop 32 [Hall 6e], the storm groups of 241st Rifle Regiment struggled to make further progress in the face of bitter German resistance from Workshop 42 [Hall 6d] and the depot, a vast yard filled with railway spurs and stored material.

section of the factory, repulsed two counterattacks but could not hold back the third…

"Just as hard was the fighting around the bakery, the school in the sector of Guriev's Division and other strongpoints. Rodimtsev's guardsmen snatched one foothold after another from the enemy on the northern slopes of Hill 107.5…"

At 2000 hours the Germans near the school counterattacked the left flank of 161st Rifle regiment with a force of 60 men but they were scattered by artillery and mortar fire and partially destroyed.

A Soviet storm group reaches Workshop 32 [Hall 6e].

– – –

To the Germans, the Soviet attacks were the ultimate exacerbation of the already horrific conditions. Artillery shells and rockets whined in throughout the day. Vast numbers of wounded congregated in the factory cellars and outlying settlements to seek food, shelter and treatment for their wounds. Bandages and medicine had run out. Barely any food was left. The predicament of the wounded weighed heavily on those still fit to fight. Front-line soldiers who had witnessed the worst humans could do to each other dreaded going down into the first-aid cellars. Major Rettenmaier reports:

> And how did it look at the dressing stations? On 28 January, a man left the command post to go to the dressing station. He had a through-and-through bullet wound in his thigh. He returned two hours later. With a tearful voice, he reported what he saw there. Wounded men lay everywhere, even out in the open, between them were many dead bodies. No-one was there to attend to the wounded, also, no-one there had the strength to carry out the dead. The doctors no longer had any bandages. 'I want to request that I be allowed to stay with my comrades. But I don't want to be a burden on them. If you help me to climb up the ladder, I'll be able to position myself as a sentry.' Moved to tears by these words, the commander said: 'Look for a little spot here and stay with me.'

The commander, Oberstleutnant Liesecke, took pity on the man.

Unteroffizier Rombach from II./Art.Rgt.305 was fortunate to only suffer light wounds but saw conditions in the dressing stations first-hand when he took a comrade for treatment:

> During the violent Russian attacks at the end of January we received a direct hit on the bunker in which we had our observation post. I was not on duty and remained in the rear corner of the bunker […] The bunker was partly destroyed. I suffered light injuries on both legs and had a large blister on my right hand. It was a real hindrance. Our Sanitätsfeldwebel Jänische treated the blister with a salve and powder. I was very lucky that the blister healed relatively quickly. The wounds on my legs were much worse because lice crawled under the bandages and prevented the wounds from healing quickly.
>
> The wounded soldiers in the pocket could barely be treated because more and more soldiers were getting wounded or becoming ill. We were lacking in dressings, medication and particularly in heated quarters for the many sick and wounded soldiers. After no more wounded and sick could be flown out – because the airfields had fallen into enemy hands – the main dressing stations overflowed and they lacked the necessary fixtures to adequately treat the many wounded and sick men.

At the end of January 1943 Leutnant Boch[17], the commander of the signals platoon to which I belonged, suffered a very severe wound to his right thigh from a Russian mortar round. I took him to the main dressing station because I hoped to get him some help there. What I saw and experienced there prompted me to bring my comrade back to our bunker because he at least had a bed and the necessary supplies there. Horrifically nightmarish scenes were played out at the main dressing station. Since the airfields had been conquered by the Russians, the wounded could no longer be flown out. The wounded were condemned to certain death. Their bandages were completely riddled with lice. At the main dressing stations the dead and wounded lay helplessly in confusion. As a result of the malnourishment of the soldiers and the deep-frozen earth, the dead could no longer be buried.

29 January, 1943

From 2200 on 28 January until 0730 hours on 29 January, three German counterattacks against 95th Rifle Division from the direction of the green fuel tank and the depths of the Barrikady factory – each with a force of 30 to 50 men – were repelled. As a result of the counterattacks, the Germans captured some dug-outs from which the approach routes to south-eastern part of the Barrikady factory could be covered by fire.

– – –

Soviet forces continued their attacks late in the morning. The divisions of 62nd Army had arrayed themselves to face north and planned to roll up the pocket from the south. General Krylov reports:

> Enemy defence remained strong and tight. The Germans clung to every fortified house. To break the desperate resistance of these condemned men, heavy guns had to be used in direct fire, flamethrowers employed and bombers sent in.
>
> During these days, artillery was used as our main source of firepower as follows: before the attack began, a 30-minute long drumfire was laid down on the entire section of the Barrikady factory occupied by the enemy. Then the artillery supported the attacking soldiers on the sectors that would be cleared of the enemy on this day. In this moment, the fire had to be guided accurately on to the front-line, just as it did throughout the entire battle. Three divisions were attacking on the grounds of the Barrikady factory, so it was important that neighbours weren't hindered and that no chaos or inaccuracy was allowed. Every division commander and even the regiment commanders found themselves at the advanced observation posts.
>
> 'When the hell will they finally give up? It's high time!' blurted out one of our staff officers.
>
> Actually, it was high time for the Germans, or at least for those who wanted to remain alive, to lay down their weapons. But our 62nd Army had for the time being taken few prisoners (from 10 to 27 January, only 139 men). That was far fewer than the other armies of the Don Front. This was probably logical in its own way. The battle that had been fought out for months in Stalingrad reached the highest levels of bitterness. Was it then astonishing that the fascists feared giving themselves up to soldiers of 62nd Army, and expected no mercy from them, even though no-one had the intention of destroying enemy soldiers and officers who had surrendered?

– – –

Relying on their system of strongpoints in the bakery and the Barrikady factory's workshops, the desperate soldiers of 305. Infanterie-Division continued to offer stubborn resistance by launching counterattacks, throwing grenades and placing intensive automatic

---

17. Boch, Oberleutnant Theodor, II./Art.Rgt.305; born 13 July, 1914. No further information known.

Orlov

The same Soviet storm group in operation around Hall 6e [Workshop 32]. This is probably a staged photo.

fire on the attacking units of 90th and 241st Rifle Regiment. Storm groups of these regiments, cooperating with units of 92nd Separate Rifle Brigade, waged fire fights in Workshop 32 during the day and repulsed the counterattacks of small Germans groups. At 1130 hours, two storm groups advanced on German dug-outs 100 metres east of the south-eastern corner of the Barrikady factory. Meeting heavy machine-gun fire from the bakery, the fuel tanks and the depths of the Barrikady factory, the storm groups suffered heavy losses and pulled back to their starting positions. The units of 90th and 241st Rifle Regiments prepared to continue their task. Losses of 90th and 241st Rifle Regiment were 3 and 8 men respectively, while 92nd Separate Rifle Brigade lost 28 men.

Carrying out Combat Order No. 019, 161st Rifle Regiment began its advance at 0800 hours towards the south-western corner of the Barrikady factory. Overcoming stubborn German resistance from the school, the bakery and the nameless gully, one storm group blasted its way forward with grenades and destroyed a group of Germans in that gully. As a result of the offensive actions three houses were captured, while barrages from ampulomets set fire to two houses and two dug-outs. Four German soldiers were taken prisoner and 2 machine-guns were captured. From 1400 hours the regiment prepared for the continuation of its combat mission. It lost 9 men killed and wounded and ended the day with 115 active bayonets, of which 13 were 82 mm mortarmen and 60 were 76mm and 45mm gunners. Soviet estimates put German losses at about 120 soldiers.

– – –

Oberarzt Dr. Konrad Schwarzkopf[18], the battalion doctor of II./Grenadier-Regiment 576, died performing a courageous and selfless act. In murderous artillery fire, Oberarzt Dr.

---

18. Schwarzkopf, Oberarzt Dr. Konrad, II./Gr.Rgt.576; born 18 June 1913 in Fischbach. Killed in action, late January, 1943 in Stalingrad.

Schwarzkopf tried to carry a severely wounded man from the Barrikady factory to a dressing station but both lost their lives when a shell landed right on them.

The unforgiving nature of the fighting can also be seen in the combat journal of 138th Rifle Division:

> At 0200 the division began its advance. At 0250 its battle formations broke through to the southern approaches of the destroyed school house and were involved in heavy bayonet and grenade fighting until 1100, beating back multiple intense enemy counterattacks. As a result of the day's fighting at the southern destroyed school house, our troops suffered heavy losses.
>
> A battalion commander of 344th Rifle Regiment, Senior Lieutenant Chizhov, and his assistant Lieutenant Koloskov, died hero's deaths. Returning from the battlefield were 19 wounded men. In 768th Rifle Regiment, of 10 men, 8 came back wounded, the fate of the other two is unknown. A battalion commander, Captain Petrenko, and two signalmen, continued to defend themselves in dug-outs 60-70 metres east of the school.
>
> Lieutenant Gusev, leader of the battle group from 650th Rifle Regiment, was wounded but continued to lead and came out of the fighting with only two men of his group left alive, while he was also wounded a second time.

– – –

At 1800 hours, Gorishny gave his troops the following order:

> On the night of 29-30.1.43 continue to improve defences of Workshop 32. From the morning of 30.1.43 241st Rifle Regiment, with one company of 348th Separate Machine-Gun and Artillery Battalion, will continue to defend Workshop 32, units of 90th Rifle Regiment – in conjunction with 92nd Separate Rifle Brigade – will continue to advance in the general direction of the south-western corner of the Barrikady factory, and 161st Rifle Regiment will seize the south-western section of the Barrikady factory from the morning of 30 January. 34th Guards Rifle Regiment, from 0300 on 30.1.43, will seize the area of the bakery, and in further cooperation with 161st Rifle Regiment, seize the southern part of the Barrikady factory.

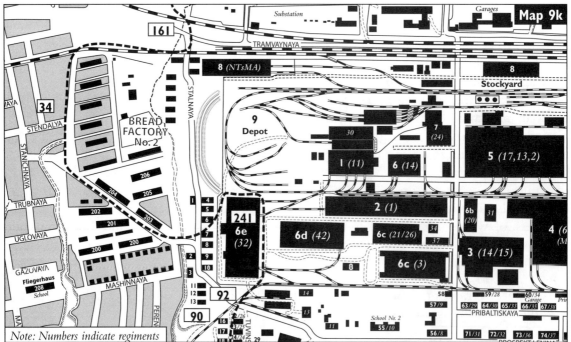

Situation in the southern section of the Barrikady, 29 January, 1943.

30 January, 1943

Hunger was causing some German units to risk their lives in foolhardy forays. To preserve the strength of the combat troops. 6. Armee stopped issuing rations to the wounded on 28 January but centralised distribution of all supplies had since collapsed and individual battalions, companies and platoons were compelled to provision themselves. Some did so by breaking out supplies that had been carefully hoarded over the previous weeks, some begged and scrounged, but most just went hungry. Their only prospect of sustenance was from supply bombs dropped by the Luftwaffe but the starving men had strict orders to hand them in or face a firing squad. The final days in Stalingrad caused base instincts to emerge: without the food in those canisters, they would die, so many Germans soldiers risked death from a kangaroo court to fill their stomachs. The first challenge, however, was to salvage the supply canisters. In impotent frustration they sometimes watched them fall into Soviet territory. Lieutenant Vasili Andreyevich Dvoryaninov, commander of a 76mm gun platoon from 295th Artillery Regiment (138th Rifle Division), recalls the following instance:

> Our battery took up firing position along a railway line. Every evening the motors of German planes were heard over our heads and we quickly got used to it. One time, however, we heard something unusual, some kind of rustling and every noise was amplified, which forced us to drop to the ground. It turned out that an unusual cargo, smelling of sausage, was dropped on our battery's position via parachute, intended for – as we discovered – the surrounded Germans. Though we were full, we could not refuse some tasty drinks, sausages and chocolate, and wished that the German pilots would drop such cargo to us more often.

Such was now the case on the southern edge of the Barrikady. Grenadiers of Regiments 212 and 576 saw a canister float down in no-man's-land and they quickly formed an assault group to retrieve it. They set out at 0030 hours with about 25-30 men. The supply parachute was about 50 metres from the front-line of 2nd Battalion of 161st Rifle Regiment, and not surprisingly, the German group was spotted. Machine-gun fire dropped a few of them and forced the rest to scatter. Undeterred, the Germans made a second attempt to retrieve it at 0430 hours but most of the 30 men were gunned down by the alert Soviet riflemen.

– – –

Storm groups of 34th Guards Rifle Regiment began an attack towards the bakery at 0300 hours, assisted by 161st Rifle Regiment which suppressed German firing points. Having advanced up to the edge of the red buildings, the guardsmen encountered heavy small-arms and machine-gun fire from the bakery and the south-western corner of the Barrikady factory and could make no further progress. At 0620 hours, 161st Rifle Regiment repelled a counterattack of 20 Germans. The regiment's units slowly moved ahead throughout the day and suffered casualties of 5 men.

On the sector of 241st Rifle Regiment, a group of 60 Germans launched an attack from the depths of the factory at 0230 hours towards Workshop 32, but were beaten off with machine-gun fire and grenades. In this workshop, a strongpoint was created under the control of the regiment's commander, Major Budarin. Four 45 mm guns were installed in and around the workshop and fired directly at German dug-outs and firing points in the depths of the factory and near the fuel tanks. Throughout the day, small groups of Germans continuously launched counterattacks against Workshop 32 but they were all repelled.

With a firm foothold in the factory, the units of 241st Rifle Regiment, 90th Rifle Regiment and 92nd Separate Rifle Brigade conducted fire fights with Germans north of

Workshop 32. Attempts to attack into the stockyard, however, did not meet with success after the storm groups were halted by organised fire coming from deeper inside the factory.

German units continued to resist stubbornly, placing accurate fire on Soviet storm groups from some dug-outs near the south-eastern corner of the Barrikady factory, from inside the factory, the south-western corner of the factory, the nameless gully and the bakery. After softening up some of these firing points, 34th Guards Rifle Regiment continued their advance at 1600 hours, overcame German resistance and slowly moving ahead.

Soviet estimates placed German losses for the day at 150 men. Four machine-guns and 10 rifles were captured, 12 dug-outs and pillboxes were destroyed by artillery fire and 8 firing points were suppressed.

Soviet attacks, 30 January, 1943.

Colonel Gorishny's ordered his units to hold the line for the night. From the morning of 31 January, units of 92nd Separate Rifle Brigade were to advance into the factory in a northern direction, 241st and 90th Rifle Regiments would advance in a north-western direction and 161st Rifle Regiment also in a northern direction

– – –

In the closing stages of the battle, every available man was thrown into the fighting, as Gefreiter Josef Zrenner of Pionier-Bataillon 305 reports:

> In the middle of January, after we had burnt our written matter and destroyed everything in our staff, the staff members were assigned to individual combat groups, and I went to a combat group in a northern direction, through the workers settlement that was the housing estate for Red October. I marched on with two comrades, towards the forwardmost strongpoint that had been indicated to us on a staff map, and there were still four infantrymen to whom we were allocated as reinforcements. We then had to hold a sector. On the left was a main road and on the right were large buildings, actually masonry buildings, designated by our units as the white houses, even though they were actually apartment blocks. And there, for the time being, we were housed in the cellars, everything was bombed out, everything, the entire street, everything bombed out. We were in a bunker from which we could survey the entire area. I then went from the shelter into the cellars of the white houses and spoke individually with comrades because I wanted to inform myself about the situation directly on the Volga and what was happening there. There were many wounded men in the cellars, half of all the men were

wounded, without medical personnel, nothing, they screamed because of their wounds, they were just left behind. To the left was another unit with a field-kitchen, they still had things to cook so I grabbed a meal from them and they also still had a radio. I knew the unit from earlier times and they gave me something to eat for my people. In the evening we had to stand guard because the Russians were on the other side of the road. They would sing and stoke up fires at night and get drunk on vodka and because they had snipers, they would fire over at us. Whenever one of us stirred, a shot rang out.

- - -

Major Poetsch, II./Grenadier-Regiment 212, knew it was almost over:

On the evening of 30 January, 1943, it was clear to every single man that only a few more days of resistance could be offered. After cleaning up the southern pocket the Soviets extracted all dispensable divisions from there and concentrated most of them around the still existent northern pocket. The Soviet command wanted to break the resistance in the northern pocket under any circumstances so that they could at last release their divisions. Located in the northern pocket at this time were the feeble remnants of 10 divisions and smaller combat groups that had fought their way through to the northern pocket after the clearance of the southern pocket.

On 30 January, 1943, Oberst Eichler, with about 13 officers of the division and an unspecified number of NCOs and enlisted men from the staff of Regiment 212, broke out of the pocket. The division subsequently consisted of only two companies that were gathered into II./212.

Unteroffizier Rombach, II./Artillerie-Regiment 305, recalls that members of 305. Infanterie-Division made the same decision as Oberst Eichler:

German soldiers pondered how they could evade captivity. The available maps were carefully studied and escape plans and escape routes set down. Despite insufficient clothing and absent march rations, several comrades undertook the attempt to get through to the German front-line. A good comrade of mine, who had been on duty with me in the observation post, set out on the path to the German front with several officers. Of these comrades, namely Leutnant Günther Lieb[19] from Stuttgart, I never heard anything about them again. He therefore didn't pull off the escape and did not survive.

While some risked the impossible odds of a break-out, others wrestled with the grim choice of suicide or Soviet captivity. Rombach continues:

Other comrades sought death by climbing out of the trenches and being immediately shot down by Russian snipers. Other comrades simply blew themselves up in their bunkers. My friend and comrade Erich Krischker and I discussed matters and came to the decision to take a chance and wait and see what happened to us when we were taken prisoner by the Russians. Our commander also decided to allow himself to be taken prisoner.

Rittmeister Giulini sums up what many were thinking:

There was not much to do in these days, so we talked. Hours-long discussions. How do we move into our 'second life' which will begin when we go into captivity? Will the Russians even take prisoners or will they knock everyone off? The boundary, the cusp, the transition to possible captivity, seemed to us to be something for which we had to prepare ourselves and with which we had to carefully proceed, as far as it was at all imaginable.

My commander swore to high heaven – and also said to anyone who wanted to listen – that he would not go into captivity. I was not so certain. One should try it at least. Hitler's instruction that 'a German officer does not go into captivity' did not please us at all. He could

19. Lieb, Leutnant Günther, II./Art.Rgt.305; born 21 May, 1917. Missing in action, January 1943 in Stalingrad.

talk, in his Wolfsschanze headquarters. We were the ones who had to take our lives, not him. In any case, I stole my commander's pistol one night and removed the firing pin. In this way, his plan to shoot himself was foiled for the time being.

Unfortunately this man, upstanding until now, disintegrated further and further. He could only sit and dully brood over the photos of his wife and daughter, and was no longer ready for reasonable discussions, possibly also no longer able to. The others repeatedly played through all scenarios of captivity – possible, conceivable and impossible. Nobody believed in miracles any more. The relief, liberation from outside that was hoped for again and again and expected any hour, was still only a utopian dream.

"We kept hoping for a miracle, namely reinforcements from the air or through a renewed attack by relief troops who would liberate us from the pocket," remembers Rombach. Feldarzt Dr. Schöpf, the doctor from Rombach's battalion, took a more pragmatic view:

> The company commander, Major K. dreamed that we would be relieved, as we all did. I doubted this, however, and declared that I would let my beard grow until the 'relief'. I did not find the beard handsome.
>
> On 30 January, 1943, Göring delivered a speech on the radio about the heroes of Stalingrad where he said that they 'would go down in history'. I said out loud: 'Go down, yes, but not in history!' Major K. screamed at me, said I was a defeatist and threatened to drag me in front of a court-martial.

Reichsmarschall Hermann Göring's so-called 'funeral oration' for 6. Armee was delivered in Berlin on the tenth anniversary of the National Socialists Party's assumption to power. In an effort to prepare the German people for the forthcoming disaster and to spin the catastrophic loss of an entire army into a modern heroic epic, Göring delivered an address befitting a funeral – except in this case, the corpse was still alive to hear the truth being distorted, to hear its deeds and sacrifice being mythologised. Many in 6. Armee were disgusted by Göring's insensitivity and everyone now realised that there was absolutely no hope of being rescued. Gefreiter Zrenner, Pionier-Bataillon 305, clearly recalls how he felt:

> I heard the radio and stood there because someone was speaking, and it was Göring's speech. Göring said […] something like future generations will remember the historic battle of our soldiers in Stalingrad, almost like the Spartans during the battle of Thermopylae. 'Wanderer, if you come to Sparta, say you have seen us lying here'. That is the meaning of what Göring said. [It was] terrible that we had been given up on by our highest military leadership. That we already no longer existed, that we had been abandoned. We had already been written off as lost.

In the darkness of his cellar, Zrenner looked around to gauge the other men's reactions. Many were wounded and displayed no outward emotion, and it was impossible to see what the few healthy men were thinking because their filthy, bearded faces were sullen masks. The 'Stalingrad heroes' in Zrenner's cellar absorbed the fact that they had been abandoned and contemplated the gloomy future.

31 January, 1943

Utilising the safety of darkness, small German groups continuously attacked the units of 92nd Separate Rifle Brigade, 90th and 241st Rifle Regiments, particularly those defending Workshop 32 and the approach routes to it. German assault groups threw grenades, smoke bombs and explosives into the workshop under cover of others spraying small-arms, submachine-gun and machine-gun fire from the western fuel tanks and the factory buildings to the north and north-west of Workshop 32. At 2340 hours, utilising a smoke screen, groups of 20-30 Germans tried to seize Workshop 32 from several directions. Grenades and submachine-gun fire killed and wounded some, others scattered. After that, Soviet 120mm mortars laid a standing barrage on the area west of the fuel tanks and north of Workshop 32.

- - -

General Krylov recounts 62nd Army's plan of attack for the day:

Bitter combat continued in the industrial district. How difficult it was to make progress there is apparent by the army's plan of engagement for 31 January. The most important units were set the following limited tasks:

Gorishny's Division, with the battalion of 92nd Rifle Brigade attached to it, would use Workshop 32 as their jumping-off position and advance to the central part of the Barrikady factory and to Pribaltiskaya street, meeting up with the troops of 156th Fortified Area (the garrison of this district, our only reserve, was sent into the attack);

Sokolov's Division, with a regiment of 13th Guards Division, would attack the enemy in the south-west section of the Barrikady factory and merge their right flank with Gorishny's troops, as a result of which the encirclement of the strongpoints in Stalnaya Street – bakery would be completed;

The divisions of Rodimtsev and Guriev would advance together and reach Tsentralnaya street…

All of this looked trivial on the large-scale city map. And I must still add that not everything we planned on this day actually eventuated. Guriev's guardsmen, for example, were only able to reach Tsentralnaya street the following day.

- - -

The staff of 95th Rifle Division communicated with their units in Workshop 32 via three wire lines that had been laid, and with those around the workshop via 4 radio sets. The telephone and radio links worked perfectly throughout the night but in the morning something odd began to happen. First, telecommunications were interrupted at 0700 hours. Five minutes later, all 4 radios went dead. A few seconds later, a tremendous explosion rang out, the stupendous blast splitting the clamour of battle and shaking the factory to its foundations. The ceiling trusses and thick masonry walls of the eastern and north-eastern sections of Workshop 32 broke apart and collapsed on the Soviet defenders below, causing grievous casualties. At that same moment, a large group of Germans rushed into the workshop shouting: "Russians, surrender!" What had happened? At some stage, either before they fell back from the workshop on 28 January or in clandestine nocturnal operations, the Germans had positioned large demolition bombs in the workhall – they must have been massive to bring down the walls – and attacked simultaneously with their detonation. Combat Report No. 62 from 95th Rifle Division described this event:

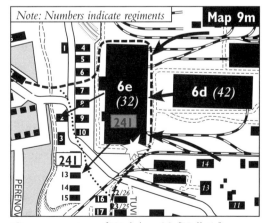

German recapture of Workshop 32 [Hall 6e].

Between 0705 and 0710, several fougasse exploded, and as a result, the ceiling and walls of the eastern and north-eastern section of Workshop 32 broke away. At this time large enemy groups attacked the workshop from several directions and captured it.

Laying down cover fire, the shell-shocked Soviet survivors abandoned the building and pulled back 100 metres, where they took up defence. Moving back with them were the tattered remnants of 1/348th Separate Machine-Gun and Artillery Battalion. The commander of 241st Rifle Regiment, Major Budarin – who had been supervising the defence of Workshop 32 – lay in a trench in a grave condition after suffering severe contusions. His soldiers had dragged him out from under the rubble before they withdrew. His chief-of-staff, Captain Suslikov, had been blinded.

This courageous attack is almost certainly the same as reported by Major Rettenmaier:

Familie Wittmann

> The final offensive actions of the division took place during the night of 30-31 January. The Russians penetrated into Hall 6. The commander in that sector was Hauptmann Wittmann, his adjutant was Leutnant Bachmann. 'No, the Russians must be kicked out,' said Bachmann. Then he asked for those still capable of taking part. He risked this operation with 12 men and succeeded. The Russians suffered heavy, bloody casualties and left behind 5 new anti-tank guns.
>
> The exemplary combat-readiness had not suffered despite misery and privation. Finally, one more thing should be said: not one case was known to me which should have been punished with discipline. This fact alone is testament to the soldierly spirit in which 305. Infanterie-Division met its end in Stalingrad.

Hauptmann Georg Wittmann, III./Gr.Rgt.577.

Leutnant Bachmann modestly recalls the division's final offensive action in Stalingrad:

> In the last weeks of the Stalingrad pocket, I led a combat group and a few days before the capitulation I destroyed a Russian assault group with my men. They had penetrated into Hall 6, held by us, and amongst other things were equipped with brand-new 4.5cm anti-tank guns.

From 0720 until 1040 hours, the men of 90th, 241st Rifle Regiment and 92nd Separate Rifle Brigade repelled four simultaneous German attacks from the green fuel tanks and Workshop 32, each with a force of 30 to 40 soldiers. Sustaining losses, the Germans fell back to their starting positions.

While these dramatic events were unfolding, two storm groups of 161st Rifle Regiment, from starting positions in Dom 83 and 84, advanced towards the south-eastern edge of the bakery at 0700 hours. Overcoming German resistance, they seized the ruins of two houses and consolidated in them. On the basis of an oral order from army staff, parts of the division switched to rigid defence from 1100 hours. Firing stopped at noon.

In the 24 hours from 1800 hours on 30 January to 1800 hours on 31 January, 95th Rifle Division incurred the following casualties: 90th Rifle Regiment – 12 men; 161st Rifle Regiment – 16 men, of them, 8 were killed and 8 wounded; 241st Rifle Regiment – 22 men. German losses were put at about 100 men. Gorishny's regiments had the following strengths: 90th Rifle Regiment – 20 active bayonets; 161st Rifle Regiment – 87 (of those, 22 were 82mm mortarmen); 241st Rifle Regiment – 49 (of those, 22 were 82mm mortarmen).

The first company of 348th Separate Machine-Gun and Artillery Battalion suffered horrific casualties when Workshop 32 was blown up: 11 killed and 20 wounded.

1 February, 1943

The continuing German opposition incensed the Soviets. Couldn't they see that further resistance was futile? That there was no chance they could win? The Soviets decided to use the sledge hammer technique to finish off the Germans, as General Krylov describes:

> To speed up the attrition of the enemy who had not surrendered and to avoid unnecessary casualties on our side, Front command prepared an artillery bombardment of particular strength – a real firestorm – for the morning of 1 February.

> The artillery of our 62nd Army was also employed within the framework of Front's plan. But both armies encircling the northern pocket from the other direction, particularly the 65th Army under Batov, had much greater striking power. As Marshall of the Artillery V.I. Kazakov[20] wrote in his memoirs, over 170 guns and mortars per kilometre were concentrated along the 6km wide sector west of the industrial district, an unparalleled density at any time.

> The heavy impact of our artillery and Katyushas was supported by the bombers and ground attack aircraft of 16th Air Army.

> 'More than enough!' I heard from our observation posts by telephone and from members of the staff who had gone out to the riverside terrace to have a look.

> The concentration of fire was truly exceptional. North of Krasny Oktyabr, in the direction of the Barrikady and tractor factories, everything seethed from numerous explosions. In the following hours, the command staff of the enemy's northern pocket apparently lost control of his troops. Individual units capitulated independently. In a few sectors the Germans displayed white flags after only 15 minutes of drumfire. But we only found out about all this later

In most sectors, however, the German troops resisted stubbornly, at least initially. Major Poetsch, Grenadier-Regiment 212, reports:

> In the morning hours of the first of February, 1943, a truly spectacular 'inferno' erupted. Among the hundreds of bombs dropped by airplanes were the detonations of shells from hundreds, even thousands, of guns, mortars and Stalin Organs. Every shot from the German side was returned a thousand-fold by the Soviets.

> Because of severe ammunition shortages, the firepower in the pocket waned almost completely, nevertheless, the Soviets only dared to launch their first attack after a continuous destructive fire preparation that lasted about 3 hours. When they then moved off to attack the southern face of the pocket with 38 tanks and several infantry regiments, they were struck by the last reserves of ammunition from what they believed was a dead front-line – a last strong burst of defensive fire from all calibres – so that the attack ground to a halt after only a few hundred metres. Despite the –30 degree cold, the crews of a 15cm cannon under an Oberwachtmeister and a flak gun

---

20. Kazakov, Marshall of the Artillery Vasili Ivanovich, HotSU; born 18 July, 1898 in Filippovo. Died 25 May, 1968.

under a young Leutnant manned theirs guns in shirtsleeves and shot directly at tank after tank. The wrath and hatred on the Soviet side rose immeasurably. The Soviets aborted their attack…

Rittmeister Giulini and his anti-tank men helped repel this attack:

The pocket in the south had already surrendered. We pulled together all the cannon which we still had around our position and shot up 24 Russian tanks on 1 February, 1943. Under normal circumstances this was a mad act and would surely have been worthy of a Knight's Cross, but here and now it was only a twitch. All-round defence. Despair.

Major Poetsch continues his account:

The Soviets […] unleashed a new inferno, even stronger and more powerful than the first. When they relaunched their attack after a further three hours, barely any resistance was offered, particularly as there was no more ammunition available and thousands of wounded suddenly rose up and stood between the lines. – 1701 hours, German time, the once-in-a-lifetime capture took place leading to captivity that would last for seven years and from which only about 3% of the prisoners would survive.

Unteroffizier Richard Trollmann[21], one of Poetsch's men, remembers the first moments of captivity as a time of brutality and callous treatment:

My battalion, with the staff, under the command of Major Poetsch, was deployed 2km west of the 'Red October' factory. I was commander of a machine-gun squad on the staff, to provide protection for them. During the previous days the Russian attacks were repulsed again and again with heavy losses for the Russians and our ammunition slowly came to an end. On 1 February, 1943, we fired off all our ammunition, so we had to pull back into our bunkers. Towards 1400 hours the Russians were at our bunkers and we had to give up. We came out of the bunkers and the Russians took receipt of us. We took with us our blankets, remaining food and cigarettes, which the battalion commander had distributed to us earlier. The Russians completely plundered us. Our watches were snatched, as was our food, identity papers and all personal belongings. Rings were torn from our fingers, and if they were not removed quickly enough, the finger was cut off, as I saw myself. Two people, an Unteroffizier whom I didn't know, and Gefechtsschreiber (clerk at a command post) Gefreiter Faber, were shot by the Russians for no reason. My battalion commander had his uniform jacket torn off and a rucksack, in which he had his meagre possessions, was ripped off his back. Warm boots and winter kit were pulled off us. We cut up our blankets and wrapped them around our feet. Oberleutnant Ries, our last adjutant, still had a pistol in his belt. They tore it from him and smashed him in the face. A Russian senior-lieutenant led Major Poetsch in front of the assembled prisoners. He was tormented on the way by the Russian soldiers without the senior-lieutenant stopping them. While we were assembling here, we received fire from our own machine-guns in the 'Red Barricades'. In the days of 31 January to 1 February, 1943 our casualties were light. Our battalion still had about 100 men. The wounded remained in the positions and continued to defend themselves. The severely wounded were shot by the Russians, as I myself witnessed. Whoever became enfeebled during the march was likewise shot. I saw for myself how 6 or 7 men were killed in this way. The motorcycle messenger, Obergefreiter Baer, was one of those comrades shot. The dead remained lying on the road and were run over by vehicles. I saw a dead officer lying, his head squashed in this way.

Because of the stiff resistance offered, German prisoners taken on this day suffered much more physical abuse than those who would go into captivity the next day.

---

21. Trollmann, Unteroffizier Richard, II./Gr.Rgt.212; born 29 December, 1920 in Danzig. Trollmann's subsequent adventures make for extraordinary reading – he was one of the very few to make it back to German lines. See Epilogue (page 487-8) for his story.

- - -

Most men of 95th Rifle Division avoided the frustration and casualties because they held the line while other units advanced. Subunits of 241st, 90th Rifle Regiment and 92nd Rifle Brigade carried out reconnaissance of German emplacements, suppressed their fire with machine-guns, mortars and artillery, and prepared to implement Combat Order No. 05. On the sector of 2/161st Rifle Regiment, however, the Germans offered stubborn resistance to the advancing storm groups from the south-east corner of the Barrikady factory and the bakery. Overcoming German resistance, 2/161st Rifle Regiment finally cleared Dom 102 and consolidated in it. It lost 2 men while doing so and the entire regiment only possessed 85 active bayonets (22 were mortarmen). Its sister regiments were far weaker: 90th Rifle Regiment had 20 men, while 241st Rifle Regiment had 49 men (including 22 mortarmen).

- - -

On 62nd Army's sector, there were no easy victories, no white flags after fifteen minutes, no mass surrenders. General Krylov reports:

> For the entire day, 116 Germans were taken prisoner. And these only now and then. The army as a whole was only able to gain a little more ground on 1 February than it did the previous day. There were minor casualties, to be sure. We had 42 dead and 105 wounded but that was less than we had on many days.
>
> The decision of the army commander for 2 February read as follows: 'The offensive will continue and the previous assignments will continue to be carried out.'
>
> Division Batyuk was transferred from the city centre (there was nothing more to do there) to the Barrikady factory. The next morning, they would attack the enemy in the direction of Arbatovskaya and Tramvaynaya streets, to the left of Division Sokolov. Toward day's end, Sokolov still only had just over 400 men. In the evening, however, reinforcements arrived from the other bank of the Volga. There was not many actually, but the division commander was very pleased: veterans of 45th Rifle Division, who had been wounded in November and December, returned to their units to take part in perhaps the last Stalingrad fighting.
>
> Then other large numbers of reinforcements began to arrive. Front command handed over to us 298th Rifle Division and 51st Guards Division from 21st Army. From the other neighbours we received a tank brigade and a Guards tank regiment.
>
> Until recently we had practically no tanks. Their use in the industrial district, which contained numerous obstacles of various types and large amounts of mines, was quite complicated. Helping the units with that was an engineer brigade subordinated to the Front. They probed literally every square metre between the jumping-off positions of the tanks on Chimitscheskaya street and the enemy's most forward line. Engineers would also be employed to escort the tanks into battle. They concluded preparations in the night of 1-2 February to support our infantry with tanks on the sectors that we deemed important for the next day.
>
> A new anti-tank regiment arrived after being freed up by the liquidation of the southern pocket. Our army commander assigned one such regiment to Batyuk and Sokolov. The Germans had almost no tanks left. In any case, none that could move, and this additional artillery was to be used, first of all, to fire directly at enemy fortifications.
>
> I will say that not everything our army now brought forward was able to be employed. That applied to the new rifle troops as much as it did to the artillery. 'Readiness for action in the allocated gun positions by 1300 hours on 2 February', said the battle instructions of the artillery commander to the commander of the last artillery regiment that reached us. Pozharski had not been able to set an earlier date. The regiment did not do it because at 1300 hours, there was no more targets for this regiment nor for the others.

2 February, 1943

The last morning of the Stalingrad battle dawned. In his post-war memoir, General Krylov describes the build-up to the final battle:

On 2 February I accompanied Chuikov and Gurov to the advanced observation post in a half-destroyed building of the Krasny Oktyabr factory's main office. As chief-of-staff, my place was at the army command post. All the same, with the turbulent development of events which did not allow themselves to be followed easily, my place next to the main communication post was not the worst.

While a day earlier, or even half a day earlier, it was still difficult to predict how long the northern group of the German 6. Armee would hold out, it was clear at dawn on 2 February that everything would end that day. The previous day's mighty pounding by the entire Front artillery had – apart from its immediate, as it were, physical effect on the enemy – seemingly demoralised the encircled Germans in a fundamental way. This had an effect on everything during the night, and the next morning experienced commanders saw by the enemy's general behaviour that they would no longer be able to offer resistance as they had previously.

Batyuk detected it first. He himself said later that he was not able to hold back his men who were straining to advance. At any rate, 284th Rifle Division advanced half an hour earlier than planned. They had nothing to fear from our artillery because shells were only fired at visible targets with direct fire. And responsibility for that lay in the hands of each division commander.

In the first one and a half hours, the Germans still returned quite strong fire from their own positions, though they never once tried to launch a counterattack. And they could in no way hold off our advance. Batyuk's troops reached the western edge of Barrikady factory's grounds in their sector almost without pause.

Lieutenant Dvoryaninov from 295th Artillery Regiment reports that Chuikov took a direct hand in the last battle against the Germans:

On the night of 1-2 February, 1943, the Germans began to surrender, but in the upper settlement of the Barrikady, they still resisted. On 2 February, crews wheeled forward their guns to place direct-fire on the Barrikady's upper settlement. Acting as gun layer on one of them this time was the commander of 62nd Army, General Chuikov, upon whose order of 'At the foe, fire', our guns and those of other batteries all fired.

After also witnessing Chuikov fire the first shot, Lyudnikov recalls what happened next:

All of our guns and mortars then joined in but our infantry did not have to attack. White flags began to flutter here and there in the upper settlement. Fixing them to their bayonets and submachine-gun barrels the Germans began to flock into imprisonment.

– – –

Gorishny's men noted that the Germans were silent, apart from the occasional snap of a rifle or brief burst of machine-gun fire. They only came to life when an hour of artillery preparation ended at 0800 hours and Soviets units went on the offensive: a barrage of small-arms and machine-gun fire struck the advancing storm groups. It was easily brushed off and the Soviet attackers coursed into the factory grounds.

At 0845 hours, the storm groups reached Workshop 32 and seized it, developed the attack further and, together with units of 45th Rifle Division, captured Workshops 42, 1, 8 and reached the northern boundary of the Barrikady factory. What was a sheer impossibility barely two days earlier – and for the previous two months – now took only a few hours.

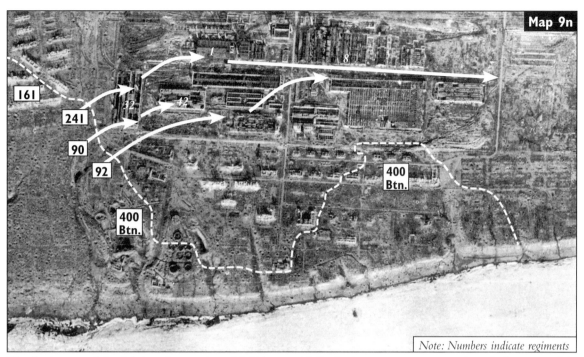

Note: Numbers indicate regiments

The final stages of the fighting, the morning of 2 February, 1943. Soviet storm groups swept through the centre of the factory, taking one workshop after another and quickly reaching its northern boundary. There was no general surrender in the Barrikady: individual German units and strongpoints only gave up when Soviet troops stood on their doorstep.

A storm group of 241st Rifle Regiment poses victoriously in front of Workshop 32 [Hall 6e]. They are well kitted out for the cold and well-armed for close quarters fighting: at least four men have pistols, the soldier in the middle (with hood up) has a spade tucked into his belt and the man on the right has a semi-automatic rifle.

– – –

At 0700 hours, however, the men of 305. Infanterie-Division had already received the order: "All fighting will cease; weapons will be destroyed; expect the Russians in about an hour!" This was the end. Oberstleutnant Liesecke made a nervous impression during the announcement of this order. He spoke hurriedly and his movements were fidgety. An inner

Later in the day, a much larger group of Soviet soldiers were gathered together for a celebratory photo in front of the ruins

concern troubled him. During the past days he had kept himself occupied again and again with thoughts of breaking out with a small group in the last phase of the battle and smuggling themselves through to the German front. The order to cease fighting may have come as too much of a surprise for him, and now, in broad daylight, nothing could be done. The Russians could appear outside the shelter at any moment and one thing was clear to everyone: any movement, even those that only indicated someone wanted to evade captivity, would mean death. And not only for the person concerned, but also for those who were nearby. The commander saw his plans thwarted. Now he only had to choose between suicide and captivity. What happened in his command post is not clear because no-one from the entire regimental staff – including orderlies – survived the subsequent captivity.

    Housed in a neighbouring room of the command post was Major Rettenmaier. He had to carry out the special order of the regiment commander. Liesecke delivered this last order personally. In addition, he added: "Assemble everyone down in the Ziegelofen[22]. I'll go there too." Rettenmaier immediately let the orderlies know about the order. The men fell silent. "Why?" This question was written on everyone's hollow, ashen faces. They seemed to be stricken by the fear of something completely sinister. Rettenmaier smiled and tried to

---

22. Trans.: 'Ziegelofen' = 'brick kiln'. Contrary to what the name suggests, the 'Ziegelofen' was not actually a blast furnace, but was some sort of storage depot. It was a long narrow building, approximately 30 to 40 metres in length with a semi-circular vaulted roof about 2.5 metres high. It was 4 to 5 metres wide and was lined with shelves. The entire building was covered with earth. When Rettenmaier returned to his unit in November 1942, his men were already calling this strange building the 'Ziegelofen' and the name stuck.

Orlov

of Workshop 32. Again, they are well-equipped with winter clothing and the only weapons visible are PPSh submachine-guns.

encourage them: "Yes, comrades, the battle is over for us. We have fulfilled our task and conducted ourselves in such a way that we can hold our own before history. We have prevailed against squalor and privation, and we did not give up, as so many of our comrades did. Forget about the danger outside for the next quarter of an hour. Everyone will prepare themselves for captivity. Protect yourselves against the Russian cold, don't take much baggage with you. We'll assemble in the Ziegelofen. I'll go there straight away. Have courage and maintain camaraderie. I'll stay with you for as long as the Russians allow it. Don't dither and follow me. Good luck, men!"

Rettenmaier went through a trench to the designated assembly point. A weird atmosphere hung over the city. All around, the weapons were quiet; the silence seemed eerie. Soldiers were not to be seen anywhere. Everything appeared to be dead. Rettenmaier suddenly felt alone and forsaken in the vast death fields of Stalingrad. But no, he was not alone. There, near the Ziegelofen, someone was exercising in the rubble. He was continually ducking up and down; he then took up a firing stance. Rettenmaier ran as fast as he was still able and called out as loud as he could: "Stop, stop, don't muck around!" It was Oberleutnant Lachmann[23]. "Tanks are coming from the tractor factory!" he called out towards Rettenmaier. Lachmann knew nothing of the cease fire order. Another calamity had been averted at the last moment. How would the Russians have dealt with them if resistance had been shown in this situation?

About 35 men assembled in the Ziegelofen. Among them were Major Krüger,

23. Lachmann, Hauptmann Herbert, 1./Nach.Abt.305; born 1 March, 1907 in Dresden. No further information known.

Hauptmann Hoyer, Stabszahlmeister Gallenz as well as a few other officers. Major Rettenmaier disclosed the order to them and reported that the regimental staff would also come there. The announcement to this circle of men was like a bombshell. Everyone fell silent and all eyes were on at Rettenmaier. There was an opportunity, however, to let a little bit of luck and joy fall into the bitter cup of suffering. Rettenmaier caught sight of the field-kitchen. Upon questioning, the man responsible for it reported that an iron reserve of Zwieback, sausage, meat, tinned vegetables and coffee was still available. There was no time to lose. Everyone packed as much as they wanted to carry and the cook opened boxes, one after another. Everyone should eat and strengthen themselves for the march into a dark fate. An almost celebratory hush dominated the room. With grateful reverence, everyone ate; nobody dared to greedily devour the delicious gifts. The Soviets were forgotten for the moment.

When their hunger was finally sated, conversation started up again, with this and that being asked. "What will it be like when the Russians come? Should epaulets and medals be taken off?" One officer spoke of suicide. "Rubbish!" Rettenmaier called out. "Should we fail in the last few minutes? Here are the men who did their duty in all the heavy fighting and – always willing to make sacrifices – would fulfil any order and stand faithfully by us in each and every situation. Are we to desert them now and escape in this last and crucial moment by shooting ourselves? No, I deem it to be our role to see to it that our men go respectably into captivity and that we remain with them for as long as the Russians permit it. If the Russians have the intention of shooting us officers, then we cannot resist any longer. The bullet that hits us, however, will not kill another German comrade. Our fate lies in the hands of a greater power. Insignia and medals will remain on uniforms. Our insignia are no longer secret for the Russians. Remain calm and level-headed. If it is somehow possible, I will go out first. If I'm not shot out of hand, then everyone else will also go into captivity unharmed. It is important that you have no weapons or ammunition. Everyone check their baggage once again."

Rettenmaier's words had a good effect. Any anxiety and hesitancy seemed to disappear. Everyone busied themselves with their baggage, and opinions were exchanged with each other. When everyone was finished, the mood resembled the impatience shown when an inspection by superiors was expected.

Not every unit in 305. Infanterie-Division, however, had the same opinion about insignia and medals, as Unteroffizier Rombach from II./Artillerie-Regiment reports:

> Because the northern pocket was relatively small, the Russians now strengthened their attacks. A man against man battle now began. In particular the Russian snipers zeroed in on every single German. They targeted officers and NCOs above all else. […] That was why openly wearing rank insignia and also medals and badges of honour in the Kessel was life-threatening. After it became clear to almost every soldier that help from the distant homeland could no longer be reckoned on, the destruction began of items and documents no longer urgently required. Medals and badges of honour, rank insignia and pay books were to be destroyed by order of the commander. Because the lack of ammunition was particularly acute, it was perfectly clear that the battle would ultimately be lost.

– – –

Emboldened by the slackening fire, storm groups raced into the German defences. Units of 161st Rifle Regiment attacked towards School No. 2 in conjunction with 400th Separate Machine-Gun and Artillery Battalion. They linked up with another company of the latter battalion stationed on Lyudnikov's Island and surrounded the German strongpoints that once filled them with dread: the Kommissarhaus, the Apotheke, Haus 79 and many others. Taken from behind, the garrisons quickly caved. Some Germans units were wiped out but most were taken prisoner. The north-east boundary of the Barrikady factory was swiftly reached. Eleven men of 161st Rifle Regiment were wounded throughout the day; 241st Rifle Regiments lost 1 dead and 1 wounded. The storm groups reportedly killed 60 German soldiers and took 354 prisoner. Two battalion staffs were also captured, complete with their

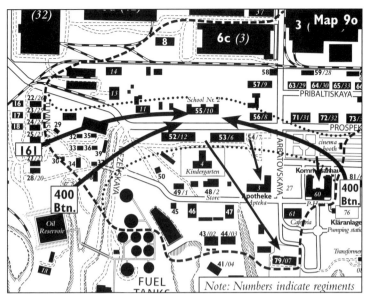

Obstinate German strongpoints finally fall, 2 February, 1943.

documents. Found on the division's sector were 3 tankettes, an anti-tank gun and 10 mortars, plus countless quantities of machine-guns, rifles and ammunition. After 11 weeks of ferocious resistance, the Red Army had finally retaken the Barrikady.

– – –

At 0814 hours, Generaloberst Strecker[24] transmitted a message to Heeresgruppe Don: "XI. Armeekorps, with its 6 divisions, has fulfilled its duty in the heaviest combat until the last." Three-quarters of an hour later, the last sign of life from 6. Armee left the pocket: "The Russians have fought their way into the tractor factory, long live Germany!" Over the next few hours, the men of the northern pocket would begin the longest and most difficult journey of their lives – captivity. The moment of capture left an indelible impression on the mind of every prisoner. Rittmeister Giulini recalls his moment:

> On 2 February, everything was at an end. I saw soldiers of my infantry division pull back past us, retreating but still firing. The Russians were directly behind them. […] Two T-34 tanks suddenly stopped outside our cellar. Two Red Army soldiers, wrapped almost only in rags, jumped off and ran down the cellar stairs, shouting. They bellowed 'Uri, Uri', fell upon us and removed our wristwatches. They weren't interested in our pistols at all. At one point, an

Generaloberst Karl Strecker, XI. Armeekorps, commanded the northern pocket in Stalingrad.

24. Strecker, Generaloberst Karl, RK, DKiG; XI. Armeekorps; born 20 September, 1884 in Radmannsdorf. Died 10 April, 1973 in Riezlern.

exceptionally tall senior-lieutenant stood in front of me, unbuttoned his long coat and pointed to the Guards star which he wore on his blouse. He reached into a pocket and gave us some of the well-known, stinking, Makhorka tobacco. He indicated that a Russian Guards officer cannot permit our watches to be removed for nothing, in such a way saying, me nothing, you nothing. Then something else happened that quite took me aback: another Russian jumped off one of the two tanks, rushed my commander and tore the gloves off his hands. 'Our' Guards senior-lieutenant wordlessly drew his pistol and shot this man. It's hard to comprehend such a thing! The senior-lieutenant again opened his coat, pointed to his Guards star and wordlessly, but with a grandiose gesture, returned the gloves to my commander. We all now headed off and prepared to face the impossible.

Oberarzt Dr. Hans Schellmann[25], battalion doctor of III./Grenadier-Regiment 578:

On Thursday, 2 February, the day of capitulation – I'd received the Iron Cross First Class the day before – some time in the morning, probably about 8 or 9 o'clock, we were working in our dressing station as usual. On this morning, however, no wounded were brought in. In a complete surprise, the Russians suddenly appeared at our entrance, which was slightly elevated above our cellar, and demanded that we come out. That was captivity. It was a cold, clear winter's day. The Russians were happy and danced about, dancing with pure joy. They were loud, well-fed, strong young men. During the first night they let loose a lunatic fireworks display with their abundantly available ammunition. It was quite depressing: we had practically nothing, no ammunition and now also nothing more to eat.

Feldarzt Dr. Karl Schöpf, II./Artillerie-Regiment 305:

Anxiety reigned in the sick bays and their surrounds during the early morning of 2 February. I said to everyone that whoever was capable of going into captivity should do that because in all probability, all of those who remained behind, meaning those who could no longer walk, would be shot. I fulfilled the request of a severely wounded Leutnant – who had a bullet wound in his thigh – to bind a small revolver into his dressings. Another soldier had stepped on a mine and the arch of his foot was destroyed. He wanted me to carry him along. I therefore applied a 'mobility' bandage made from a cut-up jacket and tent-quarter section. In the most excruciating pain, he reached the first prisoner-of-war camp after a 3 day march.

The first thing the Russians now demanded was 'Uhr yest' (Do you have a watch?). I gave my wristwatch, which I'd received from my godfather at Confirmation, to a Russian sentry at 0545 hours. Because I knew they would also take my wedding ring, I protected it with a bandage, and later, I had to stick it to my inner thigh several times. In this way – which was a rarity – I've kept my wedding ring to this day… The Russians divided us up into march columns of 100 men with 1 rifle-armed soldier at the front and the back. Whoever could not continue on was shot by the guards.

Unteroffizier Karl-August Rombach, also from II./Artillerie-Regiment 305:

Because ammunition and rations were exhausted, the division commanders, in agreement with the commander-in-chief, gave the order during the night of 1-2 February to cease fire at 0800 hours in the morning. In accordance with orders, we destroyed our telephone- and radio-equipment, as well as our pistols, and readied ourselves for the march into an unknown captivity. Apart from our mess-kits, canteen and a blanket, we took nothing else. The worst thing that can happen to a soldier, namely captivity, stood unavoidably in front of us.

A prisoner-of-war lost not only freedom through captivity. He lost everything, that is, a connection to faraway home, to his family and friends. The German prisoner in the hands of the Red Army was totally without rights. A feeling of the most utter hopelessness, which

---

25. Schellmann, Oberarzt Dr. Hans, III./Gr.Rgt.578; born 21 May, 1914 in Stuttgart. Still alive in 2006.

cannot be described, came over me. The only consolation were the few comrades with whom I was still together.

An unfamiliar silence settled along the front-line as weapons on both sides suddenly went quiet. Soldiers crawled out of their trenches, holes and dug-outs. The Russians pushed up to the infantry positions, disarmed everyone and assembled the captured German soldiers and their allies.

Towards 0800 hours the first enemy vehicle approached our bunker. It was a personnel transport towing an anti-tank gun. We took our blankets, mess-kits and canteens and tried to slip through the Russians towards the tractor factory, where out main command post was located. We intended using the underground conduits and shafts of the tractor factory to somehow avoid the feared Russian captivity and await spring with its warmer weather.

A long column of German prisoners snakes its way out of the city.

The Russian soldiers overtook us in their vehicle and ordered us to join a column of prisoners located nearby. We were checked for weapons and our watches and other valuables were brutally looted. Then they made us understand that we should form into a march column. Me and my comrades from the observation post joined a larger column of prisoners that had formed nearby. We were very lucky because in the column that we joined were our comrades from the staff of II. Abteilung of Artillerie-Regiment 305 with our commander, Major Bauer[26] from Stuttgart.

In the icy cold, we marched from Stalingrad-North via Stalingradski to Gorodische and on the evening of 2 February we found ourselves on the way towards Gumrak. By my estimate the column of prisoners consisted of about 5000 men, all undernourished and partially ill and suffering frostbite. There were no quarters for the many prisoners because the Red Army had occupied and commandeered everything.

Gefreiter Josef Zrenner, Pionier-Bataillon 305:

On 1 February, we wanted to undertake a break-out at night but that did not succeed because we barely made it 100 metres before we received machine-gun fire. Then came the morning of 2 February and we were calm, internally calm, about what lay ahead of us. There were 5 of us, and we conferred as to whether we should voluntarily emerge from our shelter, so that there was no danger of the Russian soldiers approaching and throwing hand grenades into the

26. Bauer, Major Max, II./Art.Rgt.305; born 1 October, 1897 in Stuttgart. Killed in captivity, February 1943 near Stalingrad.

bunker. Then someone said he would not go into captivity, he would shoot himself beforehand. And it is still firmly in my memory, my exact words were that I would not shoot myself, if the Russians shoot me during captivity, that was different, because I would be killed by enemy forces, enemy action, but I would not shoot myself. And then came dawn on 2 February, and at eight o'clock we heard the sounds of battle, and I said to my comrades

German prisoners move through an intact village north of Stalingrad.

that it would be better if we went outside, stood in front of our bunker and waved to the Russians. But we already saw movement in our immediate vicinity, it was Russian soldiers, and we came out as they approached. They were Siberians […]. And these Siberians came up to us and took us prisoner. We admired them for the equipment they carried. They were wide-eyed at seeing German soldiers. It was like a dream. German soldiers seeing the unimaginable, slit-eyed men with such things as fur caps, fur gloves, fur coats, everything, the best, and I simply had to say to a comrade, look at how they are equipped, and we still have no winter clothing. They treated us humanely, all 5 of us, and the first thing they did was to take our watches and the second things was our medals and decorations. They opened my coat and reached for my chest, where my medals were, took them from me, and my watch, then allowed us to get ready before leading us off, along a beaten path upon which they'd arrived. The snow was thick, a metre thick, and they led us to a command post, down on the Volga… Someone from the German side had told us that deserters were immediately shot [by the Russians] and for that reason none of us deserted. We therefore noticed that it was not as we'd been led to believe. They treated us decently. We were not struck, we were marched off, down the steep cliff to the Volga, and there we were led into a Russian command post that was built into the steep bank. We were interrogated, and all my notes – I maintained a diary – which were kept in my left breast pocket, and my Soldbuch in the right, all of that was taken away from me.

Inspektor Georg Zeller, also from Pionier-Bataillon 305, likewise ended up in a Soviet command post:

> I went into captivity with [Hauptmann] Gast. There were also two other officers. The four of us were separated from the soldiers and taken to the command post of a Russian engineer regiment, interrogated there, and spent the night in the anteroom of the shelter of two Russian captains, who were quite companionable to us. We were then incorporated into a group of prisoners.

- - -

Shortly after 1000 hours, Sokolov's 45th Rifle Division completed its combat mission. The divisions of Gorishny, Rodimtsev and Lyudnikov, divided into small combat groups, made good progress. Krylov recalls the final moments of the battle:

> The entire enemy defence collapsed. The Germans were driven out of the bread factory, out of the fortified school building, out of strongpoints in the workshops and out of the public baths in the workers settlement and pulled back in a northern and north-western direction.

It seemed absurd: attacking there were two other Soviet armies, which every German must have known. And even though our units only had dozens or hundreds of men, thousands of them fled into the opposite corners of the increasingly narrow pocket. From the 40,000 soldiers and officers of the northern group that laid down their weapons in the last two days, only a little more than 1000 surrendered to our army.

From the divisions flowed reports about attained intermediate objectives, about the encirclement of larger buildings that served as aiming points, about the capture or destruction of the garrisons and about captured weapons… And more frequently, someone who could no longer control themselves screamed excitedly into the phone that such-and-such battalion at such-and-such a place on the other side of the Barrikady factory, in the workers settlement or on the grounds of the tractor factory, had met up with units of 65th or 66th Army. What was going on there, how they were celebrating, I could already imagine by the way these reports were given.

Lyudnikov was near Chuikov when hostilities ended:

'Cease fire!' commanded Chuikov. 'And pass the cease-fire on to our neighbours!'

Army Commander congratulated us on our victory.

Guns ceased firing, flares of various colours soared into the sky and a swelling Russian 'hurra' rang out, muffling submachine-gun and rifle salutes.

The victors rejoiced.

Around midday there was no longer a front in Stalingrad. General Krylov was sitting in the army command post when the phone rang:

I was called by Gurov from the army observation post:

'Nikolai Ivanovich, haven't you had enough sitting around? Come over to us. The commander is expecting you!'

At the command post, Pozharski[27], Vainrub[28], Tkachenko[29] and almost all the division commanders were there. Everyone congratulated each other. And instructions were already issued about urgent work to de-mine, to set up a commandant service in the city, to gather the captured weapons and furthermore to take the prisoners away…

I drafted Report No. 32 to the Commander-in-Chief of the Don Front which we all – Chuikov, Gurov and myself – signed together. It began with the words: 'The troops of 62nd Army have completely fulfilled the combat mission at 1200 hours on 2 February, 1943…'

A few hours later the Moscow Broadcast issued a special bulletin of the Soviet Information Bureau which stated that the troops of the Don Front had completed the liquidation of the German troops encircled in the Stalingrad area.

– – –

Suspicious noises were heard outside the Ziegelofen again and again. Everyone listened expectantly. They were tingling seconds. Nerves were stretched to the limit. Resounding into this silence from outside was "Raus!" with the characteristic rolling Russian 'R'. Straight away Rettenmaier answered: "Ja", grabbed his satchel, said "It's happening,

27. Pozharski, Major-General Nikolai Mitrofanovich, HotSU; staff 62nd Army; born 6 May, 1899 in Klin. Died 12 September, 1945.
28. Vainrub, General-Lieutenant Matvey Grigoryevich, HotSU; staff 62nd Army; born 2 May, 1910 in Borisov. Died 14 February, 1998.
29. Tkachenko, Lieutenant-Colonel Vladimir Matveyevich, HotSU; staff 62nd Army; born 2 January, 1903 in Pomoshnaya. Died 13 May, 1983.

comrades, keep your heads high, and good luck!" And with that, he walked to the door. Outside stood three Red Army soldiers with their submachine-guns levelled. Without fear, Rettenmaier stepped up to them, stopped a few paces in front of them and saluted. The Soviets asked about weapons and superficially patted him down. Rettenmaier let the Russians know that there were still more German soldiers inside. The leader of the soldiers, a roughly 40-year-old well-fed stocky man, repeatedly requested in a loud voice for them to come out. Apparently, however, nobody wanted to be first. Rettenmaier dropped his baggage to the snowy ground and walked to the entrance. He opened the door and called: "Comrades, come out, the Russians are here!" Terror was overcome with the first step into the open when they saw Rettenmaier standing peacefully near the Soviet soldiers. They were happy that everything was happening smoothly. And happiest of all was Rettenmaier himself; he now no longer had any responsibility. From now on, the "Davai" of the Soviets meant exactly the same for him as it did for every man of his former following.

The small column crawled up the slope. With bowed heads, everyone was lost in their thoughts. Rettenmaier prayed silently. His right hand reached into his overcoat pocket. His fingers, clammy from the cold, sought the large beads of his rosary, and then he began: "The black cross was borne for us!"

From atop the hill, he cast one last glance over the Volga and the rubble of the gun factory of Stalingrad, and sent his final greetings there: "Rest in peace, comrades!"

– – – – – – – – – – – –

AFTERWORD

In his report, Unteroffizier Rombach stated his intention of using underground tunnels in the tractor factory to avoid captivity and await warmer weather. Many others had the same idea and thousands implemented their plans. None were successful in reaching German lines and no accounts from German survivors have emerged. However, a remarkable NKVD report from March 1943 is available showing the tenacity of some of these German groups:

> The mopping-up of counter-revolutionary elements in the city of Stalingrad proceeded. The German-fascist bandits – who had hidden themselves in huts and trenches – offered armed resistance after combat actions had already ended. This armed resistance continued until 15 February and in a few areas until 20 February. Most of the armed groups were liquidated by March.
>
> During this period of armed conflict with the German-fascist bandits, the brigade's units killed 2418 soldiers and officers and captured 8646 soldiers and officers, escorting them to POW camps and handing them over.

- - -

An unimaginable sense of grief and uncertainty steadily descended upon German families as letters from their soldiers ceased in mid-January and their government spun the calamitous fall of Stalingrad into an epic myth. Agnes Moosmann – whose future brother-in-law (Hans Bernhart, 1./Gr.Rgt.578) and many childhood friends were now missing – perfectly evokes the mixed feelings of utter helplessness and anger arising from this disaster that claimed their menfolk:

> How many letters may still have been written at the end of November 1942 – that most tragic of all winters – in the great bend of the Volga and 50km inland, with gritted teeth but in an attitude of true-hearted hope; in December 1942 in courage and fear; in January 1943 in sardonic laughter or helpless tears; and at the beginning of February in the knowledge of being betrayed and sold out, delivered up to an agonising destruction before life had really begun. Now nobody took their outcries back to the homeland and no postman delivered their final words – scribbled by numb fingers – to those waiting and crying at home. The great silence had begun. Silence also descended on those once so convinced of the need to confront 'world Bolshevism', on those dutifully fighting 'for Lebensraum in the East', and helplessly on those knowledgeable ones who had 'always' seen the evil disaster coming. But even those who had suspected a catastrophe did not believe – could not imagine – that German soldiers would be left in the lurch in such a disgraceful and dishonourable way.

Of the approximately 90,000 Germans captured at Stalingrad, only 5,500 ever returned home.

EPILOGUE: FATE OF INDIVIDUALS

An entire book could be written about the individual fates of the men that appear in this book but a select few will be discussed to represent the hundreds of thousands of others whose story will not – or cannot – be told. Additionally, the story of the pioneer battalion commanders will also be completed here.

BERNHART, Unteroffizier Hans (Grenadier-Regiment 578):

Moosmann

In the middle of January, a telephone call arrived for Hilde, Bernhart's wife-to-be. On the phone was one of Bernhart's regimental comrades who reported that at the end of December Hans had been promoted to Unteroffizier because of a shortage of officers and given the status of Kompanieführer at the same time. A few days later he was killed. Hilde's father, who had taken the call, was in shock and forgot to ask for the name and address of the unknown caller. The comrade never contacted the family again. Perhaps he was killed later in the war. To this day, Hans is listed as 'missing in action', just like his brothers Ludwig and Gebhard.

BONETSMÜLLER, Obergefreiter Johann (Pionier-Bataillon 305):

Familie Bonetsmüller

After being informed that her husband was still alive in January 1943, Frau Bonetsmüller endured years of silence. Finally, on 12 December 1945, she received a letter from a man just released from Soviet captivity. He said that her husband was in a camp behind the Urals, was 'relatively well' and had been put to work as a bricklayer. In 1947, another comrade told Frau Bonetsmüller that her husband had been due for release but the Soviets unexpectedly extended his sentence. In July 1948, Johann Bonetsmüller at last made it home, but he was a broken man. His wife would later write, "you have no concept of how wretched he looks, wasted away to a skeleton. After 14 days he was admitted to a sanatorium and lay there for half a year. He received over 250 injections and they did everything they could for him. To this day [July 1949] he still cannot work for one hour. The doctors say it will be at least two years until he'll be able to get up again. He was completely malnourished." His 100% war disability entitled him to a meagre pension. Over the years, as he slowly regained his health, his degree of war disability was downgraded. With great pain, he gained work as a bricklayer foreman, and continued until he retired at 65 years of age, in 1972. Amazingly, he lived to the ripe old age of 90, dying on 23 January, 1997.

BRAUN, Oberstleutnant Willi (Grenadier-Regiment 576):

The first news Braun's family received was from Hauptmann Schuboth, a fellow battalion commander. In a letter from 13 February, 1947, Braun's sister recounts what Schuboth told her:

A Hauptmann from Konstanz [Schuboth] has returned home and from him we have learned that he was with our brother in the fighting in Stalingrad. They had been a group of 200 men, they fought next to one another until they only had 16 men. Then the Hauptmann from Konstanz was heavily wounded and our brother Willi was lightly wounded in the shoulder. They were bandaged by medics. When Willi went back into the battle with the other 16 men,

Familie Braun

he (the Hauptmann from Konstanz) shook his hand and wished him a good journey into eternity. He would follow him soon because the battle was so vast that nothing different could be planned, and from then on he knows no more about Willi.

He (the Hauptmann from Konstanz) then went into hospital and managed to recover and has now returned home...

In a letter to Braun's sister, Unteroffizier Kurt Steinlen, battalion clerk of II./Grenadier-Regiment 576, describes what happened to Knight's Cross winner Braun:

> On 1 February, 1943, I went into captivity with Major Braun, alone. During the last Russian attack, he had been lightly wounded in two places by a mortar. His adjutant was killed at the same moment by a direct hit. Your brother's movement was greatly hindered by his wounds, but it was possible for me to carry him along for a few hours. On the night of 1-2 February, 1943, his condition was such that he was extremely weary and could not go on. He requested that I leave him behind at a Russian Red Cross station. I wanted to stay with him but our Russian escorts would not allow it. Despite in-depth research into every POW camp that was known to me, I have not been able to find out any more about him...

Oberstleutnant Willi Braun is still listed as 'missing in action'.

BÜCH, Hauptmann Dr. Ludwig (Pionier-Bataillon 45 & 389):
Oberleutnant Walter Heinrich, who had been wounded and flown out of the Kessel on 22 January, 1943, reported that Büch was alive and well. H. Schumann, one of the first prisoners to return home from Soviet captivity, wrote a letter to Büch's wife on 7 March, 1946:

DRK/Familie Büch

> Your husband, Hauptmann Büch, was my battalion commander. He had come through the fighting in Stalingrad quite well and on 1 February, 1943, together with Assistenarzt Dr. Wimmershof[1], Hauptfeldwebel Scheck[2] and Schirrmeister Winter[3], waited in their bunker – equipped with provisions and a radio – and allowed it to be covered with snow. They wanted to hold out for a few weeks and then attempt to break through to German lines. But because none of them are at home to this day, I must presume that they also went into captivity. However, I can give you the reassuring news that it was not too bad for officers in Russian captivity in contrast to us who had it very bad and had to work hard...

No trace was ever found of Büch, Dr. Wimmershof, Scheck or Winter. Büch was officially declared missing in action 23 January, 1943.

GAST, Hauptmann Erwin (Panzerpionier-Bataillon 50 & 305):
As reported by Inspektor Georg Zeller [see page 476], Gast went into captivity with him and spent the night of 2-3 February at the command post of a Soviet engineer regiment. They joined a column of prisoners the next day. One eyewitness states that the pioneers – both officers and enlisted men – were separated immediately after capture. However, it seems this happened much later and in a more organised fashion. Hauptmann

---

1. Wimmershof, Assistenarzt Dr. Willi, Pi.Btl.45; born 6 July 1912. Missing in action, January 1943 in Stalingrad.

2. Scheck, Hauptfeldwebel Adolf, 2./Pi.Btl.45; born 30 August, 1912 in Reute. Missing in action, January 1943 in Stalingrad.

3. Winter, Schirrmeister Karl, 1./Pi.Btl.45; born 2 January, 1915 in Ravensburg. Missing in action, 23 January, 1943 in Stalingrad.

Adelbert Holl[4], an infantryman from 94. Infanterie-Division, remembers one particular day in the Beketovka camp:

> It was 1 March, 1943. Everyone was awoken very early and we had to prepare ourselves for departure. This meant that we would be shipped to a so-called Stammlager (permanent POW camp). Everything would be better there and we could again live like normal people. Most of us took this news with scepticism. We had already been deceived so often in the few weeks of captivity; in addition, with the increasing physical weakness, we became indifferent… After we had assembled in front of the club building, it was called out: 'Everyone who is feeling particularly ill and cannot survive a long rail journey, step forward. Also, all pioneers!'

Inspektor Zeller clearly remembers this:

> I can confirm that this is what happened because I experienced it myself. We officers were in a building – I believe it was some kind of large theatre hall or something similar – and were being sorted out into the sick and the 'healthy'. Pioneers should present themselves separately. I was heavily wounded and went to the sick group. Next to me stood an officer whom I had never seen before and whom I also didn't know, even though I had been a technical supervisor in 4 battalions, and he said to me: 'Don't step forward. I think they only want the pioneers to clear mines.' Others, however, presented themselves without suspicion because they thought they might not be sent to Siberia.

Afterwards, it was clear to Zeller that the mines laid on the thoroughfares in Stalingrad by the German pioneers would now be cleared by them. Plans of the minefields had been drawn up when they were laid but they no longer existed and the work was tremendously dangerous. It seems Gast was drafted into one of these mine-clearing parties. His wife remembers that "sometime in the 1950s, an Oberst, a noblemen from Bad Godesberg, who was with Erwin in captivity, told me that Erwin had to help clear mines and probably died doing it". The use of pioneer soldiers and officers to clear mines and unexploded bombs may explain why very few survived captivity.

Gast was still officially listed as missing in action 7 January, 1943. A determination issued by the Amtsgericht (district court) of Hanau on 18 March, 1950 arbitrarily set the date of death of Hauptmann Erwin Gast as 1 February, 1943, 2400 hours.

HEINRICH, Oberleutnant Walter (2./Pionier-Bataillon 45)

After being flown out on 22 January, 1943, Heinrich remained in hospital for over 5 months. His exploits while commanding his company, particularly in Stalingrad, were legendary amongst his comrades. Heinrich was one of those rare men who thrived in war and could emerge alive from the most dire of situations. His affable but volatile personality precluded him from ever taking a passive role and his skills as a soldier were universally acknowledged. Recommendations for the Knight's Cross and the German Cross in Gold in early 1942 were denied but the Honour Roll Clasp was approved. In mid-1943, he was once again put forward for the German Cross in Gold but the lack of eyewitnesses and confirmation from his superiors (who had all been killed or captured in Stalingrad) jeopardised the justified bestowal of this

---

4. Holl, Hauptmann Adelbert, Gr.Rgt.276; born 15 February, 1919 in Duisburg. Died 6 June, 1982 in Duisburg.

high decoration. Eventually, on 21 February, 1944, Heinrich received the medal. He took commanded of his beloved Pionier-Bataillon 45 in May 1944 and received a promotion to Major in December 1944. He survived the war. One of his comrades, Karl Krauss, wrote: "For years I requested that Walter Heinrich write down his memoirs – but in vain. He no longer wanted to remember." Konni Dreier, chairman of the Pionierkameradschaft Ulm, recalls the final sad years of Heinrich's life:

> During an operation, as a result of a wartime wound, the doctors made a mistake. Kamerad Heinrich could then only walk with great difficulty and spent his last years in a wheelchair. His final years were spent in a nursing home, where in died in 1997.

KONOVALENKO, Guards Major Vladimir Anufrievich (344th Rifle Regiment):

After the Stalingrad battle, 138th Rifle Division became 70th Guards Divisions, and Konovalenko's unit was named 203rd Guards Rifle Regiment. On 23 September, 1943, Guards Major Konovalenko distinguished himself by breaking through a deep German defensive belt in the Chernobylsky district with a well-planned assault. His regiment repelled 8 hefty German counterattacks. Despite months staring death in the face while defending Stalingrad, it was for this feat that he received the coveted title of Hero of the Soviet Union, on 16 October, 1943. This vigorous and skilled young commander – beloved by his men – was killed in combat on 19 September, 1944.

KRÜGER, Major Otto (Pionier-Bataillon 162 and 305):

On 5 June, 1953, Unteroffizier Hans Krauss[5] – released from Soviet captivity in August 1945 – provided a sworn declaration:

> Major Otto Krüger from Elbing/West Prussia was commander of Pionier-Bataillon 162. I myself was Rechnungsführer (accountant and pay NCO) on the staff of this battalion. Major Krüger went into Russian captivity in Stalingrad-North, probably on 2 February, 1943. I went into Russian captivity on the same day. On the previous evening, I saw Major Krüger in the battalion's Geschäftszimmer (orderly office) bunker. It was the last time I saw him.

As we read in Major Rettenmaier's account, Krüger was with the group in the Ziegelofen taken prisoner on the morning of 2 February, 1943. Krauss continues:

> In July 1943, in Arbeitslager (labour camp) Krassnoarmeisk and in Krankenlager (sick camp) Beketovka, I learned in conversations with several officers I knew that Major Krüger had already died in a POW camp in April 1943. There were about 5 officers who told me this. They did not belong to the battalion commanded by Major Krüger [but] the details provided by these officers were unambiguous.

Krauss's statement was vital in declaring Otto Krüger dead. Although Krüger was still officially listed as missing in action 5 January, 1943, a determination issued by the Amtsgericht (district court) of Goslar on 11 January, 1954 established the date of death of Major Otto Krüger as 20 April, 1943, 2400 hours.

---

5. Krauss, Unteroffizier Hans, Stab/Pi.Btl.162; born 13 July, 1918 in Schaidt/Pfalz. Died 21 March, 1978 in Steinfeld.

LUNDT, Hauptmann Hermann (Pionier–Bataillon 336):

Lundt was officially listed as missing in action 9 January, 1943.

On 13 April, 1943, Major Pavlicek, commander of Pionier-Bataillon 336 – who had been on leave when the battalion was sent to Stalingrad, thus necessitating Lundt to take command – wrote a letter to Lundt's wife:

> Dear Frau Lundt, I have the sad duty to inform you that your husband is missing since the Stalingrad mission. Nevertheless, I have the firm hope that this courageous officer will see the homeland again. May this hope sustain you in these difficult days. All of us who knew him share in the undeserved heavy fate of this exemplary officer. Respectfully yours, Pavlicek, Major and Battalion Commander.

On 29 October, 1949, Erich Bauchspiess answered a letter from Lundt's wife:

> Dear Frau Lundt, this morning I received your card from 28 October and I thank you… I would like to give you a small description of what happened.

> On 4 November, 1942, together with our Bataillonsführer and myself as battalion paymaster, we flew from Ostrogoshk (Don position) to Stalingrad for a 14-day deployment. Our battalion had to survive fierce fighting there and suffered heavy losses. Because the Russians were extremely stubborn, however, our deployment dragged on longer than expected, and in the meantime, the Russians surrounded us on 21 November. The further fate of Stalingrad is well known to you. We filled many a quiet evening in Stalingrad with games of Skat or Doppelkopf. Also, up to the evening of 31 January, 1943, nothing had happened to your husband. It was at this moment that we saw each other for the last time. In the evening of 1 February, 1943 the incoming messages reported nothing new. On 2 February, 1943, at 0910 hours, the Russians broke in from the rear and took me prisoner, together with some lightly wounded comrades. Because our positions were only about 300 metres from the baggage train, the Russians must have also penetrated into our positions from the rear at approximately the same time.

> Day and night we trekked back and forth across the steppe around Stalingrad until on 3 February, we were finally loaded aboard trains so that we could be transported to a camp in the Urals. There, in summer 1943, I recognised an Oberleutnant whom I had come to know in Stalingrad and who also knew our Bataillonsführer, your dear husband. This man told me that on the morning of 2 February, 1943, he had seen your husband lying on a sleigh with a leg wound. Because he belonged to another prisoner trek, he could not go up to him to greet him. In the first two months of our captivity, there was as good as no medical care provided, and also hardly any food, so in the first month, approximately 50,000 of the 93,000 prisoners had already died. I am therefore afraid that in this time, your dear husband and our good comrade also closed his eyes forever. All officers captured in Russia, including those from Königsberg, congregated in the camps mentioned. Unfortunately your dear husband did not arrive there. I am the only survivor of the officer corps, perhaps even of the entire battalion which was in Stalingrad. Also, I have so far not met any of the few enlisted men who went into captivity… Since I cannot give you a definite answer about the fate of your dear husband, there still remains for you and also for me a small spark of hope because in Russia, the path of fate is unfathomable.

In a Heimkehrer-Erklärung made on 8 January, 1956, Kurt Becker stated that "Hauptmann Lundt, who was heavily wounded, went into captivity with me in Stalingrad-North on 2 February, 1943. We were separated on 3 or 4 February, 1943. Lundt should have been taken to a Russian hospital."

As with tens of thousands of others, Lundt simply disappeared.

LYUDNIKOV, Lieutenant-General Ivan Ilyich (138th Rifle Division):

Promoted to Major-General on 27 January, 1943, Lyudnikov took command of 15th Rifle Corps. During the fighting on the Kursk bulge, Lyudnikov's unit fulfilled its defensive objectives before going on the counterattack. On 22 September, 1943, his corps' forward units reached the Dnepr north of Chernobyl where they immediately began crossing the river. Having created a bridgehead on the west bank and repelled numerous German counterattacks, the corps' units continued to expand the bridgehead westward. Lyudnikov received the title Hero of the Soviet Union on 16 October, 1943.[6] He continued through the war, ending in 1945 with the storming of Königsberg. After the defeat of Germany, he participated in the brief campaign against Japan in August 1945. After the war he commanded an army and later served as the replacement commander-in-chief of East German armed forces. In 1952, he completed higher academic courses at the General Staff Military academy and later served as an instructor at various military academies. Colonel-General Lyudnikov retired from the military in 1968. He died on 22 April, 1976 and is buried at the Novodevichye cemetery in Moscow.

PECHENYUK, Guards Lieutenant-Colonel Fedor Iosifovich (650th Rifle Regiment):

Pechenyuk retained command of 650th Rifle Regiment, now renamed 205th Guards Rifle Regiment. In September 1943, his regiment crossed the Seym River east of Baturin, where it liberated Bahmach station. On 22 September, 1943, it crossed the Dnepr near the village of Domantovo (Chernobyl district). During the formation of the bridgehead, his regiment repulsed 11 German counterattacks, and for this, Pechenyuk received the title 'Hero of the Soviet Union' on 16 October, 1943. In 1945, Pechenyuk completed the General Staff military academy. In 1953, Colonel Pechenyuk became a reserve officer. He died on 26 January, 1965 and is buried in the city of Zhitomir.

PUSCHIAVO, Autiere [driver] Mariano (248° Autoreparto pesante):

The Italian drivers attached to the staff of Pionier-Bataillon 305 were not deployed in combat. They seem to have been left to their own devices. Shortly before Christmas, Puschiavo wrote to his brother: "I am in a cellar with 6 Italian comrades… The cannon fire gets ever closer, the Russians shoot without let up, there are lots of lice, everything is very difficult". In letters to his wife, however, he sugar coated the truth:

> The holy night was not too bad for me. It was quite good because I had a few things that you sent to me. We made pasta asciutta [spaghetti] and had fish fillets, which you also sent to me. There were six of us in a small shack, a nice oven gave us some warmth. Last night, a comrade

---

6. Not one member of the division received the title 'Hero of the Soviet Union' for their amazing defensive feat in Stalingrad. Perhaps defence was not considered worthy of such high recognition? As the war progressed and Soviet armies were constantly on the offensive, the title was bestowed much more readily. The overall number of 'Hero of the Soviet Union' titles awarded during or for the Stalingrad campaign was startlingly low. For forcing the crossing of the Dnepr River, Lyudnikov, Konovalenko, Pechenyuk and several other officers received the prestigious title. One wonders if this was a belated and tacit acknowledgement of their earlier actions in Stalingrad.

cooked egg noodles and we ate them for dinner. Afterwards we drank coffee with cognac, so we are going pretty well.

At the end of battle, all 50 of the Italian drivers were still alive except for 2 that had died in January 1943. The only soldier from the group that would survive captivity stated that all of his comrades died during the long train journey to the camps. This sole survivor died in 1997.

RETTENMAIER, Major Eugen (I./Grenadier-Regiment 578):

Rettenmaier returned thin and frail from Soviet captivity on 15 December, 1949. Only then did he learn of the tragedy that had befallen his family. He knew that his eldest son Ottokar had been killed in May 1942 but he was devastated to learn that two more sons had not survived the war (Gerhard, a Gefreiter, born October 1924, was missing in action, September 1943 near Smolensk; Waldemar, a Leutnant, born October 1921, was missing in action, August 1944 in Romania). Rettenmaier began work again as a teacher in 1952 but fate soon dealt his family another blow: his youngest son, Siegbert (born February 1928), passed away in July 1957, one week before his marriage. All four sons had died before their father. Rettenmaier suffered a stroke in 1964, then a second in early 1965, dying on 7 January of that year.

Above right: Rettenmaier (left) returns from Soviet captivity, 15 December, 1949 (photo taken in Moschendorf bei Hof).
Right: The full tragedy of Familie Rettenmaier is revealed on their gravestone: three sons lost to the war.
Below: Rettenmaier (with cigarette) shares a joke with his men during a training exercise near Esslingen, 1941.

TRAUB, Major Wilhelm (Pionier-Bataillon 305):

In a letter written to Traub's wife on 18 July, 1949 by the wife of Johann Bonetsmüller, the final traces of Major Traub are recorded:

Familie Traub

> I briefly want to describe to you what my husband reported about your husband. He was together with your husband until the capture on 2.2.43. They were in a very bad state. From their entire company only 8 men went into captivity, including your dear husband. Everyone else was dead or heavily wounded and remained in the pocket. He was with your husband for the first three months of captivity. After this time, officers and men were separated. The officers went to Moscow and they went to central Asia. When my husband then went to Moscow in 1946, he met a Major who had also gone into captivity with them at the same time, but came from another battalion. He asked him whether he knew the name Traub but unfortunately he couldn't provide any information. However, he told him that officers were not required to work but had to come to Moscow for political re-education. Also, they received somewhat better food supplies there. My husband cannot report anything else.

Oberstabsintendant Karl Binder, the quartermaster of 305. Infanterie-Division, kept detailed notes of who died in captivity but his secret journal was confiscated a few weeks before his release by a fellow German inmate working for the Soviets. He remembered that Traub was on the list but Frau Traub doubted the accuracy of his recall because Binder also mentioned that Max Fritz – the battalion adjutant killed on 22 December, 1942 in Stalingrad – had died in captivity. Frau Traub continued to conduct the heartbreaking search for her husband until 1954, writing letters to every conceivable government department and questioning those who had returned from captivity. All to no avail. Johann Bonetsmüller was the last person to see him alive on 8 April, 1943. Traub is still officially listed as 'missing in action'.

TROLLMANN, Unteroffizier Richard (II./Grenadier-Regiment 212)

One of the most remarkable stories to emerge from the Stalingrad battle is that of Unteroffizier Trollmann. Born in Germany in 1920, his parents moved the family to Leningrad in 1922. With war looming, Trollmann was drafted into the Red Army and sent to an NCO school in Tashkent in April 1941. He used his first opportunity in July 1942 to desert to the Germans, crossing over to the sector of 5./Gr.Rgt.212. He was initially used as an interpreter but quickly became a fully-fledged German soldier. He fought with the unit throughout the entire Stalingrad battle, until captured on 1 February, 1943. Then began a long death march. The deplorable treatment and appaling weather forced him to contemplate escape before he became too weak. He made his move on 26 March, 1943: while working on a wood-chopping commando deep in a forest, he quietly slipped away and eventually reached a small village, where he was fed, sheltered and given civilian clothes. His upbringing meant he could speak Russian fluently, so he trekked along the Don, spending nights in small villages. His luck ran out when he was picked up by Soviet troops and taken to Millerovo, where 33 other Soviet deserters had been gathered. He was interrogated by the NKVD and he told them that he had escaped from German captivity, providing the number of his pre-desertion Soviet unit as proof of his truthfulness. It worked. He was placed in the punishment company of 24th Rifle Division and sent to the front along the Mius River. Because the division suffered heavy casualties, the shtrafnikov were used as replacements: Trollmann was sent to the signals company in a rifle regiment. During an attack, his regiment was completely ripped apart: about 40% were killed and most of the others went into captivity. With the fighting swirling about him, Trollmann had crept into a bunker and awaited the arrival of German troops. This happened the next day and he was taken to a battalion command post of the Totenkopf-Division. Shortly after, he was severely wounded by a shell which later necessitated the amputation of his right leg at the thigh. His unbelievable tale was revealed in many interviews throughout August and September 1943. Several other deserters tried to convince German authorities that they were genuine survivors from Stalingrad but Trollmann provided names, dates, places and other details that could only be given by someone who was there, in Stalingrad, during the final days. For his extraordinary courage, Trollmann was awarded the Iron Cross First Class and the Wound Badge in Gold (his severe wounding was his fourth since joining the Germans). What happened to him after this point is unknown.

WEIMANN, Major Wilhelm (Pionier-Bataillon 294 & 100)

In early January 1943, after the wounding of the commander of Pionier-Bataillon 100 (100. Jäger-Division), Weimann was ordered to take command of the leaderless unit. By late January, it had been cut off in a pocket near Mamayev Kurgan and the men were taken prisoner on 30 and 31 January, 1943. An investigation by Weimann's wife showed that he had gone into Soviet captivity in early 1943 and that he was sick at the time. Her requests for information to the relevant camps as to whether her husband was still alive were either negative or not even answered. Upon application by his wife, Major Wilhelm Weimann was declared dead on 12 February, 1955.

DRK/Familie Weimann

– – – – – – – – – – – –

Pionier-Bataillon 45:

For the few months prior to being summoned to Stalingrad, Pionier-Bataillon 45 was directly subordinated to 6. Armee and had been busy carrying out many tasks, both along the Don river and in the endless steppe west of there. Two river crossings in August had given the battalion casualties, but since then, losses were almost non-existent because their main duties consisted of backbreaking digging and construction of defensive lines, all under the blistering sun. Whilst it was hard and tiring work, the men enjoyed it and at least one remembers it as "by far the most wonderful time during the entire Russian campaign". The almost peacetime atmosphere disappeared when the battalion – one of the oldest pioneer units in the Wehrmacht – received the order to head east to Stalingrad.

In October 1934, the 3rd motorised company of Pionier-Bataillon 5 was used to set up a new battalion, temporarily called Pionier-Bataillon 'B', under the command of Major Gustav Boehringer[1]. It had four companies but relinquished its 2. Kompanie in autumn 1935 so that it could be used to form a new battalion. On 15 October, 1935, Pionier-Bataillon 'B' received its official title of Pionier-Bataillon 45 (mot.) and was established as a Korps-Pionier-Bataillon. It was located in the Swabian city of Ulm, its tactical symbol was the Ulm sparrow[2] and it was garrisoned in the newly constructed Reinhardt Barracks in Neu-Ulm. The battalion was intensively schooled in obstacle construction, installation of minefields and erection of field fortifications. Oberstleutnant Walter Birkenbihl took command of the battalion in September 1936, and Major Paul Velke[3] took over on 1 April, 1938. Soon after, the battalion – minus 3. Kompanie – was employed in the Karlsruhe-Kehl area to play its part in building the Westwall fortifications. The battalion received the thanks of the Führer for its work here. In 1939 – just as in 1938 – the battalion put special emphasis on training for assaults on bunkers with live ammunition and flamethrowers, and in getting used to the detonation of demolition charges in war-like conditions. In August 1939 the unit marched out to the building of the Westwall and never returned to its garrison. During the Polish campaign in September 1939, the battalion was deployed under Armeetruppe 'S' on the Upper Rhine.

---

1. Boehringer, Generalleutnant Gustav, RK.z.Kvk.m.Schw., DKiS; Stab/Pi.Btl.45; born 7 July, 1892 in Strassburg. Died 20 February, 1974 in Konstanz.
2. 'Der Ulmer Spatz' (the Ulm sparrow), based on an old Ulm story.
3. Velke, Oberst Paul, RK; Stab/Pi.Btl.45; born 9 November, 1890 in Velpke. Died of wounds 28 July, 1942 in Verkhne-Solonovsky.

At 0535 hours on 10 May, 1940, the battalion crossed the Belgian border out of the Eifel and moved in the direction of the Meuse near Givet-Dinant. Together with the attached Strassen-Bau-Bataillon 26, they cleared obstacles of various sorts until 1500 hours, thus opening the way for the panzers. On 13 May, 1940, at Givet on the Meuse, the battalion succeeded in reconnoitring a weakly-held crossing site and brought across the reconnaissance battalion and two infantry battalions of 32. Infanterie-Division. One pioneer company had to spend 17 hours – and the relieving company 15 hours – uninterruptedly rowing inflatable floats and ferries across the 130-metre wide river. The enemy noticed this too late and his counterattack was unsuccessful. The Meuse river crossing had been the battalion's first major challenge – which it passed with flying colours – and was important to the overall advance because it was decisive for further operations by significantly easing the crossings at other places and thus indirectly helping the attack. In three days the first German forces were on the opposite bank of the Meuse. On the evening of 14 May, 1940, after personal reconnaissance by the commander, the battalion took Givet-East by storm and continued the attack across the Meuse with a company, which cleaned up French bunkers and pockets of resistance in Givet-West. Always at the front of these attacks was Leutnant Walter Heinrich, a platoon commander in 2. Kompanie, who fearlessly moved around in the open while bullets whizzed about him. For his role in crossing the Meuse and capturing Givet, he was awarded the Iron Cross Second Class on 17 May.

Still under fire from enemy infantry, the unit began building a bridge and by 1700 hours had

The battalion attends roll call in its purpose-built Reinhardt Barracks in Neu-Ulm, April 1939, in preparation for a parade in honour of the Führer's birthday.

On 14 May, 1940, assault groups of the battalion sweep the streets of Givet, a small town of strategic importance because of its bridges across the Meuse and its location at the junction of two major roads. While the other men have taken cover to avoid French sniper fire, Leutnant Walter Heinrich – pistol in hand and grenade stuffed in boot – stands out in the open, oblivious to his own safety.

Mayer/Dreier

Mark/NARA

completed the 130-metre long construction capable of bearing 16-tonnes. It was now possible to get ammunition, supplies and the necessary artillery to the infantry units on the west bank of the Meuse. The shaken enemy was soon thrown back and the way into northern France was opened up. Oberstleutnant Velke received the Knight's Cross for his unit's action. Later, the battalion took part in the fighting in Flanders, Artois and on the Somme and was also used for an attack over the Scarpe. During the fighting near La Bassé and Lille, the seemingly indestructible Leutnant Heinrich was heavily wounded on 28 May when he was sprayed by shrapnel. The battalion crossed the Somme at Abbeville. During the battles between the Somme

Oberstleutnant Paul Velke was awarded the Knight's Cross for his leadership of the battalion during the French campaign.

and the Seine the battalion was thrown into burning Rouen, where it saved the world-famous cathedral from destruction. Then, as advanced guards, reinforced by motorised artillery, it rolled onto the Loire at Nantes where it secured the bridges. Upriver from Nantes the battalion built the longest pontoon bridge of the campaign using the equipment of 14 bridging columns. This bridge over the Loire had a total length of 375 metres.

The rest of the year saw the battalion as occupation troops on the Channel coast. On 1 October, 1940 the battalion handed over its 2. Kompanie to Panzer-Pionier-Bataillon 92. The missing company was reformed from the battalion's own reserves. A fresh batch of replacements also arrived and they were trained over the next six months. One of them, 20-year-old Pionier Karl Krauss, a fit man who enjoyed sports and had been physically toughened by his stint in the labour service, remembers the training as being "extraordinarily

The bridge over the Loire was 375 metres long, had a capacity of 16 tonnes and took only 22 hours to erect on 22-23 June, 1940 with 14 bridging columns and 6 pioneer companies (1., 2. and 3./Pi.Btl.45, 2. and 3./Pi.Btl.31 and 3./Pi.Btl.2).

difficult". He also clearly recalls reading a motto inscribed above a barracks doorway: 'To be a pioneer means to be hard'. Elements of the training were practised on the grassed-over moonscape of the Somme battlefield from the First World War. Occasionally, men would crash through the ground and end up in a rotten old dug-out. Battered and rusty helmets, weapons and ammunition were also no rarity. As the training continued, the battalion went into winter quarters in Peronne sur Somme. In mid-December 1940, the much-loved and daredevilish platoon commander, Leutnant Heinrich, returned to the battalion after spending six months in various hospitals, his apparent aura of invincibility still intact.

On 1 April, 1941, the battalion was hurriedly loaded aboard trains and sent east. No-one knew where they were going. After a trip across

The graves of Gefreiter Christof Baum[4], Oberpionier Emil Gerold[5], Gefreiter Alfred Späth[6] and – in front – Leutnant Karl Rehm[7], all from 3./Pi.Btl.45, all killed on 23 May, 1940 at Feuchy, near Arras. Today, they are all buried in the Bourdon war cemetery, still in the same order.

southern Germany, through Austria and into western Hungary, the battalion was offloaded not far from the Yugoslavian border. On 11 April, the battalion moved off as part of the vanguard of Panzergruppe Kleist. There was no noteworthy resistance in Croatia and Zagreb was soon reached. The battalion then turned to the south-east and began the push towards Belgrade between the Save and Drau rivers, a fertile area where the troops were warmly welcomed by villagers of German settlements. After fighting for bridges in the Mitrovica district, near the old Turkish fortress of Sabac and in the area around Zemlin, the battalion went into quarters in the Alexander barracks in Zemlin. Casualties during the campaign had been negligible.

At the end of April, the men and vehicles were loaded aboard trains and headed north, only travelling by night. They halted in railway sidings during the day. Once darkness fell, they moved further east, across Pomerania and West Prussia, and unloaded in Schlochau, near the Polish border. On the bitterly cold first day of May, the battalion drove across the former German-Polish boundary near Konitz, then later through the Gnesen-Hohensalza area and finally set up camp in a backward Polish village south of Biala-Podlaska, about 25km west of Brest-Litovsk. It now became clear to most of the men that a war was being prepared against the Soviet Union. The appalling state of the dirt roads in the area meant that the battalion spent most of its time laying down kilometre after kilometre of corduroy roads, all running towards the east. In June, the battalion staff received cartographic material and for the first time saw its proposed route in the forthcoming attack: Brest - Slutsk - Bobruisk - Mogilev - Roslavl - Borodino - Moscow. Some staff members could not help

4. Baum, Gefreiter Christof, 3./Pi.Btl.45; born 10 April, 1914 in Gross-Bockenheim. Killed in action, 23 May, 1940 in Feuchy. Buried in Bourdon war cemetery: Block 25, Row 15, Grave 583.

5. Gerold, Oberpionier Emil, 3./Pi.Btl.45; born 6 July, 1915 in Giengen. Killed in action, 23 May, 1940 in Feuchy. Buried in Bourdon war cemetery: Block 25, Row 15, Grave 584.

6. Späth, Gefreiter Alfred, 3./Pi.Btl.45; born 16 January, 1917 in Gallenweiler. Killed in action, 23 May, 1940 in Feuchy. Buried in Bourdon war cemetery: Block 25, Row 15, Grave 585.

7. Rehm, Oberleutnant Karl, 3./Pi.Btl.45; born 17 March, 1916 in Pfullingen. Killed in action, 23 May, 1940 in Feuchy/Arras. Buried in Bourdon war cemetery: Block 25, Row 15, Grave 586.

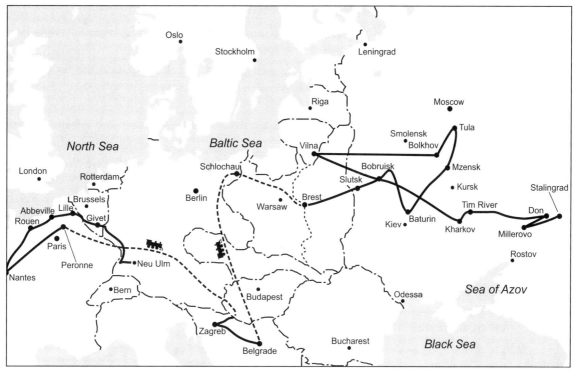

Movement of Pionier-Bataillon 45, 1939-1942.

but think that it was similar to Napoleon's advance to the Russian capital in 1812. During the night of 20 June, 1941, the battalion formed up and moved along the corduroy roads through the swampy birch forests that were thick with swarms of mosquitoes. With orders to be extremely quiet, the battalion camouflaged itself in the swamp and sat tight the entire day of 21 June in +30 degree heat. The battalion had been directly subordinated to Panzergruppe Guderian.

At 0300 hours on 22 June, 1941, thousands of guns began a barrage on the regions along and behind the Bug River. Only then did the men of Pionier-Bataillon 45 notice that they had been encamped directly in front of a well-camouflaged artillery unit. The battalion moved up to the river and began assembling their pontoons and bridging elements. Half an hour after the artillery suddenly burst to life, it just as quickly broke off. The silence was almost as eerie as the crash of the big guns. It was not long until the Soviets replied: heavy calibre shells howled in. Towering fountains of water erupted to the left and right of the bridging site. Nevertheless, work continued and the bridge was completed in an hour. The battalion crossed into the Soviet Union shortly afterwards as lines of Stukas and fighters buzzed overhead.

After breaking through the border positions on the Bug, the battalion – together with several panzer battalions – threaded their way along narrow roads through the Pripyet marshes towards Bobruisk. They were frequently attacked by Soviet Ratas that flew along the length of the columns, strafing and dropping bombs. There was no choice but to dive to the left or right, into the foetid and swampy birch forests that were already littered with abandoned Soviet materiel such as half-submerged lorries, cannon and the bloated bodies of dead horses. Buzzing over everything were dense clouds of mosquitoes. The battalion suffered its first dead and wounded. After almost a week of this, Napoleon's fateful river of Beresina was reached at

Bobruisk. The pioneers dashed over the partly burning bridge and captured the city. The first week of July was taken up by fighting forward through sand and forest near Rogachev. As part of XXIV. Korps (mot.), the battalion now came under the command of Oberstleutnant Ernst Häusele[8] and positioned itself to attack across the Dnepr. On 10 July, it crossed the broad river near Stary Bykhov and helped form a bridgehead against ever-increasing Soviet resistance which often devolved into hand-to-hand combat. As soon as a sufficiently large bridgehead had been won, a pontoon bridge capable of bearing 24 tonnes was built. Panzers and infantry threw the enemy back and a temporary bridge had to be built for all the supply traffic. The bridge was then dismantled to be used at the next river. The Stalin Line had been cracked open. For two weeks after that, the battalion was embroiled in fierce defensive fighting near Szosh. Then they crossed the Szosh at Krichev. And then the Desna at Novgorod-Seversk. Then the Seym at Kostobobre and Baturin and a number of smaller rivers in between. The battalion played its part in forming the massive Kiev pocket which eventually netted over 660,000 prisoners and seemingly endless quantities of vehicles and weapons. Swift-moving attacks alternated with weeks of defensive combat. Near Mzensk, the battalion for the first time endured the terrifying experience of a Stalin Organ bombardment and also saw the T-34s in action. Heavy casualties were suffered by the battalion around Mzensk, including Oberleutnant Reinhold Seiz[9], commander of 1. Kompanie, who was wounded.

Curious pioneers examine a T-34 for the first time. The inadequacy of German anti-tank guns meant the pioneers were often called upon to kill tanks.

Another unpleasant surprise was that despite all efforts to maintain standards of cleanliness, the men, and also the officers, had lice. Washing and cleaning of clothes did nothing.

In November 1941, 2. Panzerarmee launched an all-out attack on Tula in the direction of Kashira–Moscow. After obstinate fighting, they thrust through to the edge of Tula, a city of 300,000. On a small bridge east of the city, the pioneers – wearing their hip-waders – stood in the freezing water and built a bridge out of the trestles of the bridging equipment. In the following days, the battalion was repeatedly deployed as infantry in temperatures that fell to -30°. From a lightly forested area 2km east of Tula, the weary pioneers watched endless freight trains pull up and disgorge thousands of fresh Siberian troops well-equipped for winter warfare. The battalion received an order: "Positions are to be held until the last man". The ground was frozen solid so 'positions' consisted of holes scooped out of the snow. Violent close combat ensued. Leutnant Karl-Hermann Zehm[10], a platoon commander in 2. Kompanie, was wounded on 9 December when struck by three bullets, one passing through

8. Häusele, Oberst Ernst, Stab/Pi.Btl.45; born 11 January, 1897 in Ulm/Donau. No further information known.

9. Seiz, Oberleutnant Reinhold, 1./Pi.Btl.45; born 1918 in Reutlingen. Killed in action, early 1944 near Odessa.

10. Zehm, Oberleutnant Karl-Hermann, 2./Pi.Btl.45; born 19 February, 1921 in Stettin. Still alive in 2006.

his left wrist while the other two struck his right forearm.

When the German spearhead near Tula was forced to pull back, there were three hard days when the battalion was deployed as the pivotal point for the retreat. It lost contact on the left flank and was almost cut off but just managed to escape encirclement. The retreat continued in blisteringly cold weather: the thermometer dropped to -45°. The battalion remained as a rearguard and in this way reached the Bolkhov area, north-east of Orel. It was deployed together with elements of the Großdeutschland infantry regiment to block a Soviet breakthrough in the area of Bolkhov-Belev. On 27 December, 1941, near Vasykovo, the commander of 3. Kompanie, Oberleutnant Horst Drewitz[11], ordered an attack over a completely coverless field. Some men thought that, tactically, the attack was a crime. As predicted, the company suffered heavy casualties: amongst the dead were Leutnant Elmar Lieb[12], regarded by all as a highly intelligent man, Leutnant Karl Pfeifer[13], Obergefreiter Raimund Burkhardt[14], Obergefreiter Paul Haller[15] and Pionier Kurt Stengel[16], all men who'd been with the battalion for a long time and whose deaths were thought to be completely unnecessary. The man responsible, Oberleutnant Drewitz – who could in no way be considered inexperienced, having served as a company commander in the battalion since the war began – also paid the price: he was hit in the neck by a bullet that paralysed both arms and rendered him mute[17]. The battalion adjutant, Leutnant Fritz Karcher[18], took command of 3. Kompanie.

On 1 January, 1942 the battalion – formed into Kampfgruppe Häusele with the attached MG-Battalion 5 – pushed into the great woodlands north-west of Bolkhov to reconnoitre and secure a deep breakthrough point. Losses in officers continued: Leutnant Karcher fell ill on 12 January and was sent back to Germany. On 15 January, 1942, near Krapivna, Leutnant Karl Bauer[19] was killed while Leutnant Hans-Joachim Pietsch[20] was wounded. Both men were platoon commanders in 1. Kompanie. The next day, Leutnant Heinrich was hit in the right calf by a piece of shrapnel but remained with his men. On 18 January, the unit's commander, Oberstleutnant Häusele, received a transfer and left the battalion. A new commander was on the way but for the moment, the battalion was taken over by its highest-ranking field officer, Leutnant Heinrich, who was a pillar of strength at the front. Also still at the front at this time were Leutnant Fritz Molfenter[21], Leutnant Manfred Kimmich[22] –

---

11. Drewitz, Major Horst, 3./Pi.Btl.45; born 31 May, 1913 in Berlin. No further information known.

12. Lieb, Oberleutnant Elmar, 3./Pi.Btl.45; born 2 January, 1919 in Ulm. Killed in action, 27 December, 1941 near Vasykovo.

13. Pfeifer, Leutnant Karl, 3./Pi.Btl.45; born 20 October, 1919 in Hann.Münden. Killed in action, 27 December, 1941 near Vasykovo.

14. Burkhardt, Obergefreiter Raimund, 3./Pi.Btl.45; born 27 May, 1915 in Hettensberg. Killed in action, 27 December, 1941 near Vasykovo.

15. Haller, Obergefreiter Paul, 3./Pi.Btl.45; born 2 July, 1909 in Osterhofen. Killed in action, 27 December, 1941 near Vasykovo.

16. Stengel, Pionier Kurt, 3./Pi.Btl.45; born 24 January, 1921 in Gravelsbaum. Killed in action, 27 December, 1941 near Vasykovo.

17. After 18 months in hospital, he took command of the reformed battalion in June 1943 but signs of paralysis never completely disappeared, adversely affecting his career. He ended up commanding a pioneer battalion far from the front-line.

18. Karcher, Hauptmann Fritz, 3./Pi.Btl.45; born 2 August, 1916 in Strassburg. No further information known.

19. Bauer, Oberleutnant Karl, 1./Pi.Btl.45; born 21 February, 1917 in Bad Dürkheim. Killed in action, 15 January, 1942, near Krapivna Gorodok

20. Pietsch, Oberleutnant Hans-Joachim, 1./Pi.Btl.45; born 28 May, 1921 in Bautzen. Still alive in 2006.

21. Molfenter, Oberleutnant Fritz, 2./Pi.Btl.45; born 12 August, 1919 in Ulm. Missing in action, 23 January, 1943 in Stalingrad. See Appendix 2 (page 576) for more details.

22. Kimmich, Leutnant Manfred, 1./Pi.Btl.45; born 23 January, 1920 in Sobald Sulz a.N. Died in captivity, 20 October, 1944 in Arsk, Romania. See Appendix 2 (page 574) for more details.

who'd arrived in late December from officer's training straight into the icy hell of the Russian Front – Leutnant Erich Skutlartz[23] and Leutnant Karl Vögele[24]. At the beginning of February, the battalion finally received replacements from Pionier-Ersatz-Bataillon 5, located in its home garrison of Ulm. Amongst them were four officers, including Leutnant Anton Locherer[25], who had fought with the battalion during the French campaign as a Gefreiter. Now, after a year of training as an officer and biding his time in a replacement battalion, he returned to his 2. Kompanie comrades as a freshly-baked Leutnant. His first assignment was to construct and improve makeshift bridges, Soon, however, he was requested to help with another task: to bury the bodies of many fallen infantrymen. This proved to be impossible because the ground was as hard as steel, so the stiff corpses were stacked in empty huts. Shortly after, Locherer was informed that two of the officers that had arrived with him had been killed not far away, at Leninskoye, on 15 March, 1942. They were Leutnant Franz Häussler[26] and Leutnant Alfons Kleinheinz[27], both of 3. Kompanie.

April 1942 brought fine, warm weather which melted all the snow, dramatically raised water levels and transformed the ground into a bottomless quagmire. It was in these conditions that the battalion received an order to withdraw from the front and move to a new sector. The muck and mud were almost indescribable. Leutnant Locherer remembers that "often, I had to dismount from my horse because it was stuck up to its belly in mud". The vehicles fared much worse. The battalion limped to its objective – the small village of Zaskiewice east of Vilna – with everyone totally caked in mud and filth. The battalion was to remain in this area to rest and recover. For his performance in leading the battalion, Leutnant Heinrich was named in the Honour Roll of the German Army on 18 April, 1942. He had been proposed for the German Cross in Gold on 2 February, 1942 but it was not approved. Arriving shortly afterwards to take over was the new commander, Hauptmann Gerd Parchow[28]. Leutnant Locherer described him thus:

Familie Vögele

Leutnant Heinrich, Molfenter and Kimmich relax in Zaskiewice after months of hard winter combat.

---

23. Skutlartz, Oberleutnant Erich, 3./Pi.Btl.45; born 14 April, 1916 in Lahr-Dinglingen. Died 30 December, 2001 in Breisach. See Appendix 2 (page 578) for more details.

24. Vögele, Hauptmann Karl, 3./Pi.Btl.45; born 30 August, 1918 in Altshausen. Died 6 May, 1997 in Tübingen. See Appendix 2 (page 579) for more details.

25. Locherer, Hauptmann Anton, 2./Pi.Btl.45; born 22 June, 1920 in Ulm. Still alive in 2004. See Appendix 2 (page 575) for more details.

26. Häussler, Leutnant Franz, 3./Pi.Btl.45; born 28 February, 1918 in Ulm. Killed in action, 15 March, 1942 in Leninskoye.

27. Kleinheinz, Oberleutnant Alfons, 3./Pi.Btl.45; born 26 June, 1919 in Stuttgart. Killed in action, 15 March, 1942 in Leninskoye.

28. Parchow, Hauptmann Gerd, Stab/Pi.Btl.45; born 15 December, 1909 in Gettorf. No further information known. See Appendix 2 (page 576) for more details.

Hauptmann Parchow was a Prussian's Prussian: it was incomprehensible to me why the army personnel office had to send such a man to a purely Swabian battalion, a real 'Kommisskopf'[29] for whom nothing could be done right. He announced again and again that he would make the battalion the best in the Wehrmacht, but he'd failed to notice that we had already been that for a long time. Our battle-tested boys didn't care much about it, so the NCOs and we officers had to stomach a lot. He made a performance over every missing nail, as if the outcome of the war depended on it. Of course we knew that after a year on campaign a lot was missing and needed to be replaced, but that was why there were big supply depots where you could get everything.

Hauptmann Gerd Parchow

In June, the battalion was ordered to head east, destination unknown. They eventually reached their assigned preparation areas along the Tim river, dug in and camouflaged themselves against aerial observation. A few days later, Hauptmann Parchow was inspecting his units and he eventually reached the platoon of Leutnant Locherer:

> Our commander visited us just as a hearty salvo crashed down nearby. We already knew from the whistling of the shells where they would land; the incoming salvo was quite close, but it didn't endanger us, so the following situation arose: the commander dropped to the ground in a flash, while I remained standing and made my report to him as he was still lying there. My soldiers looked on and grinned. He then stood up, allowed me to quickly show him my platoon and enquired whether there were many such surprise artillery raids. I answered that there were at least a couple every hour, whereupon he wished us all the best and disappeared.

The summer offensive began at 0215 hours on 28 June, 1942 under an arch of artillery and nebelwerfer shells. The battalion erected a bridge over the Tim by mid-morning and traffic immediately began to roll across it. Casualties were considered light: a few men killed and wounded, including Oberleutnant Heinrich who was struck in the right thigh by a piece of shrapnel: he stayed with his company. The following month was a blur of endless slogs through dusty roads, construction of bridges and occasional firefights with enemy stragglers. Despite the enormous tracts of land being overrun, very few prisoners were being taken, but the upside was that the battalion suffered barely any casualties. In the push south into the Don area, the battalion was attached to 24. Panzer-Division and helped form the southern pincer in the encirclement battle in the great Don bend. The pincers met in the hills west of the great river. The battalion was then attached to another division to clean up the pocket. Mounted in their vehicles, they pushed north through vast graveyards of shattered Soviet tanks, leaping out again and again to engage enemy infantry in furious gun battles. The Germans tried to catch their adversary but the Soviet riflemen always melted away in the direction of the Don. On one occasion the pioneers faced a much larger enemy group, so they dug in and sent their vehicles away. Leutnant Locherer reports what happened next:

---

29. A 'Kommisskopf' is a soldier who embodies the military lifestyle in a negative way, for example, shouting like a drill sergeant, a master of the 'art' of red tape and idiotic bureaucracy, slavish obedience towards superiors and regulations, and expecting the same from subordinates.

Terrible news reached us: all of our vehicles had fallen into Russian hands. A part of our company was sent there while I held the position with my platoon, ready to fend off any attacks. We soon received word: all vehicles had been retrieved, but every driver had been shot, a cruel blow for our company. My driver was with our Horch in the workshop because of a cracked chassis, so he escaped certain death.

The battalion's men bury their earlier commander, Knight's Cross winner Oberstleutnant Paul Velke, in Oblivskaya, 30 July, 1942.

During the advance towards the Stalingrad area, Oberst Velke, commander of the battalion from 1937 to mid-1941 but now commander of Pionier-Regimentsstab 604, was killed by an enemy mine on 28 July, 1942 while reconnoitring a crossing site over the Don. On the same day, the current commander, Hauptmann Parchow, was lightly wounded, as was platoon commander Leutnant Schütz[30]. Because Velke's old battalion was in the same operational area, it was able to provide the last military honour for its highly-esteemed former commander. On 30 July, 1942, the Ulmer Korps-Pionier-Bataillon 45 took part in the funeral parade in Oblivskaya.

On 16 August, Hauptmann Parchow was admitted to hospital suffering severe bouts of dysentery. The next day he received a transfer to a replacement battalion back in Germany and the battalion was informed that a new commander was on the way, this time a Bavarian. Until his arrival, the senior company commander and former adjutant, Oberleutnant Fritz Glöckler[31], took temporary command of the unit. While Glöckler took over the reins, 1. and 3. Kompanie had been subordinated to 384. Infanterie-

---

30. Schütz, Hauptmann Günter, Pi.Btl.45; born 21 August, 1912. Died of wounds, 6 August, 1943. See Appendix 2 (page 578) for more details.

31. Glöckler, Hauptmann Fritz, Pi.Btl.45; born 11 July, 1909 in Konstanz. Killed in action, 13 November, 1943 near Nadvin/Lipuyaki. See Appendix 2 (page 572) for more details.

Flies! The NCOs of 3. Kompanie have lunch with several thousand uninvited guests. Second from left is Oberfeldwebel Hermann Tag and on the far right is Feldwebel Arthur Deuschle. Both were later declared 'missing in action' at Stalingrad.

Division to help eliminate one of the many Soviet pockets squashed up against the Don river and suffered casualties in the process: Obergefreiter Anton Haas[32] and Martin Mayer[33] were killed 4km south of Verkhne-Akatov on 16 August, while platoon commander Leutnant Karl Gebauer[34], Unteroffizier Wilhelm Segmehl[35] and Pionier Fritz Seiz[36] fell on 17 August 8km west of Vizhne-Gerassimov. Leutnant Locherer was also wounded on 16 August when a solid blow on his left upper arm knocked the submachine-gun out of his hands, but there was no pain, so Locherer thought no more of it. Only a few hours later, when it suddenly became painful, did Locherer have it looked at. Several shell splinters were dug out of his arm but he only remained in the rear for two days before returning to his company, just in time for the crossing of the Don. For this attack, the battalion was placed under Pionier-Regimentsstab 605, whose task was to get 295. Infanterie-Division across the river. Pionier-Bataillone 41 and 45, together with Pionier-Bataillon 295, would force the crossing. A light veil of fog that lay over the Don during the night disappeared and the first wave moved off into a lurid dawn on 21 August. The crossing of 295. Infanterie-Division proceeded without hiccups, a bridgehead was swiftly established and weak resistance quickly

---

32. Haas, Obergefreiter Anton, 3./Pi.Btl.45; born 20 October, 1915 in Pommertsweiler. Killed in action, 16 August, 1942 near Verkhne-Akatov.

33. Mayer, Obergefreiter Martin, 3./Pi.Btl.45; born 13 April, 1915 in Sontheim. Killed in action, 16 August, 1942 near Verkhne-Akatov.

34. Gebauer, Leutnant Karl, 1./Pi.Btl.45; born 4 April, 1919 in Sangerhausen. Killed in action, 17 August, 1942 near Vizhne-Gerassimov. See Appendix 2 (page 572) for more details.

35. Segmehl, Unteroffizier Wilhelm, 1./Pi.Btl.45; born 8 October, 1917 in Langenschemmern. Killed in action, 17 August, 1942 near Vizhne-Gerassimov.

36. Seiz, Pionier Fritz, 1./Pi.Btl.45; born 15 November, 1915 in Ulm. Killed in action, 17 August, 1942 near Vizhne-Gerassimov.

Above: Leutnant Albrecht Gläser (left), a platoon commander in 3. Kompanie, and his Zugtrupp (platoon HQ personnel), on the move in early August 1942. The shirtless man is Obergefreiter Moritz Heinle, later missing in action at Stalingrad.

Below: Leutnant Gläser and his men pose for a photo after sweeping a village for enemy stragglers. Obergefreiter Heinle is second from right. Gläser was severely wounded on 21 August during the first Don crossing and died two days later.

Right: After an exhausting day on operations, Leutnant Karl Vögele catches a quick nap, having placed his belt and pistol on the bonnet (Vögele preferred to carry his privately-owned Mauser pistol as his side-arm). The vehicles were homes to the men and carried all manner of equipment. Seen in the rack behind Vögele are two Soviet PPSh submachine-guns and four stick grenades.

Below: Attack over the Don north of Kalach on 25 August. The operation was completed by 1900 hours and involved 60 storm boats and elements of 6 pioneer battalions. Soviet forces immediately recognised the danger and began bombarding the bridge and its approaches with rockets and artillery. The Red Air Force also repeatedly bombed and strafed the bridge in low-level attacks. Despite their vigorous attempts, the bridge remained intact and traffic continued to flow across into the expanding bridgehead, as seen here on 26 August. In the background, a plume of thick smoke rises from a burning ammunition dump.

Familie Vögele

dissolved when the Soviet defenders disappeared into the thick undergrowth. The small foothold was expanded and secured, and then the attached pioneer battalions hauled forward the bridging elements. Construction proceeded rapidly and the Luchinskoi bridge was ready at 1650 hours. Columns immediately started rolling across it. During the day, Leutnant Albrecht Gläser[37], a platoon commander in 3. Kompanie, was seriously wounded and died two days later. The battalion took over protection of the bridge, together with an anti-aircraft battalion, and was only relieved on 23 August when it was sent south to force another crossing of the Don, this time north of Kalach. The battalion would support Pionier-Bataillon 171 (71. Infanterie-Division) with its 24 assault boats. The operation began before dawn on 25 August. In the vanguard of the attack was Leutnant Locherer:

> We prepared our assault boats bright and early, and after an artillery barrage, grabbed them, brought them down to the water, jumped in, gunned the motors and scooted across the Don at top speed. I kneeled in the first boat and we leapt out onto the river bank, while the assault boats returned and fetched the next wave.

Locherer was lucky: many other boats and their passengers fell victim to artillery and machine-guns as they zipped across the 300 metre wide Don. Two small bridgeheads were formed both sides of Beresov Island and these were continually strengthened by the arrival of succeeding waves. The bridgeheads were then joined together and expanded. By midday, it was 5km deep and 6km wide. When ample infantry forces had arrived in the bridgehead, the pioneers were relieved and sent back to the river to help with the vitally important bridge. Construction was hindered by fire from a solitary Soviet mortar – placed far outside the bridgehead – which landed its shells with great accuracy: the commander of a bridging column, who was standing next to Locherer, was struck in the neck by shrapnel and collapsed at Locherer's feet, dead[38]. Only after a long while did the German artillery silence the stubborn mortar and its crew. The 320-metre-long pontoon bridge, begun at 0430 hours, was completed at 1900 hours. Heavy weapons rushed across to repel Soviet attacks. The temporary commander of the battalion, Oberleutnant Glöckler, was lightly wounded during the bridging operations but remained with the troops.

On 28 August, the battalion received an order to head across the bridge to help their hard-pressed brothers from Pionier-Bataillon 171. Soviet forces had penetrated into Kalach and Pionier-Bataillon 45 was ordered to take it. Leutnant Locherer recalls:

> We hurriedly grabbed the necessary bits and pieces from our vehicles on the other bank, like hand grenades and demolition charges in great quantities. The army held this operation to be so important that Stuka operations had been arranged for our assault. We were positioned only about a hundred metres from the Russians, so we laid out swastika flags to signal to the Stukas where we were, as well as declaring this by phone. They came at the agreed time, began their dives behind us and we saw how they released the bombs, which howled directly over us and struck the designated targets. While they were still exploding, we stormed the first houses, screaming 'hurra' and dispensing hand grenades and demolition charges. Resistance was comparatively light, probably because of the Stuka attack and our 'can do' attitude. Kalach was soon in our hands. At any rate, the Wehrmacht Report the next day announced that pioneers had conquered Kalach in house-to-house fighting.

---

37. Gläser, Leutnant Albrecht, 3./Pi.Btl.45; born 13 June, 1919 in Stuttgart. Died of wounds, 23 August, 1942 near Krassny-Peskovatka.

38. Grämer, Oberleutnant, Br.Bau-Btl.134; date of birth unknown. Killed in action, 25 August, 1942 near Kalach-on-Don.

Locherer received the Iron Cross First Class for his role in the Don crossings and the capture of Kalach. After this operation, Leutnant Karl Vögele, a platoon commander in 3. Kompanie, was posted to pioneer training courses in Kursk and Minsk and would not return until well after the Stalingrad drama had begun.

On 3 September, the new battalion commander finally arrived. He was 47-year-old Hauptmann Ludwig Büch, an engineer in civilian life. He had been transferred from the Führerreserve of Heeresgruppe B. A few days later, the battalion was pulled out of the line and sent back to the Chir where it was able to rest and get everything back into shape. Mail from home arrived after a long time, as did replacements in mid-September. One of them was Gefreiter Karl Krauss who had left the battalion in February 1942 because of an injury. After recovering and undergoing more rigorous training, he returned to his 2. Kompanie as an Offizieranwärter[39]: "When I arrived at the great Don river, I was joyfully welcomed by my old company." In the following weeks the battalion was placed directly under 6. Armee's pioneer commander for special duties. In October, the battalion received a new task: construction of new defensive positions behind the allied armies holding the 500km long flank along the Don river. Gefreiter Krauss recalls:

Leutnant Locherer proudly displays his well-deserved Iron Cross First Class.

> In the sunny and warm autumnal weather, we had the task of constructing potential rearward defence positions west of the river for the coming winter. This was in the area of Millerovo – Tatsinskaya/Morosovskaya. As a squad leader I received assistance from about 90 girls and women (17 to 32 year old). With that, I was 'chieftain' of a female Russian company! The majority of them were Cossacks and Ukrainians. Discipline and respect for each other constantly provided a good understanding. With teams of horses, we headed out every morning into the vast, endless steppe. This was by far my most wonderful time during the entire Russian campaign. Mutual trust built up in a short time. During the lunch break, the girls sang in harmony, sometimes singing slightly melancholic songs – songs about the infinite steppe. At my request, they brought along their balalaikas and delighted us with their spirited Cossack dances. These steppe villages were called Olkhov and Alexandrovka.

It was into this relaxed atmosphere that the order arrived for the battalion to head to Stalingrad via Kalach. Gefreiter Krauss remembers that "the villagers very much regretted this". Leutnant Locherer would not go to Stalingrad with his battalion:

> In the evening, we received the order to drive to Stalingrad with our combat elements. The staff company would remain behind as the mission would only be for a short time. Because I became adjutant of the battalion, I would take over the staff company and remain behind. With an uneasy feeling I watched my comrades drive off the next morning – Farewell forever?!

39. Trans.: 'Offizieranwärter' = 'officer candidate'.

The men hastily gathered their equipment, climbed aboard their cars and lorries and set out from the Millerovo area in the hinterland, across the parched steppe towards Stalingrad, 350km distant. Those who had not participated in the August fighting in the Don bend were amazed by what they saw. "We passed through the steppe near Kalach and saw the results of a clash between 6. Armee and a Russian tank army", recalls Gefreiter Krauss, "about one thousand shot up and derelict Russian tanks – from T-34s up to the 152mm equipped KV2s – covered the battleground and amongst all these were countless quantities of guns and other materiel. Did Ivan still have the power to resist?"

After a dusty and gruelling drive, the battalion reached its first destination, Kalach, where it was directed into small villages on the bank of the Don river. The total number of men who made the trip was 451, which broke down to 11 officers, 1 administrative official, 43 NCOs and 396 men. Combat strength was 9 officers, 30 NCOs and 246 men equipped with 27 light machine-guns, 6 gun mounts and 6 flamethrowers. The battalion may have had more flamethrowers than officially reported because Gefreiter Krauss remembers his 2. Kompanie being equipped with 3 German flamethrowers (weighing 40kg each) and 3 Italian flamethrowers (30kg each), the latter having possibly been acquired during their brief subordination to the Italian 8. Armee.

– – –

The battalion was an excellent blend of experience and youth. Most of the officers had been soldiers or NCOs in the battalion during the Polish or French campaigns: the battalion was one of the fortunate few where men would spend their entire careers. If they were wounded, retrained or promoted, chances were very good that they would return to their beloved Pionier-Bataillon 45.

Panzerpionier-Bataillon 50:

The only panzerpioneer battalion sent to Stalingrad for the offensive was Panzerpionier-Bataillon 50 from 22. Panzer-Division. This battalion differed from the others in that it was much more heavily armed and its 3. Kompanie was equipped with Sdkfz. 250/3 command half-tracks and Sdkfz. 251/6 armoured half-tracks. Although the battalion was relatively new, it had been formed from one of the army's older pioneer units, Pionier-Bataillon 50, which had been set up on 6 October, 1936 as a Korps-Pionier-Bataillon. Its peacetime garrison was the north German city of Harburg, part of Wehrkreis[40] X, and personnel for the new battalion came from three different units: Pionier-Bataillon 20, which was also stationed in Hamburg-Harburg; Pionier-Bataillon 12 from Stettin and Pionier-Bataillon 16 garrisoned in Höxter and Holzminden a.d. Weser. The first commander of Pionier-Bataillon 50 was Major Herbert Selle who, after giving up command of the battalion in 1940, would later go on to become Armeepionierführer of 6. Armee, and at Stalingrad in November 1942, he would meet his old battalion for the last time.

---

40. Trans.: 'Wehrkreis' = 'Military district'.

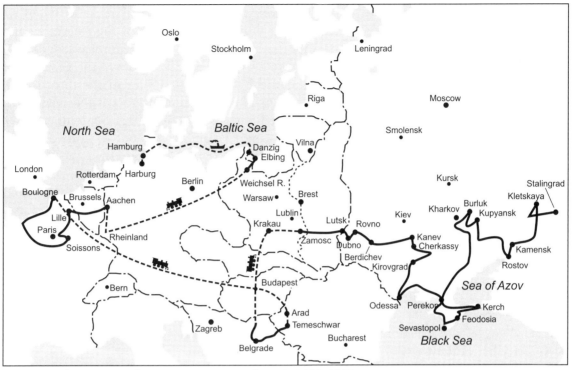

Movement of Pionier-Bataillon/Panzerpionier-Bataillon 50, 1939-1942.

Major Selle and the men of the fully-motorised Pionier-Bataillon 50 spent the pre-war years training hard in river crossings, bridge construction and other pioneering activities. Its barracks in Harburg were ideally located: a site on which to practise water activities was located near Moorburg on the Elbe River, only a fifteen minute foot-march away; its training grounds were on the edge of the city, all within thirty minutes of the barracks and consisted of various types of rough terrain to ensure a good all-round instruction for the young recruits; and finally, situated on the grounds directly opposite the barracks, was a shooting range for rifles and machine-guns. Larger training exercises meant the battalion had to leave its barracks, and in 1938, it seemed as if they were away from Harburg more than they were there. The year began with large-scale crossings of the Weser River near Nienburg-Hassbergen and the Aller River near Rethem, the swift currents[41] of both rivers making the construction of temporary crossings with ferries and bridging equipment exceedingly difficult. Having successfully completed these crossings, the battalion returned to Harburg and also passed another bridging exercise by throwing a bridge over the Kaiser-Wilhelm-Kanal. The battalion moved out a few months later and headed to the large training ground in Munster-Lager for instruction in sharpshooting. In late autumn, the battalion moved into southern Germany, in the Donaueschingen-Launigen area, for exercises in ferry construction and assault-boat driving on the Donau. In 1939, the battalion was transferred into the Eifel region along the West Wall to assist in erecting fortifications along the border. Although it was a lot of hard work, the men also enjoyed this time and remembered it fondly as a period of fun and sunny August skies. In August 1939, the battalion was ordered to down tools, return by rail to their Harburg barracks as quickly as

---

41. About 1.5 metres per second.

possible and immediately ready themselves for war. A couple of days later, when all preparations had been completed, the battalion drove out the gates of their barracks and headed in the direction of Hamburg's harbour. A large part of the battalion was loaded into an ocean-going steamer called the 'Walküre' (Valkyrie), which set off down the Elbe River, through the Kaiser-Wilhelm-Kanal and into the Baltic Sea, steaming in the direction of Danzig. The battalion was unloaded there and marched to Elbing where it received many different forms of infantry combat training over the next few days. On 1 September, 1939, the battalion moved out and passed from Elbing into Poland. It was put to immediate use in repairing destroyed bridges, one of its tasks being to erect a bridge over the Weichsel River. The battalion did not undertake other assignments because in 18 days, the Polish campaign was over. The men and equipment of Pionier-Bataillon 50 were loaded into trains and sent across Germany into the Rheinland, disembarking in the Neuß-Düsseldorf area where they spent the winter of 1939-40.

Mark/NARA

In early 1940, the battalion was transferred into the Aachen area, not far from the Dutch border. In mid-March, Major Selle gave up command of the battalion and took over Pionier-Regiment-Stabes 604. The new commander, Major Hellmuth Ermeler[42], arrived on 20 March, direct from the offices of OKH where he was a section head in the Pionier department of OKH Chef H.Rüst u. BdE[43]. Although he had been riding a desk since 1938, Ermeler had seen years of front-line service during the First World War. It had been two decades since Ermeler last felt the nerves that came with going into battle.

The battalion's campaign in the west began on 10 May, 1940 when it crossed the Meuse. For Pionier-Bataillon 50, the French campaign consisted mostly of marching and building bridges. First they moved through Holland and Belgium by crossing the Albert canal, the Gette, breaking through the Dyle position, then swiftly bouncing the Senette

Major Hellmuth Ermeler

and Dendre rivers before fighting in the Schelde for 4 days. Then, across the Lys followed by a week of combat in west Flanders and around Lille which ended on 30 May. The bulk of their assignments had been constructing dozens of small bridges and carrying out repairs on other larger crossings. After this, they were moved into position for an attack on the Somme on 5 June. On 6 June, 1940, during the breakthrough battles along the Somme, the battalion adjutant, Oberleutnant Gerhard Hoffmann[44], was shot through the thigh but remained with the troops. The battalion cross the Aisne on 8 June and continued the pursuit over the Oise and Ourcq rivers. Another river crossing, this time the Marne, and then they pushed in the direction of Paris. On 22 June, the commander of 2. Kompanie, Hauptmann Anton Lorenz[45], died in hospital from an illness. Just as the campaign was ending, the battalion moved into quarters, first in Soissons near Paris, and

---

42. Ermeler, Oberstleutnant Hellmuth, Stab/Pi.Btl.50; born 20 February, 1896 in Hannover. No further information known. See Appendix 2 (page 571) for more details.

43. Trans.: Chef H.Rüst u. BdE (Chef Heeresrüstung und Befehlshaber der Ersatzarmee) = Chief of Army Equipment and Commander of the Reserve Army.

44. Hoffmann, Major Gerhard, Stab/Pi.Btl.50; born 15 March, 1912 in Breslau. Missing in action, February 1945, in the Zichenau area.

45. Lorenz, Hauptmann Anton, 2./Pi.Btl.50; born 29 December 1898. Died of illness, 22 June, 1940.

Second platoon of 1./Pi.Btl.50 move into France, May 1940.

Above and below: Leutnant Kunze (centre), 1./Pi.Btl.50, conducts live firing exercises during a rest period in Yugoslavia, April 1941.

then into a sugar factory alongside the Somme River. Shortly thereafter, it moved to the Channel Coast as part of the occupation force and also trained for a seaborne landing against Britain. When that operation was called off, the battalion resumed normal duties.

For his role during this campaign, Major Ermeler received the clasp to both grades of his Iron Cross: for the Second Class on 31 May, 1940 and for the First Class on 5 August, 1940. Many changes in personnel took place in September 1940. At the beginning of the month, the commander of 1. Kompanie, Hauptmann Meyenburg, was transferred, and the battalion adjutant Oberleutnant Hoffmann, still recovering from the gunshot wound to his thigh, took over the company. On 29 September, 1940, Oberleutnant Paul Delius[46], who had been a platoon commander since December 1937 in both 1. and 3. Kompanien, was transferred to Pionier-Schule II[47]. In early 1941, the battalion was loaded into trains in the Boulogne-Etables area in northern France which took them through the beautiful Black Forest, Salzburg, Vienna and into Budapest. From here, they went through Szolnok to Arad in Romania and were finally offloaded in Temeschwar. On 5 April, 1941, every one of the battalion's vehicles was provided with a bright yellow sheet to be stretched over its bonnet to act as an aerial identification marking. Early the next morning, Pionier-Bataillon 50 – attached to the Großdeutschland Regiment – moved over the Yugoslavian border. The advance

46. Delius, Major Paul, RK; 3./Pi.Btl.50; born 11 December, 1912 in Versmold. DIed 5 August, 1992 in München.
47. Delius was to win the Knight's Cross on 11 March, 1945 as Major and Ia to Festungs-Kommandeur Abschnitt 44, Generalleutnant Otto Matterstock

The vast scale of warfare on the Eastern Front – and the resulting sheer brutality and devastation – stunned many German soldiers. The men of Pionier-Bataillon 50 were confronted by a slideshow of destruction on the roadsides as they moved deeper into the Soviet Union behind the armoured spearheads, ready to build bridges, clear mines or carry out one of the many other tasks demanded of the pioneers.

Top left: A Soviet BA-10 armoured car, knocked out and upended in fierce fighting. Although heavily armed (45mm gun), its armour was only sufficient to stop shell fragments and small arms fire: it was vulnerable to cannon fire, heavy machine-gun rounds and especially mines. One of the crew lies dead beside his vehicle.

Centre left: The battalion's vehicles skirt the remains of a KV-2 ripped apart by an internal explosion. This tank, weighing a hefty 53 tonnes and armed with a 152mm howitzer, was the heaviest in the Soviet arsenal in 1941 and quickly made the Germans realise their anti-tank guns and panzer armaments were inadequate. A supreme effort was required to knock out one of these armoured monsters.

Below: Every now and then, the pioneers were forced to dismount and engage bypassed enemy units. In this photo, they return (left, on the horizon) after putting down resistance and knocking out several tanks and other vehicles, including this armoured car.

progressed rapidly and on 11 April the battalion took part in the advance towards the Yugoslavian capital. Hostilities ceased on 17 April, 1941. After a short stint as occupation troops in northern Yugoslavia, the battalion again climbed into trains on 19 May and headed north-west through Krakow and ever deeper into Poland. With the sun sinking below the western horizon, the train continued on to the east. The battalion was unloaded in darkness in the Lublin countryside between Zamosc and Tomaschow and bivouacked in a forested region close to the German-Soviet border formed by the Bug River. In early June, a few weeks before Barbarossa began, the commander of 1. Kompanie, Oberleutnant Hoffmann, was transferred to another unit.

As part of the massive invasion force gathered for Operation Barbarossa, Pionier-Bataillon 50 moved towards the border in the pre-dawn greyness of 22 June, 1941. Their first order of the eastern campaign was to get a pontoon bridge erected over the Bug River, but this was no easy task: the bridging site was clearly visible to the enemy who was able to easily defend himself and upset the construction of the bridge. The battalion suffered its first deaths in the East. After more casualties and hours of dangerous work, the crossing was completed and infantry units streamed across the pontoon bridge. After several days, the battalion advanced to the east through Vladimir-Volynski, Lutsk (Luck), Dubno and Rovno. It was a haze of pioneer operations, bridge construction, mine removal and infantry-like attacks. On 14 July, 1941, while constructing a bridge across the Slucz near Czycvzka, north-west of Zwiahel – thus far enough removed from the front-line to be considered safe – the battalion was suddenly attacked by stragglers from the shattered Soviet 5th Army who were still equipped with heavy weapons. Substantial casualties were being suffered and the battalion faced a serious situation.

On 31 August, 1941, Pionier-Bataillon 50, together with other pioneer units, erected a long bridge over the Dnepr. At the same time, they operated several ferries to keep assault troops on the other side supplied with ammunition and food.

Leutnant August Elze[48], a platoon commander in 3. Kompanie, was killed. With the help of reinforcements sent by XVII. Armeekorps under the command of its Korpspionierführer, Oberst Selle – the battalion's old commander – the enemy was smashed by a counterattack and the situation restored. After that, the battalion moved on through Zhitomir, Berdichev and Belaya-Tserkov on the Dnepr as part of Panzergruppe Kleist. In late July and August, the battalion was employed to secure the operational area of 6. Armee in the Kanev-Boguslav area.

Near Cherkassy on the Dnepr, in a nocturnal operation by a powerful reconnaissance patrol in rubber rafts, the still-standing bridge span over the river – which had been partly destroyed by the enemy – was blown into the water by 3. Kompanie on its third attempt. Here, the Soviets had tried to attack and fire at the western bank from speedboats. The main body of the battalion lay in rest positions between Kremenchug and Dneprepetrovsk. A crossing of the Dnepr was in the offing. On 31 August, 1941, as pioneers from other battalions crossed the river in assault boats, Pionier-Bataillon 50, together with other units, started putting together the long bridge over the Dnepr. To keep the assault troops on the other side of the river supplied with ammunition and food, several ferries were also built. After construction of the bridge, the battalion marched across a large expanse of the

Above: After a 73 day siege, the battalion enters Odessa. October 1941.
Below: A pioneer parades around Odessa's docks with a Soviet flag.

Ukraine, occupying cities like Snamenka and Kirovgrad. A week after crossing the Dnepr, the battalion then moved into position further south, near the Romanians, and together with their allies, laid siege to the Black Sea harbour city of Odessa. The city surrendered on 16 October, 1941 after a protracted 73 day siege. The battalion then marched via Kherson and Nikolayev to the Perekop isthmus, the narrow doorway to the entire Crimea. This isthmus, a waterless, coverless, dead flat expanse of salt steppe that baked under the blazing sun, had been transformed by the Soviets into a powerful, 15km deep defence system. Over a five day period, beginning on 24 September, LIV. Armeekorps had thrashed their way forward, taking the town of Perekop and crossing the Tartar Ditch. After the capture of the strongly defended locality of Armyansk, the troops moved into slightly more open country. Ahead

48. Elze, Oberleutnant August, 3./Pi.Btl.50; born 31 July, 1916 in Graste. Killed in action, 14 July, 1941, near Czycvzka.

The Perekop isthmus, doorway to the Crimea, was fortified by Soviet forces to a depth of 15kms.

of them was the Ishun bottleneck, a parched expanse where massive salt lakes reduced the potential assault frontage to 3km. The offensive was halted due to the weakness and exhaustion of the German assault troops, the increasing number of Soviet divisions, and a massive Soviet attack between the Sea of Azov and the Dnepr which drew off German reinforcements heading for the Crimea. Only after the latter threat had been eliminated was it possible for 11. Armee to continue its advance into the Crimea. By then, however, Odessa had fallen and Soviet units evacuated from there made landfall at Sevastopol and other harbours along the west coast: they duly appeared at the battle front shortly before the renewed German offensive. This is the situation Pionier-Bataillon 50 found upon its arrival.

The attack began on 19 October. There was no room for tactical manoeuvre because with the sea on one side and the Sivash[49] on the other, only one option was open to the Germans: a purely frontal attack against the Ishun bottleneck. The commander-in-chief of 11. Armee, von Manstein[50], later described this attack as "a shining example of the aggressive spirit and self-sacrifice of the German soldier". The Soviet defence was aided by armour-plated coastal batteries. By 25 October, six days after the attack began, the troops seemed to be too exhausted to continue. A last supreme effort was called for. The unbroken aggressive spirit of the Germans eventually prevailed over the Soviets' grim determination to hold out. On 28 October, at the end of ten days of the most bitter fighting, the Soviet defence collapsed and 11. Armee could take up the pursuit. The advance continued swiftly in the direction of Simferopol, leaving only the western Crimea – from Armyansk and Mechek to Eupatoria – still to be occupied. This task fell to Pionier-Bataillon 50. During this operation, the battalion suffered numerous dead and wounded, and then they marched further along

49. The Crimea is divided from the mainland by the so-called Lazy Sea, the Sivash. This is a kind of mud-flat or brackish swamp, almost impassable for infantry and an absolute obstacle to assault boats on account of its extreme shallowness.

50. Manstein, Generalfeldmarschall, Erich von Lewinski, gen. von, Schwerter, EL, RK; 11. Armee; born 24 November, 1887 in Berlin. Died 10 June, 1973 in Irschenhausen.

the west coast to Sevastopol. By 16 November, the whole of the Crimea except for the fortified area of Sevastopol was in German hands.

Winter soon arrived all along the Ostfront, although to begin with, it was not that noticeable in the Crimea. The rains came, rendering all unpaved roads quite unusable, then, all of a sudden, the freezing weather descended upon the peninsula and the German troops found themselves without winter clothing or equipment. The battalion suffered its first cases of frostbite. Preparations for the first assault on Sevastopol dragged on as a result. Instead of beginning on 27 November, it now started three weeks later, on 17 December, 1941. The delay had allowed the Soviets to entrench even deeper. The rain quietly drizzled throughout the night before the attack, but with sunrise, the day broke clear and calm. At 0500 hours, the assault began. The German divisions moved forward in a massive wave close behind an immense artillery and nebelwerfer barrage. The first objective – some heights – were taken, but as the assault moved forward, the pioneers were struck by fearsome defensive fire. Nevertheless, they struggled on, eliminating pockets of resistance and capturing some strongpoints in the Belbek valley. During particularly stiff fighting for a well-armed fort, 3. Kompanie suffered severe casualties, including the death of its outstandingly qualified and long-time commander, Hauptmann Karl Ulrich[51]. The battalion received an order to dig in. In the meantime, the main attack by other units continued. The heights south of the Belbek valley were stormed and the assault pushed further south one pillbox at a time. The battalion members celebrated Christmas in icy foxholes hacked into the rocky ground. One of their final casualties was platoon commander Leutnant Fritz Weber[52], killed on 29 December in the Belbek valley. Shortly after, the battalion was pulled out and returned to rest positions on the Perekop isthmus.

The battalion had suffered many casualties near Sevastopol. Meanwhile, back in the siege lines, the tip of the German spearhead drew near Fort Stalin, the capture of which would have given the artillery visual command of Severnaya Bay, Sevastopol's main anchorage and port. Just then, Soviet forces landed at Kerch and then at Feodosia, effectively halting the German offensive because the attack divisions were desperately required to face this deadly threat. The battalion was formed into combat groups and sent to the threatened areas, carrying out operations near both Kerch and Feodosia. After the recapture of the latter on 18 January, the battalion mined its harbour and erected barricades, and was later inserted into the main defences. Both sides then faced each other across the Parpach position, a defensive line thrown up by the Germans across a narrow bottleneck. Heavy battles continued with unremitting violence until late March 1942. Replacements trickled in: amongst them was Leutnant Christian Geuenich[53], transferred to the battalion on 15 January, 1942 from Brücken-Bau-Bataillon 646.

– – –

On 25 September, 1941, a new panzer division – the 22nd – was established: formation of the unit continued in France throughout the rest of the year. In mid-December 1941, an armoured Panzerpionier-Kompanie – with one armoured and two motorised platoons –

---

51. Ulrich, Hauptmann Karl, 3./Pi.Btl.50; born 5 March, 1908 in Dortmund. Killed in action, 17 December, 1941 near Sevastopol.

52. Weber, Leutnant Fritz, Pi.Btl.50; born 13 August, 1914 in Witten. Killed in action, 29 December, 1941 near Sevastopol.

53. Geuenich, Oberleutnant Christian, 3./Pz.Pi.Btl.50; born 1 April, 1915 in Krauthausen. Died 4 March, 2001 in Düren. See Appendix 2 (page 572) for more details.

was set up with 4 Sdkfz. 250/3 command half-tracks and 6 Sdkfz. 251/6 half-tracks. Their drivers, together with all other half-track drivers of 22. Panzer-Division, underwent training from 19 January to 7 February. During the night of 7 February, a teletype arrived: "22. Panzer-Division will be transferred to the Ostfront." On 27 February, 1942, a few days before the division departed, an OKH order announced that the new Panzerpionier-Kompanie would be incorporated into Heeres-Pionier-Bataillon 50 as its 3. Kompanie and the battalion would then become the organic pioneer battalion of 22. Panzer-Division. Also assigned and made available by the OKH organisational department was about two-thirds of the equipment of a pioneer battalion, which was to be carried along by 22. Panzer-Division and used during the refitting of Pionier-Bataillon 50.

The divisional units arrived in Odessa via train. From there, the tracked elements were transported to the Simferopol area on the single-line railway while all wheeled units were required to drive the 500km. The situation forced von Manstein to use elements of the newly arrived division on 20 March, despite the division commander requesting to wait at least a week. In thick fog against a formidably entrenched enemy, the first attack of the new division was shattered and they suffered tremendous losses in men and materiel. Traces of this failure remained with the division's soldiers for a long time.

The two separate elements of Pionier-Bataillon 50 – the new company coming from France and the old battalion in the Crimea – only joined together in mid-March 1942. Gefreiter Ludwig Apmann, a young soldier from 2. Kompanie, remembers the arrival of the armoured company: "One day, we received replacements from France: an entire company equipped with half-tracks. Two 'old' companies were formed out of the previous three companies while the third was the 'new' one." Leading the newly-arrived 3. Kompanie was Oberleutnant Luitpold Knoerzer[54]. Around the same time, one of the battalion's senior officers, Hauptmann Dohmwirt, was transferred to Brücken-Bau-Bataillon 531.

Pionier-Battalion 50 reported for duty east of Simferopol in the middle of April, for the time being without parts of a reinforced pioneer company that had been held back near Sevastopol by the army. After a substantial argument with the administrative officers of the Pionierführer of 11. Armee, Generaloberst von Manstein ordered that Heeres-Pionier-Battalion 50 be delivered with all elements to 22. Panzer-Division and the withheld motor vehicles, as well as pioneer equipment, be exchanged accordingly. The battalion refitted, was designated Panzerpionier-Bataillon 50 and subordinated to 22. Panzer-Division. The first assignments of the new battalion were several anti-partisan sweeps, but most were without success.

With the beginning of 'Trappenjagd' (Bustard Hunt) – Manstein's bold operation to retake the Kerch peninsula – at 0315 hours on 8 May, the newly-established battalion had its first true chance to work together, although as was common to all pioneer units, it was more often used as three individual companies than as one unified battalion. Here are excerpts from the war diary of 22. Panzer-Division regarding the operations of Panzerpionier-Bataillon 50:

> 8 May, 2135 hours: Order to Pionier-Bataillon 50: be ready to move from Adshigol at 0300 hours, later attached to the panzers.

> 9 May, 0710 hours: Order to Pionier-Bataillon 50: one company will clear mines and improve the roads near Sovkhoz Arma-Eli.

54. Knoerzer, Hauptmann Luitpold; 3./Pz.Pi.Btl.50; born 14 March, 1918 in München. No further information known.

9 May, 0900 hours: The pioneer company deployed to clear mines is still lying in a trench under heavy enemy fire.

13 May, 1230 hours: Order for the pioneer battalion: staff and 2. Kompanie will be directly subordinated to the division. Mission: De-mine the Marfovka-Sultanovka road and get it ready as a supply road.

15 May, 1210 hours: Order to the pioneer battalion: the nearest available company will be immediately sent to Gruppe Rodt[55,56].

16 May, 0910 hours: Order to the pioneer battalion: mop up Bulganak with two companies.

16 May, 1300 hours: Pioneer battalion will be brought forward to collect the mass of prisoners.

17 May, 1115 hours: Order to the pioneer battalion: the battalion will support the attack of the infantry on the left wing by clearing out the caves and canyons. It is necessary to be heavily equipped with flamethrowers and hand grenades. The battalion is instructed to cooperate with the Schützen-Brigade. A company will be immediately set in march for this. The remaining companies will continue their previous tasks of road construction and gathering prisoners at assembly points. The attack will begin at 1200.

17 May, 1325 hours: Report from Brigade: The panzer spearhead has reached the lighthouse. Order: the infantry and pioneers will immediately do likewise.

1505: Fighting has flared up again around Lighthouse Mountain.

1615: Lighthouse Mountain, an immense chunk of rock, dominates in the same way as Height 175. Strongly equipped and armed. The area around the mountain was sealed off in order to prevent counterattacks from that direction.

Gruppe Rodt closes in on Lighthouse Mountain, on the peninsula north of Kerch. Pioneers escorted the panzers.

55. This company would help with a counterattack because Gruppe Rodt had no reserves of his own. At 0900, situation near Rodt: 'North edge of Bulganak in our hands. Enemy sits in deep cellars that are hewn into the cliffs and reinforced with concrete'. At 0930: 'Situation in the north has stabilised. Our troops are advancing to the north from Katerles'. At 1120: 'Bulganak still not taken but cleared by 1300'.

56. Rodt, Generalleutnant Eberhard, EL, RK, DKiG; 22.Pz.Gr.Brigade; born 4 December, 1895 in München. Died 14 December, 1979 in München.

18 May, 1240 hours: Lighthouse Mountain still in enemy hands, it should be taken by the afternoon.

19 May, 1800 hours: the pioneer battalion reports the ultimate conquest of lighthouse mountain. The battalion took over 1000 prisoners.

Combat operations at Kerch ended. Manstein's impudently named operation had been a smashing success. It was later reported that almost 170,000 prisoners had been taken and 284 tanks and 1397 guns captured or destroyed. Manstein could now devote his entire attention to the Sevastopol fortress. For their part in 'Bustard Hunt', Panzerpionier-Bataillon 50 was awarded 25 Iron Cross Second Classes and 1 Iron Cross First Class, the latter to Oberleutnant Walther Hardekopf[57], commander of 2. Kompanie. The new 3. Kompanie had performed well: eight of the Iron Crosses were bestowed upon it, likewise 1. Kompanie, while 2. Kompanie received six and the staff company three. Most of the German units were pulled back and positioned for the much more fearsome task of subjugating and capturing the might fortress of Sevastopol. Panzerpionier-Bataillon 50 and its parent division, however, were not scheduled to play a part in this mammoth undertaking: they were to be pulled out and sent north to Heeresgruppe Süd.

They were in action much sooner than expected. Most of the armoured elements of the division, including 3./Panzerpionier-Bataillon 50, were formed into Kampfgruppe Koppenburg and subordinated to III. Panzerkorps. Their task was to destroy Soviet units that had broken through near Kharkov. They moved off on 24 May and completed their mission by 28 May. On 4 and 5 June, the division marched into assembly areas south-east of Kharkov

The half-tracks of 3. Kompanie were part of Kampfgruppe Koppenburg (led by the commander of Panzer-Regiment 204) during operations to destroy Soviet units that had broken through during their Kharkov offensive in May 1942. Here, the armoured spearhead moves past a knocked-out KV-1.

57. Hardekopf, Oberleutnant Walther, 2./Pz.Pi.Btl.50; born 8 August, 1902 in Lübeck. Missing in action, January 1943 in Stalingrad. See Appendix 2 (page 573) for more details.

in preparation for Operation 'Wilhelm'. Together with 14. Panzer-Division, they thrust out of the Chuguyev area in a north-east direction and in two days had reached the Krasnoarmeiskoye area. It was here, early on the morning of 13 June, that they joined up with other units of 6. Armee and so surrounded strong enemy groups. They were soon replaced by infantry units and sent south, where they captured the decisive hills around Olkhovatka. This was the victorious conclusion to the battle on the Donets. After successfully repelling strong enemy tank attacks early on 15 June, the division was again relieved by infantry units. Six days later, from 20 June, new operations began for the pioneers and 22. Panzer-Division with the battle around Kupyansk. They attacked in a north-east direction and in five days of hard fighting reached the Oskol south of Kupyansk. For his participation in the encirclement battles at Burluk and Oskol, platoon commander Oberleutnant Gerhard Fuchs[58] was the first member of 3. Kompanie to receive the Iron Cross First Class, on 30 June, 1942. Feldwebel Herbert Griep[59] of 2. Kompanie also received the esteemed medal, while 15 others received the lower grade on 2 July, 1942. With effect from 12 July, the commander of 3. Kompanie, Oberleutnant Knoerzer, was transferred to Panzerpionier-Bataillon 16 (16. Panzer-Division) to take command of its 3. Kompanie. Taking his place was one of the platoon commanders, Oberleutnant Rindermann. On 5 July, the company reported a strength of one Sdkfz. 250/3 and six Sdkfz 251.

Oberleutnant Gerhard Fuchs

In early July, after about eight days of rest and repair work in the Artemovsk-Komsomolsk area, 22. Panzer-Division took part in the first phase of Operation 'Blau', the German summer offensive. July would be a month of constant movement. The battalion captured Lissichansk on 5 July, participated in pursuit battles north of the Donets towards Kamensk, which it reached on 16 July, before heading south towards Rostov. 22. Panzer-Division's spearheads located and crossed a ford over the Tusloff and towards 1500 hours on 23 July pushed up against a mine barrier on the northern edge of Rostov. Two hours was required for the pioneers to clear this. The division's two combat groups then pushed into central Rostov and became entangled in fierce city fighting. The pioneers were attached to assault groups that wheedled out the city's zealous defenders. During the night, the division succeeded in establishing contact in central Rostov with the advanced detachments of LVII. Panzerkorps. That night, they hedgehogged in the burning city. Nervewracking skirmishes swirled through darkened buildings and streets that were momentarily illuminated by bursting grenades and strings of tracers. The next morning, after clearing the city's main thoroughfares, the division's combat groups pushed towards Rostov's Frunze Airport at 0630 where they joined up with SS troops of 'Wiking'. In tight cooperation with these elements of LVII. Panzerkorps, the division thrust towards the Don crossing near Aksaiskaya but at the very last moment, the Soviet security detail blew the bridge up in their faces. Early on 25 July, a small bridgehead was established over the Don near Alexandrovskoye while the bulk

58. Fuchs, Oberleutnant Gerhard, 3./Pz.Pi.Btl.50; born 25 June, 1919 in Hanau a.M. No further information known. See Appendix 2 (page 571) for more details.

59. Griep, Feldwebel Herbert, 2./Pz.Pi.Btl.50; born 25 February, 1915 in Hamburg. Killed in action, 15 November, 1942 in Stalingrad.

of 22. Panzer-Division, including most of the pioneers, mopped up the eastern sector of Rostov. In the afternoon, they were relieved by units of 9. Infanterie-Division.

Apart from 35 Iron Cross Second Classes awarded to battalion members throughout July for these operations, three men were also bestowed with the Iron Cross First Class on 29 July: Oberleutnant Christian Geuenich and Unteroffizier Werner Friedrichs[60] from 2. Kompanie, and Unteroffizier Heinrich Witschen[61] from 1. Kompanie.

In a report on 27 July, the battalion stated that it had a shortfall of 120 men, including 4 officers. The battalion's armoured component was also in bad shape: of its authorised complement of 7 half-tracks, 2 were total losses, 2 were in for long-term repairs and the remaining 3 in short-term repairs. Of the bridging column's 28 vehicles, only 3 were still available while another 4 would be ready after short-term repairs. The rest required a long time in the workshops. Beginning on 28 July, the division was able to rest and refit in the Kuteinikovo-Schachty area.

Shortly before midnight on 4 August, the division was alerted by Heeresgruppe B. The first combat groups moved off five hours later, initially heading north to Kamensk, then turning east and heading into the large Don bend north-west of Kalach. They now belonged to Paulus's 6. Armee. On 7 August, 1942, the division was split into combat groups and used to suppress toughly defended Soviet resistance nests in the many gullies and to eliminate small bridgeheads holding out along the river. From 9 to 16 August, 3./Panzerpionier-Bataillon 50 – as part of Kampfgruppe Kütt[62] – cleared the Don bank in the Gromki area. Its commander, Oberleutnant Rindermann, was wounded on 11 August. Other men became casualties during various operations in the Don Bend over the next month: Leutnant Broder Petersen[63], platoon commander in 3. Kompanie, was severely wounded on 26 August and died on 4 September in hospital in Verkhne-Businovka, while Feldwebel Herbert Koepsch[64], also from 3. Kompanie, was killed on 10 September. All units of the division were relieved by 15 September and placed at the disposal of the Heeresgruppe. They assembled in Perelasovski, ready to be marched to their assigned rest areas to refit.

This resulting period of inaction was used to give furlough to the unit's soldiers, many of whom had not had home leave since 1941. One of these was Oberleutnant Willi Witt[65], the long-time adjutant who had held the same position since November 1940. Filling in for him was a fresh-faced platoon commander from 1. Kompanie, Leutnant Klaus Kunze[66]. He had been with the battalion during the entire French campaign as a Fahnenjunker-Gefreiter, been transferred to Pionier-Schule II in June 1941 for officer training, and then returned to the battalion in January 1941 as a Leutnant. He took command of a platoon in 1. Kompanie and

---

60. Friedrichs, Unteroffizier Werner, 2./Pz.Pi.Btl.50; born 6 January, 1916 in Hamburg. Killed in action, 15 November, 1942 in Stalingrad.

61. Witschen, Unteroffizier Heinrich, 1./Pz.Pi.Btl.50; born 21 March, 1917 in Hannover. Missing in action, January 1943 in Stalingrad.

62. Kütt, Generalmajor Rudolf, DKiG; Schtz.Rgt.129; born 23 June, 1896 in Fürth. Died 19 May, 1949 in Hannover.

63. Petersen, Leutnant Broder, 3./Pz.Pi.Btl.50; born 22 June, 1917 in Hattstedt. Died of wounds, 4 September, 1942 in Verkhne-Businovka. See Appendix 2 (page 577) for more details.

64. Koepsch, Feldwebel Herbert, 3./Pz.Pi.Btl.50; born 11 March, 1923 in Dresden. Killed in action, 10 September, 1942 near Logovsky.

65. Witt, Hauptmann Willi, DKiG; Stab/Pz.Pi.Btl.50; born 26 September, 1917. Died 11 May, 1947. See Appendix 2 (page 579) for more details.

66. Kunze, Oberleutnant Klaus, Stab/Pz.Pi.Btl.50; born 31 March, 1920 in Hamburg. Missing in action, 21 January, 1943 in Stalingrad. See Appendix 2 (page 575) for more details.

had led it successfully throughout the entire campaign in the east, including the brutal fighting around Sevastopol. Kunze's parents in Hamburg had been traumatised in December 1941 when they were informed of their son's death but thankfully for them – and for Kunze himself – it was simply a clerical error.

In mid-September 1942, the battalion had to say goodbye to its experienced, long-time commander, Oberstleutnant Hellmuth Ermeler. He had been called back to Germany to resume his post as a section head in the Pionier department of OKH. His previous two Beurteilungsnotizen[67] showed he had successfully fulfilled his role as a battalion commander and recommended that he was suitable for use in OKH or as a regiment commander. The new commander of Panzerpionier-Bataillon 50 was Hauptmann Erwin Gast, who had celebrated his 31st birthday eight days earlier and also just marked his tenth anniversary of entering military service. After one and a half years with a training battalion and submitting countless appeals to be sent back to a

Leutnant Klaus Kunze, battalion adjutant.

combat unit, the ambitious Gast finally received his wish in September 1942 with a posting to Panzerpionier-Bataillon 50 located deep in the Soviet Union.

On 12 October, 1./Panzerpionier-Bataillon 50 handed over 14 replacements to Pionier-Bataillon 45. A week later, 22. Panzer-Division received a replacement company comprising close to 1000 replacements, a large part of them from the division's own rear-echelon units who had willingly volunteered for front-line duty. Several dozen men from this latest draft were given to the pioneer battalion. It was noted that these recent replacements were either older men or very young recruits. Once they were incorporated, the battalion was completely up to strength.

Although their rest areas in the Mankovo – Kalitvenskaya – Chertkovo areas were in the rear, behind the Don River sector held by the German XXIX. Armeekorps and the Italian 8. Armee, shots were heard and individuals went missing or were found dead. It became very clear that partisans were operating in the area. The men had their personal weapons but the battalion's vehicles and heavy weapons were being repaired and overhauled. The situation

---

67. Trans.: 'Beurteilungsnotizen' = 'efficiency reports'.

became so bad that on 17 October, 1942, Gast requested that his pioneer companies be armed with heavy machine-guns and mortars so they could be employed against the brazen partisans. His request was granted and the battalion received all its heavy weapons the next day.

On 29 October, Gast reported about a sweep for partisans:

> The battalion reports that during the clearing action in the Kamyshnaya valley, three men were seized north of the supply road near Kuteynikov and handed over to the Feldgendarmerie of 22. Panzer-Division, while 15 civilians, detained because they did not have sufficient identity papers, were taken to the appropriate Kommandantur[68].

At the beginning of November 1942, with Gast still settling into his new role as a battalion commander, the order arrived for Panzerpionier-Bataillon 50 to start marching eastward for operations in Stalingrad. The command staff of 22. Panzer-Division were not surprised: the battalion was just the latest unit to be withdrawn from the divisional structure and sent elsewhere. With justified bitterness, the division remarked that "the clearance of 22. Panzer-Division continues". Fortunately for the division, Panzerpionier-Bataillon 50 would leave behind all armoured vehicles of 3. Kompanie – including its half-track platoon – out of which a new unit[69] would later be formed. The officers and men of this company were less fortunate than their vehicles because they were also on their way to Stalingrad with the rest of the battalion. Regardless of 22. Panzer-Division's own pressing needs regarding fuel[70], the division's quartermaster, Major Dietz von dem Knesebeck, gave his pioneers an ample supply for the march. At the beginning of November 1942, Panzerpionier-Bataillon 50 began its land march towards 6. Armee on the Volga. The distance from their positions north of Millerovo to the Don bridge at Kalach amounted to about 250 kilometres, and the battalion covered this distance within a day, arriving late on 4 November. Gefreiter Ludwig Apmann from 2. Kompanie recalls the trip:

> Mounted in our vehicles, our battalion rolled in the direction of Stalingrad, into the suburbs that were already occupied by German units. Winter was close but we still didn't have winter clothing. It looked nasty here, almost everything lying completely in ruins; we also saw many dead German soldiers…

The battalion arrived in Stalingrad with a ration strength of 10 officers, 3 administrative officials, 51 NCOs and 475 enlisted men, a total of 539 men. Its combat strength was 10 officers, 44 NCOs and 405 men.

Formed from one of the army's oldest pioneer units, the attitude of Pionier-Bataillon 50's men altered in March 1942 when they were converted to a fully motorised unit. As older commanders became casualties or were transferred, the command roles were filled by confident young officers who instilled a more aggressive spirit in the unit. Belonging to a panzer division carried some prestige and the pioneers of the battalion considered themselves elite. Embodying the new character of the battalion was its commander, Hauptmann Gast. He was by far the youngest battalion commander heading to Stalingrad and like any ambitious young officer, he wanted to demonstrate his prowess to his elders on the field of battle. There could be no more daunting arena than Stalingrad.

---

68. Trans.: 'Kommandantur' = 'commandant's office'.

69. Panzerpionier-Kompanie/Bataillon 140

70. On 27 October, the Division's quartermaster, Major von dem Knesebeck, wrote: 'Gasoline situation is intolerable! Oral requests continually come in from all units… The fuel trains are on their way'. On 28 October: 'Three wagons from the coming fuel train are absent. 22. Panzer-Division will therefore be allocated 30 cubic metres less fuel than needed…' The fuel train finally arrived on 9 November, 1942.

Pionier-Bataillon 162:

Months of constructing defensive positions along the front-line of their Italian allies had not taken the edge off the men of Pionier-Bataillon 162. Felling trees, digging trenches and erecting anti-tank obstacles kept the men in top physical condition, while their commander Major Krüger scheduled constant training and drills – combined with occasional stormtroop operations – to hone the fighting skills of his tough Silesian pioneers. The most recent operation on the night of 25 October had been small. A previous attack on 9 October had not been as successful because the infantry elements suffered heavy casualties, but the pioneers performed well. These attacks over the Don were just the latest in a long line of rivers assaulted and crossed by Pionier-Bataillon 162.

– – –

The battalion, consisting for a large part of Upper Silesians, was drawn from a stock of hardy farmers and workers, and had performed well since being formed on 26 August, 1939 in Breslau. Its first commander was Hauptmann Dr. Bennecke. As the integral pioneer battalion of 62. Infanterie-Division, it moved into Poland as a reserve of Heeresgruppe Süd but saw no action. In mid-September 1939, the entire division was transported to the west and assembled at Mosel by 20 September. The battalion wintered in the Eifel along Germany's western border. Apart from training and a few false alarms, the winter of 1939-40 passed quietly. One of the most exciting incidents for the battalion was rescuing a horse-drawn artillery piece from a swift and icy mountain brook.

The battalion was split up amongst several combat groups for the advance into France: Aufklärungs-Abteilung 162 received a motorised platoon from 3. Kompanie, Kampfgruppe von Arnim 1. Kompanie, Kampfgruppe Gulttiene the staff and 3. Kompanie (minus a platoon), Kampfgruppe von Loefen[71] 2. Kompanie while Marschgruppe Gabriel received the bridging column and light pioneer column. During the night of 9 May, the battalion gathered in forests along the border. The attack began at 0635 hours the next morning. Many roads were blocked by massive tree trunks and the pioneers were constantly being called up. After hours of hard work, the roads were cleared. The advance continued.

Throughout the campaign, the men of Pionier-Bataillon 162 – from officers down to the lowest-ranking pioneers – would display temerity and stoicism. A few examples will suffice: on 23 May, a pioneer squad led by Oberleutnant Künzel helped III./Infanterie-Regiment 164 force the Somme Canal near Buny. Preparatory fire began at 1700 hours and hand grenades were also hurled across the narrow canal to suppress French strongpoints at the crossing point. Only two small rubber boats were available (Künzel's original mission had only been to reconnoitre crossing possibilities). The first was thrown into the water despite heavy machine-gun fire. The boat was crewed by several pioneer soldiers, two officers and 1 NCO from III./164. They were halfway across when a bullet hit the boat but they kept paddling. It sunk a few metres from the enemy bank. Wading through the deep water, the boat's occupants succeeded in blowing up some enemy positions with hand grenades. The infantry NCO was killed and one of the infantry officers severely wounded. Despite

71. Loefen, Generalmajor Max-Hermann von, DKiG; Inf.Rgt.190; born 5 March, 1892 in Erfurt. Died 4 January, 1942 near Mayonovka-Ivanovka.

The battalion commander, Hauptmann Dr. Bennecke, strolls through a captured French town with one of his NCOs.

continuous artillery and mortar fire, the pioneers crossed over more infantrymen on the remaining inflatable. Pioneer Gefreiter Kaiser distinguished himself through his bold energy.

On 25 May, a heavy French tank in the northern part of Cizancourt blocked the main road west of the Somme Canal bridge. Leutnant Schuchardt and his 3. Zug of 3. Kompanie were called up to sort it out. Schuchardt immediately decided to organise a small demolition squad. He stood in front of his platoon, explained the situation, and the said: "I need a couple of volunteers". The dangerous mission appealed to most of them but Schuchardt selected only four men from the numerous volunteers. Feldwebel Michalski recalls the operation: "He selected a Gefreiter, two pioneers and myself. We quickly prepared three 10kg charges."

A three-man infantry recon troop guided the pioneers toward the enemy tank: they clambered across a destroyed bridge and leapt over fences between gardens, all the time moving parallel to the street on which the tank sat and all the time keeping their ears pricked. But there was only silence. Feldwebel Michalski continues:

> At last one of the infantrymen signalled that we were level with the tank. One after the other, we quickly peered around the corner of the house to get a grasp of the situation. There, ten metres in front of us, was a giant steel colossus that blocked the entire width of the street! I had never seen such a large thing before.

After a brief discussion with hushed voices, Schuchardt and his men quickly formulated a plan: a door upon which one of the tank's machine-guns was aimed would enable the pioneers to surprise the crew. After positioning Gefreiter Hoffmann with his machine-gun to cover the tank, Schuchardt put his simple plan into action. Feldwebel Michalski again:

> An infantry Oberfeldwebel, Pionier Zindler and myself wriggled up close to the door. I had an explosive charge in my left hand, a rifle in my right. Pionier Zindler had a charge in both

(right margin, vertical) Familie Krauss

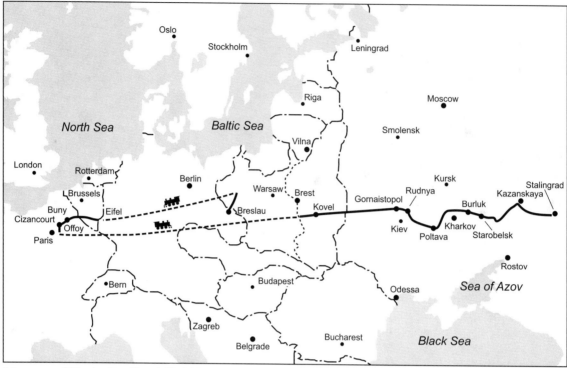

Movement of Pionier-Bataillon 162, 1939-1942.

hands. Each was armed with a 6-second fuse. This meant six seconds from ignition to detonation. This short duration was selected so that the enemy did not have time to protect the tank if he were to notice something at the last moment... We had to act as quick as lightning. I looked only at the hands of the Oberfeldwebel, who then opened the door. Go! Five quick steps – Pionier Zindler and I kneeled next to the tank. We placed our charges between the tracks and the ground – ignite! With a swift bound we disappeared back through the door. A massive detonation rocked us.

Running out onto the street, the Germans were initially sightless due to the large swathe of smoke. Then they saw the French crew bailing out. Shouting in German and French, they forced the crew to give themselves up. The pioneers then inspected their handiwork: the 32-tonne tank had been thrown 1.5 metres to the side and suffered damage to its tracks, but it was otherwise intact. Before leaving, the pioneers tossed a concentrated charge of 6 hand grenades into the turret. As they headed back to the Somme bridge, victors over the enemy behemoth, they were accompanied by the detonations of the tank's ammunition which blazed for several hours. In recognition of this feat, Leutnant Schuchardt received both grades of the Iron Cross, while Feldwebel Michalski, Gefreiter Hoffmann and Pionier Zindler received the Iron Cross Second Class.

Towards the end of May, Pionier-Bataillon 162 received the task of blowing up every bridge over the Somme in the divisional sector, apart from the one at Péronne where there was a bridgehead. On 31 May, they then received the order to reconnoitre bridging and crossing positions over the Somme and Somme Canal both sides of Ham. On 5 June, a big attack was launched. The pioneers crossed over infantry companies in their inflatable rafts. The forcing of the Somme west of Ham by Infanterie-Regiment 183 was successful but with painful casualties. East of Ham, the pioneers helped Infanterie-Regiment 190 across the

Somme by sustaining a non-stop ferrying service. They even got some anti-tank guns across. Half an hour after the beginning of the crossing, however, the boats were so shot to pieces that they were no longer 'seaworthy'. At 0740 hours, Pionier-Bataillon 162 received an order from division to bring forward new inflatable rafts to the north edge of Estovilly. Due to forceful enemy counterattacks, the attack was halted at 0800 hours by order of Infanterie-Regiment 190 and the men already across were ordered to pull back to the river and swim across, abandoning all heavy equipment. The last swimmers arrived by noon. Casualties had been very heavy. As night was falling, enemy pressure had increased to such an extent that the bridgehead of Infanterie-Regiment 183 was also abandoned and all elements of that regiment were pulled back across the river. 62. Infanterie-Division was withdrawn for employment elsewhere. Almost a month after operations commenced, the pioneer battalion was to face its toughest task during the entire French campaign: a costly water-borne assault over the Somme River on 6 June, 1940. It was the theatre in which Pionier-Bataillon 162 first truly proved itself as a tough, dependable unit.

It was now the turn of Infanterie-Regiment 164 to attempt a crossing of the Somme, this time both sides of Offoy. Supporting them was Hauptmann Wilhelm von Graevenitz[72] and his 3. Pionier-Kompanie. They had 14 large and 30 small inflatable rafts for this operation. Because it was impossible for the pioneers to bring their boats to the front in time for the 1705 start, the attack was postponed until 1900 hours. The French defenders noticed preparations and were therefore well-prepared to defend themselves. Artillery fire came down at 1900 hours and included many smoke shells. The first wave moved out five minutes later. II./Infanterie-Regiment 164 quickly crossed the canal without too much trouble but it was a different story for I. Bataillon. Pioneers carrying bulky inflatable rafts were easy targets for French mortars. Several men were killed before the attack even began. The pioneers handed over the small boats to the infantry and platoon commander Leutnant Wittig gave his men the order to head back through the danger zone to fetch the larger ones, six men per boat. The wounded cried out for medics and the battalion's assistant doctor, Unterarzt Dr. Schornak[73], moved about upright, sleeves rolled up, hands covered in blood, tirelessly going from one casualty to the next. The infantry crossing in small boats had failed utterly: they were immediately ripped to pieces. Pioneer Unteroffizier Max Giessmann[74] witnessed the carnage:

DRK

"I spoke with Leutnant Wittig – who had repeatedly instilled respect in us because of his intrepidness – about what we should do. During this discussion, Pionier Pietsch[75] suddenly collapsed after being fatally struck by a ricochet. Most of the French bullets were too high above us and smacked into the leaves."

Wittig was determined to cross the river immediately. An infantry officer from Infanterie-Regiment 164, Hauptmann Fritz Kluge[76], suddenly came up to Wittig:

Uffz. Max Giessmann

72. Graevenitz, Major Friedrich Wilhelm von, 3./Pi.Btl.162; born 18 May, 1912 in Breslau. No further information known.

73. Schornak, Stabsarzt Dr. Ludwig, Stab Pi.Btl.162; born 20 June, 1910 in Bingen. Died in captivity, 21 September, 1944 in Moldavia.

74. Giessmann, Oberfeldwebel Max, 3./Pi.Btl.162; born 2 March, 1917 in Neisse. Missing in action, January 1943 in Stalingrad.

75. Pietsch, Pionier Gerhard, 3./Pi.Btl.162; born 15 November, 1920 in Glogau, Silesia. Killed in action, 6 June , 1940 near Pithon.

76. Kluge, Hauptmann Fritz; II./Inf.Rgt.164; born 25 November, 1911 in Hassik. Killed in action, 6 June, 1940 at Offoy/ Somme.

"You want to take a chance with the crossing? When's it happening?"

"Right now, Herr Hauptmann!", replied Wittig.

The rafts kept springing new leaks as they were punctured by bullets and shrapnel. Giessmann kept plugging the holes in his boat with wooden plugs while Pionier Kinzel kept inflating it. Giessmann needed to stuff his handkerchief into a larger hole. Kinzel, who'd had a funny feeling that either Giessmann or himself would not return safely, was hit in the chest by a bullet[77]. Hauptmann Kluge, the infantry commander, crawled over to Giessmann:

"Are you the NCO who'll be crossing in the raft now?"

Giessmann answered: "Jawohl, Herr Hauptmann!"

"Good, I'll be coming with you."

All of a sudden, artillery fire from both sides swelled and German machine-guns sprayed the French bank. Giessmann and his men hauled the boat down to the water. Hauptmann Kluge, who lay flat until the boat was ready, sprang up and moved toward the water. At that moment, a bullet smacked into his head and he fell right next to the boat. Unteroffizier Giessmann continues his account:

"Nevertheless, we shoved the boat into the water... I shouted: 'Paddles in hand and go!' We quickly moved toward the enemy shore. Bullets lashed the water around us but only the man in front of me received a shot through his gas-mask container."

The men leapt onto the bank and began to combat the French defenders. Unteroffizier Giessmann had another task, however:

"Appearing back on the river bank was Pionier Kostarezyk from another squad, which still lay ready. He was going to help. Throwing himself down right next to the water and pretending to be dead, he grabbed the anchor cable we'd trailed behind us and pulled the inflatable raft back. Remaining on the enemy bank, standing up to my chest in water, I grabbed the other end of the anchor cable. In this way we quickly created a shuttle service."

Leutnant Wittig, still on the German-held bank, wanted to toss some desperately needed boxes of machine-gun ammunition into the boat but was struck by a full burst of machine-gun fire. This image remained with Giessmann:

"I can still see how his hair flew up because he'd just dropped his helmet, and how he tumbled backwards over the body of Hauptmann Kluge. He was dead immediately. Another Leutnant of the battalion fell with his messenger at the crossing point..."

The cold-bloodedness and conviction displayed in the face of grievous casualties as they struggled across the Somme earned the highest respect from all who witnessed it. The battalion never shirked in the slightest during the campaign. They always gave their all.

That evening, Hauptmann Dr. Bennecke, the battalion commander, received an order to construct a bridge over the Somme Canal during darkness and repair any other damaged bridges that could be used. The next morning, all battalions of Infanterie-Regiment 164 were across the Somme thanks to the heroism and professionalism of their pioneers.

The advance continued. At 0550 hours on 10 June, Pionier-Bataillon 162 completed a bridge over the Aisne near Vic-sur-Aisne.

As a result of a brave attack on defensive positions around Paris from 12 to 14 June, Hauptmann Dr. Bennecke was awarded the clasp to his Iron Cross First Class, while Gefreiter Kaiser was awarded the Iron Cross First Class. There was also a painful loss: on 13 June, Oberleutnant Künzel, commander of 2./Pionier-Bataillon 162, was killed near May-en-

---

77. The bullet was removed and Kinzel later recovered.

Multien, a tragedy to his unit during the final stages of the campaign.

After a short rest from the end of July to early August, the division was loaded aboard trains and sent east. Some thought they were being demobilised. The trains, however, passed right across the Reich, through their Silesian homeland, and continued on, into Poland, finally halting near the Bug River: the border with the Soviet Union. The men could see the tall Soviet observation towers in the distance. The pioneer battalion conducted reconnaissance to prepare defensive positions, to secure the border along the Bug and to install obstacles. This is where the battalion spent the winter of 1940-41 and there it remained until Barbarossa began. On 15 November, 1940, the battalion said goodbye to Hauptmann Dr. Bennecke and welcomed a new commander, Major Josef Giedl[78], a veteran soldier who had fought in pioneer units throughout the First World War.

22 June, 1941: the pioneer companies were distributed amongst the infantry regiments for the attack over the Bug near Husyne, Beresze and Dorohusk. The artillery thundered at 0315 hours. The inflatable rafts were carried to the water and paddled across the river. The red dawn lit up the eastern horizon behind the enemy bank, outlining the paddling boats against the sky reflected in the water and silhouetting the soldiers already ashore against the sunrise itself. Initially, not a

The new battalion commander, Major Josef Giedl, drinks a toast with his staff officers shortly before the commencement of Operation Barbarossa in June 1941.

shot was fired, and it seemed the Soviets had been taken completely by surprise. Soon, however, resistance flared up, unexpected in its intensity and the first considerable casualties were suffered. The attack progressed no further on this opening day of a long campaign. The daily objective of Luboml was not taken until 26 June. Casualties throughout the division were extremely high – about 30% for the first five days of fighting. Kovel was taken on 28 June. The pioneers supported the infantry in intense battles in the forests and wheatfields near Skiby. A particularly bloody day was 2 July during vicious fighting in forested areas east of Kiwerce. Soviet positions were virtually invisible behind walls of logs and foliage. The wheatfields – taller than a man – that surrounded the forests were also ferociously defended and scarcely any prisoners were taken. Fighting in forests continued for the next week between the Styr, Horyn and Slucz. On 4 July, Major Giedl was awarded the clasp to his Iron Cross First Class. A bridgehead was formed over the Styr on 5 July and the Slucz on 9 July: for the former, the pioneers constructed a footbridge using the foundations of a destroyed bridge, and for the latter, a pontoon bridge was built. On 15 July, very heavy combat took place in a forest near the village of Serby, and forceful Soviet counterattacks in the afternoon

78. Giedl, Oberst Josef, Pi.Btl.162; born 1 July, 1892 in München. Survived the war but no further information known.

caused considerable difficulties and casualties. The pioneers succeeded in removing about 500 mines there. Enemy pressure increased the next day with several counterattacks supported by a storm of artillery, the effect of which was lessened by the swampy ground which caused a disproportionately high number of duds. On 21 July, a pioneer squad helped II./Infanterie-Regiment 183 take a massive bunker east of Seredy: it was a modern construction that went several storeys underground and it had to be smoked out a floor at a time. It was just one of many which formed the Stalin Line. Leutnant Alfons Schinke, platoon commander in 3./Pionier-Bataillon 162, captured several bridges prepared for demolition. On one bridge near Serby, Schinke himself removed about 600kg of explosives. He kept a cool head despite the fact the enemy could have blown the bridge at any moment.

Division command began to feel that Major Giedl was not the right man to lead the battalion. He was described as 'nervous' and 'petulant' – characteristics not noted in previous evaluations. He was relieved of command in early August and sent to a replacement battalion in Germany. An evaluation written on 6 August by the commander of 62. Infanterie-Division, Generalleutnant Walter Keiner[79], stated that Giedl "did not always fully conform with the commitment of his battalion because he frequently lost himself in the details". On 16 August, the battalion received a new commander: Hauptmann Otto Krüger was transferred from Pionier-Bataillon 175 where he had been a company commander since the beginning of the year. Krüger was very fortunate to receive a position as battalion commander because an evaluation by his previous commander, Major Heinz Schlegel[80], was not all positive:

> A conscientious, enthusiastic and modest officer with good military service. Easily excitable, especially when there's difficulties to overcome. Sufficient tactical knowledge. Plenty of experience and good knowledge of practical duties. Despite his own adequate abilities, the performance of his company was only average. His personal performance and knowledge are perfectly sufficient for the command of a battalion, however, Hauptmann Krüger lacks the fundamental qualities from an education in the officer corps because his internal development never got beyond the early stages. Hauptmann Krüger is therefore only partially suitable as commander of a pioneer battalion.

The commander of 75. Infanterie-Division, Generalleutnant Ernst Hammer[81], added:

> Agreed! Hauptmann Krüger is a conscientious, sturdy and courageous officer. A competent company commander, though sometimes uncertain. At the moment, I think he is not yet completely suitable as a battalion commander.

In spite of these opinions, Krüger's potential was recognised and he was rewarded with his new command. After eight months in the role, in April 1942, his new division commander, Generalmajor Rudolf Friedrich[82], would describe Krüger as "personally brave", "always prepared and constantly maintains complete control" and was "fully accepted in the officer corps and by his subordinates". Finally, Friedrich wrote that "there is no more concern about his limitations noted in earlier evaluations". But that was in the future. In August 1941, Krüger still needed to prove himself to his new battalion, and he would certainly do that over the

---

79. Keiner, General der Artillerie Walter, RK; Stab 62.Inf.Div.; born 10 December, 1890 in Benshausen. Died 23 January, 1978.
80. Schlegel, Oberst Heinz, RK, DKiG; Pi.Btl.175; born 16 January, 1904 in Halle/Saale. Died 7 May, 2001.
81. Hammer, Generalleutnant Ing. Ernst, RK; Stab 75.Inf.Div.; born 20 October, 1884 in Falkenau/Eger. Died 5 December, 1957 in Wien.
82. Friedrich, Generalleutnant Rudolf, DKiG; Stab 62.Inf.Div.; born 23 August, 1889 in Zwickau. Killed in action, 9 May, 1945 in Prague.

coming months. His personnel file would later be filled with examples of his bravery[83]. The fact that he had even reached his new battalion was a sign of courage – he came straight from hospital in Zhitomir where he was having both eyes treated for damage inflicted by a mine.

On 20 August, a crossing was forced over the Shereff near Ignatopol. The railway junction of Ovrush was captured on 22 August and numerous mines were removed. On 23 August, platoon commander Oberleutnant Josef Ihrke[84] was killed at Ignatopol. On 27 August, almost 6 weeks after they began, the division successfully completed its phase of breaking through the Stalin Line near Novograd-Zwiahel. After some fighting around Korosten, it went into army reserve. It then carried out several unsuccessful sweeps for partisans in the Ovrush area. For his bravery and leadership during these actions, the new battalion commander was awarded the Iron Cross First Class on 30 August.

After rest days on 30 and 31 August, the advance was resumed, this time in the direction of Gornaistopol and the Dnepr. Other divisions forced the crossing of this mighty river and the division traversed the pontoon bridge unmolested. However, they quickly moved up to the Desna, a not insignificant tributary of the Dnepr, and the division received the task of forcing the river in the Rudnya-Koropye area. During the night of 6-7 September, the battalion commander himself personally reconnoitred for a suitable crossing point. In the pre-dawn darkness of 7 September, Krüger directed his company and platoon commanders into their sectors. Because preparations had been made extremely carefully, the river was quietly crossed in inflatable rafts, the Soviets were taken by surprise and a small bridgehead formed, almost without casualties. Immediately after the crossing began, Hauptmann Krüger gave the order to accelerate construction of a 4-tonne ferry so that heavy weapons of the infantry could be crossed over, not only to broaden the bridgehead but also to be ready to repel the expected Soviet counterattacks. The Soviets quickly discerned the danger threatening them from this position and tried to hinder further crossings with concentrated artillery fire. Impact after impact covered the small area. Riddled with holes, the inflatable pontoons were knocked out of action and ferrying traffic came to a halt, so Hauptmann Krüger leapt on to a ferry and took it under command. The pioneers and infantry were swept along by his utterly fearless example and despite the violent fire, ferrying operations started again on the river. Continued reconnaissance showed that approach roads were very bad and construction of a bridge at the crossing site would not be possible. During the night of 7-8 September, Krüger personally reconnoitred a favourable bridging site in the Koropye sector. Observation with binoculars, however, revealed that this position – the single possibility not only in the divisional sector but, as it later turned out, also in the corps' sector – was very well secured by enemy bunkers and earthen fortifications. An attack from the previously formed bridgehead was not possible because marshy ground and a dead arm of the Desna lay in between. Krüger made the extremely daring decision to capture those fortifications in a surprise raid. To reach this position, a platoon was launched much further upstream, they paddled across and then floated downstream tight against the enemy river bank. They clambered ashore under cover of thick vegetation and completely surprised the Soviets with concentrated machine-gun fire. While the rest of the river bank was cleared out in hand-to-hand fighting by the first wave, others were crossed over and the bridgehead was then broadened and secured. The Soviets redoubled their efforts with artillery, and above all,

---

83. These examples had been compiled into one document, dated 12 August, 1942, and seem to suggest that Krüger was being considered for the German Cross in Gold.

84. Ihrke, Oberleutnant Josef, Pi.Btl.162; born 18 March, 1893. Killed in action, 23 August, 1941 near Ignatopol.

aircraft, to hinder 62. Infanterie-Division's shift from one side to the other. Four pontoons, two speedboats and four inflatable rafts were shot to pieces by low-level aerial attacks. In a few hours, this important crossing site withstood 14 low-level attacks (with 3 to 6 aircraft in each attack). In these hours of extreme danger, Hauptmann Krüger controlled the crossing and employed rescue services with the greatest circumspection. Spurred on by the example of their battalion commander, the pioneers performed almost superhumanly and the crossing barely suffered a delay.

On the morning of 9 September, preparations for construction of the bridge were completed. Because the serious low-level attacks had stopped, division gave the order at 1600 hours to float sections into place for the 120-metre long bridge. The first vehicle was already using the bridge at 1645 hours. In the early morning hours of 10 September, the bridge was attacked by 14 bombers from a great height. Lengths of trestles and ramps were destroyed by a direct hit, three ferries were peppered with holes and one ammunition wagon went up in flames. Hauptmann Krüger immediately recognised the great danger and – ignoring the exploding ammunition – ran onto the bridge with a few pioneers and removed the shot-up sections from the rest of the bridge. These immediately sunk. Through this rapid and courageous intervention, not only was the rest of the bridge saved from capsizing but it ensured a swift repair with the available equipment. With the last available reserves, the bridge was made ready in the shortest time and under the most difficult conditions. Krüger had passed his most difficult test so far and demonstrated his capabilities and courage to all.

The division then played its part in the gargantuan encirclement battle of Kiev with a string of crossings, defensive battles and counterattacks. The Soviets encircled east of Kiev tried to break through to the east along a railway line with strong forces. On 19 September, 1. Kompanie was deployed to defend Ivanykovo against massive Soviet attacks. To hold the town, they needed to launch counterattack after counterattack during the night. The next day, however, many of the horsedrawn and motorised supply columns abandoned hard-pressed Ivanykovo in a wild flight and panic threatened to spread to the defenders of Vsoff. Hauptmann Krüger went up to them, pistol in hand, and made the wild-eyed drivers and supply personnel see reason again. He then organised the defence so that every dispensable officer, NCO and man lay with weapon in hand in positions he had allocated. Under Hauptmann Krüger's command, several Soviet attacks on this day –including a cavalry charge – were repulsed with bloody casualties. Thanks to his clear composure, an enemy penetration into Vsoff, which was crammed full of supply trains, was averted. Heavy combat continued for the entire division over the next five days and it suffered heavy losses of 1696 officers, NCOs and men. The immense battle of Kiev ended in victory for the Germans: about 665,000 prisoners were taken. The division was then withdrawn from the front on 1 October, subordinated directly to 6.

Schäfer

The battalion's first – and only – winner of the Knight's Cross, Unteroffizier Paul Speich.

Armee and used for various tasks in the rear areas: POW camps were built; Pionier-Bataillon 162 constructed a new bridge over the Nedra; sweeps were carried out to net Soviet stragglers.

For his bravery and courage, particularly during the defence of Ivanykovo, Unteroffizier Paul Speich[85], a squad commander from 1. Kompanie, was awarded the Knight's Cross on 18 November. It was presented to him on 30 November when the battalion was in reserve near Poltava. The whole battalion, especially the new commander Hauptmann Krüger, were proud that a Knight's Cross recipient was in their ranks.

The division remained in the Poltava area until just prior to Christmas. The winter period was a trying time for the battalion. A description of its actions are contained in 'examples of bravery' from Krüger's personnel file:

> In the heavy defensive combat during the winter, the battalion was subordinated to Gruppe Dostler[86] of 57. Infanterie-Division. The battalion put up a good showing under the prudent command of its battalion commander, Major Krüger. The sector whose defence that battalion had taken over was large but the garrisons in their individual strongpoints were thin. Despite the heaviest Russian attacks, particularly in the stormy and ice-cold nights, they succeeded time and again in bringing the assaults to a standstill, or throwing back in counterattacks the enemy who had broken through. 13 February, 1942 was a particularly difficult day. The Russians attacked the advanced strongpoint at Kusty with 15- to 20-fold superiority after heavy aerial bombardment. Artillery support could not be reckoned on because of the severe cold. Major Krüger quickly decided to pull heavy machine-guns and anti-tank guns out of the Vyshnyaya-Olshanka strongpoint and employ them under his personal leadership on the enemy flank. Under this hail of fire, the repeated attacks were repulsed, the Russians withdrew with heavy casualties and disappeared in the gully-riddled foreground. Major Krüger followed the movement of the enemy from an observation post and recognised that the Russians were slowly pushing along the gullies in the direction of Vyshnyaya-Olshanka after collecting more reserves. It was now clear that they had the aim of eliminating the troublesome menace to their flanks. Calmly and with cool consideration, Major Krüger gave his final instructions. From this distance, the artillery could again intervene and Major Krüger personally took over control of their fire. He only gave the order to fire from a distance of 400 metres: the Russians were devastatingly struck by the concentrated defensive fire of the strongpoints. With weapon in hand, Major Krüger also now participated in the almost total destruction of the enemy. It was thanks to his superior leadership, his steely composure and his tough endurance in the most difficult of situations that all of the following attacks remained without success and that our own casualties were small in comparison.

Leutnant Gambke, a platoon commander from 2. Kompanie, was heavily wounded during the repulsion of these attacks. Eight days later, on 21 February, the battalion adjutant Leutnant Stahr was killed. The battalion emerged from the winter battles thin and weary. Young replacements arrived in March. On 29 March, 1942, the average combat strength was 80 men per company but this was mostly untrained replacements. The battalion was only suitable for defence.

From 11 to 24 April, 1942, Major Krüger led a training course in Taranovka for infantry pioneers from the infantry regiments.

In May, the battalion became embroiled in the Soviet offensive near Kharkov. A report on those events comes from Krüger's personnel file:

---

85. Speich, Oberfeldwebel Paul, RK; 1./Pi.Btl.162; born 22 August, 1914 in Oberglogau. Died in 2004 or 2005.

86. Dostler, General der Infanterie Anton, DKiG; Stab 57.Inf.Div.; born 10 May, 1891 in München. Executed, 1 December, 1945 in Aversa, Italy.

During the large spring battle in May 1942, the Russians made every effort to force a breakthrough by using hundreds of tanks. Our infantry were forced to slowly retreat under the heaviest pressure. On 14 May, the battalion commander Major Krüger – with his 3. Kompanie and a subordinated construction battalion – received the order to build a rear position in the hills of Novo-Beretstky. He himself gave the responsible construction officer detailed instructions as well as ordering 3. Kompanie to speed up the manufacture of makeshift mines by using all explosives and mining every available bridge with them. Because the tanks broke through again, the infantry had to retreat further. Under his personal leadership, the railway crossing near Novo-Beretsky and the forest clearing were quickly mined shortly before the Russian tanks arrived. He observed the movements of the tanks from a tree, allowing a flak gun that was in an unfavourable position to be withdrawn. This gun then succeeded – at the closest range – in shooting several Russian tanks which had halted in front of the mine barrier. Also on 15 May, when the front-line in the Pasiki hills had to be retaken, Major Krüger was again at the front with his pioneers. The tanks soon advanced again, so with a few pioneers, he personally dug up the last available mines from in front of our infantry and used these to block the marshy spot, the narrows and the rail crossing near Pasiki. Because of these mines laid in the final seconds, two T-34s were soon completely destroyed, while four Mark IIs remained immobilised in the mine barrier as they obviously did not want to risk driving forwards or backwards because of the mines. They were later knocked out by a flak gun. Admittedly, the breakthrough of the tanks was not completely averted but the utterly fearless personal effort of Major Krüger and his pioneers held them off at the decisive moment using the last available ammunition at the only possible positions until the new front-line was systematically re-occupied.

Mark/NARA

Oberleutnant Horst Klupsch, the battalion adjutant in 1942.

The May battles around Kharkov were extremely tough for Pionier-Bataillon 162 and casualties were high. On 11 May, Oberleutnant Klupsch[87] took over as battalion adjutant. On this same day, Leutnant Kallbach, a platoon commander in 1. Kompanie, was wounded. The next day, Leutnant Ernst Arera[88], also from 1. Kompanie, was killed, and on 14 May, Oberleutnant Hahn, commander 2. Kompanie, was wounded.

At 1800 hours on 19 May, 1942, a tank destruction troop destroyed a Soviet tank behind Infanterie-Regiment 179, all that remained of a tank pack that broke through at noon.

De-mining of Taranovka and the road to Novo-Beretsky was carried out on 25 May, 1942. South of Pasiki, the pioneers disarmed 24 Soviet flamethrowers with remote ignition and disposed of an unusually large explosive charge in the unloading platform of Taranovka railway station.

On 27 May, during reconnaissance of the road from Taranovka in the area north of Smiyev, Krüger was ambushed by partisans. The partisans were beaten off in a wild shoot-out but the battalion adjutant, Oberleutnant Horst Klupsch, was severely wounded by a bullet through his right thigh. Krüger was unharmed. Oberleutnant Schinke, platoon commander in 3. Kompanie, took over as adjutant.

---

87. Klupsch, Oberleutnant Horst, Stab Pi.Btl.162; born 2 May, 1917 in Glogau. No further information known.

88. Arera, Leutnant Ernst, 1./Pi.Btl.162; born 14 March, 1917 in Breslau. Killed in action, 13 May, 1942, near Lichachevo railway station.

On 1 June, the battalion – minus 1. Kompanie – was subordinated to 297. Infanterie-Division for an attack over the Burluk to form the Donets bridgehead near Pechenegi. It was attached to Infanterie-Regiment 523 for pioneering-technical support. Major Krüger meticulously prepared his pioneer units. The attack was scheduled to begin early on 8 June but pelting rain forced a postponement until 10 June. The pioneers of 3. Kompanie moved into their assembly positions under the cover of darkness. The assault troops moved off at 0215 with artillery support. On one sector, the spearheads ran up against a mine barrier after only 100 metres. The pioneers moved forward and marked it. On another battalion sector, 780 anti-personnel and 160 anti-tank mines were cleared. In total, before reaching the river, more than 1000 mines of all types were lifted. Forward elements reached the river at 0500 hours. Because the attack could only go over the river in platoons, a thorough preparation was not possible. The small inflatable rafts, brought forward to the 10km long attack sector on panje wagons, could not reach the river bank because of heavy defensive fire. The attack threatened to stall because the Soviets had already moved fresh forces on to the opposite bank. Leutnant Schinke, commander of 2. Kompanie, swiftly decided to load the large inflatable rafts – which had already been inflated – onto lorries, three per vehicle. They were driven up to the river under the heaviest artillery fire. Two lorries and six rafts were obliterated by direct hits. Because the pioneers of 2. Kompanie could not keep up with the lorries and were left a few hundred metres behind, the men of 3. Kompanie – who were already near the river bank – began to hastily unload the rafts. Oberfeldwebel Schiwy and his 7. Gruppe (7th squad) were the first to grab a large inflatable raft and throw it into the water. They began transporting the first infantrymen across at 0530 hours. After all of 3. Kompanie and a battalion of infantry were across, 2. Kompanie quickly assembled an improvised bridge from inflatable rafts and wooden planks. More units poured across. The crossing was established. With his daredevilish acts, personal example and circumspection, Major Krüger inspired his pioneers during the crossing and then during the construction of the bridge under fire from machine-guns, anti-tank guns, tanks, artillery and low-level aircraft. By his personal instruction and advice, he spurred his people on to the utmost during the search for mines. In the shortest possible time, five infantry battalions and their heavy weapons were crossed over. In addition, the pioneers removed 2138 mines, 16 flamethrowers and 20 Geschoßminen[89]. As a result, the conditions for the construction of the bridge were produced and three panzer divisions opened the way. With a large amount of satisfaction, the pioneers learned that General der Kavallerie Eberhard von Mackensen[90], Commanding General of III. Panzerkorps, had spoken with the greatest respect for their battalion and its brave commander. During the removal of mines, 3. Kompanie lost 3 dead and 18 wounded. Casualties of 2. Kompanie were 1 dead and 7 wounded.

At 0300 on 12 June, 2. Kompanie began constructing a 16-tonne bridge over the Gnilitsa in Artemovka under the fire of Soviet tanks: the bridge was ready at 0900 hours and the company went into reserve.

On 14 June, 62. Infanterie-Division requested the return of its pioneer battalion from 297. Infanterie-Division. Elements of the battalion returned on 16 June, while the rest were still marching from Andreyevka. Upon their return, two squads of pioneers were sent to Infanterie-Regiment 179 to lay mines and construct positions.

---

89. 'Geschoßminen' = An improvised anti-tank mine made from a high explosive shell.

90. Mackensen, Generaloberst Eberhard von, EL, RK; III. Panzerkorps; born 24 September, 1889 in Bromberg. Died 19 May, 1969 in Alt-Mühlendorf bei Nortorf.

From midday on 18 June, 1. Kompanie was set in march to Volchy Yar via Lisovitsky to be subordinated to Infanterie-Regiment 190, while 2. Kompanie was sent on lorries to a forest 1km west of Ivanovka to be subordinated to Infanterie-Regiment 179. At 0900 hours on 23 June, 3. Kompanie was brought forward to Bogodorovka and re-established a river crossing there.

At 0700 hours on 24 June, Infanterie-Regiment 208 (79. Infanterie-Division) reached Miropolye and found the bridge over the Voloskaya Balakleika destroyed. The pioneers were busy with repair work along the entire route of advance; for construction of the 20-metre long bridge, one platoon of 3. Kompanie was sent to Miropolye on bicycles. All pioneering forces of the division – including the infantry regiment pioneers – had been in high demand since the beginning of the advance to clear mines. Losses were numerous from this dangerous task.

From 27 June, the pioneers began clearing mines, fixed flamethrowers and bypassed enemy stragglers from areas allocated for accommodation. Some of the mines were ingeniously rigged: on 2 July, in Yurtshenkovo, about 15km north-west of division headquarters, Pionier-Bataillon 162 dismantled four remote detonation devices fitted with 8-channel receivers and very powerful explosives. One of these remote-controlled mines had detonated the previous night and left a crater 10 metres deep and 30 metres in diameter.

On 29 July, the pioneer battalion reported the results of its reconnaissance of the Don with regards to the condition of the river bank and crossing possibilities.

On 30 July, Heeresgruppe B ordered that two mine-search troops from 3./Pionier-Bataillon 162 be set in march to Starobelsk to clear mines from the airfield there. However, fuel could not be supplied for the 150km journey. Fortunately, a diesel-powered vehicle was available and this was used to carry out the mission.

From the beginning of August, 62. Infanterie-Division – as part of XXIX. Armeekorps – built and defended positions along the Don river. Heavy Soviet attacks from mid-August until late August eventually abated and both sides settled down to positional warfare, face-to-face across the Don. On 19 August, 62. Infanterie-Division's sector was 63km wide. On 3 September, a recon patrol of Infanterie-Regiment 190, reinforced by some pioneers, crossed the Don at 2015 hours 500 metres downriver of the Kazanskaya bridge. They had a strength of two squads with 3 large and 2 small inflatable rafts. A thick wire obstacle along the enemy bank was blown up. In the south-east section of Kazanskaya, ten houses were set on fire with flamethrowers. There was only distant light machine-gun and rifle fire. The Soviets tried to attack the patrol's getaway. The assault troop returned over the Don at 2200 hours without loss.

In the five and a half week period from 1 August to 10 September, the division – whilst holding a quiet defensive sector – lost a total of 32 officers and 1266 NCOs and men to death, wounds, illness and other causes.

On the night of 12-13 September, the Soviets launched a cross-river operation 4km west of Kazanskaya. Three attempts at 2300, 0115 and 0315 hours with about ten boats were smashed by artillery fire. Boats left in the water were picked off and destroyed by mortar fire. In retaliation for this attempted raid, the Germans launched their own attack the next night at the same location. A small assault troop formed from Infanterie-Regiment 179 and Pionier-Bataillon 162 began crossing the Don at midnight and returned by 0305 hours without casualties. Three combat posts were demolished, a bunker crew and a heavy machine-gun were destroyed with flamethrowers and batches of propaganda leaflets were seized. The Soviets responded with their own small operations across the 80-100 metre wide river.

On 23 September, 62. Infanterie-Division completed another operation. It began at 0230 hours and was finished two hours later. Result: eleven houses between Baski and Saikin were set on fire. A penetration to Baski itself was not possible because of enemy machine-gun fire. At the same time, back along the river bank, 2 dwelling-bunkers and five machine-gun bunkers were blown up by the pioneers. No prisoners were taken. German casualties: two dead on the Soviet side of the river, two lightly wounded during the crossing.

These raids were occasional moments of action for the pioneers, but their main task was to build winterproof defensive positions, lay a continuous wire obstacle along the front-line and set up a second position deep in the rear. On 27 September, they were also ordered to dig a long tank trench 4 metres wide and 1.5 metres deep (2.5 metres in some place to form tank traps). The civilian population would help.

Division command ordered that at least one small assault troop operation be carried out each week. After the many small successful operations, the commanding general of XXIX. Armeekorps ordered a large raid, in battalion strength, to push deeper into the Soviet defences. The first one took place on the night of 27-28 September. Two companies – one from Pionier-Bataillon 162 and the other from III./Infanterie-Regiment 179 – crossed the Don east of Kazanskaya at 1855 hours. They broke into the depth of the Soviet defence, in some areas against tough resistance, and forced the enemy to flee. Captured: 1 officer and 8 men. Five enemy bodies were counted. Booty: 1 heavy machine-gun, 1 mortar, 1 anti-tank rifle. Destroyed weapons: 2 infantry guns, 1 anti-tank gun with explosives, 1 infantry gun through the removal of its breech block. Demolished enemy installations: 11 dug-outs, 18 dwelling-bunkers. Others demolished: 150 houses, of those, 9 were filled with shells. The assault troop returned at 2130 hours under heavy Soviet fire. Casualties: 1 man wounded.

Satisfied with the outcome, the corps commander ordered another operation. 62. Infanterie-Division proposed three, one by each infantry regiment. Infanterie-Regiment 190 proposed using three reinforced companies against Krasnoyarsky. For an operation like this, Major Krüger said he would require one pioneer company for combat support and two platoons to crew the river crossing equipment. This large 'reconnaissance in force' was being planned for early October. On 1 October, 62. Infanterie-Division received word that 22. Panzer-Division – on the order of Korps – had supplied 15 large and 15 small inflatable boats for use in an assault by Infanterie-Regiment 183. Major Krüger was ordered to arrange pick-up of the boats in Kuteynikov. Three assault boats were also supplied by 8. Italian Armee. These reached 62. Infanterie-Division on 4 October, with Italian crews, and there were four instead of the originally planned three. On 8 October, division ordered that Oberleutnant Baranski's 2./Pionier-Bataillon 162 be subordinated to Infanterie-Regiment 183 for the duration of the next day's large-scale operation over the Don.

The operation of reinforced II./183 began at 1400 hours. Their objective was to cross the river, draw out the garrisons of Baski and Saikin localities, burn down the villages, take prisoners and destroy dug-outs along the bank of the Don itself. The operation was being observed by the commanding general of XXIX. Armeekorps, General der Infanterie Hans von Obstfelder[91], the division commander Generalmajor Richard-Heinrich von Reuss[92] and an Italian staff officer from the Torino Division. Updates came in regularly.

---

91. Obstfelder, General der Infanterie Hans von, Schwerter, EL, RK, DKiG; XXIX. Armeekorps; born 6 September, 1886 in Steinbach-Hallenberg. Died 20 December, 1976 in Kassel.

92. Reuss, Generalmajor Richard-Heinrich von, RK; 62.Inf.Div.; born 23 November, 1896 in Bromberg. Killed in action, 22 December, 1942 near Novo Astashoff.

First orientation at 1505 hours: West edge of Saikin and north-east edge of Baski reached. Twelve prisoners, 10 of our own wounded. Second orientation at 1535 hours: Saikin and Baski have been traversed. The villages are burning. Resistance negligible. Twenty wounded, 2 assault boats and 6 large rafts have been knocked out by fire.

The river crossing was difficult. Despite heavy preparatory fire, an undetected bunker on the river bank flanked the boats, and as a result, 2 assault boats and 6 large inflatable rafts were knocked out by its fire.

Third orientation at 1645 hours: Our troops are pulling back from Saikin and Baski under increasing enemy pressure. Enemy reserves being brought forward and enemy artillery coming to life are being suppressed by our artillery. Fourth orientation at 1725 hours: 6. and 7./ Infanterie-Regiment 183 formed a bridgehead of 500 metres radius at the crossing site. The enemy attacked out of Saikin and Baski. A crossing back over the river has begun. The Radfahr Schwadron, which covered to one side, has 29 wounded. Fifth orientation at 1815 hours: Crossing of the wounded and 7./183 in progress. Enemy influence small at the moment. Sixth orientation at 1930 hours: Return crossing completed. About 25 prisoners. Our casualties are quite heavy.

A preliminary casualty report came in at 2145 hours: 15 dead, 92 wounded (including 2 officers, one of which was Oberleutnant Baranski) and 15 missing (this was later revised to 10 after 5 of the men originally reported MIA turned up amongst the wounded). Most casualties were not from the river crossing or the withdrawal but from heavy house-to-house fighting in the two villages with the swiftly deployed Soviet reserves. There was also 1 dead and 4 wounded amongst the Italian boat crews. Brought back were 45 prisoners, some severely wounded. Two heavy machine-guns were blown up and 2 light machine-guns were captured. It was established that there were no new enemy units opposite the division.

To give the impression of a large operation, Infanterie-Regiment 190 carried out its own Don crossing near Krassnoyarsk with a reinforced company, which included pioneers. It went according to plan. For the cost of only 4 wounded, they destroyed 17 partially occupied embrasured pillboxes, 2 dwelling-bunkers, 1 rowboat, 1 raft, 1 light and 2 heavy machine-guns, captured 1 light machine-gun and chalked up 25 enemy dead.

The two operations were in stark contrast and proved that smaller operations carried out in darkness were just as successful as large assaults – but cost far less blood. With this in mind, another operation was set for 25 October. The plan was simple: launch a surprise raid over the Don, storm and temporarily occupy two villages, destroy as many bunkers and strongpoints as possible and then withdraw back across the river, bringing all prisoners.

The sunny day gave way to a cold evening. At 1900 hours, Infanterie-Regiment 183 launched its assault across the river. An assault troop with the strength of six squads, reinforced by three pioneer demolition squads, crossed the Don river east of Podgorsky on 3 large and 10 small inflatable boats. In support were 1 heavy and 2 light batteries, as well as 2 platoons of light infantry guns. For close-in support, a light anti-tank gun and 2 heavy machine-guns were deployed right at the crossing site. The operation was a complete success: 15 dug-outs were destroyed with explosives, while 15 enemy dead were counted. German casualties were only 4 wounded.

On 26 October, a training course for pioneer company commanders was due to commence in Kursk. The division could send a participant but because of the shortage of officers in the pioneer battalion, the detachment could take place only at the expense of construction of positions.

– – –

A few weeks before being called to Stalingrad, the battalion was unfortunate to lose two very experienced company commanders, not to enemy action but instead to transfers to higher offices. Hauptmann Hans Gierth, long-time commander of 3. Kompanie, was transferred to the staff of XXIX. Armeekorps to take charge of technical engineering matters for Italian units. He had commanded 3. Kompanie since August 1940 but had been with the battalion since its formation, first as a platoon commander in 2. Kompanie and later, on 6 June – after the costly Somme River crossing took many lives – he took temporary command of the same company. A six week stint as battalion adjutant from 13 June to 31 July, 1940 was quickly followed by promotion to commander of 3. Kompanie. After more than two years in this role, he knew every man in his company by name, but only a few days before receiving the order to head for Stalingrad, Gierth was transferred. Taking his place was the current adjutant, Oberleutnant Alfons Schinke, roughly the same age as Gierth but considered much more daring. Intrepid actions had been his trademark since crossing the Soviet border in June 1941 and the men in his platoon were surprised that he had not yet been severely wounded. His promotion to commander of 3. Kompanie was seen by everyone to be a just reward.

The second old company commander to leave was Hauptmann Munz of 1. Kompanie, who was transferred back to Germany. Taking his place was a relative newcomer, Oberleutnant Kurt Barth. Two years earlier, Barth had been an Oberfeldwebel in Pionier-Bataillon 29 but a regulation allowing long-serving NCOs to be rapidly promoted propelled him into the officer ranks with a promotion to Oberleutnant. As with Major Krüger, the men trusted him just a little bit more than a career officer because he had once been 'one of them'. His old Spieß from 3./Pionier-Bataillon 29, Hauptfeldwebel Erich Kühle, remembers him:

Familie Barth

> Kurt Barth was a career NCO and was in my 3. Kompanie before the war, first as a Feldwebel, then as an Oberfeldwebel. He commanded 1. Zug and was an instructor. He was in an earlier age class and somewhat older than myself because prior to the outbreak of war he had already attended the army's technical college and passed the final examination for a civil service job in the mid- to upper-levels of the technical or administrative and supply services…

Kurt Barth as a Leutnant in 1941.

This was not a strange choice for a soldier. As a 'Zwölfender', Barth had reached the end of his time in the army and one of the benefits of being in the Reichsheer from 1919-1935 was retraining in a civilian career offered during the twelfth year of service. One of the more attractive options was to attend a training school for government officials. This allowed many old soldiers to come back into the army as civilian administrators. However, the outbreak of war in September 1939 meant that many experienced ex-soldiers were indeed called back into the service, not as civilian administrators but as soldiers. This is what happened to Kurt Barth. The army expansion program provided him with his promotion to Oberleutnant.

During Barbarossa, he commanded a platoon in Pionier-Bataillon 627 and was transferred to Pionier-Bataillon 162 on 10 May, 1942. He had led a platoon since then but his performance earned 33-year-old Barth a promotion to commander of 1. Kompanie. He headed to Stalingrad with 16 years of soldiering experience under his belt.

The commander of the remaining company – the 2nd – was Oberleutnant Arthur Baranski. He had been wounded just three weeks earlier during the stormtroop operation over the Don and was still wearing the bandages. Nevertheless, he would never think of handing his men over to another commander. So, while still on the mend, he moved toward Stalingrad at the head of his company.

Leading them all was Krüger. He had now commanded the battalion for more than a year and his officers and men trusted him implicitly. The fact that he had been a non-commissioned officer for so many years inspired confidence in the men because they all knew he was empathetic about the lot of the common soldier. His courage was beyond reproach: Major Krüger was never an officer who commanded from the rear, and this attitude was passed to his company and platoon commanders.

Around midnight on 1 November, division staff received a communique from the Ia of the German General near 8. Italian Armee ordering Pionier-Bataillon 162 to be ready by 1200 hours on 2 November for transportation by air or road. It was presumed that the battalion would be employed in Stalingrad. With this, the measures commenced the previous day to detach 2. Kompanie to the Torino Division to construct defensive positions became invalid. The removal of the pioneers adversely affected the intensity of the construction of positions, particularly the construction of a badly-needed second line. The division wrote in its diary:

> The withdrawal of the Pionier-Bataillon places further construction of positions seriously into question if at least a few men aren't left behind in every regimental sector to instruct the infantrymen. The division therefore orders that at least 2 or 3 men are to remain behind in every sector. Furthermore, the Generalkommando [XXIX. Armeekorps] requests the supply of a company from a pioneer battalion remaining in the corps area.

Major Krüger and his battalion began their long drive to Kalach early on 3 November. The staff and 3. Kompanie had their own vehicles but the two foot companies were temporarily motorised by an Italian column. Each company took along their own field-kitchen. The battalion required almost two days to reach their destination, the bulk arriving at Kalach on 4 November and the rest the next day. Its ration strength was 8 officers, 45 NCOs and 384 enlisted men, a total of 437 men, its combat strength 7 officers, 31 NCOs and 281 men with 27 light machine-guns and 6 flamethrowers.

– – –

Pionier-Bataillon 162 had one distinct advantage over the other pioneer battalions being sent to Stalingrad: because the large majority of its men came from Upper Silesia, many spoke Silesian – a dialect of Polish – and also Polish itself, and could therefore understand and communicate in Russian, a very similar Slavic language. When prisoners were taken, they could talk to them and gain knowledge that was immediately useful to their current situation rather than sending them to higher headquarters where a Sonderführer interrogated the prisoner, as happened in most other units.

Pionier-Bataillon 294[93]:

Like Pionier-Bataillon 162, this battalion also spent many months working on defensive positions along the Don River before being sent to Stalingrad. Its three companies were regularly allotted to the infantry regiments of 294. Infanterie-Division to help construct bunkers, lay minefields and erect wire obstacles. One important task they carried out was clearing trees and shrubs to produce open fields of fire. Orders made it clear that the defensive line along the Don River needed to be strong, more so than usual because large sections of it were being held by allied troops, namely the Hungarians, Romanians and Italians. The importance of this was made very clear.

Pionier-Bataillon 294 was formed on 6 February, 1940 in Weissenfels, Wehrkreis IV. Its 3. Kompanie came from 15./Infanterie-Regiment 328 (227. Infanterie-Division) but many of its officers and men came from Pionier-Bataillon 14, also stationed in Weissenfels. The battalion commander was Major Karl Back[94], former company commander of 2./Pionier-Bataillon 4, while the adjutant was Leutnant Otto-Wilhelm Heinze[95], a young platoon commander from Panzerpionier-Bataillon 4 whose career had been slightly tarnished by several incidents involving alcohol. Commander of 3. Kompanie was Hauptmann Heckmann and commander 2. Kompanie was Hauptmann Büsefeld, who only led the company during its formation. On 23 February, Oberleutnant Heinrich Bucksch[96] took over the company.

The battalion's role in the French campaign was minimal and limited mostly to building bridges, interspersed with occasional combat actions. It marched via Laon to Reims, Troyes, and further south to Clamecy. A few men were awarded medals, including Bucksch and Heinze, both being awarded the Iron Cross Second Class. In June 1940 the battalion was billeted in Belgium as part of IX. Armeekorps. It was here, approaching midnight on 27 June, 1940, that the career of Oberleutnant Bucksch almost ended. In a convivial atmosphere loosened by alcohol and surrounded by his platoon commanders and high-ranking NCOs, Bucksch allegedly called Rudolf Hess – Hitler's deputy – a 'monkey's arse'. One of the NCOs present, a committed Party member disgruntled with Bucksch for denying him a promotion, reported the incident. Only after a thorough investigation, the recording of a detailed statement by Bucksch – who denied ever uttering those words – and confirmation of Bucksch's testimony by the other officers present, was the matter put to rest. The army needed officers like Bucksch: in October 1939, Model[97] described him as a "very brave, reliable officer", someone "to keep an eye on, a promising future General Staff officer". Endorsements like this no doubt helped Bucksch out of his troubling situation.

The battalion moved toward the Channel Coast in the first half of July, reaching Le Mans on 14 July and its accommodation areas three days later. From 28 August until 7 September,

---

93. Unfortunately, very few veterans or families of deceased soldiers from this battalion could be found, so there is scant photo coverage of their activities.

94. Back, Major Karl, Pi.Btl.294; born 15 April, 1906 in Viernheim/Hessen. No further information known. See Appendix 2 (page 569) for more details.

95. Heinze, Hauptmann Otto-Wilhelm, Stab Pi.Btl.294; born 12 November, 1918 in Northeim. Died 25 May, 1983 in Osnabrück.

96. Bucksch, Major Heinrich, 2./Pi.Btl.294; born 28 July, 1913 in Charlottenhof. No further information known.

97. Model, Generalfeldmarschall Walter, Brillanten, Schwerter, EL, RK; Chef d. Gen.Stab IV. Armeekorps; born 24 January, 1891 in Genthin. Committed suicide, 21 April, 1945 in the Ruhr pocket.

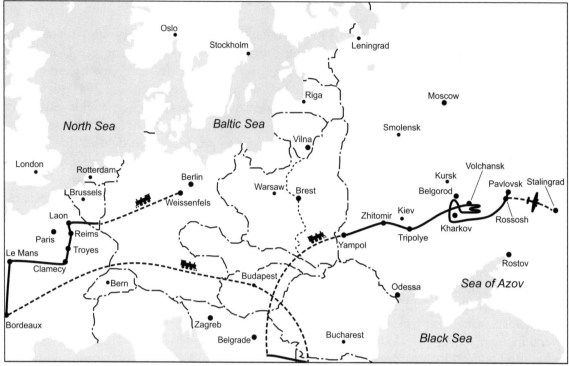

Movement of Pionier-Bataillon 294, 1939-1942.

294. Infanterie-Division exchanged positions with 6. Infanterie-Division. The former, including the pioneer battalion, now watched over the demarcation line with the unoccupied part of France. On 15 October, 1940, the battalion gave up its 1. Kompanie to Pionier-Bataillon 304 but it was reformed using the battalion's own reserves. On 1 December, the division began to be relieved of its positions along the demarcation line and then, in march groups, it was sent on to new accommodation areas with VI. Armeekorps near Bordeaux, where it remained until March the next year.

Beginning on 7 March, 1941, the battalion was moved to Bulgaria, arriving there between 21 and 25 March. It was subordinated to XI. Armeekorps for operations against Yugoslavia. The attack began on 6 April and the battalion moved across the border two days later, participating in the campaign until the surrender of Yugoslavia on 17 April. Casualties were light. Many of the battalion's soldiers were awarded Bulgarian medals for bravery. 294. Infanterie-Division remained in Yugoslavia as part of the occupation force until well after Barbarossa had begun. It left Yugoslavia on 27 June and headed for the Soviet Union where it was placed in OKH reserve in Yampol for the first half of July. It then moved to the front and for the first time experienced the ferocity of war on the Ostfront. As part of 4. Romanian Armee, the division advanced and fought its way through Zhitomir and Fastov to the Dnepr river, capturing Tripolye on 25 August. For their first month of fighting in the Soviet Union, 37 members of the battalion received the Iron Cross Second Class, one the clasp to the Iron Cross Second Class (Oberleutnant Rudolf Otto from the staff) and 3 the Iron Cross First Class (Oberleutnant Bucksch and Unteroffizier Günter Uhlig[98] from 2. Kompanie and

---

98. Uhlig, Feldwebel Günter, 2./Pi.Btl.294; born 8 January, 1915 in Plauen. Killed in action, 10 February, 1942 near Rubezhnoye.

Oberleutnant Gerhard Pohl from 1. Kompanie). In Tripolye, powerful Soviet counterattacks were repelled. The pioneers were in constant demand during the advance to establish river crossings, lift mines and knock out stubborn resistance nests. After they had established a bridgehead across the Dnepr in Tripolye, everything was undertaken to hold the precarious foothold. Strong Soviet attacks crashed against these advanced positions. The pioneers were in the front-line, reinforcing defensive positions and participating in local counterattacks. The brunt of the fighting fell upon Oberleutnant Pohl's 1. Kompanie and Oberleutnant Bucksch's 2. Kompanie. This situation continued for almost three weeks while the pincers closed around Kiev to the north. This happened on 16 September, destroying the Soviet's South-Western Front and netting around 600,000 prisoners. On 17 September the bulk of the division, together with 132. Infanterie-Division – both part of XXXIV. Armeekorps – crossed the mighty river and broke through the Soviet positions. In two days of hard fighting, the breakthrough was widened and 294. Infanterie-Division reached Yerkovsty. For the September fighting, 21 men received the Iron Cross Second Class and 3 men the First Class (Leutnant Heinze, battalion adjutant, Leutnant Karl-Hermann Ufer[99], a platoon commander from 3. Kompanie, and Feldwebel Wolfgang Kretzschmar from 2. Kompanie). Major Back received the Iron Cross First Class in early October.

In a new attack on the morning of 7 October, 294. Infanterie-Division smashed the incomplete Soviet defences along the western bank of the Merly, near Borki, and rolled further to the east. The pioneers were crucial in making the assault a success. On the morning of 17 October, the Luftwaffe pounded Soviet forces and the assault was renewed. The division, together with another, had pushed through by the evening, cracking the line along the boundary between two Soviet rifle divisions. The German units pushed on, capturing town and rivers north-west and south of Kharkov in an attempt to encircle the metropolis. Oberleutnant Viktor Piossek[100], commander of 3. Kompanie, was killed on 20 October 2km south of Mironovka. Leutnant Karl-Heinz Ufer took over the company. By the end of October, Kharkov was far in the German rear as they bounced the Donets: 294. Infanterie-Division crossed the river south of Rubezhnoye. For October, 21 men – all from 3. Kompanie – were awarded the Iron Cross Second Class while Unteroffizier Walter Lange, also from 3. Kompanie, received the Iron Cross First Class. On 9 November, a Soviet attack struck the division and after three days of fighting they were forced to pull back 15-20kms from Volchansk. The pioneers knew no rest. A security line was set up and the winter fighting along the Donets began.

In November 1941, Hauptmann Bucksch, commander of 2. Kompanie, started down the path of General Staff officer training by being detached to different units. He was with Artillerie-Regiment 294 from 12 November until 19 December, 1941, but crises at the front compelled his return to 2. Kompanie. He finally left his company in late February 1942 and only met them again in Stalingrad when he was attached to Panzer-Regiment 36.

On 24 November, elements of the battalion attacked Gnilushka and Polnaya. Most of the actions consisting of repelling frequent Soviet reconnaissance patrols and assault troop operations. Larger Soviet attacks on 5, 13 and 27 December were repulsed. On 14 December, 294. Infanterie-Division launched a surprise attack and pushed the Soviets back

---

99. Ufer, Hauptmann Karl-Hermann, 3./Pi.Btl.294; born 17 November, 1905 in Wilnsdorf. Killed in action, 8 March, 1942 in Varvarovka.

100. Piossek, Oberleutnant Viktor, 3./Pi.Btl.294; born 25 July, 1914 in Hitlersee-Oppeln. Killed in action, 20 October, 1941 near Mironovka.

to the east. Operations continued throughout the icy winter, with temperatures dropping to 45° below zero. Veterans would not easily forget the winter of 1941–42.

From the beginning of 1942, the battalion was on the defensive in the Belgorod area. On 2 January, Soviet attacks repeatedly crashed into the positions of 294. Infanterie-Division but a counterattack threw the enemy back and the division was able to improve its own position. Unteroffizier Günter Uhlig, 2. Kompanie, the first NCO in the battalion to be awarded the Iron Cross First Class during the Russian campaign, was killed on 10 February. On 7 March, the Soviets launched an offensive which struck 294. Infanterie-Division and other units to the south. 79. Infanterie-Division, positioned north of 294. Infanterie-Division, helped settle the situation on its right wing. For the next month, the pioneer battalion was split up and sent to various units. Operations in the Bolshaya-Bibka and Izbitsokye sectors continued until 12 March and losses were heavy: the commander of 3. Kompanie, Oberleutnant Karl-Heinz Ufer – promoted to Oberleutnant in February because of bravery in the face of the enemy – was killed on 8 March near Varvarovka, while one of his platoon commanders, Leutnant Karlheinz Haasper, was wounded. The NCOs and enlisted men of this company also suffered heavily: amongst the dead on 8 March were Gefreiter Ferdinand Ludewig[101], Oberpionier Peter Götz[102] and Pionier Herbert Zickler[103], while platoon commander Feldwebel Martin Israel[104] had been killed the previous day. Oberleutnant Werner Göhler[105] took command of the company. More losses hit the battalion on 10 March when Unterarzt Müller, the battalion's assistant doctor, was wounded. Elements of the battalion were then involved in combat around Pestshanoye, Nepokritaya and Peremoga from 13 to 19 March.

Oblt. Werner Göhler

On 23 March, a pioneer platoon was sent to Kampfgruppe Wolf[106] (79. Infanterie-Division) with orders only to be used for pioneering purposes. The next day, the new commander of 3. Kompanie, Oberleutnant Göhler, was wounded but could not be recovered. He was declared MIA. On 25 March, elements of the battalion attacked Fedorovka and Argunovsky.

On 30 March, the battalion was ordered to immediately send 2 NCOs and 15 men from 2. Kompanie – with pioneering materiel – to Gruppe Chales de Beaulieu[107] for blocking missions. They were needed to barricade a forested slope and de Beaulieu's Gruppe suffered from a severe lack of pioneers. Upon arrival, the pioneers immediately got to work.

The piecemeal use of 294. Infanterie-Division's units did not make its commander very happy. On 31 March, he mentioned to his corps commander that the entire 3./Pionier-Bataillon 294 had been sent to 3. Panzer-Division in Ternovaya even though this division had its own pioneer battalion, 1. Kompanie had been sent to 79. Infanterie-Division in Staritsa, and a platoon from 2. Kompanie had just been supplied to Gruppe Chales de Beaulieu. The immediate return of at least the latter was urgently requested because 3. Panzer-Division had its own pioneer battalion plus the attached 3./Pionier-Bataillon 294.

101. Ludewig, Gefreiter Ferdinand, 3./Pi.Btl.294; born 20 March, 1919 in Vietz. Killed in action, 8 March, 1942 in Varvarovka.
102. Götz, Oberpionier Peter, 3./Pi.Btl.294; born 5 March, 1917 in Weitersborn. Killed in action, 8 March, 1942 in Varvarovka.
103. Zickler, Pionier Herbert, 3./Pi.Btl.294; born 2 December, 1912 in Quohren. Killed in action, 8 March, 1942 in Varvarovka.
104. Israel, Feldwebel Martin, 3./Pi.Btl.294; born 5 July, 1913 in Schönbach. Killed in action, 7 March, 1942 in Rubezhnoye.
105. Göhler, Oberleutnant Werner, 3./Pi.Btl.294; born 26 January, 1909 in Hannover. Missing in action, 24 March, 1942 near Varvarovka.
106. Wolf, Oberst Richard; RK, DKiG; Inf.Rgt.208; born 18 March, 1894 in Simmern. Died 9 May, 1972 in Würzburg.
107. Chales de Beaulieu, Generalleutnant Walter, DKiG; Pz.Gr.Rgt.394; born 14 June, 1898 in Saalfeld. Died 26 August, 1974.

With the few shredded pioneer units available to 294. Infanterie-Division, no positive work could be successfully completed. On 29 March, the pioneer battalion had 204 men: the staff had 4 officers, 7 NCOs and 19 men, for a total of 30; 2. Kompanie had 1 officer, 16 NCOs and 96 men, for a total of 113; and the light pioneer column had 1 officer, 5 NCOs and 55 men, a total of 61 men. Most of the battalion's combat soldiers had been subordinated to other divisions.

At the end of March, 23. Panzer-Division began to relieve elements of 294. Infanterie-Division. Throughout April, as the situation settled, units gradually returned to the division. On 9 April, the pioneer platoon with Gruppe Chales de Beaulieu was ordered to return to its battalion in Nepokritaya. On 28 April, with the arrival of units of 71. Infanterie-Division, Gruppe Aulock[108] (79. Infanterie-Division) – to which many units of 294. Infanterie-Division were still subordinated – was freed up, and the division received all of them back, including elements of 1./Pionier-Bataillon 294 and all of 3. Kompanie. On 3 May, as a result of further reliefs, the rest of 1. Kompanie, a total of 120 men, was returned to the pioneer battalion. The battalion was once again complete.

While these units had been away, some major changes had affected their battalion. Their commander, Major Back, became extremely ill due to a severe liver ailment and was transferred to a hospital in Magdeburg in early April. The illness was so bad that his initial stay in hospital lasted almost 4 months, he lost 25kg and was so physically weakened and chronically afflicted that he never again took command of a combat unit. He spent the rest of the war commanding replacement battalions in the homeland. Back's place as commander was taken by Hauptmann Fritz Schwartner[109], a new arrival in the battalion. Schwartner had been transferred from the Austrian Pionier-Bataillon 80 (44. Infanterie-Division) to take command of a company but because the other two company commanders only held the rank of Oberleutnant, Schwartner took command of the battalion upon Major Back's departure. On 17 April, the newly-arrived commander arrived at division staff for a conference. All facets regarding the construction of positions in the divisional sector were discussed.

At 0200 hours on 22 April, a pioneer squad helped Gruppe Winkler implement Operation 'Hochwasser' ['Flood' or 'High Water']. The aim was to destroy Soviet positions still placed along the western bank of the Babka. The pioneer assault troop completely surprised the enemy by quickly reaching the Babka bridge along the Nepokritaya-Fedorovka road and blowing it up at 0320 hours with a 120kg charge. Infantry platoons also surprised the enemy and threw them out of their positions. At 0400 hours, the operation was over: 53 prisoners were brought in and 20 enemy dead were counted. The enemy garrison of 120 men had been eliminated. German casualties: 3 men wounded.

After recovering and regrouping in Kharkov, 1. and 3./Pionier-Bataillon 294 were brought forward on 11 May into accommodation areas in Nepokritaya and Peremoga. The next day, 12 May, packs of Soviet tanks began to break through at 0700 hours. This massive Soviet strike aimed to split and destroy the German forces near Kharkov. Tank fright affected some units. The freshly reorganised pioneer companies couldn't believe their ill fortune: they were alerted at once. One company was immediately subordinated to Gruppe Winkler. Some units began to fall back on its left flank. At 0705 hours, six Soviet tanks broke through at that

108. Aulock, Oberst Andreas von, EL, RK, DKiG; Inf.Rgt.226; born 23 March, 1893 in Kochelsdorf, Upper Silesia. Died 23 June, 2968 in Wiesbaden.

109. Schwartner, Hauptmann Fritz, Pi.Btl.294; born 7 October 1913. Killed in action, 5 July, 1943 near Alexandrovka south of Orel.

same spot. The pioneer company arrived and plugged the hole but then other infantry units started to pull back. Tank fright again spread when two Soviet tanks broke through south of Nepokritaya in the direction of Windmill Hill. To seal off this penetration, a second company of pioneers was turned to the south. Artillery pieces were used as anti-tank guns. The situation in Nepokritaya and Pestshanoye was getting critical by 1100 hours. Soviet tanks were firing directly at German resistance nests and tank-killing weapons were not available. At 1340 hours, units in Nepokritaya had used up their ammunition, so they blew up their guns and began pulling back. In the western part of town, in the westernmost houses, Hauptmann Schwartner reported at 1350 hours that the town was mostly occupied by the enemy. At 1517 hours, Hauptmann Schwartner reported from the western part of Nepokritaya for the last time. He could no longer hold out and was pulling back into a forest with the last elements. Based on Schwartner's report, Nepokritaya had been completely evacuated, but at 1545 hours, Oberst Winkler (commander of Infanterie-Regiment 514) reported from the western edge of Nepokritaya. He had assembled infantry, artillery and some pioneers and intended setting up a blocking position with those weak forces. The fighting was particularly fierce around Nepokritaya and the Germans launched three local counterattacks throughout the day. Soviet progress here was meagre compared to other sectors. During the day, Leutnant Adolf Hörner, a Zugführer in 3. Kompanie, was wounded.

In order to have a small reserve on hand, Schwartner received an order during the night to assemble fragmented groups – already collected in Kutozovka – stragglers and other incidental groups at Kolkhoz Frunze and organise them into a cohesive unit. At 0800 hours on 14 May, enemy pressure forced the weak garrison of Vesseloye to withdraw to Liptsy but Soviet movements were also seen to the north-east. Because of this situation, the combat group concentrated in Frunze under Schwartner's command was alerted and set in march to Tsirkuny. They were deployed to secure the road to the north. On 15 May, the commander of 2. Kompanie, Leutnant Scheerer, was wounded.

Oberleutnant Otto-Wilhelm Heinze

Late in the evening of 17 May, elements of the battalion were subordinated to Gruppe Zimmermann[110] (Schützen-Regiment 3 of 3. Panzer-Division). On 18 May, the long-time battalion adjutant, Oberleutnant Otto-Wilhelm Heinze, was severely wounded when struck in the back, upper and lower legs, and the back of the head with shrapnel[111]. An enemy attack on Hill 210.0 on 20 May forced the unit of feldgendarmes there to pull back their left wing after expending all of their ammunition. Hundreds of Soviet soldiers broke through the front. A counterattack immediately organised by Pionier-Bataillon 294 dispersed the enemy in tough combat and closed the hole. Leutnant Günther Panzer and Leutnant Wolff, both platoon commanders from 2. Kompanie, were wounded. At 1430 hours, the feldgendarmes were withdrawn from the hill and its defence was taken up by Pionier-Bataillon 294. The hill

110. Zimmermann, Oberst Hermann, RK, DKiG; Sch.Rgt.394; born 18 November, 1897. Died 11 January, 1978.

111. For the rest of his life, he carried numerous indented scars all over his back, as well as many pieces of shrapnel which were never removed.

was held. Over the next four days, the Soviet forces that had broken through were caught in a trap by advancing German units, and by the end of 24 May, had been successfully surrounded. Increasing pressure on the Soviet flanks finally forced a collapse. The pioneer battalion received orders to construct positions and erect obstacles and barricades. The next day saw the first major Soviet attempt to break the encirclement but all mass attacks were shattered. In four days it was over. A total of 207,000 Soviets and their armour were captured or killed. Total German losses were around 20,000 men. The Soviet offensive had turned into an utter rout. After the battle was over, elements of the battalion subordinated to 71. Infanterie-Division returned early on the morning of 4 June.

To strengthen its defences, the new division commander, Oberst Johannes Block, gave the order on 6 June to the infantry regiments and the pioneer battalion to use captured Soviet weapons to bolster their firepower: at least 8 light machine-guns in each company, at least 1 anti-tank rifle in each company sector and, as far as was possible, 7.62cm cannon should be deployed for tank defence. On 1 June, before the order, the battalion had 22 light machine-guns. On 11 June, it had 31 machine-guns (both German and Soviet), 2 Soviet heavy machine-guns, 9 heavy anti-tank rifles (28mm) and 6 Soviet anti-tank rifles, and finally, on 21 June, it had 23 German machine-guns, 14 Soviet light machine-guns, 2 Soviet heavy machine-guns, 5 heavy anti-tank rifles (28mm), 11 light mortars (50mm) and 8 Soviet anti-tank rifles. Apart from using captured enemy weapons to boost their firepower, the battalion also established a 'POW pioneer company', recruited from the mass of poorly-trained conscripts so recently taken prisoner.

June was a quiet period for the battalion. They held a calm defensive sector and their tasks consisted of building bridges, constructing defences and the occasional reconnaissance patrol. During the night of 19-20 June, in order to prepare a sector for defence, the pioneers placed demolition charges on the railway bridge over the Burluk near Mikhailovka and also on several smaller bridges. Losses were very low. The entire division suffered only 146 casualties from 5 to 30 June.

Operation 'Blau' began on 28 June but 294. Infanterie-Division did not participate until 2 July. The pioneer battalion was subordinated to Infanterie-Regiment 514 but non-existent enemy resistance meant it was recalled to act as divisional reserve. Enemy resistance increased in the afternoon and at 2230 hours, the infantry regiment requested support by the pioneers. No connection had existed with the pioneer battalion since the afternoon hours, so its 3. Kompanie – which was building a bridge in Grigoryevka – was moved forward. Early the next morning, the company supported an infantry battalion and retook Hill 195.0 in a counterattack. At 0730, a connection was re-established with Pionier-Bataillon 294 via messenger. At 1105, LI. Armeekorps ordered the battalion be sent to 79. Infanterie-Division to help them build a bridge over the Oskol. This assignment lasted for a few days and the battalion was returned to 294. Infanterie-Division at 0720 on 6 July. On 8 July, the division was placed directly under 6. Armee as a reserve, and in this role, carried out tasks behind the line. On 12 July, the pioneer swept a forest south-west of Nikolayevka for enemy stragglers but only found a few in civilian clothes. Other pioneers were sent to Losev to clear reported mine depots. They found ten 6kg wooden mines and in a depot disguised as a mass grave were 53 mortar shells fitted with an electrical ignition system. On 16 July, the battalion removed 24 mines from the Konotopovka railway bridge but did not find others along the rest of the track. Following behind the advance, various small 'clearing actions' of stragglers and partisans were carried out.

On 15 July, 1942, the battalion commander Schwartner was transferred back to Germany. The new commander, coming directly from the nearby Pionier-Bataillon 60, was the old and experienced Hauptmann Wilhelm Weimann. He was the battalion's third commander since the beginning of the year. As the eldest of the pioneer battalion commanders being sent to Stalingrad, 47-year-old Weimann had seen and endured months of terrifying trench warfare during World War One, and his Iron Cross Second and First Class from that war showed he had performed acts of bravery as a young soldier. Now, a quarter of a century later and with the acumen of a seasoned professional, he was quite comfortable letting the younger officers lead the troops in combat while he controlled them from behind. He did not lack courage: he just knew his greatest skill lay in devising strategies and suggesting tactics to be used. His battalion was on a quiet sector and enemy interference was fleeting, so Weimann had not been close to a perilous situation since taking over Pionier-Bataillon 294. Still, he knew it would be foolhardy to risk his life leading his men from the front, especially when his knowledge of stormtroop tactics and assaulting bunkers, acquired in part during the Great War, would soon be needed.

On 23 July, the division received the order to secure the Don. The next day, the pioneer battalion reached Sagrebalovka at 0730 hours with all elements. The division's sector was massive – 75km long from Krassnonorovka to Novo Kalitva – and difficult: the river bank, cut by many gullies, was overgrown with reeds and bushes. These offered the enemy the possibility of penetrating the southern bank at night, unnoticed. What's more, the Don was so shallow at some points that boats were not needed: it could be crossed on foot at several fords. The division decided to only put out weak listening and observation posts at advantageous positions while the rest of the troops remained further back in hedgehog positions, ready to counterattack and throw the enemy back into the Don. The pioneer battalion set up a new command post in Pereshchepny on 27 July. The next day, a pioneer company was sent to both Infanterie-Regiment 514 and 515. On 31 July, Soviet assault groups were able to use the terrain to their advantage and sneak up on German units. Near Deresovka, the river was so unsurveyable and the forests so thick that there was absolutely no way the companies – with their low combat strengths – could secure the river bank itself. Therefore, a pioneer company was requested to mine and wire a low mountain range south of the forest in order to make it impossible for the enemy to envelop German-held villages.

At 0430 hours on 4 August, 2. and 3. Kompanien took part in an attack to clear out a bend in the Don near Osetrovka. Progress was good but there was some stubborn resistance. The task was completed by 1300 hours and 166 prisoners and a large number of heavy machine-guns and mortar were captured, while 58 enemy bodies were counted. It was only possible to hold this position by using the two pioneer companies, previously the division's only reserve. While an infantry battalion secured to the north, the two pioneer companies held the left and right flanks, facing north-east and north-west respectively.

On 14 August, the division was ordered to prepare their sector of the Don river for defence. The pioneer battalion was to build floating mines and burning rafts to block the river. Illumination of the river bank was also to be prepared by installing headlights – taken from vehicles that would be bedded down for the winter[112]. On 18 August, the pioneer battalion gave a company to each infantry regiment to support the construction of positions.

---

112. A report from 9 September stated that these lights, powered by car batteries, were not very powerful and could only illuminate an area about 100 metres in front of them.

The pioneers would first be employed in locations where experience suggested the enemy would attack, such as gullies, villages and forests on the German side of the Don. This backbreaking work, carried out day after day, would continue for more than a month. Here are some typical examples, beginning with 18 August:

1. Kompanie constructed observation posts on elevated ground in the sector of Infanterie-Regiment 515; 2. Kompanie installed abatises[113] and booby traps, mined gullies and built dug-outs in the sector of Infanterie-Regiment 514; 3. Kompanie constructed positions on the right wing of Infanterie-Regiment 513, cleared terrain in front of the main line south-east of Karabut and installed living abatises there.

On 19 August, particular attention was given to the gullies:

2. Kompanie blocked a gully 1km north of Kuvshin with 4 pressure-board mines positioned two metres apart. In the same gully, two S-mines were installed in the slopes with trip-wires. Installation of 5 booby traps in the double-apron fence south-east of Kuvshin and construction of dug-outs and shrapnel-proof field positions in the Kuvshin locality and west of there. Two 50 metre long living abatises were set up near Duchovoye.

1. Kompanie: 1. Zug constructed positions and elevated look-out posts; 2. Zug laid mines and built bunkers; 3. Zug built a double-apron fence.

3. Kompanie: Sited a 120-metre long firing lane, 10 metres wide, in a wooded gully on the boundary between Regiments 513 and 514. The incidental timber was used for an abatis.

It was the same sort of missions, day after day. It would be repetitious to cite every day's activities here, but some tasks stand out: on 22 August, 1. Kompanie wired 250 metres south of Kulakovka, dug 54 metres of trenches (1.2 metres deep) in Strongpoint 'Condor' and buried aerial mines – 128 in all – near St. Kalitva and rigged them with trip-wires.

As would be expected with tasks like this, contact with the enemy was almost non-existent, but losses – albeit very small ones – still occurred. On 20 August, a pioneer was lightly wounded when he stumbled into a booby trap laid by the neighbouring Pionier-Bataillon 336 because it was in a different spot than shown on a sketch. A fatality occurred on 25 August when an Unteroffizier was killed in another accident.

A training course for platoon commanders was begun within 294. Infanterie-Division on 26 August. It covered many different aspects but on 8 September, an officer from the pioneer battalion conducted a 90-minute lecture entitled 'Laying and clearance of makeshift obstacles and mines', accompanied by practical demonstrations. The demonstration impressed several observers, including some Italian staff officers from the neighbouring II. Italian Korps. On 10 September, the pioneer battalion was ordered to assemble a kommando to be sent to the allied corps to run training demonstrations in Kantemirovka for Italian units. The subject was 'Fighting tanks in close combat'. It would show how to lay tank defence mines, how to defend against enemy tanks with flamethrowers and how to set up tank obstacles and anti-tank ditches. The kommando would take along any materials needed for their tenure while captured Soviet tanks were already located in Kantemirovka. Pionier-Bataillon 294 would prepare the configuration of the Lehrtruppe (instruction unit) so it could be sent to Kantemirovka on 12 September. A squad from 2. Kompanie was selected for this task. First, however, the leader of the Lehrtruppe would show the type and comprehensiveness of the proposed demonstrations to the division commander on 11 September.

---

113. Abatis = A defensive obstacle made by laying felled trees on top of each other with branches, sometimes sharpened, facing towards the enemy.

For the first time since beginning construction of positions a month earlier, the pioneers were called upon for offensive operations. The first took place on 13 September. Elements of all three pioneer companies participated but an infantry company (6./514) led the way. Supporting that company were 50 pioneers plus a pioneer assault detachment. They began crossing the Don at 0330 hours in 4 large and 15 small inflatable rafts. They were unnoticed by the Soviets. Once on the enemy bank, the assault troops moved off. The objective was to forestall an enemy attack, destroy combat installations, capture and destroy enemy weapons and grab some prisoners. At 0340, Soviet rifle and machine-gun fire started up from the southern part of Nikolayevka village. Every bunker and dug-out had to be taken by storm. The Soviet defensive system was heavily occupied and offered obstinate resistance. Artillery fire fell on the river banks. The assault troops began to disengage at 0730 hours and all elements were back across the Don by 0930. Soviet losses: 22 dead counted, numerous other casualties inflicted but not confirmed, and 22 prisoners brought back. Twelve bunkers were destroyed in close combat, as were 1 light mortar, 14 rifles, 1 submachine-gun, 1 field-kitchen, 6 rowboats and a ferry. A Maxim machine-gun and a submachine-gun were captured. German casualties: 1 NCO killed, 1 NCO and 5 men wounded, with two of the latter being pioneers: a man from 1. Kompanie was shot through the calf while another from 3. Kompanie was hit by shrapnel in the left ankle, right knee and left carpus.

The success of this operation prompted another one, named 'Sommerausgang' ['Summer's End'], on the night of 16-17 September. Most of 2. Kompanie took part. It was completed by 0430 hours with no Soviet intervention. The centre of Builovo was free of the enemy, twenty houses in the village were set ablaze and several unoccupied field positions and fortified houses were blown up. During the return crossing, however, a Soviet machine-gun 1000 metres upriver from the crossing point opened fire. Two men were severely wounded. No prisoners were brought back. That very same day, yet another cross-river attack was being planned but this time it was to be a battalion-strength operation bearing the cover name 'Herbstanfang' ['Beginning of Autumn']. It was scheduled for 21 September and would be carried out by a battalion from Infanterie-Regiment 515 and supported by artillery and pioneers. The objective was to clear a wooded area north-east of St. Kalitva, bring back prisoners and destroyed installations in the forest. Pioneer-Bataillon 294 would supply the necessary inflatable rafts and other river-crossing equipment. 'Herbstanfang' began at 0410 hours on 21 September when the first wave crossed the Don without enemy interference. The southern edge of the forest was reached at 0700 hours and several prisoners taken twenty minutes later. Resistance stiffened and the operation only ended at 1215. The Germans suffered 6 dead and 8 wounded but brought back 36 prisoners, including a political officer. They left behind 38 enemy dead. Destroyed were a 4.5cm anti-tank gun and 35 dug-outs, captured were 2 heavy and 2 light machine-guns, 4 anti-tank rifles, 3 submachine-guns and numerous rifles and ammunition. The pioneers of 1. Kompanie had no losses. The battalion suffered more losses from defensive preparations than offensive ones: on 19 September, for example, a pioneer from 2. Kompanie was wounded by an explosion while arming a mine. Niggling casualties dotted the battalion's defensive period.

294. Infanterie-Division received word that it was to be replaced by the Italian Alpini Korps. The Italians began to take over the division's sector on 20 September. The infantry regiments gradually handed over their sectors during the following days while the pioneer battalion handed over responsibility for pioneer operations to Italian engineers on 25 September. The battalion then pulled back to new accommodation areas near Ivankoff and

Sovkhoz Karayashnik. Freed from the burden of preparing defences, the battalion fulfilled requests for their expertise: on 27 September, an officer and 14 men of 2. Kompanie were sent to the Alpini Korps to lead a training course in tank destruction, while 3. Kompanie supplied a detachment of one Feldwebel and 20 men to 23. Hungarian Division to support an attack on an island in the Don taking place early the next morning. The rest of the battalion built warm accommodation in the simplest manner possible while still ensuring they were sufficient to withstand winter temperatures. Six weeks were spent on this.

For the operation with the Hungarians, the pioneers took along 11 large inflatable rafts and 6 small ones. The attack commenced at 0300 hours on 28 September and ended at 0600 with the island south of Pavlovsk being completely cleared. The Soviets lost 28 dead, 11 were taken prisoner, and captured were 1 heavy and 1 light machine-gun, 3 50mm mortars and 13 rifles. Hungarian losses: 28 men wounded (1 life-threatening, 9 severe), including an officer. Of the German pioneers, four were lightly wounded. They were Paul Völkel, Soldat Robert Kittler[114], Obergefreiter Werner Anton and Obergefreiter Willy Schubert, the latter two receiving the Iron Cross Second Class. The majority of the casualties occurred during the storming of a bunker in which the German pioneers – without having received an order to do so – willingly participated. The pioneers acquitted themselves with great bravery, so much so that the Hungarian division commander General István Kiss, who saw it as a great success, sent a letter to 294. Infanterie-Division on 29 September. In part, it said: "The enemy offered bitter resistance. Even along the river bank, he was only suppressed by the use of hand grenades. In the man versus man struggle, the German pioneers, taking the decision upon themselves, took part, whereby they demonstrated that they were energetic soldiers with aggressive impetus. As a result of the hard fighting, four of them were wounded." The letter finished by thanking 294. Infanterie-Division for sending the pioneers in the spirit of 'Waffenbrüderschaft' [brotherhood in arms]. This glowing praise was transmitted to Hauptmann Weimann.

Similar acclaim reached the division on 30 September when the commanding general of II. Italian Korps, General Giovanni Zanghieri, reported about the tank destruction course run by the pioneers:

> The pioneer Leutnant company commander and his men return to their division after excellently carrying out two consecutive short courses in the region of Sagrebalovka, each lasting 5 days, with the aim of rounding out the knowledge and expertise of Italian officers and men in combat against tanks. The activity of Leutnant Zimmer has shown him to be very effective through his technical knowledge, his experience and his exquisite tact. I therefore request that a letter of thanks be presented to him in my name…

The letter goes on to thank the commander of 294. Infanterie-Division for his collaboration in sending experienced men to instruct his Italian troops. Shortly after his return, Zimmer took over as battalion adjutant (the regular adjutant was on leave) and the newly arrived Oberleutnant Fritz Bergemann took command of 2. Kompanie.

On 29 September, the battalion had a combat strength of 7 officers, 50 NCOs and 413 men. The light pioneer column was still in Kharkov. Training continued. Weimann did not allow his men to get soft during the months of defensive construction. In fact, this attitude was fostered not just throughout the 294. Infanterie-Division, but also throughout the entire XXIX. Armeekorps. A 'syllabus' distributed in mid-August listed 18 different courses ranging

---

114. Kittler, Gefreiter Robert, 3./Pi.Btl.294; born 15 December, 1922 in Halle. Killed in action, 11 November, 1942 in Stalingrad.

from training for company and platoon commanders to instructional demonstrations of tank destruction in close combat, and more mundane but useful courses in radio operations and telephony. While a few of the higher-level courses, such as battalion and company commander training, were held in faraway France, the large majority were carried out in rear-area towns like Alexandrovka and Rossosh. In addition to these, which were available to men from other divisions, 294. Infanterie-Division also implemented Unterführer[115] training courses within its own sub-units. Pionier-Bataillon 294 held such a course from 5 to 31 October, 1942. In attendance were 24 men from all of the battalion's companies. Running the course was the popular and combat-experienced commander of 1. Kompanie, Oberleutnant Gerhard Pohl, who began the war as a Leutnant in 2./Pionier-Bataillon 14 based in Weissenfels. When Pionier-Bataillon 294 was established in the same town on 6 February, 1940, Pohl was one of the first men transferred to this new unit. He became adjutant in April 1940 and remained so for the next six months. In October 1940, with the battalion occupying a section of the Channel Coast, Pohl gave up the adjutancy and became a platoon commander in 1. Kompanie. Deep in Russia in 1941 and now an Oberleutnant, he took command of 1. Kompanie and in August was awarded the Iron Cross First Class. He continued to lead his company for the rest of the year and throughout the gruelling winter into 1942. Now, under his positive and encouraging tutelage, the Unterführer training course – full of helpful hints and rules for commanding pioneer units – produced two dozen young soldiers ready to move up the ranks. And their first opportunity to prove themselves and put their new-found knowledge to use would be in Stalingrad.

The other two company commanders, Oberleutnant Bergemann of 2. Kompanie and Oberleutnant Gerhard Menzel of 3. Kompanie, were both officers who had been at the front since the war began. Menzel had commanded first a platoon then a company in Panzerpionier-Bataillon 38 (2. Panzer-Division) during the French campaign.

On 9 October, the 23. Hungarian Division conducted another assault troop operation in the morning hours using the pioneers and their boats. The operation was either detected or, as the Hungarian division command suspected, the Soviets were launching an attack of their own – in battalion strength – at the same moment. When the Hungarian assault group landed with 3 officers and 60 men, they were immediately attacked and suffered heavy casualties. Three officers and 30 men were killed, the rest – mostly wounded – managed to get back to the west bank. Seven pioneers were wounded and two were missing. Eight boats were also lost. On 16 October, the pioneer commando from 3. Kompanie returned to its parent battalion after being attached to the Hungarians for almost three weeks. During that time, of the 1 Feldwebel and 20 men, eleven had been wounded and two were missing. Upon their return, three men from this commando were awarded the Iron Cross Second Class on 12 October: Gefreiter Reinhold Bannas, Pionier Heinz Rothe[116] and Pionier Walter Seidel.

- - -

The telephone in 294. Infanterie-Division's command post at Chkalova kolkhoz rang at 2330 hours in the night of 1 November. The telephonist on duty summoned the divisional adjutant, Hauptmann Hagenloh[117]. He listened to the caller while scribbling down the salient

---

115. Trans.: 'Unterführer' = an enlisted man tentatively selected for subsequent officer's training.
116. Rothe, Pionier Heinz, 3./Pi.Btl.294; born 19 February, 1909 in Langsdorf. Missing in action, November, 1942 in Stalingrad.
117. Hagenloh, Major Erwin, 294.Inf.Div.; born 15 January, 1912 in Königsberg. Missing in action, August 1944, near Husi.

points of the conversation. It was an advance order from XXIX. Armeekorps warning the division that Pionier-Bataillon 294 should be made ready as a Sturm-Bataillon for operations in Stalingrad. Transport would either be by lorry or by air. When Major Weimann was advised to prepare his battalion for action in Stalingrad, he protested, citing that his battalion was not ready for such a task. In his latest weekly report dated 29 October, he clearly stated that "the battalion is suitable for limited offensive tasks and for defence". He had repeatedly expressed this same opinion in previous weekly reports. The division commander, Generalmajor Johannes Block, was sympathetic but it was out of his hands because the order had come from much higher up. There were even rumours that it came directly from the top. Generalmajor Block spoke more about it when he met up with Weimann at a rather solemn occasion. On the morning of 2 November, Block took part in a commemorative service in front of German graves in Sarpina, organised by the Italians. At the conclusion of this memorial, at around 1530 hours, Block spoke with Weimann about the upcoming operation and the loading possibilities.

The definite order for the use of Pionier-Bataillon 294 in Stalingrad arrived directly from Heeresgruppe B at 1700 hours that evening and they immediately wanted to know the transport strength of the battalion. The battalion's instructions were as follows:

a) the battalion will make its way to the Rossosh airfield;

b) the commander and adjutant will be sent on ahead to Kalach in 2 passenger cars to make contact with 6. Armee;

c) a large part of the battalion's trucks, with the field-kitchens and a portion of the pioneering equipment, will also be sent to Kalach.

Division telephoned Major Weimann right away and informed him of the situation. In turn, he dispatched messengers to his company commanders. Within a matter of minutes, the billet areas of Pionier-Bataillon 294 were hives of activity. Preliminary preparations had already been carried out after the advance order had been received but no-one expected to leave in such a hurry. Due to the lateness of the hour, it was not possible to head off to the airfield, but the trucks were loaded so the battalion could move out early the next morning. At 2200 hours, however, Heeresgruppe B called again and said that the embarkation of the battalion at Rossosh airfield was delayed and would only take place on 4 November. Major Weimann and his adjutant, Leutnant Walter Zimmer, still planned to rise in darkness the next morning and drive south-east to Kalach. Upon Weimann's departure, the battalion would be in the capable hands of its senior company commander, Oberleutnant Pohl of 1. Kompanie.

The extra day created by the delay enabled the division commander to put some thought into whether all elements of the battalion really needed to be sent to Stalingrad. Fearing that his division would be left without any pioneering strength, Generalmajor Block decided to retain some units of Pionier-Bataillon 294 and the wording of his order shows the clever way in which he accomplished this. This is his order, issued at midday on 3 November, 1942:

Pi.Btl.294 will be subordinated to 6. Armee with effect from 3.11.42. In regards to this, the following is ordered:

1.) Kdr. Pi.Btl.294 and adjutant will drive in two passenger cars on 3.11. to Kalach (large Don bend) and report there to the Armeepionierschule of A.O.K.

2.) About two thirds of the Pionier-Bataillon's working trucks are to be set in march to Kalach on 3.11. Besides the baggage and equipment, 2 large field-kitchens and 3 days worth of rations are to be taken along.

3.) The supply section will provide the necessary fuel for this transfer. The map depot in Rossosh has the necessary maps ready for collection.

4.) The battalion, setting out on 4.11. under the command of Oberleutnant Pohl, will reach the Rossosh airfield before 0700 hours.

    The battalion will camouflage itself against aerial observation until it is loaded in transport planes.

    A day's worth of rations will be taken along.

5.) Remaining behind in the battalion's previous billet area as a Nachkommando are:
   the light pioneer column
   infirmary cases
   sick men on light duties
   the rest of the motorised section
   the horsedrawn section

    Men returning from leave will go to the Nachkommando until further notice. Commander of the Nachkommando is Oberleutnant Benad.

    In every village of the billet area, an Unteroffizier or Feldwebel will be assigned as a town commandant, if need be from the light pioneer column.

    The Nachkommando is to be consolidated within the villages. Equipment, including ammunition and vehicles left behind, will be collected to be respectively stored or parked. The construction of accommodation that has already been commenced will be continued by the Nachkommando until there is at least protection against the weather. Sufficient supervision of the Hilfswilligen and POWs who have been left behind with the Nachkommando is to be secured.

6.) Administration of the pioneer depot controlled by Oberleutnant Benad.

7.) Medical supplies of the Nachkommando controlled by Abt. IVb.

8.) Preparations for the muddy period are handed over to divisional supply office.

9.) Every two days, Pionier-Bataillon 294 will transmit to the division on the courier routes via Heeresgruppe B an activity report in which all types of questions and requests can be raised.

By setting up this Nachkommando, two purposes were served: firstly, Pionier-Bataillon 294 maintained a presence in the divisional structure that handled administrative matters, allowed sick men to recuperate and served as a collection point for those returning from leave and hospital; secondly, and probably more importantly, not all of the unit's men had been sent off on a dangerous and potentially costly assignment. In this way, General Block followed his orders but still retained some pioneering strength, albeit in a greatly reduced form. Oberleutnant Benad, commander of the light pioneer column, was the only pioneer officer to stay behind. The last strength report filed by Pionier-Bataillon 294 was on 29 October, 1942, four days before it left for Stalingrad, and that report shows it had a combat strength of 6 officers, 46 NCOs and 356 men, a total headcount of 408. This meant the battalion was slightly overstrength in men and a few NCOs short, but it was drastically understrength in officers... it had a shortfall of 12 officers! In that same report, Major Weimann expressed his opinion about the condition of his battalion: "Morale of the troops is good. Particular difficulties exist because of the complete lack of officers as platoon commanders..." When the battalion arrived in Stalingrad, it only had 4 officers, 29 NCOs and 275 men, plus about 20 more men not counted as combatants, including an officer (probably Weimann himself). That was a total of 328 men – 80 less than reported a few days earlier! It was these 80 men that formed the Nachkommando.

Pionier-Bataillon 294 had not been engaged in heavy combat since May 1942 when severe casualties had greatly weakened it. Several minor operations had been carried out but nothing that drastically drained the battalion's manpower. Nevertheless, it lacked officers. One thing it was not short of was weapons: captured Soviet weapons were incorporated into the battalion's arsenal, and if they were damaged, they were passed to the battalion's armourer, who was prolific in fixing weapons, both German- and Soviet-made. In addition to the many men who carried the popular PPSh submachine-gun, the battalion also had the following Soviet weapons: 1 heavy 14.5mm machine-gun, 13 light Degtyarev DP machine-guns, 5 14.5mm anti-tank rifles and 9 light mortars. This was all on top of the regular allotment of German machine-guns, in this case, 23 of them. The battalion had actually been ordered to give up some weapons on 25 October: 2 MG-34s, 6 heavy machine-gun mounts and 2 sighting mechanisms were handed over to one of the division's infantry regiments. These damaged weapons had been found and repaired by the battalion's skillful armourer and there were plans for the pioneers to use them. However, because they were not part of a pioneer battalion's standard armament as set down in the regulations, division thought they would be better utilised by the infantry, who were properly trained in their use. So they were handed over. Although many of the Soviet weapons, including the heavier weapons, and some of the German machine-guns, were left behind with the Nachkommando and the POW-Pionier company, the majority of the arsenal accompanied the battalion on the planes.

Pionier-Bataillon 336:

Many officers and men of Pionier-Bataillon 336 that were flown to Stalingrad had brand-new Iron Cross First Class medals pinned to their left breast pockets or Iron Cross Second Class ribbons in their buttonholes after participating in the most ferocious combat they had fought in since the formation of their unit on 12 December, 1940 in the Bielefeld area, Wehrkreis IV. The battalion had been formed with cadres from the East Prussian 2./Pi.Btl.161 (61. Infanterie-Division) and 2./Pi.Btl.256 (256. Infanterie-Division), units that had both participated in the French campaign and gained valuable experience there. Once this framework of more-experienced soldiers was fleshed out with young recruits, the battalion was designated as the organic pioneer battalion of 336. Infanterie-Division. Unlike many other divisions, 336. Infanterie-Division was not sent east in the hot summer of 1941 to become part of the huge invasion force ready to sweep into the Soviet Union. Instead, it was in the ranks of 15. Armee, one of the armies that moved from Belgium

Platoon commanders report to Hauptmann Borkowski, commander of 1. Kompanie, during an exercise in France in 1941.

In May 1942, the battalion's officers prepare to head east to the Russian Front. From left: Hauptmann Eduard Heiter (on special assignment with the battalion), unknown and Hauptmann Borkowski.

On the move. Hauptmann Borkowski (in front) with two of his platoon commanders.

into sunny France in May 1941 as an occupying force. The division moved into the Normandy region and was based around Le Havre on the Channel Coast where it carried out its dual role of coastal security and training. The most memorable event was when a small British force landed by parachute at Cap d'Antifere during the night of 27-28 February, 1942. This was Operation 'Biting': the Germans had erected a Würzburg radar station at Bruneval, near Le Havre, and the British wanted to get hold of this new piece of German technology. The raid was successful. Only two British paratroopers were killed and four captured. The radar set was snatched intact, and as a bonus, one of the German operators was nabbed and spirited away on a boat back across the Channel. A few of 336. Infanterie-Division's men became casualties and a few received medals. However, the relaxed atmosphere was rarely punctuated by enemy action and the officers and men savoured all the delights France had to offer, including organised trips to Paris, newspapers and magazines delivered daily, movies and regular performances by entertainment troupes.

In March 1942, the battalion moved to Brittany. On 1 April, Pionier-Bataillon 336 became the Lehrtruppe (instruction unit) at the army pioneer school in Angers, and the battalion commander, Major Pavlicek, simultaneously became head of the school. After a year of occupation duty in France, the order to transfer to the Ostfront arrived at divisional HQ in the spring of 1942. Months of continual advances and hard fighting during Operation Barbarossa, together with the near-fatal Soviet winter offensive in December 1941, had severely depleted the manpower of Germany's eastern army. Every man was needed there, particularly because a new offensive was to be launched in June 1942. News of the transfer spread like wildfire amongst all units of 336. Infanterie-Division. Rumours about being shifted to the Eastern Front were heard regularly during the past year, and many men also thought this was one of them. Instructions issued by division in May 1942 detailing the march groups and order of departure proved indisputably that the 'rumour' was true.

In late May, after weeks of seemingly endless travel by train via Warsaw, Bialystok, Rogachev and Kursk, the division was finally delivered into accommodation areas north-west of Kharkov and straight into the ranks of one of its most elite armies – Generaloberst Friedrich Paulus's 6. Armee. With an offensive only a few weeks

From left: two unidentified platoon commanders, Hauptmann Heiter, and Hauptmann Borkowski stands behind the wagon.

away, the division would not get much of a chance to settle in. On 4 June, the division began relieving units of 79. Infanterie-Division in preparation for an offensive on 10 June named Operation 'Wilhelm'. Pionier-Bataillon 336, reinforced by two construction battalions, would support the attack of the division by:

a) clearing obstacles, particularly mine barriers, in the attack sectors of the division;

b) crossing over the Donets; and

c) constructing an 8-tonne bridge.

Pioneer troops would be incorporated into the spearheads of the infantry regiments so that they could reach the Donets with the forwardmost infantry. Also, a platoon of pioneers would be deployed in the attack sector of each regiment to clear minefields.

Major Richard Pavlicek

During a preliminary inspection near Shamino early on the morning of the attack, the harsh reality of the Eastern Front was swiftly and cruelly delivered to 336. Infanterie-Division, and particularly Major Richard Pavlicek's Pionier-Bataillon 336: as many officers of the pioneer battalion inspected the front-line on reconnaissance missions, Oberleutnant Borczinski[118] stepped on a mine which exploded right amongst a large group of them. The huge explosion flung the officers in all directions. Hauptmann Eduard Heiter[119], an officer on special assignment with the battalion, was killed outright. All three platoon commanders of 2. Kompanie – Leutnant Heilmann, Leutnant Oskar Link[120] and Oberleutnant Kurt Lossius[121] – were wounded, as was Leutnant Tankred Oertel, a platoon commander in 1. Kompanie. The most unfortunate, however, was

118. Borczinski, Oberleutnant, Günther, le.pi.kol./Pi.Btl.336; born 23 March, 1910 in Kiel. Missing in action, 10 June, 1942 near Botkino.

119. Heiter, Major Eduard, z.b.V. Pi.Btl.336; born 19 August, 1898 in Mainz. Killed in action, 10 June, 1942 near Botkino.

120. Link, Oberleutnant Oskar 2./Pi.Btl.336; born 5 September, 1911 in Hainstadt. Killed in action, 18 August, 1942 near Korotoyak.

121. Lossius, Oberleutnant Kurt, 2./Pi.Btl.336; born 29 April, 1913 in Magdeburg. Killed in action, 7 January, 1943 near Goroloff Nizhne Kundrushovskaya.

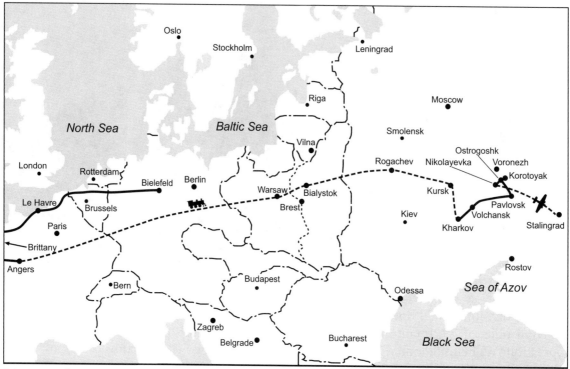

Movement of Pionier-Bataillon 336, 1939-1942.

Oberleutnant Borczinski, commander of the battalion's light pioneer column. He took the full brunt of the explosion and it tore him to pieces. Not a trace of him could be found and he was therefore listed as missing in action. This one unlucky incident had torn a huge hole in the officer ranks of the battalion – seven officers in all – and greatly weakened it even before the offensive had begun. Nevertheless, the assault began at 0255 hours and 6. Armee's units attacked the Soviet 28th Army in the Volchansk salient. It was the division's first assault and the men of Pionier–Bataillon 336 were still stunned by the earlier loss. The division threw the enemy off the west bank of the Donets, captured several intact bridges – including the main bridge at Botkino – with swift and audacious assaults, and formed several bridgeheads on the east bank of the river. At 1615 hours, the pioneer battalion was ordered to mine the east edge of the forest near Korovino up to the mouth of the Neshegoly. In the evening, the division reached the general line Krassnoarmeiskoye – Pletenevka – Novo Tavolshanka – Donets. The entire division suffered heavy casualties on their first day in action. In his order of the day, the division commander, Generalmajor Walther Lucht[122], acknowledged the performance of his green division: "The division received its baptism of fire today. It reached its assigned objectives with bold offensive impetus despite the heaviest resistance… Forward to final victory!"

The attack recommenced at 0230 the next morning. At 1130, the pioneer battalion reported that its command post was located 2km east of Botkino. At 1430, the battalion took control of the bridges near Botkino and Staraya Tavolshanka – the latter suitable only for foot traffic and vehicles under 2 tonnes – and carried out the necessary strengthening. At 0845 on 12 June, the battalion requested artillery support to help defend against constant and

---

122. Lucht, General der Artillerie Walther, EL, RK, DKiG; 336.Inf.Div.; born 26 February, 1882 in Berlin. Died 18 March, 1949 in Heilbronn.

repeated enemy thrusts out of the Shebekinsky area and the orchards south-west of there. Later that evening, the battalion was ordered to send a company to Infanterie-Regiment 685 to help cross the Neshegoly. When they arrived there early in the morning on 14 June, however, they reported back to division that they were not required because the riverbed was dried out. On 16 June the battalion was ordered to clear the heavily mined area around Krassnyanskoye. In the week since the beginning of the attack, 336. Infanterie-Division had taken 1808 prisoners and destroyed or captured 17 tanks.

At first light on 20 June, pioneers reconnoitred the road bridge over the Volchya near Mal. Volchya. It was on this sector, behind enemy lines, that the Fieseler Storch observation plane of the 23. Panzer-Division chief-of-staff, Major Reichel[123], had crashed the previous day. Against the strictest orders, Reichel took with him a memorandum regarding the upcoming 'Blau' offensive and a map showing dispositions and first phase objectives. A patrol from 336. Infanterie-Division reached the plane on 20 June and reported back what they found. Two mutilated bodies were discovered in a grave but Reichel did not seem to be one of them. This incident placed 'Blau' in jeopardy: if the Soviets knew about the forthcoming attack, they could at that very moment be bringing down reinforcements from the Moscow region. The Germans faced a dilemma but they decided to continue with the attack, scheduled to begin on 27 June.

Before then, it was business as usual. At 1730 hours on 21 June, Major Pavlicek was ordered to lay a mine barrier along the Voltsuhya river sector. Also, his pioneers were to reconnoitre other mine barriers south of Valuysk and the gully near Samornyi as defensive measures in case of an enemy breakthrough with tanks.

In preparation for 'Blau', Pionier-Bataillon 336 received the advanced order on 26 June to prepare footbridges in order to cross infantry over the river north of Oktyabriskoye. Preparations were thrown into turmoil when a torrential downpour, interspersed with hail, fell at 1500 hours. All roads flooded immediately and rivers rose. The bridge at Mal. Volchya was soon under a metre of water. Along the Volchya, weapons, bicycles, tents and even horses were washed away in the flood waters, and were only retrieved after exhausting efforts. 'Blau' was postponed until 28 June. The bridge at Mal. Volchya collapsed the next day, 27 June. Late that same evening, the pioneer battalion reported that it had constructed two 24-tonne bridges over

the sodden ground east of Oktyabriskoye. Operation 'Blau' began early the next morning with the codeword 'Aachen' but 336. Infanterie-Division – together with 23. Panzer-Division and 113. Infanterie-Division – did not move off until 0245 hours on 30 June. Two hours before departure, however, pioneers reported that the Pestshanoye-Oktyabriskoye road was probably mined: 85

Familie Borkowski

The newly arrived battalion gets a taste of conditions on the Ostfront.

123. Reichel, Major Joachim, 23.Pz.Div.; born 8 March, 1908 in Glogau. Killed in action, 19 June, 1942 near Suzkovo, north-east of Kharkov.

anti-personnel mines were eventually removed near Oktyabriskoye. The advance progressed well. At 1320, the battalion adjutant reported to division that the Budarka bridge had been blown but the village itself was enemy-free and mines were not found. At 1530, Major Pavlicek transferred his command post to Mal. Volchya. Pioneers reconnoitred the division's march routes. At 1725, Oberleutnant Ziesch's 3. Kompanie was ordered to support Hauptmann Borkowski's 1. Kompanie with all available forces, while Oberleutnant Aigner's[124] 2. Kompanie became part of a Vorausabteilung (advance detachment) being formed and led by Panzerjäger-Abteilung 336, together with Panzerjäger-Abteilung 670. They were to push towards the Oskol. Aigner's company and Panzerjäger-Abteilung 670 had still not arrived in Volchya by 2030 but the river crossing was causing troubles there anyway. The Vorausabteilung set out at 0330 hours the next morning without Panzerjäger-Abteilung 670, which could not get its vehicles over the bridge.

At 1520 on 3 July, the battalion adjutant reported that a new type of mine was found: an electrically detonated 50kg mine. To date, the battalion had removed or destroyed 743 M-32 mines, 50 wooden box mines, 600 anti-personnel mines, 7 electrical mines and 14 shell mines.

On 4 July, the battalion reported that the bridge near Yutanovka was ready at 0800 hours. The bridge near Pyatinskaya had been blown and was missing about 60 metres of its length. Four days would be needed to reconstruct it. The battalion, together with a subordinated company of Pionier-Bataillon 635, had the following casualties: 2 officers and 9 men killed, 1 officer and 20 men wounded. Near Volokonovka, 1400 mines were cleared.

The 24-tonne capacity of the bridge over the Oskol at Yutanovka – constructed by the battalion – is put to the test by a Panzer III.

On 5 July, 2. Kompanie finished reinforcing the Pokrovka bridge to 8 tonnes and that they had started to clear mines in Uspenka. The Pokrovka bridge was trafficable from 0700 hours the next morning. Over the next few days, more bridges were erected in Uspenka and Polatovka. The advance moved swiftly forward and the lead elements of the battalion reached the Don near Pavlovsk on 12 July and assumed defensive positions. The next day, the rest of the battalion assembled in areas around Kurenny and Alexandrovka.

In the time from 3 to 13 July, the battalion had built or reinforced 46 bridges, laid 210 square metres of corduroy roads, made 585 metres of road trafficable and lifted, captured or destroyed 1673 mines.

On 19 July, a pioneer company being sent to Kampfgruppe Pührer (Panzerjäger-Abteilung 336) was on its way to the sector in the Sergeyevka area when it was attacked at 0945 hours by low-flying planes using onboard weapons and shrapnel bombs. Casualties: 5 horses and 3 men wounded.

---

124. Aigner, Oberleutnant Wilhelm, 2./Pi.Btl.336; born 15 November, 1915. Killed in action, 15 August, 1942 near Korotoyak.

From 23 July onwards, Hungarian units started taking over certain sectors from the overstretched 336. Infanterie-Division. The German units were then able to condense their defensive sectors along the Don. At 1700 on 27 July, the divisional chief-of-staff spoke with Major Pavlicek about laying mine barriers in the new sector of Infanterie-Regiment 685. It was also planned to use artillery ammunition as mines. Some bridge construction was also talked about.

On 12 July near Dolzhik, Hauptmann Borkowski leads a small celebration after an awards ceremony for his company. Receiving the Iron Cross Second Class were Uffz. August Kuschel, Obergefreiter Willi Blank, Uffz. Hermann Gorziza and Gefreiter Heinz Knöbel, while Uffz. Martin Jung received the Iron Cross First Class. Borkowski is 4th from right, Feldwebel Franz Mäder is 1st from right.

From 1 to 6 August, 3. Kompanie swept the entire 10 square kilometre Voroshilovgrad airfield for mines and checked thirty building for delayed charges. The only things found were three 3kg mines, which were promptly destroyed. They also found time to level a massive bronze statue of Lenin that had withstood demolition attempts by Italian units.

The division held their sector until it received orders on 10 August to transfer to a new area of operations. 294. Infanterie-Division would take over. At 0240, the pioneer battalion was ordered to cease construction of defences and Oberleutnant Aigner and his 2. Kompanie were subordinated to Kampfgruppe Brinkmann[125] for employment in the Korotoyak area. On 16 August, the rest of the pioneer battalion reached the Goikalovo area. Towards the evening of the next day, they reached their destination: a forest 6km north of Ostrogoshk. This would be the battalion's base camp for the next two and a half months.

The battalion now became embroiled in a battle that showed how tenacious and extremely dogged Soviet soldiers could be when holding a town set along a river. Its name was Korotoyak-on-Don, a medium-sized town south of Voronezh. From 15 August until mid-September, 336. Infanterie-Division and attached units, heavily supported by Stukas, would make steady but costly headway as they pushed ever deeper into this Soviet stronghold. As always, the pioneer soldiers were in the thick of the action but the battalion was rarely employed as a single unit.

The first pioneer unit to become embroiled was 2. Kompanie. It reached its jump-off positions near Rybenskoye on 13 August. Throughout 14 August it received equipment for assault troop operations, house-to-house fighting and mine removal. At 1300 hours, a pioneer platoon was assigned to each infantry battalion scheduled for the attack: 1. Zug to III./Inf. Rgt.685, 2. Zug to II./Inf.Rgt.687 and 3. Zug to I./Inf.Rgt.686. Assembly positions were reached at 1500 hours. The attack began at 0400 hours on 15 August with II./Inf.Rgt.687 (2. Zug) on the right, I./Inf.Rgt.686 (3. Zug) on the left and III./Inf.Rgt.685 (1. Zug) in reserve. When the infantry company 2. Zug was to support had

125. Brinkmann, Oberstleutnant Robert, DKiG; commander of Infanterie-Regiment 687.

not arrived at 0400, the platoon commander decided to attack anyway. Together with a neighbouring infantry company, they pushed into the town centre towards the 'Fabrik' [factory]. The daily objective was reached. During a Soviet counterattack in the evening, the platoon commander was wounded while repelling it. Unteroffizier Philipp[126] took command of the platoon. Throughout the day, the platoon lost 1 NCO and 7 men to wounds.

After knocking out some Soviet machine-gun nests, the attack of 3. Zug moved forward. Because the Schwerpunkt of the entire attack was located there, the company commander, Oberleutnant Aigner, decided to attack at the spearhead of the infantry battalion with his Kompanietrupp and Stabsfeldwebel Piltz's[127] 3. Zug. The assault swiftly gained ground and soon moved into the centre of town. The platoon received heavy flanking fire from machine-guns and mortars, and an attempt by the enemy to cut off part of the platoon was smashed by a counterattack. Around midday, the platoon, together with I./Inf.Rgt.686, reached their objective, Korotoyak railway station, and secured it. In an advanced position, about 300 metres east of the station, Oberleutnant Aigner was killed at the spearhead of his company. Oberleutnant Link, having just returned after recovering from wounds suffered during the mine incident on 10 June, took over 2. Kompanie. After a brief redeployment, Piltz's 3. Zug was ordered to hold a strongpoint on the city's north-western outskirts. Losses of 3. Zug and the Kompanietrupp: 1 officer and 2 men killed, 2 NCOs and 3 men wounded.

1. Zug was kept in reserve and played no part in the attack on this day.

The attack continued at 1100 hours the next day. While 3. Zug held its strongpoint, the other two platoons attacked. 2. Zug stormed and occupied a house-cum-blockhouse and then used it as their own strongpoint. It was held for the rest of the day and throughout the night. Losses: 1 NCO and 1 man wounded.

Initially in reserve, 1. Zug was called upon in the afternoon to help an infantry squad approach and subdue two houses on open ground that had been turned into fortresses. The attack pushed forward to within hand grenade distance but came to a standstill because of enemy numerical superiority. The Soviet defenders also had excellent camouflage, secure shelters and fired into the flanks with tanks. Despite an in-depth reconnaissance by the platoon commander, a further operation by the assault troops was abandoned because of the falling darkness. Losses: 2 NCOs and 1 man wounded.

On 17 August, 1. and 3. Zug secured the command posts of the infantry battalions. At 0700, however, the enemy suddenly attacked, escorted by low-flying planes that paved the way with onboard guns. 3. Zug and part of 1. Zug were used for a counterattack that pushed into the enemy and quickly threw them back to their old positions. In the course of the afternoon, the Soviets attacked twice more but were immediately repelled by swiftly mounted counterattacks. Losses of 1 and 3. Zug: 3 men killed, 3 men wounded.

In the meantime, 2. Zug was having a difficult time holding its strongpoint against Soviet attacks. Because the German infantry to the left and right had pulled back, the strongpoint was far in advance of the main line and its flanks were therefore open. The enemy, in superior numbers, approached to within three paces of the strongpoint, and under their own smoke screen the platoon pulled back to the next resistance line. The tense situation caused them to leave one of their wounded behind, and despite repeated attempts, they were

---

126. Philipp, Unteroffizier Martin, 2./Pi.Btl.336; born 26 March, 1914 in Neusalza Spremberg. Killed in action, 19 November, 1942 in Stalingrad.

127. Piltz, Leutnant Gerhard, 2./Pi.Btl.336; born 4 February, 1908 in Benndorf. Died 11 December, 1985 in Remscheid.

unsuccessful in retrieving Gefreiter Fortyr[128] in the face of heavy enemy fire. Losses: 1 man missing, 5 men wounded.

At 0600 on 18 August, regiment commander Oberstleutnant Brinkmann, who controlled the attempts to capture Korotoyak, called division and informed them that he had postponed the attack scheduled for 0300 because the Soviet defenders located in houses in the north-east sector of the town were being continually reinforced. Brinkmann thereupon requested the supply of one or two pioneer companies because 2. Kompanie had been heavily crippled by losses. At 0700, the pioneer battalion commander, Major Pavlicek, received the order that the entire battalion would be used to support the attack of Kampfgruppe Brinkmann. Advanced orders were sent to 1. and 3. Kompanien at 0830: "Prepare for deployment as Stoßzüge (assault platoons)…". At 0930, Major Pavlicek, his adjutant Oberleutnant Hullen, and company commanders Hauptmann Borkowski and Oberleutnant Ziesch, attended a briefing at Brinkmann's command post: "The Russians hold the western and eastern sections of Korotoyak and attempt to take the town centre with continual counterattacks". Hauptmann Borkowski's 1. Kompanie was to support an attack of I./Inf.Rgt.687 along the railway embankment near Kopanishche at 1330, however, it did not arrive in time. Borkowski later wrote:

> After returning from the battalion command post of I./687 at 1045, preparations for the attack were immediately met. The company, loaded aboard 3 lorries, was ready at 1130 and moved off to Peski. The company reached Peski railway station at 1450 hours… The company arrived at the battalion command post at 1610. The first attack at 1330 only moved forward about 300 metres and then stalled. A second attack was planned for 1830 hours for which the company's 4 assault groups were allocated flamethrowers: two groups under the command of Oberleutnant Kaesler were to the left and two groups under the command of Oberfeldwebel Schuleit[129] were to the right of the railway embankment. The attack collapsed in the exceedingly heavy defensive fire and could move no further forward. After that, the [infantry] battalion pulled back to its starting positions.

> The battalion was assembled and redeployed with the task of setting themselves up for defence. For the connection from left to right, two passageways were created through the railway embankment and the construction of two earth bunkers was begun. Because of the loss of command, the defence was taken over by Oberleutnant Kaesler on the left and Oberfeldwebel Schuleit on the right with their platoons, to which the rest of the infantry were allotted.

Ziesch's 3. Kompanie also arrived late and could not support the opening stage of Bataillon Nöring's attack at 1400 on the north-east sector of Korotoyak. In an after-action report, Oberleutnant Ziesch wrote:

> The platoons were equipped with close combat weapons and ammunition. The 2. and 3. Zug were each allotted a flamethrower troop. The approach to the assembly positions was very difficult because the area lay under heavy fire from anti-tank guns, mortars, machine-guns and rifles. After the distribution of the company, first platoon was taken forward by a messenger from 10./Inf.Rgt.687. Because 10. Kompanie had already commenced its attack, the platoon had to follow up and in doing so walked into heavy mortar and anti-tank fire. In the process Gefreiter Paul and Pionier Lampsch[130] were severely wounded. Pionier Lampsch died a short while later

---

128. Fortyr, Gefreiter Wenzel, 2./Pi.Btl.336; born 22 February, 1912 in Briesen/Billin. Missing in action, 17 August, 1942 near Korotoyak.

129. Schuleit, Oberfeldwebel Willi, 1./Pi.Btl.336; born 24 July, 1910 in Königsberg. Killed in action, 6 September, 1942 near Korotoyak.

130. Lampsch, Pionier Heinz, 3./Pi.Btl.336; born 25 March, 1922 in Leipzig. Died of wounds, 18 August, 1942 near Korotoyak.

in an aid station. First platoon gained up to 300 metres south of the railway embankment. From then on, however, any further advance was impossible because of the fierce flanking fire…

In the meantime, 2. Zug moved up to the front-line on its own… Leutnant Ruhl then gave his platoon the order to attack. Gruppe Lang[131] advanced along the railway embankment and after crossing over it tried to push into the town. In doing so, Pionier Witschel[132] was killed by a shot to the heart. Gruppe Dutschke[133] became involved in house-to-house fighting and destroyed a small enemy strongpoint by blowing it up with a concentrated charge. Because the attack had not progressed on the right flank, these forward elements had to be pulled back at dusk.

Third platoon, which had remained at the disposal of the [infantry] battalion commander, was deployed about 1500 hours to comb through the houses taken during the attack and then push forward over the railway into the eastern district. The deployment of the platoon, however, was spotted by the enemy. The platoon received the heaviest mortar, machine-gun and rifle fire. The machine-gun of the right squad was out of action due to the wounding of all the gunners. After overcoming the mortar fire, the platoon − covered by tall grass and fruit trees − succeeded in pushing up to an intersection. A further advance over the railway embankment was no longer possible because the Russians fired on every single man and the infantry also advanced no further. Apart from that, the platoon had taken a lot of casualties. Oberleutnant Ehringhaus assembled his platoon in a factory building and informed the company commander[134] − who had arrived there − about the execution of the mission and the casualties of his platoon. Two dead, 2 severely and 7 lightly wounded, 4 of the latter remaining with the platoon. The recovery of the dead and wounded continued until nightfall. On the order of the company commander, the platoon would shelter in the factory for the night and establish defence there by placing two light machine-guns and an observer on the second floor of the factory…

During the day, Ziesch's company lost 1 NCO and 3 men killed, 1 NCO and 10 men wounded, with 5 of the latter staying with the company.

For 2. Kompanie, now led by Oberleutnant Link after the death of Aigner, the day consisted of holding defensive positions, but that does not mean it escaped casualties. At 1250, Oberleutnant Link was killed in front of the command post of Bataillon Schulz. The senior platoon commander, Stabsfeldwebel Piltz, took command of the company. A few days later, a new officer arrived to command the company. His name was Oberleutnant Karl Brockmann.

After a day of heavy fighting and painful losses, the next day (19 August) was relatively calm. Positions were held and Soviet counterattacks repulsed. Heavy fire from all types of weapons covered the German positions but casualties were low. An unfortunate man from 1. Zug of 3. Kompanie received a severe stomach wound. Early in the morning of 20 August, 1. and 2. Kompanien were pulled out of Kampfgruppe Brinkmann and returned to their old billeting areas in the forest. Oberleutnant Ziesch's 3. Kompanie stayed in the line. The Soviets did not attack but placed heavy fire on all German positions including bombing and strafing by Soviet planes. In the

The grave of Oblt. Link.

Familie Ziesch

---

131. Lang, Unteroffizier Rudi, 3./Pi.Btl.336; born 6 October, 1910 in Reichenbach. Killed in action, 13 November, 1942 in Stalingrad.

132. Witschel, Pionier Herbert, 3./Pi.Btl.336; born 15 November, 1920 in Plessa. Killed in action, 18 August, 1942 near Korotoyak.

133. Dutschke, Unteroffizier Erich, 3./Pi.Btl.336; born 5 August, 1911 in Langenfeld. Missing in action, 25 December, 1942 in Stalingrad.

134. Ziesch is referring to himself here.

evening, 1. Zug was relieved on division's order. It marched back to the company supply train around midnight. According to the divisional order, the entire company should have been relieved, but a request by the commander of Infanterie-Regiment 686 meant that 2. and 3. Zug remained in position in Korotoyak. Strangely, this probably saved some of their lives because during the night, Soviet planes bombed the company's supply train, wounding 2 men severely and 5 men lightly, as well as killing 21 horses and heavily wounding 5. Lorries arrived at 0500 on 21 August to pick up the remaining two platoons in Korotoyak but were sent away because they were still needed. Their relief was ordered at 1600 hours: 3. Zug came out about 1930 but just as 2. Zug was leaving their positions at 2000, the Soviets attacked. On his own decision, the platoon commander Leutnant Ruhl remained in position and repelled the attack, together with the infantry. During this attack, a man was severely wounded. At dawn on 22 August, 2. Zug finally left Korotoyak.

It had been a costly mission for 3. Kompanie. In total, they lost 4 dead (Unteroffizier Wildner[135], Gefreiter Schreiber[136], Pionier Lampsch and Pionier Witschel), 13 severely wounded and 12 lightly wounded.

For the battalion, their first stint in Korotoyak had resulted in the following casualties: 2 officers, 1 NCO and 11 men killed, 1 man missing, 7 NCOs and 42 men wounded (in hospital), and 4 NCOs and 33 men wounded (who remained with the troops). On top of that, 9 horses and 21 panje ponies were killed, and 7 horses and 5 panje ponies were wounded.

Most of Korotoyak still remained to be conquered. Positions were held as a new attack was prepared. The company and platoon commanders of Pionier-Bataillon 336 were ordered to attend a conference. At 0900 on 31 August, the briefing and orientation was conducted from a church in Korotoyak. Commanders of all attached weapons were briefed and missions were later laid down in a divisional order. The mission of the division was as follows: "336. Infanterie-Division will launch its attack at 0530 hours to capture the Korotoyak bridgehead from the enemy and annihilate the enemy forces defending it." Assault guns of Sturmgeschütz-Abteilung 201 were assigned to support the attack.

At about 2100 hours, the pioneers began marching towards their assembly positions but rain bucketed down and drastically impeded progress. Hauptmann Borkowski's 1. Kompanie did not reach its assigned positions until 0200 hours. While 1. Zug provided five mine-locating details – each with 1 NCO and 5 men – to each assault gun battery and company sector, 2. Zug was readied for use as assault troops and 3. Zug was kept in readiness to lay a mine barrier after the objective was reached.

The attack began at 0530 on 1 September but made no progress because every house had been turned into a bunker. Vicious Soviet mortar fire showered down. Two assault guns were out of action right at the start. The pioneers were ordered to deploy their flamethrowers. Borkowski had serious misgivings but carried out the order. Both flamethrowers, however, were knocked out on their way forward. Progress was lacking because of a vicious circle: mines prevented the assault guns from moving forward so they could fire into the bunker embrasures to suppress the heavy weapons that were pinning down the mine-clearing pioneers. Regardless, an assault group commanded by Leutnant Schmidt was deployed, and through sheer audacity, they took two bunkers. As a result, the first possibility was presented

---

135. Wildner, Unteroffizier Alfred, 3./Pi.Btl.336; born 3 September, 1913 in Markersdorf. Killed in action, 18 August, 1942 near Korotoyak.

136. Schreiber, Gefreiter Herbert, 3./Pi.Btl.336; born 8, April 1912 in Bärenstein. Killed in action, 18 August, 1942 near Korotoyak.

to push the attack forward. Despite the heaviest enemy fire, the mine-locating details cleared the heavily mined streets (85 mines were removed), and the assault guns were finally able to work over the bunkers. It was certainly not a one-sided affair: a further five assault guns were lost by 1730 hours. At 1830, Borkowski's company pulled back to rear positions 200 metres east of the church, where Borkowski was informed that for the following day, he would have two squads from 3. Kompanie and a panzerjäger company subordinated to him.

An operation to blow up the crossing over the Don with improvised floating mines, planned for the night, was postponed.

By taking the bunkers on the first day with only one pioneer assault group, the other branches of the service came to the conclusion that the bunkers could only be taken by pioneer assault groups with cooperation from all weapons. Hauptmann Borkowski now found himself organising the attack. He briefed the other commanders at 0500 on 2 September. At 0800, two assault groups under the command of Leutnant Schmidt and Feldwebel Hofstedt began the attack with the task of capturing two bunkers. They succeeded. It was recognised that the main resistance nest was on the left flank in the 'Roten Parteihaus' (Red Party House). Before this attack on the 'Red House', Borkowski held a situation conference at 1100 hours. The attack began at 1500 hours and the 'Red House' was taken by assault groups Schmidt and Hofstedt. Infantry forces then took it over. The objective had been reached with negligible casualties while the Soviets lost 60 dead and 40 prisoners, including an officer and a politruk. By 1625 hours, the division had lost 1,700 men. Army headquarters issued the following order: "The division has to be tougher than the Russians."

During the night of 2-3 September, a detachment under the command of Oberfeldwebel Milkau launched ten makeshift floating mines, each weighing 20kg, into the Don. The intention was to blow up the crossing over the river. Reconnaissance later proved that the operation had been successful. A fifty metre stretch had been blown off and swivelled downstream.

While progress had been relatively good on Borkowski's sector, it was not so on the right wing. For the first two days of the assault, two Soviet bunkers – normal buildings turned into strongpoints – could not be taken by the infantry and caused the attack to come to a stop. Borkowski proposed to capture both bunkers on 3 September. The attack on 'Bunker Weisses Haus' (White House bunker) would begin at 0900 and on 'Bunker Quadrathaus' (Square House bunker) at 1000 hours. On the left was the assault group commanded by Oberfeldwebel Schuleit, on the right the assault group of Feldwebel Schmidt. The attack began upon the agreed signal. Hauptmann Borkowski describes what happened next:

> By marvellous cooperation of all weapons, assault group Schuleit succeeded in taking and occupying the bunker so that the infantry attack was given momentum and pushed toward 'Rote Strasse' (Red Road). Because bunker after bunker was being taken by this well-planned deployment, the assault group leaders noticed that the garrisons in nearby bunkers were becoming demoralised. Recognising this immediately, assault group leader Feldwebel Schmidt, who was to be committed against the Square House, launched his attack on this strongpoint on his own initiative and captured it. Field positions near the bunker were also rolled up. With this momentum, he and his pioneer assault group continued to advance further without infantry support – again on his own initiative – and despite strong flanking fire from the north, took an occupied field position on Red Square about 50 metres behind the Square House, then advanced up to the level of the extended northern road, captured another bunker and held it. The infantry were then steadily pulled along and directed by Feldwebel Schmidt. He occupied the bunker until 1700 and then handed it over to the infantry.

At the same time, other pioneers were in action to the left of Feldwebel Schmidt's daring thrust. Three infantry companies had each been allotted a pioneer assault group, commanded by Feldwebel Hofstedt, Unteroffizier Kuschel[137] and Unteroffizier Goldbaum respectively. By taking several bunkers and punching through to the church, these three assault groups had also paved the way for the infantry and given their attack momentum. Apart from capturing several bunkers, Unteroffizier Goldbaum's assault group seized a Soviet battalion command post.

Enemy casualties amounted to 25 dead and 80 prisoners, including 2 officers. Numerous weapons of all types were also captured.

The attack continued on 4 September. At 0500, an assault group under the command of Oberfeldwebel Milkau launched an attack with the infantry, captured a bunker and took 15 prisoners. Another assault group under the command of Oberfeldwebel Schuleit had been allotted to an infantry Kampfgruppe but it was not employed because the Soviets had given up their positions. It was therefore used to clear mines until called upon at 1430 to reconnoitre enemy field positions in the Don forests and along the railway embankment. The rest of the pioneers cleared mines in the conquered sections of Korotoyak. By the end of 4 September, the pioneers had cleared a total of 390 mines, at times under heavy fire. The losses of 1. Kompanie up to the end of 4 September were as follows: 2 men killed, 4 NCOs and 7 men heavily wounded, 1 officer and 2 men lightly wounded, 1 officer, 1 NCO and 14 men lightly wounded but remained with the troops.

By this stage of the fighting, cooperation with the assault guns had been perfectly honed. Hauptmann Borkowski reported that "the first-class teamwork between the assault guns and pioneer assault groups should be mentioned because the guns are shown the resistance nests by directional shots with flare pistols, so giving the guns the possibility of suppressing the bunkers by direct fire. The pioneer assault groups can then approach the embrasures and destroy the crews in close combat."

Because the fighting in the built-up area of Korotoyak had ended on 4 September, 1. Kompanie was subordinated to Infanterie-Regiment 687 on the town's eastern outskirts. This regiment was faced with a railway line atop an embankment curving into a forested area from which the Soviets offered fierce resistance. Borkowski met the regiment commander at 1900 on 4 September and was briefed on his task: reconnoitre in order to determine direction and objectives for the assault by the storm groups within an infantry framework. The recon patrols would set out early on 5 September. Hauptmann Borkowski reports:

Reconnaissance at 0530 hours with assault group leaders Oberfeldwebel Schuleit, Milkau and Feldwebel Schmidt. Reconnaissance was carried out from company to company in view of the enemy and under their fire and then extended for accurate recognition and determination of bunkers and field positions in the entire attack sector. Also, preparations were made for an assault by the storm- and attack groups with the objective of the 'Donwäldchen' (Don Grove). The results of the reconnaissance were reported to regiment at 1600 hours. Based upon this, the assault was set for 1500 hours on 6 September... During the night, the assault groups of Oberfeldwebel Schuleit, Milkau and Feldwebel Schmidt were supplied to I./Inf.Rgt.687. The assault groups had to reach their assembly positions before daybreak, otherwise, an approach was not possible because of enemy observation. In cooperation with all weapons, the assault moved off at 1500 hours. The assault, which was well prepared, gathered momentum through the forceful verve of the assault groups and gained a good deal of ground. They set off at the same time to the right of the railway embankment in order to eliminate flanking fire from the

---

137. Kuschel, Feldwebel August; 1./Pi.Btl.336; born 6 February, 1911 in Hausdorf. Missing in action, June 1944.

right. This attack also progressed so well that the sharp bend in the railway was reached. Despite strong enemy resistance, the first objectives were taken. With two men of his group, Oberfeldwebel Schuleit reached the stream valley but was killed there in hand-to-hand combat together with both his men. Three previously recognised bunkers and several field positions were captured by assault groups Schuleit and Milkau. In tough hand-to-hand combat, assault group Schmidt rolled up about 400 metres of the stream valley, reaching the railway bend. In doing so, 6 bunkers, 2 heavy machine-gun positions, several nests of riflemen and a communications bunker were taken. Despite the attack on the right of the railway embankment pushing forward to the railway bend, the enemy held out to the left of the embankment and affected the left assault groups through flanking fire. Upon a report from Feldwebel Schmidt, an assault group was subsequently deployed on the left which would roll up the railway embankment and eliminate the flanking fire. The swift penetration of Schuleit's and Milkau's assault groups did not completely destroy the enemy to the left and right of them, so the groups had to spend nearly the entire night in grim hand-to-hand fighting to destroy the Russians to their left and right in order to create a proper defensive position for the night.

Mark/NARA

The three assault groups displayed courage and offensive elan but paid the price. With a strength of 1 NCO and 6 men each, they together suffered losses of 1 NCO and 3 men killed, 2 men missing and 2 men heavily wounded, a total of 8 men from the 21 deployed. Soviet casualties were calculated at 25 dead and 30 prisoners. Also participating in this combat was a detachment from 3. Kompanie, under the command of Stabsfeldwebel Reiter[138], deployed to the right of the embankment.

The situation with the pioneer battalion on the evening of 6 September was as follows: one platoon of 3. Kompanie was deployed as an assault group while the rest of the company was near Mutnik as divisional reserve; a platoon of 2. Kompanie was employed as a mine-clearing commando while the rest of the company was off-duty in a patch of forest; 1. Kompanie was still in the line. After a full

Otto Reiter as a Leutnant in 1943.

week of hard combat, Hauptmann Borkowski's company was relieved during the night of 6-7 September on the order of the battalion and Oberleutnant Ziesch's 3. Kompanie took over their positions. The Soviet bridgehead in the forests east of Korotoyak would never be conquered. Safe in their reserve positions, the casualties incurred by 1. Kompanie in Korotoyak were calculated: 1 NCO and 5 men killed, 4 men missing, 4 NCOs and 6 men heavily wounded, 1 officer and 3 men lightly wounded, 2 officers, 2 NCOs and 18 men lightly wounded but remained with the troops. In return, they had killed 125 enemy soldiers, taken 3 officers, 1 politruk and 200 men prisoner, and captured 14 light and 8 heavy machine-guns, 6 light and 3 heavy mortars, 19 anti-tank rifles, 45 submachine-guns, 220 rifles, 4 anti-tank guns, 1 gun and 2 radio installations. As would be expected, numerous decorations were bestowed upon the battalion after their performance in Korotoyak: 1. Kompanie soldiers received 44 Iron Cross Second Classes and 7 First Classes; 2. Kompanie received 19 Iron Cross Second Classes and 2 First Classes; 3. Kompanie received 23 Iron Cross Second Classes and 3 First Classes; and battalion staff received 2 First Classes.

On 11 September, the battalion reported that for the period 8 to 11 September, it had removed a total of 489 anti-personnel mines and 285 anti-tank mines. In the next two days, it removed another 54 mines of all types.

---

138. Reiter, Leutnant Otto; 1./Pi.Btl.336; born 18 October, 1908 in Oebisfelde. Died 30 May, 1987 in Tangerhütte.

The rest of September was fairly quiet. Towards the end of the month, there was construction of the main line, as well as switch positions, in the divisional area. Each infantry regiment was tactically responsible for defences in their sector, so to help them, a pioneer officer was assigned for technical matters: Hauptmann Borkowski to Inf.Rgt.685, Oberleutnant Brockmann to Inf.Rgt.686 and Oberleutnant Ziesch to

Rest and recuperation. Rations are received and prepared for distribution.

Inf.Rgt.687. These officers were responsible for construction of positions and for supplying the necessary tools, material and equipment. From 14 to 28 September, Borkowski's 1. Kompanie implemented an extensive mine-laying schedule in the sector of Inf.Rgt.685.

In mid-September, a new officer arrived at the battalion. His name was Hauptmann Hermann Lundt. While on home leave in August 1942, Lundt had received his new assignment: transfer to Pionier-Bataillon 336 for employment as a company commander. He joined his new unit in its reserve positions in the forest north of Ostrogoshk.

October was also a quiet month. The division still defended the Don in the Korotoyak area but its front-line was held in a strongpoint fashion. Any retreat from positions during an enemy attack was forbidden. A continuous trench along the front-line connected all strongpoints and resistance nests, and a solid line of obstacles – mostly Spanish riders and barbed wire – also ran in front of the main line. On 1 October, a switch position was built between Points 196.9 and 202.2. Construction of a Dulag[139] was also begun in Ostrogoshk on this day. Occasionally, the pioneers would be called upon to conduct anti-partisan sweeps. On 4 October, however, the pioneers were requested for a more solemn purpose: two platoons were to be provided for the funeral service of General der Panzertruppe Willibald Freiherr von Langermann und Erlencamp[140], Commanding General of XXIV. Panzerkorps, on 5 October. The service was held in a church in Shulonoye. And thus October passed.

– – –

The command structure of the battalion that would arrive in Stalingrad was significantly different to the one that emerged from Korotoyak. Their commander, Major Richard Pavlicek, had left for home leave only a few days before his battalion received the fateful order to head for Stalingrad. Command of the battalion should have passed to the senior company commander, in this case, Hauptmann Borkowski, but he was recalled to the Führerreserve of Heeresgruppe B on 1 November and then transferred to the German staff of the Hungarian 2. Armee as a liaison officer. Next in line was Hauptmann Hermann

---

139. Dulag = '<u>Du</u>rchgangs<u>lag</u>er' (POW transit camp)

140. Langermann und Erlencamp, General der Panzertruppe Willibald Freiherr von, EL, RK; XXIV. Pz.Korps; born 29 March, 1890 in Karlsruhe. Died of wounds, 3 October, 1942 near Staroshevoye.

Lundt, the former career NCO who had been transferred to Pionier-Bataillon 336 in mid-September 1942, officially for use as a company commander but instead had been kept at Bataillon HQ, ostensibly as Hauptmann z.b.V. (zur besonder Verwendung – Hauptmann on special assignment). His main role, however, was being groomed as a battalion commander. He would soon have a chance to prove his mettle.

Lundt was once described by a superior officer as a man whose military manner was "firm, energetic and soldierly" while his off-duty behaviour was "impeccable", as was his attitude towards superiors and subordinates. No embarrassing incidents blemished his military record. He was polite, popular and possessed the characteristics of a leader. An early wartime commander summed up Lundt in a few words: "a simple, forthright and reliable man. A soldierly personality through and through."

Apart from a new commander, there were other changes in the battalion. With the temporary absence of Major Pavlicek and the permanent departure of Hauptmann Borkowski forcing the 'spare' company commander – Hauptmann Lundt – to be employed as Bataillonsführer[141], the position of commander of 1. Kompanie was now vacant. The adjutant of the battalion, Oberleutnant Karl-Heinz Hullen, knew he was capable of commanding a company of pioneers, so he put his name forward for the position. When his previous experience as a platoon commander was taken into account, together with the conscientiousness he displayed as adjutant, it was apparent he would make an excellent company commander. The position of battalion adjutant was assumed by Leutnant Dr. Karl Ruhl, platoon commander from 3. Kompanie.

– – –

Like Pionier-Bataillon 294, most officers and men of Pionier-Bataillon 336 were spared the rigours of a long march: the distance to Stalingrad from their current area of operations was simply too vast and if the battalion was to arrive in time for an attack, they needed to be transported rapidly. Tight time restrictions meant preparations had to be brief: half an hour before midnight on 1 November, 336. Infanterie-Division received a communique stating that the transport of its pioneer battalion by air to another sector should be expected. The division commander called Hauptmann Lundt and gave him a heads-up. At 2030 hours the next evening, Lundt received an order to report himself at the Ilovskoye airfield near Nikolayevka at 0900 hours the next morning. He was to fly straight to 6. Armee and make his way to the army pioneer school in Kalach-on-Don where he would be briefed about an upcoming operation and make preparations for the arrival of his battalion. Two hours later, at 2230 hours on 2 November, 336. Infanterie-Division received the official order: "Transportation of the Pionier-Bataillon to Stalingrad on 4.11.1942." Hauptmann Lundt immediately had all his company commanders assembled in his command post and ordered them to prepare their men for aerial transport. He told them they needed to bring all available heavy weapons, including the flamethrowers. When asked where they were going, Lundt just needed to say one word: "Stalingrad". Oberleutnant Hullen, commander of 1. Kompanie and former adjutant, would be in charge after Lundt's departure.

Gefreiter Wilhelm Giebeler, a cook, gathered his kitchen equipment. Together with the other elements of the battalion's supply echelon, he would reach Stalingrad by road. As he packed his gear, the pioneers around him grumbled loudly about their new assignment

---

141. Trans.: 'Bataillonsführer = 'acting battalion commander'.

while they inspected flamethrowers, demolition charges and personal weapons. Giebeler had heard their griping before, on the eve of every special 'dirty job'. But since the pioneers were consummate professionals at streetfighting, he had no worries about their morale nor doubt as to their success at the Volga.

Hauptmann Lundt and his adjutant, Leutnant Dr. Ruhl, set off for the airfield around dawn. Their plane left promptly at 0900 hours and landed three hours later at the airfield north-west of the village of Pitomnik, 10km west of Stalingrad. In the meantime, back in the Korotoyak area, Oberleutnant Brockmann's 2. Kompanie climbed into nine lorries and left their billet area at midday. They too drove to the Ilovskoye airfield, arriving there as the sun was casting its long afternoon shadows. Forming themselves into squads and organising their equipment, they clambered aboard the Ju-52s supplied by Luftflotte 4. The flight went without a hitch and the company landed at Pitomnik in the darkness of a late autumn night. They were met by a small column of lorries and were driven west along the Kalach-Stalingrad railway, crossed the Don and moved into accommodation arranged for them.

Long before the sun was up on 4 November, the two remaining companies of Pionier-Bataillon 336 were packed and ready to move to the Ilovskoye airfield. The lorries pulled up just after 0300 hours, and 15 minutes later, having stowed all their gear and weapons, the men of Oberleutnant Hullen's 1. Kompanie and Oberleutnant Ziesch's 3. Kompanie squeezed into the trucks and made themselves as comfortable as possible for the long drive. They drove on to the airfield at 0700 hours, jumped down from the lorries, quickly loaded their gear in the planes and then climbed in themselves. It all happened very smoothly and very quickly. The planes were soon in the air and flew into Pitomnik airfield around 1000 hours. Trucks supplied by LI. Armeekorps picked them up and delivered them to their billet areas on the other side of the Don. In a letter to his wife, the battalion's paymaster, Oberzahlmeister Erich Bauchspiess, wrote:

> The quickest journey in my life is behind me. In two and a half hours I have covered 500km and with me, the whole battalion, other than the baggage train. It was a great experience but now the time of discomfort and strain begins again. At the moment I'm waiting with another battalion for a truck that was assigned to me to collect rations. It's already dark (it is now 1500 hours) so I must finish up. I am well.

Also at Stalingrad was the battalion's beloved doctor, Stabsarzt Dr. Horst Gallwoszus[142], whose insistence on setting up first-aid posts as close as possible to the front-line proved that his courage was beyond doubt. His life had been endangered several times because of this but there was no changing his mind. He was convinced that more lives could be saved if he was treating badly-wounded men within minutes of being hit. So far, he had been proven correct. Dozens of men wounded at Korotoyak owed their lives to the valiant doctor and his equally brave group of assistants and orderlies. His deeds were recognised on 18 September, 1942 by the bestowal of the Iron Cross First Class, a rare honour for a doctor.

Late on 5 November, the elements of the battalion that could not be transported by air – such as the field-kitchens, baggage trains and lorries with equipment, ammunition and rations – finally arrived after many hours of strenuous driving.

- - -

142. Gallwoszus, Stabsarzt Dr. Horst, Stab Pi.Btl.336; born 25 September, 1908 in Königsberg. Missing in action, January 1942 in Stalingrad.

The combat strength of the battalion on 4 November, 1942 was 8 officers, 38 non-commissioned officers and 336 men. Ration strength was about 20 men more. The battalion was up to strength, having received 69 young replacements only a few weeks earlier, on 17 October. As for weaponry, the battalion had the full complement of 27 light machine-guns, nine for each company, but it was lacking in flamethrowers, only having two per company instead of the three set down in regulations. The men carried all the standard firearms, plus a few Soviet PPSh submachine-guns, but distinguished themselves by carrying something unusual. Having been stationed in Belgium in May 1941, the battalion's men had the opportunity to pick up the Browning FN (Fabrique Nationale) High-Power pistol manufactured by the Belgian state-owned company FN Herstal in the town of Herstal, near Liege. Chambering the standard 9mm Parabellum, with 13 in the magazine and 1 in the chamber, the pioneers appreciated its greater capacity, and many men, particularly the officers and non-commissioned officers, opted to wear it as their sidearm. The pistols had stood the test in Korotoyak and now, two months later, as the battalion arrived in Stalingrad, the most experienced men preferred to carry this as their back-up weapon.

Korotoyak had melded Pionier-Bataillon 336 into a formidable unit and provided them with valuable experience in street-fighting and taking fortified buildings. They had all seen that a combination of flamethrowers, explosives and − above all − offensive elan, were effective in taking stubborn nests of enemy resistance. Of the five pioneer battalions brought in for the offensive, Pionier-Bataillon 336 was the one with the most recent experience of combat in a built-up area and, because they had succeeded with a similar mission in Korotoyak, they were confident they would again prevail. The men thought nothing in Stalingrad could compare to what they had already seen. Their recently awarded medals kept it fresh in their memories. The remarkable geographic similarities between Stalingrad and Korotoyak were immediately noted by the battalion's officers and they were somewhat taken aback when they saw that some of the Soviet strongpoints bore the same names as those in Korotoyak… 'Red House', 'White House'. But they knew this task was easily within their abilities. They were confident. Some would even say cocksure.

ACHTERBERG, Oberleutnant Kurt Hermann Wilhelm – Zugführer, Pi.Btl.45; born 19 February, 1918 in Konitz, West Prussia. FTT: Pi.Btl.2. WBK: Deutsch Krone. Wounded 29 July, 1942. Stayed with the troops. Promoted to Oberleutnant in 1943. Killed 27 July, 1944 in Liepna, Latvia.

AIGNER, Oberleutnant Wilhelm – Kompaniechef, 2./Pi.Btl.336; born 15 November, 1915. FTT: Geb.Pi.Btl.83. Adjutant Pi.Btl.336 February 1941 to June 1942. Promoted to Oberleutnant (RDA 01.04.1942). Killed 15 August, 1942 near Korotoyak-on-Don.

ANDELFINGER, Hauptmann Fritz – Bataillonsadjutant, Stab/Pi.Btl.45; born 6 December, 1916. WKK VII. WBK: Kempten/Allgau. Began the war in Pi.Btl.5. Promoted to Leutnant (RDA 01.11.1940). Adjutant May 1942 to October 1942. Promoted to Oberleutnant (RDA 01.11.1942). Died of wounds, 27 July, 1943 while in Pz.Pi.Btl.51. Posthumous promotion to Hauptmann on 6 October, 1943.

BACK, Major Karl – Bataillonskommandeur, Pi.Btl.294; born 15 April, 1906 in Viernheim/Hessen. Promoted to Hauptmann (RDA 01.10.1936). Began the war as Kompaniechef 2./Pz.Pi.Btl.4. Commanded Pi.Btl.294 from April 1940 to May 1942. Promoted to Major (RDA 01.11.1941).

BARANSKI, Hauptmann Arthur – Kompaniechef, 2./Pi.Btl.162; born 7 December, 1904 in Rastenburg, East Prussia. WBK: Bartenstein. Wounded 9 October, 1942 during a stormtroop operation. Surrounded at Stalingrad. Transferred to Stab/Pi.Btl.305 in November-December 1942. MIA 5 January, 1943 in Stalingrad as a Hauptmann.

BARTH, Hauptmann Kurt – Kompanieführer, 1./Pi.Btl.162; born 18 March, 1909 in Kassel. Began the war in Pi.Btl.29 as Oberfeldwebel and Zugführer. Promoted to Oberleutnant (RDA 01.11.1941). Transferred from Pi.Btl.627 to Pi.Btl.162 with effect from 10 May, 1942. Killed 18 November, 1942 in Stalingrad. E.K.1.Kl. 30 November, 1942. Posthumous promotion to Hauptmann (RDA 01.11.1942).

BAUCHSPIESS, Oberzahlmeister Erich – Bataillon Zahlmeister, Stab/Pi.Btl.336; born 8 January, 1913. Captured at Stalingrad and released from captivity in August 1949. Died 1989 in Hamburg-Fulsbüttel.

Familie Bauchspiess

Oberzahlmeister Erich Bauchspiess

Abbreviations used in this chapter: **A.Pi.Fü.** = <u>A</u>rmee<u>pi</u>onier<u>fü</u>hrer; **E.K.1.Kl.** = Iron Cross First Class; **E.K.2.Kl.** = Iron Cross Second Class; **FTT** = <u>F</u>riedens<u>t</u>ruppen<u>t</u>eil (peace-time unit); **MIA** = Missing in action; **MTT** = <u>M</u>obile<u>t</u>ruppen<u>t</u>eil (mobilisation unit); **RDA** = <u>R</u>ang<u>d</u>ienst<u>a</u>lter (seniority in rank); **WBK** = <u>W</u>ehr<u>b</u>ezirks<u>k</u>ommando (recruiting district headquarters); and **WKK** = <u>W</u>ehr<u>k</u>reis<u>k</u>ommando (military area headquarters)

BEIGEL, Hauptmann Ludwig – Kompaniechef, 3./Pi.Btl.305; born 19 October, 1917 in Traunstein/Mühldorf a. Inn. E.K.2.Kl. 20 June, 1942 as Leutnant in 2./Pi.Btl.305. Promoted to Oberleutnant (RDA 01.07.1942). E.K.1.Kl. 14 September, 1942. Wounded on 14 October, 1942. Promoted to Hauptmann (RDA 01.02.1944). Survived the war. Post-war career in the Bundeswehr. Died 25 January, 1991 in Traunstein.

BENAD, Oberleutnant Johannes – Stab/Pi.Btl.294; commanded Pi.Park. Outside the Kessel.

BERGEMANN, Oberleutnant Fritz – Kompaniechef, 2./Pi.Btl.294; born 22 May, 1915 in Landsberg/Warthe, Provinz Brandenburg/Neumark. WKK: Lingen. Died of wounds, 12 November, 1942 in Gorodische-Stalingrad.

BORKOWSKI, Major Herbert – Kompaniechef, 1./Pi.Btl.336; born 20 October, 1909 in Danzig/Neufahrwasser. Began the war in Pi.Btl.11. Promoted to Hauptmann (RDA 01.02.1942). Commanded 1./Pi.Btl.336 from 1940 to 31 October, 1942. Transferred to a liaison staff. Ended the war as a Major. Survived the war. Died 16 July, 1995.

BRAUN, Hauptmann Anton – Kompaniechef, 1./Pi.Btl.389; born 3 July, 1915 in Uerdingen. WBK: Krefeld. Promoted to Leutnant (RDA 01.04.1937). Began war as Adjutant Pi.Btl.49. Surrounded at Stalingrad. Possibly transferred to 1./Pi.Btl.389 in November-December 1942 from another Pi.Btl. MIA 23 January, 1943 in Stalingrad. Promotion to Hauptmann.

BROCKMANN, Oberleutnant Karl Richard – Kompaniechef, 2./Pi.Btl.336; born 18 May, 1910 in Hannover. Career soldier. Before the war, belonged to Pi.Rgt.31 in Höxter. FTT: Pi.Btl.26. Promoted to Oberleutnant (RDA 01.11.1941). Took command of 2./Pi.Btl.336 25 August, 1942. Wounded 11 November, 1942 in Stalingrad. E.K.2.Kl. 23 December 1942. Killed 12 March, 1944 near Skalat, Tarnopol (Galizien) while in Stellungsbau-Pi.Btl.737.

BÜCH, Major Dipl. Ing. Ludwig – Bataillonskommandeur, Pi.Btl.45; born 13 June, 1895 in Heydt. WBK: München. (Erk.Marke: L. Pi.Kp.316 -2-) Transferred from Führerreserve Heeresgruppe B to Pi.Btl.45 to 'assume the duties of the commander of this battalion' with effect from 22 August, 1942. Pi.Btl.45 incorporated into Pi.Btl.389 25 November; Büch took command of Pi.Btl.389. MIA 23 January, 1943 in Stalingrad as Major.

BUCHNER, Oberleutnant Peter – Zugführer, 1./Pi.Btl.305; born 29 August, 1916 in Balderhausen. E.K.2.Kl. 10 June, 1942. Promoted to Oberleutnant (RDA 01.07.1942). Wounded 15 August, 1942. In Pi.Btl.10 in March 1944. MIA February 1945.

BUNTE, Leutnant Ernst – Zugführer, 3./Pz.Pi.Btl.50; born 13 October, 1912 in Holzhausen/Post Sylbach. FTT: Pi.Btl.50. Promoted to Leutnant (RDA 01.10.1942). Killed 13 November, 1942 in Stalingrad.

BUNZ, Oberleutnant Max – Kompaniechef, 1./Pi.Btl.45; born 10 July, 1914 in Ulm/Donau. WKK V. WBK Ulm/Donau. Began the war in Pi.Btl.45. Promoted to Leutnant (RDA 01.02.1940). Promoted to Oberleutnant (RDA 01.03.1942). Surrounded at Stalingrad. Transferred to 3./Pi.Btl.389 in November-December 1942. MIA since 23 January, 1943 in Stalingrad. German Cross in Gold 10 June, 1943.

DITZEL, Oberinspektor Paul – Technisches Inspektor Pi. und K., Stab/Pi.Btl.294; born 16 April, 1903 in Dankersen/Minden. MIA 2 January, 1943 in Stalingrad. Probably survived captivity.

Leutnant Ernst Bunte

DZIUMBLA, Oberleutnant Alfons Johannes Karl Anton – Stab/Pi.Btl.305; born 16 July, 1898 in Schönau, Kreis Leobschütz, Upper Silesia. Teacher in civilian life. Surrounded at Stalingrad. Possibly transferred to Stab/Pi.Btl.305 in November-December 1942 (probably from Pi.Btl.162). MIA 5 January, 1943 in Stalingrad. Died 1 May, 1943 in Soviet captivity.

EBERHARD, Hauptmann Hans Ludwig – Kompaniechef, 2./Pi.Btl.389; born 9 June, 1917 in Shanghai, China. Promoted to Leutnant (RDA 01.09.1938). Began war in 2./Pi.Btl.15. Promoted to Oberleutnant (RDA 01.08.1940). E.K.1.Kl. 29 May, 1942. German Cross in Gold 25 January, 1943. Promoted to Hauptmann (RDA 01.02.1943). Survived the war. Died 30 November, 2002 in Rheinbach.

EHRINGHAUS, Oberleutnant Bernhard – Zugführer, 3./Pi.Btl.336; born 7 September, 1917. WKK VI. WBK Köln I. FTT: Pi.Btl.26. Began the war in Pi.Ers.Btl.16. Promoted to Leutnant (RDA 01.07.1940). Transferred to Pi.Btl.336 with effect from 1 May 1942 as Zugführer in 3./Pi.Btl.336. Promoted to Oberleutnant (RDA 01.07.1942). E.K.1.Kl. 9 July, 1942. Took command of 1./Pi.Btl.336 on 14 November, 1942. Surrounded at Stalingrad. MIA since 6 January, 1943 in Stalingrad. Probably survived captivity.

ERMELER, Oberst Hellmuth – Bataillonskommandeur, Pz.Pi.Btl.50; born 20 February, 1896 in Hannover. Promoted to Hauptmann (RDA 01.04.1934). Began the war in OKH Inspektion der Pioniere (In5). Took command of Pi.Btl.50 in March 1940. Promoted to Oberstleutnant (RDA 01.05.1942). Transferred from Pz.Pi.Btl.50 to OKH Ch.H.Rüst. u.B.d.E (In5) with effect from 15 September, 1942. Promoted to Oberst (RDA 01.08.1944). Survived the war.

FINGER, Hauptmann Edmund – Pi.Btl.336; born 7 February 1895. Promoted to Leutnant (RDA 01.10.1938). Began war as Zugführer in 2./Pi.Btl.13 (4. Inf.Div., later 14. Pz.Div.). Transferred from Pi.Btl.175 (75. Inf.Div.) to Pi.Btl.336 with effect from 1 July, 1942.

FRICKE, Hauptmann Wilhelm Franz Günther – Pz.Pi.Btl.50; born 1 July, 1916 in Rüstringen/Oldenburg. Promoted to Leutnant (RDA 01.09.1938). Began war in 1./Pi.Btl.50. Kompaniechef 1./Pz.Pi.Btl.50 in May 1942. Transferred from Stab Pi.Btl.50 to Stab A.Pi.Fü. der 6. Armee with effect from 14 August, 1942. Adjutant to Ib/Kfz (Oberst Selle). Flew into the Stalingrad pocket with Oberst Selle on 25 December, 1942. Stayed behind when Selle flew out on 22 January, 1943. MIA 29 January 1943 in Stalingrad. Promoted to Hauptmann 10 March, 1943 (RDA 01.01.1943).

FRITZ, Hauptmann Max – Bataillonsadjutant, Pi. Btl.305; born 11 March, 1918 in Stuttgart. Bachelor. WKK: Stuttgart I. Adjutant Pi.Btl.305 from May 1941. E.K.2.Kl. 10 June, 1942. On furlough in October 1942, returned 7 November, 1942. Surrounded at Stalingrad. Sent to the front to command 2./Pi. Btl.305. Killed 22 December, 1942 in Stalingrad. Posthumous promotion to Hauptmann.

FUCHS, Oberleutnant Theodor – Zugführer, 3./Pz.Pi.Btl.50; born 25 June, 1919 in Hanau a.M. Wound Badge in Black 25 December, 1939. E.K.2.Kl. 25 June, 1940. E.K.1.Kl. 30 June, 1942. Wound Badge in Silver 1 August, 1942. Zugführer in Pi. Btl.50 from 1 April to 18 October, 1942. From 13 December, 1942 until 7 October, 1943, Zugführer in Pz.Pi.E.u.A.Btl.29. Survived the war.

Familie Schaate

Max Fritz receives the Iron Cross Second Class, 10 June, 1942. From left: unknown, Lt. Heinz Schaate, Lt. Max Fritz, Gfr. Franz Rapp, Gfr. Ernst Köhle, unknown, Major Friedrich Beismann, unknown.

GALLWOSZUS, Stabsarzt Dr. Horst – Bataillonsarzt, Stab/Pi.Btl.336; born 25 September, 1908 in Königsberg, East Prussia. MIA January 1943 in Stalingrad.

GAST, Hauptmann Erwin Karl Ernst – Bataillonskommandeur, Pz.Pi.Btl.50; born 18 October, 1911 in Stolp, Pomerania. [Erk.Marke -67- 3./Pi.Btl.9] Promoted to Oberleutnant (RDA 01.10.1937). Began war commanding 3./Pi.Btl.9. Promoted to Hauptmann (RDA 01.09.1940). Transferred from Pi.Schule II to Pz.Pi.Btl.50 as Kommandeur with effect from 15 September, 1942. MIA since 7 January, 1943 in Stalingrad. (See page 582 for full career details.)

GEBAUER, Leutnant Karl-Heinz – Zugführer, 1./Pi.Btl.45; born 4 April, 1919 in Sangerhausen. WKK: Sangerhausen. Transferred from Pi.Rgt.Stab 413 to Pi.Btl.45 with effect from 10 July, 1942. Killed 17 August, 1942 8km west of Vizhne-Gerassimov.

GEUENICH, Oberleutnant Christian – Zugführer, 2./Pz.Pi.Btl.50; born 1 April, 1915 in Krauthausen. Transferred from Brückenbau-Btl. 646 to Pi.Btl.50 with effect from 15 January, 1942. E.K.1.Kl. 29 July, 1942. Wounded prior to Stalingrad. Survived the war. Died 4 March, 2001 in Düren.

GIERTH, Major Hans – Kompaniechef, 3./Pi.Btl.162; born 12 October, 1915 in Bromberg. Promoted to Leutnant (RDA 01.01.1938). Began war as Zugführer in 3./Pi.Btl.48. Took command of 3./Pi.Btl.162 1 August, 1940. On 31 October, 1942, detached from Pi.Btl.162 to staff XXIX. Armeekorps, then transferred to Führerreserve der WKK VIII with effect from 1 January, 1943. Killed 1 May, 1945 in Berlin as a Major.

GLÖCKLER, Hauptmann Hermann Albert Friedrich (Fritz) – Bataillonsadjutant, Stab/Pi.Btl.45; born 11 July, 1909 in Konstanz. Bachelor. WBK: Stuttgart I. Adjutant February to May 1942. Promoted to Oberleutnant. Bataillonsführer between Parchow's departure and Büch's arrival. Wounded 25 August, 1942 but stayed with the troops. Killed 13 November, 1943 near Nadvin/Lipuyaki as Hauptmann in Pz.Pi.Btl.32.

GOTTWALD, Leutnant Rudolf – Zugführer, 1./Pz.Pi.Btl.50; born 30 June, 1915 in Hamburg. Promoted to Leutnant (RDA 01.10.1942). Surrounded at Stalingrad. Killed 25 December, 1942 in Stalingrad.

GRÄF, Leutnant Emil – Zugführer, 1./Pi.Btl.45; born 30 October, 1915 in Hassmersheim/Baden. MIA since 12 November, 1942 in Stalingrad.

GRÄSER, Leutnant Albrecht Julius – Zugführer, Pi.Btl.45; born 13 June, 1919 in Stuttgart. E.K.2.Kl. 16 September, 1942. Died of wounds, 23 August, 1942 near Krassny-Peskovatka.

GREGOR, Leutnant Rudolf – Stab Pi.Btl.162; born 8 February, 1919 in Neudorf. Survived Stalingrad. German Cross in Gold 24 March, 1943. Promoted to Leutnant (RDA 01.12.1943). Missing in action, September 1944.

GRIEBEN, Major Olaf – Kolonneführer, Brüko K/Pz.Pi.Btl.50; born 15 April, 1898. Did not go to Stalingrad. On 3 March, 1943, took command of elements of Pz.Pi.Btl.50 outside the Stalingrad pocket. Ended war as Major z.b.V. Survived the war. Died 3 August, 1990 in Düsseldorf.

GRIMM, Hauptmann Richard – Kompanieführer, 2./Pi.Btl.305; born 17 May, 1913 in Kirchheim/Teck. WBK Stuttgart I. Began war in Pi.Btl.45. Promoted to Leutnant (RDA 01.10.1938). Promoted to Oberleutnant (RDA 01.08.1941). E.K.2.Kl. 20 June, 1942. Fell ill 11 November, 1942 in Stalingrad. Survived

Oberfeldwebel Rudolf Gregor

Stalingrad. Promoted to Hauptmann (RDA 01.12.1943). Survived the war without once being wounded. Died 24 May, 1990 in Kirchheim/Teck from prostate cancer.

HARDEKOPF, Oberleutnant Dipl.Ing. Walther – Kompaniechef, 2./Pz.Pi.Btl.50; born 8 August, 1902 in Lübeck. WKK X. WBK Hamburg I. Began war in Pi. Btl.50. Promoted to Leutnant (RDA 01.10.1939). Promoted to Oberleutnant (RDA 01.02.1942). E.K.1.Kl. 25 May, 1942. Wounded 26 August, 1942 as Chef 2./Pz. Pi.Btl.50. Surrounded at Stalingrad. MIA since 16 December, 1942 in Stalingrad as Chef 3./Pz.Pi.Btl.50.

HASSLER, Stabszahlmeister Artur – Bataillon-Zahlmeister, Stab/Pz.Pi.Btl.50; born 1 February, 1902 in Hamburg. Career soldier. Surrounded at Stalingrad. MIA January 1943 in Stalingrad.

HEILMANN, Leutnant, Zugführer in 2./Pi.Btl.336, Transferred from Pi.Ers.Btl.14 to Pi.Btl.336 as a Zugführer with effect from 1 April, 1942. Wounded 10 June, 1942.

Familie Grimm

Oberleutnant Richard Grimm and his young daughter. Photo taken early 1943.

HEINRICH, Major Walter – Kompaniechef, 2./Pi.Btl.45; born 6 April, 1918 in Ulm. Began war as Unteroffizier and Gruppenführer in 1./Pi.Btl.45. Attended 2. Offizieranwärter Lehrgang in Pi.Schule II from 15 October, 1939 to 26 January, 1940. Transferred to Pi.Btl.45 as Zugführer on 27 January, 1940. E.K.2.Kl. 17 May, 1940. Wounded 28 May, 1940 and received Wound Badge in Black the same day. After recovering from wounds, returned to Pi.Btl.45 on 10 December, 1940. Sturmabzeichen 15 December, 1940. Took command of 2./Pi.Btl.45 in September 1941. E.K.1.Kl. 14 December, 1941. Wounded 16 January, 1942 but stayed with the troops. Promoted to Oberleutnant (RDA 01.04.1942). Named in the Ehrenblatt des Deutschen Heeres on 18 April, 1942. Wounded 28 June, 1942 but stayed with the troops. Ostmedaille 15 August, 1942. Wound Badge in Silver 11 September, 1942. Wounded 13 January, 1943 and flown out 21 January, 1943. After recovery, returned to Pi.Btl.45 on 14 August, 1943. Promoted to Hauptmann (RDA 01.10.1943). German Cross in Gold 21 February, 1944. Last commander of Pi.Btl.45. Promoted to Major (RDA 01.12.1944). Survived the war. Died 13 February, 1997 in Ulm/Donau.

Pionierkameradschaft Ulm

Hauptmann Walter Heinrich, mid-1944.

HEINZE, Hauptmann Otto-Wilhelm – Bataillonsadjutant, Stab/Pi.Btl.294; born 12 November, 1918 in Northeim. FTT: Pi.Btl.4. Adjutant Pi.Btl.294 from September 1941 to June 1942. Promoted to Oberleutnant (RDA 01.10.1941). Promoted to Hauptmann (RDA 01.03.1944). Survived the war. Died 25 May, 1983 in Osnabrück. His brother, Horst, was also a pioneer officer and bearer of the Knight's Cross.

HEPP, Leutnant Alfons – Zugführer – 2./Pi.Btl.305, E.K.2.Kl. 20 June, 1942. Wounded 15 October, 1942 in Stalingrad.

HERTRAMPF, Hauptmann beim Stabe – Restkommandoführer, Stab/Pi.Btl.162; commanded Restkommando when Pi.Btl.162 went to Stalingrad. Later commanded elements of Pi.Btl.162 outside the Kessel.

HILLMANN, Oberleutnant Egon – Bataillons-ordonanzoffizier, Pz.Pi.Btl.50; born 4 July, 1918 in Bremerhaven. WBK: Wesermünde. FTT: Pi.Btl.50. Promoted to Leutnant (RDA 01.12.1940). E.K.1.Kl. 12 September, 1942. Promoted to Oberleutnant (RDA 01.12.1942). MIA January 1943 in Stalingrad.

HINGST, Oberleutnant Erwin – Zugführer, 1./Pi. Btl.305; born 14 September, 1908 in Hameln/Weser. WBK: Hameln. Wounded 16 October, 1942 in Stalingrad. Surrounded at Stalingrad. MIA 5 January, 1943 in Stalingrad. Promoted to Oberleutnant.

HINSCH, Werkmeister Walter – Stab/Pz.Pi.Btl.50; born 3 February, 1899 in Hamburg. Surrounded at Stalingrad. MIA January 1943 in Stalingrad.

HOMBURGER, Leutnant Hubert Johann – Kolonneführer, Kol./Pi.Btl.305; born 23 November, 1907 in Reiselfingen. WBK Lörrach. Surrounded at Stalingrad. Killed 22 December, 1942 in Stalingrad.

Oberleutnant Egon Hillmann as a Feldwebel.

HULLEN, Hauptmann Karl-Heinz – Kompanieführer, 1./Pi.Btl.336; born 2 June, 1917 in Wethmar. FTT: Pi.Btl.6. Transferred from Pi.Ers.Btl.16 to 3./Pi.Btl.336 with effect from 1 April, 1942. Adjutant Pi.Btl.336 from June 1942 to November 1942. Took command of 1./Pi.Btl.336 on 1 November, 1942. Wounded 14 November, 1942. Survived Stalingrad. Promoted to Hauptmann (RDA 01.11.1943). Killed 26 December, 1943 near Barishevka as Kommandeur Pi.Btl.156. Ehrenblattspange 25 January, 1944.

JAHNKE, Major Dr. Gerhard – Pz.Pi.Btl.50; born 10 October, 1911 in Usedom. Promoted to Leutnant (RDA 01.04.1937). Began war as adjutant Pi.Btl.43. Assigned to Stab A.Pi.fü. der 6. Armee in 1940. Transferred to Stab Pi.Btl.50 with effect from 14 August, 1942. Survived Stalingrad. Promoted to Major (RDA 01.07.1944). Survived the war.

KAESLER, Oberleutnant – Zugführer, 1./Pi.Btl.336; promoted to Oberleutnant (RDA 01.07.1942).

KEPPLER, Oberzahlmeister Max – Bataillon-Zahlmeister, Stab/Pi.Btl.305; born 7 March, 1909 in Kirchheim/Teck. Married with four children. Surrounded at Stalingrad. MIA January 1943 in Stalingrad. Died 25 February, 1943 in captivity.

KIMMICH, Oberleutnant Manfred – Zugführer, Pi.Btl.45; born 23 January, 1920 in Sobald Sulz. Wounded 15 November, 1942 in Stalingrad. Flown out of the Kessel. Died 20 October, 1944 in POW camp No. 3655 in Arsk, Romania.

KLEINER, Oberleutnant Engelbert – Zugführer, Pi.Btl.162; born 20 February, 1915 in Breslau. WKK: Breslau I. Killed 18 December, 1942 in Stalingrad. Posthumous promotion to Oberleutnant.

Oberzahlmeister Max Keppler

KRÜGER, Major Otto Franz Karl – Bataillonskommandeur, Pi.Btl.162; born 15 September, 1904 in Elbing. Promoted to Hauptmann (RDA 01.04.1937). Began war as Kompaniechef 3./ Pi.Btl.21. Promoted to Major (RDA 01.12.1941). Took command of Pi.Btl.305 on 26 November, 1942. Wounded in January 1943 in Stalingrad. Captured on 2 February, 1943 in Stalingrad. Died on 20 April, 1943 in Soviet captivity.

KUNZE, Oberleutnant Klaus – Bataillonsadjutant, Pz.Pi.Btl.50; born 31 March, 1920 in Hamburg. Career soldier. Began war in Pi.Btl.50. Promoted to Leutnant (RDA 01.02.1941). Surrounded at Stalingrad. MIA since 21 January, 1943 in Stalingrad. Promoted to Oberleutnant (RDA 01.02.1943).

LEHMANN, Oberarzt Dr. – Bataillonsarzt, Stab/Pz.Pi.Btl.50; in battalion from November 1940 to December 1942. Wounded and flown out of Kessel in late December 1942. Survived the war.

LINDNER, Oberleutnant Johannes – Stab/Pi.Btl.305; born 15 July, 1906 in Reddentin, East Pomerania. [Erk.Marke –358- 1./ Pi.Ers.2] WBK: Stolp. Surrounded at Stalingrad. MIA since 1 January 1943 in Stalingrad.

LOCHERER, Hauptmann Anton – Zugführer, 2./Pi.Btl.45; born 22 June, 1920 in Ulm. WKK V. WBK Ulm/Donau. Promoted to Leutnant (RDA 01.04.1941). Detached 13 November, 1942 to attend a training course in Germany. Survived Stalingrad. Promoted to Oberleutnant (RDA 01.02.1944). Promoted to Hauptmann (RDA 01.12.1944). Last Bataillonsführer Pi.Btl.45. Survived the war. Still alive in 2005 but very ill.

Oberleutnant Klaus Kunze

LOOS, Leutnant Adolf – Zugführer, 1./Pi.Btl.389; born 11 February, 1920 in Altensittenbach. E.K.1.Kl. 24 August, 1942. Killed 5 January, 1943 in Stalingrad.

LOSSIUS, Oberleutnant Kurt – Kompanieführer, 1./Pi.Btl.336; born 29 April, 1913 in Magdeburg. Wounded 10 June, 1942. Surrounded at Stalingrad? Killed 7 January, 1943 near Goroloff Nizhne Kundrushovskaya.

LUNDT, Hauptmann Hermann Johann – Bataillonsführer, Pi. Btl.336; born 14 May, 1908, in Kiel. WBK Kassel II. Began war as Stabsfeldwebel in Pi.Btl.29. Transferred from 2./Pz.Pi.Btl.39 (3. Pz.Div.) to Pi.Btl.336 on 29 July, 1942 as Kompanieführer with effect from 1 July, 1942 but was probably Offz.z.b.V. MIA since 1 January, 1943 in Stalingrad. (See page 584 for full career details.)

MÄDER, Leutnant Franz – Zugführer, 1./Pi.Btl.336; born 15 March, 1910. WKK I (Tilsit). Began war in Pi.Btl.21. Promoted to Leutnant (RDA 01.10.1942). Wounded 6 or 7 January, 1943 and flown out of the Kessel on 10 January, 1943. Survived Stalingrad and the war. Fled to West Germany after the war. Died 10 March, 1979 in Idar-Oberstein.

MATTHÄUS, Oberarzt Dr. Ulrich – Bataillonsarzt, Stab/Pi. Btl.294; born 7 November, 1915 in Görlitz. E.K.2.Kl. 28 November, 1942. MIA since 27 December, 1942 in Stalingrad.

Leutnant Franz Mäder

MEHLER, Leutnant Wilhelm – Zugführer, Pi.Btl.389; born 8 March 1913. WBK Köln II. MIA since 23 January, 1943 in Stalingrad. Probably survived captivity.

MENZEL, Hauptmann Gerhard – Kompanieführer, 3./Pi.Btl.294; born 12 February, 1907 in Oebisfelde. WKK IV. WBK Leipzig II. Promoted to Leutnant (RDA 01.04.1936). Promoted to Oberleutnant (RDA 01.07.1940). Began war in Stab/Pi.Btl.38 (2.Pz.Div.). Fell ill 15 November, 1942. E.K.2.Kl. 28 November, 1942. MIA since 5 January, 1943 in Stalingrad. Promoted to Hauptmann (RDA 01.02.1943). Captured at Stalingrad and held at Yelabuga POW Camp. Still alive on 2 July, 1943. Survived captivity but died 15 December, 1954 in Berlin.

MEYER, Leutnant Hans – Kol./Pz.Pi.Btl.50; born 24 March, 1914 in Hamburg-Blankensee. MIA January 1943 in Stalingrad. Captured at Stalingrad. Died 19 March, 1943 in Yelabuga.

MOETZK, Major Erwin – Bataillonskommandeur, Pi.Btl.389; born 18 August, 1905 in Wien. Began war in Pi.Btl.17. Took command of Pi.Btl.389 in January 1940. Promoted to Major (RDA 01.03.1942). Transferred from Pi.Ers.Btl.34 to Pi.Btl.23 with effect from 3 November, 1942. Commanded Pi.Btl.23 until 3 March, 1943. Further promotions were blocked.

MOLFENTER, Oberleutnant Friedrich (Fritz) – Zugführer, 2./Pi.Btl.45; born 12 August, 1919 in Ulm. Career soldier. Began war in Pi.Btl.45. Promoted to Leutnant (RDA 01.02.1941). MIA January 1943 in Stalingrad. Promoted to Oberleutnant (RDA 01.02.1943).

MUNZ, Hauptmann – Kompaniechef, Pi.Btl.162, transferred from Pi.Btl.162 to Führerreserve der WKK VIII with effect from 1 January, 1943. This Munz is not Ritterkreuzträger Hauptmann Johannes Munz.

OBERST, Leutnant Erich – Zugführer, 2./Pi.Btl.336; born 21 November, 1910 in Schenkendorf, East Prussia. WKK I. WBK Königsberg (Pr) II. Began war in Pi.Btl.1. Promoted to Leutnant (RDA 01.11.1941). E.K.1.Kl. 18 June, 1942. MIA January 1943 in Stalingrad.

OELSCHEN, Hauptmann Hans – Stab/Pz.Pi.Btl.50; born 31 March, 1915. WBK Lüneburg. Began war in Pi.Btl.50. Promoted to Leutnant (RDA 01.04.1939). Promoted to Oberleutnant (RDA 01.08.1941). Promoted to Hauptmann (RDA 01.10.1942). Took command of the elements of Pz.Pi.Btl.50 outside the Kessel.

Familie Vögele

Leutnant Fritz Molfenter

PALMOWSKI, Leutnant Herbert – Zugführer, 3./Pz.Pi.Btl.50; born 11 September, 1911 in Kl. Kleeberg, East Prussia. WKK Königsberg (Pr) I. Died of wounds, 13 November, 1942 in Stalingrad.

PARCHOW, Major Gerd Jacob Wilhelm – Bataillonskommandeur, Pi.Btl.45; born 15 December, 1909 in Gettorf, Prussia. Began war in Pi.Lehr-Btl.1. Took command of Pi.Btl.45 on 26 January, 1942. Wounded 28 July, 1942 but stayed with the troops. Transferred on 3 September, 1942 to Pz.Pi.Ers.Btl.5. Transferred to Pi.Lehr-Btl. and became commander on 26 January, 1943 with effect from 1 December, 1942. Promoted to Major (RDA 01.01.1944). Survived the war.

PAVLICEK, Oberstleutnant Richard – Bataillonskommandeur, Pi.Btl.336; born 3 February, 1902 in Wilten, Austria. Promoted to Hauptmann (RDA 01.05.1935). Began war with Kdr. d. Pi. XVIII. Commanded Pi.Btl.336 from February 1941 to August 1943. Had just left on furlough when his battalion was sent to Stalingrad. Promoted to Oberstleutnant (RDA 01.04.1943).

PETERSEN, Leutnant Broder – Zugführer, 3./Pz.Pi.Btl.50; born 22 June, 1917 in Hattstedt. WBK Kiel. Began war in Pi.Btl.50. Promoted to Leutnant (RDA 01.05.1942). Wounded 26 August, 1942 but died of wounds, 4 September, 1942 in Verkhne-Businovka.

PFÜTZNER, Major Ernst – Bataillonskommandeur, Pi.Btl.389; born 14 August, 1891 in Liesing bei Wien. Promoted to Hauptmann (RDA 09.03.1940). Transferred from Pi.Btl.100 to Pi.Btl.389 as Kommandeur with effect from 23 November, 1942. Captured at Stalingrad and held at Yelabuga POW Camp. Probably survived captivity.

POHL, Oberleutnant Gerhard – Kompanieführer, 1./Pi.Btl.294; born 21 April, 1915 in Hauteroda. Promoted to Leutnant (RDA 01.09.1938). Began war in 2./Pi.Btl.14. Adjutant Pi. Btl.294 from April to October 1940. Wounded 13 November, 1942. Succumbed to his wounds on 14 November, 1942 in Stalingrad.

POMPE, Stabsveterinär Dr. Rudolf – Bataillonveterinär, Stab/Pi.Btl.305; born 28 January, 1911 in Mähr. Ostrau. Captured at Stalingrad. Died 16 April, 1943 in Yelabuga POW Camp.

RINDERMANN, Oberleutnant – Kompaniechef, 3./Pz.Pi.Btl.50; wounded on 11 August, 1942.

RUDOLPH, Oberzahlmeister Arndt – Bataillon Zahlmeister, Stab/Pi.Btl.294; born 8 February, 1917 in Leipzig. MIA 22 January, 1943 in Stalingrad. Captured at Stalingrad and held in Yelabuga POW Camp. Still alive on 2 July, 1943. Probably survived captivity.

RUHL, Oberleutnant Dr. Karl – Zugführer, 3./Pi.Btl.336; born 17 November, 1913. WKK IV. WBK Leipzig II. MTT: Pz.Pi.Btl.13. Promoted to Leutnant (RDA 01.1.1941). Later in 1./Pi. Btl.336. Took over adjutancy in early November 1942. Survived Stalingrad. Adjutant Pi.Btl.336 from March 1943. Promoted to Oberleutnant (RDA 01.02.1944).

SARTORIUS, Leutnant Wolfgang – Bataillonsadjutant, Stab/Pi.Btl.45; born 12 January, 1913 in Stuttgart. WKK V. WBK Stuttgart II. Began war in Pi.Btl.45. Promoted to Leutnant (RDA 01.09.1941). Bataillonsadjutant from mid-September 1942. Surrounded at Stalingrad. MIA since 23 January, 1943 in Stalingrad. Probably survived captivity.

SCHAATE, Oberleutnant Heinz – Kompaniechef, 1./Pi. Btl.305; born 14 April, 1915 in Stuttgart. E.K.2.Kl. 10 June, 1942. Wounded 21 August, 1942. Again wounded 18 October, 1942 in Stalingrad. E.K.1.Kl. 25 October, 1942. Survived the war. Died 30 October, 1988 in Münchingen.

SCHINKE, Hauptmann Alfons – Kompaniechef, 3./Pi. Btl.162; born 24 May, 1915 in Leuber, Upper Silesia. Bachelor. WKK VIII. WBK Neustadt/O.S. Began war in Pi.Btl.8. Promoted to Leutnant (RDA 01.06.1940). With 3./ Pi.Btl.162 in July 1941. E.K.2.Kl. 15 July, 1941. E.K.1.Kl. 6 August, 1941. Promoted to Oberleutnant (RDA 01.06.1942). Surrounded at Stalingrad. Promoted to Hauptmann (RDA 01.12.1942). MIA since 2 February, 1943 in Stalingrad. German Cross in Gold 24 March, 1943.

SCHMIDT, Leutnant Karl – Zugführer, 1./Pi.Btl.336; born 11 October, 1901 in Osterhausen. WKK Wittenberg. E.K.2.Kl. and E.K.1.Kl. 18 September, 1942. MIA since 21 January, 1943 in Stalingrad. Probably survived captivity.

SCHMIDT, Leutnant Wilhelm – Zugführer, 1./Pi.Btl.336; wounded 4 September, 1942. E.K.1.Kl. 10 September, 1942.

Oberleutnant Heinz Schaate

Familie Schaate

SCHNEIDER, Oberinspektor Ernst Otto – Technisches Inspektor Pi. und K., Stab/Pz.Pi.Btl.50; born 8 March, 1903 in Tangermünde. Career soldier. Surrounded at Stalingrad. MIA since 4 January, 1943 in Stalingrad.

SCHRÖDER, Oberleutnant Wilhelm – Bataillonsadjutant, Pi.Btl.389; born 12 March, 1915 in Hamburg. WKK Hamburg VI. Adjutant Pi.Btl.389 from July 1942 until January 1943. MIA 23 January, 1943 in Stalingrad.

SCHÜTZ, Hauptmann Günter – Zugführer, Pi.Btl.45; born 21 August, 1912. Wounded 28 July, 1942 but stayed with the troops. Died of wounds, 6 August, 1943 as a Hauptmann in Pz.Pi.Btl.58.

SCHÜTZE, Oberleutnant Dr. Johannes – Zugführer, 3./Pi.Btl.162; born 1 March, 1911 in Recklinghausen. Transferred from Brück.Kol.B.80 to Pi.Btl.162 with effect from 22 May, 1942. Killed 19 November, 1942 in Stalingrad.

SCHWARTNER, Hauptmann Fritz – Bataillonskommandeur, Pi.Btl.294; born 7 October, 1913. Promoted to Oberleutnant (RDA 01.06.1938). Began war on Stab/Pi.Btl.13. Detached to Pi.Schule I. Promoted to Hauptmann (RDA 01.06.1941). Transferred from Pi.Btl.80 to Pi.Btl.294 as Kompaniechef with effect from 12 April, 1942. Took command of Pi.Btl.294 on 20 May, 1942. Transferred from Pi.Btl.294 to Führerreserve WKK IV with effect 15 July, 1942. Killed 5 July, 1943 near Alexandrovka, south of Orel, while in Pz.Pi.Kp.811.

SKUTLARTZ, Oberleutnant Erich – Zugführer, 3./Pi. Btl.45; born 14 April, 1916 in Lahr-Dinglingen. WKK V. WBK Lörrach I. Promoted to Leutnant (RDA 01.08.1941). MIA since 23 January, 1943 in Stalingrad. Promoted to Oberleutnant (RDA 01.08.1944). Captured at Stalingrad: in Beketovka-Dubovka camp February to April 1943; in Oranki camp April to December 1943; in Yelabuga camp December 1943 to September 1945; in Kazan camp September 1945 to May 1949. Released from captivity in early May 1949, arriving home on 27 May, 1949. Died 30 December, 2001 in Breisach/Baden.

STAIGER, Oberleutnant Berthold Wilfried – Kompaniechef, 3./Pi.Btl.305; born 13 March, 1914 in Rottweil. WKK V. WBK Tübingen. Began war in Pi.Btl.45. Promoted to Leutnant (RDA 01.09.1940). E.K.2.Kl. 10 June, 1942 as Zugführer in 3./Pi.Btl.305. Wounded 5 July, 1942. Promoted to Oberleutnant (RDA 01.09.1942). E.K.1.Kl. 12 December, 1942. Wounded 18 December, 1942 in Stalingrad and flown out of the Kessel. Survived Stalingrad. MIA since 17 June, 1944 near Cherbourg. Survived the war. Died 21 February, 2006 in Reutlingen.

Leutnant Erich Skutlartz

TAG, Leutnant Hermann – Zugführer, 3./Pi.Btl.45; born 10 February, 1918 in Stuttgart. WBK Calw. Began war in Pi.Btl.45. MIA 11 November, 1942 in Stalingrad. Promoted to Leutnant on 13 January, 1943 (RDA 01.11.1942).

THENEN, Oberleutnant Gottfried von – Pi.Btl.294; born 1923 or 1924. Wehrkreis VI (Moers). Began war in Pi.Btl.26. Promoted to Leutnant (RDA 01.11.1942). German Cross in Gold 9 March, 1945 as Oberleutnant in 2./Pi.Btl.119. Survived Stalingrad and the war. Died 14 March 1979.

THIELE, Leutnant Dr. phil. Gerhard – Zugführer, 2./Pz.Pi.Btl.50; born 3 August, 1907 in Berlin. WBK Berlin VIII. E.K.2.Kl. 3 December, 1942. MIA 3 January, 1943 in Stalingrad.

TRAUB, Major Dipl.Ing. Wilhelm – Bataillonsführer, Pi.Btl.305; born 14 November, 1895 in Helmstedt. WKK X. WBK Wesermünde. Began war in Pi.Btl.22. Promoted to Leutnant (RDA 15.08.1921). Promoted to Oberleutnant (RDA 01.10.1938). Promoted to Hauptmann (RDA 01.12.1940). Took command of Pi. Btl.305 on 16 October, 1942. Surrounded at Stalingrad. MIA since 5 January, 1943 in Stalingrad. Promoted to Major (RDA 01.02.1944).

VELSEN, Oberleutnant Fritz von – Pi.Btl.336; born 11 January, 1914 in Erfurt. Began war in Pi.Ers.Btl.253. Transferred to Pi.Btl.336 with effect from 1 May, 1942. Surrounded at Stalingrad. Killed 23 January, 1943 in Stalingrad as an Oberleutnant.

VÖGELE, Hauptmann Karl – Zugführer, 2./Pi.Btl.45; born 30 August, 1918 in Altshausen. Survived Stalingrad. Survived the war. Died 6 May, 1997 in Tübingen.

Familie Traub

Hauptmann Wilhelm Traub on leave, June 1942.

WALDRAFF, Oberleutnant Hans-Dietrich Zugführer, 3./Pi.Btl.45; born 10 August, 1922 in Ulm/Donau. Promoted to Leutnant (RDA 01.02.1942). Wounded 11 November, 1942 in Stalingrad. Survived Stalingrad. Promoted to Oberleutnant (RDA 01.02.1945).

WALTER, Leutnant Lothar Brotus – Zugführer, 2./Pi.Btl.45; born 1 May, 1920 in Leutkirch. WKK V. WBK Ulm. Killed 11 November, 1942 in Stalingrad. Posthumous promotion to Leutnant (RDA 01.11.1942).

WARTH, Hauptmann Eberhard – Kompaniechef, 3./Pi.Btl.45; born 8 November, 1917 in Stuttgart. WKK V. WBK Konstanz. MTT: Pi.Btl.45 Sigmaringen. Promoted to Leutnant (RDA 01.06.1940). Promoted to Oberleutnant (RDA 01.06.1942). Killed 11 November, 1942 in Stalingrad. Posthumous promotion to Hauptmann on 6 October, 1943.

WEIMANN, Major Wilhelm – Bataillonskommandeur, Pi.Btl.294; born 15 March, 1895 in Meiderich/Duisburg. [EM 1./Pi.Ers.Btl.253 -1-] WKK XVI. WBK Moers. Began war in Pi. Btl.46. Promoted to Leutnant (RDA 25.05.1921). Promoted to Oberleutnant (RDA 01.09.1937). Promoted to Hauptmann (RDA 01.08.1939). Kommandeur Pi.Btl.60. Transferred from Pi.Btl.60 to Pi.Btl.294 with effect from 15 July, 1942. Promoted to Major (RDA 01.08.1942). Surrounded at Stalingrad. Spange to E.K.1.Kl. 4 December, 1942. Took command of Pi.Btl.100 on 8 January, 1943. MIA since 5 January, 1943 in Stalingrad.

WIRTGEN, Oberarzt Dr. Theodor – Bataillonsarzt, Stab/Pi.Btl.305; promoted to Oberarzt (RDA 01.08.1942). Bataillonsarzt on 9 November, 1942. Transferred to another unit in 305.Inf. Div. Surrounded at Stalingrad. Captured at Stalingrad, 2 February, 1943. Survived captivity, returning home in 1948.

WITT, Hauptmann Willi – Bataillonsadjutant, Stab/Pz.Pi.Btl.50; born 26 September, 1917. WKK X. WBK Rendsburg. Promoted to Leutnant (RDA 01.04.1940). Promoted to Oberleutnant (01.04.1942). Adjutant Pi.Btl.50 November 1940 to October 1942. Survived Stalingrad. Promoted to Hauptmann (RDA 01.03.1944). German Cross in Gold 1 April, 1944. Died 11 May, 1947.

WOERZ, Oberstleutnant Alfred Karl – Bataillonsführer, Pi.Btl.389; born 6 January, 1903. Promoted to Hauptmann (RDA 01.11.1934). In 1938, compiled a 50-page book called 'Pioniere im Gefecht – Teil I: Einsatz der technischen Kampfmittel. Aufgaben für Trupps, Gruppen und Züge'. Began the war in Allgemeines Heeresamt (AHA), near Höh. Pi.Offz.3. Commander Geb.Pi.Btl.91 in 1940. Transferred from Führerreserve Heeresgruppe A to Pi.Btl.389 to assume command of this battalion with effect from 26 August, 1942. E.K.2.Kl. 11 October, 1942. Survived the war. Died 18 July, 1982.

Dr. Donatus Wörner

WÖRNER, Oberarzt Dr. Donatus – Bataillonsarzt, Stab/Pi.Btl.305; born 12 May, 1910 in Germersheim/Pfalz. Doctor in civilian life. Became Bataillonsarzt in October 1942. Surrounded at Stalingrad. MIA January 1943 in Stalingrad.

ZELLER, Inspektor Georg – Technisches Inspektor Pi. und K., Pi.Btl.305; born 4 December, 1915 in Alzenau. Bau-Ingenieur. Captured at Stalingrad 2 February, 1943. Survived captivity, returning home 2 June, 1948. Still alive in October 2006.

Ib Abteilung of Pi.Btl.305 in 1941. From left: Feldwebel Heinrich Bromeis, Obergefreiter Walter Lambertz, Leutnant Richard Grimm, Obergefreiter Emil Baier, Inspektor Georg Zeller and Obergefreiter Pack. Both Grimm and Zeller would survive the war but the other four men were declared 'missing in action' at Stalingrad.

ZIEGENHAGEN, Oberleutnant Wolfgang – Kompanieführer, Pz. Pi.Btl.50; born 7 September, 1917 in Mainz. Entered army 2 November, 1937. Began war in Pi.Btl.36. Promoted to Leutnant (RDA 01.04.1940). Promoted to Oberleutnant (RDA 01.04.1942). MIA 3 February, 1943 in Stalingrad.

ZIESCH, Hauptmann Bernhard – Kompaniechef, 3./Pi.Btl.336; born 19 August, 1915 in Strohschütz/Sachsen. WBK Bautzen. Ziesch was a keen hunter. Promoted to Leutnant (RDA 01.10.1938). Promoted to Oberleutnant (RDA 01.05.1941). E.K.1.Kl. 5 September, 1942. MIA since 11 January, 1943 in Stalingrad. Promoted to Hauptmann (RDA 01.09.1944).

Leutnant Ziesch with a hunting trophy.

ZIMMER, Oberleutnant Walter – Kompanieführer, 2./Pi.Btl.294; born 1 June, 1915. WKK IV. WBK Leipzig II. Began war in Pi.Btl.14. Promoted to Leutnant (RDA 01.06.1942). E.K.1.Kl. 28 November, 1942. Probably captured at Stalingrad and survived captivity. Promoted to Oberleutnant on 1 May, 1944 (RDA 01.01.1943).

ZORN, Leutnant Hans – Zugführer, 1./Pi.Btl.305; born 11 January, 1921 in Pforzheim. Entered army 29 November, 1939. Began war in Pi.Btl.5. Promoted to Leutnant (RDA 01.10.1942). Wounded 12 November, 1942 in Stalingrad. E.K.2.Kl. 19 November, 1942. Survived Stalingrad. Survived the war. Died 16 September, 1989 in Frankfurt am Main.

BEYERSDORFF, Oberleutnant Eberhard Rudolf – Führer, Sturmschwadron 24.PD; born 27 March, 1918 in Greifenhagen. FTT: Kav.Rgt. 5. E.K.1.Kl. 1941. Transferred 8 September, 1942 from Pz.Gr.Ers.Abt. 413 to Pz.Gr.Rgt.26. Führer 6. Schwadron. Wounded 11 November, 1942 in Stalingrad. Promoted to Oberleutnant (RDA 01.12.1942). German Cross in Gold 10 January, 1943. Recommended for the Knight's Cross. Survived Stalingrad. Survived the war. Died 15 September, 1974 in Oldenburg from a heart attack.

KINDLER, Hauptmann Willi – Führer, Sturmkompanie 44.ID; born 24 December, 1906 in Durlach, near Karlsruhe. Bachelor. WBK Stuttgart I. Kompaniechef 5./Inf.Rgt.132. Wounded 10 June, 1942. Upon recovery, took command of 2./Inf.Rgt.132. Wounded 14 November, 1942 in Stalingrad. E.K.1.Kl. 26 December, 1942. Survived Stalingrad. Killed 21 June, 1944 near Servery, Poland as Hauptmann and commander 5./Gr.Rgt.944 (357.Inf.Div.) when shot through the heart.

MARTIUS, Leutnant Hans-Joachim – Führer, Sturmschwadron 24.PD; born 23 May, 1920 in Bonn. Adjutant II./Pz.Gr.Rgt.26. Took command of Sturmschwadron 18 November, 1942 until it was dissolved on 21 or 22 November, 1942. Killed 25 December, 1942 in Stalingrad.

WARTBURG, Oberleutnant Hans von – Kompanieführer, 11./Inf.Rgt.131; born 20 August, 1920 in Salzburg. WBK Wien I. In Gren.Ers.Btl. II./134 from 15 January to 13 June, 1940. Transferred to Marschbtl. 44, which reached 44.Inf.Div. on 31 July, 1940. Assigned to Inf.Rgt.131 as Zugführer. Promoted to Leutnant (RDA 01.04.1941). E.K.2.Kl. 22 July, 1941. Infanterie Assault Badge 18 August, 1941. E.K.1.Kl. 18 March, 1942. Ostmedaille 15 August, 1942. Wound Badge in Black 10 October, 1942. Ill with jaundice November 1942 in Stalingrad. Promoted to Oberleutnant (RDA 01.07.1943). Still alive in August 2004.

WILLMITZER, Oberleutnant Wilhelm – Zugführer, Sturmkompanie 44.ID; born 27 January, 1918 in Krakau. WKK XVII. WBK Wien I. [Erk.Marke 11/Sch.Kp.I.R.316 -239-]. Began war in Inf.Rgt.132. Promoted to Leutnant (RDA 01.06.1942). Later Kompanieführer 11./Inf.Rgt.131. Killed in action, 13 November, 1942 in Stalingrad. Posthumous promotion to Oberleutnant 23 October, 1943.

WROBLEWSKI, Leutnant Walter Herbert Fritz – Führer, Sturmschwadron 24.PD; born 30 March, 1917 in Stettin. Entered army in 1938 in Kav.Rgt.14. From 1940, in 7./Reit.Rgt.22. E.K.2.Kl. 28 October, 1941. Assault Badge 30 November, 1941. Promoted to Leutnant (RDA 01.10.1942). Transferred 6 November, 1942 from Pz.Gr.Ers.Abt. 413 to Pz.Gr.Rgt.26. Zugführer in 7./Pz.Gr.Rgt.26 but immediately took charge of a Stosszug in the Sturmschwadron. Took command of Sturmschwadron on 11 November, 1942. Wounded 18 November, 1942 in Stalingrad. Survived Stalingrad. Wound Badge 7 January, 1943. Spent the rest of the war as a Zugführer and Schwadronsführer in Pz.Gr.Rgt.26. Severely wounded in 1945 but recovered in Lübz Lazarett in Mecklenburg. Suffered a total of 7 wounds during the war, the last being an amputation of a leg. Survived the war. Joined the Bundeswehr in 1956 and retired with the rank of Oberstleutnant. Died 26 December, 1994 in Isernhagen.

HAUPTMANN ERWIN GAST

APPENDIX FOUR

Born 18 October, 1911 in Stolp, Pomerania. Gast spent his entire childhood and teenage years in this east German town. Despite passing the Abitur [school leaving examination needed for entry to higher education] in 1932, Gast decided to pursue a military career, enlisting in the army on 15 October, 1932 and being sworn in eleven days later, on 26 October. His first unit was 2./ Pionier-Bataillon 1 based in Königsberg, Prussia. On 1 April, 1934, he was promoted to Gefreiter and attached to his battalion's 1. Kompanie for further training. The officer running the course immediately noticed Gast's enthusiasm and total lack of inhibition in voicing his opinion. An efficiency report written about Gast in 1941 stated that he "knows what he wants and gets his own way. He is sometimes brusque and obstinate in his opinion." It was put to Gast that he was suitable for officer training and on 1 July, 1934, Gast was promoted to Unteroffizier and made a Fahnenjunker [NCO officer candidate]. One week later, he was detached to an infantry school for an officer's training course beginning on 11 July. He remained there until 28 March, 1934, a total of eight and a half months. Upon completion of this course, he was promoted to Fähnrich [officer candidate] and then sent to a pioneer school for continued instruction from 4 April to 28 September, 1934. On 22 September, one week before the course ended, Gast was promoted to Oberfähnrich, and immediately upon completion, on 1 October, he received his long-coveted promotion to Leutnant. He returned to his old Pionier-Bataillon 1, now called Pionier-Bataillon Königsberg B[1]. Gast swore allegiance to the Führer on 2 August, 1934. Once the expansion of the army was out in the open, Pionier-Bataillon Königsberg B received another – and, this time, final – change of name: Pionier-Bataillon 21, and Gast was Nachrichtenoffizier [communications officer] on the staff of 2. Kompanie. On 1 August, 1936 he was attached to Pionier-Bataillon 9. His tenure was only meant to last a few months but it became permanent on 6 October, 1936. His commanding officer had been so impressed with his previous work as a communications officer that he now became adjutant of Pionier-Bataillon 9, a responsible position requiring plenty of comprehension and diligence. It was noted that Gast had a "good knowledge of official business and performed well in all branches of the service", so his proficient work was rewarded with a promotion to Oberleutnant on 1 October, 1937. After two years of deskwork, the commander of Pi.Btl.9, Major Fritz Weber, could tell that his self-assured, assertive adjutant wanted a field command, and an opportunity came in 1938 to give him one when the commander of 3. Kompanie was promoted and transferred. On 1 November, 1938, Oberleutnant Gast officially became commander of 3. Kompanie, the battalion's only motorised company. In August 1939, while most of the German army was being mobilised for the Polish campaign, Pionier-Bataillon 9, together with its parent 9. Infanterie-Division, was sent to Heeresgruppe C in the Saarpfalz to strengthen Germany's western border while the Wehrmacht overran Poland. Oberleutnant Gast got his first taste of combat when his unit participated in the battle for France in May 1940. They advanced through Luxembourg and Belgium and fought at Amiens and on the Somme River, later

---

1. To cover the secret expansion of the German army, some units received cover names. On 1 October, 1934, Pionier-Bataillon 1 was used to form three new battalions. These were Pionier-Bataillon Königsberg A (would later be called Pi.Btl.1), Pionier-Bataillon Lyck (later Pi.Btl.11 of 11.Inf.Div.) and Pionier-Bataillon Königsberg B (later Pi.Btl. 21 of 21.Inf.Div.).

Mark

Oberleutnant Gast and his 3./Pi.Btl.9 proudly pose upon a bridge they built near Kassel, 1939.

crossing the Oise and Ourcq Rivers before advancing on Paris. There was plenty of hard work for the pioneers, and Oberleutnant Gast exceeded all expectations placed upon him. His commander said that he was an "impeccable, forthright personality" with a "calm and resolute nature" and was "brave and fearless in the face of the enemy". A promotion and awards were heaped on Gast after his performance in France: he received both grades of the Iron Cross, the Sturmabzeichen [assault badge] and a promotion to Hauptmann on 17 August, 1940, effective from 1 September. After the western campaign was over, 9. Infanterie-Division went into reserve in northern France until it was transferred in April 1941 to southern Poland to prepare for the invasion of the Soviet Union. Hauptmann Gast, however, was not with them. An efficiency report written by Major Schützler, the new commander of Pionier-Bataillon 9, dramatically altered the course of Gast's career. The report was glowing in its praise and succinctly summarised Gast's personality. It also stated that Gast had fulfilled his role as company commander in a "very good" manner. However, in answering the question "Suitability for a higher position", Schützler wrote that Gast was suited to be "a battalion commander but is still too young". An alternative would be as an "instructor at a Waffenschule [service school]". And this is what happened. On 8 March, 1941, just over a month after the report was written, Gast received a transfer to Pionierschule II in Dessau-Rosslau, and although he was not thrilled by this deviation in his military career, the wisdom of this decision was apparent. Erwin Gast was a product of extensive and dedicated officer training and would now be able to give back to the system that created him. The massive expansion of the Wehrmacht meant that there was a severe shortage of well-trained leaders, and young officers fresh from the battlefield would serve to enhance the training and inject recently gained combat experience into the demonstrations. Gast threw himself into the new role with a gusto that pleased his commander, Oberst Ziebe, who described him as "hardworking and reliable" and as an "enthusiastic and successful instructor" who has "fulfilled his present role very well". The good news for Gast was that his commander would report that he was "suitable as a battalion commander". After one and a half years of endless inquiries and appeals to be sent to a combat unit, Gast finally received his wish in September 1942 with a posting to Panzerpionier-Bataillon 50 located deep in the Soviet Union. Gast was now on the path to meet his destiny in Stalingrad.

Hauptmann Hermann Lundt

Lundt was once described by a superior officer as a man whose military manner was "firm, energetic and soldierly" while his off-duty behaviour was "impeccable", as was his attitude towards superiors and subordinates. No embarrassing incidents blemished his military record. He was polite, popular and possessed the characteristics of a leader. An early wartime commander summed up Lundt in a few words: "a simple, forthright and reliable man. A soldierly personality through and through." Lundt's path to battalion commander, however, had not been straightforward. When the war began in September 1939, Lundt was an Oberfeldwebel in Pionier-Ersatz-Bataillon 9. He was nearing the end of a stint as a 'Zwölfender' [a man signed up for 12 years service] that had started way back on 1 May, 1927 when he completed his apprenticeship as a carpenter and entered the service as an 18-year-old in 1./Pionier-Bataillon 5. He was sworn in on 16 June the same year. Moving up the promotion ladder was difficult in the Reichswehr period but they occurred regularly for Lundt, roughly every two years or so: Oberpionier in May 1929, Gefreiter in May 1931 and finally, after completing a five month NCO course in March 1933, he entered the non-commissioned ranks in April 1933. During the training, Lundt received intensive instruction on the flamethrower, a fearsome weapon for which he had great respect. After Hitler came to power, a new oath of allegiance needed to be taken and Lundt did so on 3 August, 1934. A simultaneous promotion to Feldwebel and transfer to the Hann-Münden Pionier-Bataillon took place on 1 October, 1934. Two years later, on 6 October, 1936, his old unit was incorporated into a new one: it was now Pionier-Bataillon 29 and Lundt was a member of 1. Kompanie. He was also promoted to Oberfeldwebel on the same day. Lundt was with Pionier-Bataillon 29 when it moved into the Sudetenland in 1938 and remained with the unit until a few days before the outbreak of war. While his battalion readied itself for war in positions along the Polish border, Lundt received an order on 29 August, 1939 to transfer to the newly-formed Pionier-Ersatz-Bataillon 9 in Aschaffenburg. He was promoted to Stabsfeldwebel three days later, on 1 September – the same day his old unit was crossing the Polish border. His stay with the replacement battalion was brief because the role of a unit of this kind was to supply men to active units. On 19 September, Stabsfeldwebel Lundt and many others from Pionier-Ersatz-Bataillon 9 were transferred to Pionier-Bataillon 195 being formed on the training grounds in Wildflecken and Hammelburg. Months of training and drills followed. During this time, the commander of Pionier-Bataillon 195, Major Oelze, recognised the leadership qualities in Stabsfeldwebel Lundt and made him an officer candidate on 8 December 1939. Lundt was now on track to becoming an officer and on the path that would ultimately take him to Stalingrad. He was selected to become an officer on 26 December and four days later, Major Oelze submitted his recommendation for promotion not just to Leutnant d.B., but to Oberleutnant d.B.[2]. Oelze's assessment stated that Lundt had an "honest character, was tactful, reserved, comradely, and had a good military education". A simultaneous promotion would have

---

2. Trans.: 'd.B.' = 'des Beurlaubtenstandes', meaning an 'officer commissioned for the duration'. Such an officer had reserve status.

been extraordinary in most circumstances but according to the Offizierergänzungs-Bestimmungen [officer expansion regulations] set down by the Army Personnel Office, an "active career NCO who had served longer than 9 years, or a former career NCO who left the army prior to 1 September 1939 after 12 or more years service, can be proposed for promotion to Leutnant and simultaneously to Oberleutnant provided that they are suitable as a company commander without reservation. If they are suitable as a platoon commander, only a promotion to Leutnant can be decreed." Having received the proposal for Lundt's promotion, the Army Personnel Office sent a letter to Major Oelze on 19 February, 1940 that said: "A statement is requested as to whether Stabsfeldwebel Lundt, who is proposed for promotion, is completely suitable as a company commander". Oelze had no doubts. His brief reply on 3 March, 1940 said: "Stabsfeldwebel Lundt is completely suitable as a company commander." Eleven days later, Lundt received his promotion to Oberleutnant d.B., backdated to 1 February, 1940. While his promotion was being sorted out, Lundt had been transferred to the battalion that now supplied Pionier-Bataillon 195 with replacements: Pionier-Ersatz-Bataillon 253, and Lundt's transfer was effective from 26 February, 1940. A few months later, on 22 May, Oberleutnant Lundt finally received command of a company. He took over the replacement battalion's 2. Kompanie. Lundt showed he was an excellent commander who treated his subordinates with respect while still getting the best from them. After two and a half months, he was transferred to an active unit, returning to Major Oelze's Pionier-Bataillon 195 to take command of the leicht Pionier Kolonne. Although this was not a combat role, Lundt threw himself wholeheartedly into his new assignment. On 10 October, 1940, he was transferred to Pionier-Ersatz-Bataillon 16 based in the Unversagt barracks in Köln-Westhoven where he received command of its 2. Kompanie. In the final days of 1940, his battalion commander put forward a proposal for Lundt to be transferred to the active officers list. The OKH Personnel Office knocked back the proposal, stating in a letter dated 30 January, 1941 that "the promotion can only be upheld if his suitability is proven while leading combat troops. It is suggested that the officer be sent into the field." Almost half a year later, on 27 June, 1941, this finally happened when Oberleutnant Lundt was sent to Panzer-Pionier-Bataillon 39 (3. Panzer-Division) on the Eastern Front. Battles around Smolensk, the encirclement of Kiev and costly winter fighting near Tula were the furnaces in which Lundt was forged. Mistakes on the training ground earned reprimands but at the front, they cost lives. Lundt knew that, and as a platoon commander and later while commanding a company, he always bore this in mind, weighing up decisions before he made them. His men respected that. Months of constant combat, advances and losses all turned Lundt from an excellent commander of a replacement company into an excellent commander of combat pioneers, and he was recognised with both grades of the Iron Cross, an Assault Badge and in January 1942, a promotion to Hauptmann on the active officers list with effect from 1 November, 1941. Still with Panzer-Pionier-Bataillon 39, Lundt and the entire 3. Panzer-Division were transferred from Heeresgruppe Mitte to Heeresgruppe Süd in March 1942. They were in reserve as part of 6. Armee and were stationed in the Kharkov area where they remained for several months, preparing for the new summer offensive. Lundt went home on leave in May and June, then was tasked with other duties in Prague through July and August. In early September, he received a new assignment: transfer to Pi.Btl.336 for use as a company commander. He joined his new unit in mid-September 1942 as it was in reserve positions south-west of a town called Korotoyak. Lundt's letters reveal a poetic side and the idyllic days in the oak forests around Ostrogoshk were thoroughly enjoyed by Lundt and all men of Pi.Btl.336. They were busy making themselves comfortable for the coming winter by digging roomy bunkers and laying on whatever comforts they could find. In early November, the dreaded communique that would change all their lives arrived: "Transportation of the Pionier-Bataillon to Stalingrad on 4.11.1942."

19 November, 1942

Pionier-Bataillon 305 – Iron Cross Second Class

Zorn, Leutnant Hans, 1. Kompanie (w. 12.11.1942 Stalingrad)

21 November, 1942

Pionier-Bataillon 305 – Iron Cross First Class

Pauli, Feldwebel Adam, 2. Kompanie (MIA 01.1943 Stalingrad)

Pionier-Bataillon 305 – Iron Cross Second Class

Abele, Pionier Karl, 2. Kompanie

Beck, Gefreiter Josef, 2. Kompanie

Beinhardt, Obergefreiter Robert, 3. Kompanie (MIA 12.1942 Stalingrad)

Benz, Pionier Gustav, 3. Kompanie

Brixner, Unteroffizier Friedrich, 1. Kompanie

Buchholz, Stabsfeldwebel Kurt, 1. Kompanie

Bumm, Obergefreiter Johann, 2. Kompanie (MIA 12.1942 Stalingrad)

Fahrion, Obergefreiter Ernst, 1. Kompanie

Fasser, Gefreiter Karl, 2. Kompanie

Gaisser, Pionier Martin, 3. Kompanie

Gauggel, Pionier Albert, 1. Kompanie (MIA 12.1942 Stalingrad)

Geiger, Gefreiter Josef, 2. Kompanie

Glaser, Obergefreiter Gustav, 1. Kompanie

Hahn, Oberpionier Fritz, 3. Kompanie

Hartmann, Gefreiter Karl, 1. Kompanie

Hauth, Gefreiter Gustav, 3. Kompanie (MIA 10.1942 Stalingrad)

Heiduk, Unteroffizier Rudolf, 3. Kompanie († 12.11.1942 Stalingrad)

Hermann, Pionier Franz, 3. Kompanie (MIA 01.1943 Stalingrad)

Hog, Obergefreiter Friedrich, 1. Kompanie

Holzapfel, Gefreiter Karl, 3. Kompanie (MIA 01.1943 Stalingrad)

Jung, Pionier Walter, 1. Kompanie

Kaltenbach, Gefreiter Karl, 2. Kompanie (MIA 12.1942 Stalingrad)

Karpenkiel, Unteroffizier Josef, 2. Kompanie (w. 26.10.1942 Stalingrad)

Kienzler, Feldwebel Josef, Stab (w. 19.12.1942)

Kirschmann, Pionier Hermann, 3. Kompanie

Klagges, Pionier Karl, 3. Kompanie († 10.1942 Karpovka)

Knerr, Unteroffizier Georg, 1. Kompanie (MIA 11.1942 Morosovskaya)

Krieg, Pionier Walter, 3. Kompanie

Lattner, Gefreiter Max, 3. Kompanie

Lindheimer, Gefreiter Gottlob, 3. Kompanie
Lüthgen, Unteroffizier Hugo, 3. Kompanie
Lutz, Obergefreiter Johann, 1. Kompanie (MIA 12.1942 Stalingrad)
Meier, Gefreiter Karl, 3. Kompanie
Mentzel, Pionier Günter, 1. Kompanie (MIA 12.1942 Stalingrad)
Mones, Obergefreiter Engelbert, 1. Kompanie († 10.12.1942 Rostov)
Müller, Obergefreiter Adolf, 1. Kompanie
Müller, Pionier Hans, 2. Kompanie
Münd, Gefreiter Jakob, 3. Kompanie
Nastold, Gefreiter Paul, 1. Kompanie (MIA 01.1943 Stalingrad.)
Peters, Pionier Rudolf, 3. Kompanie
Prottengeier, Obergefreiter Fritz, 2. Kompanie († 24.10.1942 Stalingrad)
Reinl, Gefreiter Anton, 2. Kompanie
Rinck, Obergefreiter Heinz, 3. Kompanie (w. 04.11.1942)
Ruider, Gefreiter Johann, 2. Kompanie
Schmid, Gefreiter Heini, 3. Kompanie
Schnöll, Unteroffizier Ludwig, Stab (MIA 01.1943 Stalingrad)
Späth, Unteroffizier Heinz, 2. Kompanie (MIA 01.1943 Stalingrad)
Treu, Gefreiter Hans, 2. Kompanie
Waldbröl, Pionier Gottlieb, 1. Kompanie
Wenz, Hauptfeldwebel Kurt, 1. Kompanie (MIA 12.1942 Stalingrad)
Wild, Obergefreiter Anton, 1. Kompanie (MIA 01.1943 Stalingrad)

28 November, 1942
Pionier-Bataillon 162 – Iron Cross Second Class
Arndt, Pionier Günter, 1. Kompanie (MIA Stalingrad)
Dudek, Gefreiter Franz, 3. Kompanie
Frost, Gefreiter Bernhard, 3. Kompanie
Gabriel, Oberpionier Georg, 1. Kompanie
Gruhlke, Unteroffizier Ernst, 3. Kompanie
Halirsch, Gefreiter Franz, 2. Kompanie
Hanke, Oberpionier Walter, 1. Kompanie († 18.11.1942 Stalingrad)
Hauke, Unteroffizier Willi, Stab (MIA 01.1943 in Stalingrad)
Janetzko, Oberpionier Heinz, 1. Kompanie (MIA 01.1943 Stalingrad)
Kalinka, Obergefreiter Konrad, 1. Kompanie (MIA 01.1943 Stalingrad)
Kaluza, Unteroffizier Wolfgang, 3. Kompanie
Kirsch, Gefreiter Wilhelm, 3. Kompanie
Koblitz, Obergefreiter Josef, 2. Kompanie (MIA 10.1942 Stalingrad)
Koch, Pionier Erich, 1. Kompanie († 21.11.1942 Chir)
Maiwald, Gefreiter Leonhard, 1. Kompanie
Pietsch, Unteroffizier Emanuel, 1. Kompanie
Przybylla, Gefreiter Eduard, 3. Kompanie (MIA 25.10.1942 Stalingrad)
Ringel, Unteroffizier Franz, Stab (MIA 01.1943 Stalingrad)
Schuster, Oberpionier Paul, 1. Kompanie
Solga, Gefreiter Stanislaus, 3. Kompanie († 03.12.1942 Stalingrad
Steffan, Obergefreiter Otto, 2. Kompanie (MIA 12.1942 Stalingrad)
Steindl, Obergefreiter Franz, Stab (MIA 01.1943 Stalingrad)
Tilgner, Sanitäts-Oberfeldwebel Fritz, Stab (MIA 01.1943 Stalingrad)
Welzel, Unteroffizier Max, 3. Kompanie (MIA Stalingrad)

Pionier-Bataillon 294 – Iron Cross First Class
Dickler, Feldwebel Oskar, 2. Kompanie
Zimmer, Leutnant Walter, Stab
Pionier-Bataillon 294 – Iron Cross Second Class
Baaske, Obergefreiter Max, 2. Kompanie
Hitzke, Pionier Hermann, 1. Kompanie
Husmann, Oberschirrmeister Gerhard, 2. Kompanie (MIA 24.12.1942 Stalingrad)
Ilg, Obergefreiter Alois, 1. Kompanie (MIA 06.01.1943 Stalingrad)
Jens, Obergefreiter Werner, 1. Kompanie († 09.12.1942 Stalingrad)
Macke, Feldwebel Kurt, 1. Kompanie (MIA 26.12.1942 Stalingrad)
Matthäus, Oberarzt Dr. Ulrich, Stab (MIA 27.12.1942 Stalingrad)
Menzel, Oberleutnant Gerhard, 3. Kompanie (w. 15.11.1942 Stalingrad)
Möhring, Gefreiter Kurt, 2. Kompanie
Müller, Obergefreiter Rudi, 1. Kompanie (MIA 26.12.1942 Stalingrad)
Räumschüssel, Obergefreiter Werner, 1. Kompanie (MIA 05.01.1943 Stalingrad)
Schuldes, Obergefreiter Oswald, 1. Kompanie (MIA 28.12.1942 Stalingrad)
Seifarth, Obergefreiter Martin, 2. Kompanie (MIA 19.12.1942 Stalingrad)
Toepel, Oberfeldwebel Fritz, Stab (MIA 31.12.1942 Stalingrad)
Weber, Unteroffizier Kurt, 1. Kompanie (MIA 01.01.1943 Stalingrad)
Zimmermann, Gefreiter Max, 1. Kompanie (MIA 26.12.1942 Stalingrad)

Pionier-Bataillon 336 – Iron Cross First Class
Kampa, Obergefreiter Johann, 1. Kompanie
Reiter, Stabsfeldwebel Otto, 3. Kompanie
Pionier-Bataillon 336 – Iron Cross Second Class
Adam, Gefreiter Paul, 3. Kompanie (MIA 12.1942 Stalingrad)
Bauer, Obergefreiter Martin, 2. Kompanie († 22.11.1942 Stalingrad)
Baumann, Gefreiter Max, Stab
Besser, Obergefreiter Kurt, 2. Kompanie (w. 18.11.1942 Stalingrad)
Bieler, Stabsgefreiter Walter, 3. Kompanie (MIA 01.1943 Stalingrad)
Dannenberg, Obergefreiter Bruno, 1. Kompanie († 01.12.1942 Stalingrad)
Falk, Gefreiter Kurt, 3. Kompanie (w. 13.11.1942 Stalingrad)
Galeski, Obergefreiter Helmut, 1. Kompanie
Hoppstock, Obergefreiter Kurt, 3. Kompanie (w. 22.11.1942 Stalingrad)
Kettner, Gefreiter Herbert, 2. Kompanie
Lagies, Feldwebel Willi, 1. Kompanie
Lorenz, Obergefreiter Walter, 3. Kompanie (MIA 01.1943 Stalingrad)
Lugert, Gefreiter Karl, 2. Kompanie (w. 22.11.1942 Stalingrad
Rammelt, Obergefreiter Rudolf, 1. Kompanie (MIA 23.11.1942 Stalingrad)
Richter, Obergefreiter Richard, 3. Kompanie (w. 11.11.1942 Stalingrad)
Schatt, Obergefreiter Erich, 1. Kompanie (MIA 01.01.1943 Stalingrad)
Schramm, Obergefreiter Paul, 1. Kompanie (MIA 06.01.1943 Stalingrad)
Schütze, Gefreiter Manfred, 2. Kompanie
Seelig, Gefreiter Alfred, 3. Kompanie (w. 13.11.1942 Stalingrad)
Stache, Pionier Walter, 2. Kompanie
Walter, Obergefreiter Erich, 2. Kompanie (MIA 12.1942 Stalingrad)
Weise, Oberpionier Heinz, 1. Kompanie

30 November, 1942
Pionier-Bataillon 162 – Iron Cross First Class
Barth, Oberleutnant Kurt, 1. Kompanie († 18.11.1942 Stalingrad)

3 December, 1942
Panzerpionier-Bataillon 50 – Iron Cross First Class
Ballast, Gefreiter Karl, 3. Kompanie
Wassen, Unteroffizier Hermann, 2. Kompanie (MIA 12.1942 Stalingrad)
Panzerpionier-Bataillon 50 – Iron Cross Second Class
Arndt, Obergefreiter Paul, 3. Kompanie (MIA 01.1943 Stalingrad)
Assmann, Obergefreiter Herbert, 2. Kompanie
Baumann, Gefreiter Johann, 2. Kompanie
Behr, Obergefreiter Ludwig, 2. Kompanie
Dastig, Gefreiter Karl, 3. Kompanie
Eike, Obergefreiter Heinrich, 2. Kompanie (MIA 01.1943 Stalingrad)
Geerken, Obergefreiter Johannes, 2. Kompanie
Gnodtke, Gefreiter Werner, 2. Kompanie
Gottschlich, Gefreiter Gerhard, 3. Kompanie (MIA 12.1942 Stalingrad)
Greeck, Gefreiter Heinz, 1. Kompanie (MIA 01.1943 Stalingrad)
Guglowski, Obergefreiter Herbert, 1. Kompanie
Jess, Unteroffizier Claudius, 1. Kompanie (MIA 01.1943 Stalingrad)
Keller, Oberpionier Leonhard, 3. Kompanie
Krella, Gefreiter Erich, 1. Kompanie (MIA 01.1943 Stalingrad)
Löffler, Feldwebel Josef, 3. Kompanie
Metzner, Gefreiter Alfred, 2. Kompanie
Müller, Oberfeldwebel Wilhelm, 2. Kompanie
Oldenburg, Gefreiter Hermann, 1. Kompanie
Ostermann, Obergefreiter Heino, 1. Kompanie
Panning, Obergefreiter Heinz, 2. Kompanie (MIA 12.1942 Stalingrad)
Stein, Gefreiter Phillipp, 3. Kompanie
Thiele, Leutnant Gerhard, 2. Kompanie (MIA 01.1943 Stalingrad)
Wetter, Gefreiter Martin, 3. Kompanie (MIA 17.11.1942 Stalingrad)

4 December, 1942
Pionier-Bataillon 294 – Clasp to the Iron Cross First Class
Weimann, Major Wilhelm, Stab

12 December, 1942
Pionier-Bataillon 305 – Iron Cross First Class
Staiger, Oberleutnant Berthold, 3. Kompanie (w. 18.12.1942 Stalingrad)

15 December, 1942
Panzerpionier-Bataillon 50 – Iron Cross First Class
Hellberg, Oberfeldwebel Friedrich, 1. Kompanie (MIA 12.1942 Stalingrad)
Panzerpionier-Bataillon 50 – Iron Cross Second Class
Apmann, Gefreiter Ludwig, 2. Kompanie
Bargen, Obergefreiter Wilhelm von, 2. Kompanie († 19.11.1942 Stalingrad)

Barth, Gefreiter Helmut, 2. Kompanie
Burckhardt, Gefreiter Jakob, 1. Kompanie (MIA 12.1942 Stalingrad)
Duchene, Gefreiter Nikolaus, 1. Kompanie (MIA 01.1943 Stalingrad)
Eisemann, Obergefreiter Ludwig, 2. Kompanie
Fitschen, Gefreiter Hinrich, 1. Kompanie
Fröhlich, Pionier Hans, 3. Kompanie
Kotlinski, Obergefreiter Jonny, Stab
Kuczkowski, Pionier Stanislaus von, 3. Kompanie († 18.11.1942)
Pichmann, Gefreiter Kurt, 3. Kompanie
Schneider, Gefreiter Herbert, Stab
Scholl, Gefreiter Erich, 1. Kompanie
Seegers, Obergefreiter Wilhelm, 2. Kompanie (†22.11.1942 Stalingrad)
Stanek, Obergefreiter Alfred, 3. Kompanie
Sülter, Pionier Ernst, 1. Kompanie (MIA 01.1943 Stalingrad)
Wriede, Obergefreiter Arthur, 2. Kompanie
Zachert, Obergefreiter Johannes, 3. Kompanie

20 December, 1942
Pionier–Bataillon 162 – Iron Cross Second Class
Kügler, Gefreiter Konrad, 3. Kompanie († 11.11.1942 Stalingrad)

Pionier–Bataillon 294 – Iron Cross Second Class
Angerstein, Feldwebel Wilhelm, 1. Kompanie
Balon, Gefreiter Johannes, 1. Kompanie (MIA 10.12.1942 Stalingrad)
Ernst, Gefreiter Adolf, 1. Kompanie
Flohe, Gefreiter Wilhelm, 3. Kompanie
Friedmann, Unteroffizier Erich, 1. Kompanie (MIA 29.12.1942 Stalingrad)
Gansauge, Gefreiter Paul, 3. Kompanie (MIA 20.12.1942 Stalingrad)
Hönicke, Obergefreiter Horst, 2. Kompanie (MIA 16.11.1942 Stalingrad)
Huth, Obergefreiter Erich, Stab (MIA 03.01.1943 Stalingrad)
Kirste, Gefreiter Helmut, 1. Kompanie
Moosbauer, Obergefreiter Crostitz, 3. Kompanie
Respondek, Gefreiter Walter, 2. Kompanie (MIA 24.12.1942 Stalingrad)
Schmitz, Sanitäts-Feldwebel Fritz, Stab (MIA 10.01.1943 Stalingrad)
Trawka, Pionier Johann, 2. Kompanie
Wosch, Gefreiter Wilhelm, 1. Kompanie (MIA 26.12.1942 Stalingrad)

Pionier–Bataillon 305 – Iron Cross Second Class
Biesdorf, Unteroffizier Walter, 1. Kompanie
Bräuer, Oberpionier Fritz, 3. Kompanie
Cyranka, Gefreiter Franz, 3. Kompanie
Feist, Obergefreiter Gerhard, 2. Kompanie
Glaser, Gefreiter Alfred, 2. Kompanie (MIA 12.1942 Stalingrad.)
Götz, Gefreiter Otto, 2. Kompanie
Gwasda, Gefreiter Albert, 3. Kompanie
Hilsenbeck, Gefreiter Alois, 2. Kompanie (MIA 01.1943 Stalingrad)
Hoffmann, Gefreiter Helmut, 3. Kompanie
Jehle, Oberpionier Otto, 1. Kompanie
Kaiser, Gefreiter Johann, 2. Kompanie

Kamrad, Pionier Franz, 3. Kompanie (MIA 01.1943 Stalingrad)
Klöpfer, Pionier Paul, 1. Kompanie
König, Pionier Alfred, 3. Kompanie
Krätzi, Obergefreiter Erhard, 3. Kompanie
Kreitlow, Gefreiter Herbert, 3. Kompanie
Männle, Obergefreiter Josef, 2. Kompanie († 30.10.1942 Stalingrad)
Mattes, Unteroffizier Josef, 1. Kompanie (MIA 01.1943 Stalingrad)
May, Gefreiter Johannes, 3. Kompanie
Michel, Obergefreiter Otto, 3. Kompanie
Nätscher, Obergefreiter Josef, 1. Kompanie (MIA 01.1943 Stalingrad)
Porsch, Gefreiter Wilhelm, 3. Kompanie
Pyplatz, Pionier Johann, 1. Kompanie
Rudek, Oberpionier Josef, 3. Kompanie
Schlauch, Gefreiter Peter, 3. Kompanie
Seifert, Gefreiter Paul, 3. Kompanie
Teichelkamp, Gefreiter Peter, 2. Kompanie (w. 19.11.1942 Stalingrad)
Thanisch, Gefreiter Alfons, 2. Kompanie
Trimpe, Pionier Gerhard, 2. Kompanie
Wilde, Gefreiter Rudolf, 3. Kompanie
Winkelmann, Gefreiter Franz, 1. Kompanie
Wzelak, Obergefreiter Helmut, 3. Kompanie
Zimmermann, Gefreiter Albert, 2. Kompanie

23 December, 1942
Pionier-Bataillon 336 – Iron Cross Second Class
Aurich, Gefreiter Helmut, 3. Kompanie
Brockmann, Oberleutnant Karl, 2. Kompanie (w. 11.11.1942 Stalingrad)
Ehren, Obergefreiter Hans, 3. Kompanie (MIA 12.1942 Stalingrad)
Glessmer, Obergefreiter Herbert, 1. Kompanie (MIA 31.12.1942 Stalingrad)
Hahn, Obergefreiter Hans, 1. Kompanie (MIA 07.01.1943 Stalingrad)
Hähnel, Gefreiter Fritz, 2. Kompanie
Hanns, Gefreiter Karl, 2. Kompanie
Jahn, Pionier Kurt, Stab
Kiewel, Unteroffizier Ernst, Stab
Kraus, Obergefreiter Kurt, 1. Kompanie (MIA 11.1942)
Ludwig, Gefreiter Herbert, 3. Kompanie
Marschner, Oberpionier Herbert, 1. Kompanie (MIA 01.01.1943 Stalingrad)
Matern, Oberschirrmeister Fritz, Stab
Nagel, Arno Pionier, 2. Kompanie
Oschkinat, Obergefreiter Richard, 3. Kompanie († 23.12.1942 Stalingrad)
Reichelt, Gefreiter Otto, 3. Kompanie
Schindler, Pionier Fritz, 1. Kompanie († 12.1942 Stalingrad)
Valenta, Obergefreiter Rudolf, 2. Kompanie, (w. 11.11.1942 Stalingrad)
Warnke, Sanitäts-Unteroffizier Franz, 3. Kompanie (MIA 01.1943 Stalingrad)

Offizier-Stellenbesetzung Grenadier-Regiment 212

Appendix Seven

Rgt.Stab.

Kommandeur	Oberstlt.	Eichler	(Gren.Rgt.212)
Adjutant	Hptm.	Gordner	(Gren.Rgt.212)
Ord.Offz.	Hptm.	Till	(Gren.Rgt.208)
Offz.z.b.V.	Hptm.	Graf v. Bothmer	(Gren.Rgt.226)
Rgt.Arzt	O.Arzt	Dr. Mittag	(Gren.Rgt.212)
Rgt.Vet.	O.Vet.	Seiberlich	(Gren.Rgt.212)
Verpfl.Offz.	Hptm.	Bender	(Gren.Rgt.226)
Rgt.Zahlm.	O.Zahlm.	Ziegler	(Gren.Rgt.212)

Stabs-Kompanie

Kp.-Chef	Oblt.	Pöhler	(Gren.Rgt.212)
Fhr.Na.-Zug	Lt.	Sander	(Gren.Rgt.226)
Fhr.Pi.-Zug	Oblt.	Planz	(Pi.Btl.179)

13. (I.G.) Kompanie

Kp.-Chef	Hptm	Krah	(Gren.Rgt.212)
Zugführer	Lt.	Peter	(Gren.Rgt.208)

14. (Pz.Jg.) Kompanie

Kp.-Führer	Lt.	Hoffmann	(Gren.Rgt.212)
Zugführer	Lt.	Hansen	(Gren.Rgt.208)

I. Bataillon

Kommandeur	Hptm.	Buchholz	(Gren.Rgt.212)
Adjutant	Lt.	Nopp	(Gren.Rgt.208)
Ord.Offz.	Lt.	Schilling	(Gren.Rgt.208)
Btl.Arzt	Ass.Arzt	Dr. Gürtler	(Gren.Rgt.208)
Zahlm.	K.V.J.	Höld	(Gren.Rgt.208)

1. Kompanie

Kp.-Chef	Oblt.	Müller	(Gren.Rgt.208)
Zugführer	Lt.	Wolf	(Gren.Rgt.208)
Zugführer	Lt.	Bürgy	(Gren.Rgt.208)

2. Kompanie

Kp.-Chef	Hptm.	Brötz	(Gren.Rgt.208)
Vertreter	Hptm.	Fiedler	(Pi.Btl.179)
Zugführer	Lt.	Labonte	(Gren.Rgt.208)
Zugführer	Lt.	Rembold	(Pi.Btl.179)

schwere Kompanie (heavy company)

| Kp.-Chef | Oblt. | Schenk | (Gren.Rgt.208) |
| Zugführer | Lt. | Glasbrenner | (Gren.Rgt.208) |

Versorgungs-Kompanie (supply company)

| Führer | O.Arzt | Dr. Müller | (Gren.Rgt.208) |

II. Bataillon

Kommandeur	Hptm.	Poetsch	(Gren.Rgt.212)
Adjutant	Lt.	Hess	(Gren.Rgt.212)
Ord.Offz.	Lt.	Berger	(Pi.Btl.179)
Btl.Arzt	O.Arzt	Dr. Seufert	(Gren.Rgt.212)
Zahlm.	Zahlm.	Bockelmann	(Gren.Rgt.212)

5. Kompanie

| Kp.-Chef | Oblt. | Nittler | (Gren.Rgt.212) |
| Zugführer | Lt. | Karst | (Gren.Rgt.212) |

6. Kompanie

Kp.-Chef	Oblt.	Ries	(Gren.Rgt.212)
Zugführer	Lt.	Bäder	(Gren.Rgt.212)
Zugführer	Lt.	Hürtgen	(Pi.Btl.179)

schwere Kompanie (heavy company)

Kp.-Chef	Oblt.	Sobotta	(Gren.Rgt.212)
Zugführer	Lt.	Haug	(Gren.Rgt.212)
Zugführer	Lt.	Krützner	(Gren.Rgt.212)

Versorgungs-Kompanie (supply company)

| Führer | O.Arzt | Dr. Schostok | (Pi.Btl.179) |

III. Bataillon

Kommandeur	Rittm.	v. Zitzewitz	(Radf.Abt.179)
Adjutant	Oblt.	Braband	(Radf.Abt.179)
Ord.Offz.	Lt.	Kunz	(Gren.Rgt.226)
Btl.Arzt	U.Arzt	Weiss	(Radf.Abt.179)
Zahlm.	O.Zahlm.	Müller	(Radf.Abt.179)

9. Kompanie

| Kp.-Chef | Hptm. | Federkiel | (Gren.Rgt.226) |
| Zugführer | Lt. | Naumann | (Gren.Rgt.226) |

10. Kompanie

| Kp.-Chef | Oblt. | v. Lucke | (Radf.Abt.179) |
| Zugführer | Lt. | Tusch | (Pi.Btl.179) |

schwere Kompanie (heavy company)

Kp.-Chef	Rittm.	Rapp	(Radf.Abt.179)
Zugführer	Lt.	Lafontaine	(Gren.Rgt.226)
Zugführer	Lt.	Becker	(Radf.Abt.179)
Zugführer	Lt.	Fries	(Gren.Rgt.226)

Versorgungs-Kompanie (supply company)

| Führer | Ass.Arzt | Dr. Pfeiffer | (Gren.Rgt.226) |

Type '1125'

Displacement: 26.5 tonnes. Dimensions: 22.65 long x 3.55 metres wide. Petrol-driven internal combustion engine, 720–800 HP. Speed of 15 knots (28kph), range of 400kms. Armour plating on hull and cabin: 4-7mm. Armament: 1 x 76.2mm in a T-34 tank turret, 1 x 12.7mm and 2 x 7.62mm machine-guns. Crew: 13 men.

Armoured Boat No. 12

No. 14 (No. 12 from 12 June, 1942, 'AE-12' from 7 March, 1944).
Incorporated in 1941, launched in the spring of 1942, commissioned in June 1942 and assigned to the Onega detachment on 29 June, 1942. On 18 July, 1942 was listed in the Volga Flotilla and on 14 September, 1943 in the Dneprovskiy Flotilla. Participated in the defence of Stalingrad and the Belarus (23 June – 29 August, 1944) and East-Prussian (31 March – 25 April, 1945) offensive operations (in operational subordination to the Baltic Fleet). It was decomissioned from the Navy on 8 September, 1949.

Armoured Boat No. 13

No. 15 (No. 13 from 12 June, 1942, 'AE-13' from 7 March, 1944).
Incorporated in 1941, launched in the spring of 1942, commissioned in June 1942 and assigned to the Volga flotilla on 10 July, 1942. On 14 September, 1943 was listed in the Dneprovskiy Flotilla. Participated in the defence of Stalingrad and the Belarus (23 June – 29 August, 1944) and Berlin (16 April - 8 May, 1945) offensive operations. In 1960 it was transferred to the Volgograd State Defence Museum for installation as an exhibit.

Armoured Boat No. 53

No. 71 (No. 32 from 18 September, 1942, No. 53 from 16 November, 1942, No. 321 from 21 March, 1943, 'AE-321' from 22 March, 1944).
Incorporated in 1940, launched in the summer of 1941, commissioned in October 1941 and assigned to the Volga Flotilla on 31 October, 1942. Participated in the defence of Stalingrad. On 30 May, 1944 was part of the Azov Flotilla. Participated in Kerch-Yeltigensk landing operation (31 October – 11 December, 1943). On 13 April, 1944 was listed in the Danube Flotilla. Participated in the Budapest offensive operation (29 October, 1944 – 13 February, 1945). Sunk on 9 December, 1944 by enemy artillery in the Vukovar area.

Armoured Boat No. 61

No. 73 (No. 71 from 18 September, 1942, No. 94 from 3 October, 1942, No. 71 from 9 October, 1942, <u>No. 61 from 16 November, 1942</u>, No. 312 from 21 March, 1943).

Incorporated in 1941, launched in the summer of 1941, commissioned in October 1941 and assigned to the Volga flotilla on 31 October, 1942. Participated in the defence of Stalingrad. On 30 May, 1943 assigned to the Azov Flotilla of the Black Sea Fleet. Lost on 30 August, 1943 during a battle with enemy ships and coastal artillery at the Beglitskaya headland (Taganrog gulf).

Armoured Boat No. 63

No. 34 (No. 24 from 12 June, 1942, No. 65 from 18 August, 1942, <u>No. 63 from 18 September, 1942</u>, No. 43 from 16 November, 1942, 'AE-43' from 7 March, 1944).

Incorporated in 1941, launched in the spring of 1942, commissioned in June 1942 and assigned to the Volga flotilla on 10 July, 1942. On 14 September, 1943 was listed in Dneprovskiy Flotilla. Participated in the defence of Stalingrad and the Belarus (23 June – 29 August, 1944) and Berlin (16 April – 8 May, 1945) offensive operations. Listed as part of the Danube Flotilla on 20 April, 1951.

SOURCE NOTES

Archival sources:

BA-MA   Bundesarchiv-Militärarchiv, Freiburg im Breisgau
BA-ZNS   Bundesarchiv-Zentralnachweisstelle, Aachen
DD/WASt   Deutsche Dienststelle (Wehrmachtsauskunftstelle), Berlin
NARA   National Archives and Research Administration, Washington, D.C.
TsAMO   Tsentralniy Arkhiv Ministerstva Oborony (Central Archive of the Ministry of Defence), Podolsk
USHMM   United States Holocaust Memorial Museum, Washington, D.C.

Preface:

p. ix   "'History' is that image…', Ralph H. Gabriel, American Historical Review 36, 786 (1931)

Chapter 1:

p. 1   Story of Helmut Welz, ZDF interview, 2002; Welz, interview with Agnes Moosmann, 19.1.2005
p. 4   Casualties of 305. Inf.Div. for 17.10.42, 6. Armee, NARA T-312, Roll 1453, p. 481
p. 4   Casualties of 305. & 389.Inf.Div. for 14.10.42, 6. Armee, NARA T-312, Roll 1453, p. 360
p. 4   Casualties of 14.Pz.Div. for 14.10.42, ibid.
p. 6   'absolutely complete success', 6. Armee, NARA T-312, Roll 1688, p. 348
p. 6   Casualties of 305.Inf.Div. for 15.10.42, 6. Armee, NARA T-312, Roll 1453, p. 399
p. 6   Casualties of 14.Pz.Div. for 15.10.42, ibid.
p. 6   Casualties of 305.Inf.Div. for 16.10.42, ibid., p. 440
p. 6   Casualties of 14.Pz.Div. for 16.10.42, ibid.
p. 7   Story of Svidrov and his garrison, Lyudnikov, 'There is a Cliff on the Volga', in *Two Hundred Days of Fire*, p. 187-9; Lyudnikov's article in *Ogonyok*, No. 5, January 1968; and Svidrov interview with Evgeny Kulichenko
p. 10   Casualties of 305.Inf.Div. for 27.10.42, 6. Armee, NARA T-312, Roll 1453, p. 866
p. 10   Casualties of 305.Inf.Div. for 28.10.42, ibid., p. 927
p. 10   Casualties of 305.Inf.Div. for 29.10.42, ibid., p. 979
p. 10   a convalescent company of 260 men arrives, ibid., p. 937
p. 11   Paulus's meeting, , 'Frontfahrt des Oberbefehlshaber am 1.11.1942', ibid., p. 1079
p. 11   'Early this morning…', Goerlitz, p. 193
p. 12   'Because of the narrowness…', 6. Armee, NARA T-312, Roll 1688, p. 336
p. 13   Richthofen telephones Jeschonnek, Hayward, p. 214
p. 13   Paulus's and Schmidt's plan, 6. Armee, NARA T-312, Roll 1453, p. 1059-61
p. 13   Schmidt/Sodenstern conversation, ibid
p. 14   Paulus/Weichs conversation, ibid., p. 1062-3
p. 14   'In reference to the…', ibid., p. 1064
p. 15   'Hitler turned down…', Hillgruber, p. 83
p. 15   'At 2330 hours, an order…', 294.Inf.Div., T-315, Roll 1941, ibid., p. 1070
p. 15   'At 2330 hours, a message…', 336.Inf.Div., T-315, Roll 2093, p. 504

p. 16   'Around midnight, the…', 62.Inf.Div., T-315, Roll 1034, p. 161
p. 16   'German pioneer battalions within…', Kehrig, p. 41
p. 16   Sodenstern/Schmidt conversation, 6. Armee, NARA T-312, Roll 1688, p. 342
p. 17   Order to 294.Inf.Div., 294.Inf.Div., T-315, Roll 1941, p. 1070
p. 17   Order to Lundt (Pi.Btl.336), 336.Inf.Div., T-315, Roll 2093, p. 504
p. 17   'Pz.Pi.Btl.50 and Pi.Btl.45 (mot.)…', 6. Armee, NARA T-312, Roll 1688, p. 346
p. 17   Korpsbefehl No. 102, 79.Inf.Div., 1.11.1942, NARA T-315, Roll 1108, p. 46
p. 17   Details of attack on 2.11.42, 6. Armee, NARA T-312, Roll 1453, p. 1103 & 1106
p. 18   Paulus's front-line inspection 'Frontfahrt des Oberbefehlshaber am 3.11.1942', ibid., p. 1103
p. 19   Details of 389.Inf.Div. attack, ibid., p. 1103 & 1106
p. 19   Casualties of 389.Inf.Div. for 2.11.42, ibid., p. 1123
p. 19   Details of 305.Inf.Div. attack, ibid., p. 1103 & 1106
p. 19   Casualties of 305.Inf.Div. for 2.11.42, ibid., p. 1123
p. 19   Casualties of 14.Pz.Div. for 2.11.42, ibid.
p. 20   Details of 79.Inf.Div. attack, 79.Inf.Div., T-315, Roll 1107, p. 924-5
p. 20   Casualties of 79.Inf.Div. for 2.11.42, 6. Armee, NARA T-312, Roll 1453, p. 1123
p. 20   'clean up the enemy…', ibid., p. 1103 & 1114
p. 20   Heeresgruppe B calls 294.Inf.Div., 294.Inf.Div., T-315, Roll 1941, p. 1070
p. 20   'Transportation of the…', 336.Inf.Div., T-315, Roll 2093, p. 506
p. 21   Paulus's meeting with Seydlitz, 'Frontfahrt des Oberbefehlshaber am 3.11.1942', 6. Armee, NARA T-312, Roll 1453, p. 1155
p. 21   'A complete solution…', ibid.
p. 21   Selle and Romeis summoned, ibid.
p. 21   Sodenstern/Schmidt conversation, 6. Armee, NARA T-312, Roll 1688, p. 348 & 350
p. 21   'The Commander-in-Chief…', ibid.
p. 22   'Only once during…', ibid.
p. 22   'the army can only…', ibid.

p. 22   'The employment of the…', 6. Armee, NARA T-312, Roll 1453, p. 1153-4
p. 22   'Our assessment of…', ibid.
p. 22   'To begin with,…', ibid.
p. 22   'Regarding the employment…', ibid.
p. 23   'Pi.Btle.45 (mot.), 50…', 6. Armee, NARA T-312, Roll 1453, p. 1130
p. 23   Oberst Mikosch's tasks, ibid.
p. 23   Oberst Selle's tasks, ibid.
p. 23   Sodenstern/Schmidt conversation at 1130, 6. Armee, NARA T-312, Roll 1688, p. 351
p. 24   'Heeresgruppe is of opinion…', ibid.
p. 24   'On 4.11., Pi.Btle.336 and…', 6. Armee, NARA T-312, Roll 1453, p. 1129
p. 24   '1.) The general situation…', ibid., p. 1134-5

Chapter 2:

Pionier-Bataillon 45:

p. 25   'by far the most…', Krauss, account 18.12.2003, p. 7
p. 25   'In the evening…', Locherer, account undated, p. 10
p. 25   'We passed through…', Krauss, account 18.12.2003, p. 7
p. 26   ration and combat strengths, 6. Armee, NARA T-312, Roll 1453, p. 1204
p. 26   Italian flamethrowers, Krauss, account 21.2.2004, p. 3
p. 26   command structure, various sources such as personnel files, casualty cards, promotions lists, veterans accounts, etc.

Panzerpionier-Bataillon 50:

p. 28   'the clearance of…', Stoves, p. 43
p. 28   gave his pioneers ample fuel, ibid.
p. 28   Selle meets his old battalion, *Ursprung, Weg und Untergang des Pion. Batl. 50: Ein geschichtlicher Kurzabriss*, p. 11
p. 28   'Mounted in our vehicles…', Apmann, 'Von Harburg nach Stalingrad: Erinnerungen eines Landsers der 50er-Pioniere', in *Mitteilungsblatt des Verbandes ehemäliger Angehöriger der 23. Panzer-Division und der Traditionsverbände der 14. Panzer-Division, der 22. Panzer-Division und der Panzer-Lehr-Division*, Nr. 2/16 Jahrgang, p. 33
p. 29   ration and combat strengths, 6. Armee, NARA T-312, Roll 1453, p. 1204
p. 29   command structure, various sources such as personnel files, casualty cards, promotions lists, veterans accounts, etc.

Pionier-Bataillon 162:

p. 31   'The withdrawal of the…', 62.Inf.Div. KTB, T-315, Roll 1034, p. 163
p. 31   Italian motorised column, ibid.; and Puschiavo family archives
p. 31   ration and combat strengths, 6. Armee, NARA T-312, Roll 1453, p. 1204
p. 31   command structure, various sources such as personnel files, casualty cards, promotions lists, veterans accounts, etc.

Pionier-Bataillon 294:

p. 32   made ready as a Sturm-Bataillon', 294.Inf.Div., NARA T-315, Roll 1941, p. 1070
p. 32   'the battalion is suitable…', 294.Inf.Div., NARA T-315, Roll 1942, p. 688
p. 32   The definite order, 294.Inf.Div., NARA T-315, Roll 1941, p. 1070
p. 32   'a) the battalion will…', ibid.
p. 32   embarkation delayed, ibid.
p. 33   combat strength 4 days before departure, 294.Inf.Div., NARA T-315, Roll 1942, p. 688
p. 33   'Morale of the troops…', ibid.

p. 33   ration and combat strengths, 6. Armee, NARA T-312, Roll 1453, p. 1205
p. 33   command structure, various sources such as personnel files, casualty cards, promotions lists, veterans accounts, etc.
p. 33   the battalion's Soviet arsenal, 294.Inf.Div., NARA T-315, Roll 1942, p. 688

Pionier-Bataillon 336:

p. 34   Transfer of Borkowski, Personalakten für Herbert Borkowski
p. 34   'firm, energetic and…', Personalakten für Hermann Lundt
p. 34   'a simple, forthright…', ibid.
p. 34   336.Inf.Div. receives a communique, 336.Inf.Div., NARA T-315, Roll 2093, p. 504
p. 34   Lundt ordered to report to Ilovskoye, ibid., p. 506
p. 34   'Transportation of the…', ibid.
p. 34   Giebeler's story, Craig, p. 154, Familie Giebeler archives
p. 35   nine lorries, 336.Inf.Div., NARA T-315, Roll 2093, p. 506
p. 35   two remaining companies, ibid.
p. 35   command structure, various sources such as personnel files, casualty cards, promotions lists, veterans accounts, etc.
p. 36   ration and combat strengths, 6. Armee, NARA T-312, Roll 1453, p. 1205

Sturmschwadron 24:

p. 37   Divisionsbefehl Nr. 83, 24PD, NARA T-315, Roll 804, p. 657-9
p. 37   composition of the Sturmschwadron, ibid., p. 660-1 & 682; also see 79.Inf.Div., NARA T-315, Roll 1109, p. 10-12
p. 37   Beyersdorff given carte blanche, 'Beyersdorff Familienchronik', p. 84
p. 38   armament of the Sturmschwadron, 24PD, NARA T-315, Roll 804, p. 660; see also see 79.Inf.Div., NARA T-315, Roll 1109, p. 10-12

Sturmkompanie 44:

p. 39   6. Armee order to XI. Armeekorps 4.10.1942, 6. Armee, NARA T-312, Roll 1686, p. 922-3
p. 39   'Sturmkompanie 44.I.D., with…', 6. Armee, NARA T-312, Roll 1453, p. 894
p. 40   'Reinforced Sturmkompanie of…', 79.Inf.Div., NARA T-315, Roll 1108, p. 41
p. 40   a document dated 11 November, 6. Armee, NARA T-312, Roll 1454, p. 178
p. 42   strength of Heerespionierzug 672, 79.Inf.Div., NARA T-315, Roll 1108, p. 367
p. 42   failed attack on Martin Furnace Hall, 79.Inf.Div., NARA T-315, Roll 1107, p. 924; 79.Inf.Div., NARA T-315, Roll 1108, p. 362-4

Sturminfanteriegeschütz 33B:

p. 43   'Fighting in Stalingrad…', Jentz, p. 8-46
p. 43   'Hitler is extremely…', ibid.
p. 44   vehicle specifications, ibid., p. 8-45
p. 44   In Hitler's conference, ibid., p. 8-46
p. 44   Heeres Waffenamt reported, ibid.
p. 45   'On the Führer's orders…', 6. Armee, NARA T-312, Roll 1453, p. 605
p. 45   'Stug.Abt.244 will shortly…', ibid., p. 606
p. 45   '27.10.: Pz.K.616…', 6. Armee, NARA T-312, Roll 1450, p. 595
p. 45   '28.10.: Pz.K.627…', 6. Armee, NARA T-312, Roll 1450, p. 642
p. 45   'Stug.Abt.177 and 244…', 6. Armee, NARA T-312, Roll 1453, p. 904

p. 47   'Sturmgeschütze with s.I.G....', ibid., p. 936

p. 47   Paulus's front-line visit, 'Frontfahrt des Oberbefehlshaber am 29.10.1942', ibid., p. 943

p. 47   'The 6 s.I.G. (Sfl.) of...', 79.Inf.Div., NARA T-315, Roll 1108, p. 358

p. 47   Disappointed battery commander, 'Frontfahrt des Oberbefehlshaber am 1.11.1942', 6. Armee, NARA T-312, Roll 1453, p. 1079

p. 48   order issued by 305.Inf.Div. 1.11.42, BA-MA, RH 26-305/14, p. 93-4

p. 48   Stug.Abt.177 reports deficiencies, 6. Armee, NARA T-312, Roll 1453, p. 1126

p. 48   shortcomings of the crews, ibid.

p. 48   essential information from booklets, 'Vorläufige Schußtafel für das Sturm-Infanteriegeschütz 33 (Stu IG 33) mit der 15cm Infanteriegranate 33 und 15cm Infanteriegranate 38. Vom Oktober 1942'. BA-MA, H.Dv. 119/334

p. 49   'The 6 s.I.G. (Sfl.) of...', 6. Armee, NARA T-312, Roll 1453, p. 1194

p. 49   'I was only transferred...', Mai, report to Jaugitz, 1996

p. 49   'Lorry trip (hitchhiker)...', ibid.

p. 50   'Apparently I'd received...', ibid.

p. 50   '9.11. Attack on...', ibid.

p. 50   'The targets, such as...', ibid.

p. 50   '6 Sturmgeschütze mit s.I.G....', 6. Armee, NARA T-312, Roll 1453, p. 1344

p. 51   'The s.I.G. self-propelled...', 79.Inf.Div., NARA T-315, Roll 1108, p. 973

p. 51   'In the steel factory...', 6. Armee, NARA T-312, Roll 1453, p. 1298

p. 51   'There was a crossroads...', Wijers, *Der Kampf um Stalingrad*, p. 39

p. 52   Korpsbefehl No. 105, 79.Inf.Div., T-315, Roll 1108, p. 203-6

p. 52   'The divisions will hold...', ibid.

p. 53   'The quickest journey...', Bauchspiess, Feldpostbrief 4.11.1942

p. 54   Story of Welz and Fiedler, Welz, *Verratene Grenadiere*, p. 82-83

p. 54   'It was just...', ibid., p. 83

p. 54   '"Hubertus' is the...', Korpsbefehl No. 107, 79.Inf.Div., NARA T-315, Roll 1108, p. 207-9

p. 55   'all preparations must...', ibid.

p. 55   'For the attack...', ibid.

p. 55   Sodenstern calls Schmidt, 6. Armee, NARA T-312, Roll 1688, p. 364

p. 55   Zeitzler's questions, ibid., p. 366

p. 56   '1.) The assault on...', 6. Armee, NARA T-312, Roll 1453, p. 1228-30

p. 56   'Give us a decision...', ibid., p. 1231

p. 56   'We regard several...', 6. Armee, NARA T-312, Roll 1688, p. 370

p. 57   'We've got the decision...', 6. Armee, NARA T-312, Roll 1453, p. 1265

p. 57   'The Führer has ordered...', 6. Armee, NARA T-312, Roll 1688, p. 372

p. 57   'Operation Hubertus is postponed...', 79.Inf.Div., NARA T-315, Roll 1108, p. 56-7

p. 57   'As we approached...', Krauss, account 18.12.2003, p. 7

p. 57   Italian drivers and their trucks, Puschiavo family archives

p. 58   Korpsbefehl No. 108, 79.Inf.Div., NARA T-315, Roll 1108, p. 56-7

p. 58   LI. Armeekorps' proposal, 6. Armee, NARA T-312, Roll 1453, p. 1143

p. 58   Korpsbefehl No. 109, 79.Inf.Div., NARA T-315, Roll 1108, p. 58

p. 59   re-issued Korpsbefehl No. 109, ibid., p. 59

p. 59   'Experiences during the...', 294.Inf.Div., NARA T-315, Roll 1942, p. 724-5

p. 60   the army's intentions, 6. Armee, NARA T-312, Roll 1453, p. 1289

p. 61   Korpsbefehl No. 110, 79.Inf.Div., T-315, Roll 1108, p. 211-13

p. 61   'The enemy fights...', ibid.

p. 61   '305.I.D. and the southern...', ibid.

p. 61   '71., 295., 100.J.D. and...', ibid.

p. 62   'As a precaution...', ibid., p. 212

p. 62   Divisionsbefehl Nr. 84, 24PD, NARA T-315, Roll 804, p. 685-7

Chapter 3:

p. 63   'The leave train...', Rettenmaier, *Alte Kameraden* 1/1954, p. 3

p. 64   'I am now in a...', Rettenmaier, Feldpostbrief 6.11.1942

p. 64   Biographical details of Rettenmaier; *Aalener Volkszeitung / Ipf- und Jagst-Zeitung* Nr. 10, 14.1.1965, p. 11; and Familie Rettenmaier archives

p. 65   'My dear...', Familie Rettenmaier archives

p. 65   'From our elevated...', Winter, *Damals als die Räder rollten*, p. 29

p. 66   Biographical details of Brandt; Thomas/Wegmann, *Die Ritterkreuzträger der Deutschen Wehrmacht 1939-1945 – Teil III: Infanterie Br-Bu*, p. 29-30

p. 66   Biographical details of Braun; ibid., p. 60-61; and Familie Braun archives

p. 67   Biographical details of Pechenyuk; *Geroi Sovetskogo Soyuza*, T. 2, p. 265

p. 67   'distinguished for...', Lyudnikov, 'There is a Cliff on the Volga', in *Two Hundred Days of Fire*, p. 181

p. 67   'overcautious...', 'his calm...', ibid.

p. 67   Biographical details of Konovalenko; *Geroi Sovetskogo Soyuza*, T. 1, p. 715

p. 68   Wounding of Reutsky, Lyudnikov, *Two Hundred Days of Fire*, p. 181

p. 68   'My, what a guardian...', ibid., p. 182

p. 68   'The 344th needs...', ibid., p. 185

p. 68   'If you're sure...', ibid.

p. 69   'What are you doing...', 4.11.1942, 344 str.polk, TsAMO, p. 23

p. 69   Biographical details of Lyudnikov; *Geroi Sovetskogo Soyuza*, T. 2, p. 5; http://www.redstar. ru/2002/09/26_09/1_03.html; http://www.warheroes. ru/hero/hero.asp?Hero_id=1283; http://www.hrono.ru/ biograf/bio_l/ludnikov.html; http://www.donbass.dn. ua/2002/10/20320/20320-04.php; and http://www.pr. azov.net/archiv/2003/N_69/zna.htm

p. 70   'Kampfgruppe 578', Rettenmaier, *Alte Kameraden* 1/1954, p. 3

p. 70   Liesecke's appointment, NARA Personalakten Max Liesecke

p. 70   'You might want...', Rettenmaier, *Alte Kameraden* 1/1954, p. 3

p. 70   'The course of...', ibid., p. 4

p. 71   'I do not have...', Rettenmaier, Feldpostbrief 8.11.1942

p. 71   'Assigned by me...', Selle, *Wofür? Erleben eines führenden Pioniers bis Stalingrad*, p. 49

p. 72   Biographical details of Linden, NARA Personalakten Josef Linden; Soldbuch Josef Linden; and Hirst, 'The Cast', in *Three Scenes from Barbarossa*

p. 72   Under the command of Hans Mikosch…, Linden monograph, 'Stalingrad', p. 6 in Hirst, op. cit.

p. 72   Hundreds of T-34s…, Linden monograph, p. 6

p. 73   'The layover in Kalach…', ibid., p. 7

p. 73   'With the exception…', ibid., p. 8

p. 73   'The battalion commanders…', ibid.

p. 74   'What did the situation…', ibid., p. 8–11

p. 75   'My fellow German…', Domarus, *Hitler, Reden und Proklamationen, 1932-1945*; also http://www.adolfhitler.ws/lib/speeches/text/speeches.htm

p. 76   'If you read…', ibid.

p. 77   'It has now already…', Füssinger, Feldpostbrief 8.11.1942

p. 77   Paulus visit, 'Frontfahrt des Oberbefehlshaber am 9.11.1942', 6. Armee, NARA T-312, Roll 1453, p. 1340

p. 78   'You'll be able to…', Bauchspiess, Feldpostbrief 9.11.1942

p. 78   'Preparations for the…', Krauss, account 18.12.2003, p. 8

p. 79   'On 9 November came…', Rettenmaier, *Alte Kameraden* 1/1954, p. 4

p. 79   'The assault was planned…', ibid.

p. 82   '1.) Relief by Pionier-Bataillon 50…', Familie Grimm archives

p. 83   'After an adventurous…', Eberhard, *Inf.Div.389*, p. 62

p. 83   'During my absence…', ibid.

p. 83   'The time had come…', ibid.

p. 83   'I was glad that…', ibid., p. 63

p. 84   'On the evening of…', ibid.

p. 84   Sturmgeschütze strengths, 11.11.1942, 6. Armee, NARA T-312, Roll 1453, p. 1383

p. 84   Panzers held in reserve in the Bread Factory, 79.Inf.Div., 4.11.1942, NARA T-315, Roll 1109, p. 20-21; and 79. Inf.Div., 5.11.1942, T-315, Roll 1108, p. 957

p. 84   'Approach route…', 79.Inf.Div., NARA T-315, Roll 1109, p. 28

p. 85   Leutnant Zorn and his pioneers, Familie Zorn archives

p. 86   'With the onset…', 650 strelkovy polk, boevoy zhurnal (650 str.polk zhurnal – 650th Rifle Regiment combat journal), TsAMO, p. 27

p. 86   'the enemy hasn't…', 9.11.1942, ibid.

p. 86   'I've already written…', Ebert, *Feldpostbriefe aus Stalingrad: November 1942 bis Januar 1943*, p. 43

p. 87   'After 21 days of…', Grimm, Feldpostbriefe 9.11.1942

p. 87   'I was not a little…', Grimm, report February 1985, p. 5

p. 88   'As the last Unteroffizier…', Krauss, p. 8

p. 88   'We were warmly…', ibid.

p. 89   'On the evening of…', Eberhard, p. 63

p. 89   'The sky was clear…', Schüddekopf, 'Hans Horn' in *Im Kessel: Erzählen von Stalingrad*, p. 117

p. 89   'We marched along…', von Aaken, *Hexenkessel Ostfront*, p. 115-16

p. 90   Story of Unteroffizier Ernst Wohlfahrt, Craig, *Enemy at the Gates: The Battle for Stalingrad*, p. 156

p. 90   7 men from 2./Pi.Btl.336 wounded by a mine, DD/WASt, 'Pi.Btl.336 Namentliche Verlustmeldung Nr. 4', 16.4.1943

p. 91   'During the night, I once…', Grimm, p. 5

p. 91   'Fire with all…', 650 str.polk zhurnal, TsAMO, p. 28

p. 91   'It has been established…', 138 str.div., 'Combat Report No. 193', TsAMO, p. 151

p. 92   Bombing activity during night of 10-11.11.1942, 6. Armee, NARA T-312, Roll 1453, p. 1383

Chapter 4:

p. 93   'Beginning at 3:40…', Friedel, *Nebelwerfer-Regiment 51*, p. 303

p. 93   Details about Artillerie-Kommandeur 153, 79.Inf.Div., 8.11.1942, NARA T-315, Roll 1108, p. 211

p. 95   Successes against Soviet batteries, 6. Armee, NARA T-312, Roll 1453, p. 1401

p. 95   Successes against Soviet ships, ibid., p. 1406

p. 96   'At 0400 hours on…', Krylow, *Stalingrad: Die Entscheidende Schlacht des Zweiten Weltkriegs*, p. 321

p. 96   'The artillery fire began…', Rettenmaier, *Alte Kameraden* 1/1954, p. 4

p. 97   'I suspected that the…', Grimm, p. 5

p. 97   fired a total of 50 rounds, 295 artillerii polk, 'Combat Report No. 193', TsAMO, p. 130

p. 97   counterfire was not pre-planned, 62-armii artillerii, 'Combat Order No. 70', TsAMO, p. 96

p. 97   'The infantry and panzers…', Krylow, op. cit., p. 321

p. 97   'The five kilometre front…', Chuikov, *The Beginning of the Road*, p. 209

p. 98   Actions of 71.Inf.Div., 6. Armee, NARA T-312, Roll 1453, p. 1396

p. 98   Actions of 295.Inf.Div., ibid.

p. 98   Actions of 100.Jäg.Div., ibid.

p. 98   Actions of 79.Inf.Div., ibid.; and Mark, *Death of the Leaping Horseman*, p. 356-9

p. 98   Actions of 94.Inf.Div., 6. Armee, NARA T-312, Roll 1453, p. 1395

p. 98   Actions of 16.Pz.Div., ibid.

p. 99   'Our stormtroops have been…' ibid., p. 1397

p. 100   Braun's actions at the fuel installation, Thomas/Wegmann, *Die Ritterkreuzträger der Deutschen Wehrmacht 1939-1945 - Teil III: Infanterie Br-Bu*, p. 60-61

p. 101   Casualties of 241RR 5.11.42, 95 str.div., 'Combat Report No. 28' & 'Combat Report No. 29', TsAMO, p. 128-9

p. 101   Casualties of 241RR 7.11.42, 95 str.div., 'Combat Report No. 35' TsAMO, p. 134

p. 101   Casualties of 241RR 10.11.42, 95 str.div., 'Combat Report No. 39' TsAMO, p. 147

p. 101   'At 0400 on the…', 95 str.div., 'Combat Report No. 40' TsAMO, p. 148

p. 101   Death of Mähnert, 2./Pi.Btl.294, DD/WASt, 'Pi.Btl.294 Namentliche Verlustmeldung Nr. 14', 7.7.1944

p. 101   'concentrated on the…', 95 str.div., 'Combat Report No. 40' TsAMO, p. 148

p. 101   Actions of Kampfgruppe Seydel, 79.Inf.Div., 8.11.1942, NARA T-315, Roll 1108, p. 639

p. 101   'The night passed…', 79.Inf.Div., NARA T-315, Roll 1108, p. 986

p. 102   Death of Kerkhoff, 3./Pi.Btl.294, DD/WASt, 'Pi.Btl.294 Namentliche Verlustmeldung Nr. 17', 7.7.1944

p. 102   Deaths of Demme and Döbler, 1./Pi.Btl.294, DD/WASt, 'Pi.Btl.294 Namentliche Verlustmeldung Nr. 9', 4.7.1944

p. 102   Story of Manenkov, 'Ovrag glubokaya balka', *Putevoditel po Volgogradu*, p. 89-90; also http://region34.nm.ru/guide/volgograd/index15.html

p. 103   Leutnant Zorn's actions, Familie Zorn archives

p. 103   'The most important thing…', Rettenmaier, private report to his son Siegbert, 16.11.1942

p. 104   A total of 45 prisoners, ibid.

p. 104   'the first reports of…', Rettenmaier, *Alte Kameraden* 1/1954, p. 4

p. 104 Enemy in the Apotheke basement, Rettenmaier, report to Siegbert

p. 104 'As it became light…', Schüddekopf, op. cit., p. 117–18

p. 104 Departure positions of German assault groups, 650 str.polk zhurnal, TsAMO, p. 28

p. 104 Gast turning down infantry support, Rettenmaier, *Alte Kameraden* 1/1954, p. 4

p. 105 'Armed with mines…', Rettenmaier, report to Siegbert

p. 105 'The enemy was vigilant…', ibid.

p. 106 'On 11 November, the fascists…', Senchkovsky, report, 1.11.1967, p. 2

p. 106 Gefreiter Apmann's actions, letter from Familie Apmann to Agnes Moosmann, 29.7.2005

p. 106 'The worst thing…', Schlager, 'Mit ganz kleinen Stosstrupps…', in Zentner, *Soldaten im Einsatz*, p. 175

p. 106 'Many pioneers fell…', Rettenmaier, report to Siegbert

p. 106 Casualties of Pz.Pi.Btl.50, 6. Armee, NARA T-312, Roll 1453, p. 1428

p. 106 Death of Pischko, 3./Pz.Pi.Btl.50, DD/WASt, 'Pz.Pi.Btl.50 Namentliche Verlustmeldung Nr. 6', 29.2.1944

p. 106 Death of Stadie, 3./Pz.Pi.Btl.50, DD/WASt, 'Pz.Pi.Btl.50 Namentliche Verlustmeldung Nr. 9', 12.6.1944

p. 106 Deaths of Markus and Wilm, 2./Pi.Btl.294, DD/WASt, 'Pz.Pi.Btl.50 Namentliche Verlustmeldung Nr. 8', 12.6.1944

p. 107 Deaths of Eichhorn and Reigl, 11./Inf.Rgt.131, 'Verlusteliste 1939-1945, Inf.Rgt. - Gren.Rgt.131', BA-MA, RH37/7005, p. 26 & 68

p. 107 Death of Brock, 3./Pi.Btl.80, DD/WASt, letter to the author, 3.4.2006, p. 1

p. 107 'At 0330, the enemy…', 650 str.polk zhurnal, TsAMO, p. 28

p. 108 'Assault guns were…', Linden monograph, p. 15

p. 108 Actions of Stug.Abt.245, Rettenmaier, *Alte Kameraden* 1/1954, p. 4

p. 108 'The Germans held a…', Klyukin, 'Na 'ostrove Lyudnikova'', in *Bitva za Stalingrad*, p. 577–8

p. 109 'East of the gun factory…', 6. Armee, NARA T-312, Roll 1453, p. 1426

p. 109 Strength report for Stug.Abt.245 for 12.11.1942, 6. Armee, NARA T-312, Roll 1454, p. 11

p. 109 'I learned from the…', Grimm, p. 5

p. 110 'From 0430 650th Rifle…', '138-ya krasnoznamennaya strelkovaya diviziya v boyakh Stalingrad' (138 str.div. zhurnal – 138th Rifle Division combat journal), TsAMO, p. 24

p. 110 'during the fighting…', 650 str.polk zhurnal, TsAMO, p. 29

p. 110 'Daylight came and…', Rettenmaier, report to Siegbert

p. 110 'It did not take long…', von Aaken, op. cit., p. 116

p. 111 'I was employed on…', Staiger, interview with Agnes Moosmann, 14.1.2005

p. 112 'A Feldwebel by the…', ibid.

p. 113 'only on the lower…', Staiger, interview with Agnes Moosmann, 23.2.2005

p. 113 Pogrebnyak's Strongpoint No. 4, 9.11.1942, 344 str.polk, TsAMO, p. 22

p. 113 'On 11 November my company…', Piven, report, 15.1.1978, p. 1

p. 113 'During the war I…', Danilenko, report, undated

p. 113 'On the right flank…', 650 str.polk zhurnal, TsAMO, p. 29

p. 116 'At 0400 on 11.11.42, after…', 344 str.polk, TsAMO, p. 62

p. 116 'from 0400, 344th Rifle…', 138 str.div. zhurnal, TsAMO, p. 24

p. 116 'all enemy attacks…', 344 str.polk, TsAMO, p. 62

p. 116 'With fixed bayonets…', Krauss, p. 8

p. 117 'And now the latest…', Wiesen, *Es grüßt Euch alle, Bertold*, p. 98–99

p. 118 'on the right flank…', 344 str.polk, TsAMO, p. 62

p. 119 'The enemy has broken…', Lyudnikov, in *The Road of Battle and Glory*, p. 114–15

p. 119 'At 0340, the enemy…', 768 str.polk, 'Combat Report 11.11.1942', TsAMO, p. 53

p. 120 6. Armee Ic report about enemy strengths, 6. Armee, NARA T-312, Roll 1453, p. 1402

p. 120 'our company that was…', 768 str.polk, TsAMO, p. 52

p. 121 Attack on boundary between 768 and 118, 138 str.div., 'Combat Report No. 195', TsAMO, p. 162

p. 121 'at 0830 hours, the enemy…', ibid., p. 161

p. 121 'From 4.00, 118th Guards…', ibid.

p. 121 'The buildings on the river…', von Debschitz, 'Aufzeichnungen von den Kämpfen um Stalingrad', BA-MA MSG2-2570, p. 40

p. 122 'Everything was arranged…', Eberhard, p. 63

p. 123 'The enemy was readying…', Volostnov, *Na ognennykh rubezakh*, p. 171

p. 124 Paulus visit, 'Frontfahrt des Oberbefehlshaber am 11.11.1942', 6. Armee, NARA T-312, Roll 1453, p. 1403

p. 124 'In Stalingrad, 305. Infanterie-Division…', 11.11.1942, 6. Armee, NARA T-312, Roll 1453, p. 1388

p. 125 hastily bandaged Soviet soldiers, 95 str.div., 'Special Operational Report, 11.11.1942', TsAMO, p. 199

p. 125 Selifanov's 1st Rifle Battalion, ibid.

p. 125 'One of our best…' Kluge, *The Battle*, p. 83–5

p. 125 'During my operations…' Müller to Grimm, Feldpostbrief 21.6.1943

p. 125 'Gefreiter Müller was…' Grimm, comments February 1985

p. 126 'The flamethrower primarily…' ibid.

p. 126 Selifanov's battalion fights on, 95 str.div., 'Special Operational Report, 11.11.1942', TsAMO, p. 199

p. 126 A soldier of the security platoon, ibid.

p. 126 'I can throw these…', Beevor, *Stalingrad: The Fateful Siege*, p. 217

p. 127 'Using reserves…', 95 str.div., 'Special Operational Report, 11.11.1942', TsAMO, p. 199

p. 127 Braun's capture of the fuel tanks, Thomas/Wegmann, *Die Ritterkreuzträger der Deutschen Wehrmacht 1939-1945 - Teil III: Infanterie Br-Bu*, p. 60–61

p. 127 Four soldiers huddled in a pipe, 95 str.div., 'Special Operational Report, 11.11.1942', TsAMO, p. 199; and Beevor, p. 217

p. 127 3rd and 4th assault groups move off, Rettenmaier, *Alte Kameraden* 1/1954, p. 4

p. 128 'courageous, fair-minded…' Plaum, letter to author, 2.1.2004

p. 128 Biographical details of Kretz, Familie Kretz archive

p. 129 'You can obviously see…', Kretz, Feldpostbrief 30.10.1942

p. 130 The attack on Haus 79, Rettenmaier, *Alte Kameraden* 1/1954, p. 4

p. 130 Gorishny's appeals, 95 str.div., 'Combat Report No. 41', TsAMO, p. 150

p. 130 actions of 161RR, ibid.

p. 131 'After a short pause…', Krylow, op. cit., p. 324

p. 131n Deaths of Fiedler, Krebs and Schaarschmidt, 1./Pi.Btl.294, DD/WASt, 'Pi.Btl.294 Namentliche Verlustmeldung Nr. 9 & 10', 4.7.1944

p. 131n Deaths of Friedel, Herzog, Klötzer, Klötzer, Kubitschke, Morgenstern, Pieke, Schmarsel, Schultz and Walter, 2./Pi.Btl.294, DD/WASt, 'Pi.Btl.294 Namentliche Verlustmeldung Nr. 14 & 15', 7.7.1944

p. 131n Deaths of Bätz, Jahn, Kittler, König and Riedel, 3./Pi.Btl.294, DD/WASt, 'Pi.Btl.294 Namentliche Verlustmeldung Nr. 17, 18 & 19', 7.7.1944

p. 131n Death of Chadima, Stab/Pi.Btl.294, DD/WASt, 'Pi.Btl.294 Namentliche Verlustmeldung Nr. 1', 6.7.1944

p. 132 Advance from the Sandbank, Rettenmaier, *Alte Kameraden* 1/1954, p. 4

p. 132 241st Rifle Regiment loses its manpower, Lyudnikov, *Ognenniy Ostrov*, p. 118

p. 132 German report on Soviet air activity, 6. Armee, NARA T-312, Roll 1453, p. 1402

p. 132 'After four hours of…', von Aaken, op. cit., p. 117

p. 133 'By 0930, small groups…', 138 str.div., 'Combat Report No. 195', TsAMO, p. 162

p. 133 'Throughout the day…', 344 str.polk, TsAMO, p. 62

p. 133 'At 1540, the enemy…', 138 str.div., 'Combat Report No. 195', TsAMO, p. 162

p. 133 'On 11 November, the enemy…', 344 str.polk, 'Combat Order 11.11.1942', TsAMO, p. 61

p. 134 Casualties of Pi.Btl.336, 6. Armee, NARA T-312, Roll 1453, p. 1428

p. 134 'Wounded in the left eye…', 16.11.1942, Familie Brockmann archive

p. 134 'For over four hours…', Krauss, p. 9

p. 134 Pioneers bypass right flank of 768, 138 str.div., 'Combat Report No. 195', TsAMO, p. 162

p. 135 Story of Bushuyev, Venkov & Dudinov, *Gvardeyskaya doblest*, p. 44

p. 135 Story of Zarkayev, ibid.

p. 135 'We soon took up defence…', Lesin, report, undated, p. 6

p. 135 Actions and wounding of Beyersdorff, 'Beyersdorff Familienchronik', p. 84

p. 136 'by 1300, the enemy group…', 138 str.div., 'Combat Report No. 195', TsAMO, p. 162

p. 136 'the enemy had moved up…', 138 str.div. zhurnal, TsAMO, p. 24

p. 136 24 remaining men, ibid.

p. 136 'The Germans are attacking…', Glukhovsky, *Ostrov Lyudnikova*, p. 33–34

p. 136 'The fascists shower…', ibid., p. 34–35

p. 137 Lyudnikov and Petukhov, ibid., p. 35

p. 137 'Are you wounded…', ibid., p. 36–37

p. 138 'It was 11 November 1942…', Kamyshanov, report, 1973, p. 1

p. 138 'By evening, when we…', Volostnov, ibid., p. 171–2

p. 139 Break-out of Kolobovnikov's group, ibid., p. 172

p. 139 'After we had stormed…', Wiesen, op. cit., p. 99

p. 139 'Fortunately, dusk had…', Krauss, p. 9

p. 140 Gained a 500-metre front on the Volga, 6. Armee, NARA T-312, Roll 1453, p. 1396

p. 140 5 dug-in Soviet tanks destroyed, 6. Armee, NARA T-312, Roll 1453, p. 1428

p. 140 'The attack of the…', Eberhard, p. 64

p. 140 'I'm awfully tired…', Ebert, op. cit., p. 43

p. 141 'On 11 November, I participated…', Kirstein, *Rekonstruktion eines 'Tages-Buch': Die 295. Infanterie-Division von 1940 bis 1945*, p. 902–3

p. 142 'The balance in the…', Rettenmaier, *Alte Kameraden* 1/1954, p. 4

p. 143 'The attack of 305. and…', 11.11.1942, 6. Armee, NARA T-312, Roll 1453, p. 1396

p. 143 The new forward line…, ibid., p. 1406

p. 143 'In courageous and…', 'Korpsbefehl Nr. 111', 79.Inf.Div., NARA T-315, Roll 1108, p. 67

p. 143 'The attack will…', ibid.

p. 144 Casualties of Pi.Btl.162, 6. Armee, NARA T-312, Roll 1453, p. 1428

p. 144 Prisoners and booty taken by LI. Armeekorps, ibid.

p. 144 'Losses inflicted on…', 138 str.div., 'Combat Report No. 195', TsAMO, p. 162

p. 144 Casualties of 305. and 389.Inf.Div., 6. Armee, NARA T-312, Roll 1453, p. 1417

p. 144 Casualties of the pioneer battalions, ibid., p. 1428-9

p. 145 Casualties of 344th Rifle Regiment, 344 str.polk, TsAMO, p. 62

p. 145 Casualties of 650th Rifle Regiment, 650 str.polk zhurnal, TsAMO, p. 29

p. 145 Casualties of 138th Rifle Division, 138 str.div., 'Combat Report No. 195', TsAMO, p. 163

p. 145 138th RD Combat and numerical strength, ibid.

p. 145 138th RD armaments, ibid.

p. 146 Gorishny requests artillery fire, 95 str.div., 'Combat Report No. 41', TsAMO, p. 150

p. 146 '1. Prevent the expansion…', ibid.

p. 146 241RR launches a small attack, ibid.

p. 146 'A medic silently…', Krauss, p. 9

p. 146 'Whether by chance…', Grimm, p. 6

p. 146 'When the fire died…', Schüddekopf, op. cit., p. 118-20

p. 147 'At midnight, we gathered…', Lyudnikov, *Ognenniy Ostrov*, p. 119

p. 147 'At 0400, following a strong…', 138 str.div., 'Combat Report No. 195', TsAMO, p. 161

p. 147 'The division bravely…', Lyudnikov, *Ognenniy Ostrov*, p. 119

p. 148 German report on Soviet air activity, 6. Armee, NARA T-312, Roll 1453, p. 1440

p. 148 Capture of Haus 80, ibid., p. 1428

p. 148 night fighting near the fuel tanks, 95 str.div., 'Combat Report No. 42', TsAMO, p. 154

p. 148 marines of 3/92RB arrive, 95 str.div., 'Combat Report No. 45', TsAMO, p. 162

p. 148 'enemy assault on the…', 6. Armee, NARA T-312, Roll 1453, p. 1428

p. 148 'Parts of the Gorishny…', Krylow, op. cit., p. 326

p. 148 Zuyev captures the fuel tanks, 95 str.div., 'Combat Report No. 45', TsAMO, p. 162

p. 149 German counterattacks, 95 str.div., 'Combat Report No. 43', TsAMO, p. 156

p. 149 Shport's small group from 3/92RB, 95 str.div., 'Combat Report No. 45', TsAMO, p. 162

p. 149 'German soldiers, drunk or…', Chuikov, *The Beginning of the Road*, p. 210

p. 150 Story of Dmitriev, Koroleva, 'Neizvestny podvig', http://www.goldring.ru/podrobno.php?id_rub=5020&id_Art=5505&day=31&month=1&year=2003

p. 150 '95th Rifle Division, having…', 62-armii, boevoy zhurnal (62nd Army combat journal), TsAMO, p. 253

p. 150 strengths of 95RD's units, 95 str.div., 'Combat Report No. 45', TsAMO, p. 162

p. 150 'The pioneers felt at…', Linden monograph, p. 12

p. 151 'To achieve quick…', ibid., p. 13

p. 151   'On their first day of…', 6. Armee, NARA T-312, Roll 1454, p. 71

p. 151   'The attack will be…', 12.11.1942, 'Zusatz zum Korpsbefehl Nr. 111', 79.Inf.Div., NARA T-315, Roll 1108, p. 68-69

p. 152   'Continuation of the…', 6. Armee, NARA T-312, Roll 1453, p. 1428

p. 152   'Another large-scale…', Linden monograph, p. 14

p. 153   'clearance of the…', 6. Armee, NARA T-312, Roll 1453, p. 1428

p. 153   The story of Rolik, Glukhovsky, op. cit., p. 37-38; Venkov & Dudinov, op. cit., p. 50-51; and Lyudnikov, *Ognenniy Ostrov*, p. 131-3

p. 154   'cleaning actions in…', 6. Armee, NARA T-312, Roll 1453, p. 1443

p. 155   Leutnant Zorn's actions, Zorn Tagebuchnotizen; letter from Zorn to Pi.Btl.305, 19.2.1943

p. 155   Casualties of 1./Pi.Btl.305, ibid.

p. 155   Death of Bergemann, 2./Pi.Btl.294, DD/WASt, 'Pi. Btl.294 Namentliche Verlustmeldung', 12.2.1945; Verlustkarte, NARA T-78, Roll 951

p. 155n Deaths of Pohl and Schindler, and Claus, Lehmert, Leunert and Otto declared MIA 2./Pi.Btl.294, DD/ WASt, 'Pi.Btl.294 Namentliche Verlustmeldung Nr. 11, 12 & 15', 7.7.1944

p. 155n Deaths of Bauer, Hentzschel, Lindner, Lowin and Paula, and Zeun declared MIA 3./Pi.Btl.294, DD/WASt, 'Pi. Btl.294 Namentliche Verlustmeldung Nr. 16, 17, 18 & 22', 6.7.1944

p. 155   'A very effective…', 6. Armee, NARA T-312, Roll 1453, p. 1426

p. 156   'After the attacks in…', ibid., p. 1443

p. 156   Prisoners taken by LI. Armeekorps, 6. Armee, NARA T-312, Roll 1454, p. 49

p. 156   A riflemen from 241st Rifle Regiment, ibid., p. 59

p. 156   A soldier from 650th Rifle Regiment, ibid.

p. 156   A soldier from 768th Rifle Regiment, p. 96.

p. 157   'In the evening, Captain…', Lyudnikov, in *The Road of Battle and Glory*, p. 119-20

p. 157   'Documents from dead…', 62-armii zhurnal, TsAMO, p. 253

p. 157   Casualties of 138th Rifle Division, 138 str.div., 'Combat Report No. 189', TsAMO, p. 174

p. 157   Casualties of 305. Inf.Div., 6. Armee, NARA T-312, Roll 1454, p. 11

p. 157   'On 12 November […] holding…', Krylow, op. cit., p. 327-8

p. 157   '12 November. After the…', 138 str.div. zhurnal, TsAMO, p. 25

p. 158   'We had to find…', Chuikov, op. cit., p. 215

p. 158   'The composite regiment of…', 62-armii zhurnal, TsAMO, p. 252b

p. 158   'For the liquidation…', 685 str.polk boevoy zhurnal (685th Rifle Regiment combat journal), TsAMO, p. 8

p. 158   'With this composite…', Chuikov, op. cit., p. 215

p. 158   'Towards the end of…', Krylow, op. cit., p. 328

Chapter 5:

p. 159   'Having reached the…', 685 str.polk zhurnal, TsAMO, p. 9

p. 159   'the fighting continued…', Wiesen, op. cit., p. 98

p. 159   The attack objective remained…, Rettenmaier, *Alte Kameraden* 1/1954, p. 4

p. 159   'There were isolated ruins…', Linden monograph, p. 15

p. 160   even issued Stalin's…, 138 str.div. zhurnal, TsAMO, p. 25

p. 161   The death of Kretz…, Rettenmaier, *Alte Kameraden* 1/1954, p. 4

p. 161   'The enemy went…', 650 str.polk zhurnal, TsAMO, p. 30

p. 161   'Command posts and…', Gorbatenko, report, 6.12.1972, p. 6

p. 161   'In the morning, chemical…', ibid.

p. 162   Story of Charashvili, Charashvili, report, 18.2.1972

p. 162   'Around 4-5 November…', ibid., p. 3-4

p. 163   The German attack on Lyudnikov's HQ, 138 str.div., 'Combat Report No. 190', TsAMO, p. 175; Lyudnikov, *Ognenniy Ostrov*, p. 120-1; Venkov & Dudinov, op. cit., p. 45; and 'Grichina, Vladimir Ivanovich' in *Soldat XX veka*, p. 277

p. 163   Bestowal of Red Star and 'For Bravery' medals, TsAMO 138 krasnoznamennoi strelkovoi divizii, November 1942, TsAMO

p. 164   'It started to get…', Gorbatenko, p. 6

p. 164   'On my command…', Charashvili, report, 18.2.1972, p. 4-5

p. 164   'In the early morning…', Piven, p. 2

p. 164   'The group of…', 138 str.div., 'Combat Report No. 190', TsAMO, p. 175

p. 165n Deaths of Böhm, Bulenda, Grauer, Hackerschmied, Hoffmann, Irrgang, Kattelans, Kirsch, Schmude and Nowak, 3./Pi.Btl.162, DD/WASt, '3./Pi.Btl.162 Namentliche Verlustmeldung Nr. 1 & 1a', 18.6.1943

p. 165   Statements of German prisoners…, 138 str.div., 'Combat Report No. 190', TsAMO, p. 175

p. 165   'After a few hours…', Charashvili, p. 5-6

p. 165   Haus 79 was almost going…, Rettenmaier, *Alte Kameraden* 1/1954, p. 4

p. 166   650RR only had 90 men, 138 str.div., 'Combat Report No. 189', TsAMO, p. 174

p. 166   6 dead and 3 wounded from 3./Pi.Btl.336, 11.11.1942, DD/WASt, 'Pi.Btl.336 Namentliche Verlustmeldung Nr. 4', 16.4.1943

p. 166   German attack along Prospekt Lenina, Venkov & Dudinov, op. cit., p. 44-5; 'Combat Report No. 190', p. 175

p. 166   Bechaykin's mortarmen, 344 str.polk, 'Combat Report No. 51', TsAMO, p. 63

p. 166   They killed ten…, Venkov & Dudinov, op. cit., p. 45

p. 166   Captured 4 light and 1 heavy…, 344 str.polk, 'Combat Report No. 51', TsAMO, p. 63

p. 167   'By the end of the day…', 138 str.div., 'Combat Report No. 190', TsAMO, p. 176

p. 167   'At 0415, an enemy…', 344 str.polk., 'Combat Report No. 51', TsAMO, p. 63

p. 167   10 dead and 11 wounded from 3./Pi.Btl.336, 13.11.1942, DD/WASt, 'Pi.Btl.336 Namentliche Verlustmeldung Nr. 4', 16.4.1943

p. 168   'The resistance of the…', Rettenmaier, *Alte Kameraden* 1/1954, p. 4-5

p. 168   'succeeded by approaching…', Linden monograph, p. 15

p. 168   'From the squad that…', Rettenmaier, *Alte Kameraden* 1/1954, p. 5

p. 169   'an enemy attack of…', 79.Inf.Div., NARA T-315, Roll 1107, p. 936

p. 169   'On the sector being…', 95 str.div., 'Combat Report No. 46', TsAMO, p. 164

p. 169   'By 0900 on 13.11.42…', 685 str.polk zhurnal, TsAMO, p. 9

p. 169   'The composite regiment of…', 62-armii zhurnal, TsAMO, p. 258

p. 169   'the focal point of…', 79.Inf.Div., NARA T-312, Roll 1107, p. 936

p. 169   'Ferry traffic on…', 79.Inf.Div., NARA T-315, Roll 1108, p. 1006

p. 170   'The composite regiment of…', 95 str.div., 'Combat Report No. 47', TsAMO, p. 166

p. 170   'All attempts by the…', 62-armii zhurnal, TsAMO, p. 258

p. 170   losses of 95RD's units, 95 str.div., 'Combat Report No. 46', TsAMO, p. 164

p. 170   Pioneers were equipped with guides…, Rettenmaier, *Alte Kameraden* 1/1954, p. 4

p. 171   'Prior to the war…', Ovchinnikova, *Peredovaya nachinalas v tsekhe*, p. 154

p. 171   Construction and history of the Kommissarhaus, *Barrikadtsy: kniga pervaya*, p. 22-23; Ovchinnikova, op. cit., p. 154; and personal observations by Evgeny Kulichenko

p. 171   Underground tunnel in the Kommissarhaus, Nikolai Dontsov interview by Evgeny Kulichenko, 23.5.2003

p. 172   'At the beginning…', Ovchinnikova, op. cit., p. 154

p. 173   'The Germans stormed…', ibid., p. 154-5

p. 173   Ten German tanks thrown in…, 138 str.div., 'Combat Report No. 190', TsAMO, p. 175

p. 173   Top floor destroyed and garrison obliterated…, ibid., p. 175-6

p. 173   'A large-scale attack…', Linden monograph, p. 14

p. 173   Pioneers formed up outside the portico…, Pz.Pi.Btl.50 veteran (anonymous), letters to the author, 4.3.2004 and 8.7.2004

p. 174   Directly opposite was a thick…, ibid.

p. 174   The German plan was simple…, ibid.

p. 175   'Hitlerite submachine-gunners…', Ovchinnikova, op. cit., p. 155-6

p. 175   Using hollow charges…, Pz.Pi.Btl.50 veteran (anonymous), letter to the author, 4.3.2004 and 8.7.2004

p. 175   'the enemy has blown up…', 138 str.div., 'Combat Report No. 190', TsAMO, p. 176

p. 176   Mortarmen request artillery fire upon themselves, Lyudnikov, *Ognenniy Ostrov*, p. 121-2

p. 176   Satchel charges were crammed…, Pz.Pi.Btl.50 veteran (anonymous), letter to the author

p. 176   Use of petrol and explosives…, Rettenmaier, *Alte Kameraden* 1/1954, p. 4

p. 176   'The fascists then used…', Ovchinnikova, op. cit., p. 156

p. 177   'Something special that…', Senchkovsky, p. 2

p. 177   'Only in the evening…', Rettenmaier, *Alte Kameraden* 1/1954, p. 4

p. 177   Casualties of 80 men…, 6. Armee, NARA T-312, Roll 1454, p. 83

p. 177   Death of Bunte, 3./Pz.Pi.Btl.50, DD/WASt, 'Pz.Pi.Btl.50 Namentliche Verlustmeldung Nr. 8', 12.6.1944

p. 177   Death of Palmowski, 3./Pz.Pi.Btl.50, DD/WASt, 'Pz.Pi.Btl.50 Namentliche Verlustmeldung Nr. 3', 9.11.1943

p. 177   Death of Paelchen, 2./Pz.Pi.Btl.50, DD/WASt, 'Pz.Pi.Btl.50 Namentliche Verlustmeldung Nr. 8', 12.6.1944

p. 177   Death of Willmitzer, 11./Gr.Rgt.131, DD/WASt, 'Verlustmeldung', 13.7.1943

p. 177   'strengthened by units from…', 138 str.div., 'Combat Report No. 190', TsAMO, p. 175

p. 177   'Stormtroops of 305. Infanterie…', 6. Armee, NARA T-312, Roll 1454, p. 49

p. 177   lost 55 of its 90 men…, 138 str.div., 'Combat Report No. 190', TsAMO, p. 176

p. 178   Fresh attack by 200 Soviets…, 79.Inf.Div., NARA T-315, Roll 1108, p. 1006

p. 178   'In one of the dug-outs…', Popov, Kozlov & Usik, *Perelom*, p. 289-92

p. 179   Pi.Btl.162 relaunched its attack…, von Aaken, op. cit., p. 117; and 6. Armee, NARA T-312, Roll 1454, p. 56

p. 179   'In addition to two…', ibid.

p. 179   Prisoners taken by LI. Armeekorps, ibid., p. 89

p. 179   'clear out the conquered…', ibid., p. 53

p. 179   'fighting with grenades…', 138 str.div. zhurnal, TsAMO, p. 29

p. 179   'During the course of…', 138 str.div., 'Combat Report No. 190', TsAMO, p. 176

p. 180   allocate up to 35% of…, 138 str.div. zhurnal, TsAMO, p. 29

p. 180   Two tugboats, 'Emelyan Pugachen'…, Plekhov, Khvatov & Zakharov, *V ogne stalingradskikh pereprav*, p. 197

p. 180   Losses inflicted on the Germans…, 138 str.div., 'Combat Report No. 190', TsAMO, p. 176

p. 180   Casualties of 138th Rifle Division, ibid.

p. 180   Combat strength of 138th Rifle Division, ibid.

p. 181   'The panzer company of…', 1840 hours, 79.Inf.Div., NARA T-315, Roll 1108, p. 70

p. 181   'The panzer company of…', 2135 hours, ibid., p. 658

p. 181   'Our brief detachment…', Bauchspiess, Feldpostbrief 13.11.1942

p. 181   Story of Gefreiter Wilhelm Giebeler, Craig, op. cit., p. 162-3

p. 181   Casualties of 138th Rifle Division, 138 str.div., 'Combat Report No. 190', TsAMO, p. 176

p. 181   Casualties of 305. and 389.Inf.Div., 6. Armee, NARA T-312, Roll 1454, p. 83

p. 182   'On the morning of…', von Aaken, op. cit., p. 117

p. 182   'The enemy, having broken…', 62-armii zhurnal, TsAMO, p. 258b

p. 182   Fugenfirov's 1011th Artillery Regiment…, Krylow, op. cit., p. 312

p. 182   'Initially, it was still…', Krylow, ibid., p. 325

p. 183   '95th Rifle Division, with 3/92nd…', 62-armii zhurnal, TsAMO, p. 259

p. 183   'By the morning of 14.11.42…', 685 str.polk zhurnal, TsAMO, p. 9

p. 183   Bombardment of Pechenyuk's CP, 650 str.polk zhurnal, TsAMO, p. 31

p. 183   German attack from Halls 3 and 4 , 344 str.polk, 'Combat Report No. 54', TsAMO, p. 64

p. 184   Dom 37 defended by remnants…, 650 str.polk zhurnal, TsAMO, p. 31

p. 184   'the enemy undertook…', 138 str.div. zhurnal, TsAMO, p. 27

p. 185   Next assault began at 1100…, 344 str.polk, 'Combat Report No. 54', TsAMO, p. 64

p. 185   employed 150 men…, ibid.

p. 185   garrison of Dom 38 wiped out…, ibid.

p. 185   Pogrebnyak managed to survive…, 15.12.1942, 344 str.polk, 'Combat Report No. 108', TsAMO, p. 92

p. 185   'At 1030 Dom 38 was…', Venkov & Dudinov, op. cit., p. 45

p. 185   305.I.D. breaks into Haus 67 and 74…, 6. Armee, NARA T-312, Roll 1454, p. 89

p. 185   Tolkachev's 1st Rifle Battalion, Venkov & Dudinov, op. cit., p. 45-6

p. 186   Effective use of two and…, Pi.Btl.336 veteran (anonymous), letter to the author, 25.2.2005

p. 186   Recapture of Dom 37, 650 str.polk zhurnal, TsAMO, p. 31; and 344 str.polk, 'Combat Report No. 54', TsAMO, p. 64

p. 186   Recapture of Dom 38, 344 str.polk, 'Combat Report No. 54', TsAMO, p. 64

p. 186   artillerymen firing 200 rounds…, 138 str.div. zhurnal, TsAMO, p. 28

p. 186   'excellent use of mines…', 138 str.div., 'Combat Report No. 191', TsAMO, p. 178

p. 186   Awards for Tolkachev's 1st Rifle Battalion, Venkov & Dudinov, op. cit., p. 46

p. 186   'in the face of…', 6. Armee, NARA T-312, Roll 1454, p. 89

p. 186   Konovalenko's men captured…, 344 str.polk, 'Combat Report No. 54', TsAMO, p. 64

p. 186n 2 dead and 8 wounded from 3./Pi.Btl.336, 13.11.1942, DD/WASt, 'Pi.Btl.336 Namentliche Verlustmeldung Nr. 4', 16.4.1943

p. 186n Wounding of Hullen, 1./Pi.Btl.336, 'Soldbuch of Karl-Heinz Hullen', BA-MA PA-6554

p. 186n Ehringhaus takes command of 1./Pi.Btl.336, 336.Inf. Div., NARA T-315, Roll 2093, p. 547

p. 187   Wounding of Kindler, 2./Gr.Rgt.132, DD/WASt, letter to the author, 16.6.2005, p. 2

p. 187   'On the day of my…', von Wartburg, letters to the author, 19.5.2004, 7.8.2004 and 13.2.2005

p. 187   Casualties of 138th Rifle Division, 138 str.div., 'Combat Report No. 191', TsAMO, p. 178

p. 187   344 RR lost 1 heavy MG…, 344 str.polk, 'Combat Report No. 54', TsAMO, p. 64

p. 187   Active soldiers in rifle regiments, 138 str.div., 'Combat Report No. 191', TsAMO, p. 178

p. 187   At 1600, the Germans started…, 650 str.polk zhurnal, TsAMO, p. 31

p. 187   Pechenyuk's observers saw…, ibid.

p. 187   'At the moment, an…', 6. Armee, NARA T-312, Roll 1454, p. 89

p. 187   'In all these grim…', Lyudnikov, in *The Road of Battle and Glory*, p. 112-14

p. 188   Starenky farm and two batteries…, Venkov & Dudinov, op. cit., p. 46

p. 188   Bestowal of Red Star and 'For Bravery' medals, 138 str.div., TsAMO, November 1942

p. 188   'Located in the positions…', Krylow, op. cit., p. 326

p. 188   Stepanov's Red Star, 138 str.div., TsAMO, November 1942

p. 189   'The enemy moved closer…', Volostnov, op. cit., p. 189

p. 189   'During the night of…', Volostnov, ibid.

p. 189   'Colonel Lyudnikov was…', Krylow, op. cit., p. 326

p. 189   'The stormtroop operations…', 6. Armee, NARA T-312, Roll 1454, p. 94

p. 189   enough cartridges and grenades…, 344 str.polk, 'Combat Report No. 54', TsAMO, p. 64

p. 189   'In front of me lies…', Krylow, op. cit., p. 328-9

p. 190   'Considering that the…', 138 str.div. zhurnal, TsAMO, p. 28-9

p. 190   'The kilo package with…', Füssinger, Feldpostbrief 14.11.1942

p. 191   'Early today, after four…', Traub, Feldpostbrief 14.11.1942

p. 192   Prisoners taken by LI. Armeekorps, 6. Armee, NARA T-312, Roll 1454, p. 111

p. 192   Casualties of 138th Rifle Division, 138 str.div., 'Combat Report No. 191', TsAMO, p. 178

p. 192   Casualties of 305. and 389.Inf.Div., 6. Armee, NARA T-312, Roll 1454, p. 106

p. 192   'Today, the many…', Traub, Feldpostbrief 15.11.1942

p. 193   'After a short artillery…', 650 str.polk zhurnal, TsAMO, p. 32

p. 193   'In the morning the…', Charashvili, p. 6

p. 193   Initial penetration of Haus 81…, Rettenmaier, *Alte Kameraden* 1/1954, p. 5

p. 193   'A further surprise…', Rettenmaier, report to Siegbert

p. 194   'the enemy is employing…', 650 str.polk zhurnal, TsAMO, p. 31

p. 194   'it was necessary…', 'Zdes nasmert stoyali voiny legendarnoi 62-i armii', 1.10.2002 in http://www.novocherkassk.ru/cgi-bin/Newspap/np2.cgi?y=2002&i=2&n=40&k=10

p. 194   'The entire day had…', Rettenmaier, *Alte Kameraden* 1/1954, p. 5

p. 194   Deaths of Friedrichs, Griep and Peters, 2./Pz.Pi.Btl.50, DD/WASt, 'Pz.Pi.Btl.50 Namentliche Verlustmeldung Nr. 5', 29.2.1944

p. 194   Deaths of Brauns and Steinl, 2./Pz.Pi.Btl.50, DD/WASt, 'Pz.Pi.Btl.50 Namentliche Verlustmeldung Nr. 1 & 9, 13.7.1944

p. 194   Deaths of Ehlers and Engel, 3./Pz.Pi.Btl.50, DD/WASt, 'Pz.Pi.Btl.50 Namentliche Verlustmeldung Nr. 3 & 123', 22.8.1944

p. 194   Strength report for Stug.Abt.244, 15.11.1942, 6. Armee, NARA T-312, Roll 1454, p. 106

p. 195   'battered down', ibid., p. 113

p. 195   'Beyersdorff is now in…', Ebert, op. cit., p. 58

p. 196   Total losses of 389.Inf.Div., 6. Armee, NARA T-312, Roll 1454, p. 135

p. 196n Casualties of Pi.Btl.45, DD/WASt, individual Verlustmeldungen of Fässer, Mathieu, Rittenbacher, Sachse, Waldenmaier and Zipf (1./Pi.Btl.45); Nickel and Fischer (2./Pi.Btl.45); Böhm, Kohn and Schärr (3./Pi.Btl.45)

p. 196n Wounding of Kimmich, 1./Pi.Btl.45, NARA Personalakten für Manfred Kimmich

p. 196   Strength report for Stug.Abt.244, 16.11.1942, 6. Armee, NARA T-312, Roll 1454, p. 145

p. 196   Strength report for Stug.Abt.244, 19.11.1942, ibid., p. 243

p. 197   'Oblt. Hullen, 1. Kp…', 336.Inf.Div., NARA T-315, Roll 2093, p. 547

p. 197   'The battle for the…', Gorbatenko, p. 6-7

p. 197   'I know you have…', Rettenmaier, Feldpostbrief 15.11.1942

p. 197   Pechenyuk requests artillery…, 650 str.polk zhurnal, TsAMO, p. 32

p. 197   'In the fighting around…', 6. Armee, NARA T-312, Roll 1454, p. 111

p. 198   'In Stalingrad, storm groups…', ibid., p. 115

p. 198   'In Stalingrad, our stormtroop…', ibid., p. 113

p. 198   'In the evening,. our…', Gorbatenko, p. 7

p. 198   'The last defensive…', Dubov, report, 27.1.1978, p. 6

p. 199   Junior-Lieutenant Kalinin, Lyudnikov, *Ognenniy Ostrov*, p. 123

p. 199   Losses were 64 killed…, 138 str.div., 'Combat Report No. 192', TsAMO, p. 180

p. 199   'During the day…', ibid.

p. 199   'The enemy has been…', 138 str.div. zhurnal, TsAMO, p. 30

p. 199   Combat structure of 138th Rifle Division, 138 str.div., 'Combat Report No. 192', TsAMO, p. 180

p. 199 'Designate the front-line…', Glukhovsky, op. cit., p. 30

p. 199 'Attempts were made…', Lyudnikov, in *The Road of Battle and Glory*, p. 115-16

p. 199 'most of these bags…', ibid.

p. 200 'Our PO-2 aircraft…', Tyupa, report, 8.12.1972, p. 7

p. 200 'We experienced a…', Rettenmaier, *Alte Kameraden* 1/1954, p. 5

p. 200 'Hey, Lyudnikov's Island!…', Glukhovsky, op. cit., p. 30

p. 200 'At 1300 or 1400, in…', Charashvili, p. 6-7

p. 200 'from the officer ranks…', ibid., p. 7

p. 201 'in the afternoon…', 6. Armee, NARA T-312, Roll 1454, p. 117

p. 201 'At 1130, after half…', 62-armii zhurnal, TsAMO, p. 260

p. 201 'At 1130 on 15.11.42…', 685 str.polk zhurnal, TsAMO, p. 9-10

p. 201 'The enemy, having pressed…', ibid., p. 10-11

p. 202 'The position on the…', 62-armii zhurnal, TsAMO, p. 260

p. 202 'Night actions by units…', ibid.

p. 202 'It is reputed…', 16. Armee, NARA T-312, Roll 1454, p. 122

p. 203 '6. Armee will have…', ibid., p. 183

p. 203 Story of Kompanie Abendroth, Jaugitz, *Funklenkpanzer*, p. 104-114

p. 204 'Hitler climbed out…', ibid., p. 105

p. 204 '16 November 1942: The entire…', ibid., p. 113

p. 204 'We celebrate, we're…', ibid.

p. 205 'We are all disappointed…', ibid.

p. 205 'Stug.Abt.244 with s.I.G.…', 'Korpsbefehl Nr. 113', 79.Inf.Div., NARA T-315, Roll 1108, p. 73

p. 206 'At the end of November.…', 6. Armee, NARA T-312, Roll 1454, p. 116

p. 206 Weimann teletype message to 294.I.D., 294.Inf.Div., NARA T-315, Roll 1941, p. 1078

p. 206 'With storm groups, 305…', 6. Armee, NARA T-312, Roll 1454, p. 117

p. 206 Prisoners taken by LI. Armeekorps, ibid., p. 153

p. 207 'Of 15 supply parachutes…', ibid., p. 160

p. 207 'the help rendered…', 138 str.div., 'Combat Report No. 193', TsAMO, p. 181

p. 207 Casualties of 138th Rifle Division, 138 str.div., 'Combat Report No. 192', TsAMO, p. 180

p. 207 Casualties of 305. and 389.Inf.Div., 6. Armee, NARA T-312, Roll 1454, p. 135

p. 207 'the enemy east of…', ibid.

p. 207 'from 0130, the enemy…', 650 str.polk zhurnal, TsAMO, p. 32

p. 207 'the enemy continued to…', 138 str.div., 'Combat Report No. 193', TsAMO, p. 181

p. 207 Right wing of 305.ID, 6. Armee, NARA T-312, Roll 1454, p. 153

p. 207 captured one Soviet officer…, ibid.

p. 207 renewed attacks at 0900 and 1100…, ibid.

p. 207 '1115 hours: Everything quiet…', 79ID, NARA T-315, Roll 1107, p. 940

p. 207 Artillerie-Regiment 179 also…', ibid.

p. 207 'At midday, the enemy…', 79ID, NARA T-315, Roll 1108, p. 121

p. 208 'On the south front…', NARA T-312, Roll 1454, p. 182

p. 208 'From the line of…', 685 str.polk zhurnal, TsAMO, p. 10

p. 208 'Units of 95th Rifle…', 62-armii zhurnal, TsAMO, p. 262

p. 208 Wounding of Hering, Frau Hering, letter, 20.12.1942

p. 208 'He did not go…', ibid.

p. 208 Block the Volga shoreline with mines, 6. Armee, NARA T-312, Roll 1454, p. 158

p. 208 Death of Kochanek and Hönicke declared MIA, 2./ Pi.Btl.294, DD/WASt, 'Pi.Btl.294 Namentliche Verlustmeldung Nr. 12 & 14', 6.7.1944

p. 208 Günther declared MIA, 3./Pi.Btl.294, DD/WASt, 'Pi. Btl.294 Namentliche Verlustmeldung Nr. 17', 1.4.1944

p. 209 Gr.Rgt.576 sector handover to Gruppe Seydel, 79ID, NARA T-315, Roll 1108, p. 75

p. 209 1210 attack against 650RR, 650 str.polk zhurnal, TsAMO, p. 32

p. 209 Held position in Dom 37, ibid., p. 33

p. 209 Death of Richter and wounding of Knödel, 2./ Pi.Btl.336, DD/WASt, 'Pi.Btl.336 Namentliche Verlustmeldung Nr. 4', 16.4.1943

p. 209 Death of Rubel and wounding of Claus, 3./Pi.Btl.336, DD/WASt, 'Pi.Btl.336 Namentliche Verlustmeldung Nr. 4', 16.4.1943

p. 209 deep grumbling of engines, 650 str.polk zhurnal, TsAMO, p. 32

p. 209 'the enemy continues to…', 138 str.div. zhurnal, TsAMO, p. 30

p. 209 Small groups of German infiltrators…, 138 str.div., 'Combat Report No. 193', TsAMO, p. 181

p. 210 The story of Rolik, Glukhovsky, op. cit., p. 37-38; Venkov & Dudinov, op. cit., p. 50-51; and Lyudnikov, *Ognenniy Ostrov*, p. 131-3

p. 210 'In mid-November, our group…', Klyukin, 'Na 'ostrove Lyudnikova'', in *Bitva za Stalingrad*, p. 578-9

p. 211 'We held on to the…', Tyupa, p. 7

p. 211 'In the evening […]…', Gorbatenko, p. 7

p. 211 'I am healthy and…', Wiesen, op. cit., p. 102-3

p. 212 25 grams of bread…, 138 str.div. zhurnal, TsAMO, p. 30

p. 212 two of 18 fishing boats…, Glukhovsky, op. cit., p. 31

p. 212 Story of Lyudnikov's annoyance and vision…', ibid., p. 31-3

p. 213 Total of 800 men…, 138 str.div., 'Combat Report No. 193', TsAMO, p. 181

p. 213 Batulin and Petukhov, Venkov & Dudinov, op. cit., p. 48-9

p. 214 Story of Petukhov's and Zuyev's icy trip…, Glukhovsky, op. cit., p. 44

p. 214n one rowboat with 20 men…, 6. Armee, NARA T-312, Roll 1454, p. 158

p. 214 Commander of 107th SPB summoned, Glukhovsky, op. cit., p. 44

p. 214 'This is Politruk Zuyev…', ibid.

p. 214 'I am afraid…' Venkov & Dudinov, op. cit., p. 49

p. 215 'For several days before…', Chuikov, op. cit., p. 208-09

p. 215 'We had the task…', ibid., p. 215-16

p. 215 special armoured posts, Mereshko, interview with Mike Jones

p. 215 Of the 13 parcels dropped…, 138 str.div., 'Combat Report No. 193', TsAMO, p. 181; and 138 str.div. zhurnal, TsAMO, p. 31

p. 215 Prisoners taken by LI. Armeekorps, 6. Armee, NARA T-312, Roll 1454, p. 196

p. 215 Casualties of 138th Rifle Division, 138 str.div., 'Combat Report No. 193', TsAMO, p. 181

p. 215 Casualties of 305. and 389.Inf.Div., 6. Armee, NARA T-312, Roll 1454, p. 186

p. 216 artillery harassment fire…', 79ID, NARA T-315, Roll 1108, p. 1022 & 1023

p. 216 'The enemy throughout…', 650 str.polk zhurnal, TsAMO, p. 33

p. 216 'The army demands the…', 6. Armee, NARA T-312, Roll 1454, p. 164

p. 216 'Deployed in the…', ibid., p. 193

p. 216 'At the moment I am…', Rettenmaier, Feldpostbrief 18.11.1942

p. 217 'We received reserve…', Zrenner, interview with Dr. Manfred Oldenburg, 2002

p. 217 'I'm as fit as a…', Moosmann, *Chronik der im Zweiten Weltkrieg gefallenen und vermissten Soldaten der Gemeinde Bodnegg, 1939-1945*, p. 136

p. 217 'The following Führer…', Ziemke & Bauer, *Moscow to Stalingrad: Decision in the East*, p. 468; and 79ID, NARA T-315, Roll 1108, p. 80

p. 218 'I beg to report…', Ziemke & Bauer, op. cit., p. 468

p. 218 'I am confident…', 79ID, NARA T-315, Roll 1108, p. 80

p. 218 'After all our efforts…', von Seydlitz, *Stalingrad: Konflikt und Konsequenz*, p. 167

p. 218 Order No. 220, 17.11.1942, 62-armii zhurnal, TsAMO, p. 262b

p. 218 Foggy conditions, 6. Armee, NARA T-312, Roll 1454, p. 197

p. 218 Soviet artillery and katyusha timings, 62-armii zhurnal, TsAMO, p. 262b

p. 218 barrage on Gr.Rgt.576 and Gruppe Seydel, 79ID, NARA T-315, Roll 1108, p. 1023

p. 218 'assembly positions and…', ibid.

p. 219 stretched from the left wing…', 6. Armee, NARA T-312, Roll 1454, p. 197

p. 219 katyusha salvoes into SE section…', 62-armii zhurnal, TsAMO, p. 262b

p. 219 'our own artillery could…', 6. Armee, NARA T-312, Roll 1454, p. 197

p. 220 Gully of Death, 'Ovrag glubokaya balka', *Putevoditel po Volgogradu*, p. 87-9; also http://region34.nm.ru/guide/volgograd/index15.html

p. 220 'The regiment, with its…', 685 str.polk zhurnal, TsAMO, p. 10

p. 221 'At 1200, having gone…', 95 str.div., 'Combat Report No. 51', TsAMO, p. 210

p. 221 'After an artillery…', ibid.

p. 221 'At 1200, after an artillery…', 62-armii zhurnal, TsAMO, p. 263

p. 221 'We held a position…' Müller to Grimm, Feldpostbrief 21.6.1943

p. 222 Death of Huf, 1./Pi.Btl.294, DD/WASt, 'Pi.Btl.294 Namentliche Verlustmeldung Nr. 9', 1.4.1944

p. 222 Basan declared MIA, 2./Pi.Btl.294, DD/WASt, 'Pi.Btl.294 Namentliche Verlustmeldung Nr. 11', 1.4.1944

p. 222 'Bataillon in infantry…', 294.Inf.Div., NARA T-315, Roll 1942, p. 759

p. 222 'We were in a large…', Maier, interview with Agnes Moosmann, 21.12.2005

p. 223 Deaths of Kimmeswenger and Kuhmayer, 11./Inf. Rgt.131, 'Verlusteliste 1939-1945, Inf.Rgt. - Gren. Rgt.131', BA-MA, RH37/7005, p. 46 & 52

p. 223 'Throughout the day…', 138 str.div. zhurnal, TsAMO, p. 31

p. 223 Losses of 3 killed…', 138 str.div., 'Combat Report No. 194', TsAMO, p. 182

p. 223 Combat structure of 138th Rifle Division, ibid.

p. 223 German counterattack, 6. Armee, NARA T-312, Roll 1454, p. 210

p. 223 Rain squalls and ice, ibid., p. 197

p. 223 'Towards midday in Stalingrad…', 6. Armee, NARA T-312, Roll 1454, p. 209

p. 223 Soviet attack relaunched at 1700, ibid., p. 210

p. 223 50 barrages with rocket-launchers, ibid.

p. 224 'lied and cheated…', Löffler Tagebuchnotizen, 16.11.1942

p. 224 Wounding of Löffler, Löffler Tagebuchnotizen; interview with Agnes Moosmann, 8.1.2005

p. 224 'the takeover of the…', 79ID, NARA T-315, Roll 1108, p. 1024

p. 225 captured T-60 and T-70 tanks, Bäuerle, ZDF interview, 2002

p. 225 'I was a G-Schütze…', ibid.

p. 225 'I then went back…', ibid.

p. 226 'If the situation with…', 6. Armee, NARA T-312, Roll 1454, p. 197

p. 226 'the plan is to break…', ibid., p. 210

p. 226 'The enemy continues to…', 138 str.div. zhurnal, TsAMO, p. 31

p. 226 'The position of the…', Lyudnikov, in *The Road of Battle and Glory*, p. 116

p. 226 Numerous Soviet prisoners…', 6. Armee, NARA T-312, Roll 1454, p. 205

p. 226 Lyudnikov's 'mutiny' of wounded men, Glukhovsky, op. cit., p. 41-3

p. 228 No operational sIG33Bs…', 6. Armee, NARA T-312, Roll 1454, p. 204

p. 228 Strength reports for Stug.Abt.244 and 245, 18.11.1942, 6. Armee, NARA T-312, Roll 1454, p. 215

p. 228 Korpsbefehl Nr. 114, 17.11.1942, 79ID, NARA T-315, Roll 1108, p. 78

p. 228 Prisoners taken by LI. Armeekorps, 6. Armee, NARA T-312, Roll 1454, p. 225

p. 228 Casualties of 138th Rifle Division, 138 str.div., 'Combat Report No. 194', TsAMO, p. 182

p. 228 Casualties of 305. and 389.Inf.Div., 6. Armee, NARA T-312, Roll 1454, p. 218

p. 228 At 2330 hours, Gruppe Seydel…', 79ID, NARA T-315, Roll 1108, p. 1028

p. 230 Attempt by 327th Army…', Plekhov, Khvatov & Zakharov, op. cit., p. 203-4

p. 230 Two boats… one was completely smashed…', ibid., p. 204

p. 230 Of the five members…', ibid.

p. 230 Earlier in the day, 107th…', ibid.

Chapter 6:

p. 231 Order No. 085, 18.11.1942, 650 str.polk zhurnal, TsAMO, p. 33

p. 231 'distinguished for…', Lyudnikov, 'There is a Cliff on the Volga', in *Two Hundred Days of Fire*, p. 181

p. 231 'At night, our panzers…', Messerschmidt, report to author, 27.3.2003

p. 232 group of about 100 Germans…', 650 str.polk zhurnal, TsAMO, p. 33

p. 232 At 0420, these groups began…', ibid.

p. 233 'The attacks are helped…', ibid., p. 34

p. 233 'the German attacks are…', 138 str.div. zhurnal, TsAMO, p. 32

p. 233 'A few days ago, we…', Rettenmaier, Feldpostbrief, 20.11.1942

p. 234   'Order No. 085 received…' 650 str.polk zhurnal, TsAMO, p. 33

p. 234   'I was not a member…', Senchkovsky, p. 1

p. 235   general information…, Ishchenko, 'I was in a blocking detachment', *Voyenno-istorichesky zhurnal*, No. 11, November 1988

p. 235   'The enemy throws…', 'Order No. 227', http://www.stalingrad-info.com/order227.htm

p. 236   'Within each army…', ibid.

p. 236   'help and support in…', ibid.

p. 236n 'have the opportunity…', ibid.

p. 236   'In accordance with NKO Order…', 'Memorandum by NKVD STF to UOO NKVD of USSR in regards to activities of blocking detachments of Stalingrad and Don Fronts', 15.10.1942, Tsentralnyi Arkhiv FSB (Central Archive of Federal Security Agency), 14/4/386, p. 22-24; also http://forum.axishistory.com/viewtopic.php?t=31325

p. 237   'On 29 August, the staff…', ibid.

p. 237   'On 14 September, the enemy…', ibid.

p. 237   65% and 70% casualties…, ibid.

p. 237   'We talked about the…', Abdulin, *Red Road from Stalingrad*, p. 31

p. 238   'Cut off from the…', Senchkovsky, p. 2

p. 238   German attacks on the fuel tanks, 95 str.div., 'Combat Report No. 53, TsAMO, p. 188

p. 238   'The enemy only…', 6. Armee, NARA T-312, Roll 1454, p. 216

p. 239   '305.Inf.Div. cleaned…', 6. Armee, NARA T-312, Roll 1454, p. 225

p. 239   '95th Rifle Division…', 62-armii zhurnal, TsAMO, p. 265

p. 239   'Throughout 18.11.42, the…', 685 str.polk zhurnal, TsAMO, p. 10

p. 239   'I want to drop you…', Moosmann, op. cit., p. 138

p. 240   Bödecker and Müller declared MIA, 1./Pi.Btl.294, DD/WASt, 'Pi.Btl.294 Namentliche Verlustmeldung Nr. 5 & 7', 1.4.1944

p. 240   Death of Richter, 2./Pi.Btl.294, DD/WASt, 'Pi.Btl.294 Namentliche Verlustmeldung Nr. 15', 8.7.1944

p. 240   'Due to the heavy…', 294.Inf.Div., NARA T-315, Roll 1941, p. 1080-82

p. 241   'The Russian dug-outs…', Linden monograph, p. 15

p. 241   shifting the front-line 100-150 metres…, 6. Armee, NARA T-312, Roll 1454, p. 237

p. 241   Death of Barth, 1./Pi.Btl.162, DD/WASt, 'Pi.Btl.162 Namentliche Verlustmeldung', 16.5.1944; Familie Barth archives

p. 241   Pechenyuk lost communications…, 650 str.polk zhurnal, TsAMO, p. 34

p. 241   only 4 Soviet defenders…, ibid.

p. 241   left bank artillery ceased firing…, 138 str.div. zhurnal, TsAMO, p. 32

p. 241   650RR estimated 50 German dead…, 650 str.polk zhurnal, TsAMO, p. 34

p. 242   Deaths of Schönherr and Wilhelmy, 1./Pz.Pi.Btl.50, DD/WASt, 'Pz.Pi.Btl.50 Namentliche Verlustmeldung Nr. 5', 29.2.1944

p. 242   Death of Höbel, 2./Pz.Pi.Btl.50, DD/WASt, 'Pz.Pi.Btl.50 Namentliche Verlustmeldung Nr. 5', 29.2.1944

p. 242   Deaths of Behnke and von Kuczkowski, 3./Pz.Pi.Btl.50, DD/WASt, 'Pz.Pi.Btl.50 Namentliche Verlustmeldung Nr. 8', 12.6.1944

p. 242   'Good evening. A few…', Moorkamp, Feldpostbrief 18.11.1942

p. 242   'I am still well…', Rettenmaier, Feldpostbrief 18.11.1942

p. 242   Biographical details of von Grolman, NARA Personalakten für Friedrich von Grolman; Familie von Grolman archives; and Hirst, 'The Cast', in *Three Scenes from Barbarossa*

p. 243   'From the middle of…', Hirst, ibid.

p. 243   '305. Infanterie-Division moved…', 6. Armee, NARA T-312, Roll 1454, p. 237

p. 243   'In the evening, as darkness…', Messerschmidt, report to author, 27.3.2003

p. 244   'A reserve officer, an…', ibid.

p. 244   'Panzer Schwadron Messerschmidt…', 24.Pz.Div., NARA T-315, Roll 804, p. 931

p. 244   'The panzer schwadron…', 'Korpsbefehl Nr. 115', 79ID, NARA T-315, Roll 1108, p. 81-2

p. 244   'Throughout the entire…', 138 str.div. zhurnal, TsAMO, p. 32

p. 244   lost 6 killed…, 138 str.div., 'Combat Report No. 195', TsAMO, p. 183

p. 244   357 wounded men…, 138 str.div., 'Combat Report No. 196', TsAMO, p. 184

p. 244   shockingly low combat strengths…, 138 str.div., 'Combat Report No. 195', TsAMO, p. 183

p. 245   'Pechenyuk entrusted Tolkach…', Gorbatenko, p. 8

p. 245   'Kalinin reported that…', ibid.

p. 245   only received 5 sacks…, 138 str.div., 'Combat Report No. 196', TsAMO, p. 184

p. 245   Prisoners taken by LI. Armeekorps, 6. Armee, NARA T-312, Roll 1454, p. 263

p. 245   Casualties of 138th Rifle Division, 138 str.div., 'Combat Report No. 195', TsAMO, p. 183

p. 245   Casualties of 305. and 389.Inf.Div., 6. Armee, NARA T-312, Roll 1454, p. 243

p. 246   'enemy reconnaissance patrols…', 6. Armee, NARA T-312, Roll 1454, p. 243

p. 246   At 0430, the German attack began…, 138 str.div., 'Combat Report No. 196', TsAMO, p. 184

p. 246   'Rubble and shell craters…', Messerschmidt, report to author, 17.5.2003

p. 246   Report about use of panzers in Stalingrad, 24.Pz.Div., 15.11.1942, NARA T-315, Roll 804, p. 777-80

p. 246   'Not a misuse, but…', Messerschmidt, report to author, 28.4.2003

p. 247   'Terrain difficulties…', 'Report about use of panzers in Stalingrad', ibid.

p. 248   'Spare tracks were…', Messerschmidt, report to author, 17.5.2003

p. 248   'During an attack on…', ibid.

p. 248   'For every day of…', ibid., 9.6.2003

p. 248   'The effect of our…', ibid., 17.5.2003

p. 249   struck 344RR and the right flank…, 138 str.div., 'Combat Report No. 196', TsAMO, p. 184

p. 249   'The pioneers used…', Messerschmidt, interview with author, 11.9.2005

p. 249n 'Foolhardy!', ibid.

p. 249   'our garrison in the…', 138 str.div. zhurnal, TsAMO, p. 33

p. 249   'Fire from tanks and…', 650 str.polk zhurnal, TsAMO, p. 35

p. 249   Details of Soviet attack from Serafimovich bridgehead, Ziemke & Bauer, op. cit., p. 468-71

p. 250   Submachine-gunners and snipers active, 650 str.polk zhurnal, TsAMO, p. 34

p. 250   At 0830, on Pechenyuk's…, ibid.

p. 250 At 1130, the German storm groups…, ibid.

p. 250 An assault gun cautiously…, ibid.

p. 250 A hand grenade exploded not far…', Klyukin, report, 31.1.1978, p. 2

p. 250 Defensive line of 650RR…, 650 str.polk zhurnal, TsAMO, p. 34-5

p. 251 'Fire from tanks and…', ibid., p. 35

p. 251 'the enemy, regardless of…', ibid.

p. 251 'the daily objectives of…', 6. Armee, NARA T-312, Roll 1454, p. 263

p. 251 'In Stalingrad, storm groups…', ibid., p. 268

p. 251 a strength of 60 men…, ibid., p. 263

p. 251 'The decision of the…', Krylow, op. cit., p. 334

p. 251 'As always, we strived…', ibid.

p. 252 'at 1215 hours, the enemy…', 79ID, NARA T-315, Roll 1108, p. 1038

p. 252 Gruppe Seydel's report…, ibid.

p. 252 Deaths of Hellgoth and Schimunek, 2./Pi.Btl.294, DD/WASt, 'Pi.Btl.294 Namentliche Verlustmeldung Nr. 14 & 15', 7.7.1944

p. 252 'At 1230 the regiment again…', 685 str.polk zhurnal, TsAMO, p. 10

p. 252 'After renewed bitter…', Krylow, op. cit., p. 337

p. 252 'Units of 95th Rifle Division…', ibid.

p. 253 'at the moment, the…', 6. Armee, NARA T-312, Roll 1454, p. 263

p. 253 'In the afternoon…', ibid., p. 273

p. 253 'The enemy air force…', 138 str.div. zhurnal, TsAMO, p. 33

p. 253 Death of Szaks, 1./Pi.Btl.336, DD/WASt, 'Pi.Btl.336 Namentliche Verlustmeldung Nr. 6', 16.6.1944

p. 253 Deaths of Philipp and Petermann, and wounding of Quint and Tetzlaff, 2./Pi.Btl.336, DD/WASt, 'Pi.Btl.336 Namentliche Verlustmeldung Nr. 4', 16.4.1943

p. 253 Wounding of Köhler, 3./Pi.Btl.336, ibid.

p. 254 Story of Teichelkamp, OKW, *Geheim-Aktion über Stalingrad*, 13.2.1943, NARA T-77, Roll 1036, p. 6508199

p. 254 'For three days now…', 138 str.div. zhurnal, TsAMO, p. 33

p. 254 'War materials are…', 650 str.polk zhurnal, TsAMO, p. 35

p. 254 24 killed and 28 wounded, 138 str.div., 'Combat Report No. 196', TsAMO, p. 184

p. 254 division's strength return, ibid.

p. 254 '150 metres north…', 138 str.div. zhurnal, TsAMO, p. 32

p. 254 'The regiment, with groups…', 650 str.polk zhurnal, TsAMO, p. 35

p. 255 'Because of restricted…', Bauchspiess, Feldpostbrief 19.11.1942

p. 255 'Early today I returned…', Traub, Feldpostbrief 19.11.1942

p. 255 'Führer presentation about s.I.G.33…', 6. Armee, NARA T-312, Roll 1454, p. 292

p. 256 Wounding of Nippes, Stug.Abt.244, DD/WASt, letter to the author, 16.6.2005, p. 2

p. 256 Gefreiter Teichelkamp learned that…, OKW, *Geheim-Aktion über Stalingrad*, 13.2.1943, NARA T-77, Roll 1036, p. 6508199

p. 256 'The development of the…', Ziemke & Bauer, op. cit., p. 470

p. 256 'Korps must reckon that…', 19.11.1942, 'Korpsbefehl Nr. 116', 79ID, NARA T-315, Roll 1108, p. 84-5

p. 256 'On 20 November, 24. Panzer-Division…', ibid.

p. 257 'The assault actions in…', 6. Armee, NARA T-312, Roll 1454, p. 280

p. 257 'During the night of 19 to…', Messerschmidt, report to author, 27.3.2003

p. 257 towards 1900 hours, a motorboat…, 79ID, NARA T-315, Roll 1108, p. 1039

p. 257 Towards 2000 hours, an enemy…, ibid.

p. 257 Yeremenko order to Rogachev…, Plekhov, Khvatov & Zakharov, op. cit., p. 206

p. 257 Casualties of 138th Rifle Division, 138 str.div., 'Combat Report No. 196', TsAMO, p. 184

p. 258 Details of Soviet attack south of Stalingrad, Ziemke & Bauer, op. cit., p. 470-72; and Beevor, op. cit., p. 250-51

p. 258 'While firmly holding the…', 20.11.1942, 79ID, NARA T-315, Roll 1108, p. 86

p. 259 'in the first half…', 138 str.div. zhurnal, TsAMO, p. 33

p. 259 'The enemy, with up to…', 650 str.polk zhurnal, TsAMO, p. 35

p. 259 In the second half of…, 138 str.div., 'Combat Report No. 197', TsAMO, p. 185

p. 259 up to 50 Germans…, 138 str.div. zhurnal, TsAMO, p. 33

p. 259 'Our defence is especially…', ibid.

p. 259 4 killed and 4 wounded, 138 str.div., 'Combat Report No. 197', TsAMO, p. 185

p. 259 Combat structure, ibid.

p. 259 '95th Rifle Division…', 62-armii zhurnal, TsAMO, p. 272

p. 259 'at 2200, in accordance…', 685 str.polk zhurnal, TsAMO, p. 10

p. 259 95RD's strength figures, 95 str.div., 'Combat Report No. 57', TsAMO, p. 207

p. 260 'I'm sitting here in a…', Moosmann, op. cit., p. 139

p. 260 'First of all many thanks…', Füssinger, Feldpostbrief 20.11.1942

p. 260 'I was not a…', Rettenmaier, Feldpostbrief 20.11.1942

p. 261 'I am well-equipped…', ibid.

p. 261 Wounding of Wroblewski, NARA Personalakten für Walter Wroblewski

p. 261 'After a spin as…', Ebert, op. cit., p. 66

p. 261 Benad from Pi.Btl.294, 294.Inf.Div., NARA T-315, Roll 1941, p. 1090

p. 262 'Strong enemy forces…', 'Korpsbefehl Nr. 117', 79ID, NARA T-315, Roll 1108, p. 214

p. 262 '305. Infanterie-Division will continue…', ibid.

p. 262 'It was only proven…', Krylow, op. cit., p. 340

p. 262 Details of the first supply trip…, Plekhov, Khvatov & Zakharov, op. cit., p. 207

p. 263 When the fleet reached…, ibid.

p. 263 Rettenmaier's two 75mm anti-tank guns, Rettenmaier, *Alte Kameraden* 1/1954, p. 5

p. 264 Death of Gulko, 138 str.div. zhurnal, TsAMO, p. 34; and Glukhovsky, op. cit., p. 46

p. 264 lost 25 men and officers…, Lyudnikov, in *The Road of Battle and Glory*, p. 117

p. 264 'The Germans won't stop us…', Glukhovsky, op. cit., p. 48

p. 264 Only 45 minutes were…', Plekhov, Khvatov & Zakharov, op. cit., p. 207

p. 264 'Our greatest difficulty…, Lyudnikov, in *The Road of Battle and Glory*, p. 117

p. 264 Story of Lt. of Medical Services Ozerova, Venkov & Dudinov, op. cit., p. 51-2

p. 264 At 2120, the armoured boats…, Plekhov, Khvatov & Zakharov, op. cit., p. 207

p. 265 'Kochegar Hetman' hit, Plekhov, ibid.

p. 265 Casualties of 138th Rifle Division, 138 str.div., 'Combat Report No. 197', TsAMO, p. 185

p. 265   At 0100, the takeover of Gruppe Seydel's sector…, 79ID, NARA T-315, Roll 1108, p. 1049

p. 265   At 0430, with the strength…, 138 str.div., 'Combat Report No. 198', TsAMO, p. 186

p. 266   At 0500, the Germans threw…, 650 str.polk zhurnal, TsAMO, p. 36

p. 266   'then tried to seize…', 138 str.div., 'Combat Report No. 198', TsAMO, p. 186

p. 266   group of about 70-80 men…, 650 str.polk zhurnal, TsAMO, p. 36

p. 267   At 0900, the Germans resumed…, 138 str.div., 'Combat Report No. 198', TsAMO, p. 186

p. 267   Only at 1020…, ibid.

p. 267   25 killed and 26 wounded, 138 str.div., 'Combat Report No. 198', TsAMO, p. 186

p. 267   losses inflicted on the Germans, ibid.

p. 267   The combat structure…, ibid.

p. 268   90RR repels Germans, 95 str.div., 'Combat Report No. 58', TsAMO, p. 200

p. 268   'the Gorishny division and…', Krylow, op. cit., p. 340

p. 268   '95th Rifle Division repelled…', 62-armii zhurnal, TsAMO, p. 273

p. 268   'I got in contact…', ibid.

p. 268   Order No. 086…, 650 str.polk zhurnal, TsAMO, p. 36

p. 268   'We had a meeting …', Rettenmaier diary, 21.11.1942

p. 269   Hauptmann Lundt voiced his concerns…, 336.Inf.Div., NARA T-315, Roll 2093, p. 511

p. 269   The tugboat 'Kochegar Hetmann'…, Plekhov, Khvatov & Zakharov, op. cit., p. 208

p. 269   The command of 107th…, ibid., p. 211

p. 269   assembled 23 boats…, Glukhovsky, op. cit., p. 45

p. 269   The assistant commander for support…, Venkov & Dudinov, op. cit., p. 47

p. 269   Under incessant fire…, ibid.

p. 269   Shestopalov's crossing and installation of the beacon…, Plekhov, Khvatov & Zakharov, op. cit., p. 211-12

p. 270   Captain Korikov's 1st Pontoon Company…, Glukhovsky, op. cit., p. 45

p. 270   'Get aboard!', ibid.

p. 271   only 14 of the original 23 boats…, ibid., p. 46

p. 271   The second combat voyage of the armoured boats…, Plekhov, Khvatov & Zakharov, op. cit., p. 208-9

p. 271   'Divisional HQ personnel…', Lyudnikov, 'There is a Cliff on the Volga', in *Two Hundred Days of Fire*, p. 194

p. 271   Death of Rutkovsky…, Glukhovsky, op. cit., p. 46

p. 271   Sima Ozerov… saw the Major slump…, ibid.

p. 271   'Armoured boats moored…', Epishin, report, 21.4.1979, p. 1

p. 272   Red Star for Zuyev…, Venkov & Dudinov, op. cit., p. 48

p. 272   the boats took aboard 78 wounded…, Plekhov, Khvatov & Zakharov, op. cit., p. 209

p. 272   Rettenmaier's guns hack into the ships, Rettenmaier, *Alte Kameraden* 1/1954, p. 5

p. 272   direct hit on Armoured Boat No. 13…, Plekhov, Khvatov & Zakharov, op. cit., p. 209

p. 272   'Ivan Zlydnev doted on…', Lyudnikov, 'There is a Cliff on the Volga', in *Two Hundred Days of Fire*, p. 197-8

p. 273   the third combat voyage to Lyudnikov's Island…, Plekhov, Khvatov & Zakharov, op. cit., p. 209-10

p. 273   Casualties of 138th Rifle Division, 138 str.div., 'Combat Report No. 198', TsAMO, p. 186

p. 273   Casualties of 305. and 389.Inf.Div., 6. Armee, NARA T-312, Roll 1507, p. 571

p. 273   'At 0100, the regiment staff…', 685 str.polk zhurnal, TsAMO, p. 10

p. 273   'As a result of the…', ibid.

p. 274   At 0900, 95th Rifle Division went over…, 62-armii zhurnal, TsAMO, p. 274

p. 274   By 1600 they had captured…, ibid.

p. 274   'at 2240, the enemy…', 138 str.div., 'Combat Report No. 199', TsAMO, p. 187

p. 274   'At 0430, an enemy group…', ibid.

p. 274   Deaths of Bauer and Vopel, and wounding of Herbig, Kunz and Lugert, 2./Pi.Btl.336, DD/WASt, 'Pi.Btl.336 Namentliche Verlustmeldung Nr. 4', 16.4.1943

p. 274   Wounding of Börner, Gernegross, Hoppstock and Steier, 3./Pi.Btl.336, DD/WASt, 'Pi.Btl.336 Namentliche Verlustmeldung Nr. 4', 16.4.1943

p. 275   'Rolik is spinning…', Glukhovsky, op. cit., p. 39

p. 275   At 0430 on this morning…, 650 str.polk zhurnal, TsAMO, p. 36

p. 275   'My men are dead…', Glukhovsky, op. cit., p. 39

p. 276   German attempt to destroy Rolik, ibid.

p. 276   'The Russians were dug in…', Zrenner,

p. 277   'During my visit to…', Lyudnikov, 'There is a Cliff on the Volga', in *Two Hundred Days of Fire*, p. 197

p. 277   the Germans tossed grenades…, 650 str.polk zhurnal, TsAMO, p. 36

p. 277   The Germans patrol…, ibid.

p. 277   'One hundred and …', Rettenmaier diary, 22.11.1942

p. 277   'The assaults of 305…', Rettenmaier, *Alte Kameraden* 1/1954, p. 5

p. 277   107th IPBB sent 6 boats…, Plekhov, Khvatov & Zakharov, op. cit., p. 212

p. 277   During this dangerous task, Jnr.Sgt. S.M. Kletsko…, ibid.

p. 278   The fourth and final voyage…, ibid., p. 210

p. 278   Story of nurse Kirillov…, ibid.

p. 278   Casualties of 138th Rifle Division, 138 str.div., 'Combat Report No. 199', TsAMO, p. 187

p. 278   Pechenyuk's men noted that…, 650 str.polk zhurnal, TsAMO, p. 37

p. 279   the Germans lobbed grenades…, ibid.

p. 279   'during the day, the enemy…', 138 str.div., 'Combat Report No. 200', TsAMO, p. 188

p. 279   Small recon groups of 768RR…, ibid.

p. 279   A recon group working around…, 650 str.polk zhurnal, TsAMO, p. 37

p. 279   'On several sectors of…', Krylow, op. cit., p. 345

p. 279   '95th Rifle Division conducted…', 62-armii zhurnal, TsAMO, p. 276

p. 279   'The enemy made…', 138 str.div. zhurnal, TsAMO, p. 35

p. 279   the combat structure…, 138 str.div., 'Combat Report No. 200', TsAMO, p. 188

p. 279   losses inflicted on the Germans…, ibid.

p. 279   'The Russians heavily…', Traub, Feldpostbrief 23.11.1942

p. 281   Secret tunnel…, interview of Nikolai Dontsov by Evgeny Kulichenko, 23.5.2003

p. 281   'Kalach should be…', Rettenmaier diary, 23.11.1942

p. 281   Casualties of 138th Rifle Division, 138 str.div., 'Combat Report No. 200', TsAMO, p. 188

p. 282   In the morning, Lyudnikov's troops…, 138 str.div. zhurnal, TsAMO, p. 36

p. 282   'At 0800, after an artillery…', 62-armii zhurnal, TsAMO, p. 277

p. 282   'Along the regiment's…', 650 str.polk zhurnal, TsAMO, p. 37-8

p. 282   At 1445 hours, LI. Armeekorps…, 79ID, NARA
          T-315, Roll 1108, p. 91
p. 283n 'With a noble attitude…', von Seydlitz, op. cit., p. 203
p. 283   'Now that you have your own…', ibid.
p. 283   At 1115 hours, Paulus issued…, *Onslaught*, p. 187
p. 284   'In receipt of the…', von Seydlitz, op. cit., p. 205-6; see
          also *Onslaught*, p. 186-8
p. 284   'The OKH order, to hold…', ibid., p. 208
p. 284   'the most difficult question…, Haller, *Lieutenant General
          Karl Strecker*, p. 96
p. 284   'If the OKH does not…', von Seydlitz, op. cit., p. 210
p. 284   Combat structure, 138 str.div., 'Combat Report No.
          201', TsAMO, p. 189
p. 284   Casualties of 138th Rifle Division, ibid.
p. 284   Casualties of 305. and 389.Inf.Div., 6. Armee, NARA
          T-312, Roll 1507, p. 512
p. 285   Benad and his replacements, 294.Inf.Div., NARA
          T-315, Roll 1941, p. 1108
p. 285   'The order to 'reorganise'…', Rettenmaier diary,
          25.11.1942
p. 285   'The enemy was not active…', 138 str.div. zhurnal,
          TsAMO, p. 36
p. 285   'the regiment fires…', 650 str.polk zhurnal, TsAMO, p. 38
p. 285   destroyed about 50 soldiers…, 138 str.div., 'Combat
          Report No. 202', TsAMO, p. 190
p. 285   3 dead and 12 wounded, 6. Armee, NARA T-312, Roll
          1507, p. 553
p. 286   destroyed by artillery fire…, 138 str.div., 'Combat
          Report No. 202', TsAMO, p. 190
p. 286   Combat structure, ibid.
p. 286   Small storm groups of 95th…, 62-armii zhurnal,
          TsAMO, p. 278
p. 286   losses of 95RD's units, 95 str.div., 'Combat Report No.
          66', TsAMO, p. 235
p. 286   Casualties of 138RD, 138 str.div., 'Combat Report No.
          202', TsAMO, p. 190
p. 286   Casualties of 305. and 389.Inf.Div., 6. Armee, NARA
          T-312, Roll 1507, p. 553
p. 286   '305.Inf.Div. will disband…', 'Korpsbefehl Nr. 119',
          79ID, NARA T-315, Roll 1108, p. 95-6
p. 286   'The offensive in the Gun Factory…', Linden
          monograph, p. 15-16
p. 286   'towards the end of November…', Löffler to Frau Ell,
          Feldpostbrief 12.4.1943
p. 287   Reformation of Pi.Btl.305, 79ID, NARA T-315, Roll
          1109, p. 84
p. 287   combat strengths of Pi.Btle. 50, 294 and 336, ibid.
p. 287   'We are attached…', Puschiavo Feldpostbrief
p. 287   changes in the grenadier regiments…, ibid.
p. 288   'On the night of 25 November…', Wiesen, op. cit.,
          p. 108-9
p. 288   First task given to Pi.Btl.305, 79ID, NARA T-315, Roll
          1108, p. 699-700
p. 288   The labour force would…, ibid., p. 700

Chapter 7:

p. 289   'This morning the front…', Rettenmaier diary,
          26.11.1942
p. 289   the Germans fired on…, 138 str.div., 'Combat Report
          No. 203', TsAMO, p. 191
p. 289   threw hand grenades at the water pump…, 650 str.polk
          zhurnal, TsAMO, p. 38
p. 289   the Germans had set up 3 mortars…, ibid.

p. 290   'Order: The regiment will organise…', ibid.
p. 290   'at around 1000…', Rettenmaier diary, 26.11.1942
p. 290   '[The enemy] continued…', 138 str.div. zhurnal,
          TsAMO, p. 36
p. 290   'we have been directed…', Rettenmaier diary, 26.11.1942
p. 290   'The army, surrounded by…', 'Korpsbefehl Nr. 120',
          79ID, NARA T-315, Roll 1108, p. 99
p. 290   'For this fighting…', ibid.
p. 291   'At the moment, no regard…', ibid., p. 101
p. 291   'At 1900 hours, Oberleutnant Rominger…',
          Rettenmaier diary, 26.11.1942
p. 292   combat strengths of 305. Inf.Div., 6. Armee, NARA
          T-312, Roll 1508, p. 293
p. 292   combat strengths of 389. Inf.Div., ibid.
p. 292   with 508 men…, 138 str.div., 'Combat Report No.
          203', TsAMO, p. 191
p. 292   Casualties of 305. Inf.Div., 6. Armee, NARA T-312,
          Roll 1507, p. 493
p. 292   'It is 0500…', Rettenmaier diary, 27.11.1942
p. 293   a total of 119 flight landed…, 'Tabelle über Stärke,
          Verluste und Luftversorgung der 6. Armee in Stalingrad
          vom 20.11.1942 bis 3.2.1943' in Kehrig, *Stalingrad:
          Analyse und Dokumentation einer Schlacht*, p. 670
p. 293n By 9 December…, ibid.
p. 293   activity of 138th Rifle Division's sector…, 138 str.div.,
          'Combat Report No. 204', TsAMO, p. 192; and 650 str.
          polk zhurnal, TsAMO, p. 39
p. 293   a German Ju-88 flew over…, 138 str.div., 'Combat
          Report No. 204', TsAMO, p. 192
p. 293   Strength and armaments of 138RD…, ibid.
p. 293   'At dinner, (we get…', Rettenmaier diary, 27.11.1942
p. 294   'On 22.11, we took…', Luz to Frau Knittel,
          Feldpostbrief 4.3.1943
p. 294   'I now no longer know…', Krauss, p. 9-10
p. 295   Casualties of 138th Rifle Division, 138 str.div., 'Combat
          Report No. 204', TsAMO, p. 192
p. 295   Casualties of 305. Inf.Div., 6. Armee, NARA T-312,
          Roll 1507, p. 532
p. 295   medal presentation ceremony…, 650 str.polk zhurnal,
          TsAMO, p. 40
p. 295   'along the front of the…', 138 str.div., 'Combat Report
          No. 205', TsAMO, p. 193
p. 295   'enemy is situated in his…', 650 str.polk zhurnal,
          TsAMO, p. 39
p. 296   'East of the Gun Factory…', 6. Armee, NARA T-312,
          Roll 1507, p. 293
p. 296   Its forward defensive line…, 138 str.div., 'Combat
          Report No. 205', TsAMO, p. 193
p. 296   'the delivery of ammunition…', ibid.
p. 297   'at midday, getting…', Rettenmaier diary, 28.11.1942
p. 297   'on the opposite bank…', 79ID, NARA T-315, Roll
          1108, p. 1093
p. 297   'Our opponent is…', Rettenmaier diary, 28.11.1942
p. 297   'Stalingrad, with its positions…', 79ID, NARA T-315,
          Roll 1107, p. 950
p. 297   daily ration scale issued by LI. Armeekorps…, 79ID,
          NARA T-315, Roll 1108, p. 97
p. 298   'Because the operational measures…, ibid., p. 115-16
p. 298   'Ammunition is only to be…, ibid.
p. 298   'The enemy continues to lay…', 138 str.div. zhurnal,
          TsAMO, p. 36
p. 298   '[During the] night, the Russians…', Rettenmaier
          diary, 28.11.1942

p. 298   Casualties of 305. and 389.Inf.Div., 6. Armee, NARA T-312, Roll 1507, p. 440

p. 299   The Germans did not cease…, 138 str.div. zhurnal, TsAMO, p. 37

p. 299   'Ice floes have appeared…', ibid.

p. 299   Soviet artillery falling short…, ibid.

p. 299   activity on 650RR's sector…, 650 str.polk zhurnal, TsAMO, p. 40

p. 299   'For us, today was…', Rettenmaier diary, 29.11.1942

p. 299   'Our morale became miserable…', Staiger, interview with Agnes Moosmann, 14.1.2005

p. 300   'In the area of the transformer…, 138 str.div. zhurnal, TsAMO, p. 37

p. 300   107th IPBB, which provided…, Plekhov, Khvatov & Zakharov, op. cit., p. 212

p. 301   'veterans of 138th Red Banner…', ibid., p. 213

p. 301   activity on 650RR's sector…, 650 str.polk zhurnal, TsAMO, p. 40

p. 301   'In four weeks time…', Rettenmaier diary, 30.11.1942

p. 301   Casualties of 305. Inf.Div., 6. Armee, NARA T-312, Roll 1507, p. 408

p. 301   'At midnight, Soviet observers…, 138 str.div. zhurnal, TsAMO, p. 37

p. 301   'Close the gap…', 650 str.polk zhurnal, TsAMO, p. 41

p. 302   'The enemy continues…, 138 str.div. zhurnal, TsAMO, p. 37

p. 302   'In front of the regiment's…', 650 str.polk zhurnal, TsAMO, p. 41

p. 302   'the Führer Decree…', Rettenmaier diary, 1.12.1942

p. 302   'The fighting for Stalingrad…', 27.11.42, 6. Armee, NARA T-312, Roll 1508, p. 241

p. 302   'The army is encircled. It is…', ibid., p. 242

p. 303   'It is also said that a…', Rettenmaier diary, 1.12.1942

p. 303   'For us the night was…', ibid.

p. 303   Casualties of 305. Inf.Div., 6. Armee, NARA T-312, Roll 1507, p. 1001

p. 303   Liesecke visits Haus 79, Rettenmaier diary, 2.12.1942

p. 303   'Sturmkompanie 44.Inf.Div. will be…', 79ID, NARA T-315, Roll 1108, p. 136

p. 303   In a strength report…, 6. Armee, NARA T-312, Roll 1508, p. 293

p. 303   'returned from operations…', Schimak, Lamprecht & Dettmer, *Die 44. Infanterie-Division – Tagebuch der Hoch- und Deutschmeister*, p. 229

p. 303   Iron Cross Second Class… 'E.K. 2.Kl. Verleihungsliste Sturmkp. 44.I.D.', BA-ZNS, RH7A/885, p. 264

p. 304   Iron Cross First Class to Kindler… 'E.K. 1.Kl. Verleihungsliste Sturmkp. 44.I.D.', ibid., p. 274

p. 304   Story of Miroshchnichenko…, 650 str.polk zhurnal, TsAMO, p. 42

p. 304   The Germans continued to dig…, 138 str.div. zhurnal, TsAMO, p. 38

p. 304   'Destroy observable enemy targets…, 650 str.polk zhurnal, TsAMO, p. 41

p. 304   'The enemy ground troops…, ibid.

p. 304   'At 2100 hours, two…', Rettenmaier diary, 2.12.1942

p. 305   Casualties of 305. Inf.Div., 6. Armee, NARA T-312, Roll 1507, p. 983

p. 305   Order No. 090 sent…, 650 str.polk zhurnal, TsAMO, p. 42

p. 305   'Now in these…', Rettenmaier diary, 3.12.1942

p. 305   At 1030, small storm groups…, 138 str.div. zhurnal, TsAMO, p. 38

p. 305   grand objectives of 650RR…, 650 str.polk zhurnal, TsAMO, p. 42

p. 305   Shkarina's storm group…, ibid.

p. 305   'during the moment of our…', ibid.

p. 305   At 1100 hours, after the miscarriage…', ibid.

p. 306   'Implementing army staff's…' 95 str.div. zhurnal, TsAMO, 3.12.1942

p. 306   losses of 95RD's units, 95 str.div., 'Combat Report No. 82', TsAMO, p. 274

p. 306   Death of Kalmykov, 62-armii zhurnal, TsAMO, p. 292; and http://www.soldat.ru/kom.html

p. 306   Wounding of Dunayevsky, http://www.soldat.ru/kom.html

p. 306   Biographical details of Budarin; *Geroi Sovetskogo Soyuza*, T. 1, p. 211; http://www.omsk.edu.ru/schools/sch076/omsk_street/budarin.htm; and http://www.univer.omsk.su/omsk/City/heroes/budarin.htm

p. 306   Casualties of 138th Rifle Division, 138 str.div., 'Combat Report No. 216', TsAMO, p. 205

p. 306   Casualties of 305. Inf.Div., 6. Armee, NARA T-312, Roll 1507, p. 968

p. 307   'Last night the food…', Rettenmaier diary, 4.12.1942

p. 307   Icing over of the Volga channel…, 138 str.div. zhurnal, TsAMO, p. 38

p. 307   'carting us all…', Mereshko, interview with Mike Jones

p. 307   activity on 650RR's sector…, 650 str.polk zhurnal, TsAMO, p. 43

p. 307   one medium tank and one 'tankette'…, ibid.

p. 307   Lyudnikov ordered that the NKVD…, 138 str.div. zhurnal, TsAMO, p. 38

p. 309   'During the course of…', 650 str.polk zhurnal, TsAMO, p. 43

p. 309   'The enemy is still…', Rettenmaier diary, 4.12.1942

p. 309   Casualties of 138th Rifle Division, 138 str.div., 'Combat Report No. 221', TsAMO, p. 209

p. 309   Casualties of 305. Inf.Div., 6. Armee, NARA T-312, Roll 1507, p. 951

p. 309   replacements in the form of 120 men…, 138 str.div. zhurnal, TsAMO, p. 39

p. 309   'When the pocket formed…' Wegener, letters to author, 18.1.2003 and 9.2.2003

p. 309   'During the day…, 650 str.polk zhurnal, TsAMO, p. 43

p. 309   'Throughout the entire…', Rettenmaier diary, 5.12.1942

p. 311   'This detour to Stalingrad…', Bauchspiess, Feldpostbrief 5.12.1942

p. 311   cumulative casualty figures…, 6. Armee, NARA T-312, Roll 1507, p. 350

p. 311   Casualties of 138th Rifle Division, 138 str.div., 'Combat Report No. 222', TsAMO, p. 212

p. 311   Casualties of 305. Inf.Div., 6. Armee, NARA T-312, Roll 1507, p. 929

p. 311   'The enemy continues to fire…', 138 str.div. zhurnal, TsAMO, p. 39

p. 311   'The enemy undertook no…', 650 str.polk zhurnal, TsAMO, p. 43

p. 311   'Foggy weather…', Rettenmaier diary, 6.12.1942

p. 311   'The enemy has strengthened…' 95 str.div. zhurnal, TsAMO, 6.12.1942

p. 312   'I'm writing these…', Hering, Feldpostbrief, 6.12.1942

p. 312   'At the beginning…' Klein, report and interviews with Agnes Moosmann, April 2006 and 10.5.2006

p. 313   Casualties of 138th Rifle Division, 138 str.div., 'Combat Report No. 223', TsAMO, p. 214

p. 313   Casualties of 305. Inf.Div., 6. Armee, NARA T-312, Roll 1507, p. 913

p. 314   acquired a thick covering…, 138 str.div. zhurnal, TsAMO, p. 39

p. 314   bathhouse on Zaitsevsky Island…, Lyudnikov, 'There is a Cliff on the Volga', in *Two Hundred Days of Fire*, p. 199

p. 314   Casualties of 138th Rifle Division, 138 str.div., 'Combat Report No. 224', TsAMO, p. 219

p. 314   Casualties of 305. Inf.Div., 6. Armee, NARA T-312, Roll 1507, p. 900

p. 314   a motor boat of Lyudnikov's division…, 138 str.div. zhurnal, TsAMO, p. 39

p. 314   Novikov's recon group…, ibid.

p. 314   activity on 650RR's sector…, 650 str.polk zhurnal, TsAMO, p. 45

p. 314   'Tomorrow is my birthday…', Rettenmaier, Feldpostbrief 8.12.1942

p. 315   'Most officers showed…', Staiger, interview with Agnes Moosmann, 9.2.2005

p. 315   'I am still well and…', Rettenmaier, Feldpostbrief 10.12.1942

p. 315   Casualties of 138th Rifle Division, 138 str.div., 'Combat Report No. 225', TsAMO, p. 222

p. 315   Casualties of 305. Inf.Div., 6. Armee, NARA T-312, Roll 1507, p. 879

p. 316   'On my birthday…', Rettenmaier, Feldpostbrief 10.12.1942

p. 316   'Dear Mr. Rettenmaier…', Schwarz, letter, Familie Rettenmaier archives

p. 316   'Hope and the…', Füssinger, Feldpostbrief 9.12.1942

p. 317   'The enemy has not moved…', 138 str.div. zhurnal, TsAMO, p. 40

p. 317   'Throughout the day, the…', 650 str.polk zhurnal, TsAMO, p. 45

p. 317   the regiment's strength was…, ibid.

p. 317   Armament of 138th Rifle Division, 138 str.div., 'Combat Report No. 226', TsAMO, p. 223

p. 317   From 1830 to 2000…, 138 str.div. zhurnal, TsAMO, p. 40; and 138 str.div. artillerii, 'Operational Report No. 100', TsAMO, p. 6

p. 317   Lyudnikov presented medals…', 138 str.div. zhurnal, TsAMO, p. 40

p. 317   Casualties of 138th Rifle Division, 138 str.div., 'Combat Report No. 226', TsAMO, p. 223

p. 317   Casualties of 305. Inf.Div., 6. Armee, NARA T-312, Roll 1507, p. 862

p. 318   activity on 650RR's sector…, 650 str.polk zhurnal, TsAMO, p. 46

p. 318   The ampulomet, http://infvstanks.newmail.ru/zs/amp.html

p. 318   At 0920, there was a small…, 138 str.div. zhurnal, TsAMO, p. 40

p. 318   From 1100 to 1300, methodical…, ibid., p. 41

p. 318   'My letters […] may…', Rettenmaier, Feldpostbrief 10.12.1942

p. 319   'I am curious…', ibid.

p. 319   'The Oberst's wife requested…', Rettenmaier, Feldpostbrief 12.12.1942

p. 319   Casualties of 138th Rifle Division, 138 str.div., 'Combat Report No. 227', TsAMO, p. 228

p. 319   Casualties of 305. Inf.Div., 6. Armee, NARA T-312, Roll 1507, p. 848

p. 320   sleighs came over the ice…, 138 str.div. zhurnal, TsAMO, p. 41

p. 320   Chuikov ordered 138th and…, ibid.

p. 320   Slated for this task were…, 62-armii artillerii, 'Combat Order No. 100', TsAMO, p. 106

p. 320   Death of Hering, various documents from Familie Hering archives

p. 320   activity on 650RR's sector…, 650 str.polk zhurnal, TsAMO, p. 47

p. 321   breakdown of those numbers…, ibid.

p. 321   Reports by Soviet observers…, 138 str.div. zhurnal, TsAMO, p. 41

p. 321   'A short greeting…', Rettenmaier, Feldpostbrief 11.12.1942

p. 321   Casualties of 138th Rifle Division, 138 str.div., 'Combat Report No. 228', TsAMO, p. 229

p. 321   Casualties of 305. Inf.Div., 6. Armee, NARA T-312, Roll 1507, p. 829

p. 322   Fugenfirov's artillery grouping…, 62-armii artillerii, 'Combat Order No. 100', TsAMO, p. 106; and 138 str. div. zhurnal, TsAMO, p. 41

p. 322   The ten 122mm howitzers…, 62-armii artillerii, 'Combat Order No. 100', TsAMO, p. 106

p. 322   'We could not destroy…', Chuikov, op. cit., p. 237-8

p. 322   'the left flank group (Rolik)…', 138 str.div. zhurnal, TsAMO, p. 42

p. 322   'army artillery lay down…', 650 str.polk zhurnal, TsAMO, p. 48

p. 322   'There is nothing new…', Rettenmaier, Feldpostbrief 12.12.1942

p. 323   Fugenfirov's artillery opened…, 62-armii artillerii, 'Combat Order No. 100', TsAMO, p. 107

p. 323   Exactly 5760 rounds…, ibid.

p. 323   'Everything here is much…', Traub, Feldpostbrief 12.12.1942

p. 323   Casualties of 138th Rifle Division, 138 str.div., 'Combat Report No. 229', TsAMO, p. 233

p. 323   Casualties of 305. Inf.Div., 6. Armee, NARA T-312, Roll 1507, p. 806

p. 324   The carrying of ammunition…, 138 str.div. zhurnal, TsAMO, p. 42

p. 324   From 0600 until 1100…, ibid.

p. 324   'There is ceaseless firing…', ibid.

p. 324   'During the course of the…', 650 str.polk zhurnal, TsAMO, p. 48-9

p. 324   It had 101 men…, ibid.

p. 324   Fugenfirov's artillery replayed…, 62-armii artillerii, 'Combat Order No. 100', TsAMO, p. 107

p. 324   Casualties of 138th Rifle Division, 138 str.div., 'Combat Report No. 230', TsAMO, p. 237

p. 324   Casualties of 305. Inf.Div., 6. Armee, NARA T-312, Roll 1507, p. 795

p. 324   Paulus visit, 'Frontfahrt des Oberbefehlshaber am 14.12.1942', 6. Armee, NARA T-312, Roll 1508, p. 1123

p. 324   Also, the Unterführer…, ibid.

p. 324   'The burdens here are…', Rettenmaier, Feldpostbrief 14.12.1942

p. 325   Soviet supply runs…, 650 str.polk zhurnal, TsAMO, p. 49

p. 325   a German wearing a Red Army uniform…, ibid.

p. 325   'During the course of three…', 138 str.div. zhurnal, TsAMO, p. 42-3

p. 325   Captain Kolyakin…, ibid., p. 43

p. 325   a total of 222 men…, ibid.

p. 325   'In December, the defenders…', Dvoryaninov, report, 20.11.1972, p. 8-10

p. 327   Casualties of 138th Rifle Division, 138 str.div., 'Combat Report No. 231', TsAMO, p. 239

p. 327   Casualties of 305. Inf.Div., 6. Armee, NARA T-312, Roll 1507, p. 783

p. 327 From 2100 the previous night…, 138 str.div. zhurnal, TsAMO, p. 43

p. 327 In accordance with 62nd Army's plan…, 62-armii artillerii, 'Combat Order No. 100', TsAMO, p. 106-8

p. 327 The artillery concentration was…, 62-armii artillerii, 'Combat Order No. 028', TsAMO, p. 110

p. 328 Artillery fire schedule…, ibid.

p. 329 'We walloped first one…', Dvoryaninov, p. 10-11

p. 329 Upon seeing Konovalenko's groups…, 344 str.polk, 'Combat Report No. 108', TsAMO, p. 92

p. 329 Pogrebnyak's, Domracheva's and Sokolov's groups, ibid.

p. 329 achieved insignificant successes…, ibid.; and 138 str.div. 'Combat Report No. 232', TsAMO, p. 246

p. 329 'Throughout the day…', 344 str.polk, 'Combat Report No. 108', TsAMO, p. 92

p. 329 2 officers and 5 men killed…, ibid.

p. 330 1st Rifle Battalion began…, 650 str.polk zhurnal, TsAMO, p. 50

p. 330 2nd Rifle Battalion began…, ibid.

p. 330 'We valued winning back…', Lyudnikov, 'There is a Cliff on the Volga', in Two Hundred Days of Fire, p. 199

p. 330 casualties of 650RR were 60 men…, 650 str.polk zhurnal, TsAMO, p. 50

p. 330 'The reinforcements were…, ibid.

p. 330 Colonel Gorishny's 95th RD advanced…, 62-armii zhurnal, TsAMO, p. 312

p. 331 'Carrying out Order No. 221…' 95 str.div., 'Combat Report No. 106', TsAMO, p. 329

p. 331 'defending in front of…' ibid.

p. 331n 'Five prisoners were taken…', 62-armii zhurnal, TsAMO, p. 312

p. 331 'I request that one…', 95 str.div., 'Combat Report No. 106', TsAMO, p. 329

p. 332 'From the eastern edge of…', ibid.

p. 332 'It was noted that in…', 62-armii zhurnal, 'Enemy activity along the front of 62nd Army for the period from 11.12. to 20.12.42', TsAMO, p. 319

p. 332 Groups of 344th…, 344 str.polk, 'Combat Report No. 108', TsAMO, p. 92

p. 332 annihilated over 100 Germans and…, 138 str.div. zhurnal, TsAMO, p. 44

p. 332 'after several fruitless attacks…', 6. Armee, NARA T-312, Roll 1507, p. 776

p. 332 Casualties of 138th Rifle Division, 138 str.div., 'Combat Report No. 232', TsAMO, p. 246

p. 332 Casualties of 305. Inf.Div., 6. Armee, NARA T 312, Roll 1507, p. 774

p. 332 activity on 241RR's sector…, 95 str.div., 'Combat Report No. 108', TsAMO, p. 336

p. 332 At 0950, Soviet observers spotted…, ibid.

p. 333 activity on 90RR's sector…, ibid.

p. 333 losses of 95RD…, ibid.

p. 333 activity on 650RR's sector…, 650 str.polk zhurnal, TsAMO, p. 50-51

p. 333 two 82mm mortars only had…, ibid.

p. 333 the 15-man strong storm group…, 344 str.polk, 'Combat Report No. 110', TsAMO, p. 93

p. 333 a group of 12-15 Germans…, ibid.

p. 334 Fire from the unfinished building…, 650 str.polk zhurnal, TsAMO, p. 50

p. 334 4 killed and 21 wounded…, 138 str.div., 'Combat Report No. 233', TsAMO, p. 252

p. 334 'several attacks with strong…', 6. Armee, NARA T-312, Roll 1507, p. 774

p. 334 a machine-gunner in Haus 75…, 344 str.polk, 'Combat Report No. 111', TsAMO, p. 94

p. 334 Casualties of 138th Rifle Division, 138 str.div., 'Combat Report No. 233', TsAMO, p. 252

p. 334 Casualties of 305. Inf.Div., 6. Armee, NARA T-312, Roll 1507, p. 763

p. 334 same sleds evacuated wounded men…, 138 str.div. zhurnal, TsAMO, p. 45

p. 334 night-time counterattacks to…, 6. Armee, NARA T-312, Roll 1507, p. 762

p. 334 'Reserves that had been…', 95 str.div., 'Combat Report No. 110', TsAMO, p. 344

p. 335 'At 1200, having repelled…', ibid.

p. 335 activity on 650RR's sector…, 650 str.polk zhurnal, TsAMO, p. 51

p. 335 Soviet observers reported that…, 138 str.div. zhurnal, TsAMO, p. 45

p. 335 Pechenyuk's 1st Rifle Battalion…, 650 str.polk zhurnal, TsAMO, p. 51

p. 335 Death of Wezel, http://www.volksbund.de/graebersuche/content_suche.asp; and 'E.K. 2.Kl. Verleihungsliste Nr. 16', BA-ZNS, RH7A/885, p. 248

p. 335 'no combat activity in…', 6. Armee, NARA T-312, Roll 1508, p. 196

p. 336 'By means of a crane…', Dvoryaninov, p. 11

p. 336 'Gun No. 14042, which fell…', ibid., p. 12

p. 336 Casualties of 138th Rifle Division, 138 str.div., 'Combat Report No. 234', TsAMO, p. 254

p. 336 Casualties of 305. Inf.Div., 6. Armee, NARA T-312, Roll 1508, p. 187

p. 336 'On the sector of…', 95 str.div., 'Combat Report No. 112', TsAMO, p. 345

p. 337 reinforcements of 361 men…, 138 str.div. zhurnal, TsAMO, p. 45

p. 337 'from 0600 until 1300 there…', ibid.

p. 337 'Because of the snipers…', Staiger, interview with Agnes Moosmann, 14.1.2005

p. 338 'Some days ago…', Traub, Feldpostbrief 22.12.1942

p. 338 'The division will annihilate…', 138 str.div. zhurnal, TsAMO, p. 46

p. 338 'we decided to revise the…', Lyudnikov, 'There is a Cliff on the Volga', in Two Hundred Days of Fire, p. 199

p. 338 'Every regiment was equipped…', ibid., p. 199-200

p. 338 'Come on, Ivan…', Glukhovsky, op. cit., p. 65

p. 339 Lyudnikov prepared draft combat…, ibid., p. 66

p. 339 'Strictly observe camouflage…', ibid.

p. 339 Germans were dressing in women's clothes…, 138 str. div. zhurnal, TsAMO, p. 45

p. 339 activity on 650RR's sector…, 650 str.polk zhurnal, TsAMO, p. 52

p. 339 artillery hit Pechenyuk's CP…, ibid.

p. 340 Twenty-eight lightly wounded men…, 138 str.div. zhurnal, TsAMO, p. 45

p. 340 'in December, it had already…', Zrenner

p. 340 'In the fuel installation…', 6. Armee, NARA T-312, Roll 1508, p. 185

p. 340 'Counterattack to recapture…', ibid., p. 172

p. 340 Story of Reiner, compiled by Dieter Schäfer, 21.7.2005

p. 340 Casualties of 138th Rifle Division, 138 str.div., 'Combat Report No. 235', TsAMO, p. 260

p. 340 Casualties of 305. Inf.Div., 6. Armee, NARA T-312, Roll 1508, p. 170

p. 341 Story of Petukhov and Grigoriev…, Glukhovsky, op. cit., p. 61-2

p. 342 The 'tongue' was Heinrich Hess…, ibid., p. 54

p. 342 At 1100, a relatively…, 138 str.div. zhurnal, TsAMO, p. 46

p. 342 storm groups of Chulkov and Lyutin…, Glukhovsky, op. cit., p. 70

p. 342 Distinguishing themselves in…, 138 str.div. zhurnal, TsAMO, p. 47; and 650 str.polk zhurnal, TsAMO, p. 53

p. 342 Two dug-outs were…, 138 str.div., 'Combat Report No. 236', TsAMO, p. 262

p. 342 Contrary to what Lyudnikov…, Glukhovsky, op. cit., p. 70

p. 342 Captain Svenchkovsky…, 650 str.polk zhurnal, TsAMO, p. 53

p. 343 Comrade Geraskin…, ibid.

p. 343 Lieutenant Krashin…, ibid.

p. 343 650th RR recorded German losses…, ibid.

p. 343 64 Germans killed…, 138 str.div., 'Combat Report No. 236', TsAMO, p. 262

p. 343 'On the right wing…', 6. Armee, NARA T-312, Roll 1508, p. 156

p. 343 Grenade duels took place…, 95 str.div., 'Combat Report No. 113', TsAMO, p. 353

p. 343 At 1100, Gorishny's indomitable…, 95 str.div., 'Situation Report No. 123', TsAMO, p. 352

p. 343 deployed 17 ampulomets…, 95 str.div., 'Combat Report No. 115', TsAMO, p. 354

p. 344 sappers discovered that German corpses…, ibid.

p. 344 two men taken prisoners…, 62-armii zhurnal, TsAMO, p. 326

p. 344 'German officers also plundered…', 'Extraordinary State Commission to Investigate German-Fascist Crimes Committed on Soviet Territory from the USSR', Archive of the October Revolution records [manuscript RG-22.002M], USHMM Reel 10, Stalingrad Oblast

p. 344 'Two probes near the…', 6. Armee, NARA T-312, Roll 1508, p. 154

p. 344 Soviet riflemen noticed…, 95 str.div., 'Combat Report No. 115', TsAMO, p. 354

p. 344 Lyudnikov visits Konovalenko's CP…, Glukhovsky, op. cit., p. 69

p. 345 Lyudnikov meets Chulkov and Lyutin…, ibid., p. 70-1

p. 345 'The Russians continue to rage…', Rettenmaier, Feldpostbrief 19.12.1942

p. 346 'The change in the…', Rettenmaier, *Alte Kameraden* 2/1954, p. 3-4

p. 346 the lathe of Gustav Wagner…, ibid., p. 4

p. 346 three red rockets…, 138 str.div. zhurnal, TsAMO, p. 47

p. 346 Casualties of 138th Rifle Division, 138 str.div., 'Combat Report No. 236', TsAMO, p. 262

p. 346 Casualties of 305. Inf.Div., 6. Armee, NARA T-312, Roll 1508, p. 152

p. 347 650RR repulsed four enemy…, 138 str.div., 'Combat Report No. 237', TsAMO, p. 264

p. 347 sappers with explosives…, 650 str.polk zhurnal, TsAMO, p. 53

p. 347 From 0200 to 1600…, ibid.

p. 347 Losses of 650RR…, ibid.

p. 347 On the other sectors…, 138 str.div. zhurnal, TsAMO, p. 47

p. 347 'since 1730 hours, an enemy…', 6. Armee, NARA T-312, Roll 1508, p. 143

p. 347 Description of German defences…, 138 str.div., 'Summary Report of the operations of 138th Red Banner Rifle Division for the period from 21 December to 23 December 1942', TsAMO, p. 277-80

p. 348 344RR received the task…, 138 str.div., 'Combat Order No. 094', TsAMO, p. 257

p. 348 The mission of 650RR…, ibid.

p. 348 Gunyaga's 768RR…, ibid.

p. 348 'a surprise attack be…', 344 str.polk, 'Combat Order 18.12.1942', TsAMO, p. 30-31

p. 348 '1st Rifle Battalion…', ibid.

p. 349 'a) Storm group with 30 men…', ibid.

p. 349 'I order that…, 650 str.polk zhurnal, TsAMO, p. 54

p. 350 '1st assault group will…', ibid., p. 55

p. 350 79 men as reinforcements…, 138 str.div. zhurnal, TsAMO, p. 47

p. 350 By order of the divisional commander…, ibid.

p. 350 95th Rifle Division's preliminary operation…, 95 str.div., 'Combat Report No. 115', TsAMO, p. 354

p. 350 leaving over 60 corpses…, 95 str.div., 'Combat Report No. 117', TsAMO, p. 362

p. 350 Casualties of 138th Rifle Division, 138 str.div., 'Combat Report No. 237', TsAMO, p. 264

p. 350 Casualties of 305. Inf.Div., 6. Armee, NARA T-312, Roll 1508, p. 140

Chapter 8:

p. 351 German machine-guns and mortars…, 138 str.div., 'Combat Report No. 238', TsAMO, p. 267

p. 351 Lyudnikov's pre-attack moments, Glukhovsky, op. cit., p. 71-2

p. 352 actions of Konovalenko's storm groups…, ibid., p. 72-3; and 138 str.div., 'Combat Report No. 238', p. 267

p. 352 'I don't see the…', Glukhovsky, op. cit., p. 73

p. 352 'since 0300 hours, enemy…', 6. Armee, NARA T-312, Roll 1508, p. 140

p. 352 German troops laid…, 138 str.div., 'Combat Report No. 238', TsAMO, p. 267

p. 353 actions of Pechenyuk's storm groups, 650 str.polk zhurnal, TsAMO, p. 54-5

p. 355 'In December, the regiment…', Gorbatenko, p. 8-9

p. 356 'They destroyed over…', 138 str.div., 'Situation Report No. 252', TsAMO, p. 268

p. 356 Trophies captured, ibid.

p. 356 actions of 768RR, ibid.

p. 356 casualties of 768RR, 768 str.polk, 'Combat Report 21.12.1942', TsAMO, p. 119

p. 356 actions of 241RR, 90RR and 161RR, 95 str.div., 'Combat Report No. 117', TsAMO, p. 362

p. 357 by 1000 hours, mortars, ampulomets…, ibid.

p. 357 'Since the early hours…', 6. Armee, NARA T-312, Roll 1508, p. 135

p. 357 'break-in near 305…', ibid., p. 137

p. 357 'On 21.12., strong enemy…', ibid., p. 132

p. 357 'The repeated strong…', ibid., p. 134

p. 357 Soviet calculation of German losses, 138 str.div., 'Combat Report No. 238', TsAMO, p. 267

p. 358 '21 December, Since 0300…', Chuikov, op. cit., p. 238

p. 358 equipment captured by 95RD…', 95 str.div., 'Combat Report No. 117', TsAMO, p. 362

p. 358 Casualties of 138th Rifle Division, 138 str.div., 'Situation Report No. 252', TsAMO, p. 268

p. 358 Casualties of 305. & 389.Inf.Div., 6. Armee, NARA T-312, Roll 1508, p. 130

p. 358 At 2220 hours, storm groups of 344RR…, 138 str.div. zhurnal, TsAMO, p. 49; and 138 str.div., 'Combat Report No. 239', TsAMO, p. 270

p. 358   Berbeshkin's actions, Glukhovsky, op. cit., p. 73

p. 359   German counterattacks, ibid.; and 138 str.div. zhurnal, TsAMO, p. 49

p. 359   actions on 650RR's sector, 650 str.polk zhurnal, TsAMO, p. 56

p. 359   'further attacks during...', 6. Armee, NARA T-312, Roll 1508, p. 130

p. 359   actions on 95RD's sector, 95 str.div., 'Combat Report No. 119', TsAMO, p. 363

p. 359   9 storm groups of 241RR, ibid.

p. 360   Counterattack by 2./Pi.Btl.305' Müller to Grimm, Feldpostbrief 21.6.1943

p. 360   small groups from 90RR..., 95 str.div., 'Combat Report No. 119', TsAMO, p. 363

p. 360   Vetoshkin's story, Glukhovsky, op. cit., p. 80-1

p. 361   When Chulkov's group..., ibid.

p. 362   'Thus ended the...', Krylow, op. cit., p. 366

p. 362   'It's hard here...', Schmidt, Feldpostbrief

p. 362   actions of 768RR, 768 str.polk, 'Combat Report 22.12.1942', TsAMO, p. 121

p. 363   Ponamarev's story, ibid.

p. 363   casualties and armament of 768RR, ibid.

p. 363   'repeated attacks during...', 6. Armee, NARA T-312, Roll 1508, p. 125

p. 363   'near 305. Infanterie-Division...', ibid., p. 124

p. 363   'In Haus 83, one room...', Rettenmaier, Alte Kameraden 1/1954, p. 3

p. 363   Müller's wounding, Müller to Grimm, Feldpostbrief 21.6.1943

p. 364   'Sadly, in the last...', Traub, Feldpostbrief 27.12.1942

p. 364   Zeller recalls that Homburger..., Zeller, interview with Agnes Moosmann, 16.1.2005 and 6.2.2005

p. 364   'On 21 December, I was...', Füssinger, Feldpostbrief 23.12.1942

p. 364   The wounded from Pi.Btl.305, Familie Grimm archives, 'Vorschlagsliste für EK II für Männer, die nach dem 20.11.42 noch im Kessel waren', 7.9.1943

p. 365   'During the fighting good...', 95 str.div., 'Combat Report No. 119', TsAMO, p. 363

p. 365   'As a result of the hand...', 62-armii zhurnal, TsAMO, p. 327

p. 365   'As a result of the fierce...', 95 str.div., 'Combat Report No. 121', TsAMO, p. 370

p. 365   95RD's estimate of German losses, ibid.

p. 365   'at 1700 hours, up to a...', ibid.

p. 365   Fritz shot or clubbed to death, letter, Zeller to Grimm, 30.9.1949

p. 366   'At 1730 on 22.12...', 95 str.div., 'Combat Report No. 121', TsAMO, p. 370

p. 366   Storm groups of 344RR in Dom 37, 138 str.div., 'Combat Report No. 240', TsAMO, p. 276

p. 366   138RD's claim of German losses and trophies, 138 str.div., 'Combat Report No. 239', TsAMO, p. 270

p. 366   Casualties of 138th Rifle Division, ibid.

p. 366   Casualties of 305.Inf.Div., 6. Armee, NARA T-312, Roll 1508, p. 122

p. 366   'Since 0200 hours, enemy...', 6. Armee, NARA T-312, Roll 1508, p. 122

p. 366   'counterattacks were launched six...', 138 str.div., 'Combat Report No. 240', TsAMO, p. 276

p. 367   'The young reinforcements...', Rettenmaier, Alte Kameraden 1/1954, p. 3

p. 368   Germans leave a delayed-fuse mine, 650 str.polk zhurnal, TsAMO, p. 68

p. 368   'The enemy continued his...', 6. Armee, NARA T-312, Roll 1508, p. 116

p. 368   'Because the infantry...', Rombach, Erlebnisse eines Deutschen Soldaten im Zweiten Weltkrieg, p. 10

p. 369   344 & 650RR probe German defences..., 138 str.div., 'Combat Report No. 240', TsAMO, p. 276

p. 369   Germans were seen running..., 138 str.div. zhurnal, TsAMO, p. 49-50

p. 369   lost 31 killed..., 138 str.div., 'Combat Report No. 240', TsAMO, p. 276

p. 369   650RR was deployed as follows..., 650 str.polk zhurnal, TsAMO, p. 56-7

p. 369   'transition to a new...', 138 str.div., 'Combat Report No. 241', TsAMO, p. 281

p. 369   German prisoners and trophies..., 138 str.div., 'Combat Report No. 240', TsAMO, p. 276

p. 370   In only the two houses captured by 344RR..., 138 str. div., 'Special summary report', TsAMO, p. 277

p. 370   'Lyudnikov's division has...', Chuikov, op. cit., p. 238-9; and 62-armii zhurnal, TsAMO, p. 328

p. 370   actions of Gorishny's division..., 95 str.div., 'Combat Report No. 121', TsAMO, p. 370

p. 370   'East of the gun factory...', 6. Armee, NARA T-312, Roll 1508, p. 114

p. 370   'Along the division's front...', 138 str.div., 'Special summary report', TsAMO, p. 277

p. 372   'Within the sector of...', Steinmetz Niederschrift, p. 6

p. 372   Casualties of 138th Rifle Division, 138 str.div., 'Combat Report No. 240', TsAMO, p.276

p. 372   Casualties of 305.Inf.Div., 6. Armee, NARA T-312, Roll 1508, p. 112

p. 372   Nocturnal activity, 138 str.div. zhurnal, TsAMO, p. 50

p. 373   activity on 650RR's sector..., 650 str.polk zhurnal, TsAMO, p. 57-8

p. 373   death of Silchenko..., 138 str.div., 'Situation Report No. 257', TsAMO, p.283

p. 373   activity on 90RR's sector, 95 str.div., 'Combat Report No. 123', TsAMO, p. 373

p. 373   95RD's losses..., ibid.

p. 374   'Along the division's front...', 138 str.div., 'Combat Report No. 241', TsAMO, p. 281

p. 374   'capture stairwells...', 138 str.div. zhurnal, TsAMO, p. 50

p. 374   While 1st Battalion launched..., 650 str.polk zhurnal, TsAMO, p. 57-8

p. 375   'East of the gun factory...', 6. Armee, NARA T-312, Roll 1508, p. 106

p. 375   'in view of the fact...', Rettenmaier, Alte Kameraden 1/1954, p. 3

p. 375   'Group Toporkov seized...', 650 str.polk zhurnal, TsAMO, p. 58

p. 375   strength of 650RR, ibid., p. 57

p. 375   The wounded from Pi.Btl.305, Familie Grimm archives, 'Vorschlagsliste für EK II für Männer, die nach dem 20.11.42 noch im Kessel waren', 7.9.1943

p. 375   'It was Christmas Eve...', Bachmann, 'Die Gräber am Mamaihügel', Hessischer Rundfunk, 22.1.1993

p. 375   'Today, on Christmas Eve...', Schüsslbauer, Feldpostbrief 24.12.1942

p. 376   'Our Christmas was absolutely...', Rettenmaier, Feldpostbrief 27.12.1942

p. 376   'Today is Christmas...', Bauchspiess, Feldpostbrief 25.12.1942

p. 376   'For Christmas Eve...', Traub, Feldpostbrief 25.12.1942

p. 377   'When I visited the…', Steinmetz Niederschrift, p. 8

p. 377   'Schnapps was available…', Giulini, *Stalingrad und mein zweites Leben*, p. 14

p. 378   'We had already…', Schöpf report, p. 2

p. 378   'Many dead soldiers…', Schröter, *Stalingrad*, p. 166

p. 378   Casualties of 138th Rifle Division, 138 str.div., 'Combat Report No. 241', TsAMO, p. 281

p. 378   Casualties of 305.Inf.Div., 6. Armee, NARA T-312, Roll 1508, p. 104

p. 378   'east of the gun factory…', 6. Armee, NARA T-312, Roll 1508, p. 104

p. 378   'At 0100, supported by…', 95 str.div., 'Combat Report No. 125', TsAMO, p. 380

p. 379   trophies and losses of 95RD, ibid.

p. 379   captured a damaged German tank…, 138 str.div., 'Situation Report No. 259', TsAMO, p.285

p. 379   'no enemy attacks east…', 6. Armee, NARA T-312, Roll 1507, p. 1277

p. 379   actions of 295th Art.Rgt., 295 art.polk, 'Combat Report 25.12.1942', TsAMO, p. 189

p. 379   the 120mm mortars of…, 138 str.div. artillerii, 'Situation Report No. 115', TsAMO, p. 37

p. 379   German nebelwerfers…, 138 str.div., 'Combat Report No. 242', TsAMO, p. 287

p. 379   artillery and 120 mm mortars laid down…, ibid.

p. 379   'The enemy: remnants of…', 138 str.div. 'Combat Order No. 096', TsAMO

p. 380   'Our units must act…', ibid.

p. 380   'the Kommissarhaus was defended…', Rettenmaier, *Alte Kameraden* 1/1954, p. 3

p. 380   'The enemy stubbornly…', 650 str.polk zhurnal, TsAMO, p. 58

p. 381   strength of 650RR, ibid., p. 59

p. 381   'The enemy obstinately…', ibid.

p. 381   '138th and 95th Rifle…', 62-armii zhurnal, TsAMO, p. 332

p. 381   A storm group from 90RR…, 95 str.div., 'Combat Report No. 127', TsAMO, p. 381

p. 381   Death of Gottwald, 1./Pz.Pi.Btl.50, DD/WASt, 'Pz. Pi.Btl.50 Namentliche Verlustmeldung Nr. 9', 12.6.1944; and Verlustkarte, NARA T-78, Roll 959

p. 382   Emendörfer falls ill, Hauck, *Die 305. Infanterie-Division*, p. 74

p. 382   'In the afternoon…', Kempter, Feldpostbrief 25.12.1942

p. 383   'I had to go over…', Traub, Feldpostbrief 25.12.1942

p. 383   768RR launched its attack…, 138 str.div., 'Combat Report No. 243', TsAMO, p. 290

p. 383   Casualties of 138th Rifle Division, 138 str.div., 'Combat Report No. 242', p. 287

p. 383   Casualties of 305.Inf.Div., 6. Armee, NARA T-312, Roll 1508, p. 94

p. 383   left flank of 161RR was fired on…, 95 str.div., 'Combat Report No. 127', TsAMO, p. 381

p. 383   actions on sectors of 344 & 650RR, 138 str.div., 'Combat Report No. 243', TsAMO, p. 290

p. 383   four 76mm guns…, 138 str.div. artillerii, 'Situation Report No. 115, TsAMO, p. 39

p. 383   'exchanges of rifle…', 138 str.div. zhurnal, TsAMO, p. 50

p. 384   'exterminated two [enemy]…', 650 str.polk zhurnal, TsAMO, p. 60

p. 384   strength & armament of 138RD…, 138 str.div., 'Combat Report No. 243', TsAMO, p. 290

p. 384   3 men of 161RR wounded by own mortars, 95 str.div., 'Combat Report No. 127', TsAMO, p. 381

p. 384   'no combat activity…', 6. Armee, NARA T-312, Roll 1508, p. 88

p. 384   Wounding of Breimschmidt, Familie Grimm archives, 'Vorschlagsliste für EK II für Männer, die nach dem 20.11.42 noch im Kessel waren', 7.9.1943

p. 384   Casualties of 138th Rifle Division, 138 str.div., 'Combat Report No. 243', TsAMO, p. 290

p. 384   Casualties of 305.Inf.Div., 6. Armee, NARA T-312, Roll 1508, p. 76

p. 384   'throughout the night…', 650 str.polk zhurnal, TsAMO, p. 60

p. 384   actions on sectors of 344 & 650RR, 138 str.div., 'Combat Report No. 244', TsAMO, p. 292

p. 385   small Soviet recon groups…, ibid.

p. 385   pounding of the Kommissarhaus…, 295 art.polk, 'Combat Report 27.12.1942', TsAMO, p. 191

p. 385   Death of Birkmann, Verlustkarte, NARA T-78, Roll 951

p. 385   the Kommissarhaus was attacked…, 650 str.polk zhurnal, TsAMO, p. 60

p. 385   'At 1305 hours, after…', 6. Armee, NARA T-312, Roll 1508, p. 73

p. 385   three German Ju-52s flew…, 138 str.div., 'Combat Report No. 244', TsAMO, p. 292

p. 386   two barrels filled with 600kg…, ibid.

p. 386   'An attack against the…', 6. Armee, NARA T-312, Roll 1508, p. 69

p. 386   actions on 95RD's sector, 95 str.div., 'Combat Report No. 129', TsAMO, p. 388

p. 386   Sniper Varapayev was credited…, ibid.

p. 386   'the division's units have snipers…', 95 str.div., 'Special Report', TsAMO, p. 394 & 398

p. 386   [Table] Snipers of 95RD, ibid.

p. 387   'steps have been…', ibid.

p. 387   Death of Bofinger, Verlustkarte, NARA T-78, Roll 952; and 'E.K. 2.Kl. Verleihungsliste Nr. 17', BA-ZNS, RH7A/885, p. 223

p. 387   'Today you would…', Ziesch, Feldpostbrief 27.12.1942

p. 387   'The vermin torment us…', Rettenmaier, Feldpostbrief 27.12.1942

p. 387   'Personal hygiene was…', Rettenmaier, *Alte Kameraden* 1/1954, p. 4

p. 388   'We must hold out…', Traub, Feldpostbrief 27.12.1942

p. 388   Casualties of 138th Rifle Division, 138 str.div., 'Combat Report No. 244', TsAMO, p. 292

p. 388   Casualties of 305.Inf.Div., 6. Armee, NARA T-312, Roll 1508, p. 66

p. 388   German nocturnal activity…, 138 str.div., 'Combat Report No. 245', TsAMO, p. 299

p. 388   'Through combat, reconnaissance…', 138 str.div., 'Recon Report No. 101', TsAMO, p. 297

p. 388   'At 1910, a recon…', ibid.

p. 388   'The enemy at the…', ibid.

p. 388   Red Army man Aldoshinim…, 138 str.div., 'Situation Report No. 265', TsAMO, p. 296

p. 389   actions on 95RD's sector, 95 str.div., 'Combat Report No. 131', TsAMO, p. 390

p. 389   Death of Max Albert, 2./Pz.Pi.Btl.50, DD/WASt, 'Pz. Pi.Btl.50 Namentliche Verlustmeldung Nr. 9', 12.6.1944

p. 389   German activity during the day…, 138 str.div., 'Combat Report No. 245', TsAMO, p. 299

p. 389   'Decision of the commander…', 650 str.polk zhurnal, TsAMO, p. 61

p. 390 'East of the gun factory…', 6. Armee, NARA T-312, Roll 1508, p. 52

p. 390 Casualties of 138th Rifle Division, 138 str.div., 'Combat Report No. 245', TsAMO, p. 299

p. 390 Casualties of 305.Inf.Div., 6. Armee, NARA T-312, Roll 1508, p. 44

p. 390 '344th Rifle Regiment provided…', 138 str.div., 'Situation Report No. 267', TsAMO, p. 300

p. 390 The 4th and 5th Batteries…, 295 art.polk, 'Combat Report 29.12.1942', TsAMO, p. 193

p. 390 'during the night, two…', 6. Armee, NARA T-312, Roll 1508, p. 43

p. 390 'the enemy, placing heavy…', 650 str.polk zhurnal, TsAMO, p. 62

p. 390 'the greatest amount…', 138 str.div., 'Combat Report No. 246', TsAMO, p. 303

p. 391 actions on 95RD's sector, 95 str.div., 'Combat Report No. 133', TsAMO, p. 400

p. 391 Death of Leonhard Meissner, 2./Pz.Pi.Btl.50, DD/WASt, 'Pz.Pi.Btl.50 Namentliche Verlustmeldung Nr. 3', 9.11.1943

p. 391 650RR attacks Kommissarhaus, 650 str.polk zhurnal, TsAMO, p. 62

p. 391 3rd Battery…fired 12 rounds…, 295 art.polk, 'Combat Report 29.12.1942', TsAMO, p. 193

p. 392 'Chalykh and Konoputov…', Gorbatenko, p. 9

p. 392 'On the left flank…', 138 str.div., 'Situation Report No. 268', TsAMO, p. 302

p. 392 'fighting with grenades…', 138 str.div., 'Combat Report No. 246', TsAMO, p. 303

p. 392 'I was fortunate…', Chalykh , report, 24.11.1972, p. 1-2

p. 393 'Toporkov's group seized…', 650 str.polk zhurnal, TsAMO, p. 62

p. 393 'east of the gun factory…', 6. Armee, NARA T-312, Roll 1508, p. 39

p. 393 German mortar strike, 650 str.polk zhurnal, TsAMO, p. 62

p. 393 Casualties of 138th Rifle Division, 138 str.div., 'Combat Report No. 246', TsAMO, p. 303

p. 393 Casualties of 305.Inf.Div., 6. Armee, NARA T-312, Roll 1508, p. 30

p. 393 Loss of the 'Fliegerhaus', 95 str.div., 'Combat Report No. 135', TsAMO, p. 404; and 6. Armee, NARA T-312, Roll 1508, p. 30

p. 393 'Position east of the…', 79ID, NARA T-315, Roll 1108, p. 1283

p. 394 3./Pi.Btl.179 counterattack, ibid., p. 1281 & 1284; and 6. Armee, NARA T-312, Roll 1508, p. 21

p. 394 sappers lodge their explosives, 650 str.polk zhurnal, TsAMO, p. 63

p. 394 A group of scouts…, 138 str.div., 'Combat Report No. 247', TsAMO, p. 307

p. 395 a storm group of 161RR, 95 str.div., 'Combat Report No. 135', TsAMO, p. 404

p. 395 'Our situation in regards…', Rettenmaier, *Alte Kameraden* 1/1954, p. 4

p. 395 III/191 subordinated to 79.I.D., 79ID, NARA T-315, Roll 1108, p. 541

p. 396 'Annihilated: 9460 officers ', 138 str.div. zhurnal, TsAMO, p. 58-9

p. 396 Casualties of 138th Rifle Division, 138 str.div., 'Combat Report No. 247', TsAMO, p. 307

p. 396 Casualties of 305.Inf.Div., 6. Armee, NARA T-312, Roll 1507, p. 1195

p. 396 a demolition squad…, 650 str.polk zhurnal, TsAMO, p. 63

p. 396 'The enemy, during…', ibid.

p. 397 At 1240 hours, Soviet observers…, 138 str.div., 'Combat Report No. 248', TsAMO, p. 310

p. 397 'our formations, while…', 138 str.div. zhurnal, TsAMO, p. 51

p. 397 'Two attacks launched…', 6. Armee, NARA T-312, Roll 1508, p. 8

p. 397 'At 0430 two storm…', 95 str.div., 'Combat Report No. 137', TsAMO, p. 407

p. 397 German activity of 95RD's sector, ibid.

p. 398 'Attacks followed in…', Rettenmaier, *Alte Kameraden* 1/1954, p. 3

p. 398 Promotion of Hans Bernhart, Moosmann, op. cit., p. 147

p. 399 'Division commander, Colonel…', Glukhovsky, op. cit., p. 82

p. 399 Lyudnikov visits Chuikov…', ibid., p. 82-3

p. 401 'I invited the…', Traub, Feldpostbrief 31.12.1942

p. 401 'Bernd and I…', Bauchspiess, Feldpostbrief 31.12.1942

p. 401 Death of Kurt Wenk, 11.11.1942, DD/WASt, '1./Pi.Btl.336 Namentliche Verlustmeldung Nr. 7', 16.4.1943

p. 401 'I remember New Year'…', Steinmetz Niederschrift, p. 8

p. 401 'south-east of the…', 6. Armee, NARA T-312, Roll 1507, p. 759

p. 401 Casualties of 138th Rifle Division, 138 str.div., 'Combat Report No. 248', TsAMO, p. 310

p. 401 Casualties of 305.Inf.Div., 6. Armee, NARA T-312, Roll 1507, p. 1196

p. 402 'I was summoned…', Lesin, report, undated, p. 10-11

p. 403 'During the course…', 650 str.polk zhurnal, TsAMO, p. 64

p. 403 Losses, strength & armament of 650RR, ibid.

p. 403 actions of 241RR, 95 str.div., 'Combat Report No. 1', TsAMO, p. 2

p. 403 'It has just…', Förschner, Feldpostbrief 30.12.1942

p. 404 'As an Unteroffizier…', Steinlen, eidesstattliche Erklärung, 19.5.1950

p. 404 'I received your…', Steinlen to Frau Förschner, 19.4.1950

p. 404 storm groups from 241RR…, 95 str.div., 'Combat Report No. 1', TsAMO, p. 2

p. 404 '241st Rifle Regiment's storm…', 95 str.div., 'Situation Report No. 2', TsAMO, p. 3

p. 405 'On 1.1.43, in the…', 95 str.div., 'Combat Report No. 3', TsAMO, p. 6

p. 405 'east of the gun factory…', 6. Armee, NARA T-312, Roll 1507, p. 752

p. 405 actions of 90RR…, 95 str.div., 'Situation Report No. 2', TsAMO, p. 3

p. 405 nine rounds of 21cm Mörser ammo…, 79ID, NARA T-315, Roll 1108, p. 1292

p. 405 Casualties of 305.Inf.Div., 6. Armee, NARA T-312, Roll 1507, p. 1154

p. 405 Nocturnal activity on 95RD's sector, 95 str.div., 'Combat Report No. 3', TsAMO, p. 6

p. 405 actions on 650RR's sector…, 650 str.polk zhurnal, TsAMO, p. 65

p. 405 Losses, strength & armament of 650RR, ibid.

p. 406 At midday, a German plane…, 95 str.div., 'Combat Report No. 4', TsAMO, p. 8

p. 406 At 1600 hours, German mortars…, ibid.

p. 406 'We still haven't…', Bonetsmüller, Feldpostbrief 2.1.1943

p. 406   Johann was still alive…, Nuoffer to Frau Bonetsmüller, 3.4.1943

p. 407   Nocturnal German activity…, 138 str.div. zhurnal, TsAMO, p. 52

p. 407   Nocturnal activity on 95RD's sector, 95 str.div., 'Combat Report No. 5', TsAMO, p. 10

p. 407   'During the course of', 650 str.polk zhurnal, TsAMO, p. 65-6

p. 407   'units of 241st Rifle…', 95 str.div., 'Situation Report No. 6', TsAMO, p. 11

p. 407   Losses, strength & armament of 95RD, 95 str.div., 'Combat Report No. 6', TsAMO, p. 10

p. 407   Casualties of 305.Inf.Div., 6. Armee, NARA T-312, Roll 1507, p. 1122

p. 408   'movement over the ice…', 138 str.div. zhurnal, TsAMO, p. 52

p. 408   On Pechenyuk's sector…, 650 str.polk zhurnal, TsAMO, p. 66

p. 408   Nocturnal activity on 95RD's sector, 95 str.div., 'Combat Report No. 7', TsAMO, p. 14

p. 408   At 0600 hours, Soviet observers…, ibid.

p. 408   Losses & strength of 95RD's regiments, 95 str.div., 'Combat Report No. 8', TsAMO, p. 16

p. 409   'An event that deeply…', Rettenmaier, *Alte Kameraden* 1/1954, p. 4

p. 409   'During a meeting…', Steinmetz Niederschrift, p. 9

p. 409   'When I was admitted…', ibid.

p. 409   'Early one morning…', Bachmann, Hessischer Rundfunk, 22.1.1993

p. 410   'Oberstleutnant Brandt led his…'; Thomas/Wegmann, *Die Ritterkreuzträger der Deutschen Wehrmacht 1939-1945 - Teil III: Infanterie Br-Bu*, p. 29-30

p. 410   Wutte's story, Personalakten für Rudolf Wutte

p. 410   a modern German government agency…, DD/WASt, letter to Agnes Moosmann 29.3.2006

p. 410   'The small Leutnant…', Giulini, Feldpostbrief 8.1.1943

p. 410   'I have not received…', Füssinger, Feldpostbrief 4.1.1943

p. 411   'The little bit of…', Rettenmaier, Feldpostbrief 4.1.1943

p. 411   Casualties of 305.Inf.Div., 6. Armee, NARA T-312, Roll 1507, p. 1105

p. 411   Czimatis's story, Personalakten für Albrecht Czimatis

p. 412   activity on 138RD's sector…, 138 str.div. zhurnal, TsAMO, p. 52

p. 412   causing it to burn…, 95 str.div., 'Combat Report No. 9', TsAMO, p. 18

p. 413   'In the area of Dom 07…', 95 str.div., 'Situation Report No. 12', TsAMO, p. 23

p. 413   'we worked with decoys…', Kluge, p. 87

p. 413   'The enemy has punched…', 650 str.polk zhurnal, TsAMO, p. 67-8

p. 413   'My position still lies…', Rettenmaier, Feldpostbrief 31.12.1942

p. 413   Soviet observers spotted…, 95 str.div., 'Situation Report No. 9', TsAMO, p. 18

p. 413   Activity on 95RD's sector…, ibid.

p. 413   Losses & strength of 95RD's regiments, 95 str.div., 'Combat Report No. 10', TsAMO, p. 20

p. 414   On Lyudnikov's sector…, 138 str.div. zhurnal, TsAMO, p. 52

p. 414   three-man recon patrol of 241RR…, 95 str.div., 'Combat Report No. 12', TsAMO, p. 24

p. 414   Casualties of 305.Inf.Div., 6. Armee, NARA T-312, Roll 1507, p. 1089

p. 414   Nocturnal activity on 95RD's sector, 95 str.div., 'Combat Report No. 12', TsAMO, p. 24

p. 414   'The enemy places…', 650 str.polk zhurnal, TsAMO, p. 67

p. 414   'medium German tank…', 138 str.div. zhurnal, TsAMO, p. 52

p. 414   Strength report for Stug.Abt.245, 6.1.1943, 6. Armee, NARA T-312, Roll 1507, p. 684

p. 414   Pechenyuk's men established…', 650 str.polk zhurnal, TsAMO, p. 67-8

p. 415   'At 1250 and 1300, there…', ibid.

p. 415   Strength of 650RR…, ibid.

p. 415   'At 1430, there was…', 138 str.div. zhurnal, TsAMO, p. 52

p. 415   'For most of…', Bachmann, Feldpostbrief 6.1.1943

p. 417   'We will free up…', 6. Armee, NARA T-312, Roll 1508, p. 1206

p. 417   Freed up soldiers in 305ID, ibid., p. 1207

p. 417   Disbandment of 79ID…, 79.Inf.Div., NARA T-315, Roll 1107, p. 987-8; and 79.Inf.Div., NARA T-315, Roll 1108, p. 833-6

p. 417   Casualties of 305.Inf.Div., 6. Armee, NARA T-312, Roll 1507, p. 1077

p. 418   'in the evening hours…', 6. Armee, NARA T-312, Roll 1507, p. 1076

p. 418   'The enemy is firing…', 138 str.div. zhurnal, TsAMO, p. 53

p. 418   'three enemy thrusts…', 6. Armee, NARA T-312, Roll 1507, p. 1067

p. 418   Nocturnal activity on 95RD's sector, 95 str.div., 'Situation Report No. 13', TsAMO, p.26

p. 418   Activity on 95RD's sector, 95 str.div., 'Combat Report No. 14', TsAMO, p. 29

p. 420   'I received three new…', Ebert, op.cit., p. 281

p. 420   'It is a terrible…', Rettenmaier, Feldpostbrief 7.1.1943

p. 420   Casualties of 305.Inf.Div., 6. Armee, NARA T-312, Roll 1507, p. 1058

p. 420   Nocturnal activity on 138RD's sector, 138 str.div. zhurnal, TsAMO, p. 53

p. 420   Nocturnal activity on 95RD's sector, 95 str.div., 'Combat Report No. 15', TsAMO, p. 31

p. 420   'A mortar battery laid…', 650 str.polk zhurnal, TsAMO, p. 69

p. 421   relief in the sector of 79.I.D., 79.Inf.Div., NARA T-315, Roll 1107, p. 988

p. 421   There were 70 lucky men…, 79.Inf.Div., NARA T-315, Roll 1108, p. 841-3

p. 421   'On 7 January 1943…', Poetsch, 'Die 1. Februar 1943 in Stalingrad', in *Tapfer und Treu: Treffen der 79.I.D. am 16./17. Mai 1953 in Alzey*

p. 421   Paulus visits Steinmetz, 'Frontfahrt des Oberbefehlshaber am 8.1.1943', 6. Armee, NARA T-312, Roll 1507, p. 1045

p. 421   2/90RR moved a 45mm gun…, 95 str.div., 'Situation Report No. 16', TsAMO, p. 32

p. 421   two Romanian soldiers…, ibid.

p. 421   'In grid square 82a2…', 6. Armee, NARA T-312, Roll 1507, p. 1051

p. 422   'the machine-gun nest…', ibid., p. 1047

p. 422   Losses & strength of 95RD's regiments, 95 str.div., 'Combat Report No. 16', TsAMO, p. 33

p. 422   Casualties of 305.Inf.Div., 6. Armee, NARA T-312, Roll 1507, p. 1044

p. 422   2/241RR attacks Haus 79, 95 str.div., 'Combat Report No. 18', TsAMO, p. 37

p. 422 'Having received the…', 95 str.div., 'Combat Report No. 17'. TsAMO, p. 35

p. 422 storm groups had lost 9 dead…, ibid.

p. 422 'the enemy, firmly…', ibid.

p. 422 'animated activity…', 650 str.polk zhurnal, TsAMO, p. 70

p. 423 'particularly intensive fire…', 95 str.div., 'Combat Report No. 18', TsAMO, p. 37

p. 423 renewed attempt cost another 4 dead…, ibid.

p. 423 'two night-time attacks…', 6. Armee, NARA T-312, Roll 1507, p. 1043

p. 423 'There was never-ending…', 138 str.div. zhurnal, TsAMO, p. 53

p. 423 650RR used machine-guns…, 650 str.polk zhurnal, TsAMO, p. 70

p. 423 Medic Nikolayev…, ibid.

p. 423 a few noteworthy events, ibid.

p. 423 Strength report for Stug.Abt.245, 9.1.1943, 6. Armee, NARA T-312, Roll 1043

p. 424 '2./Stug.Abt.245 with…', 79ID KTB, T-315, Roll 1107, p. 985

p. 424 'heavy anti-tank barrages…', 6. Armee, NARA T-312, Roll 1507, p. 1034

p. 424 Gr.Rgt.578 dissolved…, ibid., p. 662

p. 424 Casualties of 305.Inf.Div., 6. Armee, NARA T-312, Roll 1507, p. 651

p. 424 400th Separate Machine-Gun…, 138 str.div. zhurnal, TsAMO, p. 53

p. 425 Details of Operation Koltso (Ring), Ziemke & Bauer, op. cit., p. 496–8

p. 426 'The enemy did not…', 650 str.polk zhurnal, TsAMO, p. 71

p. 426 'at 0600 hours, the enemy…', 6. Armee, NARA T-312, Roll 1508, p. 964

p. 426 Zabolotsky's underground tunnel…', *Voyenno-Istoricheskiy Zhurnal* No. 11, November 1982, p. 68

p. 426 'with the beginning of…', 95 str.div., 'Combat Report No. 19', TsAMO, p. 44

p. 426 Fighting around the green fuel tank…, ibid.

p. 426 Losses & strength of 90RR…, 95 str.div., 'Combat Report No. 20, TsAMO, p. 46

p. 427 Actions of 161 & 241RR…, ibid.

p. 427 'On the boundary between…', 6. Armee, NARA T-312, Roll 1508, p. 957

p. 427 Casualties of 305.Inf.Div. & 100.Jäg.Div., 6. Armee, NARA T-312, Roll 1507, p. 628

Chapter 9:

p. 429 'An enemy raid at 0200…', 6. Armee, NARA T-312, Roll 1508, p. 946

p. 429 Activity on 95RD's sector, 95 str.div., 'Combat Report No. 21 & 22', TsAMO, p. 48 & 50

p. 430 7. & 8./Gr.Rgt.576 defeated, ibid.

p. 430 'between the bread factory…', 6. Armee, NARA T-312, Roll 1508, p. 415

p. 430 'between both gullies…', ibid., p. 387

p. 430 Losses & strength of 241RR, 95 str.div., 'Combat Report No. 21 & 22', TsAMO, p. 48 & 50

p. 430 Actions of 161 & 90RR, ibid.

p. 431 According to statements extracted…, ibid.

p. 431 Gorishny's order, ibid.

p. 431 'Against the right wing…', 6. Armee, NARA T-312, Roll 1508, p. 415

p. 432 Actions of 138RD, 138 str.div. zhurnal, TsAMO, p. 54

p. 432 'Stalingrad: weakening power…', 6. Armee, NARA T-312, Roll 1508, p. 406

p. 432 Casualties of 305.Inf.Div., ibid., p. 405

p. 432 Nocturnal activity on 95RD's sector, 95 str.div., 'Combat Report No. 24', TsAMO. p. 55

p. 432 Actions of 90, 241 & 161RR, 95 str.div., 'Combat Report No. 23 & 24', TsAMO, p. 53 & 55

p. 432 German counterattacks, ibid.

p. 433 Strength report for Stug.Abt.245, 12.1.1943, 6. Armee, NARA T-312, Roll 1508, p. 395

p. 433 'During the day, the…', 95 str.div., 'Combat Report No. 24', TsAMO, p. 55

p. 433 'During the night of…', ibid.

p. 434 'After 11 weeks of…', Lyudnikov, 'There is a Cliff on the Volga', in *Two Hundred Days of Fire*, p. 205

p. 434 'During the day…', 138 str.div. zhurnal, TsAMO, p. 54

p. 434 'German soldiers, drop your…', Craig, p. 324

p. 435 'I had been in Stalingrad…', Gerecke, OKW, *Geheim-Aktion über Stalingrad*, 28.1.1943, NARA T-77, Roll 1036, p. 6508125

p. 435 'an enemy raid…', 6. Armee, NARA T-312, Roll 1508, p. 387

p. 435 Actions of 241, 161 & 90RR, 95 str.div., 'Combat Report No. 25 & 26', TsAMO, p. 59 & 61

p. 435 'The enemy pulled back…', 138 str.div. zhurnal, TsAMO, p. 54-5

p. 437 'Continuing to offer…', 95 str.div., 'Combat Report No. 27 & 28', TsAMO, p. 63 & 65

p. 437 Actions of 90, 241 & 161RR, ibid.

p. 438 'Our storm groups slowly…', 138 str.div. zhurnal, TsAMO, p. 55

p. 439 Ponamarev's story, Venkov & Dudinov, op. cit., p. 54

p. 439 Ratanova's story, ibid.

p. 439 Actions of 90, 241 & 161RR, 95 str.div., 'Combat Report No. 29 & 30', TsAMO, p. 67 & 69

p. 439 'The last units of…', Poetsch

p. 440 Actions of 161, 90 & 241RR, 95 str.div., 'Combat Report No. 31 & 32', TsAMO, p. 72 & 74

p. 441 Actions of 241, 161 & 90RR, 95 str.div., 'Combat Report No. 33 & 34', TsAMO, p. 77 & 79

p. 441 'The fate of the…', Rettenmaier, *Alte Kameraden* 1/1954, p. 4

p. 442 'On 17 January…', 138 str.div. zhurnal, TsAMO, p. 56

p. 442 German plane drops 7 parachutes, 95 str.div., 'Combat Report No. 34', TsAMO, p. 79

p. 442 'Because our allies…', Rombach, p. 9

p. 443 Wounding of Heinrich, Personalakten für Walter Heinrich

p. 443 Actions of 90, 241 & 161RR, 95 str.div., 'Combat Report No. 35 & 36', TsAMO, p. 81 & 83

p. 444 Actions of 241, 161 & 90RR, 95 str.div., 'Combat Report No. 37 & 38', TsAMO, p. 85 & 87

p. 444 'During the entire day…', 138 str.div. zhurnal, TsAMO, p. 56

p. 445 Actions of 241, 161 & 90RR, 95 str.div., 'Combat Report No. 39 & 40', TsAMO, p. 89 & 91

p. 445 'the enemy offers…', ibid.

p. 445 'The enemy is offering…', 138 str.div. zhurnal, TsAMO, p. 56

p. 445 Actions of 241, 161 & 90RR, 95 str.div., 'Combat Report No. 41 & 42', TsAMO, p. 94 & 96

p. 446 Trophies captured by 95RD, ibid.

p. 446 German bombers made two…, ibid.

p. 446   Actions of 241, 161 & 90RR, 95 str.div., 'Combat Report No. 43 & 44', TsAMO, p. 98 & 100

p. 446   'Rations exhausted…', Ziemke & Bauer, op. cit., p. 499

p. 446   'Surrender is out…', ibid.

p. 447   Actions of 241, 90 & 161RR, 95 str.div., 'Combat Report No. 46 & 46', TsAMO, p. 102 & 104

p. 447   German losses, ibid.

p. 447   'Along the division's front…', ibid.

p. 448   Actions of 241, 161 & 90RR, 95 str.div., 'Combat Report No. 48', TsAMO, p. 109

p. 448   Actions of 241, 161 & 90RR, 95 str.div., 'Combat Report No. 50', TsAMO, p. 113

p. 448   All German movements…, ibid.

p. 448   Actions of 241, 161 & 90RR, 95 str.div., 'Combat Report No. 52', TsAMO, p. 118

p. 448   'January 26 dawned…', Chuikov, op. cit., p. 258

p. 449   'It was brilliantly…', Giulini, op. cit., p. 16

p. 450   Gorishny's observers…, 95 str.div., 'Combat Report No. 52', TsAMO, p. 118

p. 451   'Search for accommodation…', Giulini, op. cit., p. 19

p. 451   Actions of 241, 161 & 90RR, 95 str.div., 'Combat Report No. 54', TsAMO, p. 124

p. 451   Observation revealed…, ibid.

p. 451   Nocturnal German attack, 95 str.div., 'Combat Report No. 56', TsAMO, p. 129

p. 452   'After the main body…', Krylow, op. cit., 405

p. 452   Actions of 241, 90 & 161RR, 95 str.div., 'Combat Report No. 56', TsAMO, p. 129

p. 452   'The enemy offers…', ibid.

p. 452   'on 28 January, we…', Krylow, op. cit., 405

p. 455   'And how did it…', Rettenmaier, *Alte Kameraden* 1/1954, p. 4

p. 455   'During the violent…', Rombach, p. 11

p. 456   Nocturnal German attacks, 95 str.div., 'Combat Report No. 58', TsAMO, p. 135

p. 456   'Enemy defence remained…', Krylow, op. cit., 407

p. 457   Storming of Workshop 32, 95 str.div., 'Combat Report No. 58', TsAMO, p. 135

p. 457   Actions of 90, 241 & 161RR, ibid.

p. 457   Death of Schwarzkopf, Steinlen archives

p. 458   'At 0200 the division…', 138 str.div. zhurnal, TsAMO, p. 57

p. 458   'On the night of…', 95 str.div., 'Combat Report No. 58', TsAMO, p. 135

p. 459   'Our battery took up…', Dvoryaninov, p. 12

p. 459   German attempts to retrieve canister, 95 str.div., 'Combat Report No. 60', TsAMO, p. 139

p. 459   Actions of 34, 161, 241 & 90RR, ibid.

p. 460   'In the middle of…', Zrenner

p. 461   'On the evening of…', Poetsch

p. 461   'German soldiers pondered…', Rombach, p. 12

p. 461   'Other comrades sought…', ibid.

p. 461   'There was not much…', Giulini, op. cit., p. 20

p. 462   'The company commander…', Schöpf report, p. 3

p. 462   'I heard the radio…', Zrenner

p. 462   German attempts to retake Workshop 32, 95 str.div., 'Combat Report No. 62', TsAMO, p. 144

p. 463   'Bitter combat continued…', Krylow, op. cit., 414

p. 463   German recapture of Workshop 32, 95 str.div., 'Combat Report No. 61 & 62', TsAMO, p. 142 & 144

p. 464   'Between 0705 and…', 95 str.div., 'Combat Report No. 62', TsAMO, p. 144

p. 464   'The final offensive…', Rettenmaier, *Alte Kameraden* 1/1954, p. 5

p. 464   'In the last weeks…', letter, Bachmann to Hirst 7.9.1981

p. 464   Actions of 90, 241, 92 & 161RR, 95 str.div., 'Combat Report No. 62', TsAMO, p. 144

p. 465   Losses of 95RD's regiments, ibid.

p. 465   Losses of 1/348 Separate…, TsAMO 156UR (156th Fortified Region), 'Situation Report No. 60', p. 65

p. 465   'To speed up…', Krylow, op. cit., 415

p. 465   'In the morning hours…', Poetsch

p. 466   'The pocket in the…', Giulini, op. cit., p. 21

p. 466   'The Soviets […] unleashed…', Poetsch

p. 466   'My battalion, with the…', Trollmann, OKH, Abwicklungsstab 6. Armee, NARA T-78, Roll 140, p. 6069800-6069839

p. 467   Actions of 241, 90, 92 & 161RR, 95 str.div. zhurnal, TsAMO, 1.2.1943

p. 467   'For the entire day…', Krylow, op. cit., 416

p. 468   'On 2 February I accompanied…', Krylow, op. cit., 417

p. 468   'On the night of…', Dvoryaninov, p. 12-13

p. 468   'All of our guns…', Lyudnikov, 'There is a Cliff on the Volga', in *Two Hundred Days of Fire*, p. 207

p. 468   Actions of 95RD, 95 str.div. zhurnal, TsAMO, 2.2.1943

p. 469   'All fighting will cease…', Rettenmaier, 'Wie ich in Stalingrad in Gefangenschaft kam' in *Kurznachrichten Reserve-Infanterie-Regiment 119*, December 1962

p. 470   'Assemble everyone…', ibid.

p. 470   Story of Rettenmaier's surrender…, ibid.

p. 472   'Because the northern…', Rombach, p. 11

p. 472   Actions of 95RD, 95 str.div. zhurnal, TsAMO, 2.2.1943

p. 473   'XI. Armeekorps, with…', Ziemke & Bauer, op. cit., p. 501

p. 473   'On 2 February, everything…', Giulini, op. cit., p. 22

p. 474   'On Thursday, 2 February…', Schellmann, interview with Agnes Moosmann, 21.2.2005

p. 474   'Anxiety reigned…', Schöpf report, p. 4

p. 474   'Because ammunition and…', Rombach, p. 13

p. 475   'On 1 February, we wanted…', Zrenner

p. 476   'I went into captivity…', Zeller, interview with Agnes Moosmann, 16.1.2005 and 6.2.2005

p. 476   'The entire enemy…', Krylow, op. cit., 418

p. 477   "Cease fire!" commanded…', Lyudnikov, 'There is a Cliff on the Volga', in *Two Hundred Days of Fire*, p. 207

p. 477   'I was called by Gurov…', Krylow, op. cit., 418

p. 477   Story of Rettenmaier's capture…, ibid.

Afterword:

p. 479   'The mopping-up…', Knopp, *Stalingrad: Das Drama*, p. 309

p. 479   'How many letters…', Moosmann, op. cit., p. 147-8

Epilogue: Fate of Individuals:

p. 480   Bernhart's story, Moosmann, op. cit., p. 147

p. 480   Bonetsmüller's story, letter, Bonetsmüller's son to Agnes Moosmann, 29.8.2004

p. 480   'you have no concept…', letter, Frau Bonetsmüller to Frau Traub, 18.7.1949

p. 480   'A Hauptmann from Konstanz…', letter, Familie Braun to Familie Steinlen, 13.2.1947

p. 481   'On 1 February 1943…', letter, Steinlen to Familie Braun, 5.1.1950

p. 481   Büch's story, letter, Büch's son to Agnes Moosmann, 17.3.2006

p. 481   'Your husband…', letter, Schumann to Frau Büch, 7.3.1946

p. 481   Gast's story, interview, Gast's niece with Agnes Moosmann, 30.8.2005

p. 482   'It was 1 March…', Holl, p. 38
p. 482   'I can confirm that…', Zeller, interview with Agnes Moosmann, 12.10.2005
p. 482   'sometime in the 1950s…', Frau Gast, interview with Agnes Moosmann
p. 482   Heinrich's story, Personalakten für Walter Heinrich
p. 483   'For years I…', Krauss, letter to author, 18.12.2003
p. 483   'During an operation…', Dreier, letter to the author, 1.11.2003
p. 483   Konovalenko's story; *Geroi Sovetskogo Soyuza, T. 1*, p. 715
p. 483   'Major Otto Krüger…', Hans Krauss, Todeserklärung, 5.6.1953
p. 483   'In July 1943…', ibid.
p. 484   'Dear Frau Lundt, I have…', letter, Pavlicek to Frau Lundt 13.4.1943
p. 484   'Dear Frau Lundt, this morning…', letter, Bauchspiess to Frau Lundt 29.10.1949
p. 484   'Hauptmann Lundt, who was…', Becker, Heimkehrer-Erklärung, 8.1.1956
p. 485   Lyudnikov's story; *Geroi Sovetskogo Soyuza, T. 2*, p. 5
p. 485   Pechenyuk's story; ibid., p. 265
p. 485   Puschiavo's story, Puschiavo family, email to Agnes Moosmann, 10.8.2006
p. 485   'I am in a cellar…', Puschiavo Feldpostbrief
p. 485   'The holy night…', Puschiavo Feldpostbrief
p. 486   Rettenmaier's story, Rettenmaier's daughter, letter to the author, 21.7.2003
p. 487   Traub's story, Traub' son; and various documents from Frau Traub's 'Suchakte'
p. 487   'I briefly want to…', letter, Frau Bonetsmüller to Frau Traub, 18.7.1949
p. 487   Trollmann's story, Trollmann, OKH, Abwicklungsstab 6. Armee, NARA T-78, Roll 140, p. 6069800-6069839
p. 488   Weimann's story, Hirst, 'The Cast', in *Three Scenes from Barbarossa*

Appendix I:

History of Pionier-Bataillon 45:

Pionier-Bataillon 45 Geschichte 1934-1939, BA-MA, RH12_5_3
150 Jahre Württembergische Pionier, Ulm 1967, p. 31-4
Ulm: Garnison und Festung, Ulm 1954, p. 162-4
Wiesen, Wolfgang (ed.). *Es grüßt Euch alle, Bertold. Von Koblenz nach Stalingrad: Die Feldpostbriefe des Pionier Bertold Paulus aus Kastel*
Die 71. Infanterie-Division im Zweiten Weltkrieg, p. 222-3
Das Kleeblatt: Nachrichtenblatt alter Regimenter und selbständigen Einheiten der ehem. 71. Infanterie-Division, Nr. 2/19 Jahrgang (93. Ausgabe), Hildesheim, Mai 1975, p. 3
Das Kleeblatt, Nr. 4/31 Jahrgang (145. Ausgabe), Hildesheim, Oktober 1987, p. 4
Personalakten für Horst Drewitz, Walter Heinrich, Walter Hettich, Fritz Karcher, Manfred Kimmich, Anton Locherer, Fritz Molfenter, Gerd Parchow, Hans-Joachim Pietsch and Karl-Hermann Zehm.
Eyewitness account by Karl Krauss, *Meine Erlebnisse beim Pionier-Bataillon 45*, 18.12.2003
Eyewitness account by Anton Locherer, undated
Interviews with Karl Krauss, 13.4.2005 and 1.10.2005
Letter from wife of Erich Skutlartz, 24.7.2005
Various documents from Pionierkameradschaft Ulm e.V.
Soldbuch Karl Vögele, Wehrpass Hartmuth Müller, Private photo album of Karl Vögele, 'Erinnerungsalbum des Oberstabszahlmeister Mayer vom 01.05.1939' and photo collections of Anton Locherer, Karl Krauss and Jason Mark

History of Panzerpionier-Bataillon 50:

22.Pz.Div., Kriegstagebuch Nr. 1 (7 February - 20 May), NARA T-315, Roll 784
22.Pz.Div., Anlagenband I, II, III & IV zum Kriegstagebuch Nr. 2 (7 February - 20 May 1942), NARA T-315, Roll 784
22.Pz.Div., Kriegstagebuch Nr. 2 (21 May - 31 August 1942), NARA T-315, Roll 784
22.Pz.Div., Anlagenband I, II & IV zum Kriegstagebuch Nr. 2 (May - 31 August 1942), NARA T-315, Roll 785
Manstein, Field Marshall Erich von. *Lost Victories*
Egger, Martin (ed.). *Die Festung Sewastopol: Eine Dokumentation ihrer Befestigungsanlagen und der Kämpfe von 1942*
Selle, Herbert. *Ursprung, Weg und Untergang des Pion. Batl. 50: Ein geschichtlicher Kurzabriss*
Apmann, Ludwig. 'Von Harburg nach Stalingrad: Erinnerungen eines Landsers der 50er-Pioniere' in *Mitteilungsblatt des Verbandes ehemäliger Angehöriger der 23. Panzer-Division und der Traditionsverbände der 14. Panzer-Division, der 22. Panzer-Division und der Panzer-Lehr-Division*, Nr. 2/16 Jahrgang, Ludwigsburg, April 1969, p. 31-3
Geschichte des Pionier-Bataillons 50, Major Reichardt, Berlin 1938
Pionier-Bataillon 50 Erfahrungsbericht Polen 1939, BA-MA, RH12_5_4
Personalakten für Hellmuth Ermeler, Theodor Fuchs, Erwin Gast, Egon Hillmann, Gerhard Hoffmann, Gerhard Jahnke, Klaus Kunze and Wolfgang Ziegenhagen.
Photo collection of Jason Mark

History of Pionier-Bataillon 162:

62.Inf.Div., Kriegstagebuch Nr. 6 (1 January - 31 March 1942), NARA T-315, Roll 1033
62.Inf.Div., Anlagen zum Kriegstagebuch Nr. 6 (4 January - 31 March 1942), NARA T-315, Roll 1033
62.Inf.Div., Kriegstagebuch Nr. 7, Buch 1 (1 April - 31 July 1942), NARA T-315, Roll 1033
62.Inf.Div., Kriegstagebuch Nr. 7, Buch 2 (1 August 1942 - 28 February 1943), NARA T-315, Roll 1034
297. Infanterie-Division Anlagen, NARA T-315, Roll 1977
Die 62. Infanterie-Division 1938-1944. Die 62. Volks-Grenadier-Division 1944-1945
Personalakten für Josef Giedl, Hans Gierth, Rudolf Gregor, Horst Klupsch and Otto Krüger.
DD/WASt, letter to Heiko Klatt, 15.2.2006, p. 1-2

History of Pionier-Bataillon 294:

294.Inf.Div., Kriegstagebuch Nr. 2 (1 April - 31 July 1942), NARA T-315, Roll 1941
294.Inf.Div., Kriegstagebuch Nr. 3 (1 August - 30 November 1942), NARA T-315, Roll 1941
294.Inf.Div., Anlagen zum Kriegstagebuch Nr. 3 (4 August - 30 November 1942), NARA T-315, Roll 1942
Personalakten für Karl Back, Heinrich Bucksch, Otto-Wilhelm Heinze and Werner Jahr.

History of Pionier-Bataillon 336:

336.Inf.Div., Kriegstagebuch Nr. 2 (14 May - 25 November 1942), NARA T-315, Roll 2093
336.Inf.Div., Anlagen A, B and C zum Kriegstagebuch Nr. 2 (14 May - 25 November 1942), NARA T-315, Roll 2094
336.Inf.Div., Anlagen zum Kriegstagebuch Nr. 2, 'Die Schlusskämpfe um Korotojak' (1-9 September 1942), NARA T-315, Roll 2094
Personalakten für Herbert Borkowski, Hermann Lundt, Richard Pavlicek, Gerhard Piltz and Otto Reiter.

Appendix 2:

Several dozen sources were used to compile these biographies: Dienstalterliste (rank seniority lists); Offizier-Stellenbesetzungen (officer staffing); Personalakten (personnel files); promotions, transfer and appointment lists; Rangliste (rank lists); Verleihungsliste (award lists) of 22.Pz. Div., 62., 294., 305., 336. and 389.Inf.Div; Verlustkarte (casualty cards); DD/WASt Verlustliste (casualty lists); DRK Vermisstenbildliste (German Red Cross photo lists of men missing in action); veterans' accounts and reports; various family documents. Also, the following published books:

Podzun, H.H. (ed.). *Das Deutsche Heer 1939: Gliederung, Standorte, Stellenbesetzung und Verzeichnis sämtlicher Offiziere am 3.1.1939.* Bad Nauheim 1953, Verlag Hans-Henning Podzun.

Scheibert, Horst. *Die Träger des Deutschen Kreuzes in Gold – Das Heer.* Friedberg, Podzun Pallas Verlag. ISBN 3-7909-0207-1

Appendix 3:

Same sources as Appendix 2

Appendix 4:

Personalakten für Erwin Gast

Appendix 5:

Personalakten für Hermann Lundt; Feldpostbriefe of Hermann Lundt and other family documents

Appendix 6:

Verleihungsliste (award lists) of 305. Infanterie-Division, BA-ZNS, RH7A/885

Appendix 7:

79.Inf.Div., 6.1.1943, NARA T-315, Roll 1108, p. 838-9

Appendix 8:

Plekhov, I.I., Khvatov, S.P. and Zakharov, G.I. *V ogne stalingradskikh pereprav.* Volgograd 1996, ISBN 5-7605-0333-2; and http://sovnavy-ww2.by.ru/small/typ_1125.htm#1125

SELECT BIBLIOGRAPHY

Unpublished accounts:

Chalykh, Ivan Gavrilovich (650RR): *Vospominaniya o Stalingradskoi bitve*

Charashvili, Ivan Georgyevich (90RR): *Vospominaniya*

Danilenko, Mikhail Andreyevich (650RR): *Vospominaniya o Stalingradskoi bitve*

Dubov, Ivan Vasilyevich (650RR): *Moya armeiskaya semiya 138-ya Krasnoznamennaya*

Dvoryaninov, Vasili Andreyevich (295AR): *Neravnyi boi* and *Po tonkomu lidu*

Eberhard, Hans Ludwig (Pi.Btl.389): *Inf.Div.389*

Epishin, Nikolai Grigoryevich (138RD staff): *Frontovaya zapisi*

Gorbatenko, Aleksei Iosifovich (650RR): *Vospominaniya kapitana Gorbatenko*

Hirst, Ronald Mac Arthur: *Three Scenes from Barbarossa*

Kamyshanov, Vasili Andreyevich (650RR): *Vospominaniya o Stalingradskoi bitve*

Klyukin, Leonid Mitrofanovich (Barrikady militia): *Vospominaniya o Stalingradskoi bitve*

Krauss, Karl (Pi.Btl.45): *Meine Erlebnisse beim Pionier-Bataillon 45*

Lesin, Fedor Anisimovich (344RR): *(untitled)*

Linden, Josef (Pi.Btl.672/305): *Stalingrad*

Locherer, Anton (Pi.Btl.45): *(untitled)*

Piven, Vasili Trofimovich (650RR): *Vospominaniya*

Rettenmaier, Eugen (Gr.Rgt.578): *(diary and reports to his son Siegbert)*

Rombach, Karl-August (II./Art.Rgt.305): *Erlebnisse eines Deutschen Soldaten im Zweiten Weltkrieg*

Selle, Herbert (Pi.Btl.50): *Ursprung, Weg und Untergang des Pion. Batl. 50: Ein geschichtlicher Kurzabriss*

Senchkovsky, Mikhail Ilyich (NKVD blocking detachment): *Dorogie rebyata!*

Steinmetz, Bernhard (305.Inf.Div.): *Meine Erinnerungen an Stalingrad und an die 305. I.D.*

Tyupa, Pavel Grigoryevich (650RR): *Vospominanie o Stalingradskoi bitve*

Published Works:

150 Jahre Württembergische Pionier. Ulm 1967. No ISBN

Aaken, Wolf van. *Hexenkessel Ostfront: Vom Smolensk nach Breslau*. Rastatt 1964, Pabel Verlag. No ISBN

Abdulin, Mansur (edited by Artem Drabkin). *Red Road from Stalingrad. Recollections of a Soviet Infantryman*. Barnsley 2004, Pen & Sword Military. ISBN 1-84415-145-X

Barrikadtsy v dvukh tomakh (collective authorship). Volgograd 1989, Nizhne-Volzhkoye knizhnoye izdatelstvo. No ISBN

Beevor, Antony. *Stalingrad – The Fateful Siege, 1942-1943*. New York 1998, Viking Penguin. ISBN 0-670-87095-1

Beshanov, V.V. *God 1942 – "Uchebniy"*. Minsk 2004, Kharvest. ISBN 985-13-0906-0

Bitva za Stalingrad (collective authorship). Volgograd 1970, Nizhne-Volzhkoye knizhnoye izdatelstvo. No ISBN

Chuikov, Vasili I. *The Beginning of the Road*. London 1963, MacGibbon & Kee. No ISBN

Craig, William. *Enemy at the Gates: The Battle for Stalingrad*. London 1973, Hodder and Stoughton. ISBN 0-340-12863-1

Danishevsky, I. (ed.). *The Road of Battle and Glory*. Moscow 1955, Foreign Languages Publishing House. No ISBN

Die 62. Infanterie-Division 1938-1944. Die 62. Volks-Grenadier-Division 1944-1945 (collective authorship). Fulda 1968, Kameradenhilfswerk der ehemaligen 62. Division e.V. No ISBN

Domarus, M. *Hitler, Reden und Proklamationen, 1932-1945*. Würzburg 1962. No ISBN

Ebert, Jens (ed.). *Feldpostbriefe aus Stalingrad: November 1942 bis Januar 1943*. Göttingen 2003, Wallstein Verlag. ISBN 3-89244-677-6

Efremov, V.S. *Eskadrili letyat za gorizont*. Volgograd 1978, Nizhne-Volzhkoye knizhnoye izdatelstvo. No ISBN

Egger, Martin (ed.). *Die Festung Sewastopol: Eine Dokumentation ihrer Befestigungsanlagen und der Kämpfe von 1942*. Bern 1995. ISBN 3-931032-32-9

Erickson, John. *The Road to Stalingrad*. London 1975, Weidenfeld and Nicolson Ltd. ISBN 0-297-76877-8

Fellgiebel, Walther-Peer. *Die Träger des Ritterkreuzes des Eisernen Kreuzes 1939-1945*. Wölfersheim-Berstadt 1996, Podzun Pallas Verlag. ISBN 3-7909-0284-5

Friedel, Hermann. *Nebelwerfer-Regiment 51, 1940-1943*. Privately published. No ISBN

Gedenkbuch des deutschen Adels. Band 3. Limburg/Lahn 1967, C. S. Starke Verlag. No ISBN

Gedenkbuch des deutschen Adels – Nachtrag. Band 6. Limburg an der Lahn 1980, C. S. Starke Verlag. No ISBN

Geroi Sovetskogo Soyuza: Kratkiy biograficheskiy slovar v dvukh tomakh. Moscow 1987, Voennoye Izdatelstvo. No ISBN

Giulini, Udo. *Stalingrad und mein zweites Leben*. Neustadt/Weinstrasse 1978, Pfälzische Verlagsanstalt GmbH. No ISBN

Glukhovsky, S.D. *Ostrov Lyudnikova*. Moscow 1961, Voennoye izdatelstvo ministerstva oborony SSSR. No ISBN

Goerlitz, Walter. *Paulus and Stalingrad*. New York, 1963, Citadel Press. No ISBN

Haller, Uli (ed.). *Lieutenant General Karl Strecker: The Life and Thought of a German Military Man*. Westport 1994, Praeger Publishers. ISBN 0-275-94582-0

Handbook on German Military Forces (U.S. War Department). Baton Rouge 1990, Louisiana State University Press. ISBN 0-8071-2011-1

Hauck, Friedrich Wilhelm. *Eine deutsche Division in Russland und Italien: 305. Infanteriedivision, 1941-1945*. Friedberg 1975, Podzun-Verlag. ISBN 3-7909-0031-1

Hayward, Joel S.A. *Stopped at Stalingrad: the Luftwaffe and Hitler's Defeat in the East, 1942-1943*. Lawrence 1998, University Press of Kansas. ISBN 0-7006-0876-1

Hillgruber, Andreas (ed.). *Von El Alamein bis Stalingrad : Aus dem Kriegstagebuch des Oberkommandos der Wehrmacht (Wehrmachfuhrungsstab)*. München 1964, Deutscher Taschenbuch Verlag. No ISBN

Himpe, Ullus. *Die 71. Infanterie-Division im Zweiten Weltkrieg*. Hildesheim 1973, Arbeitsgemeinschaft 'Das Kleeblatt'. No ISBN

Holl, Adalbert. *Was geschah nach Stalingrad: 7 1/4 Jahre als Kriegs- und Strafgefangener in Russland*. Duisburg 1965, Selbstverlag. No ISBN

Jaugitz, Markus. *Funklenkpanzer: A History of German Army Remote- and Radio-Controlled Armor Units.* Winnipeg 2001, J.J.Fedorowicz Publishing. ISBN 0-921991-58-4

Jentz, Thomas L. (ed.). *Panzer Tracts No. 8: Sturmgeschuetz (s.Pak to Sturmmoerser).* Darlington 1999, Darlington Productions, Inc. ISBN 1-892848-04-X

Kehrig, Manfred. *Stalingrad: Analyse und Dokumentation einer Schlacht.* Stuttgart 1974, Deutsche Verlags-Anstalt GmbH. ISBN 3-421-01653-4

Keilig, Wolf. *Die Generale des Heeres.* Friedburg 1983, Podzun-Pallas-Verlag. ISBN 3-7909-0202-0

Keilig, Wolf. *Rangliste des Deutschen Heeres 1944-45.* Bad Nauheim 1955, Verlag Hans-Henning Podzun. No ISBN

Kirstein, Wolfgang. *'Rekonstruktion eines Tage-Buches'. Die 295. Infanterie-Division von 1940 bis 1945.* Langelsheim 2000, privately published. No ISBN

Kluge, Alexander. *Schlachtbeschreibung.* Freiburg i.B. 1964, Walter-Verlag. No ISBN

Kluge, Alexander. *The Battle.* New York 1967, McGraw-Hill Book Company. No ISBN

Knopp, Guido. *Stalingrad: Das Drama.* München 2002, C. Bertelsmann Verlag. ISBN 3-570-00693-X

Krylow, Nikolai I. *Stalingrad. Die Entscheidende Schlacht des Zweiten Weltkrieges.* Köln 1981, Pahl-Rugenstein Verlag. ISBN 3-7609-0624-9

Lyudnikov, I.I. *Ognenniy ostrov.* Volgograd 1971, Nizhne-Volzhkoye knizhnoye izdatelstvo. No ISBN

Manstein, Field-Marshal Erich von. *Lost Victories.* Novato 1982, Presidio Press. ISBN 0-89141-130-5

Mark, Jason D. *Death of the Leaping Horseman: 24 Panzer-Division in Stalingrad, 12th August – 20th November 1942.* Sydney 2001, Leaping Horseman Books. ISBN 0-646-41034-2

Moosmann, Agnes. *Chronik der im Zweiten Weltkrieg gefallenen und vermissten Soldaten der Gemeinde Bodnegg 1939-1945.* Horb am Neckar 2003, Geiger-Verlag. ISBN 3-89570-893-3

Neidhardt, Hanns. *Mit Tanne und Eichenlaub. Kriegschronik der 100. Jäger-Division.* Stuttgart 1981, Leopold Stocker Verlag. ISBN 3-7020-0373-8

Onslaught: The German Drive to Stalingrad, Documented in 150 Unpublished Colour Photographs, London 1984, Sidgwick and Jackson Limited. ISBN 0-283-99291-3

Ot oborony k nastupleniyu. 1 iyulya – 31 dekabrya 1942 goda. Organy gosudarstvennoy bezopastnosti SSSR v velikoy otechestvennoy voine. Sbornik dokumentov. Tom tretiy Kniga 2. Moscow 2003, Izdatelstvo 'Rus'. ISBN 5-8090-0021-5

Ovchinnikova, L.P. *Peredovaya nachinalas v tsekhe.* Volgograd 1983, Nizhne-Volzhkoye knizhnoye izdatelstvo. No ISBN

Plekhov, I.I., Khvatov, S.P. and Zakharov, G.I. *V ogne stalingradskikh pereprav.* Volgograd 1996, Komitet po pechati. ISBN 5-7605-0333-2

Podzun, H.H. (ed.). *Das Deutsche Heer 1939: Gliederung, Standorte, Stellenbesetzung und Verzeichnis sämtlicher Offiziere am 3.1.1939.* Bad Nauheim 1953, Verlag Hans-Henning Podzun. No ISBN

Popov, P.P., Kozlov, A.V. and Usik, V.G. *Perelom: Po vospominaniyam uchastnikov i svidetelei Stalingradskoi bitvy.* Volgograd 2000, Gosudarstvennoye uchrezhdenie 'Izdatel'. ISBN 5-9233-0041-9

Russkiy kharakter (collective authorship). Volgograd 1981, Nizhne-Volzhkoye knizhnoye izdatelstvo. No ISBN

Samsonov, A. M. *Stalingradskaya bitva.* Moscow 1968, Izdatelstvo 'Nauka'. No ISBN

Samsonov, A. M. *Stalingradskaya epopeya.* Moscow 1968, Izdatelstvo 'Nauka'. No ISBN

Scheibert, Horst. *Die Träger der Ehrenblattspange des Heeres und der Waffen-SS.* Friedberg 1986, Podzun Pallas Verlag. ISBN 3-7909-0283-7

Scheibert, Horst. *Die Träger des Deutschen Kreuzes in Gold – Das Heer.* Friedberg, Podzun Pallas Verlag. ISBN 3-7909-0207-1

Schimak, Anton/Lamprecht, Karl & Dettmer, Friedrich. *Die 44. Infanterie-Division – Tagebuch der Hoch- und Deutschmeister.* Wien 1969, Austria Press. No ISBN

Schitaitye menya kommunistom (collective authorship). Volgograd 1982, Nizhne-Volzhkoye knizhnoye izdatelstvo. No ISBN

Schröter, Heinz. *Stalingrad. The cruellest battle of World War II.* London 1960, Pan Books Ltd. No ISBN

Schüddekopf, Carl. *Im Kessel: Erzählen von Stalingrad.* München 2002, Piper Verlag GmbH. ISBN 3-492-24032-1

Selle, Herbert. *Wofür? Erleben eines führenden Pioniers bis Stalingrad.* Neckargemünd 1977, Kurt Vowinckel Verlag. ISBN 3-87879-118-6

Seydlitz, Walther von. *Stalingrad, Konflikt und Konsequenz, Erinnerungen.* Oldenburg 1977, Verlag Gerhard Stalling AG. ISBN 3-7979-1353-2

Soldaty XX veka. Mnogotomnoye izdaniye vypusk III. Tom pervyi i vtoroy. Moscow 2003, Mezhdunarodnyi obedinennyi biograficheskii tsentr. ISBN 5-93696-007-2

Stalingradskaya bitva. Khronika, fakty, lyudi (collective authorship). Moscow 2002, Olma-Press. ISBN 5-224-03186-9

Stalingraskaya epopeya: Vpervye publikuyemye dokumenty rassekrechennye FSB RF. Moscow 2000, 'Zvonnitsa-MG'. ISBN 5-88524-050-7

Stoves, Rolf. *Die 22. Panzer-Division, 25. Panzer-Division, 27. Panzer-Division und die 233. Reserve-Panzer-Division. Aufstellung, Gliederung, Einsatz.* Friedberg 1985, Podzun-Pallas-Verlag. ISBN 3-7909-0252-7

Syny narodov vsekh (collective authorship). Volgograd 198, Nizhne-Volzhkoye knizhnoye izdatelstvo. No ISBN

Thomas, Franz. *Die Eichenlaubträger 1940-1945. Band 1: A-K.* Osnabrück 1997, Biblio Verlag. ISBN 3-7648-2299-6

Thomas, Franz. *Die Eichenlaubträger 1940-1945. Band 2: L-Z.* Osnabrück 1998, Biblio Verlag. ISBN 3-7648-2300-3

Thomas, Franz. *Sturmartillerie im Bild, 1940-1945.* Osnabrück 1986, Biblio-Verlag. ISBN 3-7648-1485-3

Thomas, Franz and Wegmann, Günter. *Die Ritterkreuzträger der Deutschen Wehrmacht 1939-1945 - Teil III: Infanterie Braake-Buxa.* Osnabrück 1993, Biblio-Verlag. ISBN 3-7648-1734-8

Two Hundred Days of Fire (collective authorship). Moscow 1970, Progress Publishers. No ISBN

Venkov, B.S. and Dudinov, P.P. *Gvardeyskaya doblest: Boyevoi Put 70-i gvardeyskoi strelkovoi divizii.* Moscow 1979, Voennoye izdatelstvo ministerstva oborony SSSR. No ISBN

Volostnov, N.I. *Gvardiya v ogne.* Gorkiy 1979, Volgo-Vyatskoye knizhnoye izdatelstvo. No ISBN

Volostnov, N.I. *Na ognennykh rubezhak.* Moscow 1983, Voennoye izdatelstvo ministerstva oborony SSSR. No ISBN

Wagner-Baumann-Lederer (eds.). *Ulm: Garnison und Festung. Festschrift zum Garnisonstreffen anläßlich der 1100 Jahrfeier am 17./18. Juli 1954.* Ulm 1954, J. Ebner. No ISBN

Welz, Helmut. *Verratene Grenadiere.* Berlin 1964, Deutscher Militärverlag. No ISBN

Wiesen, Wolfgang (ed.). *Es grüßt Euch alle, Bertold. Von Koblenz nach Stalingrad: Die Feldpostbriefe des Pionier Bertold Paulus aus Kastel.* Nonnweiler-Otzenhausen 1993, Verlag Burr. ISBN 3-9802717-1-4

Wijers, Hans (ed.). *Der Kampf um Stalingrad: Die Kämpfe im Industriegelände.* Brummen 2001, Eigen Verlag Hans Wijers. No ISBN

Winter, Franz. *'Damals als die Räder rollten'. Menschliches – Dramatisches – aber auch Heiteres aus dem Kriegsalltag eines Oberschwaben bei der Bodensee-Division im II. Weltkrieg.* Weinheim 2005, Selbstverlag. No ISBN

Zentner, Christian (ed.). *Soldaten im Einsatz: die Deutsche Wehrmacht im Zweiten Weltkrieg.* Hamburg 1977, Jahr Verlag KG. No ISBN

Ziemke, Earl F. and Bauer, Magna E. *Moscow to Stalingrad: Decision in the East.* New York 1988, Military Heritage Press. ISBN 0-88029-294-6

Periodicals:

Alte Kameraden

Bund ehemaliger Stalingradkämpfer e. V. Deutschland, Weihnachts Rundbrief

Das Kleeblatt: Nachrichtenblatt alter Regimenter und selbständigen Einheiten der ehem. 71. Infanterie-Division

Das Ritterkreuz: Mitteilungsblatt der Ordensgemeinschaft der Ritterkreuzträger e. V.

Der Sturmartillerist: Zeitschrift der 'Gemeinschaft der Sturmartillerie e. V.'

Deutsches Soldatenjahrbuch

Mitteilungsblatt des Verbandes ehemäliger Angehöriger der 23. Panzer-Division und der Traditionsverbände der 14. Panzer-Division, der 22. Panzer-Division und der Panzer-Lehr-Division

Tapfer und Treu

Voyenno-istorichesky zhurnal

Index

H

M